Praise for Leslie Beck's Books

"Canada's nutrition guru has mapped out a plan that guarantees a new you. If you follow her 12-week plan, you will lose weight. Period."

—*Calgary Herald*

"One of the most sensible 'diet books' out there."

—*The Georgia Straight*

"Adolescence is a critical period for developing healthy eating and exercise habits, and the guidance provided in this book is invaluable."
—Chris Carmichael, personal coach to eight-time Tour de France champion Lance Armstrong and author of *Chris Carmichael's Food for Fitness*

"Teenagers are constantly confronted with fast food, poor cafeteria choices and eating on the go. *Healthy Eating for Teens and Preteens* provides them with straightforward, useable tools for making the right food choices."
—Dr. Marla Shapiro, medical consultant, CTV

"Leslie Beck offers indispensable advice for healthy living."
—James F. Balch, MD, co-author of *The Prescription for Nutritional Healing*

"If you'd like to eat more healthfully, Leslie Beck is a must-read."
—*Homemakers* magazine

"Leslie Beck, one of Canada's leading authorities on nutrition, has written another well-researched, fabulously written and perfectly executed book, this time on boosting heart health. It's chock full of useful information and tips as well as scrumptious heart healthy recipes."
—Pauline Anderson, family health editor, *Canadian Living*

"[Beck's] book offers plenty of sound nutrition information and evidence-based diet strategies that can help protect you from coronary heart disease. It's all about implementing a sustainable, heart healthy lifestyle. The tools in this book will help you achieve this."

—Dr. Rob Myers, director of cardiology,
Medcan Clinic

"A comprehensive nutrition book aimed at teens that also includes terrific information for the whole family. It includes the most up-to-date information that will help your teen form a great foundation for a healthy lifestyle."

—Sally Brown, CEO, Heart and
Stroke Foundation of Canada

"Parents and teens need all the help they can get, including nutrition advice. This book is so practical and thorough that I plan to share it with my daughter and son."

—Linda Lewis, editor-in-chief,
Today's Parent

"It is a relief to have Leslie Beck's well-researched, approachable and up-to-date guide to lifelong healthful eating."

—Elizabeth Baird, *Canadian Living*

"A very sensible approach to eating, diet and nutrition."

—*The London Free Press*

"Practical, easy to follow strategies to help transform your relationship with food."

—*The Hamilton Spectator*

"Trying to eat healthfully can be a daunting task. Advice is plentiful, but often conflicting or scientifically suspect. Enter Leslie Beck and *Leslie Beck's 10 Steps to Healthy Eating*, a valuable home reference with a wealth of practical 'how-to' strategies."

—*The Vancouver Sun*

"Leslie Beck has done a superb job of rounding up all the latest nutritional information to guide women healthfully through their menopausal years. Not only does she review the current scientific literature and make sense of it—no mean feat—but she also provides you with her expert dietician's opinion on everything ... a must-have for 40-plus women who want to make informed choices."

—June Rogers, health editor, *Chatelaine*

"Finally, a map that women can use to chart their voyage through menopause the natural way."

—Marilyn Linton, health editor, *Toronto Sun*, and author of *Taking Charge by Taking Care: A Canadian Guide to Women's Health*

"Leslie Beck has written the first book that specifically outlines the relationship between nutrition and certain symptoms associated with the peri- and post-menopausal years. This book can help alleviate stressful side effects of menopause and lower the risk of disease through diet and nutrition."

—Rose Reisman, bestselling author of *The Balance of Living Well*

"A guide for women of all ages seeking to manage their health and well-being."

—Dr. Jean Marmoreo, *National Post* columnist, "Dr. Jean Marmoreo on Middle-Aged Women"

"If you believe that we are what we eat—and I do—*Leslie Beck's Nutrition Guide for Women* serves up food for thought and more to help you take charge of your own good health."

—Charlotte Empey, editor-in-chief, *Canadian Living*

"*Leslie Beck's 10 Steps to Healthy Eating* contains everything you need to know to get healthy and stay healthy by eating right. The 'Getting Ready' section is especially impressive and helpful!"

—Christiane Northrup, MD, author of *Women's Wisdom* and *The Wisdom of Menopause*

"If you are looking for a comprehensive resource *Leslie Beck's Nutrition Guide to a Healthy Pregnancy* is a must-read."

—*Toronto Sun*

PENGUIN CANADA

THE COMPLETE A–Z NUTRITION ENCYCLOPEDIA

LESLIE BECK, a registered dietitian, is Canada's leading nutri-
tionist and the bestselling author of nine nutrition books.
Leslie writes a weekly nutrition column in *The Globe and
Mail*, is a regular contributor to CTV's *Canada AM* and can
be heard one morning a week on CJAD Radio's *The
Andrew Carter Show* and on CFRB Radio's *The John
Donabie Show*.

Leslie has worked with many of Canada's leading
businesses and international food companies and runs a
thriving private practice at the Medcan Clinic in Toronto.
She also regularly delivers nutrition workshops to corporate groups across North America.

Visit Leslie Beck's website at www.lesliebeck.com.

Also by Leslie Beck

Leslie Beck's Nutrition Guide to Menopause

Leslie Beck's Nutrition Encyclopedia

Leslie Beck's Nutrition Guide for Women

10 Steps to Healthy Eating

Leslie Beck's Nutrition Guide to a Healthy Pregnancy

Healthy Eating for Preteens and Teens

The Complete Nutrition Guide to Menopause

The No-Fail Diet

Foods That Fight Disease

Heart Healthy Foods for Life

The Complete Nutrition Guide for Women

LESLIE BECK RD
The Complete A–Z
NUTRITION
Encyclopedia
A Guide to Natural Health

ASSOCIATE RESEARCHER
ANNE VON ROSENBACH, BA, MLS

PENGUIN
CANADA

PENGUIN CANADA

Published by the Penguin Group

Penguin Group (Canada), 90 Eglinton Avenue East, Suite 700, Toronto, Ontario, Canada M4P 2Y3
(a division of Pearson Canada Inc.)

Penguin Group (USA) Inc., 375 Hudson Street, New York, New York 10014, U.S.A.
Penguin Books Ltd, 80 Strand, London WC2R 0RL, England
Penguin Ireland, 25 St Stephen's Green, Dublin 2, Ireland (a division of Penguin Books Ltd)
Penguin Group (Australia), 250 Camberwell Road, Camberwell, Victoria 3124, Australia
(a division of Pearson Australia Group Pty Ltd)
Penguin Books India Pvt Ltd, 11 Community Centre, Panchsheel Park, New Delhi – 110 017, India
Penguin Group (NZ), 67 Apollo Drive, Rosedale, North Shore 0632, New Zealand (a division of Pearson New Zealand Ltd)
Penguin Books (South Africa) (Pty) Ltd, 24 Sturdee Avenue, Rosebank, Johannesburg 2196, South Africa

Penguin Books Ltd, Registered Offices: 80 Strand, London WC2R 0RL, England

First published 2010

1 2 3 4 5 6 7 8 9 10 (CR)

LIBRARY AND ARCHIVES CANADA CATALOGUING IN PUBLICATION

Beck, Leslie (Leslie C.)
The complete A–Z nutrition encyclopedia : a guide to natural
health / Leslie Beck.

Includes biographical references and index.
ISBN 978-0-14-316943-7

1. Nutrition—Encyclopedias. I. Title.

RA784.B423 2010   613.203   C2009-905512-0

Visit the Penguin Group (Canada) website at **www.penguin.ca**

Special and corporate bulk purchase rates available; please see
www.penguin.ca/corporatesales or call 1-800-810-3104, ext. 477 or 474

This book is dedicated to my number one support—
my loving and ever so patient husband, Darrell

Thank you for bringing balance, happiness and love to my life

Contents

PART TWO Herbal Remedies and Natural Health Products 115

Acknowledgments

I would like to express a sincere and heartfelt thank you to two very key people whose contributions helped make this book possible.

To my researcher, Anne von Rosenbach, B.A., M.L.S., who spent literally hundreds of hours researching the 75-plus health conditions you'll read about in this book—in 2000 for the first edition and again in 2008 for this completely revised edition. Without Anne's dedication, thoroughness and efficiency, writing this book would not have been possible—her contribution was enormous. It was a pleasure working with her as she made my job so much easier.

To Emily Kennedy, M.Sc., who has worked with me for the past 3 years, helping me research the many topics I discuss on *Canada AM* (CTV) and write about in my weekly *Globe and Mail* newspaper column. I am very thankful for Emily's diligent, thorough and organized approach to updating the statistics on disease prevalence and incidence as well as the contact information for the hundreds of resources listed in this book. Her willingness to scan the literature for my last-minute research requests doesn't go unnoticed. Her enthusiasm and keen interest in nutrition and health have been assets in helping me with this edition of the book.

And finally, I am forever grateful to my private practice clients, who over the past 20 years have inspired me to search for answers and, in the process, continue my learning. I am grateful to be able to learn every day.

Introduction

Today Canadians are faced with the very challenging task of trying to understand an overwhelming amount of health information and apply it in their daily lives. Not so easy to do given conflicting news stories, new "cure-all" supplements and a growing number of supercharged foods—it can leave the head of even the savviest consumer spinning. I understand why so many Canadians are confused, frustrated and sometimes ready to "throw in the towel" and stop caring about what they eat. I've spent my career helping my private practice clients and the public make sense of a never-ending barrage of nutrition advice, scientific jargon and research findings—it's what I love to do—and this book is no exception.

I first researched and wrote this encyclopedia in 2000. Even then it was an enormous endeavour to sift through and interpret decades of research findings on nutrition and health. As you know, the field of nutritional science evolves rapidly. Every day, it seems, there's a new study supporting or refuting earlier research findings or bringing new information to light. That's why I decided it was important—and necessary—to update and revise this encyclopedia. I wanted to provide Canadians with the latest credible scientific advice for managing health through diet and nutritional and natural health products.

Fast-forward to 2009, the year I essentially rewrote this book. Although much advice remained accurate, much had changed: nearly 10 years' worth of new scientific evidence, revised national diet and nutrient intake recommendations, and a flood of new food products in grocery stores. This revised edition of my encyclopedia is the culmination of hundreds and hundreds of hours spent researching, reading and writing. It's a comprehensive guide that translates the very latest scientific information from the fields of nutrition, herbal medicine and natural medicine into evidence-based and straightforward recommendations. This encyclopedia is for individuals of all ages—and it can benefit you even if you're completely healthy. You'll find a wealth of information that can help you prevent disease, manage a certain health condition naturally, increase your energy level, boost your immune system and achieve optimal nutritional health.

If you have a certain medical condition, the information in this book is not intended to replace conventional medicine or your doctor's advice. It's intended for educational purposes only. Under no circumstances should you discontinue a medication or put off a surgical procedure without first consulting your doctor. I advise that any recommended treatment described in this book—whether it be a vitamin supplement, an herbal remedy or another natural health product— be discussed with your doctor. Some of the therapies outlined in this book can be used effectively in place of drug treatment, while others can be used to complement conventional treatment. Although there may be exceptions, most of the food and vitamin and mineral recommendations are safe and healthy.

How to Use This Book

Part One: Nutrition and Diet gives you a crash course on nutrition. In Chapters 1 through 3, you'll learn about carbohydrates, protein and fat. You'll learn why they're important for health, how much you need of each and what types you should be eating more often. Chapter 4 is a comprehensive reference to vitamins and minerals. Not only will you find information about daily dietary requirements and the best food sources but you'll also find information that will help you take vitamin and mineral supplements safely.

Chapter 5, Elements of a Healthy Diet, helps you put all your newfound knowledge into practice. Based on the latest scientific evidence for disease prevention, I tell you what foods you should be eating more often and how to incorporate them into your diet. You'll even find a healthy eating guide that outlines recommended daily servings from each food group. And, of course, I wouldn't be doing my job if I didn't mention which foods and nutrients you should be consuming less often.

Part Two: Herbal Remedies and Natural Health Products provides in-depth information about popular supplements. Chapter 6 gives an overview of the field of herbal medicine—herbal traditions around the world, ways to take herbal remedies and guidelines to choosing a high-quality product. Chapter 7 discusses eighteen popular herbs for which there's scientific evidence to support health claims. You'll learn what these herbs are used for and how they work in the body. Potential side effects and safety issues are mentioned for each. In Chapter 8, you'll read about supplements that aren't considered vitamins or minerals or herbs. The natural health products discussed are supplements that are being actively studied for their ability to keep us healthy. I tell you what they're used for, how they work, how to take them, side effects and safety issues. I've removed supplements that were discussed in the first edition of this book that no longer have good evidence to recommend their use. I've also added natural health products for which there's now solid evidence to support their efficacy.

Part Three: The Health Conditions is where you'll find in-depth information on over seventy-five health conditions, from A to Z. For each health condition, you'll find a description of the disorder, causes, symptoms, risk factors, conventional treatments and, of course, nutritional recommendations. The recommendations are categorized as dietary strategies, vitamins and minerals, and herbal remedies and other natural health products. Once again, I provide you with information on how to safely take the supplements suggested, as well as details about who shouldn't take certain supplements. Unless otherwise specified, the recommended dietary allowances (RDAs) and dosages cited for supplements suggested in Part Three are the amounts for adults; you'll find the RDAs and appropriate suggested dosages for children in Chapter 4. I also include a list of recommended resources, including websites to visit for more information. As you read through the nutrition strategies for managing your health, you'll sometimes be directed back to Parts One and Two for a more detailed description of a certain food, vitamin, mineral or supplement.

The nutrition recommendations presented in this book are based on scientific evidence. Some recommendations are backed by stronger evidence than others, and I've tried to convey this to you in the text. If there's very little or no evidence to support using a food, nutrient or supplement, I haven't included it in this book.

Choosing Between Supplements

If you have a health condition that's described in this book, it's not my intention for you to implement every nutrition recommendation I discuss. While the dietary strategies and vitamin and mineral supplements can all be put into practice (unless a contraindication is specified), this isn't the case for the herbal remedies and natural health products. Very often, many of these supplements work in a similar way, so you'll want to choose the one that 1) isn't contraindicated for you and 2) has the strongest scientific evidence to support its use. To help you choose which supplement to take, I've compiled a brief Nutrition Strategy Checklist at the end of each health condition. This checklist tells you which strategies to implement first. Once you've decided on an herb and/or natural health product, take the supplement for at least three months to see if your symptoms improve. If you find no change after 3 to 6 months, try the next supplement on the list. It may sound like a lot of work, but it's the only way to determine if a product is working for you. Unlike conventional drugs, herbs and supplements are gentler and take longer to take effect. Be patient. At that point you're already halfway there—you've chosen a high-quality product and you've taken the correct dose. Now it's time to let healthy food and good nutrition do the rest.

I hope you find my new and revised nutrition encyclopedia a valuable reference for you and your family. Enjoy your journey to good health.

Leslie Beck, RD
Toronto

PART ONE

Nutrition and Diet

1

Carbohydrates: Sugar, Starch and Dietary Fibre

Carbohydrates often get a bad rap … they make you fat, they cause diabetes, they trigger hyperactivity in children. However, contrary to the claims of many fad diets, carbohydrate-containing foods are an important component of a healthy diet and do not cause health problems if eaten according to proper guidelines. Carbohydrates provide about half of all the energy used by your muscles, nerves and other body tissues. And carbohydrate is your brain's preferred fuel source—the brain relies on a steady supply of carbohydrate to function properly. In fact, carbohydrate-rich foods should be the major source of energy in your daily diet. And if you choose your carbohydrates wisely, these foods also supply a fair share of fibre, vitamins, minerals and protective plant chemicals.

What Is Carbohydrate?

Carbohydrate is composed of carbon, hydrogen and oxygen and is found almost exclusively in plant foods. Plants make the carbohydrate we eat from carbon dioxide, water and the sun's energy. Fruit, vegetables, whole grains, legumes and nuts are all sources of carbohydrate. The only animal foods with carbohydrate are dairy products, which contain a naturally occurring sugar called lactose. The carbohydrate family includes simple sugars, starches and dietary fibre.

Simple sugars are classified as either monosaccharides (*mono* meaning one and *saccharide* meaning sugar) or disaccharides (two sugars). Monosaccharides are the simplest form of carbohydrate because they consist of a single sugar molecule. The three monosaccharides important to nutrition are glucose (also called dextrose and blood sugar), fructose (found in fruit, honey and corn syrup) and galactose. Galactose rarely occurs by itself in foods; instead, it attaches to another sugar unit to form the disaccharide lactose. Disaccharides are pairs of monosaccharides linked together. Maltose (malt sugar), sucrose (table sugar) and lactose (milk sugar) are disaccharides we consume every day.

Starches are more complex arrangements of carbohydrate. Starches in foods are long chains of hundreds or thousands of glucose units linked together. These giant molecules are stacked side by side in a grain of rice, a slice of bread or a flake of breakfast cereal. Other starchy foods are potatoes, wheat, rye, oats, corn and legumes (including chickpeas, kidney beans and lentils).

Dietary fibres are the structural parts of vegetables, fruit, grains and legumes. Pectins, lignans, cellulose, gums and mucilages are all different forms of fibre found in these foods. Although our digestive enzymes are not able to break down the chemical bonds that link the building blocks of fibre, bacteria in our colon can digest some of these fibres.

Dietary fibre is composed of two types of fibre: *soluble* and *insoluble*. Both are present in varying proportions in the different plant foods; some foods may be rich in one or the other. Soluble fibres dissolve in water. Once consumed, they form a gel in the stomach and slow the rate of digestion and absorption. Dried peas, beans and lentils, oats, barley, psyllium husks, apples and citrus fruits are good sources of soluble fibre. Diets high in soluble fibre have been shown to stabilize blood sugar and reduce the need for insulin in some people with diabetes. And plenty of evidence supports the cholesterol-lowering effect of oat bran and psyllium.

Foods like wheat bran, whole grains and certain vegetables contain mainly insoluble fibres. These fibres have a significant capacity for retaining water and act to increase stool bulk and promote regularity. By reducing constipation, a diet high in fibre may prevent a condition called diverticulosis (see page 358). Since high-fibre diets are usually low in fat and calories, they also may help you achieve and maintain a healthy weight. To reap its health benefits, Canadians should be getting 25 to 35 grams of fibre in their diets each day. Here's a list of fibre-rich foods.

Fibre-Rich Foods

Food	Fibre (grams)
Bread and Other Grain Foods	
Bread, 100% whole-wheat, 2 slices	4.0 g
Flaxseed, ground, 2 tbsp (30 ml)	4.5 g
Pita pocket, whole-wheat, 1	4.8 g
Rice, brown, cooked, 1 cup (250 ml)	3.1 g
Spaghetti, whole-wheat, cooked, 1 cup (250 ml)	4.8 g
Wheat bran, 2 tbsp (30 ml)	2.4 g
Cereals	
100% bran cereal, 1/2 cup (125 ml)	12.0 g
All-Bran Bran Flakes, Kellogg's, 3/4 cup (175 ml)	5.0 g
All-Bran Buds, Kellogg's, 1/3 cup (75 ml)	12.0 g
Corn Bran, Quaker, 1 cup (250 ml)	6.3 g
Grape-Nuts, Post, 1/2 cup (125 ml)	6.0 g
Oat bran, 1 cup (250 ml), cooked	4.5 g
Oatmeal, 1 cup (250 ml), cooked	3.6 g
Red River Hot Cereal, 1 cup (250 ml), cooked	4.8 g
Shreddies, Post, 3/4 cup (175 ml)	4.4 g
Fruit	
Apple, 1 medium with skin	2.6 g
Apricots, dried, 1/4 cup (60 ml)	2.6 g
Banana, 1 medium	1.9 g
Blueberries, 1/2 cup (125 ml)	2.0 g
Figs, dried, 5	8.5 g
Orange, 1 medium	2.4 g
Pear, 1 medium with skin	5.1 g
Prunes, dried, 3	3.0 g
Raisins, seedless, 1/2 cup (125 ml)	2.8 g
Strawberries, 1 cup (250 ml)	3.8 g

Food	Fibre (grams)
Legumes and Nuts	
Almonds, 1/2 cup (125 ml)	8.2 g
Beans and tomato sauce, canned, 1 cup (250 ml)	20.7 g
Black beans, 1 cup (250 ml), cooked	13.0 g
Chickpeas, 1 cup (250 ml), cooked	6.1 g
Kidney beans, 1 cup (250 ml), cooked	6.7 g
Lentils, 1 cup (250 ml), cooked	9.0 g
Peanuts, dry roasted, 1/2 cup (125 ml)	6.9 g
Vegetables	
Broccoli, 1/2 cup (125 ml)	2.0 g
Brussels sprouts, 1/2 cup (125 ml)	2.6 g
Carrots, 1/2 cup (125 ml)	2.2 g
Corn niblets, 1/2 cup (125 ml)	2.3 g
Green peas, 1/2 cup (125 ml)	3.7 g
Lima beans, 1/2 cup (125 ml)	3.8 g
Potato, baked, 1 medium with skin	5.0 g
Sweet potato, mashed, 1/2 cup (125 ml)	3.9 g

Source: Adapted from the *Canadian Nutrient File*, Health Canada (2006)©. Adapted and reproduced with the permission of the Minister of Public Works and Government Services Canada, 2009.

Carbohydrates and Digestion

The process of carbohydrate digestion begins in your mouth: As you eat a carbohydrate meal or snack, an enzyme in saliva starts to break down starch. The food then makes its way into your stomach where gastric acid further breaks down the food. From your stomach, partially digested food enters your small intestine, where digestive enzymes are released to break down starches into smaller sugar units. Finally, vital enzymes on the surface of your intestinal cells dismantle disaccharides into their monosaccharide building blocks. (Inflammatory diseases, certain medications, hereditary factors and age can predispose us to deficiencies in some of these enzymes, most commonly lactase deficiency. People who don't produce enough lactase cannot break down the milk-sugar lactose into its two components, glucose and galactose. The result is cramping, bloating, gas and diarrhea. See page 529 for more on lactose intolerance.)

Once digested, the three monosaccharides—glucose, fructose and galactose—enter the bloodstream and make their way to the liver. Here, fructose and galactose are converted to glucose. Some glucose is used immediately for energy, while the rest is stored as glycogen, the body's storage form of carbohydrate (glucose), which the liver breaks down and releases as glucose according to your body's need for energy. When your blood-sugar level falls because you haven't eaten for a while, glucose is released so that body cells can use it to fuel metabolic reactions. But your liver is able to store only about one-third of your body's glucose. The rest is housed in your muscles as glycogen. During exercise, your body burns glycogen in order to keep muscles contracting. This is why low-carbohydrate diets can make exercise difficult: Since your muscles have low reserves of glycogen, you fatigue much sooner.

Carbohydrates and the Glycemic Index

By now it's apparent how important carbohydrate is for energy. Ultimately, all carbohydrate-rich foods end up in your bloodstream as glucose, which fuels your body's metabolic machinery. But the speed at which that glucose enters your bloodstream may affect your hunger, your weight and even your long-term health.

All carbohydrates do not raise your blood sugar in the same way. Some carbohydrate-rich foods are digested and absorbed into your bloodstream quickly, while others are broken down and converted to blood glucose more slowly. What effect does this have on your feeling of energy? Let's say you eat two slices of toast for breakfast. Bread (both white and whole-wheat) is digested relatively quickly, causing your blood glucose to rise quickly. This rapid rise in blood glucose triggers your pancreas to release an excessive amount of insulin (the hormone that regulates blood sugar), causing your blood glucose to drop to a very low level. The result is that you'll feel sluggish and tired, not to mention hungry, not long after eating the toast. Moreover, studies suggest that regularly eating foods that cause high blood-insulin levels may increase the risk of heart disease and cancer.

On the other hand, a bowl of high-fibre breakfast cereal with low-fat milk is digested and absorbed more slowly, causing a gradual rise in blood glucose. Because this meal doesn't result in a fast blood-sugar response, you don't get a surge of insulin. As a result, your blood-sugar level won't plummet. Instead you'll experience a smooth, steady blood-sugar level, leading to more consistent energy levels.

The rate at which a food causes your blood sugar to rise can be measured and assigned a value. This measure is referred to as the food's *glycemic index* value. The glycemic index (GI) is a ranking from 0 to 100, which indicates whether a food raises your blood glucose rapidly, moderately or slowly. Foods that are digested quickly and cause your blood sugar to rise rapidly have high glycemic-index values. Foods that are digested slowly, leading to a gradual rise in blood sugar, are assigned low glycemic-index values. All foods are compared with pure glucose, which is given a value of 100 (fast acting).

The glycemic index is used, and being studied, in athletics. After heavy exercise that depletes muscle carbohydrate stores (what muscles use for fuel during exercise), consuming a high-glycemic-index food such as a bagel or sugary drink is best since it will be more rapidly digested and converted to blood glucose. That means muscles will recover and rebuild their energy stores faster. Conversely, a low-glycemic-index food such as yogurt is best for a pre-workout snack since it will take longer to be converted to blood sugar. When you begin to exercise, your blood-glucose levels are starting to increase, giving your muscles energy for the workout.

The following tips will help you add low-glycemic foods to meals and snacks—and prevent large spikes in blood sugar:

- Unprocessed fresh foods such as whole grains, legumes, fruit and vegetables have a low GI value. High-glycemic foods are usually highly processed and may have a concentrated amount of sugar.
- Include at least one low-GI food per meal, or base two of your meals on low-GI choices. Use the list of foods below to help you choose low-GI foods.
- Pay attention to breads and breakfast cereals, since these foods contribute the most to the high glycemic load of our North American diet.
- Avoid eating high-GI snacks like pretzels, corn chips and rice cakes, as these can trigger hunger and overeating. Opt for fresh fruit, low-fat dairy products, nuts or plain popcorn.
- Choose fruit that is more acidic (e.g., oranges, grapefruit, cherries) as these have a low GI and will lower the glycemic load of a meal.
- Use salad dressings made from vinegar or lemon juice—the acidity will further reduce the GI of your meal.

Here's a list of foods ranked by their GI value, from lowest to highest. Use this table to plan your meals and snacks. Here's what the numbers mean:

Less than 55	Low GI
55–70	Medium GI
Greater than 70	High GI

Foods Ranked by GI Value

Food	GI Value
Bread and Crackers	
Pumpernickel bread, whole-grain	46
Cracked wheat	53
Sourdough rye bread	53
Linseed Rye, Rudolph's	55
Pita bread, white	57
Whole-meal rye bread	58
Rye crispbreads	64
Rye bread	65
Stoned Wheat Thins crackers	67
Breton crackers (original wheat)	67
Light rye, Silverstein's Bakery	68
Whole-wheat bread	69
Melba toast	70
White bread	70
Water crackers	71
Bagel, white	72
Kaiser roll	73
Enriched white bread, Wonder	73
Soda crackers	74
Rice cakes	82
Baguette, French	95

Food	GI Value
Breakfast Cereals	
All-Bran Original, Kellogg's	42
All-Bran Buds (with psyllium), Kellogg's	47
Red River Hot Cereal	49
Oat bran	50
Porridge made from steel-cut oats	52
Special K, Kellogg's	54
Porridge made from rolled oats, large flake	62
Cream of Wheat	66
Oatmeal, instant	66
Grape-Nuts, Post	71
Raisin Bran, Kellogg's	73
Bran flakes	74
Cheerios, General Mills	74
Cream of Wheat Instant	74
Corn Bran, Quaker	75
Shredded Wheat, Nestlé/Weetabix	75
Corn Flakes	81
Crispix, Kellogg's	87
Cookies, Cakes and Muffins	
Sponge cake	46
Banana bread	47
Oatmeal cookies	55
Blueberry muffin	59
Digestive biscuits	59
Oat bran muffin	60
Arrowroot cookies	65
Angel food cake	67
Oatmeal muffins, made from mix	69
Graham crackers	74

Food	GI Value
Pasta, Grains and Potatoes	
Barley	25
Fettuccine, egg	32
Spaghetti, whole-wheat	37
Spaghetti, white	41
Rice, white, converted, Uncle Ben's	45
Bulgur	46
Corn, sweet	53
Sweet potato, mashed	54
Rice, brown	55
Rice, long-grain, white	56
Rice, basmati	58
Potato, new, unpeeled, boiled	62
Couscous	65
Millet	71
Rice, short-grain	72
Potato, french fries	75
Potato, white-skinned, baked	85
Potato, instant, mashed	86
Rice, instant	87
Potato, red-skinned, boiled	88
Potato, red-skinned, mashed	91
Legumes and Nuts	
Peanuts	14
Soybeans	18
Kidney beans	27
Lentils	30
Black beans	31
Lentil soup, canned	34
Chickpeas, canned	42

Food	GI Value
Baked beans	48
Black bean soup	64
Split pea soup	66
Fruit and Unsweetened Juices	
Cherries	22
Grapefruit	25
Peach	28
Apricot, dried	31
Apple	34
Pear	38
Tomato juice	38
Apple juice	40
Orange	42
Grapes	43
Orange juice	46
Mango	51
Banana	52
Kiwi fruit	53
Pineapple	59
Raisins	64
Cantaloupe	65
Watermelon	72
Dates, dried	103
Milk Products and Milk Alternatives	
Yogurt, low-fat, aspartame	14
Milk, whole	27
Milk, skim	32
Soy beverage, full-fat	33
Yogurt, low-fat, sugar	33
Milk, chocolate	34

Food	GI Value
Ice cream, premium	39
Soy beverage, low-fat	44
Ice cream, regular	61
Tofu-based frozen dessert	115
Snack Foods and Sugary Drinks	
Potato chips	54
Popcorn	55
Cola	58
Energy bar, PowerBar, chocolate	58
Corn chips	72
Gatorade	78
Pretzels	83
Sugars	
Fructose (fruit sugar)	23
Lactose (milk sugar)	46
Honey	58
Sucrose (table sugar)	65
Glucose	100

Source: Foster-Powell, K, et al. International tables of glycemic index and glycemic load values: 2002. *American Journal of Clinical Nutrition* 2002, 76(1):5–56.

Carbohydrates and Weight Control

After reading about the importance of carbohydrate, you might be wondering why some fad diets shun them. Low-carbohydrate plans recommend eliminating or drastically reducing carbohydrates from your diet for a period in order to help you lose weight. Many of these diets claim that carbohydrates make you fat. However, carbohydrate-rich foods will make you gain weight *only* if you're eating a lot of them, or if you're slathering them with high-fat spreads or sauces.

It is true, however, that many people today overeat carbohydrates—high-carbohydrate foods are often fast, portable and fat free. And they're often served up in super-sized portions. Yet, although they contain very little fat, dense bagels, fat-free muffins, pretzels and bowls of pasta all add calories to your diet. Often, fat-reduced foods are not much lower in calories than the original version. Did you know that a large bagel is the equivalent of four to six slices of bread? Or that twenty pretzel sticks are equivalent to two slices? Even that restaurant portion of pasta with tomato sauce is probably worth at least four slices of bread (not to mention the bread you might eat with it!). And here's a shocker: One slice of pizza from the local walk-in pizzeria can have as much carbohydrate as seven slices of bread. When it comes to weight control, eating large portions of carbohydrates can add on the pounds, just as protein and fat can.

Added Sugars and Weight Control

Recently, added sugars have been blamed for our expanding waistlines. A steady intake of sugary foods such as sweets, candy and sugary drinks adds a surplus of calories to your diet, extra calories that sedentary folks don't burn off. And most people don't compensate for excess calories in sugary beverages by eating less food.

Added sugars are those that are added to foods during processing and preparation. They're not to be confused with naturally occurring sugars, such as lactose in milk and yogurt and fructose in fruit and sweet vegetables. Manufacturers add sugars to foods for reasons that go beyond making them taste sweet. Sugars act a preservative, enhance flavour, add bulk and texture, and aid in the browning of foods.

The most controversial added sugar is high-fructose corn syrup, an inexpensive sweetener that's added to soft drinks, fruit drinks, baked goods and canned fruit. Researchers have linked our increased use of corn syrup sweeteners over the past 20 years to rising obesity rates. This correlation doesn't prove that high-fructose corn syrup causes weight gain. But some experts contend that our body processes fructose in high-fructose corn syrup differently than glucose in cane or beet sugar. Fructose doesn't trigger hormone responses that regulate appetite and satiety, which could trick you into overeating.

Not all experts agree that our intake of high-fructose corn syrup, or any particular added sugar for that matter, is driving the obesity epidemic. Although high-fructose corn syrup might be a contributor, the real problem lies with how much added sugar we're consuming. Serving sizes of sugar-packed beverages have steadily increased from a 6.5 ounce (192 ml) serving in the 1950s to our current 20 ounce (591 ml) bottles. Super-sized sugary drinks are widely accessible in convenience stores, gas stations, movie theatres, restaurants and vending machines. Our increased reliance on processed, prepackaged foods also bumps up our intake of refined sugars.

Carbohydrates and Diabetes

It is a common misconception that consuming too much sugar will cause diabetes. As you'll read on page 343, diabetes is a disease caused by genetic and lifestyle factors. It occurs when the body doesn't produce enough insulin or doesn't use it properly. As a result, rather than entering blood cells, glucose builds up in the bloodstream and is excreted in urine, thus depriving body cells of their main source of fuel.

People with diabetes must carefully manage their carbohydrate intake. Meals need to be regularly scheduled and contain measured portions of carbohydrate foods. And contrary to what many people think, people with diabetes are allowed to eat a little bit of sugar.

Carbohydrates and Dental Caries

Dental caries is the medical term for tooth decay or cavities—and this is where sugar is a culprit. In the mouth, the enzyme amylase begins breaking down starch into smaller units of starch and the disaccharide maltose. Bacteria in the mouth then ferment starch and sugars and, in the process, produce an acid that erodes tooth enamel. The longer carbohydrate foods stay in the mouth, the greater the chance that cavities will form. Sticky foods like candy and fruit leather adhere to the teeth and will keep acid-yielding bacteria in action longer. Snacking on carbohydrate-rich foods regularly throughout the day will keep the bacteria working, too.

Eating non-sugary foods can help remove carbohydrate from the surface of your teeth. This is why, as you may have heard, eating cheese can help prevent cavities. Rinsing your mouth and brushing your teeth after eating are important strategies to help prevent dental caries.

How Much Carbohydrate Should You Eat?

Here's what you should be striving for each day:

1. Forty-five to 65 percent of your daily calories should come from carbohydrate-containing foods. This means that foods like legumes, grains, vegetables and fruit should make up one-half to two-thirds of your plate.
2. As often as possible, choose whole grains: starchy foods that have not been refined and retain important minerals, vitamins, antioxidants and fibre. (You'll read more about whole grains in Chapter 5, page 89.) Choose 100% whole-wheat bread including the germ, whole rye or whole-grain pumpernickel bread, brown rice, whole-wheat pasta, quinoa and breakfast cereals made from whole grains.
3. Limit your intake of sugary foods like candy, chocolate, soft drinks, fruit drinks, desserts and other sweets. The World Health Organization recommends that we limit added sugars to no more than 10 percent of daily calories. If you follow a 2000-calorie diet, this translates to a daily maximum of 48 grams (12 teaspoons) of added sugars.
4. Depending on your age and gender, strive to include 21 to 38 grams of dietary fibre in your daily diet (see page 320 for fibre intake recommendations). If you're like the average Canadian, you're consuming roughly 14 grams of fibre per day. Gradually add more fibre into your diet. The list of fibre-containing foods on page 4 will help you do so.
5. Remember that fibre needs fluid to work. Be sure to consume at least 1 cup (250 ml) of water with fibre-rich meals and snacks. See page 98 to learn more about how much water you need each day.

2

Protein and Amino Acids

It may be hard to believe that our ancient ancestors got most of their protein from vegetables. Animal foods entered our diet only 2.5 million years ago—a short while back in our evolutionary history. Today, foods like steak, burgers, chicken breast, eggs and dairy products occupy a central part of our dinner plates. These foods are rich in protein and supply a fair share of our daily protein intake.

Protein is essential for life. It's used to make many critical body compounds. Proteins form structural components in the body—muscle tissue, connective tissue and the support tissue inside bones—and are all derived from the protein we eat. Many of these body proteins are in a continual state of breakdown, repair and maintenance. If your diet is chronically low in protein, protein rebuilding slows down.

Body Proteins

Our bodies use proteins to produce hormones and enzymes. For example, thyroid hormones, which control metabolic rate, and insulin, which controls blood sugar, are made from proteins. Enzymes, functioning as catalysts, control virtually all chemical reactions in your cells.

Meeting your daily protein requirements also keeps your immune system in shape. Protein is used to make antibodies, white blood cells and other immune compounds that attack foreign invaders and prevent infection. Other proteins in your blood help maintain your body's fluid balance.

Your body uses protein for energy, too. In Chapter 1 I told you about the important role carbohydrate plays in providing glucose (energy) to all body tissues. If your diet doesn't supply enough carbohydrate, your liver is forced to use protein to make glucose. Metabolizing protein into glucose for energy is a normal process—it occurs when you skip a meal or don't eat for a long period. But if your usual diet is low in carbohydrate and calories, your body will break down muscle and other important body proteins to make glucose. The result can be muscle wasting, a slower metabolism and a weakened immune system.

Dietary Protein

Proteins are made up of building blocks called amino acids. There are twenty amino acids, all of which are necessary for good health. Eleven of these can be synthesized by your body and are therefore called nonessential amino acids. The remaining nine, however, must be supplied by food as your body either cannot synthesize them on its own or cannot synthesize them in sufficient quantities. They are called essential amino acids.

Essential Amino Acids	Nonessential Amino Acids
Histidine	Alanine
Isoleucine	Arginine
Leucine	Asparagine
Lysine	Aspartic acid
Methionine	Cysteine
Phenylalanine	Glutamic acid
Threonine	Glutamine
Tryptophan	Glycine
Valine	Proline
Serine	
Tyrosine	

If your diet does not supply enough essential amino acids, your body's rate of protein building will slow down. Eventually your body will break down its own protein to get these amino acids.

Animal and plant proteins have very different amino-acid profiles. Animal protein foods contain all the essential amino acids in sufficient quantities to support growth, repair and maintenance of body tissues. For this reason, animal proteins are considered complete proteins, or high-quality proteins. Plant proteins, on the other hand, are always low, or limited, in one or more of the nine essential amino acids. In some cases, a plant food may even be lacking an essential amino acid completely. The proteins from plant foods are considered incomplete proteins, or low-quality proteins.

Complementary Proteins

Many of us eat enough protein to get ample amounts of essential amino acids. But what about those who follow a strict vegetarian (vegan) diet? We used to think that vegetarians had to take care to combine their vegetarian protein foods at each meal so that the essential amino acid missing from one was supplied by another. When two or more vegetarian protein foods are combined in this way, they are called complementary proteins. The following table lists limited amino acids, the amino acids that occur in the shortest supply relative to the amount needed by the body, and offers some suggestions for complete protein meals. For instance, you'll see below that tofu (made from soybeans) doesn't provide enough methionine to meet the body's requirements. By eating tofu with brown rice (or nuts and seeds), which provide plenty of methionine, you'll end up with a complete protein meal.

We now know that as long as vegetarians eat a variety of vegetarian proteins over the course of the day, they'll meet their requirements for essential amino acids. A protein deficiency will develop, however, when grains, fruit and vegetables make up the core of the diet, severely shortchanging the quantity and quality of protein.

However, it's important for children to have combined proteins in the same meal. To support growth and development, infants and preschoolers need 35 percent of their daily protein from essential amino acids. The meals of young vegetarians must be carefully planned to ensure they get all the essential amino acids they need.

Complementary Vegetarian Proteins

Food	Limiting Amino Acids	Food to Combine	Complete Protein Meal Ideas
Legumes, soybeans	Methionine	Grains, nuts, seeds	Tofu and brown rice stir-fry
Grains	Lysine, threonine	Legumes	Pasta with white kidney beans
Nuts and seeds	Lysine	Legumes	Hummus with tahini (sesame seed paste)
Vegetables	Methionine	Grains, nuts, seeds	Bok choy with cashews
Corn	Lysine, tryptophan	Legumes	Black bean and corn salad

How Much Protein Do You Need?

As adults, we need to consume enough protein each day to make up for the amount our bodies lose through urine, skin, hair and nails. However, eating more than your daily requirements will result in excess protein being stored as body fat (not muscle!). Here's a look at your daily protein requirements.

Daily Protein Requirements for Healthy Adults

No regular exercise	0.86 gram per kilogram body weight
Regular exercise	1.2–1.7 grams per kilogram body weight
Elderly adults	0.8–1.0 gram per kilogram body weight

To calculate your actual daily protein requirements, multiply your weight (in kilograms) by your RDA of protein. If you exercise regularly, you'll need to eat more protein to compensate for that used up as energy. For example, a 135 pound (61 kg) woman who doesn't exercise needs 52 grams of protein each day (61 kg × 0.86). If that same woman jogged three or four times a week, she would need to eat 73 grams of protein per day (61 kg × 1.2). If you're a 180 pound (82 kg) male who works out with weights regularly, you need to consume 139 grams of protein each day (82 kg × 1.7).

Protein Content of Foods

Food	Protein (grams)
Meat, 3 oz (90 g)	21–25 g
Poultry, 3 oz (90 g)	21 g
Salmon, 3 oz (90 g)	25 g
Sole, 3 oz (90 g)	17 g
Tuna, canned, drained, 1/2 cup (125 ml)	30 g
Egg, whole, 1	6 g
Legumes, cooked, 1/2 cup (125 ml)	8 g
Milk, 1 cup (250 ml)	8 g
Yogurt, 3/4 cup (175 ml)	8 g
Cheese, cheddar, 1 oz (30 g)	10 g
Vegetables, 1/2 cup (125 ml)	2 g
Bread, 1 slice	2 g
Rice or pasta, cooked, 1/2 cup (125 ml)	2 g

Source: Adapted from the *Canadian Nutrient File*, Health Canada (2006)©. Adapted and reproduced with the permission of the Minister of Public Works and Government Services Canada, 2009.

For most of us, getting too little protein is likely not a problem. It's estimated that the average North American male consumes 105 grams of protein each day, while the average female consumes about 65 grams. Individuals at risk for protein deficiency include:

- those who live alone and don't often cook meat, chicken or fish
- those who frequently grab a quick meal during the day—bagels, pasta, low-fat frozen dinners
- those who skimp on calories in an effort to lose weight
- vegetarians who don't eat animal foods and don't incorporate high-quality vegetable protein sources into their daily diet
- those who engage in heavy exercise and fall into any of the above categories

At certain stages in the life cycle, the body's protein needs will increase. During pregnancy, women must eat an additional 25 grams of protein per day during the second and third trimesters. Women who are exclusively breast-feeding need to consume an additional 25 grams of protein each day—and more if they also exercise regularly. In Chapter 5, page 111, you'll find a food guide that will help you choose the right amount of protein-rich foods each day.

3

Dietary Fats and Oils

You might be surprised to learn that, when it comes to health, dietary fat actually has some virtues. In fact, some types of fat may ward off heart disease and cancer while others may ease the symptoms of arthritis and depression. It's when our diet contains too little or too much fat that ill health occurs. Today, Canadians continue to consume too many unhealthy and too few healthy fats. However, we're doing better than we were 20 years ago. Over the years, as we've been bombarded by news reports of cholesterol and heart disease, fat and obesity, our intake of unhealthy fats has decreased.

Triglycerides, made up of building blocks called *fatty acids*, are the major form of fats in our food and bodies. Fat, once consumed, is broken down into its fatty acid building blocks by digestive enzymes in the intestine. These fatty acids are then absorbed into the bloodstream, making their way to the liver, where they are repackaged into triglyceride molecules and transported to body tissues. Enzymes in cells break down these circulating triglycerides so that their fatty acids can enter the cells. Some fatty acids are used immediately for energy, while the remaining fatty acids are reformed into triglycerides and stored as body fat (adipose tissue).

Fat has many important roles. Body fat acts as a layer of insulation protecting our major organs. Stores of body fat provide a vital source of energy for the body. In fact, about half of our daily energy requirements are supplied by stored fat. Fatty acids released from muscle cells provide most of the fuel for light activity. The body's ability to store fat is almost unlimited. Fat cells can increase in size if we consume more fat than we need, and our bodies can also form new fat cells if our existing ones can't expand any further. Although stored body fat gives cells the energy they need, storing too much fat is not healthy.

Dietary fat supplies us with the fat-soluble vitamins A, D, E and K, adds flavour to foods and helps us feel satisfied after eating a meal. Because dietary fat empties from the stomach slowly, it imparts satiety, or a feeling of fullness.

Fatty acids in food consist of long chains of carbon molecules linked together, which in turn are bonded to hydrogen atoms. Each type of fatty acid has a particular chemical structure that determines how it will behave in the body. For instance, when a fatty acid is completely full of hydrogen atoms, it's considered a *saturated* fatty acid. Animal fat contains mostly saturated fatty acids. Fatty acids not saturated with hydrogen atoms, found primarily in vegetable oils and fish, are either *monounsaturated* or *polyunsaturated*. Food fats almost always contain both saturated and unsaturated fatty acids and are classified as saturated, monounsaturated or polyunsaturated depending on which fatty acids are present in the greatest concentration.

Saturated Fats

Animal foods—meat, poultry, eggs and dairy products—all contain saturated fat. Saturated fat also occurs in some plant foods, including coconut oil, coconut milk, palm kernel oil, cocoa butter and palm oil. Also called tropical oils, palm oil, palm kernel oil and coconut oil are not sold on grocery store shelves; instead they're used as ingredients in packaged foods like crackers, cookies, ice cream and non-dairy creamers.

Eating a diet high in saturated fat is widely believed to contribute to the development and progression of coronary heart disease. Many studies have consistently shown that high intakes of saturated fat raise the level of LDL (bad) blood cholesterol, a major risk factor for heart disease. Saturated fat inhibits the ability of your cells to clear cholesterol from the bloodstream.

There are many types of saturated fats, and researchers are learning that they don't all influence blood cholesterol to the same degree. For instance, the saturated fat in dairy products raises cholesterol higher than does that in meat. And the type of saturated fat found in chocolate (stearic acid) does not raise blood-cholesterol levels at all. What's more, the type of saturated fat in coconut and palm oil boosts total blood cholesterol, mostly due to its ability to increase HDL (good) cholesterol.

It's not important that you know the different types of saturated fats. What is important is that you eat only a small amount of saturated fat. It should account for less than 10 percent of your daily calories. Choosing lower-fat animal foods will help you achieve that goal. But you also need to pay attention to portion sizes. A portion size of lean meat shouldn't exceed 3 oz (90 g).

Use the following chart to help you choose foods lower in saturated fat.

Foods Lower in Saturated Fat

Food	Total Fat (grams)	Sat. Fat (grams)
Dairy Products		
Cheddar cheese, low-fat, 7% MF, 1 oz (30 g)	2.0 g	1.2 g
Cottage cheese, 1% MF, 1/2 cup (125 ml)	1.1 g	0.8 g
Cottage cheese, fat-free, 1/2 cup (125 ml)	0.5 g	0.3 g
Frozen yogurt, vanilla, 5.6% MF, 1/2 cup (125 ml)	4.0 g	2.5 g
Milk, 1% MF, 1 cup (250 ml)	2.5 g	1.7 g
Milk, skim, 0.1% MF, 1 cup (250 ml)	0.5 g	0.3 g
Mozzarella cheese, part-skim, 16.5% MF, 1 oz (30 g)	4.6 g	2.9 g
Meat and Poultry		
Beef, steak, eye of round, grilled, 3 oz (90 g)	7.7 g	2.7 g
Beef, steak, inside round, grilled, 3 oz (90 g)	3.9 g	1.4 g
Beef, steak, strip loin, broiled, 3 oz (90 g)	9.2 g	3.5 g
Beef, steak, top sirloin, grilled, 3 oz (90 g)	6.8 g	2.6 g
Beef, tenderloin, roasted, 3 oz (90 g)	7.3 g	2.3 g
Ground beef patty, extra lean, broiled, 3 oz (90 g)	7.8 g	2.1 g
Pork, back (peameal) bacon, grilled, 3 oz (90 g)	7.5 g	2.5 g
Pork, ham, lean (5% fat), 3 oz (90 g)	4.8 g	1.6 g
Pork, tenderloin, roasted, 3 oz (90 g)	3.2 g	1.0 g
Veal, grain-fed, cutlets, pan-fried, 3 oz (90 g)	2.5 g	0.8 g
Veal, grain-fed, loin chop, lean, broiled, 3 oz (90 g)	5.7 g	2.4 g
Veal, ground, broiled, 3 oz (90 g)	6.8 g	2.7 g
Veal, sirloin, roasted, 3 oz (90 g)	5.6 g	2.2 g
Chicken, dark meat, roasted, skinless, 3 oz (90 g)	8.7 g	2.4 g
Chicken, white meat, roasted, skinless, 3 oz (90 g)	4.0 g	1.1 g
Chicken breast, skinless, roasted, 3 oz (90 g)	1.9 g	0.6 g

Food	Total Fat (grams)	Sat. Fat (grams)
Turkey, dark meat, roasted, skinless, 3 oz (90 g)	2.7 g	0.9 g
Turkey, white meat, roasted, skinless, 3 oz (90 g)	0.9 g	0.2 g
Eggs		
Egg, whole, 1 large	5.3 g	1.6 g
Egg, whites only, 2 large	0.0 g	0.0 g

Source: Adapted from the *Canadian Nutrient File*, Health Canada (2006)©. Adapted and reproduced with the permission of the Minister of Public Works and Government Services Canada, 2009.

Polyunsaturated Fats

Vegetable oils supply us with most of our polyunsaturated fats. There are two types of polyunsaturated fats in foods. Omega-6 polyunsaturated fats are found in all cooking oils, including soybean, sunflower, safflower, corn and sesame. Omega-3 polyunsaturated fats are found in certain oils (flaxseed, walnut and canola), as well as in fish and shellfish. Replacing foods high in saturated fats with those rich in polyunsaturated fats will have a blood cholesterol–lowering effect—primarily because you're eating less saturated fat.

Essential Fatty Acids

Cooking oils rich in omega-3 and omega-6 fatty acids provide our bodies with two very important fatty acids they cannot produce on their own. Omega-3 oils provide *alpha-linolenic acid*, while omega-6 oils give us *linoleic acid*. These two essential fatty acids help form vital body structures and cell membranes, aid in immune function and vision, and produce powerful hormone-like compounds called eicosanoids. Without them, we would not be able to maintain good health.

The ability of alpha-linolenic acid and linoleic acid to produce eicosanoids plays an important role in health. Eicosanoids regulate our blood, immune system and hormones. Prostaglandins (you'll read about their role in health throughout the book), prostacyclins, thromboxanes and leukotrienes all belong to the eicosanoid family. The type of fat you eat determines which kind of eicosanoids your body produces. For instance, linoleic acid from omega-6 oils is used to synthesize "unfriendly" eicosanoids that cause inflammation and pain. Alpha-linolenic acid in omega-3 oils, on the other hand, produces "friendly" eicosanoids that tend to decrease inflammation and blood clotting and are thought to help prevent heart disease, ease symptoms of rheumatoid arthritis and influence brain function. (Omega-3 fatty acids in fish oil also lead to the body's production of anti-inflammatory eicosanoids.) These two essential fatty acids compete with each other for the same metabolic pathways. So if you eat a diet that contains primarily omega-6 oils, the unfriendly eicosanoids will win. If your diet is rich in omega-3 oils, more health-enhancing eicosanoids will form. It's estimated that the average Canadian currently consumes ten to twenty times more omega-6s than omega-3s. We should be consuming a ratio of 4:1 omega-6 to omega-3 fats.

Omega-3 Fats in Fish

Fish oils contain two omega-3 fatty acids: docosahexanaenoic acid (DHA) and eicosapentaenoic acid (EPA). These special fats help lower blood triglycerides, make the blood less likely to form clots, reduce inflammation and protect against irregular heartbeats that can cause sudden cardiac death. There's even evidence that fish oil can help blood vessels relax, preventing increases in blood pressure. Numerous studies have found that populations that consume fish a few times a week have lower rates of heart disease. In fact, it's estimated that eating one to two servings of fish per week is enough to reduce the risk of dying from heart attack by 36 percent. That's why Health Canada and the Heart and Stroke Foundation of Canada advise that we eat fish twice per week.

The best sources of DHA and EPA are oily fish such as salmon, trout, Arctic char, sardines, mackerel and herring. The body also produces some DHA and EPA from foods rich in alpha-linolenic acid such as flaxseed oil, canola oil, walnuts, soybeans, whole grains and leafy greens. But researchers believe that the body converts alpha-linolenic acid to DHA and EPA inefficiently, especially when the diet is rich in omega-6 fats, since these slow down the conversion process.

The health benefits of omega-3s and fish oil supplements are discussed in more detail in Chapter 8, page 162.

Monounsaturated Fats

Monounsaturated fats found in olive, canola and peanut oils and avocado are considered healthy fats. Substituting them for saturated fats can lower high levels of blood cholesterol, since your intake of saturated fat will decrease. Some studies suggest that extra-virgin olive oil helps prevent blood clots from forming and acts as an antioxidant to help protect against heart disease. Extra-virgin olive oil has been processed the least (hence the dark green colour) and contains more protective plant compounds than regular or light olive oil. Olive oil also has anti-inflammatory properties in the body, thanks to a phytochemical called oleocanthal.

Trans Fats

Trans fat is formed by partial hydrogenation, a chemical process in which hydrogen atoms are added to liquid vegetable oils. The oils become more solid and therefore more useful to food manufacturers. Packaged foods like cookies, crackers, pastries and muffins made with partially hydrogenated vegetable oils are more palatable and have a longer shelf life. Margarine made by hydro-genating a vegetable oil is firm, like butter.

Not only does partial hydrogenation make a vegetable oil more saturated and destroy the oil's essential fatty acids, the process forms a new type of fat called trans fat. Trans fats increase levels of LDL (bad) cholesterol and decrease levels of HDL (good) cholesterol, conditions that are both strongly linked to a greater risk of heart disease. Studies also indicate that a steady intake of trans fats can trigger inflammation in the body, disrupt the normal functioning of blood vessel walls and impair how the body uses insulin. Compared with saturated fats, trans fats are linked with a 2.5- to 10-fold higher risk of heart disease.

In 2002, the U.S. Institute of Medicine of the National Academies recom-mended that our intake of trans fat be as low as possible. This panel of experts did not set a safe upper intake because any increase in trans fat boosts the risk of heart disease. A year later, the World Health Organization advised that our trans fat intake be limited to a mere 1 percent of daily calories. Health Canada advises we keep trans fat plus saturated fat to a maximum of 10 percent of our daily calorie intake. If you consume 2000 calories per day, this means reducing your daily intake of trans and saturated fat combined to 20 grams at most.

Limiting or avoiding trans fat is getting easier to do in Canada. Mandatory nutrition labelling has forced food manufacturers to list the grams of trans fat on the Nutrition Facts box. Heightened consumer awareness has prompted many—but not yet all—food manufacturers and restaurant chains to reduce or eliminate trans fat from foods. Despite the progress, some baked goods, instant noodles, puddings, baby foods, pastries, microwave popcorn, hard margarines and shortenings still harbour this cholesterol-raising fat. That's why Health

Canada and the Heart and Stroke Foundation of Canada have proposed regulations for reducing trans fat in our food supply. The Trans Fat Task Force recommended that trans fat be limited to 2 percent of total fat in all vegetable oils and soft, spreadable margarines sold to consumers or used in restaurants. In other foods, trans fat should be no more than 5 percent of total fat.[1]

The Canadian government accepted these recommendations in June 2007 and called on the food industry to achieve these limits by June 2009. If significant progress had not been made by this date, Health Canada promised to develop regulations to ensure that the recommended levels would be met. From 2007 to 2009, the government has conducted three analyses of a wide variety of restaurant foods, fast foods and prepackaged foods to ensure that trans fat levels are declining. The third report, released in February 2009, concluded that food manufacturers and restaurant chains have reformulated their products and are not exceeding the trans fat limit. At that time, only 59 percent of baked goods sampled from coffee shops and doughnut shops met the criteria.

The easiest way to reduce your intake of trans fat is to pay attention to food labels. Roughly 90 percent of the trans fat in our food supply is found in cookies, cakes, pastries, doughnuts, snack foods, fried fast foods and some brands of margarine. In fact, trans fats in some of these foods may contribute as much as 45 percent of the total fat content.

- Scan the Nutrition Facts box to choose food products with little or no trans fat. You'll find the grams of trans fat listed per one serving of the food. More useful, however, is the Daily Value (DV) for saturated plus trans fat combined, which is written as a percentage. This value tells you whether there is a little or a lot of these cholesterol-raising fats in a food. The DV for saturated plus trans fat is set by Health Canada at 20 grams.
- If a packaged food does not have a Nutrition Facts box, as may be the case for foods prepared in store, read the ingredient list. Avoid buying foods that list partially hydrogenated vegetable oil, hydrogenated vegetable oil and shortening.
- If you plan on eating at a fast food or family-style restaurant, check the company's website in advance. Most fast food outlets and some family-style chain restaurants post the nutrient content of their menu items. When you're dining out, if you're uncertain, ask what kind of oil is used in cooking the food.
- If you eat margarine, choose one made with non-hydrogenated fat. This is often stated right on the label.

Dietary Cholesterol

This wax-like fatty substance is found in meat, poultry, eggs, dairy products and seafood. It's particularly plentiful in shrimp, liver and egg yolks. While high-cholesterol diets cause high blood cholesterol in animals, this is not the case in humans. Dietary cholesterol has little or no effect on most healthy people's blood cholesterol. One reason for this is that our intestines absorb only half the cholesterol we eat. The rest is excreted in the stool. Our bodies are also very efficient at secreting cholesterol into bile stored in the gallbladder. This means there's less cholesterol available for transport in your blood.

Nevertheless, too much dietary cholesterol can raise levels of LDL cholesterol in some people, especially those with hereditary forms of high blood cholesterol. People with diabetes may also be more efficient at absorbing cholesterol from foods and should control their intake. Health Canada recommends that we consume no more than 300 milligrams of cholesterol each day. If you already have high blood cholesterol, the American Heart Association advises consuming less than 200 milligrams of cholesterol each day.

Choosing animal foods that are lower in saturated fat will also help cut down on dietary cholesterol. Here's how various foods stack up in terms of cholesterol.

Cholesterol Content of Selected Foods

Food	Cholesterol (milligrams)
1 egg, whole	190 mg
1 egg, white only	0 mg
Beef sirloin, lean only, 3 oz (90 g)	64 mg
Calf's liver, fried, 3 oz (90 g)	416 mg
Pork loin, lean only, 3 oz (90 g)	71 mg
Chicken breast, no skin, 3 oz (90 g)	73 mg
Salmon, 3 oz (90 g)	54 mg
Shrimp, 3 oz (90 g)	135 mg
Milk, 2% MF, 1 cup (250 ml)	19 mg
Milk, skim, 1 cup (250 ml)	5 mg

Food	Cholesterol (milligrams)
Cheese, cheddar, 31% MF, 1 oz (30 g)	31 mg
Cheese, mozzarella, part-skim, 1 oz (30 g)	18 mg
Cream, half and half, 12% MF, 2 tbsp (30 ml)	12 mg
Yogurt, 1.5% MF, 3/4 cup (175 ml)	11 mg
Butter, 1 tsp (5 ml)	10 mg

Source: Adapted from the *Canadian Nutrient File*, Health Canada (2006)©. Adapted and reproduced with the permission of the Minister of Public Works and Government Services Canada, 2009.

How Much and What Kind of Fat Should You Eat?

Nutrition guidelines emphasize the importance of cutting back on saturated and trans fat. But you also need to ensure that you're getting essential fatty acids and omega-3 oils found in fish. To meet these recommendations, practise the following:

- Aim for a total fat intake between 20 percent and 35 percent of your daily calories to help meet daily energy and nutritional needs while reducing the risk for chronic disease. This doesn't mean that each food you eat must be low in fat. You can make up for eating one high-fat food by including plenty of low-fat foods in other meals.
- Reduce your intake of saturated and trans fats—they should contribute no more than 10 percent of your daily calories (e.g., 20 grams for a 2000-calorie diet). When choosing animal foods, make a habit of opting for those that are lower in fat. Leaner cuts of poultry and meat include skinless chicken, extra-lean ground chicken or turkey, sirloin, tenderloin, and top round and flank steak. Instead of regular full-fat cheese (31% MF), use 1% or non-fat cottage cheese, part-skim hard cheese (less than 20% MF), or skim milk cheese (7% MF or less). Vegetarian protein foods such as legumes and soy foods have very little saturated fat; try to make more of your meals vegetarian.
- To limit your intake of trans fat, read nutrition labels. Reduce your consumption of processed foods such as crackers, cookies, snack foods and toaster pastries since these foods supply most of the trans fat we consume.

- Keep your daily cholesterol intake to no more than 300 milligrams. If you have high blood cholesterol, limit your intake to 200 milligrams. If you have diabetes, research suggests it's prudent to limit your intake of egg yolks to four per week. (Egg whites are cholesterol free.)
- Eat fatty fish two times a week for its heart-protective omega-3 fats, DHA and EPA. Salmon, trout, sardines, herring, anchovies and Arctic char are good choices. You'll learn more about the health benefits of fish along with quick meal suggestions in Chapter 5, page 92.
- Meet your daily requirements for essential fatty acids by including 2 to 3 tablespoons (30 to 45 ml) of unsaturated oil in your daily diet. Include oils rich in the omega-3 fatty acid alpha-linolenic acid (ALA), such as canola, walnut and flaxseed oils. Omega-6 oils are widespread in processed foods, so most people don't have a problem meeting daily requirements for linoleic acid.

Understanding Vitamins and Minerals

Eat right, live well—so the saying goes. Your body needs more than forty-five nutrients to stay healthy. A diet that's low in fat and rich in vegetables, fruit and whole grains will give you all the vitamins and minerals you need, while offering many other natural compounds, like fibre and phytochemicals, that help your body fight disease. Yet, despite the wealth of information available on the benefits of eating healthily, many Canadians aren't getting enough vitamins and minerals in their diets. The following guide will help you choose the foods and supplements that are brimming with protective vitamins and minerals. In Chapter 5, you'll read more about the benefits of supplementing your diet with a daily vitamin and mineral pill.

Because of the lack of data needed to calculate a *recommended dietary allowance (RDA)* of some vitamins, scientists have instead established a daily *adequate intake (AI)*. Some nutrients also have been assigned an *upper daily limit*, which is the highest level of intake likely to pose no risk of adverse health effects for almost all people (adults and children).

The Vitamins

Vitamins are essential substances needed by the body in small amounts for normal growth, function and maintenance of healthy tissues. Without vitamins, we would succumb to deficiency diseases such as scurvy, rickets, pellagra and beriberi. But as scientists are learning, vitamins may also help ward off chronic conditions like heart disease, osteoporosis and certain cancers.

Since the body is not able to synthesize vitamins, they must be supplied from foods—plant or animal. Vitamins don't supply the body directly with energy. Instead, they participate in metabolic processes that generate energy for the body. Each of the thirteen vitamins has its own special role to play in maintaining health. Some vitamins dissolve in fat, others dissolve in water. Fat-soluble vitamins such as A, D, E and K are not readily excreted from the body. This means that large doses of fat-soluble vitamins have the potential to accumulate in the body and cause toxic reactions. The water-soluble vitamins, consisting of the family of Bs and C, on the other hand, are easily eliminated from the body. With the exception of vitamin B6, water-soluble vitamins have less potential to cause toxic reactions when taken in large doses because the body excretes what it doesn't need.

Because vitamins are organic, they can break down and lose their effectiveness, so cook and store your foods with care to preserve their vitamin content.

Vitamin A

Vitamin A has many important roles in the body. It supports cell growth and development; maintains healthy skin, hair, nails, bones and teeth; and supports the immune system. It's also needed for night and colour vision.

Vitamin A is found preformed in certain animal foods and also is derived from plant foods that contain beta carotene. Once consumed, some beta carotene is converted to vitamin A by the liver. Foods high in beta carotene may help prevent heart disease, cataracts, macular degeneration and possibly lung cancer. However, no official dietary requirement for beta carotene has been established as it's not considered an essential nutrient.

Recommended Dietary Allowance (RDA) of Vitamin A

Age	RDA (micrograms)
1–3 years	300 mcg
4–8 years	400 mcg
9–13 years	600 mcg
Boys, 14–18 years	900 mcg
Girls, 14–18 years	700 mcg

Age	RDA (micrograms)
Men, 19+ years	900 mcg
Women, 19+ years	700 mcg
Pregnancy	770 mcg
Breastfeeding	1300 mcg

Upper Daily Limits of Vitamin A

Age	Upper Daily Limit (micrograms)
1–3 years	600 mcg
4–8 years	900 mcg
9–13 years	1700 mcg
Boys, 14–18 years	2800 mcg
Girls, 14–18 years	2800 mcg
19+ years	3000 mcg

To date, an official recommended dietary intake for beta carotene has not been established. Experts contend that consuming 3 to 6 milligrams of beta carotene daily will maintain blood levels of beta carotene in the range that's associated with a lower risk of chronic diseases. A diet that provides 7 to 10 servings of fruit and vegetables per day and includes one bright-orange vegetable—such as carrots, sweet potato or winter squash—daily should provide sufficient beta carotene as well as other carotenoids.

Vitamin A in Foods

The best sources of vitamin A are calf's liver, oily fish, milk, cheese, butter and egg yolks. Beta carotene is found in orange and dark-green produce such as carrots, sweet potato, winter squash, broccoli, collard greens, kale, spinach, apricots, cantaloupe, peaches, nectarines, mango and papaya.

Vitamin A Supplements

Except in special circumstances, taking vitamin A supplements is not recommended. In particular, people with liver disease should not take vitamin A supplements. High dose vitamin A supplements have also been linked with a greater risk of bone loss and hip fracture. Because vitamin A is fat-soluble, the body stores it; taking too much vitamin A for a period of time can be toxic. Your diet and a one-a-day multivitamin will provide all the vitamin A you need. Pregnant women should avoid taking too much vitamin A since high doses may increase the risk of birth defects. Prenatal multivitamin and mineral formulas are safe because they have less vitamin A than regular multis.

There's also no reason to take a beta carotene supplement. Studies have found no evidence that beta carotene in pill form reduces the risk of heart disease or cancer. In fact, taking high dose beta carotene supplements (20 to 50 milligrams per day) may increase lung cancer risk if you're a smoker.

Many multivitamin and mineral supplements provide 0.5 to 5.5 milligrams of beta carotene per tablet, which is considered safe for smokers.

B Vitamins

Thiamin (Vitamin B1)

Our bodies need thiamin, one of the eight vitamins in the B family, for energy metabolism. Thiamin, or vitamin B1, also maintains normal appetite and nerve function.

Recommended Dietary Allowance (RDA) of Thiamin

Age	RDA (milligrams)
1–3 years	0.5 mg
4–8 years	0.6 mg
9–13 years	0.9 mg
Boys, 14–18 years	1.2 mg
Girls, 14–18 years	1.0 mg
Men, 19+ years	1.2 mg
Women, 19+ years	1.1 mg
Pregnancy	1.4 mg
Breastfeeding	1.4 mg
Upper daily limit	None established

Thiamin in Foods

To add a boost of thiamin to your diet, reach for pork, calf's liver, whole grains, enriched breakfast cereals, legumes and nuts.

Thiamin Supplements

People taking strong diuretic drugs (such as Lasix) for congestive heart failure may need extra thiamin, as such drugs deplete the body of this B vitamin. People with conditions that cause malabsorption of nutrients may also benefit from additional thiamin. I recommend taking a high-potency multivitamin and mineral formula that provides between 25 and 100 milligrams of thiamin.

Riboflavin (Vitamin B2)

Like the other B vitamins, riboflavin, or vitamin B2, is needed for energy metabolism. This vitamin also supports normal vision and maintains healthy skin. Evidence suggests that riboflavin may help prevent cataracts and migraine headaches.

Recommended Dietary Allowance (RDA) of Riboflavin

Age	RDA (milligrams)
1–3 years	0.5 mg
4–8 years	0.6 mg
9–13 years	0.9 mg
Boys, 14–18 years	1.3 mg
Girls, 14–18 years	1.0 mg
Men, 19+ years	1.3 mg
Women, 19+ years	1.1 mg
Pregnancy	1.4 mg
Breastfeeding	1.6 mg
Upper daily limit	*None established*

Riboflavin in Foods

Riboflavin is found in milk, yogurt, cottage cheese, fortified soy and rice beverages, meat, whole grains and enriched breakfast cereals.

Riboflavin Supplements

Studies suggest that 400 milligrams of riboflavin taken once daily can reduce the frequency of migraine attacks. Riboflavin supplements are available in 25, 50,

100, 500 and 1200 milligram doses. These supplements are nontoxic and very well tolerated by the body. However, it may take up to 3 months to notice an improvement. Riboflavin supplements may be difficult to find at a drugstore; visit your local health food or supplement store.

For possible cataract prevention, take a high-potency multivitamin and mineral formula that supplies 25 to 100 milligrams of riboflavin.

Niacin (Vitamin B3)

The body uses niacin, also known as vitamin B3 and nicotinic acid, to make two enzymes that help release energy in the form of glucose from foods. The vitamin also maintains the growth of healthy skin cells, helps nerves develop properly and keeps the digestive tract healthy.

Recommended Dietary Allowance (RDA) of Niacin

Age	RDA (milligrams)
1–3 years	6 mg
4–8 years	8 mg
9–13 years	12 mg
Boys, 14–18 years	16 mg
Girls, 14–18 years	14 mg
Men, 19+ years	16 mg
Women, 19+ years	14 mg
Pregnancy	18 mg
Breastfeeding	17 mg

Upper Daily Limits of Niacin

Age	Upper Daily Limit (milligrams)
1–3 years	10 mg
4–8 years	15 mg
9–13 years	20 mg

Age	Upper Daily Limit (milligrams)
14–18 years	30 mg
19+ years	35 mg

Niacin in Foods

Meat, poultry, fish, calf's liver, eggs, dairy products, peanuts, almonds, seeds, wheat bran, whole grains and enriched breakfast cereals are all good sources of niacin.

Niacin Supplements

Niacin is sometimes prescribed in high doses to inhibit your liver's ability to make cholesterol and triglycerides. Nutrition supplements containing niacin, or vitamin B3, are not recommended for cholesterol lowering. Not only are they ineffective, but high doses can also damage your liver. Niacin should be taken as a cholesterol-lowering medication only if prescribed by your doctor. Side effects of high dose niacin include flushing, headaches and stomach upset. The greatest risk, however, is liver damage. If your doctor prescribes this medication for you, he or she will regularly test your liver function by measuring the liver enzymes in your bloodstream.

B complex supplements and some multivitamins contain greater than 35 milligrams of niacin, a dose that can cause flushing of the face, neck and arms. This symptom is harmless and goes away within 20 minutes, but some people find it uncomfortable. Taking your supplement just after eating a meal can avert this "niacin flush." To avoid it completely, look for a formula that contains the non-flushing form of niacin called *niacinamide*.

Vitamin B6 (Pyridoxine)

The body uses vitamin B6, or pyridoxine, to perform many important functions. It's involved with more than 100 enzymes in protein metabolism. It also helps nerve cells communicate effectively and the immune system function properly. As well, vitamin B6 is necessary in the production of red blood cells and helps maintain blood sugar in the normal range.

Vitamin B6 is thought to help prevent heart disease by lowering blood levels of homocysteine, an amino acid that can damage artery walls if levels become elevated. Studies also suggest that B6 may reduce PMS-related depression and may be useful in treating morning sickness during pregnancy.

Recommended Dietary Allowance (RDA) of Vitamin B6

Age	RDA (milligrams)
1–3 years	0.5 mg
4–8 years	0.6 mg
9–13 years	1.0 mg
Boys, 14–18 years	1.3 mg
Girls, 14–18 years	1.2 mg
Men and women, adults, 19–50 years	1.3 mg
Men, 51+ years	1.7 mg
Women, 51+ years	1.5 mg
Pregnancy	1.9 mg
Breastfeeding	2.0 mg

Upper Daily Limits of Vitamin B6

Age	Upper Daily Limit (milligrams)
1–3 years	30 mg
4–8 years	40 mg
9–13 years	60 mg
14–18 years	80 mg
19+ years	100 mg

Vitamin B6 in Foods

Food	Vitamin B6 (milligrams)
Beef, flank, cooked, 3 oz (90 g)	0.3 mg
Pork, centre loin, cooked, 3 oz (90 g)	0.3 mg
Chicken, breast, cooked, 1/2 (140 g)	0.3 mg
Chicken, leg, cooked, 1 (187 g)	0.2 mg
Salmon, sockeye, cooked, 3 oz (90 g)	0.2 mg

Food	Vitamin B6 (milligrams)
Tuna, canned, drained, 3 oz (90 g)	0.4 mg
100% bran cereal, 1/2 cup (125 ml)	0.5 mg
Cereal, whole-grain flakes, 2/3 cup (150 ml)	0.5 mg
Avocado, California, 1/2 medium	0.2 mg
Avocado, Florida, 1/2 medium	0.4 mg
Banana, 1 medium	0.7 mg
Potato, baked, 1 medium with skin	0.7 mg

Source: Adapted from the *Canadian Nutrient File*, Health Canada (2006)©. Adapted and reproduced with the permission of the Minister of Public Works and Government Services Canada, 2009.

Vitamin B6 Supplements

If you want to boost your intake of vitamin B6 beyond what you can get from food, take a high-potency multivitamin and mineral pill or a B complex supplement. Both formulas will supply between 25 and 100 milligrams of vitamin B6. Do not exceed 100 milligrams per day: Too much B6 over an extended period can be toxic and cause irreversible nerve damage to the arms and legs.

People with neurologic conditions such as Parkinson's disease who take the medication levodopa are advised to not take more than 5 milligrams of B6 a day as the vitamin can interfere with the action of the drug.

Folate (Folic Acid)

This B vitamin is called folate when it occurs naturally in foods. When it's added to foods or present in a supplement, it's referred to as folic acid. Folate supports cell division and growth, which is especially important during periods of rapid growth such as infancy and pregnancy. The body uses folate to make RNA and DNA, the building blocks of cells. It's critical that women have sufficient amounts of folate before and during pregnancy in order to prevent neural tube birth defects, such as spina bifida, in the newborn.

Folate is also needed to help prevent changes in DNA that could lead to cancer, make red blood cells, and prevent anemia. Consuming adequate folate may help reduce the risk of coronary heart disease as well as breast and colon cancers.

Recommended Dietary Allowance (RDA) of Folate

Age	RDA (micrograms)
1–3 years	150 mcg
4–8 years	200 mcg
9–13 years	300 mcg
14–18 years	400 mcg
19–50 years	400 mcg
51+ years	400 mcg
Pregnancy	600 mcg
Breastfeeding	500 mcg

Upper Daily Limits of Folate

Age	Upper Daily Limit (micrograms)
1–3 years	300 mcg
4–8 years	400 mcg
9–13 years	600 mcg
14–18 years	800 mcg
19+ years	1000 mcg

Folate in Foods

The best food sources of folate include cooked spinach, lentils, asparagus, artichokes, avocadoes and orange juice. In Canada, white flour, white pasta and refined cornmeal must be fortified with folic acid. It's estimated that fortified foods add 100 to 200 micrograms (0.1 to 0.2 milligram) of folic acid to one's daily intake.

Food	Folate (micrograms)
Chicken liver, 3.5 oz (100 g)	770 mcg
Black beans, cooked, 1/2 cup (125 ml)	135 mcg
Chickpeas, cooked, 1/2 cup (125 ml)	85 mcg
Kidney beans, cooked, 1/2 cup (125 ml)	120 mcg

Food	Folate (micrograms)
Lentils, cooked, 1/2 cup (125 ml)	189 mcg
Peanuts, 1/2 cup (125 ml)	96 mcg
Sunflower seeds, 1/3 cup (75 ml)	96 mcg
Artichoke, 1 medium	64 mcg
Asparagus, 5 spears	110 mcg
Avocado, California, 1/2 medium	113 mcg
Avocado, Florida, 1/2 medium	81 mcg
Bean sprouts, 1 cup (250 ml)	91 mcg
Beets, 1/2 cup (125 ml)	72 mcg
Brussels sprouts, 1/2 cup (125 ml)	83 mcg
Romaine lettuce, 1 cup (250 ml)	80 mcg
Spinach, raw, 1 cup (250 ml)	115 mcg
Spinach, cooked, 1/2 cup (125 ml)	139 mcg
Orange, 1 medium	40 mcg
Orange juice, freshly squeezed, 1 cup (250 ml)	79 mcg
Orange juice, frozen, reconstituted, 1 cup (250 ml)	115 mcg

Source: Adapted from the *Canadian Nutrient File*, Health Canada (2006)©. Adapted and reproduced with the permission of the Minister of Public Works and Government Services Canada, 2009.

Folic Acid Supplements

Many people find it a challenge to consume 400 micrograms of folate each day. After all, cooked spinach and lentils—excellent sources of the B vitamin—aren't exactly everyday foods for most people. What's more, because folate is bound to naturally occurring compounds called glutamates, your body absorbs only about one-half of the folate in foods. But the body absorbs nearly 100 percent of folic acid from a multivitamin or fortified foods. That's why women of child-bearing age—those who could become pregnant, who are pregnant or who are breastfeeding—are advised to take a multivitamin that supplies 400 micrograms (0.4 milligrams) of folic acid. A multivitamin helps ensure that all adults meet their daily requirements for this important B vitamin.

If you're advised by your health care provider to take a folic acid supplement, be sure to choose one with vitamin B12 added. Supplementing with folic acid alone can mask a vitamin B12 deficiency, which could lead to irreversible nerve damage. Do not exceed 1000 micrograms of folic acid per day.

CONTROVERSY ABOUT FOLIC ACID SUPPLEMENTATION. Recently, there has been concern that high doses of folic acid might do more harm than good. In a randomized controlled trial of 1021 men and women who previously had precancerous polyps removed from their colon, those who took a folic acid supplement (1 milligram) got just as many new polyps as those who took placebo pills. People in the folic acid group had higher rates of advanced tumours and multiple tumours, although this could have been a chance finding (i.e., the evidence wasn't what researchers call statistically significant). This finding raised the possibility that if taken early, folic acid may prevent polyps from forming in the first place, but if taken once polyps have formed, large amounts of folic acid could accelerate their growth.[1]

Research also suggests that taking a high dose folic acid supplement (1 milligram) could raise the risk of prostate cancer.[2]

For these reasons, I advise people against taking high dose folic acid supplements or B complex supplements that provide 1 milligram of folic acid. Get your folate from your diet and a multivitamin that provides 400 micrograms (0.4 milligrams). (Note: Women at high risk of giving birth to a baby with a neural tube defect are advised to take a high dose folic acid supplement.)

Vitamin B12

Vitamin B12 helps maintain healthy nerve function and is necessary in the body to make DNA, our genetic map. The vitamin also helps keep red blood cells healthy. Some evidence suggests that vitamin B12 may help guard against heart disease and may also be beneficial in the treatment of male infertility.

Recommended Dietary Allowance (RDA) of Vitamin B12

Age	RDA (micrograms)
1–3 years	0.9 mcg
4–8 years	1.2 mcg
9–13 years	1.8 mcg
14–18 years	2.4 mcg
19–50 years	2.4 mcg

Age	RDA (micrograms)
51+ years	2.4 mcg
Pregnancy	2.6 mcg
Breastfeeding	2.8 mcg
Upper daily limit	*None established*

Vitamin B12 in Foods

Vitamin B12 is found in all animal foods, including shellfish and dairy. Many soy, rice and almond beverages are fortified with B12.

Food	Vitamin B12 (micrograms)
Beef, lean, 3 oz (90 g)	2.8 mcg
Mussels, shelled, 3 oz (90 g)	20 mcg
Salmon, sockeye, cooked, 3 oz (90 g)	4.9 mcg
Milk, 1 cup (250 ml)	1.0 mcg
Cheese, cottage, 1%, 1 cup (250 ml)	0.7 mcg
Cheese, cheddar, 1.5 oz (45 g)	0.4 mcg
Yogurt, 3/4 cup (175 ml)	1.0 mcg
Egg, 1 whole	0.6 mcg
Soy beverage, fortified, 1 cup (250 ml)	1.0 mcg

Source: Adapted from the *Canadian Nutrient File*, Health Canada (2006)©. Adapted and reproduced with the permission of the Minister of Public Works and Government Services Canada, 2009.

Vitamin B12 Supplements

Anyone over the age of 50 should be supplementing his or her diet with vitamin B12. As many as one-third of older adults are not able to properly absorb B12 from food because their bodies produce inadequate amounts of hydrochloric acid in their stomach acid. (Hydrochloric acid is needed to release B12 from the food proteins it's bound to.) For that matter, anyone taking medication to reduce stomach acid secretion should take a B12 supplement.

To boost your intake of this vitamin, take a multivitamin and mineral supplement that offers between 25 and 100 micrograms of B12. If you follow a vegetarian diet that excludes animal foods (i.e., a vegan diet), or have been diagnosed with a vitamin B12 deficiency, take a separate 500 or 1000 microgram B12 supplement. If you are B12 deficient, I advise that you take a sublingual B12 supplement (it dissolves under the tongue). (Sublingual B12 has been found to be as effective as B12 injections in replenishing body stores of the vitamin.) No adverse effects have been reported in healthy individuals taking B12 supplements.

Biotin

This B vitamin, like the others in the B family, is necessary for energy metabolism. Biotin is used to synthesize fat, amino acids and glycogen, the storage form of carbohydrate in your muscles and liver. It also plays a role in hair growth and maintaining healthy skin and nails.

Adequate Intakes (AI) of Biotin

Age	AI (micrograms)
1–3 years	8 mcg
4–8 years	12 mcg
9–13 years	20 mcg
14–18 years	25 mcg
19+ years	30 mcg
Pregnancy	30 mcg
Breastfeeding	35 mcg
Upper daily limit	*None established*

Biotin in Foods

The best sources of biotin are kidney, calf's liver, clams, oatmeal, whole grains, egg yolk, soybeans, nuts, brewer's yeast, cauliflower, mushrooms and bananas. It's also produced from bacteria in our intestinal tract. In fact, most of us likely get all the biotin we need from this source.

Biotin Supplements

Most regular multivitamin and mineral supplements provide close to 50 micrograms of the nutrient. High-potency or super-strength multivitamin formulas offer up to 100 micrograms. Some evidence suggests that supplementing with 3 milligrams of biotin daily can stimulate hair growth in patients with hair loss.

Pantothenic Acid

The body uses pantothenic acid to metabolize fat and carbohydrate for energy. In addition, the nutrient is used to make bile, a digestive aid, as well as hormones, neurotransmitters, red blood cells and vitamin D. Pantothenic acid is involved in more than 100 steps in the body's production of fats, brain chemicals (neurotransmitters), hormones, vitamin D and the iron-carrying compound called hemoglobin. It's also an important part of coenzyme A, an essential compound used by cells to generate energy.

Adequate Intakes (AI) of Pantothenic Acid

Age	AI (milligrams)
1–3 years	2 mg
4–8 years	3 mg
9–13 years	4 mg
14–18 years	5 mg
19+ years	5 mg
Pregnancy	6 mg
Breastfeeding	7 mg
Upper daily limit	*None established*

Pantothenic Acid in Foods

Pantothenic acid is found in many foods. The best sources are brewer's yeast, calf's liver, meat, fish, poultry, peanuts, soybeans, split peas, nuts, seeds, lentils, whole grains, oatmeal, buckwheat and mushrooms.

Pantothenic Acid Supplements

There is little evidence to support taking supplemental pantothenic acid since a deficiency of this B vitamin is rare. Most regular multivitamin and mineral supplements provide 10 milligrams of the nutrient. High-potency or super-strength multivitamin formulas offer up to 100 milligrams.

Choline

Although not considered a true vitamin, choline is needed in the body for fat metabolism and to maintain healthy nerve function. It's also used to make cell membranes and acetylcholine, a brain neurotransmitter that is involved in memory.

Adequate Intakes (AI) of Choline

Age	AI (milligrams)
1–3 years	200 mg
4–8 years	250 mg
9–13 years	375 mg
Boys, 14–18 years	550 mg
Girls, 14–18 years	400 mg
Men, 19+ years	550 mg
Women, 19+ years	425 mg
Pregnancy	450 mg
Breastfeeding	550 mg

Upper Daily Limits of Choline

Age	Upper Daily Limit (milligrams)
1–8 years	1000 mg
9–13 years	2000 mg
14–18 years	3000 mg
19+ years	3500 mg

Choline in Foods

Egg yolks, calf's liver, kidney, meat, brewer's yeast, wheat germ, soybeans, peanuts and green peas are foods to include in your diet to ensure that you're meeting your daily requirement of choline.

Choline Supplements

There is little evidence to support taking supplemental choline. However, if you're concerned that your daily diet doesn't contain choline-rich foods, consider taking a supplement of choline, lecithin or phosphatidylserine. Not all multivitamin supplements contain choline; check the contents list on the label.

High doses of choline from supplements may cause a fishy body odour and sweating. People with liver or kidney disease or Parkinson's disease, as well as those who suffer from depression, are at greater risk for adverse effects associated with high intakes of choline from supplements.

Vitamin C (Ascorbic Acid)

This water-soluble vitamin supports collagen synthesis and wound healing, strengthens blood vessels and helps the body absorb iron in plant foods. Its antioxidant powers may help prevent heart disease, stroke, cataracts and macular degeneration. It may also guard against osteoporosis. By supporting the body's immune system, vitamin C may lessen the severity and duration of the common cold.

Recommended Dietary Allowance (RDA) of Vitamin C

Age	RDA (milligrams)
1–3 years	15 mg
4–8 years	25 mg
9–13 years	45 mg
Boys, 14–18 years	75 mg
Girls, 14–18 years	65 mg
Men, 19+ years	90 mg
Women, 19+ years	75 mg
Pregnancy	85 mg
Breastfeeding	120 mg

Note: Smokers need an additional 35 mg.

Upper Daily Limits of Vitamin C

Age	Upper Daily Limit (milligrams)
1–3 years	400 mg
4–8 years	650 mg
9–13 years	1200 mg
14–18 years	1800 mg
19+ years	2000 mg

Vitamin C in Foods

Food	Vitamin C (milligrams)
Cantaloupe, 1/4 medium	56 mg
Grapefruit, red or pink, 1/2 medium	47 mg
Kiwi, 1 large	68 mg
Mango, 1 medium	49 mg
Orange, 1 medium	70 mg
Orange juice, fresh, 1 cup (250 ml)	131 mg
Strawberries, raw, 1 cup (250 ml)	89 mg
Broccoli, raw, 1 spear	141 mg
Brussels sprouts, cooked, 1/2 cup (125 ml)	50 mg
Cauliflower, raw, 1/2 cup (125 ml)	38 mg
Potato, with skin, baked, 1 medium	27 mg
Red pepper, raw, 1/2 cup (125 ml)	95 mg
Tomato juice, 1 cup (250 ml)	47 mg

Source: Adapted from the *Canadian Nutrient File*, Health Canada (2006)©. Adapted and reproduced with the permission of the Minister of Public Works and Government Services Canada, 2009.

Vitamin C Supplements

If you don't eat at least two vitamin C–rich foods each day, taking a supplement is a good idea. Vitamin C is available in many different forms—time released, Ester C, with bioflavonoids—but there is no evidence that one form is any better than another. Natural and synthetic forms of vitamin C are chemically identical and there are no known differences in their bioavailability (the amount that's available for the body to use) or biological activity in the body.

If you opt for a chewable vitamin C supplement, choose one that's made from a mineral salt such as sodium ascorbate or calcium ascorbate. These forms are less acidic to the enamel of your teeth. Some people also find them less irritating to the gastrointestinal tract than regular ascorbic acid supplements.

Take a 500 milligram supplement once or twice a day. Research has determined that your body can use only about 200 milligrams at one time. I've recommended 500 milligrams because this is the most common dose you'll find on the market.

People with a history of kidney stones or kidney failure should restrict their vitamin C intake to 100 milligrams per day.

Vitamin D

Vitamin D is essential for prompting calcium absorption in the intestinal tract and maintaining calcium and phosphorus levels in the blood to build strong bones and teeth. In this way, vitamin D helps reduce the risk of osteoporosis.

Mounting evidence suggests that this vitamin's benefits extend beyond bone health to cancer prevention. Vitamin D may also protect from diabetes, coronary heart disease, multiple sclerosis and rheumatoid arthritis.

The majority of our vitamin D needs are met from sunlight striking the skin, triggering vitamin D synthesis. When ultraviolet light hits the skin, it forms a pre–vitamin D. This compound then makes its way to the kidneys, where it's transformed into active vitamin D. But during our long winter, there isn't enough UVB radiation to produce any vitamin D in our skin. And in the summer, the sensible use of sunscreen blocks vitamin D production by more than 90 percent. To help you meet your vitamin D requirements, expose your hands, face and arms to sunlight without sunscreen for 10 to 15 minutes, two or three times a week.

Adequate Intakes (AI) of Vitamin D

Age	AI (International Units)
1–3 years	200 IU (5 mcg)
4–8 years	200 IU (5 mcg)
9–30 years	200 IU (5 mcg) / 400 IU*
31–50 years	200 IU (5 mcg) / 400 IU*
51–70 years	400 IU (10 mcg) / 800 IU*
71+ years	600 IU (15 mcg) / 800 IU*
Pregnancy	200 IU (5 mcg)
Breastfeeding	200 IU (5 mcg)
Upper daily limit	*2000 IU (50 mcg)*

*Note: Osteoporosis Canada advises that Canadians should consume 400 or 800 IU of vitamin D per day, depending on their age.

Vitamin D in Foods

Food	Vitamin D (International Units)
Cod liver oil, 1 tsp (5 ml)	450 IU
Mackerel, cooked, 3.5 oz (100g)	345 IU
Salmon, canned, 3.5 oz (100 g)	360 IU
Sardines, canned, 3.5 oz (100 g)	270 IU
Milk, fluid, 1 cup (250 ml)	100 IU
Rice beverage, fortified, 1 cup (250 ml)	100 IU
Soy beverage, fortified, 1 cup (250 ml)	100 IU
Egg, whole, 1 large	25 IU
Butter, 1 tsp (5 ml)	2.6 IU
Margarine, 1 tsp (5 ml)	20 IU

Source: U.S. Department of Agriculture, Agricultural Research Service, 2007. USDA National Nutrient Database for Standard Reference, Release 21. Nutrient Data Laboratory Home Page, www.ars.usda.gov/nutrientdata.

Vitamin D Supplements

The fact that very few foods contain vitamin D and our skin doesn't produce the vitamin in the fall and winter months makes it necessary to get vitamin D from a supplement. What's more, there's agreement among experts that the current "official" AIs for vitamin D are too low to reduce the risk of cancers.

Evidence that taking a vitamin D supplement reduces cancer risk prompted the Canadian Cancer Society in 2007 to recommend adults consider taking 1000 IU (International Units) of vitamin D each day throughout the fall and winter. Older adults, people with dark skin, those who don't go outdoors often and those who wear clothing that covers most of their skin should take the supplement year-round. The Canadian Cancer Society's vitamin D recommendation does not extend to children since, so far, research has focused only on adults.

It's prudent to supplement your diet with 1000 IU of vitamin D each day. (Add up how much you're already getting from your multivitamin and calcium supplements; the difference between that and the recommended 1000 IU is the dosage of vitamin D you need to buy.) Choose a vitamin D supplement that contains vitamin D3 instead of vitamin D2, which is less potent. Typically sold in 400 IU and 1000 IU doses, there is no need to be concerned if your intake exceeds 1000 IU slightly. The current safe upper limit—which vitamin D experts feel is far too low—is set at 2000 IU per day.

You can ask your doctor to test your blood for vitamin D; if you're deficient you may be advised to supplement with 2000 IU of vitamin D each day. People at risk for vitamin D deficiency include older adults (as we age, the skin cannot synthesize vitamin D as efficiently), people with limited sun exposure, people with dark skin (the pigment melanin reduces the skin's ability to produce vitamin D) and people who are obese (fat deposits under the skin sequester vitamin D and alter its release into the bloodstream).

Vitamin E (Alpha Tocopherol)

This fat-soluble vitamin acts as a powerful antioxidant to protect cells against the potentially damaging effects of free radicals, which are by-products of energy metabolism. By damaging cells, free radicals may contribute to the development of cancer and other chronic diseases. Vitamin E also plays a role in immune function, DNA repair and iron metabolism. Research suggests that vitamin E may help prevent heart disease and prostate cancer and slow the progression of Alzheimer's disease.

Recommended Dietary Allowance (RDA) of Vitamin E

Age	RDA (International Units)
1–3 years	9 IU (6 mg)
4–8 years	10 IU (7 mg)
9–13 years	16 IU (11 mg)
14–18 years	22 IU (15 mg)
19–30 years	22 IU (15 mg)
31–50 years	22 IU (15 mg)
51–70 years	22 IU (15 mg)
71+ years	22 IU (15 mg)
Pregnancy	22 IU (15 mg)
Breastfeeding	28 IU (19 mg)
Upper daily limit	*1500 IU (1000 mg)*

Vitamin E in Foods

Vegetable oils, almonds, peanuts, soybeans, whole grains, wheat germ, wheat-germ oil, avocado and green leafy vegetables, especially kale, are all good sources of vitamin E.

Vitamin E Supplements

There's some evidence that a daily vitamin E supplement might reduce the risk in healthy people of developing heart disease. But there's no evidence that supplementing with vitamin E prevents heart attacks in people with established coronary heart disease. Some research hints that high doses of vitamin E may do more harm than good, especially in people who have diabetes or heart disease.

While vitamin E supplements have not been shown to reduce cancer risk, studies have revealed that higher intakes of vitamin E from foods could help lower the risk of breast, colon and prostate cancers.

Meet your vitamin E requirements by eating a variety of foods. If you have existing cardiovascular disease or diabetes, avoid high dose vitamin E supplements. If you do take a supplement, take no more than 100 IU per day. If you're taking a blood-thinning medication like warfarin (Coumadin), don't take vitamin E without your doctor's approval. Vitamin E can act as an anticoagulant and may increase the risk of bleeding problems.

Vitamin K

Vitamin K is essential for blood clotting. It also plays an important role in the formation of new bone and may help reduce the risk of osteoporosis. Studies show that high dietary intakes of vitamin K are associated with lower risk of hip fractures.

Adequate Intakes (AI) of Vitamin K

Age	AI (micrograms)
1–3 years	30 mcg
4–8 years	55 mcg
9–13 years	60 mcg
14–18 years	75 mcg
Men, 19+ years	120 mcg
Women, 19+ years	90 mcg

Age	AI (micrograms)
Pregnancy	90 mcg
Breastfeeding	90 mcg
Upper daily limit	*None established*

Vitamin K in Foods

The best sources of vitamin K are green peas, broccoli, spinach, leafy green vegetables, Brussels sprouts, romaine lettuce, cabbage and calf's liver. Bacteria in the large intestine also produce some vitamin K.

Food	Vitamin K (micrograms)
Beet greens, cooked, 1/2 cup (125 ml)	349 mcg
Broccoli, cooked, 1 cup (250 ml)	220 mcg
Collard greens, cooked, 1/2 cup (125 ml)	418 mcg
Dandelion greens, cooked, 1/2 cup (125 ml)	102 mcg
Kale, cooked, 1/2 cup (125 ml)	531 mcg
Lettuce, leaf, raw, 1 cup (250 ml)	97 mcg
Lettuce, romaine, raw, 1 cup (250 ml)	57 mcg
Mustard greens, cooked, 1/2 cup (125 ml)	210 mcg
Spinach, cooked, 1/2 cup (125 ml)	444 mcg
Spinach, frozen, cooked, 1/2 cup (125 ml)	514 mcg
Spinach, raw, 1 cup (250 ml)	144 mcg
Turnip greens, cooked, 1/2 cup (125 ml)	265 mcg

Source: U.S. Department of Agriculture, Agricultural Research Service, 2007. USDA National Nutrient Database for Standard Reference, Release 21. Nutrient Data Laboratory Home Page, www.ars.usda.gov/nutrientdata.

Vitamin K Supplements

In Canada, vitamin K is available in a multivitamin in doses that generally range from 10 to 120 micrograms. To help reduce the risk of osteoporosis and hip fractures, adults aged 65 and older should take a multivitamin that contains vitamin K and eat one serving of leafy green vegetables each day.

Vitamin K supplements counteract the effects of anticoagulant medication such as warfarin (Coumadin). Warfarin reduces the risk of blood clots forming by decreasing the activity of vitamin K. Do not take vitamin K supplements if you take these drugs. Your doctor will also advise you to limit the frequency and quantity of vitamin K–rich foods.

The Minerals

Minerals, like vitamins, are vital to health. They are important players in many different metabolic reactions in the body. Many minerals enable enzymes (protein compounds that catalyze chemical reactions) to function. Other minerals are key components of body compounds such as hormones and hemoglobin found in red blood cells. Electrolyte minerals like sodium, potassium and chloride help maintain fluid balance throughout the body. Finally, some minerals have a critical role in the body's growth and development.

Minerals are categorized according to our daily dietary requirements. In general, if we need 100 milligrams or more (about 1/50 of a teaspoon), it's considered a major mineral. If we require less, it's referred to as a trace mineral.

The body is unable to make minerals on its own and so must get them from foods. Our diet provides a wide range of minerals, but they can vary in their availability to the body. Some foods contain naturally occurring binders that prevent much of a mineral from being released from the food during digestion. For example, phytic acid in spinach reduces the amount of calcium, iron and zinc that's available to the body. Nevertheless, a key factor in determining how much of a mineral we absorb is our body's need for that nutrient at the time.

The molecules of some minerals are roughly the same size and share the same electric charge. For instance, calcium, magnesium, iron and zinc have the same charge and so compete with each other for absorption. That's why calcium supplements can interfere with iron absorption. Mineral absorption is discussed in more detail below.

Toxicity reactions are much more likely to occur with mineral supplements than they are with vitamin pills. Take great care when supplementing with minerals. As you'll read below, single high dose supplements of many minerals are potentially dangerous and should be avoided.

The twenty-two minerals are presented below in roughly alphabetical order—first the three major minerals (calcium, magnesium and phosphorus), followed by the trace minerals and, finally, the two electrolyte minerals.

Calcium

Calcium is critical for building strong bones and teeth. It also helps muscles contract and relax, and it supports nerve function. Calcium plays an important role in blood clotting and maintaining blood pressure. An adequate intake of calcium is thought to reduce the risk of osteoporosis, high blood pressure, kidney stones and colorectal cancer. It may also help ease symptoms of premenstrual syndrome.

Recommended Dietary Allowance (RDA) of Calcium

Age	RDA (milligrams)
1–3 years	500 mg
4–8 years	800 mg
9–13 years	1300 mg
14–18 years	1300 mg
19–50 years	1000 mg
51+ years	1200 mg / 1500 mg*
Pregnancy	1000 mg
Breastfeeding	1000 mg
Upper daily limit	*2500 mg*

*Note: Canadian adults over the age of 50 who are at risk for osteoporosis are advised to consume 1500 mg of calcium per day.

Calcium in Foods

Food	Calcium (milligrams)
Dairy Foods	
Milk, chocolate, 1 cup (250 ml)	285 mg
Milk, evaporated, 1/2 cup (125 ml)	350 mg
Milk, Lactaid, 1 cup (250 ml)	300 mg
Milk, Neilson TruTaste, 1 cup (250 ml)	360 mg
Milk, Neilson TruCalcium, 1 cup (250 ml)	420 mg
Milk powder, skim, dry, 3 tbsp (45 ml)	155 mg
Carnation Instant Breakfast, Nestlé, with 1 cup (250 ml) milk	540 mg
Cheese, cheddar, 1-1/2 oz (45 g)	300 mg

Food	Calcium (milligrams)
Cheese, cottage, 1/2 cup (125 ml)	75 mg
Cheese, mozzarella, 1-1/2 oz (45 g)	228 mg
Cheese, ricotta, 1/2 cup (125 ml)	255 mg
Cheese, Swiss or Gruyère, 1-1/2 oz (45 g)	480 mg
Sour cream, light, 1/4 cup (60 ml)	120 mg
Yogurt, plain, 3/4 cup (175 ml)	300 mg
Yogurt, fruit-flavoured, 3/4 cup (175 ml)	250 mg
Non-Dairy Foods	
Baked beans, 1 cup (250 ml)	150 mg
Black beans, 1 cup (250 ml)	102 mg
Kidney beans, cooked, 1 cup (250 ml)	69 mg
Lentils, cooked, 1 cup (250 ml)	37 mg
Soy beverage, fortified, 1 cup (250 ml)	330 mg
Soybeans, cooked, 1 cup (250 ml)	175 mg
Soybeans, roasted, 1/4 cup (60 ml)	60 mg
Tempeh, cooked, 1 cup (250 ml)	154 mg
Tofu, raw, firm, with calcium sulfate, 4 oz (120 g)	241 mg
Tofu, raw, soft, with calcium sulfate, 4 oz (120 g)	133 mg
Sardines, 8 small (with bones)	165 mg
Salmon, drained, 1/2 can (with bones)	225 mg
Bok choy, cooked, 1 cup (250 ml)	158 mg
Broccoli, cooked, 1 cup (250 ml)	94 mg
Broccoli, raw, 1 cup (250 ml)	42 mg
Collard greens, cooked, 1 cup (250 ml)	357 mg
Kale, cooked, 1 cup (250 ml)	179 mg
Okra, cooked, 1 cup (250 ml)	176 mg
Rutabaga, cooked, 1/2 cup (125 ml)	57 mg
Swiss chard, cooked, 1 cup (250 ml)	102 mg
Swiss chard, raw, 1 cup (250 ml)	21 mg
Currants, 1/2 cup (125 ml)	60 mg

Food	Calcium (milligrams)
Figs, dried, 5 medium	135 mg
Orange, 1 medium	50 mg
Almonds, 1/4 cup (60 ml)	100 mg
Brazil nuts, 1/4 cup (60 ml)	65 mg
Hazelnuts, 1/4 cup (60 ml)	65 mg
Molasses, blackstrap, 2 tbsp (30 ml)	288 mg
Molasses, fancy, 2 tbsp (30 ml)	70 mg
Orange juice, calcium-fortified, 1 cup (250 ml)	300–360 mg

Source: Adapted from the *Canadian Nutrient File*, Health Canada (2006)©. Adapted and reproduced with the permission of the Minister of Public Works and Government Services Canada, 2009.

Our body does not absorb calcium from all foods equally well. While many plant foods contribute calcium to the diet, certain natural compounds in vegetables prevent some of this calcium from being absorbed. Studies show that dairy products contain the most absorbable form of calcium. The following strategies will help you enhance your body's absorption of calcium:

- Cook green vegetables in order to boost their calcium content by releasing calcium that's bound to oxalic acid.
- Don't take iron supplements with calcium-rich foods as iron competes with calcium for absorption.
- Drink tea between rather than during meals. Tannins, natural compounds in tea, inhibit calcium absorption.
- Make sure you're meeting dietary requirements for vitamin D each day (as you read earlier in this chapter, vitamin D stimulates the intestine to absorb dietary calcium).

Calcium Supplements

If you aren't getting your daily calcium from food, you need to take a supplement. You can't rely on a multivitamin and mineral supplement to provide enough calcium since most brands contain less than 200 milligrams of the mineral. Which calcium product you choose will depend on convenience, absorbability and tolerance.

CALCIUM CARBONATE AND CALCIUM CITRATE. The most common compounds used in calcium supplements are carbonate and citrate. Calcium carbonate supplements are generally the least expensive and most widely used. They also contain twice as much elemental calcium—usually 500 or 600 milligrams per tablet—as supplements made from calcium citrate. Elemental calcium is the amount of calcium in a supplement that's available for your body to absorb; since your daily calcium requirements are based on the amount you need to absorb, this information is important. Most products list the amount of elemental calcium on the label. But some brands list only the total weight (milligrams) of the tablet, that is, the weight of the calcium plus that of the carbonate or citrate compound to which it's bound.

If you need to take 1000 milligrams of elemental calcium from supplements, calcium carbonate products may be more convenient. To get the same amount of elemental calcium, you'd have to take more calcium citrate pills than calcium carbonate pills.

If you have decreased stomach acid or you're taking an acid-blocking medication, consider taking calcium citrate supplements. Calcium citrate is more readily absorbed in your intestine so it can be taken any time of day, even on an empty stomach. Calcium carbonate requires extra stomach acid for absorption so it's best taken with food or immediately after eating.

CORAL CALCIUM. These calcium supplements are made from marine coral beds off the coast of Okinawa, Japan. The U.S. Federal Trade Commission took legal action against companies making false and unsubstantiated health claims about coral calcium. Coral calcium is simply calcium carbonate. According one U.S. study, some brands may contain high levels of lead, a naturally occurring heavy metal.

OTHER CALCIUM SUPPLEMENTS. Calcium supplements made from unrefined oyster shell, bone meal and dolomite have fallen out of favour due to their higher levels of lead. Calcium citrate and refined calcium carbonate have the lowest lead content. Many experts say the exposure risk of lead in calcium supplements is relatively small and insignificant since the higher amounts of calcium present decrease intestinal absorption of lead.

Here are a few guidelines for taking calcium supplements:

• To determine how many calcium supplement tablets you need to take, look at how much elemental calcium is in each. Read the ingredient list. Spread your calcium intake over the course of the day. Absorption from supplements is best in doses of 500 milligrams or less because the percentage of calcium your body absorbs decreases as the amount in the supplement increases. Therefore, if you need to take 1000 milligrams of calcium from supplements, you should take 500 milligrams twice a day instead of 1000 milligrams of calcium at one time.

- If you're averse to swallowing pills, try a chewable, liquid or effervescent calcium supplement. These supplements are well absorbed by the body since they're broken down before they enter the stomach.

- To prevent gas, bloating and constipation, ensure your diet provides adequate fluids and fibre. If this doesn't help, try another brand or form of calcium. Increase your calcium intake gradually—take 500 milligrams per day for one week, then add more calcium slowly.

- If you take medications, check with your pharmacist about possible interactions with calcium. Calcium can interfere with the body's ability to use certain drugs, including tetracycline, bisphosphonates (Fosamax, Actonel), hypothyroid medication (Synthroid) and iron supplements.

- Don't consume more than 2500 milligrams of calcium per day from food and supplements combined. Taking too much calcium can cause stomach upset, high blood calcium levels, impaired kidney function and decreased absorption of other minerals.

Magnesium

This mineral is needed for more than 300 biochemical reactions in the body. It helps maintain normal muscle and nerve function, keeps the heart rhythm steady, supports a healthy immune system and keeps bones strong. Magnesium also helps regulate blood sugar and blood pressure. Studies suggest that magnesium may prevent migraine headaches, reduce high blood pressure and ease symptoms of premenstrual syndrome. In addition, the mineral is thought to play a role in reducing the risk of coronary heart disease and diabetes.

Recommended Dietary Allowance (RDA) of Magnesium

Age	RDA (milligrams)
1–3 years	80 mg
4–8 years	130 mg

Age	RDA (milligrams)
9–13 years	240 mg
Boys, 14–18 years	410 mg
Girls, 14–18 years	360 mg
Men, 19–30 years	400 mg
Women, 19–30 years	310 mg
Men, 31+ years	420 mg
Women, 31+ years	320 mg
Pregnancy	350–360 mg
Breastfeeding	310–320 mg

Upper Daily Limits of Magnesium*

Age	Upper Daily Limit (milligrams)
1–3 years	65 mg
4–8 years	110 mg
9+ years	350 mg

*from a supplement source

Magnesium in Foods

The best sources of magnesium include legumes, nuts and seeds, whole grains and vegetables. Green vegetables are particularly good sources of magnesium because the centre of the chlorophyll molecule—the compound that gives green vegetables their colour—contains magnesium.

Food	Magnesium (milligrams)
Wheat bran, 2 tbsp (30 ml)	46 mg
Wheat germ, 1/4 cup (60 ml)	91 mg
Almonds, 1 oz (23 nuts)	84 mg
Brazil nuts, 1 oz (8 nuts)	64 mg
Peanuts, 1 oz (35 nuts)	51 mg
Sunflower seeds, 1 oz (30 g)	100 mg

Food	Magnesium (milligrams)
Black beans, cooked, 1 cup (250 ml)	121 mg
Chickpeas, cooked, 1 cup (250 ml)	78 mg
Kidney beans, cooked, 1 cup (250 ml)	80 mg
Lentils, cooked, 1 cup (250 ml)	71 mg
Navy beans, cooked, 1 cup (250 ml)	107 mg
Soybeans, cooked, 1/2 cup (125 ml)	131 mg
Tofu, raw, firm, 1/2 cup (125 ml)	118 mg
Dates, dried, 10	29 mg
Figs, dried, 10	111 mg
Green peas, cooked, 1/2 cup (125 ml)	31 mg
Spinach, cooked, 1/2 cup (125 ml)	81 mg
Swiss chard, cooked, 1/2 cup (125 ml)	76 mg
Halibut, 3 oz (90 g)	90 mg

Source: Adapted from the *Canadian Nutrient File*, Health Canada (2006)©. Adapted and reproduced with the permission of the Minister of Public Works and Government Services Canada, 2009.

Magnesium Supplements

If a blood test indicates that you have very low magnesium stores, a daily magnesium supplement will be necessary. As well, due to a condition or age, some people may benefit from a daily magnesium supplement. Certain diuretics used to treat high blood pressure (e.g., Lasix, hydrochlorothiazide) cause magnesium to be excreted in the urine. Individuals with poorly controlled diabetes may also benefit from a magnesium supplement since increased magnesium loss in the urine is associated with elevated blood sugar. Older adults are at risk for magnesium deficiency because they tend to consume less in their diets than younger adults and magnesium absorption decreases with age.

Even if you don't fall into one of the above categories, you may feel your magnesium intake is below par despite your best efforts to eat magnesium-rich foods, and so might consider taking a magnesium supplement. But keep in mind, when it comes to reducing high blood pressure, studies show that magnesium-rich foods do the trick, not supplements. These foods also supply other nutrients and antioxidants linked to better health. While magnesium supplements may be helpful in boosting your daily intake, be sure to include magnesium-rich foods in your daily diet.

Magnesium supplements combine magnesium with another substance. You'll find supplements made of magnesium oxide, magnesium citrate, magnesium carbonate, magnesium fumarate and magnesium sulphate. It's the amount of elemental magnesium in a supplement (listed on the label) and its bioavailability that influence the mineral's effectiveness. Bioavailability refers to how much magnesium is absorbed in the intestines and is ultimately available to be used by your body's cells and tissues. Research suggests that magnesium oxide has a lower bioavailability than other forms of magnesium.

Magnesium supplements are typically sold in 200 or 250 milligram doses. Unless you have been diagnosed with a magnesium deficiency, you shouldn't need more than this amount if you're also including magnesium-rich foods in your diet.

If you take calcium supplements, a simple way to boost your intake of magnesium is to buy calcium pills with magnesium added. Calcium/magnesium supplements are sold in a 2:1 or 1:1 ratio of calcium to magnesium. A 2:1 cal/mag supplement will usually supply 300 milligrams of calcium and 150 milligrams of magnesium. If you need to take such a supplement twice daily to meet your calcium needs, you'll be consuming 300 milligrams of magnesium, close to the recommended daily intake. Supplement manufacturers often promote a 2:1 ratio as being ideal for absorption despite the fact there is no credible research to support this.

Magnesium supplements can cause diarrhea and abdominal cramping if taken in high doses. Do not exceed the safe upper limit of 350 milligrams of supplemental magnesium per day.

Phosphorus

The body uses this mineral in many different metabolic reactions. It's also part of a cell's genetic material (DNA). Phosphorus is necessary to maintain strong bones and teeth.

Recommended Dietary Allowance (RDA) of Phosphorus

Age	RDA (milligrams)
1–3 years	460 mg
4–8 years	500 mg
9–18 years	1250 mg

Age	RDA (milligrams)
19+ years	700 mg
Pregnancy	700 mg
Breastfeeding	700 mg
Upper daily limit, 1–8 years	*3000 mg*
Upper daily limit, 9+ years	*4000 mg*

Phosphorus in Foods

The best food sources of phosphorus are dairy products, meat, poultry, fish, egg yolks, legumes and wheat bran. Phosphorus is used as an additive in many processed foods, including bakery products, deli meats and soft drinks. Most people don't have a problem getting enough phosphorus in their daily diet.

Phosphorus Supplements

It's not necessary to take phosphorus supplements since the mineral is so common in foods. Too much phosphorus can interfere with calcium absorption and calcium balance in the body, especially if daily calcium requirements are not being met.

Boron

Research on this trace mineral suggests it has several important roles in the body, including helping bones develop properly and assisting with calcium, magnesium and phosphorus absorption. In addition, it may be necessary for cell membrane formation. Because of its possible role in bone health, boron may guard against osteoporosis, as well as help in the treatment of osteoarthritis. It's also thought to improve cognitive function in older adults.

Because of lack of evidence that boron is essential to humans, no recommended dietary intakes have been established. Boron intakes above the upper daily limit can cause nausea, vomiting, diarrhea and stomach pain. However, boron intake from a healthy diet does not pose a health risk. It's estimated that North Americans consume from 0.75 to 1.4 milligrams of this mineral each day from foods. Because of the part it might play in bone health, I encourage you to eat more boron-rich foods.

Upper Daily Limits of Boron

Age	Upper Daily Limit (milligrams)
1–3 years	3 mg
4–8 years	6 mg
9–13 years	11 mg
14–18 years	17 mg
19+ years	20 mg

Boron in Foods

Milk, legumes, peanuts, peanut butter, pecans, prunes, raisins, grapes, apples, avocado, potatoes, chocolate, wine and coffee all contain significant amounts of boron.

Boron Supplements

There is no evidence that boron supplements are necessary or beneficial for healthy people who eat a balanced diet. In Canada, the addition of boron to vitamin and mineral supplements is not permitted. This is not the case in the United States, where you can find boron-containing nutritional supplements.

Chromium

Chromium enhances the action of insulin, the hormone that regulates blood sugar and the metabolism of carbohydrate, protein and fat. The mineral may help people with impaired fasting glucose (pre-diabetes) or type 2 diabetes (see page 343) manage their blood-sugar levels, as well as possibly reduce elevated blood cholesterol and triglycerides in people with type 2 diabetes. Despite the hype, there's scant evidence that chromium helps increase muscle mass and reduce body fat.

Adequate Intakes (AI) of Chromium

Age	AI (micrograms)
1–3 years	11 mcg
4–8 years	15 mcg

Age	AI (micrograms)
Boys, 9–13 years	25 mcg
Girls, 9–13 years	21 mcg
Boys, 14–18 years	35 mcg
Girls, 14–18 years	24 mcg
Men, 19+ years	35 mcg
Women, 19+ years	25 mcg
Pregnancy	30 mcg
Breastfeeding	45 mcg
Upper daily limit	*None established*

Chromium in Foods

Chromium is widespread in the food supply, but most foods provide only small amounts of the minerals. The best food sources include red meat, calf's liver, chicken breast, oysters, refried beans, brewer's yeast, wheat germ, wheat bran, whole grains, blackstrap molasses, mushrooms, broccoli, green peas, grape juice and apples (with skin). Processed foods and refined starchy foods like white bread, white rice and pasta, sugar and sweets contain very little chromium.

Chromium Supplements

If you're concerned that you're not getting enough chromium in your diet, check your multivitamin and mineral formula to see how much it contains. Most brands supply 25 to 55 micrograms. If you choose to take a separate chromium supplement, do not exceed 200 micrograms per day.

Chromium supplements are available in several forms: chromium chloride, chromium nicotinate, chromium picolinate and high-chromium yeast. These are available as stand-alone supplements or in combination products. Doses typically range from 50 to 200 micrograms of elemental chromium. Bioavailability may be higher in chromium nicotinate and chromium picolinate than in chromium chloride.

If you are on medication, check with your pharmacist before taking a separate chromium supplement. If taken with chromium, certain medications (e.g., beta blockers, corticosteroids, insulin, non-steroidal anti-inflammatory drugs, ibuprofen, naproxen and aspirin) may have their effects enhanced or may increase chromium absorption.

Copper

Copper helps our bodies absorb iron. Copper also maintains nerve function and is used by the body to make connective tissue, brain neurotransmitters, red blood cells and many enzymes.

Recommended Dietary Allowance (RDA) of Copper

Age	RDA (micrograms)
1–3 years	340 mcg
4–8 years	440 mcg
9–13 years	700 mcg
14–18 years	890 mcg
19+ years	900 mcg
Pregnancy	1000 mcg (1.0 mg)
Breastfeeding	1300 mcg (1.3 mg)

Upper Daily Limits of Copper

Age	Upper Daily Limit (micrograms)
1–3 years	1000 mcg (1 mg)
4–8 years	3000 mcg (3 mg)
9–13 years	5000 mcg (5 mg)
14–18 years	8000 mcg (8 mg)
19+ years	10,000 mcg (10 mg)

Copper in Foods

The best food sources of copper are beef liver, meat, shellfish, oysters, clams, lentils, cashews, hazelnuts, sunflower seeds, almonds, prunes, wheat-bran cereal, whole grains and mushrooms.

Copper Supplements

There is no evidence that single copper supplements are necessary or beneficial for healthy people who eat a balanced diet. Copper deficiency is seldom seen in humans. Large amounts of iron or zinc can interfere with copper absorption, so if you take supplemental doses of either, you may want to increase your copper intake with a multivitamin and mineral supplement. Most brands supply 2000 micrograms (2 milligrams) of copper. Also pay attention to your copper intake if you take vitamin C supplements—those in the range of 1500 milligrams per day may decrease the activity of copper-dependent enzymes.

More than 10 milligrams of copper per day can cause nausea, vomiting, bloody diarrhea and anemia.

Fluoride

Fluoride plays a key role in the formation of healthy bones and teeth, and makes teeth resistant to decay and dental caries.

Adequate Intakes (AI) of Fluoride

Age	AI (milligrams)
1–3 years	0.7 mg
4–8 years	1.0 mg
9–13 years	2.0 mg
14–18 years	3.0 mg
Men, 19+ years	4.0 mg
Women, 19+ years	3.0 mg
Pregnancy	3.0 mg
Breastfeeding	3.0 mg

Upper Daily Limits of Fluoride

Age	Upper Daily Limit (milligrams)
1–3 years	1.3 mg
4–8 years	2.2 mg
9+ years	10.0 mg

Fluoride in Foods

Fluoride is supplied to your diet through fluoridated water, beverages made with fluoridated water, black tea, green tea and fish with the bones. Many brands of toothpaste and mouthwash also contain fluoride.

Fluoride Supplements

Fluoride supplements are available by prescription only for children who don't have access to fluoridated drinking water. The dosage is based on the concentration of fluoride present in the drinking water. (Call your local health department to find out if your water is fluoridated.) Fluoride supplements are rarely prescribed for adults.

Excessive consumption of fluoride causes fluorosis, a condition in which the teeth become yellow. Other symptoms of fluoride toxicity include nausea, vomiting, diarrhea, abdominal pain and numbness or tingling of the face and extremities.

Iodine

The body uses iodine to make thyroid hormones, which regulate growth, development, reproduction, body temperature and metabolism. Iodine may help treat fibrocystic breast conditions, especially mastaglia (cyclic breast pain).

Recommended Dietary Allowance (RDA) of Iodine

Age	RDA (micrograms)
1–8 years	90 mcg
9–13 years	120 mcg
14+ years	150 mcg
Pregnancy	220 mcg
Breastfeeding	290 mcg

Upper Daily Limits of Iodine

Age	Upper Daily Limit (micrograms)
1–3 years	200 mcg
4–8 years	300 mcg

Age	Upper Daily Limit (micrograms)
9–13 years	600 mcg
14–18 years	900 mcg
19+ years	1100 mcg

Iodine in Foods

Iodized table salt, seafood and plants grown in iodine-rich soil are good sources of iodine. (Sea salt does not contain iodine.) Most foods provide from 3 to 75 micrograms of iodine per serving. Fish and shellfish tend to be better sources of the mineral since they concentrate iodine from the ocean. Processed foods also have higher iodine content because of the added iodized salt.

Iodine Supplements

Most multivitamin and mineral supplements provide from 100 to 150 micrograms of iodine. If you use table salt and eat processed foods, you're getting more than enough iodine, perhaps even too much.

Kelp (kombu), a type of seaweed, contains very high amounts of iodine; in one study, seventeen different types of kelp supplements were reported to contain anywhere from 45 to 57,000 micrograms of iodine. Taking kelp can increase your risk of iodine toxicity.

Excessive intakes of iodine can interfere with the activity of your thyroid gland and cause hypo- or hyperthyroidism (see pages 479 and 466 for more information about these conditions). Chronic use of large quantities of iodine supplements can cause a metallic taste, sore teeth and gums, burning in the mouth and throat, increased salivation, eye irritation and headache.

Iron

Iron is used in the body to transport oxygen to all cells and tissues. It supports metabolism and helps synthesize certain brain chemicals (neurotransmitters) that aid in concentration. Most of the body's iron is found in two proteins—hemoglobin in red blood cells and myoglobin in muscles—where the mineral helps accept, carry and then release oxygen to cells and tissues. Enzymes that make amino acids and hormones also need iron.

Recommended Dietary Allowance (RDA) of Iron

Age	RDA (milligrams)
1–3 years	7 mg
4–8 years	10 mg
9–13 years	8 mg
Boys, 14–18 years	11 mg
Girls, 14–18 years	15 mg
Men, 19+ years	8 mg
Women, 19–50 years	18 mg
Women, 51+ years	8 mg
Pregnancy	27 mg
Breastfeeding	9 mg
Upper daily limit, 1–13 years	40 mg
Upper daily limit, 14+ years	45 mg

Note: If you are a vegetarian who does not eat animal foods, your recommended dietary allowance for iron is increased by a factor of 1.8.

Iron in Foods

Food	Iron (milligrams)
Beef, lean, cooked, 3 oz (90 g)	3.0 mg
Beans in tomato sauce, 1 cup (250 ml)	5.0 mg
Kidney beans, cooked, 1/2 cup (125 ml)	2.5 mg
Apricots, dried, 6	2.8 mg
Prune juice, 1/2 cup (125 ml)	5.0 mg
Spinach, cooked, 1 cup (250 ml)	4.0 mg
All-Bran Original, Kellogg's, 1/2 cup (125 ml)	4.7 mg
All-Bran Buds, Kellogg's, 1/2 cup (125 ml)	5.9 mg
Bran flakes, 3/4 cup (175 ml)	4.9 mg
Just Right, Kellogg's, 1 cup (250 ml)	6.0 mg

Food	Iron (milligrams)
Raisin Bran, Kellogg's, 3/4 cup (175 ml)	5.5 mg
Shreddies, Post, 3/4 cup (175 ml)	5.9 mg
Cream of Wheat, 1/2 cup (125 ml)	8.0 mg
Oatmeal, instant, 1 pouch	3.8 mg
Wheat germ, 1 tbsp (15 ml)	2.5 mg
Molasses, blackstrap, 1 tbsp (15 ml)	3.2 mg

Source: Adapted from the *Canadian Nutrient File*, Health Canada (2006)©. Adapted and reproduced with the permission of the Minister of Public Works and Government Services Canada, 2009.

The richest sources of iron are beef, pork, lamb, poultry and fish. These foods provide *heme* iron, the type that can be absorbed and utilized the most efficiently by your body. Sources of heme iron supply about 10 percent of the iron we consume each day. Even though heme iron accounts for such a small proportion of our intake, it is so well absorbed that it actually contributes a significant amount of iron.

The rest of our iron comes from plant foods such as dried fruits, whole grains, leafy green vegetables, nuts, seeds and legumes. These are sources of *nonheme* iron. The body is much less efficient in absorbing and using this type of iron. Vegetarians may have difficulty maintaining healthy iron stores because their diet relies exclusively on nonheme sources. The rate at which your body is able to absorb nonheme iron is strongly influenced by other factors in your diet. Practise the following to enhance your body's absorption of nonheme iron:

- Add a little animal food to your meal if you're not vegetarian. Meat, poultry and fish contain MFP factor, a special component that promotes the absorption of nonheme iron from plant foods.
- Add a source of vitamin C. Including a little vitamin C in your plant-based meal can enhance the body's absorption of nonheme iron fourfold. The acidity of the vitamin converts iron to the ferrous form for ready absorption (your stomach acid enhances iron absorption in the same way). Here are some winning combinations:
  - whole-wheat pasta with tomato sauce
  - brown rice stir-fry with broccoli and red pepper
  - whole-grain breakfast cereal topped with strawberries

- whole-grain toast with a small glass of orange juice
- spinach salad tossed with orange or grapefruit segments
• Don't take your calcium supplements with an iron-rich meal since these two minerals compete with each other for absorption.
• Drink tea between rather than during meals—tea contains tannins, compounds that inhibit iron absorption. Or add a little milk or lemon to your tea, since both inactivate its iron-binding properties.
• Cook your vegetables. Phytic acid (phytate), found in plant foods, can attach to iron and hamper its absorption. Cooking vegetables like spinach releases some of the iron that's bound to phytates.

Iron Supplements

To help you meet your daily iron requirements, taking a multivitamin and mineral supplement is a wise idea, especially for vegetarians and menstruating women. Most regular formulas provide 10 milligrams, but you can find multivitamins that provide up to 18 milligrams of the mineral.

If you're diagnosed with depleted iron stores or iron-deficiency anemia, your dietitian or doctor will prescribe single iron pills. Depending on the extent of your iron deficiency, you'll take one to three iron tablets (each containing 50 to 100 milligrams of elemental iron) per day. If you're advised to take an iron pill, take it on an empty stomach to enhance absorption. Many people find that taking their iron supplement before bed rather than during the day reduces stomach upset. Taking iron with a glass of orange juice or a vitamin C supplement helps to enhance iron absorption.

Depending on how much iron you take each day, a supplementation period of 12 weeks to 6 months is usually sufficient to treat anemia and restore your body's iron reserves. Your doctor will perform occasional blood tests to ensure that your iron supply has increased to an adequate level. Once your iron levels improve, discontinue the iron pills but continue taking a multivitamin and mineral supplement.

Too much iron may cause indigestion and constipation, though supplements of ferrous fumarate (e.g., Palafer, Eurofer) tend to be well tolerated. Excessive doses of iron can be toxic, causing damage to your liver and intestines. An iron overload can even result in death. To avoid these problems, do not take single iron supplements without having a blood test to confirm that you have an iron deficiency.

Manganese

Manganese facilitates thyroid function and blood-sugar control, and also supports healthy bone growth. The tiny amount of manganese in your body is found mostly in your bones, liver, kidneys and pancreas, where enzymes use the trace mineral to facilitate many different chemical reactions. Manganese also helps protect fats in the body from damage by free radicals.

Adequate Intakes (AI) of Manganese

Age	AI (milligrams)
1–3 years	1.2 mg
4–8 years	1.5 mg
Boys, 9–13 years	1.9 mg
Girls, 9–13 years	1.6 mg
Boys, 14–18 years	2.2 mg
Girls, 14–18 years	1.6 mg
Men, 19+ years	2.3 mg
Women, 19+ years	1.8 mg
Pregnancy	2.0 mg
Breastfeeding	2.6 mg

Upper Daily Limits of Manganese

Age	Upper Daily Limit (milligrams)
1–3 years	2 mg
4–8 years	3 mg
9–13 years	6 mg
14–18 years	9 mg
19+ years	11 mg

Manganese in Foods

Legumes, nuts, seeds, tea (non-herbal), green peas, leafy green vegetables, berries, pineapple, avocado, grape juice, whole grains, egg yolk and chocolate are good food sources of manganese.

Manganese Supplements

There is no evidence that single manganese supplements are necessary or beneficial for healthy people who eat a balanced diet. Deficiencies of manganese have not been seen in humans. Most multivitamin and mineral formulas provide 5 milligrams, more than twice the RDA.

Molybdenum

Molybdenum is used by the body to make many enzymes. It also helps the body mobilize iron stores. Deficiencies of this trace mineral are unknown, and as you'll see below, the amounts needed for good health are minuscule.

Adequate Intakes (AI) of Molybdenum

Age	AI (micrograms)
1–3 years	17 mcg
4–8 years	22 mcg
9–13 years	34 mcg
14–18 years	43 mcg
19+ years	45 mcg
Pregnancy	50 mcg
Breastfeeding	50 mcg

Upper Daily Limits of Molybdenum

Age	Upper Daily Limit (micrograms)
1–3 years	300 mcg (0.3 mg)
4–8 years	600 mcg (0.6 mg)
9–13 years	1100 mcg (1.1 mg)

Age	Upper Daily Limit (micrograms)
14–18 years	1700 mcg (1.7 mg)
19+ years	2000 mcg (2.0 mg)

Molybdenum in Foods

The best food sources are legumes, nuts, whole grains, liver and hard drinking water. The molybdenum content of plant foods depends on the molybdenum content of the soil in which they were grown. Animal foods, fruit and many vegetables tend to be low in molybdenum.

Molybdenum Supplements

There is no evidence that molybdenum supplements are necessary or beneficial for healthy people who eat a balanced diet. Most multivitamin and mineral formulas provide between 25 and 50 micrograms of the mineral.

Selenium

This trace mineral is used to make important antioxidant enzymes in the body. In doing so, selenium helps prevent free radicals from causing cellular damage—damage that may contribute to the development of certain cancers. Selenium also helps regulate thyroid function and plays a role in immune function. Research suggests that selenium may guard against prostate and lung cancers.

Recommended Dietary Allowance (RDA) of Selenium

Age	RDA (micrograms)
1–3 years	20 mcg
4–8 years	30 mcg
9–13 years	40 mcg
14–18 years	55 mcg
19+ years	55 mcg
Pregnancy	60 mcg
Breastfeeding	70 mcg

Upper Daily Limits of Selenium

Age	Upper Daily Limit (micrograms)
1–3 years	90 mcg
4–8 years	150 mcg
9–13 years	280 mcg
14–18 years	400 mcg
19+ years	400 mcg

Selenium in Foods

Brazil nuts, shrimp, salmon, halibut, crab, fish, pork, organ meats, wheat bran, whole-wheat bread, brown rice, onion, garlic and mushrooms are good sources of this mineral. The selenium content of plant foods depends on the selenium content of the soil in which they were grown.

Selenium Supplements

There's no evidence to warrant supplementing with selenium beyond the 55 micrograms that's usually provided in a multivitamin supplement. Although long thought to reduce prostate cancer risk, findings from SELECT, a randomized trial of 35,000 men done in 2008, found that 200 micrograms of selenium per day did not alter prostate cancer risk. In fact, the analysis revealed a small rise in type 2 diabetes among selenium users. This trend was not statistically significant, meaning it could have occurred by chance.[3]

Daily doses of selenium greater than 400 micrograms from food and supplements combined can cause loss of hair and fingernails, nausea, depression and anxiety.

Sulphur

Sulphur is necessary to help stabilize the shape and form of protein compounds in the body. It also maintains healthy bones and teeth, activates enzymes and regulates blood clotting. It's used to make insulin and the B vitamins biotin and thiamin (B1).

No recommended daily allowance has been established for sulphur as it's not considered an essential nutrient. All protein-containing foods, such as meat, organ meats, poultry, fish, eggs, dairy products, legumes and nuts, provide sulphur. An upper daily limit has not been established for this mineral.

There is no evidence that sulphur supplements are necessary or beneficial for healthy people who eat a balanced diet. Sulphur deficiencies have not been seen in humans.

Zinc

This trace mineral has many key functions in the body: It is necessary for growth and reproduction, it supports immunity and it is used to make the genetic material (DNA) of cells and enzymes. Zinc also helps the body transport vitamin A. Studies suggest that zinc lozenges may reduce the severity and duration of the common cold.

Recommended Dietary Allowance (RDA) of Zinc

Age	RDA (milligrams)
1–3 years	3 mg
4–8 years	5 mg
9–13 years	8 mg
Boys, 14–18 years	11 mg
Girls, 14–18 years	9 mg
Men, 19+ years	11 mg
Women, 19+ years	8 mg
Pregnancy	11 mg
Breastfeeding	12 mg

Upper Daily Limits of Zinc

Age	Upper Daily Limit (milligrams)
1–3 years	7 mg
4–8 years	12 mg
9–13 years	23 mg
14–18 years	34 mg
19+ years	40 mg

Zinc in Foods

Seafood (especially oysters and crab), red meat, poultry (dark meat), yogurt, nuts, legumes, wheat bran, wheat germ, whole grains and enriched breakfast cereals are rich in zinc. Drinking coffee with zinc-rich foods can decrease absorption of the mineral by 50 percent.

Food	Zinc (milligrams)
Beef, cooked, 3 oz (90 g)	4.5 mg
Chicken, cooked, 3 oz (90 g)	1.5 mg
Turkey, cooked, 3 oz (90 g)	1.0 mg
Lamb, cooked, 3 oz (90 g)	1.0 mg
Pork, cooked, 3 oz (90 g)	2.3 mg
Crab, king, cooked, 3 oz (90 g)	6.8 mg
Oysters, eastern, 3 oz (90 g)	40.5 mg
Milk, 1 cup (250 ml)	1.0 mg
Cheese, cheddar, 1 oz (30 g)	0.9 mg
Yogurt, 3/4 cup (175 ml)	1.4 mg
Egg, whole, 1	0.5 mg
Bran flakes, 3/4 cup (175 ml)	1.2–3.7 mg
Wheat germ, 2 tbsp (30 ml)	2.3 mg
Baked beans, 1 cup (250 ml)	4.0–7.2 mg
Black beans, cooked, 1 cup (250 ml)	3.6 mg
Garbanzo beans, cooked, 1 cup (250 ml)	5.0 mg
Green peas, cooked, 1/2 cup (125 ml)	1.0 mg
Lentils, cooked, 1 cup (250 ml)	5.0 mg
Lima beans, 1/2 cup (125 ml)	1.9 mg
Soy/rice beverage, fortified, 1 cup (250 ml)	1.0 mg
Soybeans, cooked, 1 cup (250 ml)	2.0 mg
Tofu, 1/2 cup (125 ml)	2.0 mg
Veggie burger, 1	1.1–5.5 mg
Cashews, 1/4 cup (60 ml)	1.9 mg
Pumpkin seeds, 1/4 cup (60 ml)	2.6 mg
Sunflower seeds, 1/4 cup (60 ml)	1.8 mg

Source: Canadian Nutrient File 2007b. Retrieved July 2009 from http://webprod.hc-sc.gc.ca/cnf-fce/index-eng.jsp. Adapted and reproduced with permission of the Minister of Public Works and Government Services Canada, 2009.

Zinc Supplements

Your diet plus a good multivitamin and mineral supplement should give you all the zinc you need to stay healthy. Most multivitamin and mineral formulas provide 10 to 20 milligrams of this trace mineral. Single zinc supplements are rarely appropriate. Too much zinc has toxic effects and can cause copper deficiency, heart problems and anemia. Consuming amounts greater than 40 to 50 milligrams per day can depress your immune system, making you more susceptible to infection. If you take separate zinc supplements, do not exceed 40 milligrams per day. Since large amounts of zinc can deplete the body's copper stores, buy a zinc supplement with a zinc-to-copper ratio of 10:1 (for every 10 milligrams of zinc, 1 milligram of copper is present).

To help treat a cold, take a zinc acetate or zinc gluconate lozenge, containing 10 to 20 milligrams of zinc per lozenge, every 2 to 3 hours to a maximum of five per day (see page 296 for more on treating colds).

Nickel, Silicon, Tin, Vanadium, Cobalt and Arsenic

These six trace minerals play important roles in maintaining our health, but they are not considered essential nutrients. Research to determine if such trace minerals are required in the diet is difficult because the quantities in the body are so small and human deficiencies are unknown.

Sodium (Sodium Chloride)

Sodium is essential for life. This electrolyte mineral regulates fluid balance in the body and maintains blood volume and blood pressure. Sodium is also critical for the transmission of nerve impulses, muscle contraction and heart function. Although we need a small amount of sodium for good health, excess sodium in the diet can cause and worsen high blood pressure.

Adequate Intakes (AI) of Sodium

Age	AI (milligrams)
1–3 years	1000 mg
4–8 years	1200 mg
9–13 years	1500 mg

Age	AI (milligrams)
14–18 years	1500 mg
19–50 years	1500 mg
51–70 years	1300 mg
71+ years	1200 mg
Pregnancy	1500 mg
Breastfeeding	1500 mg

Upper Daily Limits of Sodium

Age	Upper Daily Limit (milligrams)
1–3 years	1500 mg
4–8 years	1900 mg
9–13 years	2200 mg
14–18 years	2300 mg
19+ years	2300 mg

Table salt, soy sauce, processed foods, snack foods, dairy products and seafood all provide significant amounts of sodium from sodium chloride (salt).

Sodium tablets are not recommended nor are they warranted. Excess sodium can exacerbate high blood pressure, heart failure and kidney disease. Sodium's role in a healthy diet is discussed in more detail in Chapter 5, page 107.

Potassium

This electrolyte mineral maintains normal fluid balance and nerve function, promotes normal muscle function and supports cell structure and integrity. An adequate intake of potassium may help prevent and treat high blood pressure and reduce the risk of stroke, osteoporosis and kidney stones.

Adequate Intakes (AI) of Potassium

Age	AI (milligrams)
1–3 years	3000 mg
4–8 years	3800 mg
9–13 years	4500 mg
14–18 years	4700 mg
19+ years	4700 mg
Pregnancy	4700 mg
Breastfeeding	5100 mg
Upper daily limit	*None established*

Potassium in Foods

Meat, chicken, salmon, cod, lima beans, potatoes, bananas, oranges, orange juice, avocado, cantaloupe, peaches, tomatoes and tomato juice are good sources of potassium.

Food	Potassium (milligrams)
Buttermilk, 1%, 1 cup (250 ml)	391 mg
Milk, skim, 1 cup (250 ml)	404 mg
Yogurt, plain, 1%, 3/4 cup (175 ml)	410 mg
Apricots, 4, medium	362 mg
Avocado, 1 medium	345 mg
Banana, 1 medium	422 mg
Cantaloupe, cubed, 1 cup (250 ml)	440 mg
Dates, dried, 4	217 mg
Honeydew, cubed, 1 cup (250 ml)	426 mg
Nectarine, 1 medium	273 mg
Orange, 1 medium	237 mg
Orange juice, 1/2 cup (125 ml)	262 mg
Prune juice, 1/2 cup (125 ml)	373 mg
Prunes, dried, 4	245 mg

Food	Potassium (milligrams)
Raisins, 1/4 cup (60 ml)	275 mg
Spinach, cooked, 1/2 cup (125 ml)	443 mg
Sweet potato, baked, 1 small	285 mg
Swiss chard, cooked, 1/2 cup (125 ml)	508 mg
Tomato juice, 1/2 cup (125 ml)	294 mg
Winter squash, 1/2 cup (125 ml)	214 mg
Black beans, cooked 3/4 cup (175 ml)	452 mg
Chickpeas, cooked, 3/4 cup (175 ml)	353 mg
Kidney beans, cooked, 3/4 cup (175 ml)	528 mg
Lentils, cooked, 3/4 cup (175 ml)	540 mg
Nuts, mixed, 1/4 cup (60 ml)	207 mg
Molasses, blackstrap, 1 tbsp (15 ml)	518 mg

Source: Adapted from the *Canadian Nutrient File*, Health Canada (2006)©. Adapted and reproduced with the permission of the Minister of Public Works and Government Services Canada, 2009.

Potassium Supplements

Healthy people who eat a balanced diet do not need potassium supplements. Potassium is widespread in foods and deficiency is rare. However, people with high blood pressure or a potassium deficiency (often caused by a disease or medication) may benefit from potassium supplements. In this case, your doctor will determine your dose of potassium based on your blood level of the nutrient.

Excessive intakes of potassium can cause stomach upset, nausea, diarrhea, vomiting, flatulence and potentially life-threatening levels of potassium in the bloodstream.

5

Elements of a Healthy Diet

These days, we're bombarded with nutrition and food messages, some complicated and some conflicting. If you read the newspaper or watch the news, it's impossible to ignore the dozens of reports about studies linking diet to health. Some headlines leave people wondering if scientists are capable of making up their minds. From vitamin E (the heart healthy supplement that increased heart failure) to dietary fibre (the substance that did—then didn't—and then did help prevent colon cancer) to margarine (the low-saturated-fat spread that raised blood cholesterol), dietary flip-flops can make even the savviest consumer's head spin.

Conflicting news stories are frustrating, especially if you're trying to make healthy lifestyle changes. Recent controversies over fish, carbohydrates and even chocolate and coffee have raised more questions and left many people wondering what to eat. Why go to the trouble of changing your diet when today's health food or supplement might be next month's bad news?

Mixed messages in health stories are inevitable. Scientific research is a back-and-forth process and contradictions are bound to occur. With so many studies investigating the same topic in different ways, results won't always be the same. Another problem: News reports don't always capture the complexity of the research to help you determine if a study is important to you. Space in the paper and time on the air is limited so it's not always possible to provide all the supplemental information required to fully understand the research and its implications.

The key is to not react to every single study. The media often pick up on sensational or controversial studies in order to make headlines. It's important to realize that nutrition science is evolving. As it advances, it seldom follows a straight path. For every positive study, there is usually a negative study. In spite of this, we are making progress. We know far more today about how diet affects health than we did 20 years ago.

In the first few chapters of this book, I discussed the important role nutrients—both macro (big) nutrients like carbohydrate, protein and fat, and micro (tiny) nutrients like vitamins and minerals—play in our health. But we don't eat nutrients in isolation. Rather, we consume them in whole foods that provide many other protective compounds. Fruit, vegetables, whole grains, legumes and other plant foods offer fibre and many types of naturally occurring compounds known as phytochemicals. Some phytochemicals act as antioxidants, others trigger enzymes that inactivate cancer-causing substances and yet others boost the body's immune system. Some phytochemicals even mimic the beneficial effects of estrogen in our body.

Scientists are continually discovering that healthy eating means eating a variety of foods that contain these protective compounds, since phytochemicals likely work in concert with the vitamins and minerals in foods to exert their health benefits. We're also learning that certain foods, or components of them, may not be so good for our health if consumed in excess. Sodium, alcohol and caffeine fall into this category.

So what does a healthy diet look like? I don't believe in a "one size fits all" approach. Each person has a unique metabolism, unique nutrient needs and unique food preferences. But given the scientific evidence to date, I do believe that a plant-based diet is the healthiest way to eat. Repeatedly, nutrition researchers are finding that an increased intake of vegetables, fruit, whole grains and other plant foods is associated with a lower risk for high blood pressure, heart disease, stroke, osteoporosis and many types of cancer.

Eating a plant-based diet does not mean following a strict vegetarian diet. Rather, it means that your meals focus on whole grains, vegetables, fruit and legumes, with less emphasis placed on animal foods like meat and poultry. For some people, making the transition to a plant-based diet means eating a 4 ounce (120 g) portion of steak instead of their usual 10 ounce (300 g) cut. For others it means adding lentils instead of ground beef to pasta sauce, or pouring a soy beverage over breakfast cereal instead of milk.

Here's a closer look at what foods make up a healthy diet.

Fruit and Vegetables

7 to 10 servings per day
1 serving = 1 medium-sized fruit, 1/4 cup (60 ml) dried fruit, 1/2 cup (125 ml) cooked vegetables, 1 cup (250 ml) salad greens or 1/2 cup (125 ml) 100% pure juice

From a nutrition standpoint, fruit and vegetables are pretty tough to beat. They are an excellent source of dietary fibre, potassium, vitamin C and folate, nutrients that are vital for maintaining good health and guarding against disease. Indeed, a diet rich in colourful, nutrient-dense produce has been linked to a lower risk of cancer, heart disease, stroke, cataracts, macular degeneration and type 2 diabetes. Adding fruit and vegetables to your diet can also help control blood pressure and cholesterol, decrease bone loss, promote weight loss and prevent a painful intestinal condition called diverticulitis.

Despite knowing that these foods are good for us, many of us still fall short of the recommended 7 to 10 daily servings. We tell ourselves we don't have time and grab a bagel instead of an apple. Or we throw together pasta with tomato sauce instead of preparing a salad and baked potato. Perhaps we think a strawberry cereal bar counts as a fruit serving. And when it comes right down to it, some people just don't like vegetables. Well, it's time to learn to love them!

Antioxidants

Fruit and vegetables provide us with plenty of antioxidants, compounds that protect our cells from damage caused by free radical molecules. Every day, as a consequence of normal metabolism, our bodies form free radicals from oxygen. Pollution and cigarette smoke increase the number of free radicals our bodies are exposed to. Free radicals roam the body and damage the genetic material of cells, which may lead to cancer development. They can also damage protein and fat molecules.

Each cell in our body has a defence mechanism against free radicals, consisting, in part, of a system of enzymes and antioxidants. Antioxidants act as scavengers, mopping up free radicals before they cause harm. Without continuous antioxidant protection, our cells would not survive. Dietary antioxidants like beta carotene and vitamins C and E, as well as many phytochemicals, provide the body with extra ammunition against free radicals.

Choosing Fruit and Vegetables

When choosing your fruit and vegetables, consider their colour. Many of the natural chemicals in a plant that offer health benefits are the same ones responsible for the plant's vibrant colour. For instance, beta carotene is found in orange-coloured fruit and in orange and dark-green vegetables. Lycopene is plentiful in red-coloured fruit, whereas lutein is found in dark-green and orange vegetables. Other protective plant components include anthocyanins (abundant in deep-red and purple fruit; see Chapter 8, page 169), cruciferous compounds (broccoli, cauliflower and cabbage) and sulphur compounds (garlic, onions and leeks).

Protective Plant Components in Fruit and Vegetables

Beta carotene	Lycopene	Lutein
Apricots	Grapefruit, pink and red	Grapes
Cantaloupe	Guava	Kiwi
Mango	Tomatoes	Orange juice
Nectarines	Canned tomatoes	Beet greens
Papaya	Tomato sauce	Collard greens
Peaches	Tomato juice	Kale
Broccoli	Watermelon	Okra
Brussels sprouts		Red pepper
Carrots		Romaine lettuce
Rapini		Spinach
Spinach		Zucchini
Sweet potato		
Winter squash		

Anthocyanins	Cruciferous Compounds	Sulphur Compounds
Black currants	Bok choy	Garlic
Blackberries	Broccoli	Green onions
Blueberries	Cabbage	Leeks
Boysenberries	Cauliflower	Onions

Anthocyanins	Cruciferous Compounds	Sulphur Compounds
Cherries	Collard greens	Shallots
Cranberries	Kale	
Plums	Radish	
Raisins	Rutabaga	
Raspberries	Turnip	
Red grapes		
Strawberries		

Beta carotene, lutein and lycopene belong to the carotenoid family, a group of natural chemicals that act as antioxidants in many parts of our body. Dietary carotenoids aren't that well absorbed—our small intestine takes in roughly 10 percent to 30 percent of them from food. Because they are fat-soluble molecules, you'll absorb more if you eat these foods with a small amount of fat. Try a yogurt dip with carrot sticks, a splash of salad dressing on your roasted red pepper or a little olive oil in lycopene-rich pasta sauce. Heat-processed tomato products (juice, sauce, ketchup) offer a much more accessible form of lycopene than do fresh tomatoes. You'll learn more about lycopene and lutein in Chapter 8, page 171.

Here are a few tips to help you add more fresh produce to your daily diet:

- Buy pre-chopped vegetables like baby carrots or broccoli and cauliflower florets. They're ready to throw in the microwave, steamer or salad bowl.
- Pick up fresh fruit or raw veggies from the salad bar at the local super-market.
- Drink vegetable juice instead of diet drinks or coffee at lunch.
- Eat green or spinach salad for lunch (if ordering in a restaurant, ask for the dressing on the side).
- For a nutrient boost, use romaine and other dark green lettuces in salad.
- Ask for tomatoes, cucumbers and lettuce in your sandwich. When making a sandwich yourself, reach for spinach leaves as a change from lettuce.
- Add quick-cooking greens like spinach, kale, rapini or Swiss chard to soups and pasta sauces.
- Fortify soups, pasta sauces and casseroles with grated zucchini and grated carrot.
- Bake (or microwave) a sweet potato for a change from rice or pasta.

- Add slices of lemon, lime or orange to water for flavour and a little vitamin C.
- Add frozen berries to a breakfast smoothie made with low-fat milk or soy beverage.
- Top desserts such as sorbet, frozen yogurt or even chocolate cake with raspberries, blueberries or sliced strawberries.
- Out of season, reach for frozen fruit and vegetables.

Whole Grains

At least 3 servings per day
1 serving = 1 slice of bread, 1/2 cup (125 ml) oatmeal, 1 oz (30 g) cold cereal, 1/2 cup (125 ml) cooked brown rice or whole-wheat pasta

Grains provide the fuel that our brain, nervous system and muscles rely on. All grains—be it wheat, rye, oats or spelt—start out as whole-grain kernels composed of three layers: the outer bran layer, where nearly all the fibre is; the inner germ layer, which is rich in nutrients, antioxidants and healthy fats; and the endosperm, which contains most of the starch. Eating foods made from whole grains means you're getting *all* parts of the grain kernel and all the nutrients, phytochemicals and fibre they contain. In fact, the fibre content of whole grains can be four times that of refined grains! The reason whole grains are darker and chewier than refined grains is that they contain all three components of the grain kernel.

When whole grains are refined, milled, scraped and heat-processed into flakes, puffs or white flour, the bran and germ are removed, leaving only the starchy endosperm. Without bran and germ about 25 percent of a grain's protein is lost, along with at least 17 nutrients. In addition to having less protein, refined grains contain less fibre, vitamins and minerals, and 75 percent fewer phytochemicals. Refined grains are enriched with some, but not all, vitamins and minerals lost through processing. However, disease-fighting phytochemicals are not added back to refined grains.

Whole grains can be eaten whole (e.g., wheat berries, oats), cracked, split, flaked or ground. Often they're milled into flour and used to make breads, cereals, pastas and crackers. A whole grain can be a single food like oatmeal, brown rice, flaxseed, popcorn, kamut, millet or quinoa, or it can be an ingredient in another food such as bread, crackers or ready-to-eat breakfast cereal.

All grains are naturally low in fat and good sources of energy-yielding carbo-hydrate and various vitamins and minerals. But grains that haven't been refined are much better for you, thanks to their sizeable nutrient content. It's this package of nutrients—vitamins, minerals, fibre, antioxidants and phytochemi-cals—that's thought to exert health benefits. Scientists suspect the individual components of whole grains work together to guard against disease.

Studies consistently show that people who eat their grains whole instead of refined have better health outcomes. Researchers have linked a high intake of total whole grains, as well as specific whole grains (e.g., oats, flaxseed and rye), with a lower risk of many diseases.

When it comes to the beneficial health effects of whole grains, evidence is strongest in relation to heart disease. Large studies have reported that people who eat more whole grains have a lower risk for heart attack and stroke. In general, those with the highest intakes of whole grains (about 3 servings per day) had a risk of heart disease that was 20 percent to 30 percent lower than those with the lowest intakes. A steady intake of whole grains may also delay the progression of heart disease by slowing the buildup of plaque in the arteries.

There are many ways in which whole grains can protect the heart. For starters, they're good sources of nutrients that are linked to protection from heart disease, including folate, vitamin E, magnesium and potassium. Soluble fibre in oats, barley and flaxseed can also help to keep LDL cholesterol levels in the healthy range, thereby reducing heart disease risk. Phytosterols in whole grains have also been shown to help reduce elevated blood cholesterol levels.

Research also suggests that eating 3 daily servings of whole grains, compared with few or none, can significantly lower the risk of developing type 2 diabetes. One study, which followed 9702 men and 15,365 women for 7 years, found that getting more fibre from whole grains, but not fruit and vegetables, reduced the onset of type 2 diabetes. Individuals who ate the most cereal fibre (17 grams per day) were almost 30 percent less likely to develop diabetes than those who averaged only 7 grams per day.[1] Many studies have also shown that men and women who consume at least 3 servings of whole grains per day are much less likely to develop insulin resistance (when the body can't properly use insulin or blood glucose), a precursor to type 2 diabetes.

Increasing your whole-grain intake might also help reduce the risk of colon cancer. One study followed 61,433 Swedish women for almost 15 years and found that those who ate the most whole grains—at least 4.5 daily servings versus less than 1.5—were 35 percent less likely to develop colon cancer.[2]

What Counts as Whole Grain?

Consuming at least 3 servings each day isn't difficult. Consider that 1 serving is equivalent to a 30 gram slice of 100% whole-grain bread, 30 grams of whole-grain breakfast cereal, 1/2 cup (125 ml) of a cooked grain like brown rice or quinoa, or 2 tablespoons (25 ml) of ground flaxseed. Most of us know that oatmeal, brown rice or whole-wheat pasta counts as a whole grain. But it's not always easy to tell if a loaf of bread, box of crackers or package of ready-to-eat breakfast cereal contains 100% whole grains. The only way to know for sure is to read labels. You may need to look past the front of the package and examine the ingredient list to find out if a product is completely or predominantly whole grain. Here's how and what to check:

READ PACKAGE LABELS. Look for "100% whole grain" claims on food packages. The greater the percentage of whole grain, the greater the health benefit. Be skeptical if you see only the words "whole grain" or "made with whole grains" without any mention of percentage: These products may contain only tiny amounts of whole grain.

Words that always mean whole grain:
(These ingredients contain all parts of the grain.)
- whole-grain whole wheat
- whole [name of grain]
- stoneground whole [name of grain]
- brown rice
- oats, oatmeal
- wheat berries

Words that may not mean whole grain:
(These ingredients may be missing part of the grain.)
- whole wheat
- semolina
- durum wheat
- organic flour
- multigrain

Words that mean refined grain:
(These ingredients may be missing part of the grain.)
- wheat flour
- unbleached wheat flour

- cornmeal
- wheat germ

SCAN THE INGREDIENT LIST. Look for a "whole" grain to be listed first (e.g., whole-grain whole wheat, whole rye, whole spelt, brown rice, oats, flaxseed). If a whole grain is listed second, you might be getting just a little or maybe half whole grain, especially if there are only a few ingredients in the product. (Ingredients are listed by weight from most to least.)

Fish

2 servings per week
1 serving = 3 oz (90 g)

Fish is an excellent source of protein that's low in cholesterol-raising saturated fat. Ever since studies demonstrated lower rates of dying from heart disease among Greenland Inuit, North Americans have been repeatedly told to eat more fish. The cardio-protective benefits of eating fish are so clear that Health Canada and the Heart and Stroke Foundation of Canada advise people to consume fish, especially fatty fish, at least two times per week. Also, for the first time, the 2007 Canada's Food Guide recommends that Canadians eat fish at least twice weekly.

FISH AND HEART HEALTH. The cardiovascular benefits of fish have been documented in several prospective studies and randomized clinical trials. A 2006 report published in the *Journal of the American Medical Association* concluded that eating 1 to 2 servings of fish per week is enough to reduce the risk of dying from heart attack by 36 percent. Researchers from Harvard School of Public Health and Harvard Medical School based their conclusions on a review of hundreds of studies about fish and health.[3]

Scientists attribute the heart healthy properties of fish to its omega-3 fat content. Cold water fish like salmon, trout, sardines, mackerel, Arctic char and herring are particularly high in two omega-3 fats, DHA (docosahexanaenoic acid) and EPA (eicosapentaenoic acid). Omega-3 fats in fish lower blood triglycerides (fats), make the blood less likely to form clots, reduce inflammation and protect against irregular heartbeats that cause sudden cardiac death.

FISH AND BRAIN HEALTH. Omega-3 fatty acids, especially DHA found in fish, make up 60 percent of the communicating membranes of the brain. These fats help keep the lining of brain cells flexible so memory messages can pass easily between cells. All brain cell membranes continuously need to refresh themselves with a new supply of fatty acids.

Omega-3 fatty acids in fish are needed for the development and maintenance of the brain, eyes and nervous tissue throughout life, beginning in the final trimester of pregnancy. An adequate supply of DHA is vital during the periods of rapid brain development in the womb, as well as during infancy and childhood. Since the amount of DHA a developing fetus or breastfed infant receives is dependent on a mother's diet, it's important for pregnant and breast-feeding women to include fish in their diet or take a fish oil supplement.

Eating fish may also keep our brains healthy as we age. A study that followed 815 adults, aged 65 to 94 years, for almost 4 years revealed that those who ate fish at least once per week were 60 percent less likely to develop Alzheimer's disease than people who rarely or never ate fish. Total polyunsaturated fat intake and DHA intake were both associated with a lower risk of the disease.[4] Other studies have suggested that eating fish can help reduce the risk of vascular dementia, a common form of dementia caused by the narrowing and blocking of the arteries that supply blood to the brain.

FISH AND VISION. A number of studies also suggest that eating fish, especially fatty fish, one to four times per week, guards against age-related macular degeneration and reduces the risk of the disease progressing to an advanced form. Macular degeneration attacks the central part of the retina resulting in progressive loss of visual sharpness, making it difficult to drive a car, read a book and recognize faces. Macular degeneration is the leading cause of severe vision loss in older adults.

Here are some tips to help you add fish to your family's menu two times each week:

- Enjoy a whole-grain bagel topped with smoked salmon, light cream cheese and a few capers.
- Serve a grilled or baked salmon fillet on a bed of whole-grain pasta tossed with olive oil, chopped fresh dill, sliced scallions and black pepper.
- Wrap pieces of sautéed halibut or tilapia, shredded cabbage, guacamole and salsa in whole-wheat tortillas for tasty fish tacos.

- Skewer marinated chunks of fresh fish, scallops or shrimp and your favourite vegetables, and broil or grill on the barbecue.
- Make your own version of niçoise salad by combining canned light tuna with chilled cooked green peas, halved cooked baby potatoes, a sliced hard-cooked egg, capers and olives. Season to taste and drizzle with a lemon vinaigrette.

Legumes and Soy Foods

3 servings per week
1 serving = 3/4 cup (175 ml)

Legumes are low in fat and an excellent source of protein, fibre, folate, calcium and magnesium. In fact, next to bran cereal, legumes deliver more fibre per serving than any other food. Consider that 3/4 cup (175 ml) of cooked lentils or black beans packs in 12 grams of fibre—half a day's worth for women! Plus, legumes provide a source of low-glycemic carbohydrate that's digested slowly and, as a result, released gradually as blood sugar, fending off sharp rises and dips in energy.

Like other plant foods, legumes contain disease-fighting phytochemicals including saponins, protease inhibitors and phytic acid, compounds that appear to protect cells from genetic damage, which can lead to cancer.

LEGUMES AND HEART DISEASE. There's good evidence that adding legumes to your diet can help keep your heart healthy. When researchers from Tulane University School of Public Health and Tropical Medicine followed 9632 healthy men and women for 19 years, they found that those who ate dry beans, peas or peanuts at least four times weekly had a risk of coronary heart disease that was 22 percent lower than people who ate them less than once weekly.[5] Legumes can help ward off heart disease by modifying two risk factors for the disease: high blood cholesterol and high blood pressure. Numerous studies have also demonstrated the ability of soybeans to lower elevated blood cholesterol levels. As well, studies have revealed the blood pressure–reducing effect of legumes, thanks to their high magnesium content.

LEGUMES AND PROSTATE CANCER. Eating legumes may also lower the risk of prostate cancer. Some, but not all, studies have linked high intakes of soybeans with protection from the disease. A study involving 1619 men diagnosed with prostate cancer and 1618 healthy men found that those who consumed the most legumes were 38 percent less likely to develop prostate cancer. It's not only soybeans that offer protection against prostate cancer. When the researchers excluded soybeans from the analysis, the protective effects of legumes were still just as powerful.[6]

SOYBEANS AND BREAST CANCER. Breast cancer rates among women in Asian countries have long been noted as substantially lower than those among women in North America, a fact that's led researchers to speculate that diet—in particular soy—might play a role. But in addition to eating soy on a regular basis, Asians generally have a low-fat diet and eat more fish and vegetables than North Americans do.

Relatively few studies have measured soy intake and breast cancer risk among North American women. Despite this, there is some evidence that soy can reduce the risk of breast cancer in non-Asian women. Researchers from Johns Hopkins University School of Medicine combined the results of 18 studies that examined soy intake and breast cancer risk. Among all women, high soy intake (tofu and soy foods) was associated with a modest protective effect. Women who consumed the most soy had a 14 percent lower risk of breast cancer. Soy's protective effect was stronger in premenopausal women than in post-menopausal women. Premenopausal women with high soy intakes were 30 percent less likely to develop breast cancer than premenopausal women who consumed the least soy.[7]

Isoflavones in soybeans behave like weak forms of the body's own estrogen. That means that isoflavones compete for the same place on breast cells that estrogen does. By attaching to breast cell receptors, isoflavones elbow out the estrogen that can trigger the growth of breast cancer. By counteracting the action of estrogen, it's thought that soybeans and soy foods can reduce a woman's risk of breast cancer.

When it comes to preventing breast cancer, what seems most important is when you start consuming soy foods. A study of 3015 women living in China revealed that those who consumed the most soy foods during adolescence (age 13 to 15 years) had only half the breast cancer risk compared with women whose diets contained the least.[8] It's thought that soy isoflavones may confer their protective effects during puberty when breast cells are maturing and are more vulnerable to cancer-causing substances.

If soy isoflavones mimic the action of estrogen in the body, many women worry that eating soy foods could possibly promote the development of breast cancer. The concern is that soy isoflavones could increase a woman's total estrogen levels and encourage the growth of estrogen-dependent breast cancer, especially in women who already have the disease. But it's not that simple. Some studies conducted in animals and test tubes indicate that isoflavones inhibit the development of breast cancer, while others suggest they may increase breast cancer cell growth. It depends on the particular isoflavone studied (soybeans are rich in two different isoflavones) and the amount of soy foods used. There's no compelling evidence that soy foods increase breast cancer, but research is ongoing.

That said, I do advise against the use of isoflavone supplements, which offer highly concentrated doses. We just don't have data on the long-term safety of these supplements. Experts also advise women who have had breast cancer to avoid soy supplements and soy protein powders. Although it's felt that eating foods made from soybeans a few times a week is safe, many breast cancer survivors choose to avoid soy all together. It's clearly a personal decision.

- Aim to have at least three legume-based meals per week. Doing so will help lower your saturated fat intake and boost your fibre intake.
- Toss cooked legumes into leafy green and pasta salads.
- Add chickpeas to your favourite Greek salad recipe for extra protein and fibre.
- Serve soup made from dried beans or peas. Try minestrone, split pea, black bean or lentil soup.
- Add cooked legumes or chopped firm tofu to canned or homemade soups and stews.
- Add cooked chickpeas to grain dishes such as couscous or rice pilafs.
- Add black beans or pinto beans to tacos and burritos. Use half the amount of lean ground meat you normally would and make up the difference with beans.
- Sauté legumes, cubed tofu or tempeh with spinach and tomatoes and serve over cooked whole-wheat pasta.
- Add white kidney beans to a tomato-based pasta sauce for a Mediterranean-inspired meal.

Nuts

5 servings per week
1 serving = 1 oz (30 g)

There's good reason to think that adding a handful of nuts to your daily diet will help keep you healthy. Over the past decade numerous studies have tied the consumption of nuts with protection from heart attack, high blood pressure, diabetes and even Alzheimer's disease. Eating nuts on a regular basis can also help keep blood cholesterol and blood pressure numbers in check.

Nuts are cholesterol free but they are high in fat. As much as 90 percent of the calories in nuts comes from fat—but the good news is that most of the fat is the healthy unsaturated kind. Nuts contain mainly polyunsaturated and monounsaturated fats and only small amounts of saturated fat, the type that raises LDL (bad) cholesterol in the blood.

Nuts are high in protein and unusually rich in arginine, an amino acid that may improve blood vessel function. Nuts are also a good source of magnesium, a mineral shown to help maintain a healthy blood pressure. Walnuts are an excellent source of alpha-linolenic acid (ALA), an omega-3 fatty acid that's thought to protect against irregular heart rhythms. Nuts are also a good source of vitamin E, folate, B vitamins, potassium and fibre, nutrients demonstrated to have cardio-protective properties.

While nuts are nutritious, they are high in calories. A 1 ounce (30 g) serving of nuts delivers between 160 and 200 calories. That's considerably more than 1 ounce of chicken or lean meat, which contains roughly 55 calories. One ounce of nuts isn't that large—you'll need to count out 8 Brazil nuts, 18 cashews, 14 walnut halves, 24 almonds or 28 peanuts to make sure you're eating only 1 serving. To prevent weight gain, you'll also need to subtract that number of calories from your daily diet. Substitute nuts for less healthy foods like cookies, ice cream, candy, soft drinks, chips and refined starchy foods.

Aim for at least 5 servings of nuts a week, but keep your serving size to 1 ounce (30 g), or about 1/4 cup (60 ml). Try the following:

- Toss a handful of peanuts into an Asian-style stir-fry.
- Stir-fry collard greens with cashews and a teaspoon of sesame oil.
- Toss a handful of toasted nuts and seeds into green salads.
- Add toasted walnuts to whole-grain pasta tossed in olive oil.
- Add nuts to side dishes—hazelnuts to brown rice, pine nuts to couscous or slivered almonds to green beans.
- Sprinkle casseroles with seeds or chopped nuts.
- Mix sunflower or pumpkin seeds into a bowl of yogurt or hot cereal.
- Snack on a small handful of almonds and dried apricots.

Water

It's easy to forget that water is an essential nutrient. While a deficiency of other nutrients can take weeks, months or even years to develop, you can survive only a few days without water. In the body, water becomes the fluid in which all body functions occur. The fluid in your bloodstream transports nutrients and oxygen to your cells. The fluid in your urine removes waste products from your body. And the fluid in your sweat allows your muscles to release heat during physical exertion.

If you drink too little fluid or lose too much through sweat, your body can't perform these tasks properly and you won't feel your best.

Symptoms of dehydration include early fatigue during exercise, cramping, headaches, dizziness, nausea and loss of appetite. The simplest way to tell if you're replacing the fluid you lose is to check the colour and quantity of your urine. It should be clear and plentiful. If it's dark and scanty, you need to drink more fluids. However, if you're taking a multivitamin supplement containing the B vitamin riboflavin, your urine may be bright yellow; in this case, quantity is a better indicator.

Don't rely on thirst to tell you when you need to drink. Feeling thirsty is an indication that you're already dehydrated—the sensation is triggered by a high concentration of salt in your blood. But the thirst mechanism does not work as well for infants and children, people who are sick and the elderly. Nor is thirst a good indicator during exercise in warm weather. Water needs vary, depending on your age, diet, exercise and the weather.

How Much Water Do You Need to Drink Each Day?

Age	Amount
1–3 years	4 cups (1 L)
4–8 years	5 cups (1.2 L)
9–13 years	8 cups (2 L)
Girls, 14–18 years	8 cups (2 L)
Boys, 14–18 years	11 cups (2.7 L)
Women, 19+ years	9 cups (2.2 L)
Men, 19+ years	12 cups (3 L)

Age	Amount
Pregnancy	10 cups (2.5 L)
Breastfeeding	13 cups (3.2 L)

Source: National Academy of Sciences, Institute of Medicine, Food and Nutrition Board. *Dietary Reference Intakes for Water, Potassium, Sodium, Chloride, and Sulfate.* Washington, DC: The National Academy Press, 2004.

The above guidelines don't take into account factors that drive up your daily water requirements. Hot and humid weather cause your body to sweat more and increase your fluid needs. The low humidity on airplanes increases water losses through the skin and boosts your water requirements during air travel. Women who are pregnant or breastfeeding need to drink an additional 250 ml or 1 litre per day, respectively.

During exercise you do need to drink more water. Physical activity generates heat in your muscles, which your body releases through your skin as sweat. If you don't drink enough before, during and after exercise, your body can't properly release this heat. As a result your heart beats harder, your body temperature rises and, ultimately, your performance suffers.

During exercise it's important to drink 125 to 250 ml of water every 15 to 20 minutes. Sports drinks (e.g., Gatorade, Powerade) are recommended during exercise that lasts longer than 1 hour. The addition of sodium to sports drinks stimulates fluid absorption, maintains the desire to drink and helps prevent low blood sodium (hyponatremia) in prolonged exercise. Most beverages contain 6 percent to 9 percent carbohydrate in the form of liquid sugar and/or high-fructose corn syrup to provide energy for working muscles. After exercise, replenish lost fluids by consuming 500 ml of fluid for every pound of body weight lost.

Although uncommon, you can have too much of a good thing. If you drink too much water, the kidneys can't keep up and are unable to excrete the excess. Your blood becomes dilute, resulting in hyponatremia, which can lead to swelling of the brain. Even if you drink a lot of water, you're unlikely to experience hyponatremia as long as you drink it over the course of the day as opposed to drinking an enormous volume at one time. Endurance athletes such as marathon runners and triathletes, who drink large amounts of water in a short period of time, are at greater risk.

WHAT COUNTS AS WATER? All beverages—with the exception of alcoholic beverages—count towards your daily water requirements. In addition to plain drinking water, fruit juice, milk, soy beverages, soft drinks, and even coffee and tea help keep you hydrated. Older studies demonstrated caffeine to have a weak, short-term diuretic effect; from recent studies we now know the body adjusts to caffeine within 5 days of regular use, greatly reducing its mild effect of fluid loss.

Even so, some fluid choices are better than others, particularly if you're counting calories. Research suggests that our bodies don't register the calories we drink in juice, fruit drinks, soft drinks and sugared coffee drinks in the same way as the calories we eat. Calories from beverages don't trigger feelings of fullness and, as a result, liquid calories add to, rather than displace, food calories, thereby increasing our total daily calorie intake. To meet your daily water requirements, plain water outranks all other beverages because it has no calories, no sugar and no sodium and may provide some calcium, magnesium and fluoride. Ranked in order, next-best choices include unsweetened coffee and tea, low-fat milk and soy beverages, diet drinks, and calorie beverages with some nutrients (e.g., fruit juice, sports drinks).

To meet your daily water needs, practise the following:

- Drink fluids with each meal and snack and throughout the day.
- Keep a bottle of water on your desk at the office; the water cooler may be close at hand but how many times do you get up to fill your glass?
- Bring a water bottle with you when you exercise; drink 1/4 to 1/2 cup (60 to 125 ml) of fluid every 10 to 15 minutes.
- For workouts longer than 1 hour, use a sports drink like Gatorade, All Sport or Powerade. These beverages have sodium, which speeds their absorption, and carbohydrate, which your muscles use for fuel.

Do You Need Vitamin and Mineral Supplements?

There's little argument that a healthy and balanced diet helps fight disease. As you've read in the sections above, large studies have consistently shown that a diet based on whole grains, fruit, vegetables and legumes helps prevent high blood pressure, heart disease, stroke, osteoporosis, type 2 diabetes and certain cancers.

If your diet is less than stellar, you might be inclined to reach for a supplement to fill the gaps. According to Statistics Canada, nearly half (42 percent) of

Canadian adults take a vitamin and mineral supplement. Most people who pop a multivitamin supplement do so as a form of health insurance. Yet there's no evidence that taking a one-a-day formula will prevent future disease.

A 2006 review conducted by the U.S. National Institutes of Health found too few studies to give multivitamins a go-ahead for heart disease and cancer prevention.[9] Despite the lack of evidence for benefit or harm, it's still prudent for some segments of the population to reach for a multivitamin to fill nutritional gaps.

There's clear evidence that taking a multivitamin with 400 micrograms (0.4 milligrams) of folic acid (a B vitamin) before and during pregnancy prevents neural tube birth defects, which affect the brain and spinal cord. When it comes to iron, it's challenging—if not impossible—for menstruating women to meet their daily requirement (18 milligrams) from food alone. This is especially true for vegetarians and women who follow a low-calorie diet.

With age, we have more difficulty absorbing vitamin B12 from food. That's why the U.S. Institute of Medicine of the National Academies advises adults over 50 years of age to get the nutrient from a supplement or fortified foods such as soy beverages. Since B12 is found only in animal foods, strict vegetarians must also rely on a multivitamin to meet their daily needs.

A multivitamin can provide a safety net if you don't get your full complement of nutrients from diet. And despite good intentions, not all of us follow Canada's Food Guide to the letter. Stress, workplace demands and lack of time and energy are common barriers to eating healthfully.

But more is not better. A 2007 study published in the *Journal of the National Cancer Institute* found that taking a multivitamin more than seven times per week was linked with a greater risk of advanced prostate cancer and risk of death from the disease. The link was strongest in men with a family history of prostate cancer and in men who also took zinc, selenium or beta carotene supplements. Regular multivitamin use (no more than once daily) did not boost prostate cancer risk. (The researchers were unable to determine which ingredient was responsible for the association.)[10]

There's also some concern that high doses of folic acid, a B vitamin thought to guard against colon and breast cancer, might do more harm than good. Some studies hint that high dose folic acid supplements (1 milligram) may accelerate the growth of colon tumours and increase prostate cancer risk.

The following are sensible and safe strategies that can help you meet daily nutrient needs—and possibly reduce your risk of future disease.

EAT A HEALTHFUL DIET. No vitamin pill can make up for a diet that's laden with saturated and trans fats, refined sugars and sodium. Nor can a supplement offer the hundreds of naturally occurring plant chemicals thought to improve health. Ensure your daily diet includes whole grains, fruit and vegetables to get a mix of disease-fighting nutrients and phytochemicals.

TAKE A MULTIVITAMIN AND MINERAL. Choose a standard one-a-day formula that offers 100 percent of the recommended daily intake for most nutrients. Men, in particular, should avoid "mega" or "super" formulas, which can contain high amounts of zinc, selenium and/or beta carotene.

A Multivitamin Checklist

Vitamins

- Look for A, C, D, E, B1, B2, niacin, B6, folic acid and B12. Choose a formula that provides 100 percent of the RDA for B6 (1.3 to 1.7 mg), B12 (2.4 mcg) and folic acid (0.4 mg).
- Avoid products that supply more than 2500 IU of vitamin A from retinol (often called vitamin A palmitate or acetate). Excess vitamin A may increase the risk of osteoporosis and hip fracture. There's no evidence that beta carotene is harmful to bones.
- If you take prescription anticoagulants (e.g., Coumadin), speak to your doctor before taking a formula with vitamin K.

Minerals

- Look for chromium, copper, iron, magnesium, selenium and zinc.
- Premenopausal women should choose a multivitamin supplement with 10 to 18 milligrams of iron; men and post-menopausal women should look for no more than 5 to 10 milligrams of iron.
- If your diet lacks calcium, you'll need to rely on a separate supplement since the recommended daily amount is too high to fit into a multivitamin pill.

ADD EXTRA CALCIUM. Many studies have demonstrated that calcium increases bone density in post-menopausal women. In conjunction with vitamin D, calcium also reduces the risk of hip fracture. If you take calcium supplements, spread your calcium intake over the course of the day. Absorption from supplements is best in doses of 500 milligrams or less and when taken with meals. See

Chapter 4, page 56, to learn more about calcium requirements and calcium supplements.

TAKE VITAMIN D. To help guard against cancer, the Canadian Cancer Society advises taking 1000 IU of vitamin D in the fall and winter, and year-round if you're over 50, have dark skin, don't go outdoors often or wear clothing that covers most of your skin. Evidence also suggests that vitamin D may help prevent heart attack, stroke and heart failure.

Before you buy, figure out how much vitamin D you're already getting from your multivitamin and calcium supplements. Choose a supplement that contains D3 instead of the less potent D2. See Chapter 4, page 50, to learn more about vitamin D.

Foods, Beverages and Nutrients You Need to Limit

In the sections above, you've learned how certain foods and food components work to keep you healthy and to guard against disease. But it's also clear that eating certain foods on a regular basis can increase your risk for certain diseases. For example, a high intake of saturated and trans fats can raise LDL (bad) blood cholesterol, thereby increasing your risk for heart disease. (See Chapter 3, page 28, for tips to reduce saturated and trans fats in your diet.) Excess sodium—and alcohol—in the diet can boost blood pressure and increase the likelihood of heart attack and stroke. And a steady intake of refined sugars can lead to weight gain and elevated blood sugar. In the following sections, you'll learn which foods, beverages and nutrients increase the risk of health problems and how to reduce your intake.

Added Sugars

Added sugars are those added to foods during processing and preparation. You'll see them listed on food packages as a number of different ingredients, including brown sugar, corn syrup, dextrose, fructose, high-fructose corn syrup, fruit juice concentrate, glucose-fructose, honey, invert sugar, liquid sugar, malt, maltose, molasses, rice syrup, table sugar and sucrose. Manufacturers add sugars to foods to enhance flavour, add bulk and texture, and aid in the browning of foods. Added sugars are not to be confused with naturally occurring sugars, such as lactose in milk and yogurt, and fructose in fruit and sweet vegetables.

It's estimated that Canadians consume, on average, 16 teaspoons (80 g) of added sugar each day. And it's not just the usual culprits like soft drinks, cookies and candy that add sugar to your diet. Sugar also lurks in salad dressings, frozen dinners, pasta sauces, soy milk, and even peanut butter and bread.

There are several reasons why you should limit your intake of added, or refined, sugars. Eating too much sugar can increase your risk for heart disease by lowering HDL (good) cholesterol and raising blood triglycerides. A steady intake of sugar foods can also lead to overweight and obesity by adding a surplus of calories to your diet. Recent research has shown our increased use of sweeteners, especially high-fructose corn syrup, over the past 20 years correlates with rising obesity rates. This correlation doesn't prove that high-fructose corn syrup causes weight gain. But some experts contend that the body processes the fructose in high-fructose corn syrup differently than it does the glucose in cane or beet sugar. Fructose doesn't trigger hormone responses that regulate appetite and satiety, which could trick you into overeating.

Sugar-laden foods, which have a high glycemic index, can also increase your risk for insulin resistance, a condition in which the body cannot effectively remove sugar (glucose) from the bloodstream. Insulin resistance, in turn, ups your risk for developing type 2 diabetes and metabolic syndrome, two potent predictors of heart disease. (Foods with a high glycemic index are quickly digested, causing large spikes in blood sugar and an outpouring of insulin from the pancreas. Over time, the overworked pancreas can't keep up and blood sugar remains elevated. See Chapter 1, page 6, to learn more about the glycemic index.)

How Much Added Sugar?

The World Health Organization recommends we limit added sugars to no more than 10 percent of daily calories. If you follow a 2000-calorie diet, this translates to a daily maximum of 12 teaspoons (48 g) of added sugars. To me, that still sounds like a lot. But it's shocking how quickly those sugars add up if you eat processed foods. Breakfast cereals can hide as many as 15 grams of sugar per serving (almost 4 teaspoons' worth; 4 grams of sugar is equivalent to 1 teaspoon of table sugar). If you pour 1 cup (250 ml) of light vanilla soy milk over that cereal, you could be adding another 13 grams of sugar (3 teaspoons). A low-fat frozen dinner can pack as many as 10 grams of sugar. Even 2 slices of whole-grain bread can add 6 grams of sugar to your diet. And if you dress your salad with just 1 tablespoon of low-fat dressing, you could very well be drizzling a teaspoon's worth of syrup over your greens.

You need to read labels to sleuth out hidden sugars. The Nutrition Facts box on prepackaged foods discloses the grams of sugar contained in 1 serving of the food; you can do the math to convert those grams into teaspoons of sugar (4 grams equals 1 teaspoon). But keep in mind that the sugar numbers on nutrition labels include both naturally occurring sugars (e.g., fruit or milk sugars) and refined sugars added during food processing (e.g., sucrose, honey, corn syrup).

To find added sugars, you need to read the ingredient list too. You might be surprised to see how many different types of refined sugars are added to one product! The following tips will help you reduce your intake of added sugars:

- Limit sugary drinks. Replace soft drinks and fruit drinks with water, low-fat milk, unflavoured soy beverages, vegetable juice or tea.
- Satisfy your sweet tooth with natural sugars. Choose fruit, yogurt or homemade smoothies over candy, cakes, cookies and pastries.
- Reduce portion size. Avoid the temptation to choose king-sized desserts, pastries and candy bars when eating away from home. When eating sweets at home, enjoy a small serving.
- Choose breakfast cereals that have no more than 8 grams of sugar per serving. Cereals with dried fruit are an exception since the natural sugars in the fruit will increase the grams of sugar on the label.
- Sweeten foods with spices instead of sugar. Add cinnamon and nutmeg to hot cereals, a dash of vanilla to coffee and lattes, and grated fresh ginger to fruit and vegetables.
- Reduce sugar in recipes. As a rule, you can cut the sugar in most baked goods by one-third.
- Read the Nutrition Facts box when buying packaged baked goods. Compare products and choose a brand that has fewer grams of sugar per serving.

Alcoholic Beverages

No doubt you've heard that a moderate intake of alcoholic beverages—one to two drinks per day—can keep your heart healthy. Many studies have revealed that moderate alcohol consumption is linked with 20 percent to 30 percent reductions in heart disease risk. Alcohol is thought to protect against heart disease in a few ways. For starters, it increases the level of HDL (good) cholesterol in the bloodstream. There's also evidence that alcohol reduces the ability of blood cells called platelets to clump together and form clots.

Despite popular belief, there's no evidence that drinking red wine offers greater protection than any other type of alcoholic beverage. The beneficial effects on HDL cholesterol and platelets occur with wine, spirits and beer.

If you're thinking it might be wise to add a glass of wine—or pint of beer—to your daily diet, think again. First of all, the Heart and Stroke Foundation of Canada does not recommend that you drink alcohol for the purpose of reducing your risk for heart attack and stroke. That's because the harmful effects of alcohol outweigh any benefits. Drinking more than two drinks per day boosts blood pressure and increases the long-term risk of developing hypertension. Drinking alcoholic beverages can also increase blood triglycerides (fats).

But the one drink a day that may protect your heart also increases the risk of several cancers. In an ongoing study in the United Kingdom called the Million Women Study, researchers followed more than 1.2 million middle-aged women for an average of 7 years. Compared with teetotallers, women who consumed, on average, one drink per day had a higher overall cancer risk, especially for cancers of the breast, liver, rectum, mouth, throat and esophagus. What's more, each additional drink further increased the risk. The researchers estimated that alcohol could be to blame for 13 percent of these cancers—mostly breast cancer. The study also found that women who drank only wine had the same risk for developing cancer as those who drank beer, spirits or a combination of alcoholic beverages. Based on these findings, the researchers concluded that from a cancer standpoint, there is no level of alcohol consumption that can be considered safe.[11]

The link between alcohol and breast cancer risk has been extensively researched and reported on. Alcohol may increase breast cancer risk by making breast cells more permeable to carcinogens or by enhancing the liver's processing of cancer-causing substances. Alcohol may also inhibit the ability of cells to repair faulty genes and it can influence estrogen levels in the body.

How Much Alcohol?
If you do drink alcohol, limit yourself to one drink per day for women and two for men. Keep in mind that for elderly people, two drinks may be too much to be considered a low-risk intake. One drink is considered 12 ounces (340 ml) of regular beer, 5 ounces (145 ml) of wine or 1-1/2 ounces (45 ml) of 80-proof (40 percent) distilled spirits.

If you need to lower your intake of alcohol, replace alcoholic beverages with sparkling mineral water, Clamato or tomato juice, or soda with a splash of cranberry juice. Eliminate alcoholic beverages on evenings when you're not entertaining. Instead, save your cocktail or glass of wine for social occasions.

Sodium

In Chapter 4, you learned that sodium is an essential nutrient that our body needs to maintain its fluid balance. But the key is that we need only a very tiny amount. For sedentary Canadians, it takes no more than 1500 milligrams of sodium (two-thirds of a teaspoon of salt) to meet the body's requirement. If you sweat during exercise, you need a little more salt, but not much. You might have already guessed that we're unknowingly consuming far more sodium than we need. The latest survey estimates our daily sodium intakes at somewhere between 2300 and 2800 milligrams in women and between 2882 and 4066 milligrams in men.

Excess sodium in the diet contributes to high blood pressure, a major risk factor for heart attack and stroke. High blood pressure can also eventually lead to kidney disease. Studies show that, on average, blood pressure rises progressively with increasing sodium intakes. People with high blood pressure, diabetes or chronic kidney disease, older adults and African Americans are more sensitive than others to the blood pressure–raising effects of sodium.

The majority of sodium we consume each day (77 percent) is hidden in processed and restaurant foods. Only 11 percent of our daily sodium comes from salt that's added during cooking and while eating. The other 12 percent occurs naturally in foods such as milk, shellfish and tap water. Some of the worst sodium culprits include soups, canned vegetables, frozen dinners, processed meats and snack foods. Many restaurant meals also deliver a hefty dose of salt, especially breakfasts, Chinese entrées and deli sandwiches. Consider these facts: Denny's Country Scramble packs 3995 milligrams of sodium, a typical order of chow mein delivers roughly 3600 milligrams and a Rueben sandwich has about 3200 milligrams!

Sodium is added to food as sodium chloride (table salt), monosodium glutamate (MSG), sodium nitrite, sodium bicarbonate and sodium benzoate. However, sources of sodium other than sodium chloride may have a lesser effect on blood pressure. In addition to enhancing flavour, sodium is added to foods to help control the growth of bacteria and moulds, to preserve texture and to extend shelf life.

How Much Sodium?

As a general rule, you should eat foods low in sodium (less than 200 milligrams per serving) and stick to a daily total of no more than 1500 milligrams. If you'll recall from Chapter 4, we need only 1200 to 1500 milligrams each day, depending on our age. The upper daily limit—the maximum amount of sodium we should be consuming each day—is 2300 milligrams. Some foods you eat, such as tomato juice or pasta sauce, might be high in sodium. That's okay, as long as you balance your daily intake by choosing lower-sodium foods at other meals and as snacks.

To de-salt your diet, one key strategy is to eat fewer processed foods and restaurant meals. The following tips will help you reduce your sodium intake.

- Read the Nutrition Facts box on packaged foods. Sodium levels vary widely across different brands of like products. The number of milligrams listed for sodium in the Nutrition Facts table is the amount per one serving of the food. When comparing brands of similar foods for sodium levels, make sure the serving size is the same for both products. For some packaged foods, serving sizes on nutrition labels can vary across brands. Remember that adults need no more than 1500 milligrams of sodium per day. You can also look at the % Daily Value (DV) of sodium to get a sense of whether one serving of food supplies a little or a lot of sodium. Foods with a DV of sodium of 5% or less are low in sodium. (The daily value for sodium on nutrition labels is set at 2400 milligrams, which is too high.)
- Pay attention to portion size. Sodium numbers on a nutrition label will underestimate your intake if you consume more than the serving size indicated.
- Limit your intake of processed meats such as bologna, ham, sausage, hot dogs, bacon, deli meats and smoked salmon.
- Limit your use of bouillon cubes, soy sauce, Worcestershire sauce, soy sauce and barbecue sauce.
- Rely less on convenience foods such as canned soups, frozen dinners and packaged rice and pasta mixes. Choose pre-made entrées or frozen dinners that contain no more than 200 milligrams of sodium per 100 calories.
- When possible, choose lower-sodium products. Many sodium-reduced brands contain 25 percent less sodium than the original version and some, like V8 juice, contain 75 percent less. If you can't find low-salt products in your supermarket, ask your grocer to stock them.

- Substitute herbs and spices for salt when cooking—try garlic, lemon juice, salsa, onion, vinegar and herbs.
- Remove the saltshaker from the table to break the habit of salting food at the table.

Caffeine

When you think of caffeine, no doubt coffee comes to mind. If you enjoy your daily cup—or two—of coffee, it seems there's no reason to stop. Mounting evidence suggests that, for most people, drinking coffee does more good than harm. Research suggests that if you drink enough of it, you'll lower the risk of developing type 2 diabetes, heart disease, asthma, gallstones, Parkinson's disease, liver cancer and possibly colon cancer. And you'll feel more alert and work out harder at the gym.

Researchers suspect that some of coffee's benefits are linked to its anti-oxidants, a number of which become more potent during roasting. Antioxidants in both caffeinated and decaffeinated coffee are thought to reduce inflammation in the body and improve how the body uses insulin, the hormone that lowers blood sugar. Coffee also contains magnesium, a mineral linked to blood-sugar regulation.

Caffeine is also thought to play a helpful role in treating asthma symptoms, enhancing physical performance and boosting mental alertness. As well, coffee's protective effects against gallstones and Parkinson's disease are attributed to caffeine.

But caffeine isn't for everyone. Studies suggest that excess caffeine can boost blood pressure and heart rate, a concern for people with high blood pressure and heart disease. In post-menopausal women who don't get enough calcium, consuming 450 milligrams of caffeine per day—about three 8 ounce cups of coffee—has been linked to lower bone density. (Caffeine increases the amount of calcium your kidneys excrete in the urine.) And some studies suggest that high intakes of caffeine during pregnancy can increase the risk of miscarriage.

Caffeine is a stimulant drug that's mildly addictive. If you're a habitual coffee drinker and you miss your daily dose, you can experience indigestion, muscle soreness, headache, irritability and even slight depression. Caffeine sensitivity—the amount it takes to elicit an effect—varies from person to person. In general, the smaller the person, the less caffeine it takes to produce side effects. But regardless of body size, the more caffeine you consume, the less sensitive you become to its effects: In other words, it takes more caffeine to feel its jolt.

How Much Caffeine?

Based on a review of the evidence, Health Canada contends that healthy adults are not at risk for adverse effects from caffeine, provided you limit your daily intake to 450 milligrams. During pregnancy, women are advised to consume no more than 300 milligrams per day, but some experts suggest a stricter limit of 200 milligrams. Having high blood pressure, insomnia and osteoporosis are other sensible reasons to limit your caffeine intake. Start by avoiding caffeine in the afternoon. Replace these beverages with caffeine-free or decaffeinated beverages like herbal tea, mineral water, fruit and vegetable juice or decaffeinated coffee.

Caffeine Content of Beverages, Foods and Medications

Beverage/Food or Medication	Caffeine (milligrams)
Beverage or Food	
Coffee, brewed, 8 oz (250 ml)	100 mg
Coffee, instant, 8 oz (250 ml)	66 mg
Coffee, decaffeinated, 8 oz (250 ml)	3 mg
Espresso, 2 oz (60 ml)	54 mg
Second Cup coffee, large, 20 oz (600 ml)	391 mg
Starbucks coffee, venti, 20 oz (600 ml)	415 mg
Tim Hortons coffee, large, 20 oz (600 ml)	270 mg
Tea, green, 8 oz (250 ml)	30 mg
Tea, black, 8 oz (250 ml)	45 mg
Cola, 1 can, 12 oz (355 ml)	37 mg
Diet cola, 1 can, 12 oz (355 ml)	50 mg
Red Bull Energy Drink, 1 can, 8 oz (250 ml)	80 mg
Dark chocolate, 1 oz (30 g)	20 mg
Medication (2 tablets)	
Anacin	64 mg
Excedrin	130 mg
Midol	64 mg

Putting It All Together: A Healthy Eating Plan

To make sure you get your daily share of nutrients, antioxidants and the many protective chemicals plant foods have to offer, follow the food plan below. Adjust your daily number of servings according to your exercise level and body-weight goal (i.e., maintain, lose or gain). If you work out every day, the number of servings you need to eat is at the upper end of the recommended range. If you engage in heavy exercise, you may find you need to eat even more than what's outlined below. Add more whole grains, fruit, vegetables and vegetarian foods to provide extra calories. If you're trying to lose weight, stick to the lower end of the range.

Before you start down the road to healthy eating, there are a few pointers to keep in mind:

- **Make one change at a time**. There's no need to do everything at once. You'll be surprised to find that small changes make a big difference. Set one new goal each week.
- **Plan ahead whenever you can**. Most of my clients report that their biggest roadblock to eating well is a lack of time. Plan your weekly meals in advance. Shop for groceries once a week so you have healthy foods in your fridge and cupboards. You'll find that taking the extra time to plan ahead actually saves you time during your busy week.
- **All foods can be part of a healthy diet**. The occasional splurge on ice cream or deep-fried chicken wings won't upset your healthy eating plan. It's the overall picture that counts.
- **Periodic overeating or eating of junk food does not mean you have failed**. We're all human. Just return to your usual healthy diet at the next meal.

A Healthy Eating Plan

Food Group	Food Choices	Recommended Daily Servings
Grain Foods Source of carbohydrate, iron, fibre.	Choose whole grain as often as possible.	*4 to 8**
	Whole-grain bread, 1 slice	
	Bagel, large, 1/4	
	Roll, large, 1/2	

Food Group	Food Choices	Recommended Daily Servings
	Pita pocket, 1/2	
	Tortilla, 6-inch (15 cm), 1	
	Cereal, cold, 3/4 cup (175 ml)	
	Cereal, 100% bran, 1/2 cup (125 ml)	
	Cereal, hot, 1/2 cup (125 ml)	
	Crackers, soda, 6	
	Corn, 1/2 cup (125 ml)	
	Popcorn, plain, 3 cups (750 ml)	
	Grains, cooked, 1/2 cup (125 ml)	
	Pasta, cooked, 1/2 cup (125 ml)	
	Rice, cooked, 1/3 cup (75 ml)	

*Children aged 2 to 3 years require 3 daily servings.

Fruit and Vegetables   *7 to 10**
Source of carbohydrate, fibre, vitamins, minerals, phytochemicals.

	Food Choices	
	Fruit, whole, 1 piece	
	Fruit, small (plums, apricots), 4 pieces	
	Fruit, cut up, 1 cup (250 ml)	
	Berries, 1 cup (250 ml)	
	Raisins, 2 tbsp (30 ml)	
	Juice, unsweetened, 1/2 cup (125 ml)	
	Vegetables, cooked or raw, 1/2 cup (125 ml)	
	Vegetables, leafy green, 1 cup (250 ml)	

*Children aged 2 to 3 years need 4 servings per day; 4- to 8-year-olds require 5 servings; 9- to 13-year-olds should consume 6 servings per day.

Milk and Milk Alternatives   *2 to 3**
Source of protein, carbohydrate, calcium, vitamin D, vitamin A, riboflavin, zinc.

	Food Choices	
	Milk, 1 cup (250 ml)	
	Yogurt, 3/4 cup (175 ml)	
	Cheese, 1-1/2 oz (45 g)	
	Soy beverage, calcium fortified, 1 cup (250 ml)	

*Preteens and teenagers need 3 to 4 servings per day; children aged 2 to 8 require 2 daily servings.

Food Group	Food Choices	Recommended Daily Servings
Meat and Alternatives Source of protein, vitamin B6, magnesium, iron, zinc.		*6 to 10**
	Fish, lean meat, poultry, 1 oz (30 g)	
	Egg, whole, 1	
	Egg, whites only, 2	
	Legumes (beans, chickpeas, lentils), 1/3 cup (75 ml)	
	Soy nuts, 2 tbsp (30 ml)	
	Tempeh, 1/4 cup (60 ml)	
	Tofu, firm, 1/3 cup (75 ml)	
	Texturized vegetable protein, 1/3 cup (75 ml)	
	Veggie dog, small, 1	

*Children aged 2 to 8 years need to include 2 to 3 servings in their daily diet.

Food Group	Food Choices	Recommended Daily Servings
Fats and Oils Source of fat, essential fatty acids, vitamin E. To include more health-enhancing essential fatty acids, choose canola oil, walnut oil, flaxseed oil and nuts and seeds more often as your fat servings.		*6 to 9*
	Butter, margarine, 1 tsp (5 ml)	
	Avocado, 1/8 medium	
	Mayonnaise, 1 tsp (5 ml)	
	Mayonnaise, fat-reduced, 2 tsp (10 ml)	
	Nuts/seeds, 1 tbsp (15 ml)	
	Peanut and nut butters, 1-1/2 tsp (7 ml)	
	Salad dressing, 2 tsp (10 ml)	
	Salad dressing, fat-reduced, 4 tsp (20 ml)	
	Vegetable oil, 1 tsp (5 ml)	

Food Group	Food Choices	Recommended Daily Servings
Water Source of fluid. Plain water, juice, milk, coffee, tea, herbal tea and even diet soft drinks all count towards your daily water requirements.		*8 to 12*
	Water, 1 cup (250 ml)	

Note: All serving sizes are based on measures after cooking.

PART TWO

Herbal Remedies and Natural Health Products

6

Herbal Medicine

Simply put, the term *herb* refers to a plant that is used for medicinal purposes (it may also be used for flavouring food and for its scent). Herbal medicine may be relatively new to North America, but it's certainly not new to the rest of the world. According to the World Health Organization, 80 percent of the world's population relies on herbs to stay healthy. In countries such as Germany, France, Italy, China, Japan and India, herbal remedies have been integrated into the national health care systems. And in Africa, Latin America and North America, herbs have been used for hundreds of years as folk medicines.

Many North Americans are now turning to this alternative form of therapy. But there is a lot we still need to learn. Although we may know that a certain plant has a beneficial effect on our health, we might not know what compounds are responsible for those effects. Nor do we know all the possible ways an herb may interact with prescription medications. Most studies on herbal medicines have lasted less than a year, so the effects of taking herbs for a longer period are largely unknown. And very little research has been done on herbs and pregnant women and children.

Despite the unknowns, the majority of Canadians feel that natural health products have a role to play in managing health. According to a 2005 survey conducted by Health Canada, 71 percent of Canadians regularly take vitamins and minerals, herbal products, homeopathic medicines and the like—products that have come to be known as natural health products (NHPs). Not surprisingly, 77 percent agree that these supplements can be used to maintain or promote health or treat illness.[1]

In this day and age, an increasing number of people are taking a more active role in their health care. Furthermore, scientists have discovered that some herbal extracts may be just as effective as drug treatment. Many clients I see in my private practice are leery about taking prescription drugs and would rather first try an herbal remedy. They feel it's safer or more natural. In fact, one-half of Canadians (52 percent) think that natural health products are safe because they are made from natural ingredients.

It's true that, in general, herbs have far fewer side effects than prescription drugs. They are gentler in their action and, as a result, take longer to work. But it's important to realize that just because something is deemed "natural" does not necessarily mean it's safe. Herbal therapies, like drugs, must be treated with respect and taken wisely. As you'll read in the next two chapters, herbal remedies and natural health products can have side effects, they can interfere with medication, they can cause serious allergic reactions, and some can be dangerous for people with certain health conditions.

How Are Herbal Remedies Regulated in Canada?

Herbal remedies—as well as all other natural health products—are regulated by Health Canada's Natural Health Products Directorate. Natural health products are defined as vitamins and minerals, herbal remedies, homeopathic medicines, traditional medicines such as traditional Chinese medicine, probiotics and other products such as amino acids and essential fatty acids. The mission of the Natural Health Products Directorate is to ensure that we have ready access to natural health products that are safe, effective and of high quality. The Natural Health Products Regulations of the Food and Drugs Act came into effect on January 1, 2004, and set out requirements for the manufacture, packaging, labelling, storage, importation, distribution and sale of natural health products in Canada as well as for clinical trials involving human subjects.

You can identify licensed natural health products by looking for the eight-digit Natural Product Number (NPN) or Homeopathic Medicine Number (DIN-HM) designation on the label. These numbers assure you that the product has been reviewed by Health Canada and found to be safe, effective and of high quality under its recommended conditions of use.

Before I tell you what you might use certain herbal remedies for, and how to take them safely, let's take a closer look at the world of plant medicine.

Herbal Traditions Around the World

Herbs play an important role in the medical systems of many cultures and have done so for thousands of years. In traditional Chinese medicine (TCM), herbs have been used for more than 2000 years. In North America, interest in Chinese medicine is relatively recent and has been growing over the past 20 years. Ayurveda medicine developed on the Indian subcontinent some 3000 to 5000 years ago.

Traditional Chinese Medicine (TCM)

Four main disciplines make up traditional Chinese medicine: acupuncture, herbology, massage and manipulation (called Tui Na), and diet therapy. Doctors of TCM are concerned with the person as a whole. Both physical and psychological characteristics are viewed as important determinants of health and disease. From a detailed examination and the history of signs and symptoms, practitioners of TCM piece together a pattern of disharmony, which is used to make a diagnosis and develop a personalized treatment plan. TCM aims to alleviate symptoms and treat the underlying causes of disease. The goal of TCM is to return the body, mind and spirit to a balanced state.

Concepts important to TCM include yin and yang (cold/passivity/interior and heat/vigour/exterior); substances such as qi (energy), blood, jing (a congenital essence inherited from one's parents and vitality obtained from food) and other body fluids; organs such as the heart and spleen; meridians or channels that connect the organs and circulate blood and qi throughout the body; and conditions that cause disharmony in the body (wind, heat, cold, dampness). Mastering the art and science of TCM takes years of practice. Traditional Chinese herbal remedies, which are combinations of herbs, are called patent medicines and are used to treat specific syndromes. The doses are quite high and are typically taken in the form of strong-smelling soups.

Ayurveda

This complex traditional Hindu healing system focuses on healing from within, rather than on treating individual symptoms. Ayurveda recognizes that there are unique constitutional differences between individuals and therefore different treatments are needed for different types of people: Although two people may share the same symptoms, their energetic constitutions may differ and call for very different remedies.

Three fundamental principles guide an Ayurvedic practitioner in diagnosis and the development of a treatment plan: Vata (movement, breathing, activity), Pitta (energy released from biochemical process, digestion, vision) and Kapha (stability, mental strength, resistance to disease). According to Ayurveda, these three principles control all human biological and psychological functions.

Treatments include the use of herbal medicines, minerals, animal products, strict dieting, yoga, meditation, exercise and surgery. Ayurvedic herbal remedies involve the use of more than 1000 medicinal plants. The system has over 8000 recipes for medicines, the majority of which are made from herbs and minerals. Ayurvedic medicines are given as pills, infusions, tinctures, powders and oils. Both the choice and dose of an herbal medicine are influenced by the disease, the patient's constitution and the environment.

There are Ayurvedic practitioners in North America, but they can be difficult to find. Your local health food retailer that sells Ayurvedic herbal formulas may be able to help you locate one.

Herbalism and Phytotherapy

As I mentioned earlier, it's only recently that herbal medicine has come to be appreciated by the Western world. Over the past 20 years, there has been an enormous amount of research on herbs and their role as medicines. Today in North America, you'll find two distinct philosophies among practitioners who recommend herbal therapies. Traditional herbalists practise what is often referred to as herbalism. They believe that the sum of the plant parts is greater than the individual parts. Herbalists believe that the constituents of the plant work in synergy with each other. They also believe that the plant has both a drug-like and an energy aspect. Herbalists rarely prescribe one herb; rather, they prescribe a combination of herbs to treat a disorder.

Modern practitioners who prescribe herbs believe that a plant's medicinal action is determined solely by its active components. This approach is commonly referred to as *phytotherapy*, the science of using herbs to treat illness. Countries such as Germany, Italy and France have adopted this model of herbal medicine and have combined it with conventional medical practice. It's in the field of phytotherapy that we're seeing an explosion of scientific research. Throughout the rest of this book, I discuss the use of herbal remedies using this model—remedies made from plants with active ingredients that can be used to treat or prevent a health condition.

Forms of Herbal Remedies

Like vitamins and minerals, herbs can be taken in several forms. Here's a look at the various ways an herbal remedy might be prepared:

TEAS (INFUSIONS AND DECOCTIONS). Infusions are made by steeping the delicate part of an herb (leaves, flowers) in hot water. Boiling roots, barks and stems results in a decoction. Some herbs taste unpleasant in tea form. As well, many herbs have components that are not soluble in water (saw palmetto and valerian are two examples). You're better off buying a standardized extract of those herbs in pill form. A variety of herbs, such as chamomile and echinacea, are available in tea bags at health food stores. Some stores also sell bulk herbs that you can steep in boiling water for a specified time, then strain. Bulk herbs are also available from reputable herbalists.

TINCTURES. These are made by soaking the herb in a mixture of alcohol and water for as little as a few hours or as long as a few weeks, depending on the plant. The herbal material is then removed: The remaining liquid is the tincture. Usually packaged in small bottles with droppers, tinctures are readily available in health food stores. They're great for people who don't like to swallow pills, especially children. Alcohol-free tinctures are also available and are recommended for children or anyone with a health condition for which alcohol in contraindicated. To take a tincture, add the specified amount to a glass of water.

The strength of a tincture is determined by its concentration. This information may be on the label, though manufacturers are not required to state it. Tinctures usually range in concentration from 1:3 to 1:10. This means that, in the case of the former, one part herb was soaked in three parts solvent (water and alcohol) and in the case of the weaker-concentration tincture, there is ten times more solvent than herb. Your health care provider should advise you on the concentration of tincture to buy.

FLUID EXTRACTS. These liquid herbal remedies are more concentrated than tinctures. They are usually a 1:1 or 1:2 concentration.

SOLID EXTRACTS. These are the strongest form of herb you can buy and are made by removing all the solvent, leaving only the solid material (which looks like thick molasses). Solid extracts of herbs are sold as capsules, pills and tablets, and their strength is expressed as a concentration. A concentration of 4:1 means that one part of extract is equivalent in strength, or potency, to four parts of the dried herb. The label's statement of concentration, however, does not tell you the amount of active ingredients present, often an important factor if the herb is to be effective.

STANDARDIZED EXTRACTS. These are solid extracts guaranteed to have a specific amount of a specific ingredient(s) in the final product. This amount is expressed as a percentage. For example, the label on my bottle of echinacea says it contains 4 percent echinacosides. All the components of the plant may be present in a standardized extract but often not in the proportions in which they occur naturally in the plant. Some manufacturers standardize their products to contain a certain amount of a marker compound. This compound is not the active ingredient but a characteristic component of the plant. By standardizing to such a marker, manufacturers can ensure quality of the product, guaranteeing the correct plant was used to make the herbal remedy.

Clearly, the biggest advantage of buying a standardized herbal product is assurance of quality. Many proponents of standardized extracts also believe that they enable health care professionals to recommend a more accurate dose, based on a measured amount of specific ingredients, and that, in turn, standardized products are more likely to be effective in treating a health condition. But there are a few caveats. First, we don't yet know all the active ingredients responsible for an herb's effect. A case in point is feverfew, an herb used to prevent migraine headaches. Scientists isolated what they thought was the active ingredient and made a standardized extract from it, but the standardized extract turned out to be ineffective in preventing migraines. It turns out that, in order to be effective, feverfew products need to be made from the whole leaf, rather than from a standardized extract. And while standardized extracts do offer an assurance of quality, it's important to keep in mind that some non-standardized products may also be of high quality and effective.

How to Choose a High-Quality Product

The following list will help you shop for a high-quality herbal supplement:

- Look for Health Canada's seal of approval on product labels: Use products that bear a DIN (Drug Identification Number), NPN (Natural Product

Number) or DIN-HM (Homeopathic Medicine Number). On herbal products, look for the eight-digit NPN.

- If you don't see an NPN (not all products will bear one), choose a supplement manufactured by a company with a strong reputation for producing high-quality products. Ask your dietitian, naturopath, doctor, pharmacist or health food retailer for a list.
- Consider buying an herbal remedy manufactured by a company that also produces pharmaceuticals, since it should have very high quality-control standards.
- If possible, always buy a standardized extract that clearly states the percentage of active ingredient or marker on the label.
- Ask the retailer or manufacturer if the product was manufactured according to good manufacturing practices (GMP) if this is not indicated on the label.
- Look for a product that discloses all the ingredients, including binders and fillers.
- Check the expiry date; make sure the product will not expire during the period you intend to use it.
- Check to see if the product has a safety seal.
- Don't be afraid to ask the supplement manufacturer or health food retailer questions, including: How is one product different from another? What measures does the retailer take to make sure it stocks high-quality products? How does the manufacturer ensure that it uses high-quality raw ingredients?

Consulting an Expert

As you can see, there's a lot to consider before using an herbal remedy. I certainly do not recommend self-diagnosing your condition and rushing off to the health food store to buy an herb that seems to match. Take the time to consult with a professional who can properly assess your symptoms and guide you in the right direction. Herbalists are not officially recognized as health professionals in Canada and so are not regulated. When choosing an herbalist, it's important to ask about his or her credentials, training and clinical experience. Here's what you need to know to choose a competent practitioner (the following applies to practitioners in both Canada and the United States):

- Herbalists with a science degree in phytotherapy have completed a 4-year university or college program.
- Herbalists with the MNIMH designation (Member of the National Institute of Medical Herbalism) have completed a 4-year university program.
- North American–trained herbalists with the Clinical Herbalist (ClH) designation have completed a 3- or 4-year university program.
- Master herbalists (MH) have usually completed a 6- to 12-month program, or a self-directed course through correspondence. Courses can vary, so ask questions!
- Naturopathic doctors (ND) have completed a 4-year program that includes many courses on herbal medicine. Some naturopaths choose to specialize in this area and may have more expertise than others.
- Doctors of traditional Chinese medicine (DTCM) have completed at least 4 years of training.

Recommended Resources

American Botanical Council
www.abc.herbalgram.org
Incorporated in November 1988 as a nonprofit education organization, the American Botanical Council (ABC) aims to educate the public about beneficial herbs and plants and to promote the safe and effective use of medicinal plants. ABC disseminates responsible, science-based information on herbs and phytomedicines on a subscription or one-time basis.

Health Canada—Natural Health Products
www.hc-sc.gc.ca/dhp-mps/prodnatur/index-eng.php
This section of Health Canada's website provides information on how natural health products are regulated in Canada as well as tips on how to use natural health products safely. You can also access the Licensed Natural Health Products Database, which contains specific information on those natural health products that have been issued a product licence by Health Canada.

Herb Research Foundation
www.herbs.org
The Herb Research Foundation (HRF) is an excellent source of accurate, science-based information on the health benefits and safety of medicinal plants. Founded in 1983 with a mission of herb research and public education, HRF has a vast storehouse of information resources, including a specialty research library containing over 300,000 scientific articles on thousands of herbs. HRF is a non-profit organization.

7

Popular
Herbal Remedies

Scientific research suggests that the eighteen herbs discussed in this chapter may be effective in helping to treat or prevent certain health conditions. These remedies are widely available in health food stores and pharmacies. Lesser-known herbs that may be useful in managing certain health conditions are discussed in Part Three.

Herbal remedies are not a substitute for other medical treatments. If you have a health condition that persists or worsens, seek the advice of your doctor. Many serious medical conditions are not appropriate for self-diagnosis and require the supervision of a qualified health professional. Never substitute an herbal supplement for a prescription medication without first consulting your doctor.

It's important to note that the safety of most herbal remedies has not been evaluated in children, in pregnant and breastfeeding women and in people with liver or kidney disease. Seek the advice of a health professional if you fall into one of these categories.

Some herbal remedies, including ginkgo biloba, can be incompatible with surgery because of their blood-thinning effect. You should stop taking such supplements 2 weeks prior to scheduled surgery.

Bilberry *(Vaccinium myrtillus)*

Used for visual acuity (cataracts, macular degeneration [see page 547], eye complications of diabetes and hypertension, night vision), menstrual cramps, hemorrhoids

A relative of the American blueberry, the bilberry plant grows in Canada, the United States and northern Europe. Bilberry is an excellent source of naturally occurring compounds called flavonoids, or, more specifically, of anthocyanins. These compounds help the body form strong connective tissue and blood capillaries.

Traditionally, bilberry has been used for diabetes and gastrointestinal disorders. It was during the Second World War that British pilots noticed that their night vision improved after eating bilberry jam. Since then, two studies found that, compared with placebo treatment, bilberry significantly improved eye health in people with eye complications caused by diabetes or hypertension.[1-3] One study revealed that the herbal extract improved night vision in air traffic controllers and pilots.

The anthocyanins in bilberry are thought to improve blood flow in the tiny capillaries of the eye. Bilberry's effect on circulation may also be responsible for its ability to reduce symptoms of dysmenorrhea, including breast tenderness, painful periods, nausea and headache.[4] Preliminary evidence suggests that bilberry might also have triglyceride-, cholesterol- and blood-glucose-lowering properties, with the chromium in the herb thought to play a role in lowering blood glucose.

Bilberry Supplements

Only the ripe fruit of bilberry plants is used in medicinal extracts. Don't confuse bilberry extract with bilberry leaf or bog bilberry. If you're taking bilberry supplements to improve vision, choose a product standardized to contain 25 percent to 36 percent anthocyanins. Clinical studies of bilberry's effectiveness have used formulations containing 25 percent anthocyanins. Take 160 milligrams twice daily. One- to 6-month use is usually recommended for improvement in visual disorders.

For dysmenorrhea, take 50 to 160 milligrams twice daily for the 3 days before your period and during your period. Stop on day 7. It may take up to three menstrual cycles for bilberry to have an effect on dysmenorrhea.

No adverse effects have been reported on the use of bilberry supplements. Theoretically, bilberry might lower blood glucose. As a result, if you have diabetes and take medication to lower your blood glucose, be cautious using bilberry.

Black Cohosh *(Cimicifuga racemosa)*

Used for perimenopause (see page 601): hot flashes, mood swings, vaginal dryness

Also known as black snakeroot, bugbane and baneberry, black cohosh has a long tradition of being used to treat gynecological conditions. This perennial shrub is native to North America, growing up to two feet high, with white flowers. The root of the plant is used for medicinal purposes. The herb was first used by Native Americans, who introduced it to European colonists. In Germany, physicians have been prescribing this herb for more than 50 years to millions of women.

In studies lasting 6 months to 1 year, black cohosh extracts seem to modestly reduce symptoms of menopause, such as hot flashes. The most consistent evidence is for a specific commercial extract called Remifemin (by Phytopharmica/Enzymatic Therapy). This extract is standardized to contain 1 mg triterpene glycosides, calculated as 27-deoxyactein per 20 milligram tablet. Studies have found that, compared with a placebo, it significantly reduces menopausal symptoms and hot flash frequency. Preliminary evidence suggests that the herbal remedy is comparable to low-dose transdermal estradiol (Estraderm) for relieving menopausal symptoms. Research using other formulations of black cohosh is less consistent. [1-3]

Exactly how the herb works is still under scientific debate. It exerts estrogen-like effects, but its active ingredients do not bind to estrogen receptors or influence estrogen levels in the blood. The herb may exert its effect by interacting with certain brain receptors. Experiments in animals have demonstrated that black cohosh does not stimulate the growth of estrogen-dependent tumours.

The herb contains triterpene glycosides, naturally occurring compounds thought to be responsible for its effect. It may take up to 4 weeks to notice improvement in symptoms.

Black Cohosh Supplements

Buy a product standardized to contain 2.5 percent triterpene glycosides. The typical dose is 40 milligrams taken twice daily. In virtually all the scientific research, the type of black cohosh used is sold under the name Remifemin. This product is sold in 20 milligram strength, since a recent study has shown that a lower dose of the herb is equally effective.

Mild stomach upset and headache have been reported in a small number of women. Other potential side effects include rash, dizziness, weight gain, feeling of heaviness in the legs, cramping, breast tenderness and vaginal spotting or bleeding. There is concern that black cohosh might cause liver disease. Although adverse effects on the liver have not been documented in clinical studies, several case reports of liver toxicity have been described in women taking black cohosh products alone or in combination with other herbs. Over 49 cases of liver toxicity related to black cohosh have now been reported; however, most of these cases are unpublished and poorly documented. Most reports don't indicate that black cohosh is the probable or certain cause. While these cases don't provide conclusive evidence that black cohosh is responsible for liver disease, some countries require cautionary labelling on black cohosh products suggesting a risk of liver toxicity.

Because preliminary evidence in animals suggests that black cohosh might increase the risk of metastasis in existing breast cancer, women with a history of breast cancer or women at risk for breast cancer should avoid using black cohosh.

Chasteberry *(Vitex agnus-castus)*

Used for premenstrual syndrome (see page 618), amenorrhea, breast pain, mood swings

Some 2000 years ago, a Greek physician first mentioned the use of chasteberry as a medicinal plant, noting that a drink made from the plant's seeds reduced sexual desires. It has also been reported that the herb helped medieval monks keep their vow of chastity. Its Latin name, *agnus-castus*, means "chaste lamb." In modern times, European physicians have been prescribing chasteberry to women for more than 40 years to regulate the menstrual cycle and ease symptoms of premenstrual syndrome (PMS).

Taking chasteberry seems to decrease some symptoms of PMS, especially breast pain or tenderness (mastalgia), edema, constipation, irritability, depressed mood or mood alterations, anger and headache in some women.[1-5]

Chasteberry also appears to be effective in treating Premenstrual Dysphoric Disorder (PMDD). In an 8-week study, the herb was comparable to the drug fluoxetine in relieving overall symptoms. However, chasteberry seems to be somewhat more effective for physical symptoms such as breast tenderness, swelling, cramps and food cravings, while the medication seems to be somewhat more effective for psychological symptoms such as depression, irritability, insomnia, nervous tension and feeling out of control.[6]

Less vigorous research has been done in the area of amenorrhea and infertility, though a few studies do support the use of chasteberry for these conditions.

The active ingredients in chasteberry—including compounds called aucubin and agnuside—are believed to act on the pituitary gland in the brain to cause the release of a neurotransmitter called dopamine. Herbalists believe that chasteberry increases the production of progesterone, leading to a normal balance of estrogen and progesterone. Studies show that through its action on dopamine in the brain, chasteberry also suppresses the release of prolactin, thereby lowering excessive levels—which is considered the main reason for the herb's effectiveness.

Chasteberry Supplements

Choose a product standardized to contain 6 percent agnuside since this is what has been used in most of the clinical trials. The recommended dose varies and will depend on the formulation of chasteberry. Extracts typically used are in doses of 20 to 240 mg per day. Keep in mind that it takes at least 4 weeks for noticeable effects. Mild side effects occasionally reported include nausea, headache and skin rash.

Historically, chasteberry has been used to promote lactation; however, since the herb inhibits prolactin secretion (prolactin is necessary for milk production), you should not use it if you are breastfeeding unless you have been advised to do so by a health care practitioner. The herb has not been evaluated in pregnant women.

If you're on a medication that interacts with the neurotransmitter dopamine (e.g., the antidepressants Wellbutrin and Effexor), be sure to tell your doctor that you're taking chasteberry. He or she should monitor you closely to ensure the herb doesn't interact with your medication and make it less effective. If you're taking birth control pills or hormone replacement therapy, use caution. Although there have been no case reports, chasteberry could theoretically interfere with the effectiveness of these medications because of its hormone-regulating activity.

Cranberry *(Vaccinium macrocarpon)*

Used for urinary tract infections (see page 674)

Cranberry is native to the marshland of northern Europe, eastern Canada and the eastern United States. It's a small evergreen shrub with characteristic shiny red berries and pale pink flowers. Cranberry juice has a long history of use among American Indian tribes, primarily for urinary tract conditions. It was used to prevent kidney stones and was even thought to remove "toxins" from the blood.

For the past two decades, much of the focus on cranberry has been related to urinary tract infections, especially the prevention of recurrent infections. Clinical research has demonstrated that, compared with a placebo, drinking 300 millilitres of (Ocean Spray) cranberry juice cocktail daily significantly reduced the risk of recurrent urinary tract infections in elderly women. Studies have also found that drinking 16 ounces (500 ml) of cranberry juice cocktail daily reduces the amount of bacteria found in the urine and the number of urinary tract infections in pregnant women.[1-2]

If you're concerned about the extra calories from juice, some evidence supports the use of cranberry-containing capsules. In one small clinical trial, a 400 milligram cranberry capsule taken twice daily for 6 months was effective at reducing the risk of infection in women with recurrent urinary infections. In a larger study, taking 500 milligrams of a specific cranberry extract (Cran-Max, Buckton Scott Health Products) daily for 6 months was found to be comparable to certain medications used to prevent recurrence in women with recurrent urinary tract infections.[3-4]

The anti-infective properties of cranberries are attributed to compounds called anthocyanins. These phytochemicals "wrap" around *Escherichia coli* *(E. coli)*, which causes most urinary tract infections, and prevent the bacteria from adhering to the urinary tract wall; however, cranberry doesn't seem to have the ability to release bacteria that has already adhered to urinary tract cells. Lab studies suggest that fructose in cranberries might also contribute to the berry's anti-infective action.

Cranberry Juice and Supplements

Cranberry juice cocktail is approximately 26 percent to 33 percent pure cranberry juice, sweetened with sugar or artificial sweetener. An 8 ounce

(250 ml) serving of cranberry cocktail is equivalent to 2 tablespoons (25 ml) of pure cranberry juice. Pure cranberry juice is very tart as it contains no refined sugars or sweeteners, so I suggest you dilute it with water to decrease the tartness. It's available in natural food stores and many grocery stores.

For preventing urinary tract infections, drink 10 to 16 ounces (300 to 500 ml) of cranberry juice cocktail daily. To avoid the extra sugar calories, use 2 tablespoons (30 ml) of cranberry juice once or twice daily. Alternatively, take a 400 milligram cranberry capsule twice daily.

Cranberry is usually well tolerated. However, in very large doses, for example 96 to 128 ounces (3 to 4 L) of juice per day, cranberry can cause stomach upset and diarrhea. One study reported nausea, vomiting and diarrhea in pregnant women who drank 16 ounces (500 ml) of cranberry juice cocktail daily, the equivalent of about 4 ounces (125 ml) of pure cranberry juice.

Consuming more than 32 ounces (1 L) of cranberry juice cocktail per day over a prolonged period of time could also increase the risk of uric acid kidney stone formation.

Devil's Claw *(Harpagophytum procumbens)*

Used for osteoarthritis (see page 578), rheumatoid arthritis (see page 646), low back pain

Devil's claw is native to southern Africa. Its botanical name, Harpagophytum, means "hook plant" in Greek and refers to the appearance of its fruit, which is covered with barbed hooks meant to attach onto animals in order to spread the seeds.

Indigenous people have long used the plant's roots as a tea to relieve digestive and joint complaints. Devil's claw didn't become popular in the Western world until 1976, when an estimated 30,000 arthritis patients in the United Kingdom were taking the herbal remedy.

Devil's claw has been reputed to have anti-inflammatory and anti-rheumatic properties, which scientific studies have confirmed. Research conducted in patients taking devil's claw alone or in conjunction with non-steroidal anti-inflammatory drugs (NSAIDs) found the herb helped decrease osteoarthritis-related pain of the knee and hip. Study participants taking devil's claw also seemed to be able to decrease use of NSAIDs for pain relief.[1-4]

In addition, studies point to the ability of devil's claw to ease non-specific low back pain. Some evidence even suggests that a certain extract of devil's claw may be as effective at decreasing low back pain as 12.5 milligrams of rofecoxib (Vioxx).[5,6]

The active ingredients in devil's claw are known collectively as glycosides. Among them, one called harpagoside is thought to contribute the most to the herb's anti-inflammatory properties.

Devil's Claw Supplements

The dose of devil's claw will depend on the formulation of the product. Buy a supplement standardized to contain a certain amount of harpagoside; check the ingredient list for milligrams per tablet. For reducing the joint pain of osteoarthritis, 57 to 60 milligrams of harpagoside has been used in clinical studies. For treating low back pain, clinical studies have given patients 50 to 100 milligrams of harpagoside daily.

Devil's claw is generally well tolerated. The most common side effect is diarrhea, but other complaints include nausea, vomiting and abdominal pain. It can cause allergic skin reaction in susceptible individuals. Devil's claw should be avoided or used cautiously by people taking warfarin.

Echinacea *(Echinacea purpurea, Echinacea angustifolia, Echinacea pallida)*

Used for colds (see page 294) and flu, ear infections (see page 363), candidiasis (see page 254), sinusitis (see page 657), urinary tract infections (see page 674)

This plant, also known as purple coneflower, is native to North America. You may even have this tall daisy-like flower growing in your summer garden. Historically, the herb was used by North American Natives and early settlers as a topical treatment for burns, wounds and snake and insect bites. The root of the herb was chewed to cure toothache, and preparations were ingested to cure a host of ailments. Today, three species of echinacea are found in products; all have medicinal benefits.

Many studies in the laboratory have shown the ability of echinacea to enhance the body's production of white blood cells, which fight infection. The herb also appears to prevent the recurrence of *Candida albicans*, the organism responsible for vaginal yeast infections.[1] Studies in humans have not been consistent in their findings. Despite the positive results in the laboratory, clinical trials in adults taking echinacea to treat a cold or flu have not conclusively shown that the herb is effective.[2-5] Studies have not only used different echinacea species and a wide variety of preparation methods but have also used different patient populations and study designs. Given these variances among studies, it's not surprising that they have had different results.

However, a review of studies conducted to date finds that most report a positive effect on infection. The research suggests that taking echinacea can reduce the severity and duration of the common cold by 10 percent to 30 percent. One review of fourteen studies concluded the echinacea lowered the odds of developing a cold by 58 percent.[6,7]

Echinacea contains many different compounds, and the amounts present differ depending on whether the plant's flower, leaf or root is being used. At this point, scientists are uncertain as to which particular plant components are most responsible for the herb's immune-stimulation effect. It's thought that these ingredients work together to exert their effects in the body.

Echinacea Supplements

To ensure quality, buy a product standardized to contain 4 percent echinacosides *(Echinacea angustifolia)* and 0.7 percent flavonoids *(Echinacea purpurea)*, two of the herb's active ingredients.

You can choose from several forms of the herb to treat active colds, flu and infection:

- *Standardized extracts made from echinacea root:* a total of 900 milligrams three to four times daily
- *Fluid extracts (1:1):* 0.25 to 1.0 millilitres three times daily
- *Tinctures (1:5):* 1 to 2 millilitres three times daily
- *Teas:* 125 to 250 millilitres three to four times daily

Take until symptoms are relieved, then continue taking two to three times daily for 1 week. Some experts recommend taking the herb once every 2 hours (300 milligram standardized extract or 3 to 4 millilitre tincture) until symptoms have subsided, then up to three times daily for a week. To prevent infection, take two to three times daily for 2 weeks of every month.

Doses for children are based on their body weight. For children under the age of 12, a general guideline is as follows:

- Adult dose (milligrams) × (age of child ÷ 12) = child's dose, or
- Adult dose (milligrams) × (body weight in pounds ÷ 150) = child's dose

For older children who are at acceptable percentiles for height and weight, half the recommended adult dosage can be used. Studies have not yet determined appropriate doses for children.

Daily use should be limited to 8 consecutive weeks because of concern that long-term use of echinacea might depress the immune system.

Adverse effects are rare but can include allergic skin and respiratory reactions. High doses of the herb can cause nausea and dizziness. Echinacea also appears to increase blood concentrations of caffeine by 30 percent; if you're sensitive to the effects of caffeine, be cautious using echinacea.

Don't use echinacea if you're allergic to plants in the Asteraceae/ Compositae family (ragweed, daisy, marigold and chrysanthemum). Although there is controversy among experts, the herb is generally not recommended for use by people with autoimmune diseases (HIV, lupus), multiple sclerosis, diabetes or asthma. People on immune-suppressing drugs (corticosteroids, cyclosporin) should not take the herb.

Evening Primrose *(Oenothera biennis)*

Used for cyclic breast pain (mastalgia) (see fibrocystic breast conditions, page 383), premenstrual syndrome (see page 618), eczema, rheumatoid arthritis (see page 646), schizophrenia, cystic fibrosis (page 323)

Also known as King's cure-all, evening primrose is a wildflower native to North America. Once its bright-yellow flowers die, pods are left that contain brown seeds rich in oil. It's this oil that is used medicinally.

Evening primrose oil is abundant in a special type of fatty acid called gamma-linolenic acid (GLA). The body uses GLA to make prostaglandins (PGs), powerful hormone-like compounds that regulate our blood, immune system and hormones. PGs can either increase or decrease inflammation. Using GLA, the body makes friendly, or less inflammatory, PGs.

There is very little GLA in food and so GLA must be made from other types of fat in the diet, such as vegetable oils (the body converts linoleic acid in these oils to GLA). Some researchers think that women with PMS may have difficulty converting linoleic acid in food into GLA and that this can cause symptoms such as breast pain and tenderness, irritability, depression and headache. By taking supplemental evening primrose oil, women with PMS may get adequate GLA to produce friendly PGs and as a result experience fewer uncomfortable symptoms.

Studies in the 1980s showed that daily supplements of evening primrose oil outperformed the placebo pill in improving PMS symptoms of breast tenderness, irritability and depression. In a few studies, the difference between evening primrose oil and placebo was statistically significant. However, studies performed over the past 10 years have not found any beneficial effects for evening primrose oil treating PMS as a whole. Lack of an effect may be because these studies were of short duration (evening primrose oil may take up to 8 months to reach its peak effectiveness). Studies have also found that supplementing with evening primrose oil has no effect on menopausal hot flashes and night sweats.

Evening primrose oil appears to offer most promise in treating breast pain and tenderness. Some studies have found the supplement to be as effective as certain drugs used to treat cyclic breast pain. Researchers from the University of Wales in Great Britain concluded that evening primrose oil was the best first-line therapy for cyclic breast pain.[1-3]

GLA is used to make other anti-inflammatory PGs, one of which appears to ease the itchiness of atopic eczema. When British researchers analyzed the results from a number of studies, they found that evening primrose oil does relieve eczema symptoms.[4] But two other studies found that evening primrose oil was no better than the placebo treatment. It is possible, however, that the duration of these studies was not long enough to detect effects.

A handful of studies show that evening primrose oil combined with fish oil may be a promising treatment for easing symptoms of rheumatoid arthritis.[5] In arthritis, painful and inflamed joints are caused by an excess production of inflammatory, or unfriendly, PGs. Consuming more GLA (and fatty acids in fish oil) may help the body make more anti-inflammatory PGs, thereby relieving joint swelling and pain.

Although preliminary, there is some research to suggest that people suffering with alcoholism may be deficient in GLA, and that supplementing with evening primrose oil may help improve their tolerance to alcohol. Studies show that alcohol administration changes the fatty-acid profile of brain cells and that evening primrose oil can reverse these effects.[6,7]

Evening primrose oil has also been shown to reverse a deficiency of PGs in brain cells in people with schizophrenia.[8] Increasing the levels of GLA and anti-inflammatory PGs may help improve symptoms in these patients.

Evening Primrose Supplements

Buy a supplement standardized to contain 9 percent GLA. For cyclic breast pain, take 3 to 4 grams per day, split in two equal doses. Start by taking three 500 milligram capsules at breakfast, and repeat at dinner. For PMS, take 2 to 4 grams per day in divided doses. For eczema, adults should take 4 to 6 grams per day, split in two equal doses. For rheumatoid arthritis, studies have found daily doses of 540 milligrams to 2.8 grams to be effective. For other conditions, the effective dose has not been determined. Treatment for at least 3 months is usually required to notice an effect.

Evening primrose supplements may cause indigestion, headache and soft stools in some people. Large doses can lead to diarrhea. Evening primrose oil may increase the risk of pregnancy complications and so should be avoided by pregnant women. However, the herb is safe to take while breastfeeding. People with epilepsy and those taking the schizophrenia medication phenothiazine should use evening primrose oil with caution.

Feverfew *(Tanacetum parthenium)*

Used for migraine headache prevention (see page 556)

This plant, once native to Europe, can now be found throughout most of the world. Its use dates back to ancient Greek times, when it was often used to treat fever, headache, gynecological problems and stomach upset. The use of feverfew for migraines became popular in England in the 1970s after a doctor's wife noticed that her migraines were greatly relieved once she started chewing fresh feverfew leaves. As the story goes, after one year of faithfully taking the leaves daily, she almost forgot that she ever suffered from migraines.

A number of studies suggest that taking feverfew orally can reduce the frequency of migraine headaches and reduce symptoms of pain, nausea, vomiting and sensitivity to light and noise. But the herbal supplement may be more effective in patients with more frequent migraine attacks. In one randomized, controlled trial from England, 76 people who experienced migraines were given either whole feverfew leaf or placebo daily for 4 months. The treatments were then reversed for another 4-month period. Without knowing which treatment they received when, 59 percent of the people taking feverfew identified the feverfew period as more effective, compared with 24 percent who chose the placebo period. The herbal remedy reduced the number of classic migraines (with aura) by 32 percent and common migraines (without aura) by 21 percent.[1-4]

Researchers believe that feverfew reduces the frequency and intensity of migraines by preventing the release of prostaglandins, which dilate blood vessels and cause inflammation. It was once thought that parthenolide, one of the herb's active ingredients, was responsible for feverfew's beneficial effect. But an alcohol extract containing only parthenolide was found to have no effect on migraine headaches. It seems that parthenolide is only one of the compounds in feverfew leaf responsible for preventing migraines.

Feverfew Supplements

Don't buy an alcohol extract containing parthenolide only. Instead, buy capsules of powdered feverfew leaf. Take 50 to 100 milligrams daily. You can also try taking the herb at the onset of a migraine to ease the symptoms.

Feverfew rarely causes side effects other than mild gastrointestinal upset. The herb may cause an allergic reaction in people sensitive to members of the Asteraceae/Compositae plant family (ragweed, daisy, marigold and chrysanthemum). The safety of feverfew in pregnant or nursing women or those with liver or kidney disease has not been studied. Feverfew should not be used during pregnancy (historically, it was used to induce abortions).

Garlic *(Allium sativum)*

Used for lowering blood cholesterol (see page 429) and blood pressure (see page 461), colds (see page 294) and flu, ear infections (see page 363), Helicobacter pylori infection (see ulcers, page 669), colon cancer prevention (see page 304)

This herb has a long tradition of healing powers. Ancient Egyptians ate garlic as part of their daily diet. In fact, well-preserved cloves of garlic were found in King Tutankhamen's tomb. In Biblical times, garlic was thought to preserve strength and was given to slaves to increase their fitness. In ancient Greece, athletes took garlic before competing in the Olympic games to enhance strength and vigour. Historically, garlic has been used worldwide to fight bacterial infections. The French chemist Louis Pasteur was the first to describe the antibacterial effect of garlic. Today, garlic is still taken to fight infection, but it is also being praised by scientists for its protective effects against heart disease and cancer.

Laboratory studies have shown garlic and garlic's sulphur compounds inhibit the action of HMG-CoA reductase in the liver, a critical enzyme involved in cholesterol synthesis. As a result, more than 40 clinical trials have examined the effects of raw garlic and garlic supplements on blood cholesterol. The results of many trials suggest that garlic supplements modestly lower total cholesterol, LDL (bad) cholesterol and blood triglycerides over the short term (1 to 3 months). However, similar cholesterol-lowering effects have not been found in studies lasting 6 months.

Garlic contains many different sulphur compounds, and one in particular, S-allyl cysteine (SAC), has been shown to lower LDL cholesterol by up to 10 percent in humans.[1-4] SAC is present in small amounts in raw garlic, increasing in concentration as the garlic ages. The scientific studies that have found a cholesterol-lowering effect have used an aged garlic extract (Kyolic brand from Wakunaga).

Garlic may protect us from heart disease in other ways. Studies have shown the herb can thin the blood by reducing the stickiness of platelets.[5] Platelet stickiness or aggregation is one of the first steps in the formation of blood clots that can lead to a heart attack or stroke. Garlic's sulphur compounds have also been shown to have antioxidant powers and prevent damage to LDL choles-terol.[6,7] As well, garlic may help reduce inflammation, a process thought to play an important role in the development of heart disease. Some, but not all, studies also suggest that garlic might help lower blood pressure.[8]

Much of the research on cancer prevention has looked at stomach and colon cancer. Population-based studies have found that eating raw and cooked garlic may reduce the risk of stomach cancer by as much as 60 percent. The Iowa Women's Health Study, which followed 42,000 women for 5 years, found that those who consumed 0.7 grams of raw or cooked garlic each day (less than one clove) had a 32 percent lower risk of colon cancer than women who did not consume garlic.[9] A Swiss study found that men who consumed raw or cooked garlic had a 23 percent lower risk of colon cancer.[10]

Some research suggests that eating garlic may also offer protection from prostate cancer. A study from the United Kingdom found that, compared with men who never consumed garlic, those who consumed garlic in foods and supplements at least twice a week had a 40 percent reduced risk of prostate cancer.[11] Men who consumed garlic one to four times per month had a 30 percent reduced risk. The more garlic the men consumed, the greater the protection.

There are three possible reasons for the potential anti-cancer effect of garlic's sulphur compounds. First, these compounds help the liver detoxify and get rid of cancer-causing substances. Second, some sulphur compounds may have a direct toxic effect on certain cancer cells. And third, studies have shown that sulphur compounds in aged garlic extract can stimulate the body's immune system.

Helicobacter pylori (*H. pylori*) is a bacterium that's implicated in the development of stomach cancer and ulcers. Laboratory studies show that garlic, especially aged garlic extract, inhibits the growth of the organism. However, studies conducted in humans have not found a beneficial effect.[12,13]

Garlic Supplements

As little as half a clove of raw or cooked garlic each day is thought to offer general health benefits. Raw garlic contains very little SAC, but researchers at Pennsylvania State University found that allowing crushed garlic to sit at room temperature for 10 minutes before using it in cooking will increase the concentration of SAC.[14]

Most studies related to garlic and lowering of high cholesterol have used a standardized garlic powder extract containing 1.3 percent alliin (Kwai, Lichtwer Pharma)—300 milligrams taken three times daily. A specific aged garlic extract (Kyolic, Wakanuga)—7.2 grams per day—has also been used. As well, a specific garlic powder product (Garlicin, Nature's Way) has been studied.

For treating hypertension, garlic powder, 600 to 900 milligrams daily, has been used—in most studies, a specific garlic powder formulation (Kwai, Lichtwer Pharma). An aged garlic extract, 2400 milligrams daily, has also been found effective.

For the prevention of colorectal and stomach cancer, consuming 3.5 to 29 grams (1 to 10 cloves) of fresh or cooked garlic each week seems to be protective.

When taken in large amounts, garlic may cause stomach upset, heartburn, flatulence, nausea and diarrhea. Certain people are more sensitive to the sulphur compounds in garlic, and these effects are more pronounced when eating raw garlic. Garlic supplements in high doses may be unsafe during pregnancy. Garlic (both fresh and supplements) may enhance the effects of blood-thinning medications like warfarin (Coumadin). If you're taking this type of drug and garlic at the same time, be sure to inform your pharmacist and doctor. Since garlic can prolong bleeding time, stop taking it 1 week prior to scheduled surgery.

Ginger *(Zingiber officinale)*

Used for motion sickness (see page 559), morning sickness (pregnancy), post-operative nausea and vomiting, vertigo

This perennial plant has been cultivated for thousands of years in China and has been a part of traditional Chinese medicine for more than 2500 years. Historically, ginger was prescribed for abdominal distension, vomiting, diarrhea and coughing. Ginger has also played an important healing role in the medical systems of India, Nigeria and the West Indies. Ginger became popular as an herbal remedy in the Western world in the early 1980s when a scientist with the flu noticed that taking capsules of ginger cured his nausea. Since then, ginger has been widely accepted as a treatment for nausea. The ginger root you can buy at the supermarket is the underground stem (rhizome) of the plant, and the part used for medicinal purposes.

A number of studies have found ginger an effective agent in reducing motion sickness. In one Swedish study of 79 naval cadets, ginger reduced vomiting and cold sweats.[1] Another study, conducted among almost 1500 people aboard a ship, found ginger to be just as effective as various medications for seasickness.[2] Despite these positive findings, a few studies have reported no effect of ginger on nausea associated with travel.[3,4]

A number of studies have also assessed the effectiveness (and safety) of ginger supplements in pregnant women with morning sickness. A study from Thailand gave 70 pregnant women experiencing nausea and vomiting either 1 gram of ginger or a placebo pill daily for 4 days. Among the women receiving ginger, 87 percent had less nausea. As well, episodes of vomiting decreased significantly in the group taking ginger. Another study from Denmark looked at 27 pregnant women suffering from severe morning sickness and revealed that ginger taken 4 times a day significantly reduced nausea and vomiting. The effects of ginger became apparent after 4 days of treatment.[5-9]

Studies support the use of ginger for reducing nausea and vomiting that occurs after surgery. Two out of three studies found ginger to be superior to placebo and equally effective as metoclopramide, the standard medication given to patients.

Researchers have also found that taking ginger seems to reduce symptoms of vertigo, including nausea.[10,11]

Ginger contains many ingredients: As the precise active ingredient remains unknown, all may play a role in the herb's beneficial effects. Scientists believe that ginger acts on the stomach and improves the motility of the intestinal tract. Shogaol and gingerol are two compounds that give ginger its pungent smell; the latter may improve appetite and digestion because of its ability to reduce gastric secretions and increase the release of important digestive aids.

Ginger Supplements

Buy powdered ginger pills. For treating morning sickness, 250 milligrams of ginger four times daily, or 500 milligrams twice daily, has been used. For motion sickness, take 1 gram of dried powdered ginger root 30 minutes to 4 hours before travel. To reduce post-operative nausea and vomiting, take 1 to 2 grams of powdered ginger root 1 hour before induction of anesthesia. For reducing chemotherapy-induced nausea and vomiting, studies have found an effective dose to be 1 gram daily started on the first day of chemotherapy and continued for 5 days. A ginger tea has also been used and is typically prepared and taken on the day of chemotherapy and continued for as long as needed.

Mild intestinal upset is the only adverse effect that has been reported from taking ginger at the recommended doses. Ginger does have a slight blood-thinning effect and may possibly interact with blood-thinning medications like warfarin (Coumadin), though no studies have reported this effect. The safety of taking ginger supplements during pregnancy has not been proven and therefore its use during pregnancy remains controversial. The effect of ginger on the developing fetus is unknown. Ginger may also increase bleeding time and should be used with caution if taking before scheduled surgery. (Discuss with your surgeon the use of ginger to reduce post-operative nausea prior to taking it.)

Ginkgo *(Ginkgo biloba)*

Used for dementia, Alzheimer's disease (see page 201), age-related memory loss, intermittent claudication (peripheral vascular disease)

Ginkgo biloba is the world's oldest living species of tree—its fossil records date back more than 200 million years. The ginkgo tree lives as long as 1000 years and grows over 100 feet high. Ginkgo extracts used in herbal medicine come from the tree's characteristic fan-shaped bilobed leaves. The use of ginkgo as a medicinal plant dates back almost 5000 years, to the beginning of Chinese medicine. Scientific research into ginkgo's active ingredients started in the late

1950s. A standardized extract of ginkgo was produced some 20 years later. It's this special extract, EGb 761, that continues to be used in much of the scientific research today.

More than two decades of research on ginkgo have not produced convincing evidence that the herb is helpful in slowing cognitive decline. The vast majority of studies have been conducted in adults who already have cognitive impairment or dementia and only a few have turned up positive results. Findings from these studies suggest taking ginkgo can modestly improve some measures of cognitive function, particularly short-term visual memory and possibly speed of cognitive processing, in non-demented patients with mild cognitive impairment. (Individuals with mild cognitive impairment have memory problems not severe enough to warrant a diagnosis of Alzheimer's disease. Studies suggest that some people with mild cognitive impairment have an increased risk of progressing to Alzheimer's disease.) Researchers have learned that taking ginkgo does not improve memory in people over the age of 60 with normal mental function.[1-3]

Studies do suggest that gingko might improve some measures of cognitive function in healthy young to middle-aged people. Ginkgo has been found to improve memory, speed of cognitive processing and concentration in people with no complaints of memory impairment.

Studies conducted in older adults who do not have cognitive impairment have yielded mixed results at best. In a 2008 study—the largest and longest trial performed to date—researchers assigned 3069 adults aged 75 years or older to take *Ginkgo biloba* (120 milligrams twice daily) or a placebo pill for 7 years to determine whether the herb could delay the onset of dementia due to any cause, including Alzheimer's disease. (Dementia describes progressive symptoms such as memory loss, mood changes and a decline in the ability to talk, read and write caused by damage or changes to the brain. After Alzheimer's disease, the most common cause of dementia is stroke, referred to as vascular dementia.)

At the study's outset, participants were either not cognitively impaired or had mild cognitive impairment. After an average of 6.1 years of follow-up, the study found that taking *Ginkgo biloba* did not prevent dementia and had no effect on the risk of developing Alzheimer's disease. Because the delay from initial brain changes to clinical dementia is known to be long, it's possible that ginkgo's effect—positive or negative—may take many more years to show up.[4]

Some clinical trials have demonstrated a significant improvement or delay in the progression of Alzheimer's disease when standardized extracts of ginkgo leaf were given over several weeks to one year. A 52-week American clinical trial conducted with 309 patients with mild to moderate dementia as a result of Alzheimer's disease or stroke compared the effects of 40 milligrams of ginkgo (EGb 761) taken three times daily to a placebo pill. After one year, the placebo group showed a decline in cognitive function, whereas the ginkgo group did not. When the researchers looked at Alzheimer's patients only, there were modest but statistically significant changes in memory and other brain functions.[5]

Ginkgo has been shown to be an effective treatment for relief from intermittent claudication, a condition in which the arteries supplying the legs with blood may become blocked because of hardening of those arteries. Because the muscles in the legs can't get enough oxygen, walking more than a short distance causes cramps and pain. One study of 79 patients suffering from this condition found that leg pain was reduced and walking distance increased after taking a standardized extract of ginkgo.[6] A smaller study found that ginkgo (the EGb 761 extract) improved the health of the blood vessels in people with intermittent claudication.[7]

The active ingredients thought to be responsible for ginkgo's beneficial effects are terpene lactones and ginkgo flavone glycosides. A number of studies suggest that ginkgo increases circulation and oxygen delivery to the brain. The herb's active ingredients also make platelets less sticky, thus making circulation more efficient. In addition, ginkgo has a strong antioxidant effect in the brain. (Free radical damage to brain cells may be a contributing factor in Alzheimer's disease.)

Ginkgo Supplements

Choose a product that is standardized to contain 24 percent ginkgo flavone glycosides and 6 percent terpene lactones. For dementia syndromes, take 120 to 240 milligrams daily, in divided doses. To improve cognitive function in healthy adults, take 120 to 240 milligrams daily, in divided doses. To relieve walking pain in people with intermittent claudication, take 120 to 240 milligrams daily, in divided doses.

For all indications, start at a lower daily dose—not more than 120 milligrams—to avoid stomach upset. Increase the dose if needed, but do so slowly.

On rare occasions, ginkgo may cause gastrointestinal upset, headache or an allergic skin reaction in susceptible individuals. Ginkgo seems to alter insulin secretion and might affect blood-sugar levels in people with type 2 diabetes; this appears to occur only in people with diabetes who are taking oral medications to control blood glucose. If you're taking medication to control diabetes, be cautious about using ginkgo.

Ginkgo has a slight blood-thinning effect, so it has the potential to enhance the effects of other blood-thinning medications (warfarin, aspirin). If you're on anticoagulant medication, let your pharmacist and doctor know if you start taking ginkgo. In fact, ginkgo has the potential to interact with a number of prescription drugs; if you take medication, consult your pharmacist before taking ginkgo. The herb's safety during pregnancy and breastfeeding has not been established.

Ginseng *(Panax ginseng* and *Panax quinquefolius)*

Used for stress (see page 663) and fatigue, immune enhancement (see common cold, page 294), type 2 diabetes (see page 343) (American ginseng only)

Ginseng is a perennial herb with a taproot. *Panax ginseng* goes by many names, including Asian ginseng, Korean ginseng and Chinese ginseng. It grows in northern China, Korea and Russia. American ginseng *(Panax quinquefolius)* grows in the United States. The herb takes 5 years to grow; as a result, high-quality ginseng root is extremely expensive. White ginseng is ginseng root that has been dried but is unprocessed; red ginseng refers to the herb when it has been steamed and heat-dried. Both are thought to have unique characteristics.

A part of Chinese medicine for more than 2000 years, ginseng root is known as an adaptogenic herb: It increases the body's resistance to stress and balances functions of the immune, nervous and cardiovascular systems.

Evidence suggests that *Panax ginseng* has strong immune-enhancing properties. Studies done in test tubes, in animals and in humans found that ginseng increases the body's production of a number of different immune cells. Ginseng also seems to be able to help certain cells engulf foreign compounds that invade the bloodstream.

A well-designed Italian study tested the theory that regular use of *Panax ginseng* helps prevent colds and flus.[1] The researchers enrolled 227 people, giving half the participants 100 milligrams of a standardized ginseng extract (G115) and the remaining volunteers a placebo pill. Four weeks later, all participants received a flu vaccine. Those individuals taking ginseng had significantly higher levels of antibodies in response to the flu shot than those who did not take the herb. Killer white blood cells (an important part of the body's defence against viruses and foreign molecules) were nearly twice as high in the ginseng group after 8 weeks of supplementation. As well, the ginseng users had significantly fewer episodes of cold or flu compared with the placebo group.

Panax ginseng contains several active ingredients. Those thought to be of most importance are referred to collectively as ginsenosides or panaxosides, compounds found in the root. (*Ginsenosides* is the term developed by Asian researchers; *panaxosides* was coined by early Russian researchers.) These active ingredients are thought to reduce stress by stimulating the body's adrenal glands. These triangular-shaped glands sit above the kidneys and regulate the release of stress hormones. Chronic fatigue or stress can compromise adrenal function, affecting the body's release of hormones and immune compounds, as well as diminishing one's overall feeling of energy. Ginsenosides also appear to stimulate the production of immune compounds that help fight infection.

American ginseng may help control blood-sugar levels in people with type 2 diabetes. Studies have found that taking American ginseng up to 2 hours before a meal can lower post-meal blood-glucose levels in people with type 2 diabetes.[2-3]

You might already be familiar with a specific extract of American ginseng called COLD-fX (Afexa Life Sciences Inc.). Evidence suggests that taking 200 milligrams of COLD-fX twice daily over a 3 to 4 month period during flu season can reduce the risk of getting a cold or flu. This ginseng extract also seems to reduce the severity and duration of symptoms when infections do occur. COLD-fX might not reduce the chance of getting the first cold of the season, but it seems to reduce the risk of getting repeated colds in a season.[4-6]

Ginseng Supplements

PANAX GINSENG. To reduce the risk of getting the common cold or flu, take 100 milligrams of *Panax ginseng* daily for the 4 weeks prior to getting a flu vaccination and continue for 8 weeks thereafter. To help treat an acute attack of chronic bronchitis, take 100 milligrams twice daily for 9 days in combination with antibiotic therapy. Take ginseng for 3 weeks to 3 months and follow with a 1 to 2 week rest period before you resume taking the herb.

Sometimes you'll hear people refer to *Panax ginseng* as red or white ginseng. This distinguishes how some ginseng roots are prepared. Red ginseng is produced by steam-curing the root. This heat treatment causes increased production of certain ginsenosides that are usually absent or present in only small amounts in preparations of white ginseng. White ginseng is air-dried in the sun and contains less of the therapeutic constituents. Some think that the process of drying causes enzymes contained in the root to break down these constituents.

AMERICAN GINSENG. To reduce postprandial blood-glucose levels in patients with type 2 diabetes, take 3 grams of American ginseng up to 2 hours before a meal. There is no added benefit to taking more than 3 grams. American ginseng should be taken within 2 hours of a meal to avoid potential hypoglycemia (low blood sugar).

If you take medication to lower blood glucose, use American ginseng with caution as it could increase the likelihood of a low blood-sugar reaction. If you take warfarin, do not take American ginseng as the herb reduces the effectiveness of the drug.

For preventing upper respiratory tract infections such as the common cold or influenza, take COLD-fX (Afexa Life Sciences Inc.), 200 milligrams twice daily, during cold and flu season.

Ginseng is relatively safe at the recommended dosage. In some people, it may cause mild stomach upset, irritability and insomnia. To avoid overstimulation, start with 100 milligrams a day and avoid taking the herb with caffeine. Ginseng should not be used during pregnancy or breastfeeding or by individuals with poorly controlled high blood pressure.

Siberian Ginseng (Eleutherococcus senticosus)

Siberian ginseng is a completely different herb from American gingseng or *Panax ginseng*. Unlike *Panax ginseng*, this herb has a much milder effect and fewer reported side effects. Pregnant and nursing women can safely take Siberian ginseng, and it's much less likely to cause overstimulation in sensitive individuals. To ensure quality, choose a product standardized for eleutherosides B and E. The usual dosage is 300 to 400 milligrams once daily for 6 to 8 weeks, followed by a 1 to 2 week break.

Horse Chestnut *(Aesculus hippocastanum)*

Used for varicose veins (see page 679) and chronic venous insufficiency

This herb comes from trees that are native to Asia and northern Greece but now grow in North America and other parts of Europe. The fruit of the tree consists of a capsule that contains up to three large seeds, known as horse chestnuts. It's these seeds that are used to make medicinal extracts of horse chestnut. Traditionally, the herb was used both internally and externally to treat a host of ills, from arthritis to varicose veins. Today, horse chestnut has received much attention from scientists as an effective remedy for discomfort caused by varicose veins.

The seed of the horse chestnut tree contains active compounds called saponins. One compound in particular, aescin, enhances circulation through the veins. Studies have demonstrated aescin's ability to constrict and promote normal tone in the veins so that blood returns to the heart. The compound also has anti-inflammatory properties and may reduce swelling in the legs.[1,2]

After a comprehensive review of all horse chestnut studies, researchers from the United Kingdom concluded that the use of the herb is associated with a "decrease of the lower-leg volume and a reduction in leg circumference at the calf and ankle."[3] The herbal remedy was found to ease symptoms such as leg pain, fatigue and tenseness. Five studies even found that horse chestnut was as effective as standard drug therapy for varicose veins.[4] Another study suggests that taking horse chestnut seed extract is as effective as wearing compression stockings.[5]

Horse Chestnut Supplements

Buy a product standardized to contain 16 percent to 21 percent aescin. Studies have used a 300 milligram horse chestnut seed extract, containing 50 milligrams of aescin, twice daily.

In rare instances, horse chestnut seed extract can cause stomach upset, nausea and itching. Use is not recommended during pregnancy and breast-feeding since there is insufficient information available about its safety at these times. Horse chestnut should not be taken by people with liver or kidney disease.

Milk Thistle *(Silybum marianum)*

Used for liver disorders: chronic hepatitis (see page 445), acute hepatitis, alcoholic liver disease (see alcoholism, page 192), liver cirrhosis (see page 288); type 2 diabetes (see page 343)

Often referred to as wild artichoke or holy thistle, this native European plant has characteristic spiny leaves and thistle-shaped flowers. It has a long history of use as both a food and a medicine. In the early 1900s, milk thistle leaves were tossed into salads and often substituted for spinach. The seeds and leaves were used to treat jaundice and promote the production of breast milk. It wasn't until 1960 that German researchers began the process of identifying the plant's active compounds. By 1986, milk thistle had become accepted by German physicians as a treatment for liver disease.

Milk thistle has three active ingredients, known collectively as silymarin. This active complex appears to protect the liver in a number of ways. First, silymarin can prevent toxic substances from penetrating liver cells, possibly by preventing the binding of harmful compounds to the liver.[1,2] Second, silymarin has been shown to help liver cells regenerate more quickly. And finally, milk thistle may act as an antioxidant and, as such, protect liver cells from damage caused by unstable oxygen molecules (free radicals).[3]

Studies conducted in people with chronic viral hepatitis found that milk thistle can improve symptoms such as poor appetite, fatigue and stomach upset.[4–6] As well, liver-function blood-test results improve (liver enzyme levels are reduced) with milk thistle.[7] A handful of studies looking at the effects of milk thistle in alcoholic liver disease have found the herb able to improve both liver-function blood-test results and the health of liver cells.[8,9]

Two studies suggest that milk thistle may improve survival in patients with cirrhosis of the liver.[10,11] One study of 146 people with liver cirrhosis looked at the effect of taking milk thistle for 3 to 6 years. At the end of 4 years, the survival rate was 58 percent in the herb-treated group compared with 38 percent in the placebo group. The herb might also inhibit liver damage caused by certain prescription drugs such as acetaminophen, Dilantin (phenytoin) and phenothiazines.[12]

While numerous studies have suggested that milk thistle might be beneficial for decreasing mortality and improving liver-function blood tests in patients with alcoholic liver disease, a recent analysis of high-quality milk thistle studies suggested that the herb does not significantly affect mortality or liver-function tests in patients with alcohol-related liver disease.[13]

The herbal remedy might also help people with type 2 diabetes control blood-glucose levels. One study found that taking 200 milligrams of silymarin three times daily for 4 months, in combination with conventional treatment, significantly decreased fasting blood glucose, hemoglobin A1c (a measure of one's blood-sugar control for the past 12 weeks), LDL cholesterol and triglycerides.[14]

Milk Thistle Supplements

Buy a product standardized to contain 70 percent to 80 percent silymarin. For liver cirrhosis, the recommended dose is 420 milligrams per day. For diabetes, 200 milligrams of silymarin, taken three times daily, has been used in combination with conventional treatment.

Milk thistle is very safe in the recommended doses. A mild laxative effect may occur in some individuals. Use milk thistle with caution if you're allergic to plants in the Asteraceae/Compositae family (ragweed, daisy, marigold and chrysanthemum). Although the herb is thought to have no harmful effects, safety during pregnancy and breastfeeding has not been established so pregnant and breastfeeding women should use milk thistle with caution. Milk thistle may reduce the effectiveness of oral contraceptives.

St. John's Wort *(Hypericum perforatum)*

Used for mild to moderate depression (see page 330); seasonal affective disorder

This plant is native to Europe but can be found growing in Canada and the United States along roadsides and in meadows and woods. It produces bright-yellow flowers that are said to be most vivid in colour on June 24, the birth date of St. John the Baptist. The medicinal use of St. John's wort dates back more than 2000 years, when it was used to ease pain and promote wound healing. Today, St. John's wort is regarded as an effective treatment for mild depression. As well, new research is emerging regarding its potential antiviral activity against HIV and herpes simplex virus. The above-ground parts of the plant are used to make extracts of St. John's wort.

Many experts believe that St. John's wort works by keeping brain serotonin levels high for a longer period, just like the popular antidepressant drugs Paxil,

Zoloft and Prozac. Serotonin is a neurotransmitter, a natural brain chemical associated with feeling happy, relaxed and calm. St. John's wort also appears to alter levels of dopamine and norepinephrine in the brain, two other neurotransmitters involved in mood. Researchers believe the power of St. John's wort lies in two main active ingredients: hypericin and hyperforin. Although hypericin was originally thought to be responsible for the herb's antidepressant effects, it's now understood that hyperforin is the primary active ingredient.[1,2]

Studies clearly suggest that St. John's wort is likely as effective as low dose tricyclic antidepressants (e.g., Amitriptyline, Nortriptyline) and selective serotonin reuptake inhibitors (e.g., Prozac, Zoloft, Paxil) in treating depression. Taking St. John's wort improves mood, decreases anxiety and reduces insomnia caused by mild to major depression.

A 2008 review of studies conducted in 1200 patients suffering from mild depression concluded that St. John's wort provided a beneficial effect and led to a substantial increase in rates of remission.[3] In fact, clinical guidelines from the American College of Physicians–American Society of Internal Medicine suggest that St. John's wort can be considered an option along with conventional antidepressants for short-term treatment of mild depression. However, because the herbal remedy interacts with so many different medications (see below), this might not be a viable option for people who take other conventional medications.

St. John's Wort Supplements

Buy a St. John's wort supplement that is standardized to 0.3 percent hyperforin content, the extract used in most clinical studies of mild and moderate depression. The recommended dose is 300 milligrams taken three times daily.

St. John's wort is generally well tolerated. Side effects may include insomnia, restlessness, irritability, stomach upset, fatigue, skin rash and headache. Insomnia can be relieved by decreasing the dose, or taking St. John's wort in the morning. When the herb is taken in high doses for a long period, it may cause sensitivity to sunlight in very light- or fair-skinned individuals. St. John's wort has the potential to interact with many prescription medications, including anti-cancer agents (imatinib and irinotecan), anti-HIV agents (e.g., indinavir, lamivudine and nevirapine), anti-inflammatory agents (e.g., ibuprofen and fexofenadine), anti-microbial agents (e.g., erythromycin and voriconazole), heart drugs (e.g., digoxin, ivabradine, warfarin, verapamil, nifedipine and talinolol), and certain antidepressants, oral contraceptives and statins (e.g., atorvastatin and pravastatin). If you take medication, be sure to consult with your pharmacist and doctor before taking St. John's wort.

St. John's wort is not recommended for use during pregnancy and breast-feeding. If you're taking a prescription antidepressant drug, do not take it concurrently with St. John's wort, and always consult your physician before stopping any medication.

Saw Palmetto *(Serenoa repens, Sabal serrulata)*

Used for prostate enlargement (benign prostatic hyperplasia) (see page 629)

This plant, sometimes referred to as sabal in Europe, is native to North America and can be found growing in Atlantic Canada. Historically, the wrinkled, dark-coloured berries were used for food and to treat medical conditions affecting the bladder, urinary tract and prostate. It was once believed that saw palmetto increased sperm production and libido in men. Today, the berries of this plant are used to relieve symptoms associated with benign prostate enlargement.

Benign prostatic hyperplasia (BPH) affects roughly half of all men over 40 years of age. BPH is an enlargement of the prostate gland due to an over-production of the hormone dihydrotestosterone (an active form of testosterone) in the prostate.

The active ingredients in saw palmetto berries are thought to be fatty acids (a group of fat-soluble compounds), sterols and esters. Saw palmetto berries have been shown to lower the level of dihydrotestosterone in the prostate. The active ingredients appear to block the conversion of testosterone to dihydrotestosterone and to prevent the binding of dihydrotestosterone to prostate cells. As well, saw palmetto might have anti-inflammatory and anti-estrogenic properties.

Numerous clinical trials lasting up to 1 year have demonstrated that saw palmetto provides mild to moderate improvement in urinary symptoms, including frequent urination, painful urination, hesitancy and urgency. The herb has also been found to decrease nighttime urination. In a recent review of twenty-one randomized controlled studies, American researchers concluded that compared with the standard drug treatment Proscar, saw palmetto was equally effective at improving urinary tract symptoms and improving urinary flow.[1-3] And use of the herb was associated with fewer side effects.

Saw Palmetto Supplements

Buy a product standardized to contain between 80 percent and 90 percent fatty acids. Take 160 milligrams twice daily or 320 milligrams once per day. Significant symptom improvement may take up to 2 months of treatment. Teas made from saw palmetto berries are not likely to be effective, since adequate amounts of the fat-soluble active ingredients may not be released from the herb.

On rare occasions, saw palmetto may cause stomach upset, dizziness and headache. No interactions with medications have been found in clinical trials.

Valerian *(Valeriana officinalis)*

Used for insomnia (see page 507)

Over 200 species of valerian can be found growing around the world. The species used for medicinal purposes grows wild in Europe, but most of the plants used for making herbal extracts are cultivated. Ancient Greek physicians recommended valerian as a healing aid for stomach upset, liver problems and urinary tract disorders. The herb was not used to treat sleep problems until some time late in the 16th century. By 1940, mention of valerian could be found in American medical textbooks. Today, many European countries have approved its use as an over-the-counter medication for insomnia. It's starting to gain popularity in North America among consumers and within the medical profession.

Valerian root acts like a mild sedative on the central nervous system. Scientists have learned that valerian promotes sleep by weakly binding to two brain receptors, GABA receptors and benzodiazepine receptors. Many active components, including volatile oils and valepotriates, are believed to be responsible for the herb's sedating effect. The herb also appears to have anti-anxiety and mood-enhancing properties.

Several small studies conducted among patients with sleep disorders have found valerian reduces the time to fall asleep and improves the quality of sleep. In one double-blind study conducted in Germany, 44 percent of patients taking valerian root reported perfect sleep and 89 percent reported improved sleep compared to those taking the placebo pill. Another small study found that individuals with mild insomnia who took 450 milligrams of valerian before bedtime experienced a significant decrease in sleep problems. The same researchers studied 128 individuals and found that compared with the placebo,

400 milligrams of valerian produced a significant improvement in sleep quality in people who considered themselves poor sleepers.[1-4]

A recent review of 16 studies conducted with 1093 patients concluded that valerian improved sleep quality without producing side effects.[5] Unlike commonly prescribed sleeping pills, valerian does not lead to dependency or addiction. Nor does it produce a morning drug hangover.

Valerian Supplements

The recommended dose is 400 to 900 milligrams in capsule or tablet form, 2 hours before bedtime for up to 28 days. For tinctures (1:5), take 1 to 3 millilitres (15 to 20 drops) in water several times per day, or try 5 millilitres before bedtime. The herb works best when used over a period of time.

Do not take valerian with alcohol or sedative medications. The herb is not recommended for use during pregnancy and breastfeeding.

8

Other Popular
Natural Health Products

Alpha Lipoic Acid

Used for type 2 diabetes (see page 343), peripheral neuropathy (a nerve complication of diabetes)

Alpha lipoic acid is a sulphur-containing fatty acid found in liver, yeast and, to a lesser extent, spinach, broccoli, potatoes and kidney. There is no dietary requirement for alpha lipoic acid as the body is able to make its supply. However, supplements are necessary to achieve the amounts of alpha lipoic acid used in clinical studies. Alpha lipoic acid was first identified and isolated from food in 1950. Since then, it has been actively studied for its potential to help control blood-sugar levels and complications of diabetes.

Alpha lipoic acid helps enzymes turn the carbohydrate we eat into a useable source of energy for the body. It's needed by cells to generate ATP (adenosine triphosphate), energy molecules used in all cellular reactions. Alpha lipoic acid is also an antioxidant, able to neutralize free radicals, compounds naturally produced by the body that, if produced in excess, damage many types of body cells. Unlike other well-known antioxidants, such as vitamins C and E, alpha lipoic acid works in both a water and fat environment, which allows it to have a broad effect. Because of antioxidant effects in fat tissue, alpha lipoic acid is able to enter nerve cells, where it may offer protection. In addition, the body uses alpha lipoic acid to regenerate vitamins C and E.

Alpha lipoic acid has been shown to improve how the body uses insulin and to lower blood-glucose levels in people with type 2 diabetes after 4 weeks of supplementation. However, studies have not found the supplement to improve hemoglobin A1c levels.[1-3] (Hemoglobin [Hb] A1c is a blood test that provides an average of a person's blood-glucose measurements over the past 6 to 12 weeks. If someone's blood-glucose levels have been high over recent weeks, the HbA1c result will be higher.)

Furthermore, taking supplements of alpha lipoic acid appears to be effective in improving symptoms of diabetes neuropathy (nerve damage caused by high blood-sugar levels), including pain, tingling and numbness of the arms and legs.[4-8] One study of people with diabetes suggests that alpha lipoic acid supplements can also help reduce nerve damage caused to the body's internal organs.

Alpha Lipoic Acid Supplements

For type 2 diabetes and peripheral neuropathy, doses of 600 or 1200 milligrams per day have been used. In one of the largest studies on the use of alpha lipoic acid, 181 people took 600, 1200 or 1800 milligrams of alpha lipoic acid a day or a placebo. After 5 weeks, alpha lipoic acid improved nerve symptoms. The dose that was best tolerated while still providing benefit was 600 milligrams once daily. For maximum absorption, the supplement should be taken on an empty stomach.

Alpha lipoic acid may improve blood-sugar control, so people with type 2 diabetes who are taking medication, such as metformin or glyburide, to lower blood sugar should only take alpha lipoic acid under the supervision of a qualified health professional and should have their blood-sugar levels carefully monitored.

The safety of alpha lipoic acid in pregnant or nursing women, children, or people with kidney or liver disease is unknown.

Chondroitin Sulphate

Used for osteoarthritis (see page 578)

Chondroitin sulphate belongs to the glucosaminoglycan family of compounds. These compounds are a normal part of cartilage—a tough, elastic tissue in joints that covers the ends of bones, tendons and ligaments. Cartilage allows bones to glide smoothly over one another when they move. In osteoarthritis, the cartilage breaks down and disintegrates, the bones rub painfully against each other and movement is restricted.

Early research from the 1980s until 2001 showed that, after several weeks of treatment, taking chondroitin sulphate along with conventional painkillers or non-steroidal anti-inflammatory drugs (NSAIDs) significantly reduced pain and improved mobility in patients with osteoarthritis of the hip and knee.[1-6] But more recent research published since 2005 has not been positive. In one large trial, taking chondroitin sulphate alone or in combination with glucosamine hydrochloride did not reduce pain in most patients with osteoarthritis of the knee; however, the combination did reduce pain in a subgroup of patients with moderate to severe osteoarthritis of the knee.[7]

One report that pooled the findings of all chondroitin studies concluded that chondroitin significantly reduced osteoarthritis pain. But when only the largest, highest-quality trials were included in the analysis, chondroitin did not appear to significantly reduce pain. The reason for these mixed findings could be due to differences in patient populations, different products used or other variances in study design.[8]

Overall, the evidence shows that some people with osteoarthritis of the knee can experience some benefit from taking chondroitin; however, pain relief is likely to be modest.

Scientists believe that chondroitin supplementation can slow the progression of this "wear and tear" disease. When researchers looked at the effects of chondroitin in people with osteoarthritis, they found that those using chondroitin experienced less joint damage over time compared with those not taking the supplement. Taking supplemental chondroitin may offer joints the building blocks they need to repair cartilage. Some experts believe that chondroitin increases the amount of hyaluronic acid in the joints. (Hyaluronic acid is the fluid that keeps the joints lubricated.) Chondroitin may also inhibit enzymes that break down cartilage.

Chondroitin Sulphate Supplements

The typical dose for chondroitin sulphate supplements is 200 to 400 milligrams three times daily or 1000 to 1200 milligrams once daily. Chondroitin sulphate and glucosamine sulphate are frequently sold together in combination products, but there is no evidence from studies on humans that this combination works better than either product alone. It may take 2 to 4 months of treatment to notice significant improvement in osteoarthritis symptoms.

Occasionally, chondroitin supplements may cause stomach upset and nausea. No serious side effects have been reported. There is a potential for allergic reaction in some individuals from chondroitin supplements made from animal sources.

Beware of chondroitin and glucosamine combination products that also contain manganese. When taken in doses higher than recommended, chondroitin products can sometimes supply more than the 11 milligrams per day tolerable upper limit for manganese, which might cause toxic effects to the central nervous system.

The potential risk of transmission of bovine spongiform encephalopathy (BSE, or mad cow disease) is raising people's concerns about products containing chondroitin, which is produced from bovine trachea. Although bovine trachea tissue does not seem to carry a high risk of BSE infection, in some cases, manufacturing methods might lead to contamination from diseased animal tissues. So far there are no reports of BSE or other disease transmission to humans from dietary supplements containing animal materials, and the risk of potential disease transmission is thought to be quite low. If you are concerned, call the manufacturer and ask what steps are being taken to ensure that its chondroitin is not contaminated.

Coenzyme Q10 (CoQ10)

Used for congestive heart failure (see page 311), high blood pressure (see page 458), migraine headaches (see page 553)

Coenzyme Q10 (CoQ10) is a fat-soluble, vitamin-like substance that's made by every cell in the body. Because the body makes CoQ10, it's not considered an essential nutrient and, therefore, there is no recommended daily intake. It's found in cell membranes, with the highest concentrations being in heart, liver, kidney and pancreas cells. It's also found in lipoproteins that transport cholesterol and fat in the bloodstream.

CoQ10 works with many different enzymes in the body and thus is needed for many important metabolic reactions. One very important function of CoQ10 is the production of the body's energy compounds, ATP (adenosine triphosphate). CoQ10 also has antioxidant properties and has been demonstrated to protect LDL cholesterol particles from becoming oxidized in the body. (Oxidized LDL cholesterol is thought to adhere more readily to artery walls.)

CoQ10 also prolongs the effects of vitamin E, another powerful antioxidant.

The compound was first identified in 1957 by researchers at the University of Wisconsin. In the 1960s, Japanese scientists began studying its health benefits. Today, CoQ10 is widely used in Japan, Europe and Russia. In fact, the Japanese government approved the use of CoQ10 for the treatment of congestive heart failure in 1974.

Adding a CoQ10 supplement to conventional treatments has been shown to improve quality of life, decrease hospitalization rates and reduce symptoms of heart failure such as edema, enlarged liver and insomnia in patients with mild to severe congestive heart failure. There is no evidence that CoQ10 can help heart failure when taken alone, but it might be helpful when taken with other heart failure drugs.[1-6]

Three studies have also found that CoQ10 taken in addition to blood pressure medications provided a further blood pressure–lowering effect and might allow dosage reduction or discontinuation of some antihypertensive medications.[7-9]

CoQ10 appears to help prevent migraine headaches. Research suggests that CoQ10 decreases the frequency of headaches by about 30 percent and the number of days with headache-related nausea by about 45 percent in adults. However, taking CoQ10 at the onset of a migraine doesn't seem to reduce the headache's duration or severity.[10,11]

CoQ10 levels in the body decline with age and stress. Some medications can also interfere with the body's production of CoQ10 or may hamper its action. Cholesterol-lowering medications such as atorvastatin (Lipitor), lovastatin (Mevacor), simvastatin (Zocor) and pravastatin (Pravachol) have been shown to reduce blood levels of CoQ10. Statins' effect on CoQ10 appears to be dose-related. Taking a 10 milligram daily dose of Lipitor doesn't significantly decrease levels of circulating CoQ10 in healthy people. However, a daily Lipitor dose of 80 milligrams for 1 month has been shown to reduce CoQ10 levels by 52 percent.[12-15] Whether this affects heart health is not yet known, but it may be wise to take CoQ10 supplements if you are on these drugs. There is also preliminary research that CoQ10 might decrease adverse muscular effects caused by statin drugs.

CoQ10 Supplements

Coenzyme Q10 (CoQ10) supplements are made by fermenting beets and sugar cane with special strains of yeast. Buy a CoQ10 supplement in an oil base (instead of dry-powder tablets or capsules) as this is more available to the body.[16] There is no consensus on how much CoQ10 is beneficial for health. The amounts used in clinical studies that have reported beneficial effects are as follows:

- For treating symptoms of congestive heart failure, most studies have used 100 milligrams per day divided into 2 or 3 doses, but benefits have also been found with 60 milligrams per day.
- For reducing the risk of future heart problems in patients who suffered a recent heart attack, a dose of 60 milligrams taken twice daily has been used.
- For treating high blood pressure, researchers have given study participants 120 to 200 milligrams per day in divided doses (e.g., 60 milligrams twice per day).
- To prevent statin-induced muscle pain, studies have given patients 100 to 200 milligrams per day.
- For preventing migraine headache, 100 milligrams three times daily has been used.

CoQ10 supplements are very safe; no significant side effects have been reported. However, when taken in daily doses of 300 milligrams or more, CoQ10 can interfere with liver enzyme blood tests. CoQ10 can decrease blood pressure and might have additive blood pressure–lowering effects when used with antihypertensive drugs; if you are taking medication to treat hypertension, use CoQ10 with caution. The supplement may also interfere with the blood-thinning effects of warfarin (Coumadin).[17,18] If you are taking this medication, don't take CoQ10 unless monitored by your doctor.

Conjugated Linoleic Acid (CLA)

Used for weight loss (see page 569)

Conjugated linoleic acid (CLA) is a naturally occurring fatty acid found in dairy products and red meat and, in lesser amounts, in pork and chicken. It's estimated that non-vegetarians consume about 1 gram of CLA each day. Since the body does not manufacture CLA, the only way to get it is through foods or supplements. But because there is no evidence that CLA is essential to our body, no official daily recommended intake has been established.

The health benefits of CLA have been studied for some time. Research on animals and experiments using human breast cancer cells suggest that CLA may be protective from breast cancer.[1-4] CLA is also an antioxidant: It can protect cells from damage caused by free radicals and therefore may help ward off heart disease by keeping cholesterol levels in check.

Recently, however, studies are indicating that CLA supplements may play a role in weight control.[5-10] Taking supplemental CLA seems to improve body composition in people who are overweight or obese. The supplement has been shown to significantly decrease body fat and might increase lean body mass (muscle) in some people. CLA is thought to facilitate weight loss by inhibiting the action of lipoprotein lipase, an enzyme that breaks down dietary fat so it can be absorbed by the body. CLA is also believed to increase the activity of the enzyme responsible for breaking down body fat stores. In one study, CLA supplements also increased feelings of fullness, but this effect didn't lead to reduced food intake or improved weight maintenance after weight loss.

CLA Supplements

To assist with body fat loss, the recommended dose is 1 gram (1000 milligrams) taken three times a day with meals.

CLA supplements may cause mild stomach upset in some people. There's some concern about CLA's long-term safety. Some studies have found increased insulin levels and insulin resistance—risk factors for type 2 diabetes—in people with abdominal obesity who are taking a specific isomer of CLA. (Isomers are compounds that have an identical molecular formula but different structures of atoms and therefore different properties.) Most CLA supplements contain a mixture of CLA isomers; it's unknown whether these mixed CLA products harbour the same risk.

DHEA (Dehydroepiandrosterone)

Used for impotence (erectile dysfunction) (see page 485), adrenal insufficiency in women, lupus (see page 481)

DHEA (dehydroepiandrosterone) is a hormone produced by the adrenal glands, two small triangular-shaped glands that sit above the kidneys. DHEA levels are higher in men than in women, and they naturally decline with age: By the age of 60, we produce 5 percent to 15 percent of what we did when we were 20. Some experts attribute this decline in DHEA to the aging process, although this remains to be proven.

Once your adrenal glands secrete DHEA, it's used as a building block to make estrogen and testosterone. DHEA supplementation seems to change circulating levels of estrogen and progesterone. In men, DHEA supplements appear to increase estrogens, but not the male sex hormones. In women, the opposite is true: DHEA increases blood levels of androgens, but not estrogens. The effect of DHEA on circulating hormone levels may be responsible for its health benefits.

Researchers have found that compared with healthy volunteers, DHEA levels are lower in men with erectile dysfunction. One study involving 40 men with erectile dysfunction revealed that a daily 50 milligram supplement of DHEA taken for 6 months was associated with improved sexual performance. DHEA seems to help men with erectile dysfunction that's caused by high blood pressure or that's due to an unknown cause. It doesn't seem to improve erectile dysfunction related to diabetes or neurological disorders.[1,2]

Failure of the adrenal glands can occur because of an illness or surgical removal of the glands. People with adrenal failure are given medications that provide the body with the hormones the adrenal glands are no longer producing. Studies show that when DHEA supplements are taken along with standard medications, women with adrenal failure report increased energy, libido and feelings of well-being.[3,4] Keep in mind that adrenal failure is not the same as "tired adrenal glands," a condition often diagnosed by natural health practitioners. DHEA supplements are not warranted for so-called adrenal weakness.

A number of studies have shown DHEA supplements improve symptoms of lupus, an autoimmune disease that affects mostly women in their childbearing years.[5-13] DHEA may be helpful in easing symptoms of fatigue and sore joints. It may also reduce flare-ups of the disease.

DHEA Supplements

DHEA supplements consist of a hormone manufactured from compounds found in soybeans. It is sold as a dietary supplement in the United States but is not allowed for sale in Canada.

For impotence, take 50 milligrams per day. For adrenal failure, take 50 milligrams per day. For lupus, take 200 milligrams per day as an adjunct to conventional medication. Keep in mind that DHEA supplements have been plagued by quality-control problems. In tested products, DHEA content ranges from 0 percent to 150 percent of the labelled amount. If you decide to purchase DHEA, make sure you buy from a reputable manufacturer.

Short-term use of 50 milligrams of DHEA per day is considered safe and reported side effects are mild. However, at doses of 200 milligrams per day, DHEA frequently causes adverse effects such as acne and hirsutism (excessive hair growth on the face or body) in women. DHEA can also cause hair loss, voice-deepening, insulin resistance, changes in menstrual pattern, hepatic dysfunction, abdominal pain and hypertension. DHEA may increase testosterone levels and worsen conditions such as polycystic ovary syndrome (see page 613). DHEA may also increase or decrease your body's sensitivity to insulin, the hormone that regulates your blood sugar. If you have diabetes, be sure to have your doctor closely monitor your blood-glucose levels. There is also some concern that long-term use in amounts that raise DHEA levels above normal might increase the growth of cancerous cells.

Because DHEA is converted to estrogen and testosterone, women with an estrogen-sensitive disease (breast cancer, uterine cancer, endometriosis) should avoid using this supplement.

Fish Oil

Used for high blood triglycerides, high blood pressure (see page 458), prevention of heart disease, Crohn's disease (see inflammatory bowel disease, page 499), attention deficit hyperactivity disorder (see page 226), clinical depression (see page 330), rheumatoid arthritis (see page 646)

Fish oil supplements contain two omega-3 fatty acids: DHA (docosahexanaenoic acid) and EPA (eicosapentaenoic acid). You can also get DHA and EPA directly by eating oily fish such as salmon, trout and sardines. The body needs fatty acids to make eicosanoids, a family of powerful compounds, including prostaglandins, prostacyclins, thromboxanes and leukotrienes, that regulate our blood, immune system and hormones. Omega-3 fatty acids like DHA and EPA are used to make "friendly" eicosanoids, which reduce inflammation and blood clotting and are believed to offer a number of other health benefits. Animal fats and omega-6 fatty acids (found in corn, sunflower and safflower oils), on the other hand, are used to make inflammatory eicosanoids, compounds that have been linked to a number of ill-health effects.

Once consumed, omega-3 and omega-6 fats compete with each other in the body. Experts agree that it's important to eat several times more omega-3 fats than omega-6 fats so that healthy eicosanoids are formed. However, by some estimates, the typical North American diet provides twenty times more omega-6s than omega-3s. Fish oil supplements are one way to help balance your fat intake in favour of omega-3 fatty acids.

Omega-3 fats in fish act in several ways to protect the heart. DHA and EPA make the blood less likely to form clots, reduce inflammation and protect against irregular heartbeats that cause sudden cardiac death. Fish oil also seems to help blood vessels relax, preventing increases in blood pressure. Fish oil may help raise HDL cholesterol and increase the size of LDL cholesterol particles, resulting in larger, fluffy LDLs that are less damaging to artery walls. One trial, which enrolled 11,323 subjects who survived their first heart attack, demonstrated that even a small amount of omega-3 fatty acids (1000 milligrams per day) was effective at reducing overall death and the risk of sudden cardiac death by 20 percent and 45 percent respectively. Another study, from Finland, conducted in post-menopausal women with heart disease found that higher levels of DHA in the blood—consistent with their reported fish intake—was associated with slowed progression of the disease.[1,2]

It's well documented that omega-3 fish oil can reduce elevated blood triglycerides by 20 to 50 percent. It's thought that DHA and EPA reduce the liver's secretion of triglycerides and increase their clearance from the bloodstream. A pooled analysis of eighteen randomized trials including 823 people with type 2 diabetes concluded that fish oil can significantly lower blood triglycerides.[3] Studies conducted in people with mild hypertension have found that supplementation with fish oil provided a modest, but significant, reduction in blood pressure.[4-6]

Omega-3 fats are important components of nerve and brain cell membranes, where they help cells communicate messages effectively. Omega-3 fats may also be crucial for the formation of brain hormones that help stabilize mood. Scientists have found that people with major depression have lower levels of omega-3 fats in their body.[7,8] Taking fish oil supplements also seems to improve response to conventional antidepressants in patients with major depression.[9,10] Observational studies have also linked eating fish with lowering the risk of depression and suicide. In countries where fish intake is high, rates of depression are lower.

As well, Attention Deficit Hyperactivity Disorder (ADHD) is thought to be linked with a deficiency of omega-3 fats.[11] Omega-3 fats are necessary for proper brain development and function in growing children. Preliminary research shows that taking fish oil improves cognitive function and behaviour in children aged 8 to 12 years with ADHD. One study also found that taking a specific supplement containing fish oil and evening primrose oil improves cognitive function, hyperactivity, inattentiveness and behaviour in children aged 7 to 12 years with ADHD.[12,13]

By helping the body form friendly prostaglandins, DHA and EPA also have anti-inflammatory effects, which are thought to be responsible for helping to relieve joint pain, soreness and stiffness associated with rheumatoid arthritis. Studies have found that levels of these two fatty acids are lower in people with rheumatoid arthritis. Studies show that when used in people with rheumatoid arthritis who are also taking the medication naproxen (Naprosyn), supplementing with fish oil significantly relieves the duration of morning stiffness. Evidence also suggests that the use of fish oil might allow people to reduce their dose of non-steroidal anti-inflammatory drugs (NSAIDs). A recent study combined and analyzed the results of seventeen randomized, controlled trials assessing the pain-relieving effects of fish oil in patients with rheumatoid arthritis or joint pain caused by inflammatory bowel disease and dysmenorrhea (painful menstruation). Supplementation with fish oil for 3 to 4 months reduces joint pain intensity, minutes of morning stiffness, number of painful or tender joints, and the use of NSAIDs. The results suggest fish oil is an effective adjunctive treatment for joint pain associated with rheumatoid arthritis, inflammatory bowel disease and dysmenorrhea.[14-19]

Some, but not all, studies suggest that the anti-inflammatory effects of fish oil may help reduce symptoms and flare-ups of Crohn's disease, a condition in which parts of the digestive tract are severely inflamed.

Fish Oil Supplements

Fish oil supplements are made from a variety of fatty fish, including mackerel, herring, tuna, halibut and salmon, as well as seal blubber. Supplements vary in the amounts and ratios of DHA and EPA, the active ingredients in fish oil. For instance, most omega 3-6-9 supplements provide very little DHA and EPA, and some contain omega-3 fat from flaxseed oil rather than fish oil. Many fish liver oil supplements also provide little or no DHA and EPA. I don't advise using supplements made from fish liver oil for another reason: Fish liver oil is a concentrated source of vitamin A, which has been linked with a higher risk of hip fracture when taken in large supplemental amounts for long periods.

(Some fish liver oil products are low in vitamin A; this will be stated on the label.)

The typical dosage of fish oil is 2 to 9 grams of fish oil per day, often taken in divided doses. Check the product label to see how much fish oil each capsule provides (most products provide 1000 milligrams or 1 gram of fish oil per capsule). In most clinical studies, participants took enough fish oil capsules to provide a minimum of 1800 milligrams of EPA and 900 milligrams of DHA.

For the prevention of coronary heart disease, take a fish oil capsule that supplies 500 to 600 milligrams of DHA and EPA combined. If you don't eat oily fish twice per week, take 2 capsules daily. For the prevention of cardiac events in people with established heart disease, the recommended dose is 1000 milligrams of DHA and EPA combined.

When taken in doses of 3 to 4 grams per day or less, fish oil is very well tolerated. Fish oil supplements can cause belching and a fishy taste. To minimize this, buy an enteric-coated product or try taking fish oil during dinner, rather than breakfast. High doses can cause nausea, heartburn, loose stools and rash. Because fish oil has a blood-thinning effect, use caution if you're taking blood-thinning medication such as aspirin, warfarin (Coumadin) or heparin. It's possible that high doses of fish oil could increase the risk of bleeding. However, some research shows that taking 3 to 6 grams per day does not affect blood clotting in people also taking warfarin. Nevertheless, if you take these drugs, it's a wise idea to consult your physician before taking fish oil supplements.

Flaxseed

Used for high blood cholesterol (see page 424), menopausal symptoms (see page 601), lupus (see page 541), breast cancer prevention (see page 235)

Flax is a blue-flowered plant crop that has been grown since ancient times for both its seeds and fibre. In North America, flax is primarily grown for its seed. In Canada, the crop is grown mainly in the cool, northern climate of the western Canadian prairies. Flaxseed contains three ingredients that provide health benefits: soluble fibre, an omega-3 fatty acid called alpha-linolenic acid (ALA) and natural compounds called lignans.

The soluble fibre and omega-3 fatty acids in flaxseed are responsible for its cardio-protective properties. Flaxseed in various forms—raw, ground, in muffins and breads—helps reduce total and LDL cholesterol in people with normal and elevated cholesterol levels. Consuming 40 to 50 grams of flaxseed per day (about 6 tablespoons of ground flaxseed) has been shown to lower total cholesterol by 5 percent to 9 percent and LDL cholesterol by 8 percent to 18 percent.[1-6] Alpha-linolenic acid in flaxseed also reduces the stickiness of platelets, cells that clump together to form blood clots. (When a blood clot blocks the flow of blood through a coronary artery—a blood vessel that feeds the heart muscle—a heart attack can occur.)

Flaxseed may also be helpful for improving mild menopausal symptoms. In one study that compared flaxseed to wheat germ, as the placebo, flaxseed reduced reported hot flashes by 35 percent and night sweats by 44 percent. (In this study, wheat germ seemed to similarly improve symptoms.)[7]

Flaxseed is an excellent source of lignans, plant compounds that have a weak estrogen-like effect in the body and can help block the action of the hormone estrogen on breast cells, thereby helping to reduce the risk of breast cancer. (It's believed that the body's own estrogen can promote the growth and development of mutated breast cells.) Studies in animals have demonstrated the ability of lignans in flaxseed to reduce the size of breast tumours. In a study of post-menopausal women with newly diagnosed breast cancer, consuming 25 grams of flaxseed per day in the form of a muffin versus a placebo muffin significantly slowed the growth of breast tumours.[8-10]

Research also suggests that consuming flaxseed improves kidney function in people with lupus. Lupus can cause inflammation of the kidneys, which can impair their ability to function properly. Studies have shown that taking supplemental flaxseed is effective in lowering blood levels of creatinine, a measure of kidney function. (When the kidneys aren't functioning properly, an increased level of creatinine can accumulate in the blood.)[11,12]

Flaxseed Supplements

You can buy flaxseed in bulk, in vacuum-packed bags or in capsules. To obtain the health benefits from flaxseed, you must first grind it because whole seeds will pass through your system undigested. Grinding, or milling, breaks the tough outer skin of the seed, creating a light-coloured powder. Milled flaxseed is sold in a vacuum package, or you can prepare it yourself in a coffee grinder. To keep flaxseed fresh, grind it as you need it. Ground flaxseed can be refrigerated in an airtight, opaque container for up to 30 days. (Flaxseed oil is sold in bottles or capsules. The oil is extracted from whole flaxseeds using a cold-press process. Flaxseed oil provides alpha-linolenic acid, but no soluble fibre or lignans, and it doesn't lower blood cholesterol.)

To help lower cholesterol or improve menopausal symptoms, a daily intake of 40 to 50 grams (5 to 6 tablespoons) of ground flaxseed is recommended. To help reduce the risk of breast cancer, 25 grams (3 tablespoons) of ground flaxseed is recommended. To improve kidney function in people with lupus, studies have used 15 grams (2 tablespoons) of ground flaxseed per day.

Add ground flaxseed to your diet gradually. Like other sources of fibre, flaxseed can cause digestive symptoms including bloating, flatulence, abdominal pain, diarrhea, constipation and stomach upset.

Glucosamine Sulphate

Used for osteoarthritis (see page 578)

The body uses glucosamine to make a family of compounds called mucopolysaccharides. These compounds are a normal part of cartilage—a tough, elastic tissue found in joints that covers the ends of bones, tendons and ligaments. Cartilage allows bones to glide smoothly over one another when they move. In osteoarthritis, the cartilage breaks down and disintegrates, the bones rub painfully against each other and movement is restricted.

Foods do not directly supply glucosamine. Instead, your body makes this compound from glucose found in foods. Studies show that glucosamine stimulates the production of glycosaminoglycons, important compounds of cartilage in your joints. Research suggests that glucosamine supplements stop and possibly even reverse this degenerative disease of the joints.

Findings from studies lasting 3 years have found that glucosamine sulphate significantly relieved pain and improved mobility in people with osteoarthritis of the knee. Some studies have found the supplement to be as effective as ibuprofen and piroxicam (Feldene), two non-steroidal anti-inflammatory drugs used to manage osteoarthritis. Other research suggests glucosamine is more effective than acetaminophen.[1-9] However, whereas conventional medications take 2 weeks to improve symptoms, glucosamine takes 4 to 8 weeks for symptom relief.

There's also evidence that glucosamine may actually slow joint degeneration in people with osteoarthritis of the knee. Patients taking glucosamine for up to 3 years appear to have significantly less joint degeneration, less joint space narrowing and significant symptom improvement compared with those taking the placebo. A combined analysis of studies lasting at least 1 year and conducted in patients with knee osteoarthritis concluded that taking glucosamine sulphate might reduce the risk of disease progression by up to 54 percent.[10]

Although glucosamine sulphate appears to reduce pain and improve joint mobility, it may not prevent disease flare-ups. While most studies have evaluated the effectiveness of glucosamine for knee osteoarthritis, some evidence suggests it might also help osteoarthritis of the hip and spine.

Glucosamine Sulphate Supplements

Glucosamine supplements are made from the outer shell of shrimp, lobster and crab. For osteoarthritis, the typical dose is 1500 milligrams once daily, or 500 milligrams taken three times daily. Glucosamine sulphate is often combined with chondroitin in supplements; however, it's not known if this combination is any more effective than taking glucosamine or chondroitin alone.

No serious side effects have been reported. Glucosamine supplements may cause mild gastrointestinal upset, including nausea, heartburn, diarrhea or constipation. In one early study, glucosamine sulphate was reported to elevate blood-glucose levels in people with diabetes. Since then, clinical studies indicate that glucosamine has little or no effect on blood-glucose levels. In studies lasting 3 months to 3 years, glucosamine did not affect blood-sugar control in people with and without type 2 diabetes.

Because glucosamine supplements are made from shellfish, there is a concern that they can cause a problem for people with a shellfish allergy. However, such allergies are reactions to the protein, or meat, of shellfish, not the shell. There have been no documented reports of allergic reaction to glucosamine in people who have a shellfish allergy.

Grapeseed Extract

Used for heart disease prevention (see page 428), chronic venous insufficiency (intermittent claudication), varicose veins (see page 679), hemorrhoids (see page 441)

Grapeseed extract is most often derived as a by-product of wine manufacturing. Grapeseed is a rich source of anthocyanins, naturally occurring compounds also found in red wine, tea leaves, blueberries, cranberries, black currants and bilberry (see Chapter 7, page 125). In Europe, grapeseed extract is widely used to treat conditions related to fragile blood capillaries. It's also used to help reduce the risk of heart disease.

Anthocyanins are thought to keep blood vessels healthy by inhibiting the action of enzymes that break down connective tissue. Research suggests that a daily supplement of grapeseed extract can significantly reduce symptoms of peripheral venous insufficiency, including leg pain and swelling. In one study of patients with chronic venous insufficiency, taking a specific grapeseed extract sold in Europe significantly decreased leg swelling after 6 weeks of treatment compared with a placebo. Daily doses of 360 milligrams and 720 milligrams daily were both effective, but the higher dosage produced a slightly greater effect. After 12 weeks of supplementation, study participants also reported significant decreases in symptoms such as tired or heavy legs, tension, tingling and pain.[1]

The heart-protective effects of grapeseed extract are inferred from the antioxidant powers of anthocyanins. While no study has looked at whether grapeseed extract can ward off a heart attack, studies in the laboratory show that anthocyanins can prevent free radical damage to LDL cholesterol. (Free radicals oxidize LDL cholesterol; the oxidized form is thought to be more dangerous because it sticks more readily to artery walls.) One study found grapeseed anthocyanins to be superior to vitamins C and E in antioxidant capacity. Anthocyanins have been shown to reduce the likelihood of blood clot formation and to help blood vessels relax.[2-5]

Grapeseed Extract Supplements

For venous insufficiency, some experts recommend taking 75 to 300 milligrams for 3 weeks, followed by a maintenance dose of 40 to 80 milligrams daily. The specific grapeseed extract used in the study described above—Antistax (Boehringer Ingelheim)—is sold in continental Europe and the United Kingdom. The recommended dose of Antistax for chronic venous insufficiency is 360 milligrams or 720 milligrams once per day.

For a general antioxidant effect, take 50 milligrams of grapeseed extract once daily. It's considered extremely safe: No adverse effects are known.

A supplement called Pycnogenol offers the same effects as grapeseed extract and can be used to prevent or treat the same conditions, but it's more expensive than grapeseed extract. Rich in anthocyanins, Pycnogenol is the U.S.–registered trademark for an extract made from the bark of French Maritime pine trees. The dose used in clinical studies has ranged from 50 to 300 milligrams per day, in divided doses.

Inositol

Used for panic disorder, polycystic ovary syndrome (see page 613)

Although not recognized as a vitamin, inositol is closely related to the B vitamin family (see Chapter 4, page 32). It's found in foods mainly as phytic acid, a fibrous compound. Our diet provides approximately 1000 milligrams of inositol each day, mainly from citrus fruits, whole grains, legumes, nuts and seeds. When you eat these foods, bacteria in your intestine liberate inositol from phytic acid.

Once in the body, inositol is an essential component of cell membranes. It promotes the export of fat from cells in the liver and intestine. Inositol is also abundant in the central nervous system and contributes to the healthy functioning of nerves and muscles.

Researchers think that inositol might improve the sensitivity of serotonin receptors in the brain. Serotonin is a natural brain chemical that's associated with feelings of happiness, calmness and relaxation. Some evidence suggests that inositol may have benefits similar to serotonin reuptake inhibitor drugs (Prozac, Effexor, Paxil, Zoloft, Serzone) in conditions such as panic disorder and depression.[1]

One small study found that, compared with placebo treatment, daily inositol supplementation significantly improved depressive symptoms based on the Hamilton Depression Rating Scale.[2] When the researchers followed up with these patients after the study, they found a rapid relapse in symptoms once inositol was discontinued.[3]

Inositol seems to be helpful for treating panic disorder with or without agoraphobia. (Agoraphobia is a condition that causes people to become anxious in environments that are unfamiliar or in which they feel they have little control. Triggers may include crowds, wide-open spaces or travel.) One study found that inositol significantly reduced the severity and rate of panic attacks and the severity of agoraphobia over 4 weeks of treatment. Some research even suggests that inositol may be as effective as fluvoxamine (Luvox) for treatment of panic disorder.[4,5]

Inositol is thought to improve the action of insulin in women with polycystic ovary syndrome (PCOS). One study found that inositol, taken once daily for 6 weeks, increased the effectiveness of insulin and, as a result, decreased blood triglycerides and testosterone levels, reduced blood pressure and caused ovulation in obese women with PCOS.[6] Previous studies have suggested that people with insulin resistance and type 2 diabetes might be deficient in inositol.

Inositol Supplements

Inositol supplements may be difficult to find as few companies manufacture them. For panic disorder, the recommended dose is 12 to 18 grams per day. For polycystic ovary syndrome, buy D-chiro-inositol; take 1200 milligrams (1.2 grams) per day.

No adverse effects have been reported from taking inositol supplements; however, no long-term studies have been conducted. Because the recommended dosage of inositol is high (grams versus milligrams), be sure to buy a product made by a reputable manufacturer. When taking products in high doses, there is a greater risk for ill effects from contaminants, even if the contaminant is present in small amounts.

Lutein

Used for age-related macular degeneration (see page 547), cataracts (see page 264)

Lutein, Latin for "egg yolk" and "yellow," is a member of the carotenoid family, a group of chemicals found in dark-green and orange vegetables. The best dietary sources of lutein are spinach, kale, collard greens, dandelion greens, mustard greens, green peas, sweet yellow corn, Brussels sprouts and broccoli. Although lutein is not considered an essential nutrient, scientists have learned that this natural chemical is important to eye health.

High dietary intakes of lutein are associated with up to a 40 percent lower risk of age-related macular degeneration, the leading cause of blindness in adults over 65. Most cases of macular degeneration are dry macular degeneration, a condition that occurs when the tissues in the eye called the macula—the small part of the retina that's responsible for fine, detailed vision—gradually thin out. Lutein, which is concentrated in the macula, acts as a filter, protecting structures of the eye from the damaging effects of the sun's ultraviolet (UV) light. Lutein contributes to the density, or thickness, of the macula. The denser the macula, the better it can absorb incoming light.

A handful of studies have shown that adding lutein-rich foods or a lutein supplement to your daily diet can increase the density of the macula. In fact, researchers have noted significant increases in macular density within as little as 3 months. Research has found supplemental lutein to increase macular density in patients with macular degeneration and improve eye symptoms such as glare recovery, near-vision acuity and contrast sensitivity. In one study from the Veterans Administration Medical Center in Chicago, lutein in the form of 1/2 cup (125 ml) of sautéed spinach or a supplement, taken 4 to 7 times per week, improved visual function in men with age-related macular degeneration.[1-8]

Lutein also acts as an antioxidant, protecting the retina from oxidative damage caused by UV light. UV light can also lead to the development of cataracts, a disease in which the lens of the eye becomes yellow, making vision cloudy and blurry. Two large studies from Harvard University found that men and women with the highest intakes of lutein had a 20 percent lower risk of cataracts compared with those who consumed the least. Broccoli, spinach and kale were the foods most often associated with protection.[9-11] It's not known if lutein supplements offer the same benefit.

There's some evidence to suggest that lutein may also help protect from breast and colon cancer. Both low intakes and low blood levels of lutein are linked with a higher risk of these cancers. Studies in the lab have shown that a lutein extract from marigold flowers can halt the growth of cancer cells in animals.

Lutein Supplements

For reducing the risk of developing cataracts and age-related macular degeneration, 6 to 10 milligrams of lutein per day, either through diet or supplementation, is recommended. In the studies, people consuming 6 to 11.7 milligrams of lutein per day through diet had the lowest risk of developing these conditions. (One-half cup of cooked spinach has 10 milligrams of lutein; the same-sized serving of cooked kale contains 12 milligrams.) For reducing symptoms of macular degeneration, the recommended dose is 10 milligrams of supplemental lutein per day.

Choose a supplement made with FloraGLO, a high-quality patented lutein extract purified from marigold flowers that has been used in clinical studies.

Lutein is best absorbed when consumed with fat in a meal. No adverse reactions or drug interactions have been reported. Some multivitamins have added lutein; read ingredient lists before buying. Some brands contain only 0.25 milligrams per dose—not enough to offer a health benefit.

Lycopene

Used for prostate cancer prevention (see page 630), cervical dysplasia (see page 275)

Lycopene, belonging to the same family of carotenoid compounds as beta carotene, is found in red-coloured fruit and vegetables. It's the natural chemical that gives these foods their bright colour. Tomatoes are the richest source of lycopene, but you'll also find some in pink grapefruit, watermelon, guava and apricots. There is no daily recommended intake for lycopene as it isn't an essential nutrient.

Lycopene is an antioxidant, a compound that defends the body against free radical damage. Free radicals, toxic by-products formed in the body from oxygen, can destroy the genetic material of cells, which in turn may lead to cancer development. Compared with its cousin beta carotene, lycopene is twice as potent an antioxidant.[1,2]

The evidence that lycopene helps prevent prostate cancer is mixed. A number of studies have found that men with high lycopene intakes from foods such as tomato products have a lower risk of developing prostate cancer compared with men who consume little lycopene. However, one large-scale study found that lycopene in the diet only offered protection to men with a family history of prostate cancer.[3–7]

In a study from Harvard University that followed 47,365 men for 12 years, lycopene was clearly linked with protection from prostate cancer. Men with the highest lycopene intake were 16 percent less likely to be diagnosed with prostate cancer than their peers who consumed the least. Consuming tomato sauce, the primary source of bioavailable lycopene, at least twice per week versus less than once per month was linked with a 23 percent lower risk of prostate cancer. Studies have also related low blood and tissue lycopene levels with higher rates of prostate cancer.[8–10]

Lycopene may also have a role in the treatment for prostate cancer. Results of a study of 40 men with high-grade prostate intraepithelial neoplasia (PIN) suggest that taking a 4 milligram lycopene supplement twice daily might delay or prevent progression to prostate cancer. (PIN is a microscopic lesion in the prostate that is thought to be a precursor to prostate cancer.) Other preliminary research suggests that taking 15 milligrams of lycopene twice daily for 3 weeks before surgery for prostate cancer might decrease tumour growth.[11,12]

A handful of studies have suggested that consuming foods rich in lycopene protects women from cervical dysplasia, a condition in which cells lining the surface of the cervix grow abnormally. One study from the University of Pennsylvania School of Medicine found that women with the highest intake of lycopene were significantly less likely to have dysplasia compared with those who consumed the least.[13] Cervical dysplasia is caused by infection with certain strains of human papillomavirus (HPV). HPV is a common virus spread through sexual contact. In most cases, HPV leaves the body naturally, but some of the strains linked with cervical cancer can persist. Interestingly, research suggests that women with higher lycopene levels in their blood have a faster rate of clearing HPV from their body than women with lower lycopene levels.[14]

Some evidence also suggests that a higher intake of lycopene from foods and higher blood levels of lycopene may reduce the risk of cardiovascular disease as well as breast, ovarian and lung cancers.

Lycopene Supplements

Lycopene supplements may be useful in treating prostate cancer. The recommended dose is 15 milligrams twice daily. Choose a supplement that's made with the Lyc-O-Mato or LycoRed extract. This source of lycopene comes from Israel and is derived from whole tomatoes. It's also the extract that has been used in clinical studies.

When it comes to reducing the risk of cancer, it's best to get lycopene from foods. Studies suggest a daily intake of 6 to 12 milligrams offers cancer protection. Heat-processed tomato products like tomato paste, tomato juice, tomato sauce and ketchup contain the highest concentrations of bioavailable lycopene. (Lycopene is tightly bound to fibre in foods; processing breaks down some of the fibre thereby releasing lycopene and making more available to the body.) Excellent food sources include tomato juice (22 milligrams of lycopene per 1 cup), marinara pasta sauce (21 milligrams per 1/2 cup), tomato soup (12 milligrams per 1 cup) and stewed tomatoes (5 milligrams per 1/2 cup).

Absorption of lycopene is enhanced by the presence of some dietary fat. Lycopene is considered very safe. No adverse reactions or serious side effects have been reported.

Lysine

Used for herpes simplex labialis virus (cold sores) (see page 450)

Lysine is an essential amino acid, a building block of protein foods, which the body must get from the diet. Lysine is found in animal protein foods, including meat, poultry, dairy products and eggs. It's also found in dried peas, beans and lentils. It's estimated that the body needs about 1 gram (1000 milligrams) of lysine each day for good health. The body uses it to form collagen, a fibrous protein that holds together various structures in the body.

Studies in the lab show that lysine inhibits the growth of the herpes simplex virus.[1] Lysine seems to block the action of arginine, an amino acid the virus needs in order to replicate.

Herpes simplex remains dormant in nerve cells until periods of stress, when the virus can reappear, causing symptoms such as cold sores or genital sores. Studies lasting 6 months to 1 year found that supplemental lysine reduced the number of herpes flare-ups.[2-7] Lysine also lessened the severity of symptoms during a herpes attack and sped the rate of healing.

Lysine Supplements

For preventing cold sore flare-ups, take 1000 milligrams once daily (although one study found effects with 1000 milligrams taken three times daily). Taking lysine with a calcium supplement may increase calcium absorption and prevent calcium loss in the urine.[8]

High daily doses (10 grams per day) of lysine may cause diarrhea and stomach pain.

Melatonin

Used for insomnia (see page 507), jet lag

Melatonin, a hormone produced in the tiny pineal gland located in the brain, regulates the body's wake-sleep cycles. Its release from the brain is stimulated by darkness: The darker the room, the more melatonin your body produces. The hormone induces sleep by interacting with melatonin receptors in the brain. Once in the bloodstream, melatonin lowers body temperature, alertness and performance.

Contrary to popular belief, melatonin production does not appear to decline as we age. However, studies have found decreased melatonin production in people suffering from insomnia.[1] For insomnia, short-term melatonin treatment appears to help reduce the time it takes to fall asleep (sleep latency). Some patients also report minor improvement in subjective feelings of sleep quality. Some evidence suggests that melatonin might benefit elderly patients with insomnia who could be melatonin deficient compared with younger adults or children. In children with insomnia due to delayed onset of sleep, melatonin seems to shorten the time that it takes to fall asleep and to increase the duration of sleep. In addition, melatonin may be helpful to people who are trying to discontinue prescription sleeping aids.[2-9]

Taking melatonin also helps improve sleep in people diagnosed with circadian rhythm sleep disorders.[10-12] This family of sleep disorders affects the timing, not the quality, of sleep. People with this condition are unable to sleep and wake at the times required for normal work, school and social activities. They are generally able to get enough sleep if allowed to sleep and wake at the times dictated by their body clocks.

Research further suggests that melatonin is useful in relieving the effects of jet lag, such as reduced alertness and physical and mental fatigue, when travelling eastward through many time zones. Melatonin also seems to improve, but to a lesser extent, jet lag effects such as daytime sleepiness and fatigue. Taking melatonin in advance of travel doesn't help prevent jet lag. The usefulness of melatonin for westward travel or over fewer time zones is less clear.[13-19]

Melatonin Supplements

Melatonin is sold as a dietary supplement in Canada and the United States. It's also available by prescription in a number of countries. For insomnia, a typical dose is 0.3 to 5 milligrams at bedtime. In children with insomnia due to delayed sleep onset, a dose of 5 milligrams taken at 6:00 P.M. has been used in studies. Both immediate-release and sustained-release melatonin preparations have been found to be effective. For jet lag, 0.5 to 5 milligrams taken at bedtime on the arrival day at the destination is recommended and should be continued for 2 to 5 days. Lower doses of 0.5 to 3 milligrams are often used to avoid drowsiness associated with higher doses.

The most commonly reported side effects of melatonin include daytime drowsiness, headache and dizziness. Do not drive or operate machinery for 5 hours after taking melatonin. Long-term use of melatonin supplements should be avoided; studies have been brief in duration and long-term safety has not been evaluated. Because melatonin is a hormone, its effects, if any, may take years to develop. People taking immunosuppressive drugs and women who are pregnant or breastfeeding should not use melatonin. People with depression should avoid this supplement as it can worsen symptoms.[20] Since melatonin is metabolized in the liver, people with liver disease should avoid using it.

Keep in mind that not all melatonin products are safe. Most commercial melatonin is synthesized in the laboratory. However, in some cases it can be derived from the pineal glands of animals. Melatonin from animal sources should be avoided due to the possibility of contamination of bovine spongiform encephalopathy (BSE, or mad cow disease). Some preparations of synthetic melatonin contain contaminants that are associated with eosinophilia-myalgia syndrome, a sometimes fatal flu-like disease that causes severe pain, inflammation of the tendons, fluid build-up in the muscles and skin rash.

Phosphatidylserine

Used for Alzheimer's disease (see page 201), age-related memory impairment

Phosphatidylserine belongs to a family of chemical compounds known as phospholipids, which are components of cell membranes and essential to their healthy functioning. Phospholipids derived from phosphatidylserine give cell membranes structural integrity and also regulate the nutrients and waste products that pass in and out of cells.

Phosphatidylserine is not an essential nutrient and only a very tiny amount is found in foods. The body manufactures its own phosphatidylserine from other phospholipid building blocks. The only way to get the amounts of phosphatidylserine used in clinical studies is to take a supplement.

Phosphatidylserine is routinely used in European countries to help preserve mental function in patients with Alzheimer's disease and dementia. A number of studies have shown that supplements of phosphatidylserine improve cognitive function and behaviour in people with Alzheimer's disease after 6 to 12 weeks of treatment. Compared with patients taking placebo pills, phosphatidylserine users do significantly better on tests of cognitive function.[1-5] It's thought that phosphatidylserine is most effective in patients with less severe Alzheimer's symptoms. The supplement also seems to lose its effectiveness when taken for longer than 12 weeks.

Phosphatidylserine may also be useful for people with mild cognitive impairment. Memory loss is a normal part of the aging process. However, mild cognitive impairment is a transition stage between the cognitive decline of normal aging and the more serious problems caused by Alzheimer's disease. Individuals with mild cognitive impairment have memory problems not severe enough to warrant a diagnosis of Alzheimer's disease. Studies suggest that some people with mild cognitive impairment have an increased risk of progressing to Alzheimer's disease. Clinical studies show that phosphatidylserine improves attention, arousal, verbal fluency and memory in aging people with cognitive deterioration. People with the greatest memory impairment appear to show the most improvement.[6–9]

Phosphatidylserine Supplements

Most clinical studies used phosphatidylserine derived from bovine (cow) cortex. However, most products now contain phosphatidylserine derived from soy or cabbage due to the risk—albeit very low risk—of transmission of bovine spongiform encephalopathy (BSE, or mad cow disease). Keep in mind that studies have not yet evaluated the effectiveness of phosphatidylserine from plant sources. It's unknown if phosphatidylserine from soy or cabbage is as effective as bovine-derived products, especially for Alzheimer's disease. There is, however, preliminary evidence that plant-derived phosphatidylserine improves memory in people with age-associated memory impairment.[10]

For Alzheimer's disease and mild cognitive impairment, the recommended dose is 100 milligrams taken three times daily.

Phosphatidylserine supplements are typically well tolerated. Some people can experience gastrointestinal upset, such as flatulence, or insomnia when taking high doses (300 milligrams for gastrointestinal upset and 600 milligrams for insomnia).

Probiotics (Lactic Acid Bacteria)

Used for diarrhea (see page 354), vaginal yeast infections and candidiasis (see page 254), irritable bowel syndrome (see page 518), inflammatory bowel disease (see page 499)

The term *probiotic*, the opposite of antibiotic, literally means "to promote life" and refers to living organisms that, upon ingestion in certain numbers, improve microbial balance in the intestine and exert health benefits. Such "friendly" bacteria are known collectively as lactic acid bacteria. Probiotics can be found in both supplement form and as ingredients in foods and beverages. The main types of probiotics in foods and supplements are *Lactobacillus* and *Bifidobacterium*. Within these main types there are dozens of species and strains such as *Lactobacillus acidophilus*, *Lactobacillus GG*, *Lactobacillus rhamnosus*, *Bifidobacterium lactis* and *Bifidobacterium bifidus*.

Probiotics are also normally found in your digestive tract as part of the intestinal flora, a community of hundreds of strains of beneficial bacteria. Here, probiotic bacteria help inhibit the growth of unfriendly, disease-causing bacteria by preventing their attachment to the intestinal wall and by producing substances that suppress their growth. Consuming foods or supplements that are rich sources of these so-called good bacteria is believed to maintain a healthy balance of bacteria in the body. Numerous studies have shown that consuming probiotic foods or supplements increases the number of lactic acid bacteria in the intestinal tract and can exert a number of health benefits.

Probiotics may do more than promote a barrier against germs and viruses. Studies suggest that consuming probiotics regularly can stimulate the immune system, prevent allergies, reduce symptoms of lactose intolerance, help treat inflammatory bowel disease (e.g., ulcerative colitis, Crohn's disease) and possibly lower elevated cholesterol levels. Emerging research also hints that probiotics may guard against colon cancer.

The most compelling evidence for their effectiveness is in the prevention of diarrhea and helping with regularity. Studies conducted in adults and children show that many strains of *Lactobacillus* and *Bifidobacteria* help reduce the risk of developing traveller's diarrhea. (Consuming food or water contaminated with disease-causing bacteria causes traveller's diarrhea.) An analysis of thirty-one studies also reported that taking probiotics along with antibiotics prevented diarrhea associated with antibiotic therapy. (Antibiotics kill not only disease-causing organisms but also helpful lactic acid bacteria.) Several well-controlled clinical studies have shown that lactic acid bacteria, when taken as a supplement or as yogurt, speed recovery from diarrhea in children and adults.[1-12]

Taking a special probiotic supplement may also help manage inflammatory bowel disease. In people with ulcerative colitis, a specific combination of *Lactobacillus*, *Bifidobacteria* and *Streptococcus* (called VSL#3) has been shown to prevent increases in disease-causing bacteria and flare-ups of the disease. Additional evidence suggests that adding VSL#3 to the treatment regime of patients with active mild to moderate ulcerative colitis who don't adequately respond to conventional treatment can induce remission in up to 53 percent of patients. Furthermore, there is evidence that combining VSL#3 with the conventional drug balsalazide (Balzide) significantly prolongs remission rates compared with treatment with the drug alone.[13-15]

Some strains of *Lactobacillus* may also improve symptoms of irritable bowel syndrome. One clinical trial shows that taking heat-killed *Lactobacillus acidophilus* capsules for 6 weeks significantly improved abdominal pain, bloating, and number and quality of stools compared with the placebo. Studies have also found the probiotic supplement VSL#3 improved symptoms in patients with diarrhea-dominant irritable bowel syndrome. Studies using other products have not yielded positive results.[16,17]

Lactic acid bacteria can inhibit the growth of *Candida albicans*, a yeast organism responsible for vaginal yeast infections.[18] Two studies have found that women who consumed 3/4 to 1 cup (175 to 250 ml) of *L. acidophilus* yogurt each day for 6 months had a significant decrease in vaginal *Candida* infections compared with women who did not eat the yogurt.[19,20]

Probiotic Supplements

The strength of a probiotic supplement is usually quantified by the number of living organisms, or colony-forming units (CFUs), per capsule. Typical doses usually range from 1 billion to 10 billion viable organisms taken daily, in 3 to 4 divided doses. Children's probiotic products are available; these usually contain one-quarter to one-half of the adult dose. Probiotic supplements may cause flatulence, which usually subsides as you continue treatment. There are no safety issues associated with taking these supplements.

For convenience, choose a product that is stable at room temperature and does not require refrigeration. This allows you to conveniently continue taking your supplement while travelling or at the office. Good manufacturers will test their products to ensure that they maintain their viability over a long period.

If possible, take your probiotic supplement with food. After a meal, stomach contents become less acidic because of the presence of food, allowing live bacteria to withstand stomach acid and reach their final destination in the intestinal tract. To reduce antibiotic-related diarrhea, take the supplement when you start your antibiotic therapy and continue taking it for 5 days after antibiotics are stopped. To prevent antibiotic medication from killing a significant number of probiotic bacteria in the supplement, take your probiotic supplement 2 hours after taking antibiotics.

For ulcerative colitis and irritable bowel syndrome, a combination probiotic supplement called VSL#3 is recommended. VSL#3 comes in a flavoured or unflavoured powder that is mixed with at least 4 ounces (125 ml) of cold water and then consumed. The recommended dose for adults is as follows:

- For reducing bloating and flatulence associated with irritable bowel syndrome, take 1/2 to 1 packet of VSL#3 per day (225 billion to 450 billion bacteria).
- For maintaining remission of ulcerative colitis, take 1 to 2 packets of VSL#3 per day (450 billion to 900 billion bacteria).
- For treating active ulcerative colitis that is not responding to conventional therapy, take 4 to 8 packets of VSL#3 per day (1800 billion to 3600 billion bacteria).
- VSL#3 is available in some pharmacies or can be ordered by phone at 1-866-438-8753 or online at www.vsl3.com.

SAMe (S-Adenosyl-Methionine)

Used for depression (see page 330), fibromyalgia (see page 388), osteoarthritis (see page 578)

SAMe (S-Adenosyl-Methionine) is a compound our body makes naturally from certain amino acids in high-protein foods like fish and meat. It's found in virtually all body tissues and fluids. The production of SAMe is closely linked with folate and vitamin B12. Deficiencies in these two B vitamins can lead to depressed levels of SAMe in the brain and nervous system. In the body, SAMe is used to synthesize hormones, brain neurotransmitters, proteins and cell membranes. SAMe donates a part of itself, a methyl group, to surrounding body tissues, especially the brain.

SAMe is approved as a prescription drug in fourteen countries and is available as a dietary supplement in the United States. European physicians use SAMe to treat patients with depression. SAMe is associated with higher levels of brain neurotransmitters, natural chemicals that influence mood. It may also work by favourably changing the composition of cell membranes in the brain, enabling neurotransmitters and cell receptors to work more efficiently.

Research suggests that taking SAMe supplements reduces symptoms of major depression, a form of depression characterized by a sustained and severely depressed mood, feelings of worthlessness and guilt, and sleep and appetite disturbances. Several studies conducted in small numbers of patients have reported that SAMe supplements are possibly as effective as tricyclic antidepressants in trials lasting up to 42 days. Well-designed, large-scale studies are still needed to clarify the benefit of SAMe supplements in major depression.[1–8]

SAMe also has analgesic and anti-inflammatory properties, which are thought to be responsible for its beneficial effects in treatment of osteoarthritis and fibromyalgia. Some evidence even suggests that SAMe might stimulate the growth and repair of cartilage. Several studies lasting from 2 weeks to 2 years have found SAMe to be significantly better than a placebo and comparable to non-steroidal anti-inflammatory drugs (NSAIDs) for decreasing joint pain and improving mobility in osteoarthritis.[9–20] Significant symptom relief may take up to 30 days of supplementation. Two studies also found that fibromyalgia patients who took SAMe had significant improvement in their symptoms.[20,21]

SAMe Supplements

SAMe is sold as a dietary supplement in the United States but has not been approved for sale in Canada. If you are shopping on the Internet or while visiting the United States, look for an enteric-coated supplement to help SAMe withstand the acidity of your stomach. There are several forms of SAMe available: sulphate, sulfate-p-toluenesulfonate (tosylate) and butanedisulfonate. Some experts believe butanedisulfonate is more stable than tosylate.

For depression, take 800 to 1600 milligrams per day, in divided doses. Start with one 400 milligram tablet twice daily, working up to two tablets three times daily. It may take 30 days of treatment to notice significant improvements in mood. For osteoarthritis, take 200 milligrams three times daily. For fibromyalgia, take 400 milligrams twice daily. Be sure to take SAMe on an empty stomach.

The supplement is very well tolerated at the recommended doses, but daily doses greater than 1600 milligrams may cause nausea, gastrointestinal upset, dry mouth, nervousness and headache.

If you are currently taking medication for depression and are considering trying SAMe, do not discontinue your medication without first speaking to your doctor. When taken with certain antidepressant drugs, SAMe may have an additive effect causing potentially dangerous side effects. Discuss with your doctor before using.

PART THREE

The Health Conditions

Acne *(Acne vulgaris)*

Acne is the most common skin disease to affect North Americans. Almost everyone experiences the annoying pimples and inflammation of acne to some degree during their lifetime. The condition flares up most often during the ages 10 through 40. Women are particularly prone to developing adult acne in their mid- to late 20s because of hormonal changes associated with the menstrual cycle and pregnancy.

Acne can appear on the skin as congested pores (comedones), whiteheads, blackheads, pimples, pustules or cysts (deep pimples or boils). These blemishes occur wherever there are many oil (sebaceous) glands, mainly on the face, chest and back. Common acne is not a serious threat to health and usually subsides after 5 or 10 years. However, acne can cause vulnerable teenagers to suffer from embarrassment, social withdrawal and reduced self-esteem. With modern medical treatment, most symptoms can be alleviated.

What Causes Acne?

Acne is a disorder of the sebaceous glands of the skin. The sebaceous glands produce an oily substance called sebum. Normally, sebum empties onto the surface of the skin through microscopic canals called hair follicles. In acne, these canals become plugged with dead cells, trapping the sebum inside the follicle. This mixture of cells and oil provides just the right environment to encourage the growth of bacteria, resulting in an inflammation or irritation of the skin. This inflammation is called a pimple. Deeper inflammation results in a cyst. If the oil breaks through the skin's surface, it's called a whitehead.

Acne is most often associated with puberty because it's stimulated by the production of androgens, male sex hormones. When children reach the ages of between 10 and 14 years, their bodies produce increased levels of androgens, which in turn cause the sebaceous glands to enlarge. Acne seems to develop when androgens overstimulate these glands, causing them to produce excess sebum. As sebum production increases, hair follicles become blocked more easily and pimples are the result.

Younger women often find that acne flare-ups coincide with their menstrual cycles. The hormonal changes of menstruation upset the normal relationship between sebaceous glands and androgen hormones. Acne tends to develop in the areas where sebaceous glands are most numerous—the face, neck, back, upper arms, shoulders and scalp.

For some people, women especially, acne does not start until age 20 or even 40. If you develop acne at an older age, it will probably be a type known as *acne rosacea*. Rosacea does not cause the whiteheads and blackheads of common acne. Instead, you'll experience redness, tiny pimples and broken blood vessels, usually on the central area of your face. Your nose may also become bumpy and your skin will flush much more easily.

The cause of rosacea is not known, but it's more common among women and in people with fair complexions. Acne rosacea becomes worse if you drink hot beverages or alcohol, eat spicy foods, smoke or are exposed to excessive sunlight or extreme temperatures. Symptoms tend to go in cycles, with periods of remission and flare-up. Rosacea is a chronic disorder that will become more severe without treatment.

Symptoms

There are several types of acne pimples. A plugged hair follicle is called a comedo or comedone. If the comedone stays beneath the skin, it appears as a small white or yellowish bump—a whitehead. If the comedone accumulates melanin pigment or becomes oxidized, the oil changes from white to black and a blackhead forms. Other types of pimples include papules, small pink bumps on the skin; pustules, inflamed, pus-filled sores; and nodules, large pus-filled cysts or abscesses that extend deep into the skin.

In most cases, acne doesn't leave any scars. In more serious cases of acne, deep cysts or abscesses develop, which are much more likely to rupture and cause scarring. Squeezing, picking or in some way opening pimples can make the acne worse by promoting infection and inflammation. This will increase the risk of scarring.

Who's at Risk?

Acne affects people of all races and ethnic groups, but it seems to be more common among Caucasians. It's safe to say that nearly 100 percent of youths between the ages of 12 and 17 have an occasional pimple or acne breakout. If you are this age and have acne, you can expect it to last for 5 to 10 years and to disappear sometime during your early 20s. Unfortunately, acne can sometimes persist well into adulthood.

Women are very likely to develop acne during their adolescent years in response to the hormonal changes of menstruation. As well, the elevated hormone levels caused by pregnancy and birth control pills can stimulate acne symptoms. In general, adolescent boys are more likely than girls to develop severe, long-lasting forms of acne.

Some people are born with a predisposition to certain types of acne. If your parents or older siblings had severe acne, the chances are greater that you'll have it too. Other factors that may influence the development of acne include these:

- **Stress.** Severe or prolonged emotional tension may aggravate acne, especially if medications are prescribed to alleviate your stress symptoms.
- **Diet.** Chocolate, pizza or french fries are not thought to cause acne. However, there is some evidence that milk and milk products may aggravate acne. If you think you're sensitive to certain foods, try eliminating them from your diet for several weeks. Then add them back to see if they do have an effect on your acne. Eating a healthy balanced diet always has a good effect on your general health—including the health of your skin.
- **Cosmetics.** Certain cosmetics and toiletries may contain ingredients that can clog pores. To prevent this problem, look for products labelled *noncomedogenic*.
- **Sunlight.** The drying and scaling effect of sunlight can help lessen acne. Many people find that their acne symptoms improve during summer and worsen during winter.
- **Medications.** Certain drugs, including lithium, barbiturates and androgens, can cause acne.
- **Friction.** Rubbing the skin or pressure from bike helmets, backpacks or tight collars can cause irritation and trigger acne breakouts.
- **Environmental irritants.** Pollution, high humidity or scrubbing with harsh soaps may provoke acne.

Conventional Treatment

Your doctor will prescribe the appropriate treatment. If your acne is more severe or does not respond to basic treatment, you may be referred to a dermatologist, a doctor who specializes in skin disorders. However, acne usually responds well to treatment and almost every case can be improved or cleared completely with the right medication.

- Wash your skin gently with a good soap twice daily. Avoid overwashing or using antibacterial soaps that may cause irritation and aggravate the acne. Use a gentle astringent, or toner, to wipe way oil produced by your skin. Antibacterial pads containing benzoyl peroxide can also help remove excess oil. Products containing glycolic acid or other alpha hydroxy acids might be helpful in cleaning the skin by exfoliating its superficial layer.
- Comedos can be carefully removed from the skin using a sterile needle or a specialized tool, but this should be done only with the approval of your doctor.
- For mild or moderate acne, there are many over-the-counter medications that will limit the formation of whiteheads and blackheads and reduce inflammation. The most common topical medications contain benzoyl peroxide, resorcinol, salicylic acid or sulphur. These products are applied either directly on the pimples or over the entire affected area. It can take 4 to 8 weeks before you see improvement in your skin, so be patient.
- Women may benefit from prescription oral contraceptives as these medications contain female hormones that suppress the production of androgens.

For more severe cases, prescription antibiotics are usually the treatment of choice. These products can be applied directly onto the skin in a topical gel or lotion or may be taken orally, in pill form. Oral antibiotics are more effective in treating severe acne because they circulate through the body and penetrate the sebaceous glands.

Prescription medications usually contain antibiotics such as clindamycin, erythromycin or tetracycline and may also include retinoids, which are vitamin A derivatives. Using products with retinoids may increase your sensitivity to sunlight, making you prone to sunburn. Tetracycline is not usually given to pregnant women or children under 12 because it can cause discoloration in developing teeth. Since some antibiotics may reduce the effectiveness of oral contraceptives, it's wise to use a backup form of birth control when you're taking these medications. Some oral contraceptives are also effective in treating acne symptoms.

In the case of severe acne that doesn't respond to standard treatment, your doctor may prescribe an oral retinoid called isotretinoin (Accutane and other generic versions). This drug is very effective in treating deep cysts and abscesses and will prevent extensive scarring. However, it has numerous side effects, including birth defects in the developing fetus of pregnant women. It's crucial that you do not become pregnant while taking this drug. You must use appropriate birth control 1 month before starting the treatment, during the entire course of your prescription and for at least 1 month after the treatment stops. Consult your doctor for further information on this medication.

Managing Acne
Dietary Strategies
A Healthy Diet

It has long been thought that certain foods cause acne. Although there's little scientific evidence to support this notion, it is true that oily foods and sugary foods may exacerbate acne symptoms. As well, foods high in iodine, such as shellfish, table salt and milk, can worsen some cases of acne. Certain vitamins and minerals, by altering the balance of healthy bacteria in the intestinal tract, have also been implicated in acne. Alcohol and cigarette smoking can also worsen acne. A diet low in fat and refined sugars and high in nutrients can boost the body's immune system, reduce inflammation and improve symptoms. (Chapter 5, page 84, discusses overall healthy dietary guidelines.) In some cases, food allergies may trigger acne. If you suspect this is the case, it may be worthwhile to speak to your doctor about allergy testing.

Dairy Products

Recent studies have hinted that high intakes of milk might be associated with teenage acne. In studies conducted in teenage boys and girls, consuming more than 2 servings of milk per day, especially of skim milk, has been found to significantly increase the likelihood of acne. In another study, researchers surveyed 47,355 women to evaluate whether dairy intake during high school was linked with physician-diagnosed severe teenage acne. After accounting for factors such as age of menstruation, body weight and calorie intake, the researchers found that total dairy products, whole milk, low-fat milk and skim milk were all positively related to having teenage acne. Consumption of instant breakfast drinks, sherbet, cottage cheese and cream cheese also increased the risk of acne. Researchers speculate that dairy's effect on the skin may be due to its content of hormones and bioactive molecules.[1-3]

If you have a teenager who suffers from acne, try eliminating dairy products for 2 to 3 weeks to see if symptoms subside. But ensure your child is meeting his or her daily requirement for calcium (1300 milligrams). See Chapter 4, page 57, for more information on calcium-rich foods and calcium supplements. If removing dairy products does not improve skin complexion, they can be added back to the diet.

Essential Fatty Acids

It has been suggested that abnormalities in the body's metabolism of essential fatty acids may play a role in acne. Studies have shown that in people with acne, the acne sebum has lower levels of an essential fatty acid called linoleic acid.[4] Linoleic acid is needed to suppress the inflammatory effects of white blood cells involved in acne. One Japanese study found that linoleic acid significantly decreased inflammation and the production of free radical molecules by white blood cells (free radicals may worsen acne symptoms).[5]

Linoleic acid is an omega-6 fatty acid found in all vegetable oils. Some linoleic acid is also found in meat. The body cannot produce linoleic acid on its own so it must be supplied by the diet. With our high intake of processed foods, most Canadians are not at risk for getting too little linoleic acid. But you should pay attention to your intake of these fats if you suffer from acne or you eat a very low-fat diet. Aim to include 1 tablespoon (15 ml) of an oil rich in linoleic acid in your daily diet.

Alpha-linolenic acid is also very important for health. This omega-3 essential fatty acid is found in flaxseed, walnut and canola oils. Alpha-linolenic acid is used by the body to produce anti-inflammatory immune compounds that may help prevent or reduce acne. Aim to get 1 to 2 tablespoons (15 to 30 ml) of these oils per day. Other sources of alpha-linolenic acid include soybeans and foods fortified with flaxseed oil such as soy beverages, yogurt, fruit juice and omega-3 eggs.

To get both essential fatty acids in one oil, consider adding Udo's Choice Oil Blend to your daily diet. It contains oils from organic flaxseed, sesame and sunflower seeds, wheat germ, rice germ and oat germ—and has a balance of both alpha-linolenic and linoleic acid fatty acids. The oil is sensitive to light, air and heat, so it should not be used for frying, deep-frying or sautéing, but can otherwise replace most oils in food preparation. Use it for making salad dressings, serve it on steamed vegetables or baked potatoes, stir it into soups after cooking or add it to fresh vegetable juices or homemade smoothies. You'll find this product in health food stores.

Carbohydrates: Low Glycemic Index

Studies suggest that the glycemic index (GI) of your diet may play a role in acne development and severity. A number of studies have found that diets based on carbohydrate-rich foods with a low glycemic index help improve acne symptoms. Low-glycemic foods are digested slowly, leading to a gradual rise in blood sugar. One study conducted among 43 males, aged 15 to 25, demonstrated that a low-glycemic diet that derived 25 percent of calories from protein and 45 percent from low-glycemic carbohydrates significantly reduced the number of acne lesions after 12 weeks compared with a control diet that did not emphasize low-glycemic foods. Studies evaluating the effect of low-glycemic diets have found that these diets improve how the body uses the blood-sugar-clearing hormone insulin and promote weight loss, both of which may play a role in acne improvement. A diet based on high-glycemic foods is thought to augment the activity of male sex hormones and of compounds called insulin growth factors, which may aggravate acne development.[6–9]

Choose unprocessed fresh foods such as whole grains, legumes, fruit and vegetables, which have a low GI value. High-glycemic foods, such as white bread, white rice, refined breakfast cereals and soft drinks, are usually highly processed and many have a concentrated amount of sugar. Include at least one low-GI food per meal, or base two of your meals on low-GI choices. See Chapter 1, pages 8–12, for a list of low-GI foods.

Vitamins and Minerals

Vitamin A

This vitamin may influence the activity of sebaceous glands in a way that reduces sebum production. The nutrient also helps reduce inflammation around sebaceous glands. Research has found that patients with acne have significantly lower blood levels of vitamin A than those without acne—and the lower the blood level, the more severe the acne condition.[10] To meet your daily vitamin A requirement, reach for oily fish, milk, cheese and whole eggs. Beta carotene, a compound found in orange and dark-green produce, is converted to vitamin A in the body and helps you meet your daily requirements. Foods rich in beta carotene include carrots, sweet potato, winter squash, broccoli, collard greens, kale, spinach, apricots, cantaloupe, peaches, nectarines, mango and papaya.

Keep in mind that most studies have investigated the effects of very high doses of vitamin A on acne. It's best to get your vitamin A from foods and a multivitamin supplement. Avoid taking a separate vitamin A supplement unless advised by your physician. Because vitamin A is fat soluble, the body stores it, and too much vitamin A taken for a period can be toxic. An excessive intake of vitamin A from supplements has been linked to lower bone densities and a greater risk of hip fracture. However, there is no evidence associating beta carotene intake and increased risk of osteoporosis. Vitamin A supplements should not be taken with vitamin A–derivative acne drugs as this will increase the likelihood of a toxic reaction. Pregnant women must avoid vitamin A supplements since high doses can cause birth defects.

Vitamins C and E

Because white blood cells involved in the inflammation of acne can produce free radical molecules, getting plenty of dietary antioxidants may help reduce inflammation. Vitamins C and E may also boost the body's immune system, which can help reduce the chances of infection. Studies have revealed that acne sufferers have lower levels of vitamin E in their blood. Vitamin C–rich foods include citrus fruit, strawberries, kiwi, cantaloupe, broccoli, bell peppers, Brussels sprouts, cabbage, tomatoes and potatoes. Vitamin E is found in vegetable oils, almonds, peanuts, soybeans, whole grains, wheat germ, avocado and green leafy vegetables, especially kale.

It can be difficult to obtain large amounts of these nutrients from a normal diet, so supplements may be useful. Take 500 milligrams of vitamin C once or twice daily. Take 200 to 400 international units (IU) of a natural source vitamin E once daily. To learn more about vitamin C and E supplements, see Chapter 4, page 49.

B Vitamins

This family of vitamins helps to maintain healthy skin. Vitamin B6, found in animal foods, whole grains, avocado and potatoes, may help reduce acne associated with the menstrual cycle. Studies in women have used supplemental doses of 50 milligrams once daily.[11] In supplemental doses, vitamin B6 has also been shown to reduce inflammatory acne lesions. Vitamin B6 is found in a wide variety of foods, including fortified breakfast cereals, salmon, tuna, pork, chicken, bananas, legumes, peanut butter and many vegetables. Niacin (vitamin B3) can help improve blood flow to the skin and may be useful in acne management. Food sources of niacin include meat, poultry, dairy products, peanuts, almonds, seeds, whole grains, enriched breakfast cereals and wheat bran.

To ensure that you are meeting your daily requirements for the B vitamins, eat a healthy diet and take a multivitamin and mineral supplement. High-potency multivitamins provide B vitamins in amounts similar to those found in a B complex supplement. If you decide to add a B6 supplement to your regime, do not exceed 100 milligrams per day. Too much vitamin B6 can result in nerve damage to the arms and legs. High doses of vitamins B6 and B12 may also aggravate symptoms of acne rosacea and should be used with caution in women with this form of acne.

Chromium

Some experts suggest that the mineral chromium may be effective in treating acne, although little research has been done on this. Since many dermatologists have reported that the diabetes medications insulin and tolbutamide have been effective in acne, it's been hypothesized that chromium might be beneficial, since chromium works with insulin to regulate the blood sugar. One study did find that a chromium supplement derived from yeast was effective.[12]

The best food sources of chromium include brewer's yeast, calf's liver, blackstrap molasses, wheat germ, wheat bran, whole grains, mushrooms, apples with skin, green peas, chicken breast, refried beans and oysters. If you're concerned that you're not getting enough chromium in your diet, check your multivitamin and mineral supplement to see how much it contains. Most brands supply 25 to 50 micrograms. If you choose to take a separate chromium supplement, do not exceed 200 micrograms per day. High doses of chromium can cause cognitive impairment, anemia and kidney damage.

Selenium

This trace mineral is an essential component of an antioxidant enzyme called glutathione peroxidase, so selenium helps the body fight free radicals that are formed during normal metabolism. Excess free radicals can contribute to the inflammation of sebaceous glands in the skin. Selenium works very closely with vitamin E in the body. Researchers have noted depressed levels of glutathione peroxidase in people with acne.[13] One study found that a daily supplement of selenium (200 micrograms) and vitamin E (10 milligrams) taken for 6 to 12 weeks increased glutathione peroxidase levels and improved pustular acne symptoms.[14]

To boost the selenium content of your diet, reach for seafood, meat, organ meats, wheat bran, whole grains, nuts, Brazil nuts, onion, garlic, mushrooms, Swiss chard and orange juice. Most multivitamins supply 55 micrograms, the recommended daily intake for adults. If you decide to supplement, take 200 micrograms per day. Supplements made from organic forms of selenium (selenomethionine and high-selenium yeast) are absorbed more efficiently than inorganic forms. Since vitamin E and selenium work in tandem, consider buying a supplement that combines the two nutrients. Look for a broad-based antioxidant supplement that contains selenium, vitamin E and vitamin C.

Do not exceed 400 micrograms of selenium per day. Higher doses can cause loss of hair and fingernails, nausea, depression and anxiety.

Zinc

This nutrient may be useful in treating acne, especially in boys. Studies have shown that zinc levels in the skin cells and blood are often low in adolescent males who are more prone to acne.[15] Zinc has many roles in the body that may affect the symptoms of acne. This mineral helps transport vitamin A, assists in wound healing, supports immune function and regulates the activity of oil glands. High concentrations of zinc may reduce oil gland secretion by preventing the conversion of testosterone to its active form. Studies found that 30 milligrams of supplemental zinc significantly reduced inflammation in patients with acne.[16–18]

The best food sources of zinc include oysters, seafood, red meat, poultry, yogurt, milk, wheat bran, wheat germ, whole grains and enriched breakfast cereals. A healthy diet and a good multivitamin and mineral supplement will give you all the zinc you need to stay healthy. Taking too much zinc from supplements has toxic effects, including copper deficiency, heart problems and anemia. Excess zinc can also depress your immune system, making you more susceptible to infection. If you take a separate zinc supplement, do not exceed 40 milligrams per day.

Herbal Remedies

In addition to ensuring your diet contains adequate amounts of the vitamins and minerals listed above, you may want to use one of the following topical herbal creams to help improve acne symptoms. These creams may be sold over the counter in certain supplement stores or they may be made by compounding pharmacists. Contact your provincial pharmacist's association to locate a compounding pharmacist in your community.

Echinacea

Many laboratory studies have shown that echinacea enhances the body's production of white blood cells, which fight infection. The herb also has weak antibacterial and antiviral activity. Three species of echinacea have medicinal benefits: *Echinacea purpurea*, *Echinacea angustifolia* and *Echinacea pallida*. *Echinacea purpurea* may be effective in promoting healing of acne. Apply a cream or liquid preparation that contains 15 percent *Echinacea purpurea* juice to affected areas.

Goldenseal (*Hydrastis canadensis*)

Historically, this herb was used by Native Americans to treat a variety of skin disorders and wounds. The plant name is derived from the golden-yellow scar on the base of its stem: When the stem is broken, the scar resembles a gold letter seal. One of the active ingredients in goldenseal, berberine, possesses strong antibacterial activity. The herb is most effective when used topically because the plant's active ingredients are poorly absorbed by the intes-tinal tract. Apply a sufficient amount of a goldenseal cream to affected areas.

Tea Tree Oil (*Melaleuca alternifolia*)

Many studies have demonstrated the antiseptic and antibiotic properties of tea tree oil. In one study, 60 patients with mild to moderate acne were treated with either a topical 5 percent tea tree oil gel or a placebo. After 45 days, the use of tea tree oil gel was 3.55 times more effective at reducing acne lesions and 5.75 times more effective at decreasing acne severity. It appears to kill many types of bacteria and fungi, including some that are resistant to antibiotic therapy. Tea tree oil comes from the aromatic leaves of a plant native to Australia, where the oil had been used for hundreds of years to prevent infection and treat wounds. A recent review of four well-controlled trials found the topical use of tea tree oil to be an effective treatment for acne.[19-21]

Buy a preparation that contains 5 percent tea tree oil. Tea tree oil can irritate the skin, so apply only a little to start. High-quality products are made from the oil of the *alternifolia* species of the plant. They should be standardized to contain not more than 10 percent cineole and at least 30 percent terpinen-4-ol. Apply the oil or gel two or three times per day to affected areas until the acne symptoms resolve. Avoid contact with the eyes. Do not ingest tea tree oil. Topical use of tea tree oil may cause allergic skin reactions in some individuals.

Nutrition Strategy Checklist for Acne

☐ Low-fat, low-sugar diet
☐ Low-GI carbohydrate-rich foods
☐ Limit alcohol and salty foods

- ☐ Limit dairy, but get calcium
- ☐ Healthy oils
- ☐ Vitamin A
- ☐ Vitamin B6, niacin
- ☐ Vitamin C
- ☐ Vitamin E
- ☐ Chromium
- ☐ Zinc
- ☐ Herbal creams/oils: Tea tree oil* OR Echinacea OR Goldenseal

*Strongest evidence—start here.

Recommended Resources

Alberta Health Services
www.crha-health.ab.ca/
700 Manulife Place
10180–101 Street
Edmonton, AB T5J 3S4
Tel: 780-342-2000
Fax: 780-342-2060

American Academy of Dermatology
www.skincarephysicians.com/acnenet
930 E. Woodfield Road
Schaumburg, IL, USA 60173
Tel: 847-330-0230
Fax: 847-330-0050

National Institute of Arthritis and Musculoskeletal and Skin Diseases
National Institutes of Health
www.niams.nih.gov/Health_Info/Acne/default.
  asp
1 AMS Circle
Bethesda, MD, USA 20892-3675
Tel: 301-495-4484 or 1-877-22-NIAMS
  (64267)
Fax: 301-718-6366
Email: NIAMSinfo@mail.nih.gov

An online information resource on acne, this website is a collaborative effort by Roche Laboratories Inc. and the American Academy of Dermatology.

Alcoholism

Drinking alcohol has become an integral part of North American culture. Recent statistical surveys indicate that nearly 79 percent of Canadians reported consuming alcohol over a 12-month period.[1] Most Canadians drink in moderation—one or two drinks per day. When used in moderation, alcohol is not harmful for most adults. (Keep in mind, however, that a moderate intake of alcohol is associated with a slightly higher risk of cancers, including cancers of the breast and colon.) Moderate alcohol use is defined as no more than two drinks a day for men and no more than one drink a day for women and older adults. A standard drink is 12 ounces (340 ml) of regular beer, 5 ounces (145 ml) of wine or 1-1/2 ounces (45 ml) of 80-proof (40 percent) distilled spirits.

However, because social drinking is such a popular activity, it's easy to overlook the fact that alcohol is a depressant drug with powerfully addictive properties. If used excessively, it can have harmful effects on almost every system in the body. Despite its general acceptance, alcohol is one of the most abused drugs in our society. Steady drinking over time can produce a physical dependence on alcohol. Men who drink more than 15 drinks per week and women who consume more than 12 are at increased risk of becoming dependent on alcohol. Sadly, it's estimated that 2.6 percent of Canadians aged 15 and older have an alcohol dependency.

Effects of Alcohol
Physical Effects

Alcohol is quickly absorbed into the blood-stream through the stomach and the small intestine. While even small amounts of alcohol will produce physical changes, the overall effects of alcohol on the body are dependent on several factors, including the drinker's size, gender and metabolism. For example, after drinking the same amount of alcohol, women will usually have higher blood alcohol concentrations (BAC) than men. Women may have lower levels of alcohol dehydrogenase, a stomach enzyme that helps the body metabolize alcohol. Female hormones may also influence a woman's ability to metabolize alcohol.

Alcohol slows down the nervous system and alters the functions of almost every organ in the body. It depresses centres in the brain that are responsible for inhibiting or restraining behaviour. After only one drink, people will report feeling more relaxed, friendly and self-confident. Higher levels of alcohol consumption will impair thinking, judgment and physical reaction time. Even a small amount of alcohol in the bloodstream is enough to impair performance skills, greatly increasing the risk of accident when driving a car or operating machinery.

Other short-term effects of alcohol use include:

- dilation of blood vessels in the skin, causing loss of body heat
- increased urine production
- increased stomach secretions
- accumulations of fat in the liver cells

Although moderate alcohol use has been reported to have a protective effect against heart disease, eating sensibly, exercising regularly and quitting smoking provide better alternatives to good heart health.

Excessive use of alcohol over an extended period can result in serious, long-term health problems, such as:

- brain injury, resulting in severe dysfunction
- sleep disruptions
- movement disorders
- serious diseases of the liver (alcoholic hepatitis and cirrhosis)
- serious disease of the pancreas (pancreatitis)
- damage to the stomach and intestines
- nutritional deficiencies
- anemia
- deterioration of the heart muscle, leading to sudden death
- impotence, sterility and breast enlargement in men
- early menopause and menstrual irregularities in women
- osteoporosis
- increased risk of having babies with birth defects for women who drink during pregnancy, the most serious defect being fetal alcohol syndrome
- depression of the immune system, leading to pneumonia, tuberculosis and cancer

Alcohol has been proven to react negatively with over 150 medications. Death may occur when even moderate amounts of alcohol are combined with other depressant drugs, such as tranquilizers and sleeping pills. Excessive consumption of alcohol can also lead to death by overdose.

Social Effects

Drinking alcohol has the potential to interfere with interpersonal relationships. Problems that may develop include:

- arguments with spouse or family members, eventually leading to violence
- difficult relationships with co-workers
- lateness or absence from work
- loss of employment because of decreased productivity
- becoming the victim of violence
- suicide

Symptoms of Alcoholism

Alcoholism, also known as alcohol dependence syndrome, is characterized by:

- **Craving:** the strong need or compulsion to drink
- **Loss of control:** the inability to stop drinking once a person has begun
- **Physical dependence:** the development of withdrawal symptoms, such as nausea, sweating, shakiness and anxiety, when heavy drinking is stopped
- **Tolerance:** a need for increasing amounts of alcohol to obtain the desired effect or to get "high"

Alcohol abuse differs from alcoholism in that there is not a strong craving to drink, nor is there loss of control or physical dependence. Alcohol abuse is a pattern of drinking that is accompanied by one of the following for a 12-month period:

- failure to meet professional or family obligations

- drinking while driving or operating machinery
- recurring alcohol-related legal problems
- continued drinking despite ongoing relationship problems that are worsened by alcohol use

Who's at Risk?

Men are more likely than women to be heavy drinkers, and heavier drinking is more prevalent at lower education and income levels. People who began drinking by age 16 are at a higher risk of alcohol dependence or abuse. Children of alcoholics are more likely to develop alcoholism than are children whose parents are not alcoholics. Studies have found that women who suffer from bulimia nervosa are more susceptible to alcohol abuse, and that people who are single, separated or divorced drink more than do people with partners. Adults with attention deficit hyperactivity disorder may also be more likely to become dependent on alcohol. Environmental influences, such as peer pressure and availability of alcohol, may increase risk.

Conventional Treatment

Alcoholism is a treatable disease, but at this time there is no cure. Treatment depends on the degree of alcohol abuse or alcoholism and the availability of community resources. Treatment may include:

- socio-behavioural counselling on an in- or outpatient basis; psychotherapy
- family therapy and marital counselling
- detoxification in a hospital or residential treatment centre or on an outpatient basis
- medications to ease withdrawal symptoms or to help prevent a return to drinking

- involvement in support groups, such as Alcoholics Anonymous

Nutritional Care for Alcoholism

Nutrient deficiencies are common in alcoholism and are caused by many different factors. Many people with the disease have nutritionally poor diets, which contributes to malnutrition. But alcohol-induced damage to the gastrointestinal tract and the liver affects the body's ability to absorb, process and store a wide range of nutrients. Heavy drinking also causes certain minerals to be lost in the urine. Alcohol inactivates some vitamins needed to metabolize energy. And finally, people who suffer from alcoholism have an increased need for many nutrients to detoxify and metabolize alcohol, as well as to help heal damaged body tissues. The nutritional strategies listed below are intended to prevent or correct nutrient deficiencies and reduce the severity and length of withdrawal symptoms.

Dietary Strategies

A Healthy Diet

The importance of eating a nutrient-dense, well-balanced diet cannot be overemphasized. Research shows that nutritional therapy helps in the recovery from alcoholism.[2] Follow the healthy eating guide outlined in Chapter 5, page 111. Not only does a regular intake of food supply energy, vitamins, minerals and protective plant chemicals, but it can also minimize the symptoms of alcohol withdrawal. Both appetite loss and a ravenous appetite are rebound symptoms of quitting alcohol. Food cravings, especially for carbohydrates, and

insomnia can also occur during the alcohol-withdrawal stage. Heavy drinking may result in damage to the liver or pancreas, making people with alcoholism susceptible to fluctuations in blood sugar. The following strategies can help manage these symptoms.[3]

To stimulate appetite:

- Eat small meals, every 2 to 3 hours.
- Drink plenty of fluids such as juice, milk, sports drinks, even ginger ale.
- Use commercial meal replacement beverages such as Ensure or Boost. These provide protein, carbohydrates, vitamins and minerals in a relatively small volume.
- Limit your intake of fatty foods; these foods can depress appetite because they are emptied from the stomach slowly.
- Limit caffeine intake; caffeine further depresses appetite so aim for less than 450 milligrams per day (see Chapter 5, page 110).

To control ravenous hunger and food cravings:

- Eat meals and snacks at regular intervals throughout the day.
- Consume protein-rich foods at each meal and snack as these foods are digested slowly and promote a feeling of fullness.
- Limit intake of sweets and caffeine.

To prevent blood sugar fluctuations:

- Eat once every 3 to 4 hours.
- Include a source of protein with each meal and snack.
- Choose low-glycemic carbohydrates that are more slowly digested and converted to blood glucose. (For a list of these foods, see Chapter 1, page 8.)

- Consume plenty of chromium-rich foods, which can help regulate blood sugar levels (see Chapter 4, page 65).
  To combat insomnia:
- Eat a carbohydrate-rich snack (milk, toast) 1 hour before bedtime.
- Eliminate or limit caffeine intake 5 to 8 hours before bedtime.

Alcohol in Foods

If you're taking a protective drug such as Antabuse or Temposil, you must avoid consuming foods made with alcohol. Studies have shown that very little alcohol is lost in the cooking process: As much as two-thirds may still be present after 20 minutes of cooking. If alcohol is added after cooking, all of the alcohol will be present. The following foods, food ingredients and supplements may contain alcohol and should be avoided:

- flavour extracts
- mirin (used in mock crab)
- cooking wines
- cakes and pastries made with liqueur
- Angostura aromatic bitters
- hollandaise, Béarnaise and bordelaise sauces
- herbal tinctures
- Madeira and Marsala sauces
- liqueur-filled chocolates and candies
- some soups (black bean, onion)
- nonalcoholic beer and wine
- aspic
- apple cider
- fondues
- malt vinegar, cider vinegar, red wine vinegar
- chocolate mousse
- wine-flavoured cheese and pâté
- liquid vitamin supplements
- some brands of Dijon mustard
- flambé desserts
- commercial eggnog
- teriyaki sauce
- wine sauerkraut
- lobster bisque

Essential Fatty Acids

Chronic alcohol ingestion causes alterations in fat metabolism, and this is worsened if liver damage is present. Studies consistently find that individuals with alcoholism have depressed levels of important fatty acids in their blood cells, where these acids play a vital role in maintaining healthy cell membranes.[4-6] People who drink alcohol in excess have also been reported to have diets that are low in essential fatty acids. Some experts hypothesize that fatty acid deficiency, especially a deficiency of the omega-3 fatty acid DHA, may contribute to depression that occurs in alcoholism.

The omega-3 and omega-6 oils in our diet each provide a different essential fatty acid that our body cannot make on its own. Omega-3 oils (flaxseed, canola, walnut) provide alpha-linolenic acid, and omega-6 oils (corn, sunflower, safflower, soybean) give us linoleic acid. These two essential fatty acids are used to form vital body structures and cell membranes, aid in immune function and vision, and produce powerful compounds called eicosanoids that help regulate inflammation, hormones and nerve and brain function.

Aim to include 2 tablespoons (30 ml) of some combination of the following oils in your daily diet: flaxseed, walnut, canola and Udo's Choice Oil Blend (available in health food stores). With the exception of canola oil, these oils should not be used for high-heat cooking. Use them for salad dressings or add them to hot foods after cooking.

To increase your intake of DHA, eat fatty fish two times a week. Salmon, trout, sardines,

Arctic char, herring, pickerel and light tuna are the best choices.

Vitamins and Minerals

B Vitamins

Deficiencies of many B vitamins are common with chronic heavy drinking. Blood levels of thiamin (B1), niacin (B3), folate, B6 and pantothenic acid have all been found to be lower in people with alcoholism.[7-12] B vitamin deficiencies are due to an inadequate dietary intake; the toxic effects of alcohol that reduce absorption, metabolism and storage of these nutrients; and the increased amounts of these vitamins needed to metabolize large quantities of alcohol.

One of the most serious consequences of alcoholism is Wernicke-Korsakoff syndrome, a disease caused by thiamin deficiency. This disease is often seen in people who have consumed alcohol heavily for several weeks and have eaten very little.[13,14] Symptoms of Wernicke-Korsakoff syndrome include confusion, stupor, memory impairment and vision abnormalities. If left untreated, it can lead to permanent brain damage and death. Because alcohol requires thiamin for its metabolism, this serves to only further deplete body stores.

The following is recommended to replenish body stores of the B vitamins during alcohol withdrawal:

- Take a 50 to 100 milligram thiamin supplement once daily.
- Take a multivitamin and mineral supplement once daily.
- Emphasize foods rich in B vitamins: wholegrain breads and cereals, lentils and lean meats and poultry. You'll find a list of each B vitamin and food sources in Chapter 4, page 35.

If a thiamin deficiency has caused nerve damage, B vitamin treatment may be necessary for months or years. If you have alcoholic liver damage, do not take doses of vitamins (except thiamin) or minerals beyond what is provided in a regular multivitamin and mineral supplement. Excessive consumption of certain nutrients (vitamin A, niacin, iron) can lead to toxicity in the presence of impaired liver function. Higher doses should be taken under the direction and supervision of your doctor.

Antioxidants

Chronic alcohol drinking increases free radical production in the body. Free radicals are unstable oxygen molecules that can harm virtually every cell in the body and promote the development of heart disease and cancer. Furthermore, alcoholism is associated with depressed blood levels of many important antioxidants—the very compounds that seek and destroy free radicals. Studies show that compared with healthy adults, levels of vitamins C and E, beta carotene and selenium are lower in people with alcoholism.[15-19] To get more dietary antioxidants, focus on the following foods.

VITAMIN C. The recommended dietary allowance (RDA) of this vitamin is 75 and 90 milligrams for women and men respectively (smokers need an additional 35 milligrams). Best food sources include citrus fruit, citrus juices, cantaloupe, kiwi, mango, strawberries, broccoli, Brussels sprouts, cauliflower, red pepper and tomato juice. To supplement, take 500 or 600 milligrams of vitamin C once daily. The upper daily limit for adults is 2000 milligrams.

VITAMIN E. The RDA for vitamin E is 22 international units (IU) from foods and/or natural source supplements. Best food sources include wheat germ, nuts, seeds, vegetable oils, whole grains and kale. To supplement, take 200 to 400 IU of natural source vitamin E once daily. The upper daily limit is 1500 IU.

SELENIUM. The RDA for this trace mineral is 55 micrograms. Best food sources are seafood, chicken, organ meats, whole grains, nuts, Brazil nuts, onions, garlic and mushrooms. To supplement, take 200 micrograms of selenium-rich yeast per day. Check how much your multivitamin and mineral formula gives you before you buy a separate selenium pill. The upper daily limit is 400 micrograms.

BETA CAROTENE. There is no established RDA for beta carotene. Best food sources are orange and dark-green produce, including carrots, sweet potato, winter squash, broccoli, collard greens, kale, spinach, apricots, cantaloupe, peaches, nectarines, mango and papaya. Choose a multivitamin and mineral supplement with beta carotene added.

Calcium and Vitamin D

Chronic alcohol consumption can induce bone loss, a risk factor for osteoporosis. Alcohol hampers the activity of vitamin D in the body, making it less effective at maintaining bone health. Heavy drinking also increases urinary excretion of magnesium, calcium and zinc, all important minerals in preserving bone mass. Studies have revealed that men and women being treated for alcohol abuse often have low bone densities and report a higher prevalence of past bone fractures.[20-22] To slow down bone loss, it's especially important to meet your daily requirements for calcium and vitamin D.

The RDA for calcium is 1000 to 1500 milligrams. Best food sources are milk, yogurt, cheese, fortified soy and rice beverages, fortified orange juice, tofu, salmon (with bones), kale, bok choy, broccoli and Swiss chard. If you take calcium supplements, buy calcium citrate with vitamin D and magnesium added.

The recommended intake for vitamin D is 1000 IU per day (from a supplement) in the fall and winter. Older adults, people with dark skin, those who don't go outdoors often and those who wear clothing that covers most of their skin should take the supplement year-round. To determine the dose of vitamin D you need to buy, start with the RDA, subtract how much you're already getting in your multivitamin and calcium supplements and then make up the difference. Choose a vitamin D supplement that contains vitamin D3 instead of vitamin D2, which is less potent.

Magnesium

Alcohol causes a rapid loss of magnesium in the urine; alcoholism is associated with depleted body stores of this mineral. It's believed that magnesium deficiency induced by heavy drinking may increase the risk of high blood pressure, stroke, sudden death and osteoporosis.[23] Studies have shown that short-term magnesium supplementation can improve liver cell function, muscle strength and body fluid balance in chronic alcoholics.[24,25]

The RDA for magnesium is between 320 and 420 milligrams per day (see the RDA chart in Chapter 4, page 60). Best sources of magnesium include nuts, seeds, legumes, prunes, whole grains, leafy green vegetables, brewer's yeast, cheddar cheese and shrimp. If you decide to supplement your diet and you don't take supplemental calcium with magnesium added, buy a separate magnesium supplement made from magnesium citrate. The body absorbs this form of the mineral more efficiently than magnesium oxide. Taking more than 350 milli-grams of magnesium in a supplement can cause diarrhea, nausea and stomach cramps.

Zinc

Chronic alcoholism is associated with low blood zinc levels. Some researchers hypothe-size that low levels of zinc in the brain enhance susceptibility to alcohol withdrawal seizures.[26] Zinc deficiency can also promote nerve damage by increasing the formation of harmful free radicals.

To prevent a zinc deficiency, focus on choosing zinc-rich foods every day: oysters, seafood, red meat, poultry, yogurt, wheat bran, wheat germ, whole grains and enriched break-fast cereals. A multivitamin and mineral supplement will provide 10 to 20 milligrams of the mineral. If you choose to take a separate zinc supplement, buy one with added copper and do not exceed a daily intake of 40 milligrams of zinc. Too much zinc can cause a copper deficiency, heart problems and anemia.

Herbal Remedies

Milk Thistle (Silybum marianum)

The active ingredients of this herb, known collectively as silymarin, can support and enhance liver function. Silymarin can prevent toxic substances from penetrating liver cells, and it may even help liver cells regenerate more quickly. Milk thistle also seems to act as an antioxidant, protecting liver cells from damage caused by free radicals. Studies conducted in people with alcoholic liver cirrhosis suggest the herbal supplement results in an increase in the antioxidant glutathione and a decrease in oxidation of fats in the liver. A recent review of sixty-five papers concluded that silymarin may be a supportive therapy in the treatment of alcoholic cirrhosis.[27-31]

Buy a milk thistle product that's standard-ized to contain 70 percent to 80 percent silymarin. The recommended dose is 420 milligrams daily. Use milk thistle with caution if you're allergic to plants in the Asteraceae/Compositae family (ragweed, daisy, marigold and chrysanthemum).

Other Natural Health Products

Lecithin (Phosphatidylcholine)

Lecithin and phosphatidylcholine supplements are thought to exert their health benefits by supplying the body with choline, a B vitamin. Once ingested, choline is incorporated into the membranes of cells. Phosphatidylcholine supplements are used in Europe to treat alcoholic liver disorders. Studies suggest that phosphatidylcholine supplements can oppose alcohol-induced liver damage.[32-34]

Most lecithin supplements contain 10 per-cent to 20 percent phosphatidylcholine. Others, however, are almost pure phos-phatidylcholine and are labelled as such. Most clinical studies have been done with phosphatidylcholine supplements. Buy a supplement labelled phosphatidylcholine. Take 1200 to 2220 milligrams per day, in divided doses.

SAMe (S-Adenosyl-Methionine)

SAMe is a compound that our body makes naturally from certain amino acids in high-protein foods like fish and meat. It's found in virtually all body tissues and fluids. The production of SAMe is closely linked with folate and vitamin B12, so deficiencies of these B vitamins can lead to depressed levels of SAMe. The body uses SAMe to synthesize hormones, brain neurotransmitters, proteins and cell membranes.

A number of studies have found SAMe to reduce the signs and symptoms of liver disease caused by alcohol. Supplementation with SAMe has been shown to normalize liver enzymes and reduce bilirubin, a compound in the blood that results from the breakdown of hemoglobin. (Bilirubin is measured to monitor liver problems.) It's thought that SAMe acts as an essential nutrient by restoring biochemical compounds that are depleted in people with alcoholic liver disease.[35,36] People with liver disease lose the ability to form SAMe, and this leads to deficiencies in choline, a B vitamin, and glutathione, an enzyme that plays a critical role in liver detoxification and antioxidant reactions.

To supplement, take 400 milligrams three times daily. Studies evaluating the effectiveness of SAMe in alcoholic liver disease have used a daily dose of 1200 to 1600 milligrams. Buy an enteric-coated supplement product and take SAMe on an empty stomach.

Nutrition Strategy Checklist for Alcoholism

- [ ] Low-fat, high-fibre diet
- [ ] Avoid alcohol in foods
- [ ] Healthy oils
- [ ] Fish
- [ ] Multivitamin/mineral
- [ ] B complex supplement
- [ ] Thiamin
- [ ] Antioxidants: C, E, selenium, beta carotene
- [ ] Calcium
- [ ] Vitamin D
- [ ] Magnesium
- [ ] Foods rich in zinc
- [ ] Milk thistle
- [ ] Lecithin (phosphatidylcholine)
- [ ] SAMe

Recommended Resources

Alberta Alcohol and Drug Abuse Commission/Alberta Health Services
www.aadac.com/default.asp
10302–107 Street NW
Edmonton, AB T5J 1K2
Tel: 780-342-2000
Fax: 780-342-2060

Centre for Addiction and Mental Health
www.camh.net
There are three locations in Toronto
Tel: 416-535-8501 or 1-800-463-6273

Alcoholics Anonymous World Services
www.aa.org/?Media=PlayFlash
P.O. Box 459
New York, NY, USA 10163
Tel: 212-870-3400

National Association for Children of Alcoholics
www.nacoa.org
11426 Rockville Pike, Suite 301
Rockville, MD, USA 20852
Tel: 1-888-554-2627
Email: nacoa@nacoa.org

National Clearinghouse for Alcohol and Drug Information
http://ncadi.samhsa.gov/
P.O. Box 2345
Rockville, MD, USA 20847-2345
Tel: 1-800-729-6686

National Institute on Alcohol Abuse
and Alcoholism
National Institutes of Health
www.niaaa.nih.gov
5635 Fishers Lane, MSC 9304
Bethesda, MD, USA 20892-9304
Tel: 301-443-3860

Alzheimer's Disease

Alzheimer's disease is the leading cause of dementia in older people. In Canada, 450,000 people over the age of 65 are suffering from the condition. It's projected that by 2031, more than three-quarters of a million Canadians will be victims of Alzheimer's disease.[1] Unfortunately, as our population ages, the situation is expected to only become worse. Alzheimer's disease is likely to become one of the greatest public health problems in the coming decades.

What Causes Alzheimer's Disease?

Although Alzheimer's disease is often associated with getting older, it's not a normal part of the aging process. Rather, it's a medical condition that disrupts brain function by destroying vital nerve cells. Alzheimer's disease develops slowly, resulting in a gradual loss of motor skills and a general decline in intellectual ability. The disease targets the centres in the brain that control memory, thought and language. It causes changes in mood and behaviour, as well as loss of memory, judgment and reasoning. The massive brain-cell death associated with Alzheimer's disease is permanent, and there is no known cure at this time.

Alzheimer's disease causes abnormal clumps or plaques and tangled bundles of fibres to develop in the brain. A buildup in the brain of a protein called beta amyloid has been associated with the disease. While the exact cause of Alzheimer's disease is still unknown, researchers are investigating a number of different possibilities, including genetic factors, viruses, vitamin and hormone deficiencies, and head injuries. An accumulation of toxic substances in the brain (aluminum is a primary suspect) may also contribute to the degenerative brain changes associated with the disease.

Scientists have identified two types of Alzheimer's disease. Sporadic Alzheimer's disease is the most common type and is responsible for over 90 percent of the cases diagnosed. The second type, Familial Autosomal Dominant Alzheimer's disease (FAD), has a genetic basis and is clearly passed from generation to generation. If a parent has the mutated gene responsible for this type of the disease, each child has a 50 percent chance of inheriting it. People with the mutated gene will inevitably develop Alzheimer's disease at some point in their lives. FAD accounts for 5 percent to 10 percent of all cases of Alzheimer's disease.

Symptoms

Symptoms of Alzheimer's disease include changes in intellectual abilities. Those with the disease:

- gradually become unable to learn new things and make decisions
- forget how to do simple, familiar tasks
- have trouble remembering names, appointments, daily routines

- have difficulty understanding what has been said
- have difficulty communicating, forget simple words, use words inappropriately
- lose track of time and place; become lost and disoriented easily
- may remember past events more clearly than current events
- are no longer interested in normal activities; demonstrate no initiative

The disease also affects mood. Those with Alzheimer's disease:

- have less expression; may eventually have little or no reaction to people or surroundings
- are more withdrawn
- have difficulty controlling moods and emotions
- have rapidly changing moods and emotions
- may worry excessively over small things
- may become suspicious or easily angered

Changes in behaviour and physical functioning may include:

- pacing, agitation, wandering and restlessness
- repetitive actions
- physical outbursts
- swearing, arguing and aggressiveness
- hiding things; constantly searching
- difficulty feeding, dressing and bathing
- loss of bowel and bladder control
- loss of mobility

The symptoms of Alzheimer's disease vary from person to person. So too does the speed at which the condition progresses. Some people with the disease live relatively normal lives for many years, whereas others experience rapid progression of their symptoms. No matter what the speed of onset, Alzheimer's disease will eventually lead to complete dependence on caregivers and, inevitably, death.

Who's at Risk?

Twice as many women as men have Alzheimer's disease. The risk of Alzheimer's disease increases as you age. After the age of 65, risks double every 5 years; by the age of 80, 20 percent of men and women suffer from the disease. It's estimated that 50 percent of people over 85 years of age have Alzheimer's. Those with a family history of Alzheimer's disease are also at higher risk.[2] As well, an individual with a family history of Alzheimer's disease may face an increased risk of developing the condition when exposed to suspected trigger factors, such as viruses or environmental toxins.

Conventional Treatment

The management of Alzheimer's disease may include:

- medications (usually tacrine, donepezil or rivastigmine) that treat memory loss and cognitive symptoms by increasing the brain's supply of acetylcholine, a nerve-communication chemical
- modification of the home environment to eliminate factors that may trigger behaviour problems (noise, colours, lighting)
- establishment of daily routines
- creative leisure activities to improve behaviour and mood
- anti-psychotic or antidepressant medications to treat behaviour and mood changes
- family education and counselling to help both the patient and caregivers deal with the symptoms of the disease

Managing Alzheimer's Disease

Dietary Strategies

A Healthy Diet

Ensuring that a loved one with Alzheimer's disease eats a nutritious diet can be a challenge. People with Alzheimer's often have difficulty staying focused on the task of eating. As well, the ability to use utensils deteriorates because of the progressive loss of cognitive function and motor skills. To help patients maintain good nutrition, it's important to alter the eating environment and provide a variety of foods.

People with Alzheimer's disease are at risk for developing protein and calorie malnutrition because of poor food intake and increased energy needs. As the disease progresses, a loss of weight and muscle mass is common. However, one study found that patients were able to maintain their weight if they were given a diet that provided 35 calories per kilogram of body weight.[3] Emphasis must be placed on providing meals and snacks that supply adequate calories throughout the day.

There is good evidence that dietary factors that help maintain a healthy cholesterol level and blood pressure, thereby preserving the health of blood vessels, are important for the prevention of Alzheimer's disease. It may be possible to reduce your risk or postpone the onset of the disease by adopting a healthy diet that is low in saturated fat, trans fat and sodium and that includes fatty fish.

MEDITERRANEAN DIET. Research does suggest that following a Mediterranean-style diet may help prevent Alzheimer's disease. In a 2009 study of 1188 healthy elderly adults living in the United States, those who adhered most closely to a Mediterranean-style diet had a 32 to 40 percent reduced Alzheimer's risk. (Adherence to a Mediterranean-style diet was scored as low, medium and high.)

What's more, the risk of Alzheimer's gradually decreased with more exercise and higher diet adherence. Individuals with the highest scores for both physical activity and Mediterranean-type diet were 67 percent less likely to be diagnosed with Alzheimer's during the study.[4]

A Mediterranean-style diet combines several foods and nutrients—such as fish, monounsaturated fat, vitamins B12 and folate, vitamin E and flavonoids—that may reduce free radical damage and inflammation, two factors that contribute to the development of Alzheimer's.

The Mediterranean diet may also keep your brain healthy through its protective effects on blood vessels. It has been shown to provide protection from obesity, type 2 diabetes and hypertension, risk factors that damage blood vessels and that have also been linked to a greater risk of Alzheimer's disease. The following tips will help you incorporate elements of the Mediterranean diet into your own eating plan:

- **Grains, vegetables and fruit.** These should be eaten at most meals. Choose whole grains that are minimally processed such as brown rice, barley and whole grain pasta. While all vegetables are nutritious, spinach, eggplant, tomatoes, broccoli, peppers, mushrooms, garlic and green beans are staples in Mediterranean cuisine. Fruit is typically served for dessert; choose whole fruit over fruit juice.
- **Olives and olive oil.** This monounsaturated fat is the principal fat in the Mediterranean diet, replacing butter and margarine. Choose extra virgin olive oil, which is

higher in phytochemicals, compounds thought to reduce inflammation.

- **Fish and shellfish.** These high-protein foods are low in saturated fat. Salmon, tuna, sardines and herring are rich in omega-3 fatty acids. Eat grilled, sautéed or baked fish or shellfish two times per week.
- **Cheese and yogurt.** These dairy products are eaten daily in the Mediterranean diet, but in low to moderate amounts.
- **Legumes, nuts and seeds.** These foods add protein, healthy fats, fibre, vitamins and minerals to the diet. Use them to add flavour and texture to dishes.
- **Eggs.** The Mediterranean diet includes up to four eggs per week, including those used in cooking and baking.
- **Meats.** Lean cuts of meat are eaten only a few times a month. In Mediterranean cuisine, veal and lamb are most often consumed. Poultry is also a lean-protein choice.
- **Sweets.** Dessert, such as sorbet and gelato, is served only a few times per week in small portions.
- **Wine.** Although wine is consumed regularly, it is consumed moderately, usually with meals. Limit your intake to one glass (5 ounces) per day for women and one to two glasses per day for men.

Fish and Fish Oil

The brain is especially rich in DHA (docosahexanaenoic acid), an omega-3 fatty acid that is plentiful in oily fish. DHA contributes to the fluidity of brain cell membranes, allowing nutrients to pass in and out. DHA is also used to produce eicosanoids, powerful compounds that regulate the blood, hormones and immune system and have anti-inflammatory effects. Research has revealed that patients with Alzheimer's disease often have lower levels of DHA in the brain and bloodstream. What's more, studies have shown that DHA-rich diets help limit brain cell damage caused by beta amyloid peptides. Free radical molecules can damage DHA in cell membranes, so it's important to constantly supply the body with these fatty acids.

In a study of 174 patients with mild to moderate Alzheimer's disease receiving conventional drug treatment, researchers found that a daily supplementation of 1.7 grams of DHA and 0.6 grams of EPA improved cognition scores in patients with very mild Alzheimer's. (A beneficial effect was not observed in patients with moderate disease.)[5] Studies have also suggested that an optimal balance of omega-3 and omega-6 fats can help improve mood, co-operation, appetite, sleep and short-term memory in people with Alzheimer's disease.[6]

To help prevent Alzheimer's disease, it's also important to increase your intake of omega-3 fatty acids from fish and fish oil and limit your intake of cholesterol-raising saturated fat. Studies have revealed that a diet high in saturated animal fat increased the risk of Alzheimer's disease, whereas consuming polyunsaturated and monounsaturated fats reduced it. Several studies have reported a lower risk of Alzheimer's disease among people who consume fish once or twice weekly compared with rarely.[7,8]

The ideal intake of omega-3 fatty acids to prevent and possibly help treat Alzheimer's is unknown. However, experts advise a daily intake of at least 500 milligrams of DHA and EPA combined to help prevent heart disease. (Keep in mind the same factors that increase the risk for heart disease—high cholesterol, high blood pressure and poorly controlled diabetes—are also linked to a greater likelihood of Alzheimer's disease and vascular dementia.) To increase your intake of omega-3 fats, especially DHA, eat fish two times a week. Salmon, trout, mackerel, sardines, Arctic char, herring and pickerel are the best choices. If you don't like fish, take a fish oil capsule that provides 500 milligrams of DHA and EPA combined once or twice daily. Aim to include 2 tablespoons (30 ml) of one or a combination of the following unsaturated oils in your daily diet: flaxseed, walnut, canola and Udo's Choice Oil Blend (available in health food stores). With the exception of canola oil, these oils should not be used for high-heat cooking. Use in salad dressings and smoothies or add them to hot foods after cooking.

Vitamins and Minerals

Vitamin B12 and Folate

Studies consistently find that low levels of these two B vitamins are associated with Alzheimer's disease.[9,10] An adequate intake of vitamin B12 and folate helps prevent blood levels of an amino acid called homocysteine from rising; a high homocysteine level is thought to damage artery walls and increase the risk of Alzheimer's and other forms of dementia. Vitamin B12 is also crucial for maintaining healthy nerves. Some of the signs of a B12 deficiency are similar to those of Alzheimer's disease. Without adequate B12, the body is unable to use folate (folic acid) and, eventually, a folate deficiency will occur.

All animal foods contain B12: meat, poultry, fish, clams, eggs and dairy products. Fortified soy and rice beverages are also a good source of the vitamin. Adults over the age of 50 are advised to get their vitamin B12 from a supplement or fortified foods, since these are well absorbed by the body. (After age 50, many adults produce insufficient amounts of the gastric acid necessary to absorb B12 from foods.) Folate-rich foods include cooked spinach, lentils, orange juice, whole grains, fortified breakfast cereals, asparagus, artichoke, avocado and sunflower seeds. In addition to choosing foods rich in B vitamins, take a multivitamin and mineral pill. Most formulas will supply anywhere from 25 to 100 micrograms of B12 and 400 to 800 micrograms of folic acid. While research has found multivitamins useful in lowering homocysteine levels in patients with mild to moderate Alzheimer's disease, this has not resulted in improvements in cognitive function.[11]

Vitamin E

This potent antioxidant nutrient appears to prevent free radical damage to the brain caused by beta amyloid, the protein structures abundant in the brains of patients with Alzheimer's disease. The brain contains a high level of fat that is readily oxidized by free radicals. It is thought that this free radical damage contributes to the progressive decline in brain function seen in Alzheimer's patients and, therefore, antioxidants may be an important tool in the prevention and treatment of the disease. Despite the ability of vitamin E to protect nerve cells in the brain by combating harmful free radicals, only one study, lasting for 2 years, has shown that high dose vitamin E supplementation (2000 IU per day) can slow the progression of Alzheimer's disease. Another trial conducted among people with mild cognitive impairment found no difference in the rate of progression of Alzheimer's disease among those taking 2000 IU of vitamin E daily and those taking a placebo.[12-14]

Based on these contradictory results—and recent findings that high dose vitamin E might do more harm than good in some people (see Chapter 4, page 53)—vitamin E supplements are not recommended for the treatment or prevention of Alzheimer's disease. Instead, get your vitamin E from foods and a multivitamin, some of which provide up to 100 IU per day. Good food sources of vitamin E include vegetable oils, almonds, peanuts, soybeans, whole grains, wheat germ, avocado and green leafy vegetables. If you decide to supplement with vitamin E in the hopes of reducing your risk of Alzheimer's, do not take more than 400 IU per day. (People with existing heart disease and diabetes should not consume more than 100 IU per day.) When taken with anti-coagulant medications, very high doses of vitamin E may increase the risk of bleeding.

Vitamin D and Calcium

Patients with Alzheimer's disease have lower bone mass and are at increased risk for falls and hip fractures.[15] The fact that most patients are deprived of sunlight and do not get adequate vitamin D in their diet puts them at a high risk for vitamin D deficiency. Elderly patients require 1500 milligrams of calcium (the amount found in 4 to 5 cups of milk) and 1000 IU of vitamin D each day. For a detailed list of food sources of these two nutrients, see Chapter 4, page 56.

Supplements are recommended to help prevent bone loss caused by poor dietary intakes of vitamin D and calcium. Choose a calcium supplement made from calcium citrate (about 300 milligrams per tablet) or calcium carbonate (about 500 milligrams per tablet). Take a calcium supplement two or three times per day, depending on your calcium intake from foods. Take calcium carbonate with meals; calcium citrate can be taken with food or on an empty stomach.

Get 1000 IU of vitamin D per day from a supplement. (To know how much to buy, determine how much you're already getting from a multivitamin and calcium supplement and make up the difference to reach your RDA.) Buy a vitamin D supplement made with vitamin D3 instead of vitamin D2. Older adults should take vitamin D year-round. People diagnosed with insufficient blood levels of vitamin D should take 2000 IU per day.

Herbal Remedies

Ginkgo Biloba *(Ginkgo biloba)*

This herb is said to improve memory loss and slow the progression of Alzheimer's disease. A 52-week study looked at the effects of ginkgo in 309 patients with mild to moderate dementia as a result of Alzheimer's disease or stroke.[16] Patients were given either 40 milligrams of ginkgo (a special extract called EGb 761) three times daily or a placebo pill. After 1 year, the placebo group showed a decline in cognitive function whereas the ginkgo group did not. When the researchers looked at Alzheimer's patients only, there were modest but significant positive changes in memory and other brain functions. Other studies lasting 3 to 6 months have also found ginkgo to be an effective treatment in mild to moderate Alzheimer's dementia. Gingko is not effective, however, at reducing the risk of developing Alzheimer's disease in older adults who are not cognitively impaired or who have mild cognitive impairment.[17–19]

A number of studies suggest that ginkgo increases circulation and oxygen delivery to the brain.[20] The herb's active ingredients make blood cells called platelets less sticky, and circulation therefore becomes more efficient. In addition, ginkgo has a strong antioxidant effect in the brain, which may also have a positive effect in Alzheimer's disease.

Choose a product that is standardized to contain 24 percent ginkgo flavone glycosides and 6 percent terpene lactones. For dementia, the recommended dose is 120 to 240 milligrams daily, in three divided doses.

Ginkgo biloba has slight blood-thinning effects. When combined with medications (e.g., aspirin) and/or supplements with similar effects (e.g., vitamin E, garlic), there is a potential for bleeding problems. Be sure to inform your primary caregiver about any supplement you're taking.

Gotu Kola *(Centella asiatica)*
This herb may help improve memory, although it has not been studied to the same extent in Alzheimer's disease as has *Ginkgo biloba*. Some evidence suggests that the herb's active ingredients, asiaticosides, can protect nerve cells from the toxic effects of beta amyloid structures and therefore may have a role in treating Alzheimer's dementia.[21]

Buy a product standardized to 40 percent asiaticoside and 30 percent asiatic acid. The usual dosage is 20 to 60 milligrams three times daily. To make the herbal tea, steep 600 grams of dried leaves in 150 millilitres of boiling water for 5 to 10 minutes. Drink three times daily. High doses of gotu kola may cause sun sensitivity and high blood pressure in some individuals. Pregnant women should not use this herb.

Other Natural Health Products
Acetyl-L-Carnitine
Carnitine is an amino acid found in all body cells, where it is used to metabolize fatty acids into energy. Carnitine also clears toxic accumulations of fatty acids from cells and serves as a building block for acetylcholine, a memory neurotransmitter. A number of studies involving more than 1400 people have found that one form of carnitine, acetyl-L-carnitine, can slow the rate of disease progression, improve memory and improve some measures of cognitive function and behavioural performance in some patients with Alzheimer's disease. It's more likely to show some effect in those with early-onset Alzheimer's disease who are less than 66 years of age and in those who have a faster rate of disease progression and mental decline. However, acetyl-L-carnitine has not been compared with drugs, such as donepezil (Aricept), used to treat Alzheimer's.[22-28]

In Alzheimer's disease, a daily dose of 1500 to 4000 milligrams has been used, divided into two or three doses during the day. Acetyl-L-carnitine is generally well tolerated but can cause stomach upset and restlessness. It may also cause the urine, breath and sweat to have a fishy odour. People taking anticoagulant medication should use the supplement cautiously as it may increase the effects of these drugs. Acetyl-L-carnitine is available in the United States but is not approved for sale in Canada. However, some health food stores do stock it. Do not take D-carnitine or DL-carnitine, which can cause heart and muscle dysfunction.

Phosphatidylserine
Phosphatidylserine belongs to a family of chemical compounds known as phospholipids, important structural components of all cell membranes. Phospholipids also regulate the passage of nutrients and waste products in and out of cells.

There is some evidence for using this supplement in Alzheimer's disease. A number of studies have shown that supplements of phosphatidylserine improve cognitive function and behaviour in people with Alzheimer's disease after 6 to 12 weeks of treatment. Compared with patients taking placebo pills, phosphatidylserine users do significantly better on tests of cognitive function. These supplements also seem to help ease feelings of depression in people with Alzheimer's disease.[28-31] The standard dosage is 100 milligrams taken three times daily.

Nutrition Strategy Checklist for Alzheimer's Disease

☐ Three meals plus two to three snacks to maintain weight

☐ Fish and fish oil

☐ Healthy oils

☐ Multivitamin/mineral

☐ Foods rich in vitamin E

☐ Vitamin D

☐ Calcium

☐ *Ginkgo biloba** OR Gotu kola

☐ Phosphatidylserine

*Strongest evidence—start here.

Recommended Resources

Alzheimer Society of Canada
www.alzheimer.ca
20 Eglinton Avenue W, Suite 1600
Toronto, ON M4R 1K8
Tel: 416-488-8772 or 1-800-616-8816
   (Canada only)
Fax: 416-488-3778
Email: info@alzheimer.ca

Alzheimer's Association
www.alz.org
225 N. Michigan Ave., Fl. 17
Chicago, IL, USA 60601-7633

Tel: 312-335-8700 or 1-800-272-3900
Fax: 312-335-1110
Email: info@alz.org

Alzheimer's Disease International
www.alz.co.uk/
64 Great Suffolk Street
London, U.K. SE1 0BL
Tel: +44 20 79810880
Fax: +44 20 79282357
Email: info@alz.co.uk

Anemia (Iron-Deficiency Anemia)

Anemia, a Latin word, literally means "too little blood." It refers to any condition in which too few red blood cells are present, or the red blood cells are too small or contain too little hemoglobin, the pigment that transports oxygen throughout the body. Anemia lowers the oxygen-carrying capacity of the blood and starves tissues in your body of the energy they need to function properly. Anemia affects the whole body, causing fatigue, shortness of breath, lack of energy and many other complications.

What Causes Anemia?

There are several kinds of anemia, but the most common and severe type is iron-deficiency anemia. The mineral iron is essential for making hemoglobin, the main component of red blood cells. Your body uses its iron supply very efficiently. It recycles the mineral from dead red blood cells to produce new ones. While vegetarians, menstruating women and pregnant women often don't meet their daily iron requirements from diet alone, a healthy, well-balanced diet generally provides some or all of the iron your body needs to ensure healthy red blood cell production.

However, there are circumstances when normal dietary intake is not sufficient to maintain your iron stores. In adults, the main cause of iron deficiency is blood loss. Conditions that result in chronic or repeated bleeding, such as nosebleeds, hemorrhoids, certain cancers, ulcers or other gastrointestinal problems, will deplete iron stores and may eventually lead to anemia. Anemia can also develop because of a sudden blood loss caused by an injury or surgery.

Anemia is often a side effect of chronic disease, especially in the elderly. Health conditions such as infection, inflammation and cancer will suppress red blood cell production and deprive the developing cells of much-needed iron. Deficiencies of folate and vitamin B12 can also cause anemia. Shortchanging your body of these vitamins affects your red blood cells differently than does a lack of iron.

Symptoms

Iron-deficiency anemia is a progressive condition. It usually develops in stages, so it can be months or even years before symptoms appear. Anemia ranges from mild to severe, and the symptoms vary accordingly. The main symptoms include fatigue, weakness, loss of appetite, loss of energy, shortness of breath, cold hands and feet, difficulty concentrating, hair loss, pale skin and increased susceptibility to infection. It's important to keep in mind that you may feel these symptoms even if you aren't classified as "anemic." A marginal iron deficiency, measured by a low level of ferritin in the blood, can affect your energy levels too, although not as severely. (Ferritin is one of the chief forms in which iron is stored in the body.)

Tongue irritation, cracks at the side of the mouth and spoonlike deformities in the fingernails also may result from iron deficiency. Some people with anemia develop pica, a craving for non-food substances such as ice, dirt or pure starch. In young children, iron deficiency may cause irreversible abnormalities in brain development, resulting in impaired attention span, cognitive function and learning ability.

Who's at Risk?

If you fall into any of the following categories, you're at risk for developing iron-deficiency anemia:

- menstruating female
- pregnant
- vegetarian
- engage in regular endurance exercise (e.g., long-distance running, triathlons)
- follow a low-calorie diet (less than 1400 calories daily)
- have an intestinal disorder that affects nutrient absorption in the small intestine (e.g., Crohn's disease, celiac disease)

All women of reproductive age are at risk of developing iron deficiency, even more so if their diet lacks iron-rich foods. Women who are pregnant or breastfeeding are predisposed to anemia because of the additional demands of the growing baby and placenta. Female runners or triathletes lose iron through sweat and can become iron deficient, especially if their diet lacks iron. Any woman who reduces her calorie intake to lose weight or eats an unbalanced vegetarian diet is also at risk. In fact, the daily recommended iron intake for vegetarians—male or female—is 1.8 times higher than for non-vegetarians.

Infants are born with sufficient stores of iron, but this supply becomes depleted during the first few months of life. For this reason, pediatricians recommend that infants receive additional iron from iron-fortified cereals or formulas from the time they are 6 months of age.

Conventional Treatment

Anemia is treated by stopping the source of blood loss (if determined to be the cause) and by rebuilding the body's nutrient stores through diet and supplements. In most cases, iron supplements are prescribed as a short-term therapy for iron deficiency (you'll read more about this below).

When anemia is severe or the blood loss is rapid, a blood transfusion may be required to immediately replenish iron supplies. If excessive menstrual bleeding or another uterine problem is causing your anemia, your doctor may prescribe oral contraceptives to reduce your monthly blood flow.

The other types of vitamin-deficiency anemia are treated with a daily regimen of vitamin supplements. In some cases, people with vitamin B12– and folic acid–deficiency must take supplements for their entire lives. Anemia caused by medical disorders or chronic disease usually disappears once the underlying cause of the condition is addressed.

Preventing and Treating Iron-Deficiency Anemia
Vitamins and Minerals
Iron

You learned above how iron helps carry oxygen throughout the body and releases it to tissues, where it is used for energy. To help prevent iron deficiency, it's critical that everyone, especially women, consume adequate amounts of iron every day. To learn your daily requirements, see Chapter 4, page 71.

The richest sources of iron are beef, fish, poultry, pork and lamb. These are heme sources of iron, the type that can be absorbed and utilized the most efficiently by your body. Though heme sources of iron contribute about 10 percent of the iron we consume each day—a relatively small proportion of our intake—it is so well absorbed that it actually contributes a significant amount of iron.

The rest of our iron comes from plant foods such as dried fruit, whole grains, leafy green vegetables, nuts, seeds and legumes. These are nonheme sources of iron, which the body is much less efficient in absorbing and using. Strict vegetarians may have difficulty maintaining healthy iron stores because their diet relies exclusively on nonheme sources.

IRON SUPPLEMENTS. To help you meet your daily iron requirements and prevent iron deficiency, a daily multivitamin and mineral supplement is prudent. Most formulas provide 10 milligrams, but you can find multivitamins that provide up to 18 milligrams of the mineral. Menstruating women and vegetarians should choose a formula that supplies 10 to 18 milligrams of iron; men and post-menopausal women should look for 5 to 10 milligrams of iron in a multivitamin. During pregnancy, women are advised to take a prenatal formula that supplies 27 to 30 milligrams of iron.

If you're diagnosed with iron-deficiency anemia, your doctor will prescribe single iron pills. Depending on the extent of your iron deficiency, you may take 1 to 3 iron tablets (each containing 50 to 100 milligrams of elemental iron) per day. If you're advised to take an iron pill, take it on an empty stomach to enhance absorption. Taking your iron supplement with a vitamin C pill or a glass of orange juice can further enhance iron absorption. A supplementation period of 12 weeks is usually sufficient to treat anemia. However, you may need to take the supplements for up to 6 months to completely restore your body's iron reserves.

When it comes to iron supplements, more is *not* better. Excessive doses of iron can be quite toxic, causing damage to the liver and intestines, and even death. Do not take iron supplements without having a blood test to confirm that you're suffering from an iron deficiency or anemia.

NONHEME IRON. The following enhance absorption of nonheme iron:

- **Animal foods.** Meat, poultry and fish contain not only the most bioavailable heme iron but also a special component, called MFP factor, that promotes the absorption of nonheme iron from other foods eaten with them. So, to absorb more iron from your brown rice stir-fry, throw in a little lean beef.
- **Vitamin C.** Adding a vitamin C–rich food to a plant-based meal can enhance the body's absorption of nonheme iron fourfold. Vitamin C is the most potent promoter of nonheme iron absorption. The acidity of the vitamin converts iron to the ferrous form that's ready for absorption (your stomach acid enhances iron absorption in the same way).
- **Calcium.** Calcium and iron are absorbed the same way in the gut, so they compete with one another for transport across the intestinal tract. However, research has shown that, for up to 6 months, taking a calcium supplement with meals does not affect iron levels in healthy adults. But if you're taking

calcium supplements and iron pills to treat anemia, take them at separate times. Likewise, don't take an iron supplement with a calcium-rich meal.

- **Tea.** Natural compounds in teas called tannins can bind with iron and make it unavailable for absorption. However, a recent study found no evidence that drinking 3 cups (750 ml) or more of black tea per day reduced iron stores in non-iron-deficient adults.[1] If you are iron deficient and a tea drinker, it's wise to enjoy your tea between rather than during meals. Or add a little milk or lemon to your cup of tea, since both inactivate the iron-binding properties of tannins.
- **Phytate-rich foods.** Phytates are natural compounds found in dietary fibre, nuts, spinach and other leafy vegetables and can bind to iron, inhibiting its absorption. The recommended intake for dietary fibre (21 to 38 grams per day, depending on your age) is not associated with impaired iron absorption. You would have to be eating a diet that is extremely high in fibre (50 grams or more each day) before you would interfere with the body's absorption of minerals. Cooking vegetables like spinach releases some of the iron that's bound to phytates. For this reason, cooked vegetables are always a better source of minerals than their raw counterparts.

Preventing and Treating Other Types of Anemia
Vitamins and Minerals
Folate

An ongoing deficiency of this important B vitamin leads to what is known as macrocytic or megaloblastic anemia. When your body lacks folate as a result of poor diet, impaired absorption or an unusually high need for the vitamin, metabolism of rapidly dividing red blood cells is slowed down. The red blood cells that do form are immature and cannot efficiently carry oxygen and travel through the tiny blood vessels.

You're at risk for folate deficiency if you are pregnant, have Crohn's or celiac disease, abuse alcohol or are taking certain medications that block folate absorption (e.g., some anti-seizure drugs), or if your diet lacks fresh fruit and vegetables.

To help prevent anemia associated with a folate deficiency, aim to meet your recommended dietary allowance (RDA) of 400 micrograms of folate (see Chapter 4, page 41). The best food sources include cooked spinach, lentils, orange juice, whole grains, fortified breakfast cereals, asparagus, artichoke, avocado and seeds.

FOLIC ACID SUPPLEMENTS. Folate refers to the B vitamin in its natural form in foods. Folic acid describes the synthetic version found in supplements or in fortified foods such as white flour, white pasta and enriched cornmeal. It can be challenging to meet your daily folate requirements through diet alone. To make sure that you're meeting your requirement, take a daily multivitamin and mineral pill. Select a product that has 0.4 milligrams (400 micro-grams) of folic acid. I don't recommend taking a separate folic acid supplement (1 milligram) unless you've been diagnosed with folate deficiency. Recent study findings have hinted that folic acid, when consumed in amounts of 1 milligram or greater per day, may be linked with an increased risk of cancer.

If you're advised to take a separate folic acid supplement, buy one with vitamin B12, since these two nutrients work closely together. The body uses folic acid to activate B12 and vice versa. So a deficiency of one vitamin will eventually lead to a deficiency of the other. If you supplement with folic acid and don't pay attention to meeting your B12 requirements, this can mask an underlying B12 deficiency: A high folic acid intake can correct the anemia, but not the nerve and cognitive deterioration that occurs with vitamin B12 deficiency. Without the indication of anemia on a blood test, vitamin B12 deficiency may not be suspected and neurological deterioration may continue untreated.

Vitamin B12

A B12–related condition called pernicious anemia is caused by impaired absorption rather than by poor dietary intake of this vitamin. After you consume B12 in your diet, the acid in your stomach helps to release the vitamin from proteins in food. B12 then binds to a protein known as intrinsic factor that enables the vitamin to be absorbed from the small intestine into the bloodstream. (Some people produce an insufficient amount of hydrochloric acid in their stomach. This condition is particularly common in older adults. Without enough stomach acid, B12 can't be released from food proteins, and it won't be absorbed into the blood. A B12 deficiency can result, but it isn't pernicious anemia.)

In pernicious anemia, people inherit a defective gene for intrinsic factor and don't produce this necessary protein that attaches to B12 and delivers it into the bloodstream. Without enough vitamin B12, your red blood cells don't divide normally and are too large. Pernicious anemia is characterized by a deficit of red blood cells, muscle weakness and nerve damage. Most doctors prefer to treat pernicious anemia with injections of vitamin B12, although oral supplements taken under the tongue (sublingual) may also be effective. A recent study found that taking a B12 supplement twice daily that dissolved under the tongue was as effective as shots in restoring B12 levels.[2]

Vitamin B12 is found naturally exclusively in animal foods and seafood: meat, poultry, fish, clams, eggs and dairy products. Fortified soy and rice beverages also supply vitamin B12.

VITAMIN B12 SUPPLEMENTS. If you're a strict vegetarian who eats no animal products and who doesn't drink fortified soy or rice beverages, take a B12 supplement. Anyone over the age of 50 should be getting vitamin B12 from a supplement or fortified foods, since up to one-third of older adults produce insufficient amounts of the gastric acid needed to release B12 from food proteins.

If you take certain medications, you should consider taking extra B12. For example, if you suffer from reflux or ulcers and take acid blockers, your body may not absorb enough B12 (as well as iron and calcium). Metformin, used to manage type 2 diabetes and polycystic ovary syndrome, can also deplete B12 levels. If you take these medications, your doctor should monitor your blood periodically for signs of B12 deficiency.

To get adequate B12, take a good multivitamin and mineral supplement. If you take a single B12 supplement, take 500 to 1000 micrograms once daily. If you're a vegetarian relying on diet for vitamin B12, avoid taking a vitamin C supplement at mealtime. Preliminary evidence suggests that vitamin C supplements can destroy vitamin B12 in foods. However, other components of food, such as iron, might counteract this effect. It isn't clear whether this interaction can result in a reduced amount of B12 being absorbed from foods; however, the possibility can be avoided by taking your vitamin C supplement at least 2 hours after a meal.

Nutrition Strategy Checklist for Preventing Anemia

☐ Foods rich in iron
☐ Foods rich in vitamin C, taken with nonheme iron
☐ Animal foods with nonheme iron (non-vegetarians)
☐ Multivitamin/mineral
☐ Foods rich in folate
☐ Foods rich in vitamin B12
☐ B12 supplement

Recommended Resources

The College of Physicians and Surgeons of Canada
The College of Family Physicians of Canada
www.cfpc.ca/English/cfpc/programs/
    patient%20education/anemia/default.asp
2630 Skymark Avenue
Mississauga, ON L4W 5A4
Tel: 905-629-0900 or 1-800-387-6197

American Academy of Family Physicians
www.aafp.org/online/en/home.html
11400 Tomahawk Creek Parkway
Leawood, KS, USA 66211-2672
Tel: 913-906-6000
Fax: 913-906-6075

Merck & Co., Inc.
www.merck.com

Angina *(Angina pectoris)*

As coronary heart disease narrows the arteries that feed the heart, the flow of oxygen-rich blood is gradually reduced. One of the first indications that your heart is not receiving enough oxygen is often a recurring chest pain. This pain is known as angina. Angina feels like a squeezing, pressing or aching pressure that starts behind your breastbone. The pain may travel to your jaw, left shoulder, down your left arm or through your back. In most cases, symptoms last less than 5 minutes and are relieved by rest or medication such as nitroglycerine taken under the tongue.

There are two types of angina: stable and unstable. These are discussed in more detail below. (See also Heart Disease and High Blood Cholesterol, page 424.)

What Causes Angina?

The underlying cause of angina is atherosclerosis, or hardening and narrowing of the arteries. When angina symptoms are mild to moderate and develop fairly predictably at a certain level of exertion, you have what is known as stable angina. Stable angina is usually triggered by physical activity, when the heart is working harder than usual and requires more oxygen. The pain usually lasts less than 5 minutes and eases off when you rest or stop exerting yourself. Emotional stress, heavy meals, alcohol, cigarette smoking or rapid changes in temperature can also provoke angina. Although angina pain may be worrisome, it does not mean that you're having a heart attack. Episodes of angina rarely cause permanent or irreversible damage to your heart muscle. However, angina does indicate that you are feeling the early effects of coronary heart disease and that fatty deposits may be building up on your coronary arteries.

Unstable angina is less common and more serious. The symptoms are more severe, last longer (up to 30 minutes) and are less predictable than the pattern of stable angina. Chest pain often comes as a surprise while at rest or sleeping at night, or with little physical exertion. Unlike stable angina, the pain of unstable angina is not relieved with rest or medication and may mean that a heart attack will happen soon. You should seek medical attention immediately.

Symptoms

Symptoms of angina include:

- squeezing pressure in the chest, behind the breastbone
- discomfort in the left arm, left shoulder, back, throat, jaw or teeth
- pain during exercise or physical activity
- pain that becomes worse after heavy meals, changes of temperature, drinking alcohol, smoking cigarettes or during times of emotional stress
- pain lasting only a few minutes and easing off when you rest
- indigestion, heartburn, fatigue, nausea, cramping and shortness of breath

There is some indication that men and women experience angina symptoms quite differently. Men tend to describe angina pain as crushing or squeezing, while women feel it more as a vague discomfort that doesn't go away, even with rest. Women are more likely to feel discomfort in their back, shoulders and abdomen. Women may also experience fatigue or shortness of breath during exercise or exertion, rather than feeling actual pain or discomfort. As a result, heart disease in women is harder to detect and often is not diagnosed until the disease is advanced.

Who's at Risk?

People with elevated levels of blood cholesterol and triglycerides are at risk for angina, as are those who smoke cigarettes. People who have established heart disease as well as those with a family history of coronary heart disease are also at greater risk.

Conventional Treatment

Any lifestyle modification that helps lower the risk of heart disease can help treat angina—quitting smoking, reducing alcohol intake, eating a low-fat diet, controlling your weight and controlling diabetes. Following a moderate exercise program will improve heart function. Keep in mind that you should increase exercise gradually and avoid sudden bursts of effort. If you have angina, exercise should only be undertaken with the approval of your physician. Medications may be prescribed to reduce blood pressure. Medications to reduce angina pain include:

- nitroglycerine to relieve pain by widening blood vessels
- beta blockers to slow the heart rate and reduce the force of the heart's pumping action
- calcium channel blockers to reduce the frequency and severity of angina attacks

Managing Angina
Dietary Strategies
Dietary Fat

Eating a diet that's low in animal (saturated) fat can help prevent the buildup of fatty deposits on artery walls. Diets high in saturated fat raise your risk for heart disease by increasing your level of LDL (bad) blood cholesterol. Animal foods contain mostly saturated fat, a type of fat that inhibits the activity of receptors on cells so that LDL cholesterol is not cleared efficiently from the bloodstream. To reduce your intake of saturated fat, choose lean cuts of meat, poultry breast, 1% or skim milk, yogurt with less than 2% milk fat and cheese with less than 20% milk fat. Use butter sparingly.

The other type of fat to avoid is trans fat, found in foods made with partially hydrogenated vegetable oils. The chemical process of partial hydrogenation makes what starts out as an unsaturated fat more saturated, and along the way trans fats are formed. Trans fat raises LDL (bad) cholesterol and lowers HDL (good) cholesterol. (See Chapter 3, page 27, for more on trans fat.) The easiest way to reduce your intake of trans fat is to read nutrition labels. As much as 40 percent of the fat in foods like french fries, fast food, doughnuts, pastries, snack foods and commercial cookies is trans fat. Choose packaged foods that supply a Daily Value for saturated fat plus trans fat of 5% or less. This means that one serving of the food is low in these so-called bad fats. If you eat margarine, choose one that's made with non-hydrogenated fat. You'll find more dietary strategies to keep your cholesterol levels in check under Heart Disease and High Blood Cholesterol, page 424.

Vitamins and Minerals

B Vitamins

These nutrients won't lower your cholesterol, but they will help keep your blood homocysteine from rising to an unhealthy level. (A high blood level of homocysteine is associated with a higher risk of heart attack.) To prevent homocysteine from accumulating and damaging blood vessels, the body uses three B vitamins—folate, B6 and B12—to convert it into other harmless compounds. One simple strategy to lower elevated homocysteine levels is to boost your intake of these three B vitamins. You'll learn your daily requirements and good food sources of B6, B12 and folate in Chapter 4, page 38.

If you have difficulty eating a varied diet, I recommend taking a good-quality multivitamin and mineral supplement to ensure that you're getting your daily B vitamins. If you're looking for more B vitamins than a regular multi will give, choose a high-potency formula that contains 25 to 100 milligrams of B vitamins (or micrograms in the case of folic acid and B12). However, as discussed in Chapter 4, page 42, unless you're pregnant or have a folic acid deficiency, I do not recommend taking more than 400 micrograms (0.4 milligrams) of folic acid from a supplement.

Vitamin C

Vitamin C may protect from heart disease by acting as an antioxidant. The vitamin is able to neutralize harmful free radical molecules before they can damage your bad LDL cholesterol. This means that LDL cholesterol is less likely to accumulate on artery walls. Studies also suggest that vitamin C may inhibit the formation of blood clots by reducing the stickiness of platelets. Despite vitamin C's heart

healthy actions in the body, there is no evidence that taking a vitamin C supplement will guard against heart disease. In the Physicians' Health Study II, researchers from Harvard Medical School assigned 14,461 healthy men aged 50 and older to take 400 international units (IU) of vitamin E every other day or 500 milligrams of vitamin C daily or a placebo pill. After 8 years, neither supplement lowered the risk of cardiovascular disease. Compared with men taking the placebo treatment, vitamin E and vitamin C users were just as likely to suffer a heart attack, total stroke or die from heart disease.[1]

The recommended dietary allowance (RDA) is 75 and 90 milligrams for women and men, respectively (smokers need an extra 35 milligrams). The best food sources include citrus fruit, citrus juices, cantaloupe, kiwi, mango, strawberries, broccoli, Brussels sprouts, cauliflower, red pepper and tomato juice. If you do decide to take a supplement because your diet lacks fruit and vegetables, take 500 or 600 milligrams of vitamin C once or twice daily. The upper daily limit for vitamin C is 2000 milligrams.

Vitamin E

This vitamin is a potent antioxidant that protects LDL cholesterol particles from oxygen damage caused by free radicals. (Oxidized LDL cholesterol is considered more dangerous because it adheres more readily to artery walls.) Vitamin E may also inhibit blood clot formation and preserve the health of blood vessels that feed the heart. Some studies have suggested that vitamin E supplements can lower the risk of heart attack in healthy men and women; the evidence for its protective effect is less clear in individuals with established heart disease.[2-4]

Two large trials conducted in individuals with previous heart attack, stroke or evidence of heart disease found that a daily vitamin E supplement did not change the risk of subsequent heart attack or stroke. What's more, some trials suggest that high dose vitamin E supplements may actually cause health problems in people with existing heart disease.[5-8]

Get the vitamin E you need by eating a variety of foods such as nuts, seeds, wheat germ, vegetable oils and leafy greens. If you have existing cardiovascular disease or diabetes, avoid high dose vitamin E supplements. If you do decide to take a supplement, take no more than 100 IU per day. If you're a post-menopausal woman who does not have heart disease, recent evidence does suggest that taking 600 IU of vitamin E every other day may help prevent a heart attack and reduce the risk of dying from heart disease.

If you're taking a blood-thinning medication like warfarin (Coumadin), don't take vitamin E without your doctor's approval, since it has slight anti-clotting properties.

Vitamin D

There's growing evidence that the vitamin D might guard against heart disease. Vitamin D is needed to maintain normal immune function, reduce inflammation in the body, assist in keeping heart cells healthy and help maintain normal blood pressure. Studies have linked low blood vitamin D levels to greater inflammation, impaired fasting glucose, metabolic syndrome and hypertension—all risk factors for heart disease. Recent studies have also revealed that people who are deficient in vitamin D have a higher risk of heart attack and coronary heart disease.[9,10]

Vitamin D is found in foods such as fortified milk, oily fish and egg yolks, but the amount we consume from diet is considered to be insufficient to maintain good health. And during the fall and winter, when there's little sunlight, our skin produces little or no vitamin D.

At this time, there is no evidence that taking a daily vitamin D pill will lower the odds of developing heart disease that could cause angina. However, it's prudent to supplement your diet with 1000 IU of vitamin D each day. Not only might it guard against heart disease, it might also cut your risk of developing osteoporosis and certain cancers. To determine the dose of vitamin D you need to buy, make up the difference between the RDA and how much you're already getting from your multivitamin and calcium supplements. Choose a vitamin D supplement that contains vitamin D3, instead of vitamin D2, which is less potent.

Magnesium

Many studies have reported lower magnesium levels in people with angina. Some studies have even found that the greater the degree of deficiency, the more severe the angina attacks. While most studies have given patients magnesium through intravenous administration, a few have used oral supplements and reported fewer angina attacks and improved exercise tolerance. One study conducted in people with stable heart disease found that, compared with the placebo treatment, magnesium supplementation (365 milligrams taken twice daily) improved exercise tolerance and exercise duration during an exercise stress test. Those taking magnesium supplements were also less likely to experience chest pain. If you have heart disease, consuming more magnesium may improve your prognosis.[11-14] Furthermore, there's evidence that low body stores of magnesium increase the likelihood of abnormal heart rhythms (arrhythmia), a potentially fatal complication of heart attack.

It's thought that magnesium helps maintain the normal functioning of blood vessels during exercise by allowing vessels to dilate, or relax. Magnesium is also thought to act like a calcium channel drug (a prescription heart medication), although much less powerfully. Magnesium is able to block calcium from entering heart cells.

The best food sources of magnesium are nuts, seeds, legumes, prunes, figs, whole grains, leafy green vegetables and brewer's yeast. (See Chapter 4, page 61, for a list of magnesium-rich foods.) Magnesium supplements are typically sold in 200 or 250 milligram doses. To supplement, buy a product made from magnesium citrate. In addition to dietary magnesium, take a 250 milligram supplement once daily. Taking more than 350 milligrams of magnesium in a supplement can cause diarrhea, nausea and stomach cramps. If you have severe heart disease, do not take magnesium without your doctor's approval.

Other Natural Health Products

Coenzyme Q10

This substance, manufactured by the body, is found inside virtually every cell. Coenzyme Q10 (CoQ10) is a powerful antioxidant and helps cells produce important molecules of energy called ATP (adenosine triphosphate). Research hints that CoQ10 supplements may help improve heart health in people with heart disease. Studies have examined the effect of adding CoQ10 to conventional medical therapy in patients with chronic stable angina (chest pain) and have found that the supplement (60 to 600 milligrams per day) improved exercise tolerance during an exercise stress test and reduced or delayed electrocardiographic changes associated with angina. Research has found that supplemental CoQ10 can improve exercise tolerance in people with stable angina.[15,16]

In addition to what's synthesized in the body, we also consume roughly 10 milligrams of CoQ10 each day from a wide variety of foods. For managing angina, take 50 milligrams three times per day. Cholesterol-lowering statin medications such as lovastatin (Mevacor), simvastatin (Zocor), atorvastatin (Lipitor) and pravastatin (Pravachol) have been shown to reduce blood levels of CoQ10. Whether this affects heart health is not yet known, but it may be wise to take CoQ10 supplements if you're on these drugs.

L-Carnitine

Carnitine is an amino acid found in all body cells, where it is used to metabolize fatty acids into energy. Carnitine appears to help the heart produce energy more efficiently and, as a result, use less oxygen. A number of studies have found that individuals with chronic stable angina who took L-carnitine supplements improved in several measures of heart function, including the ability to exercise without chest pain. Some studies found that people were able to reduce the dose of their heart medications.[17-22]

Most studies use the form of carnitine called L-carnitine. L-carnitine is available in the United States but not legally available in Canada. For stable angina, the dose used in clinical studies is 1000 milligrams (1 gram) twice daily. L-carnitine is generally well tolerated but can cause stomach upset and restlessness. It may also cause the urine, breath and sweat to have a fishy odour. People taking anti-coagulant medication should use the supplement cautiously as it may increase the effects of these drugs. Do not take D-carnitine or DL-carnitine, which can cause heart and muscle dysfunction.

Nutrition Strategy Checklist for Angina

- ☐ Low–saturated fat and –trans fat diet
- ☐ Multivitamin/mineral
- ☐ Vitamin C
- ☐ Vitamin D
- ☐ Foods rich in vitamin E
- ☐ Magnesium
- ☐ Coenzyme Q10
- ☐ L-carnitine

Recommended Resources

Heart and Stroke Foundation of Canada
www.heartandstroke.ca
222 Queen Street, Suite 1402
Ottawa, ON K1P 5V9
Tel: 613-569-4361
Fax: 613-569-3278

American Heart Association
www.americanheart.org
7272 Greenville Avenue
Dallas, TX, USA 75231
Tel: 1-800-AHA-USA1 (242-8721)

National Heart, Lung and Blood Institute
National Institutes of Health
www.nhlbi.nih.gov
P.O. Box 30105
Bethesda, MD, USA 20824-0105
Tel: 301-592-8573
Fax: 240-629-3246

Asthma

Asthma is one of the most commonly diagnosed illnesses in North America and its prevalence has been increasing over the last 20 years, affecting 3 million Canadians.[1] It is a chronic inflammatory lung condition that causes breathing difficulties such as wheezing, coughing and shortness of breath. In almost all cases, the disease has its onset in early childhood, with the vast majority of cases being diagnosed before the age of 6 years. There is no cure for asthma, although it can be effectively controlled with medication and other management strategies.

What Causes Asthma?

People with asthma have very sensitive airways that become swollen and inflamed when exposed to irritants. During an asthmatic episode, the airways or bronchial tubes tighten, making it difficult for the lungs to force air in and out. This tightening and narrowing of the airways is known as bronchoconstriction and can be caused by contraction of the small muscles surrounding the bronchial tubes, swelling of airway linings or production of excess mucus.

Asthma attacks are often provoked by triggers or stimuli that irritate the airways. These triggers usually vary from person to person and can include:

- cold air or changes in weather or temperature
- respiratory viral infections
- exercising, crying, laughing
- allergies to mould, animal dander, pollen, cockroaches and dust mites
- food allergies
- stress or emotional upset
- cigarette smoke
- strong odours, strong chemical fumes or other inhaled irritants
- certain medications (aspirin, beta blockers)

Although triggers may irritate the bronchial tubes, they usually don't cause the airways to become inflamed. Asthma symptoms that result from exposure to triggers tend to be immediate, short-lived and easy to reverse.

Asthmatic episodes may also be provoked by factors that cause both irritation *and* inflammation in the airways. Symptoms resulting from inflammation will usually last longer and are harder to reverse than those caused by triggers. The most common causes of airway inflammation are allergens:

- pollen, especially from grasses, weeds and trees
- animal dander and secretions
- moulds
- dust mites

Some allergens provoke an immediate asthmatic reaction by irritating the overly sensitive airways. However, in most cases, exposure to allergens is also accompanied by inflammation, which tends to develop over a longer period. This delay can make it very difficult to identify the factors causing the asthma. Asthmatic symptoms may not appear until 4 to 8 hours after initial contact with the allergen or may reappear several hours after the initial asthma attack has been successfully treated. Respiratory infections such as colds and flu can also inflame the airways and cause an asthma attack.

Symptoms

Signs of an asthma attack include:

- wheezing
- coughing
- shortness of breath or laboured breathing
- chest tightness

Who's at Risk?

Most cases of asthma are diagnosed in childhood but the disease can develop at any age. The following people are more susceptible to developing the condition:

- individuals with a family history of asthma and/or allergy such as eczema
- those exposed to high levels of dust mites during infancy
- those exposed to cigarette smoke or chemical irritants in the workplace
- those who are obese—being overweight or obese is thought to increase the risk of asthma by 50 percent[2]; obesity is also associated with more severe asthma
- young boys—during childhood, asthma affects twice as many boys as girls
- teenage girls—during adolescence, more girls than boys develop asthma
- babies born to women who smoke during pregnancy

Conventional Treatment

It is very important to minimize exposure to triggers of asthma. Washing sheets and blankets weekly in hot water, enclosing your mattress and box spring in plastic, not smoking in the house, not allowing pets in the house, reducing humidity in the house to keep dust mites and moulds under control and avoiding the outside air during times of high pollen counts all help reduce the chance of an asthma attack.

There are two types of medications used to manage asthma. *Controllers*, also called "preventers," are used to treat airway inflammation and swelling and are taken every day. Doctors generally prescribe inhaled controllers over oral (tablet or liquid) controllers because the inhaled medication is more targeted to the lungs where it's needed. It's important to continue these medications because if they're discontinued the airway inflammation may return. These anti-inflammatory drugs—both in steroid (e.g., Beclovent, Vanceril, Becloforte, Pulmicort, Flovent) and non-steroidal (e.g., Intal, Tilade) form—don't have an immediate effect and will not help in an asthma emergency. Steroid drugs may cause side effects, such as hoarseness and sore throat and thrush (oral yeast infections), which can be prevented by rinsing the mouth or gargling after use. Leukotriene receptor antagonists (e.g., Accolate, Singulair) are oral medications that help prevent inflammation and protect against bronchoconstriction when taken before exercise or exposure to a trigger.

Relievers help relieve or alleviate symptoms such as coughing, wheezing or shortness of breath quickly. Relievers are a short-term solution to breathing problems as they treat the bronchoconstriction but do not treat the underlying airway inflammation. It is important to monitor how often relievers are used since increased use over time indicates that asthma symptoms are worsening. Bronchodilators (e.g., Ventolin, Berotec, Bricanyl, Atrovent, Theo-Dur) relax the muscles around the airways and may be used just before exercising or before exposure to known triggers. Bronchodilators may produce side effects such as trembling, nervousness and flushing.

Managing Asthma

Dietary Strategies

Asthma rates have nearly doubled in North America over the past two decades and many researchers believe our changing diet may be partly to blame. Studies suggest that eating fewer and fewer fruits and vegetables and more processed foods is increasing the risk of developing asthma.

While diet can't cure asthma, studies suggest the following foods and nutrients can help manage—and possibly prevent—the condition.

Fruit and Vegetables

Evidence suggests that children and adults who have higher intakes of fruit and vegetables have lower rates of asthma. And it seems the earlier their introduction into the diet, the better. In a study of 502 children aged 6 to 16 years, those who consumed fruit and vegetables daily during infancy were 43 percent less likely to develop asthma after 1 year of age than children who ate fruit and vegetables less often. Asthma sufferers who eat plenty of fruit and vegetables also tend to have their condition under better control.

One study of 690 preschoolers found that those who adhered closely to a Mediterranean diet—high in grapes, oranges, apples and fresh tomatoes—were 66 percent less likely to have asthma symptoms than children who ate few of these foods. Following such a diet during pregnancy has also been shown to protect the child from asthma symptoms and allergic disease later in childhood.

Fruit rich in vitamin C is especially helpful in reducing wheezing in children and adults with asthma. A study of 12-year-old asthma sufferers revealed that following a vegetarian diet for 1 year provided a significant decrease in asthma symptoms and allowed medication to be drastically reduced or discontinued.[3–10]

Fruit and vegetables may help prevent asthma in a few ways. These foods offer important vitamins, minerals and antioxidants needed for healthy lung function. Studies suggest that lycopene, an antioxidant in heat-processed tomato products such as tomato juice, can reduce asthma symptoms. Vitamin C, a key antioxidant abundant in the fluid lining the lungs, has also been shown to reduce wheezing in people with asthma. People who eat more produce also tend to eat more fibre and less fat, two habits that can help maintain a healthy body weight. Studies conducted among women found that weight gain in early adulthood significantly increases the risk of developing adult-onset asthma. What's more, researchers have learned that when obese individuals with asthma lose weight, their asthma symptoms improve.[11-13] To learn about healthy body weights for adults, see Obesity and Weight Loss, page 569.

Aim for at least 7 servings of fruit and vegetables in your daily diet. Children aged 2 to 3 need at least 4 servings and 4- to 8-year-olds need 5 servings. One serving is equivalent to 1 medium-sized fruit, 1/4 cup (50 ml) of dried fruit, 1/2 cup (125 ml) of vegetables or 1 cup (250 ml) of salad greens.

Fish

Eating oily fish may also help prevent asthma and improve symptoms of asthma. Fish contains the omega-3 fatty acids DHA (docosahexanaenoic acid) and EPA (eicosapentaenoic acid), which the body uses to produce anti-inflammatory compounds. Studies show that people who consume fish as a regular part of their diet have improved lung function and lower rates of asthma.[14] Aim to eat fish two times a week. The best choices are salmon, trout, herring, mackerel, Arctic char and sardines.

Avoid consuming large amounts of omega-6 fats found in corn, soybean and safflower oils, as well as margarines and processed foods. There's evidence these fats may promote inflammation and worsen asthma.

Sodium

A low-sodium diet may also help provide symptom relief, since many asthmatics, especially males, appear to be salt-sensitive.[15] Evidence suggests that a high intake of sodium may trigger spasms in the bronchial smooth muscle and that a low-salt diet may even reduce the need for asthma medications.[16,17] Research has shown that adopting a low-sodium diet for 2 to 5 weeks can improve lung function and reduce bronchial constriction in adults with asthma.[18] However, a 2008 study of 200 asthmatics aged 18 to 65 found no evidence that a low-sodium diet improved lung function.[19]

Whether or not reducing sodium intake improves asthma symptoms, it has other important health benefits. Consume no more than the safe upper limit of 2300 milligrams of sodium each day. See Chapter 4, page 80, and Chapter 5, page 107, for more on sodium. As often as possible, avoid eating processed foods and adding salt to foods.

Food Allergies

Food-triggered asthma occurs among 6 to 8 percent of children with asthma and less than 2 percent of adults. Foods that have been confirmed to trigger asthma include milk, eggs, peanuts, tree nuts, soy, wheat, fish and shellfish. Food additives that can worsen asthma include sulphites and sulphating agents added to foods such as dried fruit, prepared potatoes, wine, bottled lemon and lime juice and shrimp. To determine if a food allergy triggers your or your child's asthma, try an elimination/challenge diet as outlined below. You may want to seek the help of a registered dietitian (www.dietitians.ca) to help determine if you have a food allergy.

1. **Elimination phase.** For a period of 2 weeks, eliminate common food allergens—dairy products, soy foods, nuts, peanuts, wheat, shellfish, fish, eggs and sulphite food additives. Read ingredient lists on food labels to identify the presence of food allergens in packaged foods.

2. **Challenge phase.** After 2 weeks, start introducing one food every 3 days. Keep a food and symptom diary in which you record everything you eat, amounts eaten and what time you ate the food or meal. Document any symptoms, the time of day you started to feel the symptom and the duration of time you felt the symptom. If symptoms recur when a particular food is added back, you or your child may be allergic. Consult your doctor for further food allergy testing.

Vitamins and Minerals

Vitamin B12

Since a deficiency of vitamin B12 may increase the body's reactivity to sulphite preservatives in food, this vitamin has been proposed as a possible treatment for asthma. To prevent a deficiency, ensure you are meeting your daily requirements by eating animal foods and seafood such as meat, poultry, fish, clams, eggs, dairy products and fortified soy and rice beverages and taking a multivitamin and mineral supplement. Separate B12 pills are very safe. The recommended dose for vegetarians who consume no animal products (vegans) is 500 to 1000 micrograms per day.

Vitamin C

A number of studies point to the protective effects of vitamin C in asthma. This antioxidant vitamin is concentrated in the fluid that lines the lungs, protecting them from free radical damage.

Studies show that people with asthma tend to have lower levels of vitamin C in their lung fluid.[20,21] However, a recent review of vitamin C studies concluded there isn't enough evidence to make a vitamin C recommendation for the treatment of asthma. Among the nine studies reviewed, only one found that 2 grams of supplemental vitamin C reduced exercise-induced asthma in children and young adults.[22,23]

While there is no conclusive evidence that vitamin C improves asthma symptoms, increasing your intake of the nutrient has numerous other health benefits, among them maintaining a healthy immune system. The best food sources of vitamin C include citrus fruit, strawberries, kiwi, cantaloupe, broccoli, bell peppers, Brussels sprouts, cabbage, tomatoes and potatoes. To supplement, take 500 milligrams of vitamin C once or twice daily. For more information on vitamin C, see Chapter 4, page 48.

Vitamin E

Studies have revealed that increased vitamin E intakes are linked with a lower risk of asthma and that low intakes of the nutrient increase the likelihood of developing asthma. However, research has found that vitamin E supplements offer no benefit in the treatment of asthma. In addition to its antioxidant properties, vitamin E helps maintain the proper function of immune cells called mast cells. When mast cells react and accumulate in an uncontrolled manner, inflammatory compounds are released that can contribute to asthma.

The best food sources of vitamin E include vegetable oils, almonds, peanuts, soybeans, whole grains, wheat germ, wheat germ oil, avocado and green leafy vegetables. For more information on vitamin E, see Chapter 4, page 52.

Magnesium

This mineral plays an important role in lung function by influencing the contraction and relaxation of bronchial smooth muscle. Studies show that low dietary intakes of magnesium are linked with impaired lung function, spasms of the bronchial passageway and wheezing.[24] In one study, 40 percent of patients with asthma were deficient in magnesium. Another study found that supplementing the diet with magnesium can help reduce asthma symptoms in people who are magnesium deficient.[25,26] Research conducted in children and teenagers with asthma found that taking a 300 milligram magnesium supplement once daily was associated with reduced bronchial constriction, fewer asthma flare-ups and reduced use of medication.[27]

To help meet your daily magnesium requirements, include the following foods in your diet: nuts, seeds, legumes, prunes, whole-grain cereals, leafy green vegetables, brewer's yeast and dairy products. Keep in mind that much magnesium is lost in refining foods, so a diet high in refined or processed food will be lacking magnesium.

To supplement, take 150 to 250 milligrams of magnesium citrate once daily. See Chapter 4, page 63, to learn the safe upper daily limits for children and adults. Taking more than the upper daily limit can cause diarrhea.

Herbal Remedies

Boswellia (Boswellia serrata)

This herbal product is derived from the resin of the Indian Boswellia tree. Although very few studies have been conducted using this herb, one double-blind trial found that, when taken for 6 weeks, it reduced the frequency of asthma attacks and improved breathing capacity in adults with mild asthma.[28] Seventy percent of people taking the herb experienced improvement. Boswellia is thought to work by reducing inflammation.

The effective dosage was 300 milligrams three times daily. Buy a product standardized to contain 37.5 percent boswellic acids. It may take up to 8 weeks to notice improvement in asthma symptoms once you start taking the herb. Boswellia has not been evaluated for safety in children or in pregnant or breast-feeding women.

Other Natural Health Products

Fish Oil Supplements

Evidence suggests that taking a fish oil supplement during pregnancy may, after birth, reduce the risk of asthma in the young child. A handful of studies conducted in children with asthma have also demonstrated the ability of a fish oil–enriched diet to improve oxygen flow, lessen wheezing and reduce the need for medication. One study conducted in adults with asthma showed that daily fish oil supplementation significantly improved asthma symptoms before and during exercise.[29–34]

Fish oil capsules are a concentrated source of DHA and EPA, two omega-3 fatty acids that have anti-inflammatory functions in the body. Some research suggests that fish oil may help lessen asthmatic symptoms resulting from airborne triggers. Fish oil appears to benefit children with asthma more than it benefits adults with the condition.

The dosage of fish oil used in children with asthma is based on body weight: 17 to 26 milligrams of EPA per kilogram and 7.3 to 11.5 milligrams of DHA per kilogram, taken in divided doses. In adults, a daily dose of 5.2 milligrams of DHA and EPA combined has been used. Buy a fish oil capsule with a combination of DHA and EPA. Avoid fish *liver* oil capsules. Fish liver oil is a concentrated source of vitamin A, which can be toxic when taken in large amounts for long periods.

Probiotics

It's thought that people with asthma have alterations in the composition of bacteria resident in the intestinal tract. Probiotic bacteria may reduce the risk of developing asthma by helping the immune system mature after birth. Preliminary evidence hints that consuming a probiotic supplement during pregnancy and breastfeeding may protect children from asthma.[35,36] In one study of women with at least one first-degree relative with eczema or asthma, those who took a probiotic supplement (*Lactobacillus GG*) during pregnancy and for 6 months after delivery halved the likelihood of subsequent development of eczema in their child during the first 2 years of life. (Chronic recurring eczema is the main sign of allergic disease in infancy and early childhood.)

For preventing allergic diseases in infants with a family history of allergy, the dose used in clinical research with pregnant women was 20 billion live *Lactobacillus GG* daily for 4 weeks prior to delivery and then for 3 to 6 months during breastfeeding.

Nutrition Strategy Checklist for Asthma

- ☐ Fruit and vegetables
- ☐ Fish
- ☐ Low-sodium/salt diet
- ☐ Food allergy identification
- ☐ Foods rich in vitamin B6
- ☐ Vitamin C
- ☐ Foods rich in vitamin E
- ☐ Magnesium
- ☐ Fish oil capsules
- ☐ Probiotics

Recommended Resources

Allergy/Asthma Information Association
www.aaia.ca
111 Zenway Boulevard, Unit 1
Vaughan, ON L4H 3H9
Tel: 905-265-3322
Fax: 905-850-2070
Email: admin@aaia.ca

The Asthma Society of Canada
www.asthma.ca
4950 Yonge Street, Suite 2306
Toronto, ON M2N 6K1
Tel: 1-866-787-4050
Fax: 416-787-5807
Email: info@asthma.ca

The Canadian Lung Association
www.lung.ca
1750 Courtwood Crescent, Suite 300
Ottawa, ON K2C 2B5
Tel: 1-888-566-LUNG (5864)
Fax: 613-569-8860
Email: info@lung.ca

American Lung Association
www.lungusa.org/asthma
1301 Pennsylvania Avenue, NW
Suite 800
Washington, DC, USA 20004
Tel: 212-315-8700

National Heart, Lung and Blood Institute
National Institutes of Health
www.nhlbi.nih.gov
P.O. Box 30105
Bethesda, MD, USA 20824-0105

Tel: 301-592-8573
Fax: 240-629-3246
Email: nhlbiinfo@nhlbi.nih.gov

Attention Deficit Hyperactivity Disorder (ADHD)

Attention deficit hyperactivity disorder (ADHD) is a neurobiological disability that can have a profound and disruptive effect on daily life. People with ADHD have difficulty sitting still, paying attention and controlling impulsive behaviour. They tend to be hyperactive and easily distracted, and they often act before they think. These negative and persistent behaviour patterns can create long-term problems at home, work and school, as well as in social settings.

ADHD affects approximately 8 to 10 percent of males and 3 to 4 percent of females under the age of 18.[1] Symptoms usually appear before the age of 7 and cause significant problems in school, at home and in social settings. It's estimated that 60 percent of children with ADHD will continue to have symptoms as adults.[2]

What Causes ADHD?

While considerable research has been conducted into ADHD, the cause of the condition is still unknown and no cure has been found. However, researchers believe both genetics and environmental factors play a role. ADHD frequently runs in families. Smoking, drinking alcohol and exposure to toxins such as PCBs (polychlorinated biphenyls) during pregnancy have been linked to later ADHD in a child. Chemical changes that affect brain function and brain injuries are other possible explanations that are currently under investigation.

Symptoms

ADHD can be difficult to pinpoint because nearly everyone experiences periods of restless behaviour and a short attention span during his or her lifetime. The diagnosis is further complicated by the fact that ADHD symptoms are very similar to those of other disorders, such as anxiety, depression and certain learning disabilities. As a result, the guidelines for identifying ADHD are quite specific. Symptoms must persist for at least 6 months and to a degree that is maladaptive and inconsistent with the developmental level of the child. Symptoms must affect the ability to function in two or more settings, including home, school, work or social life.

There are three types of ADHD symptoms and each type may vary from person to person.

INATTENTION
- makes careless mistakes
- does not seem to listen when spoken to
- does not maintain an attention span
- is disorganized
- is easily distracted
- has difficulty following instructions
- is forgetful

HYPERACTIVITY
- fidgets or squirms constantly
- runs around excessively
- has difficulty sitting still for any length of time
- has difficulty behaving quietly
- talks excessively

IMPULSIVITY
- blurts out answers before questions have been completed
- has difficulty waiting or taking turns
- interrupts or intrudes on others

Children with ADHD usually do not perform well at school, have trouble making friends and experience family conflicts. With adolescents, the problems become more severe, often causing low self-esteem, mood swings, higher injury rates, drug abuse, poor school performance and, in the case of females, early pregnancy. Adults with ADHD often experience career difficulties, are disorganized, have difficulty planning ahead and struggle with interpersonal relationships.

Who's at Risk?

Research indicates that there is a genetic basis to ADHD; children are at increased risk for ADHD if the disorder has been diagnosed in other close relatives. Several studies have demonstrated that children with ADHD usually have at least one close relative (child or adult) that also has ADHD. At least one-third of fathers with ADHD will produce a child with the condition. ADHD may be more common in very low birth-weight infants (1500 grams or less). And boys are more likely than girls to develop ADHD.

On average, one child in every classroom in North America needs treatment for ADHD. While the number of children identified and treated for ADHD has risen in recent years, this is most likely the result of increased media attention and heightened awareness of the condition. There is no scientific evidence to prove that the prevalence of ADHD has actually increased.

Conventional Treatment

While ADHD can't be cured, it can be managed. Currently, the only therapies proven effective in scientific studies are medications and/or behavioural therapy. Conventional treatments for children with ADHD include:

- behaviour management
- educational assistance in the classroom
- educational program modification
- special placement outside regular classrooms
- parent education
- psychostimulant medications
- antidepressant and antihypertensive medications
- psychotherapy
- vocational counselling for adults

Although many children continue to demonstrate symptoms of ADHD into adulthood, studies indicate that those who receive adequate treatment at an early age will have fewer problems at school, will interact more appropriately with their peer group and will generally function better in their daily life.

Many parents have tried a number of nutritional interventions claimed to improve ADHD symptoms in their children. Nutritional factors such as food additives, food allergies, refined sugar, fatty acid and deficiencies have all been linked to ADHD. Despite this, there are no well-established nutritional treatments that have been consistently demonstrated to be effective in helping a large number of children with the condition. Below, I describe nutritional approaches that studies suggest may benefit some children. (Dietary modification and nutritional supplements should not be used instead of the usual medication without a doctor being involved.)

Managing ADHD
Dietary Strategies
Amino Acids and Protein

Since many amino acids in protein-rich foods provide the building blocks for brain chemicals called neurotransmitters, it has been hypothesized that supplementing the diet with some of these could improve ADHD symptoms. Indeed, some research has found that compared with healthy children, those with ADHD have lower levels of tyrosine and tryptophan, two amino acids that help the brain synthesize neurotransmitters that regulate mood and cognitive function.[3] What's more, when researchers depleted tryptophan levels of males with ADHD, aggressive behaviour increased. However, studies have found no effect on symptoms when children and adults with ADHD were given large doses of these amino acids.[4,5]

Although supplement studies have not shown positive results, it is crucial that children and adults with ADHD meet their daily protein requirements. Tryptophan is considered an essential amino acid because it cannot be made by the body and so must be supplied by the diet. Once inside the brain, tryptophan is used to make serotonin, a brain chemical believed to have a calming, relaxing effect. Tyrosine serves as a building block for dopamine, a neurotransmitter associated with improved alertness and sharpened thinking. In Chapter 5, you'll find a food guide that will help you choose the right amount of protein-rich foods each day.

Breakfast

Many studies of both children and adults have shown that, compared with breakfast eaters, individuals who skip the morning meal do not score as well on tests of mental performance that same morning.[6] What seems to be affected the most is the speed of information retrieval (a component of memory). Breakfast foods supply glucose in the bloodstream, which the brain cells use for energy. After a night of sleeping, we wake up in a fasting state. That means blood-glucose levels are low and need to be replenished.

Breakfast also supplies key nutrients in the diet, including important B vitamins, calcium and iron. Research has shown that when breakfast is skipped, these missing nutrients are usually not made up for later in the day. Below you'll read about the important role that iron plays in brain function.

The best breakfast includes carbohydrates for blood glucose and a little protein to help sustain energy levels longer. This is partly because protein takes longer to digest. That means the carbohydrate you eat with protein gets converted to glucose more slowly. Here are a few combinations to ensure that your diet provides both nutrients:

- whole-grain cereal with low-fat milk or calcium-fortified soy beverage; top with fruit or have a small glass of citrus juice
- whole-grain toast with a poached or hard-boiled egg and a fruit salad
- homemade breakfast smoothie made with soy beverage or milk, orange juice and a banana; add soy protein powder or egg whites for a protein boost
- a piece of fruit, a whole-grain cereal bar and a low-fat yogurt for protein for breakfast-on-the-run as you're dashing out the door

Fatty Acids

It has been suggested that children with ADHD have altered fatty acid metabolism, since some symptoms of ADHD are similar to those observed in people with a fatty acid deficiency. The omega-3 and omega-6 oils in our diet provide two essential fatty acids that our body cannot make on its own. Omega-3 oils (flaxseed, canola, walnut) provide alpha-linolenic acid and omega-6 oils (corn, sunflower, safflower, soybean) give us linoleic acid. These two essential fatty acids are used to form vital body structures and cell membranes, to aid in both immune function and vision and to produce powerful compounds called eicosanoids that help regulate inflammation, hormones and nerve and brain function. One study conducted in children with ADHD found that supplementation with ALA-rich flaxseed oil significantly improved hyperactivity symptoms.[7]

Children and adults should consume 2 table spoons (30 ml) of oil rich in alpha-linolenic acid per day. Flaxseed, walnut and canola oil are the best sources. A commercial product called Udo's Choice Ultimate Oil Blend is available in health food stores. Udo's oil contains a balance of both alpha-linolenic and linoleic fatty acids from organic flaxseed, sesame and sunflower seeds, wheat germ, rice germ and oat germ. Flaxseed oil, walnut oil and Udo's oil should not be used for sautéing or frying as their essential fatty acids are easily destroyed by heat. Store the oil in the refrigerator and use in salad dressings, dips and smoothies or add to foods like pasta sauces and soups after cooking.

Food Additives and the Feingold Diet

In 1975, Dr. Benjamin Feingold, an allergist from California, suggested that avoidance of artificial colours, flavours and preservatives as well as naturally occurring salicylates (compounds found in fruit and vegetables) could dramatically improve ADHD symptoms in kids. A few studies do suggest that salicylates influence the activity of phenol sulfotransferase, an enzyme needed by the brain but also used in the gut to metabolize artificial colours and flavours.[8-10] Salicylates can be found in natural flavouring, natural colouring and aspirin. In addition, they occur naturally in a number of foods, including almonds, apples, apricots, nectarines, berries, cherries, grapes, currants, raisins, chili powder, cider, cloves, coffee, cucumbers, bell peppers, tomatoes and tea.

Yet most studies have failed to find improvements in learning and attention problems in children on the Feingold Diet. A few early studies, however, did suggest that eliminating food additives may be beneficial for some children, particularly with respect to irritability, restlessness and sleep disturbances. A 1986 review of the Feingold Diet determined that only 1 percent of children consistently improved on the diet and 10 percent developed symptoms when dyes were consumed.[11-18]

Since then, numerous well-designed studies have found that the behaviour of some children improved when food colouring and common food allergens (corn, milk, fish, eggs, peanuts, soy, wheat, oranges) were removed, and significantly worsened when reintroduced. A 2008 British study of 300 children between the ages of 3 and 9 who did not have ADHD found that consuming food dyes added to fruit drinks— equivalent to two or four 56 gram bags of candy—significantly exacerbated hyperactive behaviours. The additives studied (also permitted for use in Canada) included sodium benzoate (a preservative); tartrazine, quinoline yellow and sunset yellow (yellow food dyes); and allura red (a red food dye).[19]

Elimination diets are thought to benefit only 5 percent of kids with ADHD. Children most likely to respond are those with a history of allergic conditions such as asthma or eczema, a family history of migraine and/or a family history of food sensitivities. If you think certain foods or food additives affect your child's behaviour, eliminate them one at a time to see if symptoms improve. Elimination diets that remove many suspect foods should be used under the guidance of a registered dietitian to ensure nutritional needs are met.

The Feingold Diet promotes the elimination of most food additives (e.g., colouring and flavouring agents and preservatives) and foods that contain salicylates. Beyond foods, any toiletries, cleaning supplies and art supplies that contain such ingredients are to be avoided. As a first step, advocates of the diet recommend avoiding perfume, corn syrup, molasses, caramel colour, MSG (monosodium glutamate), HVP (hydrolyzed vegetable protein), natural flavouring, processed foods containing oil, processed foods containing fruit concentrates, nitrites and sulphites. For more information about the Feingold Diet, log on to www.feingold.org. This website defines the diet and food restrictions and lists a number of books that you may find useful.

Sugar and Sweeteners

Whether the elimination of sugars and artificial sweeteners from the diet can help reduce ADHD symptoms remains a controversial issue, especially since the evidence does not support the notion that sugar causes hyperactivity.[20,21] Studies in which children were given high amounts of refined sugar and aspartame (NutraSweet) found that their behaviour was not negatively affected.[22,23] Despite the fact that sugar does not seem to trigger or worsen symptoms, there may be a small number of children who react to sugary foods. One study did find that sugar, but not aspartame, exacerbated inattention in children with ADHD but had no effect in children without the disorder.[24] In this study, sugar did not worsen aggressive behaviour.

For overall good nutrition, it is wise to minimize the consumption of table sugar, soft drinks, fruit drinks, fruit leather, candy and other sweets. Sugary foods may also contain preservatives and dyes linked with hyperactive behaviour. Parents should help children understand that these foods are considered treats and so should not be eaten on a regular basis.

Vitamins and Minerals

Iron

The body needs iron to carry oxygen to the brain cells. It is also used to make brain neurotransmitters, especially the ones that regulate the ability to pay attention, which is crucial to memory and learning. A deficiency of iron can directly affect mood, attention span and learning ability.

Existing data suggest that iron deficiency contributes to ADHD and that children with the condition could benefit from iron supplementation. A number of studies have found that low blood ferritin levels, a measure of the body's iron stores, is common in children with ADHD. In one study of 53 children with ADHD, aged 4 to 14 years, 84 percent had abnormal ferritin levels. In ADHD children who were not anemic but had low ferritin, researchers found that iron supplementation resulted in a progressive and significant improvement in ADHD symptons.[25–27]

It is extremely important for children and adults to meet their daily iron requirements (see Chapter 4, page 71). Good food sources of this mineral include lean beef, whole-grain breakfast cereals, whole-grain breads, raisins, dried apricots, legumes, bean dips and bran muffins. Iron in plant foods (nonheme iron) is not absorbed as well as iron in animal foods (heme iron). To enhance the body's absorption of nonheme iron from plant foods, include a vitamin C–rich food with the meal. A children's multivitamin and mineral supplement with iron taken once daily will also help ensure your child's iron needs are met. Avoid single iron pills unless your dietitian or doctor has recommended them to treat an iron deficiency.

Magnesium

Based on a number of studies that show depressed magnesium levels in the red blood cells and hair of children with ADHD, it's been suggested that magnesium supplements may be useful in treatment.[28] Magnesium is needed to help brain neurotransmitters function properly. In one study, 50 children with ADHD and magnesium deficiency were given 200 milligrams of supplemental magnesium daily for 6 months. At the end of the trial, the researchers noted an increase in magnesium levels in hair and a significant decrease in hyperactivity.[29]

Good food sources of magnesium include nuts, seeds, legumes, prunes, whole grains, leafy green vegetables, brewer's yeast, cheddar cheese and shrimp. For a detailed listing and daily requirements, see Chapter 4, page 61. If you opt for a supplement, buy one made from magnesium citrate, a form of magnesium that the body absorbs more efficiently. Take 150 to 200 milligrams once daily in addition to eating magnesium-rich foods. Taking more than 350 milligrams of supplemental magnesium can cause diarrhea, nausea and stomach cramps.

Zinc

A zinc deficiency may play a role in the development of ADHD. Two studies have revealed that children with ADHD have lower blood levels of zinc than those without ADHD. One small study also found that school-aged children taking the stimulant medication Ritalin, along with a 15 milligram zinc supplement, had greater improvement than those who took their medication alone.[30-32]

The body relies on zinc for the activity of brain chemicals, fatty acids and melatonin (a naturally occurring hormone related to sleep), all of which are related to behaviour. To prevent a zinc deficiency, reach for the following foods: oysters, seafood, red meat, poultry, yogurt, wheat bran, wheat germ, whole grains and enriched breakfast cereals. You'll find recommended daily intakes and a detailed food list in Chapter 4, page 79.

Children with ADHD should take a children's multivitamin and mineral supplement that contains zinc. Single zinc supplements are rarely appropriate for adults and should not be taken by children. Too much zinc has toxic effects, including copper deficiency, heart problems, anemia and depressed immunity.

Other Natural Health Products

Evening Primrose Oil (Oenothera biennis)

Evening primrose oil contains a fatty acid called gamma-linolenic acid (GLA) that might help children with ADHD. The essential fatty acid called linoleic acid is converted in the body to GLA with the help of an enzyme. GLA is then transformed into prostaglandins, compounds that regulate our blood, immune system and hormones. Some researchers believe that children with ADHD may have difficulty carrying out this conversion. Dietary components such as animal fat and hydrogenated vegetable oils can interfere with this conversion. To function properly, the enzyme responsible for making GLA requires zinc, magnesium and vitamins B6 and C. A high-fat diet that's missing important vitamins and minerals can hamper GLA production and contribute to low levels of fatty acids in the body. It's also thought that the amount of GLA actually made may not be enough to cope with the requirement for prostaglandin formation.

Evening primrose oil is a concentrated source of GLA. Two studies found no effect on ADHD symptoms with a daily evening primrose oil supplement, possibly because the dosage used was too low and/or the duration of the study too short (only 4 weeks) to notice improvements.[33,34] However, findings from a more recent double-blind study suggest that a supplement containing a mixture of fish oil and evening primrose oil might improve ADHD symptoms.[35] Evening primrose oil is very safe; very few side effects are reported in studies. Buy a product standardized to 9 percent GLA. The dosage of GLA used in combination with fish oil is 96 milligrams per day.

Fish Oil

Omega-3 fatty acids, called DHA (docosahexanaenoic acid) and EPA (eicosapentaenoic acid), are found in salmon, trout, sardines, mackerel, herring and fish oil capsules. Concentrated in our brain—in fact, 60 percent of our brain's solid matter is composed of these essential fatty acids, especially DHA—they play an essential role in cognition and behaviour. Omega-3 fatty acids make up a large portion of the communicating membranes of the brain. Because these fats are needed for proper brain development in growing children, a number of studies have investigated their relationship to ADHD.

Children with ADHD are more likely to have lower levels of omega-3s in their blood than children without ADHD.[36–38] Studies have also shown that children with lower levels of these fatty acids demonstrate significantly more behavioural problems, temper tantrums and learning and sleep problems. It is unclear why some children with ADHD are lacking essential fatty acids. Factors such as poor dietary intake and faulty metabolism of these fats in the body have been proposed. Some, but not all, clinical studies using supplements of DHA and EPA have demonstrated improvement in symptoms of inattention and hyperactivity.[39–42]

Individuals with ADHD should also supplement their diet with DHA and EPA from a fish oil supplement. Look for a fish oil supplement or liquid fish oil that contains 250 to 500 milligrams of DHA plus EPA combined. Children who have an allergy to fish or a bleeding disorder, or who are taking anti-coagulant medications, should not take fish oil.

Herbal Teas

The use of herbal teas may have a calming effect in children and adults with ADHD. Lemon balm, lavender and chamomile all have mild sedative and relaxing properties. Tea bags can be purchased at health food stores or you can obtain dried herbs from a licensed herbalist.

To make herbal tea, use 1 teaspoon (5 ml) of dried herb per 1 cup (250 ml) of hot water. Steep, covered, for 5 to 10 minutes for leaf or flowers, 10 to 20 minutes for roots. Drink 1 cup of tea two or three times a day. If the taste of the tea is a deterrent, speak to your natural health care provider about the availability of these herbs as alcohol-free tinctures. (See Chapter 6, page 120, for more on teas and tinctures.)

Nutrition Strategy Checklist for ADHD

☐   Eat breakfast daily
☐   Flaxseed oil
☐   Avoid food additives
☐   Limit sugar and sweeteners
☐   Foods rich in iron
☐   Foods rich in magnesium
☐   Foods rich in zinc
☐   Evening primrose oil
☐   Fish oil

Recommended Resources

Attention Deficit Disorder Association (ADDA)
www.add.org
PO Box 7557
Wilmington, DE, USA 19803-9997
Tel/Fax: 800-939-1019
Email: adda@jmoadmin.com

Children and Adults with Attention Deficit/Hyperactivity Disorder (CHADD)
www.chadd.org
8181 Professional Place, Suite 201
Landover, MD, USA 20785
Tel: 301-306-7070
Fax: 301-306-7090

National Institute of Mental Health
National Institutes of Health
NIMH Public Inquiries
www.nimh.nih.gov/publicat/adhd.cfm
6001 Executive Boulevard, Room 8184,
   MSC 9663
Bethesda, MD, USA 20892-9663
Tel: 301-443-4513
Fax: 301-443-4279

National Institute of Neurological Disorders and Stroke
National Institutes of Health
www.ninds.nih.gov/disorders/adhd/adhd.htm
P.O. Box 5801
Bethesda, MD, USA 20824
Tel: 301-496-5751

Breast Cancer

Breast cancer is the most common type of cancer among Canadian women, affecting 22,700 women in 2009. One in nine women will develop breast cancer in her lifetime. This lifetime risk represents the average risk for the population of Canadian women.[1] If you have certain risk factors for breast cancer, like a family history or a poor diet, this number underestimates your risk. If you have no risk factors at all for the disease, this lifetime risk overestimates your chances of getting breast cancer.

Sadly, 102 Canadian women die from breast cancer every week.[2] But the good news is that the death rate from breast cancer has decreased since the mid-1990s. This is largely because more and more women are having mammograms, enabling earlier detection and treatment.

Breast cancer can also occur in men, although rarely; it's most commonly diagnosed in men over 60. In Canada, less than 1 percent of all breast cancers occur in men. Breast cancer risk factors, diagnosis and treatment are the same for both men and women.

What Causes Breast Cancer?

Simply put, cancer is a disease in which abnormal cells grow out of control. When enough of these cells accumulate, a tumour forms. Finally, if the cancer cells are able to break away from the tumour, they can spread to the lymph nodes or to other parts of the body and take up residence in another organ, a process called metastasis.

Every cell has a genetic blueprint called DNA (deoxyribonucleic acid). The DNA of cells contains genes that program cell reproduction, growth and repair of all body processes. Sometimes genes can become damaged by a mutation that occurs during normal cell division or by exposure to cancer-causing agents (carcinogens). Such damage can result in cancer. Flawed genes can be inherited from your parents. However, very few cancers are the result of inherited genes. Only 5 to 10 percent of breast cancers are inherited. Families that have genetic defects in one of two genes—breast cancer gene 1 (BRCA1) or breast cancer gene 2 (BRCA2)—have a much greater risk of developing both breast and ovarian cancer.

Breast cancer is not explained by genetics alone. Experts agree that cancer is the result of an interaction between genes and environmental factors. For instance, you might have a mutated gene that predisposes you to breast cancer, but, because you eat a low-fat diet with plenty of fruit and vegetables, the cancer may never express itself.

Who's at Risk?

The clearest risk factors for breast cancer are associated with hormonal and reproductive factors. It is thought that a woman's own estrogen promotes the growth and development of mutated breast cells. It seems that the longer breast tissue is exposed to the body's circulating estrogen, the greater the risk for breast cancer. Some risk factors you can't change, such as age and family history; others, including weight and poor diet, are within your control. The following risk factors make a woman more susceptible to breast cancer. Keep in mind, however, that just because you have one or more risk factors doesn't mean you'll get the disease.

- **Age.** Breast cancer risk increases with age. Close to 80 percent of breast cancers occur in women older than 50.
- **Previous breast cancer.** A history of breast cancer increases the odds that a woman will get breast cancer again, in the same breast or in the other breast.
- **Family history of breast cancer.** If you have a first-degree relative (a mother, sister or daughter) with breast or ovarian cancer, you have a greater chance of also developing breast cancer. In general, the more relatives you have who were diagnosed with breast cancer before menopause, the higher your own risk. If you have one first-degree relative who developed breast cancer before the age of 50, your own risk is doubled.
- **Genetic predisposition.** Defects in one of several genes, especially BRCA1 or BRCA2 genes, increase your risk of developing breast (and ovarian) cancer. Normally, these genes inhibit cancer development by making proteins that keep cells from growing out of control. Mutated genes are less effective at protecting from cancer.
- **Age of first pregnancy.** Women who have children before 30 years of age have a lower risk of breast cancer. Women who have their first child after 30 have a higher risk, and women who never have children are at an even greater risk.
- **Age of first period (menarche).** Onset of your period before 12 years of age is associated with a slightly higher risk of breast cancer.

- **Late menopause.** Women who menstruate for longer than 40 years have a slightly higher risk of breast cancer.
- **Exposure to radiation.** Ionizing radiation from X-rays or chest radiation therapy at a young age may increase the risk for breast cancer later in life.
- **Use of hormones.** Short-term use of hormone replacement therapy (HRT) for menopausal symptoms is considered safe. But taking the hormone combination of estrogen and progesterone for more than 4 years increases the risk of breast cancer. HRT also makes breast tumours harder to detect on a mammogram, leading to a cancer that is more advanced and difficult to treat. Estrogen-alone hormone therapy has not been shown to increase the risk of breast cancer in post-menopausal women.
- **Diet.** A growing body of research is finding a link between certain dietary factors and the risk of breast cancer. Diet may affect breast cancer development by either initiating cancer growth or promoting the growth of cancerous cells.
- **Alcoholic beverages.** Women who drink more than one alcoholic beverage per day have a greater risk of breast cancer than women who do not drink. Even consuming one drink per day is thought to slightly increase one's risk.
- **Excess weight.** Carrying extra body weight increases the risk of breast cancer, especially if that weight was gained during adolescence. The risk is even greater if weight gain occurs after menopause. Carrying excess weight around the abdominal area (i.e., apple shape) also increases the risk.

Preventing Breast Cancer

Beginning at age 20, all Canadian women should be performing monthly breast self-exams to detect physical changes in their breasts. Use the pads of your fingers to examine the tissue in your breasts and in your armpits. Be sure to also look carefully at your breast for any noticeable physical changes, such as a lump in the breast or underarm area, unusual breast swelling, change in colour or texture of skin on the breast, blood leakage from the nipple or inversion of the nipple. Any of these changes should prompt a visit to your family doctor.

Women aged 40 to 49 should have a clinic breast examination by a trained health care professional every 2 years. If you have a higher than average risk for breast cancer, you'll likely be screened more often and earlier (before age 40).

It's recommended that all Canadian women between the ages of 50 and 69 years have a mammogram every 2 years in addition to a clinic breast exam. A mammogram is a special X-ray of the breast that can catch breast cancer early and lead to a significant improvement in the chance of survival. Mammograms show detailed images and views of the breast taken from different angles.

Your doctor may advise a diagnostic procedure such as an ultrasound or biopsy to further characterize an abnormality found on a screening mammogram. An ultrasound uses sound waves to create an image of the breast. In a biopsy, a small sample of breast tissue is removed for analysis in a laboratory.

Dietary Strategies

Dietary factors such as fat, alcohol, fibre, fruit and vegetables have all been well studied.

Below, I list nutrition recommendations based on the current body of scientific evidence. Some of these strategies have strong research to support their adoption; others have evidence to suggest that they *may* be helpful.

Dietary Fat

It's long been thought that dietary fat may increase breast cancer risk by affecting estrogen metabolism. Studies have found that women who follow a low-fat, high-fibre diet have lower levels of circulating estrogen and less breast cancer.[3,4] A high-fat diet may lead to breast cancer by promoting weight gain and body fat accumulation, which in turn increases the risk of breast cancer.

While the hypothesis that a low-fat diet guards against breast cancer has existed for decades, only recently was it tested in a randomized controlled trial. The Women's Health Initiative Dietary Modification Trial, the largest long-term trial ever conducted, followed 48,835 post-menopausal women from across the United States, aged 50 to 79, for 8 years. Researchers assigned 40 percent of the women to a low-fat diet (20 percent of calories from fat) and an increased amount of fruit and vegetables (at least 5 servings per day) and grains (6 or more servings per day). The remaining women were assigned to the comparison group and were asked to not make any changes to their diets. After 8 years of follow-up, there was no overall difference in risk of breast cancer between women in the low-fat diet group and women in the comparison group. There were, however, signs that a woman's risk of disease could be modified by dietary change. Women in the low-fat group were 9 percent less likely to develop breast cancer than their peers in the comparison group, although this finding was not deemed statistically significant (it could

have been due to chance). A 9 percent reduction in breast cancer risk means that out of 10,000 women, 42 following the low-fat diet and 45 following their normal diets developed breast cancer each year.

The researchers did find, however, that the low-fat diet was associated with a 15 percent reduction in circulating levels of the hormone estradiol, the form of estrogen that increases the risk of breast cancer. Significant results were seen among women in the low-fat diet group who consumed the most fat at the beginning of the study. Women in these categories were 15 to 22 percent less likely to be diagnosed with breast cancer than women following their normal diets. Adopting a low-fat diet may help guard against breast cancer, especially among women who have a relatively high fat intake to begin with.[5]

A low-fat diet has also been shown to improve survival in women diagnosed with breast cancer. The Women's Intervention Nutrition Study, conducted among 2,437 women aged 48 to 79 with early-stage breast cancer, demonstrated that a low-fat diet consisting of 15 percent fat calories, or 33 grams of fat per day, can influence body weight and decrease breast cancer recurrence in women with estrogen receptor (ER)–negative breast cancer.[6] Cells with estrogen receptors grow and multiply when estrogen attaches to the receptors. After a breast cancer is removed, the cancer cells are tested to see if they have hormone receptors. If either estrogen or progesterone receptors are present, a response to hormonal therapy is very possible. About 75 percent of breast cancers are estrogen receptor (ER)–positive and 25 percent are ER–negative.

While the evidence is not concrete that reducing your fat intake will reduce breast cancer risk, it's prudent to limit your fat intake to 20 percent of daily calories if you're a post-menopausal woman. Women who have been diagnosed with ER–negative breast cancer should consume no more than 15 percent of daily calories from fat.

SATURATED FAT. Some studies show that higher meat intakes are linked with a greater risk of breast cancer. The harmful effect of meat may be because of its saturated fat content or because of the way it's prepared. Cooking meat at high temperatures forms compounds called heterocyclic amines, which have been shown to cause breast tumours in animals. This may hold true for women too. A University of Minnesota study found that women who ate hamburger, steak and bacon cooked well done were more than four times as likely to have breast cancer than women who enjoyed their meat cooked rare or medium done.[7] Until we know more about the effect of cooked meat, breast cancer experts advise that we consume no more than 3 ounces (90 g) of meat each day.

OMEGA-3 FATTY ACIDS. Research suggests that consuming plenty of fish for many years is associated with a lower risk of breast cancer. Studies conducted in the laboratory and in animals have demonstrated the ability of omega-3 fatty acids from fish to slow the growth of breast cancer and increase the effectiveness of certain chemotherapy drugs.[8] Three studies have reported lower risks of breast cancer among women who consume the most fish.[9] Aim to eat fatty fish like salmon and trout two times a week. If you don't like fish, consider taking a fish oil capsule that supplies 500 milligrams of DHA and EPA, the two omega-3 fatty acids found in fish.

Low Glycemic Index

Some evidence suggests that eating a low-glycemic diet guards against breast cancer. (The glycemic index is a measure of the rate at which a carbohydrate-containing food—starchy foods, fruit, milk and yogurt—is converted to glucose in the bloodstream. Low-glycemic foods release their sugar slowly and are linked with better health. See Chapter 1, page 6, for more information on the glycemic index.) A Canadian study of 49,613 women who were followed for nearly 17 years revealed that post-menopausal women who followed a high-glycemic diet were 87 percent more likely to develop breast cancer than women whose diet included mainly low-glycemic foods.[10] Glycemic index did not alter the risk of breast cancer among premenopausal women. It's thought that diets rich in high-glycemic carbohydrates lead to higher blood-glucose and insulin levels, which in turn increase breast cancer risk. Insulin may affect breast cells directly or increase the growth of cancerous cells.

Reduce your intake of foods with a high glycemic index such as white bread, white rice, white potatoes, refined breakfast cereals, cookies, cakes and candy. Instead choose low-glycemic options such as stone-ground whole-wheat bread, steel-cut oats, brown rice, pasta, legumes, citrus fruit, apples, pears and yogurt.

Soy Foods

Epidemiological studies reveal that Asians, who eat a high soy diet, have lower rates of breast cancer. Researchers attribute soy's possible protective effect to naturally occurring compounds called isoflavones. Once in the body, isoflavones behave like weak estrogen compounds and are able to attach to estrogen receptors in the breast. In so doing, they can block the ability of a woman's own estrogen from taking that spot. This means that breast cells have less contact with estrogen. A handful of studies have shown that a regular intake of soy isoflavones may lower circulating levels of estrogen, and this might reduce a woman's future risk of breast cancer. Other studies show that consuming a soy-rich diet can lengthen a woman's menstrual cycle, thereby influencing how much estrogen her breast cells are exposed to.

Whether an increased intake of soy foods will reduce the risk of breast cancer in Canadian women remains to be seen. Keep in mind that Asians generally have a low-fat diet and eat more fish and vegetables than North Americans do. It's also thought that Asian women might be more responsive to the effects of soy. But what might be most important is when you start consuming soy. Research conducted among women living in China and the United States suggests that consuming soy during childhood and adolescence is associated with a lower risk of breast cancer in adulthood. Soy isoflavones may confer their protective effects during puberty when breast cells are maturing and are more vulnerable to cancer-causing substances.[11,12]

Yet many women worry that because isoflavones have estrogen-like effects in the body, consuming soy may increase breast cancer risk. The concern is that soy isoflavones could increase a woman's total estrogen levels and encourage the growth of estrogen-dependent breast cancer, especially in women who already have the disease. Some studies conducted in animals and test tubes indicate that isoflavones inhibit the development of breast cancer, while other studies suggest they may increase breast cancer growth. It depends on the particular isoflavone studied (soybeans are rich in two different isoflavones) and the amount used. There's no compelling evidence that soy foods increase breast cancer, but research is ongoing.

Because we lack sufficient reliable information about the effect of soy foods in women with breast cancer, a history of breast cancer or a family history of breast cancer, soy should be used cautiously. Until more is known, avoid consuming large amounts of soy each day, and avoid using soy protein powders and isoflavone supplements. Consuming soy foods three times a week as part of a plant-based diet is considered safe. For ways to include soy in your diet, see Chapter 5, page 94.

Flaxseed

These tiny whole-grain brown and golden seeds contain natural plant estrogens called lignans. Once in the body, phytoestrogens from flaxseed have a weak estrogen action, and they are able to bind to estrogen receptors (just like soy isoflavones). In so doing, they appear to block the action of our body's own estrogen on breast cells. Animal studies conducted at the University of Toronto found that flaxseed has anti-cancer properties.[13,14] Researchers have demonstrated that giving women 1 or 2 tablespoons (15 to 30 ml) of ground flaxseed each day significantly lowered circulating estrogen levels.[15] In a study of post-menopausal women with newly diagnosed breast cancer, consuming 25 grams of flaxseed per day in the form of a muffin, versus a placebo muffin, significantly slowed the growth of breast tumours.[16] Lignans in whole grains may also inhibit the action of enzymes that are involved in the body's production of estrogen. To date, research on flaxseed has focused on estrogen receptor–negative breast cancers. The effect of flaxseed on estrogen receptor–positive breast cancer is unknown.

Aim to get 1 to 2 tablespoons (15 to 30 ml) of ground flaxseed each day. Grind your flaxseed in a clean coffee grinder or use a mortar and pestle. You can also buy pre-ground flaxseed at supermarkets and natural food stores. Once you grind flaxseed, store it in an airtight container in the fridge or freezer since the natural fats in flaxseed go rancid quickly if exposed to air and heat; it will keep for several months. Ground flaxseed can be added to many foods and recipes; for tips, see Chapter 5, page 89.

Vegetables

Hundreds of studies from around the world have shown that a diet high in vegetables lowers the risk of many cancers, including breast cancer. Researchers from Harvard University studied more than 89,000 women and found that those who ate more than 2.2 servings of vegetables a day had a 20 percent lower risk of breast cancer compared with those who ate less than 1 serving a day.[17] Another study in premenopausal women found that high total vegetable intake lowered the risk of breast cancer by 54 percent.[18]

Several studies hint that cruciferous vegetables such as broccoli, cauliflower and cabbage might be especially protective. Researchers have reported that women diagnosed with breast cancer have significantly lower intakes of cruciferous vegetables than their cancer-free peers. Triggered by the observation that breast cancer risk of Polish women rose threefold after they immigrated to the United States, scientists from Michigan State University recently decided to evaluate the diets of Polish immigrant women living in Chicago and Detroit. They found that women who ate at least 3 servings of raw or lightly cooked cabbage and sauerkraut per week had a significantly lower risk of breast cancer than those who ate only 1 serving per week.

Interestingly, consuming cabbage that had been cooked for a long time had no bearing on breast cancer risk.[19]

Cruciferous vegetables contain phytochemicals called glucosinolates, potent protectors against cancer development. When you eat cruciferous vegetables, glucosinolates are broken down by bacteria in the digestive tract and transformed into compounds called isothiocyanates and indole-3-carbinol. Isothiocyanates help eliminate cancer-causing substances by regulating the body's detoxification enzymes. Researchers suspect that the various compounds in cruciferous vegetables work together to promote a greater cancer-fighting effect.

Make sure you get at least 7 to 10 servings of fruit and vegetables each day. One serving is 1/2 cup (125 ml) of cooked or raw vegetable, 1 cup (250 ml) of raw greens or 1 piece of whole fruit. Aim for a minimum of 5 vegetable servings. Include 1 serving of cruciferous vegetable in your diet five times per week. Cruciferous vegetables include bok choy, broccoli, broccoli sprouts, broccoflower, broccolini, Brussels sprouts, cabbage, cauliflower, rutabaga and turnip.

Dietary Fibre

Evidence suggests that a high-fibre diet may offer protection from breast cancer. Toronto researchers found that 20 grams of fibre per day (the amount found in about 1 cup of 100% bran cereal) was associated with lower risk.[20] Fibre may help lower the risk of breast cancer by binding to estrogen in the intestine and causing it to be excreted in the stool. Every day, your intestine reabsorbs estrogen from bile, the compound that's released into your intestine from your gallbladder to help digest fat. If dietary fibre can attach to this estrogen and facilitate its removal from the body, your body has to take estrogen out of your bloodstream to make more bile. The net result is a lower level of circulating estrogen. It's possible that following a high-fibre diet for many years could lower your risk for breast cancer.

High-fibre diets also tend to be higher in antioxidant nutrients and lower in fat, both of which might help protect from breast cancer. People who eat plenty of fibre also tend to maintain a healthy weight. The studies suggest that dietary fibre works best if you follow a low-fat diet. So adding foods rich in wheat bran to a diet that's high in fat and low in fruit and vegetables probably won't do you much good.

Foods like wheat bran, whole grains and some vegetables contain mainly insoluble fibres (see Chapter 1 for more on insoluble fibre). Wheat bran has been studied the most in relation to breast cancer risk. To boost your intake of insoluble fibre and wheat bran, try the following:

- Strive for at least 7 servings of fruit and vegetables every day.
- Leave the peel on fruit and vegetables whenever possible.
- Eat at least 5 servings of 100% whole-grain foods each day.
- Buy a high-fibre breakfast cereal. Gradually add 1/2 to 1 cup (125 to 250 ml) of 100% bran cereal to your morning meal. One-half cup (125 ml) of 100% bran cereal contains 12 grams of fibre.
- Add 2 tablespoons (30 ml) of natural wheat bran or oat bran to cereals, yogurt, casseroles and soup.
- Add nuts and seeds to salads.
- Reach for high-fibre snacks like popcorn, nuts, dried apricots or dates.

To avoid intestinal distress, build up your fibre intake gradually. Be sure to drink 8 ounces of fluid with every high-fibre meal and snack.

Green Tea

There is a growing body of evidence to suggest that drinking green tea protects from certain cancers, including breast cancer. Recently, scientists combined the results from four studies examining the link between green tea and breast cancer—three from Japan and one from Los Angeles—and concluded that green tea is indeed protective. Compared with women who consumed less than 1 cup of green tea per day, those who drank at least 5 cups daily were 22 percent less likely to develop breast cancer.[21]

Drinking green tea might also improve a woman's prognosis once diagnosed with breast cancer. Japanese researchers discovered that among women with stage 1 and 2 breast cancer, drinking 5 or more cups daily lowered the risk of the cancer coming back by 46 percent. The researchers suspect that phytochemicals in green tea somehow modify breast cancer, making treatment easier and more successful.[22]

Like fruit and vegetables, green tea is a plant food and, as such, it contains natural chemicals that act as powerful antioxidants. The antioxidants in green tea leaves belong to a special class of compounds called catechins. By mopping up harmful free radical molecules in the body, catechins in tea may prevent damage to the genetic material of breast cells. Aim to drink 1 to 3 cups of green tea each day.

Alcoholic Beverages

The evidence is convincing that drinking alcoholic beverages increases the risk of breast cancer before and after menopause. A pooled analysis of 98 studies concluded that 1 drink per day increased a woman's risk by 10 percent.[23] Studies have also determined that the more drinks consumed, the greater the risk of breast cancer. The Million Women Study published in 2009 found that for every additional drink regularly consumed per day, the risk of breast cancer increased by 12 percent. All forms of alcoholic beverage—wine, beer and spirits—increased the risk equally.[24]

Alcohol may increase breast cancer risk in a number of ways. One of its metabolic by-products, acetaldehyde, may be carcinogenic. Alcohol may also make breast cells more vulnerable to the effects of carcinogens or it may enhance the liver's processing of these substances. Alcohol may inhibit the ability of cells to repair faulty genes and may also increase estrogen levels in the body.

Nutrition and cancer experts recommend that women not drink alcohol. If consumed at all, alcoholic drinks should be limited to 1 a day or 7 per week. If you do drink, ensure you are meeting your daily requirements of folate, a B vitamin that may help protect your breast cells from alcohol's harmful effects. See Chapter 4, page 41, for more information on folate requirements and best food sources.

Weight Control

Gaining weight after menopause is clearly linked with a higher risk of breast cancer. Among post-menopausal women, those who are obese have a risk of breast cancer about 50 percent higher than that of lean women. Women who are overweight and sedentary have an even greater risk. In a study of 38,660 women aged 55 to 74 years, those with the highest calorie intake, the highest body mass index (BMI) and the least physical activity had double the risk of breast cancer than women with the lowest calorie intake, the lowest BMI and the most physical activity.[25–31] The relationship between excess weight and breast cancer risk is most clearly seen after the age of 60. Obesity is thought to influence breast cancer risk by increasing circulating estradiol, the most potent form of estrogen in the body. Estradiol is positively associated with the risk of breast cancer in post-menopausal women.

World cancer experts advise maintaining your weight within a healthy BMI throughout adulthood. Steps should be taken to avoid adult weight gain and increases in waist circumference. If you are overweight or have gained excess weight since menopause, I strongly advise that you take action to lose weight. Start by determining your BMI (see Obesity, Overweight and Weight Loss, page 569).

Vitamins and Minerals

Carotenoids

A number of studies show that women who get the most beta carotene in their diet have a lower risk of breast cancer. The Harvard Nurses' Health Study found that premenopausal women who ate 5 or more servings of high-carotenoid fruit and vegetables per day had a lower risk of breast cancer than women who ate less than 2 servings per day.[32]

More recently, the Women's Health Initiative Observational Study from Los Angeles, California, revealed that among nearly 85,000 women, those with the highest intakes of beta carotene and lycopene were less likely to develop estrogen receptor–positive breast cancer than those who consumed the least. Other research has shown that women with higher blood levels of beta carotene and lycopene—a reflection of dietary intake—had about half the risk of breast cancer compared with women who had the lowest blood levels.[33,34] A diet rich in beta carotene fruit and vegetables may improve breast cancer survival.

More than 600 types of carotenoid compounds exist in plants, beta carotene in carrots, sweet potato and winter squash being the most plentiful. Other important carotenoids include alpha carotene, lycopene and lutein. Beta carotene and lycopene have an antioxidant effect in the body, which can help protect our genes from oxidative damage caused by free radicals. Some beta carotene is also converted to vitamin A inside the body. This vitamin is essential for proper cell growth and development and the normal function of the body's immune system. Research also suggests that these two carotenoids may trigger cancer cell death and inhibit the growth of breast cells.

To boost your intake of carotenoid-rich fruit and vegetables, use the list in Chapter 5, page 87. Aim for at least 1 serving per day.

Vitamin C

Although the research findings on vitamin C are less consistent than they are for beta carotene, evidence suggests you should be getting more vitamin C in your diet. This vitamin may keep women healthy by acting as an antioxidant, or it may work by enhancing the body's immune system. Vitamin C also plays an important role in synthesizing collagen, an important tissue in the breast.

The best food sources of vitamin C are citrus fruit, strawberries, kiwi, cantaloupe, broccoli, bell peppers, Brussels sprouts, cabbage, tomatoes and potatoes. To supplement, take 500 milligrams once or twice daily. Vitamin C is discussed in more detail in Chapter 4, page 48.

Vitamin D

Many studies have reported that higher levels of vitamin D in the bloodstream are linked with a lower risk of breast cancer. A study of 34,321 post-menopausal women also found that consuming more than 800 international units (IU) of vitamin D daily—versus less than 400 IU—was associated with protection from breast cancer.[35] Once consumed from foods or synthesized in the skin from sunlight, vitamin D acts like a hormone in the body and has been shown to have anti-cancer effects. In 2007, the first randomized controlled trial demonstrated vitamin D's cancer-fighting properties in women. In the 4-year study of 1179 healthy, post-menopausal women, researchers found that those taking 1110 IU of vitamin D per day, in conjunction with calcium, were 60 percent less likely to get cancers than their peers taking placebos.[36]

This finding—and the fact that Canadians don't produce enough vitamin D from sunlight from October to March—prompted the Canadian Cancer Society to recommend adults take 1000 IU of vitamin D per day in the fall and winter. Older adults, people with dark skin, those who don't go outdoors often and those who wear clothing that covers most of their skin should take the supplement year-round. To learn more about vitamin D supplements, see Chapter 4, page 50.

Folate

If you drink alcohol, be sure to meet your daily requirement for the B vitamin folate. A Harvard study found that among women who consumed 15 grams of alcohol per day (about a glass and a half of beer or wine), those with the highest daily intake of folate (600 micrograms) had a 45 percent lower risk for breast cancer than women who consumed the least folate (150 to 299 micrograms a day).[37] It's thought that alcohol interferes with the transport and metabolism of folate and may deprive body tissues of this B vitamin, which is essential to DNA synthesis.

The best food sources of folate include spinach, lentils, orange juice, asparagus, artichokes and whole-grain breads and cereals. To supplement, take a multivitamin and mineral that supplies 400 micrograms (0.4 milligrams) of folic acid. I don't advise taking more than 400 micrograms from a supplement since some research hints that high intakes of folic acid might stimulate the growth of certain pre-cancerous lesions. For more information about folate and folic acid, see Chapter 4, page 40.

Nutrition Strategy Checklist for Preventing Breast Cancer

☐ Eat a low-fat diet
☐ Limit meat intake; avoid well-cooked meat
☐ Fish
☐ Low-glycemic foods
☐ Soy foods
☐ Flaxseed
☐ Fruit and vegetables
☐ Foods rich in beta carotene and lycopene
☐ Dietary fibre
☐ Green tea
☐ Vitamin D
☐ Multivitamin/mineral
☐ Avoid alcohol
☐ Manage your weight

Recommended Resources

Canadian Breast Cancer Foundation
www.cbcf.org
This website is primarily advocacy related; however, it does provide useful links and bulletin boards for women to access.
375 University Avenue, 6th Floor
Toronto, ON M5G 2J5
Tel: 416-596-6773 or 1-800-387-9816

Canadian Breast Cancer Network
www.cbcn.ca
This website is primarily advocacy related; however, it does provide useful links and bulletin boards for women to access.
331 Cooper Street, Suite 602
Ottawa, ON K2P 0G5
Tel: 613-230-3044
Fax: 613-230-4424
Email: cbcn@cbcn.ca

Canadian Cancer Society
www.cancer.ca
10 Alcorn Avenue, Suite 200
Toronto, ON M4V 3B1
Tel: 416-961-7223 or 1-888-939-3333 (Cancer Information Service)
Fax: 416-961-4189
Email: ccs@cancer.ca

Sunnybrook and Women's College Health Sciences Centre and The Centre for Research in Women's Health
www.womenshealthmatters.ca
Women's College Hospital
76 Grenville Street
Toronto, ON M5S 1B2
Email: info@womenshealthmatters.ca

National Cancer Institute (www.nci.nih.gov)
www.cancer.gov
6116 Executive Boulevard
Room 3036A
Bethesda, MD, USA 20892-8322
Tel: 1-800-332-8615 or 1-800-422-6237

Bronchitis

Bronchitis is a common respiratory condition that affects most people at least once in their lives. It's caused by viruses or bacteria and often develops after a bout of the common cold (see page 294). Normally, bronchitis is a mild illness that heals completely in a few weeks. However, it can be a serious problem for the elderly or for people with heart or lung disease.

What Causes Bronchitis?

Bronchitis results from an inflammation of the tiny bronchial tubes that line the main air passages of the lungs. Infections produced by viruses or bacteria will damage these tubes, causing swelling and excess mucus production. The inflammation narrows the airways, which rapidly become clogged with mucus. These obstructions reduce the movement of air in and out of the lungs, limiting the amount of oxygen that can enter the bloodstream to nourish vital organs. The swollen bronchial tubes also are responsible for the telltale wheezing and coughing that is so characteristic of bronchitis.

Most cases of infectious, or acute, bronchitis clear up within 6 weeks. (Acute bronchitis is generally caused by lung infections—90 percent are viral in origin and 10 percent are bacterial.) The bronchial tubes will take longer to heal if there is additional damage caused by cigarette smoking. Allergies, inhaled irritants, air pollution and chronic conditions such as sinusitis may also cause recurring bronchial infections.

For some people, bronchitis develops when stomach acids back up into the esophagus and enter the lungs, a condition known as gastroesophageal reflux disease (see page 405). In children, bronchitis may be the result of enlarged tonsils and adenoids.

Sometimes, inflammation of the bronchial tubes becomes a permanent condition reoccurring frequently. This is known as chronic bronchitis and is a serious health problem that endangers the lungs and can be potentially life threatening. Chronic bronchitis is a cough that persists for 2 to 3 months each year for at least 2 years. Unlike acute bronchitis, chronic bronchitis does not clear up in a matter of weeks. It is caused by inflammation that scars the lungs, limiting the exchange of old air for new. Chronic bronchitis is characterized by an ongoing, irritating cough and excessive mucus production that can last for months at a time, sometimes requiring hospitalization. Cigarette smoking is the most common cause of chronic bronchitis but industrial pollution is another culprit.

Symptoms

Symptoms of bronchitis include:

- persistent cough that is frequent and produces mucus, or sputum, which may be clear, yellow or green (indicating a secondary bacterial infection) or blood-streaked
- shortness of breath
- wheezing sound when breathing may or may not be present
- chest pain, soreness or rattling in the chest
- fever may or may not be present
- sore throat
- lack of energy
- back and muscle aches

The symptoms of acute bronchitis can also be confused with those of asthma or pneumonia. If coughing and wheezing persist for more than 2 weeks or are accompanied by a high fever and shortness of breath, specific testing by your doctor may be necessary to determine which condition is responsible for your respiratory problems.

Who's at Risk?

People who smoke are more likely to get bronchitis and to take longer to recover from it than non-smokers. Children of cigarette smokers are also more prone to bronchitis. Others at risk include:

- people who are exposed to others suffering from acute bronchitis
- people suffering from chronic conditions that compromise the immune system
- people suffering from gastroesophageal reflux disease
- people who are exposed to lung irritants at work, especially dust particles and chemical fumes

Conventional Treatment

There are several ways to treat bronchitis, including:

- bed rest
- increased fluid intake
- over-the-counter cough medicine only if prescribed by your doctor (coughing is productive in ridding the lungs of excess mucus)
- use of a humidifier to loosen mucus and relieve coughing
- antibiotics if a bacterial infection is present (evidenced by yellow or green sputum) or in cases of pre-existing lung disease
- acetaminophen or aspirin to reduce fever

- avoidance of exposure to cold, damp environments
- avoidance of exposure to air pollution and inhaled irritants
- reduction or cessation of cigarette smoking

Managing Bronchitis
Dietary Strategies
Fruit and Vegetables
Fruit and, particularly, vegetables contain many vitamins, minerals and antioxidants that may protect the lungs. One study conducted among 46,000 people over the age of 15 found that those who had the highest intake of vegetables had a 31 percent lower risk of bronchitis than those who ate the least.[1] Aim to consume at least 4 vegetable servings per day. Evidence suggests that vegetables rich in vitamin C may offer the most protection. Try to include at least two 1/2 cup (125 ml) servings of broccoli, Brussels sprouts, cabbage, bell peppers, tomato juice or potatoes in your daily diet.

Food Allergies
Chronic bronchial infections may be caused by food allergies. In one study, patients with bronchitis who eliminated problematic foods identified by allergy testing experienced a 70 percent improvement in symptoms.[2] To determine if food allergies trigger ongoing bouts of bronchitis, try an elimination/challenge diet as outlined below. You may want to seek the help of a registered dietitian (www.dietitians.ca) to help determine food allergies.

1. **Elimination phase.** For a period of 2 weeks, eliminate common food allergens: dairy products, soy foods, citrus fruit, nuts, wheat, shellfish, fish, eggs, corn and sulphite food additives.

2. **Challenge phase.** After 2 weeks, start introducing one food every 3 days. Keep a food and symptom diary in which to record everything you eat, amounts eaten and time you ate the food or meal. Document any symptoms, the time of day you started to feel the symptom and the duration of time you felt the symptom. If symptoms recur when a particular food is added back, you or your child may be allergic. Consult your doctor for further food allergy testing.

Vitamins and Minerals

Vitamin A
This vitamin plays an important role in maintaining healthy lung tissue and immune function. Some research suggests that a diet poor in vitamin A increases the risk of airway obstruction.[3] To prevent this, ensure you are meeting your daily vitamin A requirements by including liver, oily fish, milk, cheese and egg yolks in your diet. Some beta carotene, a natural compound found in dark-green and orange produce, is converted to vitamin A in the body. Consuming foods rich in beta carotene also contributes to your daily vitamin A. Reach for carrots, sweet potato, winter squash, broccoli, collard greens, kale, spinach, apricots, cantaloupe, peaches, nectarines, mango and papaya.

Your diet and a multivitamin and mineral supplement will provide all the vitamin A you require each day. High dose vitamin A supplements are not recommended, since too much vitamin A taken for an extended period can produce toxic effects. If you smoke, do not take high dose beta carotene supplements; doing so has been linked with a greater risk of lung cancer. The amount of beta carotene added to a multivitamin is considered safe.

Vitamin C
Oxidative damage to the lungs caused by air pollution and cigarette smoke can contribute to bronchitis. Consuming adequate amounts of the antioxidant vitamin C can reduce such damage. Vitamin C is also needed for the production of infection-fighting compounds in the body. Studies have revealed that lower levels of vitamin C in the body were associated with bronchitis symptoms in adults.[4,5] Researchers have also found that supplementing with vitamin C can help treat symptoms of acute bronchitis, especially in the elderly, who may have low dietary intakes of the vitamin.[6]

The best food sources of vitamin C are citrus fruit, strawberries, kiwi, cantaloupe, broccoli, bell peppers, Brussels sprouts, cabbage, tomatoes, tomato juice and potatoes. To supplement, take 200 to 500 milligrams of vitamin C once or twice daily. For more information on vitamin C, see Chapter 4, page 48.

Magnesium
It is thought that a low intake of magnesium is somehow related to the development of chronic bronchitis. Magnesium appears to influence the contraction–relaxation state of bronchial smooth muscle. One study conducted in over 2600 adults found that individuals who consumed the most magnesium from foods reported less wheezing in the previous year.[7] Higher magnesium intakes were also associated with a reduction in hyperactivity of the bronchial passages.

To prevent a magnesium deficiency, include the following foods in your diet: nuts, seeds, legumes, prunes, whole-grain cereals, leafy green vegetables and brewer's yeast. Magnesium is lost when grains are refined, so a diet high in refined or processed foods will be lacking magnesium.

To supplement, take 200 to 250 milligrams of magnesium citrate once daily. If you take calcium supplements, buy one with added magnesium. To learn more about magnesium supplements, see Chapter 4, page 62.

Zinc

This mineral plays an important role in maintaining a healthy immune system, and a deficiency can increase the chances of respiratory infections. One large study found that a lower level of zinc in the bloodstream was associated with bronchitis in adults.[8] A recent review of 17 studies conducted in children under 5 years of age found that zinc supplementation was associated with fewer episodes of respiratory tract infections.[9]

The best food sources of zinc include oysters, seafood, red meat, poultry, yogurt, wheat bran, wheat germ, whole grains and enriched breakfast cereals. Your diet and a good multivitamin and mineral supplement will give you all the zinc you need to stay healthy. Single supplements of zinc in high doses can have toxic effects, including copper deficiency, heart problems and anemia. Consuming more than 40 milligrams of zinc per day can depress your immune system, making you more susceptible to infection. If you do take a separate zinc supplement, be sure it has copper added and do not exceed 40 milligrams of zinc per day.

Herbal Remedies

Echinacea

Many studies in the laboratory have shown the ability of echinacea to enhance the body's production of white blood cells, which fight infection. To treat acute bronchitis, buy a product made from echinacea root. To ensure that you're buying a high-quality product, look for a statement of standardization.

Take a total of 900 milligrams three to four times daily. For tinctures (1:5), take 1 to 2 millilitres three times daily. Take echinacea until your symptoms are relieved, then continue taking two to three times daily for 1 week. Some experts recommend taking the herb once every 2 hours (300 milligram standardized extract or 3 to 4 millilitres of a tincture) until symptoms have subsided, then up to three times daily for a week. See Chapter 7, page 132, for more information about echinacea.

Garlic (*Allium sativum*)

Garlic contains many different sulphur compounds, and one in particular, S-allyl cysteine (SAC), has been shown to stimulate the body's immune system and help ward off infection. Use one-half to one clove of garlic per day in cooking. If raw garlic irritates your stomach, use an aged garlic extract supplement. This type of garlic is concentrated in S-allyl cysteine and has lost the irritating sulphur compounds during the aging process; it is also odourless. Take 2 to 6 capsules per day, in divided doses.

Myrtol (Essential Oils)

This standardized combination of three essential oils has been studied for its effectiveness in acute and chronic bronchitis. The product contains cineole from eucalyptus, d-limonene from citrus fruit and alpha-pinene from pine. Short-term use of this essential oil supplement in acute bronchitis has been shown to result in a more rapid recovery compared with placebo pills and to a comparable recovery compared with standard prescription medications.[10,11] In chronic bronchitis, 4 weeks of myrtol use has been associated with a reduced frequency and severity of coughing and expectoration and a reduced need for antibiotics. The usual dose is 300 milligrams taken three or four times daily.

Other Natural Health Products

N-Acetyl Cysteine

This supplement is a modified form of cysteine, an amino acid found in protein-rich foods. N-acetyl cysteine is used by the body to make glutathione, a potent antioxidant that protects cells from the harmful effects of free radicals. Studies suggest that it may be very helpful for cigarette smokers with chronic bronchitis. A review of nine well-controlled studies on N-acetyl cysteine and bronchitis concluded that the supplement could indeed reduce flare-ups.[12] It was originally believed that N-acetyl cysteine may help break up mucus; however, scientists now feel that it may work in other ways to help treat bronchitis, such as killing bacteria that cause lung infection.[13]

The recommended dose is 400 to 1200 milligrams per day. The supplement is well tolerated but occasional side effects may include nausea and diarrhea. Safety of this supplement has not been evaluated in young children or pregnant and breastfeeding women.

Nutrition Strategy Checklist for Bronchitis

- ☐ Vegetables and fruit
- ☐ Identify food allergies
- ☐ Foods rich in vitamin A and beta carotene
- ☐ Vitamin C
- ☐ Magnesium
- ☐ Zinc
- ☐ Echinacea
- ☐ Garlic
- ☐ N-acetyl cysteine

Recommended Resources

The Canadian Lung Association
www.lung.ca
1750 Courtwood Crescent, Suite 300
Ottawa, ON K2C 2B5
Tel: 1-888-566-LUNG (5864)
Fax: 613-569-8860
Email: info@lung.ca

American Academy of Family Physicians
www.familydoctor.org

Mayo Foundation for Medical Education and Research
www.mayoclinic.com
This website is produced by a team of writers, editors, health educators, nurses, doctors and scientists, and is one of the best patient-education sites on the Internet. The information is reliable, thorough and clearly written.

Burns

The entire surface of your body is covered with a vital, sensitive tissue that we know as skin. Composed of three main layers—the epidermis, the dermis and the subcutis—skin acts as a protective barrier against toxins, bacteria and injury. Although skin is normally a strong defender of the body, skin cells and tissue can be easily burned and damaged when exposed to heat at temperatures higher than 50°C (120°F). The most common causes of burn are contact with fire, hot liquids and steam, but contact with sun exposure, electricity and chemicals can also result in burn.

When skin tissue is burned, the blood vessels in the tissue leak fluid, causing swelling. If burns are extensive, large amounts of fluid may be lost, triggering the body to go into shock. Shock can be a life-threatening condition because it causes a dangerous drop in blood pressure, which restricts blood flow to the brain and other vital organs.

In some cases, internal organs can be burned, even when the skin is not affected. For example, inhaling smoke or hot air during a fire can burn the lungs. Swallowing hot liquids or chemical substances can injure the esophagus and stomach. Electrical burns are particularly deceiving. While burning of the skin may be quite minimal, the damage to tissue and organs underneath the skin may be extensive. Electrical shocks can also injure the heart and may paralyze breathing or disturb the heart rhythm, leading to cardiac arrest.

The severity of a burn depends on the amount of tissue affected and the depth of the injury. Burns are classified as first, second or third degree, depending on the amount of damage to body tissues. Healing depends on the location and the depth of the burn. Approximately 85 percent of all burns are minor and can be treated at home or at a doctor's office.

Symptoms
First Degree Burns

This is the least serious type of burn. Only the outer layer of skin (epidermis) is affected. The skin may redden and there may be swelling and pain. First degree burns heal quickly; the dead layers of skin drop off in a few days and the epidermis regrows to cover the layers of tissue below the skin surface. Little or no scarring results from first degree burns.

Second Degree Burns

These burns cause deeper damage than first degree burns. They affect the epidermis and some of the second layer (dermis) of skin. The skin becomes intensely reddened and splotchy. Blisters, severe pain and swelling develop. A minor second degree burn covers an area no larger than 2 to 3 inches (5 to 7.5 cm) in diameter. It is not serious and will heal in a short time. A major second degree burn covers a larger area or is on the hands, feet, face, groin, buttocks or a major joint. It is serious and requires immediate medical attention.

Third Degree Burns

This type of burn is always serious as it involves all three layers of the skin. Nerves, fat tissue, muscle and bone may also be affected. The burned area may appear white and soft or black, charred and leathery. Generally these burns aren't painful because nerve endings in the skin have been destroyed. Deep burns injure the dermis and may be life threatening. Healing is very slow and scarring is considerable.

Burned areas are more susceptible to infection. Signs of infection include increased pain, fever, redness, swelling or oozing. If infection develops, medical attention is necessary immediately.

Who's at Risk?

Children and the elderly are most likely to experience serious burns because their skin is thinner. In fact, children in North America account for more than 35 percent of all fire and burn injuries and deaths. Fires and burns are the second-leading cause of accidental death for children under age 4, and the third-leading cause of death for all children under age 19.

Conventional Treatment
First and Second Degree Burns

- Cover the burned area with cold water or cold, wet cloths for 10 to 15 minutes or until the pain lessens.
- Do not apply ice—putting ice directly on a burn can cause frostbite, further damaging the skin.
- Do not apply creams or lotions to the area as they may interfere with proper healing.
- Do not apply pressure to the burned area.
- Cover the burned area with a light, dry, sterile dressing.
- Non-prescription pain relievers, such as aspirin, ibuprofen or acetaminophen, may help relieve temporary discomfort.
- Do not attempt to remove burned clothing that has become stuck to the skin.
- Do not break blisters or peel off damaged skin. Exposing tissues underneath the burned area increases the risk of infection.
- If blisters break, wash the area with mild soap and water, then apply an antibiotic cream and cover with a dry, sterile dressing. Change the dressing daily.

Third Degree Burns

- Call 911 for emergency medical services.
- Before the tissues swell, remove tight clothing that is not stuck to the skin, plus all jewellery, belts and shoes. Do not remove burnt clothing.
- Do not apply ointments or antiseptic creams.
- Cover the burned area with a clean, dry dressing.

- Elevate injured areas higher than the heart to reduce swelling.
- If breathing has stopped, check for blocked airways and perform CPR.
- To prevent a life-threatening loss of body fluids, intravenous fluids are essential. If medical assistance is delayed, give the burn victim frequent, small cold drinks to replace fluid loss.
- Skin grafting, plastic surgery and physical therapy may be necessary to complete the healing process.

Prevention Strategies

Burns are frequently caused by preventable accidents in the home. Studies indicate that death from fires is less common in homes equipped with smoke detectors. Take the following safety precautions to protect yourself and your family from injury:

- Equip each floor in your home with a smoke detector.
- Check smoke detector batteries annually.
- Practise fire drills and escape routes regularly.
- Keep a fire extinguisher in the kitchen.
- Keep hot foods and drinks out of reach of young children.
- When cooking, turn pot handles towards the back of the stove.
- Avoid holding young children in your lap when drinking hot liquids or smoking cigarettes.
- Keep young children safe by covering electrical outlets and blocking access to electrical devices.
- Check appliances regularly for frayed electrical wiring.
- Store potentially dangerous chemicals in childproof cabinets.

Managing Burns
Dietary Strategies

Nutrition plays a critical role in burn treatment. A healthy diet is needed to provide an adequate amount of nutrients in order to replace losses, promote the healing of burns and reduce the chances of infection. Certain nutrients and antioxidants are able to lessen the inflammation and compromised immune function that result from burns. Diet should also provide enough calories and protein to minimize the muscle wasting associated with serious burns and caused by the body's healing response.

A High-Calorie, High-Protein, Low-Fat Diet

Burns cause the body to go into a hypermetabolic state (in which the body burns calories at a much faster than normal rate). The degree of increased calorie burning depends on the severity of the burn, the degree of inflammation, body composition and age. It has been reported that adults who are severely burned need to increase their daily calorie needs by twice the normal amount, and young children suffering from serious burns can need up to four times more calories.[1,2] The more serious the burn, the faster the body uses nutrients. In the case of major burns, muscle protein tissue is used by the body for energy, and this leads to a progressive loss of muscle mass. Diets should provide 1.5 to 2 grams of protein per kilogram of body weight per day. (Healthy sedentary people require 0.8 grams of protein per kilogram of body weight.)

Many studies show that low-fat diets (where fat makes up only 15 percent of daily calories) can help promote healing and shorten the length of hospital stays.[3-5] Too much fat can depress the body's immune system, increasing the likelihood of infection. It is also important that a large portion of daily fat comes from omega-3 fats found in oily fish.[6,7] Once consumed, these fats are used by the body to produce anti-inflammatory immune compounds that help speed healing.

Major burns require hospitalization. A registered dietitian working in the burn unit will ensure that burn patients receive the appropriate amount of protein, carbohydrate and fat from a special diet or, in cases when eating by mouth is not possible, by tube feeding or intravenous feeding. Often, liquid supplements such as Ensure or Boost and nutrient-dense snacks are necessary to maintain a high-calorie intake during the day.

Vitamins and Minerals
Multivitamin and Mineral Supplement

Since wound healing increases the body's need for many nutrients, a multivitamin and mineral supplement is recommended for adults and children suffering from minor or major burns.

Vitamin A

This fat-soluble vitamin is important for wound healing as it helps the layers of the skin fight infection by preventing the invasion of bacteria and viruses. Vitamin A also promotes cell division in the skin. The best sources of vitamin A include liver, oily fish, milk, cheese, butter and egg yolks. Foods rich in beta carotene, such as orange and dark-green produce (carrots, sweet potato, winter squash, broccoli, collard greens, kale, spinach, apricots, cantaloupe, peaches, nectarines, mango and papaya), also provide the body with some vitamin A.

For major burns, a daily vitamin A supplement is advised: 10,000 international units (IU) for adults and 5000 IU for children.

High-potency multivitamin and mineral supplements often provide 5000 IU per day.

Vitamins C and E

Vitamin C has three important roles in wound healing: It is needed for healthy scar formation, it acts as an antioxidant and protects the body from inflammatory free radical damage, and it enhances the immune system. Research in patients with major burns shows that vitamin C can decrease free radical damage caused by burns and reduce tissue swelling.[8]

Some of the best food sources of vitamin C are citrus fruit, strawberries, kiwi, cantaloupe, broccoli, bell peppers, Brussels sprouts, cabbage, tomatoes and potatoes. Include at least two of these foods in your daily diet to promote healing of minor and major burns. In the case of major burns, take a vitamin C supplement: adults, 500 milligrams twice daily and children, 250 milligrams twice daily.

Like vitamin C, vitamin E also acts as an antioxidant in the skin and can protect cell membranes from damage induced by burns.[9] Food sources include vegetable oils, almonds, peanuts, soybeans, whole grains, wheat germ, avocado and green leafy vegetables. To get higher amounts of vitamin E, a supplement is necessary. Take 200 to 400 IU natural source vitamin E per day to help promote burn healing.

Zinc, Selenium and Copper

These trace minerals are involved in scaveng-ing harmful free radicals and are needed in increased amounts following a burn. They also play an important role in supporting the body's immune system. Studies suggest that including these minerals in dietary treatment of major burns can reduce infection, lessen protein breakdown in the skin and shorten hospital stays.[10-14] Good food sources are as follows:

- **Zinc:** Oysters, seafood, red meat, poultry, yogurt, wheat bran, wheat germ, whole grains, enriched breakfast cereals
- **Selenium:** Seafood, meat, organ meats, wheat bran, whole grains, nuts, Brazil nuts, onion, garlic, mushrooms, Swiss chard, orange juice
- **Copper:** Liver, meat, shellfish (especially oysters), legumes, nuts, prunes, whole grains, dark green vegetables, sweet potatoes

For minor first degree burns, diet and a multivitamin and mineral pill will provide you with adequate amounts of these minerals. For major burns, research suggests that supplemental doses help speed healing: 40 milligrams of zinc with 4 milligrams of copper once daily; 200 micrograms of selenium once daily.

Herbal Remedies

Gotu Kola (*Centella asiatica*)

This herb has long been used in India and Indonesia to promote wound healing. It seems to promote the formation of healthy connective tissue. Although no randomized controlled studies have been conducted, a number of clinical reports and small studies suggest that the herb does help burns heal.[15]

Buy a product standardized for 40 percent asiaticoside, 30 percent asiatic acid, 30 percent madecassic acid and 1 percent to 2 percent madecassoside. Take 20 to 60 milligrams three times daily. The herb is not associated with any side effects other than the occasional skin rash. Safety in pregnant and breastfeeding women and young children has not been established.

Aloe Vera

The gel made from this plant has a long history of use in wound and burn healing; current science suggests it be used for the treatment of first and second degree burns. A 2007 review of four studies enrolling 371 patients concluded that burn healing time among those using aloe vera was almost 9 days shorter than patients in the control group.[16-19]

The active ingredients in the aloe vera inhibit the activity of bradykinin, a pain-producing substance. Aloe vera also seems to reduce inflammation and to possess antibacterial and antifungal properties.

For burns, buy a gel or cream that contains 0.5 percent aloe. Apply liberally as needed three to five times per day.

Calendula (Calendula officinalis L.) and Chamomile (Matricaria recutita L.)

Both of these herbs have an anti-inflammatory action and creams made from them have been used to promote the healing of minor burns. Apply one of these creams to the affected area one to four times daily.

Other Natural Health Products

Ornithine Alpha-Ketoglutarate (OAK)

This compound is made in the body from two amino acids—ornithine and glutamine—found in high-protein foods such as meat, poultry, fish, eggs and dairy products. Studies in burn patients show that when taken as a supplement, OAK results in reduced muscle breakdown and better wound healing.[20-22] This supplement is not intended for the treatment of a major burn—an injury that causes the body to go into a catabolic, or tissue breakdown, state.

Based on the research, the recommended dose for adults is 10 grams taken twice daily. Be sure to buy a product from a reputable manufacturer.

Nutrition Strategy Checklist for Burns

☐ High-calorie, high-protein, low-fat diet (major burns)
☐ Multivitamin/mineral
☐ Foods rich in vitamin A and beta carotene
☐ Vitamin C
☐ Vitamin E
☐ Zinc and copper
☐ Selenium
☐ Aloe vera gel
☐ Ornithine alpha-ketoglutarate

Recommended Resources

Canadian Paediatric Society
www.cps.ca
This site offers good general tips on safety in the home.
2305 St. Laurent Blvd.
Ottawa, ON K1G 4J8
Tel: 613-526-9397
Fax: 613-526-3332

Mayo Foundation for Medical Education and Research
www.mayoclinic.com
This website is produced by a team of writers, editors, health educators, nurses, doctors and scientists, and is one of the best patient-education sites on the Internet. The information is reliable, thorough and clearly written.

Shriners Hospital for Children
www.shrinershq.org/
2211 North Oak Park Ave.
Chicago, IL, USA 60707
Tel: 773-622-5400
Fax: 773-385-5453

Candidiasis

Your body is home to a wide variety of micro-organisms. Invisible to the naked eye, microscopic colonies of bacteria and fungi live on or in your skin, intestines and genitals—actually, they can be found almost anywhere in the body. Many of these micro-organisms are essential to maintaining good health. An intricate system of checks and balances keeps the size of these microbial colonies under control and ensures that all the normal flora in your body live in harmony.

If something disturbs this natural harmony, certain bacteria or fungi colonies can grow out of control, overwhelming your immune system and causing infections or other health problems. The *Candida* group of fungi is a prime example of a harmless micro-organism that can cause persistent health problems if its growth is not kept in check.

Candida is a type of yeast that normally lives in the mouth, vagina and gastrointestinal tract and on the skin. Bacteria that live in the same areas of the body as candida control growth of this yeast. If these bacteria are harmed or destroyed in any way, such as with antibiotic use, candida colonies can grow to unusually high levels. The overgrowth of candida disrupts natural bodily functions, causing a fungal infection known as candidiasis.

Candida albicans, a common type of candida yeast, is the usual culprit behind candidiasis, but several other types of candida can also cause the infection. *Candida albicans* is considered an opportunistic organism because it spreads only when the conditions for growth are ideal. The most common types of candidiasis are:

ORAL: an infection affecting the mucus membranes of the mouth and tongue, commonly known as oral thrush

VAGINAL: a yeast infection that often develops during pregnancy or when taking oral contraceptives with high estrogen content

CUTANEOUS: an infection of the skin; in infants, it often causes diaper rash

But candidiasis can develop on the surface of almost any mucus membrane. In most cases, the infection does not penetrate very far into the body. However, under certain conditions, the candida yeast can enter the bloodstream, where it causes a condition known as invasive or systemic candidiasis. Once in the bloodstream, the fungus is carried to all parts of the body, spreading deep into joints, muscles and organs such as the liver, heart, kidneys or eyes. If not properly treated, it can cause serious harm, such as blindness, heart damage, eating problems and organ failure. In rare instances, it may even lead to death. People at risk of developing invasive candidiasis are surgical patients, low-birth-weight babies and people with malfunctioning immune systems, particularly those with HIV, AIDS or leukemia.

Scientists are beginning to explore the possibility that candidiasis may be linked to chronic fatigue syndrome (see page 280), a serious medical condition that has been associated with other systemic infections, such as Epstein-Barr syndrome. At this time, however, there is no evidence to prove that the two conditions are connected.

What Causes Candidiasis?

Factors that have been blamed for candidiasis include intestinal disorders such as "leaky gut syndrome," inadequate stomach acid and digestive enzymes, vitamin and mineral deficiencies and a weakened immune system. Until further research has been completed, it is difficult to say for certain that these factors result in candidiasis.

What is becoming clear, however, is the strong association between yeast infections and antibiotic use. Antibiotics disrupt or destroy the healthy bacteria that naturally keep the candida fungus under control. By changing the normal balance between these two organisms, antibiotics encourage the overgrowth of candida.

There is also a strong connection between yeast infections and the hormone estrogen. Over 75 percent of all women experience a yeast infection at least once during their reproductive years. Vaginal infections are a common complaint among pregnant women and among women who take oral contraceptives with a high estrogen content. An increased level of estrogen produces changes in the internal environment of the vagina, creating conditions that encourage candida to grow and flourish.

Like all types of fungi, candida thrives in warm, moist environments. It flourishes under diapers, in the folds of skin (particularly the skin of obese people) and in the areas between fingers and toes. Candida is an infectious condition and can be passed from one person to another. A pregnant woman with a vaginal yeast infection may transfer the infection to her newborn baby, leaving the baby with oral thrush or a yeast diaper rash. A vaginal yeast infection may also be transferred to a male sexual partner, where the organisms can cause an itchy rash on the penis. Swimming pool surfaces, showers, clothing or combs all provide easy routes for transferring the infection. In some cases, invasive candidiasis may enter the bloodstream through medical instruments or other devices used in surgical or hospital treatment.

While most episodes of candidiasis can be cleared up fairly easily with medications or over-the-counter treatments, sometimes the infection can be very persistent and recur frequently—candida organisms that have become resistant to antibiotic treatment may cause such infections.

Symptoms

VAGINAL CANDIDIASIS (VAGINAL YEAST INFECTION). Symptoms include:

- abnormal vaginal discharge, which may be white and watery or thick and chunky, like cottage cheese
- itching and burning sensations in the vaginal area
- red, inflamed skin around the vaginal area
- pain during intercourse and urination

ORAL CANDIDIASIS (THRUSH). Symptoms include:

- cracks in the corner of the mouth
- white patches on the mouth and tongue and inside the cheeks
- small pinpoints of bleeding when patches are rubbed
- in an infant, fussiness and irritability and possibly difficulty feeding

CUTANEOUS CANDIDIASIS (SKIN INFECTION/ DIAPER RASH). Symptoms include:

- itching that may be quite intense
- red, tender rash

- spots or lesions may be scaly or blistered and pimple-like
- rash usually develops in skin folds, around the buttocks or genitals, or under the breasts

SYSTEMIC CANDIDIASIS. Symptoms are not specific and will vary depending on which area of the body is affected. They may include:

- fever and chills that don't improve after antibiotic treatment (these are the most common symptoms)
- fatigue and a general feeling of ill health
- memory loss, short attention span
- depression, mood swings

Who's at Risk?

The following may be more likely to develop candidiasis:

- females, especially those who use high-estrogen oral contraceptives
- pregnant women
- people taking broad-spectrum antibiotics or corticosteroid medications or corticosteroid inhalers
- elderly individuals
- people in poor general health
- people with diabetes
- people with a medical condition that compromises the immune system, such as HIV, AIDS or leukemia
- patients undergoing chemotherapy
- infants born to mothers with vaginal yeast infections
- obese people (cutaneous candidiasis)
- people who have been hospitalized (systemic candidiasis is the fourth most common bloodstream infection among hospitalized patients in the United States)
- people who wear dentures (oral candidiasis)

- people using antibacterial mouthwash excessively (oral candidiasis)
- people taking medications that cause dry mouth (oral candidiasis)

Conventional Treatment

Topical antifungal treatments, used directly on the skin or inside the mouth or vagina, are the most common way to clear up a candida infection. These include mouthwashes, lozenges, shampoos and creams or vaginal inserts. Topical treatments may be messy to use and may take slightly longer to produce results but they have almost no side effects. Oral antifungal medications or injections also may be prescribed to treat candidiasis. They are more convenient and act faster but may cause side effects. Invasive candidiasis is treated with intravenous or oral medications.

Improving the health of the immune system, particularly for people with diabetes, may help control the infection and prevent recurrences.

Preventing Candidiasis

Because the *Candida* fungus lives naturally in our bodies, it is impossible to avoid. However, the following suggestions may help keep the fungus under control and prevent future infections.

VAGINAL CANDIDIASIS. Suggestions for control and prevention include:

- Wear underwear and pantyhose with a cotton crotch; synthetic fabrics don't breathe as well as cotton and keep moisture trapped in the genital area.
- Avoid wearing tight-fitting slacks, which block air circulation and keep the genital area excessively moist.

- Don't wear wet bathing suits or sweaty exercise clothes for long periods; wash them after every use.
- Keep the vaginal area clean by washing with unscented soap. Avoid using vaginal sprays or douches.

CUTANEOUS CANDIDIASIS. The following may help:

- Follow good hygiene practices to keep the skin clean, dry and clear of infection.
- Wear loose-fitting clothing made of natural fibres to allow air to circulate over the skin.
- Wash hands thoroughly after contact with any fungal infection.
- Obese people may find that exercise and weight loss reduce the number of skin infections.

ORAL CANDIDIASIS. Suggestions that may help:

- If you wear dentures, leave them out overnight, or for at least 6 hours daily. Constant wearing of dentures, and not taking them out at night, is thought to be one of the commonest causes of oral thrush. Clean and disinfect dentures daily. See a dentist if your dentures don't fit well.
- Sip water frequently during the day if you take medication that causes a dry mouth.
- Regularly sterilize all soothers, mouth toys and bottles used by your baby.

TO PREVENT DIAPER RASH. Suggestions include:

- Always change wet or soiled diapers immediately.
- Rinse cloth diapers several times to remove traces of soap, and avoid using fabric softeners that can irritate the skin.

- If possible, let your baby go without a diaper for a few hours every day to allow the skin to dry thoroughly.
- Protect your baby's skin with a diaper cream or ointment.

Dietary Strategies

Natural health practitioners recommend many of the nutritional strategies listed below. With the exception of fermented milk products, no published studies could be found to show that the following foods and supplements are effective in the treatment and/or prevention of candida yeast infections. Most of the recommendations below are based on laboratory studies and clinical experience. The rational and appropriate use of nutritional supplements for managing candidiasis should be determined in consultation with your health care provider.

Dietary Sugar

Since the *Candida* organism thrives on sugar, the first step to recovering from a candida infection is to eliminate all simple sugars and refined starchy foods from your diet.[1,2] Avoid table sugar, cookies, cakes, desserts, candy, chocolate, fruit drinks, soda pop, syrup, corn syrup, jam, fruit juice, dried fruit and large portions of sweet fruit such as bananas and grapes. Refined starchy foods made with white flour should also be avoided, including white bread, crackers, low-fibre breakfast cereals, cereal bars, granola bars and white pasta.

Dietary Fibre

An anti-candida diet should consist of whole grains (brown rice, whole-wheat pasta, whole-grain breads and cereals), legumes (lentils, kidney beans and chickpeas), vegetables and small quantities of whole fruits (not fruit juice). These foods provide dietary fibre, which will help ease bloating, constipation, diarrhea and gas. As you increase your fibre intake, be sure to drink at least 8 to 10 glasses of water per day.

Psyllium–seed-husk powder is a water-soluble fibre that helps keep the intestinal tract healthy. It is available in health food stores. Mix 1 to 2 tablespoons (15 to 30 ml) into 2 cups (500 ml) of water before consuming to prevent bloating and constipation.

Fermented Milk Products

Yogurt, kefir and acidophilus milk are referred to as probiotic foods because they all contain friendly lactic acid bacteria that are normally resident in the intestinal tract. There, they prevent disease-causing microbes from attaching by taking up space and producing substances that prevent microbe growth. A number of studies have shown that women who consume yogurt or fermented milk beverages each day have a significant reduction in vaginal yeast infections.[3-7] (Some studies have found a yogurt douche helps treat these yeast infections.) Most trials support the effectiveness of two specific probiotic bacteria called *Lactobacillus acidophilus* and *Lactobacillus rhamnosus*. A 16-week randomized controlled trial conducted in 276 elderly people found that consuming 50 grams of a probiotic cheese—versus a placebo cheese—once daily significantly decreased the prevalence of oral candida infections.[8]

Consume 1 cup (250 ml) of plain yogurt or kefir each day to restore the microbial balance of your intestinal tract. You can also take a daily supplement that contains lactic acid bacteria (see Chapter 8, page 180, for information on probiotic supplements).

Eat foods that contain fructo-oligosaccharides (FOS), a type of carbohydrate that promotes the growth of lactic acid bacteria, especially bifidobacteria, in the gut. Jerusalem artichokes, asparagus and soybeans contain these compounds, which pass undigested through the small intestine to the colon, where they are fermented and exert their health effects. Supplements of FOS are available. A typical dose is 4 to 10 grams per day.

Food Allergies

Candida infections are often associated with food allergies, especially allergies to foods containing yeast or fermented foods that contain fungi, such as cheese, breads and beer. Alternative health practitioners frequently suggest avoiding these foods to help clear up symptoms of candida infections. Despite a great deal of discussion and several books on the subject, there is still no scientific proof to support these claims or to establish a clear link between candidiasis and food allergies.

However, many people do find that avoiding certain foods reduces symptoms, especially gastrointestinal discomfort from bloating, constipation, diarrhea and gas. Try staying clear of yeast and mould-containing foods (e.g., leavened breads, brewer's yeast, beer, cheese, tomato paste) to see if you feel better. Alcohol and caffeine-containing foods and beverages may also aggravate symptoms.

You might consider getting tested for food allergies. ELISA and RAST blood tests are used by many nutritional physicians to assess food sensitivities.

Vitamins and Minerals

The following nutrients are important for a healthy immune system and may help treat and prevent candida infections:

VITAMIN C. Food sources include citrus fruit, strawberries, kiwi, cantaloupe, broccoli, bell peppers, Brussels sprouts, cabbage, tomatoes and potatoes. To supplement, take 500 milligrams of vitamin C once or twice daily.

VITAMIN E. Food sources include vegetable oils, almonds, peanuts, soybeans, whole grains, wheat germ, avocado and green leafy vegetables, especially kale. To supplement, take 100 to 400 international units (IU) of natural vitamin E per day. Buy a vitamin E supplement made with "mixed tocopherols."

ZINC. Food sources include oysters, seafood, red meat, poultry, milk, yogurt, wheat bran, wheat germ, whole grains and enriched breakfast cereals. To supplement, take a multivitamin and mineral once daily. Most brands supply 10 to 15 milligrams of zinc.

Herbal Remedies

Garlic (Allium sativum)

A daily intake of fresh garlic, with its accompanying sulphur compounds, has been used to enhance the body's immune system and kill many types of bacteria and fungi.[9-12] One-half to one clove per day is recommended. Crushed garlic can also be combined with yogurt and used as a vaginal douche to treat candida infections.

Supplements made from aged garlic extract have been shown to stimulate immunity. You can purchase liquid drops or capsules of aged garlic (Kyolic brand) at health food stores and drug stores. Take 300 to 600 milligrams three times daily with meals. If you don't like to swallow pills, add drops of aged garlic to your foods.

Echinacea

Laboratory studies have shown that active compounds in echinacea called polysaccha-

rides have anti-candida properties. The herb may prevent the recurrence of candida once it is treated with antifungal drugs. Echinacea also enhances the body's production of white blood cells that fight infection.

To treat a candida infection, choose a standardized extract of echinacea to ensure quality. For products made from echinacea root, take a total of 900 milligrams three to four times daily. For tinctures (1:5), take 1 to 2 millilitres three times daily. For teas, take 125 to 250 millilitres three to four times daily. Take until symptoms are relieved, then continue taking two to three times daily for 1 week.

Don't use echinacea if you're allergic to plants in the Asteraceae/Compositae family (ragweed, daisy, marigold and chrysanthemum). Although the issue is controversial among experts, the herb is not recommended for use by people with autoimmune diseases (HIV, lupus), multiple sclerosis, diabetes or asthma.

Other Natural Health Products

Acidifying Supplements

These products are thought to help treat candida infections by enhancing the acidity of the stomach. Try one of the following supplements with each meal (do not take on an empty stomach):

- **Grapefruit seed extract**
- **Betaine hydrochloride**, 325 to 650 milligrams taken with each meal
- **Apple cider vinegar**, 1 tablespoon (15 ml) mixed into water, sipped with each meal
- **Glutamic acid**
- **Vitamin C**, 500 milligrams three times per day with meals

Excess stomach acid can lead to heartburn and possibly ulcers. Try these supplements only after consultation with your natural health care provider.

Digestive Enzymes
Digestive enzymes help break down carbohydrate, protein and fat. They may help people who suffer from gastrointestinal distress after eating. But they may also help digest candida in the intestinal tract, thereby controlling its growth. Take 1 capsule after each meal for 3 days. If your symptoms don't improve, increase your dose to 2 capsules. Some people require 3 capsules per meal. I highly recommend Sisu brand digestive enzymes. Sisu products are plant-based enzymes that are active in a wide pH range.

Do not take digestive enzymes if you have ulcers or an inflammatory bowel disease (Crohn's disease, ulcerative colitis).

Nutrition Strategy Checklist for Candidiasis

- ☐ Eliminate sugars and sweets
- ☐ Foods rich in fibre
- ☐ Psyllium seed husks
- ☐ Fermented milk products
- ☐ Probiotic supplement
- ☐ Vitamin C
- ☐ Vitamin E
- ☐ Zinc
- ☐ Multivitamin/mineral
- ☐ Garlic
- ☐ Echinacea
- ☐ Digestive enzymes

Recommended Resources
National Candida Society (UK)
www.candida-society.org.uk
This site is not scientifically based and is member-run, but you may find it helpful.
P.O. Box 151
Orpington
Kent, UK BR5 1UJ
Tel: +44 (0)1689-813039
Email: info@candida-society.org

Canker Sores

Canker sores are small, shallow lesions or ulcers that appear on the inside of the mouth. Irritating and painful, they usually develop on the tongue, the inside of the cheeks or lips, and at the base of the gums. Canker sores are not contagious. They are quite different from cold sores, which are highly contagious and caused by the herpes simplex virus (see page 450).

Simple canker sores are the most common type of mouth ulcer. They appear singly or in clusters and typically last 7 to 14 days. You may develop simple canker sores as often as three or four times a year. Complex, or major, canker sores are less common but more problematic. People suffering from major canker sores will have large ulcers in their mouths almost constantly, with new sores developing as old ones heal. The large canker sores often heal with extensive scarring.

What Causes Canker Sores?

In any given year, up to 50 percent of the population will experience at least one outbreak of canker sores. Yet despite the fact that it afflicts so many people, the precise cause of this annoying ailment is still unknown. Current thinking indicates that the following factors may be responsible for depressing the body's immune system and triggering an outbreak:

- stress
- an impaired immune system
- tissue injuries caused by biting the tongue or the inside of the mouth, dental appliances, sharp tooth surfaces, hot food, toothbrushes or eating utensils
- food allergies or sensitivities to specific types of food, such as citrus fruits, strawberries, pineapple, tomatoes, cheese, chocolate, coffee, almonds, peanuts or wheat
- nutritional deficiencies such as B12, zinc, folate or iron
- disease of the gastrointestinal tract such as celiac disease and inflammatory bowel disease

Symptoms

A tingling or burning sensation will be felt at the affected spot before the actual sore develops. A sore then appears as a round, white spot with a red border. Canker sores can be very painful, and the discomfort can become worse if you rub the sore with your tongue or eat hot or spicy food. Complex canker sores may cause fever, fatigue and swollen lymph nodes.

The following symptoms may be signs of more serious conditions that require medical treatment. Contact your doctor if:

- your sores last 3 weeks or longer
- you have persistent, multiple or unusually large mouth sores
- you have signs of spreading infection or spreading sores
- you have recurring sores, with new ones developing before the old ones heal

- you develop high fever with new canker sores

Who's at Risk?

Females are twice as likely as males to develop canker sores. Teenagers suffer from canker sores more often than do adults, possibly because their immune systems are not fully developed. Most people experience their first outbreak between 10 and 40 years of age. As well, those with a family history of canker sores are at higher risk—more than 42 percent of people with canker sores have a first-degree relative with the condition. If both parents are affected, the likelihood of their children developing canker sores is 90 percent. Susceptibility to the ailment seems to run in families either because of genetics or shared food or environmental allergies. People who are under stress and run down are also at higher risk.

Conventional Treatment

Canker sores will usually heal by themselves. There is no really effective treatment, but there are some things you can do to help ease the pain:

- Avoid spicy, acidic or abrasive foods.
- Brush teeth gently to avoid irritating the sores.
- Rinse your mouth with salt water or baking soda and water (1 teaspoon/5 ml of baking soda per 1/2 cup/125 ml warm water).
- Apply ice to the affected area.
- Apply an ointment containing topical anesthetic.
- Apply an ointment that provides a protective coating, such as glycerine.
- Cover lesions with a paste made of baking soda and water.

- Severe outbreaks may be treated with a prescription mouthwash, corticosteroid ointment, prednisone tablets or a lidocaine anesthetic solution.

Managing Canker Sores
Dietary Strategies
Food Allergies

Since food sensitivities may trigger the development of canker sores, it may be helpful to be tested for allergies if you have recurring sores. In one study of patients with canker sores who were previously diagnosed as sensitive to food additives, half showed improvement when certain foods were removed from the diet.[1] If you suspect certain foods may be causing your mouth sores, speak to your doctor about food allergy testing. If you have already determined likely culprits in your diet, follow the elimination/challenge diet below to confirm your suspicions. Keep in mind, though, that some foods may trigger a canker sore only in the presence of stress or some other factor that contributes to canker development.

1. **Elimination phase.** For a period of 2 weeks, eliminate suspected food allergens, such as citrus fruits, nuts, wheat or corn.
2. **Challenge phase.** After 2 weeks, start introducing one food every 3 days. Keep a food and symptom diary in which you record everything you eat, amounts eaten and what time you ate the food or meal. Document any symptoms. If the food causes a canker to develop, omit it from your diet.

Gluten-Free Diet

Some people with recurrent mouth ulcers may benefit from a gluten-free diet. In fact, mouth sores may be the only presenting symptom of celiac disease, a condition in which the gluten protein in wheat, rye and barley is toxic to the body. Removing gluten from the diet has also been found to improve symptoms in people without celiac disease.[2,3] For more information about the gluten-free diet, refer to Celiac Disease, page 269.

Vitamins and Minerals
B Vitamins

Several studies have shown that deficiencies of a number of B vitamins, including B1, B2, B6, B12 and folate, are associated with recurring canker sores. Replacement of the deficient nutrients has improved symptoms in some people.[4-8] To determine if such a deficiency is the cause of your canker sores, ask your doctor about testing your blood for these nutrients. In the meantime, ensure that your daily diet contains adequate amounts of these B vitamins:

B1 (THIAMIN). Food sources include pork, liver, whole grains, enriched breakfast cereals, legumes and nuts.

B2 (RIBOFLAVIN). Food sources include milk, yogurt, cottage cheese, fortified soy and rice beverages, meat, whole grains and enriched breakfast cereals.

B6. Food sources include meat, poultry, fish, liver, legumes, nuts, seeds, whole grains, green leafy vegetables, bananas and avocados.

B12. Food sources include animal foods such as meat, poultry, fish, eggs and dairy products as well as fortified soy and rice beverages.

FOLATE. Food sources include spinach (cooked), lentils, orange juice, whole grains, fortified breakfast cereals, asparagus, artichoke, avocado and seeds.

To ensure that you're meeting your daily requirements (see Chapter 4, page 32), take a multivitamin and mineral supplement. If a blood test indicates you're deficient in one or more B vitamins, you may also take a B complex supplement that contains the whole family of B vitamins in higher amounts than a regular multivitamin pill.

Iron
Some research shows that an iron deficiency may trigger canker sores. To prevent a deficiency of this mineral, make sure you're eating iron-rich foods such as lean red meat, seafood, poultry, eggs, legumes, whole grains, enriched breakfast cereals and blackstrap molasses. If a blood test reveals you have an iron deficiency or you are anemic, your doctor or dietitian will recommend a single iron supplement to replenish your stores. The dose and duration of iron supplementation will depend on the extent of your iron deficiency. For more information about iron supplementation to treat an iron deficiency, see Anemia, page 208.

A daily multivitamin and mineral will usually supply 10 milligrams of iron. If a blood test reveals that you're deficient in this mineral, your doctor will recommend single iron supplements for 6 to 12 weeks to replenish your body's stores.

Herbal Remedies
Licorice (*Glycyrrhiza glabra*)
This herb may be useful in treating canker sores as it has anti-inflammatory and anti-

allergic properties. Licorice contains many active ingredients, but one, called glycyrrhizin, can cause fluid retention, high blood pressure and potassium loss when taken in high amounts. However, an altered form of licorice, deglycyrrhizinated licorice (DGL), doesn't appear to have these negative side effects and is believed to be safe. Studies have shown that DGL can reduce the pain and speed the healing rate of canker sores.[9]

To treat cankers, chew one to three 380 milligram DGL tablets before each meal and at bedtime. Be forewarned: The taste may be unpleasant to some people.

A randomized controlled trial has also shown that using a dissolving adhesive mouth patch treated with licorice root extract is effective at reducing lesion size and pain. After 8 days, 81 percent of people using the patch reported no pain compared with 40 percent of people who did not get the treatment.[10] These patches, or discs, can be purchased over the counter as Cankermelts-GX.

Other Natural Health Products
Probiotics
Supplements of friendly bacteria known collectively as lactic acid bacteria may help clear up and prevent canker sores. Lactic acid bacteria such as L. *acidophilus* and bifidobacteria normally reside in the intestinal tract, where they prevent disease-causing microbes from attaching. Many studies have found that supplementing with these bacteria protects the gastrointestinal tract and boosts the body's immune system.

To supplement, take 1 billion to 10 billion viable cells, in three or four divided doses, with meals. For more information about probiotic supplements, see Chapter 8, page 180. Lactic acid bacteria are found in fermented dairy products such as yogurt, kefir and acidophilus milk.

Nutrition Strategy Checklist for Canker Sores

☐ Identify food allergies
☐ Multivitamin/mineral
☐ Foods rich in B vitamins
☐ Foods rich in iron
☐ Deglycyrrhizinated licorice
☐ Probiotic supplement

Recommended Resources

Mayo Foundation for Medical Education and Research
www.mayoclinic.com
This website is produced by a team of writers, editors, health educators, nurses, doctors and scientists, and is one of the best patient-education sites on the Internet. The information is reliable, thorough and clearly written.

Cataracts

Imagine processing over one and a half million messages, all at the same time. Your eyes—those complex, sensory organs hard-wired to your brain—are capable of accomplishing this difficult feat. Containing over 70 percent of the body's sensors, your eyes gather visual images and send them directly to the brain, providing you with much of the information you need to perceive and understand the world around you.

Your eyes are designed to be extremely light sensitive because they need light to create clear, sharp visual images. Light enters through the cornea, the transparent outer surface of the eye, and passes through the pupil to reach the lens. The lens then focuses the light on the retina at the back of the eye, creating a visual message that is transmitted to the brain. To keep the light properly focused on the retina, the lens changes shape, becoming flatter or rounder depending on the distance between the eye and the viewed object.

Normally, the lens of the eye is clear and transparent, allowing light to travel directly to the retina. The lens must be clear for the retina to receive a sharp image. When the lens is cloudy due to a cataract, the passage of light to the retina is obstructed, causing vision to become blurry. Cataracts can develop in one or both eyes and usually progress very slowly and painlessly. They are the leading cause of blindness throughout the world, especially among older people.

What Causes Cataracts?

Cataracts are a natural part of the aging process and are most common in people over 65 years of age. While people can develop cataracts in their 40s and 50s, it's not until after the age of 60 that the majority of cataracts impair vision. Almost all cataracts are caused by a change in the chemical composition of the lens. Proteins within the lens become damaged and clump together, producing the characteristic clouding of vision. Some of these chemical changes are caused by free radicals, unstable oxygen molecules that are created through normal bodily functions. Free radicals can damage proteins in the eye and are thought to play a major role in cataract development.

Other factors that can contribute to cataracts include:

• diabetes (one study found that women with diabetes were four times more likely to develop cataracts than women with normal blood-glucose levels[1])

- atopic dermatitis or prolonged eye inflammation
- cigarette smoking and alcohol use
- injuries or blows to the eye
- prolonged use of corticosteroid medications
- a hereditary predisposition to cataracts
- prolonged exposure to sunlight, ultraviolet light or infrared rays
- a diet lacking in protective nutrients

The degree of vision loss that accompanies a cataract depends on where the cataract occurs and how mature or dense it is. If the cataract develops on the outer edge of the lens, it may not cause any vision problems for a long time. If it develops in the centre of the lens, then your vision will become hazy, fuzzy and blurry. Eventually, a cataract will interfere with your ability to read, drive or work. Some people reach this stage faster than others, depending on their sensitivity to the changes in their vision.

With improvements in technology and surgical techniques, cataracts can usually be successfully removed and replaced with a clear artificial lens. More than 90 percent of people who have cataract surgery end up with improved vision.

Symptoms

Symptoms of cataracts include:

- blurry or hazy vision; double vision
- colours appear faded
- sensitivity to light and glare
- seeing halos around lights
- poor night vision
- need for brighter light when reading and working

- frequent changes in eyeglass prescriptions
- change in pupil colour from the normal black to yellowish or white

Occasionally, swelling in the lens and increased pressure in the eye may develop.

Who's at Risk?

Adults 65 years of age or older are at greater risk of developing cataracts, as are those people with a family history of cataracts. Other factors that may increase risk are, as mentioned above, eye injuries or blows to the eye; prolonged use of medications, such as corticosteroids; excessive exposure to sunlight, ultraviolet light or radiation; cigarette smoking; and alcohol consumption.

Conventional Treatment

Surgery is the most effective treatment. Two types of cataract surgery are most common:

1. **Phacoemulsification or phaco.** A special instrument breaks up the cataract with ultrasound waves; the fragmented pieces are then vacuumed out of the eye.
2. **Extracapsular surgery.** Through a small incision in the lens capsule, the central portion of the lens is removed and smaller portions are vacuumed out.

After the cataract is removed, an artificial lens implant (intraocular lens) is inserted into the eye to focus light on the retina. Vision improves within 1 to 2 days and improvement continues for approximately 4 weeks. Most people who needed eyeglasses before cataract surgery will still need them after. In some cases, instead of an implanted intraocular lens, contact lenses or eyeglasses replace the natural lens. The procedure is usually very safe and quite successful.

Preventing Cataracts

Since cigarette smoking generates free radicals, one of the most important ways to prevent cataracts is to quit smoking. Research has shown that compared with nonsmokers, those who smoke at least 20 cigarettes per day have almost a threefold higher risk for cataracts.[2] Giving up the habit may reverse some of the damage to the lens of the eye. Researchers from Harvard University found that, compared with male smokers, former male smokers had almost a 25 percent reduced risk for cataract.[3]

It's also important to protect your eyes from sunlight whenever possible by wearing a hat and sunglasses that offer UVA and UVB protection.

Dietary Strategies

Weight Control

Studies find that people who are overweight have a higher risk of cataract formation.[4-7] People with a body mass index (BMI) of 27.8 or greater have twice the risk for cataracts compared with those whose BMI is 22 or less. Even being moderately overweight with a BMI of 25 to 27 appears to increase one's risk. And carrying extra weight around the middle seems to be more predictive of cataracts than lower body fat. Researchers believe that restricting your calorie intake may in some way slow the development of cataracts.

Excess body fat may contribute to cataract formation by increasing the level of blood uric acid and, as a result, the risk of gout (see Gout, page 414). Obesity also increases inflammation in the body, which is thought to increase the risk of cataract. Finally, carrying excess weight

also increases the risk of type 2 diabetes, a condition strongly related to early cataract formation.

To calculate your BMI, see Obesity, Overweight and Weight Loss, page 569. If your BMI is greater than 25, take steps to reduce excess weight.

Carbohydrates: Low Glycemic Index

Studies suggest that diets made up of predominantly high glycemic carbohydrate–rich foods (e.g., a high glycemic load diet) increase the risk of developing cataracts. In one study of 3654 healthy men and women aged 49 years and older, those whose diet had the highest glycemic load were 77 percent more likely to develop cataracts over 10 years than their peers who consumed a low glycemic diet. As well, research suggests that consuming a high quantity of carbohydrates may also boost cataract risk.[8-10] Diets with a high glycemic load are associated with elevated blood glucose. Once glucose passes into the lens of the eye, it is used very slowly for metabolic reactions. High blood-glucose levels in the lens may increase cataract risk by causing oxidation and damaging proteins.

To reduce the glycemic load of your diet, choose foods that have a low glycemic index such as whole-grain breads, brown rice, pasta, steel-cut oats, legumes, nuts, citrus fruit, yogurt, milk and soy beverages. See Chapter 1, page 6, for more on the glycemic index.

Omega-3 Fatty Acids

There's some evidence that consuming a higher intake of omega-3 fatty acids from diet reduces the risk of cataract. The Blue Mountains Eye Study found that among 3654 men and women, those who consumed the most—versus the least—omega-3 fatty acids were 42 percent less likely to develop a cataract.[11] Omega-3 fatty acids, especially DHA, are critical for proper visual development in infants. Also, deficiencies of these fats in adults can lead to impaired vision. Studies suggest that prolonged deficiencies may increase the risk of damage to the retina. Omega-3 fatty acids may also play a role in helping eye fluids drain, which helps regulate intraocular pressure.

To increase your intake of omega-3 fatty acids, eat oily fish such as salmon, trout, sardines and herring at least twice per week. If you don't like fish, consider taking a fish oil capsule that supplies 300 to 600 milligrams of DHA plus EPA combined.

Lutein- and Zeaxanthin-Rich Foods

Lutein and zeaxanthin are naturally occurring plant compounds related to beta carotene, the carotenoid found in carrots. Once consumed, they make their way to the eye where they act as antioxidants and protect both the lens and retina from oxidative damage. Studies have found that people who consume the most lutein from their diet have a 20 percent to 50 percent lower risk of developing cataracts or having cataract surgery compared with those who consume the least. Two large studies from Harvard University found that men and women with the highest intakes of lutein had a 20 percent lower risk of cataracts compared with those who consumed the least.[12–14] Broccoli, spinach and kale were most often associated with protection.

Scientists speculate that an intake of 6 to 15 milligrams of lutein plus zeaxanthin per day is optimal for eye health. Average intakes of lutein and zeaxanthin in North America, however, are below levels associated with cataract prevention. The best sources of lutein and zeaxanthin include kale, Swiss chard, collard greens, green peas, broccoli, romaine lettuce, Brussels sprouts, nectarines and oranges.

There is some evidence that supplementing with 15 milligrams of lutein per day can improve vision in people with age-related cataracts.[15] Choose a supplement made with FloraGLO, a high-quality, patented lutein extract purified from marigold flowers that's been used in clinical studies. For more information about lutein and lutein supplements, see Chapter 8, page 171.

Sodium

Research suggests that a high-sodium diet can increase the risk of cataracts by as much as twofold.[16] Aim to consume no more than 2300 milligrams of sodium (equivalent to 1 teaspoon/5 ml of table salt) per day. Avoid processed foods and salty snacks and limit your consumption of restaurant meals. See Chapter 5, page 108, to learn the sodium content of selected foods.

Alcohol

For reasons that aren't clear, drinking alcohol is linked with a higher risk of cataracts, particularly in men. Studies show that compared with no drinking, daily drinking or consuming more than seven drinks a week is associated with a significantly higher likelihood of cataracts.[17–19] A recent study conducted in almost 80,000 women did not find that drinking up to two drinks per day was associated with cataracts.[20] That said, I recommend limiting your intake of alcohol to no more than one drink per day, whether you're male or female.

Vitamins and Minerals

Multivitamin and Mineral Supplements

A few studies have linked regular use of a multivitamin and mineral pill to a lower risk of cataracts. In the Blue Mountains Eye Study, use of multivitamin supplements was linked with a 40 percent lower risk of cataracts. A study of 478 Boston women also found that those whose diets provided the most vitamins C and E, folate, riboflavin, beta carotene and lutein had a significantly lower risk of cataracts than women who consumed the least.[21–25]

Broad-based multivitamin and mineral supplements can help you meet your recommended daily intakes for antioxidant nutrients, including vitamins C and E, selenium and B vitamins. Take one multivitamin and mineral pill each day with a meal.

Vitamin C

This antioxidant nutrient is concentrated in the eye, where it protects the lens from oxidative damage caused by free radicals. Studies show that high blood vitamin C levels are linked with a lower risk of cataract disease.[26–28] A Tufts University study of 492 healthy American women found that a high vitamin C intake and long-term use of vitamin C supplements offered substantial protection from cataracts. Women under the age of 60 who consumed at least 362 milligrams of vitamin C per day—versus less than 140 milligrams— were 57 percent less likely to develop cataracts. Taking a vitamin C supplement for at least 10 years was associated with a 60 percent lower risk.[29]

Based on the evidence available, it appears that intakes higher than the official recommended intake are required to help prevent cataracts. To increase your intake, aim to include three vitamin C–rich foods in your daily diet. To supplement, take 500 milligrams of vitamin C once or twice daily. There is some concern that high dose vitamin C supplements might induce kidney stones in people with a history of stones or in individuals with kidney disease. In these cases, it's prudent to limit your dose to 100 milligrams per day. See Chapter 4, page 49, for more information on vitamin C–rich foods and supplements.

Vitamin E

Diets rich in vitamin E and vitamin E supplements may also help lower the odds of cataract development. Vitamin E works with vitamin C and other antioxidant compounds in the eye to ward off free radical damage. Research has shown that low blood levels of vitamin E are linked with almost a fourfold increase in the risk of early cataract formation. One study determined that regular use of a vitamin E supplement reduced the risk of cataract by one-half.[30–33] However, vitamin E may not help you if you're a current smoker. A study from Finland found that extra vitamin E made no difference to cataract risk in older men who smoked at least twenty cigarettes per day.[34]

To increase your dietary intake of vitamin E, reach for vegetable oils, almonds, peanuts, soybeans, whole grains, wheat germ, wheat germ oil, avocado and green leafy vegetables. To supplement, take 100 to 400 international units (IU) of natural vitamin E per day. If you have existing cardiovascular disease or diabetes, avoid high dose vitamin E supplements.

Herbal Remedies

Bilberry (Vaccinium myrtillus)

This herbal remedy contains anthocyanins, antioxidant compounds that may help preserve eye health. The anthocyanins in bilberry are thought to improve blood flow in the tiny capillaries of the eye. A handful of well-controlled studies found that compared with the placebo treatment, bilberry significantly improved eye health in people with diabetes-related eye complications.[35,36]

Buy a product standardized to 25 percent to 36 percent anthocyanins. Take 160 milligrams twice daily. For more information on bilberry, see Chapter 7, page 125.

Other Natural Health Products

Grapeseed Extract and Pycnogenol
Like bilberry, both grapeseed extract and Pycnogenol contain potent antioxidants called anthocyanins that may be helpful in protecting the eye. Grapeseed extract is more readily available than Pycnogenol, and it's less expensive. For general antioxidant protection, take 50 milligrams once daily.

Lutein
If you don't eat 7 to 10 servings of fruit and vegetables (combined) each day, you may want to consider taking lutein supplements. Buy a high-quality product that's made with the FloraGlo extract. Take 5 to 10 milligrams once daily with a meal that contains some fat (carotenoids are best absorbed in the presence of dietary fat). See Chapter 8, page 171, for more on this carotenoid.

Nutrition Strategy Checklist for Cataracts

- ☐ Quit smoking
- ☐ Maintain a healthy weight
- ☐ Low-GI carbohydrate-rich foods
- ☐ Omega-3 fatty acids
- ☐ Limit sodium
- ☐ Limit alcohol
- ☐ Multivitamin/mineral
- ☐ Vitamin C
- ☐ Vitamin E
- ☐ Lutein
- ☐ Lycopene
- ☐ Bilberry
- ☐ Grapeseed extract

Recommended Resources

Canadian Ophthalmological Society
www.eyesite.ca
610–1525 Carling Avenue
Ottawa, ON K1Z 8R9
Tel: 613-729-6779 or 1-800-267-5763
Fax: 613-729-7209
Email: cos@eyesite.ca

American Academy of Ophthalmology
www.aao.org
P.O. Box 7424
San Francisco, CA, USA 94120-7424
Tel: 415-561-8500
Fax: 415-561-8533

National Eye Institute
National Institutes of Health, HHS
www.nei.nih.gov
2020 Vision Place
Bethesda, MD, USA 20892-3655
Tel: 301-496-5248

Celiac Disease (Gluten Intolerance)

The simple pleasures that most of us take for granted, such as enjoying a slice of bread, a plate of pasta or the sweet temptation of cookies, can be the source of acute discomfort for people suffering from celiac disease. This autoimmune digestive disorder is caused by sensitivity to gluten, a protein found in wheat, barley and rye. Even a small indulgence in forbidden foods can trigger cramps, diarrhea, abdominal pain and fatigue. A lifetime of vigilance is necessary to keep the debilitating effects of celiac disease under control.

As many as 300,000 Canadians suffer from celiac disease, although many of them don't know it, since the condition often goes undiagnosed. Experts commonly refer to it as an "iceberg" disease: Visible at the tip are individuals whose symptoms include diarrhea, abdominal pain, weight loss and, in children, delayed growth; the rest of the iceberg consists of those with more subtle symptoms, such as bloating or excess gas that may go unrecognized as a sign of celiac disease. According to a 2007 survey of the Canadian Celiac Association's more than 5,000 members, it took an average of 12 years to get diagnosed. Many respondents had consulted three or more doctors before getting their diagnosis.

Celiac disease is considered a malabsorption syndrome because it deprives the nervous system and vital organs of essential nourishment. If left untreated, celiac disease increases the risk of osteoporosis (because of poor absorption of calcium and vitamin D), infertility, certain digestive tract cancers and other autoimmune disorders such as type 1 diabetes and thyroid disease. There is no cure for celiac disease, but it can be effectively treated and controlled by following a gluten-free diet.

What Causes Celiac Disease?

When people with celiac disease eat foods containing gluten, the protein triggers a malfunction in the immune system. Normally, the nutrients from digested food are absorbed into the bloodstream through thousands of tiny projections, called villi, which line the surface of the small intestine. In celiac disease, gluten in the diet provokes the immune system to attack the intestinal lining. The resulting swelling and inflammation damages the small intestine by causing the hair-like villi to shrink and flatten. This reduces the surface area of the intestinal lining, interfering with digestion and limiting the absorption of vitamins, minerals and other vital nutrients.

There is clear evidence that celiac disease is an inherited condition. Five percent to 10 percent of the immediate relatives (parents, children, siblings) of people diagnosed with this condition also eventually develop the disease. For those with a genetic predisposition, the onset of the disease is often stimulated by specific triggers, such as pregnancy, severe stress, viral infections or a physical injury.

Symptoms

While stomach pain, abdominal distention and diarrhea are considered the classic symptoms of celiac disease, they're often not present in adults. Constipation and bloating may be the only outward signs. Symptoms such as fatigue, weakness, joint pain and migraines—ones typically not recognized as gut-related—are also commonly reported.

Symptoms of celiac disease include:

- iron deficiency or iron-deficiency anemia
- gas, bloating, abdominal pain and cramping
- diarrhea
- weight loss
- fatigue
- irritability
- pale, foul-smelling, bulky stools
- loss of menstrual periods

- unexplained infertility
- dermatitis herpetiformis, which causes severe rashes on the arms, elbows, back, knees and buttocks

Children with the disease may stop growing normally and may have abnormally bowed long bones, wasted buttocks and potbellies.

There is no typical case of celiac disease. Symptoms and reactions vary considerably from person to person and may develop at any age. Screening tests that measure the level of antibodies in the blood are available. (People with celiac disease have higher than normal levels of antibodies to gluten.) Health Canada recently approved the Biocard Celiac Test, an at-home test kit that measures gluten antibodies from a fingertip blood sample. A blood test, however, is only the first step in diagnosing celiac disease: It's used to detect people who are likely to have the condition. Confirming a diagnosis requires that a doctor who specializes in gastrointestinal disorders take a biopsy of the small bowel. In this procedure, an endoscope is passed through the mouth into the stomach and upper intestine so that the lining can be examined and a biopsy taken.

Who's at Risk?

Women are at greater risk of celiac disease than men. While most people think celiac disease afflicts mainly children, it can occur at any age. In fact, two-thirds of those diagnosed are adults. Later in life, the disease can be triggered by pregnancy, surgery, gastrointestinal infection or severe emotional stress. People of northwestern European descent or with a family history of celiac disease are at greater risk. Individuals with type 1 diabetes or thyroid disease are also at increased risk.

Conventional Treatment

Following a gluten-free diet for life is the only effective treatment. Once gluten is removed from the diet, healing of the intestinal lining begins fairly quickly, though full recovery of the villi can take several months to years in adults with celiac disease. Consultation with a registered dietitian (www.dietitians.ca) will help ensure the nutritional quality of a gluten-free diet.

Gluten is widely used in the production of processed and packaged foods. As well, many commercial foods contain hidden sources of gluten, such as hydrolyzed vegetable protein (HVP) and hydrolyzed plant protein (HPP), malt, spelt and kamut. Because it is such a pervasive ingredient in our food supply, eliminating gluten from the diet can be a challenging task. People with celiac disease must pay careful attention to the ingredients list on food labels in order to avoid inadvertently consuming gluten. And since ingredients of commercial foods change frequently, labels must be checked with each purchase. If an ingredients list is not present, contact the manufacturer for product information.

People with celiac disease who do not maintain a gluten-free diet have a greater chance of developing osteoporosis and certain types of cancer, especially intestinal lymphoma.

Managing Celiac Disease
Dietary Strategies
A Gluten-Free Diet

Lifelong adherence to a gluten-free diet is essential for managing celiac disease. Use the following list to avoid gluten-containing grains:

Not Allowed	Allowed
Barley	Amaranth
Bulgur	Arrowroot
Couscous	Buckwheat
Eikorn	Corn
Emmer	Corn bran
Faro	Flaxseed
Kamut	Legumes
Mir	Millet
Oat bran	Nuts
Rye	Plantain
Semolina	Potato
Spelt	Psyllium
Triticale	Pure, uncontaminated oats
Wheat, wheat flour, wheat starch	Quinoa
	Rice, rice bran, rice polishings
	Sweet potato

Oats, previously on the list of gluten-containing foods to avoid, has now been given the green light for people with celiac disease. The Canadian Celiac Association maintains that eating pure, uncontaminated oats—up to 3/4 cup (175 ml) dry oats a day for adults and 1/4 cup (125 ml) for children—is safe. The problem is that oats may become contaminated with other gluten-containing grains during processing. Pure, uncontaminated oats are trademarked "Pavena" to ensure accurate identification. Still, a small number of people may not be able to tolerate oats and should follow up with their dietitian or doctor when adding them to a gluten-free diet.

Gluten can also be a hidden ingredient in many foods such as soups, sauces and salad dressings. In addition to the grains listed above, the following should be avoided: bran, caramel colour, cereal binding, durum, emulsifiers, edible starch, filler, food starch, germ, graham flour, gum base, hydrolyzed plant protein (HPP), hydrolyzed vegetable protein (HVP), icing sugar, malt, malt extract, malt flavouring, malt syrup, natural flavour, stabilizers, wheat germ and wheat starch.

For more information about gluten-containing foods, obtain a copy of *Acceptability of Foods and Food Ingredients for the Gluten-Free Diet*, a pocket dictionary available from the Canadian Celiac Association (see contact information below).

Gluten-Free Commercial Foods

Today, with the influx of products in supermarkets and natural food stores, it's getting easier to follow a gluten-free diet. Manufacturers of gluten-free products available in Canada include El Peto, Glutino, Kinnikinnick, Enjoy Life, Kaybee, Rizopia and Tinkyada. The following is a selection of organizations that specialize in producing or selling gluten-free foods. Their product lists are posted on their websites.

El Peto	1-800-387-4064	www.elpeto.com
Glutino	1-800-363-3468	www.glutino.com
Kingsmill Foods	416-755-1124	www.kingsmillfoods.com
Kinnikinnick	1-877-503-4466	www.kinnikinnick.com
Specialty Food Shop	1-800-737-7976	www.specialtyfoodshop.com

Dietary Fibre

A gluten-free diet may be low in fibre, since wheat bran and oat bran must be avoided. Some people might experience constipation. However, many of the allowed grains are good sources of fibre and should be added to your daily diet to promote bowel regularity.

Psyllium seed husks, ground flaxseed, corn bran, rice bran and rice polishings are all gluten-free sources of fibre. Legumes such as kidney beans, black beans, navy beans, chickpeas and lentils are very good sources of fibre and should regularly be included in the gluten-free diet. Drinking 9 to 12 glasses (2.2 to 3 L) of fluid per day and getting regular exercise will also help prevent constipation.

Lactose

In the initial stages of celiac disease, avoidance of lactose-containing foods can help minimize symptoms of abdominal pain, bloating, gas and diarrhea. Lactose is a natural sugar found in dairy products and some commercial foods. It's digested by an enzyme called lactase that is present on the intestinal villi. Damage to the intestinal tract caused by gluten can impair lactose digestion and absorption.

Lactose intolerance usually normalizes within a few months of starting the gluten-free diet, once the intestinal lining has healed. However, some people find that a lactose intolerance persists; they will benefit from a lactose-free diet (see Lactose Intolerance, page 529).

Vitamins and Minerals

Multivitamin and Mineral Supplements

Untreated celiac disease causes malabsorption of many nutrients, including calcium, magnesium, fat-soluble vitamins (A, D, E, K), folate, vitamin B12 and iron.[1] In cases of severe malabsorption, vitamin and mineral supplements may be required for several months until the intestinal cells regenerate. Taking a one-a-day multivitamin and mineral supplement is a good way to get the recommended daily amounts for most nutrients. It's wise to continue taking a multivitamin and mineral supplement even after the intestine has healed, since many gluten-free grains tend to be lower in B vitamins, especially folate, an important B vitamin for women of childbearing age. The synthetic version of folate, called folic acid, is added to white flour and white pasta in Canada in an effort to help prevent spinal cord defects in newborns. Since white pasta and foods made with white flour are not permitted on a gluten-free diet, a multivitamin and mineral supplement can help you meet your daily folate requirements.

Your registered dietitian will assess the need for additional vitamin or mineral supplements based on the degree of malabsorption and resulting nutrient deficiencies.

Calcium, Magnesium and Vitamin D

Osteoporosis is a common condition in adults with celiac disease.[2] Many children and teenagers with celiac disease have also been shown to have lower bone densities than peers who do not have the disease. Impaired absorption of calcium, magnesium and vitamin D may play a role in developing low bone density. Studies do show, however, that strict following of a gluten-free diet promotes recovery of bone loss.[3-6] Despite this, it's crucial to ensure that you're meeting your daily requirements for these bone-building nutrients. Young children, teens and women should pay very close attention to the adequacy of their diets, especially if they are lactose intolerant. The following are good food sources of these nutrients.

CALCIUM. Food sources include milk, yogurt, cheese, fortified soy and rice beverages, fortified orange juice, tofu, salmon (with bones), kale, bok choy, broccoli and Swiss chard.

MAGNESIUM. Food sources include nuts, seeds, legumes, figs, prunes, leafy green vegetables, brewer's yeast, cheddar cheese and shrimp.

VITAMIN D. Food sources include fluid milk, fortified soy and rice beverages and oily fish.

If you determine that you need to supplement to meet your daily calcium needs, buy a calcium citrate pill, since calcium in this form is absorbed more efficiently. Choose a product with added magnesium. Research has shown that many people with celiac disease who have followed a gluten-free diet for many years are deficient in magnesium due to poor dietary intake. Choose a calcium/magnesium supplement that supplies 300 to 350 milligrams of calcium with 150 milligrams of magnesium (a 2:1 formula). Take this supplement one to three times per day depending on the amount of calcium you consume from foods. Keep in mind that taking more than 350 milligrams of magnesium from a supplement may cause loose stools or diarrhea. If you take a calcium/magnesium supplement three times daily and experience this, replace one supplement with a calcium citrate supplement that doesn't contain magnesium.

For bone health (and cancer prevention) ensure you're consuming 1000 to 2000 international units (IU) of vitamin D each day. You can't rely on foods to provide adequate vitamin D. Nor can you rely on sun exposure to produce vitamin D in your skin during the fall and winter. Vitamin D must come from a supplement to ensure that your needs are met. To determine how much vitamin D you need, add up how much is supplied by your multivitamin and calcium supplements and make up the difference between that total and the RDA by taking 400 or 1000 IU of supplemental vitamin D.

For detailed information about calcium, magnesium and vitamin D, see Chapter 4.

Nutrition Strategy Checklist for Celiac Disease

☐   Gluten-free diet
☐   Dietary fibre
☐   Low-lactose diet
☐   Multivitamin/mineral
☐   Calcium
☐   Vitamin D
☐   Magnesium

Recommended Resources

Canadian Celiac Association
www.celiac.ca
5170 Dixie Road, Suite 204
Mississauga, ON L4W 1E3
Tel: 905-507-6208 or 1-800-363-7296
Fax: 905-507-4673

Celiac Disease Foundation
www.celiac.org
13251 Ventura Boulevard, Suite #1
Studio City, CA, USA 91604-1838
Tel: 818-990-2354
Fax: 818-990-2379
Email: cfd@celic.org

Celiac Sprue Association/USA Inc.
www.csaceliacs.org
P.O. Box 31700
Omaha, NE, USA 68131-0700

Tel: 402-558-0600
Fax: 402-558-1347

Cervical Dysplasia

If you're diagnosed with cervical dysplasia, it means that abnormal changes are beginning to take place in the cells lining the surface of your cervix, the part of your reproductive system that forms the entrance to your uterus. If left untreated, cervical dysplasia could progress to become cervical cancer. The only reliable way to detect this pre-cancerous condition is to have an annual Pap smear, a laboratory test of a small sample of your cervical tissue.

What Causes Cervical Dysplasia?

Scientists know that specific persistent strains of human papillomavirus (HPV) are definitively linked with cervical cancer. About one-third of HPV strains are sexually transmitted and some types cause genital warts. Two strains, HPV-16 and HPV-18, are linked to cervical dysplasia and cervical cancer. Researchers now believe that most young people who engage in sexual activity carry HPV viruses. In most cases, HPV leaves the body naturally. But some of the strains linked with cervical cancer can persist, especially in women over 30 years of age. It's estimated that about 75 percent of sexually active men and women in Canada will have at least one HPV infection in their lifetime. Young women 20 to 24 years old generally have the highest rates of cancer-causing HPV infection.[1]

There are three stages of cervical dysplasia. If abnormal cells are found only on the surface of the cervix, the condition is considered mild. This is the most common form, and up to 70 percent of mild dysplasia cases regress on their own without treatment. But unfortunately, sometimes these pre-cancerous cells can spread deeper into the tissue of the cervix lining. When this happens, cervical dysplasia is labelled as moderate or severe, depending on the extent of the tissue penetration. Moderate and severe cervical dysplasia are less likely to self-resolve and have a higher risk of progressing to cancer within the next 10 years.

Symptoms

There are no warning signs or symptoms of cervical dysplasia. Without the appropriate medical testing, you probably won't realize that anything is wrong until the disease is well advanced. If you have regular medical checkups, your doctor may notice a growth, sore or suspicious area on your cervix during a routine pelvic examination.

In most cases, identifiable symptoms don't appear until the cervical dysplasia has progressed to cervical cancer. At that time, a woman may experience some pain or some intermittent bleeding or spotting between menstrual cycles. To prevent cervical cancer, it's critical that you get tested for cervical dysplasia by having a Pap smear on an annual basis. The Pap smear identifies pre-cancerous changes of cervical cells and also indicates the presence of invasive cancer cells. But an abnormal result doesn't always mean your health is at risk. Sometimes a virus may cause temporary cell changes that will disappear in a short period of time.

Who's at Risk?

While it can occur at any age, cervical dysplasia most often occurs in women between the ages of 25 to 35. Women at greater risk include those who begin having sexual intercourse at an early age (16 years or younger) and those who have multiple sexual partners. Women who have a history of sexually transmitted disease, especially HPV infection, are also at increased risk for cervical dysplasia. Eighty percent to 90 percent of women with cervical dysplasia have an HPV infection. Other conditions that may increase the risk for cervical dysplasia include:

- smoking cigarettes or exposure to second-hand smoke
- using oral contraceptives for more than 10 years (oral contraceptives can interfere with folic acid metabolism in the cells around the cervix; women who use oral contraceptives may have increased exposure to sexually transmitted diseases)
- having a history of a gynecological cancer
- following a diet that's low in vitamin A, beta carotene and folate; a poor diet may also result in a weakened immune system, decreasing the body's ability to fight HPV

Women who are sexually active and do not have regular Pap smears to test for cervical dysplasia have a greater chance of developing cervical cancer. Two vaccines have been developed to prevent HPV-16 and HPV-18 infections. One is available in Canada; the other is currently being reviewed by Health Canada.

Conventional Treatment

The treatment for cervical dysplasia varies, depending on the extent and severity of the condition. If a woman is diagnosed with mild dysplasia and has no other risk factors for cervical cancer, her doctor will probably monitor the condition and wait to see if the affected cells return to normal. A second Pap smear will be performed in 4 to 6 months and, if cell growth is normal at that time, no treatment will be necessary. It's recommended that women with mild dysplasia return for a pelvic examination and Pap smear twice a year for at least 2 years.

A diagnosis of moderate or severe dysplasia is treated differently. The surface of the cervix is examined for abnormalities in a procedure called a *colposcopy*. Using a viewing tube with a magnifying lens, your doctor will inspect your cervix and take a biopsy of tissue from the abnormal area. The tissue samples are then sent to a laboratory to determine the extent of changes to cervical cells.

Once the severity of the cervical dysplasia is known, the treatment will involve removing all the abnormal growth that can potentially turn into cervical cancer. Your doctor may perform a surgical procedure called *cervical conization*, which removes a cone-shaped area of tissue. Other ways of removing the abnormal area include cauterizing the tissue with heat, freezing it with cryosurgery, vaporizing it with lasers or removing it using an electrified wire loop procedure known as LEEP. Because cervical dysplasia can return, it's important for women to have Pap smears every 3 months for the first year after surgery and every 6 months after that.

In more severe cases, a hysterectomy to remove the uterus may be necessary.

The sooner cervical dysplasia is detected and treated, the lower a woman's risk for developing cervical cancer. The following dietary and nutritional strategies may help prevent cervical dysplasia from developing in the first place. Some of the strategies I discuss below might even reverse the dysplasia.

Preventing Cervical Dysplasia
Vitamins and Minerals
Antioxidants

Many studies have found a link between cervical dysplasia and low blood levels of antioxidant nutrients, especially beta carotene and vitamin C. Women with cervical dysplasia are also more likely to have poor dietary intakes of these and other antioxidants. Antioxidants are vitamins, minerals or natural plant chemicals that protect cells in the body from damage caused by free radicals—highly reactive oxygen molecules produced by normal body processes. Excess free radicals can also be formed by pollution, cigarette smoke and heavy exercise. These compounds can damage the genetic material of cells, which in turn may lead to cancer development. Antioxidants neutralize free radicals, preventing them from causing damage to cells.

The body has built-in antioxidant enzymes for keeping free radical activity in check, but levels decline as we age. Scientists are learning every day that a daily supply of dietary antioxidants is important for reducing the risk of certain cancers. When it comes to cervical dysplasia (a precursor to cervical cancer), a handful of dietary antioxidants have been identified that may prevent free radical damage to cervical cells.

BETA CAROTENE. This antioxidant is plentiful in dark-green vegetables and orange fruit and vegetables. It's been hypothesized that beta carotene may protect from cervical dysplasia and cervical cancer in a few ways. First of all, we know that beta carotene is a potent antioxidant and may therefore protect cervical cells from free radical damage. Beta carotene is also used to synthesize some vitamin A in the body. Vitamin A is essential for normal cellular growth and development. A number of laboratory studies have shown the ability of vitamin A to prevent abnormal cell growth. Researchers have found that, compared with women free of cervical dysplasia, those with the condition have significantly lower blood levels and dietary intakes of beta carotene.[2] Despite this consistent finding, studies, including a 2-year randomized controlled trial, have not found that beta carotene supplements are able to enhance the regression of severe cervical dysplasia, especially in women with HPV.[3-5]

Currently, there is no daily recommended intake for beta carotene, but many experts believe that 3 to 6 milligrams per day offers protection from disease. A diet containing plenty of fruit and vegetables—at least 7 to 10 servings per day—will help you consume an adequate amount of beta carotene. Orange and dark-green produce, including carrots, sweet potato, winter squash, broccoli, collard greens, kale, spinach, apricots, cantaloupe, peaches, nectarines, mango and papaya, contain the most beta carotene. The body doesn't absorb the beta carotene in raw foods efficiently. To enhance absorption, cook the vegetables and eat them along with a little fat in your meal.

LYCOPENE. This antioxidant belongs to the same family of carotenoid compounds as beta carotene. But lycopene is twice as potent an antioxidant as beta carotene. A few studies have suggested that lycopene protects women from cervical dysplasia. A study from the

University of Pennsylvania School of Medicine found that women with the highest intake of lycopene were one-third as likely to have dysplasia as those who consumed the least.[6]

Lycopene is found in red-coloured fruit and vegetables. It's the natural chemical that gives these foods their bright colour. Heat-processed tomato products such as tomato juice, pasta sauce and cooked tomatoes are the richest source of lycopene, but you'll also find some in fresh tomatoes, pink grapefruit, watermelon, guava and apricots. Based on the research, it appears that a daily intake of 5 to 15 milligrams offers protection from chronic disease. Lycopene is a fat-soluble compound and is better absorbed in the presence of a little fat.

Lycopene supplements are available in health food stores and drug stores. Choose a brand that's made with the Lyc-O-Mato or LycoRed extract, which is the lycopene source used in clinical studies. Most supplements offer 5 milligrams of lycopene per tablet. Take 5 to 10 milligrams once daily with a meal. For more information about lycopene, see Chapter 8, page 173.

VITAMIN C. Less research has been done on this antioxidant vitamin and its potential role in protection from cervical dysplasia. A few studies have determined that women with low blood levels of vitamin C have a greater risk of cervical dysplasia than women with higher levels. Furthermore, cigarette smoke decreases the level of vitamin C in the body. One American study found a strong association between a woman's history of smoking and her level of vitamin C, whether or not she had cervical dysplasia.[7]

Citrus fruit, strawberries, kiwi, cantaloupe, broccoli, bell peppers, Brussels sprouts, cabbage, tomatoes and potatoes are all good

sources of vitamin C. Mango, cantaloupe, red grapefruit and tomato juice also contain beta carotene and/or lycopene. Aim to eat at least two foods rich in vitamin C per day.

If you decide to supplement your diet, take 500 milligrams of vitamin C once or twice a day. There's little point in taking much more than that at once, since your body can use only about 200 milligrams at one time.

VITAMIN E. As with vitamin C, only a little research has been done in the area of vitamin E and cervical dysplasia. Nevertheless, observational studies have found a link between the risk of dysplasia and blood levels of this vitamin. For instance, one study from the Cancer Research Center of Hawaii revealed that women with the highest blood vitamin E levels had a 70 percent lower risk of cervical dysplasia than women with the lowest blood levels of the vitamin.[8] The researchers also noticed what's called a dose response effect: the higher the level of vitamin E, the lower the risk of dysplasia.

Wheat germ, nuts, seeds, soybeans, vegetable oils, corn oil, whole grains and kale are all good sources of vitamin E. To supplement, take 200 to 400 IU of a natural source vitamin E per day. Do not take vitamin E supplements if you have diabetes or coronary heart disease.

Folate

This B vitamin appears to have a very important role in preventing the development of dysplasia. Research shows that as one's intake of folate-rich foods decreases, the risk of cervical dysplasia increases. An American study found that women consuming less than 400 micrograms of folate each day were 2.6 times more likely to develop dysplasia than women who consumed more than 400 micrograms.[9] Studies have found that many women with dysplasia have normal blood levels of folate but low levels of the vitamin in cervical tissue.[10] Research also suggests that in women with HPV infection, those with low blood levels of folate are significantly more likely to be diagnosed with moderate or severe cervical dysplasia than women with higher blood folate levels.[11]

A lack of folate may promote the development of dysplasia in a number of ways. Folate may act in some way to protect cervical cells. For example, a deficiency of folate is thought to promote the incorporation of HPV into the DNA of cervical cells, causing cancerous transformations.

Folate is critical for the synthesis of DNA (deoxyribonucleic acid), the genetic material of all cells. Low levels of folate in cervical tissue can make cellular DNA more susceptible to damage. Even a marginal folate deficiency can cause damage to DNA in cells, damage that resembles cervical dysplasia. It's possible that this alteration to DNA is an early step in the progression of cervical dysplasia and cervical cancer. Furthermore, this damage to a cell's genetic material may be stopped or reversed with supplements of this B vitamin. Two trials have found that folic acid supplements improved dysplasia in women taking birth control pills.[12,13] However, in trials conducted in women not taking oral contraceptives, folic acid supplements did not alter the course of dysplasia. The researchers concluded that a deficiency of this B vitamin may be involved in the initiation of dysplasia, but once you have the disease, supplements do not appear to reverse it.

The best sources of folate are cooked spinach, lentils, orange juice, whole grains, fortified breakfast cereals, asparagus, artichoke, avocado and seeds.

Folic Acid Supplements

Folic acid is the synthetic form of folate, whether in a supplement or fortified foods like white flour and white pasta. For many women, consuming the recommended daily intake of 400 micrograms of folate can be challenging. To supplement your diet, take a multivitamin and mineral supplement once daily. Look for a brand that supplies 0.4 milligrams (400 micrograms) of folic acid. If you take a separate folic acid supplement, buy one that has vitamin B12 added. High doses of folic acid taken over a period of time can hide a B12 deficiency and result in progressive nerve damage.

Nutrition Strategy Checklist for Cervical Dysplasia

☐ Beta carotene
☐ Lycopene
☐ Vitamin C
☐ Vitamin E
☐ Folate
☐ Multivitamin

Recommended Resources

The Johns Hopkins University School of Medicine
Barbara A. Biedrzycki, Adult Nurse Practitioner
www.hopkinsmedicine.org

Mayo Foundation for Medical Education and Research
www.mayoclinic.com
The Mayo Foundation for Medical Education and Research provides one of the best patient-education websites on the Internet. The

information is reliable, thorough and clearly written.

National Cancer Institute
www.cancer.gov
This is a gateway to recent, accurate cancer information from the National Cancer Institute.
6116 Executive Boulevard
Room 3036A
Bethesda, MD, USA 20892-8322
Tel: 1-800-4-CANCER (226237)

Women's Health Channel
www.womenshealthchannel.com
This U.S.-based website, developed and monitored by physicians, provides comprehensive, trustworthy information about conditions that affect women.

Chronic Fatigue Syndrome (CFS)

Chronic Fatigue Syndrome (CFS) is an enigma—a largely misunderstood illness that saps vitality and steals mental acuity. Very little is known about the causes of CFS and even less about the possible cures. CFS is a disease characterized by a profound fatigue that is not improved with bed rest and may be worsened with physical or mental activity. People with CFS have a substantially reduced level of activity compared with what they were capable of before the onset of the condition. In some cases, CFS can persist for years, dramatically altering the lives of those who suffer from it.

What Causes CFS?

There doesn't seem to be one single cause for CFS. Instead, nearly 20 years of research indicate there are likely a number of different factors—working alone or in combination—that might cause CFS. Initially, CFS was thought to be produced by a viral infection. Scientific attention was focused on the Epstein-Barr virus, herpes-type viruses and infections that cause polio. But extensive studies were unable to establish a direct connection between CFS and these or any other infectious agents. Despite this, scientists still speculate that a virus may help trigger the disease.

Much of the ongoing research into the cause of CFS has focused on the roles of the immune, hormonal and nervous systems. CFS may be caused when an infection or virus attacks someone with a weakened immune system. Once the infection has passed, the immune system doesn't return to its normal state. Instead, it remains active, continuously producing excess immune-activating factors. As these factors circulate through the bloodstream, they may cause profound fatigue. Studies do find that many people with CFS have chronically overactive immune systems, with white blood cells that are less able to fight off viruses.

It's also thought that oxidative stress caused by free radicals in the body may play a role in the development and progression of CFS.

People with CFS often have a history of allergies, which, for some unknown reason, seems to predispose them to the disease. There is also the possibility that a severe metabolic dysfunction may be the culprit behind CFS. Many sufferers show evidence of extreme shifts in metabolism that limit heart and lung functions, making it difficult and even physically damaging to carry out normal activities. Research has also linked CFS with brain abnormalities, especially those associated with sleep-related disorders.

Certain malfunctions of the nervous system can produce racing heartbeats or sudden drops in blood pressure. These conditions seem to be associated with the development of CFS in ways that are not yet fully understood. Periods of physical or emotional stress also have an impact on the nervous system. Stressful events stimulate the brain to produce cortisol and other stress hormones, which affect the immune system by suppressing inflammation. Because stress may be a trigger for the development of CFS, it's possible that there is a connection between the disease and altered levels of stress hormones.

CFS is not caused by depression. Although the two illnesses often appear together, many people with CFS do not suffer from depression or other psychiatric disorders.

Symptoms

There are no diagnostic laboratory tests for CFS. A physician must carefully evaluate individuals who may be suffering from CFS in order to rule out other treatable medical conditions that have similar symptoms. CFS is marked by extreme fatigue that has lasted at least 6 months and is not relieved by rest. The fatigue of CFS goes far beyond the exhausted, overtired feeling that we all get from time to time. The fatigue that characterizes CFS is relentless and causes a substantial reduction in daily activities. In addition to fatigue, CFS includes the following eight characteristic symptoms:

- relapse of symptoms after physical or mental exertion
- sleep disturbances; non-refreshing sleep
- impaired thinking, forgetfulness, confusion, difficulty concentrating
- muscle pain and weakness
- joint pain, often in multiple joints
- headaches

- sore throat
- tender lymph nodes in the neck or armpits

Because the disease involves a faulty immune system, it's also common for people with CFS to experience food allergies, other fungal infections (e.g., yeast infections) and frequent bouts of the common cold.

CFS symptoms and their duration vary widely from individual to individual. Approximately 50 percent of people with CFS return to a fairly normal lifestyle within 5 years. The other half will still be dramatically ill even after 10 years. Some people recover from the disease in 2 to 3 years, only to suffer a relapse at a later time. CFS can be cyclical, producing alternating periods of illness and relatively good health.

Who's at Risk?

CFS is thought to affect 350,000 to 480,000 Canadians.[1] CFS can affect people of every age, gender, ethnicity and socioeconomic group. Despite this, the condition is most common in people in their 40s and 50s. Research also indicates that women report the condition four times more often than men, possibly because women are more willing to seek medical treatment for fatigue.[2]

Conventional Treatment

Since there is no known cure for CFS, medications and treatments prescribed are intended to provide relief of symptoms. In treating this disease today, doctors use a combination of drug and nondrug therapies and a gradual approach to rehabilitation.

Low-dose *tricyclic antidepressants* seem to have a positive effect on some people with CFS, possibly because they improve the quality of sleep. Another form of antidepressant, *SSRIs (selective serotonin reuptake inhibitors)*, also provides treatment benefits. In some cases, *benzodiazepines*, a type of drug used to treat anxiety and sleep problems, will improve the quality of life for CFS sufferers. *NSAIDs (non-steroidal anti-inflammatory drugs)* will help fight the aches and pains, and *antihistamines* may relieve the allergy symptoms associated with the condition.

Lifestyle changes such as prevention of overexertion, reduced stress, gentle stretching, yoga and physical therapy are also used to treat CFS. Learning to manage your fatigue will help you improve the ability to function. Behaviour therapy can help you find effective ways to plan daily activities so that you can take advantage of peak energy levels. Exercise is also important in the management of CFS. Although exercise may seem to aggravate the symptoms, it's essential to maintain some muscle strength and conditioning. Throughout the course of this disease, it's important to learn to pace yourself physically, emotionally and mentally since extra stress can exacerbate symptoms.

Managing CFS

Nutrition plays an important role in the recovery to good health. Scientists have identified a number of vitamins and minerals that are deficient in many people with CFS. This seems to be mostly due to the illness itself, rather than a poor diet. Even marginal nutrient deficiencies can contribute to fatigue symptoms. Lacking important nutrients can also delay the healing process.

Dietary Strategies

Follow a wholesome, healthy and well-balanced diet. The quality of the foods eaten seems to be most important in helping to restore energy levels. Some practitioners recommended a low-sugar, low-yeast diet; however, research has not shown this eating plan to be any more effective at improving energy levels and quality of life than an overall healthful diet.[3] Beneficial strategies include:

1. **Emphasize plant foods.** Fill your plate with grains, fruit and vegetables. If you eat animal protein foods like meat or poultry, they should take up no more than one-quarter of your plate. Try vegetarian sources of protein, like legumes and soy.
2. **Choose foods and oils that are rich in essential fatty acids.** Fish, nuts, seeds, flaxseed and flaxseed oil, canola oil, omega-3 eggs, wheat germ and leafy green vegetables are examples.
3. **Choose foods rich in vitamins, minerals and protective plant compounds.** Reach for whole grains as often as possible. Eat at least three different coloured fruits and three different coloured vegetables every day.
4. **Eliminate sources of refined sugar whenever possible.** Opt for healthier choices in place of cookies, cakes, pastries, frozen desserts, soft drinks, sweetened fruit juices, fruit drinks, candy, etc.
5. **Buy organic produce** or **wash fruit and vegetables** to remove pesticide residues.
6. **Limit foods with chemical additives.**
7. **Avoid caffeine.** (It can worsen fatigue by interrupting sleep patterns.)
8. **Drink at least 9 to 13 cups (2.2 to 3.2 L) of water every day.**

9. **Avoid alcohol.** If you drink, limit your alcohol intake. Women should consume no more than one drink a day, or seven per week, men no more than two drinks per day, or nine per week.

10. **Take a multivitamin and mineral supplement each day.** You want to ensure that you're meeting your needs for most nutrients. Buy a product that contains no artificial preservatives, colours or flavours and no added sugar, starch, lactose or yeast. This should be declared in small print below the ingredients list. If you experience gastrointestinal upset when taking a multivitamin, try a "professional brand" supplement available at certain health food stores. These products contain no binding materials and are suitable for people with food sensitivities. However, they're expensive, and you have to take at least three to six capsules a day to meet your recommended intake levels. Brand names include Genestra and Thorne Research.

To help you follow these principles, reread Chapter 5. You'll learn what foods you should be eating more often. You'll also learn how many servings of these foods you should be striving for each day.

If you experience bloating, cramps, gas, diarrhea or skin rashes after eating, it's a good idea to be tested for food allergies. Ask your family doctor for a referral to an allergy specialist.

Omega-3 Fatty Acids

A number of studies have shown that patients with CFS have depressed levels of the omega-3 fatty acids DHA and EPA in their blood cells. Scientists also speculate that a persistent viral infection may impair the body's ability to synthesize omega-3 fatty acids. Since DHA and EPA are used to help regulate the immune system and reduce inflammation in the body, lower levels of these fats may contribute to the symptoms of CFS.

Researchers have reported symptom improvements in many patients treated with omega-3 fatty acid supplementation. Patients given high dose EPA showed improvement within 8 to 12 weeks.[4-6]

Aim to eat oily fish rich in omega-3 fatty acids twice per week. In addition, take a fish oil supplement that supplies both EPA and DHA. Refer to Fish Oil Supplements later in this section.

Vitamins and Minerals
Antioxidants
Since CFS is often accompanied by signs of oxidative stress and by decreased antioxidant levels in the body, individuals with the condition may benefit from increasing their intake of antioxidant nutrients. Start by adding the following antioxidant-rich foods to your daily diet. To learn more, see Chapter 4.

VITAMIN C. The recommended daily intake is 75 milligrams per day for women and 90 milligrams for men. The best food sources include citrus fruit, citrus juices, kiwi, mango, cantaloupe, strawberries, broccoli, Brussels sprouts, red pepper and tomato juice.

VITAMIN E. The recommended daily intake for adults is 15 milligrams of alpha tocopherol, equivalent to 22 international units (IU) of natural source or 33 IU of synthetic vitamin E. The best food sources include vegetable oils, sunflower seeds, almonds, hazelnuts, peanuts and kale.

BETA CAROTENE. There is no recommended daily intake for beta carotene. Research suggests that consuming 3 to 6 milligrams daily will maintain blood levels of beta carotene in the range linked with disease prevention. The best food sources include carrots, winter squash, sweet potato, kale, spinach, turnip greens, collard greens, romaine lettuce, broccoli, apricots, cantaloupe, peaches, nectarines, mango and papaya.

SELENIUM. Adults need 55 micrograms of selenium per day. The best food sources include Brazil nuts, seafood, tuna, cod, beef, turkey breast and chicken breast.

B Vitamins

Without B vitamins, our bodies would lack energy. These eight nutrients are indispensable for yielding energy compounds from the foods we eat. Many B vitamins serve as helpers to enzymes that release energy from fat, protein and carbohydrate. Compared with healthy people, patients with CFS often have lower levels of B vitamins in their blood.[7-10] One study also found that enzymes dependent on B vitamins were less active in people with CFS. No published studies have assessed the effect of vitamin B supplements on fatigue symptoms.

In Chapter 4, I discuss in detail each B vitamin, daily requirements and food sources. To ensure that you're getting your daily B vitamins, it's wise to take a good-quality multi-vitamin and mineral supplement each day.

Magnesium

Magnesium is a part of adenosine triphosphate (ATP), the active energy compound that's used by every cell in your body. It's believed that a deficiency in magnesium can lead to the decreased energy and weakness seen in CFS.

Some investigations have found low levels of magnesium in the red blood cells of patients with CFS.[11,12] When these patients are regularly given magnesium by injection, they reported more energy, less pain and more balanced emotions.

Researchers have also learned that many CFS patients who are deficient in magnesium have a decreased antioxidant status in their body. Supplementing the diet with magnesium has been shown to improve the body's magnesium stores and antioxidant levels.[13]

Many Canadians do not meet their daily magnesium requirements. Some of the best food sources include nuts, seeds, legumes, prunes, figs, whole grains, leafy green vegetables and brewer's yeast.

If you decide to supplement, choose a product made from magnesium citrate, a form that's more easily absorbed by the body. No definite dose has been established for CFS. Doses of 200 to 300 milligrams have been used to reduce the muscle pain and joint tenderness associated with fibromyalgia. (Like CFS, fibromyalgia is a chronic disorder that causes muscle pain, fatigue, sleep disturbances and other symptoms. See Fibromyalgia, page 383.) The upper daily limit for supplemental magnesium is 350 milligrams. Doses higher than this can cause diarrhea and stomach upset.

Herbal Remedies

The following herbs have been shown to boost the body's production of infection-fighting immune compounds. Of the three I discuss, echinacea and *Panax ginseng* have been shown to enhance the activity of immune cells in people with CFS.[14] Echinacea can be beneficial in helping to treat bothersome colds, while ginseng and aged garlic extract can be used longer term for immune stimulation.

Echinacea

Studies have found that this herb can reduce the duration of cold symptoms by as much as 50 percent. Echinacea's active ingredients enhance the body's immune system by increasing production of certain white blood cells that fight off viruses and bacteria. Three species of echinacea are found in products— *Echinacea purpurea, Echinacea angustifolia* and *Echinacea pallida*—and all have medicinal benefits.

To ensure that you're getting a quality product, buy one that's standardized. Take a total of 900 milligrams of echinacea three to four times daily at the first sign of cold or flu. Limit daily use to 8 consecutive weeks; there is some concern that long-term use of echinacea might depress the immune system. Do not use echinacea if you're allergic to plants in the Asteraceae/ Compositae family (ragweed, daisy, marigold and chrysanthemum).

Panax Ginseng

This ginseng goes by many names, including Asian, Korean and Chinese. Studies have shown the herb to have strong immune-enhancing properties. A large Italian study found that individuals taking 100 milligrams of a standardized ginseng product (G115 extract) had significantly higher levels of antibodies in response to a flu shot than those who did not take the herb. Killer white blood cell counts were nearly twice as high in the ginseng group after 8 weeks of supplementation. These and other white blood cells are an important part of the body's defence against viruses and foreign molecules.

The typical dosage of a standardized extract is 100 milligrams once daily. Take ginseng for 3 weeks to 3 months and follow with a 1- to 2-week rest period before you resume taking the herb. In some people, it may cause mild stomach upset, irritability and insomnia. To avoid overstimulation, start with 100 milligrams a day and avoid taking the herb with caffeine. Ginseng should not be used during pregnancy or breastfeeding, or by individuals with poorly controlled high blood pressure.

Siberian Ginseng *(Eleutherococcus senticosus)*

In a study of 96 patients, those assigned to take Siberian ginseng versus a placebo reported less fatigue after 2 months of supplementation. Treatment was most effective for patients with less severe fatigue.[15]

Unlike *Panax ginseng*, this herb has a much milder effect and fewer reported side effects. It's also been used in clinical studies of CFS. Pregnant and nursing women can safely take Siberian ginseng, and it's much less likely to cause overstimulation in sensitive individuals. To ensure quality, choose a product standardized for eleutherosides B and E. The usual dosage is 300 to 400 milligrams once daily for 6 to 8 weeks, followed by a 1- to 2-week break.

Garlic *(Allium sativum)*

A daily intake of garlic and its accompanying sulphur compounds has been used to enhance the body's immune system and kill many types of bacteria and fungi (including the *Candida* organism that causes yeast infections). One-half to one clove a day is recommended.

To supplement, buy aged garlic extract. The aging process used to make this supplement increases the concentration of the special sulphur compounds that stimulate the immune system. In fact, animal studies have found that an amount of garlic equivalent to three aged garlic extract capsules dramatically increases activity of white blood cells (killer cells, macrophages and leukocytes). Generally, two to six capsules a day (one or two with meals) are recommended. You can also buy aged garlic in a liquid form (Kyolic brand) that you then add to foods.

Other Natural Health Products

Fish Oil Supplements

Based on the finding that CFS patients have depressed essential fatty acids in their blood cells, Scottish researchers had 63 adults with CFS take either fish oil (eight 500 milligram capsules per day) or placebo capsules for 3 months.[16] When the study was over, 85 percent of patients taking the fish oil had a significant improvement in their symptoms. As would be expected, there was also an increase in cellular levels of essential fatty acids. Researchers from the United Kingdom tried to replicate these results among 50 patients with CFS and found no difference in symptoms between those taking fish oil and those taking a placebo.[17] Other studies have reported beneficial effects of fish oil supplementation.

Buy a product that contains both omega-3 fatty acids, EPA and DHA. The brand used in clinical studies was Efamol Marine. You might also consider using a liquid fish oil supplement rather than a capsule. Per teaspoon, most brands of liquid fish oil supply twice the amount of omega-3 fatty acids as one capsule. Avoid fish *liver* oil capsules. Most supplements made from fish liver are a concentrated source of vitamin A; too much of this nutrient can be toxic when taken in large amounts for long periods.

Fish oil has a blood-thinning effect. If you take anti-clotting medication, consult your physician first. Follow your health care practitioner's advice for dosage.

Acetyl-L-Carnitine (ALC)

This compound is not considered an essential nutrient because the body makes it in sufficient quantities. The body obtains some carnitine from the diet, primarily from red meat and dairy products. The body can also synthesize carnitine from amino acids. In the body, ALC is converted to L-carnitine, a compound that helps all cells in the body generate energy, especially muscle cells. In addition, ALC is used to synthesize acetylcholine, a brain chemical that aids in memory. It's possible that a deficiency of this compound can cause the fatigue associated with CFS. Studies have shown that CFS patients tend to have lower levels of carnitine in their blood, and higher levels are linked with less severe symptoms.[18,19]

Two studies suggest that supplementing with ALC can reduce CFS symptoms. In one study of 96 elderly patients with fatigue, ALC treatment significantly outperformed the placebo treatment for improving muscle pain, prolonged fatigue after exercise, sleep disorders, physical fatigue and mental fatigue.[20] Another study conducted in 90 patients with CFS found ALC reduced mental fatigue—50 percent of patients on the supplement showed considerable improvement in attention and concentration. In this study the researchers also tested the effectiveness of another form of carnitine called propionyl-L-carnitine. Among patients who received this treatment, 63 percent reported significant improvement in general fatigue. Patients in the study who were given a combined supplement of ALC and propionyl-L-carnitine reported less improvement.[21]

Based on the clinical research, a dose of 2 grams of ALC or propionyl-L-carnitine has been used. If symptoms of mental fatigue trouble you most, supplement with ALC. If feelings of general fatigue are most bothersome, take propionyl-L-carnitine. Supplement for 6 months to evaluate its effectiveness on improving energy.

Both supplements are considered safe and are generally well tolerated; however, gastrointestinal upset can occur. Propionyl-L-carnitine may cause the urine and breath to have a fishy odour.

Avoid products that contain D-carnitine or DL-carnitine. These forms compete with L-carnitine in the body and could lead to a deficiency.

Melatonin

This hormone regulates the body's wake-sleep cycles. Its release from the brain is stimulated by darkness: the darker the room, the more melatonin your body produces. The hormone induces sleep by interacting with melatonin receptors in the brain. Based on the observation that many patients with CFS have wake-sleep cycle disturbances, researchers have investigated the effectiveness of melatonin supplements in treating CFS.

One study conducted in 29 patients with CFS found that taking 5 milligrams of melatonin in the evening for 12 weeks improved measures of fatigue, concentration, motivation and activity.[22] However, another study reported no benefit from melatonin supplementation. These studies used different methods for assessing symptoms, which might explain the difference in findings.

To improve sleep disturbances associated with CFS, take a daily dose of 5 milligrams of melatonin at bedtime. The most commonly reported side effects of melatonin include daytime drowsiness, headache and dizziness. See Chapter 8, page 176, for more information about melatonin supplements.

Nutrition Strategy Checklist for Chronic Fatigue Syndrome

☐   Healthy, balanced diet
☐   Identify food allergies
☐   Fish
☐   Multivitamin/mineral
☐   B vitamins
☐   Magnesium
☐   Echinacea
☐   *Panax ginseng*
☐   Siberian ginseng
☐   Garlic
☐   Carnitine
☐   Melatonin

Recommended Resources

The CFIDS (Chronic Fatigue and Immune Dysfunction Syndrome) Association of America, Inc.
www.cfids.org
P.O. Box 220398
Charlotte, NC, USA 28222-0398
Tel: 704-365-2343 (resource line) or
   1-800-442-3437 (voice mail)
Fax: 704-365-9755

National Institute of Allergy and Infectious Diseases
National Institutes of Health
NIAID Office of Communications and Government Relations
www3.niaid.nih.gov
6610 Rockledge Drive, MSC 6612
Bethesda, MD, USA 20892-6612
Tel: 301-496-5717
Fax: 301-402-3573

Cirrhosis of the Liver

Weighing in at three pounds and roughly the size of an American football in adults, the liver is the largest internal organ in the body. Every minute, one-quarter of the body's blood supply flows into the liver, where it's processed and cleaned to remove all harmful substances before flowing out again. The liver performs countless other functions essential for maintaining good health. It stores energy to fuel your muscles, produces over a thousand different enzymes, manufactures bile and cholesterol, regulates hormones and processes waste products. Because the liver plays such a crucial role in supporting your bodily functions, you cannot survive if your liver stops functioning.

Cirrhosis is a term that describes scarring of the liver. It's caused by several chronic diseases and conditions that damage healthy liver tissue, replacing it with scar tissue. The scar tissue restricts the flow of blood and prevents the liver from performing its many essential tasks. In mild cirrhosis, the liver can repair itself and continue to function. But with advanced cirrhosis, more and more scar tissue forms, reducing the ability of the liver to perform its vital functions.

What Causes Cirrhosis?

In North America, the most common cause of cirrhosis is alcohol abuse. Heavy drinkers are nearly thirty times more likely to develop cirrhosis than non-drinkers. Alcoholic cirrhosis usually develops in people who have been heavy drinkers for more than 10 years. The amount of alcohol necessary to damage the liver varies from person to person. Because men are more inclined than women to drink excessively, alcoholic liver disease is twice as common in men as it is in women. However, even though women drink less, they are more easily affected by alcohol and more susceptible to alcohol-related liver injury. (For more on alcohol abuse, see page 194.)

Not everyone who drinks excessively will develop cirrhosis. Approximately 15 percent of alcoholics acquire the condition, while others experience less serious forms of liver damage.

Even social drinkers have been known to develop cirrhosis. Frequency and regularity of alcohol intake are the greatest risk factors influencing the prognosis of this disease. In alcoholics, nutritional deficiencies caused by a poor diet may also trigger the development of cirrhosis.

Hepatitis B ranks as a major cause of cirrhosis worldwide, although it's not as common a problem in North America. In the Western world, hepatitis C is the culprit behind cirrhosis. Both of these viral diseases provoke low-grade inflammation of the liver that often continues over several decades. The long-term damage to liver tissue associated with this type of inflammation often leads to cirrhosis.

Several inherited diseases, including hemochromatosis and glycogen storage diseases, interfere with the way the liver produces and stores a variety of essential substances, such as proteins, metals and enzymes. Blocked bile ducts cause bile to back up into the liver, resulting in serious tissue damage. Non-alcoholic fatty liver disease, the fastest-growing liver ailment in Canada, is another cause of cirrhosis. Environmental toxins, reactions to prescription drugs and parasitic infections are additional factors that can cause scar tissue to develop in the liver.

No matter how it's caused, liver damage associated with chronic cirrhosis is irreversible.

Early diagnosis and treatment is essential to prevent long-term damage. It's important to have regular medical checkups because a significant portion of the liver may have stopped functioning before any signs or symptoms of cirrhosis become apparent. While there are some treatments that can delay the progression of the scar tissue and reduce complications, there is no cure for this disease.

Symptoms

Most people with cirrhosis feel no symptoms until liver damage is extensive. Common symptoms include fatigue, easy bruising, loss of appetite, nausea, fluid retention in the abdomen, leg swelling and weight loss. As well, the liver may feel larger and harder. As the disease progresses, complications may develop due to loss of liver function, including:

- frequent infections
- malnutrition caused by the liver's inability to efficiently process nutrients
- yellowing of the skin (jaundice), gallstones and itching
- impaired mental function, personality changes, coma or death caused by toxins that accumulate in the blood and brain because the liver can no longer process the blood to remove them
- high blood pressure in the veins that run from the intestine to the liver
- enlarged blood vessels (varices) in the lower end of the esophagus (varices have thin walls and are more likely to burst under high pressure, resulting in serious bleeding problems)
- bacterial infections
- kidney dysfunction and possible kidney failure

- increased sensitivity to medications and drugs
- increased risk of liver cancer

Who's at Risk?

The following may be more likely to develop cirrhosis:

- individuals who drink more than two alcoholic drinks a day for more than 10 years (women are more susceptible to alcohol-related liver damage than men)
- individuals who suffer from chronic viral hepatitis types B, C and D, autoimmune hepatitis and non-alcoholic steatohepatitis
- individuals with prolonged obstruction of the bile ducts or diseases of the bile ducts
- individuals with an inherited disease such as hemochromatosis, glycogen storage diseases, Wilson's disease and alpha-1 antitrypsin deficiency
- individuals exposed to environmental toxins or parasitic infections

Conventional Treatment

The treatment for cirrhosis depends on the cause of the disease and the complications that have developed. A healthy, wholesome diet is always necessary to provide the body with essential nutrients. The following are common treatments for the causes and complications of cirrhosis:

- **Alcoholic cirrhosis:** avoid alcohol to prevent further liver damage and to allow for some improvement in liver function
- **Hepatitis-related cirrhosis:** medications, such as interferon and corticosteroids, to treat the hepatitis

- **Edema and ascites**: low-sodium diet or diuretics (medication to remove fluid from the body)
- **Infections**: antibiotics
- **Itching**: medication
- **Toxins**: protein-restricted diet to reduce buildup of toxins in the blood and brain
- **Portal hypertension**: beta-blocker medication
- **Varices**: injection with anti-clotting agents

Severe cases of liver damage require a liver transplant: The diseased liver is replaced with a healthy one from an organ donor. Survival rates have improved and 80 percent to 90 percent of liver transplant patients now survive the surgery.

Early intervention with nutrition and diet therapy can improve response to treatment, alleviate symptoms and improve quality of life for individuals with cirrhosis. Nutritional therapies are individualized for each person, depending on the cause of the disease and its severity. A registered dietitian who specializes in liver disease should be consulted to develop an appropriate nutritional care plan. The following guidelines are general and should be tailored to each patient's specific condition.

Managing Cirrhosis
Dietary Strategies
Dietary Calories and Protein

Weight loss is common in people with severe liver disease, so following a diet that contains adequate calories and protein is important to help prevent muscle breakdown. Protein-calorie malnutrition occurs in as many as 60 percent of patients with cirrhosis and is often associated with the development of complications such as hepatic encephalopathy. Individuals with liver cirrhosis should increase their intake of protein-rich foods. The recommended intake of protein for healthy people is 0.8 grams protein per kilogram of body weight. This should be almost doubled to 1.2 to 1.5 grams per kilogram of body weight for people with cirrhosis.[1,2] A registered dietitian will help you plan a diet that provides sufficient protein. A list of foods and their protein content can be found in Chapter 2.

Evidence supports the use of vegetable protein foods (legumes, soy, unsalted nuts) in people with cirrhosis who develop mental confusion, a condition called hepatic encephalopathy.[3] It's believed that an imbalance in circulating amino acids and high levels of ammonia in the bloodstream contribute to an altered mental state. In one study of 153 patients with cirrhosis, a high-calorie (30 calories per kilogram body weight per day), high-protein (1.2 grams protein per kilogram body weight per day) diet improved the mental status of 80 percent of patients. The diet supplied better-tolerated vegetable and milk (casein) proteins.[4] When diets containing mainly vegetable protein rather than animal protein were consumed along with lactulose medication to lower blood ammonia levels, improvements in mental status symptoms resulted.

Some research suggests that people with cirrhosis fare better by eating four to seven smaller meals per day, including a good breakfast and a late-evening meal.[5] A grazing pattern of eating appears to minimize some of the muscle breakdown that accompanies cirrhosis.

In people who experience impaired fat absorption because of decreased production and secretion of bile, the digestive aid that helps absorb dietary fat, a low-fat diet is required.

Branched Chain Amino Acids (BCAAs)

Branched chain amino acids (BCAAs) such as isoleucine, leucine and valine are found naturally in protein-rich foods. Based on how they are metabolized in the body, they have been shown to normalize blood amino acids and lower ammonia levels in people with hepatic encephalopathy. Studies have shown that adding BCAAs to the diet can also decrease muscle breakdown and improve energy metabolism in liver cirrhosis.[6-9] BCAAs may also reduce the risk of liver cancer in patients with advanced cirrhosis. On balance, prescribing supplementation with BCAAs as a maintenance therapy appears to be associated with a lower frequency of complications of cirrhosis and improved liver function tests and nutritional status.

The typical dose of BCAAs used in studies is 240 milligrams per kilogram of body weight per day or a daily dose of up to 25 grams. These products are found in health food and supplement stores. Special BCAA formulas can be used for hospitalized patients. If you decide to supplement your diet with BCAAs, be sure to inform your physician.

Carbohydrates

Liver disease leads to malfunctions in carbohydrate metabolism and can result in elevated (hyper) blood-sugar and insulin levels as well as low (hypo) blood-sugar levels. Choosing carbohydrate-containing foods that are digested and converted to blood sugar slowly may help minimize symptoms of carbohydrate intolerance. Researchers have found that a low-glycemic-index diet had beneficial effects in individuals with cirrhosis.[10,11] For a list of low-glycemic-index foods see Chapter 1, page 8.

Sodium

Restricting the intake of sodium is necessary to alleviate fluid retention that occurs with leg or abdomen swelling.[12-14] A diet containing no more than 2 grams (2000 milligrams) of sodium is usually adequate to reduce swelling. In cases of severe fluid retention, your dietitian may prescribe a lower-sodium diet. For the sodium content of many foods see Chapter 5, page 108.

Vitamins and Minerals

Multivitamin and Mineral Supplements

Since the liver is responsible for activating vitamins into forms the body can use, nutrient deficiencies are common in people with liver disease, especially if alcoholism is the cause. Deficiencies of B vitamins occur often, particularly deficiencies of folate, B1 (thiamin), B6 and B12. A daily multivitamin and mineral pill can help correct these nutrient deficits. A B complex supplement can also be used; it contains the whole family of B vitamins in greater amounts than a standard multivitamin pill.

Antioxidants

Studies reveal that liver cirrhosis is accompanied by deficiencies in vitamins C and E, beta carotene and selenium, important antioxidants that protect cells from damage caused by free radicals.[15,16] Free radicals are unstable oxygen molecules that cause damage to virtually every cell in the body, including liver cells. Research suggests that higher levels of free radical activity may be present in people with liver cirrhosis, especially when heavy drinking is the cause.[17] In addition to alcohol metabolism, increased iron storage in the liver can also cause excess oxidative stress. Despite the rationale for supplementation with antioxidant nutrients, most studies have failed to show a benefit on fatigue or other liver-related symptoms. Some research conducted in people with non-alcoholic fatty liver disease—which can progress to cirrhosis—has found vitamin C and E supplements helpful in improving liver function.[18,19] Supplementation with vitamin E and selenium has also been shown to improve nutrient status.[20,21] The following antioxidant nutrients should be included in the diet.

VITAMIN C. The recommended dietary allowance (RDA) of this vitamin is 75 and 90 milligrams for women and men respectively (smokers need an additional 35 milligrams). Best food sources include citrus fruit, citrus juices, cantaloupe, kiwi, mango, strawberries, broccoli, Brussels sprouts, cauliflower, red pepper and tomato juice. To supplement, take a 500 or 600 milligram supplement of Ester C once daily. The upper daily limit for vitamin C is 2000 milligrams.

VITAMIN E. The RDA for vitamin E is 22 international units (IU). Best food sources include wheat germ, nuts, seeds, vegetable oils, whole grains and kale. To supplement, take 200 to 800 IU of natural source vitamin E. The upper daily limit is 1500 IU. Do not take vitamin E supplements if you have diabetes or heart disease. See Chapter 4, page 53, for more information about the safety of vitamin E supplements.

BETA CAROTENE. No RDA has been established for beta carotene as it isn't considered an essential nutrient. Best food sources are orange and dark-green produce, including carrots, sweet potato, winter squash, broccoli, collard greens, kale, spinach, apricots, cantaloupe, peaches, nectarines, mango and papaya. There's no evidence that beta carotene supplements improve symptoms of cirrhosis.

SELENIUM. The RDA for this trace mineral for adults is 55 micrograms. Best food sources are seafood, chicken, organ meats, whole grains, nuts, onions, garlic and mushrooms. To supplement, take 200 micrograms of selenium-rich yeast per day. There's no evidence that beta-selenium supplements improve symptoms of cirrhosis. Meet your daily requirement from diet and a multivitamin and mineral supplement; most multivitamins supply 55 micrograms per daily dose.

Calcium and Vitamin D

People with chronic liver disease are twice as likely to suffer bone fractures caused by osteoporosis as healthy individuals. Research has also revealed that two-thirds of patients with moderately severe cirrhosis are deficient in vitamin D, a critical nutrient for maintaining bone density. However most reports have not found that vitamin D deficiency plays a significant role in the development of osteoporosis in patients with cirrhosis. Despite the lack of evidence for a therapeutic effect of vitamin D supplements, individuals with cirrhosis and low bone density should supplement their diet with calcium and vitamin D. To ensure that you're meeting recommended intakes of each nutrient, refer to Chapter 4.

Herbal Remedies
Milk Thistle (*Silybum marianum*)

The active ingredients of this herb (known collectively as silymarin) can support and enhance liver function.[22-24] Silymarin can prevent toxic substances from penetrating liver cells and may even help liver cells regenerate more quickly. Milk thistle also seems to act as an antioxidant, protecting liver cells from damage caused by free radicals. Studies suggest that milk thistle may improve survival in patients with cirrhosis of the liver.[25,26] One study of 146 people with liver cirrhosis looked at the effect of taking milk thistle for 3 to 6 years. At the end of 4 years, the survival rate was 58 percent in the herb-treated group compared with 38 percent in the placebo group.

Buy a product standardized to contain 70 percent to 80 percent silymarin. For liver cirrhosis, the recommended dose is 420 milligrams per day. Use milk thistle with caution if you're allergic to plants in the Asteraceae/ Compositae family (ragweed, daisy, marigold and chrysanthemum). For more information on milk thistle, see Chapter 7, page 148.

Other Natural Health Products

Grapeseed Extract

Individuals with liver cirrhosis tend to bruise and bleed easily because the liver slows or stops production of the proteins needed for blood clotting. Grapeseed extract contains natural chemicals called anthocyanins, which are thought to keep blood vessels healthy by inhibiting the action of enzymes that break down connective tissue. In Europe, grapeseed extract is widely used to treat conditions related to fragile blood capillaries.

While no studies have assessed the effectiveness of grapeseed extract in patients with cirrhosis, it is a very safe supplement and it may be beneficial. The typical maintenance dose is 40 to 80 milligrams daily.

SAMe (S-Adenosyl-Methionine)

SAMe is a compound that our body makes naturally from certain amino acids in high-protein foods like fish and meat. It's found in virtually all body tissues and fluids. The production of SAMe is closely linked with folate and vitamin B12, so deficiencies of these B vitamins can lead to depressed levels of SAMe. In the body, SAMe is used to synthesize hormones, brain neurotransmitters, proteins and cell membranes. It's also used to make glutathione, the main antioxidant found inside cells.

It's thought that SAMe acts as an essential nutrient by restoring biochemical compounds that are depleted in people with alcoholic liver disease. People with liver disease lose the ability to form SAMe, and this leads to deficiencies in choline and glutathione, an enzyme that plays a critical role in liver detoxification and antioxidant reactions.[27–30] One study conducted on patients with alcoholic liver cirrhosis found that, compared with the placebo, SAMe resulted in improved survival and reduced the need for liver transplants among subjects with severe cirrhosis.[31] A review of nine studies on the use of SAMe in alcoholic liver disease found no evidence to support—or refute—the beneficial effects of the supplement with regard to death from liver disease, rate of liver transplantation or transplant complications. However, the authors noted their conclusions were based mostly on only one trial that used adequate research methods.[32]

For alcoholic liver disease and cirrhosis, the dose used is 400 milligrams three to four times daily, taken on an empty stomach. Buy an enteric-coated product. See Chapter 8, page 181, for more information.

Nutrition Strategy Checklist for Cirrhosis

- ☐ Diet high in calories and vegetable protein
- ☐ Frequent small meals
- ☐ Branched chain amino acids
- ☐ Low-GI carbohydrate-rich foods
- ☐ Limit sodium
- ☐ High-potency multivitamin/mineral OR B complex
- ☐ Vitamin C
- ☐ Vitamin E
- ☐ Foods rich in beta carotene
- ☐ Foods rich in selenium
- ☐ Calcium and vitamin D
- ☐ Milk thistle
- ☐ Grapeseed extract
- ☐ SAMe

Recommended Resources

Canadian Liver Foundation
www.liver.ca
2235 Sheppard Avenue E., Suite 1500
Toronto, ON M2J 5B5
Tel: 416-491-3353 or 1-800-563-5483
Fax: 416-491-4952
Email: clf@liver.ca

American Liver Foundation
www.liverfoundation.org
75 Marden Lane, Suite 603
New York, NY, USA 10038
Tel: 212-668-1000
Fax: 212-483-8179

National Digestive Diseases Information Clearinghouse
National Institutes of Health
www2.niddk.nih.gov
Building 31, Rm 9A06

31 Center Drive, MSC 2560
Bethesda, MD, USA 20892-2560
Tel: 301-496-3583

Colds and Influenza

Cold is the common name for a viral infection of the upper respiratory tract, which includes the sinuses, the lining of the nose, the throat and the large airways. Most adults suffer from two to four colds per year and children six to ten, most often in the winter months. Current estimates indicate that the North American population suffers more than 1 billion colds annually, making this pesky condition a leading cause of doctor visits and school and work absenteeism. While colds may be annoying, they are fairly harmless and usually cause nothing more than an inconvenience in our busy lives.

Influenza, or the flu, is an infection of the entire respiratory system caused by influenza viruses. The flu is typically more severe than the common cold and is responsible for considerable illness worldwide. The influenza virus mutates rapidly, making it difficult for researchers trying to develop effective vaccines. In Canada, the flu season stretches from fall to spring, with peak activity from December through early March.

What Causes Colds and Flu?

There are over 100 viruses that can cause a cold, with rhinoviruses causing 50 percent of them. Because these viruses are so widespread and varied, conventional medicine has been unable to cure or prevent the common cold. Cold viruses are spread by direct person-to-person contact, contact with contaminated surfaces (e.g., telephone, door handles, stair rails, toys, used tissue) and inhalation of contaminated air droplets. When someone coughs or sneezes, or even talks, viruses are spread through the air. Inhaling the contaminated droplets allows viruses that have entered the nose to infect the nasal membranes. Cold viruses can remain infective for several hours outside the body. Rubbing your nose or eyes after touching an object that has been contaminated with saliva or nasal secretions will transfer the virus. Even shaking hands with someone who has a cold can expose you to infectious secretions.

Cold symptoms occur within 1 to 2 days after infection and peak 2 to 4 days later. However, some people report symptoms within 24 hours after exposure to the virus. A cold will usually last from 4 to 10 days and is most contagious shortly after symptoms first appear, approximately 2 to 3 days after the infection was contracted. People seem to suffer from colds more often during the winter months. This is probably because the winter temperatures keep people indoors, where they are more likely to come into prolonged contact with other people suffering from cold viruses. As well, the many rhinoviruses survive better when humidity is low, which is usually during the colder months. It's also possible that cold weather dries out the lining of the nasal passages, making them more susceptible to infection.

The flu is caused by influenza viruses A and B. Influenza A viruses are usually responsible for flu epidemics whereas influenza B viruses generally cause milder illness and do not undergo mutation as quickly as influenza A viruses. After infection, the incubation period for flu viruses is 1 to 4 days. Mild cases of the flu present much like the common cold; however, a flu is typically accompanied by chills, fever, aches and pains. Symptoms usually subside within 2 to 3 days although

fever may last for 5 days. The flu usually resolves in 3 days to 1 week. However, cough and general malaise can last for weeks.

Symptoms

Symptoms of the common cold include:

- sore, scratchy throat; cough
- husky voice
- sneezing; runny nose
- mild feeling of illness
- tired and achy
- mild headache
- watering eyes

Cold symptoms may be complicated by other illnesses that develop when the body's defences are weakened. For instance, children often suffer from middle ear infections during or after a cold. Bacterial infections of the sinuses may also follow a bout with a cold virus. Complications such as these increase the severity of cold symptoms and may be dangerous for some people. Contact a doctor if you develop a high fever that lasts longer than 2 days; if you experience chest pains, wheezing, hard coughing spells or earache; if you cough up thick green, yellow or bloody sputum; if your symptoms last more than a week or if you feel more ill than usual with a cold.

Symptoms of influenza include:

- chills and high fever
- cough; chest congestion
- body aches and pains
- headache
- sensitivity to light
- fatigue and weakness
- extreme exhaustion

The flu can also cause the complications observed for the common cold. However, the influenza virus can spread to the lungs, causing pneumonia, a serious complication that can lead to death. As well, on rare occasions, influenza can result in encephalitis (inflammation of the brain); symptoms can include fever, severe headache, neck stiffness, drowsiness, muscle weakness or seizures.

Who's at Risk?

Children have colds more often than adults. Women are also at high risk, possibly because of their often close contact with children or as an effect of their menstrual cycle. People who are fatigued, are stressed or have allergies are also more susceptible.

Certain people are at increased risk for influenza and its potential complications. They include adults aged 65 and older, children under the age of 2, children on long-term aspirin therapy, pregnant women, long-term care residents and those with cardiovascular disease or a respiratory illness.

Conventional Treatment

Colds and flu are caused by viruses and therefore cannot be treated with antibiotics. Antibiotic treatment is prescribed only if colds or flu are complicated by secondary bacterial infections. Because these illnesses usually resolve on their own in a short period of time, treatment focuses on reducing the severity and duration of symptoms and minimizing the risk of complications.

To help ease symptoms of the common cold:

- Stay warm and comfortable.
- Drink fluids to help keep mucus membranes moist.

- Rest at home if you have a fever or severe symptoms.
- Try nasal decongestants to provide temporary relief.
- Take antihistamines to reduce allergic reactions that may accompany colds.
- Use cough suppressants for severe coughs. (Coughing helps clear secretions and mucus from the airways and should be left untreated, if possible.)
- Use a vaporizer to loosen secretions and ease chest tightness.

Because the flu is often accompanied by high fever, aspirin or acetaminophen is often added to the over-the-counter pain relievers and anti-inflammatory agents used for symptom relief. (Note: Children and adolescents should not take aspirin because of increased risk of Reye's syndrome, a potentially fatal condition.)

Influenza vaccines are considered the standard of care for preventing the flu and its complications. Flu vaccines are typically modified each year to include the most prevalent strains from the previous season. The vaccine is only effective against three particular viral strains in any given season. Flu vaccines are available in the late fall. If you're at greater risk for succumbing to the flu and its complications, speak to your doctor about the benefits and drawbacks of vaccination. (Because there are so many types of cold viruses, it's impossible to prevent most colds with a vaccine.)

Preventing and Managing Colds and Flu

Although colds and flu can't actually be prevented, good personal hygiene will help protect you, your family and your co-workers from these viruses:

- Wash hands thoroughly and frequently.
- Cover your mouth when coughing or sneezing, preferably with a tissue.
- Clean surfaces that you touch with germ-killing disinfectant.
- Avoid rubbing your eyes and nose with dirty hands.
- Eat a nutritious diet.
- Get plenty of sleep.
- Avoid drinking alcohol.
- If possible, avoid crowded places or close contact with people who have colds or flu.
- Aim to get 30 to 60 minutes of light to moderate activity most days of the week. Studies show that physically active people get fewer colds each year than do their sedentary peers. Moderate exercise seems to improve immune function. But don't overdo it. High-intensity or prolonged endurance exercise steps up the production of stress hormones, which can hinder the body's ability to fight infection.

Dietary Strategies

Fluids

During a cold or the flu, drink at least 9 to 12 cups (2.2 to 3 L) of fluid per day to prevent dehydration and constipation. Hot fluids are most effective for alleviating nasal congestion. Drink hot water, hot tea, soups and broths. Fluid also helps keep the lining of the respiratory tract moist, which can ease the symptoms of a sore throat.

Drinking plenty of fluids each day is an important way to help prevent the common cold. When you're dehydrated, tiny cracks form in your nasal membranes. These cracks let in virus-filled droplets that promote infec-

tion. Always consume 9 to 12 cups (2.2 to 3 L) of fluid daily.

Chicken Soup

Research from Mount Sinai Hospital in Miami, Florida, suggests that chicken soup may help treat a cold.[1] A compound in the soup called cystine appears to have a decongestant effect. And it's thought that the spicier the soup, the better. Hot peppers contain capsaicin, a natural compound that acts as a decongestant.

Fermented Milk Products

Fermented milk products such as yogurt, kefir and acidophilus milk contain lactic acid bacteria, healthy bacteria that may help prevent the common cold and flu. Once ingested, these microbes take up residence in the gastrointestinal tract, where they exert their health benefits. A number of studies have shown that regular consumption of probiotic foods, such as fermented milk products, as well as probiotic supplements enhances the activity of the immune system.[2,3] Recent research suggests that a deficiency of lactic acid bacteria in the intestinal tract of children may be responsible for viral infections of the respiratory tract.[4] Include one fermented milk product in your daily diet. If you don't consume dairy products, consider taking a probiotic supplement as discussed later in this section.

Vitamins and Minerals

Vitamin C

Numerous studies have examined the effects of large doses of vitamin C on the common cold. While few studies support the notion that vitamin C supplements prevent a cold, many have demonstrated the ability of vitamin C to reduce the duration and severity of symptoms in adults and children. A review of thirty randomized trials involving 11,350 participants concluded that vitamin C consistently provided benefit in reducing the duration of colds. Among the thirty studies, six were conducted in people under physical stress, such as marathon runners, skiers and soldiers on subarctic exercise. In these individuals, vitamin C supplementation cut the risk of developing the common cold in half.[5-8]

Studies have tested doses of 200 milligrams and higher; however, the greatest benefit is seen when a daily dose of 2000 milligrams (2 grams) or more is taken. Children, people under physical stress and people with low dietary intakes of vitamin C tend to respond best to supplements of the nutrient.

Vitamin C promotes the body's production of immune compounds, including interferon, a natural antiviral agent that fights infection. Vitamin C also has a slight antihistaminic effect. To treat a cold, take a 500 milligram vitamin C pill four times daily. High doses of vitamin C can cause diarrhea, but this side effect resolves after continued use. You may have to build up to 2000 milligrams per day. Once your cold symptoms have subsided, return to a typical supplemental dose of 500 milligrams per day.

Large doses of vitamin C may not be safe for everyone. Vitamin C supplementation of 1000 milligrams (1 gram) appears to increase the risk of oxalate kidney stones, the most common type of kidney stones. Individuals with a history of oxalate kidney stones or kidney failure should restrict their intake to 100 milligrams per day. There's also some evidence that taking 500 milligrams of vitamin C for 18 months can increase the rate of carotid inner wall thickening in male smokers and former smokers. (The carotid arteries supply your head and neck with oxygen-rich blood. The thickness of carotid arteries is a marker of atherosclerosis or hardening of the arteries.) If you're a male with risk factors for heart disease—including cigarette smoking—use high-dose vitamin C cautiously.

Vitamin E

Vitamin E doesn't treat a cold, but it may play a role in preventing one. Research in healthy older adults determined that a daily vitamin E supplement taken for 1 month improved the responsiveness of the immune system. A study of 617 elderly nursing home residents found that a daily 200 international units (IU) vitamin E supplement versus a placebo reduced the number of colds (all study participants also took a daily multivitamin and mineral supplement).[9-11] Vitamin E appears to help certain white blood cells, called natural killer cells, fight infection.

Foods rich in vitamin E include wheat germ, nuts, seeds, vegetable oils, whole grains and leafy green vegetables. To supplement, take 200 to 400 IU of natural source vitamin E. The upper daily limit is 1500 IU. Avoid vitamin E supplements if you have diabetes or existing heart disease. See Chapter 4, page 53, for more information about the safety of vitamin E supplements.

Zinc

Studies support the use of zinc lozenges to reduce the duration of cold symptoms. Compared with cold sufferers taking placebo pills, those taking zinc gluconate or zinc acetate lozenges experienced faster recovery from coughing, sore throat, runny nose and headache.[12-15] However, not all studies have found zinc lozenges to be effective. It has been suggested that this may be because of the chemical form of zinc used or the addition of certain flavouring agents that may interfere with zinc's activity.[16–18]

When zinc lozenges are dissolved in the mouth, the zinc is released and attaches to cold viruses. Now unable to bind to cells in the mouth and throat, the virus cannot cause infection.

To treat a cold, take one zinc lozenge made of zinc gluconate or zinc acetate every 2 to 3 hours, for a total of five per day. More is *not* better, since taking high doses of zinc can cause toxic effects. Once your cold symptoms have disappeared, discontinue the use of zinc lozenges.

Since this mineral is vital to a healthy immune system, it's important to ensure that your daily diet contains zinc-rich foods. These include oysters, seafood, red meat, poultry, yogurt, wheat bran, wheat germ, whole grains and enriched breakfast cereals. Your diet and a multivitamin and mineral supplement will provide all the zinc you need to stay healthy.

Herbal Remedies

Echinacea

The majority of studies have shown this herbal remedy to be safe and possibly effective in treating an upper respiratory tract infection. Many studies in the laboratory have shown the ability of echinacea to enhance the body's production of white blood cells that fight infection. Despite the positive results in the lab, clinical trials in adults taking echinacea to treat a cold or flu have not conclusively shown that the herb is effective, perhaps because so many different brands were used. However, the most recent review of sixteen randomized trials conducted with 3396 participants found that most studies report a positive effect, most notably when supplements of *Echinacea*

purpurea were used. The beneficial effects of other echinacea preparations have not been consistently demonstrated in studies.[19]

To ensure quality, buy a product that's standardized to contain 4 percent echinacosides (*Echinacea angustifolia*) and 0.7 percent flavonoids (*Echinacea purpurea*), two of the herb's active ingredients. Take a total of 900 milligrams three to four times daily. For fluid extracts (1:1), take 0.25 to 1.0 millilitre three times daily. For tinctures (1:5), take 1 to 2 millilitres three times daily. For teas, take 125 to 250 millilitres three to four times daily. Take until symptoms are relieved, then continue taking two to three times daily for 1 week. Guidelines for doses in children can be found in Chapter 7, page 133. Don't use echinacea if you're allergic to plants in the Asteraceae/ Compositae family (ragweed, daisy, marigold and chrysanthemum).

Garlic (*Allium sativum*)

The sulphur compounds in garlic have been shown to stimulate the body's immune system, making garlic a potential agent in the prevention of colds.[20–22] In one study, researchers gave 146 volunteers one allicin-containing garlic supplement or a placebo daily for 12 weeks between November and February. Individuals in the garlic group reported significantly fewer colds than those in the placebo group. If infected, garlic users recovered faster than those taking the placebo.[23] Other studies have focused on the specific sulphur compounds in aged garlic extract, a special supplement that is aged for up to 20 months.

To help boost your immune system, use one-half to one clove of garlic each day in cooking. To supplement, buy a product made with aged garlic extract. Take two to six capsules a day, in divided doses. Aged garlic extract is odourless and less irritating to the gastrointestinal tract than other forms of garlic supplement (garlic oil capsules, garlic powder tablets).

Ginseng: *Panax* (Asian) or North American

This herbal remedy may help prevent colds through its ability to stimulate the immune system. A well-controlled trial in Italy found that 100 milligrams of *Panax ginseng* (G115 extract) taken daily resulted in a significant decline in the frequency of colds and flu.[24]

There's also evidence that a special extract made from North American ginseng, sold as COLD-fX (Afexa Life Sciences Inc.), can treat colds and flu. One study, published in 2008 in the *Canadian Medical Association Journal*, was conducted among 323 healthy adults aged 18 to 65 who had suffered at least two colds in the previous year. Compared with those who were given the placebo pill, participants who took two daily capsules of COLD-fX were 26 percent less likely to get a cold, and among those who did get colds, 56 percent were less likely to get a second one. This ginseng extract also seems to reduce the severity and duration of symptoms when infections do occur.[25-27] While COLD-fX shows promise for healthy adults, it has not been tested in children or the elderly.

To supplement with *Panax*, or Asian, ginseng, take 100 milligrams daily for 4 weeks prior to getting a flu vaccination and continue for 8 weeks thereafter.

To supplement with North American ginseng, take 200 milligrams COLD-fX (Afexa Life Sciences Inc.) twice daily during cold and flu season. Note: Do not take both *Panax* and North American ginseng. If you decide to give ginseng a try during cold and flu season, take only one form of the herb.

Ginseng is relatively safe at the recommended dosage. In some people, it may cause mild stomach upset, irritability and insomnia. Ginseng should not be used during pregnancy or breastfeeding or by individuals with poorly controlled high blood pressure.

Other Natural Health Products

Probiotic Supplements

Research suggests that taking a supplement containing lactobacilli and bifidobacteria can ease the severity and duration of colds and flu. In one study, 479 healthy adults supplemented daily with a multivitamin and mineral, and either with or without probiotic bacteria. Adding the probiotic supplement did not prevent colds, but it did significantly shorten the duration by almost two days, reduce the intensity of symptoms and lead to greater increases in immune compounds in the body.[28]

To supplement, buy a product that contains 1 billion to 10 billion live cells per dose (capsule). Choose a probiotic supplement that contains both lactobacilli and bifidobacteria strains. Take 1 billion to 10 billion viable cells three times daily with food. Children's products are available on the market; these usually contain one-quarter to one-half of the adult dose.

Nutrition Strategy Checklist for Treating and Preventing Colds and Influenza

- ☐ Hot fluids
- ☐ Chicken soup
- ☐ Fermented milk products
- ☐ Vitamin C

☐   Vitamin E

☐   Zinc lozenges

☐   Echinacea

☐   Garlic

☐   *Panax* OR North American ginseng

☐   Probiotic supplement

Recommended Resources

The Canadian Lung Association
www.lung.ca/diseases/common_cold.html
1750 Courtwood Crescent, Suite 300
Ottawa, ON K2C 2B5
Tel: 1-888-566-LUNG (5864)
Fax: 613-569-8860
Email: info@lung.ca

Food and Drug Administration
Department of Health and Human Services
www.fda.gov/ForConsumers/default.htm
Tel: 1-800-216-7331 or 301-575-0156

National Institute of Allergy and Infectious
Diseases
National Institutes of Health
NIAID Office of Communications and
Government Relations
www3.niaid.nih.gov
6610 Rockledge Drive, MSC 6612
Bethesda, MD, USA 20892-6612
Tel: 301-496-5717
Fax: 301-402-3573

Colorectal Cancer

In 2009, approximately 22,000 Canadians were diagnosed with colorectal cancer—on average, 423 Canadians every week[1]—and 9100 will die of it. Overall, colorectal cancer is the second-leading cause of death from cancer in men and women combined.

Colorectal cancer targets the cells of the large intestine, which is made up of the colon and the rectum, two essential components of your digestive system. When you eat, food passes from the stomach into the small intestine, where digestive juices break down the food into individual nutrients. Once nutrients are absorbed from food in the small intestine, the remaining watery mass passes into the colon, where excess water is removed. The remaining solid waste, or stool, is moved into the rectum and then passed out of the body in a bowel movement.

Cancer develops when the cells in the lining of the colon or rectum begin to grow out of control. These cells divide and multiply at abnormal rates, forming small clumps or growths known as polyps. When polyps first form, they are non-cancerous (benign). Eventually some of the polyps can change to become cancerous (malignant). Polyps smaller than 1 centimetre (0.5 inch) rarely become malignant, but the cancer risk increases as the polyps grow in size. There's almost a 50 percent chance of cancer developing from polyps that are larger than 2 centimetres (about 1 inch). Several different types of polyps can grow in the intestine, but those called adenomatous polyps are most likely to cause cancer.

What Causes Colorectal Cancer?

Scientists don't know what triggers polyps to develop. A hereditary factor may be involved. Studies indicate that people with a family history of colorectal cancer are much more likely to develop malignant growths in their intestinal tract. Colon cancer may also be stimulated by familial adenomatous polyposis, a rare hereditary genetic disorder that causes thousands of polyps to develop in the intestinal tract. People with the condition frequently develop colon cancer before the age of 40. Other risk factors for colorectal cancer include inflammatory bowel diseases such as ulcerative colitis and Crohn's disease.

Diet and lifestyle also play important roles in the development of colorectal cancer. Studies show that people at greater risk eat red meat and processed meat, and drink more alcohol. People who exercise regularly and who eat high-fibre diets, with plenty of fruit and vegetables, have a lower risk of colon cancer.

Colorectal cancer develops very slowly, usually over a period of 7 to 10 years. By reacting quickly to certain warning signs, it's possible to prevent cancer from developing. There are also several screening tests that can detect the presence of polyps. Removing polyps is the best way to prevent colorectal cancer. Screening tests can also find cancer in the early stages, when treatment is more effective and the disease is curable. Colorectal cancer often develops with no symptoms, which makes screening even more important.

Screening Tests

There are several screening options for colorectal cancer and each one has benefits and drawbacks. Screening options include:

- fecal occult blood test (FOBT)
- flexible sigmoidoscopy
- double-contrast barium enema
- colonoscopy
- virtual colonoscopy

The Canadian Cancer Society recommends that men and women age 50 and over who are at average risk of colorectal cancer have a fecal occult blood test at least every 2 years. This simple test requires collecting a stool sample at home for analysis at a laboratory. The test checks for blood in the stool that is not visible to the naked eye. If blood is found, more testing will be necessary to determine if the blood was caused by cancer. Beginning at age 50, your doctor will also recommend a screening sigmoidoscopy or colonoscopy every 3 to 5 years. If you have a higher risk for colorectal cancer, regular screening will begin at an earlier age and be done more frequently. A flexible sigmoidoscopy lets a gastroenterologist, a doctor who specializes in the gastrointestinal tract, examine the lining of the rectum and the lower one-third of the colon, called the sigmoid colon. The procedure involves inserting a soft, flexible, lighted viewing tube into the rectum and lower colon. During a sigmoidoscopy, the doctor can remove polyps and also take samples from abnormal-looking tissues to biopsy with a microscope for signs of disease.

A double-contrast barium enema checks for polyps using an x-ray of the entire colon, which is filled with a barium solution. However, biopsies cannot be taken during a barium enema.

A colonoscopy is a procedure that allows a gastroenterologist to look at the lining of the entire colon: A flexible, lighted viewing tube (a colonoscope) is inserted through the rectum. Biopsies can be taken and polyps can be removed during this screening test. A virtual colonoscopy—known as computerized tomography (CT) colonography—uses a CT scanner to produce hundreds of cross-sectional images of your abdominal organs. These images provide a detailed view of the interior of your colon without having to insert a colonoscope or use sedation. Doctors may use virtual colonoscopy when conventional colonoscopy or other screening exams can't be done.

Symptoms

Colorectal cancer can be present for several years before symptoms develop. Symptoms can be numerous and non-specific and can vary depending on where in the large intestine the tumour is located. Consult your doctor if you have any of these warning signs:

- a change in normal bowel habits for more than 2 weeks, such as constipation or diarrhea or both
- narrow, pencil-thin stools
- bright- or dark-red blood in or on your stools on more than one occasion
- constant abdominal pain, cramping or bloating
- frequent gas pain
- a feeling that your bowel doesn't empty completely
- weight loss for no apparent reason
- constant fatigue, which may be caused by iron-deficiency anemia due to slow blood loss over a long period of time

These symptoms may be caused by other conditions, such as ulcers or hemorrhoids. However, changes in your stools or bowel habits should not be ignored and require immediate medical attention. People with a family history of colorectal cancer should be screened regularly for the disease.

Who's at Risk?

While there is no single cause of colorectal cancer, the following factors are known to increase the risk of developing it:

- age—risk rises as we get older, especially after 50

- family history of colorectal cancer—especially if the relative (parent, sibling, child) developed the disease before the age of 45
- inflammatory bowel disease (ulcerative colitis, Crohn's disease)
- genetic disorders such as Gardner's syndrome, familial adenomatous polyposis (FAP) or hereditary non-polyposis colorectal cancer (HNPCC)
- ethnic background—people of Eastern European Jewish descent have a greater risk
- obesity
- physical inactivity
- smoking
- alcohol consumption
- diet high in red and processed meat

Conventional Treatment

Surgery is the most common treatment for colorectal cancer. The tumour, a small margin of the surrounding healthy bowel and nearby lymph nodes are removed. The surgeon then reconnects the healthy sections of the intestine. In cases of rectal cancer, the rectum is permanently removed and the surgeon creates a colostomy, an opening on the abdominal wall for elimination of waste material into an external bag. In patients with early-stage colon cancer, surgery is often the only treatment needed. After surgery for early-stage colorectal cancer, the long-term survival rate is 80 percent or higher.

The long-term prognosis for colorectal cancer after surgery depends on whether the cancer has spread (metastasized) to other organs. The risk of metastasis depends on how deeply the cancer spread into the bowel wall. In patients with advanced colon cancer where the tumour has penetrated beyond the bowel wall, chemotherapy is used after surgery to kill remaining cancer cells and improve survival. Radiation therapy is used to treat cancers of the rectum.

Preventing Colorectal Cancer

Dietary Strategies

Carbohydrates: Low Glycemic Index

High intakes of refined starches, especially foods made with white flour, seem to increase the risk of colorectal cancer. There is also evidence that sucrose-containing foods increase the risk. High blood levels of the sugar-clearing hormone insulin have been associated with a greater risk of colorectal cancer. As a result, researchers have investigated whether a high glycemic diet that increases blood sugar and causes elevated insulin levels can increase the risk of colorectal cancer. Some, but not all, research supports a relationship between glycemic index and colorectal cancer risk. In one study that followed 38,451 women for almost 8 years, those on a diet with the highest glycemic load had almost a threefold greater risk of developing colorectal cancer that those on a diet with the lowest.[2] It's thought that insulin and insulin-like growth factors in the blood can stimulate the development of colorectal cancer cells.

As often as possible, avoid consuming too much table sugar, cookies, cakes, desserts, candy, chocolate, fruit drinks, soft drinks, syrup, corn syrup and jam. Refined foods with a high glycemic index, such as white bread, crackers, pre-sweetened breakfast cereals, cereal bars, granola bars, white pasta and white rice, should be limited. For meals and snacks, choose foods containing low glycemic carbo-hydrates to prevent large rises in insulin. Examples of low glycemic foods include lentils, kidney beans, barley, 100% stone-ground bread, large flake oatmeal, 100% bran cereal, pasta, yogurt and soy milk. For foods listed with their corresponding glycemic-index value, see Chapter 1, page 8.

Dietary Fibre

It's long been thought that a diet high in fibre prevents colorectal cancer in a number of ways. Dietary fibre can bind bile acids before they can enter colon cells (certain bile acids are toxic to colon cells). A high fibre intake can increase stool bulk and dilute the concentration of cancer-causing substances. By speeding the rate at which waste products are removed from the colon, dietary fibre can prevent carcinogens from making contact with colon and rectal cells. Finally, bacterial fermentation of fibre in the colon produces short-chain fatty acids, substances that have anti-cancer properties.

A combined analysis of 13 studies involving 735,628 healthy men and women who were followed for 6 to 20 years found that a high intake of fibre was associated with a reduced risk of developing colorectal cancer. However, once the researchers accounted for other risk factors, the protective effect of fibre was no longer evident.[3] Three large randomized controlled trials revealed that when people at high risk for colon cancer (they have adenoma-tous polyps) were given a high-fibre diet or daily fibre supplements for a number of years, there was no reduction in the growth of polyps.[4-6] Cancer is a slow process and these studies may have been too short to detect a protective effect. It's also possible that fibre may affect cancer development before polyps occur. It may be that fibre works with other compounds in foods to lower your risk. Some research also suggests that men may experience greater benefit from fibre. In one trial, there was no overall association between fibre supplementation and the recurrence of polyps. But when the researchers analyzed the results for men and women separately, fibre supplementation significantly reduced the risk of polyp recurrence in men but not women.[7]

The relationship between a high-fibre diet and colon cancer risk remains unclear. However, because dietary fibre is associated with so many other health benefits, current recommendations are to consume between 21 and 38 grams per day depending on your age. See Chapter 1, page 4, for a list of fibre-rich foods.

Evidence does suggest that eating more whole grains can lower the risk. In a 2007 study of almost 500,000 men and women, aged 50 to 71, whole-grain intake—but not total fibre—was protective. Participants who ate the most whole grains were one-fifth as likely to develop colorectal cancer compared with those who ate the least.[8] Whole grains such as barley, brown rice, oats, whole wheat, whole rye and quinoa contain a "package" of nutrients and phytochemicals that are thought to work together to guard against cancer. For more information on whole grains, see Chapter 5, page 89.

Fish and Omega-3 Fatty Acids

Results from animal and lab studies suggest that omega-3 fatty acids in fish oil may reduce the risk of colon cancer by inhibiting normal cells from becoming cancerous and by inhibiting the growth of cancerous cells. In studies conducted in people, fish consumption was shown to slightly reduce colorectal cancer risk—in one study by as much as 50 percent.[9,10] Some research has also demonstrated that fish oil supplements, when taken for up to 6 months, can actually improve the health of colon cells in people at high risk for colorectal cancer. While it's premature to recommend fish oil capsules for the prevention of colon and rectal cancer, it makes sense to add fish to your weekly menu.

Aim to eat oily fish at least two times per week. Salmon, trout, Arctic char, herring, sardines and mackerel are good choices. If you don't eat fish, consider taking a fish oil capsule. For information on omega-3 fatty acid supplements see Chapter 8, page 163.

Fruit and Vegetables

Research suggests that many types of vegetables can reduce the risk of polyp recurrence and, possibly, colorectal cancer. Raw vegetables, dark-green leafy vegetables, cruciferous vegetables (broccoli, cauliflower, cabbage, turnip), deep-yellow vegetables, onions and garlic seem to offer protection.[11] A recent study that followed 452,755 men and women for almost 9 years found that those with the highest intake of fruit and vegetables had a significantly lower risk of colorectal cancer, most notably colon cancer. Interestingly, the protective effect of fruit and vegetables was observed only in people who never smoked or who had quit smoking.[12] Researchers suspect that cigarette smoke may negate the beneficial effects of fruit and vegetables.

Fruit and vegetables contain many substances that may keep the bowel healthy. Beta carotene, lutein, B vitamins, vitamin C and other natural phytochemicals may all have anti-cancer properties. Produce is also rich in fibre. And certain vegetables such as asparagus and Jerusalem artichokes may promote the growth of health-enhancing bacteria in the intestinal tract.

Aim to include 7 to 10 servings of fruit and vegetables combined in your daily diet. See

Chapter 5 for serving sizes and a list of vegetables categorized by their predominant phytochemicals (e.g., beta carotene, lutein).

Milk and Milk Products

Many studies have revealed that greater intakes of low-fat dairy products are associated with a lower risk of colorectal cancer. A large study of Swedish men found that a high dairy intake versus low consumption was associated with a 54 percent reduced risk of colorectal cancer. Calcium intake from dairy foods was also shown to lower the risk. Compared with those who consumed the least calcium from milk and milk products, individuals who consumed the most were 32 percent less likely to develop colorectal cancer.[13] When researchers pooled the results from ten large studies conducted in 534,536 individuals, milk intake was clearly linked with a lower risk of colorectal cancer. Compared with those who consumed less than 70 ml (about 1/3 cup) of milk per day, people whose diets included at least 250 ml (1 cup) were 15 percent less likely to develop colorectal cancer. Calcium intake from foods and supplements was also protective.[14] It's thought that once calcium is ingested, the mineral binds with bile acids in the intestinal tract, thereby preventing their toxic effect on colon cells.

Be sure to meet your daily calcium requirements by eating three to four 1 cup servings of low-fat milk or yogurt. If you don't eat dairy foods, calcium-fortified soy beverages can be substituted. Supplements can also help increase your calcium intake. I discuss calcium supplements and colorectal cancer risk further on.

Meat (Red) and Processed Meat

The evidence is convincing that a high intake of red meat and processed meat increases the risk of colorectal cancer. A review of twenty-nine large studies, published in 2006, summarized the risk of colorectal cancer based on red meat and processed meat consumption. The researchers concluded that compared with people with lower meat intakes, those with the highest intake of red meat and processed meat had a 28 percent and 20 percent increased risk, respectively, of developing the cancer. Red and processed meat increased the risk of both colon and rectal cancer, although the link to red meat was stronger for rectal cancer.[15-17]

Meat might increase colorectal cancer risk in a few ways. Cooking meat at a high temperature forms heterocyclic amines, compounds that laboratory studies have found to be cancer causing. Studies in humans also suggest that heterocyclic amines and meat cooked well done increase colorectal cancer risk. A recent study of 25,540 men and women found that a high versus low intake of heterocyclic amines from the diet increased the risk of colorectal adenoma (polyps) by 47 percent. As well, the risk of pre-cancerous polyps increased with the consumption of strongly or extremely browned meat.[18,19] The form of iron in red meat—heme iron—may also damage colon cells and trigger cancer growth. And it's thought that nitrites, used as colour additives and preservatives, in processed meats may form cancer-causing compounds.

Limit your intake of red meat (beef, veal, pork, lamb, goat) to less than 18 ounces (500 g) per week. Choose fish, chicken, turkey, legumes, tofu and soy foods more often than red meat. Eat very little, if any, processed meats. "Processed meats" commonly refers to meats (usually red meats) preserved by smoking, curing, salting or the addition of preservatives. Ham, bacon, pastrami, salami, bologna, hot dogs and sausages are processed meats. Burgers sometimes fall into the processed meat category if they are preserved with chemicals. A few studies have defined turkey and chicken slices as processed meat. On sandwiches, enjoy tuna, salmon or fresh-cooked chicken and turkey.

Green Tea

Research suggests that antioxidant compounds in green tea may prevent colon cells from becoming cancerous. Population studies have shown that drinking green tea is associated with lower rates of colon and rectal cancer. A review of twenty-five studies conducted in eleven countries concluded that drinking green tea is associated with an 18 percent lower risk of colorectal cancer.[20] Laboratory studies have demonstrated the ability of antioxidants in green tea to powerfully inhibit cancer growth by triggering the death of cancer cells, halting the growth of blood vessels in tumours and shutting off genes in cancer cells. Green tea antioxidants also have anti-inflammatory effects that may play a role in preventing colorectal cancer.

Add at least 2 cups of green tea to your daily diet—drink it in place of coffee, soft drinks and fruit drinks. I recommend brewing green tea from loose tea leaves rather than tea bags. The tea is much better tasting and also contains more antioxidants. (Whole tea leaves have more surface area for hot water to extract the flavour and the antioxidants in the leaf. Tea bags, which contain tea fannings and dust, don't have as much surface area for this extraction.)

Alcoholic Beverages

There is plenty of evidence that all types of alcoholic beverages increase the risk of colorectal cancer. A pooled analysis of sixteen studies involving more than 6300 people found that alcohol significantly increased cancers of the colon and rectum. Compared with those consuming the least alcohol, individuals who reported the highest intake had a 50 percent greater risk of colon cancer and a 63 percent increased risk of rectal cancer.[21]

Alcohol may stimulate the growth of colorectal cancer cells, activate cancer-causing substances and help transform polyps into cancer. Alcohol also interferes with the body's use of folate, a B vitamin needed for the repair of DNA in cells. If you do drink alcohol, increase your intake of folate-rich foods such as cooked spinach, lentils, asparagus, avocado and oranges.

Cancer experts do not recommend the consumption of alcohol. If you drink, limit yourself to no more than two drinks per day and a maximum of nine per week (men) or no more than one drink per day and a maximum of seven per week (women).

Weight Control

There is ample and convincing evidence that excess abdominal fat and body weight increases the risk of colorectal cancer. What's more, as abdominal fat increases, so does colorectal cancer risk. Increasing body fat may elevate colorectal cancer risk by promoting inflammation in the body, influencing circulating hormones and increasing insulin levels.

During adulthood, maintain a healthy body mass index (BMI) and waist circumference. Be proactive to avoid weight gain and increases in waist circumference throughout adulthood. See Obesity, Overweight and Weight Loss, page 570, to learn what your BMI and waist circumference should be.

Physical Activity

Many studies show a strong relationship between increased physical activity and protection from colorectal cancer. Regular exercise has been shown to reduce the risk of colon cancer by 30 percent to 40 percent. A 2009 published analysis of fifty-two studies reported a significant protective effect of physical activity in men and women.[22] Regular exercise stimulates peristalsis, wave-like muscular contractions that help move waste through the colon. As well, regular exercise of moderate intensity can lower levels of certain hormones and insulin that can promote cancer growth.

To reduce the risk of colon cancer, experts advise being moderately physically active, equivalent to brisk walking, for at least 30 minutes every day. As fitness improves, aim for 60 minutes or more of moderate or 30 minutes or more of vigorous physical activity every day. Limit sedentary habits such as watching television.

Vitamins and Minerals

Folate

A deficiency of this B vitamin has been linked with colorectal cancer. Folate is essential for the production within cells of a cell's genetic material, DNA (deoxyribonucleic acid). DNA is the blueprint that controls individual cell division and all body processes. Without enough folate, the ability of colorectal cells to repair faulty DNA can be impaired, increasing the risk of cancer development. A lack of folate may also make the harmful effect of alcohol on colon cells more pronounced. A handful of studies have found that an increased intake of folate from foods and a multivitamin may guard against colorectal cancer.[23–26] Research suggests that a folate-rich diet may be most protective for women with a family history of colorectal cancer.

However, supplements of folic acid (the synthetic form of folate) have not been shown to reduce the risk of colon and rectal cancers.

In a study of 1021 men and women who had a previous pre-cancerous colon polyp, taking a daily 1 milligram folic acid supplement did not reduce the risk of recurrent polyps. In fact, compared with those in the placebo group, individuals in the folic acid group had a higher risk of having three or more adenomatous polyps and of having other types of cancer.[27] Scientists speculate that if taken early in life, folic acid supplements may reduce the risk of colorectal cancer, but if taken later in life, folic acid may stimulate the growth of pre-cancerous polyps.

Meet your daily folate requirements by adding folate-rich foods such as spinach, lentils, orange juice, whole grains, fortified breakfast cereals, asparagus, artichoke, avocado and seeds to your diet. To supplement, take a multivitamin and mineral that contains 400 micrograms of folic acid. Avoid taking higher doses of folic acid from a supplement.

Vitamin D

Over the past several decades, studies have supported the notion that higher levels of vitamin D in the body may lower the risk of colorectal cancer. Research has even suggested that sufficient vitamin D blood levels at the time of diagnosis and treatment may improve survival from colorectal cancer. Vitamin D production in the skin seems to reduce the risk of several cancers, including those of the colon and rectum. The evidence to date suggests that a daily intake of 1000 to 2000 international units (IU) could reduce the risk of colorectal cancer.

The fact that very few foods contain vitamin D and our skin doesn't produce the vitamin in the fall and winter months makes it necessary to get vitamin D from a supplement. The Canadian Cancer Society recommends adults take 1000 IU of vitamin D each day in the fall and winter. Older adults, people with dark skin, those who don't go outdoors often and those who wear clothing that covers most of their skin should take the supplement year-round. For more information on vitamin D supplementation, see Chapter 4, page 51.

Vitamin E

An intake of foods rich in vitamin E has been linked with a lower risk of colorectal cancer. A study conducted among Iowa women found that those with the highest intake of vitamin E had a 68 percent lower risk of the cancer than those who consumed the least. Vitamin E was most protective in women under 65 years of age.[28] Another study found some suggestion that 300 IU of vitamin E offered men, but not women, protection from colon cancer.[29] One Finnish study found that vitamin E supplements offered men protection from colorectal cancer.[30]

Vitamin E is a strong antioxidant, able to protect the genetic material of cells from damage caused by free radical molecules. Cells with faulty genetic material may progress to polyps and eventually cancer. Studies have revealed that the colon cells in patients with colorectal cancer have a diminished antioxidant capacity.

The best food sources of vitamin E include wheat germ, nuts, seeds, vegetable oils, whole grains and leafy greens. To learn more about vitamin E, see Chapter 4, page 52.

Calcium

Earlier I discussed study findings linking higher intakes of dairy products with a lower risk of colorectal cancer. Studies have also determined that calcium—from food sources and from supplements—helps guard against the cancer. Two randomized controlled trials revealed that supplemental calcium in doses of 1200 and 2000 milligrams per day reduced the development of recurrent colorectal adenomatous polyps. When the results from both trials were combined, the risk of recurrent polyps was reduced by 26 percent with calcium supplementation.[31]

If you don't meet your calcium intake from your diet—and many Canadians don't—take a calcium supplement. To learn more about calcium requirements, food sources and how to supplement safely, see Chapter 4, page 58.

Selenium

This trace mineral is needed to form a selenium-containing enzyme called gluta-thione peroxidase. As a part of glutathione peroxidase, selenium acts as an antioxidant, protecting the genetic material of cells from free radical damage. Studies show that, compared with people free of colorectal cancer, individuals with the disease have lower levels of selenium and glutathione peroxidase in their body.[32-34]

An American study investigated the daily use of a 200 microgram selenium supplement and the risk of colorectal adenomas in 1312 people. Selenium supplementation was associated with a reduced risk of pre-cancerous polyps, but only in smokers and people with a low blood selenium level at the start of the study. In these individuals, taking a selenium supplement reduced the risk of pre-cancerous polyps by 73 percent.[35]

Selenium-rich foods include Brazil nuts, shrimp, salmon, halibut, crab, fish, pork, organ meats, wheat bran, whole-wheat bread, brown rice, onion, garlic and mushrooms. To supplement, take 100 to 200 micrograms of selenium per day. Check how much your multivitamin and mineral pill gives you before you buy a separate selenium pill since some multis contain as much as 100 micrograms of the mineral.

Herbal Remedies

Garlic (*Allium sativum*)

A daily intake of raw and cooked garlic and its accompanying sulphur compounds is associated with a lower risk of colon and rectal cancer. A recent review of published studies found that a high intake of raw and cooked garlic reduced the risk of colon cancer by 30 percent.[36] The Iowa Women's Health Study, which followed 42,000 women for 5 years, found that women who consumed 0.7 grams of garlic per day (less than one clove) had a 32 percent lower risk of colon cancer than those who did not consume garlic.[37] Research has also demonstrated that in patients with colorectal adenomas, supplementation with aged garlic extract can reduce the number and size of adenomas after 1 year of treatment.[38,39]

Garlic may help prevent cancer in a number of ways. Like vitamin E, garlic possesses antioxidant properties, which may keep DNA healthy. The sulphur compounds in garlic may also help the liver detoxify cancer-causing substances. Garlic may have a direct toxic effect on certain types of cancer cells. And finally, studies have shown that garlic, in particular the allyl sulphides in aged garlic extract, stimulate the body's immune system.

Include one to two cloves of cooked or raw garlic in your daily diet. To supplement, buy aged garlic extract. The aging process used to make this supplement increases the concentration of the sulphur compounds that stimulate the immune system. Aged garlic is also odour free and gentler on the stomach. Generally, two to six capsules a day (one or two with meals)

are recommended. You can also buy aged garlic in a liquid form (Kyolic brand) that you add to foods.

Nutrition Strategy Checklist for Preventing Colorectal Cancer

☐ Low-GI carbohydrate-rich foods
☐ Limit sugar and sweets
☐ Dietary fibre
☐ Whole grains
☐ Fish
☐ Milk and milk products
☐ Limit red meat
☐ Avoid processed meat
☐ Fruit and vegetables
☐ Green tea
☐ Limit alcohol
☐ Control weight
☐ Folate
☐ Vitamin D
☐ Vitamin E
☐ Calcium
☐ Selenium
☐ Garlic

Recommended Resources

Canadian Cancer Society
www.cancer.ca
10 Alcorn Avenue, Suite 200
Toronto, ON M4V 3B1
Tel: 416-961-7223
Fax: 416-961-4189
Email: ccs@cancer.ca

Colorectal Cancer Association of Canada
www.colorectal-cancer.ca
60 St. Clair Avenue East, Suite 204
Toronto, ON M4T 1N5
Tel: 1-877-50-COLON (26566)
Fax: 416-920-3004
Email: information@colorectal-cancer.ca

American Cancer Society
www.cancer.org
Tel: 1-800-ACS-2345 (227-2345)

National Cancer Institute
www.cancernet.gov
6116 Executive Boulevard, Room 3036A
Bethesda, MD, USA 20892-8322
Tel: 301-435-3848 or 1-800-4-CANCER
   (226237) (help-line)

Colon Cancer Alliance, Inc.
www.ccalliance.org
1200 G Street, NW, Suite 800
Washington, DC, USA 20005
Tel: 202-434-8980
Fax: 866-304-9075

Congestive Heart Failure (CHF)

Congestive heart failure (CHF) is a serious medical disorder that requires monitoring by a physician. The term *heart failure* can be misleading: This condition doesn't actually cause your heart to fail or stop beating, but rather your heart becomes weakened and can no longer deliver enough oxygen-rich blood to the body to meet its needs. CHF is generally a progressive disease with periods of stability and episodes of exacerbation.

The heart is a hollow, muscular organ that circulates blood to all parts of your body. Blood is pumped by the right side of your heart to the lungs, where it becomes loaded with oxygen, a fuel essential for maintaining your bodily functions. The oxygenated blood then returns to the heart, where the chambers on the left side circulate the blood to your brain and other vital organs and through the body's whole circulatory system. Once your cells have absorbed the oxygen and nutrients, the blood returns to the heart and the cycle begins again.

When your heart becomes damaged and weak, its ability to pump blood is compromised. Less blood is forced into your system, causing a backup of fluid (congestion) in your lungs and other tissues. Your organs become deprived of the oxygen and vital nutrients they need for fuel, which means that they can no longer function properly. Congestive heart failure can leave you feeling tired and short of breath after even the slightest exertion.

As the damage from CHF progresses, the heart must work harder to compensate for its reduced pumping power. This extra workload causes the heart to undergo significant changes. Over time, the heart may become enlarged and stretched so that it can pump larger quantities of blood. Or the heart muscle may thicken, building extra strength to increase the force of each pump. In some cases, the heart may beat faster, attempting to compensate for its shortcomings by pumping blood more frequently. These changes weaken the heart even more by causing it to strain and overwork.

Congestive heart failure also affects the kidneys. The kidneys, which normally eliminate excess water from your body, begin to retain salt (sodium) and water, increasing the volume of blood circulating in your system. Initially, this improves the heart's performance. However, the excess fluid eventually accumulates in various parts of the body, causing swelling (edema) in your legs and feet when you're standing or in your back and abdomen when you're lying down. Weight gain is frequently a result of this increased retention of sodium and water.

What Causes Congestive Heart Failure?

Any disease that weakens or stiffens the heart muscle can lead to congestive heart failure. Diseases that increase oxygen demand by the body tissue beyond the capability of the heart to deliver can also lead to CHF. The most common causes include:

- coronary artery disease—fatty deposits that narrow the arteries supplying blood to your heart
- heart attack
- high blood pressure
- heart valve problems—damage to tiny valves in your heart that keep the blood flowing in the right direction
- cardiomyopathy—damage to the heart muscle caused by viral infections or drug and alcohol abuse
- congenital heart disease—heart damage that may occur at birth
- arrhythmias—abnormal heart rhythms may cause the heart to beat too fast
- other medical conditions—diabetes, extreme obesity or an overactive thyroid gland
- long-standing alcohol abuse

CHF is an incurable disease. However, symptoms can be managed and progression of the disease can be controlled with medications and lifestyle changes. Unfortunately, only 20 percent of people diagnosed with this condition survive longer than 8 to 10 years and nearly one in five dies within the first year after diagnosis.

Symptoms

CHF progresses gradually and symptoms such as the following develop slowly:

- shortness of breath when you exert yourself
- shortness of breath when lying down
- wheezing or coughing, accompanied by shortness of breath
- fatigue and weakness
- swelling in your legs, ankles, feet or abdomen
- increased urination, especially at night
- swollen neck veins
- rapid weight gain
- dizzy spells
- nausea, abdominal pain, decreased appetite (caused by fluid accumulation in the liver and intestines)

Who's at Risk?

Because older people tend to suffer most often from diseases that cause congestive heart failure, they are the most susceptible to developing CHF. The risk is higher for people with poorly controlled high blood pressure, coronary heart disease, kidney disease and diabetes. The disease affects men and women equally.

Conventional Treatment

The following lifestyle modifications can ease symptoms and help prevent CHF from becoming worse:

- **Increase daily exercise:** Moderate exercise helps your heart pump more efficiently; try

20 to 40 minutes of moderate walking 3 to 5 days per week.[1-4]

- **Stop smoking:** Smoking damages your heart muscle and reduces the amount of oxygen in your blood.
- **Manage stress:** Chronic stress can make your heart beat faster.
- **Restrict sodium and fluid intake:** Sodium causes an increase in fluid accumulation in the body's tissues.

The following medications may be used to treat heart failure:

- **ACE (angiotensin-converting enzyme) inhibitors** to lower blood pressure and help blood flow more easily
- **Diuretics** to keep fluids from accumulating in your body by increasing urination
- **Digoxin** to slow the heartbeat and increase the power of each beat
- **Beta blockers** to slow your heart rate and reduce blood pressure

Surgery may be necessary to replace faulty heart valves or repair damage caused by coronary artery disease. A heart transplant may be needed in severe cases of CHF.

Managing Congestive Heart Failure

Dietary Strategies

Your heart doesn't have to work as hard when you make certain alterations to your diet. If you have congestive heart failure, the following strategies can help lessen your symptoms:

- **Monitor fluids.** Individuals with severe heart failure may need to restrict daily fluids to 1000 to 2000 millilitres (1 to 2 L) to prevent fluid retention. To monitor fluid gain, weigh yourself daily before breakfast (after urinating). A rapid weight gain of more than 3 pounds (1.3 kg) may indicate that you're retaining fluid and may require additional treatment. Notify your doctor if you gain weight suddenly.
- **Avoid alcohol and caffeine.** Alcohol can reduce your heart's ability to pump effectively and can interact with heart medications.[5] As well, limit or avoid beverages and foods containing caffeine, which can potentially increase the heart rate and cause abnormal heart rhythms. (See Chapter 5, page 110, for the caffeine content of selected foods.)
- **Eat often.** Eating small, frequent meals may increase appetite, improve your intake of calories and nutrients, and help reduce the workload of the heart. Calorie needs for people with CHF are higher because of the additional workload of the heart and an increased metabolism. By eating five or six times a day, you'll be more likely to meet your energy needs.

Sodium

Sodium restriction is the primary dietary intervention for treating CHF. Too much salt (sodium chloride) causes the body to retain water, making your heart work harder. This causes shortness of breath and fluid accumulation in body tissues. For mild to moderate heart failure, reduce your intake to no more than 2000 milligrams (2 g) of sodium per day. Some individuals will require further sodium restriction as recommended by a registered dietitian. To reduce sodium intake, practise the following:

- Eliminate salty processed foods and restaurant meals (see Chapter 5, page 108).
- Read food labels to see how much sodium is present. Foods with a daily value of 5% or less are low in sodium.
- Remove the saltshaker from the table; don't add salt when cooking.
- Avoid beverages high in salt: vegetable juice, tomato juice, some mineral waters and hot malt beverages.
- Use herbs and spices for seasonings: pepper, garlic powder, onion powder and lemon juice.
- When dining out, ask that no salt be added to meals.
- Discuss the use of salt substitutes with your dietitian. Some brands should not be used if you are taking certain diuretic medications.

Vitamins and Minerals

Multivitamin and Mineral Supplements

Many people with advanced heart failure are deficient in certain nutrients and can benefit from a daily multivitamin and mineral supplement. People with CHF often have difficulty eating enough food to meet their increased energy requirements. In addition to nutrient deficiencies due to reduced food intake, impaired absorption can cause increased loss of nutrients from the body. Some evidence also suggests that supplementing with a multivitamin and mineral supplement might improve heart function in elderly individuals with CHF. Furthermore, ensuring an adequate intake of vitamins B6, B12 and folic acid from a multivitamin can help prevent accumulation in the blood of an amino acid called homocysteine. Elevated homocysteine is thought to increase the risk of CHF by damaging artery walls.

To help prevent nutrient deficiencies, take one multivitamin and mineral pill daily. Look for a supplement that provides 0.4 milligrams (400 micrograms) of folic acid. Avoid larger doses of this B vitamin.

Antioxidants

It is a well-accepted assertion that damage caused by free radicals contributes to the development and progression of CHF.[6-8] Free radicals are unstable oxygen molecules generated by normal body processes. If produced in excess, they can damage virtually every cell in the body. A regular intake of dietary antioxidants (vitamins C and E, beta carotene, selenium) helps the body keep free radical activity under control.

Whether antioxidant supplements help treat CHF remains to be seen. It's possible that they may help prevent a worsening of heart failure. A few studies have shown that supplementation with vitamins C and E can reduce free radical activity in CHF.[9,10] Therefore, be sure to include the following antioxidants in your daily diet:

VITAMIN C. Best food sources include citrus fruit, citrus juices, cantaloupe, kiwi, mango, strawberries, broccoli, Brussels sprouts, cauliflower, red pepper and tomato juice. To supplement, take 500 or 600 milligrams of vitamin C, once daily.

VITAMIN E. Best food sources include wheat germ, nuts, seeds, vegetable oils, whole grains and kale. Avoid taking vitamin E supplements. There is no evidence that supplemental vitamin E delays disease progression or improves the quality of life in patients with CHF. What's more, research suggests that taking 400 international units (IU) of vitamin E once daily can increase the risk of heart failure in individuals with diabetes and coronary heart disease.[11]

SELENIUM. Best food sources are seafood, chicken, organ meats, whole grains, Brazil nuts, nuts, onions, garlic and mushrooms. To supplement, take 200 micrograms of selenium-rich yeast per day.

BETA CAROTENE. Best food sources are orange and dark-green produce, including carrots, sweet potato, winter squash, broccoli, collard greens, kale, spinach, apricots, cantaloupe, peaches, nectarines, mango and papaya. There is no evidence to warrant taking a beta carotene supplement for managing CHF.

Thiamin (Vitamin B1)
Long-term use of a diuretic called Lasix (furosemide) leads to a loss of thiamin in the urine, and a deficiency of this B vitamin may worsen heart performance. Many studies have found that patients with heart failure who take these diuretics are deficient in thiamin.[12–14] Thiamin deficiency leads to impaired metabolism, retention of fluid and sodium, and swelling. Researchers have also found that a daily thiamin supplement can replenish the body's supply of the vitamin and improve the functioning of the heart.[15]

If you're taking Lasix, your doctor should monitor your thiamin status. To treat a deficiency, take 100 milligrams of thiamin twice daily. Thiamin is very safe and rarely causes an adverse reaction.

Vitamin D
Preliminary research suggests that vitamin D may help prevent the development and progression of CHF. Among its many important roles in the body, vitamin D has anti-inflammatory actions and is needed for proper immune function. A study conducted in 123 men with CHF and an average age of 55 found that taking 2000 IU of vitamin D daily for 15 months led to a significant reduction in inflammatory compounds and an increase in anti-inflammatory immune compounds. This finding suggests that vitamin D has protective effects on the heart itself.[16]

If diet or sun exposure cannot be relied on to provide adequate vitamin D, adults aged 50 and older should take 1000 IU of vitamin D year-round to ensure sufficient blood levels. If you have CHF, consider taking 2000 IU of vitamin D per day. Choose a supplement that contains vitamin D3 instead of D2, as D3 is more biologically active in the body. See Chapter 4, page 51, for more information on vitamin D supplementation.

Magnesium
This mineral is essential for the functioning of heart cell membranes, and many enzymes that catalyze reactions in the heart muscle use it. A number of medications used to treat CHF can alter magnesium levels in the body.[17] A decrease in magnesium in patients with CHF has been linked to heart arrhythmias and a poorer prognosis.[18,19] Studies have shown that supplementation of magnesium increases mineral levels in the body, improves vascular function and reduces heart arrhythmias.[20–23]

Good food sources of magnesium include nuts and seeds (choose unsalted varieties), legumes, prunes, figs, whole grains, leafy green vegetables and brewer's yeast. Your heart specialist will monitor your magnesium levels and determine if magnesium supplements are required. If you decide to take magnesium supplements to prevent a deficiency, take 200 to 250 milligrams twice daily. Buy a supplement made from magnesium gluconate, citrate, aspartate, succinate or fumarte—the body absorbs these forms of the mineral more efficiently. Magnesium gluconate is less likely to cause diarrhea than other forms of the mineral. It may take 6 months to see improvement.

Potassium

Certain diuretic drugs can cause potassium to be excreted in the urine. Because this mineral helps maintain normal blood pressure and heart functioning, your doctor may recommend supplements if you take potassium-wasting diuretics such as Lasix (furosemide) or Hydrodiuril (hydrochlorothiazide).

Include potassium-rich foods in your daily diet. Raisins, prunes, dates, dried apricots, bananas, oranges, citrus juices, strawberries, watermelon, beets, greens, spinach, tomatoes, legumes and peas are good choices. See Chapter 4, page 82, to learn more about potassium requirements and food sources.

Herbal Remedies

Hawthorn (species *Crataegus*)

There is a substantial amount of evidence for hawthorn's beneficial effects in congestive heart failure. A 2008 review of ten randomized controlled trials conducted in 855 patients with chronic heart failure concluded that hawthorn, when used with conventional medication, was significantly better than a placebo at improving exercise tolerance, increasing oxygen consumption and reducing symptoms such as shortness of breath and fatigue.[24–27]

The active components in this plant—flavonoids and procyanidins—act on the heart by increasing the force of contraction, lengthening the period between heartbeats, reducing oxygen use and increasing nerve transmission.

The herb may also improve blood flow by dilating blood vessels.

Hawthorn should only be used early on in heart failure, when symptoms aren't too severe and before the medication digoxin is required. There's no benefit to taking hawthorn if you're already taking digoxin.

To supplement, buy a product standardized to 2 percent to 3 percent flavonoids or 18 percent to 20 percent procyanidins. The recommended dose is typically 200 to 500 milligrams taken three times daily. It can take 6 to 8 weeks of supplementation before there is maximal benefit. Hawthorn can interact with certain heart medications, so check with your pharmacist. If you're on certain heart drugs, take hawthorn only under your physician's supervision. Do not take hawthorn with digitalis.

Other Natural Health Products

Coenzyme Q10 (CoQ10)

Coenzyme Q10 (CoQ10) works with many different enzymes in the body and so is needed for many important metabolic reactions. One very important function of CoQ10 is the production of the body's energy compounds, ATP (adenosine triphosphate). Studies have shown that CoQ10 levels are much lower in the heart cells of individuals with CHF than they are in healthy people.

Many clinical trials have shown that CoQ10 supplements (along with medication) improve cardiac function, blood vessel integrity and quality of life in patients with CHF.[28–33] Studies show that supplementation with CoQ10 can reduce hospitalization and significantly decrease many of the symptoms associated with heart failure. CoQ10 also acts as an antioxidant.

Choose an oil-based CoQ10 supplement. The recommended dose for treating symptoms of congestive heart failure is 100 mg per day, divided into two or three doses. However, benefits have also been found with 60 milligrams once per day.

Creatine Monohydrate

Creatine is found in the diet and can be synthesized by the liver, pancreas and kidneys. Approximately 95 percent of the body's creatine is stored in muscles, where it's used to generate energy compounds called ATP (adenosine triphosphate) that fuel exercise. Creatine is also found in the heart, brain, retina and other tissues. In CHF, creatine levels in both heart and skeletal muscle are depressed.

Some research have found creatine supplementation in addition to standard medication to be effective at increasing body weight and improving muscle strength and exercise tolerance in patients with CHF.[34] Creatine is usually given at a loading dose of 20 grams daily for 2 to 5 days, and then reduced to a maintenance dose of 2 grams daily. Creatine supplementation can impair the function of kidneys in people with renal disease. If you have kidney disease or have an increased risk for kidney problems, do not use creatine supplements.

L-Propionyl-Carnitine

Carnitine is an amino acid found in all body cells, where it's used to metabolize fatty acids into energy. Carnitine helps the heart contract and produce energy more efficiently and, as a result, use less oxygen. A handful of studies have found that L-carnitine supplementation improves exercise tolerance and duration, oxygen uptake and heart functioning in patients with CHF.[35–40]

Most studies use the form of carnitine called L-propionyl-carnitine. The dose used in clinical trials of CHF is 500 milligrams three times daily. The supplement is considered to be very safe. Do not take D-carnitine or DL-carnitine, which can cause heart and muscle dysfunction.

L-Taurine

This is an amino acid that's used to make many different proteins in the body. It's found in meat, poultry, eggs, fish and dairy products. The body can also make taurine from vitamin B6 and other amino acids in food.

It's believed that taurine helps the heart beat and maintains healthy cell membranes. Studies have found that supplementation of taurine (2 grams three times daily) improved shortness of breath, edema and heart palpitations in patients with CHF.[41,42] Taurine supplements are considered to be very safe. However, be sure to buy a product made by a reputable manufacturer (particularly if you're taking large doses, i.e., grams, of the supplement).

Nutrition Strategy Checklist for Congestive Heart Failure

- ☐ Restrict fluids and sodium
- ☐ Avoid alcohol and caffeine
- ☐ Eat small, frequent meals
- ☐ Multivitamin/mineral
- ☐ Vitamin C
- ☐ Vitamin D
- ☐ Foods rich in vitamin E
- ☐ Foods rich in beta carotene
- ☐ Thiamin (vitamin B1)
- ☐ Magnesium
- ☐ Hawthorn
- ☐ Coenzyme Q10
- ☐ Creatine

☐ L-propionyl-carnitine

☐ L-taurine

Recommended Resources

Heart and Stroke Foundation of Canada
www.heartandstroke.ca
222 Queen Street, Suite 1402
Ottawa, ON K1P 5V9
Tel: 613-569-4361
Fax: 613-569-3278

American Heart Association
www.americanheart.org
7272 Greenville Avenue
Dallas, TX, USA 75231
Tel: 1-800-AHA-USA1 (242-8721)

National Heart, Lung and Blood Institute
National Institutes of Health
www.nhlbi.nih.gov
P.O. Box 30105
Bethesda, MD, USA 20824-0105
Tel: 301-592-8573
Fax: 240-629-3246

Constipation

An increasingly sedentary lifestyle and a growing preference for a diet of refined and over-processed foods that lack fibre can make us more susceptible to constipation. But many people worry unnecessarily about their bowel habits, expressing concern if they don't have a bowel movement every day. Bowel habits are highly individualized and frequency can vary considerably. In healthy adults, it's quite normal for bowel movements to range in frequency from three times a day to three times a week.

A person who is suffering from acute or chronic constipation usually has fewer than three bowel movements a week and produces small, hard stools that are difficult to pass. Bloating, gas pains, cramps and sluggishness often accompany constipation. Some people may also have the feeling that their rectum is not fully emptied. Fortunately, most cases of constipation are temporary and can be treated by making simple lifestyle changes.

What Causes Constipation?

Acute constipation comes on suddenly and is usually triggered by medications, illness or recent changes in diet. Chronic constipation takes a longer time to develop and can last for months or years. Under normal circumstances, your bowel functions very efficiently. During the digestive process, a series of wave-like muscle contractions called peristalsis move the waste products of digestion through the intestinal tract. Once in the large intestine (colon), fluid and electrolytes, such as sodium and potassium, are removed and most of the water content is absorbed. Muscle contractions move the remaining semi-solid waste material into the rectum, where it collects and is passed out of the body as a bowel movement.

Constipation usually develops when the muscles of the colon contract sluggishly or too slowly, allowing waste material to linger in the bowel. As a result, the colon absorbs excessive amounts of water, leaving the stool hard, dry and difficult to pass. Often, constipation is caused by a diet that is low in fibre and/or fluids or by a lack of physical activity. Factors that may slow the movement of food through the intestine and cause constipation include:

• medications, such as painkillers and iron supplements

- changes in routine, such as travel, stress or irregular sleeping habits
- life changes, such as pregnancy or aging
- frequent use or abuse of laxatives
- ignoring the urge to have a bowel movement
- irritable bowel syndrome or other problems affecting the intestines, colon or rectum
- illness or diseases, such as hypothyroid, stroke, diabetes or Parkinson's disease

While constipation is not a life-threatening condition, it can sometimes lead to complications. Straining and excessive pushing to pass the stool may lead to hemorrhoids or small tears around the anus (anal fissures). Too much straining may also cause a small portion of the intestinal lining to push out through the rectum, a condition called a rectal prolapse. Less often, the hard stool may pack so tightly into the intestine and rectum that the normal contractions of the colon cannot move it out of the body; this is called a fecal impaction. In rare cases, constipation may be a sign of colorectal cancer, heart disease or kidney failure.

Symptoms

Symptoms of constipation include:

- small, hard, dry stools
- thin, pencil-like stools
- difficult bowel movements that require excessive straining
- bowel movements occurring more than 3 days apart
- abdominal cramps, gas pain, bloating
- a feeling of incomplete evacuation after a bowel movement

Who's at Risk?

Constipation is the most common gastro-intestinal complaint in North America, affecting almost everyone at one time or another. Women, children and adults over age 65 report constipation most often. Pregnant women also tend to experience constipation. As well, people who are sedentary or bedridden, those undergoing chemotherapy or individuals who have recently had surgery are more likely to experience constipation.

Conventional Treatment

To prevent constipation, always respond to your body's urge to have a bowel movement. If constipation persists, laxatives, stool softeners or enemas may be recommended for a short period. These include:

- **Bulking agents,** such as wheat bran or psyllium, to add volume and draw fluid into the stool so that it can be passed more easily
- **Stool softeners** to allow water to penetrate the stool and soften it, triggering natural contractions of the colon
- **Mineral oil** to soften the stool
- **Glycerine suppositories** to lubricate the rectum, making it easier to pass a hard, dry stool
- **Magnesium salts** to pull large amounts of water into the intestine, making the stool soft and loose and stretching the intestinal walls to stimulate contractions
- **Bowel stimulants** to irritate the intestine, causing it to contract and move the stool through more quickly
- **Enemas** to fill the bowel with fluid, stimulating a bowel movement

Excessive use of constipation medications may damage the nerve cells and interfere with the normal muscle contractions of the colon, leading to lazy bowel syndrome. Use laxatives only when necessary. Instead, rely on the dietary strategies listed below to promote regular bowel movements. It's also important to increase physical activity to stimulate bowel function. Aim to be active for at least 30 minutes most days of the week.

Preventing and Managing Constipation
Dietary Strategies

Develop regular eating habits and try to eat at regular intervals during the day. This helps to promote bowel motility. If your busy schedule interferes with your ability to respond to your body's defecation signals, revise your schedule. Go to bed earlier in order to rise earlier, allowing time for breakfast and a bowel movement. And remember, try not to worry excessively about your bowel movements: Anxiety can aggravate constipation.

Dietary Fibre

Foods contain varying amounts of insoluble fibres and soluble fibres. Foods that have a greater proportion of insoluble fibres, such as wheat bran, whole grains, nuts, seeds and certain fruit and vegetables, are used to treat and prevent constipation.[1-5] Once consumed, insoluble fibres make their way to the intestinal tract, where they absorb water, help form bulkier, softer stools and speed evacuation. Psyllium, a type of soluble fibre, also adds bulk to stools and can be used to treat constipation.

It's recommended that adults up to age 50 be getting 25 (women) to 38 grams (men) of fibre per day; children 2 years and older should be getting 5 grams plus their age in years (e.g., a 7-year-old should be consuming 5 + 7 for a total of 12 grams per day). After age 50, daily fibre requirements are reduced to 21 and 30 grams, respectively, for women and men. In addition to the list below, see Chapter 1, page 4, which outlines the fibre content of selected foods.

Despite the advice of health professional to increase fibre intake, the average Canadian consumes between 11 and 17 grams of fibre each day—half the amount that's recommended to reap health benefits. Popular foods like bagels, cereal bars, pasta, pizza and fast food tend to be low in fibre. And usual serving sizes of whole grains, fruit and vegetables provide only 1 to 3 grams of fibre.

To treat constipation, add high-fibre foods to your daily diet. Below is a list of selected foods and their fibre content.

Food	Fibre (grams)
100% bran cereal, 1/2 cup (125 ml)	12 g
All-Bran Buds (with psyllium), Kellogg's 1/3 cup (75 ml)	12 g
Natural wheat bran, 2 tbsp (30 ml)	2.4 g
Flaxseed, ground, 2 tbsp (30 ml)	4.5 g
Almonds, 1/4 cup (60 ml)	4.8 g

Also choose higher-fibre fruit and vegetables:

Fruit	Vegetables
High Fibre (5+ grams)	*High Fibre (5+ grams)*
Apple, with skin	Green peas, 1/2 cup (125 ml)
Blackberries, 1/2 cup (125 ml)	Snow peas, 10
Blueberries, 1 cup (250 ml)	Swiss chard, 1 cup (250 ml)

Fruit	Vegetables
Figs, dates, dried, 10	
Kiwi, 2 medium	
Mango, 1 medium	
Pear, 1 medium	
Prunes, dried, 5	
Prunes, stewed, 1/2 cup (125 ml)	
Raspberries, 1/2 cup (125 ml)	
Medium Fibre (2 to 4 grams)	*Medium Fibre (2 to 4 grams)*
Orange, 1 medium	Bean sprouts, 1/2 cup (125 ml)
Raisins, 2 tbsp (30 ml)	Beans, string, 1/2 cup (125 ml)
Rhubarb, cooked, 1/2 cup (125 ml)	Broccoli, 1/2 cup (125 ml)
Strawberries, 1 cup (250 ml)	Brussels sprouts, 1/2 cup (125 ml)
Tangerine, 1 medium	Carrots, raw, 1/2 cup (125 ml)
	Eggplant, 1/2 cup (125 ml)
	Parsnips, 1/2 cup (125 ml)
	Vegetables, mixed, 1/2 cup (125 ml)

Increase your fibre intake gradually to prevent intestinal discomfort. To minimize possible side effects such as bloating and gas, spread your fibre intake over the course of the day, rather than consuming it all at once. It's normal to experience some flatulence upon starting a high-fibre diet. This usually resolves within a few weeks, once the bacteria residing in your large intestine adjust to a higher fibre intake.

Dietary fibre needs to absorb fluid in the intestinal tract in order to add bulk to stool.

Drink 9 to 13 cups (2.2 to 3 L) of fluid every day. Always include 1 cup (250 ml) of fluid with high-fibre meals and snacks.

Fibre Supplements

It's best to get your fibre fix from whole foods rather than supplements. Unlike fibre supplements, fibre-rich foods provide vitamins, minerals and many natural compounds that help to keep you healthy in other ways. However, for some people fibre supplements may be useful for treating and preventing constipation. People who don't like high-fibre foods, or who find they cause cramping or flatulence, often turn to fibre supplements available as wafers, capsules, tablets or powders.

PSYLLIUM. Bulk-forming supplements like Metamucil contain psyllium, a soluble fibre that comes from the crushed seeds of a plant most commonly grown in India. While insoluble fibre in wheat bran generally works best for treating constipation, psyllium is effective for some individuals.[6-10] You can buy psyllium husk powder, which you mix into water, at health food stores. One tablespoon provides roughly 3 grams of fibre. Metamucil (Procter and Gamble) comes in wafers, capsules and powdered drink mix. For bowel regularity, recommended use is three times per day with at least 8 ounces (250 ml) of water.

Regular use of psyllium is considered safe but excessive amounts can cause bloating, gas, diarrhea and intestinal blockage. Not drinking enough water with the psyllium can cause choking and blockage of the esophagus and throat. Psyllium may also slow the absorption of certain medications (e.g., tetracycline, digoxin, aspirin, some diuretics), so they should be taken 1 hour before or 2 hours after consuming psyllium.

OTHER FIBRE SUPPLEMENTS. Some fibre supplements are made with natural fruit and vegetable fibres. Genuine Health Satisfibre+ delivers 10 grams of fibre from oats, flaxseeds, fenugreek, prunes, raisins, pears and apple per two-scoop serving.

Comparing Fibre Supplements

Supplement	Fibre (grams)
Benefibre, 1 tsp (5 ml)	3
Bowel Buddy, 1 wafer (25 g)	4
Genuine Health Satisfibre+, 2 scoops	10
Metamucil, 6 capsules	3
Metamucil, orange-flavoured, original, 1 tbsp (15 ml)	3
Metamucil, unflavoured, original, 1 tsp (5 ml)	3
Metamucil, 2 wafers	3
Metamucil Fibresure, 1 tsp (5 ml)	5
Ultra Fibre, 4 capsules	3
Prunes, stewed, 5	3.8

Prunes contain fibre (1 gram of fibre per prune) but they also provide a natural laxative substance called dihydroxyphenyl isatin. Eat four dried or stewed prunes as a snack. Drink prune juice for a concentrated source of prune's natural laxative. For a morning bowel movement, drink prune juice at bedtime. If an evening bowel movement is preferred, drink prune juice at breakfast.

Probiotics

Foods and supplements that contain friendly lactic acid bacteria (e.g., lactobacilli, bifidobacteria) can help prevent constipation. These bacteria normally reside in the intestinal tract, where they perform a number of tasks that keep the bowel healthy. Numerous studies conducted in adults with irritable bowel syndrome and children suffering from constipation have shown probiotic supplements to be effective in increasing the frequency of bowel movements.[11–15]

Eat 1 cup (250 ml) of a fermented dairy product daily—yogurt, kefir or acidophilus milk. All yogurts in Canada are made with lactic acid bacteria, whether or not they are labelled as such. However, some brands, such as Astro BioBest and Danone Activia, have included additional strains of probiotic bacteria. Supplements provide a higher dose of probiotic bacteria; take 1 billion to 10 billion live cells (per capsule) with one to three meals daily. See Chapter 8, page 180, for more about probiotic supplements.

Herbal Remedies

If dietary strategies have failed, short-term use of one of the following herbal remedies may be tried. Seek medical attention for unresolved constipation.

Aloe (*Aloe vera, Aloe barbadensis*)

Components in the aloe leaf known as anthraquinones cause a laxative effect in the large bowel when these molecules interact with intestinal bacteria. To treat constipation, the typical dose is 100 to 200 milligrams of aloe or 50 milligrams of aloe extract taken in the evening for a maximum of 10 days. If used longer, aloe can cause diarrhea and deplete body potassium.

Cascara (*Rhamnus purshiani cortex*)

Cascara bark is high in cascarosides, compounds that induce the large intestine to increase its muscular contraction, resulting in bowel movement. Use only the dried form of cascara. It can be taken as a tea by steeping 2 grams of finely chopped bark in 2/3 cup (160 ml) of boiling water for 5 to 10 minutes. As a tincture, cascara liquid extract is given in a dose of 2 to 5 millilitres three times daily. Use the smallest dosage necessary to maintain soft stools.

Cascara should be taken for a maximum of 10 days. It should not be taken long term. Long-term use or abuse of cascara may cause a loss of potassium in the body, thereby strengthening the action of certain heart medications, with fatal consequences. Long-term use of this herb may also weaken the colon. Women who are pregnant or lactating should not use cascara without the advice of a physician. Do not use this herb if you have abdominal pain or diarrhea.

Nutrition Strategy Checklist for Constipation

☐ Eat on a regular schedule
☐ Insoluble fibre
☐ Fluids
☐ Psyllium
☐ Prunes
☐ Regular physical activity

Recommended Resources

Alberta Health Services
www.crha-health.ab.ca/
700 Manulife Place
10180–101 Street
Edmonton, AB T5J 3S4
Tel: 780-342-2000
Fax: 780-342-2060

Hospital for Sick Children
www.sickkids.on.ca
555 University Avenue
Toronto, ON M5G 1X8
Telehealth Ontario info line: 1-866-797-0000

National Digestive Diseases Information Clearinghouse
National Institutes of Health
www2.niddk.nih.gov
Building 31, Room 9A06
31 Center Drive, MSC 2560
Bethesda, MD, USA 20892-2560
Tel: 301-496-3583

Cystic Fibrosis (CF)

Cystic fibrosis is a progressive, potentially fatal, inherited disorder that affects the glands in the body that produce sweat and mucus. The disease affects mainly the lungs, pancreas, liver, intestines, sinuses and sex organs. The defective cystic fibrosis genes produce an abnormal protein that interferes with the ability of the body to move sodium chloride and water through the cells. This causes the exocrine glands (the glands that produce sweat, saliva, mucus and tears) to malfunction. The fluids or secretions from the exocrine glands are used as lubricants in the body and are normally quite thin and slippery. By altering the transportation of chloride and water, the defective cystic fibrosis genes cause the glands to produce secretions that are abnormally thick and sticky.

The problems caused by cystic fibrosis are most evident in the respiratory and digestive systems. The thick secretions block the passages of the lungs, clogging the airways and creating an ideal environment for infection-causing bacteria to flourish. Breathing difficulties, recurrent infections and permanent lung damage are typical symptoms of cystic fibrosis.

The sticky mucus can also block the ducts of the pancreas, which prevents digestive enzymes from reaching the intestinal tract. As a result of this mucus buildup, the body is unable to break down and absorb adequate nutrition from food. Chronic diarrhea, abdominal pain and nutritional deficiencies are common problems associated with cystic fibrosis.

People with cystic fibrosis tend to lose excessive amounts of salt through their sweat and saliva. This salt loss can upset the mineral balance in the body and may cause abnormalities in heart rhythms or shock. Cystic fibrosis also affects the reproductive system of both men and women. Men with the disease are usually infertile and women may have difficulty conceiving or may have more complications during pregnancy.

The severity of cystic fibrosis varies from person to person and usually depends on the degree of lung damage caused by the disease. Improved treatments can postpone some of the lung damage associated with cystic fibrosis, and many people with the disorder now have a life expectancy of 30 years or longer. Research in gene therapy is promising and may eventually prevent the progression of cystic fibrosis. However, at this time there is no cure for cystic fibrosis, and the disorder inevitably leads to death, usually as a result of lung disease and heart failure.

What Causes Cystic Fibrosis?

Cystic fibrosis is one of the most common inherited diseases among Caucasians. Approximately one in every 3600 children born in Canada has the disease.[1] To be born with cystic fibrosis, a child must inherit two defective cystic fibrosis genes, one from each parent. Most people have two normal genes; however, approximately 5 percent of all Caucasians who don't show any signs of cystic fibrosis are carriers of the disease. That means they are born with one normal gene and one defective cystic fibrosis gene.

If a child's mother and father are both carriers of a defective gene, then there is a

- 25 percent chance the child will be born with cystic fibrosis
- 50 percent chance the child will not have cystic fibrosis but will be a carrier
- 25 percent chance the child will not have cystic fibrosis and will not be a carrier

Most babies are diagnosed with the disease before they are 1 year old. In some cases, symptoms of the disease may not become apparent until the child is a teenager or even an adult.

Symptoms

Symptoms of cystic fibrosis include:

- constant cough that expels thick mucus or phlegm
- recurring bouts of respiratory infection, such as pneumonia or bronchitis
- growths (polyps) in the nose due to excess fluid in the mucus lining of the nasal passages
- skin that tastes salty
- ongoing diarrhea or bulky, foul-smelling, greasy stools
- failure (for children) to grow, despite a large or normal appetite
- stomach pain and discomfort caused by intestinal gas

- barrel-shaped chest
- clubbing of the fingers and toes and bluish skin, caused by lack of oxygen
- night blindness, rickets, anemia and bleeding disorders caused by vitamin deficiencies
- delayed puberty, slowed growth and declining physical stamina in teenagers
- collapsed lung, coughing up of blood, impaired reproductive function, liver disease and heart failure in adults

Who's at Risk?

Cystic fibrosis occurs mainly in Caucasians, especially those of Northern European heritage. The disease is also common in Latinos and Native Americans. It affects boys and girls equally. Long-term survival is better in males, in people without pancreatic problems and in people who have only digestive problems in the early stages of the disease.

Conventional Treatment

Treatment programs are usually tailored to individual needs, depending on the severity of the disease and the organs affected. Home treatments include:

- chest physical therapy—clapping or tapping the chest vigorously (percussion or vibration) and postural drainage to loosen the mucus clogging the lungs (mechanical devices are available to assist with this process)
- taking enteric-coated pancreatic enzymes with meals to aid digestion
- taking nutritional supplements to improve general nutrition
- taking salt supplements during a fever, exercise or exposure to hot weather

- aerobic exercise to loosen mucus, encourage coughing to expel mucus and improve physical health

Medications may be prescribed to treat various symptoms:

- antibiotics to fight bacteria causing lung infections
- a bronchodilator to prevent narrowing of the airways
- mucus-thinning drugs to make the secretions thinner and easier to cough up
- anti-inflammatory drugs to reduce lung inflammation
- routine immunizations and influenza vaccines to prevent viral infections that can damage lungs

Oxygen therapy may be required for those patients with low oxygen levels. Surgery may be necessary for specific complications of the disease.

Managing Cystic Fibrosis
Dietary Strategies

Nutrition is a crucial component of the management of cystic fibrosis. Optimizing growth and nutritional status is directly related to both lung function and survival. Dietetic care by a registered dietitian who specializes in cystic fibrosis is necessary to ensure adequate calories and nutrients are provided from food and supplements.

High-Calorie Diet

The impaired digestion caused by cystic fibrosis results in weight loss and may, in children, result in improper growth. It's estimated that 23 percent of children are below the tenth percentile for weight based on age and sex, and 22 percent of adults are underweight. When food isn't digested properly, calories and nutrients are lost. To support weight maintenance in adults and weight gain in children, cystic fibrosis patients require 110 percent to 200 percent more calories than healthy individuals. These calories should come from fat, protein and carbohydrate. A registered dietitian who specializes in cystic fibrosis can help develop a diet with adequate calories for both children and adults. Children with impaired growth and adults who are underweight may benefit from nutritional supplements to increase calorie intake.

Essential Fatty Acids

Many studies have revealed that patients with cystic fibrosis are deficient in both alpha-linolenic and linoleic acid because of poor absorption of dietary fat and faulty metabolism of these fatty acids.[2] A deficiency of these essential fatty acids may contribute to the kidney complications, lung damage and liver disease seen in patients with cystic fibrosis.[3,4]

Children and adults should consume at least 2 tablespoons (30 ml) of oil rich in essential fatty acids (your dietitian will determine how much fat is required for an optimal calorie intake). Flaxseed oil, walnut oil and canola oil are good sources of ALA. A commercial product called Udo's Choice Ultimate Oil Blend is available in health food stores. It contains a balance of both alpha-linolenic and linoleic fatty acids from organic flaxseed, sesame and sunflower seeds, wheat germ, rice germ and oat germ. Flaxseed oil, walnut oil and Udo's oil should not be used for sautéing or frying since their essential fatty acids are easily destroyed by heat. Store these oils in the refrigerator and use in salad dressings, dips and smoothies or add to foods like pasta sauces and soups after cooking.

ESSENTIAL FATTY ACID SUPPLEMENTS. Supplements of essential fatty acids may help correct imbalances that occur in cystic fibrosis. One study found that borage oil that contained the fatty acid gamma-linolenic acid (GLA), taken daily for 4 weeks, improved essential fatty acid levels in patients with the disease.[5] While supplements of borage oil and evening primrose oil, which also contains GLA, may help, it's very important to get these healthy oils from your daily diet in order to provide extra calories.

To supplement with evening primrose oil, take 1000 to 1500 milligrams twice daily. Buy a product standardized for 9 percent GLA.

OMEGA-3 FATTY ACIDS. In addition to alterations in essential fatty acid metabolism, it's also common for patients with cystic fibrosis to have reduced circulating levels of DHA, an omega-3 fatty acid found in fish and fish oil. Several studies have investigated the effect of DHA supplementation in cystic fibrosis patients. While most trials have resulted in an increase in blood levels of DHA, significant clinical improvement has not been demonstrated. Although more studies are needed, it's thought that increasing levels of DHA in the body can produce an anti-inflammatory effect that could possibly improve quality of life for individuals with cystic fibrosis. In cystic fibrosis, inflammation occurs in response to ongoing infection of the airways and can contribute to complications from the disease, including bone loss, diabetes and blood vessel inflammation.

Studies have used DHA doses ranging from 300 milligrams to 5 grams per day. To supplement, buy a liquid fish oil. The dose, usually in teaspoons, will vary depending on the amount of DHA provided by one teaspoon of fish oil.

Food Sensitivities

Some children continue to have diarrhea and fail to thrive despite adequate dietary treatment. These children should be evaluated for possible food allergies. Studies have found that when allergenic foods are removed from the diet, diarrhea stops and weight gain occurs.[6,7] Your doctor should consider the possibility of food allergies if improvement doesn't occur with standard treatment. Ask for a referral to an allergy specialist for testing.

Vitamins and Minerals

Multivitamin and Mineral Supplements

Because of impaired absorption of nutrients, people with cystic fibrosis should take a multivitamin and mineral supplement twice daily with meals. This supplement will provide many of the nutrients that are commonly depressed in people with cystic fibrosis: beta carotene, zinc, copper and vitamins A, D, E and C. Of particular significance is the malabsorption of fat-soluble nutrients—vitamins A, D, E and K—as a result of a deficiency of the pancreatic enzyme called lipase. (Lipase is needed to break down fat in the intestine and release fat-soluble vitamins so they can be absorbed into the bloodstream.) As a result, vitamin deficiencies are common and can have important implications for the long-term health of people with the disease.

Vitamin A

Vitamin A levels should be monitored routinely in adults with cystic fibrosis who drive cars, since a deficiency causes night blindness.[8-11] Inflammatory lung flare-ups may also increase the risk for vitamin A deficiency. The best food sources of vitamin A include liver, oily fish, milk, cheese, butter and whole eggs. Your doctor will measure your blood level of vitamin A to determine if it's necessary take a supplement. Excessive supplementation of vitamin A may harm bone development and the respiratory system of children.

Vitamin D

Vitamin D is necessary for bone health, and a deficiency can increase the risk of bone loss and osteoporosis, two conditions often seen in people with cystic fibrosis.[12-16] Vitamin D also has anti-inflammatory effects in the body. The majority of adults with cystic fibrosis have insufficient levels of vitamin D in their bloodstream. Research has shown that vitamin D supplementation—together with calcium—can reduce bone loss in adult patients.[17] Good food sources of vitamin D include milk, oily fish, margarine and whole eggs; however, dietary sources are ineffective at maintaining optimal vitamin D levels in the body. A daily supplement providing 1000 international units (IU) of vitamin D3 is recommended.

Children and adults with cystic fibrosis should get regular blood tests to evaluate their vitamin D status. Higher dosing of vitamin D may be required to increase blood levels to an acceptable range. Based on your blood test results, your doctor or dietitian will recommend an appropriate vitamin D dose.

Vitamin E

As with levels of other fat-soluble nutrients, those of vitamin E are also often reduced in cystic fibrosis, primarily because of poor absorption.[18-21] This antioxidant vitamin plays an important role in scavenging harmful free radical molecules whose damage can reduce lung function and increase the risk of heart disease. Vitamin E is also needed for proper immune function. In cystic fibrosis, levels of many antioxidant nutrients are depressed (E, C, beta carotene) and levels of free radicals are increased by inflammatory reactions of the disease. As a result, people with cystic fibrosis may have inadequate antioxidant defences to protect their health. Oxidative stress caused by harmful free radicals is associated with the progression of cystic fibrosis lung disease.

Studies of patients with the disease have found that vitamin E supplements improve vitamin E levels and prevent free radical damage to blood cholesterol.[22-25] To supplement, take 200 to 400 IU per day of water-soluble vitamin E. The best food sources of vitamin E include wheat germ, nuts, seeds, vegetable oils, whole grains and leafy greens.

Vitamin K

Vitamin K status may also be impaired in people with cystic fibrosis because of poor fat absorption.[26,27] Vitamin K is essential for blood clotting and healthy bone growth. Risk factors for vitamin K deficiency include lipase deficiency, repeated antibiotic use and liver disease—problems encountered in most individuals with cystic fibrosis. While experts agree that vitamin K should be supplemented in patients with cystic fibrosis, the optimal effective dose is not yet known. Regular blood tests will detect a vitamin K deficiency and your doctor may recommend supplements. Good food sources of this vitamin include green peas, broccoli, spinach, leafy green vegetables, Brussels sprouts, romaine lettuce, cabbage and liver. Many multivitamins also contain a small amount of vitamin K.

Beta Carotene

Studies show that people with cystic fibrosis tend to be deficient in beta carotene.[28-30] This nutrient is found in orange and dark-green produce, including carrots, sweet potato, winter squash, broccoli, collard greens, kale, spinach, apricots, cantaloupe, peaches, nectarines, mango and papaya. Once consumed, some beta carotene is converted to vitamin A in the body. Beta carotene also acts as an antioxidant and can help protect the body from oxidative stress.

To get additional beta carotene, choose a multivitamin and mineral supplement with the nutrient added.

Vitamin C

Ensuring an optimal intake of vitamin C can help mitigate some of the free radical damage that occurs in cystic fibrosis. Researchers have found that patients who did not take a multivitamin supplement had low blood vitamin C levels and evidence of increased lung inflammation.[31] In patients who received low dose vitamin C from a multivitamin pill, vitamin C levels were normal and levels of certain compounds in the blood that are markers of inflammation were much lower.

Foods rich in vitamin C include citrus fruit and juices, cantaloupe, kiwi, mango, strawberries, broccoli, Brussels sprouts, cauliflower, red pepper and tomato juice. To supplement, take 500 or 600 milligrams with meals once or twice daily.

Calcium

Many adults and adolescents with cystic fibrosis have evidence of bone loss.[32,33] Low bone mass and osteoporosis are caused by a deficiency of vitamin D and poor intake of calcium. It's very important to ensure an adequate intake of calcium, since critical periods of bone growth occur throughout childhood and adolescence. To determine your calcium requirements, see Chapter 4, page 56. If your bone density has been tested and found to be low, a daily calcium intake of 1500 milligrams from foods and supplements combined is recommended.

Calcium-rich foods include milk, yogurt, cheese, fortified soy and rice beverages, fortified orange juice, tofu, salmon (with bones), kale, bok choy, broccoli and Swiss chard. To supplement, take 300 milligrams of calcium citrate with added vitamin D one to three times daily. Your dose will depend on how much calcium your diet provides. See Chapter 4, page 56, for detailed information about calcium-rich foods and supplementation.

Zinc

Increasing zinc intake may help people with cystic fibrosis fight bacterial lung infections. This mineral is needed to activate thymulin, a hormone that enhances the immune system. Zinc is also needed for proper growth and development. Research suggests that zinc metabolism is altered in cystic fibrosis and that people with the disease may have lower blood levels of the mineral. Research conducted in children with cystic fibrosis has also found that a daily zinc supplement of 30 milligrams reduced the number of days of taking antibiotics to treat respiratory infections.[34-39]

Zinc-rich foods include oysters, seafood, red meat, poultry, yogurt, wheat bran, wheat germ, whole grains and enriched breakfast cereals. Most adult multivitamin and mineral supplements provide 10 milligrams of this mineral; children's formulas may or may not contain zinc. Take single zinc supplements only on the advice of your doctor. Too much zinc taken for long periods has toxic effects and may suppress the immune system.

Other Natural Health Products
Digestive Enzymes

In cystic fibrosis, insufficient amounts of digestive enzymes enter the intestine because the ducts from the pancreas are blocked with mucus. As a result, carbohydrates, proteins and especially fats are not completely broken down and nutrients cannot be absorbed into the bloodstream. Taking a digestive enzyme supplement can help the body digest food and can increase nutrients available for absorption.

With supplements, the amount of digestive enzymes is expressed in activity units rather than milligrams. These units refer to the enzyme's potency. The amount of enzymes needed for proper nutrition varies from person to person. Your doctor will decide which dose is best for you or your child. The recommended dose of pancreatic enzymes for individuals with cystic fibrosis is as follows:[40]

- 500 to 2000 units of lipase per kilogram body weight per meal OR
- <10,000 units of lipase per kilogram body weight per day OR
- <4,000 units of lipase per gram of dietary fat per day

Digestive enzymes sold in health food stores and pharmacies may be different in type and potency from those prescribed by your doctor. In order for the supplement to withstand the acidity in the stomach, enteric-coated enzymes are recommended.

Nutrition Strategy Checklist for Cystic Fibrosis

- ☐ High-calorie diet
- ☐ Healthy oils
- ☐ Omega-3 fatty acids
- ☐ Identify food allergies
- ☐ Multivitamin/mineral
- ☐ Vitamin A
- ☐ Vitamin D
- ☐ Vitamin E
- ☐ Vitamin K
- ☐ Beta carotene
- ☐ Vitamin C
- ☐ Calcium
- ☐ Zinc
- ☐ Pancreatic enzymes (lipase)

Recommended Resources

Canadian Cystic Fibrosis Foundation
www.cysticfibrosis.ca
2221 Yonge Street, Suite 601
Toronto, ON M4S 2B4
Tel: 416-485-9149 or 1-800-378-2233
Fax: 416-485-0960
Email: info@cysticfibrosis.ca

The Cystic Fibrosis Foundation
www.cff.org
6931 Arlington Road, Suite 200
Bethesda, MD, USA 20814
Tel: 301-951-4422 or 1-800-344-4823
Fax: 301-951-6378
Email: info@cff.org

National Heart, Lung and Blood Institute
National Institutes of Health
NHLBI Health Information Network
www.nhlbi.nih.gov

P.O. Box 30105
Bethesda, MD, USA 20824-0105
Tel: 301-592-8573
Fax: 240-629-3246

Depression

At any given time, as many as 3 million Canadians have serious depression.[1] In fact, at some point in their lives, one in every ten Canadians will experience a degree of depression serious enough to require treatment. When faced with life's stresses and losses, it's only natural to feel sadness and grief. Everyone experiences emotional highs and lows and it's very normal to suffer through a bout of the "blues" once in a while. But depressive illness goes beyond these reactions.

Depression becomes an illness, or clinical depression, when feelings of sadness, emptiness and worthlessness are severe, last for several weeks and begin to interfere with one's work, personal and social life. Depressive illness changes the way a person thinks and behaves, and how his/her body functions. Without treatment, symptoms can last for months or even years. There are three types of depression.

MAJOR DEPRESSION (CLINICAL OR UNIPOLAR DEPRESSION). This diagnosis is made if symptoms of deep despair persist and consistently interfere with normal functioning during a 2-week period.

DYSTHYMIA. This milder form of depression is a chronic mood disorder that lasts for at least 2 years. Those who suffer from dysthymia are usually able to function adequately but might seem consistently unhappy.

MANIC DEPRESSION (BIPOLAR DISORDER). Less common than the other forms of depression, this condition involves disruptive cycles of elation or euphoria alternating with depressive episodes, irritable excitement and mania.

What Causes Depression?

The actual causes of depression are not fully understood. It's thought that several factors—including a genetic or family history of depression; psychological or emotional vulnerability to depression; body chemistry, such as hormone levels; and major life stress—may play a part in the onset of depression. Modern brain imaging technologies reveal that specific neural circuits in the brain don't function properly during depression, impairing the performance of crucial brain chemicals called neurotransmitters. Another theory holds that depression is caused by an imbalance in the body's response to stress, which results in an overactive hormonal system. Some studies also suggest that low levels of certain brain chemicals, known as amines, may slow down the nervous system and impair brain function enough to cause depression.

In women, there is evidence that the hormonal fluctuations of menstruation and pregnancy can trigger mental disorders. That women suffer depression twice as often as men also may be related to the fact that women synthesize serotonin, a brain chemical that carries messages between brain cells, at a lower rate than men. Melatonin, a chemical involved in regulating certain bodily functions, is also produced at different levels in women and men. Both differences may predispose women to become depressed with a lack of sunlight, a condition known as seasonal affective disorder (SAD).

Symptoms

Symptoms of depression develop gradually, over a period of days or weeks. The severity of symptoms can vary from person to person. To be diagnosed with depression, you must be experiencing at least four of the following indicators consistently over a period of at least 2 weeks:

- general sluggishness or agitation
- loss of interest in daily activities
- withdrawal
- acute sadness or feeling of emptiness
- demoralization, despair, feelings of worthlessness and hopelessness
- anxiety
- frequent outbursts of anger and rage
- concentration difficulties, memory loss, unusual indecisiveness
- self-criticism, self-deprecation
- changes in eating habits
- sleep disorders (insomnia, frequent awakening)
- chronic fatigue, lack of energy
- physical discomfort, such as constipation, headaches
- thoughts of death or suicide

In dysthymia, these symptoms are present in a milder form. People with manic depression often appear elated, uncontrollably enthusiastic and intrusively friendly. But they may just as easily become irritable or hostile. As the condition progresses, mental activity speeds up and the need for sleep decreases. A manic person is easily distracted, shifting constantly from one task or project to another, and may indulge in inappropriate sexual or personal behaviours or may have delusions of power and wealth.

A typical depression can last for 6 to 9 months, and episodes may recur several times over a lifetime. Symptoms rarely go away on their own, but with professional diagnosis and treatment, depression can be managed and controlled very successfully.

Who's at Risk?

Depression can affect anyone, at any time. Some of the main risk factors associated with depression include:

- **Family history.** If you have an immediate family member with depression, your risk for depression is greater.
- **Traumatic life events.** Early childhood events, such as the loss of a parent, sexual abuse or divorce, increase the risk of adult depression.
- **Stress.** Work-related pressures, the loss of a loved one, divorce, financial problems or a move to a new location might trigger depression.
- **Marital and work status.** Depression is highest among divorced, separated or widowed people. Unemployment lasting more than 6 months is also a factor.
- **Physical illness.** Cancer, heart disease, AIDS/HIV, hormonal disorders and thyroid conditions are associated with depression.
- **Medications.** Many medications, including sedatives and those for pain, produce mood disorders as a side effect.
- **Gender and age.** Women suffer from depression and attempt suicide more often than men. Children, adolescents and the elderly experience stressful life events that may predispose them to depression.
- **Alcohol or drug use.** Alcohol is a depressive drug and will aggravate the symptoms of depression. Mood-altering drugs tend to complicate depression and interfere with its treatment.

Conventional Treatment

Depression is one of the most common and treatable mental disorders. It's usually treated without hospitalization, using a combination of medications and psychotherapy. The earlier treatment begins, the more effective it is and the more likely it will prevent serious recurrences. However, even when treatment is successful, depression may recur. Results of any treatment should be apparent within 2 to 3 months.

Several different types of antidepressant drugs are available. They work by influencing the activity of brain neurotransmitters—primarily serotonin, norepinephrine and dopamine—and must be taken for several weeks before they begin to work. Anti-depressant drugs include:

- **Selective serotonin reuptake inhibitors (SSRIs):** Prozac (fluoxetine), Paxil (paroxetine), Zoloft (sertaline). These drugs raise serotonin levels in the brain. (It's thought that reduced serotonin levels in the brain play a role in depression.) SSRIs have fewer side effects and are often the first choice of treatment for depression. They may cause mild nausea, diarrhea and headaches that usually subside over time. SSRIs commonly cause sexual dysfunction as a side effect.
- **Monoamine oxidase inhibitors (MAOIs):** Nardil (phenelzine), Parnate (tranylcypromine). Monoamine oxidase is an enzyme that breaks down neurotransmitters. Monoamine oxidase inhibitors inactivate this enzyme, leaving more of the

neurotransmitter to produce an antidepressant effect. This medication may be helpful for people with atypical symptoms such as overeating, excessive sleeping and anxiety, panic attacks and phobias, or for those who failed to improve on other types of medication. People who take MAOIs must avoid foods and beverages that contain tyramine (such as red wine, beer, aged cheeses, soy sauce and yeast extracts). Though occurrence is rare, combining MAOIs with tyramine can lead to severe high blood pressure or even a stroke or heart attack.

- **Tricyclic antidepressants:** Elavil (amitriptyline), Tofranil (imipramine), Pamelor (nortipyline). These drugs inhibit the reabsorption of two neurotransmitters, norepinephrine and serotonin, into brain cells (neurons). As a result, the neurons receiving the drug get extra stimulation, which helps counter depression. While useful in treating depression, these drugs bring with them a host of unpleasant side effects such as weight gain, drowsiness, dizziness and an increased heart rate. They are not usually used to treat mild to moderate depression because the side effects are often worse than the disorder.

Psychotherapy—individual and group—can help to gradually change negative attitudes and feelings of hopelessness and can provide guidance in adjusting to the normal pressures of life. It's often used in conjunction with antidepressant drugs. Electroconvulsive therapy (ECT) is used for severe cases of depression. An electric current is applied to the head to induce a seizure in the brain. For reasons not completely understood, the seizure will quickly and very effectively alleviate depression.

Managing Depression
Dietary Strategies
Carbohydrates
Carbohydrate has been one of the most widely studied nutrients with respect to mood. High-carbohydrate meals have been associated with a calming, relaxing effect and even drowsiness.[2,3] Carbohydrate-rich meals allow an amino acid called tryptophan to enter the brain, where it's used to make the neurotransmitter serotonin. Many studies associate high serotonin levels with happier moods and low levels with mild depression.

If you're feeling depressed, try a high-carbohydrate meal that contains very little protein. Protein-rich foods like chicken, meat or fish provide many different amino acids that compete with tryptophan for entry into the brain, which means that less serotonin will be produced. Good food choices include pasta with tomato sauce, whole-grain toast with jam or a bowl of whole-grain cereal with skim milk. High-carbohydrate beverages such as unsweetened fruit juice and sports drinks may also help increase serotonin levels.

Omega-3 Fatty Acids
Low blood levels of two omega-3 fatty acids—DHA and EPA—are common in people who are depressed. It has been established that DHA plays a fundamental role in brain structure and function: As an important component of nerve and brain cell membranes, it helps cells communicate messages effectively. DHA may work to ease depression by altering the structure of cell membranes in the brain, making them more responsive to the effects of serotonin. DHA may also have anti-inflammatory effects in the brain, which can also influence mood. Many studies have found

omega-3 supplementation—alone or in combination with other medication—is effective in treating clinical depression. Omega-3 fatty acids also seem to improve a person's response to conventional antidepressants. As well, one study of omega-3 fatty acids combined with medication showed positive effects in treating depression in patients with bipolar disorder.[4-9]

The best food sources of DHA are cold-water fish such as salmon, trout, Arctic char, mackerel, herring, sardines and fresh tuna. Aim to eat fish at least two times a week. (Women of childbearing age and young children should avoid tuna steaks as they are high in mercury.)

If you have clinical depression, you'll need to take a fish oil supplement to get the required amount of DHA and EPA. The doses used in clinical research are as follows:

- For treating depression: Along with conventional antidepressants, 9.6 grams of fish oil have been used. Take three fish oil capsules three times per day or use 1 teaspoon (5 ml) of liquid fish oil two to three times per day.
- For treating bipolar disorder–related depression: Daily supplementation of 6.2 grams of EPA and 3.4 grams of DHA has been used.

Buy an omega-3 fatty acid supplement that contains both EPA and DHA. A good-quality fish oil supplement should also contain vitamin E, which is added to help stabilize the oils. Avoid fish *liver* oil capsules. Fish liver oil supplements often contain only small doses of DHA and EPA. As well, supplements made from fish livers are a concentrated source of vitamin A: Too much vitamin A can be toxic when taken in large amounts for long periods.

High doses of fish oil can have side effects, such as leaving an unpleasant taste in the mouth. Fish oil also has a blood-thinning effect. If you take medication that thins the blood, consult your physician before taking any supplements. Fish oil supplements should never replace your medication. Always discuss any alternative or complementary treatment with your doctor first.

Vitamins and Minerals

Vitamin B6

Even marginal deficiencies of certain B vitamins have been associated with irritability, depression and mood changes. The body uses B6 to form an important enzyme that's needed to convert tryptophan to serotonin in the brain. Vitamin B6 has been the focus of study in more than 900 women suffering from depression related to premenstrual syndrome (PMS). Based on the evidence available, a daily supplement of B6 seems likely to balance emotions in women suffering from PMS-related depression.[10]

The best sources of B6 include meat, fish, poultry, whole grains, bananas and potatoes. To supplement, a daily dose of 50 to 100 milligrams has been used to treat PMS-related depression. Do not exceed 100 milligrams per day as too much vitamin B6 taken for an extended period of time can cause irreversible nerve damage.

Folate (Folic Acid)

People with depression have consistently been found to have lower blood levels of folate than those who do not have depression. Reduced folate levels have been associated with poorer response rates to serotonin reuptake inhibitor drugs (Prozac, Paxil, Zoloft). A number of studies have shown that taking a daily supplement of folic acid (the synthetic version of folate) improves medication response, which may help patients keep the condition in remission.[11-18]

A folate deficiency can contribute to depression by lowering levels of serotonin. In most, but not all, studies of patients with depression, folate deficiency is accompanied by low levels of serotonin in the central nervous system. Research has also shown that supplementing with folic acid restored serotonin levels. The link between low folate and low serotonin is not fully understood but researchers speculate that a compound called S-adenosyl-methionine (SAMe) is involved (see below and also Chapter 8, page 181). Folate deficiency reduces SAMe, which has known antidepressant effects because it increases serotonin in the brain.

The best food sources of folate include cooked spinach, artichokes, asparagus, lentils, dried peas and beans, chicken liver, orange juice and wheat germ. Folic acid (the synthetic version of folate) is added to white flour and white pasta in Canada. To enhance the response to antidepressant medications, a daily folic acid supplement of 200 to 500 micrograms (0.2 to 0.5 milligrams) has been used in studies. If you take a single supplement of folic acid, ensure that it has B12 added.

Chromium

In patients with atypical depression who are overweight or obese and who also have severe carbohydrate cravings, supplementing with chromium may be beneficial. Research has found that a daily supplement can help reduce appetite, overeating and carbohydrate cravings.[19,20] There's also preliminary evidence that chromium might improve the response to antidepressants in people with dysthymia by maintaining brain levels of serotonin and improving how the body uses the hormone insulin to regulate blood sugar.

Chromium-rich foods include calf's liver, chicken breast, oysters, refried beans, brewer's yeast, wheat germ, wheat bran, whole grains, blackstrap molasses, mushrooms, broccoli, green peas, grape juice and apples (with skin). To reduce carbohydrate cravings in depressed patients, studies have used a supplemental dose of 600 micrograms of chromium picolinate. To improve mood in patients with dysthymia, take 200 micrograms of chromium picolinate or chromium nicotinate once or twice daily. A daily dose of 600 micrograms or more of chromium picolinate has been associated with adverse effects, so use cautiously. Be sure to inform your doctor if you decide to take chromium in addition to your medication.

Zinc

More than three hundred enzymes in the body require zinc and the highest amounts of this trace mineral are found in the brain. Low blood levels of zinc have been linked to major and minor depression. Furthermore, supplementing with zinc has been shown to have an antidepressant effect. Studies conducted in healthy older adults suggest that getting adequate zinc from a variety of foods or a supplement may help reduce the likelihood of depression.[21,22] Research has also found that adding a daily zinc supplement to standard antidepressant therapy significantly improves symptoms of depression.[23,24]

To ensure an adequate intake of zinc, include the following foods in your diet: seafood (especially oysters and crab), red meat, poultry (dark meat), yogurt, nuts, legumes, wheat bran, wheat germ, whole grains and enriched breakfast cereals. A daily multivitamin and mineral supplement will also supply 10 to 20 milligrams of zinc. (See Chapter 4, page 78, to determine your daily zinc requirement.) To augment the effects of standard antidepressant medication in people with unipolar depression, a daily zinc supplement of 25 milligrams has been used. Do not take more than 40 milligrams of zinc per day.

Herbal Remedies

St. John's Wort (*Hypericum perforatum*)

For years, this herb has been used in Europe to treat both mild depression and seasonal affective disorder. Findings from numerous clinical trials have concluded that St. John's wort is an effective treatment for mild depression.[25,26] It can be considered an option along with conventional antidepressants for short-term treatment of mild depression. Experts believe that St. John's wort keeps brain serotonin levels high for a longer period, just like the popular antidepressant drugs Paxil, Zoloft and Prozac. St. John's wort also appears to alter levels of dopamine and norepinephrine in the brain, two other neurotransmitters involved in mood.

Buy a St. John's wort supplement that is standardized to 0.3 percent hyperforin content, the extract used in most clinical studies of mild and moderate depression. The recommended dose is 300 milligrams taken three times daily.

When taken in high doses for a long period, the herb may cause sensitivity to sunlight in very light-skinned individuals. St. John's wort has the potential to interact with a number of medications (see Chapter 7, page 149). The herb is not recommended for use during pregnancy and breastfeeding. If you're currently taking a prescription antidepressant drug, do not take it concurrently with St. John's wort. Always consult your physician before stopping any medication.

Other Natural Health Products

SAMe (S-Adenosyl-Methionine)

SAMe is a compound the body makes naturally from certain amino acids found in high-protein foods like fish and meat. The production of SAMe is closely linked with folate and vitamin B12, and deficiencies of these two nutrients can lead to depressed levels of SAMe in the brain and nervous system.

The results of recent well-controlled studies show that SAMe is significantly better than a placebo in treating depression, and it may even be more effective than tricyclic antidepressant medication.[27-34] In patients taking SAMe, symptoms improve in as few as 4 to 5 days. Exactly how SAMe works to treat depressive symptoms is not entirely clear. It's associated with higher levels of brain neurotransmitters. But it may also work by favourably changing the composition of cell membranes in the brain, enabling neurotransmitters and cell receptors to function more efficiently.

SAMe is sold as a dietary supplement in the United States, but it has not been approved for sale in Canada. If you are shopping on the Internet or visiting the United States, look for an enteric-coated supplement to help SAMe withstand the acidity of your stomach. There are several forms of SAMe available: sulphate, sulphate-p-toluenesulphonate (tosylate) and butanedisulphonate. Some experts believe butanedisulphonate is more stable than tosylate.

For depression, take 800 to 1600 milligrams per day, in divided doses. Start with one 400 milligram tablet twice daily, working up to two tablets three times daily. Take SAMe on an empty stomach. It may take 30 days of treatment to notice significant improvements in mood. If you're currently taking medication for depression and you're thinking about trying SAMe, do not discontinue your medication without first speaking to your doctor. When taken with antidepressant drugs, SAMe may cause potentially dangerous side effects.

Nutrition Strategy Checklist for Depression

☐ Foods rich in carbohydrate

☐ Omega-3 supplement (DHA, EPA)

☐ Vitamin B6

☐ Folate

☐ Chromium

☐ Zinc

☐ St. John's wort

☐ SAMe

Recommended Resources

Canadian Mental Health Association
www.cmha.ca
Phenix Professional Building
595 Montreal Road, Suite 303
Ottawa, ON K1K 4L2
Tel: 613-745-7750
Fax: 613-745-5522
Email: info@cmha.ca

Mental Health America
www.nmha.org
2000 N. Beauregard Street, 6th Floor
Alexandria, VA, USA 22311
Tel: 703-684-7722 or 1-800-969-NMHA
   (6642) (Mental Health Information Center)
Fax: 703-684-5968

National Depressive and Manic Depressive Association
www.ndmda.org

730 N. Franklin Street, Suite 501
Chicago, IL, USA 60601
Tel: 1-312-642-0049 or 1-800-826-3632
Fax: 312-642-7243

National Institute of Mental Health
National Institutes of Health
www.nimh.nih.gov
6001 Executive Boulevard, Room 8184,
   MSC 9663
Bethesda, MD, USA 20892-9663
Tel: 301-443-4513
Fax: 301-443-4279

Dermatitis and Eczema

Dermatitis is a general term used to describe an inflammation of the skin. There are several types of dermatitis, including eczema, and most cause swollen, reddened and itchy skin. The common types of dermatitis include:

CONTACT DERMATITIS. This condition develops when allergy-causing substances (allergens) come in contact with the skin, triggering redness, itchiness, burning sensations and blisters on the skin surface. Perfumes, cosmetics, metal jewellery, household-cleaning products, preservatives in creams and lotions, and plants such as poison ivy are examples of allergens known to cause contact dermatitis. The reaction usually disappears when contact with the allergen is avoided.

SEBORRHEIC DERMATITIS. Yellowish, oily, scaling patches appear on the scalp, face and other areas of the body where the sebaceous (oil-producing) glands are numerous. It often appears as a stubborn, itchy form of dandruff. It tends to be an inherited condition and is treated with medicated shampoos and hydro-cortisone creams or lotions.

NEURODERMATITIS. This condition develops when a skin irritant, such as a tight garment or an insect bite, triggers a cycle of constant rubbing or scratching. Scaly patches appear on the affected area and become thickened and leathery (lichenified) because of the persistent scratching. Treatment usually involves applying dressings over the irritated spot to prevent further scratching or rubbing, plus topical hydrocortisone creams or ointments to soothe the skin.

NUMMULAR ECZEMA. Round, coin-shaped patches of irritated skin develop on the arms, backs, lower legs and buttocks. These patches may become crusty, dry, red and leathery. It's common in older adults and children and is often triggered by stress or extremely dry or humid climates.

STASIS DERMATITIS. This condition occurs when fluid gathers in the tissues under the skin. People with varicose veins or other circulatory problems in the legs are prone to developing this condition. It causes the skin on the ankles to become fragile, discoloured, thickened and itchy. Treatment focuses on correcting the condition that causes the fluid buildup. Elastic support hose or varicose vein surgery may be necessary.

Atopic Dermatitis (Eczema)

One of the most prevalent types of dermatitis is atopic dermatitis, commonly known as eczema. *Atopic* refers to a group of allergic diseases that are hereditary and often affect several members of a family. Asthma and hay fever are part of this group, as are the skin eruptions that are characteristic of atopic dermatitis.

Atopic dermatitis is thought to affect 20 percent of children and 1 percent to 2 percent of adults. It's a chronic, recurrent condition that causes the skin to become extremely itchy, inflamed, swollen, dry and cracked. Atopic dermatitis occurs most often in infants and children. One-third of all cases appear in the first year of life and 90 percent of patients show symptoms before the age of 5.[1] The disease rarely develops after the age of 30. Eczema usually permanently resolves by the age of 3 in about half of all affected infants. In others, the disease tends to recur throughout life.

The cause of atopic dermatitis is unclear. It's not a contagious condition and cannot be spread from one person to another. It seems to be associated with a malfunction of the immune system, triggered in response to infectious or irritating conditions. Current research also indicates that it may be linked to a defect in the conversion of linoleic acid, an essential fatty acid the body must get from food. Atopic dermatitis is often aggravated by a combination of hereditary and environmental factors such as:

- inherited tendencies to allergies or asthma
- dry skin
- extremely high or low temperatures
- irritants such as household cleaning products, detergents, perfumes and cosmetics, wool and other rough or synthetic fabrics, cigarette smoke, dust and sand
- allergens such as pollen, dog or cat dander, or foods known to trigger allergic reactions (peanuts, eggs, soy products, fish, milk and wheat)
- emotional issues, anxiety and stress
- bacterial or viral skin infections

Symptoms

The symptoms of atopic dermatitis vary from person to person and include:

- dry, itchy skin
- cracks behind the ears
- rashes on the cheeks, arms and legs; small red bumps (papules) may develop, becoming crusty and infected when scratched
- red and scaly skin; skin may become thick and leathery (lichenified) due to constant scratching
- extra fold of skin around eyes (atopic pleat)
- darkened skin on the eyelids due to inflammation
- sparse and patchy eyebrows and eyelashes due to rubbing

Who's at Risk?

The incidence of atopic dermatitis has increased dramatically since 1970, possibly because of our changing diet (reduced fruit, vegetables and omega-3 fatty acids), increased exposure to environmental irritants, allergens and emotional stress. The skin condition affects men and women equally and tends to run in families. Atopic dermatitis occurs most often in infants and children. It's estimated that up to 20 percent of all infants suffer from atopic dermatitis and nearly 50 percent outgrow it by adulthood.[2]

Conventional Treatment

To keep the skin healthy, it's important to develop a proper skin-care routine. Avoid hot or long showers and use mild soaps or non-soap cleansers to prevent drying of the skin. After bathing, gently pat skin dry—avoid rubbing briskly. Moisturize the skin with creams or ointments immediately after bathing or showering.

If the skin shows signs of infection such as oozing areas or crusty or pus-filled blisters, begin medical treatment immediately. Commonly prescribed treatments include the following:

- **Corticosteroid creams and ointments** may be prescribed to treat flare-ups. Oral or systemic corticosteroid medications may be necessary for more severe episodes.
- **Antibiotics** may be needed to treat skin infections.
- **Antihistamines** may be prescribed to cause drowsiness to reduce nighttime scratching.
- **Phototherapy** with ultraviolet A or B light may be helpful.
- **Immunosuppressive drugs** may be used in adults to treat attacks that are not responding to other forms of therapy.
- **Topical immunomodulators**, new drugs under development, are offering hope for an improved, steroid-free approach to management of atopic dermatitis.

The most effective strategy for preventing eczema in high-risk infants is exclusive breastfeeding for the first 6 months of life. (An infant is considered to be at risk if one or both parents have an atopic illness.) Breast milk contains many protective compounds that can bolster an infant's developing immune system. Finnish researchers studied 236 high-risk infants at ages 1, 3, 5, 10 and 17 to determine the effect of breastfeeding on atopic disease. They found that the prevalence of atopic eczema, food allergy and respiratory illness was lowest for those who were breastfed for longer than 6 months and highest in those who had little or no breastfeeding.[3]

If breastfeeding is not possible, a hypoallergenic infant formula should be used for the first 4 to 6 months. It's also important to delay the introduction of potentially allergenic foods. In particular, put off introduction of cow's milk until after 12 months of age. It's preferable to use hydrolyzed formula first (e.g., Nutramigen, Alimentum, GoodStart) because the milk protein has been altered, making it less allergenic. Egg whites should not be added to the diet until 2 years of age. The introduction of nuts, fish and shellfish should be delayed until 3 years of age. Avoiding eggs, peanuts, nuts, fish and shellfish in the diet while breastfeeding may also help prevent atopic disease in an infant.

Managing Atopic Dermatitis

Dietary Strategies

Food Allergies

Certain food proteins known to cause allergic reactions may be involved in the development of eczema or may exacerbate its condition. In fact, it's estimated that food allergies contribute to atopic eczema in as many as one-third of children with the skin condition.[4] Common food allergens that can cause eczema include eggs, fish, milk, nuts and wheat. It's important to be tested for food allergies by a trained doctor to avoid dietary limitations that may be unnecessary and even harmful. Studies have shown that once food allergies are confirmed by testing, elimination of these foods results in improvement of skin symptoms.[5-8]

To determine if a food allergy is triggering your or your child's atopic eczema, try an elimination/challenge diet as outlined below. A registered dietitian (www.dietitians.ca) can help you identify problematic foods and plan a healthy diet that avoids them.

1. **Elimination phase.** For a period of 2 weeks, eliminate common food allergens—dairy products, soy foods, citrus fruits, nuts, wheat, shellfish, fish, eggs, corn and sulphite food additives.
2. **Challenge phase.** After 2 weeks, start introducing one food every 3 days. Keep a food and symptom diary. Record everything you eat, amounts eaten and what time you ate the food or meal. Document any skin symptoms. If symptoms recur when a particular food is added back, you may be allergic to it. Consult your doctor for further food allergy testing.

Essential Fatty Acids

People with atopic dermatitis are thought to have impaired fatty acid metabolism.[9-12] The body uses essential fatty acids in food to produce compounds called eicosanoids, which have a wide range of health effects in the body. Linoleic acid, an essential fatty acid found in vegetable oils, is converted in the body to gamma-linolenic acid (GLA), which in turn is used to make anti-inflammatory eicosanoids.

Some experts believe that the conversion of linoleic acid to GLA is impaired in people with atopic dermatitis. A diet that is high in saturated fat and processed vegetable oils further slows down this conversion. Some, but not all, studies have found that supplementing the diet with oils rich in essential fatty acids or omega-3 fatty acids in fish oil improves symptoms of eczema.[13-16] There is also some evidence that taking a fish oil supplement during pregnancy might reduce the severity of eczema in infants at risk for allergic diseases.[17]

To promote the production of anti-inflammatory immune compounds (eicosanoids) in the body, ensure your diet includes foods and plant oils that supply essential fatty acids. Include 1 to 2 tablespoons (15 to 30 ml) of an oil rich in essential fatty acids, such as hempseed oil, flaxseed oil or Udo's Choice Ultimate Oil Blend. Limit your intake of fatty foods that increase the production of inflammatory immune compounds. Choose lean cuts of meat, poultry breast and low-fat dairy products. Avoid processed foods that contain partially hydrogenated vegetable oils. If you use margarine, choose one that is non-hydrogenated. If you don't have an allergy to fish, eat fish rich in omega-3 fatty acids twice per week. Good choices—which are also low in mercury—include salmon, trout, Arctic char, sardines and herring.

Flavonoids

Flavonoids are natural compounds found in fruit, vegetables, tea and red wine that have anti-inflammatory effects in the body. Lab studies have demonstrated that flavonoids inhibit the release of histamine (a protein involved in many allergic reactions) and reduce the production of other inflammatory immune compounds. Research has also shown that giving flavonoids to eczema-prone mice was effective in preventing the skin condition. Interestingly, observational studies have also reported a significantly lower incidence of asthma in populations with a high intake of flavonoids.[18]

To increase your intake of flavonoids, include 7 to 10 servings of fruit and vegetables combined in your daily diet. (One serving is equivalent to 1 medium fruit, 1/4 cup/60 ml of dried fruit, 1/2 cup/125 ml cooked or raw vegetables, and 1 cup/250 ml of salad greens.) Good sources of flavonoids include berries, cherries, red grapes, apples, citrus fruit, broccoli, kale and onions.

Vitamins and Minerals

Vitamin E

There is compelling evidence that oxidative stress caused by free radicals is involved in inflammatory skin conditions. Vitamin E is a potent antioxidant that can help protect skin cells from free radical damage. In a study of 96 adults who suffered from eczema, taking 400 international units (IU) of vitamin E daily for 8 months was associated with substantial improvement in skin symptoms compared with taking a placebo. Many participants taking vitamin E experienced complete remission of eczema. Those in the vitamin E group also had a marked reduction in blood levels of IgE antibodies, immune compounds that play an important role in allergic diseases.[19]

The best food sources of vitamin E include vegetable oils, almonds, peanuts, soybeans, whole grains, wheat germ, wheat germ oil, avocado and green leafy vegetables, especially kale. To supplement, take 400 IU of vitamin E once daily. If you have existing cardiovascular disease or diabetes, do not take vitamin E supplements. (See Chapter 4, page 53, to learn more about vitamin E supplements.)

Zinc

A deficiency of this mineral leads to a number of health problems, including a weakened immune system and atopic dermatitis.[20,21] Scandinavian researchers have found that compared with healthy children, those with allergies tend to have lower zinc levels.[22] To prevent a deficiency, include zinc-rich foods in your daily diet. Zinc is abundant in red meat, oysters, seafood, poultry, wheat bran, wheat germ, whole grains, enriched breakfast cereals and yogurt. Adult multivitamin and mineral supplements provide 10 to 20 milligrams of the mineral. Children's products may or may not contain zinc because of its potential toxicity when consumed in large amounts; if they do have zinc, very small amounts are present (e.g., 2 milligrams).

If you have been diagnosed with a zinc deficiency, take 10 to 40 milligrams of zinc once daily. Children under 10 years of age should take no more than 10 milligrams of zinc. Buy a zinc supplement with 1 milligram of copper for every 10 milligrams of zinc (large amounts of zinc deplete the body's copper stores). Consuming more than 40 milligrams per day can depress the immune system and cause toxic effects. Do not exceed 40 milligrams of zinc per day.

Herbal Remedies

Herbal Creams

Topical creams of calendula, chamomile and licorice, alone or in combination, are often used in Europe to ease the symptoms of eczema. When used topically, these creams have anti-inflammatory properties. Researchers from Germany found the use of chamomile cream equally effective or superior to hydrocortisone creams.[23,24] Apply one of these creams to the affected areas one to four times daily.

Other Natural Health Products

Probiotics

A group of health-enhancing microbes called lactic acid bacteria may be useful in treating eczema. Researchers from Finland evaluated the effect of lactobacilli and bifidobacteria supplemental infant formula in 27 infants with atopic eczema.[25,26] After 2 months of treatment, the infants receiving the probiotic formula experienced a significant improvement in their skin condition, whereas those on regular

formula did not. A review of thirteen randomized controlled trials concluded that probiotics, in particular *Lactobacillus rhamnosus GG*, is effective in preventing atopic dermatitis in high-risk infants. In these studies, mothers took the probiotic supplement during pregnancy and this was followed by treatment of their infants with the same probiotic supplement for the first 6 months of life. Probiotics were also found to reduce the severity of eczema in half of all the trials reviewed.[27]

Lactic acid bacteria exert their health benefits in the intestinal tract. Here they may help treat eczema by enhancing the body's immune system, preventing the attachment of harmful microbes to the intestinal tract and secreting substances that destroy infection-causing bacteria.

A supplement of *Lactobacillus rhamnosus GG* is sold in the United States and on the Internet under the brand name Culturelle and Culturelle for Kids (ConAgra Foods). Culturelle supplies 10 billion live cells per dose; Culturelle for Kids provides 1 billion per dose. When children reach a body weight of 100 pounds (45.5 kg), they can use the adult product. Culturelle can be taken with or without food at any time during the day. The capsule can also be opened and the contents mixed with any cool food or beverage. For more information, visit www.culturelle.com.

Nutrition Strategy Checklist for Dermatitis and Eczema

☐ Identify food allergies
☐ Essential fatty acids
☐ Limit saturated fat
☐ Fish
☐ Flavonoids

- ☐ Vitamin E
- ☐ Zinc
- ☐ Chamomile cream
- ☐ Probiotic supplements

Recommended Resources

The Eczema Society of Canada
www.eczemahelp.ca
417 The Queensway South
P.O. Box 25009
Keswick, ON L4P 2C4
Tel: 905-535-0776
Email: director@eczemahelp.ca

American Academy of Allergy, Asthma and Immunology
www.aaaai.org
555 E. Wells Street, Suite 1100
Milwaukee, WI, USA 53202-3823
Tel: 414-272-6071

American Academy of Dermatology
www.aad.org
1350 I Street, NW, Suite 870
Washington, DC, USA 20005-3305
Tel: 202-842-3555
Fax: 202-842-4355

National Institute of Arthritis and Musculoskeletal and Skin Diseases
National Institutes of Health
www.niams.nih.gov
1 AMS Circle
Bethesda, MD, USA 20892-3675
Tel: 301-495-4484 or 1-877-226-4267
Fax: 301-718-6366
Email: NIAMSinfo@mail.nih.gov

Diabetes Mellitus (Type 2 Diabetes)

Today it's estimated that 246 million people worldwide have diabetes. More than 2 million Canadians have diabetes, a number that's expected to rise to three million by the end of 2010.[1] Diabetes is a condition in which your blood sugar (glucose) is higher than it should be. This happens either because the body's pancreas doesn't secrete enough insulin, the hormone that removes sugar from the bloodstream, or because cells in the body don't use insulin properly. Sometimes diabetes results from both circumstances. Over time, excess sugar in the blood damages blood vessels by increasing fat deposits on vessel walls, which can lead to atherosclerosis and blocked arteries.

The following describes the types of diabetes that one can develop, and the condition that precedes the most common form of diabetes, called type 2.

TYPE 1 DIABETES, formerly called insulin-dependent diabetes, typically occurs in childhood or the teen years and requires daily insulin injections. Most cases of type 1 diabetes are caused by the body's immune system destroying the insulin-producing cells of the pancreas. Type 1 diabetes accounts for 10 percent of all diabetes cases in Canada.

TYPE 2 DIABETES, previously known as non-insulin-dependent diabetes, is the form of the disease experienced by the vast majority of people with diabetes (90 percent). Type 2 diabetes usually develops after the age of 40, but it's increasingly being diagnosed in children and adolescents. The underlying cause of type 2 diabetes is thought to be insulin resistance, a condition whereby your cells are unable to use insulin properly. In the early stages, the body responds by telling the pancreas to produce more insulin to clear sugar from the bloodstream. But over time, the pancreas can't keep up with demands, blood sugar rises and diabetes results. Unlike type 1 diabetes, which cannot be prevented, it's possible to prevent or delay the onset of type 2 diabetes through healthy lifestyle choices such as physical activity, healthy eating, weight control and not smoking.

GESTATIONAL DIABETES develops only during pregnancy and disappears when the pregnancy is over. In Canada, it affects approximately 3.7 percent of all pregnancies in the non-Aboriginal population and 8 percent to 18 percent of all pregnancies in the Aboriginal population, and involves an increased risk of developing diabetes for both mother and child.

PREDIABETES (IMPAIRED FASTING GLUCOSE) is a condition that precedes type 2 diabetes. If you have been diagnosed with impaired fasting glucose this means your fasting glucose (your blood-glucose measurement after fasting for 8 to 12 hours) is higher than normal but not high enough to be diagnosed as type 2 diabetes. Regular exercise and losing excess body weight can lower your fasting blood sugar to the normal range and prevent full-blown type 2 diabetes.

During its insidious progress, diabetes can damage both large and small blood vessels and nerves. This usually leads to a number of associated health problems, including:

- **Eye disease.** People with diabetes are four times more likely to become blind—in fact, diabetes is the leading cause of adult blindness in North America. Diabetic retinopathy is caused by a deterioration of the blood vessels in the eyes. It affects almost everyone with type 1 diabetes and 60 percent of people with type 2 diabetes. People with diabetes are also at greater risk of developing glaucoma, cataracts and damage to the macula of the eye. Regular visits to an ophthalmologist can prevent the progression of diabetic retinopathy and preserve eyesight.

- **Kidney disease.** As many as 20 percent to 30 percent of people with diabetes develop kidney disease within 15 years of their diagnosis. Damage to the kidneys can ultimately lead to kidney failure, requiring treatment with dialysis or organ transplant.

- **Nerve damage.** Diabetes can generate nerve damage (neuropathy) that will cause numbness and tingling sensations, especially in the feet. Nerve damage can also result in insensitivity to pain or extreme sensitivity to touch. Nerves also control gastrointestinal function and the ability to achieve an erection. Neuropathy can affect all of these bodily functions.

- **Heart disease.** People with diabetes are six times more likely to have heart disease or stroke than those without the condition. Sadly, 80 percent of people living with diabetes will die as a result of cardiovascular disease. Chronic high blood-sugar levels lead to narrowing of the arteries, high blood pressure, heart attack and stroke.

- **Infections.** Poor blood supply and nerve damage caused by diabetes can lead to ulcers on the skin and slow healing of wounds. Chronic high glucose levels increase the risk of infection and interfere with the body's immune system.

- **Impotence.** Because of blood vessel blockage, impotence affects between 8 percent and 13 percent of all men with diabetes.
- **Pregnancy complications.** Women with diabetes have a higher risk of delivering babies with birth defects and often have complications in their pregnancies.

These long-term complications usually develop after more than 10 years of diabetes and are related to the level of blood-sugar control and hereditary factors. Cigarette smoking, high blood pressure, and high blood cholesterol and triglycerides can further increase the chances of complications. These statistics may sound bleak, but two large intervention studies have demonstrated that tight control of blood sugar can significantly reduce the risk of eye, nerve and kidney disease.[2,3] Early diagnosis of diabetes and tight control of blood sugars are essential to help delay or prevent the complications of this disease.

The following sections will discuss mainly type 2 diabetes, since this disease is largely preventable.

Symptoms

Symptoms of type 1 and type 2 diabetes include the following. However, some people with type 2 diabetes may have no symptoms at all.

- extreme thirst
- frequent urination
- unusual weight loss
- excessive hunger
- extreme fatigue or lack of energy
- blurred vision
- recurring infections, especially of the skin, gums and bladder
- cuts and bruises that are slow to heal
- tingling or numbness in the hands or feet
- for men, trouble getting or maintaining an erection

Who's at Risk?

Researchers don't fully understand why some people develop type 2 diabetes and others don't. A person's genetic makeup plays a role, as do numerous environmental factors. The following factors are thought to increase the risk:

- **Aging.** Becoming older increases the odds of developing type 2 diabetes, largely because with age, people tend to exercise less and to gain weight. However, these lifestyle factors are also causing an increase of type 2 diabetes in children.
- **Genetics.** If you have a parent, brother or sister with diabetes, you're at increased risk for developing diabetes yourself. Being a member of a high-risk population, such as Aboriginal, Hispanic, Asian, South Asian or African, also increases the likelihood of developing diabetes. Unfortunately, you can't change your genes but there are other important risk factors you can control.
- **Being overweight.** Carrying excess body weight, especially around the middle, is the main risk factor for type 2 diabetes. The more body fat you have, the more resistant your cells become to the action of insulin. The good news: Losing weight can reverse insulin resistance.
- **Sedentary lifestyle.** Physical inactivity boosts the risk of diabetes by making you more likely to gain weight. Regular exercise also uses glucose in your body for energy, thereby making your cells more sensitive to insulin.

- **Impaired fasting glucose**. Having an elevated fasting blood sugar, even slightly higher than normal, often progresses to type 2 diabetes if it's not managed through healthy lifestyle behaviours and, in some cases, medication.
- **Metabolic syndrome**. This disorder is characterized by a cluster of risk factors in one person. A person is thought to have metabolic syndrome if he or she has a large waist circumference plus two or more of the following: high blood triglycerides, high blood pressure, impaired fasting glucose and low HDL (good) cholesterol. Having metabolic syndrome is thought to increase the likelihood of developing type 2 diabetes by fivefold.
- **Gestational diabetes**. This type of diabetes occurs during pregnancy, usually during the second trimester. While gestational diabetes usually disappears after childbirth, it increases a woman's future risk for type 2 diabetes. As well, giving birth to a baby weighing 9 pounds (4.1 kg) or more increases the chances of developing diabetes.

Conventional Treatment

Controlling blood sugar is the most important goal of treatment. Type 1 diabetes always requires daily injections of insulin administered by needle or an insulin pump. Type 2 diabetes may require oral medications to increase insulin secretion by the pancreas (drugs such as Amaryl, Starlix, Diabeta, Diamicron, GlucoNorm) or to enhance the action of insulin (drugs such as Glucophage, Glumetza, Avandamet, Actos, Avandia). Some people with type 2 diabetes may require insulin injections or a combination of insulin and oral medications to lower their blood sugar.

Managing diabetes includes eating healthy foods on a regular schedule, managing carbohydrate intake, exercising regularly, achieving and maintaining a healthy weight, and reducing stress. Exercise improves the body's sensitivity to insulin and lowers blood sugar to the same extent as some type 2 diabetes medications.

Self-monitoring with a home blood-glucose meter (glucometer) is essential to keep a check on sugar levels and, for people with type 1 diabetes, to help adjust diet and insulin accordingly. Maintaining blood glucose at optimal levels can significantly reduce the risk of long-term complications such as eye problems, nerve damage and heart disease.

Recommended Targets for Blood-Glucose Control[4]

HbA1c (%)	Fasting Blood Glucose	2-Hour Post-Meal Glucose
Type 1 and Type 2 diabetes	≤7	4.0–7.0 5.0–10.0 5.0–8.0 if HbA1c targets are not being met

The level of hemoglobin A1c (HbA1c) in your blood is a measure of how well your diabetes is being controlled. Hemoglobin is a pigment within red blood cells that carries oxygen throughout the body. When diabetes is not controlled, sugar (glucose) builds up in your blood and combines with your hemoglobin, making it "glycated" or sticky with sugar. The HbA1c test provides an average of your blood-glucose measurements over the past 6 to 12 weeks. If your blood-glucose levels have been high over recent weeks, the HbA1c result will be higher.

Once you're diagnosed with diabetes, proper education by registered dietitians, nurses and certified diabetes educators is crucial to learn how to manage your blood glucose through medication, eating habits, exercise regimen and stress levels. Diabetes education centres in hospitals offer intensive training programs for those newly diagnosed with the disease and their families.

Managing Diabetes
Dietary Strategies

The cornerstone of diabetes management is diet therapy. Dietary advice for people with diabetes follows the principles of Canada's Food Guide.[5,6] A registered dietitian is a key member of the diabetes health care team and will help develop a healthy eating plan that is tailored to your food preferences, medication and lifestyle. Research shows that following the advice of a dietitian trained in diabetes management results in significant improvements in blood-sugar control.[7]

An appropriate meal plan can help achieve and maintain optimal blood-sugar and blood-fat levels and prevent or delay the long-term complications of diabetes. Depending on the type of diabetes, your education level and whether or not medications are used, your dietitian may develop a meal plan using either Canada's Food Guide or the Canadian Diabetes Association's meal planning guide/manual. Both provide the number of servings per day and appropriate serving sizes for food choices. They also outline which food groups and specific foods affect blood sugar the most.

The Canadian Diabetes Association's recently revised *Beyond the Basics: Meal Planning for Healthy Eating, Diabetes Prevention and Management* contains informa-tion on a wide variety of topics, from eating out to recipe makeovers to physical activity. The meal planning guide is based on the association's clinical practice guidelines and current scientific evidence. It can be downloaded from the association's website, www.diabetes.ca.

Carbohydrates: Low Glycemic Index

Carbohydrate-containing foods such as cereals, breads, grains, legumes, fruit, vegetables and milk products are all digested and converted to blood glucose. Contrary to what some people might think, diabetic diets are not low in carbohydrate. It's recommended that a person with diabetes, just like a healthy individual, consume 50 percent to 60 percent of daily calories from carbohydrates. But with diabetes, it's important to manage the total amount and type of carbohydrate eaten at each meal and snack. Carbohydrates should be spread evenly over the day, as part of slowly digested meals. A dietitian will determine the appropriate amount of carbohydrate you need to consume, and distribute it evenly throughout the day (refer to Carbohydrate Counting, below).

Both the type of carbohydrate and the amount eaten affect blood-sugar levels. Not too long ago, dietitians used the terms simple and complex to classify carbohydrates, with simple carbohydrates such as table sugar resulting in a rapid rise in blood sugar and complex carbohydrates such as starchy foods leading to a gradual rise in glucose. However, these terms are no longer used because they don't indicate the impact that a food has on blood-glucose levels. For instance, some starchy foods that were considered complex, such as white bread, white potatoes and white rice, result in a fast rise in blood sugar.

The glycemic index (GI) is used to express the rise in blood sugar caused by a carbohydrate-rich food. Studies have found that incorporating foods with a low glycemic-index value into meals of people with type 2 diabetes results in a slow, gradual rise in blood sugar, which improves blood-sugar control.[8–11] Lentils, kidney beans, barley, whole-grain pumpernickel bread, steel-cut and large-flake oatmeal, 100% bran cereals, pasta, yogurt and soy milk are all low-glycemic-index foods that can help optimize blood glucose control. Meal planning with the GI involves choosing foods that have a low or medium GI. However, if you're eating a food with a high GI, you can combine it with low GI foods to help balance the meal. For a list of selected foods with their corresponding glycemic-index value, see Chapter 1, page 8.

Carbohydrates: Carbohydrate Counting

Some dietitians may help their patients manage blood-sugar levels through carbohydrate counting. By setting a limit on how much carbohydrate you can eat at meals and snacks and then keeping track of your intake in relation to that maximum amount, you can help maintain blood-glucose levels in your target range. Finding the right amount of carbohydrate depends on many things, including how active you are and what, if any, medications you take. A good starting point is about 45 to 60 grams (1.5 to 2 ounces) of carbohydrate at a meal. You may need more or less carbohydrate at different meals, depending on how you manage your diabetes. Reading food labels is an important way to know how much carbohydrate is in one serving of a food. For foods that don't have a label, you have to estimate the amount of carbohydrate in it— keeping general serving sizes in mind will help you do that.

For example, there is about 15 grams of carbohydrate in:

- 1 small piece of fresh fruit
- 1/2 cup (125 ml) of canned or frozen fruit
- 1 slice of bread (1 oz) or 1 (6-inch) tortilla
- 1/2 cup (125 ml) of cooked oatmeal
- 1/3 cup (75 ml) of cooked pasta or rice
- 1/2 English muffin or small hamburger bun
- 1/2 cup (125 ml) of black beans or starchy vegetable (e.g., corn, potato)
- 2/3 cup (150 ml) of plain yogurt, fat-free or sweetened with sugar substitutes
- 2 small cookies
- 2 inch square brownie or cake without frosting
- 1/2 cup (125 ml) sherbet
- 1 tbsp (15 ml) syrup, jam, jelly, sugar or honey
- 1 cup (250 ml) of soup

You and your registered dietitian will determine the total amount of carbohydrate to be consumed at each meal and snack, then you'll be taught how to determine the amounts of carbohydrate in different portions of carbohydrate foods (e.g., milk, yogurt, cereal, bread, fruit) in order to count your carbohydrate intake.

As you master carbohydrate counting, you'll be able to make adjustments to medication, food and exercise. This involves learning how to read nutrition labels and, with regard to your blood sugar, learning to identify patterns, interpret the causes for fluctuations and determine appropriate strategies to achieve blood-glucose targets.

Carbohydrates: Sugars

In the past, people with diabetes were told to avoid sugar in order to control their blood-glucose levels. However, researchers have now determined that natural sugars in fruit, milk and vegetables are an acceptable part of a healthy diabetic diet.[12,13] Added sugars such as sucrose (table sugar), syrup, jam, honey, molasses, maltose, dextrose and fruit juice are also allowed in small quantities. When developing a personal meal plan, a dietitian can include these sugars as part of your total daily carbohydrate intake.

Dietary Fibre

The recommendation is that people with diabetes achieve an intake of 25 to 38 grams of fibre per day (see Chapter 1, page 4, for a list of fibre-rich foods). Good sources of soluble fibre, such as legumes, barley, oats, oat bran, psyllium-enriched breakfast cereals and salba, have been shown to improve blood-sugar control in people with type 2 diabetes and should be included in the diet.[14-17] This type of fibre slows the absorption of sugar from the digestive tract, causing a slower rise in blood glucose. A daily intake of soluble fibre combined with a low-fat diet can also lower LDL (bad) blood cholesterol levels by 9 percent.

Increasing your intake of insoluble dietary fibre from cereals and whole grains is also thought to reduce the risk of developing type 2 diabetes. Studies consistently support increasing whole-grain intake for the prevention of type 2 diabetes. To learn more about whole grains, refer to Chapter 5, page 89.

Dietary Fat

It's recommended that, like all Canadians, people with diabetes consume 25 percent to 35 percent of their daily calories from fat. Since people with diabetes have a greater risk of developing coronary heart disease than individuals without diabetes, it's critical to limit your daily intake of saturated plus trans fat to 10 percent of calories. A number of studies have found that diets high in these fats impair glucose tolerance, promote obesity and cause high LDL (bad) blood cholesterol levels.[18,19] Scientists have learned that limiting the amount of saturated fat by choosing lower-fat animal foods and avoiding packaged foods made with partially hydrogenated vegetable oil (a.k.a. trans fat) can improve blood-sugar abnormalities. To help reduce your saturated and trans fat intake, see Chapter 3, page 28.

The majority of your fat should come from unsaturated fats. Polyunsaturated fat found in fish and fish oil and monounsaturated fats help lower elevated blood triglycerides, an abnormality common in people with diabetes. Emphasizing monounsaturated fats can also help lower high LDL cholesterol. The best sources of monounsaturated fats are olive oil, canola oil, peanut oil, avocado and almonds. Your dietitian will help you balance your daily fat and oil servings to achieve a fat intake that contains proportionately more monounsaturated fat than polyunsaturated and saturated fat.

Caffeinated Beverages

Although drinking 4 to 6 cups of coffee per day has been associated with protection from type 2 diabetes, if you already have the condition, caffeine might negatively influence blood-glucose control. One small study conducted in men and women with type 2 diabetes found that consuming 250 milligrams of caffeine at breakfast (the amount found in two 8 ounce cups of coffee) versus none resulted in a higher daytime blood-glucose level and a sharper rise in blood glucose after eating. It's thought that caffeine could hamper the ability of glucose to enter cells in the body. Or caffeine could stimulate the release of hormones that boost blood-glucose levels.[20,21] If you have type 2 diabetes and your glucose measurements are higher than they should be, it's possible that eliminating caffeinated beverages, especially coffee, could improve your blood-sugar control. See Chapter 5, page 110, to learn the caffeine content of various beverages and foods.

Alcoholic Beverages

You may have heard that a moderate intake of alcohol can help reduce the risk of heart disease. Although this may be true, consuming one or two alcoholic beverages can be dangerous for some people with diabetes. It's important to know that if you use insulin or take oral diabetes medications, delayed hypoglycemia (low blood glucose) can occur up to 24 hours after drinking alcohol. Symptoms of hypoglycemia include hunger, dizziness, nervousness, anxiety, shakiness, weakness, sweating, light-headedness and confusion. People with type 1 diabetes should be aware of the risk of morning hypoglycemia if alcohol is consumed 2 to 3 hours after the previous evening's meal. Alcohol can impair the liver's ability to release glucose in the bloodstream. Combining alcohol with exercise and a lack of food will further increase the risk of hypoglycemia.

Never drink on an empty stomach. If your blood glucose is well controlled, limit your intake of alcoholic beverages to one per day for women and two per day for men. If you take medication, speak to your doctor or diabetes educator about the use of alcohol.

Weight Control

The majority of people with type 2 diabetes are overweight. Experts believe that managing body weight can prevent most cases of type 2 diabetes. Carrying excess body fat around the abdomen is linked with higher levels of insulin in the blood and insulin resistance, and a greater risk of developing type 2 diabetes.[22,23] Having an "apple-" rather than a "pear-"shaped figure increases the risk of diabetes. Large studies conducted in people with impaired fasting glucose have demonstrated that losing as little as 7 percent of body weight can dramatically reduce the risk of developing full-blown diabetes.[24] If you have diabetes, losing 5 percent to 10 percent of body weight can enhance the body's sensitivity to insulin and improve blood-glucose levels.[25] Some people with type 2 diabetes who take oral hypoglycemic medications are able to decrease or discontinue medication once they have lost weight.

To determine if your body weight and waist circumference are within acceptable limits, see Obesity, Overweight and Weight Loss, page 569. If you are overweight and have been newly diagnosed with type 2 diabetes, your dietitian will develop a meal plan that promotes gradual weight loss. Weight loss is best achieved by a combination of reduction in calorie intake and increase in physical exercise. Obesity, Overweight and Weight Loss, page 569, also includes strategies to help you lose weight.

The following sections discuss nutrients and supplements that may be helpful in preventing diabetes complications or possibly even controlling blood sugar in people with type 2 diabetes. Keep in mind that research in these areas is limited and in no circumstances should the following be used as a sole therapy for diabetes. The only effective ways to lower and control blood sugar are through diet, exercise and, in many cases, medication. If your diabetes is not well controlled, the strategies below will not help you lower your blood sugar.

Vitamins and Minerals

Antioxidants

Diabetes is associated with an increased production of free radicals, unstable oxygen molecules that are generated by normal body processes. Free radicals damage cells and increase the risk of many health problems. It has also been found that people with diabetes have decreased levels of antioxidants in the body; these compounds neutralize free radicals and prevent them from doing harm. Some researchers have found that diabetic patients have lower levels of vitamin E and beta carotene, two antioxidant nutrients that neutralize free radicals, rendering them harmless.[26-29]

Oxidative stress caused by free radicals plays a key role in the development of long-term diabetes complications. Free radical damage to LDL cholesterol particles can increase the risk of heart disease in diabetes. Oxidative stress is also thought to cause diabetic retinopathy, a disease of the retina that can cause vision loss. Evidence suggests that vitamin C works with insulin to maintain tight blood-sugar control. Some studies have found that a daily vitamin C supplement can help decrease blood glucose, thereby lowering the risk of diabetes complications.[30-33]

To help combat free radicals, incorporate foods rich in the following antioxidants into your diet:

VITAMIN E. The recommended dietary allowance (RDA) is 22 international units (IU). Best food sources include wheat germ, nuts, seeds, vegetable oils, whole grains and kale. If you have diabetes, do not take high dose vitamin E supplements. See Chapter 4, page 53, about the safety of vitamin E supplementation.

BETA CAROTENE. No RDA has been established for beta carotene; however, experts think an intake of 3 to 6 milligrams is optimal for health. To achieve this level, include 7 to 10 servings of fruit and vegetables combined in your daily diet. Best food sources are orange and dark-green produce, including carrots, sweet potato, winter squash, broccoli, collard greens, kale, spinach, apricots, cantaloupe, peaches and nectarines. There's no good evidence that single beta carotene supplements are useful in the management of diabetes.

VITAMIN C. The RDA for women and men is 75 and 90 milligrams respectively (smokers need an additional 35 milligrams). Best food sources include citrus fruit, cantaloupe, kiwi, mango, strawberries, broccoli, Brussels sprouts, cauliflower, red pepper and tomato juice. To supplement, take 500 milligrams once or twice daily. The upper daily limit is 2000 milligrams.

Even if you don't have diabetes, it's important to increase your intake of antioxidant-rich foods. Research does suggest that higher intakes are linked with a lower risk of developing type 2 diabetes.[34]

Vitamin D

A lack of vitamin D during early childhood may increase the risk of developing type 1 diabetes. Vitamin D plays an important role in immunity and may inhibit the development of autoimmune diseases such as type 1 diabetes.[35] Too little vitamin D is also thought to increase the likelihood of type 2 diabetes by altering the synthesis and release of insulin in the body. A vitamin D deficiency may hamper the insulin's ability to clear sugar from the bloodstream, thereby increasing the risk of type 2 diabetes. Furthermore, some research has found that taking a vitamin D supplement to increase blood levels of the nutrient improves blood-vessel function in patients with type 2 diabetes.[36-38]

Take 1000 to 2000 international units (IU) of supplemental vitamin D each day. You can't rely on foods to provide adequate vitamin D, nor can you rely on sun exposure to produce vitamin D in your skin during the fall and winter months. Add up how much vitamin D you're getting from your multivitamin and calcium supplements. To get 1000 to 2000 IU per day, make up the difference by taking a separate vitamin D supplement, available in 400 or 1000 IU doses. See Chapter 4, page 51, to learn more about vitamin D supplementation.

Magnesium

Numerous studies indicate that lower intakes of magnesium and lower blood levels of the mineral play a role in the development of metabolic syndrome, insulin resistance and type 2 diabetes. Magnesium is thought to regulate blood-sugar control by influencing the release and activity of insulin. A few short-term studies have found that a daily magnesium supplement improved both the body's sensitivity to insulin and glucose removal from the blood.[39-41]

To prevent a magnesium deficiency, be sure to include foods rich in the mineral in your daily diet. Nuts, seeds, legumes, prunes, figs, whole grains, leafy green vegetables and brewer's yeast are all good sources. See Chapter 4, page 61, for an extensive list of foods rich in magnesium.

If you find it a challenge to meet your daily requirement from diet alone, take a magnesium supplement. If you take calcium pills, buy one with magnesium added (look for a 2:1 ratio of calcium to magnesium). If you don't need to take calcium supplements, take 200 to 250 milligrams of magnesium citrate once daily. Taking more than 350 milligrams of supplemental magnesium may cause diarrhea, nausea and stomach cramps.

Chromium

A deficiency of this trace mineral is associated with reduced glucose tolerance.[42] Chromium is used to make glucose-tolerance factor, a compound that interacts with insulin and helps maintain normal blood-sugar levels. With adequate amounts of chromium present, the body uses less insulin to do its job. Some studies suggest that with aging and in the presence of type 2 diabetes, chromium is lost from the body at an increased rate.[43-45] Many studies have looked at the effect of chromium supplements on blood-glucose control in people with type 2 diabetes, and most report a beneficial effect. Taking a supplement of chromium picolinate has been shown to reduce blood glucose and insulin, lower LDL choles-terol and triglycerides, and decrease the need for oral diabetes medication.

The best sources of chromium include brewer's yeast, calf's liver, blackstrap molasses, wheat germ, wheat bran, whole grains, mushrooms, apples with the skin, green peas, chicken breast, refried beans and oysters. Processed foods and refined starchy foods like white bread, white rice and pasta, sugar and sweets contain very little chromium.

If you're concerned that you're not getting enough chromium in your diet, check your multivitamin and mineral supplement to see how much it contains. Most brands supply 25 to 50 micrograms. If you choose to take a separate chromium supplement, do not exceed 200 micrograms per day. High doses of chromium can cause cognitive impairment, anemia and kidney damage. Supplements made from chromium picolinate and chromium nicotinate are thought to be absorbed more efficiently than those made from chromium chloride.

Herbal Remedies

American Ginseng (*Panax quinque-folius L*)

Preliminary research conducted at the University of Toronto suggests that this herb may be useful in helping people with type 2 diabetes manage their blood sugar.[46-47] Researchers gave people with type 2 diabetes 3 grams of ground American ginseng root or a placebo pill either 40 minutes before or together with a glucose drink. Significant reductions in blood glucose were observed in those who had been given the ginseng, whether it had been taken before or with the sugary drink.

Ginseng contains active ingredients called ginsenosides; American ginseng contains primarily a ginsenoside called Rb-1. No adverse reactions have been reported with the use of American ginseng (see Chapter 7, page 144). If you have type 2 diabetes and decide to try American ginseng, take the herb with a meal to avoid a possible low-blood-sugar reaction. Because the herb may enhance the action of diabetes medication, monitor your blood-glucose levels closely if you take oral hypoglycemic agents. Be sure to inform your health care practitioner that you're taking ginseng.

Other Natural Health Products

Alpha Lipoic Acid

Since 1950, alpha lipoic acid has been actively studied for its potential to help control blood-sugar levels and complications of diabetes. Alpha lipoic acid helps enzymes turn carbohy-drate from foods into a usable source of energy for the body. But alpha lipoic acid is also an antioxidant and, as such, is able to neutralize harmful compounds called free radicals. Unlike other well-known antioxidants such as vitamins C and E, alpha lipoic acid works in both a water and fat environment, allowing it to have a broad effect. Because of its antioxidant effects in fat tissue, alpha lipoic acid is able to enter nerve cells where it may offer protection. The body also uses alpha lipoic acid to regenerate vitamins C and E.

Studies have found that alpha lipoic acid supplementation can improve—and may even prevent—symptoms of diabetes neuropathy (nerve damage), including pain, tingling and numbness of the arms and legs.[48-51] Alpha lipoic acid also seems to help people with type 2 diabetes control their blood-sugar level. German researchers found that a daily alpha lipoic acid supplement taken for 1 month improved insulin sensitivity and glucose removal from the bloodstream in people with type 2 diabetes.[52-54]

To supplement, take 600 milligrams of alpha lipoic acid once or twice daily on an empty stomach. Alpha lipoic acid supplements appear to have no significant side effects. If you decide to supplement, monitor your blood-sugar levels closely. Because of its potential to lower blood glucose, alpha lipoic acid could have additive effects when taken together with diabetes medications.

Nutrition Strategy Checklist for Diabetes

☐   Diabetic diet

☐   Low-GI carbohydrate-rich foods

☐   Soluble fibre

- [ ] Low saturated and trans fat
- [ ] Monounsaturated fat
- [ ] Limit or avoid alcohol
- [ ] Weight control (type 2)
- [ ] Antioxidants
- [ ] Vitamin D
- [ ] Magnesium (type 2)
- [ ] Chromium (type 2)
- [ ] Alpha lipoic acid

Recommended Resources

Canadian Diabetes Association
www.diabetes.ca
1400–522 University Avenue
Toronto, ON M5G 2R5
Tel: 1-800-226-8464
Email: info@diabetes.ca

American Diabetes Association
www.diabetes.org
Attn: Customer Service
1701 N Beauregard Street
Alexandria, VA, USA 22311
Email: AskADA@diabetes.org

National Diabetes Information Clearinghouse
National Institutes of Health
www.diabetes.niddk.nih.gov
1 Information Way
Bethesda, MD, USA 20892-3560
Tel: 1-800-860-8747
Fax: 703-738-4929
Email: ndic@info.niddk.nih.gov

Diarrhea

Few people manage to get through life without experiencing at least one bout of diarrhea. In fact, most healthy adults can expect to have as many as four episodes every year.[1] Fortunately, diarrhea is usually just a temporary condition that goes away without any special treatment.

Diarrhea typically means more frequent trips to the washroom and a greater volume of stool. In most cases, acute diarrhea lasts less than a few weeks and is associated with short-term conditions, such as bacterial, viral or parasitic infections. Chronic diarrhea is most often related to intestinal disorders and generally persists longer than 4 weeks. People who travel, especially in developing countries, will often experience bouts of diarrhea, called traveller's diarrhea. This is commonly caused by contaminated food or water.

One of the most serious complications of diarrhea is dehydration, which occurs when the body loses excessive amounts of water and electrolytes (sodium, potassium, chloride) in the stool. Dehydration can cause a rapid drop in blood pressure and lead to fainting and heart problems. Dehydration is particularly dangerous for young children, the elderly and people who are physically debilitated.

What Causes Diarrhea?

Diarrhea can be triggered by many different conditions, including:

- **Bacterial infections.** Consuming contaminated water or food can cause diarrhea due to bacterial infections. *Salmonella* and *Escherichia coli (E. coli)* are two well-known culprits.
- **Viral infections.** An invading virus, such as rotavirus or Norwalk virus, can irritate the lining of the intestine, interfering with fluid absorption in the digestive process.

- **Parasites.** Contaminated food or water can carry parasites into the digestive system, where they can cause bloody, watery diarrhea, often accompanied by a high fever.
- **Food allergies or intolerance.** Some people have difficulty digesting certain components of the food they eat, resulting in intestinal irritation and diarrhea.
- **Medications.** Some medications, including antibiotics, may cause adverse reactions, including diarrhea.
- **Intestinal diseases and bowel disorders.** Diarrhea is a frequent symptom of chronic medical conditions such as inflammatory bowel disease or irritable bowel syndrome.

Symptoms

Along with the possible nausea, vomiting and fever, symptoms of diarrhea are:

- frequent loose, watery stools
- urgent need to have a bowel movement at least three times a day or more
- abdominal pain, cramping and bloating

Although diarrhea is usually a temporary condition, it may sometimes be a symptom of more serious problems. Contact your doctor if you have any of the following symptoms:

- severe pain in the abdomen or rectum
- fever of 39°C (102°F) or higher
- signs of dehydration, including thirst, less-frequent urination, light-headedness, dry skin and dark-coloured urine
- blood in the stool (possibly caused by a bacterial or parasitic infection)

Who's at Risk?

Diarrhea is most common among people who:

- have direct exposure to others suffering from gastrointestinal infections
- consume food or drinking water contaminated with bacteria, viruses or parasites
- take certain medications, especially antibiotics and magnesium-containing antacids
- suffer from food allergies or food intolerance
- suffer from chronic intestinal disorders
- are in hospital receiving feedings by nasogastric (nose to stomach) tube

Conventional Treatment

Diarrhea will usually resolve on its own without medical treatment. In most cases, drinking enough fluids to prevent dehydration and consuming electrolytes is the only treatment necessary. Some over-the-counter medications may reduce the frequency of bowel movements and of having to go to the bathroom and slow down physical movement through the body (basically "hold it in" longer), but they won't speed recovery. Do not use these medications if the diarrhea is caused by a bacterial or parasitic infection: They trap the organisms inside the gut, prolonging the problem. Antibiotics are usually prescribed to shorten the duration of diarrhea caused by bacterial infections. Diarrhea caused by a virus is either treated with medication or left to run its course, depending on the severity and type of virus.

Managing Diarrhea
Dietary Strategies

To prevent dehydration, drink 9 to 13 cups (2.2 to 3.2 L) of water or other fluids each day.

Fluids that help replace lost electrolytes include broth, clear sodas, weak tea, fruit juice and sports drinks.

To treat mild diarrhea, it may be helpful to allow your intestine time to rest by temporarily following a liquid diet. Gradually add semi-solid, low-fibre foods such as crackers, toast, rice, bananas, cooked carrots, boiled potatoes and chicken. For children, doctors often prescribe the BRAT diet: bananas, rice, apple-sauce and toast.

Avoid foods and food ingredients that can make diarrhea worse, such as milk, fatty foods, high-fibre foods, grapes, figs, dates, prune juice, gassy vegetables (broccoli, cauliflower, Brussels sprouts, cabbage), nuts, sweets and sugars, chocolate, sugar-free gum, honey, soft drinks, spicy foods, caffeine and alcohol. Avoid nicotine.

Fruit Juice

Excessive consumption of fruit juice, especially apple juice and pear nectar, is often the cause of so-called toddler's diarrhea.[2-4] In one study from the David Geffen School of Medicine at UCLA, elimination of these fruit juices immediately stopped diarrhea in all cases of chronic, non-specific diarrhea.[5] These juices contain higher amounts of fructose and sorbitol, types of carbohydrate that may be poorly absorbed.

Preschoolers should drink no more than 4 ounces (1/2 cup/125 ml) of unsweetened juice per day, and older children no more than 6 to 8 ounces (3/4 to 1 cup/175 to 250 ml) per day. Encourage your child to drink water when thirsty. Excessive juice consumption (12 ounces/1-1/2 cups/360 ml per day or more) can displace other important nutrients in the diet and cause failure to thrive in small children. In older children, too much juice has been linked with overweight.

Fermented Milk Products

To help recover from diarrhea, include 1 serving of yogurt or kefir in your daily diet. These foods contain live bacterial cultures that help recolonize the digestive tract with friendly, protective bacteria (probiotics). These bacteria are known collectively as lactic acid bacteria and, in numerous studies, have been shown to reduce the duration of antibiotic-associated diarrhea, traveller's (E. coli) diarrhea and viral diarrhea in both adults and children.[6-13] *Lactobacillus* and *Bifidobacterium* are the most researched types of bacteria.

Lactic acid bacteria are thought to help treat diarrhea by preventing the attachment of harmful microbes to the intestinal tract, secreting substances that destroy infection-causing bacteria and enhancing the body's immune system. Fermented milk products are appropriate for people with a mild to moderate lactose (milk sugar) intolerance (see Lactose Intolerance, page 529), since they have lower lactose content and take longer to be digested than plain milk.

Food Allergies

Research suggests that persistent diarrhea in infants and young children may indicate a food allergy to cow's milk.[14-16] Whereas many food allergy symptoms are dramatic and can be linked to eating a certain food, others are not. Some signs of sensitivity to cow's milk are chronic, less acute and more difficult for doctors to diagnose. These types of food allergies usually occur in infants between 1 week and 3 months of age. Vomiting and diarrhea are signs of a cow's milk sensitivity. A thorough examination and medical history by a pediatrician will help diagnose a food allergy (skin tests are not useful in these types of allergies).

Eliminating the problematic food is the only way of dealing with the allergy.

If formula made from cow's milk is causing your infant gastrointestinal distress, switch to one of the two hypoallergenic formulas available. Cow's milk proteins in extensively hydrolyzed formulas are broken down into small particles so they're less allergenic than the whole proteins in regular formulas. Amino acid–based infant formulas, which contain protein in its simplest form, may be recommended for infants who don't improve on a hydrolyzed formula. The majority of infants will outgrow their symptoms sometime between 1 month and 3 years of age. However, older children and adults are less likely to outgrow their sensitivity.

Vitamins and Minerals

Zinc

Many studies have linked diarrhea to a lack of zinc.[17–20] This deficiency suppresses the body's immune system and increases the intestine's susceptibility to toxin-producing bacteria or viruses. It's thought that one of the first target areas where a zinc deficiency manifests itself may be the gastrointestinal tract. The deficiency may also impair the gut's absorption of water and electrolytes, prolonging diarrhea.

Many studies conducted in children in developing countries have shown short-term zinc supplementation improves immunity and reduces the duration of diarrhea. While zinc malnutrition is most often seen in developing countries, cases of zinc deficiency have been reported among children and adolescents in Canada and the United States. Zinc is abundant in red meat, which is common in the North American diet. Other good sources include seafood, poultry, wheat bran, wheat germ, whole grains, enriched breakfast cereals and yogurt.

Although North Americans consume adequate amounts of zinc, there are some people who are at increased risk for a deficiency:

- **Children who follow a vegan (no animal products) diet.** Zinc in plant foods is less available to the body than the zinc in animal foods. Therefore, in order to meet their daily requirement, strict vegetarians may need to consume twice as much zinc-rich (plant) food as non-vegetarians.
- **People who don't eat enough protein.** High-protein foods are the best sources of zinc.
- **The elderly.** Older people absorb zinc less efficiently and tend to have a poor intake of high-protein foods.

To ensure that you and your family members are meeting your daily zinc needs, see Chapter 4, page 78, for recommended dietary allowances and food sources. If your doctor identifies a zinc deficiency as the cause of diarrhea, take 10 to 40 milligrams of zinc once daily. Children under 10 years of age should take no more than 10 milligrams of zinc. Buy a zinc supplement with 1 milligram of copper for every 10 milligrams of zinc (large amounts of zinc deplete the body's copper stores). Consuming more than 40 milligrams of zinc per day can depress the immune system and cause toxic effects: Do not exceed 40 milligrams per day.

Other Natural Health Products

Probiotics

Many studies support taking lactic acid bacteria in doses higher than what can be consumed from fermented milk products. Studies conducted in adults and children show that many strains of *Lactobacillus* and

Bifidobacterium help reduce the risk of developing traveller's diarrhea. An analysis of thirty-one studies also reported that taking probiotics along with antibiotics prevented diarrhea associated with antibiotic therapy.[21] (Antibiotics kill not only disease-causing organisms but also helpful lactic acid bacteria.)

Many experts believe that probiotic supplements are needed to ensure that sufficient numbers of live bacteria survive the acidic contents of the stomach and reach the intestine. Typical doses usually range from 1 billion to 10 billion viable organisms taken daily with food, in three to four divided doses. To reduce antibiotic-related diarrhea, take the supplement when you start your antibiotic therapy and continue taking for 5 days after antibiotics are stopped. To prevent antibiotic medication from killing a significant number of probiotic bacteria in the supplement, take antibiotics and probiotic supplements 2 hours apart.

Children's probiotic products are available. These usually contain one-quarter to one-half the adult dose.

Probiotic supplements may cause flatulence, which usually subsides as you continue treatment. There are no safety issues associated with taking these supplements.

Nutrition Strategy Checklist for Diarrhea

- ☐ Fluids and electrolytes
- ☐ Limit fruit juice
- ☐ Fermented milk products
- ☐ Identify food allergies
- ☐ Zinc
- ☐ Probiotic supplements

Recommended Resources

Caring for Kids, The Canadian Pediatric Society
www.caringforkids.cps.ca
2305 St. Laurent Boulevard
Ottawa, ON K1G 4J8
Tel: 613-526-9397
Fax: 613-526-3332

Mayo Foundation for Medical Education and Research
www.mayoclinic.com
The Mayo Foundation for Medical Education and Research provides one of the best patient-education websites on the Internet. The information is reliable, thorough and clearly written.

National Digestive Diseases Information Clearinghouse
National Institutes of Health
www.digestive.niddk.nih.gov
2 Information Way
Bethesda, MD, USA 20892-3570
Tel: 1-800-891-5389
Fax: 703-738-4929
Email: nddic@info.niddk.nih.gov

Diverticulosis and Diverticulitis

Almost 50 percent of North Americans over the age of 60 have diverticulosis, a condition that develops when small, bulging pouches, called diverticula, form in the gastrointestinal tract. Although diverticula can appear almost anywhere in the body, they typically develop in the walls of the large intestine, particularly in the colon. As we age, the walls of our intestines gradually become weaker. Over time, the lining of the bowel can force its way out through the weakened areas, forming these tiny, sac-like bulges.

Diverticulosis rarely displays any physical symptoms. However, feces and food particles can become trapped in the diverticula, resulting in diverticulitis, a condition in which the pouches become inflamed or infected. Tenderness in the abdomen, crampy pain, fever and possibly nausea and colonic obstruction can result. Approximately 10 percent to 25 percent of people with diverticulosis will go on to develop diverticulitis.

What Causes Diverticular Disease?

Scientists have linked diverticular disease to aging and to low-fibre diets. With advancing age, the outer walls of the intestine become thickened, narrowing the passageway through the colon. This makes it increasingly difficult for the muscles in the intestine to move waste products through the colon. When waste products linger in the colon too long, the stool becomes hard and dry, often resulting in constipation. The muscle straining associated with constipation puts increased pressure on the intestinal walls and may force the bowel lining to bulge through any weak spots.

A diet low in fibre is often a contributing factor in constipation and may increase the pressure inside the digestive tract. The incidence of diverticulitis has steadily increased as North Americans have added more refined and processed food to their diets.

While diverticulitis is usually not a serious disease, it can lead to medical complications. Infected diverticula can cause an abscess, or collection of pus, to form on the intestinal wall. If the abscess is small and remains in the wall of the colon, it can clear up with antibiotic treatment. If the abscess doesn't clear up with antibiotics, it may need to be drained using a catheter—a small tube—placed into the abscess through the skin. If the inflamed diverticula rupture, pus and bacteria can leak into the abdominal cavity causing the lining of the cavity to become inflamed. This is called peritonitis and is considered a medical emergency. Immediate surgery is necessary to clean out the infection and remove the damaged areas of the colon. Infection may also cause damaged tissue from neighbouring organs to stick together, forming a fistula. (A fistula is an abnormal connection that occurs between different parts of your intestine, between your intestine and your bladder or vagina, or between your intestine and abdominal wall.) The most common type of fistula occurs between the bladder and the colon. Fistulas are more common in men than women and can result in serious, long-term infections. Finally, scar tissue that often develops after an infection can cause a blockage in the intestinal tract and prevent normal bowel movements.

Symptoms

Most people with diverticulosis don't have symptoms or discomfort. Mild cramps, bloating and constipation may develop in some cases. However, symptoms of diverticulitis include:

- abdominal pain that may develop quite suddenly
- tenderness on the lower left side of the abdomen

- fever, nausea, vomiting, cramps and constipation
- rectal bleeding that is caused by burst blood vessels in the diverticula

Who's at Risk?

Those at risk for diverticulosis include older adults, especially those who follow a low-fibre diet. One-half of all North Americans between the ages of 60 and 80 have diverticulosis and nearly everyone over 80 has the condition.[1] As many as one-quarter of people with diverticulosis go on to develop diverticulitis.

Conventional Treatment

Many people with diverticulosis don't require any treatment beyond a high-fibre diet to prevent constipation and the formation of additional diverticula. During an attack of diverticulitis, the following may help the colon heal faster:

- a liquid diet followed for a short time to allow the bowel to rest
- bed rest
- antibiotic medications to treat infection
- anti-spasmodic medications to relieve abdominal discomfort
- surgery may be necessary to remove the diseased part of the intestine

If you have diverticulosis, it's important to avoid constipation, which can increase the risk of a diverticulitis flare-up. Respond to your body's urge for bowel movements. Exercise regularly to promote normal bowel functions. If you have diverticulosis, the nutritional strategies below can help prevent diverticulitis.

Managing Diverticulitis
Dietary Strategies

Many practitioners tell their patients to avoid certain foods that may irritate the diverticula, such as nuts, seeds, corn, popcorn, raspberries, strawberries, figs, grapes with seeds and cucumbers with seeds. The recommendation to avoid nuts and seeds appears to have originated from one single study. There is little evidence to support the link between nuts and seeds and diverticulitis. A 2008 study that followed 47,228 healthy men aged 40 to 75 years for 18 years found that consuming nuts, corn and popcorn did not increase the risk of diverticulosis or diverticular complications.[2] In fact, people following a low-fibre diet tend to have more symptoms than people on a liberal diet. Despite this, some individuals may find that certain foods cause inflammation and pain; these foods should be avoided.

Dietary Fibre

It is well accepted that a high-fibre diet prevents diverticulitis.[3,4] The role of fibre in gastrointestinal health was recognized when researchers observed much lower rates of colonic problems in South African blacks who followed a diet that was very high in fibre compared with North Americans who consumed dramatically less fibre.

Since that time, many studies have linked higher-fibre diets to a lower incidence of diverticulosis.[5-7] A study from Harvard University followed almost 48,000 men for 4 years and found that, compared with men with the lowest fibre intake, those who consumed the most fibre had a 42 percent lower risk of diverticulitis.[8] Fibre from fruit and vegetables offered the most protection. In the same study, men who followed a high-fat, low-fibre diet had a 2.3-fold higher risk of the disease, and men on a high red-meat, low-fibre diet had a 3.3-fold greater chance of having diverticulitis.

Over the past 30 years, fibre supplementation has received widespread acceptance in the management of diverticulitis. Patients treated with fibre develop fewer complications and require less surgery compared with those on low-fibre diets. Insoluble fibres in whole grains, fruit and vegetables have a significant water-retaining capacity, which helps to increase stool bulk and softness and promote regularity. By speeding the removal of waste material, dietary fibre lowers pressure in the colon.

To prevent diverticulitis, gradually increase daily fibre intake to 21 to 38 grams, depending on your age and gender. See Chapter 1, page 4, for a list of fibre content of selected foods. Include some of the following high-fibre foods in your daily diet (all have 5 or more grams per serving).

High-Fibre Foods

Starchy Foods	Fruit	Vegetables
100% bran cereals	Apple, with skin	Green peas
All-Bran Buds cereal	Blackberries	Snow peas
Corn-bran cereal	Blueberries	Swiss chard
Fiber One cereal	Figs and dates	
Oat bran	Kiwi	
Red River Hot Cereal	Mango	
Barley	Pear, raw and canned	
Rye crackers	Prunes	
Whole-wheat pasta	Raspberries	
Dried peas, beans, lentils		
Popcorn		

Almonds are also high in fibre; add a few to your daily diet.

Bulk-forming fibre supplements may be used to promote regularity. Psyllium-husk powder and Metamucil may be purchased at health food stores and pharmacies.

Drink at least 9 to 13 cups (2.2 to 3.2 L) of water or other liquids daily to help fibre produce soft stools. Water, juices, milk, soups, coffee, teas and herbal teas all contribute to your fluid intake.

Fermented Milk Products

Consuming 1 cup (250 ml) of yogurt or kefir per day can help the body fight infection during diverticulitis and may prevent bacterial overgrowth in unaffected diverticula. These foods contain live bacterial cultures (lactic acid bacteria) that help recolonize the digestive tract with friendly, protective bacteria; they are often referred to as probiotics. Once consumed, lactic acid bacteria make their way to the colon where, after colonizing, they prevent the attachment of harmful microbes to the intestinal tract, secrete substances that destroy infection-causing bacteria and enhance the body's immune system.

Lactic acid bacteria are especially important if you're taking antibiotics to treat infection in the diverticula. Antibiotics destroy both the harmful and beneficial bacteria in the gut. Probiotic foods and supplements (see below) re-establish the growth of healthy bacteria in the intestine.

Vitamins and Minerals

If an attack of diverticulitis includes an infection, your body's immune system will need many nutrients. Vitamins A, C and E and zinc are all important. To learn the best food sources for these nutrients, see Chapter 4, page 32. A daily multivitamin and mineral supplement will help ensure that you meet your daily requirements.

Herbal Remedies

Garlic (*Allium sativum*)

This herb may be a worthwhile addition to your daily nutritional regime if an infection is present during diverticulitis. Natural sulphur compounds in garlic have been shown to enhance the activity of infection-fighting white blood cells. Laboratory studies have also shown garlic to inhibit the growth of a number of bacteria and yeast organisms.

Add one-half to one clove of garlic to your meals each day. If you choose to supplement, buy a product made with aged garlic extract. Take two to six capsules a day, in divided doses. Aged garlic extract is odourless and less irritating to the gastrointestinal tract than other forms of garlic supplements (e.g., garlic oil capsules, garlic powder tablets). You'll find more information about garlic in Chapter 7, page 137.

Other Natural Health Products

Probiotics

Lactic acid bacteria are available in supplements that provide doses higher than what can be consumed from fermented milk products alone. Probiotic supplements may be useful in shortening the course of diverticulitis and perhaps in preventing recurrences. In a study of thirty patients affected by uncomplicated diverticulitis, taking a probiotic supplement called VSL#3 with conventional medication was effective in preventing a relapse over 12 months.[9] To prevent a recurrence of diverticulitis, take VSL#3 (450 billion live cells) once daily for 15 consecutive days every month.

More information about VSL#3 is available at www.vsl3.com. Some research supports the use of other probiotic strains in preventing recurrence of diverticulitis, in particular *Lactobacillus casei*. Choose a probiotic supplement that includes this strain of *Lactobacillus*. Take 1 billion to 10 billion viable cells, in three or four divided doses, with food. A probiotic supplement is also recommended if you are prescribed antibiotics, since the medication also kills lactic acid bacteria in the gut. To reduce antibiotic-related diarrhea, take the supplement when you start your antibiotic therapy and continue taking it for 5 days after antibiotics are stopped.

Nutrition Strategy Checklist for Diverticulitis

☐   Insoluble fibre

☐   Psyllium

☐   Fluids

☐   Fermented milk products

☐   Multivitamin/mineral

☐   Probiotic supplements

Recommended Resources

Mayo Foundation for Medical Education and Research
www.mayoclinic.com

The Mayo Foundation for Medical Education and Research provides one of the best patient-education websites on the Internet. The information is reliable, thorough and clearly written.

National Digestive Diseases Information Clearinghouse
National Institutes of Health

http://digestive.niddk.nih.gov
2 Information Way
Bethesda, MD, USA 20892-3570
Tel: 1-800-891-5389
Fax: 703-738-4929
Email: nddic@info.niddk.nih.gov

Ear Infections (Otitis Media)

By the time the majority of children reach the age of 3, they will have had at least one ear infection. Although ear infections can affect anyone, they're most common among children, particularly those between 3 months and 3 years of age. Although ear infections typically cause children discomfort, most clear up on their own within a few days. In general, children stop having ear infections by the age of 5.

The ear is divided into three main parts: the inner ear, middle ear and outer ear. The inner ear contains a highly sensitive hearing sense organ known as the cochlea, as well as the fluid-filled semicircular canals that control balance. The middle ear is the passageway between the eardrum and the Eustachian tube. The Eustachian tube conducts sound vibrations from the outer ear to the eardrum and connects the middle ear to the nose and the back of the throat. The outer ear is the area connecting the external opening of the ear to the eardrum. Earaches usually originate in the outer or middle ear.

What Causes Ear Infections?

An ear infection is a symptom that may be caused by a variety of medical conditions. In most cases, earaches are the result of a bacterial or viral infection, often developing as a compli-cation of the common cold. Allergies, mumps, tonsillitis or other illnesses that cause nasal congestion or sore throat will also trigger earache symptoms. Occasionally, ear pain may occur even though there is nothing wrong with the ear. The head is a very nerve-rich area of the body, and many of the structures in the jaw, face and neck share the same sensory nerve pathways to the brain. As a result, even a mild inflammation in the nose, sinus, teeth, throat or tonsils can refer severe pain and tenderness to the ear.

The most common cause of earache in children is a bacterial infection of the middle ear known as otitis media. Normally, the middle ear is filled with air and the Eustachian tube acts like a vent to maintain a constant air pressure. During an illness, bacteria travel from the nose and throat, along the Eustachian tube, to the middle ear. The bacteria inflame the lining of the Eustachian tube, causing it to become swollen and filled with mucus. This blocks the flow of air into the middle ear, decreasing the pressure and allowing fluid to build up. The fluid remains trapped inside the ear and can deaden sound, resulting in hearing loss in one or both ears. The fluid accumulation also puts increased pressure on the eardrum, causing intense pain. Children are particularly susceptible to otitis media because their Eustachian tubes are smaller and narrower than those of adults and are more easily blocked by inflammation.

Skin infections of the outer ear are also frequent sources of earaches. Popularly referred to as swimmer's ear, they are often caused by an accumulation of moisture in the outer ear canal. When water enters the ear during swimming or showering, the dampness creates an ideal breeding ground for bacteria. The bacteria enter the skin through tiny cuts or scratches caused by activities such as rubbing or cleaning the ears too vigorously or poking the ear with Q-tips or dirty fingernails.

Ear infections are not contagious, but the respiratory illnesses that lead to earache symptoms are infectious. Although children with earaches may suffer some temporary loss of hearing, most ear infections do not lead to permanent damage. However, infections that aren't treated can spread to the inner ear, where they can harm delicate hearing structures and cause permanent hearing loss. Children with otitis media may develop complications such as *secretory otitis media*, which is a persistent accumulation of fluid in the middle ear; *mastoiditis*, an infection of the bone behind the ear; or occasionally *spinal meningitis*. Recurring ear infections may also affect a child's speech and language development by causing frequent, short-term hearing losses.

Most ear infections will clear up by themselves, often through a harmless rupture of the eardrum. A break in the eardrum releases the pressure and fluid in the middle ear and usually ends the painful symptoms immediately. A ruptured eardrum will normally heal over without any further difficulty, but repeated ruptures may cause serious scarring and some hearing loss.

Symptoms

Ear infections can be hard to detect in young children who can't link their discomfort to their ear. The following signs may indicate your child is experiencing an ear infection:

- pain or feeling of pressure in the ear
- temporary hearing loss
- symptoms of the common cold, including cough or sore throat

- irritability
- dizziness
- sudden loss of appetite
- fever of 100°F (38°C) or higher
- nausea or vomiting
- headache
- fluid or pus draining from the ear
- in children, pulling or tugging on the ear
- in young children, crying frequently, especially during the night

Who's at Risk?

Ear infections can develop in people of all ages, but they are most common in children, particularly those between the ages of 3 months and 3 years. Ear infections occur more often in boys than girls. Estimates indicate that up to 95 percent of all children in North America will have an ear infection before the age of 7.[1] Ear infections are more prevalent during the fall and winter. Children who are more susceptible to ear infections include those who:

- have brothers or sisters with a history of recurring ear infections
- have their first ear infection before they are 4 months old
- are in group childcare situations
- are exposed to cigarette smoke
- have frequent upper respiratory infections or seasonal allergies
- were bottle-fed rather than breastfed

Conventional Treatment

Many cases of ear infection do not require treatments with antibiotics and the majority of children with ear infections recover without the use of these drugs. In children who are older than 6 months and otherwise healthy, if a bacteria-caused infection does not clear up on its own, doctors may prescribe antibiotics. Symptoms will usually subside within 72 hours after the medication is started. If antibiotics are prescribed, they must be taken as directed, for the course. This will prevent recurring infections and the development of drug-resistant strains of bacteria. Other treatments that may be recommended include:

- acetaminophen or ibuprofen for fever or pain relief (aspirin should not be used by children or teens)
- antihistamines for children with allergies
- decongestants to relieve feelings of pressure in the ear
- soothing ear drops to ease swimmer's ear
- a warm, moist towel or a hot water bottle wrapped in a towel applied to the ear to reduce pain

Persistent ear infections lasting more than 3 months may be treated with a *myringotomy*, a procedure that makes a small hole in the eardrum to release the fluid. Children with persistent secretory otitis media may be treated with a *tympanotomy*, which involves inserting small plastic tubes into the blocked ear to help equalize the pressure and improve airflow.

Although most ear infections clear up without treatment, children must be seen by a doctor if they have:

- an earache that becomes worse, despite treatment
- a fever that lasts more than 3 days or is higher than 39°C (102°F)
- fluid (blood or pus) leaking from the ear
- a headache, fever and stiff neck
- a skin rash

- rapid or difficult breathing
- hearing loss or dizziness
- periods of excessive sleepiness, irritability or unusual fussiness

Preventing and Managing Ear Infections

The following strategies will help reduce the risk of ear infections in your child:

- Breastfeed rather than bottle-feed your baby for at least 6 months.
- Hold your baby in a semi-sitting position when breast- or bottle-feeding.
- Avoid exposure to tobacco smoke.
- Avoid exposure to children and adults with upper respiratory tract illnesses such as cold or flu.
- Teach your child good handwashing techniques to prevent the transfer of bacteria that may cause upper respiratory tract infections.
- Teach your child to blow his or her nose gently and not to block the flow of air during a sneeze. Blowing the nose forcefully or blocking a sneeze may cause bacteria to travel up the Eustachian tubes to the ear.

Dietary Strategies
Food Allergies
There is some evidence that food allergies can cause recurrent ear infections in children.[2-6] One American study found a significant association between food allergies and recurrent otitis media in 78 percent of the children studied, and also found that a food-elimination diet led to significant improvement in 86 percent of the children identified as allergic. Researchers have found that once food allergies are diagnosed,

appropriate food-elimination diets resolve symptoms and prevent recurrent infections.

It's thought that immune compounds formed in the body in response to an allergic food can block the Eustachian tubes by changing pressure and increasing fluid in the middle ear. If your child suffers from recurrent ear infections, discuss the possibility of food allergies with his or her pediatrician. Skin tests, RAST testing and food challenges are all methods used to identify food allergies.

If allergy testing indicates certain foods need to be avoided, consult a registered dietitian (www.dietitians.ca) for advice on how to ensure that your child is meeting his or her nutrient needs. For more information on food allergies, see Food Allergies, page 395.

Probiotics

Fermented milk products such as yogurt, kefir and acidophilus milk contain lactic acid bacteria (e.g., *Lactobacillus*, *Bifidobacterium*, *Streptococcus* strains) that may help prevent recurrent ear infections. Foods and supplements that contain these live bacteria are referred to as probiotics. Once ingested, lactic acid bacteria take up residence in the gastrointestinal tract, where they exert their health benefits. A number of studies have shown that regular consumption of probiotic foods as well as probiotic supplements enhances the activity of the immune system. One trial conducted in 309 otitis-prone children found that although a mixed probiotic supplement did not prevent ear infection, children in the probiotic group tended to experience fewer recurrent infections.[7] Research also suggests that a deficiency of lactic acid bacteria in the intestinal tract of children may be responsible for viral infections of the respiratory tract.[8]

Healthy bacteria belonging to the streptococci family also reside in the nose, throat and ear, where they protect the body from bacteria that cause ear infection. Studies have found that children prone to otitis media have reduced numbers of these protective bacteria. A recent study conducted among 130 children prone to ear infections found that those treated with an oral spray containing streptococci bacteria experienced a significantly reduced number of ear infections compared with those receiving the placebo treatment.[9]

Include one fermented milk product in your daily diet. (If your child is at risk for allergic disease, do not introduce cow's milk until 1 year of age.) Probiotic supplements are available for children with a milk allergy. Take one capsule one to three times daily with a meal.

Vitamins and Minerals

Vitamin C

This nutrient is well known for its ability to reduce the duration and severity of cold symptoms. Children, people under physical stress and people with low dietary intakes of vitamin C tend to respond best to the nutrient.[10,11] Vitamin C promotes the body's production of interferon, an immune compound that helps the body fight infection. Based on its ability to enhance the immune system, vitamin C is important for a child's overall health. It's also thought that inflammation of the middle ear causes increased production of free radicals, which could play a role in the course of otitis media.[12]

The best food sources of vitamin C include citrus fruit and juices, cantaloupe, kiwi, mango, strawberries, broccoli, Brussels sprouts, cauliflower, red pepper and tomato juice. Most children's multivitamin formulas contain 20 to 60 milligrams of vitamin C.

Vitamin E

Vitamin E may play a role in preventing ear infections. The vitamin appears to help certain white blood cells, called natural killer cells, fight infection. Vitamin E's role as an antioxidant may also help combat the inflammation involved in otitis media. Russian researchers investigated the effects of vitamin E (and vitamin C) in children with ear infections and found beneficial effects.[13]

Foods rich in vitamin E include wheat germ, nuts, seeds, vegetable oils, whole grains and leafy green vegetables. Children and adults should be encouraged to get their vitamin E from nutrient-dense foods like nuts and seeds, nut butters, vegetable oils and avocado.

Zinc

It's important to ensure that your child's daily diet contains zinc-rich foods, since this mineral is vital to a healthy immune system. Scandinavian researchers found that children susceptible to recurrent ear infections had significantly lower blood levels of zinc compared with healthy children.[14]

Zinc-rich foods include oysters, seafood, red meat, poultry, yogurt, wheat bran, wheat germ, whole grains and enriched breakfast cereals. If a blood test identifies that your child has a zinc deficiency, short-term zinc supplementation will likely be prescribed. Children under 10 years of age should take 10 milligrams of zinc with 1 milligram of copper added, once daily. Consuming amounts greater than 40 milligrams per day can depress the immune system and cause toxic effects. See Chapter 4, page 78, for more information on zinc.

Herbal Remedies

Echinacea

Many studies in the laboratory have shown the ability of echinacea to enhance the body's production of white blood cells that fight infection. Based on this, many natural health practitioners recommend echinacea to treat ear infections in children. In view of the controversy over antibiotic use and the development of drug-resistant bacteria, there may be value in alternative therapies such as echinacea.[15,16] Buy an alcohol-free echinacea tincture for children. The adult dose of a 1:5 tincture is 1 to 2 milligrams three times daily. Doses for children are based on their body weight. For children under the age of 12, a general guideline is as follows:

- Adult dose (milligrams) × (age of child ÷ 12) = child's dose, or
- Adult dose (milligrams) × (child's body weight in pounds ÷ 150) = child's dose

For older children who are at acceptable percentiles for height and weight, use half the recommended adult dosage. Because of concern that long-term use of echinacea might depress the immune system, limit daily use to 8 consecutive weeks. Children allergic to plants in the Asteraceae/Compositae family (ragweed, daisy, marigold and chrysanthemum) should not use echinacea.

Garlic (*Allium sativum*)

The sulphur compounds in garlic have been shown to stimulate the body's immune system, making garlic a potential preventative agent for recurrent ear infections. Laboratory studies have determined that garlic's sulphur compounds are able to kill the major bacteria that cause otitis media. Studies have focused on the many types of sulphur compounds found in raw garlic and specific sulphur compounds present in aged garlic extract.

Use one-half to one clove each day in cooking. To supplement, buy a product made with aged garlic extract. Take two to six capsules a day, in divided doses; children should take one to three capsules per day. Aged garlic extract is odourless and less irritating to the gastrointestinal tract than other forms of garlic supplements (e.g., garlic oil capsules, garlic powder tablets).

Other Natural Health Products
Xylitol
This natural sugar found in plums, strawberries and raspberries is used as a sweetener in some sugarless gums, syrups and lozenges. Xylitol is known to inhibit the growth of two bacteria that cause otitis media: *Streptococcus pneumoniae* and *Haemophilus influenza*. Based on this, researchers have evaluated the ability of xylitol-sweetened chewing gums, syrups, lozenges and oral solutions to prevent ear infections in children.

Two studies conducted with over 1200 children attending daycare found that xylitol significantly reduced the number of ear infections and the need for antibiotics.[17,18] The greatest success was found with the chewing gum and the syrup. The children chewing the gum received 8.4 grams of xylitol per day, while those taking the syrup received 10 grams per day.

Nutrition Strategy Checklist for Ear Infections
- ☐ Identify food allergies
- ☐ Fermented milk products
- ☐ Probiotic supplements
- ☐ Vitamin C
- ☐ Foods rich in vitamin E
- ☐ Zinc
- ☐ Echinacea
- ☐ Garlic
- ☐ Xylitol

Recommended Resources
Mayo Foundation for Medical Education and Research
www.mayoclinic.com
This website is produced by a team of writers, editors, health educators, nurses, doctors and scientists, and is one of the best patient-education sites on the Internet. The information is reliable, thorough and clearly written.

National Institute on Deafness and Other Communication Disorders
National Institutes of Health
www.nidcd.nih.gov
31 Center Drive, MSC 2320
Bethesda, MD, USA 20892-2320
Email: nidcdinfo@nidcd.nih.gov

Eating Disorders

We live in a society that's dominated by the cult of thinness. Everywhere we look, we're bombarded with the message that thin is beautiful. The waifish looks of ultra-thin models and Hollywood actors have become our ideal—establishing standards of beauty that are not only unattainable, but unhealthy as well. It's no wonder that so many North Americans, particularly women, struggle with their body image. By the time they reach adulthood, nearly half of all North American females have concerns about their weight and many have already begun the vicious cycle of dieting and weight gain. While the most common age of onset is between 14 and 25 years of age, eating disorders occur in a wide range of ages, and are increasingly seen in children as young as 10. It's estimated that 3 percent of women will be affected by eating disorders in their lifetime.[1]

Anorexia nervosa, bulimia nervosa and *binge eating disorder* are the three main types of eating disorders. Individuals who suffer from these conditions experience physical, psychological and social symptoms that eventually threaten their well-being, their overall health and even their lives. Eating disorders can be treated with long-term therapy but usually require the intervention of a variety of health professionals, including registered dietitians, physicians and mental-health specialists.

Because the treatment for each type of eating disorder is unique and involves a multidisciplinary approach, it's beyond the scope of this chapter to outline all possible nutrition recommendations. Instead, I've presented important information about each condition to help you better understand the causes, risk factors and symptoms. I also provide a list of treatment programs across Canada. If your eating disorder is not serious enough to warrant this type of intervention, seek the advice of a registered dietitian (www.dietitians.ca) to help you normalize your eating patterns and correct any nutritional deficiencies. This is imperative to prevent long-term health problems associated with eating disorders.

Anorexia Nervosa

This eating disorder is characterized by an extreme fear of gaining weight. People with anorexia nervosa are obsessed with being thin and have an unrealistic concept of their body image. Even though they are noticeably underweight, anorexics always believe they're fat. To achieve their goal of weight loss, they eat very little and may exercise excessively. Sometimes they'll even engage in self-induced vomiting or they may misuse laxatives or diuretics as part of a binge-purge cycle. Anorexia nervosa is an extremely dangerous and potentially life-threatening condition. People suffering from this eating disorder can literally starve themselves to death.

People with anorexia nervosa often ritualize food preparation and will sometimes hide food in special places, but never eat it. They get pleasure from controlling their eating and, as they begin to starve, they may even achieve a sense of euphoria from being so disciplined and successful in achieving their goals.

There's no precise cause of anorexia nervosa, but it's thought to be an illness of psychological origin. What begins as a normal desire to lose a few pounds rapidly becomes a compulsive obsession with body image. Anorexia nervosa primarily affects women, particularly young women. Often, women with anorexia nervosa have very low self-esteem. In an attempt to change their self-image, these women may take their interest in dieting and weight loss to an extreme. For these women, anorexia nervosa is a means of taking control of their lives. By taking rigid control of their eating, they are able to maintain a sense of control over some aspect of their lives. This response is frequently triggered by stress, anxiety or anger towards family members or in other personal relationships.

In many cases, women who suffer from anorexia are perfectionists and overachievers. They are overly critical of themselves, set unreasonable standards of performance and have a compulsive need to please others. Having low self-confidence and setting unrealistic goals often result in feelings of ineffectiveness that may lead to abnormal eating behaviours.

Studies indicate that certain brain chemicals, known as neurotransmitters, are at lower levels in people with anorexia. Reduced levels of serotonin, a powerful neurotransmitter, are known to be associated with depression, and it's thought that there may be a link between anorexia and depression. Higher levels of cortisol, a brain hormone released in response to stress, and vasopressin, a brain chemical associated with obsessive-compulsive disorders, have also been identified with anorexia nervosa.

Symptoms

The warning signs of anorexia nervosa include:

- preoccupation with food and weight: excessive dieting, counting calories, checking body weight several times a day
- feeling fat, even when weight is below normal; distorted body image
- significant weight loss, with no evidence of related illness
- depression
- denial of hunger, despite an extreme reduction in eating
- strange eating habits: cutting food into small pieces, preferring food of specific texture or colour, refusing to eat in front of others
- excessive exercise habits
- withdrawal from social activities
- complaints of feeling cold because of dropping body temperatures
- appearance of long, fine hair on the body as a way of conserving body heat
- brittle hair and broken fingernails

- dry, yellow skin
- cessation of menstrual periods for 3 consecutive months

As anorexia nervosa progresses, the symptoms of starvation become increasingly evident. Eventually, every major organ in the body will be affected. The heart becomes weaker and pumps less blood through the body. Dehydration sets in and fainting spells are common. Electrolyte imbalances develop as the body loses potassium, sodium and chloride; this results in fatigue, muscle weakness, irritability, muscle spasms and depression. In severe cases, these physical changes will cause irregular heartbeats, convulsions and death due to kidney or heart failure. Approximately one in ten women suffering from anorexia will die—a death rate that is among the highest for a psychiatric disease.

Who's at Risk?

Not surprisingly, women suffer from eating disorders far more often than men, representing nearly 90 percent of all cases. In Canada, it's estimated that 200,000 to 300,000 women between the ages of 13 and 40 suffer from anorexia nervosa. It's a condition that usually surfaces during the teenage years, when girls are between 14 and 18 years old.

In many cases, the incidence of anorexia is influenced by social environment. Girls with a peer group or family network that emphasizes physical attractiveness and thinness are more likely to acquire eating disturbances. Girls and women with low self-esteem or depressive tendencies are also very susceptible to the condition, especially if they are dealing with high levels of stress or traumatic events such as rape or abuse. There are also indications that anorexia nervosa may run in families.

In our society, there are certain professions or activities that emphasize thinness and appearance to an exceptional degree. People who participate in dancing, gymnastics, wrestling, modelling, acting and long-distance running are likely to be very aware of their weight or body image and may be particularly susceptible to developing anorexia nervosa.

Conventional Treatment

In the early stages, anorexia nervosa may be treated without hospitalization. But when weight loss is severe, hospitalization is necessary to restore weight and prevent further physical deterioration. A structured approach that involves careful observation of all eating and elimination (urinating, bowel movements and vomiting) is the first stage of treatment. Once weight is restored and symptoms are stabilized, some type of psychotherapy is required to deal with the underlying emotional issues triggering the abnormal eating patterns. Family therapy is especially helpful for younger girls, and behavioural or cognitive therapy is also effective in helping replace destructive attitudes with positive ones. A nutritionist will add support by providing advice on proper diet and eating regimens. In some cases, antidepressant medications may be prescribed, but they should not be used as a substitute for appropriate psychological treatment.

Unfortunately, many people with anorexia nervosa have a tendency to relapse and return to dysfunctional eating habits. Long-term therapy and regular health monitoring are essential for a successful result. A strong network of love and support from family and friends is also crucial to the recovery process.

Bulimia Nervosa

Bulimia nervosa is the most common type of eating disorder in North America. A person with this condition will eat large amounts of high-calorie food in a very short period, then use vomiting, diuretics or laxatives to eliminate the food before the body can absorb it. Fasting or excessive exercising are other methods that bulimics may use to counteract the weight gain caused by binge eating.

People suffering from bulimia will binge as often as several times a day, sometimes consuming 10,000 calories or more in a matter of minutes or hours. Comfort foods that are sweet, soft and high in calories, such as ice cream, cake or pastry, are favourite choices for bingeing. Immediately after the binge comes the purge, when some bulimics will use as many as twenty or more laxatives a day to rid their bodies of these huge quantities of food.

Like people with anorexia nervosa, bulimics are extremely afraid of becoming fat and are obsessed with body image. People with bulimia usually look quite normal and often show few signs of their condition. Their weight may fluctuate, but it usually stays within normal ranges. They may even be slightly heavy. Because bulimics are often very secretive about their abnormal behaviour, the presence of bulimia can be hard to identify.

People with bulimia nervosa are very aware of their behaviour and feel guilty or remorseful. Nearly half of all people with anorexia go on to develop some symptoms of bulimia.

Studies have shown that bulimics are particularly prone to impulsive behaviour. They have difficulty dealing with anxiety, have little self-control and often indulge in drug or alcohol abuse or sexual promiscuity. They're also susceptible to depression, anxiety disorders and social phobias. People with bulimia have lower levels of brain neurotransmitters, such as serotonin, which may predispose them to developing these psychological disturbances.

Symptoms

In addition to the preoccupation with food and weight characteristic of most eating disorders, symptoms of bulimia may include:

- evidence of binge eating, such as large amounts of food missing, stealing money or food
- eating of huge amounts of food but no weight gain
- food cravings
- complaints of stomach pain (caused by frequent vomiting)
- evidence of purging, such as excuses to go to the bathroom immediately after meals
- development of "chipmunk cheeks" (caused when the salivary glands permanently expand from frequent vomiting)
- erosion of tooth enamel and other dental problems (caused by frequent vomiting)
- feelings of shame, self-reproach and guilt
- emotional changes such as depression, irritability or social withdrawal

The purging behaviour associated with bulimia can cause physical complications that are dangerous to long-term health. Vomiting and purging can lead to imbalances in fluids and electrolytes. When potassium levels fall too low, abnormal heart rhythms develop. Some bulimics use a medication called ipecac to induce vomiting. Overuse of this substance has been known to cause sudden death.

Who's at Risk?

Like anorexia, bulimia is primarily a women's disorder. Nearly twice as many women suffer from bulimia as anorexia and, in Canada, estimates run as high as 600,000 women affected by this eating disorder. Bulimia tends to develop in later adolescence, often striking young women between the ages of 18 and 20. However, it can appear in earlier adolescence.

As with other eating disorders, bulimia surfaces most often in people who have low self-confidence and are insecure about their appearance. Girls reporting sexual or physical abuse are very susceptible to developing bulimia nervosa. Studies also indicate that the disorder may have a genetic element and may run in families. As well, bulimia may be triggered by elevated stress levels and often affects women who are intelligent and high achievers.

Conventional Treatment

In most cases, people with bulimia are treated without hospitalization. Because it's a psychological condition, cognitive and behaviour therapy are necessary to deal with the emotional issues underlying the symptoms of this disorder. As with anorexia nervosa, a multidisciplinary approach to treatment works best. Physicians, nutritionists and mental health professionals work together to address the many different facets of this eating disorder. In particular, long-term psychotherapy is needed to help reduce destructive tendencies and develop better coping strategies. Antidepressant medication has proven to be an effective psychological intervention.

Binge Eating Disorder (BED)

Binge eating disorder (BED) is a newly recognized condition that has many similarities to bulimia nervosa. People with BED frequently eat huge quantities of food and feel that they have no control over their eating. Unlike bulimia, however, they don't purge afterwards with vomiting or laxatives.

There is no known single cause for binge eating. Experts believe that a combination of factors is responsible, including genetics, emotional issues and learned behaviours. Some scientists feel that some people are more prone to overeating because the part of the brain that controls appetite fails to send proper messages about hunger and satiety. Serotonin, the brain chemical involved in mood, may also be involved in the development of BED. Patterns of overeating can also begin in childhood when food may be overused to comfort, reward or punish. Some children may grow up thinking that negative emotions should be suppressed and may turn to food to deal with their feelings.

Symptoms

Symptoms of BED include:

- frequently eating an abnormally large amount of food
- feeling unable to control what or how much food is eaten
- eating more rapidly than usual
- eating until uncomfortably full
- eating large amounts of food, even when not hungry
- feelings of disgust, guilt or depression after overeating
- eating alone because of embarrassment at the quantity of food being eaten

Who's at Risk?

BED occurs most often in people who are obese (with a BMI greater than 27), and becomes more prevalent as body weight increases. It's estimated that between 30 percent and 90 percent of all people who are obese have binge eating problems. Obese people with BED become overweight at an earlier age than those without the disorder and may suffer more frequent bouts of losing and regaining weight. However, it's not uncommon for people with normal, healthy weight to suffer from BED. It occurs slightly more often in women than in men and tends to appear in later years, affecting an older population than does either anorexia or bulimia nervosa.

Conventional Treatment

Many of the medical problems related to obesity are also associated with binge eating disorder. Treatment may be necessary for conditions such as high cholesterol, high blood pressure, diabetes, gallbladder disease and heart disease. Other than the appropriate therapies for obesity-related disorders, there are no standard treatments for BED. As with most eating disorders, an approach that involves psychotherapy and antidepressant drugs seems to be most effective. It's essential to deal with the emotional issues of the illness. Because people with BED find it very difficult to stay on a treatment regimen and frequently return to unhealthy eating behaviours, long-term therapy is always recommended.

Recommended Resources

National Eating Disorder Information Centre
www.nedic.ca
200 Elizabeth Street
ES 7-421
Toronto, ON M5G 2C4
Tel: 416-340-4156
Fax: 416-340-4736
Email: nedic@uhn.on.ca

National Association of Anorexia Nervosa and Associated Disorders (ANAD)
www.anad.org
P.O. Box 7
Highland Park, IL, USA 60035
Tel: 847-831-3438
Fax: 847-433-4632

www.something-fishy.org
The Something Fishy website on eating disorders is an extensive resource on eating disorders posted by a recovering sufferer of anorexia nervosa.

Endometriosis

Endometriosis develops in women when uterine-type cells grow outside of the uterus. These cells may travel throughout the body and attach to a number of different areas, including the intestines. The misplaced cells develop into nodules, lesions, implants or growths that are affected by the hormonal fluctuations of the menstrual cycle. These growths cause pelvic pain, pain during intercourse, infertility and other problems.

What Causes Endometriosis?

The uterus, a reproductive organ located within the abdominal cavity, is lined with a type of tissue called endometrium. When you have endometriosis, tissue that looks and acts like endometrium is found living outside the uterus. In most cases, the misplaced tissue is discovered growing somewhere within the abdominal cavity, attached to the ovaries, bowel, bladder, fallopian tubes or cervix. Endometrial growths can vary in size and in penetration of the surrounding tissue. Endometrial growths are generally not cancerous; rather, they are normal types of tissue found growing outside the normal location.

During the course of a normal menstrual cycle, the endometrial lining of the uterus gradually builds up in preparation for pregnancy. If a woman does not become pregnant, the lining breaks down, bleeds and is discharged from the body during a menstrual period. Unfortunately, the endometrial tissue living outside of the uterus responds to the hormonal cycles of menstruation in exactly the same way. But, unlike the menstrual flow from the uterus, the blood from the misplaced tissue has no place to go. This causes episodes of internal bleeding and inflammation that can result in internal scarring, severe pain and infertility.

Scientists still don't know what causes endometriosis. The most commonly held view is the *retrograde menstruation theory*, which suggests that menstrual tissue occasionally flows backwards through the fallopian tubes during menstruation. The tissue is discharged from the fallopian tubes into the abdomen, where it becomes implanted and develops into endometrial growths. Another theory proposes that the lining of the pelvic organs (vagina, rectum, uterus and bladder) possesses primitive cells that are able to grow into endometrial cells. It's also possible that endometrial tissue may be distributed from the uterus to other parts of the body through the lymph glands or blood vessels. In some cases, endometrial tissue may be accidentally transplanted into distant sites during surgical procedures.

Women with endometriosis have a slightly increased risk for certain types of cancer of the ovary known as epithelial ovarian cancer. The risk seems to be highest in women with endometriosis and primary infertility (women who have never given birth to a child), but the use of oral contraceptives appears to significantly reduce the risk of cancer.

Symptoms

Most women who have endometriosis do not have symptoms. However, among those who do experience symptoms, they include:

- pelvic pain just before and during menstruation that lessens after menstruation
- severe menstrual cramps
- irregular vaginal bleeding
- pelvic pain
- painful sexual intercourse
- painful bowel movements
- pain with exercise
- painful and frequent urination
- backache
- constipation or diarrhea
- fatigue
- infertility

The pain intensity of endometriosis can change from month to month and varies greatly among affected women. Some women experience progressive worsening of pain while others find their symptoms resolve without treatment. Pelvic pain depends partly on where the implants of endometriosis are located. Deeper implants and implants in areas with many pain-sensing nerves are likely to cause more intense pain. Endometrial implants can also produce substances that circulate in the bloodstream and cause pain. As well, pain can result when implants form scar tissue. Symptoms usually start after the onset of menstruation and subside after menopause, when the growths tend to shrink or disappear.

Many women with endometriosis experience ongoing gastrointestinal discomfort, including diarrhea, painful bowel movements and general intestinal distress. Studies have revealed that endometriosis is associated with changes to the intestinal tract, such as altered motility and bacterial overgrowth. Women with endometriosis experience bowel problems as a result of endometrial growths that develop directly on the bowel, usually in the latter part of the large intestine. Most specialists carefully check the bowel for the presence of endometriosis, but because the intestine is so long, it's possible for growths to be missed. As well, adhesions, resulting from the endometriosis itself, or from past surgeries, can also cause bowel symptoms. (Adhesions are fibrous bands of tissue that bind organs together.) These adhesions pull on the bowel and cause pain.

Women with endometriosis are often told by their doctor that they have irritable bowel syndrome (IBS). Unfortunately that diagnosis isn't very helpful, because it doesn't indicate the underlying problem. IBS is an umbrella term used to describe gastrointestinal distress when no other diagnosis can be made. Having your doctor thoroughly investigate the cause of your bowel problems is important for effective treatment.

Laparoscopy is the most common surgical procedure used to diagnose endometriosis. It's performed under anesthesia. The abdomen is inflated with carbon dioxide through a small incision made in the navel. A laparoscope is then inserted to inspect the abdomen and pelvis for endometrial implants. At the same time, biopsies can be done for a diagnosis.

Who's at Risk?

It's estimated that 3 percent to 18 percent of North American women and teenaged girls have endometriosis.[1] The disease generally appears between the ages of 15 and 50; however, it has been diagnosed in girls as young as 11. The disease is believed to run in families; you're at higher risk if you have a first-degree relative (e.g., mother, sister) with endometriosis. Other risk factors include being of Caucasian descent, having your first child after the age of 30, having a low body mass index and having an abnormal uterus.

Conventional Treatment

The choice of treatment is guided by the extent of your symptoms, your age and your plans to have a family. For mild cases, your doctor may choose to simply wait and see how the disease progresses. The only treatment may be pain relief medication such as aspirin or ibuprofen. Exercise, heat from a bath or heating pad, massage and relaxation may also help ease painful symptoms.

If a woman with endometriosis is not planning to have children, hormone suppression treatment may be recommended. This involves taking a combination of drugs to prevent ovulation and limit the amount of estrogen that stimulates the endometrial growths. This will hopefully slow the growth of the misplaced tissue and minimize injury to surrounding organs. Drugs commonly prescribed include:

- **Birth control pills** to control irregular vaginal bleeding and diminish pain with a regulated, low-dose combination of estrogen and progesterone.
- **Progestins** to prevent ovulation and reduce estrogen levels.
- **Gonadotropin-releasing hormone (GnRH) agonists** (such as Lupron or Synarel) to create a temporary and reversible menopause by suppressing estrogen production by the ovaries. Side effects include hot flashes, mood swings, headache, vaginal dryness and some bone loss.
- **Danazol (danocrine)**, a synthetic testosterone, to reduce the production of estrogen from the ovaries and stop menstruation. Possible side effects include water retention, weight gain, oily skin, muscle cramps, mood changes and hot flashes. Occasionally a rash, facial hair or deepening of the voice may occur, in which case treatment with danazol should be stopped.

For cases of moderate or severe endometriosis, surgery may be necessary. As much misplaced tissue as possible is removed, while preserving the woman's ability to have children by retaining the ovaries and uterus. This type of surgery usually provides only temporary relief of symptoms, since endometriosis recurs in most women.

A complete hysterectomy, which removes all reproductive organs, will be considered only for women not planning to become pregnant and those who have severe pelvic pain that is not relieved by medication. After surgery, estrogen replacement therapy may be prescribed to counteract the menopausal symptoms that will develop.

Managing Endometriosis

There's some evidence that diet therapy is as effective as hormonal suppression and more effective than surgery in reducing endometrial pelvic pain.[2] The nutritional approaches listed below are aimed at easing endometriosis-associated pain, improving fertility and minimizing the side effects of certain medications. While these are not cures for endometriosis, nor intended as stand-alone treatments for the condition, they can help women feel better.

Dietary Strategies

Essential Fatty Acids and Omega-3 Fats

Dietary fats are made up of building blocks called fatty acids. These fatty acids are incorporated into cell membranes, where they affect the integrity and fluidity of the membrane. The body is able to make all but two fatty acids: linoleic and alpha-linolenic. Because these two are indispensable to health, they must be obtained from food and, therefore, are called essential fatty acids (see Chapter 3, page 25). The body uses these two essential fatty acids to produce hormone-like compounds called prostaglandins (PGs), which are sometimes referred to as eicosanoids.

Prostaglandins regulate our blood pressure, blood-clot formation, blood fats, immune compounds and hormones. They are produced by the lining of the uterus, by endometrial lesions and by immune compounds called macrophages. Researchers have learned that prostaglandin formation is altered in women with endometriosis. Studies have revealed that these women have significantly higher levels of prostaglandins compared with women who are free of endometriosis.[3-8] A high level of prostaglandins can alter the contractility of the uterus and fallopian tubes, resulting in painful menstrual periods and infertility. Some of these PGs can enter the bloodstream and affect smooth muscle in other parts of the body. PGs can stimulate the gastrointestinal tract, causing it to contract in an uncontrolled manner.

The body makes different types of prostaglandins, which can either increase or decrease inflammation. In the case of endometriosis, two inflammatory prostaglandins called PGE and PGF appear to be involved. A diet that's high in fatty acids from animal foods and processed fat favours the production of prostaglandins that cause inflammation. A diet that's high in omega-3 fatty acids, such as those found in flaxseed oil, canola oil, walnuts, soybeans and fish, favours the formation of anti-inflammatory prostaglandins.

The balance of omega-6 to omega-3 oils in the diet is important for proper prostaglandin formation. The optimal ratio is thought to be 4:1, or four times the amount of omega-6 oils to omega-3 oils. It's estimated that we currently follow a diet that has over twenty times more omega-6 oils than omega-3 oils. That kind of imbalance will lead to a greater production of inflammatory PGs.

To achieve a better balance of omega-6 oils to omega-3 oils, practise the following:

- **Reduce the amount of animal fat in your diet.** Findings from Italian researchers revealed that women with the highest intakes of red meat are twice as likely to have endometriosis as women who consume the least.[9] Limit your intake of meat to once per week. Choose lean cuts of meat and poultry (e.g., flank steak, inside round, sirloin, eye of round, extra-lean ground beef, venison, centre-cut pork chops, pork tenderloin, skinless chicken breast, turkey breast, lean ground turkey). Choose 1% or skim milk, cheeses made with less than 20% milk fat and yogurt with less than 2% milk fat.

- **Avoid foods with trans fat.** This unhealthy fat is formed when manufacturers partially hydrogenate vegetable oils for commercial foods such as certain margarines, baked goods, snack foods and deep-fried fast foods. Read nutrition labels on food packages and choose foods that do not contain trans fat.
- **Add 1 to 2 tablespoons (15 to 30 ml) of flaxseed oil to your daily diet.** This oil is one of the richest sources of the omega-3 fatty acid called alpha-linolenic acid (ALA). Flaxseed oil is easily broken down by heat, so don't cook with it. If you want to add it to a hot dish such as pasta sauce, stir it in at the end of cooking. Use the oil in salad dressing and dip recipes. Store flaxseed oil in the fridge. You'll find flaxseed oil in the refrigerator section of health food stores and supermarkets. Supplements of flaxseed oil are also available. Keep in mind that it takes four capsules (4 grams) to give you a teaspoon of oil. It may be more convenient—and less expensive—to use the bottled oil.
- **Eat fatty fish at least two times a week.** Salmon, trout, sardines, Arctic char, herring and mackerel are the richest sources of the omega-3 fatty acids called DHA and EPA.

Fruit and Vegetables

Women who report higher intakes of green vegetables and fruit have a lower risk of developing endometriosis.[10] It's speculated that natural compounds in fruit and vegetables, called flavonoids, might be responsible. These plant compounds have been shown to suppress a process called angiogenesis, the formation of new blood vessels from existing blood vessels. Uncontrolled angiogenesis is a major contributor to a number of diseases, including endometriosis.[11]

To increase your intake of flavonoids, include 7 to 10 daily servings of fruit and vegetables combined in your diet. (One serving is equivalent to 1 medium fruit, 1/4 cup/60 ml of dried fruit, 1/2 cup/125 ml of cooked or raw vegetables or 1 cup/250 ml of salad greens.) The best sources of flavonoids include berries, cherries, red grapes, apples, citrus fruit, broccoli, kale and onions.

Dietary Fibre

Getting enough fibre each day is an important way to help regulate bowel habits and ease gastrointestinal symptoms of endometriosis. It's estimated that Canadians are getting roughly 14 grams of fibre each day, only one-half of the daily recommendation. Experts agree that a daily intake of 25 to 35 grams of dietary fibre is needed to reap its health benefits. Good food choices include whole-grain breads, breakfast cereals with at least 5 grams of fibre per serving (check the Nutrition Facts box), dried fruit, nuts and legumes. To add higher-fibre foods to your daily diet, see Chapter 1, page 4.

When adding fibre to your diet, gradually build up to the recommended 25 grams. Too much too soon can cause bloating, gas and diarrhea. Spread high-fibre foods out over the course of the day. And aim to drink a minimum of 8 ounces (250 ml) of fluid with each high-fibre meal and snack.

Probiotics

Research suggests that women with endometriosis may have bacterial or yeast overgrowth in their gastrointestinal tract, which may aggravate bloating, stomach pain, early satiety, diarrhea and/or constipation. In one study conducted at the Women's Hospital of Texas in Houston, forty out of fifty women studied had excessive levels of bacteria.[12]

The term *probiotic* literally means "to promote life" and refers to living organisms that, upon ingestion in certain numbers, improve microbial balance in the intestine and exert health benefits. Such friendly bacteria are known collectively as lactic acid bacteria and include *L. acidophilus, L. bulgaricus, L. casei, S. thermophilus* and bifidobacteria. The human digestive tract contains hundreds of strains of bacteria making up what is called the normal intestinal flora. Among the intestinal flora are lactic acid bacteria, which inhibit the growth of unfriendly, or disease-causing, bacteria by preventing their attachment to the intestine and by producing lactic acid and other antibacterial substances that suppress harmful bacteria. Numerous studies have shown that consuming probiotic foods or supplements increases the number of lactic acid bacteria in the intestinal tract. Lactic acid bacteria have been shown to help treat diarrhea and constipation and also inhibit the growth of *Candida albicans* (see Candidiasis, page 254).

Lactic acid bacteria are found in fermented milk products. Include 1 serving of yogurt or kefir in your daily diet. See the section on probiotic supplements below.

Prebiotics

It's possible to eat foods that promote the growth of protective lactic acid bacteria in your intestinal tract. These foods are called prebiotics and contain components called fructo-oligosaccharides (FOSs). The human intestine does not digest FOSs; instead, they remain in the intestinal tract and feed lactic acid bacteria, supporting their growth. Good food sources include Jerusalem artichokes, asparagus, onions and garlic. A number of commercial food products found in grocery stores, such as breads, pasta and fruit and vegetable juices, contain inulin, a prebiotic isolated from chicory root.

Food Sensitivities

Certain foods and spices may aggravate the bowel discomfort of endometriosis. To help you determine food sensitivities, keep a food and symptom diary over the course of at least one menstrual cycle. Record everything you eat, how much of the food you eat, when you eat and any symptoms you feel. If you're working with a consulting dietitian, he or she will use this tool to identify potential food culprits.

It can be difficult to detect foods that are causing you grief because a particular food may not bother you all the time. Sometimes it isn't what you ate but how much of the food you ate, or how quickly you ate, or how many aggravating foods you ate in one day or how much stress you were under at the time. Use your food diary to look for patterns, not just specific foods.

The following foods may cause intestinal problems in women with endometriosis:

- **Caffeine and alcohol.**
- **Artificial sweeteners.**

- **High-fat and/or high-calorie meals.** Both dietary fat and large meals have a greater stimulating effect on colon contractions.
- **Excessive sugar** from soft drinks, fruit drinks, candy and sweets.
- **Dairy products.** Some women don't produce enough of an enzyme called lactase in the intestinal tract. Lactase breaks down the natural milk sugar, lactose. If lactose remains undigested in the intestinal tract, it will cause bloating, gas and diarrhea. Women who have moderate lactose intolerance can usually tolerate yogurt, since it has less lactose than milk. Hard cheeses contain even less lactose. If you are symptomatic, try lactose-free milk or low-lactose yogurt. Alternatively, you can purchase Lactaid enzyme pills at the pharmacy; take a pill before a meal that contains dairy. Alternatives to dairy include calcium-fortified soy beverages.
- **Wheat.** In some women with endometriosis, bloating, distension and gas are caused by an intolerance to wheat-based foods such as bread, bagels, muffins, pasta, ready-to-eat breakfast cereals and crackers as well as baked goods made from wheat flour. If you are unsure whether wheat is causing your gas and bloating, try eliminating it from your diet for 1 month to see if your symptoms improve. Then, slowly add wheat back to your diet. Every 2 days, add one new wheat food. If your symptoms recur, consider alternatives to wheat such as rice, rice pasta, rice crackers, quinoa, quinoa pasta, millet, potato, sweet potato, corn, 100% rye breads and oats. Natural food stores and many large grocery stores often stock many products—breakfast cereals, pasta, crackers, cookies and breads—that are made from wheat-free grains.

- **Raw vegetables.** Be sure to cook your vegetables; cooked vegetables are less likely to cause gas than raw vegetables. Vegetables that have a greater potential to cause gas include bok choy, broccoli, Brussels sprouts, cabbage, cauliflower, kale, radishes, rutabaga, onions and raw garlic.
- **Legumes** such as kidney beans, chickpeas and black beans. Natural sugars called ogliosaccharides, found in dried peas, beans and lentils, often cause gas and bloating. To reduce potential symptoms, rinse canned beans before adding them to recipes and eat a smaller portion. You may also want to try Beano; available at pharmacies and health food stores, this natural enzyme breaks down ogliosaccharides so they can be absorbed in the intestinal tract.
- **Certain fruit,** such as berries, apple with the peel, melon and prunes.
- **Nuts and seeds.**
- **Spices** such as chili powder, curry, ginger, garlic and hot sauce.

Caffeinated Beverages

A study from the Harvard School of Public Health found that women with endometriosis who consumed 5 to 7 grams of caffeine per month (one to two cups of coffee per day) had almost double the risk of not conceiving compared with women who didn't drink any caffeinated beverages.[13] This study suggests that caffeine may delay conception and therefore further aggravate fertility in women with endometriosis.

Women taking a gonadotropin-releasing hormone (GnRH) drug like Lupron (leuprolide) or Synarel (nafarelin) should limit their consumption of caffeine, because these drugs cause bone loss, as does caffeine. If you don't want to eliminate caffeine completely from your diet, ensure you're meeting your daily requirement of 1000 to 1500 milligrams of calcium.

Caffeine can also aggravate gastrointestinal symptoms. It can stimulate the intestinal tract and cause more frequent bowel movements and diarrhea.

Assess your current caffeine intake using the list of caffeine-containing beverages and foods in Chapter 5, page 110. Gradually cut back over a period of 2 to 3 weeks to minimize withdrawal symptoms such as headaches, tiredness or muscle pain. Switch to low-caffeine beverages like tea or hot chocolate or caffeine-free alternatives such as decaf coffee, herbal tea, cereal coffee, juice, milk or water.

Alcoholic Beverages

When it comes to fertility, alcohol consumption should be minimized or avoided altogether. The same researchers from the Harvard School of Public Health who investigated caffeine and conception in women with endometriosis examined the effect of alcohol.[14] They determined that women who consumed one or two drinks a day had a 60 percent higher risk of infertility compared with non-drinkers. And like caffeine, alcohol can also increase bowel discomfort.

Vitamins and Minerals

Vitamin E

Some researchers theorize that oxidative damage caused by free radical molecules contributes to endometriosis by promoting the growth of endometrial tissue. Free radicals are highly reactive oxygen molecules that are produced by normal body processes, including the body's own inflammatory immune response. It's thought that damaged red blood cells and misplaced endometrial tissue signal the recruitment and activity of immune compounds in the abdominal cavity. In the process of engulfing foreign particles and protecting the body, these activated immune compounds generate harmful free radicals, which cause oxidation.

Studies conducted in women with endometriosis have shown that, in the fluid of the abdominal cavity, compounds called lipoproteins do indeed have lower levels of vitamin E, an important antioxidant.[15] Certain vitamins, minerals and natural plant chemicals have antioxidant properties that can protect cells in the body from damage caused by free radicals.

The best food sources of vitamin E include vegetable oils, nuts, seeds, soybeans, olives, wheat germ, whole grains and leafy green vegetables like kale. To supplement, take 200 to 400 international units (IU) of natural source vitamin E per day. If you have diabetes or coronary heart disease, avoid taking single supplements of vitamin E. See Chapter 4, page 52, for more information on vitamin E.

Calcium

If you're taking a GnRH drug such as Lupron (leuprolide) or Synarel (nafarelin), bone health is a concern. These drugs suppress estrogen production, resulting in accelerated bone loss. A review of studies of women taking GnRH drugs determined the average bone loss to be 1 percent per month or 6 percent in total.[16] If you compare that with an average bone loss of 3 percent in the first year of menopause, it seems considerable. Due to the negative effect of GnRH drugs on bone density, Health Canada limits its continuous use to 6 months; frequency of medication depends on the condition being treated.

Ensure that you are meeting your daily requirement of 1000 to 1500 milligrams of calcium by choosing foods listed in Chapter 4, page 56. If you are not meeting your daily targets for calcium, take a supplement. One serving of milk or calcium-fortified beverage (1 cup/250 ml) or plain yogurt (3/4 cup/ 175 ml) or cheese (45 grams) supplies roughly 300 milligrams of calcium. If you require 1000 milligrams, your diet should provide three milk or milk alternative servings. For every serving you're missing and not making up with other calcium-rich foods, take a 300 milligram calcium citrate supplement. See Chapter 4, page 58, for information on calcium supplements.

Vitamin D

This nutrient is also critical for bone health. As well, vitamin D has anti-inflammatory effects in the body. The current recommended intake for adults is 1000 international units (IU) per day, an amount that can only be achieved by taking a supplement. (Many experts recommend 2000 IU per day.) To determine the dose of vitamin D you need to take, calculate how much vitamin D you're already consuming from a multivitamin and calcium supplements and then make up the difference to reach your RDA. Vitamin D comes in 400 IU or 1000 IU doses. Choose a supplement made with vitamin D3 rather than vitamin D2; the former is more biologically active in the body. You'll find more information about vitamin D recommendations and supplements in Chapter 4, page 51.

Other Natural Health Products

Fish Oil Supplements

There's some evidence that taking fish oil reduces menstrual pain in women who suffer endometriosis and dysmenorrhea.[17,18] (Dysmenorrhea is pain and discomfort associated with menstruation.) It's well established that the two omega-3 fatty acids found in fish oil, DHA and EPA, have anti-inflammatory effects in the body. To treat painful menstruation, a daily dose of fish oil supplying 1080 milligrams of EPA and 720 milligrams of DHA has been used. This dose of omega-3 fatty acids is best achieved by using a high-potency liquid fish oil supplement such as Carlson's MedOmega Fish Oil (one teaspoon/5 ml provides 1200 milligrams of EPA and 1200 milligrams of DHA).

Probiotic Supplements

If you don't eat dairy products, probiotic capsules or tablets are a good alternative. In fact, many health experts believe that taking a high-quality supplement is the only way to ensure that you're getting a sufficient number of friendly bacteria to the intestinal tract. Use the following guide when choosing a product:

- **Buy a product that offers 1 billion to 10 billion live cells per dose.** Taking more than this may result in gastrointestinal discomfort.
- **Choose a product that's stable at room temperature.** It's more convenient and, since it doesn't require refrigeration, you can continue taking your supplement while travelling.
- **Always take your supplement with food.** When eating a meal, the stomach contents become less acidic due to the presence of food. This allows live bacteria to withstand stomach acids and reach their final destination in the intestinal tract.

Nutrition Strategy Checklist for Endometriosis

☐   Limit saturated and trans fat

☐   Flaxseed oil

- ☐ Fatty fish
- ☐ Fruit and vegetables
- ☐ Dietary fibre
- ☐ Fermented milk products
- ☐ Identify food sensitivities
- ☐ Limit caffeine and alcohol
- ☐ Vitamin E
- ☐ Calcium
- ☐ Vitamin D
- ☐ Fish oil supplement
- ☐ Probiotic supplement

Recommended Resources

Endometriosis Association
www.endometriosisassn.org
8585 N 76th Place
Milwaukee, WI, USA 53223
Tel: 414-355-2200
Fax: 414-355-6065

Endometriosis Awareness and Information
www.hcgresources.com/endoindex.html

Mayo Foundation for Medical Education and Research
www.mayoclinic.com
This website is produced by a team of writers, editors, health educators, nurses, doctors and scientists, and is one of the best patient-education sites on the Internet. The information is reliable, thorough and clearly written.

Eunice Kennedy Shriver National Institute of Child Health and Development
NICHD Clearinghouse
National Institutes of Health
www.nichd.nih.gov/health/topics/
   Endometriosis.cfm
Building 31, Room 2A32, MSC 2425
31 Center Drive
Bethesda, MD, USA 20892-2425
Tel: 1-800-370-2943
Fax: 1-866-760-5947
Email: NICHDInformationResourceCenter@
   mail.nih.gov

Fibrocystic Breast Conditions

Formerly called fibrocystic breast disease, this disorder may include breast nodules, breast swelling, tenderness and pain. These symptoms are collectively referred to as fibro-cystic breast conditions, and are not considered a disease at all. Breast pain and tenderness are also called cyclic mastalgia. A woman with fibrocystic breast conditions may experience breast pain only, lumpiness only or both. Doctors often refer to this condition as nodular or glandular breast tissue. Although these fibrocystic breast changes can be painful and suspicious lumps can cause anxiety, most are perfectly normal and do not increase a woman's risk of breast cancer.

What Causes Fibrocystic Breast Conditions?

The exact cause of this disorder is not known but hormones, especially estrogen, are thought to play a role. Breast changes usually appear during the years a woman menstruates and regress with the onset of menopause. In most cases, the small, round lumps appear in the breasts because of hormonal changes associated with menstruation. The hormones estrogen and progesterone, which control the menstrual cycle, trigger physical responses that can make breasts become lumpy, or fibrocystic, and painful. It's thought that a deficiency of progesterone and an excess of estrogen in the last 14 days of a woman's menstrual cycle are responsible for breast changes. A woman will find that her breasts become increasingly tender and painful as her body prepares for menstruation. The discomfort normally subsides once her period starts. Over time, breast lumps may develop into cysts, which fill with fluid, causing swelling and pain.

Some researchers believe that hormone-like compounds called prostaglandins are responsible for breast changes. Studies indicate that the development of lumpy breasts may also be stimulated by a diet that includes higher levels of caffeine and dietary fat. Despite these theories, most of the clues about the cause of fibrocystic breast conditions suggest that estrogen is the key.

Symptoms

One of the main symptoms of fibrocystic breast conditions is breast lumpiness. A woman may discover only one lump, but it's more common to have multiple lumps. The lumps are tender, come in different sizes and usually move freely within the breast tissue. A woman may also experience some breast pain and swelling, which becomes worse just before her menstrual period.

Some women who are severely affected by this condition complain of continuous discomfort. Up to 50 percent of women with breast pain report that it interferes with their sex life and physical activity. Occasionally, a woman may develop breast cysts that require medical attention.

Who's at Risk?

Fibrocystic breast conditions can affect women from puberty to old age. However, they most often affect women between the ages of 30 and 50. Breast symptoms usually disappear with menopause, and it's quite rare to find the disorder in post-menopausal women unless they are taking hormone replacement therapy.

Conventional Treatment

If fibrocystic breast changes don't cause symptoms or cause only mild symptoms, no treatment is required. Women who suffer from painful breasts at certain times during the month may find that applying cold compresses on the tender areas and wearing a well-fitting, supportive bra both day and night will relieve some of the discomfort. Your doctor may recommend pain relievers to treat the aches and pains. If fibrocystic breast conditions cause severe pain, medications such as danazol, a mild synthetic male hormone, may be used. Because these drugs can produce side effects, they should be used for a short time only. Oral contraceptives, which lower menstrual cycle hormones, may also be prescribed. Fine needle aspiration, which removes fluid from the cyst, is used to treat some breast cysts. In rare cases, surgery may be required to remove a persistent cyst that doesn't resolve after other treatment.

Managing Fibrocystic Breast Conditions

At this time, there is only weak evidence pointing to dietary factors as the cause of fibrocystic breast conditions. However, certain food and food components may very well aggravate symptoms. And since a high level of estrogen, or an increased sensitivity to estrogen, seems to be the dominant theory, any dietary modification that is able to reduce the circulating level of estrogen may help lessen your symptoms.

Dietary Strategies

Dietary Fat

Reducing the amount of fat you eat, from the typical North American intake of 30 percent to 35 percent of your calories to 15 percent to 20 percent, may be beneficial.[1] Although studies have not investigated the effect of a low-fat diet on fibrocystic breast conditions per se, there is indirect evidence to support this strategy. Research in women with breast dysplasia (abnormal growth of breast cells) has found that a low-fat diet has a positive effect on the density of breast tissue and the composition of breast fluid.[2]

A high-fat diet is also associated with higher levels of circulating estrogen. Studies reveal that when women reduce their fat intake, their levels of blood estrogen and prolactin, a hormone that may be involved in fibrocystic breast conditions, also decline. In two small studies, women with fibrocystic breast conditions who followed a 21 percent–fat diet for 3 months experienced a significantly lower level of circulating estrogen, prolactin and cholesterol.[3,4]

To help you follow a 20 percent–fat diet:

- **Choose lower-fat animal foods.** Buy lean meat, skinless poultry breast, skim milk, non-fat yogurt and skim-milk cheese made with 7% milk fat.
- **Use added fats and oils sparingly.** Replace butter on toast with sugar-reduced jam; try mustard instead of high-fat spreads on sandwiches; mix tuna with non-fat yogurt instead of mayonnaise; top a baked potato with salsa instead of butter; order salad dressing on the side. Use oil sparingly in cooking. Invest in a few high-quality non-stick pans. Use chicken broth, apple juice or water to prevent sticking in stir-fry dishes.
- **Read nutrition labels on packaged foods** like crackers, frozen entrées, snack foods, cookies and cereals. A food that provides no more than 20 percent of calories from total fat will have no more than 2 grams of total fat per 100 calories.

Dietary Fibre

Like dietary fat, fibre may also influence a woman's circulating estrogen levels. Most of the research on fibre intake and estrogen levels has focused on breast cancer risk, but the findings may be relevant to fibrocystic breast conditions. Two studies conducted among premenopausal women suggest that diets high in wheat bran are effective in lowering circulating estrogen.[5,6] In one study, both a 10 and 20 gram wheat-bran supplement significantly lowered estrogen after 4 weeks. The total daily fibre intake of these women was between 20 and 32 grams.

Wheat bran belongs to a class of fibres known as insoluble, which means they're unable to dissolve in water. They pass through the intestinal tract intact and, in the process, are able to bind compounds, including estrogen, preventing their absorption in the bloodstream. Soluble fibres found in oatmeal, oat bran, dried beans, lentils and psyllium-enriched breakfast cereals also have this ability, even though they have not been specifically studied for their effect on estrogen levels.

Use the list in Chapter 1, page 4, to gradually add higher-fibre foods to your diet. Spread fibre-rich foods out over the course of the day. Since fibre needs fluid to work, be sure to drink at least 8 ounces (250 ml) of fluid with each high-fibre meal and snack.

Flaxseed

Ground flaxseed is a rich source of lignans, natural plant compounds that help to lower circulating levels of estrogen and, as a result, may help ease breast symptoms. A Canadian review of treatment strategies for fibrocystic breast conditions concluded that flaxseed should be considered as a first-line treatment for cyclic mastalgia.[7]

Add 2 tablespoons (30 ml) of ground flaxseed to your daily diet. Add ground flaxseed to hot cereal, smoothies, yogurt, applesauce, casseroles, muffin and pancake batters, and other baked-good recipes.

Soy Foods

Research findings on soy intake and estrogen levels provide indirect evidence that this food may be beneficial in preventing fibrocystic breast conditions. Many studies have found that a diet rich in soy foods lowers the level of circulating estrogen in women.[8-11] Soybeans contain natural chemicals called isoflavones, a class of plant compounds that have weak estrogen activity in the body. One of the main isoflavones in soybeans, called genistein, is able to compete with a woman's own estrogen for binding to estrogen receptors. In so doing, soy isoflavones are able to reduce the amount of estrogen that contacts breast cells. One study found that women who added soy isoflavones to their diet experienced significantly less breast tenderness compared with women who added a milk-protein placebo. Another study of 64 premenopausal women revealed that after 1 year of daily supplementation with a soy protein powder, women and their physicians reported a consistent reduction in breast tenderness and fibrocystic breast changes.[12,13]

Aim to include one soy food in your daily diet. Use an unflavoured soy beverage on cereals and in smoothies. Add chopped firm tofu to stir-fries, soups and salads. Buy canned soy beans—drain, rinse and toss them in soups, salads and chilies. Instead of a beef burger, grill a soy-based burger. Use soy ground round in pasta sauce and chili recipes.

Caffeine

It's long been thought that caffeine plays a role in fibrocystic breast conditions. The interest in caffeine dates back to the late 1970s and early 1980s, when researchers noted higher intakes of caffeine in women with fibrocystic breast conditions. It has been hypothesized that caffeine causes an abnormally high level of energy compounds called cAMP in cells, which may lead to symptoms.

Studies over the past decade have failed to find a relationship between caffeine intake and the development of fibrocystic breast conditions. Drinking coffee may, however, make your symptoms worse. A study from Duke University in Durham, North Carolina, asked 147 women with fibrocystic breast conditions to abstain from caffeine-containing foods, beverages and medication.[14] Among those women who successfully removed caffeine from their diet for 1 year, 69 percent reported a decrease or absence of breast pain.

Currently, Health Canada recommends a daily maximum of 450 milligrams of caffeine. While your goal should be to avoid caffeine as much as possible, use this amount as a benchmark when you look at how much you're consuming now. Eliminate caffeine for 3 months before you assess its effect on reducing your breast symptoms. A list of caffeine-containing foods and beverages can be found in Chapter 5, page 110.

Vitamins and Minerals

Vitamin E

The use of vitamin E for treating fibrocystic breast conditions dates back to the 1960s. It has been claimed that vitamin E alters blood levels of certain hormones, especially progesterone, but this has not yet been proven. A few small studies from the early 1980s did find that vitamin E was effective in reducing symptoms.[15,16] However, subsequent well-designed studies that looked at the effect of 150, 300 and 600 international units (IU) of vitamin E in larger numbers of women found no effect on breast pain or lumps. These studies lasted only 2 or 3 months, and it's possible that vitamin E might be beneficial if taken for a longer period.

While the balance of evidence does not support the use of vitamin E supplements for managing fibrocystic breast conditions, it's certainly worth a try. Take 400 IU of natural source vitamin E per day. (If you have heart disease or diabetes, do not take high-dose vitamin E supplements.) Foods rich in vitamin E include vegetable oils, nuts, seeds, wheat germ and leafy green vegetables. For more information about vitamin E, see Chapter 4, page 52.

Herbal Remedies

Evening Primrose Oil (*Oenothera biennis*)

The oil from the evening primrose plant is a rich source of a fatty acid called gamma-linoleic acid (GLA). GLA is an omega-6 fatty acid that our bodies produce from linoleic acid, an essential fatty acid found in corn, sunflower and safflower oils.

By providing the body with GLA, evening primrose oil (EPO) is thought to help ease breast pain and tenderness in two ways. GLA is a polyunsaturated fat, which means it belongs to a class of fats with a different chemical structure than saturated fats (found in meat and dairy products). As a result, it behaves differently in the body. Taking EPO is thought to increase the ratio of polyunsaturated to saturated fats in the body. Some experts believe that if saturated fats dominate, your body will be overly sensitive to hormones like estrogen. That's because hormones made from saturated fat are more potent and attach more readily to receptors. What's more, a diet that's high in saturated fat is also believed to impair the conversion of dietary linoleic acid to GLA inside the body. Interestingly, research has found abnormally high levels of saturated fatty acids in women with fibrocystic breast conditions.

Supplementing with EPO may also alter your body's production of hormone-like compounds called prostaglandins. Many prostaglandins are made in the body; some are inflammatory and may cause breast pain, while others are considered friendly as they do not lead to inflammation. GLA produces a special class of friendly prostaglandins called PGE1. These prostaglandins are also thought to reduce the activity of prolactin, a hormone possibly involved in fibrocystic breast conditions.

An early review of studies conducted in 291 women with persistent breast pain found EPO to be beneficial in easing symptoms.[17] However, more recent trials have not found EPO to be any more effective at reducing breast tenderness and pain than the placebo treatment.[18] Despite this, many women do find supplementing with EPO eases their symptoms. If you experience cyclic breast pain, EPO is worth trying.

The recommended dose of EPO is 3 to 4 grams daily. Take two 1000 milligram capsules twice daily. EPO capsules are available in 500 milligram and 1000 milligram (1 gram) capsules. Buy a supplement that is standardized to 9 percent to 10 percent GLA. It may take three menstrual cycles before you feel the effects of EPO and up to 8 months for the supplement to reach its full effect.

Ginkgo (Ginkgo biloba)

French researchers studied 143 women with PMS and found that Ginkgo biloba significantly reduced PMS-related breast tenderness (as well as abdominal bloating and swollen hands, legs and feet).[19] The women took ginkgo on day 16 of their cycle and continued until day 5 of the next cycle, at which time they stopped. They resumed taking the herb again on day 16.

The recommended dose of ginkgo is 80 milligrams taken twice daily. Start on day 16 (counting from the first day of your period) and continue until day 5 of the next cycle. This means you will take ginkgo for roughly 18 days each month. To buy a high-quality product, choose one standardized to 24 percent ginkgo flavone glycosides. On rare occasions, ginkgo may cause gastrointestinal upset, headache or an allergic skin reaction in susceptible individuals. Ginkgo should not be taken with blood-thinning drugs such as Coumadin (warfarin) or heparin without medical supervision. Ginkgo may enhance the blood-thinning effect of other natural health products (like vitamin E or garlic), so be sure to inform your physician and pharmacist if you are taking a number of these supplements.

Nutrition Strategy Checklist for Fibrocystic Breast Conditions

☐ Low-fat diet
☐ Dietary fibre
☐ Ground flaxseed
☐ Soy foods
☐ Avoid caffeine
☐ Vitamin E
☐ Evening primrose oil
☐ Ginkgo biloba

Recommended Resources

American Cancer Society
www.cancer.org
Tel: 1-800-ACS-2345

Mayo Foundation for Medical Education and Research
www.mayoclinic.com
This website is produced by a team of writers, editors, health educators, nurses, doctors and scientists, and is one of the best patient-education sites on the Internet. The information is reliable, thorough and clearly written.

Fibromyalgia (FM)

Fibromyalgia (FM) is a chronic, debilitating disorder characterized by widespread, persistent pain, stiffness and tenderness of the joints, tendons and muscles. The disease is also characterized by restless sleep, fatigue, anxiety, depression and bowel-function disturbances. Although pain symptoms are similar to those of arthritis, fibromyalgia doesn't cause inflammation of the joints or joint deformity. In rheumatoid arthritis, tissue inflammation is the major cause of joint pain and stiffness.

What Causes Fibromyalgia?

The cause of fibromyalgia is unknown, but many experts think that it's a biological response to stress. People with fibromyalgia experience pain in response to stimuli that are normally not perceived as painful. Researchers have identified abnormalities in brain chemical activities that may be responsible for fibromyalgia symptoms. People with FM have lower levels of brain chemicals such as serotonin and tryptophan and higher levels of a growth hormone known as somatomedin C. As well, patients tend to have elevated levels of a chemical called substance P that signals nerves. These chemical imbalances have been linked to heightened pain sensitivity in other stress-related disorders such as depression and migraine.

Scientists are beginning to suspect that certain people may be susceptible to stressful conditions if they are genetically predisposed to chronic pain disorders. Post-traumatic stress disorder, an anxiety disorder that emerges after traumatic events such as sexual or physical abuse, has been known to cause changes in brain activity that can be linked to FM syndrome. Physical traumas, such as accidents, injuries or severe illness, also seem to promote the onset of fibromyalgia by affecting the central nervous system. This response is especially prevalent in injuries that involve the neck.

Another popular theory suggests that FM may be an autoimmune disease that develops when a defect in the immune system stimulates antibodies to attack the body's own tissue. Studies have indicated that inadequate or disturbed sleep patterns very often trigger immune system reactions, causing inflammation and pain. Almost all FM sufferers experience chronic sleep disturbances, and many people report that their FM pain is much worse after a night of disturbed sleep.

Symptoms

Although symptoms vary from person to person, the universal symptom of FM is widespread pain. In most cases, the disorder causes burning or aching pain that begins in a specific "tender spot" and radiates outward through the body. The pain can change location and vary in severity from day to day. Weather changes, physical activity and stressful events can affect the degree of FM pain symptoms.

Ninety percent of people with FM feel fatigued, sometimes to the point of exhaustion. Fatigue may be related to abnormal sleep patterns commonly observed in FM patients. Energy levels may be low, and the ability to concentrate and remember things may be impaired. Numbness and tingling in parts of your body and occasional muscle spasms are also common symptoms. Your body may feel stiff and tight after you wake up in the morning or after long periods of standing or sitting. Digestive problems, including diarrhea, constipation, abdominal pain, gas and heartburn, as well as bladder pain and frequent urination, may all be associated with FM. Women with fibromyalgia often experience pelvic pain and may have pain during menstrual periods or during sexual intercourse.

Fibromyalgia is associated with a number of other symptoms and syndromes. At least 25 percent of all people who suffer from FM are prone to depression or mood disorders. In addition, sleep disturbances are very common. Fibromyalgia sufferers are given to migraines and other types of headaches. Sensitivities to temperature and to environmental conditions such as light, noise and weather patterns are also common in FM.

Because of its complex nature, fibromyalgia is very difficult to diagnose and is often confused with other psychological or autoimmune disorders, such as depression, arthritis or sleep disturbances caused by other conditions.

Who's at Risk?

Fibromyalgia affects 2 percent to 6 percent of all Canadians.[1] Women are four times more likely than men to develop fibromyalgia, especially after the age of 50. Evidence suggests that fibromyalgia runs in families and is inherited through the female line. The risk of developing fibromyalgia may also increase if you are exposed to high levels of stress or suffer a physical injury or accident, especially one that involves the neck.

Conventional Treatment

Treatment of fibromyalgia usually involves a combination of therapeutic approaches including education, stress reduction, exercise and medications. A regular program of low-impact aerobic exercise has been shown to be very effective, yet many people with the disease avoid physical activity because it seems to aggravate pain. However, without physical activity, your muscles will become weak, and, as the muscles weaken, it takes less and less physical activity to produce painful symptoms. This vicious cycle of inactivity and muscle weakness can prolong and heighten the exhausting symptoms of FM. Swimming, water-exercise programs, walking and stationary biking are all good activity choices. When undertaking any physical activity, it is important to incorporate stretching at the beginning and end of the exercise.

Learning to cope with the disease is an important component to healing. Respecting the limitations of your body and recognizing circumstances that aggravate the condition are important lifestyle management skills. Reducing stress and adopting a positive approach to pain management can help establish better control over FM symptoms. Psychological therapy may help in gaining such life skills.

Various physical rehabilitation therapies, massage, heat applications and relaxation techniques have all been useful in managing FM symptoms. In some cases, medication, including the following, may be required to treat symptoms:

- **Tricyclic antidepressants** to improve sleep and reduce muscle pain. Only small doses are needed to provide effective relief. Side effects such as blurred vision, drowsiness and dry mouth are often associated with these drugs.
- **Selective serotonin reuptake inhibitors (SSRIs)** to increase the level of serotonin in the brain. They're often prescribed for people with FM who are also suffering from a major depression. Side effects can include agitation, nausea and sexual dysfunction.
- **Pain relievers** such as non-steroidal anti-inflammatories for relief of pain symptoms.
- **Estrogen therapy** to improve sleep for women who develop fibromyalgia during menopause. It helps reduce fatigue associated with FM.

None of the treatments for fibromyalgia offer a cure for the disease. It can take months or even years to become symptom-free. Occasional relapses and recurrence of symptoms are bound to happen along the path to recovery.

Managing Fibromyalgia
Dietary Strategies

There is no evidence so far that any one dietary factor is effective in managing fibromyalgia. It is important to eat a healthy, low-fat diet that provides plenty of fibre and fresh fruit and vegetables. Dietary recommendations for fibromyalgia are similar to those for chronic fatigue syndrome, since the two conditions share many of the same clinical features. In fact, 75 percent of patients fit the diagnosis for both fibromyalgia and chronic fatigue. The following dietary guidelines should be followed:

1. **Emphasize plant foods in your daily diet.** Fill your plate with grains, fruit and vegetables. More often, substitute vegetarian protein foods such as legumes, soy and tofu for animal protein. If you eat meat or poultry, limit your portion size to 3 ounces (90 g); 1 serving of meat should take up no more than one-quarter of your plate.
2. **Choose foods and oils that are rich in essential fatty acids and fish that are rich in omega-3 fatty acids.** Nuts, seeds, flaxseed and flaxseed oil, canola oil, omega-3 eggs, wheat germ and leafy green vegetables are sources of essential fatty acids. Salmon, trout, sardines and herring are excellent sources of DHA and EPA, the two omega-3 fatty acids found in fish.
3. **Choose foods that are rich in vitamins, minerals and protective plant compounds.** Pick whole grains as often as possible. Eat at least three different-coloured fruits and three different-coloured vegetables every day.
4. **Eliminate sources of refined sugar** as often as possible: cookies, cakes, pastries, frozen desserts, soft drinks, fruit drinks, candy, etc.
5. **Buy organic produce** or **wash fruit and vegetables** to remove pesticide residues.
6. **Limit foods with chemical additives.**
7. **Avoid caffeine.** It can worsen fatigue by interrupting sleep patterns.
8. **Drink at least 9 to 13 cups (2.2 to 3.2 L) of water every day.**
9. **Avoid alcohol.** If you drink, consume no more than one drink a day and no more than seven or nine per week for women and men, respectively.

Vitamins and Minerals
Multivitamin and Mineral Supplements

A broad-based supplement will ensure that you are meeting your daily requirements for most nutrients. Some evidence suggests that a daily multivitamin and mineral pill, when combined with a supplement of freeze-dried fruit and vegetables (Phyt-Aloe by Mannatech Inc., www.mannatech.com) and medical treatment, may help reduce the severity of pain symptoms.[2]

Buy a product that contains no artificial preservatives, colours, flavours or added sugar, starch, lactose or yeast. This should be declared in small print below the ingredients list. If you experience gastrointestinal upset when taking a multivitamin, try a "professional brand" supplement available at certain health food stores. These products contain no binding materials and are suitable for people with food sensitivities. However, they are expensive and you will need to take more than three to six capsules a day to meet your recommended intake levels. Brand names include Genestra and Thorne Research.

Calcium and Vitamin D

According to a small study from the Osteoporosis Prevention and Treatment Center in Santa Monica, California, women with fibromyalgia may be at increased risk for osteoporosis.[3] Among women aged 33 to 60 years with fibromyalgia, all had lower bone densities of the spine than healthy women. It is especially important to meet your daily requirements for calcium and vitamin D to slow down bone loss. A number of studies have also linked suboptimal vitamin D levels in the blood to persistent, non-specific muscle pain. However, a recent trial of 104 participants with diffuse muscle pain concluded that low vitamin D levels weren't associated with pain and, furthermore, treatment with high dose vitamin D supplementation didn't reduce pain.[4]

Ensure that your daily diet provides an adequate amount of calcium, a crucial nutrient for bone health. Vitamin D also plays a key role in maintaining bone density.

The recommended dietary allowance (RDA) for calcium is 1000 to 1500 milligrams, depending on your age. Best food sources are milk, yogurt, cheese, fortified soy, rice and almond beverages, fortified orange juice, tofu, salmon (with bones), kale, bok choy, broccoli and Swiss chard. If you take calcium supplements, buy calcium citrate with vitamin D and magnesium added.

Health experts advise a daily intake of 1000 international units (IU) of vitamin D, an amount higher than the current official recommended dietary allowance (RDA). (At the time of writing, vitamin D recommendations are under revision based on the evidence that higher intakes are required to guard against disease.) The fact that very few foods contain vitamin D and our skin doesn't produce the vitamin in the fall and winter months makes it necessary to get vitamin D from a supplement. To determine the dose of vitamin D you need to buy, add up how much you're already getting from your multivitamin and calcium supplements, subtract that from your RDA and make up the difference. Choose a vitamin D supplement that contains vitamin D3 instead of vitamin D2, which is less potent. Vitamin D is typically sold in 400 IU and 1000 IU doses.

See Chapter 4, page 56, for more information about calcium and vitamin D.

Magnesium

This mineral plays an important role in muscle contraction and the transmission of nerve impulses. Muscle pain is associated with magnesium deficiency, and some studies have linked fibromyalgia with low body stores of magnesium, despite normal blood tests.[5,6] One study found that supplemental magnesium combined with malic acid (Super Malic, see below) provided significant reductions in the severity of pain and tenderness.[7] You may want to consider taking Super Malic to correct a magnesium deficiency.

The RDA for magnesium is 310 to 420 milligrams per day (see Chapter 4, page 60). The best food sources include nuts, seeds, legumes, prunes, figs, whole grains, leafy green vegetables and brewer's yeast. If your daily diet falls short in magnesium, as is the case for most Canadians, take a supplement. If you do not take supplemental calcium with magnesium, single supplements of magnesium are available. Take 200 to 250 milligrams of magnesium citrate. Taking more than 350 milligrams of magnesium in a supplement may cause diarrhea, nausea and stomach cramps.

Other Natural Health Products

Capsaicin

This natural compound, responsible for the heat of chili peppers, has a long history of use as a topical agent for pain disorders. One study suggests that capsaicin cream might help relieve fibromyalgia pain and tenderness.[8] Individuals with fibromyalgia who applied the cream to tender points four times per day for 1 month reported less tenderness than those using the placebo cream. The researchers found no difference in overall pain or sleep quality. Other studies have found capsaicin (or capsicum) cream very effective in the treatment of chronic, non-specific low back pain.[9,10]

Capsaicin creams are available in health food stores and pharmacies. Buy a cream with 0.025 to 0.075 percent capsaicin (the higher strength may be more effective). Capsaicin cream will produce a burning sensation, which will diminish after several applications. Use a small amount to begin. When you no longer feel burning upon application, increase the amount of cream you use. Be careful not to touch your eyes or other sensitive tissues after applying capsaicin cream. Wash your hands with soap after using the product.

Malic Acid

Malic acid is a compound produced by the body. It's also abundant in citrus fruit, apples and apple juice, grapes and sour milk. Some researchers theorize that people with fibromyalgia have difficulty producing or using

malic acid and that this may impair muscle function. To date, only one small study supports this theory. Researchers from Texas gave 24 individuals with fibromyalgia a supplement called Super Malic, which combined 200 milligrams of malic acid from apples with 50 milligrams of magnesium, or a placebo. After 6 months, those taking Super Malic experienced significant reductions in pain and tenderness compared with the placebo group. Improvements were seen after 2 months of taking six tablets twice daily (2400 milligrams of malic acid, 600 milligrams of magnesium).[11] It's not clear how the combination of malic acid and magnesium hydroxide seems to decrease pain and tenderness.

To treat fibromyalgia, take 600 to 1200 milligrams of malic acid twice daily with 150 to 300 milligrams of magnesium twice daily; for convenience, they can be taken at the same time. This is equivalent to three to six Super Malic tablets, taken twice daily. This amount of magnesium may cause diarrhea, in which case you should reduce the dose. Since this product is recommended for treating a magnesium deficiency, it shouldn't be used indefinitely. Take it for 3 months, and then taper off use to see if symptoms return. Do not take Super Malic with magnesium-containing antacids; it may also interfere with antibiotic absorption. Be sure to inform your physician if you start using this product.

Melatonin

Preliminary evidence suggests that melatonin supplements are useful in the management of fibromyalgia symptoms. In a study of nineteen patients with the disease, taking melatonin at bedtime for 1 month significantly reduced the number of painful joints and pain severity, and improved sleep.[12] Numerous studies conducted in healthy people have found melatonin effective in treating sleep disturbances.

Melatonin is a hormone produced in the body's pineal gland, a tiny gland located in the brain. Melatonin regulates the body's wake-sleep cycles. The hormone induces sleep by interacting with melatonin receptors in the brain. Once in the bloodstream, melatonin lowers body temperature, alertness and performance. Interestingly, researchers have observed low melatonin levels in women with fibromyalgia.

To help manage joint pain and sleep disturbances in people with fibromyalgia, a dose of 3 milligrams, taken at bedtime, has been used. For more information on melatonin supplements, see Chapter 8, page 176.

SAMe (S-Adenosyl-Methionine)

SAMe is a compound the body makes naturally from certain amino acids found in high-protein foods like fish and meat. As a supplement, it's well known as a treatment for depression. SAMe is associated with higher levels of brain neurotransmitters, and it also appears to change the composition of cell membranes in the brain, enabling neurotransmitters and cell receptors to work more efficiently.

Some evidence suggests that SAMe may be useful in treating fibromyalgia. A handful of studies have found SAMe effective in managing symptoms when it was given by injection. Although these findings cannot be generalized to oral supplements, one study using SAMe in pill form did find the supplement beneficial. In the study, individuals with fibromyalgia who took SAMe for 6 weeks fared better in terms of pain, fatigue and morning stiffness than those taking the placebo.[13] It's unclear exactly how SAMe works to help ease fibromyalgia symptoms.

Take 800 milligrams once daily on an empty stomach. Buy an enteric-coated product.

Nutrition Strategy Checklist for Fibromyalgia

☐ Low-fat, plant-based diet
☐ Healthy oils
☐ Avoid caffeine and alcohol
☐ Multivitamin/mineral
☐ Calcium
☐ Vitamin D
☐ Magnesium
☐ Capsaicin cream
☐ Melatonin
☐ SAMe

Recommended Resources

The Arthritis Society
www.arthritis.ca
393 University Avenue, Suite 1700
Toronto, ON M5G 1E6
Tel: 416-979-7228
Fax: 416-979-8366
Email: info@arthritis.ca

Chronic Fatigue Syndrome and Fibromyalgia Information Exchange Forum
www.co-cure.org

Fibromyalgia Network
www.fmnetnews.com
P.O. Box 31750
Tucson, AZ, USA 85751
Tel: 1-800-853-2929

National Institute of Arthritis and Musculoskeletal and Skin Diseases National Institutes of Health
www.niams.nih.gov
1 AMS Circle
Bethesda, MD, USA 20892-3675

Tel: 301-495-4484
Fax: 301-718-6366
Email: NIAMSinfo@mail.nih.gov

Food Allergies

It's estimated that 4 percent of Canadian adults and 6 percent of Canadian children suffer from food allergies, numbers that are on the rise.[1] People with food allergies must avoid certain foods such as nuts, shellfish and eggs and must scrutinize ingredient lists to make sure packaged foods are safe to eat. For some, accidentally consuming even one bite of the wrong food can be life threatening.

An allergic reaction to food develops when the immune system mistakenly responds to a food. Thinking that the food, or an ingredient in the food, is harmful, the immune system produces immunoglobulin E (IgE), a type of protective antibody. The IgE antibodies circulate in the bloodstream, ready to defend the body against this foreign invader. The next time the particular food is consumed, it interacts with the IgE antibodies, triggering the release of massive quantities of chemicals such as histamine. The defensive actions of histamine and other chemicals provoke a wide range of allergic symptoms that can affect the skin, cardiovascular system, gastrointestinal tract or respiratory system.

Food allergies are not to be confused with food intolerances, reactions that don't involve the body's immune system or the release of histamine (see Lactose Intolerance, page 529). Some of the symptoms may be similar, but only a true food allergy can provoke potentially fatal reactions.

Experts believe that the number of people with food allergies is rising, as is the number of foods to which they become allergic. One popular theory is the "hygiene hypothesis," which states that keeping kids germ-free and our environment clean increases the body's susceptibility to allergy by somehow altering its immune system. It's thought that, to develop properly, a healthy immune system needs early exposure to micro-organisms. Our global food supply may also play a role by exposing us to foods we've never had before. Kiwi allergies are now increasingly diagnosed in North America as are peanut allergies in countries that have introduced peanut butter. Food manufacturing might also be to blame. Dry roasting of peanuts, common in North America, increases their allergic potential compared with boiling or frying, as is commonly done in China. The Chinese eat just as many peanuts as North Americans yet have lower rates of peanut allergy.

What Causes Food Allergies?

Allergists believe that many food allergies in children are the result of immature immune systems. In other words, their bodies aren't developed enough to properly process certain foods. Children will sometimes outgrow a food allergy, especially those involving dairy products or eggs. However, allergic reactions to peanuts, fish and shellfish are usually considered lifelong problems. The older a person is when a food allergy develops, the less likely that he or she will outgrow it.

Some evidence suggests that breastfeeding infants for the first 6 to 12 months of life may help avoid milk or soy allergies, especially if the parents are allergic and the baby is likely to be more prone to allergies.[2-5] In some cases, a food eaten by a mother may enter the breast milk and may cause an allergic reaction in the child, so caution should be exercised during this time.[6]

Delaying the introduction of foods that are known to cause allergies until the second or third year of life may also help to avoid or postpone the development of food allergies in high-risk infants. (An infant is considered to be at high risk for developing allergies if he or she has a parent or sibling with an allergic disease such as food allergy, asthma or eczema.) According to a consensus report of the American College of Allergy, Asthma and Immunology, for high-risk infants, the optimal introduction of various foods includes:[7]

- solid foods, 6 months
- dairy products, 12 months
- egg, 2 years
- peanuts, tree nuts, fish, seafood, at least 3 years

Foods That Cause Allergy

The vast majority—95 percent—of food allergies are caused by the following:

- cow's milk
- egg whites
- peanuts
- wheat
- soybeans
- fish
- shellfish
- tree nuts

Sesame seeds and certain fruits and vegetables can also trigger allergic reactions. Sulphites, chemicals used to maintain colour, prolong shelf life and prevent bacterial growth, can also cause severe reactions in sensitive people. Although sulphites don't trigger a true allergic reaction, sensitive people may react to them with allergy-like symptoms ranging from nausea, stomach pain and diarrhea to seizures,

asthma and anaphylactic shock. Some people with asthma are extremely sensitive to sulphites. Sulphites are added to foods such as dried fruit, commercially prepared potatoes, wine, bottled lemon and lime juice, and shrimp. Other food additives may cause adverse reactions, but are not true allergens; aspartame, monosodium glutamate (MSG) and yellow food colouring can sometimes cause mild and transitory reactions in people who are sensitive to them.

In some cases, people with an allergy to one type of food may also be allergic to other foods of a similar nature. This is known as cross-reactivity. For example, someone allergic to lobster may also be allergic to shrimp or crab and may have severe reactions to these foods if eaten unsuspectingly. Some pollen allergies, such as those to ragweed or birch tree pollen, have been associated with allergies to specific foods.

Symptoms

Allergic reactions range from mild to severe and may even be life threatening. In food allergy, certain proteins in an offending food cause the body's immune system to react by releasing chemicals such as histamine. Histamine can trigger swelling, hives, eczema, nasal congestion, wheezing, asthma, nausea and vomiting. Signs and symptoms usually develop within a few minutes to 1 hour after eating the food. Anaphylaxis is a severe allergic reaction that occurs rapidly, involves only a trace amount of food and affects the whole body. Without immediate attention, death can result.

Though the theory is controversial, some experts believe that certain food allergies are more delayed in their onset. Such allergies may cause gastrointestinal symptoms, rash or headache over days or weeks, making it difficult to trace your reaction to a particular food.

Symptoms of food allergy include:

- running nose, sneezing
- itchy eyes, mouth or face
- wheezing or coughing or dry throat
- rashes or hives or eczema
- nausea, vomiting, diarrhea
- abdominal pain

Symptoms of anaphylaxis include:

- rash
- swelling of the throat and mouth
- laboured breathing
- sudden drop in blood pressure
- dizziness
- rapid pulse
- loss of consciousness

Who's at Risk?

Children are far more likely to have a food allergy than adults. The risk of food allergy increases if someone in your family has allergies such as hay fever, asthma or eczema. For instance, if one parent has an allergic disease, the child has roughly a 50 percent chance of developing an allergy. Food allergies are also more common in infants and young children whose digestive systems are not fully developed. Although children typically outgrow allergies to milk, soy, wheat and eggs, their allergies to nuts, fish and shellfish are usually lifelong.

Diagnosing Food Allergies

In combination with a patient's history and his or her diet and symptom diary, a doctor may use one of the following tests to identify food allergies:

- **Skin testing.** A small amount of the food is scratched into the skin using a needle. Swelling or redness indicates an allergy. Skin testing can't be used in extremely allergic people who have a history of anaphylactic reactions. This testing isn't reliable for delayed food allergies.
- **RAST blood test** (radioallergosorbent tests) and **ELISA blood test** (enzyme-linked immunosorbent assay). Both tests measure the presence of food-specific IgE antibodies. They're expensive and, unlike skin testing, results aren't available immediately. Blood tests aren't reliable for delayed food allergies.
- **Controlled food challenge.** Various foods, including the suspected allergen, are placed in opaque capsules. The patient swallows the capsules one at a time and is watched to see if a reaction occurs. In a true food challenge, neither the doctor nor the patient knows which capsule contains the allergen. This is considered the gold standard of allergy testing.

Conventional Treatment

Desensitization or allergy shots may be recommended for some immediate-type food allergies. Antihistamines (e.g., Benadryl) may help reduce or prevent allergic symptoms by blocking the release of histamine by the immune system. Some topical creams and ointments may help soothe skin symptoms.

Injectable epinephrine is required to treat an anaphylactic reaction. This synthetic version of the naturally occurring hormone adrenaline is injected directly into a thigh muscle or vein. It constricts blood vessels thereby reversing throat swelling and improving breathing. Individuals with a severe allergy should wear a medical alert bracelet and carry an injectable epinephrine kit with them at all times.

Managing Food Allergies
Dietary Strategies
The Elimination/Challenge Diet
If you're having difficulty identifying which foods are causing you grief, use the elimination diet to pinpoint your trigger foods. It may be a short-term hassle, but it's worth the effort. This process should help you determine what foods to avoid and what foods you can continue to enjoy. (Important note: This diet should not be followed if you have experienced an anaphylactic reaction.)

The purpose of this diet is to demonstrate relief of symptoms upon removal of a given food item (elimination diet) and recurrence of symptoms upon its reintroduction (challenge diet). You might consider enlisting the help of a registered dietitian to help you follow this diet.

Because milk, soybeans, eggs, wheat, peanuts, nuts, fish, shellfish, corn and sulphites are the main culprits for the majority of food allergies, these foods are usually not included in the starting diet. However, if you suspect any other foods cause symptoms, eliminate them from your diet too. Make sure that these foods are not in other foods you eat—for example, egg or milk may be in mayonnaise or salad dressings. You'll need to read ingredient lists of packaged foods. Stay on this elimination diet for 7 days. You should notice a drastic reduction or cessation of symptoms during this period. If you don't feel better, your body chemistry may recover more slowly after eating a trigger food; you will need to stay on the elimination diet for an additional 7 days.

During this period, keep a food and symptom diary. Record everything you eat, amounts eaten and what time you ate the food or meal. Document any symptoms, the time of day you started to feel the symptom and the duration of the symptom. You might want to grade your symptoms: 1 = mild, 2 = moderate, 3 = severe. If your symptoms don't subside, eliminate additional foods until all of your symptoms stop.

Once your symptoms disappear, suspect foods are reintroduced to the basic diet until symptoms reappear. Do this gradually, introducing the foods one at a time. Use the following procedure for testing foods in the challenge phase of this diet:

Day 1: Introduce the test food in the morning, at or after breakfast. If you don't experience symptoms, try the food again in the afternoon or with dinner.

Day 2: Don't eat any of the test food. Follow your elimination diet. If you don't experience a reaction today, the food is considered safe and can be included in your diet. If you do experience a reaction to a tested food on Day 1 or 2, don't continue eating it and don't reintroduce any other foods until your symptoms have resolved.

Day 3: If no symptoms occurred on Day 1 and 2, try the next food on your list, according to the above schedule.

Food Avoidance
Once a food allergy is diagnosed, eliminating the food from the diet is the most effective treatment. If allergy testing or an elimination/challenge diet reveals that you need to avoid certain foods, consult a registered dietitian in your community (www. dietitians.ca) to plan a healthy diet that is nutritionally complete. A

dietitian can teach you how to read food labels for hidden ingredients and how to avoid restaurant-prepared foods that may contain ingredients that trigger reactions. It's especially important for parents and caregivers to learn how to protect children from foods they are allergic to, especially if the food causes an anaphylactic reaction.

When dining out, don't rely on the menu description. Ask whether the dish contains the specific food you are allergic to and how the food is prepared. While a dish might not contain peanuts, the fact that it's fried in peanut oil might be overlooked. If the server is unsure about ingredients, ask the chef.

Label Reading

If you have a food allergy, reading the label is the only way to know if a food is safe. Yet reading labels can be frustrating. A voluntary warning of "may contain traces of peanut or tree nuts" means it's impossible to know whether a food accidentally contains the allergen. Label reading is expected to become easier for Canadians with food allergies: New regulations announced in July 2008 require food manufacturers and importers to declare food allergens on ingredient lists. Tree nuts, peanuts, sesame seeds, wheat, eggs, milk, soy, shellfish, fish, sulphites—and their derivatives—will be disclosed as an ingredient or in a statement immediately following the ingredient list.

Become familiar with terms on ingredient lists that indicate allergenic foods. For example, if you're allergic to milk protein, foods made with casein, whey and lactalbumin must be avoided. Since manufacturers often change ingredients, always read labels—even for products you've purchased before.

Nutrition Strategy Checklist for Food Allergies

☐ Elimination/challenge diet
☐ Avoidance of certain foods
☐ Label reading
☐ Vitamin and/or mineral supplements as required

Recommended Resources

Allergy and Asthma Information Association
www.aaia.ca
111 Zenway Boulevard, Unit 1
Vaughan, ON L4H 3H9
Tel: 1-800-611-7011
Fax: 905-850-2070
Email: admin@aaia.ca

Health Canada
www.hc-sc.gc.ca

The Food Allergy and Anaphylaxis Network
www.foodallergy.org
11781 Lee Jackson Highway, Suite 160
Fairfax, VA, USA 22033-3309
Tel: 1-800-929-4040
Fax: 703-691-2713
Email: faan@foodallergy.org

International Food Information Council
www.ific.org
1100 Connecticut Avenue NW, Suite 430
Washington, DC, USA 20036
Tel: 202-296-6540
Fax: 202-296-6547

National Institute of Allergy and Infectious Diseases
National Institutes of Health
www3.niaid.nih.gov
6610 Rockledge Drive, MSC 6612

Bethesda, MD, USA 20892-6612
Tel: 301-496-5717
Fax: 301-402-3573

Gallstones

Gallstones are solid deposits that form in the gallbladder or nearby bile ducts. Nearly one in ten people has gallstones, but many will never experience symptoms or need medical treatment. However, gallstones may travel out of the gallbladder and into the digestive system, where they create a blockage that can lead to inflammation and intense pain. If left untreated, complications caused by gallstone obstructions can be serious, even fatal.

The gallbladder's main job is to store bile produced by the liver from cholesterol. Bile is necessary for digestion and assists in the absorption of dietary fat, fat-soluble vitamins and minerals such as iron and calcium. Bile flows from the liver through a series of ducts (bile ducts) to the gallbladder, where it's stored until needed for digestion. When food enters the digestive tract, the gallbladder contracts and releases bile into the small intestine to assist with digestion and absorption.

What Causes Gallstones?

Bile contains large amounts of cholesterol, which normally remains in a liquid form. However, when bile contains more cholesterol than normal, the cholesterol changes into a sludgy substance that collects in the gallbladder. Eventually, this sludge becomes hard deposits called gallstones. Occasionally, gallstones can be formed from calcium or bile salts that accumulate in the gallbladder, but most often they are cholesterol based. Gallstones can range in size from smaller than a pinhead to as much as 3 inches (7.5 cm) in diameter.

When gallstones form in the gallbladder, the condition is known as *cholelithiasis*. These stones normally don't cause any symptoms, especially if they remain in the gallbladder. Gallstones may also be passed from the gallbladder into the bile ducts, a condition known as *choledocholithiasis*. The stones may then travel into the small intestine without ever causing symptoms.

If gallstones become trapped in the bile ducts, causing a blockage or obstruction, symptoms will occur. A persistent obstruction will cause inflammation of the gallbladder (*acute cholecystitis*) or the pancreas (*pancreatitis*). The blockage may also cause a backup of bile, which can result in liver damage. In rare cases, large gallstones may erode the wall of the gallbladder and enter the intestine, where they cause an obstruction called a *gallstone ileus*.

Factors that can contribute to the development of gallstones include too much cholesterol in bile, a condition that has no relation to the amount of cholesterol in your bloodstream. Incomplete or infrequent emptying of the gallbladder can also increase the risk of gallstones. This can occur during pregnancy or by going for long periods of time without eating. Skipping meals and eating too little fat can result in fewer contractions of the gallbladder, thus preventing it from emptying completely.

Symptoms

Fortunately, nearly 80 percent of all gallstones cause no symptoms at all. In fact, many people only discover they have gallstones during a medical test done for other reasons. Gallstones that temporarily block the bile ducts will cause minor attacks of pain that are usually brief and infrequent, occurring weeks, months or even years apart. You may also feel bloated, full, gassy and nauseated, especially after eating fried or fatty foods. It's very easy to confuse gallstone symptoms with those of indigestion.

If the gallstones are fully obstructing the bile ducts and causing an inflammation of the gallbladder, the symptoms will become much more acute. You'll feel severe, recurrent pain that's focused beneath the right lower rib cage. This is one of the most reliable symptoms of gallbladder disease and often develops between midnight and 3 A.M. The pain may last from 30 minutes to several hours and may be accompanied by nausea and vomiting. Over time, the pain can radiate to the back or right shoulder blade. As the condition worsens, your urine becomes tea- or coffee-coloured. Fever, chills and jaundice may also develop.

Who's at Risk?

The following have an increased likelihood of developing gallbladder disease:

- **Females.** Women aged 20 to 60 are three times more likely to have gallstones than men. The female sex hormone estrogen stimulates the liver to remove greater amounts of cholesterol from the blood, which then accumulates in the gallbladder. Pregnancy, oral contraceptives and hormone therapy are also associated with higher estrogen levels and increased cholesterol-containing bile.
- **Older adults.** People over the age of 60 are more likely to have gallstones than those who are younger.
- **Related family.** Individuals with family members who have had gallstones are at higher risk of developing the condition.
- **Overweight individuals.** Even a small weight gain can raise cholesterol levels in the bile and cause the gallbladder to contract and empty less frequently. As a result, the bile becomes more concentrated, creating ideal conditions for gallstones. However, you should be careful in your attempts to lose weight. Rapid weight loss as a result of very low-calorie or crash diets can also upset your bile chemistry and encourage gallstone development.
- **People who don't exercise regularly.**
- **People who eat a high-fat, high-sugar diet.**

Conventional Treatment

People who experience occasional gallbladder pain can reduce or prevent the number of attacks by following a diet that limits or eliminates fatty foods.

If pain continues despite the dietary changes, gallbladder surgery may be required. A procedure called a *cholecystectomy* involves making small incisions in the abdominal wall for inserting a miniaturized video camera (laparoscope) for monitoring and specialized surgical instruments to completely remove the gallbladder. Occasionally, conventional abdominal surgery may be necessary. The removal of your gallbladder has little effect on overall health and imposes no dietary restrictions. You may find that you have more frequent bowel movements and looser stools after the surgery.

When surgery is inadvisable, your doctor may recommend dissolving the gallstones with oral doses of bile salts. However, results may take months and the stones may recur once you discontinue the drug. Dissolving the stones with methyl tert-butyl ether or fragmenting them with sonic shock waves are also techniques that have been used with varying degrees of effectiveness.

Preventing and Managing Gallstones

The strategies below are intended to prevent the formation of gallstones, or reduce the risk of "silent" gallstones becoming symptomatic. While many of the recommendations are healthy for all individuals, it's important to seek medical attention if you have gallbladder pain. Using alternative therapies to postpone surgery for symptomatic gallstones can result in rupture of the gallbladder or other serious complications. If gallbladder pain is only occasional, the following strategies may help, but medical supervision is necessary.

Dietary Strategies

Meal Frequency
It's important to eat meals at regular intervals throughout the day. Skipping meals or prolonged fasting causes the gallbladder to contract less frequently, which concentrates bile and may encourage stones to form.

Dietary Fat and Cholesterol
Reducing your intake of animal fat and dietary cholesterol can change the composition of bile, making gallstone formation less likely.[1,2] One study found that a diet high in saturated fat increased the risk of gallstones in men and women by threefold.[3] Choose lean cuts of meat, skinless poultry breast and low-fat dairy products. Avoid processed foods that contain hydrogenated vegetable oils (a source of saturated fat). Choose a margarine made with non-hydrogenated oil.

There's also evidence that consuming certain types of fat on a regular basis may favourably influence the composition of bile in a way that reduces the risk of gallstone formation. Some research suggests that consuming olive oil, rather than sunflower oil, at meals can reduce the cholesterol content of bile.[4,5] It's also thought that olive oil enhances gallbladder emptying. Use extra-virgin olive oil and canola oil, which contain mainly monounsaturated fats and very little saturated fat.

Health Canada recommends consuming no more than 300 milligrams of cholesterol each day. Choosing animal foods that are lower in saturated fat will help you to reduce dietary cholesterol intake. Other cholesterol-rich foods are egg yolks, shrimp and liver (see Chapter 3, page 29, for a list of cholesterol-containing foods).

While lower-fat diets may help prevent gallstones, some fat is necessary for the proper functioning of the gallbladder. Scientists have determined that 10 grams of fat (2-1/2 teaspoons/22 ml of oil) should be consumed at each meal to ensure efficient gallbladder emptying of bile.[5] Very low fat intakes can decrease gallbladder contractions, encouraging the formation of gallstones.

Weight Control
Obesity, especially of the abdomen, is an established risk factor for gallstones. Research has found that men with a waist circumference greater than 40 inches (102 cm) were more than twice as likely to develop gallstones as men whose waist measurement was less than 34 inches (86 cm).[6] Obese women are also more likely to develop gallstones than healthy-weight women. It's thought that carrying excess weight around the abdomen increases

the amount of bile in the gallbladder and may also cause impaired gallbladder motility.

Although being overweight increases the likelihood of developing gallstones, it's crucial to lose excess weight gradually. Low-fat, very low-calorie diets (1000 calories per day or less) that cause rapid weight loss of more than 3 pounds (1.5 kg) per week substantially increase the risk of gallstones. Studies have found that up to 25 percent of obese people on such diets develop gallstones.[7-10] Crash dieting causes a shift in the balance of bile acids and cholesterol in the bile, favouring a cholesterol-rich bile. Fasting, long periods without eating and very low fat intakes all encourage cholesterol to accumulate in the bile.

Diets that promote gradual weight loss (1200 to 2000 calories per day) and that provide some fat at each meal will lessen the risk of gallstones. As well, achieving a slow, steady weight loss of 1 to 2 pounds (0.5 to 1 kg) per week will reduce the risk of weight regain. See Obesity, Overweight and Weight Loss, page 574, for strategies for safe weight loss. Research has found that weight cycling among women increases the risk of gallstones requiring surgery.[11]

Physical activity may play an important role in the prevention of gallstones and should be a component of a weight-loss program. Harvard University researchers found that 34 percent of symptomatic gallstone cases in men could be prevented with 30 minutes of aerobic exercise (brisk walking, jogging, biking, stair climbing) five times per week.[12]

Dietary Fibre

A number of studies have revealed that people who eat high-fibre diets have a lower risk of gallstones.[13-15] Once fibre reaches the intestinal tract, it binds to cholesterol and a bile acid called deoxycholic acid, causing their removal from the body. Both cholesterol and deoxycholic acid contribute to gallstone formation.

Gradually increase your fibre intake to 20 to 38 grams per day. Foods rich in soluble fibre may be the most beneficial because of their cholesterol-binding properties. Oatmeal, oat bran, psyllium-enriched breakfast cereals, legumes, citrus fruit, apples and carrots are good sources of soluble fibre. Be sure to drink at least 9 cups (2.2 L) of fluid per day to help fibre work properly.

A diet providing 7 to 10 daily servings of fruit and vegetables (not as juice) combined will also help increase fibre intake. One serving is equivalent to 1 medium-sized fruit, 1/4 cup (60 ml) of dried fruit, 1/2 cup (125 ml) of raw or cooked vegetables or 1 cup (250 ml) of salad greens.

Simple Sugars

Diets high in refined sugars have been linked to gallstones. It's thought that refined sugars can influence the composition of bile by altering the metabolism of fat in the body. Many sweets, such as muffins, pastries, cookies and cakes, are also high in fat—another risk factor for gallstones. Minimize your consumption of table sugar, syrups, soft drinks, fruit drinks, candy and other sweets.

Caffeine

According to a Harvard University study, drinking coffee may protect you from developing symptomatic gallstones.[16] Among 46,000 men, those who consumed 2 to 3 cups (500 to 750 ml) of coffee per day had a 40 percent lower risk of gallstones compared with men who were not regular coffee drinkers. And the risk was slightly less for men who drank 4 or more cups (1 L) of coffee per day.

Animal studies show that caffeine causes the gallbladder to contract, which can help flush out cholesterol-rich bile. While coffee may reduce the risk, people who already have gallstones should avoid it, since caffeine can aggravate symptoms.

Vitamins and Minerals

Vitamin C

Low vitamin C intakes may increase the risk of gallstones by causing cholesterol to concentrate in the bile. Without vitamin C, the enzyme that breaks down cholesterol into bile acids can't work efficiently. Studies have also found that people with gallstones tend to have reduced levels of vitamin C in their blood.[17,18] Swedish researchers gave sixteen gallstone patients a 500 milligram vitamin C supplement daily for 2 weeks before surgery and found that the vitamin influenced the composition of the bile.[19]

The daily requirement for vitamin C for women and men is 75 and 90 milligrams, respectively (smokers need an additional 35 milligrams). The best food sources include citrus fruit, citrus juices, cantaloupe, kiwi, mango, strawberries, broccoli, Brussels sprouts, cauliflower, red pepper and tomato juice. To supplement, take 500 milligrams once daily.

Calcium

Like dietary fibre, calcium binds to deoxycholic acid (the bile acid that tends to form gallstones) and causes its excretion from the body. This means that deoxycholic acid cannot be reabsorbed into the bloodstream and contribute to gallstone formation. One study conducted among 860 men found that those who consumed the most calcium had a 70 percent lower risk of gallstone development than those who consumed the least.[20]

The recommended dietary allowance (RDA) is 1000 to 1500 milligrams. Calcium-rich foods include milk, yogurt, cheese, fortified soy beverages, fortified orange juice, tofu, salmon (with bones), kale, bok choy, broccoli and Swiss chard. If your diet does not provide the calcium your body needs each day, take a calcium supplement. See Chapter 4, page 58, for information on calcium supplements.

Magnesium

Magnesium in foods and supplements may also help guard against gallstones. In a study of 42,705 healthy men, those with the highest intake of total magnesium were 28 percent less likely to develop gallbladder disease than men who consumed the least.[21] Like calcium, magnesium may help remove the bile acids that form in the intestinal tract so they can't be reabsorbed into the bloodstream.

Women and men need 320 and 420 milligrams, respectively, of magnesium each day. The best food sources include nuts, seeds, legumes, figs, prunes, leafy green vegetables and brewer's yeast. Many Canadians fall short in meeting daily magnesium requirements. Consider taking a magnesium citrate supplement providing 200 to 250 milligrams per day. Alternatively, if you take calcium supplements, you might choose one with magnesium added.

Nutrition Strategy Checklist for Gallstones

☐　Eat at regular intervals
☐　Limit animal fat and dietary cholesterol
☐　Olive oil

☐   Control weight
☐   Avoid very low-calorie diets
☐   Regular exercise
☐   Dietary fibre
☐   Limit sugar
☐   Caffeine
☐   Vitamin C
☐   Calcium
☐   Magnesium

Recommended Resources

American Gastroenterological Association
www.gastro.org
4930 Del Ray Avenue
Bethesda, MD, USA 20814
Tel: 301-654-2055
Fax: 301-654-5920
Email: member@gastro.org

Mayo Foundation for Medical Education
and Research
www.mayoclinic.com
This website is produced by a team of writers, editors, health educators, nurses, doctors and scientists, and is one of the best patient-education sites on the Internet. The information is reliable, thorough and clearly written.

National Digestive Diseases Information
Clearinghouse
National Institutes of Health
www.digestive.niddk.nih.gov
2 Information Way
Bethesda, MD, USA 20892-3570
Tel: 301-654-3810

Gastroesophageal Reflux Disease (GERD; see also Hiatal Hernia)

Most of us experience a queasy stomach or heartburn now and then after eating a large meal. But for people with gastroesophageal reflux disease, or GERD, these uncomfortable symptoms persist and can disrupt daily life. GERD is a condition where the liquid, acidic contents of the stomach regurgitate, or reflux, into the esophagus. The constant acid reflux can irritate the lining of the esophagus and cause inflammation. Over time, complications can occur, such as narrowing of the esophagus, ulcers and even a slightly increased risk of esophageal cancer. GERD is a chronic condition; once it develops, it's usually lifelong. However, lifestyle modifications and, in many cases, medications can successfully manage GERD symptoms.

What Causes GERD?

There are many causes of GERD and they affect individuals differently. Although some people with GERD produce abnormally large amounts of stomach acid, this isn't the case for most. More common contributing factors include the action of the lower esophageal sphincter, hiatal hernias and emptying of the stomach.

By far, the most important cause of GERD is the action of the lower esophageal sphincter (LES). The esophagus is a muscular tube that extends from your lower throat into your stomach. The LES is a ring of muscles that sits at the very end of the esophagus where it joins the stomach. Normally, the LES is working all the time. It contracts to close off the passage from the esophagus into the stomach, preventing the reflux of stomach contents into the esophagus. When you swallow food, the LES relaxes, allowing food to enter the stomach from the esophagus. Once this happens, the LES closes again.

With GERD, the LES contracts very weakly, which impairs its ability to prevent reflux. Some cases of GERD are caused by abnormal relaxation of the LES, called transient LES relaxations. These happen separate from the swallowing of food and last for several minutes, allowing reflux to occur more easily.

It's been found that about one in five people with GERD has a stomach that empties abnormally slowly after eating. This results in prolonged distention of the stomach, which can trigger LES transient relaxations. Delayed emptying of food from the stomach into the small intestine means there is more time for reflux to occur.

Hiatal hernias can also contribute to GERD by pushing the LES out of place and interfering with the muscles that control contraction and relaxation of the valve.

Factors such as fatty foods, spices, alcohol, cigarette smoking and certain medications can make GERD worse.

Symptoms

Hallmark symptoms of GERD include heartburn—a burning pain in the middle of the chest that can extend to the back—and acid regurgitation in the mouth. Some people also experience nausea, dry cough, sore throat, hoarseness in the morning, difficulty swallowing and bad breath. Constant acid reflux can irritate the lining of the esophagus and cause inflammation. Over time, complications such as the following can occur: ulcers in the esophagus, narrowing of the esophagus and, although uncommon, Barrett's esophagus—a condition in which the colour and composition of the cells in the lower esophagus change. Barrett's esophagus is brought on by long-term exposure to stomach acid and is associated with an increased risk of esophageal cancer.

Who's at Risk?

It's estimated that as many as 20 percent of Canadians have GERD, and its occurrence is believed to be on the rise. It's thought that shifts in diet towards fattier foods, later mealtimes and higher rates of obesity are among the factors to blame. Risk factors for GERD include:

- **Obesity.** Excess weight puts added pressure on your stomach and diaphragm, forcing open the LES and causing reflux.
- **Hiatal hernia.**
- **Pregnancy.** A higher production of the hormone progesterone during pregnancy relaxes the LES. As well, the extra pressure placed on the stomach can contribute to reflux.
- **Asthma.** It's thought that coughing and difficulty breathing can trigger reflux. Certain asthma medications may also relax the LES.
- **Diabetes.** A complication of diabetes is delayed stomach emptying, which increases the likelihood of reflux.

As well, connective tissue disorders, such as scleroderma, can cause muscular tissues to thicken and prevent digestive muscles from relaxing and contracting normally.

Conventional Treatment

The most common treatment for GERD involves medication. Over-the-counter antacids are used to neutralize the acid in the stomach so there is no acid to reflux and irritate the esophagus. However, antacids have drawbacks, including their brief action and their potential to cause constipation (aluminum-containing antacids) or diarrhea (magnesium-containing antacids). Prescription medications are commonly used to treat GERD. Histamine antagonists, such as cimetidine (Tagamet), block the production of gastric acid in the stomach. Proton pump inhibitors such as iansoprazole (Prevacid) and esomeprazole (Nexium) also block acid production in the stomach, but they do so more completely and for a longer time than histamine antagonists. Other medications may be used to increase the pressure of the LES and strengthen its contractions.

Medications are generally very effective in managing GERD. In some cases, however, surgery may be required for people with a large hiatal hernia, a severely inflamed esophagus with bleeding, narrowing of the esophagus or GERD that can't be controlled by standard medications.

Preventing and Managing GERD

Some of the simplest and most effective treatments for GERD are lifestyle modifications that eliminate or reduce the frequency of reflux and heartburn. Avoid activities that involve stooping or bending for long periods, especially after eating. Avoid lying down for at least 3 hours after a meal. Some people benefit by raising the head of their bed about 6 to 9 inches (15 to 23 cm). Reflux occurs less often when you sleep on your left rather than right side. If you smoke, give serious consideration to stopping. Nicotine weakens the esophageal sphincter muscle, which can increase the

likelihood of stomach contents refluxing into the esophagus. Managing GERD also involves making certain changes to your eating habits.

Dietary Strategies
Weight Control
Studies have found a very strong link between increasing body mass index (BMI) and GERD.[1,2] In a report published in *The New England Journal of Medicine*, researchers studied more than 10,000 healthy women and found that those who were overweight had a two-and-a-half-times greater risk of developing GERD than those with healthy BMIs. In women with BMIs over 30, the risk of GERD almost tripled. Even moderate weight gain among women of normal weight caused or worsened reflux symptoms.[3] (BMI is calculated as your weight in kilograms divided by the square of your height in metres. For adults, a BMI of 25 to 29.9 signals overweight; 30 or more indicates obesity.)

It's thought that carrying extra weight around your abdomen creates pressure that can cause GERD. It's also possible that excess body fat releases chemicals that alter the normal function of the esophagus.

If your BMI is over 25, take steps to gradually reduce your weight. You'll find tools to assess your current body weight—and strategies to help achieve a healthy weight—under Obesity, Overweight and Weight Loss, pages 569–577.

Smaller Meals
Eating smaller, more frequent meals results in less distension of the stomach and reduces the likelihood of reflux. By bedtime, a smaller and lighter meal is more likely to have emptied from the stomach than a large one. To help

reduce stomach distension, drink fluids apart from meals.

Trigger Foods

It's estimated that as many as 90 percent to 95 percent of people with heartburn or esophageal disorders can link their symptoms to specific foods.[4] Chocolate, peppermint, spearmint, caffeinated beverages, alcohol and fatty foods can lower the pressure of the esophageal sphincter and, as a result, promote reflux. Alcoholic beverages and coffee—both caffeinated and decaf—also stimulate stomach acid secretion.

Citrus fruit and juices, tomatoes and tomato-based products, garlic, onions, carbonated beverages, chili pepper and black pepper can irritate an inflamed esophagus and worsen heartburn.

Not all foods affect people the same way. The best way to identify foods that cause grief is to keep a food and symptom diary for 1 week.

Vitamins and Minerals

Vitamin B12

By reducing or suppressing gastric acid secretion, histamine antagonists and proton pump inhibitors may interfere with the absorption of vitamin B12 from foods, a process that's dependent on the presence of gastric acid. Clinical studies have shown that dietary vitamin B12 malabsorption can occur during treatment with these medications, particularly proton pump inhibitors, although the likelihood of developing a B12 deficiency over time is unknown.

If you take acid-blocking medication to manage GERD, take a vitamin B12 supplement. Since it's not known if these medications also reduce the absorption of B12 from oral supplements, I recommend taking a sublingual (dissolves under the tongue) B12 supplement, available in many health food stores and pharmacies. Sublingual B12 has been found to be as effective as B12 injections in replenishing body stores of the vitamin.

Iron

The powerful action of proton pump inhibitors in blocking the production of gastric acid may impair the absorption of nonheme iron, which is found in plant foods and which relies on stomach acid for absoprtion. Heme iron, found in meat, poultry and fish, isn't dependent on gastric acid for absorption. You'll find a list of foods rich in heme iron in Chapter 4, page 72.

If you have low iron stores or you are a vegetarian who does not eat animal foods that provide heme iron, long-term use of proton pump inhibitors could increase the risk of iron-deficiency anemia. If a blood test identifies an iron deficiency or iron-deficiency anemia, oral iron supplements may not be useful in replenishing your iron stores. Speak to your doctor about iron injections.

Nutrition Strategy Checklist for GERD

☐ Weight control
☐ Small meals
☐ Fluids between meals
☐ Avoid trigger foods
☐ Vitamin B12
☐ Iron

Recommended Resources

**Mayo Foundation for Medical Education
and Research**
www.mayoclinic.com
This website is produced by a team of writers, editors, health educators, nurses, doctors and scientists, and is one of the best patient-education sites on the Internet. The information is reliable, thorough and clearly written.

MedicineNet.com.
www.medicinenet.com

Glaucoma

Known as the "sneak thief of sight," glaucoma develops slowly and painlessly, giving no hint of its presence until the major nerve of vision, the optic nerve, is irreversibly damaged and vision loss has occurred. Glaucoma, which refers to a group of eye diseases that cause damage to the optic nerve, is the second leading cause of blindness in the world.

What Causes Glaucoma?

Increased pressure within the eye, a condition referred to as elevated intraocular pressure (IOP), is the main cause of glaucoma. In a healthy eye, the front part of the eyeball (anterior chamber) is filled with a thin, clear fluid called the aqueous humor. This fluid circulates through the eye, nourishing eye tissues and maintaining the eye shape. In order to keep the fluid fresh and the internal pressure constant, the eye produces a continuous supply of aqueous humor. Once the aqueous humor has circulated through the eye tissues, it leaves the anterior chamber through a drainage angle, located where the iris and cornea meet,

and then flows out of the eye through drainage channels called the trabecular meshwork.

This drainage system prevents a dangerous buildup of pressure within the eye. However, when the aqueous humor doesn't drain properly, the fluid backs up into the anterior chamber, raising the internal eye pressure. This increased pressure slowly damages the optic nerve fibres, causing a gradual loss of peripheral vision and eventual blindness.

The drainage system in the eye can malfunction in a number of different ways, each resulting in a different form of glaucoma.

PRIMARY OPEN-ANGLE GLAUCOMA accounts for 90 percent of all cases. Although the drainage angle in the eye is open and functional, the fluid drains out through the trabecular meshwork much too slowly. Pressure inside the eye gradually rises as the fluid accumulates, resulting in a slow, progressive vision loss. Vision loss begins at the sides or edges of your field of vision and gradually spreads until you are completely blind. The causes are unknown.

CLOSED-ANGLE GLAUCOMA is relatively rare and occurs when the drainage angle between the iris and the cornea is narrowed or blocked. The aqueous humor can't reach the angle; prevented from leaving the eye, the fluid causes a sudden and intense buildup of pressure. Attacks usually occur only in one eye and are extremely painful. Blockage of the drainage angle can be triggered by anything that causes the pupil of the eye to dilate. Dim lighting, emotional stress, eye drops given before an eye examination and certain medications have been known to trigger these attacks. Closed-angle glaucoma is considered a medical emergency because it can destroy the optic nerve very quickly and cause blindness within a few days.

CONGENITAL GLAUCOMA occurs in children who are born with a defect in the drainage angle that slows the normal drainage of the aqueous humor.

SECONDARY GLAUCOMA develops as a complication of other medical conditions such as:

- eye injuries
- eye surgery
- cataracts
- eye tumours
- eye inflammation
- diabetes
- corticosteroid drugs

People with normal IOP have also been known to develop glaucoma. The cause of glaucoma is not yet fully understood. It cannot be prevented, and the damage it causes cannot be reversed. Regular, complete eye examinations are the best way to monitor changes in your eyesight. Early detection and treatment is essential to prevent blindness. Healthy adults should schedule an eye examination:

- age 19 to 40, at least every 10 years
- age 41 to 55, at least every 5 years
- age 56 to 65, at least every 3 years
- over age 65, at least every 2 years

If you have a tendency towards high intraocular pressure or have a family history of glaucoma, see an eye doctor as follows:

- over age 40, at least every 3 years
- over age 50, at least every 2 years
- over age 60, at least once a year

There's growing interest in glaucoma as a neurodegenerative disease since vision loss occurs even when increased ocular pressure is treated. In some cases, glaucoma is diagnosed in people who have normal intraocular pressure but poor aqueous humor circulation, resulting in damage to the optic nerve. Scientists are currently exploring therapies aimed at protecting the vision cells (neurons) from damage that leads to progressive vision loss.

Symptoms

Open-angle glaucoma may not cause any symptoms until irreversible damage has been done. It tends to affect both eyes, though symptoms may appear in only one eye at first. These symptoms include:

- gradual vision loss beginning at the sides or edges of your field of vision
- difficulty focusing on close work
- mild headaches
- visual disturbances, such as difficulty adjusting to darkness or seeing a rainbow-coloured halo around electric lights
- frequent need to change prescription glasses

Early warning signs of closed-angle glaucoma include:

- recurrent blurry vision
- pain around the eyes after watching TV or leaving a darkened room
- morning headaches
- sudden and severe pain in the eye and head
- rapid loss of vision
- nausea and vomiting
- eyelid swells
- eye becomes watery and red
- pupil dilates and does not respond to bright light in a normal manner

Who's at Risk?

You are at greater risk of glaucoma if you:

- are over 45 years of age
- are of African ancestry (compared with Caucasians, black people are three to four times more likely to get glaucoma, are six times more likely to suffer permanent blindness and will experience the onset of the disease 10 years earlier)
- have an immediate relative with glaucoma
- have diabetes
- have a history of elevated intraocular pressure
- have extreme nearsightedness, high blood pressure or heart disease
- have suffered an eye injury, inflammation and abnormally high intraocular pressure
- use oral corticosteroids for a long period

Conventional Treatment

Glaucoma is a chronic disease and must be treated for a lifetime. Treatment is more successful if it's started early and maintained regularly. Treatments vary from person to person and can include:

- **Beta blockers** in eye drops to decrease fluid production
- **Miotic medications** to constrict the pupil, causing the iris to pull away from the drainage angle and increase fluid drainage
- **Carbonic anhydrase inhibitors** or alpha-2-adrenergic agonists to decrease the production of aqueous humor
- **Prostaglandins,** hormone-like substances produced by your body, to increase fluid outflow
- **Laser therapy** to cut a hole in the iris to increase drainage (glaucoma drugs will still be needed after the surgery as the effects are not permanent)
- **Conventional surgery** to create a new opening for fluid drainage (usually done after medication and laser therapy have failed to solve the problem)
- **Regular exercise** to reduce eye pressure and modify associated risk factors such as diabetes and high blood pressure
- **Avoiding head-down or inverted positions** (common in yoga or recreational exercises) because of the risk of increasing IOP
- **Relaxation** and **biofeedback** to help control cases of open-angle glaucoma

Preventing and Managing Glaucoma

Dietary Strategies

Weight Control

Achieving and maintaining a healthy weight may help prevent or delay glaucoma. Research suggests that glaucoma is more likely to develop in individuals with a high body mass index (BMI).[1] To determine whether or not you're at an acceptable weight, turn to Obesity, Overweight and Weight Loss, page 569, to calculate your BMI. A BMI from 25 to 29.9 indicates overweight, and a BMI of 30 or greater is defined as obese.

People who are overweight are more susceptible to diabetes and high blood pressure, two factors that can increase the risk of glaucoma. If you have hypertension, losing weight is one of the most effective ways to lower blood pressure and intraocular pressure. See High Blood Pressure, page 458, for specific nutrition recommendations.

Fruit and Vegetables

A higher intake of certain fruit and vegetables has been linked with protection from glaucoma. A study of 1155 women found that the odds of developing glaucoma were reduced by 69 percent among women who consumed leafy greens (collard, kale) at least once per month compared with those who ate less. Women whose diets provided 2 servings per week of carrots were 64 percent less likely to have glaucoma than their peers who consumed less than 1 serving per week. Canned or dried peaches were also protective.[2] Fruit and vegetables are an excellent source of antioxidants such as vitamin E, beta carotene, lutein and flavonoids, all of which may protect the optic nerve from oxidative damage.

Aim to consume 7 to 10 servings of fruit and vegetables combined each day. Include one dark-green vegetable and one orange fruit or vegetable to increase your intake of beta carotene. See Chapter 5, page 87, for a list of antioxidant-rich fruit and vegetables.

Caffeine, Alcohol and Fluids

If you have glaucoma, limit or avoid caffeine intake. Caffeine can elevate intraocular pressure and reduce blood flow to the retina.[3-5] If you do consume caffeinated beverages, keep your intake to less than 200 milligrams per day. Sources of caffeine include coffee, tea, iced tea, chocolate, soft drinks and certain medications (see Chapter 5, page 110, for a list of the caffeine content of selected items). Switch to decaffeinated coffee and tea, herbal teas or malt beverages.

Women should drink no more than one alcoholic beverage per day (to a limit of seven per week) and men no more than one or two per day (to a limit of nine per week). Moderate consumption of alcohol can raise levels of HDL (good) cholesterol, which may help protect from glaucoma. However, too much alcohol damages artery walls and increases the risk of developing high blood pressure.

Drink fluids (water, juices, milk, herbal tea) in small amounts throughout the day. Consuming large quantities of water in a short period of time can elevate intraocular pressure.

Vitamins and Minerals

B Vitamins

There is some evidence to support taking a B vitamin supplement to prevent or delay the damage caused by glaucoma. Italian researchers gave thirty glaucoma patients a nutritional supplement containing the family of B vitamins, vitamin E and DHA, a fatty acid found in oily fish.[6] After 3 months of treatment, there were significant improvements in the visual field.

Vitamin B12 may be particularly important in glaucoma.[7] It maintains healthy nerve function in the body and therefore may protect the optical nerve fibre from damage. Vitamin B12 is found exclusively in animal foods such as meat, poultry, eggs and dairy products. Fortified soy and rice beverages also contain B12. Adults over 50 should be meeting their daily B12 requirements from fortified foods or a supplement, since the vitamin is absorbed from food less efficiently as we age. To supplement, take a multivitamin and mineral pill.

Vitamin C

This nutrient appears to play an important role in the healing process after glaucoma surgery. Unlike surgery on other parts of the body, successful glaucoma surgery depends on the incomplete healing of the surgical wound. Laboratory tests suggest that the high level of vitamin C normally present in the aqueous humor inhibits wound healing and contributes to successful surgery outcomes.[8,9] (During surgery, a piece of tissue in the drainage angle of the eye is removed, creating an opening. Though partially covered with a flap of tissue, the new hole needs to remain open, not heal shut, to allow fluid [aqueous humor] to drain out of the eye.)

Vitamin C taken as a supplement has also been shown to lower intraocular pressure.

Vitamin C's role as an antioxidant may also serve to protect from optic nerve damage. While the main cause of glaucoma is elevated intraocular pressure, some experts believe that free radical damage contributes to glaucoma by harming the optic nerve, especially in people who have normal eye pressure.

To ensure that you meet your daily vitamin C requirements (see Chapter 4, page 48), include the following foods regularly in your diet: citrus fruit, citrus juices, cantaloupe, kiwi, mango, strawberries, broccoli, Brussels sprouts, cauliflower, red pepper and tomato juice. To supplement, take 500 milligrams of vitamin C once daily.

Vitamin E

Like vitamin C, vitamin E may be important for successful glaucoma surgery. Failure of glaucoma surgery is mostly due to scar formation from fibroblasts. Preliminary research in the laboratory found that vitamin E was able to prevent scar formation in human eye tissue.[10] Vitamin E is also an antioxidant and may act to protect the optic nerve from free radical damage.[11]

The best food sources of vitamin E include wheat germ, nuts, seeds, vegetable oils, whole grains and kale. To supplement, take 400 international units (IU) of natural source vitamin E. If you have heart disease or diabetes, avoid taking more than 100 IU of vitamin E daily.

Magnesium

One type of drug used for glaucoma is a calcium channel blocker, which prevents calcium from entering cells and helps maintain healthy blood vessels. The mineral magnesium is a natural calcium channel blocker, though much less powerful than drugs. A small study from Switzerland found that 121 milligrams of magnesium taken twice daily improved visual field and peripheral circulation in glaucoma patients.[12]

The best sources of magnesium include nuts, seeds, legumes, prunes, figs, whole grains, leafy green vegetables and brewer's yeast. If you decide to supplement your diet and you don't already take supplemental calcium with magnesium, buy a separate magnesium citrate supplement. Take 200 to 250 milligrams once daily. Taking more than 350 milligrams of magnesium in a supplement can cause diarrhea, nausea and stomach cramps.

Herbal Remedies

Ginkgo (*Ginkgo biloba*)

Ginkgo can increase blood flow to the eye and may be useful in glaucoma.[13] American researchers gave healthy individuals 40 milligrams of ginkgo three times daily for 2 days.[14] The herb has been shown to significantly increase ocular blood flow. It's also been found to improve pre-existing vision damage in patients with normal pressure glaucoma.[15] Ginkgo also acts as an antioxidant and helps to thin the blood, two actions that may preserve the health of the optic nerve.

Choose a product standardized to 24 percent ginkgo flavone glycosides and 6 percent terpene lactones. The typical dose is 120 to 240 milligrams, divided into three doses. Start at a lower daily dose of not more than 120 milligrams (e.g., 60 milligrams twice daily) to avoid stomach upset. Increase the dose if needed, but do so slowly.

On rare occasions, ginkgo may cause headache or an allergic skin reaction. Ginkgo has the potential to enhance the effects of blood-thinning medications (warfarin, aspirin). If you're on blood thinners, let your doctor know if you start taking ginkgo.

Nutrition Strategy Checklist for Glaucoma

- ☐ Weight control
- ☐ Fruit and vegetables
- ☐ Avoid/limit caffeine
- ☐ Limit alcohol
- ☐ Vitamin B12
- ☐ Vitamin C
- ☐ Vitamin E
- ☐ Magnesium
- ☐ *Ginkgo biloba*

Recommended Resources

Canadian National Institute for the Blind (CNIB)
National Communications
www.cnib.ca
1929 Bayview Avenue
Toronto, ON M4G 3E8
Tel: 416-480-7644
Fax: 416-480-7019

The Canadian Ophthalmological Society
www.eyesite.ca
610–1525 Carling Avenue
Ottawa, ON K1Z 8R9

American Academy of Ophthalmology
www.eyenet.org
P.O. Box 7424
San Francisco, CA, USA 94120-7424
Tel: 415-561-8500
Fax: 415-561-8533

Glaucoma Research Foundation
www.glaucoma.org
251 Post Street, Suite 600
San Francisco, CA, USA 94108
Tel: 415-986-3162 or 1-800-826-6693

National Eye Institute
National Institutes of Health
www.nei.nih.gov
2020 Vision Place
Bethesda, MD, USA 20892-3655
Tel: 901-496-5248

Gout

Gout is a form of arthritis marked by sudden attacks of painful, inflamed joints—usually the big toe. Referred to throughout history as "the disease of kings," gout was once thought to be a disorder that affected only wealthy, older men—those privileged enough to afford rich foods and plenty of alcohol. Scientists now know that diet is only a contributing factor to this chronic condition. The real culprit behind the painful symptoms of gout is uric acid, a waste product formed naturally in the body.

Uric acid is produced when the body breaks down purines, naturally occurring substances found in the body. Purines are also present in many foods, including organ meats, dried peas, beans, herring, mackerel and trout. As the body breaks down cells and forms new ones, the bloodstream carries uric acid to the kidneys, where it's excreted as urine.

Gout develops when the body either makes too much uric acid or does not excrete it efficiently. As the level of uric acid rises above normal, crystals form and are deposited in the joints. These needle-sharp uric acid crystals inflame the joints, causing pain, redness, swelling and tenderness. The joint most commonly affected is the big toe, but gout can also affect your feet, ankles, knees, hands and wrists.

Gout attacks occur more often in the lower limbs and, typically, only one joint is affected. With proper treatment, attacks will usually last only 3 to 10 days; however, more than half of the people who have one go on to experience another within a year. Over time, the attacks can become more frequent, last longer and may involve more than one joint.

Gout may become chronic, damaging tendons and restricting joint movement. Uric acid crystals may also form hard lumps, called tophi, under the skin. Tophi occur most often in the fingers and toes but can also develop under the skin around the ears, the elbows and in the kidney or urinary tract. If left untreated, tophi may break through the skin and discharge masses of crystals.

What Causes Gout?

A number of factors contribute to the development of gout. Genetics, obesity, heavy alcohol and caffeine consumption, and a purine-rich diet (see below) all play a role. Medical conditions and certain medications, especially diuretics, may interfere with the body's ability to produce or excrete uric acid efficiently, thereby increasing the risk of gout. Surgery, heart attacks, strokes, fatigue and stress have also been known to trigger gout attacks.

Symptoms

The onset of gout is often rapid and unexpected. Attacks frequently occur during the night and become progressively worse over time. The following symptoms are often more severe in people who develop the disease before the age of 30:

- acute, intense, ongoing pain in one joint, usually the big toe (sometimes, even the weight of a bedsheet is unbearable)
- hot, red swollen skin and a feeling of tightness and pressure in the affected area
- feeling of stretching or tearing in the skin
- fever, chills and a general feeling of illness

Research suggests that gout can do more than damage your joints—it has also been shown to increase the risk of angina (chest pain) and heart attack if you already have risk factors for heart disease. It's thought that having too much uric acid in the blood creates oxidative stress, a state that damages LDL (bad) cholesterol, causing it to oxidize. (Oxidized LDL cholesterol is considered more dangerous because it causes hardening and narrowing of artery walls.) High uric acid is also associated with higher levels of C-reactive protein in the blood, an inflammatory compound linked to atherosclerosis and heart attack.

Who's at Risk?

One in thirty Canadians has gout, with men four times more likely than women to develop the condition. It usually shows up between the ages of 30 and 50 in men and after menopause in women.[1] Women have lower levels of uric acid until after menopause, at which time their uric acid levels increase to equal those of men.

Others at higher risk of gout are those who have a family member with gout, overweight people, those with poorly controlled high blood pressure and people who consume excessive alcohol, coffee and purine-rich foods.

Conventional Treatment

Conventional treatment of gout may include:

- **Non-steroidal anti-inflammatory drugs (NSAIDs)** to reduce the pain, inflammation and swelling of an acute attack
- **Medications such as allopurinol** to slow the production and speed up the elimination of uric acid
- **Colchicine** to treat acute gout attacks (can cause side effects such as nausea, vomiting and diarrhea)
- **Corticosteroid injections** to treat severe pain and inflammation
- **Applying ice packs** to the affected joint to help reduce inflammation

Preventing and Managing Gout

Some simple lifestyle changes may prevent recurrent attacks of gout:

1. **Maintain a healthy weight.** Weight loss will lessen the pressure on affected joints and may decrease levels of uric acid.
2. **Exercising regularly** may help strengthen your joints and keep your weight under control.
3. **Avoid certain foods rich in purines,** such as meat and seafood (see below).
4. **Limit the amount of alcohol you drink.** Alcohol interferes with the excretion of uric acid, leading to a buildup of this waste product.
5. **Drink plenty of fluids** to dilute the levels of uric acid in your blood.

Dietary Strategies

Fluids

Drink 9 to 13 cups (2.2 to 3.2 L) of fluids per day to help your body excrete uric acid. Avoid sugar-sweetened soft drinks and fruit juice, which have been linked to a higher risk of gout. Drinking coffee may help prevent gout. A recent study found the risk of gout was 40 percent lower for men who drank 4 to 5 cups (1 to 1.25 L) of coffee per day compared with non–coffee drinkers.[2] Coffee drinking is associated with lower levels of uric acid, an effect likely due to antioxidants in coffee rather than caffeine.

Weight Control

People who are overweight and obese are more susceptible to developing gout. People with gout who are overweight have higher blood uric acid levels and suffer from attacks more frequently. Excess weight also puts more stress on your joints. Studies show that losing weight can reduce gout symptoms and the number of monthly attacks.[3-8] Losing weight is protective from gout because it helps to lower elevated levels of blood triglycerides (elevated levels are common in people with gout).

To determine if you're at a healthy weight, see Obesity, Overweight and Weight Loss, page 569, to calculate your body mass index (BMI). A BMI of 25 to 29.9 indicates overweight, and a BMI of 30 or greater is defined as obese.

If you need to lose excess weight, do so gradually at a rate of 1 to 2 pounds (0.5 to 1 kg) per week. Rapid weight loss and fasting can increase uric acid levels in the blood. Avoid low-carbohydrate, high-protein diets since they can elevate uric acid levels. Use the strategies outlined in Obesity, Overweight and Weight Loss, page 574, to promote safe, gradual weight loss.

Purine-Rich Foods

Certain foods contribute to the overproduction of uric acid in the body. By limiting the intake of these foods—particularly those containing purines, a natural compound that breaks down into uric acid—it's possible to keep uric acid levels low. Purines are found in organ meats, beef, pork, lamb, sardines, anchovies, mackerel, clams, asparagus, mushrooms, spinach, green peas, cauliflower, beans and lentils. Historically, people with gout were told to avoid all purine-rich foods. However, a 2004 Harvard University study involving 47,150 men found that although high intakes of meat and seafood increased the odds of developing gout by as much as 50 percent, intakes of purine-rich vegetables did not.[9]

Reduce your intake of meat and seafood. Each day, consume no more than 2 to 3 servings of meat, fish, poultry, eggs and meat alternatives such as soy and legumes. Eating larger portions may increase uric acid and the risk of gout. (One serving equals 2.5 oz/75 g of meat, fish or poultry, 2 eggs or 3/4 cup/175 ml cooked legumes or tofu.)

A diet low in purine-containing foods should be combined with medication to prevent attacks of gout. Purines occur mainly in animal foods, with the exception of dairy products and eggs, which do not contain purines. The following foods are high in purine and should be limited:

- organ meats
- meat: beef, pork, lamb, game
- anchovies
- canned tuna
- sardines
- herring
- mackerel
- lobster
- scallops
- shrimp
- legumes

Dairy Products

The Harvard University study discussed above also found that men who drank at least two 8 ounce (250 ml) servings of skim milk each day were 44 percent less likely to develop gout than men who drank less than one serving per month.[10] It's thought that the proteins in dairy help reduce uric acid levels. Aim to include 2 to 3 servings of low-fat dairy products in your daily diet. One serving is equivalent to 1 cup (250 ml) skim milk or 3/4 cup (175 ml) 1% or non-fat yogurt.

Alcoholic Beverages

Alcohol interferes with the body's excretion of uric acid, and some types of alcoholic beverages also contain purines. Studies have found that beer-drinking in particular increases the risk of gout because it raises uric acid levels to a greater extent.[11–17] Beer, unlike wine and spirits, also contains purines. A heavy intake of any type of alcohol also increases body weight and blood triglycerides, two factors implicated in gout. Alcohol may also interfere with gout medications. If you're unsure, speak to your doctor about alcohol consumption.

Cherries and Celery Juice

Cherries have long been used as a folk remedy for gout. One study did find that eating half a pound of cherries each day reduced uric acid levels and gout attacks. Cherries contain compounds called anthocyanidins, which have anti-inflammatory properties in the body.

Celery juice is another folk remedy that is used widely in Australia. If you are experiencing a gout attack, consider drinking celery juice throughout the day.

Vitamins and Minerals

Vitamin B12

If you take the medication colchicine for gout, add a vitamin B12 supplement to your daily nutrition regime; the drug is known to impair the body's ability to absorb B12. Vitamin B12 is found exclusively in animal foods such as meat, poultry, eggs and dairy products as well as in fortified soy and rice beverages. However, with the exception of eggs and dairy, these foods should be limited because of their purine content. Fortified soy and rice beverages also contain B12. To supplement, take a multivitamin and mineral pill.

Vitamin C

High intakes of vitamin C are thought to guard against gout. A recent study that followed 46,994 healthy men for 20 years found that compared with men who consumed less than 250 milligrams of vitamin C per day, a daily intake of 500 to 999 milligrams reduced the risk of gout by 17 percent. The higher the intake of vitamin C from foods and supplements combined, the lower the risk of gout. Men who consumed a daily total of 1500 milligrams or more of vitamin C were 45 percent less likely to develop gout. Vitamin C is thought to protect from gout by reducing uric acid levels. Research has demonstrated that a daily 500 milligram vitamin C supplement, taken for 2 months, significantly reduces serum uric acid levels in men and women.[18–20]

Increasing your intake of vitamin C rich foods *and* taking a daily vitamin C supplement may not only help prevent gout, it might also be beneficial in the management of gout. The best food sources of vitamin C include citrus fruit, cantaloupe, strawberries, kiwi, broccoli, cabbage, bell peppers and tomato juice. Take 500 milligrams of vitamin C twice daily. To learn more about vitamin C supplementation, see Chapter 4, page 49.

Nutrition Strategy Checklist for Gout

- ☐ Fluids
- ☐ Weight control
- ☐ Limit purine-rich foods
- ☐ Dairy products
- ☐ Avoid beer
- ☐ Cherries
- ☐ Celery juice
- ☐ Vitamin B12
- ☐ Vitamin C

Recommended Resources

The Arthritis Society
www.arthritis.ca
393 University Avenue, Suite 1700
Toronto, ON M5G 1E6
Tel: 416-979-7228
Fax: 416-979-8366
Email: info@arthritis.ca

American College of Rheumatology
www.rheumatology.org
1800 Century Place, Suite 250
Atlanta, GA, USA 30345
Tel: 404-633-3777
Fax: 404-633-1870

National Institute of Arthritis and
Musculoskeletal and Skin Diseases
National Institutes of Health
www.niams.nih.gov
1 AMS Circle
Bethesda, MD, USA 20892-3675
Tel: 301-495-4484 or 1-877-22-NIAMS
   (64267)
Fax: 301-718-6366

Gum Disease

Most people worry that cavities will cause tooth loss. However, very few adult teeth are lost because of cavities. Rather, gum disease is the leading cause of tooth decay. At least 90 percent of Canadians suffer from some form of gum disease, which could be avoided and controlled through good oral hygiene and regular visits to the dentist.[1] Unfortunately, less than half of all Canadians visit a dentist on a regular basis and fewer still practise daily brushing and flossing.

What Causes Gum Disease?

Gum disease describes the events that begin with bacterial growth in the mouth and end—if not treated—with tooth loss due to destruction of tissue that surrounds the teeth. In its early stages, gum disease is commonly referred to as *gingivitis*. Gingivitis develops when a sticky film called plaque builds up on the teeth and irritates the gums. Within just minutes of you brushing your teeth, plaque begins to form. If left on the teeth for more than 72 hours, plaque hardens into tartar or calculus, a tough, discoloured deposit that cannot be completely removed by brushing or flossing. As the bacteria accumulate on your teeth, they release toxins that irritate your oral

tissues. The body responds by triggering inflammation, making your gums red and swollen. Tender gums that bleed easily are a common sign of gingivitis. Left untreated, gingivitis can advance to *periodontitis* or *periodontal disease.*

Untreated gingivitis leads to a buildup of plaque and tartar along the gum line at the base of your teeth, an area known as the gingiva. Gradually, tartar extends below the gum line, causing the gums to pull away from the teeth. In the airless environment below the gums, bacteria flourish and pockets of infection form, slowly deepening as the disease progresses. Eventually, periodontitis can destroy the tissue and bone that keep your teeth in an upright position, causing them to loosen and fall out. It's estimated that three-quarters of adults have some form of periodontal disease. What's more, in approximately 10 percent of affected adults, the disease is severe enough to cause tooth loss.[2]

Oral bacteria may do more than cause tooth loss. These bacteria can enter your bloodstream whenever you brush, floss or even chew. Preliminary studies have linked oral bacteria to blood clots and clogged arteries. Early results suggest that people with periodontal disease seem to be more susceptible to heart attack and stroke than those with healthy mouths. Oral bacteria may also influence blood-sugar levels in people with diabetes and may lead to pneumonia if inhaled by people with lung disease. In addition, these microbes have been linked to osteoporosis and preterm births.

Gum disease usually develops as a result of inadequate brushing and flossing, but there are other conditions that can increase one's risk. Many women suffer from gingivitis during pregnancy, a response triggered primarily by hormonal changes. Deficiencies in certain vitamins, particularly vitamin C, are known to cause bleeding gums and mouth infections. Diabetes, Crohn's disease, leukemia, Down syndrome and AIDS can all provoke periodontitis.

Symptoms

The warning signs of gum disease include:

- red, swollen, tender gums that bleed easily
- recessed gums; gums that are pulled away from the teeth
- pus between the teeth and gums when you press your gums with a finger
- unpleasant taste in the mouth
- bad breath
- teeth that seem loose or change position
- a change in your bite or the way that dentures fit

Who's at Risk?

Some people are more susceptible than others to the bacteria that cause gum disease and this predisposition may be inherited. Women are especially at risk of gum disease during times of hormonal change, such as during puberty, menstruation, pregnancy and menopause. People who take medications that decrease saliva production (saliva helps wash away plaque from the teeth) or cause an overgrowth of gum tissue may find plaque buildup is stimulated. Medications for high blood pressure and arthritis as well as birth control pills can increase the risk. People who smoke cigarettes and drink alcohol are at a higher risk for gum disease, as are those whose medical conditions reduce their immunity and make them prone to infection. An unbalanced diet lacking fruit and vegetables has also been associated with a greater risk of gum disease.

Conventional Treatment

The best treatment for gum disease is prevention. Brush your teeth after every meal and floss daily to prevent buildup of harmful bacteria. Soft toothbrushes are best for removing plaque. Toothbrushes should be replaced as soon as the bristles become matted or splayed. Choose a toothpaste containing fluoride to help protect against plaque buildup. Even if you brush regularly, it's possible to miss areas. Consider using a disclosing agent (a harmless dye) to show you which areas you need to concentrate on. Regular dental visits and professional dental cleaning (scaling) are critical to remove tartar that has built up on the teeth.

Antibiotic therapy may be required to reduce the levels of oral bacteria. In more advanced cases of periodontal disease, surgery may be needed to remove a section of the infected gum tissue and/or graft new bone to replace the bone destroyed by the disease.

Preventing and Managing Gum Disease

In addition to the nutrition strategies discussed below, other lifestyle changes—such as maintaining good oral hygiene, stopping smoking and managing stress—can help guard against gum disease. (Stress can impair your body's immune system, making it difficult to fight off infection.)

Dietary Strategies

A Healthy Diet

A well-balanced diet that provides adequate protein, vitamins and minerals is essential to maintaining the health of the gums and preventing disease. Protein, vitamins A, C and D, the B vitamins, calcium, magnesium and antioxidants all play a critical role in maintaining the health of gum tissue and its supporting structures. Foods such as lean meat, poultry, dairy products and whole grains supply the body with B vitamins, nutrients indispensable for the production of new cells during development and healing. The most common symptom of a B vitamin deficiency is a decline in the integrity of gum tissue. Fruit and vegetables are excellent sources of antioxidants and vitamins A and C, key nutrients in maintaining oral health. To ensure that your daily diet supplies ample nutrients to support gum health, include the following:

- **Meat and meat alternatives**, 2 to 3 servings per day
  1 serving = 3 ounces (90 g) lean meat, poultry or fish; 3/4 cup (175 ml) legumes or tofu; 1 soy-based veggie burger
- **Milk and milk alternatives**, 2 to 4 servings per day
  1 serving = 1 cup (250 ml) low-fat milk or soy beverage; 3/4 cup (175 ml) low-fat yogurt; 1.5 ounces (45 g) part-skim cheese
- **Whole-grain foods**, 6 to 8 servings per day
  1 serving = 1 slice of bread; 1 ounce (30 g) ready-to-eat cereal; 1/2 cup (125 ml) oatmeal; 1/2 cup (125 ml) cooked rice, pasta or quinoa
- **Fruit and vegetables**, 7 to 10 servings per day
  1 serving = 1 medium-sized fruit; 1/2 cup (125 ml) dried fruit; 1/2 cup (125 ml) 100% fruit or vegetable juice; 1/2 cup (125 ml) raw or cooked vegetables; 1 cup (250 ml) salad greens

Take a daily multivitamin and mineral supplement to help ensure your nutrient needs are met. If you are being treated for periodontal disease, research suggests that taking a multivitamin supplement can help reduce gum inflammation and bleeding.[3]

Omega-3 Fatty Acids

Periodontal disease is a chronic inflammatory disease and many studies have investigated the use of omega-3 fatty acid supplements that have anti-inflammatory actions in the body. Research suggests these fats, found in oily fish, flaxseed oil, walnut oil and canola oil, may reduce gum inflammation and may help treat bone destruction in periodontal disease. French researchers examined 105 patients, 78 of whom had periodontal disease, and found that, compared with healthy individuals, those with bone loss had increased levels of omega-6 fatty acids and reduced levels of omega-3 fatty acids in their blood.[4] (Higher levels of omega-6 fatty acids, found in many vegetable oils, can lead to inflammation in the body.) Another study found that fish oil supplements tended to reduce gingivitis in men who abstained from brushing their teeth for 3 weeks.

Include fish in your diet two times per week. The best sources of omega-3 fats include salmon, trout, Arctic char, sardines, herring and mackerel. If you don't like fish, take a fish oil supplement daily (see Chapter 8, page 164).

Weight Control

Studies conducted in adults and teenagers have identified being overweight and having an elevated waist circumference as risk factors for periodontal disease.[5,6] Research conducted among 12,110 individuals also revealed that those who maintained a healthy weight, exercised regularly and had a high-quality diet were 40 percent less likely to have periodontitis than people who did not engage in these healthy behaviours.[7] It's believed that abdominal fat cells actively secrete a variety of chemicals and hormones that cause inflammation, which contributes to a number of health problems, including periodontal disease.

To assess your body weight and waist circumference, see Obesity, Overweight and Weight Loss, page 569.

Vitamins and Minerals

Vitamin C

The role of vitamin C in maintaining healthy teeth and gums is unchallenged. This vitamin helps form collagen, the supportive network on which bones and teeth are formed. It also helps maintain the integrity of blood vessels. Without adequate vitamin C, gums become inflamed and bleed easily around the teeth. And because the nutrient is important for a strong immune system, it can help reduce the risk of oral infections. Studies have revealed that people with periodontal disease have lower intakes of vitamin C: the less vitamin C consumed in the daily diet, the greater the risk of serious gum disease.[8-14] One study found that supplementation of 250 milligrams of vitamin C daily decreased gum inflammation and bleeding in healthy adults.[15]

The recommended dietary allowance (RDA) for vitamin C for women and men is 75 and 90 milligrams, respectively (smokers need an additional 35 milligrams). The best food sources include citrus fruit, citrus juices, cantaloupe, kiwi, mango, strawberries, broccoli, Brussels sprouts, cauliflower, red pepper and tomato juice. To supplement, take 250 to 500 milligrams of vitamin C once or twice daily. The upper daily limit is 2000 milligrams.

Calcium and Vitamin D

Since these two nutrients are so critical to bone health, it's not surprising that a lack of either can increase the risk of periodontal disease. Higher intakes of calcium and vitamin D are associated with a lower risk of periodontal disease and tooth loss. A survey of Americans found that men and women with the lowest calcium intakes had the greatest risk of periodontal disease. As dietary intake of calcium declined, the risk increased. Women with the lowest calcium consumption had a 54 percent higher risk of the disease.[16] In a study of 145 healthy adults aged 65 and older, researchers found that calcium and vitamin D supplementation to prevent bone loss from the hip significantly reduced tooth loss.[17]

It's especially important to meet your daily requirements for calcium and vitamin D to slow bone loss.

The RDA for calcium is 1000 to 1500 milligrams, depending on your age. The best food sources are milk, yogurt, cheese, fortified soy and rice beverages, fortified orange juice, tofu, salmon (with bones), kale, bok choy, broccoli and Swiss chard. If your diet doesn't supply enough calcium to meet your daily requirement, take a supplement once or twice per day. See Chapter 4, page 58, to learn about calcium supplements.

It's recommended that adults take 1000 IU of vitamin D from a supplement in the fall and winter months. If you're over the age of 50, have dark-coloured skin or don't expose your skin to sunlight in the summer months, take vitamin D year-round. You'll get some vitamin D from fluid milk, fortified soy and rice beverages, oily fish, egg yolks, butter and margarine, but not enough to meet the recommended intake. To determine the dose of vitamin D you need to buy, calculate how much you're already getting from your multivitamin and calcium supplements, subtract that from your RDA and make up the difference. Vitamin D comes in 400 and 1000 IU doses. For more information, see Chapter 4, page 50.

Magnesium

Low magnesium levels in the body have been linked to a greater risk of periodontitis. In one study of 4290 adults aged 20 to 80, individuals with higher blood-magnesium levels showed fewer signs of periodontal disease and less tooth loss. As well, those taking magnesium-containing drugs, such as antacids, displayed fewer signs of periodontal disease compared with their counterparts who didn't use medications containing magnesium. This suggests that supplementing the diet with magnesium could prevent tooth loss in the middle-aged and delay tooth loss in the elderly.[18]

Magnesium plays an important role in bone health. Magnesium deficiency can lead to low bone mass. In the oral cavity, decreased bone density is seen as a loss of bone height and tooth loss, which stimulates the release of inflammatory compounds.

The RDA for magnesium is 310 to 420 milligrams per day (see Chapter 4, page 60). The best food sources include nuts, seeds, legumes, prunes, figs, whole grains, leafy green vegetables and brewer's yeast. If your daily diet falls short in magnesium, as is the case for most Canadians, take a supplement. If you don't take supplemental calcium with magnesium, single supplements of magnesium are available. Take 200 to 250 milligrams of magnesium citrate. Taking more than 350 milligrams of magne-

sium in a supplement may cause diarrhea, nausea and stomach cramps.

Other Natural Health Products

Coenzyme Q10 (CoQ10)

This supplement is known for its antioxidant ability and is thought by some experts to prevent or treat periodontal disease. Most of the studies on CoQ10 in dental health are published in a language other than English. In Japan, practitioners have used CoQ10 topically to improve periodontitis.[19] At this time, it's not clear whether oral supplements of CoQ10 can help gum disease, though it's possible that the antioxidant properties of CoQ10 may be beneficial.

CoQ10 is very safe. If you decide to supplement, buy CoQ10 in an oil base (instead of dry-powder tablets or capsules) as these are more available to the body. Take 50 to 60 milligrams once daily. For more information on CoQ10, see Chapter 8, page 157.

Lycopene

Preliminary evidence suggests that consuming an adequate amount of lycopene each day can help treat gingivitis. In a study of 20 healthy adults with gingivitis, those who took an 8 milligram lycopene supplement for 2 weeks, in addition to following standard oral hygiene practices, had significant improvement in gum health.[20]

Lycopene is an antioxidant, a compound that defends the body, including gum tissue, from free radical damage. The best food sources are heat-processed tomato products such as tomato juice (22 milligrams of lycopene per 1 cup/250 ml), marinara pasta sauce (21 milligrams per 1/2cup/125 ml), tomato soup (12 milligrams per 1 cup/250 ml) and stewed tomatoes (5 milligrams per 1/2 cup/125 ml). For more on lycopene, see Chapter 5, page 87.

Nutrition Strategy Checklist for Gum Disease

☐ Healthy diet

☐ Omega-3 fatty acids

☐ Weight control

☐ Vitamin C

☐ Calcium

☐ Vitamin D

☐ Magnesium

☐ Coenzyme Q10

☐ Lycopene

Recommended Resources

Canadian Dental Association
www.cda-adc.ca/en/cda/index.asp
1815 Alta Vista Drive
Ottawa, ON K1G 3Y6
Tel: 613-523-1770
Fax: 613-523-7736
Email: reception@cda-adc.ca

American Dental Association
www.ada.org
211 E Chicago Avenue
Chicago, IL, USA 60611
Tel: 312-440-2500
Fax: 312-440-2800

American Dental Hygienists' Association
www.adha.org
444 N Michigan Avenue, Suite 3400
Chicago, IL, USA 60611
Tel: 312- 440-8900

Mayo Foundation for Medical Education and Research
www.mayoclinic.com
This website is produced by a team of writers, editors, health educators, nurses, doctors and scientists, and is one of the best patient-education sites on the Internet. The information is reliable, thorough and clearly written.

Heart Disease and High Blood Cholesterol

Heart disease isn't just one condition. There are many types of heart disease that affect the ability of the heart to function properly. The term *cardiovascular disease* refers to a group of diseases that affect the blood vessels throughout the entire body, including the heart, brain, lungs and legs. Coronary artery disease, heart valve disease, heart rhythm disorders, heart failure, hypertension, peripheral vascular disease and congenital heart disease are all included under the umbrella term *cardiovascular disease*.

The most common type of cardiovascular disease is *coronary artery disease*, often referred to as coronary heart disease, or simply heart disease. This section discusses only coronary heart disease, a disease that affects the blood vessels that feed the heart.

What Causes Heart Disease?

The most common cause of heart disease is a disorder called *atherosclerosis*. Simply put, atherosclerosis is the buildup of fatty plaques (collections) on the inner lining of the arteries, like the accumulation of rust in a water pipe. These cholesterol-rich plaques cause hardening of the arteries and narrowing of the inner channel (called the lumen) of the artery. Narrowed coronary arteries can't deliver enough blood and oxygen to maintain normal function of the heart. Reduced blood flow to the heart can cause angina, heart attack, sudden death, abnormal heart rhythms and heart failure.

Atherosclerosis is a progressive disease that can begin in childhood: Fatty streaks can appear on the lining of arteries when cholesterol sticks to the arteries. The next stage of atherosclerosis is an injury to the lining of an artery. An infection or virus, high blood pressure, cigarette smoking or diabetes may cause this damage. The body attempts to heal itself, just like it would with any wound. Immune cells are attracted to the injured artery wall and accumulate. Over time, the fatty streaks enlarge and become hardened with minerals, tissue, fat and cells, forming plaques. As plaques form beneath the artery wall, they stiffen arteries and narrow the passage through them. Most people have well-developed plaques by the time they are 30 years old. If atherosclerosis progresses, it can restrict blood flow to the heart.

Blood cells called platelets respond to damaged spots on blood vessels by forming clots. A clot may stick to a plaque and gradually enlarge until it blocks blood flow to an area of the heart. That portion of the heart may slowly die and form scar tissue. But a clot can also break loose and circulate in the blood until it reaches an artery too small for it to pass through. When a clot that's wedged in such a vessel cuts off the supply of oxygen and nutrients to a part of the heart muscle, a heart attack results.

Who's at Risk?

Risk factors for heart disease are usually classified as either modifiable or non-modifiable.

You can't change non-modifiable factors, but you can help prevent heart disease by changing modifiable risk factors.

Non-Modifiable Risk Factors

- **Aging.** As you get older, the heart's function tends to weaken, our arteries get stiffer and the artery walls become thicker. As well, other known risk factors for heart disease—high blood pressure, elevated cholesterol and diabetes—become more prevalent with increasing age.
- **Family history.** If a male member of your immediate family developed heart disease before the age of 55 or a female relative was diagnosed before age 65, you then have a higher risk of developing the disease.
- **Gender.** Men are more likely than women to have heart attacks and to have them at a younger age. On average, men develop heart disease 10 years earlier than women, although the reasons for this are unclear. Although heart disease was once seen as a man's disease, the gap between men and women has narrowed.

Modifiable Risk Factors

- You have high LDL ("bad") blood cholesterol.
- You have high blood triglycerides (fats).
- You have low HDL ("good") cholesterol.
- You have high blood pressure.
- You smoke cigarettes. Smokers are two to four times more likely to develop heart disease than non-smokers. Smoking damages the lining of the arteries, increasing the likelihood of plaque formation. Inhaling cigarette smoke also produces free radicals in the body, which then damage LDL cholesterol, making it stick to the

artery walls. Finally, smoking increases blood pressure and makes blood-clot formation more likely.

- You don't exercise regularly. Regular exercise helps you maintain a healthy weight. It lowers LDL cholesterol, raises HDL cholesterol, helps keep blood pressure in check and strengthens the heart and blood vessels.
- You have diabetes or prediabetes. In diabetes, fatty plaques develop and progress much more rapidly. In the 35 to 64 age group, people with diabetes are six times more likely to have heart disease or stroke than those without the condition.
- You're overweight or obese. Carrying extra weight puts stress on your heart and circulatory system. Being overweight can also cause high blood pressure and elevated blood cholesterol. Excess weight around the waist, called abdominal obesity, is much more dangerous to your heart than excess lower body fat.
- You have a poor diet. The foods and nutrients you consume—or don't consume—can increase the likelihood of developing risk factors such as high cholesterol and triglycerides, elevated blood pressure, type 2 diabetes and obesity.
- You're stressed. The way in which you cope with stress can contribute to your risk of developing heart disease.

Lipid Profile

The lipid profile is a group of blood tests, often ordered together, that measure the amount of lipids (fats) in your bloodstream. The profile includes total cholesterol, HDL cholesterol, LDL cholesterol and triglycerides. It can also include a calculated value for the total cholesterol/HDL ratio or a risk score based on lipid profile results, age, sex and other risk factors.

Men aged 40 and older should have a lipid profile every 1 to 3 years, as should women who are post-menopausal or 50 years of age or older. Younger adults should have a lipid profile at least once every 5 years.

LDL CHOLESTEROL. Cholesterol is a waxy substance that can't dissolve in your blood. That means it needs to piggyback on carriers called lipoproteins in order to circulate in your bloodstream. Low-density lipoprotein (LDL) cholesterol is referred to as "bad" cholesterol because too much of it in your bloodstream causes the buildup of fatty plaques on artery walls. The higher your LDL cholesterol, the greater your risk for heart disease.

What's a desirable LDL cholesterol level? That all depends on your risk for developing heart disease over the next 10 years. Your doctor will add up points for your age, LDL cholesterol, HDL cholesterol, blood pressure and whether or not you smoke to calculate what's called the Framingham Risk Score. The points used to determine this 10-year risk for heart disease are weighted differently for men and women. Your risk is determined as a percentage based on the following:

Framingham Risk Score

	Risk Factors	10-Year Risk
High	Those who have had a cardiac event or have been diagnosed with heart disease or diabetes	>20%
Moderate	2 or more risk factors	10–20%
Low	Zero to one risk factor	<10%

Your Framingham Risk Score determines the target value for your LDL cholesterol. As you'll see in the chart below, if you're "low risk" for developing heart disease, your target LDL cholesterol should be less than 5.0 millimoles per litre (mmol/L). If you're at high risk for heart disease (e.g., you have diabetes), your doctor will want your LDL cholesterol level to be less than 1.8 mmol/L. If your LDL value is higher than the desirable level, your doctor will recommend treatment with lifestyle changes such as diet and exercise, and possibly medication.

RISK RATIO. The ratio of your total cholesterol to HDL cholesterol is helpful in predicting the risk of developing atherosclerosis. The risk ratio is simply the number obtained by dividing your total cholesterol value by the value of the HDL cholesterol. A high ratio indicates a higher risk of heart attack, whereas a low ratio denotes a lower risk. Having a high total cholesterol and low HDL cholesterol increases the ratio and is undesirable. Conversely, low total cholesterol and high HDL cholesterol lowers the ratio and is desirable.

The following chart outlines LDL cholesterol and risk ratio targets based on the Framingham Risk Scores.

LDL Cholesterol and Risk Ratio Targets

Framingham Risk	10-Year Risk of Heart Disease	LDL Cholesterol Target	Risk Ratio Target (Total Cholesterol/ HDL)
High	≥20%	<1.8 mmol/L	<4.0
Moderate	10–19%	<3.5 mmol/L	<5.0
Low	<10%	<5.0 mmol/L	<6.0

HDL CHOLESTEROL. High-density lipoproteins (HDL) carry cholesterol away from the arteries towards the liver where it's broken down. HDL cholesterol keeps the arteries open and blood flowing through them. The higher your HDL level, the lower the risk for heart disease. That's why HDL cholesterol is called the "good" cholesterol.

Reference Ranges for HDL Cholesterol

	Desired	Increased Risk
Males to age 19	0.90–1.60 mmol/L	<0.90 mmol/L
Males, 20+ years	≥1.0 mmol/L	<1.0 mmol/L
Females to age 19	0.90–2.40 mmol/L	<0.90 mmol/L
Females, 20+ years	≥1.30 mmol/L	<1.30 mmol/L

TOTAL CHOLESTEROL. This is a sum of your blood's cholesterol content. A high level can put you at increased risk of heart disease. Desired total cholesterol is <5.2 mmol/L.

TRIGLYCERIDES. Triglycerides are fats that are made in the liver from the food you eat. They are transported in your blood on very low-density lipoproteins (VLDL). High triglyceride levels usually mean you eat more calories than you burn or you drink too much alcohol. High triglyceride levels increase your risk of heart disease. Desired triglyceride level is <1.7 mmol/L.

High Blood Pressure

The higher your blood pressure is above normal, the greater your risk for heart disease. Blood pressure is the force on your artery walls that's generated by your heart as it pushes blood through your arteries. When your heart beats, blood pressure in your arteries rises. Between beats, when your heart relaxes, blood pressure falls. Your blood pressure rises and falls throughout the day, but when it remains elevated over time it's called high blood pressure, or *hypertension*.

Blood pressure is recorded in millimetres of mercury (written as mmHg). It's composed of two measurements: systolic blood pressure and diastolic blood pressure. You may have heard someone say their blood pressure is 115 over 75. The first (top) number is the systolic pressure, created when your heart is pumping out blood. The second (bottom) number is the diastolic pressure, created when your heart muscle is relaxing and filling with blood.

Adults should have a blood pressure of less than 120/80. Hypertension is defined as a systolic pressure of $\geq$140 mmHg or a diastolic pressure of $\geq$90 mmHg. One in five Canadians falls into the category between, called prehypertension (130–139/85–89 mmHg). Unless lifestyle changes are made to bring blood pressure down, 60 percent of people with prehypertension will develop hypertension within 4 years.

Do You Have High Blood Pressure?

	Millilitres of Mercury (mmHg)
Normal blood pressure	$\leq$120 / $\leq$80
Prehypertension	130–139 / 85–89
Hypertension	$\geq$140 / $\geq$90

Because prehypertension and hypertension usually don't cause symptoms, it's important to have your blood pressure checked regularly—at least once every 2 years and more often if your blood pressure is high. If you have prehypertension you should have your blood pressure monitored once a year. High blood pressure is treated by weight loss, dietary modifications and, often, medication (see High Blood Pressure, page 458).

Homocysteine

Homocysteine is an amino acid normally produced by the body to help build and maintain tissues. However, although the body needs homocysteine to function properly, too much is not a good thing. An elevated level of homocysteine in the bloodstream is linked with a greater risk of atherosclerosis, heart attack and stroke. High homocysteine damages artery walls and promotes the buildup of fatty plaques.

Homocysteine is transformed into harmless compounds with the help of folic acid (a B vitamin also called folate), vitamin B12 and vitamin B6. A lack of these vitamins in the body can hamper the natural breakdown of homocysteine, causing it to accumulate in the bloodstream. Studies show that higher intakes of folic acid and higher blood levels of the B vitamin are associated with lower blood homocysteine levels. Although it's well established that B vitamins can lower elevated homocysteine, it's not clear if doing so can actually ward off a heart attack. Even so, your doctor may order a homocysteine blood test if you've had heart problems or if you have a family member who developed heart disease at a young age. The normal range for homocysteine is 5 to 15 micromoles per litre (umol/L)

Preventing Heart Disease

Many of the risk factors for heart disease are influenced by what you eat. The nutrition and herbal recommendations below can keep your blood cholesterol at a healthy level, prevent damage or oxidation to your LDL cholesterol and promote weight loss.

Dietary Strategies

Saturated Fat

When it comes to heart health, the evidence is pretty clear that what's most important is the type of fat you eat, rather than the total amount. Dietary fats are named according to their chemical structure. Saturated fats are solid at room temperature. This is the type of fat found in animal foods—meat, poultry, eggs and dairy products. Studies have consistently demonstrated that excess saturated fat in the diet raises total and LDL cholesterol levels, a major risk factor for heart disease. What's more, there is clear evidence that reducing your intake of these so-called bad fats can lower blood cholesterol, helping to guard against heart attack. Saturated fat seems to inhibit the activity of LDL receptors on cells so that this type of cholesterol accumulates in the bloodstream.

Foods contain many types of saturated fats, and not all of them influence blood-cholesterol levels to the same degree. For instance, the saturated fat in dairy products is more cholesterol-raising than the saturated fat in meat. What's most important is to eat less saturated fat, period. Saturated fat should account for less than 10 percent of your daily calories. Make a habit of choosing animal foods that are lower in fat. Lean cuts of meat (sirloin, tenderloin, flank steak, eye of round), skinless poultry breast, 1% or skim milk, 1% or non-fat yogurt, and part-skim or skim milk cheese are examples of animal foods lower in saturated fat. See Chapter 3, page 24, for a list of selected foods and their saturated fat content. And don't forget to pay attention to portion size. For instance, when you eat lean meat, your portion size should not exceed 3 ounces (90 grams), about the size of a deck of cards.

Butter is a concentrated source of saturated fat. If your blood-cholesterol levels are normal, there's no reason why you should avoid butter. Just use it sparingly. People with high blood cholesterol can also continue to use a little butter. Many people have made the switch to margarine because, unlike butter, margarine is made from a vegetable oil that doesn't contain saturated fat. However, if you opt for margarine over butter, be sure you choose a healthy one (see Chapter 3, page 23).

Trans Fat

Trans fats are formed during partial hydrogenation, a process used by the food industry to harden and stabilize liquid vegetable oils. The vegetable oil becomes saturated *and* it forms a new type of fat called trans fat. Roughly 90 percent of the trans fat in our food supply is found in commercial snack foods and baked goods including cookies, cakes, pastries and doughnuts, as well as in fried fast foods and some brands of margarines.

Compared to saturated fats, trans fats are linked with a 2.5- to 10-fold higher risk of heart disease. Trans fats increase levels of LDL cholesterol and decrease levels of good, HDL cholesterol, both of which are strongly linked to a greater risk of heart disease. Studies also indicate that a steady intake of trans fats can trigger inflammation in the body, disrupt the normal functioning of blood vessel walls and impair the body's use of insulin. When it comes to the development of heart disease itself, researchers have found that higher intakes of trans fat are linked with a greater risk of developing coronary heart disease.[1-3]

To help reduce your intake of trans fat, read nutrition labels. You'll find the grams of trans fat listed per one serving of the food. More useful, however, is the Daily Value (DV) for saturated plus trans fat combined, which is written as a percentage. This value tells you whether there's a little or a lot of these cholesterol-raising fats in a food. The Daily Value for saturated plus trans fat is set at 20 grams, 10 percent of the calories in a standard 2000-calorie diet. Foods with a Daily Value for saturated plus trans fat of 5 percent or less are low in these fats.

If a packaged food doesn't have a Nutrition Facts box, as may be the case for foods prepared in-store, read the ingredient list. Avoid buying foods that list partially hydrogenated vegetable oil, hydrogenated vegetable oil and shortening. When buying margarine, choose one that is made from non-hydrogenated vegetable oil since it will be trans fat free.

Cut down on your consumption of processed foods such as crackers, cookies, snack foods and toaster pastries; these foods supply most of the trans fat we consume.

Trans fats also occur naturally at low levels in foods from ruminant animals, such as beef, lamb, goat and dairy products. However, unlike industry-produced trans fat, naturally occurring trans fats are not considered harmful.

Polyunsaturated Fat and Omega-3 Fatty Acids

This type of dietary fat is liquid at room temperature. Omega-6 polyunsaturated fats are found in all plant oils, such as corn, soybean, canola, grapeseed, sunflower, safflower, sesame and flaxseed oils. Omega-3 polyunsaturated fats are found in fish and seafood. Replacing foods that provide mostly saturated fat with those rich in polyunsaturated fat can help you lower your cholesterol level.

Omega-3 fatty acids, called DHA and EPA, found in fish and fish oil, also help lower high levels of blood triglycerides and reduce the stickiness of platelets, the cells that form blood clots in arteries. They also may increase the flexibility of red blood cells, enabling them to pass more readily through tiny blood vessels. Many studies have found that populations that consume fish a few times each week have lower rates of heart disease than those that rarely or never eat fish.

To increase your intake of DHA and EPA, eat fish two times per week. Choose oilier fish such as salmon, trout, Arctic char, sardines, herring, mackerel and sea bass.

Consuming foods rich in alpha-linolenic acid (ALA) is an alternative way to ensure that you're consuming omega-3 fatty acids. ALA is an omega-3 fatty acid plentiful in flax, canola and walnut oils as well as soybeans. While the evidence for ALA's cardio-protective properties isn't nearly as abundant or compelling as it is for DHA and EPA, numerous studies do suggest this omega-3 fat may offer some protection. A large study of healthy women revealed that after 18 years of follow-up, a greater ALA intake was linked with significant protection from sudden cardiac death. Women who consumed 1.16 grams of ALA per day were 40 percent less likely to suddenly die of cardiac arrest than women whose diets provided only 0.66 grams per day. In this study, a greater intake of ALA didn't reduce the risk of non-fatal heart attacks.[4]

Women require 1.1 grams (1100 milligrams) of ALA per day and men need 1.6 grams (1600 milligrams). The richest sources of ALA are flaxseed, walnut and canola oil as well as ground flaxseed and salba. For instance, 1 teaspoon (5 ml) of flaxseed oil contains 2400 milligrams of ALA as does 2 tablespoons (30 ml) of ground flaxseed or ground salba. ALA is also found to a lesser extent in soybean oil, tofu and food products fortified with flaxseed oil such as yogurt and juice. Flaxseed oil capsules sold in drugstores and health food stores supply 500 milligrams of ALA per capsule.

Monounsaturated Fat

These fats, which are liquid at room temperature but become semi-solid when stored in the fridge, are abundant in olive, canola and peanut oils as well as in avocados and almonds. Many studies have demonstrated that replacing saturated and trans fats with monounsaturated fats helps to lower the risk of heart disease. Higher intakes of monounsaturated fat are linked with lower death rates from heart disease. Research suggests that extra-virgin olive oil helps prevent blood clots from forming and has anti-inflammatory properties in the body. (Extra-virgin olive oil is extracted from olives using minimal heat and no chemicals, resulting in a higher concentration of protective plant compounds.) As a general guideline, one-third to two-thirds of your daily fat (10 percent to 20 percent of calories) should come from monounsaturated fats.

Dietary Cholesterol

This wax-like fatty substance is found in meat, poultry, eggs, dairy products, fish and seafood. It's particularly plentiful in shrimp, liver and egg yolks. While there's compelling evidence that high cholesterol intakes can cause hardening of the arteries in rabbits, pigs and mice, there's little evidence that this is so in humans. For most people, only a small amount of cholesterol in food passes into the bloodstream. A number of short-term studies have demonstrated that feeding healthy people as many as three whole eggs per day doesn't raise LDL cholesterol. In fact, some research has even found that an egg-rich diet increases HDL cholesterol. What's more, so far, 30 years of research have not turned up a connection

between eating eggs and heart disease risk. Studies have determined that healthy people who eat one egg per day don't have an increased risk of coronary heart disease or stroke.[5-9]

Too much dietary cholesterol can raise levels of LDL cholesterol in some people, especially those with hereditary forms of high cholesterol. There's also evidence that people with diabetes are more efficient at absorbing cholesterol from foods, which may increase their risk of heart disease. Health Canada recommends that we consume no more than 300 milligrams of cholesterol each day. If you have high blood cholesterol, it's wise to limit your daily intake to 200 milligrams. Choosing animal foods that are lower in saturated fat also helps to cut down on dietary cholesterol. A list of selected foods and their cholesterol content can be found in Chapter 3, page 29.

Legumes and Soy Foods

Numerous studies have demonstrated the cardio-protective properties of legumes and foods made from soybeans. A regular intake of these foods has been shown to help lower LDL cholesterol and elevated blood pressure as well as guard against type 2 diabetes. Researchers attribute the cardio-protective properties of legumes to their vegetarian protein, B vitamin, potassium, calcium, magnesium, potassium and phytochemical content. Rather than just one nutrient, it's the unique package of nutrients and phytochemicals in legumes and soy that works synergistically to reduce the risk of heart disease.

To increase your intake of legumes and soy, include at least 3 servings in your diet each week. One serving is equivalent to 3/4 cup (175 ml) of cooked legumes or tofu or 1 soy-based veggie burger. See Chapter 5, page 94, for tips on adding these foods to your diet.

Nuts

There's compelling evidence that eating nuts on a regular basis can lower your risk of developing heart disease and dying from it. To date, four large studies involving 172,000 men and women have found that those who eat nuts at least four times per week are almost 40 percent less likely to succumb to heart disease than those who eat nuts less than once per week.[10–13] Nuts—all types—can help control certain risk factors for heart attack such as high cholesterol and high blood pressure. A regular intake of nuts has also been found to reduce the risk of developing type 2 diabetes, a strong risk factor for heart disease.

Nuts are rich sources of unsaturated fat, vitamin E, folate, B vitamins, magnesium, potassium and fibre, nutrients demonstrated to have cardio-protective properties. Add 1/4 cup (60 ml) of plain, unsalted nuts to your diet five times a week.

Whole Grains

In general, studies have revealed that people with the highest intake of whole grains (about 3 servings per day) have a risk of heart disease or stroke that is 20 percent to 40 percent lower than those whose diets contained little or no whole-grain foods. Some research even hints that a steady intake of whole grains may delay the progression of heart disease by slowing the buildup of plaque in the arteries.

Whole grains such as 100% whole-grain breads and cereals, whole rye, oats, brown rice, quinoa and millet have many protective ingredients that might help lower the risk of heart disease. Whole grains are important sources of fibre, vitamin E, magnesium, zinc, selenium, copper, iron, manganese and phytochemicals. Many of these natural compounds have antioxidant properties and may offer protection from heart disease by keeping LDL cholesterol levels in check, maintaining the health of blood vessels and reducing the risk of type 2 diabetes.

Include at least 3 servings of whole grains in your daily diet. One serving is equivalent to 1 slice of bread, 1/2 cup (125 ml) of cooked oatmeal, 1 ounce (30 g) of cold cereal or 1/2 cup (125 ml) of cooked brown rice or whole-wheat pasta. A list of whole grains can be found in Chapter 5, page 91.

Soluble Fibre

Plant foods contain a mix of two types of fibre, soluble and insoluble, but will have more of one than the other. Soluble fibre, which dissolves in water, has been shown to lower high LDL blood-cholesterol levels. Numerous studies have demonstrated the ability of foods rich in soluble fibre, such as legumes, oats and oat bran, and psyllium, to lower elevated LDL blood cholesterol in adults and children. Most of the research suggests that including a good source of soluble fibre in your daily diet can lower LDL cholesterol by 9 percent. A combined analysis of eight clinical trials involving people with high blood cholesterol concluded that, in conjunction with a low-fat diet, consuming 10.2 grams of psyllium per day lowered total cholesterol by 4 percent and LDL cholesterol by 7 percent.[14–16]

When soluble fibre reaches the intestine, it attaches to bile, causing it to be excreted in the stool. Bile is a digestive aid that's released into the intestine after you eat. The liver makes bile from cholesterol and sends it to your gallbladder to be stored until it's needed. Since soluble fibre causes your body to excrete bile, your liver has to make more of it from cholesterol in the bloodstream. The end result is a lower blood-cholesterol level. When unabsorbed fibre reaches your colon, bacteria degrade it and form compounds called short chain fatty acids. These fatty acids may also hamper the liver's ability to produce cholesterol.

To lower elevated LDL cholesterol, consume at least 3 grams of soluble fibre each day. You'll find this amount in the following foods:

Sources of Soluble Fibre

Food	Total Fibre (grams)	Soluble Fibre (grams)
Barley, cooked, 1-1/2 cups (375 ml)	12	3
Flaxseed, ground, 1/4 cup (60 ml)	8	2.6
All-Bran Buds w/psyllium, Kellogg's, 1/3 cup (75 ml)	12	3
Guardian cereal, Kellogg's, 1 cup (250 ml)	6	4
SmartBran cereal, Nature's Path, 2/3 cup (150 ml)	13	3
Oatmeal, cooked, 1-1/2 cups (375 ml)	6	3
Oatmeal, instant, unflavoured, 3 packs	8.4	3
Oat bran, cooked, 1 cup (250 ml)	6	3
Baked beans, cooked, 1/2 cup (125 ml)	6	3
Black beans, cooked 3/4 cup (175 ml)	8.2	3
Kidney beans, cooked, 1/2 cup (125 ml)	6	3
Lentils, cooked, 1-1/2 cups (375 ml)	24	3

Tea

Many studies have shown clear evidence that drinking at least 3 cups (750 ml) of tea per day reduces the risk of developing coronary heart disease. In combined analysis of seventeen studies, the researchers found that a 3 cup (750 ml) increase in daily tea consumption was associated with an 11 percent lower risk of heart attack. A 7-year study of U.S. women found the risk of heart attack and stroke and of death from heart disease was significantly lower in women who drank at least 4 cups (1000 ml) of black tea per day. In a study of 4807 Dutch men and women aged 55 and older, those who drank more than 1-1/2 cups (375 ml) of black tea per day were 43 percent less likely to suffer a heart attack than non-tea drinkers. Drinking black tea on a regular basis might also safeguard people with existing heart disease.[17-20]

Tea leaves contain antioxidants called catechins. Studies in the lab have demonstrated the ability of catechins in tea to reduce blood clotting, shield LDL cholesterol from oxidation, reduce inflammation and improve blood vessel function. Catechins are found in green tea, black tea and oolong tea, but not herbal teas. To incorporate tea into your diet, replace coffee and soft drinks with your favourite type of tea, be it green or black. Tea brewed from loose leaves will have a higher concentration of antioxidants than that brewed from tea bags.

Alcoholic Beverages

Moderate alcohol consumption—one to two drinks per day—is linked with 20 percent to 30 percent reductions in heart disease risk. Alcohol is thought to protect against heart disease by increasing the level of HDL (good) cholesterol in the bloodstream and by reducing the ability of blood cells called platelets to clump together and form clots. However, alcohol's protective effects are limited to middle-aged and older adults. Alcohol's protective effects are attributed to all types of alcoholic beverages, including wine, beer and spirits.

The Heart and Stroke Foundation of Canada doesn't recommend that you drink alcohol for the purpose of reducing your risk for heart attack and stroke. Drinking more than two drinks per day boosts blood pressure and increases the long-term risk of developing hypertension. Drinking alcoholic beverages can also increase blood triglycerides. Even just one drink a day can increase these blood fats in susceptible people. If you have elevated triglycerides, limiting or avoiding alcohol is strongly advised. A moderate alcohol intake also increases the risk for several cancers, including breast and colon cancers.

If you drink alcohol, limit yourself to one drink per day for women and two for men. Avoid binge drinking, which can elevate blood pressure. (For elderly people, two drinks per day may be too much to be considered a low-risk intake.)

Vitamins and Minerals

B Vitamins

The theory that these nutrients help ward off heart disease and heart attack stems from the fact that three B vitamins in particular—folic acid, B6 and B12—lower homocysteine levels in the blood. Homocysteine is an amino acid made by the body during normal metabolism. A high homocysteine level in the blood is considered by many experts to be a risk factor for heart disease and stroke. Many studies have suggested that excess homocysteine in the bloodstream increases the likelihood of developing heart disease by damaging the lining of the arteries. Studies in the lab have demonstrated the ability of homocysteine to cause oxidative stress, inflammation, blood clotting and blood vessel dysfunction.

Folic acid and vitamins B6 and B12 help break down homocysteine in the body so it doesn't accumulate. Even marginal deficiencies of these nutrients—the result of poor dietary intake or the inability of the body to absorb the vitamins—can lead to a high homocysteine level. Numerous studies have clearly shown that taking a supplement of folic acid, alone or in combination with vitamins B6 and B12, lowers homocysteine levels. Studies have used daily doses of folic acid ranging from 0.5 to 5 milligrams, although 0.8 to 1 milligram appears to provide maximal homocysteine lowering. (The recommended daily intake of folate for men and women is 0.4 milligram. Folate is often used to describe folic acid. Folate refers to the B vitamin found naturally in foods; folic acid is the synthetic version added to vitamin pills and fortified foods.)

Although consuming adequate amounts of these B vitamins can help keep blood homocysteine in the normal range, large randomized controlled trials have failed to show that taking a B vitamin supplement actually prevents heart attack. It's unclear why the B vitamin homocysteine-lowering trials conducted to date have not demonstrated any benefit. One possibility is that since the introduction of mandatory folic acid food fortification in 1998, B vitamin supplements have a lesser effect on homocysteine levels than expected. It's also possible that B vitamins simply have no effect on your risk of heart disease. Keep in mind that all trials have been conducted in high-risk individuals—people with documented heart disease or kidney disease. The effect of long-term folic acid supplementation on the risk of heart disease in healthy people is unknown.

The Heart and Stroke Foundation of Canada doesn't feel there's enough evidence to recommend an amount of folic acid, B6 or B12 for the prevention of heart disease. It's important, however, that you increase your intake of B vitamins from food sources to help meet your daily-recommended intakes.

The best food sources of folate include cooked spinach, lentils, orange juice, asparagus, artichokes and whole-grain breads and cereals. Foods rich in vitamin B6 include meat, poultry, fish, liver, legumes, nuts, seeds, whole grains, green leafy vegetables, bananas and avocados. Vitamin B12 is found in animal foods such as meat, poultry, fish, eggs and dairy products, and also in fortified soy and rice beverages.

If you have difficulty eating a varied diet, take a multivitamin and mineral supplement to ensure that you're meeting your B vitamin requirements (see Chapter 4, page 35).

Vitamin C

Many studies have reported a link between high dietary intakes and high blood levels of vitamin C and a lower risk of heart disease. American researchers observed that rates of heart disease were 27 percent lower in the men and women with the highest vitamin C levels compared with those with the lowest.[21] The level of vitamin C in your bloodstream is a good indicator of the amount of vitamin C in your diet. A Portuguese study conducted among 194 adults determined that, compared with those individuals with marginal vitamin C intakes, those who consumed the most vitamin C had an 80 percent lower risk of heart attack.[22] Vitamin C supplements have not been shown to reduce the risk of heart disease.

Dietary vitamin C may protect from heart disease by acting as an antioxidant; it neutralizes harmful free radical molecules that damage your LDL cholesterol. Studies also suggest vitamin C may inhibit the formation of blood clots by reducing the stickiness of platelets.

Include two vitamin C–rich foods in your daily diet. The best sources of vitamin C include citrus fruit, citrus juices, cantaloupe, kiwi, mango, strawberries, broccoli, Brussels sprouts, cauliflower, red pepper and tomato juice. See Chapter 4, page 48, to learn about your daily vitamin C requirements.

Vitamin D

There's growing evidence that vitamin D guards against heart disease. In most populations studied, death rates from cardiovascular disease rise at higher latitudes (e.g., Canada and the northern United States), increase during the winter months and are lower at high altitudes. This pattern fits with the observation that vitamin D deficiency is more common at higher latitudes, during long, dark winters and at lower altitudes. (Our main source of vitamin D comes from sunshine. Vitamin D is synthesized in the skin when it's exposed to the sun's UVB rays for short periods of time.) While vitamin D is found in foods such as fortified milk, oily fish and egg yolks, the amount we consume from diet is considered insufficient to maintain good health.

Recent studies have revealed that people who are deficient in vitamin D have a higher risk of heart attack and coronary heart disease. In a study of 18,255 healthy men aged 40 to 75 years who were followed for 10 years, men who were vitamin D deficient were twice as likely to suffer a heart attack as those with sufficient vitamin D levels, even after controlling for other risk factors such as blood cholesterol, body weight and family history of heart disease. Even men with intermediate blood–vitamin D levels were at increased risk of a heart attack.[23]

Vitamin D helps maintain normal immune function and reduces inflammation in the body. It also assists in keeping heart cells healthy and maintaining normal blood pressure. Studies have linked low blood–vitamin D levels to greater inflammation, impaired fasting glucose, metabolic syndrome and hypertension—all risk factors for heart disease.

At this time, there is no evidence that taking a daily vitamin D pill will lower the odds of developing heart disease. We'll have to wait for the results of randomized controlled trials to give us this answer. In the meantime, there are other reasons that you should be taking a daily vitamin D supplement. First, foods don't supply much vitamin D to aid in maintaining adequate blood levels of the nutrient. Second, Canadians don't produce enough vitamin D from sunlight from October through March. Third, there's now strong evidence that vitamin D helps reduce the risk of certain cancers, which prompted the Canadian Cancer Society to recommend in 2007 that adults consider taking 1000 international units (IU) of vitamin D each day in the fall and winter. Older adults, people with dark skin, those who don't go outdoors often and those who wear clothing that covers most of their skin should take the supplement year-round.

To determine the dose of vitamin D you need to buy, add up how much you're already getting from your multivitamin and calcium supplements, subtract that from your RDA and make up the difference. Choose a vitamin D supplement than contains vitamin D3 instead of vitamin D2, which is less potent. Vitamin D is typically sold in 400 IU and 1000 IU doses, which can make it difficult to hit the 1000 IU dose on the nose. See Chapter 4, page 51, for more on vitamin D supplements.

Vitamin E

Studies conducted in the 1990s hinted that taking a vitamin E supplement can help lower the odds of developing heart disease. More recently the Women's Health Study, a long-term randomized trial, investigated the effect of a 600 international unit (IU) vitamin E supplement, taken every other day, on the prevention of heart disease in almost 40,000 healthy American women aged 45 or older. Overall, vitamin E had no effect on dying from any cause. But among women 65 and older, those taking vitamin E were 26 percent less likely to have a heart attack or die from heart disease than women not taking the vitamin supplement.[24]

There's little evidence, however, that vitamin E is effective in preventing heart attacks in people with existing heart disease. Two large trials conducted in individuals with a previous heart attack or stroke or evidence of heart disease found that a daily vitamin E supplement didn't change the risk of a subsequent heart attack or stroke.[25,26]

Some trials have found that high-dose vitamin E supplements may actually cause health problems in people with existing heart disease or diabetes.[27,28] It's possible that high doses of vitamin E might actually cause oxidative stress instead of reducing it. Excess vitamin E might also displace other fat-soluble nutrients, disrupting the body's natural balance of antioxidants. Some researchers believe that other forms of vitamin E, such as gamma-tocopherol found in walnuts, nuts, pecans and sesame oil, may be more important for cancer prevention than alpha-tocopherol (the main type of vitamin E found in supplements).

To meet your daily vitamin E requirements, add vitamin E–rich foods such as vegetable oils, avocado, nuts, seeds, wheat germ, whole grains and leafy greens to your daily diet. If you have existing cardiovascular disease or diabetes, avoid high dose vitamin E supplements. If you do take a supplement, take no more than 100 IU per day.

Magnesium

Among its many important roles, magnesium keeps your heart rhythm steady, maintains normal blood pressure and helps regulate blood sugar—all of which influence your heart health. Studies have revealed that higher magnesium intakes and higher body stores of the mineral are linked with protection from type 2 diabetes and heart disease. Consuming more magnesium may improve the prognosis of heart disease by helping to maintain the normal functioning of blood vessels during exercise by allowing vessels to dilate, or relax.[29-34]

Many Canadians don't consume the recommended amount of magnesium (see Chapter 4, page 60). Although symptoms of magnesium deficiency are rarely seen in Canada, many experts have expressed concern about the prevalence of marginal, or suboptimal, magnesium stores in the body. The best way to increase your intake of magnesium and to maintain normal body stores is to boost your intake of magnesium-rich foods, including whole grains, nuts, legumes, leafy green vegetables and dried fruit.

If a blood test indicates you have very low magnesium stores, increasing your intake of heart healthy foods may not be enough to restore normal magnesium levels. In this case, a daily magnesium supplement will be necessary. Older adults are at risk for magnesium deficiency because they tend to consume less of the mineral in their diets than younger adults and, as well, magnesium absorption decreases with age. If you feel your magnesium

intake is below par despite your best efforts to eat more heart healthy foods, consider taking a magnesium supplement. Take 200 to 250 milligrams of magnesium citrate once daily. Magnesium supplements can cause diarrhea and abdominal cramping if taken in high doses. Do not exceed the safe upper limit of 350 milligrams of supplemental magnesium per day.

And keep in mind, when it comes to promoting healthy blood pressure, studies show that magnesium-rich foods do the trick, not supplements. What's more, magnesium-rich foods also supply other nutrients and antioxidants linked to heart health.

Herbal Remedies

Garlic (*Allium sativum*)

Interest in garlic's potential to guard against heart disease began when researchers noticed that people living near the Mediterranean—where garlic is a common ingredient in meals—had lower rates of death from cardiovascular disease. Since then, many studies have investigated garlic's effect on such risk factors for heart disease as blood cholesterol, blood pressure and blood clot formation. Some, but not all, trials suggest that garlic supplements modestly lower total cholesterol, LDL (bad) cholesterol and blood triglycerides over the short term (1 to 3 months). However, similar cholesterol-lowering effects have not been found in studies lasting six months.

The heart disease–fighting property of garlic is attributed to a variety of powerful sulphur-containing chemicals, in particular allicin and allyl sulphides. Many of these sulphur compounds are responsible for garlic's distinctive smell. In addition to sulphur compounds, fresh and cooked garlic also add vitamin C, B6, manganese and selenium to your diet.

Many studies show garlic and garlic supplements can significantly impede the ability of platelets in the blood to clump together (aggregate). Platelet aggregation is one of the first steps in the formation of blood clots, which can lead to a heart attack or stroke. A few studies also suggest that garlic might help lower blood pressure. Furthermore, in test tube studies, garlic's sulphur compounds have been shown to have antioxidant powers and reduce the oxidation of LDL cholesterol. In addition, garlic may help reduce inflammation, a process thought to play an important role in the development of heart disease.

If you have high blood cholesterol, a garlic supplement might help—at least in the short term. Several types of garlic supplements are available, each providing differing amounts and types of sulphur compounds, depending on how they are manufactured.

Supplements of powdered or dehydrated garlic are made from garlic cloves that are sliced and dried at a low temperature to preserve an enzyme that triggers the production of allicin, which in turn stimulates the production of other active sulphur compounds. The most commonly used doses range from 600 to 900 milligrams per day.

Supplements of aged garlic extract are made by aging garlic cloves for up to 20 months in a water and ethanol solution. This aging process reduces the content of allicin and sulphur compounds that cause garlic's strong odour. Aged garlic extract is usually standardized to contain a guaranteed amount of S-allyl-L-cysteine, a powerful sulphur compound believed to lower LDL cholesterol and inhibit blood clotting. Doses typically used in studies range from 2.4 to 7.2 grams per day.

When it comes to *fresh garlic*, 4 grams (roughly one clove) per day have been used in cholesterol-lowering studies.

Consuming high amounts of garlic—from supplements or raw—can have side effects, the most common including breath and body odour. More uncomfortable and potentially serious adverse effects include irritation of the digestive tract, heartburn, flatulence, nausea, vomiting and diarrhea. As well, a high dose of garlic may increase the risk of bleeding. If you're planning to have surgery, avoid using fresh garlic and garlic supplements for the 7 days prior to the procedure. There's also potential for garlic to enhance the blood-thinning effects of some prescription drugs (e.g., warfarin (Coumadin) and of other supplements (e.g., fish oil, vitamin E, *Ginkgo biloba*). Be sure to inform your health care provider if you're taking a garlic supplement, especially if you're taking an anticoagulant medication.

Other Natural Health Products
Coenzyme Q10 (CoQ10)
Coenzyme Q10 (CoQ10) is a fat-soluble, vitamin-like substance made by every cell in the body and stored in cell membranes. Highest concentrations are in heart, liver, kidney and pancreas cells, but CoQ10 is also found in lipoproteins that transport cholesterol and fat in the bloodstream.

CoQ10's role in producing energy in cells and its antioxidant powers have led researchers to study its effectiveness in preventing and treating heart disease. Studies conducted in test tubes have demonstrated the ability of CoQ10 to inhibit the oxidation of LDL cholesterol. It's also thought that CoQ10 works with vitamin E in the fight against oxidation.

Research hints that CoQ10 supplements may help improve heart health in people with heart disease. Studies have examined the effect of CoQ10 in addition to conventional medical therapy in patients with chronic stable angina (chest pain) and have found that the supplement (60 to 600 milligrams per day) improved exercise tolerance during an exercise stress test and reduced or delayed electrocardiographic changes associated with angina.[35] Several small studies also suggest that taking a CoQ10 supplement could be beneficial in treating hypertension. Some, but not all, research suggests that a daily 200 milligram CoQ10 supplement can improve the functioning of the inner lining of blood vessels (the endothelium) in patients who have both diabetes and high blood cholesterol.[36-38]

A number of studies have shown that statins decrease blood levels of CoQ10. There's also preliminary research that supports a role for CoQ10 in decreasing muscle pain caused by statins. Despite the fact that more research is needed to confirm if CoQ10 supplements might be beneficial for those taking cholesterol-lowering statins, many people take the supplement as a safeguard. Supplements might also offset the natural decline of CoQ10 in the body due to aging.

There is no consensus on how much CoQ10 is beneficial for heart health. In clinical studies that have reported beneficial effects among participants, the following amounts of CoQ10 were used:

- for angina, a dose of 50 milligrams three times per day
- for reducing the risk of future heart problems in patients who suffered a recent heart attack, a dose of 60 milligrams twice daily
- to prevent statin-induced muscle pain, 100 to 200 milligrams per day
- for treating high blood pressure, 120 to 200 milligrams per day in divided doses (e.g., 60 milligrams twice per day)

There have been no reports of adverse effects from taking CoQ10 supplements. However, there have been reports that concurrent use of warfarin (Coumadin) and CoQ10 reduced the blood-thinning effect of warfarin. If you take warfarin, don't take CoQ10 supplements without first consulting your doctor.

Fish Oil Supplements
If you don't eat fatty fish twice per week, consider taking a fish oil capsule to get your DHA and EPA. Experts advise a daily intake of at least 500 milligrams of DHA and EPA combined to help prevent heart disease. The American Heart Association recommends that people who have coronary heart disease consume 1000 milligrams of DHA + EPA combined each day, an amount that requires taking a daily supplement.

Randomized controlled trials have found fish oil reduces the risk of heart attack, stroke, sudden cardiac death and dying from all causes. Findings from studies conducted in people without documented heart disease also suggest that fish oil supplements benefit the heart. One study conducted in overweight men who had high blood pressure and high cholesterol or elevated triglycerides found that a daily fish oil supplement and regular exercise resulted in lower triglycerides, higher levels of HDL cholesterol and a loss of body fat.[39,40] In addition, it's well documented that taking fish oil lowers elevated triglycerides by 20 percent to 50 percent.

Fish oil supplements are made from salmon, anchovies, sardines, herring and mackerel, species of fish rich in omega-3 fatty acids. Most fish oil capsules (1 gram each) provide 300, 500 or 600 milligrams of DHA + EPA combined (check the label to be sure).

For triglyceride lowering, studies have used 1 to 4 grams (1 to 4 capsules) per day. Because fish oil thins the blood, taking high doses may increase the risk of bleeding in people taking prescription anticoagulants such as heparin or warfarin (Coumadin). If you take such a medication, check with your doctor before taking a fish oil supplement.

Red Yeast Rice

Red yeast rice is made by fermenting rice with a red yeast called *Monascus purpureus*. In China, it has been used for centuries as a food preservative, food colouring, spice and ingredient in rice wine. Today, red yeast rice is sold as a natural health product to lower LDL blood cholesterol and triglycerides. Studies lasting 8 to 12 weeks have demonstrated that taking red yeast rice significantly lowers total and LDL cholesterol levels.[41,42] Some research suggests that red yeast rice might be as effective as the statin drug simvastatin (Zocor) in improving lipid profiles.

Red yeast rice contains compounds called mevinic acids, which, like statin drugs, inhibit the action of HMG-CoA reductase, the enzyme that synthesizes cholesterol in the liver.

The dose used most commonly is 1.2 grams taken twice daily, but a dose of only 1.2 grams per day may also provide some benefit. Most studies used a specific red yeast rice product called Cholestin manufactured by Pharmanex.

Taking red yeast rice supplements can cause abdominal discomfort, heartburn and flatulence. Since it contains HMG-CoA reductase inhibitors similar to "statin" drugs, red yeast rice is likely to cause similar side effects, including elevated liver enzymes and muscle damage. If you decide to take red yeast rice to lower your LDL cholesterol, be sure to inform your physician so he or she can monitor your liver function through blood tests.

Nutrition Strategy Checklist for Heart Disease and High Blood Cholesterol

☐ Low saturated and trans fat
☐ Fish
☐ Legumes and soy
☐ Nuts
☐ Whole grains
☐ Soluble fibre
☐ Tea
☐ B vitamins
☐ Vitamin C
☐ Vitamin D
☐ Vitamin E
☐ Magnesium
☐ Garlic
☐ Coenzyme Q10
☐ Fish oil supplement
☐ Red yeast rice

Recommended Resources

Heart and Stroke Foundation of Canada
www.heartandstroke.ca
222 Queen Street, Suite 1402
Ottawa, ON K1P 5V9
Tel: 613-569-4361
Fax: 613-569-3278

American Heart Association
www.americanheart.org
7272 Greenville Avenue
Dallas, TX, USA 75231
Tel: 1-800-AHA-USA1

National Heart, Lung, and Blood Institute Information Center
www.nhlbi.nih.gov

P.O. Box 30105
Bethesda, MD, USA 20824-0105
Tel: 301-592-8573 (publications) or
    1-800-575-9355 (blood pressure and
    cholesterol information)
Fax: 301-592-8563

Hemorrhoids

Hemorrhoids, or piles, are large, swollen and inflamed veins that develop in the anus and lower rectum. Very similar to varicose veins in the legs, hemorrhoids occur when the blood vessels in the anal area swell and stretch under pressure. At some time in their lives, more than half of North Americans have experienced the itching, burning and pain associated with hemorrhoids.

Although not dangerous or life threatening, hemorrhoids can be persistent, annoying and sometimes quite painful. There are two types of hemorrhoids.

INTERNAL HEMORRHOIDS develop in the upper area of the anal canal. They cannot be seen and, normally, cause little discomfort. Sometimes you may detect an internal hemorrhoid by the sensation of fullness that you feel in your rectum after a bowel movement.

If you strain too much during a bowel movement, you can inadvertently push an internal hemorrhoid out through the anal opening. This is known as a protruding hemorrhoid. Once the delicate tissue of the blood vessel is exposed in this way, it can become very irritated and painful and can bleed easily. While protruding hemorrhoids will usually return to their internal position without any help, it may be necessary to gently push them back into the anal canal after a bowel movement.

EXTERNAL HEMORRHOIDS are swollen, skin-covered blood vessels, occurring outside the anus, which can be itchy, painful and tender. When blood pools in these veins, a blood clot may form, producing a hard, inflamed lump around the anus.

What Causes Hemorrhoids?

Human beings are particularly prone to hemorrhoids because our erect posture puts extra pressure on the tissues surrounding the anus and rectum. Conditions such as pregnancy or obesity increase this pressure and are frequent causes of hemorrhoids. Hemorrhoids can also develop as a result of straining during a bowel movement, straining during childbirth, lifting heavy objects and sitting or standing in one position for a long time. Some people are genetically predisposed to hemorrhoids, due to an inherited weakness in the walls of the anal blood vessels.

Symptoms

An internal hemorrhoid may be felt protruding out of the anus after a bowel movement, whereas an external hemorrhoid may be felt as a hard lump near the anus. Other signs of hemorrhoids include:

- itching and burning in the anal area
- pain or discomfort around the anus and rectum
- rectal bleeding

Rectal bleeding may be noticed as blood on the toilet paper, blood in the toilet bowl, streaks of blood on your stool or spots of blood on your underwear. It may also be a sign of other, more serious medical conditions such as diverticular disease, colon or rectal polyps, colitis, bowel cancer or an anal fissure. Don't ignore rectal bleeding, even if you're convinced that it's a symptom of hemorrhoids. When you detect any sign of bleeding from your rectum, consult your doctor.

Who's at Risk?

Hemorrhoids are rare before the age of 30 and become more frequent after the age of 50. People prone to constipation often have hemorrhoids. Pregnant women are also susceptible to developing this condition. Poor bowel habits, such as withholding stool or reading while on the toilet, are contributing factors to hemorrhoids.

Conventional Treatment

Hemorrhoids require very little treatment and will usually go away on their own within a few days. The following may help relieve the discomfort of hemorrhoids:

- cold compresses applied to the affected area
- avoidance of prolonged standing or sitting
- witch hazel or other soothing lotions applied directly to reduce itching
- over-the-counter preparations to relieve itching
- warm sitz baths taken two or three times daily
- acetaminophen to relieve pain (avoid codeine as it causes constipation)
- stool softeners or psyllium to relieve constipation

Hemorrhoids may be destroyed by:

- **Tying off.** Tiny rubber bands are tied around the base of the hemorrhoid to cut off circu-

lation; within 10 days, the hemorrhoid withers and falls off.
- **Laser therapy.** A laser beam vaporizes the affected tissue.
- **Injection sclerotherapy.** A shrinking agent is injected to stop bleeding.
- **Infrared photocoagulation.** A burst of infrared light is used to cut off circulation to an internal hemorrhoid.
- **Cryosurgery.** The affected tissue is frozen to cut off circulation.
- **Electric current.** A burst of electric current is used to shrink a hemorrhoid.

Preventing and Managing Hemorrhoids
Dietary Strategies

Maintaining a healthy weight is important in the prevention and management of hemorrhoids. Excess weight can add to the pressure on your anal veins. Preventing constipation is also key.

Dietary Fibre
A high-fibre diet is considered the first line of therapy in the management of hemorrhoids. A high-fibre diet—along with adequate fluids—is necessary to produce soft, well-formed and regular bowel movements. In fact, a review of seven trials involving 378 patients found a consistent beneficial effect of fibre for treating the symptoms of hemorrhoids.[1] Constipation causes straining, which promotes the development of hemorrhoids. To treat and prevent constipation, gradually increase your daily fibre intake to 21 to 38 grams.

Foods contain varying amounts of insoluble fibres and soluble fibres. Foods that have a greater proportion of insoluble fibres, such as wheat bran, whole grains, nuts, seeds and certain fruit and vegetables, are used to treat and prevent constipation. Insoluble fibres absorb water and thus help form larger, softer stools and speed evacuation. Psyllium, a type of soluble fibre, also adds bulk to stools and may be effective in preventing and treating constipation in some people.

Studies have shown that adding 10 grams of fibre to the diet helps reduce bleeding from internal hemorrhoids and speeds the removal of stool from the intestinal tract.[2,3] Use the following guide to add bulk-forming fibre to your diet:

Fibre Content of Selected Foods

Food	Fibre (grams)
100% bran cereal, 1/2 cup (125 ml)	12.0 g
All-Bran Buds (with psyllium), Kellogg's, 1/3 cup (75 ml)	12.0 g
Natural wheat bran, 2 tbsp (30 ml)	2.4 g
Flaxseed, ground, 2 tbsp (30 ml)	4.5 g
Almonds, 1/4 cup (60 ml)	4.8 g

Choose higher-fibre fruit and vegetables. You'll find a list of fibre-rich fruit and vegetables under Constipation, page 320. Increase your fibre intake gradually to prevent intestinal discomfort, and spread your fibre intake over the course of the day rather than consuming it all at once.

Bulk-forming fibre supplements may be used to promote regularity. Psyllium-husk powder and Metamucil may be purchased at health food stores and pharmacies.

Dietary fibre needs to absorb fluid in the intestinal tract in order to add bulk to stool. Drink 9 to 13 cups (2.2 to 3.2 L) of fluid every day. Always include 1 cup (250 ml) of fluid with high-fibre meals and snacks.

Hot Chili

If you require surgery to treat hemorrhoids, avoid consuming chili powder and red chili flakes for at least 1 week after surgery. Two studies have found that consuming hot chili powder twice daily significantly increased post-operative pain, burning, bowel frequency and the use of pain medication.[4,5]

Probiotics

Foods and supplements called probiotics contain friendly lactic acid bacteria (e.g., *Lactobacillus*, *Bifidobacterium*) and can help promote regularity. These bacteria normally reside in the intestinal tract, performing a number of tasks that keep the bowel healthy. Probiotics must be consumed regularly to have a health benefit.

Include 1 cup (250 ml) of fermented dairy product in your daily diet: yogurt, kefir or acidophilus milk. All yogurts in Canada are made with lactic acid bacteria, whether or not they are labelled as such; however, some brands have additional probiotic strains that increase the number of live bacteria per serving (examples include Astro BioBest and Danone Activia yogurts). To supplement, take 1 billion to 10 billion live cells (per capsule) with one to three meals daily. See Chapter 8, page 180, for information about probiotic supplements.

Herbal Remedies

Horse Chestnut (*Aesculus hippocastanum*)

Studies have found horse chestnut effective in treating varicose veins in the legs; it may be useful for hemorrhoids as well. This herb contains active compounds called saponins that enhance circulation through the veins. Studies have demonstrated horse chestnut's ability to constrict and promote normal tone in veins so that blood returns to the heart.

Buy a product standardized to 16 percent to 21 percent aescin. Take one capsule up to three times per day. In rare instances, horse chestnut seed extract can cause stomach upset, nausea and itching. Its use is not recommended during pregnancy and breastfeeding as insufficient information is available about its safety. People with liver or kidney disease should not take horse chestnut.

Other Natural Health Products

Citrus Bioflavonoids

These compounds are found in the inner peel of citrus fruit; when consumed, they help strengthen blood capillaries. A number of studies have shown that a special formulation of two bioflavonoids, diosmin and hesperidin, is effective in reducing the duration and severity of hemorrhoid episodes.[6-11] Another citrus bioflavonoid called oxerutins may also be useful.

Bioflavonoids are very safe and may have a range of other health benefits. The typical dose is 500 milligrams twice daily. Oxerutins have been used in doses of 500 to 1000 milligrams up to three times daily.

Grapeseed Extract

This supplement is rich in flavonoids called anthocyanins, natural compounds that help keep blood vessels healthy. Grapeseed extract is thought to work by inhibiting the action of enzymes that break down connective tissue. Another anthocyanin-rich supplement is Pycnogenol, the U.S. registered trademark for an extract made from the bark of pine trees. This supplement has the same effect as grapeseed extract and can be used to prevent and/or treat the same conditions.

A number of studies have found a daily flavonoids supplement effective in the treatment of hemorrhoids. Patients taking flavonoids, compared with those taking placebos, have significantly less pain, itching, bleeding and hemorrhoid recurrence.[6-11] Anthocyanins may also help reduce blood clots.

Experts recommend taking 150 to 300 milligrams for 3 weeks, followed by a maintenance dose of 40 to 80 milligrams daily. Grapeseed extract is considered extremely safe. Pycnogenol is more expensive than grapeseed extract; the usual dose is 50 to 300 milligrams daily, taken in divided doses.

Nutrition Strategy Checklist for Hemorrhoids

☐ Weight control
☐ Dietary fibre
☐ Fluids
☐ Fermented milk products
☐ Probiotic supplements
☐ Horse chestnut
☐ Citrus bioflavonoids
☐ Grapeseed extract

Recommended Resources

Mayo Foundation for Medical Education and Research
www.mayoclinic.com
This website is produced by a team of writers, editors, health educators, nurses, doctors and scientists, and is one of the best patient-education sites on the Internet. The information is reliable, thorough and clearly written.

National Digestive Diseases Information Clearinghouse
National Institutes of Health
www2.niddk.nih.gov
2 Information Way
Bethesda, MD, USA 20892-3570
Tel: 301-654-3810

Hepatitis (see also Cirrhosis of the Liver)

Hepatitis is an infection or inflammation of the liver. Scientists have identified six hepatitis viruses, but three—known as A, B and C—cause about 90 percent of acute hepatitis cases in Canada. Hepatitis attacks the liver silently, with few, if any, obvious symptoms. Often, people don't even know they have been exposed to the disease until liver damage becomes apparent many years later. Because symptoms are so frequently overlooked, hepatitis can be easily and unknowingly transmitted to others.

The liver is the largest internal organ in the body, responsible for more than five hundred different functions. In addition to processing nutrients and manufacturing essential chemicals, the liver removes toxins from the blood and processes waste products. Inflammation caused by a hepatitis virus interferes with normal liver function and, in some cases, may lead to serious liver disease, cancer or liver failure. Hepatitis can be acute, which means that the virus lasts less than 6 months, or it can become a chronic, long-term condition. Hepatitis B and C are the viruses most likely to develop into chronic hepatitis.

The characteristics of viral hepatitis vary according to the differing viruses that cause the disease.

Hepatitis A

Hepatitis A is highly contagious and is usually transmitted from the stool of one person to the mouth of another; it's often associated with poor hygiene. Water-borne and food-borne epidemics of hepatitis A are common, especially in developing countries where sewage-polluted water and food are prevalent. The disease can also be transmitted by eating contaminated raw shellfish. Hepatitis A doesn't lead to chronic hepatitis.

Hepatitis B

Hepatitis B is transmitted by contact with blood or body fluids of someone who is infected. In Canada and the United States, measures are taken to ensure a safe blood supply, so transmission by blood transfusion is unlikely. The disease frequently spreads through sexual contact and the exchange of body fluids by heterosexual and homosexual partners, and may be transmitted by drug users sharing needles or by improperly sterilized implements used for tattoos, body piercing, ear piercing or acupuncture. Mothers can infect their infants, possibly through breast milk.

The hepatitis B virus is very tough; it will survive and remain infective for days on household items such as toothbrushes and razors.

Approximately 10 percent of people with hepatitis B continue to carry the virus in their blood and may infect others without realizing it.[1] As many as 60 percent to 90 percent of children and 10 percent of adults with hepatitis B go on to develop chronic hepatitis.[2]

Hepatitis C

In Canada, an estimated 242,500 individuals are infected with hepatitis C and, because there are often no symptoms, nearly 20 percent of those individuals remain undiagnosed and unaware.[3] Like hepatitis B, hepatitis C is primarily spread by contact with blood and blood products. Transmission through blood transfusion has been virtually eliminated in North America by routine blood screening for hepatitis C–virus antibodies. Transmission is most common through drug users sharing contaminated needles or through improperly sterilized implements used for tattooing, body or ear piercing, or acupuncture. However, unlike hepatitis B, hepatitis C is less likely to be spread through sexual contact. The disease is one of the main causes of chronic liver disease; the majority of acute cases develop into chronic hepatitis.

Symptoms

Acute viral hepatitis may cause no symptoms at all. Symptoms that do develop usually begin suddenly:

- flu-like feeling of illness
- nausea and vomiting, poor appetite
- low-grade fever
- fatigue
- muscle and joint pain
- liver tenderness

- darkened urine
- jaundice (yellowing of the skin and eyes)
- pale stools

The symptoms usually last only 1 to 2 weeks. Most people usually recover in 4 to 8 weeks, even without treatment.

Who's at Risk?

Those at highest risk of contracting hepatitis include:

- health care workers exposed to blood, blood products or body fluids
- users of illegal intravenous or intranasal drugs, such as cocaine
- individuals with multiple sexual partners
- babies born to mothers who are carriers of the hepatitis B virus
- people sharing a household with a hepatitis carrier
- people who have had blood transfusions or organ transplants or who have received clotting factor concentrates prior to blood screening (1992 in the United States, 1990 in Canada)
- people who travel to countries where hepatitis is common
- people who get tattoos or piercings

Conventional Treatment

There's no effective treatment for viral hepatitis, so prevention is the best strategy. Vaccines exist for hepatitis A and B, but there's no vaccine for hepatitis C. Infants born to mothers who are carriers of hepatitis B are vaccinated and given hepatitis B immune globulin, which prevents chronic hepatitis in approximately 70 percent of those infants.

For hepatitis C, interferon combined with broad-spectrum antiviral agents is successful in approximately 40 percent of cases. Interferon may not be used in people who have untreated thyroid disease, low blood-cell counts, an autoimmune disease or those who drink alcohol or take drugs. Other treatments for hepatitis include:

- eliminating alcoholic beverages, since alcohol speeds the progression of liver disease
- avoiding medications known to cause liver disease
- maintaining a healthy lifestyle
- exercising regularly and getting plenty of rest

Preventing and Managing Hepatitis

A vaccine is available to protect against hepatitis B. Three injections of the vaccine over a period of time will protect most people from this disease. To prevent infection, it's also critical to practise good hygiene at all times, especially when travelling to foreign countries. Avoid unprotected sex with multiple partners or with a partner who may have been exposed to the hepatitis virus. Don't share needles or drug paraphernalia and avoid intranasal drugs such as cocaine. When considering body piercing, ear piercing, tattooing or acupuncture, make certain that all implements are properly sterilized.

Dietary Strategies

A Healthy Diet
Good nutrition, in the form of a healthy, well-balanced diet, may help regenerate liver cells damaged by the hepatitis virus. Healthy eating is an important part of treatment for hepatitis as it helps protect the liver from further damage. The guidelines in Chapter 5, page 111, should be followed.

Avoid overeating carbohydrate-rich foods, since excess amounts can cause fatty deposits in the liver. Include foods rich in soluble fibre in your daily diet. The soluble fibre found in legumes, oats, psyllium, apples and citrus fruit binds toxic bile acids (a product of digestion) in the intestine and removes them from the body.

Alcohol must be avoided to allow the liver to heal and rebuild.

Green Tea
There's some suggestion that the antioxidants in green tea may help protect from liver disease. Japanese researchers found that men who drank green tea, especially more than 10 cups (2.5 L) per day, had decreased liver enzymes as measured by blood tests.[4] Animal research has also found that natural compounds called flavonoids, extracted from green tea, are able to protect from chemically induced liver damage.[5] An extract of green tea has also been shown to inhibit the growth of hepatitis B virus in laboratory studies.[6]

The antioxidants in green tea have a half-life in your body of only a few hours, so it's best to drink several cups of green tea throughout the day to get the most benefit. (Half-life refers to the time it takes for one-half of the antioxidants to be broken down and eliminated from your body.)

Whey Protein
Whey is a protein complex derived from milk. It contains a number of active components, including lactoferrin, beta-lactoglobulin, alpha-lactalbumin and immunoglobulins,

which have been shown to demonstrate a range of immune-enhancing effects. (Lactoferrin, purified from milk, has been shown to decrease the blood level of the virus in hepatitis C patients when combined with interferon treatment. Lab studies as well have demonstrated the ability of lactoferrin to inhibit the hepatitis C virus.) Whey protein is also a source of gamma-glutamylcysteine, a compound needed by the body to synthesize a potent antioxidant called glutathione.

In one study conducted in twenty-five patients with hepatitis B or C, 12 grams of whey protein supplement, called Immunocal, taken for 12 weeks resulted in improved immune scores in patients with hepatitis B. There were no significant immune changes in patients with hepatitis C.[7]

If you have hepatitis B, consider taking 12 grams of whey protein each day. Add whey protein to homemade smoothies, milk and soy beverages or mix it into hot cereal. Check the nutrition label to determine the serving size you need in order to get 12 grams of protein; most products supply 25 grams of protein per scoop. Choose a whey protein powder that contains no artificial ingredients or sweeteners, such as Genuine Health Proteins+. Immunocal is not sold in health food stores; it's available for purchase online (www.immunotec.com).

Vitamins and Minerals

Antioxidants: Vitamin E and Selenium

Scientists believe that oxidative damage caused by free radical molecules may be involved in the initiation and progression of viral hepatitis.[8-11] Free radical damage may make the liver more susceptible to viruses, and it may continue to destroy liver cells after the onset of hepatitis. Free radical damage may be due to a deficiency of antioxidants such as vitamin E and selenium and/or an overproduction of free radicals by damaged and inflamed liver cells.

In the body, vitamin E and selenium work closely together to neutralize harmful free radicals. Both nutrients also boost the body's immune system. Although antioxidant supplements, taken alone or in combination, have improved levels of antioxidants in patients with viral hepatitis, most studies have failed to show beneficial effects on liver function tests. One small study did find that a daily vitamin E supplement taken for 3 months improved liver function tests in patients with chronic hepatitis B.[12]

Researchers from China found that daily selenium supplementation reduced the risk of liver cancer among hepatitis B carriers.[13] A German study conducted among hepatitis C patients found that vitamin E, when combined with interferon therapy, reduced the amount of virus in the liver.[14] Case reports of individuals infected with hepatitis C also document improved liver tests and recovery rates when supplemented with antioxidants.[15]

The recommended dietary allowance (RDA) for vitamin E is 22 international units (IU). Best food sources include wheat germ, nuts, seeds, vegetable oils, whole grains and kale. To supplement, take 200 to 400 IU of natural source vitamin E. Buy a "mixed" vitamin E supplement if possible. The upper daily limit is 1500 IU.

The RDA for selenium is 55 micrograms. Best food sources are seafood, chicken, organ meats, whole grains, nuts, onions, garlic and mushrooms. To supplement, take 200 micrograms of selenium-rich yeast per day. The upper daily limit is 400 micrograms.

Iron: Low Iron Diet

The liver plays an important role in the metabolism of iron since it's the primary organ in the body that stores this mineral. Only about 10 percent of the iron we consume each day is eliminated from the body. People with chronic hepatitis C sometimes have difficulty excreting iron from the body. This can result in an overload of iron in the liver, blood and other organs. Excess iron can be very damaging to the liver and is thought to play a role in the progression of the disease. Studies suggest that high iron levels reduce the response rate of patients with hepatitis C to interferon.

Phlebotomy, removing blood from a vein, is often used to reduce body iron stores in people with hepatitis C. While this method is very effective at removing iron from the body and protecting the liver, some evidence suggests that a low iron diet offers additional protection.[16]

Avoid taking iron supplements if you have chronic hepatitis C and your iron stores are elevated. Choose an iron-free multivitamin and mineral supplement. Restrict the amounts of iron-rich food, such as red meat, liver, trout and iron-fortified breakfast cereals, in your diet. You'll find a list of iron-rich foods in Chapter 4, page 71.

Drink coffee or tea with meals to help reduce iron absorption. These beverages contain tannins, which inhibit the absorption of iron from plant foods. Limit supplemental vitamin C to 200 milligrams since this nutrient enhances iron absorption from plant foods.

Herbal Remedies

Milk Thistle (*Silybum marianum*)

This herbal supplement contains three active ingredients known collectively as silymarin, which appears to protect the liver in a few ways. It can prevent toxic substances from penetrating liver cells, possibly by preventing the binding of harmful compounds to the liver. Silymarin has also been shown to help liver cells regenerate more quickly. Milk thistle may act as an antioxidant and thus protects liver cells from damage caused by free radicals.

Studies conducted in people with chronic viral hepatitis found that milk thistle can improve symptoms such as poor appetite, fatigue and stomach upset. As well, liver-function blood-test results improve (liver enzyme levels are reduced) with milk thistle.[17,18]

Buy a product that's standardized to 70 percent to 80 percent silymarin. For liver cirrhosis, the recommended dose is 420 milligrams per day. Use milk thistle with caution if you're allergic to plants in the Asteraceae/Compositae family (ragweed, daisy, marigold and chrysanthemum). For more information on milk thistle, see Chapter 7, page 148.

Other Natural Health Products

Coenzyme Q10 (CoQ10)

This antioxidant may help the body respond better to the hepatitis B vaccine. Researchers gave healthy individuals either 90 or 180 milligrams of coenzyme Q10 (CoQ10) daily for 2 weeks prior to vaccination and for 3 months afterward.[19] The study found that CoQ10 was able to increase production of antibodies to the hepatitis B virus, with the higher dose having a greater effect.

CoQ10 may also help combat free radical damage caused by hepatitis. Japanese researchers found a significant increase in the blood levels of oxidized CoQ10 among chronic hepatitis patients compared with healthy people.[20] This suggests that the compounds may be important in protecting liver cells.

Choose a CoQ10 supplement in an oil base (instead of dry-powder tablets or capsules), since this is more available to the body. Take 50 milligrams twice daily. When taken in daily doses of 300 milligrams or more, CoQ10 can interfere with liver-enzyme blood tests.

Phosphatidylcholine

Phosphatidylcholine supplements are thought to exert their health benefits by supplying the body with choline, a member of the B vitamin family. Once ingested, choline is incorporated into the membranes of cells, where it appears to have an anti-inflammatory effect.

Research suggests that phosphatidylcholine may be beneficial for people with hepatitis C. German researchers showed that when taken with interferon therapy and continued for 24 weeks after, phosphatidylcholine taken daily improved liver function to a greater extent than interferon alone.[21]

Buy a supplement labelled phosphatidylcholine. For hepatitis C treatment in conjunction with interferon, take 1800 milligrams per day, in divided doses.

Nutrition Strategy Checklist for Hepatitis

- ☐ Healthy diet
- ☐ Green tea
- ☐ Soluble fibre
- ☐ Whey protein
- ☐ Avoid alcohol
- ☐ Vitamin E
- ☐ Selenium
- ☐ Low iron (hepatitis C)

- ☐ Milk thistle
- ☐ Coenzyme Q10 (hepatitis B)
- ☐ N-acetyl cysteine (hepatitis C)
- ☐ Phosphatidylcholine (hepatitis C)

Recommended Resources

Canadian Liver Foundation
www.liver.ca
2235 Sheppard Avenue E, Suite 1500
Toronto, ON M2J 5B5
Tel: 416-491-3353 or 1-800-563-5483
Fax: 416-491-4952
Email: clf@liver.ca

American Liver Foundation
www.liverfoundation.org
75 Maiden Lane, Suite 603
New York, NY, USA 10038
Tel: 1-212-668-1000
Fax: 1-212-483-8179

Hepatitis Foundation International
www.hepfi.org
504 Blick Drive
Silver Spring, MD, USA 20904
Tel: 1-301-622-4200
Fax: 1-301-622-4702

Herpes (Cold Sores and Genital Herpes)

The herpes simplex virus (HSV) is responsible for two common and painful infections: cold sores and genital herpes. A different type of herpes virus causes each infection. Cold sores, the irritating little blisters that often appear on your lips and gums and on the outside of your mouth, nose or cheeks, are usually triggered by *HSV type 1* (HSV-1), known as herpes labialis.

HSV type 2 (HSV-2) is associated with genital herpes, a highly contagious, sexually transmitted disease that causes sores to develop on the penis, in and around the vaginal opening, around the anal opening, on the buttocks or on the thighs. It's important to understand, however, that either type of herpes virus can trigger cold sores and genital lesions.

The herpes virus lurks deep within the nerve cells at the base of your spine, where it may remain inactive for months or even years at a time. Every so often, something will activate the virus, causing it to travel along the nerves to the skin, where it triggers an outbreak. Usually, the first eruption of sores is the worst, with later episodes becoming milder. HSV remains in your nerve cells for life and cannot be cured.

Most outbreaks of HSV are unpredictable. Physical or emotional stress, fatigue, fever, colds, the flu, menstruation, certain foods, dental treatment or exposure to sunlight may reactivate the virus. Sometimes, however, the virus can recur with no apparent cause. The frequency of recurrent attacks can vary considerably. Some people have only one or two outbreaks in a lifetime, while others deal with several attacks in a year.

Contracting the Virus

Herpes simplex is a highly contagious virus. Both cold sores and genital herpes can be passed from one person to another through skin-to-skin contact. Cold sores are spread by contact with the open sores or the saliva of an infected person. The virus is often contracted during infancy, through exposure to an adult with a cold sore. People who are exposed to oral herpes for the first time as adults frequently suffer more severe symptoms.

Genital herpes is usually transmitted through sexual intercourse with someone who is having a herpes outbreak. The sores that appear in the genital area during an active outbreak will shed viruses that can infect a sexual partner. In some instances, a person can have an HSV-2 outbreak without any visible sores. However, the virus can still be transmitted even when blisters aren't present. Unfortunately, many cases of genital herpes are contracted when someone has intercourse with a partner who doesn't know that he or she is infected.

If you have genital herpes or a cold sore, you may also transmit the virus to a partner during oral sex. Because the virus is so contagious, it's possible to transfer the virus to other parts of your body by touching the open sores and then accidentally rubbing or touching your genitals, eyes, mouth or other skin surfaces. If the herpes virus spreads to your eyes, it can cause corneal blindness.

A pregnant woman with genital herpes can spread the infection to her baby as the infant passes through the birth canal. Genital herpes is very dangerous during pregnancy, as babies born with it may die, suffer from nerve damage or have serious problems affecting the brain, skin or eyes. Herpes can also cause life-threatening illness in people suffering from eczema, AIDS, cancer or a suppressed immune system.

Symptoms
Cold Sores

A painful, tingling or itching sensation (called the prodome) may precede the blisters by 1 or 2 days. Then fluid-filled blisters or painful red sores appear on or near the mouth or lips. These blisters form in clusters, before joining together into a larger single sore. After the blisters break and ooze, a yellow crust or scab forms. The dead skin then sloughs off and the area heals without a scar. During this time, your gums may be swollen and sensitive.

The first attack may also cause swollen lymph nodes, fever and flu-like symptoms. The sores normally last 7 to 10 days.

Genital Herpes

The symptoms of genital herpes may develop 1 to 3 weeks after sexual contact with an infected person. Sometimes symptoms don't appear until weeks or months after contact.

An itching or burning sensation in the genital or anal area precedes the blisters. The legs, buttocks or genital area will also be painful. Gradually, small red bumps appear, which join together to form fluid-filled blisters.

These blisters break to become painful open sores. As a crust or scab forms over the scar, dead skin sloughs off and the area heals, though it may be scarred.

The first outbreak may also be accompanied by fever, headache, muscle aches, painful urination, vaginal discharge and swollen glands. Sores normally last 2 to 3 weeks.

Who's at Risk?

Cold sores are very common. Estimates indicate that 80 percent of the North American population suffers from HSV-1. The virus is easily spread within families, with infants being most susceptible to infection. Outbreaks occur most often during adolescence and tend to decrease after age 35.

It's believed that 60 percent of sexually active adults carry HSV-2. The genital herpes virus affects both men and women. People who have unprotected sex with an infected partner are most at risk.

Conventional Treatment
Cold Sores

Cold sores usually clear up without treatment. Antiviral medications, in ointment or oral drug form, may shorten the duration of the outbreak but won't prevent recurrent attacks. Anesthetic mouthwashes or mouthwashes containing baking soda may ease the discomfort. Do not squeeze or pinch the blister. Keep the cold sore area dry to prevent the infection from worsening.

If you have burning pain in the eye or a rash near the eye, see your doctor immediately to prevent an infection that may lead to corneal blindness.

Genital Herpes

Antiviral medications (such as acyclovir, famciclovir and valacyclovir) in ointment or oral drug form may help genital herpes sores heal faster and reduce the number of recurrent outbreaks. Wear cotton underwear; synthetic fabrics hold moisture and may make the infection worse. Soaking in a shallow tub of salty water may ease discomfort. Eating a healthy diet, managing stress and getting enough rest and exercise may reduce the number of outbreaks.

To prevent the spread of further infection, you should tell anyone whom you've had sexual intercourse with in the past 2 years that you have genital herpes so that they can be examined and treated.

Preventing and Managing Herpes

If you have HSV-1, use sun protection on your lips and face before exposure to the sun to help prevent outbreaks. Avoid spicy foods, as they may trigger a cold sore. To prevent spread of the virus, avoid skin contact (kissing, touching, oral sex) with other people when blisters are present. And always wash your hands carefully after touching a cold sore.

To prevent the spread of HSV-2, abstain from sexual intercourse (including oral sex) during an active outbreak. Use a latex condom during all sexual contact, since you may infect your partner even when blisters are not present.

Avoid touching other parts of your body after touching a genital sore and wash your hands carefully after contact with a sore.

Dietary Strategies

A nutritious, well-balanced diet provides vitamins and minerals that are important for wound healing and a strong immune system. Focus on low-fat animal-protein foods such as skinless poultry breast, lean meat and low-fat dairy products. Be sure to eat whole-grain starchy foods, legumes and 7 to 10 servings of fruit and vegetables each day. Include zinc-rich foods such as yogurt, wheat bran, wheat germ and enriched breakfast cereals to support immunity. Eat oily fish two times a week to get health-enhancing omega-3 fatty acids. Use cooking oils that support a healthy immune system, such as flaxseed, walnut and canola oils.

Minimize your intake of foods that can undermine the immune system and increase your susceptibility to infection. Limit animal fats, refined sugars and alcoholic beverages. You'll find guidelines for a healthy diet in Chapter 5, page 111.

Vitamins and Minerals

Vitamin A

This vitamin is essential for a healthy immune system and for healing of the skin. Some research suggests that people with HSV may be deficient in vitamin A.[1] The best food sources of this vitamin include liver, oily fish, milk, cheese and egg yolks.

Beta carotene in foods also contributes to your vitamin A intake. Once daily, eat orange and dark-green produce such as carrots, sweet potato, winter squash, broccoli, collard greens, kale, spinach, apricots, cantaloupe, peaches, nectarines, mango and papaya.

Your diet and a multivitamin will provide your daily requirement of vitamin A. Most multivitamins offer 2000 to 5000 international units (IU) of vitamin A. Because high doses of vitamin A can be toxic if taken over a period of time, separate vitamin A supplements should be taken only under the guidance of your health care provider. Do not take extra vitamin A during pregnancy. While beta carotene supplements are considered safe for non-smokers, there is no evidence to warrant taking a beta carotene supplement. (High dose beta carotene supplements may increase the risk of lung cancer in smokers.)

Vitamins C and E

Both these nutrients are needed for proper immune function and wound healing. One study found that vitamin C combined with flavonoids was effective in treating genital herpes.[2] (Interestingly, many of the herbs used in developing countries to treat herpes contain flavonoids, natural compounds found in fruit and vegetables.)

VITAMIN C. It's plentiful in citrus fruit, citrus juices, cantaloupe, kiwi, mango, strawberries, broccoli, Brussels sprouts, cauliflower, red pepper and tomato juice. During a herpes outbreak, take 200 to 600 milligrams of vitamin C with 200 milligrams of bioflavonoids five times daily. To help prevent a recurrence, take 500 to 600 milligrams of vitamin C (with added bioflavonoids) once daily.

VITAMIN E. Food sources include wheat germ, nuts, seeds, vegetable oils, whole grains and kale. For immune system support, take 400 IU of natural source vitamin E. Buy a "mixed" vitamin E supplement if possible. People who have heart disease or diabetes should not take high dose vitamin E supplements. However, the amount provided by most multivitamins, less than 100 IU per daily dose, is considered safe.

Herbal Remedies

Aloe Vera
Researchers have found that applying aloe vera gel or cream to genital herpes reduces the time needed for lesions to heal.[3] Some evidence suggests that the cream is better absorbed than the gel and therefore may be more effective. Apply aloe vera cream (containing 0.5 percent aloe) three times daily.

Lemon Balm (Melissa officinalis)
As a topical cream or oil, this herb is widely used in Europe to treat cold sores and genital herpes, both at the first sign of symptoms and on a regular basis to prevent attacks. Studies have found that lemon balm cream significantly reduces the pain, number of blisters and size of blisters caused by HSV-1.[4-7] It's thought that active components in the plant interfere with the ability of the herpes virus to attach to cells and replicate.

Apply lemon balm cream (70:1 extract) two to four times daily at the first sign of an outbreak of a cold sore and for a few days after the lesion has healed.

Siberian Ginseng (Eleutherococcus senticosus)
Taking this herbal supplement appears to reduce the frequency, severity and duration of HSV-2 infections. One study found that, compared with the placebo, this mild form of ginseng reduced the frequency of herpes outbreaks by 50 percent.[8]

To ensure quality, choose a product standardized for eleutherosides E. The usual dose is 400 milligrams once daily. See Chapter 7, page 146, for more information about Siberian ginseng.

Other Natural Health Products

Lysine
Lysine is an amino acid plentiful in meat and dairy products. Supplemental doses of lysine have been found to significantly reduce the severity of symptoms of HSV-1 outbreaks as well as the healing time.[9,10] There's also evidence that lysine can reduce or even prevent recurrences of attacks.[11] When 1543 people were surveyed after taking lysine for 6 months, 84 percent said that the supplement prevented recurrence or decreased the number of outbreaks. Among people not taking lysine, 79 percent said their symptoms were intolerable, whereas only 8 percent of those taking lysine described their symptoms as intolerable. Studies in the laboratory have determined that lysine inhibits the growth of HSV-1.

Buy a supplement of L-lysine monohydrochloride. Studies have used varying dosages. To treat cold sores (HSV-1), take 1200 milligrams daily for 6 months or 1000 milligrams three times daily for 6 months. Doses less than 1000 milligrams per day have not been effective. No side effects have been reported with these amounts.

Nutrition Strategy Checklist for Herpes

☐ Healthy diet
☐ Vitamin A
☐ Vitamin C
☐ Vitamin E
☐ Herbal creams: aloe vera OR lemon balm
☐ Siberian ginseng
☐ Lysine

Recommended Resources

Ontario Ministry of Health Promotion
www.healthyontario.com
777 Bay Street, 18th Floor
Toronto, ON M7A 1S5
Tel: 416-326-8475
Fax: 416-326-4864

American Social Health Association
www.ashastd.org
P.O. Box 13827
Research Triangle Park, NC, USA 207709
Tel: 919-361-8400
Fax: 919-361-8425

National Institute of Allergy and Infectious Diseases
National Institutes of Health
NIAID Office of Communications and Government Relations
www3.niaid.nih.gov
6610 Rockledge Drive, MSC 6612
Bethesda, MD, USA 20892-6612
Tel: 301-496-5717
Fax: 301-402-3573

Hiatal Hernia (see also Gastroesophageal Reflux Disease)

A hernia forms when one part of an organ protrudes or bulges through the wall of the cavity that contains it. A hiatal hernia develops at the opening in your diaphragm where your esophagus joins your stomach. The diaphragm, the muscle used for breathing, separates the chest from the abdomen. Normally, the esophagus, or food pipe, joins the stomach by passing through a small opening in the diaphragm, called the esophageal hiatus. When the muscle tissue surrounding your hiatus becomes weak, the upper part of your stomach can herniate, or push through, forming a hiatal hernia. There are two types of hiatal hernia.

SLIDING HERNIA. This is the most common. The stomach pushes into the chest only when you swallow. As the muscle of the esophagus contracts during a swallow, the stomach is pulled up through the hiatus opening. When the swallow is finished, the esophageal muscle relaxes and the stomach falls back into the abdomen.

PARA-ESOPHAGEAL HERNIA. This type develops less often, but is more serious. Rather than sliding up and down with each swallow, the stomach bulges into the chest and remains there. If the para-esophageal hernia becomes large enough, it can interfere with the passage of food into the stomach and may cause food to actually become stuck in the esophagus. An accumulation of stomach acid or damage caused by trapped food may also cause ulcers to form in the herniated part of the stomach.

What Causes a Hiatal Hernia?

Anything that puts intense pressure on your abdomen may lead to a hiatal hernia. Pregnancy, obesity and lifting heavy objects are risk factors for this condition. Even severe coughing, vomiting or straining during a bowel movement may generate enough pressure to push the stomach through the hiatus opening.

Symptoms

Very often, a hiatal hernia will cause no symptoms at all, especially if it's small. However, in some cases, a hernia may cause reflux of the stomach contents into the esophagus, heartburn, belching, chest pain and nausea. A hiatal hernia can interfere with the action of a small band of muscle that surrounds the bottom of the esophagus, called the lower esophageal sphincter. During normal digestion, this sphincter muscle acts like a valve, opening to allow food to pass into the stomach and closing to prevent food and stomach acid from flowing back into the esophagus.

As the stomach herniates into the chest, it may push the sphincter out of place, interfering with the muscles that control the valve. If the sphincter opens and closes at the wrong times, stomach acid may back up into the esophagus, causing heartburn, burping, pain and sometimes bleeding. Discomfort may be worse after eating, when lying down or after stooping over. Sometimes pain can spread into the upper chest, back and neck, similar to the pain of a heart attack, and should be assessed by a doctor. In most cases, symptoms will clear up with dietary and lifestyle changes.

Who's at Risk?

It's estimated that 10 percent of Canadians have hiatal hernias. The prevalence climbs to 40 percent in people over the age of 50.[1] Women appear to be at greater risk for developing a hiatal hernia than men. Pregnant women and people who are overweight are at higher risk. Smoking as well as sustaining an injury to the abdomen may also increase the risk. Other risk factors include severe coughing, weightlifting, vomiting or straining.

Conventional Treatment

Treatment isn't necessary unless you're experiencing symptoms. Lifestyle changes may help ease heartburn symptoms that often accompany a hiatal hernia. Dietary changes (see below) as well as the following strategies are useful:

- Avoid lying down after you eat to reduce the risk of food and stomach acid entering the esophagus; avoid eating 2 to 3 hours before bedtime.
- Elevate the head of your bed 6 to 8 inches (15 to 20 cm) to prevent stomach acid from moving up into your esophagus while you sleep.
- Avoid strenuous exercise immediately after eating.
- Avoid clothing that is tight around the abdominal area.
- Avoid certain medications, such as NSAIDs, sedatives, tranquilizers and calcium channel blockers, which may cause heartburn.
- Stop smoking.
- Avoid stress, which slows down digestion and encourages esophageal reflux; try relaxation techniques to help reduce heartburn.

Certain medications may reduce heartburn, including antacids, H-2 blockers that decrease the amount of acid produced by the stomach and proton pump inhibitors that block acid production. In severe cases, surgery may be necessary to repair the hernia.

Preventing and Managing a Hernia

Dietary Strategies

Trigger Foods

Dietary changes will help reduce heartburn by preventing reflux and irritation of a sensitive or inflamed esophagus. Fatty foods and high-fat meals often cause symptoms because they remain in the stomach longer and increase the time the esophagus is exposed to the acidic stomach contents. Cream, ice cream, milkshakes, fatty desserts and pastries, gravies, butter, margarine, vegetable oil, fried meats, sausage, cream soups, french fries and potato chips are often poorly tolerated.

Chocolate and coffee can cause distress as well. Chocolate contains methylxanthine, a compound that relaxes the esophageal sphincter and increases the likelihood of reflux. Coffee also relaxes the esophageal sphincter and stimulates acid secretion by the stomach, which can make symptoms worse. If your esophagus is not inflamed, coffee may be allowed as tolerated. Alcohol, carbonated beverages, spearmint, peppermint, spicy foods, tomatoes, citrus fruit, onions and garlic can also irritate the esophagus.

Eating smaller meals and drinking fluids between meals rather than with meals can help prevent heartburn.

Weight Control

People who are overweight and have an elevated waist circumference are at increased risk of developing a sliding hernia and esophageal reflux.[2-6] Weight loss helps to lessen abdominal pressure and can eliminate symptoms of heartburn.

To determine if you're at a healthy weight, see Obesity, Overweight and Weight Loss, page 569, to calculate your body mass index (BMI). Having a BMI of 25 to 29.9 indicates overweight and a BMI of 30 or greater is defined as obese. Men and women are advised to maintain a waist circumference of less than 37 and 31.5 inches (94 and 80 cm), respectively. If you are overweight or have an elevated waist circumference, use the strategies outlined in Obesity, Overweight and Weight Loss, page 574, to promote safe, gradual weight loss.

Vitamins and Minerals

Vitamin B12

People on acid-blocking medication are at risk for developing a vitamin B12 deficiency and so should supplement this vitamin. Stomach (gastric) acid is required to release vitamin B12 from food proteins so that it can be absorbed into the bloodstream. Without adequate gastric acid, the intestine cannot absorb B12 from foods.

Because the absorption of other nutrients, such as iron and zinc, can be affected by insufficient gastric acid, a daily multivitamin and mineral supplement is recommended. These formulas will provide 25 to 100 micrograms of B12. Separate B12 supplements are also available in 500 and 1000 microgram doses. Vitamin B12 is extremely safe.

Iron

Some people with a large hiatal hernia may develop an iron deficiency because of slow bleeding of the hernia.[7-10] You should take care to eat an iron-rich diet. The richest sources of iron are beef, fish, poultry, pork and lamb (see Chapter 4, page 72). These foods contain heme iron, the type that can be absorbed and utilized most efficiently by your body. Iron in plant foods such as dried fruits, whole grains, leafy green vegetables, nuts, seeds and legumes is called nonheme iron, and the body is much less efficient at absorbing it. To enhance absorption, eat foods containing nonheme iron with non-irritating vitamin C–rich foods such as red pepper, broccoli, Brussels sprouts, cantaloupe and strawberries.

To help you meet your daily iron requirements, a multivitamin and mineral supplement is a wise idea. Most formulas provide 10 milligrams, but you can find multivitamins that provide up to 18 milligrams of the mineral.

If you're diagnosed with iron-deficiency anemia, your doctor will prescribe single iron pills. See Anemia, page 208, for more information on using iron supplements safely.

Nutrition Strategy Checklist for Hiatal Hernia

- ☐ Avoid food triggers
- ☐ Small, frequent meals
- ☐ Fluids between meals
- ☐ Weight control
- ☐ Vitamin B12
- ☐ Iron

Recommended Resources

Mayo Foundation for Medical Education and Research
www.mayoclinic.com
This website is produced by a team of writers, editors, health educators, nurses, doctors and scientists, and is one of the best patient-education sites on the Internet. The information is reliable, thorough and clearly written.

MedicineNet.com
www.medicinenet.com

High Blood Pressure (Hypertension)

High blood pressure, or hypertension, is one of the "big three" major risk factors for heart disease (along with high cholesterol and cigarette smoking). The higher your blood pressure is above normal, the greater your risk of coronary artery disease, congestive heart failure, stroke, dementia and kidney disease. Hypertension is called the silent killer because it develops slowly, over a number of years, and usually displays no symptoms until a vital organ is irreversibly damaged.

Blood pressure is the force on your artery walls that's generated by your heart as it pushes blood through your arteries. When your heart beats, blood pressure in your arteries rises. Between beats, when your heart relaxes, blood pressure falls. Your blood pressure rises and falls throughout the day, but when it remains elevated over time it's called high blood pressure, or hypertension.

Blood pressure is recorded in millimetres of mercury (written as mmHg). It's composed of two measurements: systolic blood pressure and diastolic blood pressure. The first (top) number in a blood-pressure reading is the systolic pressure, created when your heart is pumping out blood. The second (bottom) number is the diastolic pressure, created when your heart muscle is relaxing and filling with blood.

Adults should have a blood pressure of less than 120/80. Hypertension is defined as a systolic pressure of ≥140 mmHg or a diastolic pressure of ≥90 mmHg. One in five Canadians falls into the category between, called prehypertension (130–139/85–89 mmHg). Unless lifestyle changes are made to bring blood pressure down, 60 percent of people with prehypertension will develop hypertension within 4 years.

Do You Have High Blood Pressure?

	Millilitres of mercury (mmHg)
Normal blood pressure	≤120 / ≤80
Prehypertension	130–139 / 85–89
Hypertension	≥140 / ≥90

Because prehypertension and hypertension usually don't cause symptoms, it's important to have your blood pressure checked regularly—at least once every 2 years, and more often if your blood pressure is high. If you have prehypertension you should have your blood pressure monitored once a year. Even children should have their blood pressure measured, beginning at the age of 2. Blood pressure is measured—when you're relaxed and rested—by putting a cuff around your arm, inflating the cuff and listening to the flow of blood. If you're under emotional or physical stress, your blood pressure may be elevated.

One high blood pressure reading doesn't mean you have hypertension. Your doctor will measure your blood pressure at more than one visit to determine if you have hypertension; however, if your blood pressure is extremely high, your doctor may diagnose hypertension after one reading.

If high blood pressure is complicated by hardening of the arteries (atherosclerosis), the condition becomes much more serious. Arteries that are hardened and stiff strain as blood pumps through; they can't expand to accommodate the blood flow and blood pressure rises. This prolonged stress damages the arteries and causes cholesterol to accumulate on the artery walls, narrowing the arteries even further. This usually leads to a reduction in the blood flowing to the kidneys. The kidneys respond by retaining sodium to increase blood volume and blood pressure.

The higher your blood pressure and the longer it remains uncontrolled, the greater the damage it can cause. Complications from high blood pressure include aneurysm (an enlarged, bulging blood vessel), stroke, kidney disorders and vision loss.

What Causes High Blood Pressure?

In 95 percent of all cases, the cause of high blood pressure is unknown. In these cases, the condition is referred to as *primary or essential hypertension*. Scientists suspect that high blood pressure is caused by several changes in the heart and blood vessels brought about by an interaction of genetic, lifestyle and social factors. The role of lifestyle factors such as obesity, alcohol consumption, smoking, inactivity, poor diet and stress have been well documented.

In the remaining 10 percent of cases, the cause of high blood pressure can be identified.

Causes include kidney disease, hormonal disorders such as thyroid disease, certain medications, pregnancy and drug abuse. When the cause of high blood pressure is known, the condition is referred to as *secondary hypertension.*

Symptoms

Uncomplicated high blood pressure usually occurs without symptoms and can remain unnoticed for many years, even decades. However, some people may experience the following signs or symptoms:

- headaches, dizziness and nosebleeds
- damage to the eyes, kidneys, brain and heart, causing fatigue, nausea, vomiting, shortness of breath, restlessness and blurred vision
- drowsiness or coma from swelling in the brain in severe cases

Who's at Risk?

One in five Canadians has high blood pressure. Because as many as 43 percent of Canadians don't even know they have high blood pressure, the prevalence of hypertension may be much higher than estimated. What's more, the number of Canadians with high blood pressure is increasing, due in large part to rising obesity rates. From 1995 to 2005, the number of adults in Ontario with hypertension more than doubled and the prevalence of high blood pressure was slightly higher among younger adults than older adults.[1]

The following factors may increase your risk of developing the condition:

- **Age.** The risk of hypertension increases as we get older. Middle-aged men are more likely to develop high blood pressure, but after menopause, women are at greater risk.
- **Genetics.** If you have a family member with hypertension, you're at increased risk for developing the condition. High blood pressure is more common in people of South Asian and African American descent, and develops at a younger age than in Caucasians.
- **Overweight and obesity.** As your body weight increases, your blood pressure rises too. That's because a larger body mass requires more blood to supply oxygen and nutrients to your tissues. As more blood circulates through your blood vessels, the pressure on your artery walls increases.
- **Lack of exercise.** People who are sedentary tend to have higher heart rates, causing the heart to work harder with each contraction, which puts extra pressure on your artery walls.
- **Diet.** Excess sodium in your diet can cause fluid retention and increased blood pressure, especially if you're sodium sensitive. A lack of potassium-rich fruits and vegetables can also contribute to hypertension, since potassium helps balance the amount of sodium in your cells.
- **Excess alcohol.** Consuming more than two drinks per day can increase blood pressure and, over time, damage your heart.
- **Smoking.** Cigarette smoking damages the lining of your artery walls, causing them to narrow. As result, blood pressure rises.

Conventional Treatment

The health problems associated with high blood pressure—heart attack, stroke, kidney disease—can be prevented by controlling your blood pressure. Lowering your blood pressure can cut your risk of stroke by up to 40 percent and of heart attack by as much as 25 percent. Treating hypertension involves lifestyle changes such as weight loss, diet, exercise, smoking cessation, stress management and usually two or more medications. The following medications are sometimes prescribed to lower blood pressure:

- **Diuretics,** or water pills, to help the kidneys eliminate salt and water, which helps to relax the blood vessel walls
- **Beta blockers** to reduce the nerve impulses to the heart and blood vessels, which causes the heart to beat slower and with less force
- **ACE (angiotensin converting enzyme) inhibitors** to block the formation of a hormone called angiotensin II (normally, angiotensin II causes blood vessels to narrow), which helps the blood vessels relax
- **Angiotensin antagonists** to shield blood vessels from the action of angiotensin II
- **Calcium channel blockers (CCBs)** to prevent calcium from entering the heart muscle cells and blood vessels, which keeps the blood vessels dilated and relaxed
- **Renin inhibitors** to inhibit the action of a kidney enzyme called renin, which can act to raise blood pressure

Preventing and Managing High Blood Pressure

Dietary Strategies

Weight Control

People who are overweight have an increased risk of developing high blood pressure. Study after study has determined overweight and obesity to be strong risk factors for elevated blood pressure.[2-5] Weight loss should be the first line of treatment in hypertension. Even a moderate weight loss of 5 percent to 10 percent of body weight will cause a drop in blood pressure. In some cases, achieving and maintaining a healthy weight can reduce or eliminate the need for blood pressure medication.

To determine if you're at a healthy weight, see Obesity, Overweight and Weight Loss, page 569, to calculate your body mass index (BMI). A BMI of 25 to 29.9 indicates overweight; a BMI of 30 or greater is defined as obese. If you determine your BMI is greater than 25, use the strategies outlined on page 574 for safe, gradual weight loss.

The DASH Diet

The DASH (Dietary Approaches to Stop Hypertension) diet is the result of randomized controlled trials that demonstrated eating a combination of certain foods—a dietary pattern—can lower blood pressure dramatically. The DASH diet is low in saturated fat, cholesterol and total fat and rich in carbohydrate in that it emphasizes fruit, vegetables, whole grains and low-fat dairy products.

In the first DASH trial, 459 adults with prehypertension or hypertension were randomized to follow one of three diets for 8 weeks: 1) a control diet (i.e., a typical North American diet); 2) a diet rich in fruit and vegetables; or 3) a "combination" diet rich in fruit, vegetables and low-fat dairy products, with reduced saturated fat and total fat (i.e., the DASH diet). Sodium intake and body weight were maintained at a constant level during the study.

The DASH diet significantly lowered blood pressure compared to the control diet and reduced blood pressure to a greater extent than the fruit and vegetable diet. Individuals on the DASH diet who had mild hypertension achieved a reduction in blood pressure similar to that obtained by drug treatment. The DASH diet resulted in substantial blood pressure lowering in the absence of weight loss. The 2100-calorie DASH diet was not designed to promote weight loss, but rather examine the impact of a dietary pattern on blood pressure.[6]

The DASH-Sodium trial tested effects of the DASH diet at three different sodium levels—3300, 2400 and 1500 milligrams per day. A total of 412 participants were assigned to eat either a control diet or the DASH diet at high, intermediate or low sodium levels for 30 days. The DASH eating plan resulted in significantly lower systolic blood pressure readings at each sodium level. The lowest sodium DASH diet (1500 milligrams) produced the greatest reduction in blood pressure. Although people with hypertension lowered their blood pressure the most, those with normal blood pressure also had big reductions.[7]

This DASH diet provides food choices that are high in fibre, calcium, magnesium and potassium, all of which have been associated with lower blood pressure. The key foods that supply these nutrients are low-fat dairy products, fruit, vegetables, legumes and nuts. The DASH diet is also low in refined carbohydrates and saturated fats, which can cause salt retention and elevated blood pressure.

If you have high blood pressure and would like to follow the DASH diet, use the following as your guide:

DASH Eating Plan
Number of Daily Servings for 1600, 2600 and 3100 Calories

Food Group	Servings/Day		
	1600	2600	3100
Whole grains	6	10–11	12–13
Vegetables	3–4	5–6	6
Fruit	4	5–6	6

Food Group	Servings/Day		
	1600	2600	3100
Non-fat or low-fat	2–3	3	3–4
Milk and milk products			
Lean meats, poultry, fish	3–6	6	6–9
Nuts, seeds, legumes	3/week	1/day	1/day
Fats and oils	2	3	4
Sweets and sugars	0	£2	£2

The DASH diet and serving sizes can be found at www.nhlbi.nih.gov/health/public/heart/hbp/dash/new_dash.pdf.

Fish
There's evidence that fish oil can help blood vessels relax, preventing increases in blood pressure. Studies have shown that eating fish once a day lowers blood pressure in people with hypertension.[8,9] Two studies found that adding fish to a weight-loss diet produced a greater blood pressure–lowering effect than weight loss alone.[10,11] The body uses omega-3 fatty acids from fish to produce anti-inflammatory compounds called eicosanoids (prostaglandins, leukotrienes, prostacylcins, thromboxanes). These compounds are thought to protect from hypertension.

The best sources of omega-3 fats are salmon, trout, Arctic char, sardines, herring and mackerel. These fish are also low in mercury. Aim to include 1 serving of fish in your daily diet. Fish oil capsules are an alternative for people who don't like fish or don't want to eat it daily (see below).

Nuts
The DASH trials demonstrated that eating nuts (and legumes) four times per week helped lower elevated blood pressure in people with

mild hypertension. Nuts are unusually rich in arginine, an amino acid thought to improve blood vessel function. Nuts are also a good source of magnesium and potassium, minerals that help maintain a healthy blood pressure.

Include 1 serving of nuts in your diet four times per week. One serving is roughly 1/4 cup (60 ml) or 28 grams (slightly less than 1 ounce). Use the following guide to determine portion size:

Portion Size for Nuts

	Number of Nuts per 28 Gram Serving
Almonds	24
Brazil nuts	6–8
Cashews	18
Hazelnuts	20
Macadamia nuts	10–12
Peanuts	28
Pecans	20 halves
Pine nuts	157
Pistachios	49
Walnuts	14 halves

Alcohol and Caffeine

An excessive intake of alcohol—more than two drinks per day—damages blood vessel walls and increases the risk of hypertension.[12–14] Women should limit their intake of alcohol to no more than one drink per day (or seven per week) and men, to no more than two drinks per day (to a maximum of nine per week). A drink is considered 12 ounces (340 ml) of regular beer, 5 ounces (145 ml) of wine or 1-1/2 ounces (45 ml) of 80-proof (40 percent) distilled spirits.

Caffeine does increase blood pressure, but its effect is short lived. However, if your blood pressure is poorly controlled, it's wise to limit caffeine. If you're under stress, which increases blood pressure, the effect of caffeine can be additive. Older adults with hypertension may be more sensitive to the effect of caffeine and should limit their intake to no more than a small cup (6 ounces/180 ml) of regular coffee per day.[15–18] If your blood pressure is well controlled, keep your caffeine intake to no more than 450 milligrams per day (see Chapter 5, page 109). Avoid caffeinated beverages, especially coffee, if you're under stress or your blood pressure is poorly controlled. Switch to decaffeinated coffee or herbal tea.

Vitamins and Minerals

Vitamin C

Some evidence suggests that the formation of free radicals increases in people with hypertension and that this may impair the ability of blood vessels to relax and dilate.[19,20] As an antioxidant, vitamin C is thought to inhibit the production of free radicals in vessel walls, thereby preserving their health. Studies have found that taking a vitamin C supplement along with antihypertensive medication helps lower systolic blood pressure in people with hypertension. In people with type 2 diabetes, a daily vitamin C supplement taken for 4 weeks, in conjunction with conventional medication, lowered blood pressure and reduced the stiffness of artery walls. However, taking vitamin C without antihypertensive drugs doesn't seem to reduce elevated blood pressure. Studies have also found that a low dietary vitamin C intake is associated with increased blood pressure.[21–25]

The recommended dietary allowance (RDA) is 75 and 90 milligrams for women and men, respectively (smokers need an additional 35 milligrams). Foods rich in vitamin C include citrus fruit, citrus juices, cantaloupe, kiwi, mango, strawberries, broccoli, Brussels sprouts, cauliflower, red pepper and tomato juice. If you take medication to lower blood pressure, supplement with 500 milligrams of vitamin C once daily. The upper daily limit is 2000 milligrams.

Calcium

This mineral is important in both preventing and treating high blood pressure. Low calcium intakes from diet are associated with hypertension, and higher intakes have been shown to lower blood pressure.[26,27] Low-fat dairy products are an important component of the DASH diet. Calcium might help lower blood pressure by causing the kidneys to excrete sodium. Calcium supplements do not help lower elevated blood pressure.

To ensure that you're meeting your daily recommended intake for calcium, include calcium-rich foods in your daily diet. Low-fat milk, yogurt, fortified soy beverages, fortified orange juice, tofu, salmon (with bones), kale, bok choy, broccoli, Swiss chard and almonds are all good choices. You'll find more information about calcium requirements and calcium-rich foods in Chapter 4, page 56.

Magnesium

Low levels of magnesium in the diet and the blood are believed to contribute to the development of hypertension.[28,29] Magnesium influences the excitability of the heart and the reactivity of blood vessels. While studies show that magnesium-rich diets are important in preventing high blood pressure, clinical studies using magnesium supplements to treat hypertension have been less than convincing.[30] The Canadian Hypertension Society doesn't recommend magnesium supplements to treat or prevent high blood pressure.

The best strategy is to eat magnesium-rich foods, as outlined in the DASH diet (see above). For most people this is quite a change, since a diet of refined, processed foods contains little magnesium.

The best food sources of magnesium include nuts, seeds, legumes, lentils, prunes, figs, whole grains, leafy green vegetables and brewer's yeast. See Chapter 4, page 60, for a detailed food list and recommended magnesium intakes.

Potassium

Low daily intakes of dietary potassium (less than 1560 milligrams) are linked with high blood pressure.[31] The DASH diet provides abundant potassium, which contributes to its blood pressure–lowering effect. Potassium is thought to make blood vessels less sensitive to hormones that normally cause them to constrict. Potassium may also act on blood vessels directly, causing them to relax. A higher potassium intake also causes the kidneys to excrete more sodium, thereby preventing blood pressure from rising.[32,33]

Adults need 4.7 grams (4700 milligrams) of potassium each day. Meat, chicken, salmon, cod, lima beans, potatoes, bananas, oranges, orange juice, avocado, cantaloupe, peaches, tomatoes and tomato juice are good sources of potassium. The best way to increase your potassium intake is to eat more fruit and vegetables. Although you can get potassium in a supplement, research has shown that potassium in foods is far superior in keeping blood pressure in the normal range. (Before increasing your intake of potassium, check with your doctor. Some people, for example, those with kidney disease, may need to avoid potassium-rich foods.) See Chapter 4, page 82, to learn the potassium content of selected foods.

Sodium

Study after study has linked excess sodium with elevated blood pressure. Research shows that, on average, blood pressure rises progressively with increasing sodium intakes. The DASH-Sodium trial, described above, demonstrated that reducing sodium intake substantially lowered blood pressure in a directly proportionate fashion—the greater the sodium reduction, the greater the effect. People with high blood pressure, diabetes, chronic kidney disease, older adults and African Americans are more sensitive than others to the blood pressure–raising effects of sodium and respond well to a sodium-reduced diet.

Canadians of all ages, from young to old, are consuming too much sodium. Estimated daily sodium intakes range between 2300 and 2800 milligrams for women and between 2882 and 4066 milligrams for men—amounts in excess of what our bodies need. (One teaspoon/5 ml of table salt—sodium chloride—contains 2300 milligrams of sodium.) Adults aged 19 to 50 require only 1500 milligrams of sodium per day; older adults need 1300 milligrams. The upper daily limit is 2300 milligrams.

For tips to help you reduce your sodium intake, see Chapter 5, page 108.

Herbal Remedies

Garlic (*Allium sativum*)

Some studies have shown that garlic supplements can lower elevated blood pressure by 5 percent to 10 percent.[34-36] Garlic is thought to work by relaxing the smooth muscle of blood vessels and activating compounds that dilate vessels. Both Kwai garlic powder and Kyolic aged garlic extract supplements have shown

beneficial effects. Studies using Kwai gave 600 to 900 milligrams daily, in divided doses. With Kyolic a large dose—7.2 grams—achieved a reduction in blood pressure.

Garlic supplements in high doses may be unsafe during pregnancy. Garlic may also enhance the effects of blood-thinning medications like warfarin (Coumadin). Since garlic can prolong bleeding time, stop taking it 1 week prior to scheduled surgery.

Other Natural Health Products

Coenzyme Q10 (CoQ10)

Reports from several research studies deem this antioxidant to be a moderately effective treatment for hypertension. Studies have found that taking coenzyme Q10 (CoQ10) with antihypertensive medications seems to provide an additional blood pressure–lowering effect and might allow for the dosage of blood pressure medications to be reduced.[37-39] CoQ10 may lower blood pressure by increasing the production of anti-inflammatory compounds formed in artery walls, or by increasing the sensitivity of artery walls to their effects.

The recommended dose for treating high blood pressure is 60 milligrams twice daily. CoQ10 is very safe and no significant side effects have been reported. For more information about CoQ10, see Chapter 8, page 157.

Fish Oil Supplements

A handful of studies have found that fish oil supplements reduce blood pressure in people with mild hypertension and with or without type 2 diabetes.[40-43] Omega-3 fatty acids in fish oil have anti-inflammatory properties that are thought to help dilate blood vessels, thereby preventing increases in blood pressure and maintaining kidney function.

Buy a product with a combination of EPA and DHA, two omega-3 fatty acids found in fish. Avoid fish *liver* oil capsules. Many fish liver oil products contain large amounts of vitamin A, which can be toxic when taken in large amounts for an extended period.

The typical dosage to lower blood pressure is 4 grams per day, often taken in divided doses. Studies have used 4 grams of fish oil providing 2 grams of EPA and 1.4 grams of DHA. To achieve this amount of EPA and DHA, a liquid fish oil supplement is advised. Carlson MedOmega Fish Oil provides 1200 milligrams of EPA and 1200 milligrams of DHA per 1 teaspoon (5 ml).

Fish oil supplements can cause belching and a fishy taste. Because fish oil has a thinning effect on the blood, you should use caution if you're taking blood-thinning medication such as aspirin, warfarin (Coumadin) or heparin. See Chapter 8, page 162, for more information on fish oils.

Nutrition Strategy Checklist for High Blood Pressure

- ☐ Weight control
- ☐ DASH diet
- ☐ Fish
- ☐ Nuts
- ☐ Limit alcohol and caffeine
- ☐ Vitamin C
- ☐ Calcium
- ☐ Magnesium
- ☐ Potassium
- ☐ Restrict sodium
- ☐ Garlic
- ☐ Coenzyme Q10
- ☐ Fish oil supplement

Recommended Resources

Blood Pressure Canada
www.hypertension.ca

American Heart Association
National Center
www.americanheart.org
7272 Greenville Avenue
Dallas, TX, USA 75231
Tel: 1-800-AHA-USA1 (242-8721)

American Society of Hypertension
www.ash-us.org
515 Madison Avenue, Suite 1212
New York, NY, USA 10022
Tel: 212-644-0650
Fax: 212-644-0658

National Heart, Lung, and Blood Institute
NHLBI Health Information Network
National Institutes of Health
www.nhlbi.nih.gov
P.O. Box 30105
Bethesda, MD, USA 20824-0105
Tel: 301-592-8573
Fax: 301-592-8563

Hyperthyroidism (Graves' Disease)

Hyperthyroidism, or overactive thyroid, occurs when your thyroid gland produces too much of a thyroid hormone called thyroxine. The thyroid gland is a tiny butterfly-shaped gland that weighs only an ounce. It produces a steady supply of two major thyroid hormones: triiodothyronine (T3) and thyroxine (T4). When you're healthy, the pituitary gland located in your brain releases thyroid stimulating-hormone (TSH), which triggers the release of T3 and T4. These thyroid hormones travel in your bloodstream to various organs in the body and determine the speed of all your internal chemical processes. In a nutshell, thyroid hormones act to control your body's metabolic rate (the speed at which you burn calories). When T3 and T4 are at normal levels, the amount of TSH in your blood will level off.

When the thyroid gland becomes overactive it secretes excessive T4, causing your cells to work harder and your metabolism to speed up by 60 percent to 100 percent. This condition is known as hyperthyroidism and is characterized by a high metabolic rate.

What Causes Hyperthyroidism?

Several factors may trigger hyperthyroidism, but in North America, Graves' disease causes 90 percent of all cases. This disorder is named after the Irish physician Robert Graves, who first described it in 1835. The condition is also referred to as diffuse toxic goiter, thyrotoxicosis or Basedow's disease.

Graves' disease is an autoimmune condition. Under normal circumstances, the immune system produces antibodies that protect the body from foreign invaders, such as bacteria and viruses. In Graves' disease, the immune system malfunctions and produces a protein called thyroid-stimulating antibody that causes the thyroid gland to overproduce thyroid hormones.

Little is known about the exact causes of Graves' disease. It's thought that several factors, including a genetic predisposition, may be involved. Severe emotional stress may also be a factor. Stress can increase the blood levels of cortisone and adrenaline, two hormones that help prepare the body for a stressful event. Cortisone and adrenaline may also affect the production of antibodies in the immune system. It's possible that environmental conditions may cause immune system malfunctions, triggering the problems of an overactive thyroid.

Symptoms

Hyperthyroidism causes a range of symptoms, including:

- anxiousness, nervousness and irritability
- fast heartbeat
- sleeplessness
- fatigue
- heat intolerance
- high blood pressure
- profuse sweating
- shakiness and tremors
- muscle weakness, especially in the upper arms and thighs
- confusion
- increased appetite
- weight loss
- frequent bowel movements
- eye changes, including puffiness and a constant stare
- sensitivity to light, increased tear formation
- fine, brittle hair
- thinning skin
- lighter or less frequent menstrual periods

In addition to the symptoms of hyperthyroidism listed above, Graves' disease is characterized by three other distinctive symptoms:

- The thyroid gland may become quite enlarged, causing a bulge in the neck. This is called a goitre.
- Sometimes people with Graves' disease develop a lumpy, reddish thickening of the skin in front of the shins. This condition is called pretibial myxedema.
- Fifty percent of people with Graves' disease will have eyes that protrude out of their sockets due to a buildup of deposits and fluid in the orbit of the eye. As a result, the muscles that move the eye are not able to function properly, causing double or blurred vision. Eyelids may not close properly because they are swollen with fluid, exposing the eye to injury from foreign particles. Eyes will be red and watery, and will hurt.

Thyroid hormones also have an effect on the reproductive system. Women with Graves' disease may find that their menstrual periods are decreased and younger girls may experience a delay in the onset of menstruation. For many women, an overactive thyroid gland is connected with infertility. Fortunately, once the condition has been treated successfully, fertility is usually quickly restored.

Who's at Risk?

About 75 percent of all autoimmune diseases occur in women, hitting them most often between the ages of 30 and 40.[1] In North America, hyperthyroidism (from all causes) affects more women than men. In Canada, Graves' disease affects approximately one in every one hundred people, and it looks like it's becoming more common.[2] You may be at risk of developing Graves' disease if you:

- are a woman between the ages of 20 and 40
- are a woman who has given birth within the last 6 months
- have experienced thyroid disease before
- have been overtreated for hypothyroidism
- have other autoimmune conditions (e.g., Hashimoto's thyroiditis, diabetes mellitus, rheumatoid arthritis, lupus, pernicious anemia or vitiligo)

Diseases of the immune system tend to run in families. Graves' disease has been identified as an inherited condition, although not every member of an afflicted family will develop the disorder. Cigarette smoking and stress may also increase the risk for Graves' disease.[3]

Conventional Treatment

The treatment for hyperthyroidism varies according to the needs and symptoms of each person. In developing a treatment plan, your physician will consider your age, the severity of your illness, the symptoms you're experiencing and other medical conditions you may have.

There are three main approaches to treating the problems associated with hyperthyroidism and Graves' disease.

1. **Medication.** Antithyroid drugs such as Tapazole (methimazole) and Propyl-Thyracil (propylthiouracil) are most commonly used to treat hyperthyroidism. They slow down the activity of the thyroid gland by suppressing the release of thyroid hormones. The doses of these medications are adjusted according to the level of thyroid hormone in your blood. Antithyroid drugs are usually prescribed in mild cases of hyperthyroidism and for children, young adults or the elderly with the disease.

2. **Radioactive iodine.** Since antithyroid drugs don't cure hyperthyroidism, you may be treated with radioactive iodine to achieve a long-term solution. A small dose of radioactive iodine is taken by mouth and travels from your stomach to your thyroid gland, where it destroys some of the cells. Treatment is usually designed to destroy only enough thyroid cells to bring thyroid hormone production back to a normal level. Treatment with radioactive iodine usually causes your thyroid gland to slow down to the point where it underproduces thyroid hormones, creating a condition known as hypothyroidism. Hypothyroidism is easily treated by taking a daily thyroid hormone pill called Synthroid (levothyroxine) to restore normal blood levels.

3. **Surgery.** Hyperthyroidism can be permanently cured by surgically removing the thyroid gland in a procedure called a *thyroidectomy*. This may be considered if you have a large goitre, if you have a negative reaction to antithyroid medication or if you are in a younger age group. Once the thyroid gland is removed, the cause of hyperthyroidism is eliminated. However, you'll probably become hypothyroid and thus require thyroid replacement medication for the rest of your life.

In addition to one or more of these treatments, your doctor will usually prescribe beta-blocking drugs such as Inderal (propranolol), Tenormin (atenolol) and Lopressor (metoprolol). Beta blockers don't control abnormal thyroid function but are useful in managing symptoms such as increased heart rate, elevated blood pressure and nervousness until other forms of treatment can be started. These drugs block the action of the thyroid hormone circulating in your bloodstream, slowing your heart rate and reducing feelings of nervousness and irritability. They are not suitable for people who have asthma or heart failure as they may cause these conditions to worsen.

Eye Symptoms

Any eye changes you experience because of Graves' disease will usually improve once the hyperthyroidism is under control. In some cases, however, the condition progresses despite all thyroid gland treatments. In these situations, strong drugs such as oral steroids (prednisone) or immunosuppressants (cyclosporin) may be used to minimize swelling and reduce pressure on the optic nerve.

Your specialist may consider radioactive treatments and surgery to remove some bone from the eye orbit to reduce swelling and prevent nerve damage. Simple ways to help you cope with your eye changes include using eye drops and eye lubricants, sleeping with the head of your bed elevated and wearing eyeglasses with prisms to improve double vision. If you're a cigarette smoker, bear in mind that smoking makes eye symptoms worse and reduces your response to treatment.

Managing Graves' Disease

The nutritional approaches recommended below are intended to help offset side effects associated with various types of treatment for Graves' disease. In addition to keeping you well during and after your course of therapy, these strategies will improve your overall health and feeling of well-being.

Dietary Strategies

Weight Control

If you have been treated for hyperthyroidism, you're at risk for gaining weight. Research suggests that up to 50 percent of women with hyperthyroidism report weight problems after therapy.[4-7] To prevent weight loss, many women increase their food intake when they are experiencing the disease. When thyroid hormones return to lower, normal levels, metabolic rate slows down. This means your body will burn fewer calories each day. If you don't reduce your food intake to match your lower metabolism, you'll gain weight.

If you have finished your treatment program and you now weigh more than you did before you were diagnosed with Graves' disease, examine your eating habits to determine where you're going wrong. Keep a food diary for 2 weeks. Writing down what you eat often highlights dietary discrepancies. In Obesity, Overweight and Weight Loss, page 574, I outline many strategies to help promote weight loss.

To improve your chances of long-term success, consider working one-on-one with a registered dietitian. To find a nutritionist in private practice in your area, log on to www.dietitians.ca.

Vitamins and Minerals

Antioxidants

Research suggests that hyperthyroidism is associated with a decrease in antioxidants and an increase in oxidative stress brought on by free radical molecules. It's also thought that oxidative stress caused by free radicals can contribute to the tissue damage caused by hyperthyroidism.[8-11] Free radicals are highly reactive oxygen molecules that are produced by normal body processes. Dietary antioxidants such as vitamins C and E, beta carotene and selenium quench harmful free radicals and prevent them from causing damage to body cells.

Studies that measured levels of antioxidant nutrients in the blood and thyroid tissue of women with Graves' disease have observed decreased levels of beta carotene and vitamin E.[12,13] Another study looked at the effect of a daily vitamin C supplement in twenty-four women undergoing antithyroid drug therapy for Graves' disease.[14] At the beginning of the study, the researchers found that, compared with healthy women who served as controls, those with hyperthyroidism had higher levels of oxidized compounds and lower levels of antioxidant enzymes in their blood. After taking 1000 milligrams of vitamin C for 1 month, these women had significant increases in antioxidant enzymes.

Research conducted in women taking Tapazole (methimazole) for Graves' disease found that a mixed antioxidant supplement (vitamins C and E, beta carotene and selenium) increased antioxidant enzymes in the body and was associated with achieving normal thyroid hormone levels at a faster rate than medication alone.[15,16]

If you're undergoing antithyroid drug treatment for Graves' disease, increase your intake of antioxidants from diet and supplements. As an alternative to supplementing antioxidants singly (see below), mixed antioxidant supplements are available (e.g., SISU Supreme Antioxidant 6, SISU Ester ACES Plus and Jamieson Formula NT-OX).

VITAMIN C. The recommended dietary allowance (RDA) is 75 and 90 milligrams for women and men, respectively (smokers need an additional 35 milligrams). Best food sources include citrus fruit, citrus juices, cantaloupe, kiwi, mango, strawberries, broccoli, Brussels sprouts, cauliflower, red pepper and tomato juice. To supplement, take 500 milligrams of vitamin C once daily. The upper daily limit is 2000 milligrams.

VITAMIN E. The RDA is 22 international units (IU). Best food sources include wheat germ, nuts, seeds, vegetable oils, whole grains and kale. To supplement take 400 IU of natural source vitamin E. Buy a "mixed" vitamin E supplement if possible. The upper daily limit is 1500 IU.

BETA CAROTENE. No RDA has been established for beta carotene. Best food sources are orange and dark-green produce, including carrots, sweet potato, winter squash, broccoli, collard greens, kale, spinach, apricots, cantaloupe, peaches, nectarines, mango and papaya. Most beta carotene supplements supply 10,000 to 25,000 IU of beta carotene. If you're a smoker, don't take high dose beta carotene supplements.

SELENIUM. The RDA is 55 micrograms. Best food sources include Brazil nuts, shrimp, salmon, halibut, crab, fish, pork, organ meats, wheat bran, whole-wheat bread, brown rice, onion, garlic and mushrooms. To supplement take 100 to 200 micrograms per day. The upper daily limit is 400 micrograms.

Calcium and Vitamin D

It's well documented that hyperthyroidism causes a higher rate of bone breakdown. Some studies, but not all, have found that antithyroid medication has a harmful effect on bone density. To further explore the effect of anti-thyroid medication on bone loss, French researchers summarized the results from forty-one studies in 1250 patients.[17] Their results showed that medications like Tapazole (methimazole) and Propyl-Thyracil (propylth-iouracil), which suppress thyroid hormone secretion, cause significant bone loss in the lower spine and hip in post-menopausal women.

There's also evidence that women with Graves' disease are more susceptible to calcium and vitamin D deficiency during the winter months.[18] Deficiencies of these two nutrients are linked with a higher risk of tetany following surgery for Graves' disease. Tetany—usually caused by very low calcium levels in the blood—is characterized by pain, twitching, cramps and spasms of the muscles. Mild tetany is typified by tingling in the fingers, toes, lips and tongue. Low calcium levels can be caused by a lack of vitamin D. Fortunately, tetany can be successfully treated with adequate calcium and vitamin D.

To protect your bones and lower the risk of post-operative tetany, make sure you meet your daily requirements for each nutrient (see Chapter 4, page 56, for more information on food sources and supplements).

CALCIUM. Consume 1500 milligrams of calcium per day to help offset increased bone loss. Best food sources are milk, yogurt, cheese, fortified soy and rice beverages, fortified orange juice, tofu, salmon (with bones), kale, bok choy, broccoli and Swiss chard. Take a calcium supplement once or twice daily to ensure that you reach an intake of 1500 milligrams.

VITAMIN D. Consume 1000 IU of vitamin D daily from a supplement. Best food sources are fluid milk, fortified soy and rice beverages, oily fish, egg yolks, butter and margarine; however, diet will not provide enough vitamin D to meet your needs. To determine how much vitamin D you need to buy, calculate how much you're already consuming from your multivitamin and calcium supplements, subtract that from your RDA and make up the difference. Vitamin D is available in 400 and 1000 IU doses.

Iodine

This trace mineral is an integral part of T3 and T4, the two thyroid hormones released by the thyroid gland. When the body is faced with an ongoing lack of iodine, production of thyroid hormones declines. This can lead to hypothyroidism, which produces symptoms such as weight gain and sluggishness (see Hypothyroidism, page 479).

While a deficiency of iodine doesn't lead to Graves' disease, shortchanging your diet of this indispensable mineral might influence your remission rate after treatment with antithyroid drugs. One American study of sixty-nine patients who took antithyroid medication for Graves' disease suggests that the more iodine in the diet, the longer the rate of remission (i.e., the longer the disease remained dormant).[19]

The major source of iodine is the ocean— seafood and seawater are excellent sources of the mineral. As you move farther inland, the amount of iodine in foods varies and generally reflects the amount of this mineral in the soil that plants grow in or animals graze on. Land that was once under the ocean contains plenty of iodine. In Canada and the United States the soil around the Great Lakes is iodine-poor. However, in Canada and the United States the fortification of table salt with iodine has eliminated the health problems associated with iodine deficiency.

The daily recommended intake of iodine for adults is 150 micrograms. Women need to consume an additional 70 and 140 micrograms each day during pregnancy and breastfeeding, respectively. North Americans are estimated to be getting approximately 200 to 500 micrograms of iodine per day, well above the requirements. Some of this excess may be coming from a diet increasingly reliant on fast foods, which add a generous amount of iodized salt to the diet. Besides salt, other food sources of iodine include seafood, bread, dairy products, plants grown in iodine-rich soil and meat and poultry from animals raised on iodine-rich soil.

If antithyroid drugs are a part of your treatment regime, make sure you include iodine-rich foods in your diet. This is particularly true if you live in an area with iodine-poor soil, if you avoid fast food and salty foods and if you don't add table salt to your meals. Consider bringing back the saltshaker to the table—a little is all you need.

Nutrition Strategy Checklist for Hyperthyroidism

- ☐ Weight control
- ☐ Vitamin C
- ☐ Vitamin E
- ☐ Beta carotene
- ☐ Selenium
- ☐ Calcium
- ☐ Vitamin D
- ☐ Iodine

Recommended Resources

Thyroid Foundation of Canada
www.thyroid.ca
1669 Jalna Boulevard, Suite 803
London, ON N6E 3S1

Tel: 519-649-5478 or 1-800-267-8822
Fax: 519-649-5402

Graves' Disease Foundation
www.ngdf.org
400 International Drive
Williamsville, NY, USA 14221
Tel: 716- 631-2310
Fax: 716-631-2822
Email: gravesdiseasefd@gmail.com

Hypoglycemia

Most of us have experienced that difficult time of day when energy dips, concentration wanes and our stomach grumbles for food. But for some people, the effects of too little sugar (glucose) in the bloodstream are more debilitating—headache, shakiness, weakness, rapid heartbeat, anxiety, confusion, blurred vision—and they often occur without warning. Hypoglycemia is the medical term for low blood sugar (glucose). Low glucose or blood sugar can cause many body organs to malfunction. The brain is the most susceptible because glucose is its main energy source.

Your body relies on glucose as its main source of fuel for daily activities. During the process of digestion, the carbohydrates (sugars and starches) that you eat are broken down in the intestine into glucose. Glucose is absorbed by your bloodstream and then carried to every cell in your body. Unused glucose is stored in your muscles and liver as glycogen. Your body draws on these sugar stores for energy when your blood sugar drops.

Normally, blood-glucose levels range from 4.0 to 6.0 millimoles per litre (mmol/L) of blood before eating and rise to 5.0 to 8.0 mmol/L in the 2 hours following a meal. Whenever you eat food, the breakdown of carbohydrates into glucose causes your blood-sugar level to rise. This triggers your pancreas, an organ located in your upper abdomen, to release a hormone called insulin. Insulin helps glucose enter body cells, where it supplies the energy to fuel most bodily functions. As glucose is absorbed into the cells, your blood-sugar level gradually drops back to a normal range.

A few hours later, when most of the available glucose supply is consumed, your blood-sugar levels start to fall below normal, indicating that your body needs more fuel. Your pancreas responds to the falling glucose levels by releasing a different hormone, called glucagon. Glucagon stimulates your liver to release its stored supply of glucose into the bloodstream, where it's circulated to the cells. Once again, your blood-sugar levels rise back to normal. Adrenaline and cortisol, hormones released by your adrenal glands, also help keep blood-glucose levels up. By relying on insulin, glucagon and several other hormones, your body keeps your blood-glucose levels under constant control and regulates your daily energy supply.

What Causes Hypoglycemia?

Hypoglycemia occurs when your blood-glucose levels drop too low and you no longer have enough energy to fuel your daily activities. It can be a concern for people with diabetes who are taking certain blood sugar–lowering medications, but it can also affect people who don't have diabetes. Two types of hypoglycemia can occur in people without diabetes: fasting and reactive. *Fasting hypoglycemia* happens when a person hasn't had anything to eat or drink for 8 or more hours. It's usually related to an underlying illness; to hereditary hormone or enzyme deficiencies; to taking certain medications; or to binge drinking (alcohol interferes with your liver's attempts to raise blood glucose).

More common is *reactive hypoglycemia*, which happens when blood glucose drops abnormally low within 1 to 4 hours after eating a meal. This type of low blood-sugar reaction occurs when the pancreas releases too much insulin at once, causing your blood-sugar level to plummet below normal. If you're prone to reactive hypoglycemia, eating too many refined starchy or sugary foods can aggravate the condition. That's because large portions of processed carbohydrate-rich foods cause your blood sugar to rise very rapidly, triggering excessive insulin production and a dramatic drop in your glucose level, leaving you feeling sweaty, anxious, hungry and shaky.

Other possible causes of hypoglycemia include:

- stress and anxiety
- an unbalanced diet that's high in refined grains and/or sugars
- drinking alcohol
- early pregnancy
- prolonged fasting
- long periods of strenuous exercise
- exercising while you're on beta-blocker medication (e.g., propranolol)
- liver disease
- gastric surgery that disrupts the balance between digestion and insulin release
- hereditary intolerance of foods that contain the natural sugars fructose and galactose (rare childhood conditions)

Although there are many conditions that may cause hypoglycemia, only 1 percent of hypoglycemia cases occur in people who do not have diabetes. Studies indicate that it's actually quite a rare disorder.

Symptoms

When your blood-sugar level falls, your body responds by releasing a hormone called epinephrine (adrenaline) from your adrenal glands. This hormone stimulates your liver to release its stored glucose into your bloodstream. But this adrenaline rush also produces the symptoms that are characteristic of hypoglycemia, such as sweating, nervousness, rapid heartbeat, hunger, faintness and trembling.

If your blood-sugar level continues to fall, the reduced glucose supply will begin to affect your brain. Symptoms include headache, dizziness, confusion, blurred vision, difficulty concentrating, anxiety, agitation and abnormal behaviour that could be mistaken for drunkenness. If your condition continues to worsen, convulsions, loss of consciousness and coma may result. Such life-threatening symptoms are usually caused by too much medication in people with diabetes.

If you have symptoms of hypoglycemia and you don't have diabetes, your doctor may conduct some simple blood tests to measure your blood-sugar and insulin levels. Ideally, this test will be done while you're experiencing an episode of hypoglycemic symptoms. The diagnosis of hypoglycemia will be confirmed if the blood test indicates that your blood-sugar levels are below normal and your symptoms improve when you consume sugar. If your blood glucose is less than 4.0 mmol/L and your symptoms disappear when food is eaten, hypoglycemia is likely the cause.

For years, doctors used the oral glucose tolerance test to diagnose hypoglycemia; however, it's no longer used because it can trigger symptoms. (The oral glucose tolerance test measures blood-glucose levels after an overnight fast, and then 2 hours after consumption of a sugary solution.) One of the most useful ways to determine if you suffer from hypoglycemia is to assess your symptoms. In general, when symptoms appear 3 to 4 hours after eating and disappear after you've consumed food, hypoglycemia is a likely cause.

Who's at Risk?

You may be more likely to develop hypoglycemia if you fall into one of the following categories:

- people who take medication for diabetes
- people who fast or follow a low-calorie diet
- pregnant women
- people who drink alcohol after a long period without eating food

Conventional Treatment

In most cases, the symptoms of hypoglycemia will quickly improve when you consume sugar in any form. Eating candy, sugar cubes, glucose or dextrose tablets or drinking a glass of fruit juice, milk or sugar water will immediately raise your blood-sugar levels, making you feel much better. If you do experience a low blood-sugar reaction, treat it immediately by consuming 10 to 15 grams of carbohydrate, such as five Life Savers candies, 4 teaspoons (20 ml) of sugar, half a banana or 1/2 to 3/4 cup (125 to 175 ml) of fruit juice.

If you have diabetes or are prone to recurring episodes of hypoglycemia, you should always carry some candy or other type of sugar. Dextrose tablets are widely available in drugstores. In severe cases of hypoglycemia, an injection of glucagon or intravenous glucose may be necessary to restore blood-sugar levels.

Hypoglycemia that develops after gastrointestinal surgery can often be managed by eating small, frequent meals and following a high-protein, low-carbohydrate diet. A hereditary intolerance of fructose (fruit sugar) or galactose (milk sugar) is treated by eliminating the foods that cause hypoglycemic symptoms.

Managing Hypoglycemia

The section below focuses on nutritional strategies that will help you maintain a consistent blood-sugar level so that you're less vulnerable to experiencing hypoglycemia. Over the years, I have had many clients seek my help for managing their hypoglycemia. They have learned that following a proper diet is key to preventing low blood-sugar reactions. Instead of relying on fast-acting carbohydrates to treat a low blood-sugar reaction, use the strategies below to prevent a sugar low from occurring in the first place. The following strategies can help to ensure glucose enters your bloodstream at a steady, even pace during the day. (If you have diabetes, ask your dietitian for a diabetic meal plan that helps manage your blood-sugar level.)

Dietary Strategies

Meal Timing

One of the first and most important ways to prevent a low blood-sugar reaction is to eat regularly throughout the day. Your blood sugar will peak 45 to 90 minutes after you eat a meal. After this point, your sugar level starts its decline. If you suffer from hypoglycemia, you should eat every 3 hours—that means eating *three meals and three snacks*. Here's what a daytime meal and snack schedule might look like (the time span is the approximate time of the meal or snack, not the duration):

Breakfast:	7:00–8:00 A.M.
Snack:	10:00–10:30 A.M.
Lunch:	12:00–1:00 P.M.
Snack:	3:00–4:00 P.M.
Dinner:	6:00–7:00 P.M.
Snack:	9:00–10:00 P.M.

Once you get into a consistent pattern of eating, you'll feel much better. And if you choose the right foods at your meals and snacks, chances are you'll forget that you're vulnerable to hypoglycemic reactions.

Carbohydrates: Low Glycemic Index

Carbohydrate-containing foods, such as starches, fruit, milk and sugars, eventually wind up as glucose in your bloodstream. But not all carbohydrates behave the same way when it comes to raising your blood sugar. Some carbohydrate-rich foods are digested and absorbed into the bloodstream quickly, while others are broken down and converted to glucose more gradually.

Foods that are converted to blood glucose quickly (e.g., white bread, white rice) trigger your pancreas to release an excessive amount of insulin, causing your blood-glucose level to drop to a very low level. On the other hand, foods such as high-fibre breakfast cereals, grainy breads, steel-cut oatmeal and yogurt are digested and absorbed more slowly, causing a gradual rise in blood sugar. This means your pancreas doesn't release as large an amount of insulin, so your blood-sugar level won't plummet. Instead, you experience a smooth,

steady blood-sugar level, leading to more consistent energy levels.

The rate at which a food causes your blood sugar to rise can be measured and assigned a value. This measure is referred to as the glycemic-index value. The glycemic index (GI) is a ranking from 0 to 100. The number tells you whether a food raises your blood glucose rapidly, moderately or slowly. Foods that are digested quickly and cause your blood sugar to rise rapidly have high glycemic-index values. Foods that are digested slowly, leading to a gradual rise in blood sugar, are assigned low glycemic-index values. All foods are compared with pure glucose, which is given a value of 100 (fast acting). Choosing fibre-rich low-glycemic carbohydrates also helps people with diabetes reduce the number of hypoglycemic episodes.[1]

- Choose carbohydrate foods that do not cause large increases in blood sugar.
- Choose low GI foods at your meals and snacks.
- Avoid eating high GI foods as snacks, since they can trigger a low blood sugar.
- Combine a high GI food with a low GI food to result in a meal with a medium GI value.

You'll find a list of foods ranked by their GI value in Chapter 1, page 8.

Soluble Fibre

Many of the foods with a low glycemic-index value tend to be higher in soluble fibre. Dried peas, beans, lentils, oats, barley, psyllium husks, apples and citrus fruit are all good sources of soluble fibre and, as you'll see from the GI table in Chapter 1, page 8, these foods also have a low GI. When you eat these foods, the soluble fibre forms a gel in your stomach and slows the rate of digestion and absorption.

That means your blood sugar will rise at a slower rate and your pancreas won't produce excessive amounts of insulin.

To help sustain your blood glucose longer after eating, choose low-GI foods that are rich in soluble fibre:

Low-GI Foods Rich in Soluble Fibre

Food	Good Sources of Soluble Fibre
Cereals	100% bran cereal, Kellogg's All-Bran Buds, steel-cut or large-flake oatmeal, oat bran, Red River Hot Cereal
Grains	Barley, wild rice, brown rice
Legumes	All (baked beans, bean soups, black beans, chickpeas, kidney beans, lentils, soybeans, etc.)
Fruit	Apples, cantaloupe, grapefruit, oranges, pears, strawberries
Vegetables	Carrots, green peas, sweet potato

Adding a source of protein to meals slows the rate at which your stomach empties its contents into the small intestine. As a result, the carbohydrate in your meal will enter your bloodstream at a slower rate. Choose lean protein foods such as lean beef, skinless chicken breast, turkey, pork tenderloin, centre-cut pork chops, seafood and eggs. If you're a vegetarian, include vegetarian protein foods in your meals—tofu, beans, veggie ground round and tempeh. Dairy products such as milk, yogurt and cheese also contribute protein to a meal.

To help manage your blood sugar, distribute your protein throughout the day. If you need to eat 60 grams of protein each day, aim for 20 grams at each meal. You'll find a list of foods and their protein content in Chapter 2, page 20.

If you enjoy a green salad with your meal, continue doing so—but toss it with a vinaigrette dressing. Studies have found that vinegars, especially red wine vinegar, also slow the rate at which food leaves your stomach.

Caffeine and Alcohol

Caffeine is known to cause a low blood-sugar reaction, especially if it has been a few hours since you last ate. Researchers from the Yale School of Medicine found that consuming 400 milligrams of caffeine triggered hypoglycemia when blood-sugar levels were in the low–normal range, as might occur 2 to 3 hours after a meal.[2]

If you're sensitive to caffeine, switch to low-caffeine or caffeine-free beverages. Replace coffee with decaf coffee, cereal-based beverages (e.g., Postum), herbal tea, weakly brewed black tea or green tea. If you don't want to part with your daily cup of coffee, drink it with a meal so that the caffeine will be less likely to trigger a low blood-sugar reaction. Between meals, stick to vegetable juice, water, milk, herbal tea or decaf lattes.

Drinking alcoholic beverages can also impair blood-sugar control and trigger a hypoglycemic reaction in susceptible individuals, especially if consumed on an empty stomach. Alcohol can induce reactive hypoglycemia by interfering with glucose uptake and promoting the release of insulin from your pancreas. The drop in blood sugar that follows leads to a craving for foods, especially sweets. If you reach for sugary foods in response to this low blood sugar, you'll only aggravate your symptoms. Drinking alcohol can also cause delayed hypoglycemia up to 14 hours later in people with type 1 diabetes.

If you have hypoglycemia, avoid drinking alcohol on an empty stomach. Instead, enjoy your drink with a meal. The presence of food in your stomach delays the absorption of alcohol. If you do drink, limit yourself to seven alcoholic drinks per week (women) or nine per week (men) for health protection.

Vitamins and Minerals

Chromium

Supplements of this trace mineral have been promoted to manage hypoglycemia, but unfortunately research studies are few and far between. One small study was conducted in the late 1980s with eight women who had reactive hypoglycemia.[3] Those who took 200 micrograms of chromium for 3 months experienced significantly fewer low blood-sugar symptoms and had higher blood-glucose levels 2 to 4 hours after eating. Another small study conducted among twenty patients with hypoglycemia found similar results using 125 micrograms of the mineral.[4] A larger number of studies have investigated the use of chromium in individuals with type 2 diabetes.

Chromium plays an important role in regulating blood glucose. It's used by the body to make glucose tolerance factor (GTF), a compound that interacts with insulin and helps maintain normal blood-sugar levels. With adequate amounts of chromium present, your body uses less insulin to do its job.

The recommended intake for chromium is 25 and 35 micrograms per day for women and men, respectively. Chromium-rich foods include apples with the skin, green peas, chicken breast, refried beans, mushrooms, oysters, wheat germ and brewer's yeast. Processed foods and refined (white) starchy foods like white bread, instant rice, white pasta, sugar and sweets contain very little chromium.

If you're concerned that you're not getting enough of this mineral through your diet, check your multivitamin and mineral supplement to see how much it contains. If it's less than 50 micrograms, consider taking a separate 100 or 200 microgram supplement each day. Studies show that chromium picinolate and chromium nicotinate are absorbed more easily than other forms (such as chromium chloride). The safe upper limit is 400 micrograms per day.

Other Lifestyle Factors

Regular Exercise

Exercise improves many aspects of blood-sugar control. Working out enhances the body's sensitivity to insulin, improves glucose uptake by your cells and increases the concentration of chromium in your tissues. (If you have type 1 diabetes, however, it's critical to know how to manage insulin dosage and food intake to prevent an exercise-induced low blood-sugar reaction.)

You don't need to exercise vigorously to reap benefits. In fact, working out too intensely may bring on hypoglycemia. If you exercise with someone, you should be able to carry on a conversation (though you should be a little breathless). If you work out at a gym, consult with a certified personal trainer to help you find your target heart-rate zone. Staying within this range while you exercise will prevent you from overdoing it. Good activities include brisk walking, jogging, stair climbing, swimming, rowing and cycling. Aim to exercise four times per week, with each session at least 30 minutes long. If you're not exercising this much, gradually work up to it.

Plan your snacks around your exercise session. If you eat lunch at noon and exercise at 3 P.M., you'll want a snack about 30 minutes before you begin. At 2:30 P.M., eat an apple, some yogurt or a sports energy bar. Depending on what time you eat dinner, you'll likely need to eat another small snack around 4:30 P.M., after your workout session.

Nutrition Strategy Checklist for Hypoglycemia

☐ Eat every 3 hours
☐ Low-GI carbohydrate-rich foods
☐ Soluble fibre
☐ Foods rich in protein
☐ Avoid or limit caffeine
☐ Avoid or limit alcohol
☐ Chromium
☐ Regular exercise

Recommended Resources

The Hypoglycemia Support Foundation, Inc.
www.hypoglycemia.org
P.O. Box 451778
Sunrise, FL, USA 33345
This website was founded by an author on the subject.

Mayo Foundation for Medical Education and Research
www.mayoclinic.com
This website is produced by a team of writers, editors, health educators, nurses, doctors and scientists, and is one of the best patient-education sites on the Internet. The information is reliable, thorough and clearly written.

National Diabetes Information Clearinghouse
National Institutes of Health
www.diabetes.niddk.nih.gov
1 Information Way
Bethesda, MD, USA 20892-3560
Tel: 301-654-3327

Hypothyroidism

Hypothyroidism develops when your thyroid gland doesn't produce enough thyroid hormones to meet your body's needs. An underactive thyroid gland will cause your metabolic rate to slow down, making you feel slow, sluggish and constantly tired. Thyroid deficiencies have also been known to cause infertility or miscarriages in early pregnancy.

What Causes Hypothyroidism?

The thyroid gland is a small organ with a big job. Located in your neck, just below your Adam's apple, the thyroid controls and coordinates your body's main body functions, or metabolism. It produces two thyroid hormones, triiodothyronine (T3) and thyroxine (T4), which circulate through your bloodstream and act on almost every organ in your body. These hormones maintain a healthy metabolic rate by controlling the speed at which your body burns calories for energy.

A well-functioning thyroid gland is essential to normal growth and development. If your gland doesn't produce enough thyroid hormones, all your bodily functions will slow down. An underactive thyroid seldom produces symptoms in the early stages, but over time you may feel sluggish and tired and may develop a variety of other uncomfortable symptoms. As the condition becomes more advanced, you could experience serious health problems.

The most common type of hypothyroidism is *Hashimoto's thyroiditis*, or *chronic thyroiditis*. It's an autoimmune disease caused by a malfunction of your immune system. In this case, the immune system begins to produce antithyroid antibodies that attack the thyroid gland. The damage caused by these antibodies prevents the thyroid from producing adequate levels of thyroid hormones. People with Hashimoto's thyroiditis often develop a painless thyroid lump or goitre that can be seen at the lower front of their throat.

Hypothyroidism can also be caused by:

- surgery to remove the thyroid gland (usually a treatment for thyroid cancer or, in some cases, for overactive thyroid)
- radioactive iodine therapy (usually used to treat overactive thyroid conditions)
- X-rays, especially of the head and neck
- treatment with certain medications, such as lithium
- obesity
- pregnancy and postpartum conditions
- iodine deficiencies
- absence of a thyroid gland at birth (all babies in Canada are screened for hypothyroidism to detect this condition)
- genetic predisposition

Another version of the disorder, *secondary hypothyroidism*, may develop if you have an abnormality in an area of your brain called the hypothalamic-pituitary axis. The pituitary gland helps the thyroid gland regulate the production of T3 and T4 by releasing thyroid-stimulating hormone (TSH). The hypothalamus gland performs a similar function by producing thyrotropin-releasing hormone (TRH). If these two glands don't secrete enough hormones to trigger your thyroid gland to function, you may experience the hormonal deficiencies that lead to hypothyroidism.

Symptoms

The symptoms of hypothyroidism vary in severity, depending on the decrease in thyroid

hormone levels and the length of time a deficiency has been present. Most of the time, the symptoms are fairly mild. In the early stages of the disorder, symptoms may not be noticeable at all and you may still feel quite well. However, research indicates that people with mild hypothyroidism go on to develop more severe thyroid problems in later years.

When you have more severe hypothyroidism, you may begin to feel slow, sluggish, tired and rundown. You may also feel depressed and lose interest in daily activities. Additional symptoms include:

- increased sensitivity to cold
- muscle swelling or cramps, especially in your arms and legs
- weight gain
- dry, itchy skin
- constipation
- increased menstrual flow
- tingling or numbness in your hands and feet
- coarseness or loss of hair
- memory loss and mental impairment
- infertility or miscarriages
- a slow heart rate
- dull facial expression, droopy eyelids and hoarse voice
- high blood pressure

Because hypothyroidism progresses gradually, worsening over a period of months or years, you may not even realize how unwell you feel until your thyroid condition is corrected with a hormone medication.

Who's at Risk?

Two out of every 100 Canadians have an underactive thyroid gland.[1] Thyroid disease can affect anyone, but hypothyroidism is ten times more common in women than in men. The risk of hypothyroidism increases considerably as you age. It usually strikes after age 40 and is common in elderly women. In fact, up to 10 percent of women over the age of 65 show evidence of hypothyroidism.[2] Although the condition most often affects middle-aged and older adults, it can develop in infants and teenagers.

Hashimoto's thyroiditis has been associated with a genetic component, so your risk may be greater if you have a close relative, such as a parent or grandparent, with a related autoimmune disease.

Some women also develop thyroid conditions during or immediately after pregnancy. Thyroiditis is especially common during the period following the birth of the baby, when it can often be confused with postpartum depression.

If you have had surgery or received radioactive iodine therapy to treat thyroid conditions such as hyperthyroidism, Graves' disease or thyroid cancer, you may be predisposed to hypothyroidism. Irradiation of the head and neck through X-rays or cancer treatment may also predispose you to thyroid problems.

In countries outside North America, one of the most common causes of hypothyroidism is iodine deficiency. This mineral is an essential component of thyroid hormones. People who don't have natural sources of iodine in their diet, such as fish and other seafood, are at high risk of developing hypothyroidism. In Canada and the United States, the problem has been virtually eliminated because iodine has been added to table salt.

Conventional Treatment

In most cases, hypothyroidism is a permanent condition that requires a lifetime of treatment. The goal of treatment is to provide the body with enough thyroid hormones to maintain an efficient metabolic rate. At present, the prescription of a thyroid hormone called levothyroxine (Synthroid) is the only effective treatment for this disorder.

Your doctor will determine your daily dosage of levothyroxine based on your age, sex, weight, thyroid function and other medications you're taking. Usually, you'll start with a low dose and increase it gradually until your blood levels of T4 and TSH are within the normal range. Hypothyroidism is an ongoing process, and your dosage may change as your thyroid function continues to deteriorate. Regular blood tests will help your doctor adjust your thyroid hormone medication to suit your needs. If you become pregnant, the dose may need to be increased. Older people need less T4, so your dosage may be lowered as you age.

Managing Hypothyroidism
Dietary Strategies
Weight Control

A deficiency of thyroid hormones leads to a general decline in the rate at which the body burns calories from carbohydrate, protein and fat for energy. As a result, weight gain is common in hypothyroidism. And it can be more difficult to lose weight if your thyroid hormone levels are not in a correct balance—but it's not impossible! In my private practice I have helped hundreds of women with an underactive thyroid successfully lose excess weight.

If you're suffering from hypothyroidism and experiencing difficulty controlling your weight, examine your eating habits to pinpoint areas that require modification. Keep a food diary for 2 weeks. Writing down what you eat often highlights dietary discrepancies. For weight-loss strategies, see Obesity, Overweight and Weight Loss, page 574.

High Blood Cholesterol

Hypothyroidism is linked with a greater risk of early heart disease, since thyroid hormones influence the level of blood cholesterol. Many studies find that patients suffering from a deficiency of thyroid hormones, whether they have overt symptoms or not, have higher levels of total cholesterol, LDL (bad) cholesterol and triglyceride levels.[3-9] The more severe the hypothyroidism, the higher the cholesterol levels.

Researchers have also learned that people with a sluggish thyroid gland have LDL cholesterol particles that are more readily oxidized by harmful free radical molecules.[10-12] Free radicals are reactive oxygen molecules that roam the body and damage cells. LDL cholesterol oxidized by free radicals has a greater tendency to stick to your artery walls. Your body does have ways of protecting itself from free radicals, though. Special enzymes in the body and certain nutrients in foods, such as vitamins C and E, act as antioxidants and help keep free radical activity in check.

If you have high blood cholesterol, see Heart Disease and High Blood Cholesterol, page 424, for nutritional strategies to prevent heart disease.

Soy Foods

You may have heard that eating large amounts of soy can block the production of thyroid hormones and result in an underactive thyroid and goitre (an enlarged thyroid gland). It's true that raw soybeans contain compounds that prevent the body's ability to use iodine. But heating soybeans eliminates these effects, and all soy foods, from tofu to soy nuts, are manufactured using heat. Goitre appears to occur only in people who are iodine deficient (the mineral is needed for normal thyroid function). In developed countries, salt is fortified with iodine to prevent deficiency. It's possible, however, that people who eat soy foods and who don't get enough iodine from their diet could be at risk for goitre.

Over the past 15 years, a handful of studies have found no effect of soy foods on thyroid function or thyroid hormone levels in healthy adults and people with hypothyroidism who are not iodine deficient.[13-15]

Vitamins and Minerals

B Vitamins

Some, but not all, studies have found that people with hypothyroidism may have higher blood levels of homocysteine, a known risk factor for early heart disease.[16-18] Homocysteine is an amino acid that everyone produces. Under normal circumstances it's converted to other harmless amino acids with the help of three B vitamins: folate, B6 and B12. When this conversion doesn't occur rapidly enough because of a deficiency of B vitamins or a genetic defect, homocysteine can accumulate in the blood. High levels of homocysteine can damage blood vessel walls and promote the buildup of cholesterol deposits. Research suggests that elevated homocysteine levels seen in patients with hypothyroidism are accompanied by low blood-folate levels.

Getting adequate amounts of B vitamins is an important way to keep your blood homocysteine at a healthy level. The best food sources for each B vitamin are as follows:

Vitamin B Food Sources

B Vitamin	Good Food Sources
Folate	Spinach (cooked), orange juice, lentils, wheat germ, broccoli, artichokes, asparagus, leafy greens and whole grains
Vitamin B6	Whole grains, bananas, potatoes, legumes, fish, meat and poultry
Vitamin B12	All animal foods, including meat, poultry, fish, dairy products and eggs, as well as fortified soy and rice beverages

Including good food sources of B vitamins and taking a daily multivitamin and mineral pill will ensure that you meet your requirements for all B vitamins. A standard multivitamin will provide 100 percent to 300 percent of the recommended dietary allowance (RDA) for each nutrient.

If your blood-homocysteine level is elevated, your doctor may advise you to take a single supplement of folic acid. A daily dose of 0.8 to 1 milligram of folic acid is sufficient to lower elevated blood homocysteine. Choose a folic acid supplement with vitamin B12 added. I don't recommend taking single folic acid supplements indefinitely. Once your homocysteine level is lowered to the acceptable range, discontinue. A multivitamin that supplies 0.4 milligrams of folic acid is sufficient. (See Chapter 4, page 42, for information on folic acid supplementation.)

Many B complex supplements also supply a higher dose of folic acid than standard multivitamins. One word of warning if you opt for a high-potency B vitamin supplement: Vitamin B3, or niacin, can cause flushing when taken in amounts greater than 35 milligrams. This is a harmless reaction that causes your face, chest and arms to feel hot and tingly. The reaction usually passes within 20 to 30 minutes. To avoid this niacin flush: 1) take your supplement right after eating a meal, 2) buy a supplement with less than 35 milligrams of niacin or 3) buy a multivitamin or B complex that contains niacinamide rather than niacin (niacinamide is non-flushing).

Iodine

This trace mineral is an integral part of T3 and T4, the two thyroid hormones released by the thyroid gland. The major source of iodine is the ocean—seafood and seawater are excellent sources of the mineral. As you move farther inland, the amount of iodine in foods varies and generally reflects the amount of iodine that's in the soil plants grow in or animals graze on. Land that was once under the ocean contains plenty of iodine. In Canada and the United States, the soil around the Great Lakes is iodine-poor. However, the fortification of table salt with iodine in Canada and the United States has eliminated health problems caused by iodine deficiency.

If the body is shortchanged of iodine on an ongoing basis, the production of thyroid hormones slows down and eventually hypothyroidism develops. But if you eat processed foods, restaurant meals and/or fast foods, or you add table salt to your meals, you're not at risk for consuming too little iodine.

Excess iodine in the diet can also cause hypothyroidism by halting the activity of enzymes needed for production of thyroid hormones. There have been cases of people developing hypothyroidism by taking in too much iodine in the form of iodine-rich seaweed and kelp supplements on a daily basis.[19]

The daily recommended intake for iodine is 150 micrograms per day. North Americans are estimated to be consuming 200 to 600 micrograms of iodine per day—well above requirements. Some of this iodine excess may come from our growing dependence on fast and processed foods, since these foods contribute a generous amount of salt to our daily diet. Besides iodized salt, other food sources of iodine include seafood, bread, dairy products, plants grown in iodine-rich soil and meat and poultry from animals raised on iodine-rich soil.

Selenium

This trace mineral is an important component of an enzyme that produces the thyroid hormone T3. Researchers have learned that a selenium deficiency in older adults is strongly associated with lower levels of the T3 hormone.[20] The relationship between impaired selenium status and reduced thyroid hormone levels may be partially responsible for the hypothyroidism that's often diagnosed in elderly women. Despite this, a recent study of 501 adults aged 60 to 74 living in the United Kingdom failed to show an effect of selenium supplements on thyroid function.[21] However, a study conducted in pregnant women with thyroid antibodies in their bloodstream found that taking 200 micrograms of selenium versus a placebo during and after pregnancy was associated with reduced inflammation of the thyroid and a lower risk of developing hypothyroidism (pregnant women who test positive for thyroid antibodies are more prone to develop hypothyroidism after pregnancy).[22] Other research suggests that a daily selenium supplement can reduce thyroid antibodies in patients with autoimmune thyroidosis (e.g., Hashimoto's thyroiditis).[23]

The best food sources of selenium include seafood and meat. Whole-wheat bread, wheat bran, wheat germ, oats, brown rice, Brazil nuts,

Swiss chard and garlic are other good sources. Dietary intake from plant foods will vary according to the selenium content of the soil in which the foods were grown.

People at greatest risk for a selenium deficiency are those who eat a vegetarian diet based on plant foods grown in low-selenium areas. But because most of us eat supermarket foods that have been transported from areas throughout Canada, the United States, Mexico or South America, selenium deficiency is uncommon.

If you're considering a supplement, check your multivitamin first. Some high-potency brands contain up to 100 micrograms of selenium. If you're using single selenium supplements, a 200 microgram dose is plenty. You might want to choose one that contains selenomethionine or selenium-rich yeast, since these organic forms of the mineral appear to be more available to the body.

The upper daily limit for selenium from foods and supplements is 400 micrograms per day. Consuming too much selenium over a period has toxic effects, including hair and nail loss, gastrointestinal upset, skin rash, garlic breath odour, fatigue, irritability and nervous-system abnormalities.

Iron and Calcium Supplements

If you're taking levothyroxine (Synthroid) and also being treated for an iron deficiency, take your medication and your iron pill 2 to 3 hours apart rather than at the same time. Studies have found that iron supplements can reduce the body's absorption of levothyroxine.[24,25] It's possible that impaired absorption of your medication could make you hypothyroid and increase your medication requirements.

If you're taking iron supplements to correct an iron deficiency, your doctor will monitor your thyroid hormone levels closely. Iron pills should be taken only if your doctor has diagnosed you with iron deficiency. If you're taking them of your own accord, be sure to let your physician know.

Calcium supplements can also interfere with the absorption of levothyroxine, primarily when the two are taken at or near the same time. To avoid an interaction, take your calcium supplements at least 4 hours before or after taking levothyroxine.

Nutrition Strategy Checklist for Hypothyroidism

☐ Weight control
☐ Manage blood cholesterol
☐ B vitamins
☐ Iodine
☐ Selenium

Recommended Resources

Thyroid Foundation of Canada
www.thyroid.ca
1669 Jalna Boulevard, Suite 803
London, ON N6E 3S1
Tel: 519-649-5478 or 1-800-267-8822
Fax: 519-649-5402

Impotence (Erectile Dysfunction)

For most men, impotence, or erectile dysfunction, can be a great source of embarrassment, anxiety and fear. It's defined as the inability to achieve or sustain an erection satisfactory for sexual intercourse. Impotence is different from other conditions that interfere with sexual intercourse, such as lack of sexual desire and problems with ejaculation. Erectile dysfunction varies in severity: Some men have a total inability to achieve an erection; others can do so inconsistently, and can sustain only brief erections.

Almost all men experience occasional episodes of erectile dysfunction. As men age, their sexual abilities change. Erections may take longer to achieve and may be slightly softer. More direct stimulation may be needed to produce an erection, orgasms may be less intense and recovery time between erections may be longer. These changes are a natural part of the aging process and not a cause for concern. Although a man's sexual responses may slow down over time, impotence is not an inevitable part of growing older.

Producing and sustaining an erection is a complex process. A precise sequence of events must take place, beginning with the sensory and mental stimulation provoked by sight, sound, touch, smell and thought. This state of sexual arousal triggers the brain to communicate with the nervous system, increasing blood flow to the penis. Surrounding muscles, tissues, arteries and veins respond to the message of sexual excitation by relaxing and expanding. This process allows the penis to engorge with blood. If this delicately balanced sequence of events is interrupted at any point, impotence can be the result.

What Causes Impotence?

Once thought to be primarily a psychological problem, impotence is often caused by a physical or medical condition. The most common cause of erectile dysfunction is damage to the arteries, tissues and muscles in the area of the penis. Diseases that may be responsible for the damage include diabetes, metabolic syndrome, multiple sclerosis, atherosclerosis, vascular diseases and kidney disease.

Prostate surgery or other surgical procedures can harm nerves and arteries near the penis. Impotence can also develop as a result of injuries to the penis, prostate gland, spinal cord or bladder, especially if there's damage to the surrounding muscles, nerves and tissue. Medications such as antihistamines, antidepressants, tranquilizers and high blood pressure drugs list impotence as a side effect. Cigarette smoking, obesity and an inadequate production of testosterone or other male hormones may also contribute to erectile dysfunction. Chronic alcoholism, substance abuse and smoking often increase the risk of impotence by lowering sexual drive or by interfering with the blood flow necessary to achieve an erection.

Although most cases of erectile dysfunction have an underlying medical cause, approximately 10 percent to 20 percent develop as a result of psychological factors.[1] Men who fail to achieve an erection because of a physical condition may find that anxiety only makes the situation worse. What may begin as an occasional physical problem can easily turn into an ongoing psychological issue. Other factors associated with impotence include stress, fatigue, guilt, depression, low self-esteem and loss of interest in a partner.

Symptoms

Signs of impotence include:

- total inability to achieve an erection
- inconsistent or sporadic inability to achieve an erection
- inability to maintain an erection

Who's at Risk?

It's estimated that 34 percent of Canadian men suffer from erectile dysfunction regularly.[2]

Impotence can affect men at any age after puberty, but the incidence increases with age. About 52 percent of men between the ages of 40 and 70 suffer from some type of erectile difficulty, with five in every one hundred men experiencing impotence after age 40.[3,4] Diseases account for over 70 percent of all cases of impotence. In fact, 35 percent to 50 percent of men with diabetes have erectile dysfunction.[5] Psychological factors account for up to 20 percent of all cases of impotence.

Conventional Treatment

Treatment is necessary if erectile dysfunction lasts longer than 2 months or is a recurring problem. Treatment may vary according to the cause and severity of the problem. Treatments include:

- **Viagra (sildenafil)** to relax the smooth muscles in the penis during sexual stimulation, increasing blood flow necessary to achieve an erection
- **Prostaglandin E (alprostadil)** to relax the smooth muscles in the penis, increasing blood flow necessary to achieve an erection
- **Testosterone** replacement therapy used in men with hormone deficiency
- **Binding devices** to slow the outflow of blood from the penis to achieve and sustain an erection
- **Vacuum devices** to create a vacuum pressure that draws blood into arteries in the penis
- **Vascular surgery** to improve blood flow to the penis (used when blood flow has been affected by an injury or a vascular blockage)

- **Penile implants** to place inflatable devices or rods into the sides of the penis to create a permanent erection; usually used after other approaches have been unsuccessful
- **Psychological counselling** to help deal with impotence problems caused by anxiety, stress or other psychological factors; most successful when both partners receive counselling
- **Behavioural sex therapy**

The following lifestyle changes may help prevent occasional episodes of erectile dysfunction:

- Quit smoking. The Massachusetts Male Aging Study found that smoking cigarettes almost doubles the likelihood of moderate or complete erectile dysfunction. Cigar smoking and secondhand smoke also increased the risk.[6]
- Limit use of alcohol or other drugs.
- Exercise regularly and eat a balanced diet.
- Reduce stress and anxiety.
- Get adequate sleep.
- Improve communication with your partner. Work on the relationship rather than the sexual intercourse.
- Create a relaxed, private and comfortable environment for intercourse.
- See your doctor for regular checkups.

Managing Impotence

Dietary Strategies

Weight Control

Many large studies have found a direct link between obesity and erectile dysfunction. In men reporting symptoms of erectile dysfunction, 79 percent have been found to be overweight or obese. Research suggests that erectile dysfunction is associated with having a body mass index (BMI) of 28 or greater. What's more, the results of weight-loss intervention studies point towards reduced weight improving sexual function. Men who exercise regularly also have a lower risk of becoming impotent.[7-10]

It's thought that carrying excess body fat increases inflammation in the body, which interferes with the normal functioning of blood vessel walls. Being overweight may also contribute to erectile dysfunction by causing reduced levels of male sex hormones.

To assess your current body weight see Obesity, Overweight and Weight Loss, page 569. If you determine your BMI is too high, modify your eating and exercise habits to promote a gradual, safe weight loss.

Mediterranean Diet

Research suggests that men who have metabolic syndrome and erectile dysfunction can improve their symptoms by following a Mediterranean-style diet. (Metabolic syndrome is a risk factor for erectile dysfunction. A person is thought to have metabolic syndrome, which is a clustering of risk factors in one person, if he or she has a large waist circumference plus two or more of the following: high blood triglycerides [blood fat], high blood pressure, elevated fasting blood glucose and low HDL [good] cholesterol.) In a 2-year study of sixty-five men, those following a Mediterranean diet had fewer symptoms, improved blood-vessel function and lower levels of inflammatory compounds in the bloodstream compared with those on the control diet.[11]

Adopt the principles below for a Mediterranean-style diet:

- Eat fruit, vegetables, grains, beans, nuts and seeds daily.
- Consume extra-virgin olive oil as your predominant source of added fat.
- Eat dairy products, fish and poultry in moderate amounts.
- Eat eggs at most four times weekly.
- Eat red meat infrequently.
- If you drink wine, consume it in low to moderate amounts and with meals.

Dietary Fat: Saturated and Trans Fats

Since achieving and maintaining an erection involves the arteries in the penis, it's logical that a diet high in saturated and trans fats might increase the risk of erectile dysfunction by increasing LDL (bad) cholesterol and damaging blood vessel walls. In fact, the Massachusetts Male Aging Study found that dietary fat and cholesterol were linked with erectile dysfunction.

Reduce your intake of saturated and trans fats, the types of fat that raise LDL blood cholesterol. Trans fat is found in foods made with partially hydrogenated vegetable oil—commercial bakery goods, snack foods, fast food and certain margarines. Read nutrition labels and choose foods that contain zero trans fats. Foods with a Daily Value of 5% or less for saturated plus trans fat are considered low in these cholesterol-raising fats.

Saturated fat is found in animal foods. Use the following list to help you minimize your intake of saturated fat.

Saturated Fat in Selected Animal Foods

Food	Lower-Fat Choices or Substitutes
Milk	Skim, 1% milk fat (MF)
Yogurt	Products with less than 2% MF

Food	Lower-Fat Choices or Substitutes
Cheese	Products with less than 20% MF
Cottage cheese	Products with 1% MF
Sour cream	Products with 7% or less MF
Cream	Evaporated 2% or evaporated skim milk
Red meat	Flank steak, inside round, sirloin, eye of round, extra-lean ground beef, venison
Pork	Centre-cut pork chops, pork tenderloin, pork leg (inside round, roast), baked ham, deli ham, back bacon
Poultry	Skinless chicken breast, turkey breast, lean ground turkey or chicken
Eggs	Egg whites (2 whites replace 1 egg). You can buy these beside the fresh eggs at your grocery store.

To learn more about dietary fats and how much you should be eating, see Chapter 3, page 22.

Vitamins and Minerals

Vitamin E

Ensuring your daily diet includes vitamin E–rich foods helps guard against artery damage that could lead to erectile dysfunction. Vitamin E is a potent antioxidant and, as such, it prevents LDL (bad) cholesterol from becoming damaged, or oxidized, by unstable oxygen molecules called free radicals. Oxidized LDL cholesterol is considered more dangerous because it sticks readily to artery walls.

Vitamin E supplements might benefit men with early stage Peyronie's disease, an uncommon condition resulting from trauma to the penis. Injury causes inflammation, scarring and, in a low percentage of men, erectile dysfunction. Studies have found that taking 400 and 800 international units (IU) of vitamin

E daily helps to promote healing and prevent scarring.[12,13]

The recommended dietary allowance (RDA) for vitamin E is 22 IU. The best food sources include wheat germ, nuts, seeds, vegetable oils, whole grains and kale. To supplement, take 400 IU of natural source vitamin E. The upper daily limit is 1500 IU.

Zinc

This mineral is essential for growth, sexual development and sperm production. A zinc deficiency may lead to low testosterone levels and, as a result, may contribute to impotence. Certain medications can deplete the body of zinc and may cause sexual dysfunction. A South African study found that compared with healthy men, those who were taking a diuretic drug called hydrochlorothiazide for high blood pressure had lower zinc levels and a higher incidence of sexual dysfunction.[14] When these men were given supplemental zinc, symptoms of sexual dysfunction improved in some, but not all, of the men.

Men require 11 milligrams of zinc per day. The best food sources include oysters, dark turkey meat, lentils, ricotta cheese, tofu, yogurt, lean beef, wheat germ, spinach, broccoli, green beans and tomato juice. If using a supplement, choose one that offers 15 to 30 milligrams of zinc (many multivitamin and mineral formulas offer this amount). Make sure your zinc supplement has 1 milligram of copper for every 10 milligrams of zinc, since supplemental zinc depletes the body's stores of copper. Don't exceed 40 milligrams per day; a prolonged high intake of zinc can have toxic effects.

Herbal Remedies

Ginkgo (Ginkgo biloba)

The active ingredients in this herb can improve blood flow to the extremities by increasing the availability of nitric oxide, a compound formed in the cells that line blood vessel walls. Nitric oxide dilates blood vessels and improves circulation. Some, but not all, studies have found ginkgo to be useful in the treatment of sexual dysfunction caused by antidepressant drugs known as serotonin reuptake inhibitors (e.g., Prozac, Effexor, Paxil, Zoloft).[15–17] Although there is minimal evidence for the use of ginkgo in treating erectile dysfunction, it may improve overall blood flow.

Choose a product that is standardized to 24 percent ginkgo flavone glycosides and 6 percent terpene lactones. The recommended starting dose to reverse sexual dysfunction is 120 milligrams daily. Take 40 milligrams three times daily or 60 milligrams twice daily with meals. If needed, the dose of ginkgo can be increased, but gastrointestinal upset may occur.

Panax Ginseng

This herb goes by many names, including Asian, Korean and Chinese ginseng. A handful of studies have shown that taking Korean red ginseng improves sexual function in men with erectile dysfunction.[18–20] The active constituents in ginseng, called ginsenosides, are thought to relax blood vessels by stimulating the release of nitric oxide.

Buy a product standardized to contain 4 percent to 7 percent ginsenosides. The typical dosage for treating erectile dysfunction is 900 milligrams three times daily.

In some people, ginseng may cause mild stomach upset, irritability and insomnia.

Ginseng should not be used if you have poorly controlled high blood pressure.

Herbs to Avoid

Two herbs in particular should be avoided by men with erectile difficulties or dysfunction. Licorice may reduce testosterone levels in men and may therefore interfere with libido and cause impotence.

Yohimbe, a herb from the bark of an evergreen tree native to Africa, may be effective when used to treat impotence, but it has a number of dangerous side effects, including tremors, insomnia, anxiety, high blood pressure, increased heart rate, nausea and vomiting. Yohimbe is not appropriate for self-treatment.

Other Natural Health Products

DHEA (Dehydroepiandrosterone)

The hormone DHEA is produced by the two adrenal glands, which sit one above each kidney. The body uses DHEA as a building block to make estrogen and testosterone, but production declines with age. Austrian researchers have found DHEA levels to be lower in men with erectile dysfunction compared with healthy volunteers.[21] Research has shown that taking DHEA for 24 weeks improves sexual function in men with erectile dysfunction. One study involving 40 men with erectile dysfunction revealed that a daily 50 milligram supplement of DHEA taken for 6 months was associated with improved sexual performance.[22] Another study suggests that DHEA is effective in men with erectile dysfunction who have hypertension and in those who have erectile dysfunction of unknown cause.[23]

The dose used to treat erectile dysfunction is 50 milligrams per day. Avoid supplements made from wild yam or soy labelled as "natural DHEA." These products cannot be converted to DHEA in the body.

DHEA is considered safe and well tolerated when taken for the short term and at a lower dose of 50 milligrams. There's some concern that long-term use of DHEA might increase cancer risk; however, preliminary research suggests it might protect against cancer.

L-Arginine

This amino acid is a building block for protein. It's found in dairy products, meat, poultry, fish, nuts and chocolate. Along with its many other functions in the body, arginine is used to make nitric oxide, a compound that relaxes blood vessels. Nitric oxide is considered an important factor in achieving an erection. The majority of studies using L-arginine to treat erectile dysfunction have reported positive results. Studies have found that taken alone, or in combination with Pycnogenol, L-arginine significantly improves sexual function in men with erectile dysfuntion.[24–26]

The dose used to treat erectile dysfunction is 5 grams per day. Although L-arginine is considered safe, side effects can include abdominal pain and bloating. L-arginine may also cause airway inflammation and worsen asthma symptoms.

Nutrition Strategy Checklist for Impotence

- ☐ Weight control
- ☐ Mediterranean diet
- ☐ Low saturated and trans fat
- ☐ Vitamin E
- ☐ Zinc
- ☐ Ginseng
- ☐ DHEA

- ☐ L-arginine
- ☐ Quit smoking

Recommended Resources

Mayo Foundation for Medical Education and Research
www.mayoclinic.com
This website is produced by a team of writers, editors, health educators, nurses, doctors and scientists, and is one of the best patient-education sites on the Internet. The information is reliable, thorough and clearly written.

National Kidney and Urologic Diseases Information Clearinghouse
The National Institute of Diabetes and Digestive and Kidney Diseases
National Institutes of Health
www.kidney.niddk.nih.gov
3 Information Way
Bethesda, MD, USA 20892–3580
Tel: 1-800-891-5390
Fax: 703-738-4929
Email: nkudic@info.niddk.nih.gov

Infertility

Defined as the inability to conceive after one year of frequent, unprotected intercourse, infertility affects approximately one in six couples. Throughout North America, infertility is on the rise, possibly because of the increase in sexually transmitted diseases and the decision of a growing number of women to delay having children until later in life.

Once thought to be solely a woman's problem, failure to conceive can be caused by reproductive difficulties in both men and women. Thirty percent of all cases of infertility originate with the woman, 30 percent originate with the man, 30 percent are the result of combined factors and the remaining cases are unexplained.[1] For women, infertility is often associated with ovarian disorders, and for men, it's usually linked to problems with sperm production.

What Causes Infertility?

Conception

A woman's lifetime supply of over 7 million eggs, or ova, is created during her growth in the womb. After birth, as she grows and matures, millions of these eggs disintegrate, leaving only about 300,000 eggs available for fertilization by the time she reaches puberty. A woman becomes fertile once her menstrual cycle begins, usually between the ages of nine and sixteen. From this point onward, an egg will ripen inside her ovaries once every month until she reaches menopause.

Stimulated by a sequence of hormones, the egg matures inside a tiny, sac-like structure called a follicle and is released into the fallopian tube. For conception to take place, a sperm must fertilize the egg as it travels from the ovaries and through the fallopian tubes to reach the uterus.

A man produces sperm in his testicles on a continuous basis throughout his lifetime. Sperm are shaped like tadpoles, carrying genetic material in their "heads" and lashing their "tails" to move in a swimming motion. During intercourse, a man will ejaculate millions of sperm into a woman's vagina. Ideally, because both the sperm and egg deteriorate fairly quickly, the sperm will fertilize the egg within 24 hours of ovulation. To reach the egg, the sperm must travel through the acidic environment of the vagina into the uterus and up the fallopian tubes. Although millions of sperm begin this difficult journey, only one will penetrate the tough outer membrane of the egg.

Once the first sperm has entered the egg, a chemical reaction makes the egg impenetrable to other sperm. The genetic material in the head of the sperm then combines with the genetic material in the egg, completing the process of conception. The fertilized egg travels down through the fallopian tube into the uterus, where it implants on the thickened lining of the uterus wall, called the endometrium. The woman's uterus will nurture this tiny collection of cells for 9 months as it grows and develops into a fully formed fetus.

Female Infertility

At any stage along the way, from the development of a woman's eggs to the journey of a fertilized egg into the uterus, the female reproductive process can go astray. Approximately one-third of female infertility is caused by a failure to ovulate, a condition known as *anovulation*. Unless ovulation takes place, no egg is available for the sperm to fertilize. A balance of hormones is necessary for ovulation to occur successfully. Two small glands located in the brain, the hypothalamus and the pituitary gland, regulate most of these hormonal responses.

The hypothalamus secretes gonadotropin-releasing hormone (GnRH), which stimulates the pituitary gland to relay hormonal messages to the ovaries. In response to these messages, the ovaries nurture an egg to maturity and release it into the fallopian tubes, ready to be fertilized. Emotional stress, extreme exercise, dieting, poor nutrition, low body fat, anorexia, medications and environmental toxins can interfere with the performance of the hypothalamus, preventing it from sending the correct signals to the pituitary gland and disrupting conception.

The pituitary gland produces two hormones, follicle-stimulating hormone (FSH) and luteinizing hormone (LH), that stimulate the follicles in the ovaries to grow and release mature eggs. These hormones also tell the ovaries to produce estrogen and progesterone. The pituitary gland may malfunction because of a tumour, an injury, surgical complications or various medical disorders. A defective pituitary gland can over- or under-produce FSH and LH, resulting in ovulation failure.

The pituitary gland also produces prolactin, a hormone involved in the production of breast milk. Prolactin has the effect of suppressing ovulation, acting as a natural form of birth control during pregnancy and breastfeeding. The pituitary gland may secrete too much prolactin due to severe kidney disease, adrenal gland disorders, hypothyroidism and the effect of certain medications.

Other glands also affect hormones involved in conception. For instance, the thyroid gland establishes your metabolic rate by circulating hormones to control the speed and efficiency of bodily functions. A thyroid gland that is overactive (hyperthyroid) or underactive (hypothyroid) can interfere with the body's ability to use hormones and thus cause infertility.

Every woman has small amounts of male sex hormones, called androgens, circulating through her bloodstream. These hormones are secreted by the adrenal glands and are necessary for normal sexual development. If the adrenal glands malfunction, elevated levels of male hormones can suppress ovulation.

In addition, a variety of ovarian disorders, including cysts, tumours, infections and medical conditions, can cause infertility. For some women, their ovaries simply fail to function. Because of surgery, injury, radiation or chromosomal problems, their ovaries run out of eggs too early, sending them into premature menopause. In rare instances, women are born without ovaries or without a normal supply of eggs, making ovulation impossible.

Several disorders of the uterus can also hamper conception. During a normal reproductive process, progesterone and luteinizing hormone stimulate the uterine lining to thicken into a nourishing bed for the fertilized egg. If the uterus is unable to respond to these hormones, the egg cannot implant properly. The result is usually a spontaneous abortion or miscarriage. Some women find it difficult to carry a fetus to full term because their uterus is structurally abnormal. Others discover that they are infertile because they were born without a uterus.

Sexually transmitted diseases such as gonorrhea, chlamydia and pelvic inflammatory disease affect the reproductive tract and are another cause of infertility. These infections can go undetected for long periods and, if left untreated, can scar the uterus, block the fallopian tubes and cause the formation of pelvic adhesions.

Many women fail to realize that diet, nutrition and lifestyle can also influence fertility. Excessive exercise, low-calorie diets, eating disorders, obesity, certain medications and elevated stress levels are all factors that will interfere with the reproductive process. Fortunately, these are among the easiest fertility problems to correct.

Male Infertility

Men are considered to be infertile when they don't produce enough sperm or when their sperm are of poor quality. Each time a man ejaculates, he releases approximately 50 million sperm in each millilitre of seminal fluid. If his sperm count drops below 20 million sperm per millilitre of ejaculate, his fertility will be impaired. The quality of the sperm is also important. Normal sperm have oval heads and long tails. Poor-quality sperm have large heads and deformed tails. These abnormalities interfere with the motility of the sperm, making them unable to swim to the egg in a vigorous, forward motion.

Problems with sperm production can result from:

- medical illnesses, including mumps and sexually transmitted diseases
- injury to the testicles, an undescended testicle or testicular cancer
- certain drugs, including recreational drugs such as marijuana
- cigarette smoking or drinking alcohol
- antibodies that are produced by the immune system to attack or disable the sperm
- vasectomy (surgical sterilization)
- overheating the sperm by wearing tight clothes, taking too many long baths or using saunas
- environmental toxins
- defects in the sperm-producing cells

Combined Infertility Factors

One of the main reasons behind the increased rate of infertility in North America is age. Many couples are waiting until they are well into their 30s or 40s before attempting to have children. However, the quality and numbers of both sperm and eggs deteriorate as men and women grow older.

Sometimes infertility arises because the man's sperm is incompatible with the woman's cervical mucus. Normally, the cervix secretes thick mucus to protect the vagina from foreign invaders, such as bacteria. During ovulation, chemical changes take place to thin the mucus consistency, allowing the sperm to enter the reproductive tract. For some couples, the chemistry between the sperm and the cervix just isn't right. The mucus remains thick, creating an environment that can block or damage the sperm, preventing conception.

Approximately 10 percent of all infertile couples discover that their infertility has no apparent cause. Both partners appear to be normal, healthy and able to reproduce. However, they simply cannot conceive together.

Symptoms

The main symptom of infertility is the inability to conceive a child after 1 year of unprotected, frequent intercourse. Each specific medical disorder, hormonal disruption or anatomical abnormality produces additional symptoms in the woman that may indicate infertility. These symptoms may include:

- history of recent weight loss or gain
- irregular menstrual periods
- absent menstrual periods (amenorrhea)
- prolonged or heavy periods
- spotting between periods
- abnormal vaginal discharge
- discomfort in the lower abdomen
- pain during sexual intercourse

Who's at Risk?

One in six couples experiences infertility problems. Many of the risk factors for female and male infertility are the same. You may be at

increased risk of developing fertility problems if you:

- are a female over 32 years old or a male over 35
- are a smoker
- are a female who is overweight or underweight
- are a male who is obese
- have irregular or absent periods
- have a history of or have a partner with a history of sexually transmitted diseases (STDs), pelvic infections or genital infections
- are a woman with polycystic ovary syndrome (PCOS)
- have a history of using an intrauterine device (IUD) for birth control
- have had a surgical sterilization reversed or if your partner has undergone this procedure
- have had abdominal surgery or your partner has undergone this type of surgery
- have endometriosis
- have a history of emotional stress

Conventional Treatment

For the majority of couples, giving nature enough time is usually the only treatment required for successful conception. Most healthy couples under 35 years of age have a 25 percent chance of becoming pregnant in the first month of trying to conceive. That rate rises to 60 percent after 3 to 6 months and reaches 85 percent after 1 year.

In many cases, mistimed intercourse is the only reason for infertility. For a woman, detecting the changes in your body that signal the beginning of ovulation is often the first step towards solving your fertility problems.

Keeping a record of your basal temperature will help determine your most fertile days. (There is a slight rise in the body's basal temperature when ovulation occurs. Recording your temperature each morning will help pinpoint this crucial time in your menstrual cycle.) A urine test, indicating the presence of luteinizing hormones, is another method of establishing ovulation. By planning intercourse to maximize the chances of a mature egg meeting a viable sperm, you considerably increase the possibility of conception.

Since the primary cause of infertility is anovulation, the major objective of most fertility treatments is to stimulate ovulation. The fertility drug clomiphene citrate (Clomid) is often used to trigger ovulation by affecting the release of luteinizing hormone. Some women benefit from supplements of the hormones FSH, LH or GnRH to restore a normal menstrual cycle and stimulate egg production.

In some instances, surgery may be necessary to repair damage caused to reproductive organs by infections or endometriosis. Surgery is also helpful in correcting certain uterine abnormalities and removing polyps and fibroids.

Assisted reproductive technologies (ART), such as in vitro fertilization, are proving to be very successful in treating a wide variety of infertility problems. During this process, fertility drugs are prescribed to stimulate the ovaries to produce many eggs. When they mature, several eggs are retrieved from the ovaries and fertilized in a laboratory. Three to five embryos are then implanted in your uterus, in the hope of establishing a successful pregnancy. In vitro fertilization is used most frequently for women who have fallopian tube damage, endometriosis, antisperm antibodies and unexplained infertility.

Enhancing Fertility
Dietary Strategies
Weight Control

A woman's body weight can affect her chances of becoming pregnant. If a woman is obese, fat cells can produce enough estrogen to interfere with her ability to conceive. High estrogen levels tell the brain to stop stimulating the development of follicles and, as result, ovulation doesn't occur. Studies show that losing weight can lead to ovulation and pregnancy.

Weighing too little is not healthy either. Menstruation occurs at a critical level of "fatness." If you lose too much weight, or you're already thin, your body fat diminishes and hormone levels are affected. This, in turn, can lead to the inability to ovulate.

Obesity also contributes to male infertility. Studies have shown that obese men tend to have a lower testosterone levels, which can result in reduced sperm count and sperm density.[2]

To find out if you're at a healthy weight, see Obesity, Overweight and Weight Loss, page 569. If you're overweight and have polycystic ovary syndrome (PCOS), follow the recommendations given in the section on PCOS. If you're underweight, read healthy eating guidelines in Chapter 5, page 111. Incorporating some of these suggestions will help you ensure that you're getting enough calories and nutrients in your daily diet. If you recognize that your low body weight is caused by an eating disorder, read Eating Disorders, page 368, for information on how to begin your recovery process.

Vitamins and Minerals

B Vitamins: Folate and Vitamin B12

There's a growing body of evidence demonstrating a relationship between B vitamin deficiencies and impaired sperm production, reduced ovarian reserve and male and female infertility. A deficiency of B vitamins, especially folate and B12, can lead to elevated blood levels of an amino acid called homocysteine. High homocysteine levels are thought to contribute to infertility. (B vitamins are needed to break down homocysteine into other harmless amino acids.) Two case reports also revealed that when women with a B12 deficiency who were having trouble conceiving were given supplemental B12, pregnancy occurred.[3-5]

One study looked at the effects of B12 supplements among infertile men. Supplementing the diet with extra B12 helped only those men with low sperm counts and impaired sperm motility.[6]

The best food sources of folate include cooked spinach, lentils, orange juice, asparagus, artichokes and whole-grain breads and cereals. Vitamin B12 is found in animal foods such as meat, poultry, fish, eggs and dairy products and also in fortified soy and rice beverages.

If you have difficulty eating a varied diet, take multivitamin and mineral supplement to ensure that you're meeting your B vitamin requirements (see Chapter 4, page 35). Women of childbearing age should take a multivitamin that contains 0.4 milligrams (400 micrograms) of folic acid to help reduce the risk of neural defects in their newborns. (Folic acid is the synthetic form of folate that's added to vitamins and fortified foods.)

Antioxidants (Male Infertility)

It appears that certain vitamins and minerals affect the health and motility of sperm. Most research attention has been paid to the antioxidant nutrients, in particular vitamin E, vitamin C and selenium. It's widely accepted that oxidative stress caused by free radicals is involved in male infertility. Free radicals are unstable oxygen molecules produced in the body that damage cells. Cigarette smoking increases the formation of free radical compounds. Free radicals can damage sperm as well as decrease their motility and ability to fuse with a woman's egg. Oxidative stress can also alter the DNA of sperm, resulting in defective sperm. Antioxidant nutrients neutralize these harmful chemicals, rendering them inactive in the body.

Studies have found that the vitamin C level of seminal fluid is significantly lower in infertile men than in those who are fertile. Cigarette smokers also have lower levels of vitamin C in seminal fluid.[7,8] Furthermore, studies have found that compared with fertile men, infertile men have significantly lower levels of selenium in their semen.[9,10] In addition to its role as an antioxidant, selenium is required for sperm maturation and motility.

Some research has shown that vitamin E supplements, taken in doses of 100 and 200 international units (IU), improved sperm activity in infertile men and increased the rate of pregnancy in their partners. Preliminary research suggests that vitamin C may improve sperm count and sperm motility.[11,12] Although studies are not conclusive, consuming adequate dietary antioxidants may help prevent male infertility that's caused by oxidative stress.

VITAMIN C. The recommended dietary allowance (RDA) for men is 90 milligrams (smokers need 125 milligrams). Best food sources include citrus fruit, citrus juices, cantaloupe, kiwi, mango, strawberries, broccoli, Brussels sprouts, cauliflower, red pepper and tomato juice. To supplement, take 500 milligrams of vitamin C once daily. The upper daily limit is 2000 milligrams.

VITAMIN E. The RDA is 22 IU. Best food sources include wheat germ, nuts, seeds, vegetable oils, whole grains and kale. To supplement, take 200 to 400 IU of natural source vitamin E. Buy a "mixed" vitamin E supplement if possible. The upper daily limit is 1500 IU.

SELENIUM. The RDA is 55 micrograms. Best food sources are fish, seafood, chicken, organ meats, whole grains, nuts, onions, garlic and mushrooms. To supplement, take 200 micrograms per day. Check how much your multivitamin and mineral formula gives you before you buy a separate selenium pill. The upper daily limit is 400 micrograms.

Zinc (Male Infertility)

This mineral is essential for growth, sexual development and sperm production. Many studies have found a link between infertility in men and a low zinc concentration in seminal fluid. A zinc deficiency may also lead to low testosterone levels. One study found that a daily zinc supplement improved sperm motility. Another small study conducted in men with low testosterone levels found that zinc supplements increased their sperm count and the rate of pregnancy in their partners.[13,14]

Zinc-rich foods include oysters, dark turkey meat, lentils, ricotta cheese, tofu, yogurt, lean beef, wheat germ, spinach, broccoli, green beans and tomato juice. If supplements are used, take from 15 to 30 milligrams (many multivitamin and mineral formulas offer 15 milligrams). A zinc supplement should have 1 milligram of copper for every 10 milligrams of zinc. Don't exceed 40 milligrams of zinc per day.

Herbal Remedies

Chasteberry (*Vitex agnus-castus*) (Female Infertility)

Preliminary research suggests that taking chasteberry can increase the chances of getting pregnant in women who are infertile due to a progesterone deficiency. The herb is believed to increase the pituitary gland's production of luteinizing hormone (LH). LH in turn boosts the secretion of progesterone during the last 14 days of the menstrual cycle. Chasteberry also lowers excessive levels of prolactin.

European studies suggest that when taken daily, chasteberry can restore progesterone and prolactin levels to normal and result in pregnancy. Researchers from Stanford University in California found that a nutritional supplement containing chasteberry, green tea, L-arginine, vitamins and minerals increased progesterone levels and increased the rate of pregnancy in women taking the supplement. (The supplement used in the study is called FertilityBlend, manufactured by The Daily Wellness Company, Honolulu, Hawaii.)[15]

Buy a product that is standardized to 6 percent agnuside, one of the plant's active ingredients. The recommended dose varies and will depend on the formulation of chasteberry. Research and clinical experience suggest that it takes 5 to 7 months to restore regular menstrual periods. In women who haven't had a period for more than 2 years, it can take up to

18 months to have an effect. If you become pregnant, stop taking chasteberry as it may stimulate the uterus.

Other Natural Health Products

L-Carnitine (Male Infertility)

This compound isn't an essential nutrient because the body makes it in sufficient quantities. Carnitine helps the body generate energy by transporting fat into cells. Most of the body's carnitine is located in muscles and in the heart, but some is also found in sperm and seminal fluid. A number of studies have found a positive relationship between sperm count and motility and their concentration of L-carnitine. The higher the concentration of L-carnitine, the higher the sperm count. Researchers have also found that infertile men have much lower levels of L-carnitine in their semen than fertile men.[16]

An Italian study revealed that 3 grams per day of supplemental L-carnitine taken for 3 months increased sperm count and sperm motility in thirty-seven out of forty-seven men.[17] A recent review of randomized clinical trials found that, compared with taking placebo, taking L-carnitine for 6 months improved sperm motility and pregnancy rate.[18]

L-carnitine is found in meat and dairy products, but to get 3 grams a day, you'll need to take supplements. To supplement, take 1 to 3 grams per day. L-carnitine is available in the United States but is not legally available in Canada. Avoid products that contain D-carnitine or DL-carnitine as they compete with L-carnitine in the body and may lead to a deficiency. Occasional side effects of gastrointestinal upset have been reported.

Nutrition Strategy Checklist for Infertility

Females:

☐ Weight control
☐ Folate
☐ Vitamin B12
☐ Multivitamin
☐ Chasteberry

Males:

☐ Weight control
☐ Folate
☐ Vitamin B12
☐ Vitamin C
☐ Vitamin E
☐ Selenium
☐ Zinc
☐ L-carnitine

Recommended Resources

Infertility Awareness Association of Canada, Inc. (IAAC)
www.iaac.ca
2100 Marlowe Avenue, Suite 342
Montreal, QC, H4A 3L5
Tel: 514-484-2891 or 1-800-263-2929
Fax: 514-484-0454
Email: info@iaac.ca

Infertility Network
www.infertilitynetwork.org
160 Pickering Street
Toronto, ON M4E 3J7
Tel: 416-691-3611
Fax: 416-690-8015

American Society for Reproductive Medicine
www.asrm.org
1209 Montgomery Highway
Birmingham, AL, USA 35216-2809
Tel: 205-978-5000
Fax: 205-978-5005

The International Council on Infertility Information Dissemination, Inc.
www.inciid.org
P.O. Box 6836
Arlington, VA, USA 22206
Tel: 703-379-9178

Mayo Foundation for Medical Education and Research
www.mayoclinic.com
This website is produced by a team of writers, editors, health educators, nurses, doctors and scientists, and is one of the best patient-education sites on the Internet. The information is reliable, thorough and clearly written.

Inflammatory Bowel Disease (Ulcerative Colitis and Crohn's Disease)

Inflammatory bowel disease is a term used to describe two lifelong conditions that affect the digestive tract: ulcerative colitis and Crohn's disease. These disorders cause the intestine to become inflamed, bleed easily and form sores or scars. It's estimated that 201,000 Canadian men and women are affected with inflammatory bowel disease.[1] Although there is no known cure for this condition, treatments are available to reduce the symptoms and keep the disease in remission.

Ulcerative colitis affects only the inner-most layer of the colon (large bowel) and rectum. It always starts in the rectum and may extend into the rest of the colon. The inflammation of ulcerative colitis is continuous—unlike Crohn's disease, there are no areas of normal tissue. Ulcers form in the affected areas, which may then bleed and become infected.

Crohn's disease can affect any part of the digestive tract, from the mouth to the anus. Patches of inflammation occur, with areas of healthy tissue in between. The inflammation of Crohn's disease can spread deep into layers of affected bowel tissue.

Although they differ in some ways, these disorders do share common characteristics. Both are unpredictable. People may experience multiple flare-ups, followed by weeks or years of quiet periods, or remissions. Abdominal pain, cramping, fatigue and diarrhea are typical symptoms of both Crohn's disease and ulcerative colitis.

What Causes Inflammatory Bowel Disease?

The cause of inflammatory bowel disease remains unknown. Some scientists think that a virus or bacterial infection may trigger the immune system, causing inflammation of the intestine. Researchers are investigating the involvement of certain bacteria in the development of inflammatory bowel disease. Heredity also plays a role—you're more likely to develop Crohn's disease or ulcerative colitis if you have a parent, sibling or child who also has the disease.

Symptoms

The symptoms of inflammatory bowel disease can vary considerably in severity. Some people have only mild symptoms that can be managed with dietary modifications and medication. Others experience severe symptoms, requiring treatment with intravenous nutrition, stronger drugs, hospitalization and, in some cases, surgery.

Ulcerative Colitis

The symptoms of ulcerative colitis will depend on where the inflammation occurs. Symptoms include:

- diarrhea, which may be violent and urgent
- frequent bowel movements, as many as 6 to 10 a day
- stool may be watery, bloody and filled with pus and mucus
- painful rectal spasms
- abdominal pain and cramping
- mild fever
- fatigue
- loss of appetite
- anemia
- weight loss and malnutrition
- rectal bleeding
- skin ulcers on the lower legs

Crohn's Disease

Signs of Crohn's disease can develop gradually or appear suddenly, without warning. They include:

- diarrhea, sometimes bloody
- abdominal pain and cramping
- mild fever
- fatigue

- nausea, vomiting and bloating
- sores around the anus
- painful or swollen joints
- slow growth and delayed puberty in children
- anemia
- a lump or swelling in the abdomen, often on the right side
- reduced appetite and weight loss
- skin rash on the legs

Who's at Risk?

Inflammatory bowel disease affects both men and women equally. It can strike at any age; however, most people are diagnosed before the age of 30. People of Jewish or European descent are five times more likely to develop inflammatory bowel disease than other people. Both Crohn's disease and ulcerative colitis run in families. In fact, 20 percent of those affected with Crohn's disease have a close relative with the disease. People who use isotretinoin (Accutane) to treat cystic acne may also be at increased risk of inflammatory bowel disease.

People who live in cities rather than rural areas are more likely to develop Crohn's disease or ulcerative colitis, perhaps because environmental factors, such as diet, play a role. One study found that children whose diet was characterized by meat, fatty foods and desserts were almost five times more likely to develop Crohn's disease than children whose diet emphasized vegetables, fruit, olive oil, fish, grains and nuts.[2]

Conventional Treatment

In most cases, ulcerative colitis can be controlled with medication and may be cured completely through surgical removal of the colon. Crohn's disease cannot be cured with either drugs or surgery, but these and other treatments make the disease more manageable and relieve some of the discomfort. The following treatments may be used to manage inflammatory bowel disease:

- anti-inflammatory drugs such as tablets, enemas or suppositories
- corticosteroids to reduce inflammation
- immune system suppressors to reduce the immune system response, possibly preventing further damage to digestive tissues
- antibiotics to help heal fistulas and abscesses, complications of ulcerative colitis
- bulking agents to relieve diarrhea
- laxatives to treat constipation that may develop from a narrowing of the intestine
- pain relievers to manage pain and discomfort
- iron supplements to treat anemia
- vitamin and mineral supplements to treat nutritional deficiencies caused by impaired absorption
- exercise to relieve stress, which can worsen symptoms during a flare-up, and to help achieve normal bowel movements
- surgery to remove damaged portions of the digestive tract, close fistulas or remove scar tissue

Managing Inflammatory Bowel Disease

Dietary Strategies

During a Flare-Up

When symptoms of inflammatory bowel disease flare up, bowel rest and a low-fibre, low-fat diet can help minimize discomfort and speed healing. Medication may also be necessary. If the flare-up doesn't require hospitalization, liquid supplement drinks such as Ensure or Boost (both lactose free) provide energy, protein, vitamins and minerals in an easy-to-digest form. These products are readily available in drugstores in different formulations, such as high protein and extra calories.

Many people find they cannot tolerate milk products when the disease is active.[3-5] Lactase, the enzyme necessary to digest the milk sugar lactose, is located on the lining of the small intestine. In Crohn's disease, damage to the intestinal lining causes a loss of lactase. As a result, lactose remains undigested in the intestinal tract, causing abdominal pain, bloating, gas and diarrhea. In people with ulcerative colitis, lactose intolerance is due more to age and ethnicity than the disease itself. You should avoid dairy products and lactose-containing foods during such a flare-up (see Lactose Intolerance, page 529). Once the bowel heals, tolerance to lactose typically improves.

Your diet therapy during the healing process will be based on your own specific food intolerances, the portion of your gastrointestinal tract affected and the severity of the flare-up. A deficiency of certain vitamins and/or minerals may occur if you have severe or long-standing disease activity. The intestine's absorption of iron, calcium, selenium, B vitamins, zinc, magnesium and vitamins A, D and E can all be affected by inflammatory bowel disease. As well, many people find that they experience digestive problems with corn, soy foods, chocolate, fats and fatty foods, and artificial sweeteners.[6] A registered dietitian who specializes in inflammatory bowel disease can advise you on dietary modifications. If you don't already have a dietitian, ask your gastroenterologist for a referral.

WHEAT GRASS JUICE. Some research suggests certain food and supplements may help speed recovery during a flare-up. Findings from a randomized controlled trial suggest that wheat grass juice may be effective in managing ulcerative colitis. In the study, people drinking 100 ml (about 1/3 cup) of wheat grass juice daily for 1 month had fewer signs of disease activity such as rectal bleeding than those taking the placebo drink.[7] Wheat grass juice contains chlorophyll and vitamins A, C and E, all of which have strong antioxidant properties. One component of wheat grass juice, apigenin, is believed to exert both anti-inflammatory and antioxidant actions in the body.

During Remission

DIETARY FIBRE. When the bowel has healed and inflammatory bowel disease is in remission, a high-fibre diet will help stimulate bowel motility and improve the muscle tone of the intestinal walls, especially in the colon. High-fibre diets also produce compounds called short chain fatty acids in the colon. These fatty acids, called acetate, propionate and butyrate, are created during bacterial fermentation of undigested fibre and play an important role in maintaining the health of colon cells. Butyrate is thought to have anti-inflammatory effects in the colon. As well, short chain fatty acids are the main source of fuel for colon cells. Fibre also binds to compounds that may irritate the colon, causing their removal from the body.[8]

Gradually increase your fibre intake to 21 to 38 grams per day, depending on your age. A list of fibre-rich foods can be found in Chapter 1, page 4. To help fibre work in the body, drink 9 to 13 cups (2.2 to 3.2 L) of water a day. Drinking plenty of fluids is especially important for people with ulcerative colitis who take the medication sulfasalazine (Asacol) to help prevent kidney stones.

Food intolerances often don't persist during remission.[9] Avoiding foods can limit the nutritional quality of your diet and may contribute to nutrient deficiencies.

DIETARY FAT. The type of fat you eat may affect symptoms of inflammatory bowel disease. Higher intakes of omega-6 fatty acids found in corn, soy, sunflower and safflower oils and red meat are linked with a greater risk of inflammatory bowel disease. Once consumed, omega-6 fatty acids enter a metabolic pathway and are converted to inflammatory compounds in the body. However, omega-3 fatty acids in fish, fish oil and flaxseed compete with omega-6 fatty acids in this metabolic pathway. If more omega-3 fats than omega-6 fats are consumed, anti-inflammatory rather than inflammatory compounds are formed. Numerous studies have found that increasing the intake of omega-3 fats has a positive effect on inflammatory bowel disease. (See the section on fish oil supplements below.)

Include sources of omega-3 fats in your daily diet. Use omega-3–rich plant oils such as flaxseed, walnut and canola. Buy eggs enriched with omega-3 fatty acids from fish oil (e.g., Naturegg Omega Pro) or flaxseed (e.g., Naturegg Omega 3). The body uses fat to produce eicosanoids, powerful hormone-like compounds that regulate our blood, immune system and hormones. Aim to eat oily fish at least twice weekly. Good choices include salmon, sardines, trout, herring and mackerel. To reduce omega-6 fatty acid intake, limit your intake of meat to twice per week and keep your portion size to no more than 3 ounces (90 g). Choose lean cuts of meat and poultry breast. See Chapter 3, page 24, for a list of lower-fat animal foods.

Vitamins and Minerals

Antioxidants

When the intestinal cells are inflamed, they can produce free radicals, molecules that can cause further damage to the intestinal lining. Studies have found that people with active inflammatory bowel disease often have lower levels of dietary antioxidants such as vitamins A, E and C and beta carotene.[10-15] The body's antioxidant stores can become depleted from impaired absorption of nutrients in the intestine. Research suggests that people with Crohn's disease who have had part of the small intestine removed are more prone to a selenium deficiency.[16] Without a sufficient supply of antioxidants, the intestine is vulnerable to further damage. To ensure an optimal intake of dietary antioxidants, include the following foods in your daily diet:

VITAMIN C. The recommended dietary allowance (RDA) is 75 and 90 milligrams for women and men, respectively (smokers need an additional 35 milligrams). Best food sources include citrus fruit, citrus juices, cantaloupe, kiwi, mango, strawberries, broccoli, Brussels sprouts, cauliflower, red pepper and tomato juice. To supplement, take 500 milligrams of vitamin C once daily. The upper daily limit is 2000 milligrams.

VITAMIN E. It's found in wheat germ, nuts, seeds, vegetable oils, whole grains and kale. To supplement, take 400 international units (IU) of natural source vitamin E. Buy a "mixed" vitamin E supplement if possible. The upper daily limit is 1500 IU. See Chapter 4, page 53, for information about the safety of vitamin E supplements.

SELENIUM. Food sources include seafood, chicken, organ meats, whole grains, nuts, onions, garlic and mushrooms. To supplement, take 200 micrograms of selenium-rich yeast per day. Check how much your multivitamin and mineral formula gives you before you buy a separate selenium pill. The upper daily limit is 400 micrograms.

BETA CAROTENE. It's found in orange and dark-green produce, including carrots, sweet potato, winter squash, broccoli, collard greens, kale, spinach, apricots, cantaloupe, peaches, nectarines, mango and papaya.

Depending on the severity of a flare-up, some of these foods may be poorly tolerated; for vitamin C and beta carotene, try juices or soups instead of whole fruit and vegetables.

Folate

People with long-standing ulcerative colitis often have a deficiency of the B vitamin folate. A lack of folate can lead to DNA damage and can increase the risk of colon cancer.[17] In fact, 5 percent of people with ulcerative colitis develop colon cancer. The risk increases if the disease has affected the entire colon and has lasted more than 8 to 10 years.[18] Studies suggest that folate supplements may reduce the risk of abnormal growth of colon cells.[19,20] In one study, patients with ulcerative colitis who took a folic acid supplement had a 66 percent lower risk for colon cancer than non-supplement users. Folate absorption may also be impaired in people with Crohn's disease.

Folate-rich foods include cooked spinach, lentils, orange juice, whole grains, fortified breakfast cereals, asparagus, artichoke, avocado and seeds. Folate is the B vitamin in its natural form in foods. Folic acid is the synthetic vitamin found in supplements or fortified foods like breakfast cereal. To ensure that you're meeting your daily requirements for folate, take a daily multivitamin and mineral supplement that has 0.4 milligrams (400 micrograms) of folic acid.

Vitamin B12

People with Crohn's disease who have had a portion of their ileum, the lower part of the small intestine, removed are at risk for B12 deficiency, since this vitamin is absorbed through the ileum into the bloodstream.[21] Depending on the length of intestine removed, B12 supplements or injections may be required. Your doctor should monitor levels of vitamin B12 in your blood.

B12 is found in all animal foods: meat, poultry, fish, eggs and dairy products. Fortified soy and rice beverages have vitamin B12 added to them. To boost your intake of B12, take a multivitamin and mineral pill that supplies 25 to 100 micrograms of B12. Or consider taking a single B12 supplement of 500 or 1000 micrograms. Supplements that are dissolved under the tongue (sublingual) and absorbed through the mouth have been shown to be as effective as injections in replenishing B12 stores.[22]

Calcium and Vitamin D

It's estimated that as many as 30 percent of people with inflammatory bowel disease have osteoporosis, a disease characterized by weak bones more likely to fracture. Malabsorption of calcium and vitamin D, nutrients critical for bone health, and intestinal nutrient losses through an inflamed intestine put people with inflammatory bowel disease at greater risk for low bone mass and osteoporosis. People who are undergoing corticosteroid drug therapy must pay special attention to their daily calcium and vitamin D intake. Corticosteroids cause bone loss and their use is associated with the development of low bone density and osteoporosis in patients with Crohn's disease and ulcerative colitis.[23-26]

There's another important reason to increase your intake of vitamin D: In addition to building strong bones, vitamin D helps regulate the immune system of the gut and acts as an anti-inflammatory. Researchers have found suboptimal vitamin D levels in the blood of many adults with inflammatory bowel disease, likely from poor absorption as well as inadequate synthesis of the vitamin in the skin during the fall and winter months. (Exposure to sunshine triggers the formation of vitamin D in the skin.) Interestingly, inflammatory bowel disease is more common among people who live in the northern hemisphere. Preliminary research suggests that vitamin D may even have a role in the treatment of active inflammatory bowel disease.

Ensure that you meet your daily requirements for calcium and vitamin D.

CALCIUM. The recommended dietary allowance (RDA) is 1000 to 1500 milligrams, depending on your age. Best food sources are milk, Lactaid milk, yogurt, cheese, fortified soy beverages, fortified orange juice, tofu, salmon (with bones), kale, bok choy, broccoli and Swiss chard. If you don't meet your calcium requirements from your diet, take a calcium supplement once or twice per day. (See Chapter 4, page 58, for more information about calcium supplements.)

VITAMIN D. The recommended intake is 1000 international units (IU) daily for adults and 400 IU daily for children. Best food sources are fluid milk, fortified soy and rice beverages, oily fish, egg yolks, butter and margarine. However, it's not possible for adults to consume 1000 IU each day from foods alone. For this reason, it's necessary to take a vitamin D supplement in the fall and winter, and year-round if you are over the age of 50, have dark-coloured skin or don't expose your skin to sunshine in the summer months. (See Chapter 4, page 51, to learn about vitamin D supplements.)

Magnesium

A deficiency of this mineral may occur in people with inflammatory bowel disease because of impaired absorption, a decreased intake from foods and increased losses from the body. Include in your daily diet magnesium-rich foods such as nuts, seeds, legumes, prunes, figs, whole grains, leafy green vegetables and brewer's yeast.

If you decide to supplement your diet and you don't take supplemental calcium with magnesium, buy a separate magnesium supplement made from magnesium citrate. The body absorbs this form of the mineral more efficiently. Taking more than 350 milligrams of supplemental magnesium can cause diarrhea, nausea and stomach cramps.

Iron

Iron-deficiency anemia is one of the most common complications of inflammatory bowel disease. It's caused by impaired absorption of iron due to inflamed intestinal cells and by loss of iron due to intestinal bleeding. If your doctor has diagnosed you with an iron deficiency or anemia, you'll need to take a single iron supplement to replenish your stores. Iron supplements that are well tolerated include Palafer (available over the counter from a pharmacist) and TriFerrix (available

with a doctor's prescription). Iron supplements are effective and well tolerated in treating anemia related to inflammatory bowel disease. However, in a tiny minority of people with ulcerative colitis, iron supplements might worsen symptoms.[27] For more information about treating iron-deficiency anemia, see Anemia, page 208.

Other Natural Health Products
Fish Oil Supplements

Since fish oil capsules are a concentrated source of anti-inflammatory omega-3 fatty acids, many studies have investigated their effectiveness on the treatment of inflammatory bowel disease. Although some studies have found beneficial effects, others have not. Research does suggest that taking enteric-coated fish oil (3 grams) in addition to treatment with medication is effective for maintaining remission of Crohn's disease. Other studies have found that supplementing the diet with fish oil can help prevent a relapse of Crohn's disease and may even reduce the dose of corticosteroid medication that's needed to keep the disease in remission. Based on the mixed findings, researchers have concluded that more studies are needed.[28–33]

Fish oil supplements are a concentrated source of the two omega-3 fatty acids DHA (docosahexanaenoic acid) and EPA (eicosapentanoic acid). These acids inhibit the body's production of inflammatory compounds called leukotrienes.

There's no recommended dosage for treating inflammatory bowel disease or keeping it in remission. Studies have used 2 to 9 grams of fish oil daily. Although fish oil may not be effective in managing inflammatory bowel disease, it's important for other health reasons to ensure that you're consuming 500 to 1000 milligrams of DHA + EPA combined per day. Most fish oil capsules supply 300, 500 or 600 milligrams of DHA and EPA in a 1 gram capsule. Most liquid fish oil supplements supply roughly 1300 milligrams per 1 teaspoon (5 ml).

Fish oil supplements can cause belching and a fishy taste, and high doses can cause nausea and diarrhea. Because fish oil thins the blood, caution should be used if you're taking blood-thinning medication such as aspirin, warfarin (Coumadin) or heparin.

Probiotics

Foods such as yogurt and nutritional supplements that contain certain live bacteria known to enhance health are called probiotics. Lactobacilli, bifidobacteria and streptococci strains of bacteria have been shown to exert health benefits in the bowel. Once consumed, these bacteria make their way to the intestinal tract, where they take up residence and protect the body from disease-causing microbes through a number of mechanisms, including enhancing the body's immune system. It's thought that a disturbance in the bacteria that normally reside in the intestinal tract is responsible for the immune reaction that causes inflammatory bowel disease. Many studies have found that probiotics can help reduce chronic intestinal inflammation.

Studies suggest that probiotic supplements can help keep ulcerative colitis in remission, and may prevent a relapse of pouchitis, an inflammation of a pouch that's created in the intestine during surgery for ulcerative colitis.[34-38] More recently, scientists have learned that a specific combination of lactobacilli, bifidobacteria, and streptococci (called VSL#3) has been shown to prevent increases in

disease-causing bacteria and flare-ups of ulcerative colitis. Additional evidence suggests that adding VSL#3 to the treatment regime of patients with active mild-to-moderate ulcerative colitis who don't adequately respond to conventional treatment can induce remission in up to 53 percent of patients. Combining VSL#3 with the medication balsalazide (Balzide) was also shown to significantly prolong remission rates compared to treatment with the drug alone.[39-41]

The strength of a probiotic supplement is usually quantified by the number of living organisms, or colony-forming units (CFUs) per capsule. Typical doses usually range from 1 billion to 10 billion viable organisms taken daily, in three or four divided doses.

For ulcerative colitis, a combination probiotic supplement called VSL#3 is recommended. VSL#3 comes in a flavoured or unflavoured powder that's intended to be mixed with at least 4 ounces (125 ml) of cold water and then consumed. For maintaining remission of ulcerative colitis, take 1 to 2 packets of VSL#3 per day (450 billion to 900 billion bacteria). For treating active ulcerative colitis that's not responding to conventional therapy, take 4 to 8 packets of VSL#3 per day (1800 billion to 3600 billion bacteria). To help manage pouchitis (reduce stool frequency), 2 to 4 packages (900 billion to 1800 billion bacteria) per day is recommended.

VSL#3 is available in some pharmacies or can be ordered online at www.vsl3.com or by calling 1-866-438-8753.

Prebiotics

Prebiotics are non-digestible foods that make their way through our digestive system and help good bacteria grow and flourish. Once they reach the colon, prebiotics also produce short chain fatty acids, which help to keep colon cells healthy. Prebiotics that feed the beneficial bacteria in your gut mostly come from carbohydrate fibres called oligosaccharides. Sources of oligosaccharides include fruit, legumes and whole grains. Inulin, a fibre derived from chicory root, is also a prebiotic. It's sold as a fibre supplement that can be added to foods and beverages (e.g., Metamucil Fibresure). Manufacturers have also added inulin to certain foods such as breads, juices and pastas. Research has demonstrated the ability of germinated barley, a prebiotic, to reduce disease activity, including blood in stools and nighttime diarrhea, in patients with ulcerative colitis.[42]

Include prebiotic foods in your daily diet to support the growth and beneficial effects of probiotic bacteria.

Nutrition Strategy Checklist for Inflammatory Bowel Disease

☐ Dietary fibre (during remission)
☐ Diet low in meat and animal fat
☐ Omega-3 fatty acids
☐ Antioxidants
☐ Folate (ulcerative colitis)
☐ Vitamin B12 (Crohn's disease)
☐ Calcium
☐ Vitamin D
☐ Magnesium
☐ Fish oil
☐ Probiotics
☐ Prebiotics

Recommended Resources

Crohn's and Colitis Foundation of Canada
www.ccfa.ca
600–60 St. Clair Avenue E
Toronto, ON M4T 1N5
Tel: 416-920-5035 or 1-800-387-1479
Fax: 416-929-0364

Crohn's and Colitis Foundation of America
www.ccfa.org
386 Park Avenue S, 17th Floor
New York, NY, USA 10016-8804
Tel: 212-685-3440 or 1-800-932-2423
Email: info@ccfa.org

National Digestive Diseases Information Clearing House (NDDIC)
National Institutes of Health
www.digestive.niddk.nih.gov
2 Information Way
Bethesda, MD, USA 20892–3570
Tel: 1-800-891-5389
Fax: 703-738-4929
Email: nddic@info.niddk.nih.gov

Insomnia

Sleep is a basic human need. When we sleep, our minds and bodies rest and restore vital energy. Adults need between 7 and 8 hours of restful sleep each night to maintain good health and to feel mentally alert during the day. Children and teenagers need 9 to 10 hours each night. A lack of sleep can result in decreased productivity, increased motor vehicle and job-related accidents and higher rates of mental and physical illness. Insomnia, the inability to sleep, is a term that refers to a number of different sleep disruptions and disturbances, including:

- difficulty falling asleep
- waking up early in the morning and being unable to return to sleep
- waking up frequently during the night or having difficulty staying asleep
- waking up after a full night's sleep and not feeling well rested

What Causes Insomnia?

Chronic insomnia occurs when sleep habits are disturbed regularly for more than 3 weeks. Usually, insomnia is a symptom of a medical condition or emotional disorder. Often associated with psychiatric disturbances, it's common in people with depression and anxiety disorders. Alzheimer's disease and other forms of dementia can also disturb sleep and cause repeated nighttime awakening. People suffering from arthritis, kidney or thyroid disease, asthma, restless leg syndrome, sleep apnea and gastrointestinal disorders will frequently experience pain and discomfort severe enough to interfere with normal sleep patterns. As well, medications used to treat these and other health conditions may trigger insomnia as an unwanted side effect.

Our sleep patterns also change as we age. Sleep efficiency is known to decrease from a high of 95 percent in adolescence to less than 80 percent in old age.[1] Consequently, older people have more difficulty falling asleep or staying asleep and often find that sleep is not as refreshing as it used to be. Many lifestyle and environmental factors can also lead to chronic insomnia, such as:

- drinking excessive amounts of alcohol or taking recreational drugs
- drinking coffee or caffeinated beverages before bedtime
- smoking cigarettes before bedtime
- taking long naps in the daytime or evening
- engaging in shift work that disrupts the day/night (or wake/sleep) cycle or in ongoing work travel that results in jet lag
- experiencing chronic tension or stress
- sleeping in a noisy environment
- sleeping in a room that is too warm or too cold

Who's at Risk?

It's estimated that 3.3 million—one in 10 Canadians—suffer from insomnia.[2] Although people of all ages can experience insomnia, it seems that women experience it more frequently than men, and are more willing to seek treatment. Insomnia is also common among the elderly. Studies indicate that people coping with stressful situations, such as divorce or unemployment, or who have medical or emotional conditions, are much more prone to insomnia.

Conventional Treatment

The treatment of insomnia depends, of course, on its underlying cause. Making simple lifestyle changes is often the best way to treat insomnia. Here are some recommendations for improving sleep habits:

- **Exercise.** Regular, moderate-intensity exercise is known to improve sleep quality. Take a brisk walk, do some gardening or join an exercise class. Avoid exercise in the late evening before bedtime because it may overstimulate the body.

- **Change your diet**. Avoid large meals late at night and limit the use of alcohol and tobacco. Foods high in sugar or caffeine should also be restricted. Avoiding spicy or high-fat foods in the evening may improve sleep. Limiting fluid intake may reduce the need to go to the bathroom during the night, allowing for a more restful sleep.
- **Control your weight.** If obstructive sleep apnea is the cause of your sleep disturbances, losing excess weight can help you get a good night's sleep. Obstructive sleep apnea—the most common form of sleep apnea—occurs when the upper airway gets completely or partially blocked during sleep and breathing momentarily stops. These breathing pauses, or apneas, can last up to 30 seconds and can happen many times throughout the night. The brain senses this breathing difficulty and briefly rouses you from sleep to reopen your airway. Symptoms of sleep apnea include excessive daytime sleepiness, loud snoring, memory loss and difficulty staying asleep. Fat deposits around the upper airway can obstruct breathing during sleep. Losing 10 percent of your body weight—22 pounds for a 220 pound man—can greatly reduce the number of sleep apnea episodes each night.
- **Control your sleep environment.** Keep your bedroom dark and quiet and make sure it isn't too warm or cold. Use your bedroom as a place to sleep; don't use it for watching television, eating, exercising, working or other activities associated with wakefulness.
- **Establish a regular bedtime routine.** Go to bed at the same time each night, and try to get up at the same time in the morning. Following a regular evening routine of brushing your teeth, washing your face and setting your alarm will help set the mood for sleep. Avoid daytime naps that might interfere with nighttime sleep.
- **Relax.** Stress and worry can trigger insomnia. Relax at bedtime by taking a warm bath, enjoying a cup of herbal tea or reading until sleepy. Try to avoid worrying about daytime problems. Some people find that alternative therapies, such as biofeedback, muscle relaxation, behavioural therapy or psychotherapy help them achieve a more restful sleep.

If your insomnia can't be managed using these techniques, medications may be prescribed. Sleeping aids include sedatives, barbiturates and tranquilizers. All carry a risk for overdose, addiction, tolerance and withdrawal symptoms. Use hypnotic drugs only a few times a week and only for a short time (2 to 4 weeks) to avoid future problems. Hypnotic drugs should be discontinued gradually to avoid rebound insomnia, the return of sleep problems after abruptly stopping medications.

Managing Insomnia
Dietary Strategies
Caffeine
Caffeine stimulates the central nervous system and increases the metabolic rate. Researchers have found that older adults suffering from insomnia report higher caffeine intakes. Studies have reported increased sleep problems in people consuming 240 to 400 milligrams of caffeine versus abstainers.[3-8] Although one or two cups of coffee in the morning can boost your mental alertness, drinking more can overstimulate your body and cause insomnia. Health Canada's safe daily limit for caffeine, 450 milligrams, is based on studies that have investigated the effect of caffeine on blood

pressure and other health conditions, not your ability to sleep soundly. Studies have shown that less caffeine (one or two small cups of coffee), consumed in the morning, can affect the quality of sleep that same night.[9,10] Caffeine blocks the action of adenosine, a natural sleep-inducing brain chemical.

If you have insomnia, aim for no more than 200 milligrams of caffeine a day, and preferably none. (One 8 ounce/250 ml cup of coffee has 80 to 175 milligrams of caffeine; the same serving size of tea has 45 milligrams.) See Chapter 5, page 110, for a detailed list of caffeine-containing beverages and foods. Avoid caffeine in the afternoon. Replace caffeinated beverages with caffeine-free or decaffeinated beverages such as herbal tea, mineral water, fruit and vegetable juice or decaf coffee.

Alcohol

Consuming alcoholic beverages worsens insomnia and breathing disturbances during sleep.[11] Once absorbed into the bloodstream, alcohol is metabolized at a set rate by the liver. If you drink more alcohol than your liver can keep up with (more than one standard drink an hour), alcohol arrives in the brain, where it interferes with brain chemicals called neuro-transmitters. (One standard drink is equivalent to 5 ounces/145 ml of wine, 12 ounces/340 ml of beer, or 1-1/2 ounces/45 ml of spirits.) Alcohol has been shown to impair REM (rapid eye movement) sleep, the portion of sleep associated with dreaming and thought to be important for memory.

Alcohol also dehydrates you, which can make you feel fatigued the following day. By depressing the brain's ability to produce a hormone called antidiuretic hormone, alcohol causes the body to lose water through the kidneys. And if you have sleep apnea, drinking alcohol can make your throat muscles relax more than normal, increasing the chance that airways get blocked.

A review of sixty studies suggests that up to two to three standard drinks consumed before bedtime initially promotes sleep, but that these effects diminish in as few as 3 continuous days of such alcohol consumption. The vast majority of studies support a relationship between sleep disturbances and alcohol use.[12]

If you have insomnia, abstain from drinking alcohol. If you do drink, avoid drinking before going to bed and only drink alcohol with a meal or snack to lessen alcohol's effect on your sleep. When alcohol is consumed on an empty stomach, about 20 percent is absorbed directly across the walls of the stomach, reaching the brain within a minute. When the stomach is full of food, alcohol has a lesser chance of touching the walls and passing through, so the effect on the brain is delayed.

Don't drink more than one alcoholic beverage per hour. Alternate one alcoholic drink with a non-alcoholic drink or a glass of water.

Carbohydrate Before Bed

A carbohydrate-rich snack, such as a glass of milk, a small bowl of cereal or a slice of toast, provides the brain with an amino acid called tryptophan. The brain uses tryptophan as a building block to manufacture a neurotrans-mitter called serotonin. Serotonin has been shown to facilitate sleep, improve mood, diminish pain and even reduce appetite.

Vitamins and Minerals
Vitamin B12

Many studies have found that vitamin B12 promotes sleep in people who suffer from sleep disorders. In a randomized double-blind study,

Japanese researchers determined that a daily dose of 1.5 to 3 milligrams of the vitamin restored normal sleep patterns in such patients.[13] German researchers have also found that sleep quality, concentration and "feeling refreshed" were significantly correlated with the blood level of vitamin B12 in healthy men and women.[14]

B12 may promote sleep by working with melatonin, a natural hormone in the body that's involved in maintaining the body's internal clock, which regulates the secretion of various other hormones. In so doing, melatonin helps control sleep and wakefulness. Secretion of this hormone is stimulated by darkness and suppressed by light. Vitamin B12 appears to directly influence the action of melatonin, and the vitamin may prevent disturbances in melatonin release.

Vitamin B12 is found exclusively in animal foods; meat, poultry, eggs, fish and dairy products are all good sources. Fortified soy and rice beverages also have vitamin B12. To get additional B12, take a multivitamin and mineral or single supplement of the vitamin (these come in 500 or 1000 microgram doses). For sleep disorders that are due to a deficiency of vitamin B12 (have your doctor measure your B12 stores), a dose of 500 to 1000 micrograms three times daily can be used.

Vitamin B12 is considered safe and non-toxic, even in large amounts. However, there have been some reports of B12 supplements causing diarrhea, itching, swelling, hives and, rarely, anaphylactic reactions.

Herbal Remedies

Valerian (*Valeriana officinalis*)
This native North American plant acts like a mild sedative on the central nervous system.

Studies show that valerian root makes getting to sleep easier and increases deep sleep. Valerian promotes sleep by interacting with certain brain receptors called GABA receptors and benzodiazepine receptors. Compared to drugs like Valium and Xanax, valerian binds very weakly to these receptors. And unlike conventional sleeping pills, the herb doesn't lead to dependence or addiction.

In one double-blind study from Germany, 44 percent of those taking valerian root reported perfect sleep, and 89 percent reported improved sleep compared with those taking the placebo pill.[15] Another small study found that individuals with mild insomnia who took 450 milligrams of valerian experienced a significant decrease in sleep problems.[16] The same researchers studied 128 individuals and found that compared with the placebo, 400 milligrams of valerian produced a significant improvement in sleep quality in people who considered themselves poor sleepers.[17]

The recommended dose is 400 to 900 milligrams in capsule or tablet form, 2 hours before bedtime for up to 28 days. For tinctures (1:5), take 1 to 3 millilitres (15 to 20 drops) in water several times per day, or try 5 millilitres before bedtime. The herb works best when used over a period of time; it may take 2 to 4 weeks to notice an improvement in sleep.

Don't take valerian with alcohol or sedative medications. The herb is not recommended for use during pregnancy and breastfeeding.

Other Natural Health Products
Melatonin
This hormone is produced in the body's tiny pineal gland, located in the brain, and regulates the body's wake-sleep cycles. Its release is stimulated by darkness: The darker the room,

the more melatonin your body produces. The hormone induces sleep by interacting with melatonin receptors in the brain. Once in the bloodstream, melatonin lowers body temperature, alertness and performance.

Studies have found decreased melatonin production in people suffering from insomnia.[18] For insomnia, short-term melatonin treatment appears to help reduce the time it takes to fall asleep (sleep latency). Some patients also report minor improvement in subjective feelings of sleep quality. Some evidence suggests that melatonin might benefit elderly patients with insomnia who could be melatonin deficient compared to younger adults or children. In children with insomnia due to delayed onset of sleep, melatonin seems to shorten the time that it takes to fall asleep and to increase the duration of sleep. In addition, melatonin may be helpful to people who are trying to discontinue prescription sleeping aids.[19–26]

For insomnia, take 0.3 to 5 milligrams of melatonin at bedtime. Both immediate-release and sustained-release melatonin preparations have been found to be effective. The most commonly reported side effects of melatonin include daytime drowsiness, headache and dizziness. Don't drive or operate machinery for 5 hours after taking melatonin. Long-term use of melatonin supplements should be avoided. For more information about melatonin, see Chapter 8, page 175.

Nutrition Strategy Checklist for Insomnia

☐ Weight control
☐ Avoid large, late-night meals
☐ Avoid caffeine
☐ Avoid alcohol
☐ Carbohydrate bedtime snack
☐ Vitamin B12
☐ Valerian OR melatonin

Recommended Resources

National Heart, Lung and Blood Institute Information Center
National Institutes of Health
U.S. Department of Health and Human Services
www.nhlbi.nih.gov/health/public/sleep/
    insomnia.htm
P.O. Box 30105
Bethesda, MD, USA 20824-0105
Tel: 301-592-8573
Fax: 301-592-8563

National Sleep Foundation
www.sleepfoundation.org
1522 K Street NW, Suite 500
Washington, DC, USA 20005
Fax: 202-347-3472

Interstitial Cystitis

Interstitial cystitis is a chronic inflammatory condition that affects mainly women. It's characterized by bladder pain, bladder pressure and sometimes pelvic pain that can be mild or severe. Although the symptoms are often very similar to those of a urinary tract infection, interstitial cystitis is not a true urinary tract infection as it isn't caused by infection and is resistant to conventional antibiotic therapy.

What Causes Interstitial Cystitis?

The bladder is an important part of the urinary tract that's connected to the kidneys by two small tubes called ureters. The kidneys produce urine, and as urine accumulates, it flows through the ureters into the bladder, which acts as a storage tank for the fluid waste. The bladder gradually expands to hold a larger quantity of urine. When maximum bladder capacity is reached, urine is released into another tube, the urethra, where it flows out of the body in a process called urination.

In interstitial cystitis, small areas on the walls of the bladder become irritated by constant inflammation. This causes the bladder wall to become scarred and stiff, impairing its normal function. The inflammation can also cause the bladder to spasm, which can reduce its capacity to store urine, causing an urgent need to urinate. As the irritation becomes more pronounced, small spots of pinpoint bleeding, called glomerulations, develop on the bladder walls. In rare cases, ulcers appear behind the bladder lining.

The exact cause of this disabling disorder remains a mystery. Because the symptoms are varied, most experts believe interstitial cystitis represents a spectrum of disorders rather than one single disease. One theory suggests a defective defence barrier in the bladder lining is responsible. It's thought this protective layer of the bladder is "leaky," allowing toxins or infective agents in the urine to permeate the lining and irritate the bladder wall, triggering interstitial cystitis. Some researchers are investigating the possibility that reduced levels of protective compounds called glycosaminoglycans in the bladder wall cause this condition. It has also been speculated that interstitial cystitis is an autoimmune disorder and that the chronic inflammation is the body's response to an earlier bladder infection.

Symptoms

Fortunately, interstitial cystitis isn't a progressive disease and symptoms don't usually become worse over time. They may go into remission for extended periods, only to recur months or years later. Symptoms vary among individuals and even in the same person. The most common symptoms of interstitial cystitis include:

- **Frequent urination.** People with interstitial cystitis feel the urge to urinate more often, both during the day and at night. In mild cases, this may be the only symptom of the disorder.
- **Urgent urination.** Another symptom is the pressure to urinate immediately; this sensation may be accompanied by pain and bladder spasms.
- **Pain.** People with the condition may feel mild to severe pressure, pain and tenderness in the lower abdomen or vaginal area. Interstitial cystitis makes sexual intercourse quite painful for women and sex drive may be reduced as a result. In men, interstitial cystitis can cause discomfort or pain in the penis and scrotum.
- **Other disorders.** Muscle and joint pain, gastrointestinal discomfort, allergies and migraine headaches may also occur in some people with interstitial cystitis. There appears to be some unknown connection between the condition and other chronic disease and pain disorders such as fibromyalgia, lupus, endometriosis and irritable bowel syndrome.

Who's at Risk?

Very little is known about the risk factors of interstitial cystitis, but research indicates that it's much more prevalent than was previously reported. Ninety percent of people with interstitial cystitis are women. Although the condition affects post-menopausal women most frequently, it's becoming evident that interstitial cystitis can attack people at any age.

Conventional Treatment

At this time there's no cure for interstitial cystitis. Nor is there a single treatment that works effectively in all people who have the disease. The earlier a diagnosis is made, the better one's chances are of responding to medical treatment, which is aimed mainly at relieving symptoms.

One of the more effective treatments is the oral drug Elmiron (pentosan polysulfate sodium or PPS). This medication provides a protective lining to the bladder wall and is believed to repair the wall's defence barrier. Symptoms may continue for some time after therapy with Elmiron has begun. Because sensory nerves in the bladder have been hyperactive, it takes time for the nerves to return to their normal state of activation—which is why doctors recommend continuing the drug for 1 year, in cases of mild interstitial cystitis, and 2 years, in severe cases, before deciding if treatment is effective. Most people taking the medication improve within 3 months. Side effects of Elmiron may include upset stomach, diarrhea and hair loss, which disappear when the medication is discontinued.

Pain medications such as aspirin and ibuprofen are often helpful in treating the discomfort. Antidepressants and antihistamines are sometimes prescribed to ease chronic pain and psychological stress associated with the condition. If pain is quite severe, narcotic drugs may be necessary to control symptoms.

Another treatment that can be effective is a bladder installation, or bladder wash. A solution of PPS, heparin or dimethyl sulfoxide (DMSO) is passed into the bladder and held for a few seconds or up to 15 minutes before being expelled. The washes are done regularly for 6 to 8 weeks, usually in the doctor's office. They are thought to be effective because they reach the bladder tissue more directly, reducing inflammation and pain.

If all treatment methods have failed and pain is severe, surgery may be considered. Unfortunately, the results of surgery can be unpredictable, and many people continue to have symptoms even after the surgery.

Several alternative treatments have proven to ease the chronic pain of interstitial cystitis. Transcutaneous electrical nerve stimulation (TENS) uses mild electrical pulses to relieve daily discomfort. The electrical pulses may work by increasing blood flow to the bladder, strengthening the pelvic muscles that control the bladder or triggering substances that block pain. Self-help techniques such as exercise, bladder retraining, biofeedback and stress reduction may reduce the severity and frequency of symptom flare-ups.

Managing Interstitial Cystitis
Dietary Strategies
Food Triggers

Many people with interstitial cystitis develop painful symptoms after eating certain foods. Eliminating these foods from the diet can help control symptoms and flare-ups. No two interstitial cystitis sufferers are alike when it comes to food sensitivities. Doctors compile food avoidance lists based on patient case histories; they should be used as a general guideline to help you pinpoint your triggers. Below is a list of foods that have been reported to trigger pain in people with interstitial cystitis. Many of these foods are acidic and can irritate the bladder.

Food List for People with Interstitial Cystitis

PRESERVATIVES AND ADDITIVES
Avoid: benzol alcohol, citric acid, monosodium glutamate (MSG), aspartame (NutraSweet), saccharin, artificial colours; tyramine-containing foods including wine, beer, aged cheese, nuts, yogurt, bananas, soy sauce, brewer's yeast and chocolate

FRUIT
Avoid: apples, citrus fruit, figs, cranberries, cantaloupe, grapes, guava, mango, strawberries, pineapple, peaches, nectarines, plums, prunes, rhubarb
Okay: melons (except cantaloupe), pears

VEGETABLES
Avoid: asparagus, beets, eggplant, mushrooms, pickles, tomatoes, tomato-based sauces, raw onion, spinach, parsley, beet greens, peppers, corn, sauerkraut, sweet potatoes, dandelion greens, artichokes, turnip greens, Swiss chard, purslane
Okay: other vegetables, homegrown tomatoes (tend to be less acidic)

MEATS AND FISH
Avoid: aged, canned, cured, processed or smoked meats and fish; anchovies, caviar, chicken livers, corned beef and meats that contain nitrates or nitrites
Okay: other meats, fish and poultry

DAIRY PRODUCTS
Avoid: aged and natural cheeses, sour cream, yogurt, goat's milk
Okay: cottage cheese, frozen yogurt, milk

GRAIN FOODS
Grain products are usually not well tolerated; try them in small quantities.
Avoid: yeast-based products such as leavened bread; wheat, corn, rye, oats and barley
Okay: rice, potatoes, rice pasta, pasta

LEGUMES
Avoid: lentils, lima beans, fava beans, soybeans, tofu
Okay: all other beans

NUTS AND SEEDS
Avoid: most nuts
Okay: almonds, cashews and pine nuts

EGGS
Eggs may aggravate symptoms.

HERBS, SPICES AND CONDIMENTS
Avoid: BBQ sauce, cocktail sauce, mayonnaise, miso, spicy foods, ketchup, salsa, hot sauce, relish, soy sauce, salad dressing, vinegar, Worcestershire sauce
Okay: garlic and other seasonings

BEVERAGES
Avoid: alcohol (especially beer and wine), carbonated drinks, tea, coffee, cranberry juice
Okay: bottled still (flat) water, decaffeinated coffee or tea, some herbal teas

OTHER
Avoid: caffeine (chocolate, especially dark chocolate; certain medications), junk foods,

tobacco, diet pills, all vitamins that contain starch fillers

Painful symptoms often occur up to 4 hours after eating, making it relatively easy to pinpoint problem foods. But sometimes symptoms don't appear until the following day. In these cases, identifying foods that trigger your condition can be challenging and frustrating.

Elimination/Challenge Diet
The steps below outline an elimination diet for identifying food sensitivities.

1. **Elimination phase**. For a period of 2 weeks, eat only foods identified above as Okay, unless you already know that one of these foods causes you bladder or pelvic pain.
At the same time, keep a *food and symptom diary*. Record everything you eat, amounts eaten and what time you ate the food or meal. Document any symptoms, the time of day you started to feel the symptom and the duration of time you felt the symptom. You might want to grade your symptoms: 1 = mild, 2 = moderate, 3 = severe.
2. **Challenge phase**. After 2 weeks, start introducing foods from the Avoid section. Do this gradually, introducing them one at a time. I recommend the following procedure for testing foods:
Day 1: Introduce the test food in the morning, at or after breakfast. If you don't experience symptoms, try the food again in the afternoon or with dinner.
Day 2: Don't eat any of the test food. Follow your elimination diet. If you don't experience a reaction today, the food is considered safe and can be included in your diet. If you do experience a reaction to a tested food on

Day 1 or 2, don't continue eating it and don't reintroduce any other foods until your symptoms have resolved.
Day 3: If no symptoms occurred on Day 1 and 2, try the next food on your list, according to the above schedule.

You may find that you can tolerate some foods if you eat them once every few days, but not if you eat them every day. You may also learn that some troublesome foods are better tolerated if eaten in small portions.

Some people with interstitial cystitis have food allergies that contribute to their symptoms.[1] Allergies to wheat, corn, rye, oats and barley are common. If you suspect you have a food allergy, speak to your family doctor about allergy testing. The elimination diet outlined above will also help determine allergenic foods.

Low-Acid Foods
Many of the foods in the Avoid section of the food list above are acidic and can cause bladder pain and urinary urgency in people with interstitial cystitis. If your list of troublesome foods leaves you little to eat, you might want to try a dietary supplement called Prelief (by AkPharma in the United States). This supplement reduces the acid in foods and beverages so that they don't have to be excluded from your diet. Two studies of more than 200 interstitial cystitis sufferers found that Prelief reduced the pain and discomfort associated with consuming foods such as pizza, tomatoes, spicy foods, coffee, fruit juices, alcohol and chocolate.[2,3]

The supplement is made of calcium glycerophosphate. It's available in tablet form to be taken with food or as granules that can be mixed into foods. The supplement isn't available in Canada, but can be ordered directly from the manufacturer by calling 1-800-994-4711 or visiting www.akpharma.com. In the United States, it's sold in the antacid section of drugstores. It's important to use the correct amount of Prelief to reduce the amount of acid in certain foods; the company offers a free pocket guide to help you do this.

If eating a certain food brings on bladder symptoms, you can neutralize the acid in your urine by drinking a glass of water mixed with 1 teaspoon (5 ml) of baking soda. Practising this as a precautionary measure when you're dining out may also help prevent bladder irritation. To prevent a flare-up after eating, drink plenty of water to help dilute the urine.

Other Natural Health Products

L-Arginine
Supplementing your diet with the amino acid L-arginine can help lessen symptoms of interstitial cystitis. L-arginine is used to make an enzyme necessary for the formation of nitric oxide, a compound that relaxes the smooth muscle of the bladder. Research suggests that patients with interstitial cystitis have reduced levels of nitric oxide in their urine.[4] Women with a larger bladder capacity and/or a history of recurrent urinary infections may respond more favourably to this amino acid.

A handful of studies have found that 500 to 1500 milligrams of L-arginine taken orally can significantly reduce voiding discomfort, urinary frequency, lower abdominal pain and pelvic pain in as little as 5 weeks of treatment.[5-8]

Although we consume L-arginine from protein-rich foods in our diet, a supplement is required to achieve an intake of 500 to 1500 milligrams per day.

Nutrition Strategy Checklist for Interstitial Cystitis

☐ Identify food triggers
☐ Low-acid foods
☐ Prelief dietary supplement
☐ L-arginine

Recommended Resources

Interstitial Cystitis Association
www.ichelp.org
100 Park Avenue, Suite 108A
Rockville, MD, USA 20850
Tel: 800-435-7422
Fax: 301-610-5308
Email: icamail@ichelp.org

The Interstitial Cystitis Network
www.ic-network.com
P.O. Box 2159
Healdsburg, CA, USA 95448
Tel: 707-538-9442
Fax: 707-538-9444
Orders: 707-433-0413

National Kidney and Urologic Diseases Information Clearinghouse
National Institutes of Health
www.kidney.niddk.nih.gov
3 Information Way
Bethesda, MD, USA 20892-3580
Tel: 301-654-4415 or 1-800-891-5390
Fax: 301-907-8906
Email: nkudic@info.niddk.nih.gov

Irritable Bowel Syndrome (IBS)

Most people have suffered an occasional bout of bloating, gas, constipation and even diarrhea. But for people who suffer from irritable bowel syndrome (IBS), these uncomfortable—and often painful—symptoms persist, often interfering with daily life. IBS is a relatively common disorder of the gastrointestinal tract that often develops during periods of stress or emotional conflict. IBS causes changes in bowel habits that result in constipation, diarrhea, gassy pain and bloating. IBS doesn't cause any permanent harm to the gastrointestinal tract, nor does it lead to serious diseases, such as cancer. In most cases, IBS symptoms can be managed with simple changes to lifestyle and diet.

What Causes Irritable Bowel Syndrome?

Doctors refer to IBS as a functional disorder, since there's no sign of any abnormality when a person's large bowel, or colon, is examined. Although the symptoms can be painful and persistent, there's usually no evidence of disease, injury or structural damage to the gastrointestinal tract in people with IBS—the large bowel just doesn't work as it should. So far, researchers haven't identified the exact cause of IBS. It's thought that symptoms result from overly reactive and/or extra-sensitive nerves that control muscles in the bowel. People with IBS appear to have very sensitive colons. Even the mildest stimulation can cause the colon muscle to overreact, triggering cramps and spasms. For some people, these muscle spasms delay the passage of food through the intestine, causing constipation. In others, the muscle spasms cause urgent diarrhea by forcing food through the intestine much too quickly.

It's not known what causes IBS to develop in the first place, but hormones, stress, bacterial infection, antibiotic use, food sensitivities and disorders that affect intestinal muscle contractions are among the list of suspects. It is known, however, that certain foods can stimulate reactions in the gut. If you have IBS, eating too much of these foods might bring on or worsen your symptoms.

Symptoms

The main symptoms of IBS are abdominal pain or discomfort and altered bowel habits. Most people experience either diarrhea (IBS-D or diarrhea predominant) or constipation (IBS-C or constipation predominant), but some people experience both and alternate between diarrhea and constipation (IBS-A). Other symptoms include mucus in the stool, abdominal bloating and a feeling of incomplete emptying after a bowel movement. Headaches, fatigue, depression and anxiety can also occur in people with IBS.

Who's at Risk?

It's estimated that as many as 20 percent of Canadians have IBS. Women are affected three times more often than men. IBS symptoms may increase during a woman's menstrual period. The disorder usually begins in late adolescence or early adulthood, and rarely appears for the first time after the age of 50. IBS often surfaces during times of emotional stress.

Conventional Treatment

The treatment for IBS varies from person to person. Since emotional stress is often a trigger for the condition, learning how to cope with stress is an important way to help prevent a flare-up. Learning relaxation techniques, exercising regularly and stress-management counselling may all be helpful.

Dietary modifications (see below) can lessen IBS symptoms and prevent a flare-up. Occasionally, medications are prescribed to relieve IBS symptoms, including:

- bulk fibre supplements or laxatives to treat constipation
- drugs to control muscle spasms in the colon
- drugs to slow the passage of food through the digestive system
- tranquilizers or antidepressants
- alosetron to slow intestinal movement and reduce nerve problems (used in women)

Managing Irritable Bowel Syndrome

Dietary Strategies

To get relief from IBS, the best place to start is with your diet. The influence of diet on IBS is unique to each person and there's no single piece of dietary advice that will work for everyone. Whether only a few prove effective in individual cases, all of the following strategies may help ease IBS symptoms.

Eat at Regular Intervals

To help regulate bowel function, don't skip meals. Eat well-balanced, low-fat meals at the same time each day. People with IBS-D may find eating smaller meals more frequently reduces symptoms. It's also important to eat slowly. Poorly chewed foods are more difficult to digest and may lead to impaired absorption and intestinal discomfort. Eating too quickly can also lead to swallowed air and gas. Chew foods thoroughly: Aim to take at least 20 minutes to finish a meal.

Food Intolerances

Foods may trigger or worsen the symptoms of IBS. Many people with IBS, especially those who suffer from diarrhea, report adverse reactions to certain foods and improvement once these foods are removed from their diet. People with IBS have also been shown to have higher levels of certain immune compounds in their blood, indicating specific food sensitivities. One study found that people with IBS tended to be more sensitive to wheat, beef, pork and lamb.[1-7]

Before making dietary changes—especially unnecessary ones—keep a daily food and symptom journal for 2 weeks to identify what foods, or patterns of eating, set off your symptoms. Keep track of meal and snack times, the types of foods eaten and portion sizes, symptoms, as well as what time your symptoms start and end. Keep in mind that factors such as stress, certain medications (e.g., magnesium-containing antacids), the menstrual cycle and a lack of physical activity may also aggravate symptoms. A registered dietitian (www.dietitians.ca) can help you identify trigger foods and make changes to your diet.

Although dietary intolerance varies from person to person, the following foods may cause distress:

- **Lactose-containing foods** such as milk, yogurt and soft cheeses. These foods often cause symptoms in individuals with IBS.[8-13]

When the milk sugar lactose cannot be properly absorbed in the intestine, the result can be abdominal pain, bloating, gas and diarrhea. Lactose-free milk and yogurt (e.g., Lacteeze, Lactaid) are available, and taking lactase pills with a meal that contains milk will also help if you're lactose intolerant. Many people with a mild or moderate lactose intolerance can eat yogurt and cheese without experiencing any discomfort, since these foods contain much less lactose than milk. See Lactose Intolerance, page 531, for lactose-reduced diet guidelines.

- **Fructose- and sorbitol-containing foods** such as fruit drinks, fruit juices, dried fruit, honey, hard candies, cough drops, throat lozenges and dietetic cookies and wafers. Colonic bacteria will ferment the sugar fructose when it's in the colon, causing gas and bloating. Sorbitol, a sugar alcohol found naturally in fruit and fruit juices and used to sweeten many "diet" foods, isn't absorbed as readily as sugar, which means some sorbitol reaches the colon and may exacerbate IBS symptoms. Numerous studies have found that these sugars trigger symptoms in some people with IBS. One study conducted in forty-eight patients with IBS also noted significant improvement in symptoms after following a low-fructose diet.[14-21] High-fructose fruit include prunes, pears, cherries, peaches, apples, plums, apple-sauce, apple juice, pear juice, apple cider, grapes and dates. Fruit lower in fructose content include pineapples, strawberries, raspberries, blackberries, lemons, limes, avocado, bananas, rhubarb and oranges.
- **Gas-producing foods** such as dried peas and beans, lentils, bell peppers, cucumber, onions, chives, garlic, broccoli, cauliflower, cabbage, turnip, melon, pickles, eggs, carbonated beverages and chewing gum. If beans bother you, trying using Beano, a commercial enzyme sold in pharmacies that helps break down the gas-producing starches in beans. Gassy vegetables are usually better tolerated cooked rather than raw, and if eaten in small portions.
- **Alcoholic beverages and caffeine**, found in coffee, tea, colas, chocolate and certain medications (see Chapter 5, page 110, for sources of caffeine).

Dietary Fat

Meals that are high in fat and/or calories can bring on symptoms of IBS.[22-24] A low-fat diet can normalize bowel function by reducing contractions in the colon that occur in response to a meal. Avoid fatty foods such as whole milk, cream, cheese, butter, margarine, fatty cuts of meat (rib eye steak, spareribs, sausage, salami) and deep-fried foods. Use smaller portions of healthy fats such as avocado, peanut butter and vegetable oils.

Eating large volumes of food at one time can cause abdominal distension and discomfort. It's better to eat small, frequent meals than three large ones. Avoid skipping meals, since this is likely to trigger overeating at the next meal.

Dietary Fibre

A high-fibre diet adds bulk to stool, reduces pressure in the colon, promotes normal bowel motility and can relieve constipation in IBS.[25-28] For many people with IBS, increasing fibre helps control symptoms. Fibre reduces constipation by softening the stool, making it easier to pass. People with IBS-C should include sources of insoluble fibre such as wheat bran, whole-grain cereals, fruit and vegetables. Too much wheat bran, however, can worsen diarrhea. If you have IBS-D, it's best to consume more soluble fibre, which takes longer to leave the digestive tract. Sources of soluble fibre include oat bran, barley, psyllium husks, citrus fruit and legumes.

Gradually increase your fibre intake to 21 to 38 grams per day, depending on your age. See Chapter 1, page 4, to learn your daily fibre requirement and the fibre content of various foods. Refer also to Constipation, page 318.

Regardless of the type of fibre you experiment with, increase your intake gradually over a period of weeks. Drink at least 9 cups (2.2 L) of water each day, preferably 1 hour before or 1 hour after meals. Drinking water with meals may make food move through the gut faster.

Add higher-fibre foods to your diet slowly to avoid an aggravation of abdominal pain and bloating. For instance, if you're adding a bran cereal to your diet, do so in 1/4 cup (60 ml) increments.

Herbal Remedies

Peppermint Oil (Menthae piperitate aetheroleum)

This herbal remedy is widely used to ease the symptoms of IBS. A number of studies have found it significantly reduces bloating, pain, distension, stool frequency and flatulence in IBS sufferers.[29-32] The volatile oils in peppermint directly affect the smooth muscle of the digestive tract and reduce spasms. As well, flavonoid compounds in peppermint stimulate the secretion of bile, aiding in the digestive process.

To ease bowel spasms, the recommended dose is 0.2 to 0.4 millilitre in enteric-coated capsules taken three times daily, 15 to 30 minutes before meals. For children aged 8 years and older with IBS, the usual dose is 0.1 to 0.2 millilitre three times daily. Peppermint

oil can cause heartburn, so be sure to buy an enteric-coated product.

Peppermint tea may help ease digestion and can be consumed with and between meals. Steep 1 tablespoon (15 ml) of dried peppermint leaf in 2/3 cup (150 ml) boiling water for 10 minutes and then strain.

Don't use peppermint oil or peppermint tea to treat infant colic as it can cause jaundice and a choking sensation.

Other Natural Health Products

Psyllium and Flaxseed

The seeds from both of these plants may help treat constipation in people with IBS.[33,34] A 2004 review of seventeen studies comparing soluble (psyllium, oats) versus insoluble (wheat bran, corn) fibres concluded that people taking soluble fibre tended to have symptom improvement and those who took insoluble fibre were more likely to have pain. Flaxseed and psyllium seeds are bulk-forming laxatives high in both insoluble and soluble fibres. The laxative properties of psyllium and flaxseed are due to the swelling of the fibres when they come in contact with water. Once consumed, they form a gelatinous mass that keeps the feces hydrated and soft. The increased bulk stimulates a reflex contraction of the walls of the bowel and prompts evacuation.

- **Psyllium seed husks.** Mix 1 to 2 tablespoons (15 to 30 ml) into 2 cups (500 ml) water; take one to three times per day. Or try Metamucil (Procter and Gamble), a bulk-forming fibre supplement made from psyllium. Metamucil comes in wafers, capsules and powdered drink mix. For bowel regularity, recommended use is three times per day with at least 8 ounces (250 ml) of water. Regular use of psyllium is considered safe, but excessive amounts can cause bloating, gas, diarrhea and intestinal blockage. Not drinking enough water when taking psyllium can cause choking and blockage of the esophagus and throat. Psyllium may also slow the absorption of certain medications (e.g., tetracycline, digoxin, aspirin, some diuretics), so take them 1 hour before or 2 hours after taking psyllium.

• **Ground flaxseed.** Take 2 tablespoons (30 ml) once daily. Mix into hot cereal, yogurt, applesauce or smoothies. Add ground flaxseed when preparing baked goods and casseroles.

Probiotics

Foods and supplements that contain lactic acid bacteria are called probiotics, which means "to promote life." The most widely studied of the health-friendly lactic acid bacteria are the *Lactobacillus* and *Bifidobacterium* species. Once consumed, these bacteria make their way to the intestinal tract, where they take up residence and prevent the attachment of harmful bacteria and yeasts. It's thought that people with IBS may have an imbalance in their intestinal bacteria (called the intestinal flora), which can lead to gastrointestinal symptoms. Changing the intestinal flora by taking probiotic supplements may ease or prevent IBS.

In a recent review of sixteen randomized controlled trials, researchers from Northwestern University in Chicago concluded that *Bifidobacterium infantis* 35624 was the only probiotic strain out of thirteen different individual strains or preparations reviewed to significantly improve symptoms of IBS, including abdominal pain, bloating and bowel

movement difficulty.[35] Align (Procter and Gamble) is a probiotic supplement made with *Bifidobacterium infantis* 35624. It's sold in pharmacies across the United States.

Research has also shown that a combination probiotic supplement called VSL#3, available in Canada, improved symptoms in patients with diarrhea-dominant irritable bowel syndrome.[36]

The recommended dose of Align is one capsule per day. The recommended dose of VSL#3 is 1/2 to 1 packet per day. VSL#3 comes in a flavoured or unflavoured powder that's to be mixed with at least 4 ounces (125 ml) of cold water and then consumed. See Chapter 8, page 178, for further information on probiotics.

Nutrition Strategy Checklist for Irritable Bowel Syndrome

☐ Eat at regular intervals
☐ Identify food intolerances
☐ Low-fat diet
☐ Dietary fibre
☐ Psyllium
☐ Flaxseed
☐ Peppermint oil
☐ Probiotics

Recommended Resources

American College of Gastroenterology
www.acg.gi.org
4900 B South 31st Street
Arlington, VA, USA 22206-1656
Tel: 703-820-7400
Fax: 703-931-4520

International Foundation for Functional Gastrointestinal Disorders (IFFGD)
www.iffgd.org
P.O. Box 170864
Milwaukee, WI, USA 53217
Tel: 1-888-964-2001

The Irritable Bowel Syndrome Self Help and Support Group
www.ibsgroup.org (online self-help)

National Digestive Diseases Information Clearinghouse
The National Institute of Diabetes and Digestive and Kidney Diseases
National Institutes of Health
www.digestive.niddk.nih.gov
2 Information Way
Bethesda, MD, USA 20892-3570
Tel: 1-800-891-5389
Fax: 703-738-4929
Email: nddic@info.niddk.nih.gov

University of North Carolina Center for Functional GI and Motility Disorders
www.med.unc.edu/wrkunits/2depts/medicine/
    fgidc/welcome.htm
CB #7080, 778 Burnett-Womack Building
Chapel Hill, NC, USA 27599-7080
Tel: 919-966-0144
Fax: 919-966-8929

Kidney Stones

The urinary system is made up of the kidneys, the ureters, the bladder and the urethra, which help eliminate waste products from the body in the form of urine. Your kidneys play a critical role in removing waste products that are created through digestion and the breakdown of muscle tissue. These waste materials are carried through the bloodstream to the kidneys, where impurities are removed from the blood and converted into urine. Then the kidneys return clean, purified blood to the body. The ureters carry urine from the kidneys to the bladder, where it's stored until you urinate, at which point it passes out of the body through a tube called the urethra. Every day, your kidneys process nearly 200 quarts (190 L) of fluid, removing approximately 2 quarts (1.9 L) of waste and excess water. Without this cleansing process, toxic wastes would build up and cause extensive damage to your body.

A kidney stone forms when chemicals in your urine create crystals that clump together. Kidney stones vary in size and can form within the kidney or urinary tract. Very small stones pass through the urine without causing symptoms. Large stones can cause blood in the urine and severe pain in the abdomen or groin.

What Causes Kidney Stones?

Sometimes, substances in the urine can cause crystals to form that then build up on the inner surfaces of the kidneys. These solid masses are called stones. Normally, the urine contains compounds that prevent crystals from forming, but these chemical inhibitors don't seem to work effectively for everyone.

Kidney stones can vary considerably in size. Some are as small as a grain of sand; others can grow to be the size of a golf ball. There are four main types of kidney stones:

1. **Calcium oxalate** and **calcium phosphate** stones are the most common types. In fact, 70 percent to 80 percent of kidney stones are made of calcium oxalate, two chemicals that are part of a normal diet.

2. **Struvite stones** usually form after a urinary tract infection.
3. **Uric acid stones** can occur when there's too much acid in the urine.
4. **Cysteine stones** are quite rare and are usually caused by an inherited disease.

The exact cause of kidney stones remains unknown. Genetic predisposition, diet and lifestyle factors appear to play a role. Dehydration through reduced fluid intake or strenuous exercise without adequate fluid replacement as well as obstruction to the flow of urine can lead to stone formation. Scientists have also identified tiny bacteria called nanobacteria inside kidney stones that are thought to trigger stone development.

Symptoms

Although some stones, known as "silent" stones, cause no discomfort, many cause the following symptoms:

- cramping or extreme pain in the low back, groin or abdomen—the pain may come and go, lasting for minutes or hours at a time
- blood in the urine
- nausea and vomiting if pain is severe
- fever and chills
- burning sensation during urination
- urge to urinate frequently
- cloudy or foul-smelling urine

Who's at Risk?

It's estimated that one out of ten Canadians will have a kidney stone at some point in his or her life.[1] Those more susceptible to stone formation include:

- men; they suffer from kidney stones more often than women
- people with a family history of kidney disease
- middle-aged adults; the risk of kidney stones increases when men reach their 40s and continues to rise into their 70s
- people who live in hot climates and don't drink enough fluids
- people who have recurrent urinary tract infections, kidney disorders and metabolic disorders such as gout and hyperparathyroidism
- people who take certain medications such as diuretics and calcium-containing antacids

Conventional Treatment

Most kidney stones pass out of the body on their own. Your doctor will prescribe pain medication as needed and suggest you drink plenty of water to help move the stone through your system. The passed stone is usually saved for testing and analysis. This helps your doctor determine the type of crystals that are forming and suggest appropriate treatment to prevent a recurrence. If a stone won't pass by itself, treatment options include:

- **Extracorporeal shock wave lithotripsy (ESWL).** Shock waves are pinpointed to the area and sent through the body to break the large stone into smaller stones that will pass through the urinary tract system with the urine.
- **Percutaneous nephrolithotomy.** A small incision is made in the back, creating a narrow tunnel under the skin and through tissue to the stone in the kidney. The doctor uses a special instrument to shatter or remove the stone.

- **Ureteroscopy.** The doctor inserts an instrument, shaped like a long wire and with a miniature camera attached, into the urinary tract. This allows the doctor to see the stone and shatter or remove it.
- **Open or incisional surgery.** This is conventional surgery to remove kidney stones, but it's used less frequently now because of the newer technologies available.

Preventing and Managing Kidney Stones

Dietary Strategies

In as many as 50 percent of cases, kidney stones will recur after 5 years.[2] If you have kidney stones, making lifestyle modifications can minimize crystal formation and help prevent a future attack. In fact, it's estimated that 85 percent of all people with kidneys stones could anticipate a lower risk of recurrence by altering their dietary and lifestyle habits.[3] Your nephrologist (a doctor who specializes in kidney disorders) will give you very specific nutrition advice based on the type of kidney stone you produce and the results of a 24-hour urine collection. You may also be referred to a dietitian who specializes in diets for patients with kidney stones.

Fluids

This is one of the simplest and more important measures you can take to reduce the risk of kidney stone formation. Drinking fluids—water or other beverages—helps flush away substances that can cause crystals to form in the kidneys. When you're not drinking enough fluids, your urine is less dilute and more concentrated in chemicals that can crystallize into stones. If you've already had a kidney

stone, drink 12 cups (3 L) of water in divided doses throughout the day. If you have cysteine kidney stones, aim for 14 cups (3.5 L) per day. In hot weather, drink an additional 2 to 4 cups (0.5 to 1 L) to make up for fluid lost through sweating.

Depending on what kind of kidney stones you have, the type of fluid you drink may increase or decrease the chances of stone formation. (This may also be true for people with a family history of kidney disease who are at risk for stones.) Hard tap water and some bottled waters contain higher amounts of calcium and sodium (see below), two minerals that may increase the risk of stone formation. Whether or not you need to drink soft tap water or low mineral-content bottled water remains controversial. Although one small study found soft water preferable to hard water, others suggest that mineral waters with a higher calcium content may protect from calcium oxalate stones by reducing the amount of oxalate in the urine.[4,5] The most important strategy is to be drinking more water in general. If you're concerned, ask your doctor or dietitian, who can advise you on choice of water based on the type of stones you have.

Certain beverages may lower the risk of kidney stone recurrences. Coffee, decaffeinated coffee, tea, beer and wine have been shown to prevent stone formation, presumably by increasing the flow of a more dilute urine.[6,7] Drinking cranberry juice has been shown to alter the composition of the urine to help reduce the risk of calcium oxalate stone formation.[8] Grapefruit juice and apple juice may also reduce the risk of calcium oxalate kidney stones by increasing citric acid secretion.[9,10] Some research suggests that lemonade made from 4 ounces (125 ml) of reconstituted lemon juice may be beneficial for some people with calcium kidney stones. Lemonade increases citrate in the urine, thereby reducing calcium oxalate formation.[11-13]

Low Oxalate Diet

Oxalate, or oxalic acid, is a compound found naturally in plant foods that can crystallize with calcium in the urine. If you have calcium oxalate kidney stones, restricting your intake of foods that contain oxalate is advisable, especially if a urine test reveals you excrete high amounts of oxalate.[14] Although present in many foods, only a fraction of dietary oxalate is available for absorption. As a result, food sources don't contribute much oxalate to the urine. However, studies do show that spinach, rhubarb, nuts, chocolate, tea, wheat bran and strawberries increase oxalate excretion the most and should be avoided if you're at risk for kidney stones.[15]

The following foods contain moderate or high amounts of oxalate and should be limited:[16]

Foods Containing Moderate or High Amounts of Oxalate

Type of Food	Limit (Eat Less Often and in Small Portions)
Beverages	Draft beer, chocolate beverage mixes, cocoa, instant coffee
Breads & Cereals	Grits (white corn), wheat germ, whole-wheat flour
Fruit	Berries, Concord grapes, red currants, damson plums, lemon, lime, orange peel, tangerines
Vegetables	Beets, celery, eggplant, endive, escarole, leeks, parsley, summer squash, sweet potatoes, Swiss chard, wax beans

Type of Food	Limit (Eat Less Often and in Small Portions)
Legumes	Dried peas, beans, lentils, baked beans with tomato sauce, tofu
Desserts	Fruitcake, desserts containing fruit listed above
Other	Chocolate, cocoa, carob powder

If you have a history of calcium oxalate kidney stones, be sure to include a source of calcium (food or supplement) with meals to reduce oxalate absorption (see Calcium below).

Dietary Protein

Overeating protein foods like meat, poultry, eggs and dairy products can increase the amount of calcium excreted in the urine. A handful of studies have shown that a moderately low-protein diet reduces the amount of calcium, sodium, phosphates and uric acid in the urine, components known to cause kidney stones.[17,18]

If you have calcium kidney stones, limit your protein intake to between 0.8 and 1.0 gram per kilogram of body weight per day (see Chapter 2, page 17). Keep your portion size of meat and poultry to 3 ounces (90 g). If you don't have a history of kidney stones, replace animal protein with legumes and soy foods more often, since vegetable proteins may reduce the risk of kidney stones.[19] (If you have a history of calcium oxalate stones, these foods must be limited due to their oxalate content. People with kidney stones are advised to avoid a strictly vegetarian diet in order to reduce the risk of stone recurrence.)

Limiting portion size of animal-protein foods is also important to reduce the risk of uric acid stone recurrence. Animal-protein foods contain purines, compounds that increase the amount of uric acid in the bloodstream and in the urine. The main purine-rich foods to limit in your diet include seafood, canned anchovies, sardines and herring, fish roe, meat, organ meats, consommé soup and gravies (made from meat).

Each day, consume no more than 2 to 3 servings of meat, fish, poultry, eggs and meat alternatives such as soy and legumes. (One serving equals 2-1/2 ounces/75 g of meat, fish or poultry, 2 eggs or 3/4 cup/175 ml cooked legumes or tofu.)

Alcoholic Beverages

If you have uric acid kidney stones, alcoholic beverages, especially beer and spirits, prevent uric acid from leaving your body and may trigger stone formation. Furthermore, beer, unlike wine and spirits, contains purines. Avoid beer and limit your intake of other alcoholic beverages. Speak to your doctor about the amount of alcohol consumption that's safe for you.

Weight Control

Studies suggest that overweight and obesity increase the risk of developing kidney stones. If you're overweight, losing weight may help prevent gout attacks. Excess weight is associated with altered acidity of the urine and elevated blood uric acid levels, two factors that can trigger stone formation. In people with gout, high levels of uric acid may precipitate in the kidneys and form uric acid stones.

If you need to lose weight, do so gradually at a rate of 1 to 2 pounds (0.5 to 1 kg) per week. Rapid weight loss and fasting can increase uric acid levels in the blood and may affect stone formation. Avoid low-carbohydrate, high-protein diets since they can elevate uric acid levels. See Obesity, Overweight and Weight Loss, page 574, for strategies to reduce weight safely.

Vitamins and Minerals

Vitamin C

When vitamin C is consumed in high doses, some is converted to oxalate in the body. Indeed, studies have shown oxalate excretion to increase with vitamin C supplementation.[20-24] For this reason, people with recurrent calcium oxalate kidney stones are often advised to consume no more than 100 milligrams of vitamin C per day.

However, not all research suggests that restricting vitamin C intake is warranted. A large Harvard Medical School study conducted among 85,500 women revealed that vitamin C intake was not associated with the risk of kidney stones.[25] Despite these findings, another large American study conducted in men found that those who consumed 1000 milligrams or more of vitamin C each day—compared to 90 milligrams—were 40 percent more likely to be diagnosed with kidney stones.[26]

If your doctor has determined that you have high levels of oxalate in your urine, focus on meeting your daily vitamin C requirement through foods (see Chapter 4, page 49, for a list of vitamin C–rich foods). Limit your intake to no more than 100 milligrams per day. Avoid taking single vitamin C supplements.

Vitamin B6

The same Harvard study mentioned above found that higher doses of vitamin B6 (40 milligrams or more per day) reduced the risk of kidney stones in women. Vitamin B6 decreases the amount of oxalate produced in the body and therefore reduces the amount available for stone formation in the urine.

If you have calcium oxalate stones caused by high oxalate excretion in your urine, consider supplementing your diet with 50 milligrams of B6. Don't take more than 100 milligrams of B6 per day; supplementing with too much B6 for an extended period can lead to toxic effects, including irreversible nerve damage.

Calcium

For years the standard prescription for kidney stones has been a low-calcium diet. The assumption was that if you reduce the amount of calcium that ends up in your urine, there's less of it available to form stones with other substances such as oxalate. However, if you have calcium-containing kidney stones, it's not necessary to limit your intake of calcium-rich foods. In fact, restricting dietary calcium is no longer recommended. Many studies have found that eating a calcium-rich diet is associated with a lower risk of stone formation in men and women. One study of 51,529 healthy men aged 40 to 75 years revealed that those with the highest calcium intake were 36 percent less likely to develop kidney stones than those with the lowest intake. Similar results were found in an 8-year study of 96,245 women aged 27 to 44 with no history of kidney stones. Compared to women with the lowest daily calcium intakes (less than 626 milligrams), those who consumed at least 1126 milligrams each day had a 27 percent reduced risk of developing kidney stones. What's more, calcium supplements weren't associated with a higher risk.[27-34]

Researchers have learned that consuming enough calcium helps to decrease the amount of oxalate that's excreted in the urine.[35,36] Calcium in foods binds to oxalate in the intestine, preventing its absorption. Many calcium-rich foods also contain potassium and magnesium, two nutrients that might help prevent kidney stones.

A low calcium intake may not only increase the risk of kidney stones but also be detrimental to bone health. Ensure that you're meeting your daily calcium requirements of 1000 to 1500 milligrams.

If you don't meet your calcium requirements from food, take a supplement. Because calcium reduces the absorption of oxalate, the timing of ingestion is important. Studies show that taking your calcium supplement with rather than apart from meals reduces oxalate excretion in the urine.[37,38] If you've had a calcium oxalate kidney stone, be sure to include a source of calcium—dietary or supplement—with each meal to reduce oxalate absorption.

Some people with calcium kidney stones may absorb too much calcium from their intestine. Specific tests will reveal this, and your doctor may advise that you limit your calcium intake to 800 milligrams daily. This means consuming no more than two milk-product servings per day (e.g., 1 cup/250 ml milk, yogurt or calcium-fortified beverage or 45 grams of cheese). See Chapter 4, page 56, for the calcium content of selected foods.

Magnesium

Higher magnesium intakes have been linked with a lower risk of kidney stones.[39] Magnesium is thought to bind to oxalates in the gut and inhibit their absorption into the bloodstream. Be sure to include magnesium-rich foods such as whole grains and leafy green vegetables in your daily diet. If you take a magnesium supplement, take it with a meal so that the mineral can bind with and remove oxalates from the body. See Chapter 4, page 61, for more information about magnesium food sources and supplements.

Sodium

A high-salt diet causes more calcium to be excreted in the urine and makes the urine more acidic, two factors that increase the likelihood of calcium salts crystallizing to form kidney stones. If your calcium kidney stones are caused because you excrete too much calcium in your urine, limit your sodium intake to less than 2300 milligrams per day.

To help cut back on sodium, avoid the saltshaker at the table, minimize the use of salt in cooking and buy commercial food products that are low in added salt. See Chapter 5, page 108, for strategies to reduce your sodium intake.

Nutrition Strategy Checklist for Kidney Stones

☐ Fluids
☐ Low oxalate-rich foods
☐ Limit animal protein
☐ Limit or avoid alcohol
☐ Weight control
☐ Reduce vitamin C
☐ Vitamin B6
☐ Calcium
☐ Magnesium
☐ Low-sodium diet

Recommended Resources

The Kidney Foundation of Canada
www.kidney.ca
300–5165 Sherbrooke Street W
Montreal, QC H4A 1T6
Tel: 514-369-4806 or 1-800-361-7494
Fax: 514-369-2472
Email: info@kidney.ca

National Kidney and Urologic Diseases Information Clearinghouse
The National Institute of Diabetes and Digestive and Kidney Diseases
National Institutes of Health
www.kidney.niddk.nih.gov
3 Information Way
Bethesda, MD, USA 20892-3580
Tel: 1-800-891-5390
Fax: 703-738-4929
Email: nkudic@info.niddk.nih.gov

National Kidney Foundation
www.kidney.org
30 E 33rd Street
New York, NY, USA 10016
Tel: 1-800-622-9010 or 212-889-2210
Fax: 212-689-9261

Lactose Intolerance

Lactose intolerance is the most common type of food intolerance. The fact that 70 percent of the world's population has difficulty digesting lactose, the natural sugar found in milk, has led some researchers to hypothesize that lactose intolerance is in fact normal and tolerance is the abnormal condition. Although not dangerous, the symptoms of lactose intolerance can be uncomfortable for many people. Luckily, the symptoms can be avoided by making dietary modifications.

Food intolerance is much more common than food allergy. An intolerance often develops when the body can't properly digest a certain type of food because the digestive system lacks the necessary enzyme to break down food into individual nutrients. Other causes of food intolerance include:

- digestive disorders, such as celiac disease or irritable bowel syndrome
- injuries to the small intestine
- an excess of acid in the stomach
- foods contaminated by a toxin
- certain types of bacteria growing in the intestine
- recurring stress or psychological disorders

What Causes Lactose Intolerance?

Lactose is primarily found in dairy products, including milk, yogurt, kefir, cheese and ice cream. Before it can be absorbed into the bloodstream, lactose must first be broken down into smaller sugar units by an enzyme called lactase, located on the lining of the small intestine. When the lactase enzyme is deficient, undigested lactose remains in the intestine. Fluid is drawn into the small intestine by the high concentration of lactose, causing diarrhea. When the unabsorbed lactose reaches the large intestine, it's fermented by bacteria, producing excess gas, bloating and abdominal cramps. Although the symptoms may be similar, lactose intolerance is very different from a true milk allergy.

Nearly 75 percent of all adults lack sufficient quantities of the lactase enzyme to digest milk or other dairy products properly.[1] Most infants are born with adequate levels of lactase, but these levels seem to decline after the age of two. Normally, lactase production declines as your diet becomes varied and less reliant on dairy. This gradual loss of lactase may lead to a lactose intolerance in some people. In the majority of cases, symptoms of lactose intolerance develop before the age of 20 and intensify over time.

The inability to digest lactose can also occur as a result of an illness or a disease that injures the intestinal lining, such as celiac disease, inflammatory bowel disease, parasitic infections and antibiotic therapy. In these cases, the intolerance is often temporary and will disappear when bowel health returns to normal, usually a few days to several months.

Symptoms

Common complaints include nausea, cramps, bloating, gas pain and diarrhea. These occur 30 minutes to 2 hours after eating or drinking a food containing lactose. The severity of the symptoms will depend on the amount of lactose you can tolerate. Some people have mild or moderate lactose intolerance and can handle some lactose without gastrointestinal distress, whereas others, who have a severe intolerance and severe symptoms, must avoid all lactose-containing foods and products.

Who's at Risk?

Lactose intolerance is more common among Asians, African-Americans, Hispanics, First Nations Americans and people of Jewish descent. Age is also a risk factor—lactose intolerance usually starts after the age of five. It's very uncommon for babies and young children to be lactose intolerant. However, babies born prematurely may be at increased risk since the enzyme lactase increases in the developing fetus during the third trimester.

Conventional Treatment

A lactose intolerance may be diagnosed based on your symptoms and your response to eliminating dairy from your diet. Or your doctor may perform a lactose intolerance test or a hydrogen breath test to confirm a diagnosis. Both tests require you to drink a liquid solution that contains a high level of lactose. If you do have a lactose intolerance, the only treatment is to reduce or, in severe cases, avoid lactose in your diet since you can't improve your body's ability to produce lactase.

Managing Lactose Intolerance
Dietary Strategies
Low-Lactose Diet

If you experience adverse reactions to lactose, a lactose-restricted diet will prevent or reduce symptoms of bloating, flatulence, cramps, nausea and diarrhea. Living without lactose doesn't necessarily mean following a dairy-free diet. In fact, research suggests that people with lactose intolerance who include milk and other lactose-containing foods in their diet may actually improve their tolerance to lactose.[2] Most people with mild or moderate lactose intolerance can consume milk in small portions (1/2 to 3/4 cup/125 to 175 ml).[3] The smaller the serving of milk, the less likely it is to cause symptoms. Yogurt is generally well tolerated because it has less lactose than milk; the live bacteria present break down some of the lactose. Yogurt is also emptied from the stomach more slowly than milk, giving the enzyme lactase more time to break down lactose.

In general, eating solid foods with milk improves lactose digestion because food enters the small intestine at a slower rate.[4] Consuming lactose-containing foods with foods rich in soluble fibre (oats, beans, psyllium-enriched breakfast cereals) may also ease symptoms of intolerance.[5]

Below is a list of foods according to their lactose content. Depending on the severity of your symptoms, you may need to avoid some or all of these foods.

Lactose is found primarily in dairy products, but it may also be present as an ingredient or component of various food products. Read labels carefully to identify sources of lactose.

Selected Foods According to Lactose Content

High Lactose	Moderate Lactose	Low Lactose	Lactose-Free Alternatives
Buttermilk	Cottage	Blue cheese	Astro BioBest
Condensed	cheese	Brie cheese	Lactose
milk	Cream	Butter	Reduced
Evaporated	Feta cheese	Cheddar	Yogurt
milk	Goat's milk	cheese	Lactaid milk
Ice milk	Ice cream	Cream cheese	(99% lactose
Milk: whole,	Ricotta cheese	Parmesan	free)
2%, 1%, skim	Sour cream	cheese	Rice bever-
Whipping		Swiss cheese	ages
cream			Soy beverages
Yogurt			

Lactose is found in milk, milk solids, sweet or sour cream, whey, lactose, curds, cheese flavours and non-fat milk powder. Possible food sources of lactose include breads, candy, cookies, sport energy bars, cold cuts, hot dogs, processed meats, commercial sauces and gravies, dessert mixes, some ready-to-eat breakfast cereals, frostings, margarines, salad dressings and sugar substitutes. People with severe lactose intolerance must avoid lactose in medications. Ask your dietitian for a list of lactose-free equivalents.

LACTASE-TREATED PRODUCTS AND LACTASE SUPPLEMENTS. Lactose-reduced dairy products are readily available in the dairy section of supermarkets. Products such as Lactaid milk have been pretreated with lactase enzyme and are 99 percent lactose-free.

You can also reduce the lactose content of dairy products yourself by using commercial supplements such as Lactaid lactase enzyme (McNeil Consumer Healthcare, Inc.). Lactase enzyme preparations come in tablets and liquid. Tablets are taken before eating foods that have lactose; the liquid can be added to regular milk. Read the package instructions before using these products.

Because the lactose content of dairy products can vary, you may have to adjust the number of Lactaid drops you add to the food. Lactaid enzyme supplements are available over the counter in the pharmacy department of most groceries and drugstores.

Vitamins and Minerals

Calcium and Vitamin D

If you avoid milk and other dairy products, your intake of calcium and vitamin D will be inadequate, which can increase your risk for osteoporosis. Use fortified soy beverages in place of milk, since they provide the same amount of calcium and vitamin D (as well as protein) as an equivalent amount of milk. One cup (250 ml) of a fortified soy beverage will provide roughly 300 milligrams of calcium and 100 international units (IU) of vitamin D.

Other sources of calcium appropriate for a lactose-reduced diet are yogurt, calcium-fortified orange juice, leafy green vegetables, almonds and tofu. Keep in mind, however, that these foods lack vitamin D. See Chapter 4, page 58, for lists of foods rich in calcium and vitamin D.

If you don't use fortified soy beverages, or you don't consume enough of them to supply your daily calcium, take a calcium supplement. Calcium citrate supplements supply 300 milligrams of calcium; calcium carbonate pills offer 500 to 600 milligrams. If you take a medication that blocks or reduces stomach acid, choose calcium citrate, since the body absorbs this form of the mineral more efficiently. Depending on the amount of calcium in your diet, you may need to take a calcium pill two to three times a day.

You'll need to take a vitamin D supplement. It's recommended that Canadian adults take 1000 IU of vitamin D each day in the fall and winter, and year-round if you're over 50, if you have dark-coloured skin or if you don't expose your skin to sunlight in the summer months. (Exposure to sunlight—without the use of sunscreen—triggers the synthesis of vitamin D in the skin.) Children should get 400 IU of vitamin D each day. This recommendation not only protects your bones, but may also reduce your risk of certain cancers.

To determine the amount of vitamin D you need to buy, add up how much you're already getting from your multivitamin and calcium supplements, subtract that from your recommended dietary allowance (RDA) and make up the difference with a single vitamin D supplement. Vitamin D is sold in 400 and 1000 IU doses. Buy a supplement that provides vitamin D3, instead of vitamin D2; vitamin D3 is more active in the body. The upper daily limit is 2000 IU per day.

Riboflavin (Vitamin B2)

Milk provides much of our daily intake of this B vitamin, an important nutrient for energy metabolism, vision and healthy skin. If you drink fortified soy beverages each day, your riboflavin requirements will be met. Other sources of the vitamin include breakfast cereals, whole grains and meat.

If you're concerned that you aren't getting enough riboflavin in your daily diet, take a multivitamin and mineral supplement each day. Separate riboflavin supplements are also available in 25, 50, 100, 500 and 1200 milligram doses, although they're rarely necessary if you eat a varied diet and take a multivitamin.

Other Natural Health Products

Probiotics

Probiotics are living bacteria that reside in your intestinal tract, where they help maintain a healthy digestive system and strong immune system. Probiotics are found in fermented dairy products such as yogurt and kefir and they're also sold as supplements. Evidence suggests that probiotics can help reduce diarrhea and symptoms of irritable bowel syndrome. They also help your body break down lactose. In fact, a number of studies have shown that consuming probiotics helps reduce symptoms of lactose intolerance.[6-8]

The main types of probiotics in foods and supplements are *Lactobacillus* and *Bifidobacterium*. Within these main types there are dozens of species and strains such as *Lactobacillus acidophilus*, *Lactobacillus GG*, *Lactobacillus rhamnosus*, *Bifidobacterium lactis* and *Bifidobacterium bifidus*.

If you have a mild to moderate lactose intolerance, include kefir or yogurt in your daily diet. All yogurts in Canada are made with two probiotic bacteria, *Lactobacillus bulgaricus* and *Streptococcus thermophilus*. Some yogurt manufacturers have added other strains such as *Bifidobacterium* and *L. acidophilus* to boost the probiotic content of their products.

The strength of a probiotic food or supplement is usually quantified by the number of living organisms, or colony-forming units (CFUs), per capsule. When buying probiotic foods, choose a product with at least 1 billion active, or live, cells per dose or serving.

Typical daily doses for supplements range from 1 billion to 10 billion viable organisms taken in three to four divided doses. If you decide to supplement, take your probiotic supplement with food. After eating a meal, stomach contents become less acidic because of the presence of food, allowing live bacteria to withstand stomach acid and reach their final destination in the intestinal tract.

Prebiotics

There are ways to increase the amount of good bacteria in your gut without taking probiotics. Eating prebiotics—foods that contain non-digestible carbohydrates—can increase the growth and activity of beneficial bacteria in your gut. Prebiotic food sources include oatmeal, flaxseed, onions, garlic, leeks, asparagus and Jerusalem artichokes.

Nutrition Strategy Checklist for Lactose Intolerance

☐ Low-lactose diet
☐ Lactaid products
☐ Calcium
☐ Vitamin D
☐ Vitamin B2
☐ Probiotics
☐ Prebiotics

Recommended Resources

International Food Information Council
www.ific.org
1100 Connecticut Avenue NW, Suite 430
Washington, DC, USA 20036
Tel: 202-296-6540
Fax: 202-296-6547

National Digestive Diseases Information
Clearinghouse
National Institutes of Health
www.digestive.niddk.nih.gov
2 Information Way
Bethesda, MD, USA 20892-3570
Tel: 301-654-3810
Fax: 703-738-4929
Email: nddic@info.niddk.nih.gov

Mayo Foundation for Medical Education
and Research
www.mayoclinic.com
This website is produced by a team of writers, editors, health educators, nurses, doctors and scientists, and is one of the best patient-education sites on the Internet. The information is reliable, thorough and clearly written.

Lung Cancer

Lung cancer is one of the most preventable types of cancers. And yet, in Canada, it's the leading cause of cancer death for both men and women. It's estimated that 23,400 Canadians will be diagnosed with lung cancer in 2009, and 394 people will die of the disease every week.[1] Nearly 90 percent of all lung cancers develop as a direct result of cigarette smoking. The more cigarettes you smoke, the higher your risk of developing this devastating disease. Studies have indicated that even secondhand cigarette smoke can be dangerous to your respiratory system.

Lung cancer develops when mutated or abnormal cells grow out of control, dividing and multiplying much more rapidly than normal cells. When the abnormal cells accumulate faster than the body can use them, they begin to clump together to form a tumour. The cancerous cells will often spread outward from the main tumour, invading and destroying normal tissue and travelling to other parts of the body, a process called metastasis.

The vast majority of all lung cancers begin in the bronchi, the large airways that supply the lungs. Lung cancer can take several different forms, but there are two main types. *Small-cell lung cancer* grows quickly and often spreads to other parts of the body. *Non-small cell lung cancer* is the most common type of lung cancer and grows more slowly than small cell lung cancer.

Cancerous cells in the lungs can quickly invade a large number of blood vessels and lymph nodes. These systems can carry the cancer cells to nearby or distant organs and to tissues almost anywhere in the body. This is particularly true of small-cell cancer, which spreads aggressively and often causes death within a matter of months.

What Causes Lung Cancer?

By far the biggest danger to lung health is cigarette smoking. Tobacco smoke contains over 4000 chemicals, many of which have been shown to be cancer causing. The two main carcinogens in cigarette smoke are called nitrosamines and polycyclic aromatic hydrocarbons. When you inhale smoke from cigarettes or other forms of tobacco, you damage the ability of the lungs to protect themselves from injury. As smoke travels through the bronchi to the lungs, the mucus coating that lines the airways thickens to protect the delicate lung tissue. Cancer-causing chemicals then become trapped in the thick mucus. The smoke also destroys the tiny mechanisms that normally clean these substances out of the bronchi. Although eventually dislodged by coughing, the toxins remain in the airways long enough to be absorbed by the cells. The harmful chemicals gradually alter the normal body cells, beginning a process that eventually leads to cancer.

Passive smoking, or the inhalation of smoke from other smokers, is also a known risk factor for lung cancer. Research has shown that non-smokers who live with smokers have a 24 percent increased risk of developing lung cancer compared with other non-smokers. Smokers continue to put others at risk, making secondhand smoke one of the major environmental health problems in today's society.

Although smoking rates have declined among men and women of all age groups, it's estimated that 19 percent of the population aged 15 and older (slightly less than 5 million Canadians) still smoke an average of 15 cigarettes per day.[2] Some research indicates that women who smoke may be more vulnerable to the cancer-causing agents in tobacco and may have a higher risk of developing lung cancer than men who smoke. Equally worrisome is a growing interest in smoking among youths. When smoking starts in adolescence, the risk of developing lung cancer at an early age increases substantially.

Toxic substances in the environment such as radon gas, asbestos, coke-oven emissions, arsenic, chromate and chromium, nickel and polycyclic aromatic hydrocarbons cause a small percentage of lung cancers. Other types of industrial emissions, air pollution and motor vehicle emissions have also been linked with lung cancer.

Some people develop lung cancer without any known cause.

The best way to prevent lung cancer is to never start smoking. However, if you do smoke, it's never too late to quit. The moment you stop smoking, your lung cancer risk begins to slowly decline. In former smokers, the risk of developing lung cancer begins to approach that of a non-smoker about 15 years after quitting.

Symptoms

There are often no signs of lung cancer until the disease reaches an advanced stage. The following symptoms may be present once the disease is advanced:

- a cough that gets worse or doesn't go away
- coughing up mucus and traces of blood
- chest pain, especially when you cough
- shortness of breath or wheezing
- frequent chest infections such as pneumonia
- persistent hoarseness in your voice
- unexplained weight loss
- loss of appetite
- fatigue and weakness
- difficulty swallowing

Who's at Risk?

People at high risk for lung cancer are:

- cigarette smokers; female smokers may be at greater risk than male smokers
- people who are regularly exposed to secondhand smoke
- people who are exposed to workplace or household toxins such as industrial emissions, asbestos and radon gas
- people with a family history of lung cancer
- people who have had lung cancer before

Lungs that have been damaged by cigarette smoke are more vulnerable to injury from other types of inhaled pollutants. The length of time that you have smoked, the number of cigarettes you smoke and how deeply you inhale the smoke also influence the risk for lung cancer. Among those who smoke two or more packs per day, one in seven will die of lung cancer.

Conventional Treatment

Treatment for lung cancer varies, depending on the type and stage of the cancer and on your general health. Early detection is important to improve prognosis. The following treatments may be recommended:

- quitting smoking and trying not to be with other people who smoke
- supplemental oxygen to relieve shortness of breath
- corticosteroids to relieve symptoms of fever, coughing and shortness of breath
- regular exercise, a healthy diet and reducing stress to maintain your strength and vigour
- chemotherapy alone or chemotherapy in combination with radiation therapy
- surgery, generally done for non-small cell lung cancer, especially in the early stages
- radiation therapy or a combination of chemotherapy and radiation therapy for advanced lung cancer
- targeted therapy that uses certain drugs that specifically target cancer cells or block the development of blood vessels within a tumour
- narcotics to control pain in the final stages of the disease

Preventing Lung Cancer
Dietary Strategies
Alcohol

The relationship between alcohol intake and lung cancer has been examined in a number of studies. Because alcohol drinking is strongly associated with smoking, many studies have controlled for cigarette smoking and have still found an increased risk. The findings from several studies suggest that drinking one or more drinks per day is associated with a higher risk for lung cancer.[3-7] One review of studies concluded that drinking one beer or more per day increased the risk of lung cancer in men and women, consuming one or more liquor drinks increased the likelihood of lung cancer in men but not women, and modest wine drinking was not found to increase lung cancer risk.[8]

Alcohol may act as a solvent for cancer-causing agents in cigarette smoke. Alcohol has been shown to induce changes in the lining of the lungs that might increase susceptibility to cancer-causing substances. Alcohol may also impair the ability of liver enzymes to metabolize tobacco carcinogens, resulting in increased activation of these compounds. Finally, alcohol may bind to DNA, the genetic material of cells, enhancing the damage caused by cigarette smoke.

Cancer experts don't recommend the consumption of alcohol. Men should limit themselves to no more than two drinks per day (to a maximum of nine per week), and women should have no more than one drink per day. One drink is considered 12 ounces (340 ml) of regular beer, 5 ounces (145 ml) of wine or 1-1/2 ounces (45 ml) of 80-proof (40 percent) distilled spirits.

Dietary Fat and Cholesterol

Some, but not all, studies suggest that a high intake of fat, especially saturated fat, and dietary cholesterol increases the risk of lung cancer in smokers and non-smokers.[9-16] It's thought that cancer-causing substances in cigarette smoke are more easily activated by a high-fat diet. A high-fat diet may also promote the development of lung cancer by influencing cell membranes, the immune system and circulating levels of hormones. Specific foods found to increase the risk include fried foods, fatty meat, dairy products and rich desserts.

To reduce your intake of saturated fat and cholesterol, choose lower-fat animal foods, such as lean meat, poultry breast and milk and yogurt with 1% or less milk fat. Limit or avoid processed meats such as sausage, bacon, bologna, hot dogs and salami. Use added saturated fat such as butter and cream cheese sparingly. Avoid margarines and packaged foods made with hydrogenated vegetable oil, another source of saturated fat. You'll find a list of sources of saturated fat and cholesterol in Chapter 3, page 22.

Substituting vegetable oils for animal fats such as butter may help prevent lung cancer in women. American researchers found that women who had the highest intake of vegetable fat had a 30 percent to 40 percent lower risk of lung cancer compared with those who were consuming more animal fat.[17]

Although limited, there is some evidence to suggest that omega-3 fats in fish may protect from lung cancer, especially in men who smoke or in those who have high intakes of animal fat.[18] Animal research has also demonstrated anti-cancer properties of fish-oil diets fed to mice with lung cancer.[19] Aim to include oily fish such as salmon, trout and sardines in your diet two times per week. Eating more fish also means you'll be consuming fewer animal-based meals, which are higher in saturated fat.

Fruit and Vegetables

There's substantial evidence for the protective effect of a high intake of vegetables and fruit on lung cancer. The Second Expert Report of the World Cancer Research Fund/American Institute for Cancer Research, published in 2007, summarized the results of sixty-four studies investigating fruit intake and lung cancer risk. Most studies reported a lower risk of lung cancer with increased fruit intake.[20] One study conducted in 478,000 healthy adults showed a 40 percent reduced risk among people who ate the most fruit.[21]

Fruits are excellent sources of vitamin C and other antioxidants, such as beta carotene, that trap harmful free radicals and thus protect lung cells from oxidative damage. As well, phytochemicals in fruit called flavonoids have been shown to help liver enzymes break down toxins that have been associated with lung cancer, especially in smokers.

A high consumption of all types of vegetables—but especially green vegetables, carrots and tomatoes—has been shown to lower the risk of lung cancer.[22-26] Scientists believe that a high intake of carotenoid compounds (beta carotene, lycopene and lutein) are responsible for the protective effects of vegetables. In fact, most studies have revealed that people who get the most beta carotene from foods have a lower risk of lung cancer than those who consume the least. Beyond its antioxidant activity in the body, some beta carotene is converted to vitamin A, a nutrient necessary for maintaining healthy body tissues, especially epithelial and mucus tissues, the body's first line of defence against invading organisms and toxins.

Cruciferous vegetables, including broccoli, cabbage, cauliflower and bok choy, may also reduce the risk of lung cancer. Two studies that followed large groups of healthy men and women for a number of years linked a higher cruciferous vegetable intake (3 or more servings per week) with strong protection from lung cancer.[27,28] Cruciferous vegetables have a strikingly high concentration of cancer-fighting chemicals calls glucosinolates, which are broken down by bacteria in the digestive tract and transformed into compounds called isothiocyanates. As well, enzymes in cruciferous vegetables convert glucosinolates to isothiocyanates when they're chopped or chewed. Isothiocyanates help eliminate cancer-causing substances by regulating your body's detoxification enzymes. They also act as antioxidants by preventing DNA, the genetic material of your cells, from being damaged by harmful free radicals.

Eating a diet plentiful in fruit and vegetables is one of the most important strategies to lower the risk of lung cancer—second only to quitting smoking. Be sure to eat at least 7 to 10 servings of vegetables and fruit each day. One serving is equivalent to 1 medium-sized fruit, 1 cup (250 ml) of fruit salad, 1/2 cup (125 ml) of unsweetened juice, 1/2 cup (125 ml) of cooked or raw vegetables or 1 cup (250 ml) of salad greens.

Choose different-coloured vegetables and different-coloured fruits to get a wide range of vitamins, minerals and protective plant chemicals. Eat at least one orange and one dark-green vegetable every day to increase your beta carotene intake. Include 5 servings of cruciferous vegetables in your diet each week.

Use the following table to add a variety of fruit and vegetables to your diet that are plentiful in cancer-fighting compounds:

Beta Carotene	Lycopene	Lutein	Cruciferous Chemicals
Broccoli	Canned tomatoes	Beet greens	Bok choy
Brussels sprouts	Tomato juice	Collard greens	Broccoli
Carrots	Tomato sauce	Kale	Cabbage
Rapini	Tomatoes	Okra	Cauliflower
Spinach	Grapefruit, pink and red	Red pepper	Collard greens
Sweet potato	Guava	Romaine lettuce	Kale
Winter squash	Watermelon	Spinach	Radishes
Apricots		Zucchini	Rutabaga
Cantaloupe		Grapes	Turnip
Mango		Kiwi fruit	
Nectarines		Orange juice	
Papaya			

See Chapter 5, page 88, for tips on how to incorporate more vegetables and fruit into your daily diet.

Flavonoids

Eating more flavonoid-rich foods may lower your chances of developing lung cancer. Plant foods contain hundreds of different flavonoids. These natural chemicals act as antioxidants and inhibit the action of liver enzymes that activate cancer-causing substances.

Two large studies found that men and women who ate the most apples, onions and white grapefruit had a significantly lower risk of lung cancer compared with those who consumed the least.[29,30] Apples and onions contain a flavonoid called quercetin and white grapefruit contains one called naringin.

Green Tea

Populations that drink green tea have lower rates of cancer, including lung cancer. And a number of laboratory studies have determined that extracts of green tea have anti-cancer properties.[31-34] The natural chemicals in green tea have been shown to protect the genetic material of lung cells from free radicals and to inhibit the growth of lung tumours in mice. Green tea leaves are a rich source of phyto-chemicals called catechins (a class of flavonoids), which have potent antioxidant properties. The primary catechin found in green tea is called epigallocatechin gallate (EGCG). Green tea is also a good source of another class of flavonoids called flavonols, including kaempferol, quercetin and myricitin.

Although the evidence is limited that drinking green tea guards against lung cancer, adding it to your daily diet may have other potential health benefits such as reducing the risk of breast cancer and heart disease. Green tea brewed from loose leaves contains more antioxidants. Whole tea leaves, compared to teabags, offer more surface area from which hot water can extract the antioxidants.

Vitamins and Minerals

Folate

This B vitamin is essential for the formation of DNA, the genetic material of all cells. Research suggests that higher intakes of folate from foods may lower the risk of lung cancer.[35] One study from Tufts University in Boston found that higher blood levels of the B vitamin were associated with better survival rates in patients who had surgery for small-cell lung cancer.[36]

Vegetables and fruit are the major sources of folate, which might account, in part, for their protective effect. To increase your intake of folate, reach for cooked spinach, lentils, orange juice, whole grains, fortified breakfast cereals, asparagus, artichoke, avocado and seeds. Supplemental folate (folic acid) has not been shown to reduce lung cancer risk.[37]

Antioxidants

Numerous studies have found that a high intake of antioxidants, especially beta carotene, from fruit and vegetables protects from lung cancer. Some studies have even found that lung cancer is associated with a lower level of certain antioxidants in the blood.[38-41] However, when researchers have examined the effect of antioxidant supplements on lung cancer risk, the findings are disappointing. Studies have found that supplements of vitamins C and E and beta carotene didn't protect from the disease.[42-45] In fact, two of these trials found an increased risk of lung cancer among beta carotene–users who smoked. One study also hinted that vitamin E supplementation might slightly increase the risk of lung cancer.[46]

Avoid taking single supplements of beta carotene, especially if you smoke. There's no evidence that the small amount of beta carotene in a multivitamin supplement is harmful.

There's no evidence yet that antioxidant supplements will protect from lung cancer. An overwhelming amount of evidence points to the protective effects of antioxidants when they are consumed as food. When it comes to cancer prevention, the biological properties of nutrients from supplements may be different from those in foods. Aim to get more antioxidants in your daily diet.

VITAMIN C. The recommended dietary allowance (RDA) is 75 and 90 milligrams for women and men, respectively (smokers need an additional 35 milligrams). Best food sources include citrus fruit, citrus juices, cantaloupe, kiwi, mango, strawberries, broccoli, Brussels sprouts, cauliflower, red pepper and tomato juice.

VITAMIN E. The RDA is 22 international units (IU). Best food sources include wheat germ, nuts, seeds, vegetable oils, whole grains and kale.

BETA CAROTENE. No RDA has been established. Best food sources are orange and dark-green produce, including carrots, sweet potato, winter squash, broccoli, collard greens, kale, spinach, apricots, cantaloupe, peaches, nectarines, mango and papaya.

Selenium

Most published studies have shown a reduced risk of lung cancer with higher intakes of the mineral selenium. Researchers have also found that people with low levels of selenium in their blood are at increased risk of lung cancer compared to those with higher blood levels. A deficiency of selenium reduces the body's production of selenium-containing proteins, many of which have antioxidant and anti-inflammatory properties. Four of these proteins form enzymes that play a critical role in protecting cell DNA from oxidative damage; others are needed to regenerate vitamin C in the body to its active antioxidant form.

Men and women require 55 micrograms of selenium each day. The best food sources include Brazil nuts, shrimp, salmon, halibut, crab, fish, pork, organ meats, wheat bran, whole-wheat bread, brown rice, onion, garlic and mushrooms. A daily multivitamin and mineral supplement will also help ensure you meet your daily selenium requirements. There's sparse evidence, however, that taking a single supplement of selenium reduces the risk of developing lung cancer. It's possible that selenium supplements may help lower the risk in people who are deficient in the mineral.

Nutrition Strategy Checklist for Preventing Lung Cancer

- ☐ Quit smoking
- ☐ Limit or avoid alcohol
- ☐ Limit animal fat
- ☐ Fish
- ☐ Fruit and vegetables
- ☐ Foods rich in flavonoids
- ☐ Green tea
- ☐ Foods rich in folate
- ☐ Foods rich in antioxidants
- ☐ Selenium

Recommended Resources

Canadian Cancer Society
www.cancer.ca
10 Alcorn Avenue, Suite 200
Toronto, ON M4V 3B1
Tel: 416-961-7223
Fax: 416-961-4189
Email: ccs@cancer.ca

National Cancer Institute
National Institutes of Health
NCI Public Inquiries Office
www.cancer.gov
6116 Executive Boulevard, Room 3036A
Bethesda, MD, USA 20892-8322
Tel: 1-800-4-CANCER (1-800-422-6237)

Mayo Foundation for Medical Education and Research
www.mayoclinic.com
This website is produced by a team of writers, editors, health educators, nurses, doctors and scientists, and is one of the best patient-education sites on the Internet. The information is reliable, thorough and clearly written.

Lupus

Lupus is the name of a group of chronic autoimmune diseases that target mainly women during their childbearing years, causing inflammation in many different body systems. An autoimmune disease develops when the body begins to harm its own healthy cells and tissues. Normally, your immune system protects your body from germs, viruses and bacteria by producing antibodies to fight these dangerous invaders. With lupus, the immune system malfunctions and begins to produce antibodies that attack its own body parts. This causes inflammation and tissue damage that results in a wide variety of disabling symptoms.

Systemic lupus erythematosus (SLE) is the most common and serious type of lupus. It has been identified as a systemic disease because it can target any tissue in the body, including the skin, muscles, blood, joints, lungs, heart, kidneys or brain. SLE affects each person differently and symptoms vary depending on which tissues and body organs become inflamed. The disease is chronic and is characterized by recurring periods of illness, called flares, which alternate with periods of wellness or remission.

Other types of lupus include:

DISCOID LUPUS ERYTHEMATOSUS (DLE) primarily affects the skin, causing a red, scaly rash on your face, scalp, ears, arms and/or chest. Extreme sun sensitivity is a common symptom of this disease.

SUBACUTE CUTANEOUS LUPUS (SCLE) causes rashes and sun sensitivity. However, the rashes develop only on the arms and upper body, and the disease rarely affects other organs.

DRUG-INDUCED LUPUS ERYTHEMATOSUS is very similar to SLE and the symptoms usually disappear when the medication is discontinued.

NEONATAL LUPUS affects infants born to women with immune disorders such as SLE.

What Causes Lupus?

Lupus is caused by the body's immune system attacking healthy tissue. This can result in inflammation in the joints, skin, kidneys, heart, lungs, blood vessels and brain. Current research indicates that lupus doesn't have a single cause but, rather, is triggered by a combination of genetic, environmental and hormonal factors. High levels of estrogen may accelerate the progress of the disease. Lupus also seems to run in families, which may indicate a hereditary basis for the illness.

Symptoms

Lupus affects each person in a different way, with symptoms ranging from fairly mild to severe, disabling or even fatal. Generally, lupus develops slowly, with symptoms appearing over a period of weeks, months or years. Initially, the disease is quite active and symptoms will steadily increase in severity, often requiring medical attention and treatment. This phase is known as a flare. After a flare, lupus will frequently move into a chronic phase, in which symptoms are less severe, though they don't disappear entirely. Women with lupus may also experience periods of remission, when the disease is inactive and symptoms subside.

The following symptoms may be early warning signs of SLE:

- **fatigue:** often extreme and overwhelming
- **weight changes:** an unexpected weight loss of more than 5 pounds (2.3 kg) may signal SLE activity; a sudden weight gain may be caused by swelling associated with SLE damage to heart and kidney tissue
- **fever**
- **swollen glands:** a sudden, unexplained swelling of the lymph glands might be an immune system response triggered by SLE
- **joint pain, stiffness and swelling**

There are also a number of specific symptoms that indicate the presence of lupus. Although the list of lupus symptoms below is extensive, it's rare for anyone to experience more than a few of these complications:

- **Photosensitivity.** At least 50 percent of people with lupus develop an abnormal skin reaction to sunlight, causing a rash on exposed skin.
- **Butterfly rash (Malar rash).** A red rash appears on the cheeks and over the nose of nearly 50 percent of all people with SLE.
- **Mucosal ulcers.** Small sores often appear on the mucus lining of the mouth or nose.
- **Arthritis.** Almost all women with SLE eventually develop arthritis. The arthritis associated with lupus doesn't usually cause crippling or deformities in the joints.
- **Pleuritis or pericarditis.** Inflammation of the lining of the lungs (pleuritis) or inflammation of the lining of the heart (pericarditis) affects nearly half of all people with SLE, causing chest pain and painful breathing.
- **Kidney damage.** Lupus can cause serious kidney damage; in fact, one of the leading causes of death among people with lupus is kidney failure.

- **Seizures.** SLE-caused damage to the central nervous system can produce problems such as epileptic seizures, delusions, hallucinations and behavioural changes.
- **Blood cell disorders.** The immune system may produce antibodies that will attack the red blood cells, causing a type of anemia. It can also reduce the number of white blood cells and may interfere with blood clotting.
- **Discoid rash.** This is a raised, red, scaly rash that appears on the chest, arms, face, scalp or ears of approximately one-quarter of people with lupus. The rash will worsen if exposed to sunlight.

Who's at Risk?

Lupus mainly strikes women between the ages of 15 and 45. Systemic lupus erythematosus (SLE) is eight to ten times more common in women than men.[1] Women who have a relative with some type of autoimmune disease are also at greater risk of developing lupus. Lupus is more common in blacks and Asians than in Caucasians. Long-term use of certain prescription drugs may also trigger a form of lupus called drug-induced lupus erythematosus in a small percentage of people.

Conventional Treatment

The treatment for lupus varies from person to person, depending on the severity of the disease and the type of symptoms involved. Because there's no cure, the goal of treatment is to bring the disease under control so that patients can lead a relatively normal life. Women with a mild case of lupus may not require any medical treatment. If the disease is more advanced, a variety of treatment options is available.

The most important factor in managing lupus is avoiding circumstances that trigger flares, such as excessive fatigue and high levels of stress. Following a healthy diet, quitting smoking and engaging in regular exercise can help keep the disease under control. As well, it's important that you learn to recognize the warning signs of a flare, such as increased fatigue, pain, rash, stomach upset, headache and dizziness.

In some cases, medications are used to manage the symptoms of lupus; one of the primary drugs is a corticosteroid called prednisone. Because corticosteroids act rapidly to suppress inflammation in your tissues, they're usually prescribed when symptoms are severe or life-threatening. Corticosteroids are potent drugs with serious side effects such as high blood pressure, osteoporosis, weight gain, acne and stomach ulcers.

Non-steroidal anti-inflammatory drugs (NSAIDs) are helpful in decreasing the inflammation that causes joint pain, fever and swelling. The arthritis pain often associated with SLE can usually be controlled with a mild pain-relief medication such as acetaminophen. Some people also find that their lupus symptoms respond well to antimalarial drugs, which suppress some of the immune responses that cause joint pain, fatigue, skin rashes and lung inflammation. If the nervous system or kidneys are affected, immunosuppressive drugs may be prescribed to restrain an overactive immune system.

Managing Lupus

Once medication brings lupus under control, a number of lifestyle changes can minimize the possibility of future flares. Whereas a poor diet, excessive use of alcohol and smoking can contribute to lupus flares, regular exercise can help prevent them, as well as reduce pain and help you manage stress.

Dietary Strategies

It's important to eat a healthy, low-saturated-fat diet that provides plenty of fibre and fresh fruit and vegetables. These foods contain protective vitamins, minerals and antioxidants that can keep you healthy. The following dietary guidelines should be followed:

1. Emphasize plant foods in your daily diet. Fill your plate with grains, fruit and vegetables. If you eat animal-protein foods like meat or poultry, choose lean sources and make sure they take up no more than one-quarter of your plate. Eat vegetarian sources of protein, like beans and soy, more often.

2. Eat fish twice per week. Oily fish such as salmon, trout, Arctic char, sardines and herring are rich in omega-3 fatty acids, which may help reduce the inflammation of lupus. (See Fish Oil Supplements below.)

3. Choose foods and oils rich in essential fatty acids. Nuts, seeds, flaxseed and flaxseed oil, canola oil, omega-3 eggs, wheat germ and leafy green vegetables are good choices.

4. Choose foods rich in vitamins, minerals and protective plant compounds. Choose whole grains as often as possible. Eat 7 to 10 servings of fruit and vegetables every day. Select a variety of different-coloured fruit and vegetables in your daily diet to increase your intake of phytochemicals, many of which have anti-inflammatory properties.

5. As often as possible, eliminate sources of refined sugar: cookies, cakes, pastries, frozen desserts, soft drinks, sweetened fruit juices, fruit drinks and candy.
6. Buy organic produce or wash fruit and vegetables to remove pesticide residues.
7. Limit foods that contain chemical additives.
8. Limit or avoid caffeine (caffeine can worsen fatigue by interrupting sleep patterns).
9. Drink at least 9 cups (2.2 L) of water every day.
10. Avoid alcohol. If you drink, consume no more than one drink per day, or seven per week.

Alfalfa

Alfalfa seeds contain an amino acid called L-canavanine that has been shown to provoke lupus in animals.[2-5] There have also been reports that alfalfa can worsen symptoms or cause a flare in women with lupus. Avoid eating alfalfa sprouts and don't use any herbal supplements that contain alfalfa.

Flaxseed

The seed of the flax grain contains plant estrogens called lignans and the essential fatty acid alpha-linolenic acid. Research indicates that flaxseed may inhibit the action of platelet-activating factor, a substance involved in SLE kidney disease. Two small studies found that women with lupus who consumed 30 grams of flaxseed each day experienced improved kidney function, less inflammation and reduced blood cholesterol levels.[6,7] Add 1 to 2 tablespoons (15 to 30 ml) of ground flaxseed to yogurt, breakfast smoothies, applesauce, hot cereal and baked goods.

Vitamins and Minerals

Vitamin C

There's some evidence that higher intake of vitamin C from the diet may reduce the risk of a lupus flare. In a study of 279 women with SLE, those who consumed the most vitamin C from foods were significantly less likely to have active lupus.[8]

The recommended daily intake of vitamin C is 75 milligrams for women and 90 milligrams for men. If you smoke, you need an additional 35 milligrams each day. The best food sources of vitamin C include citrus fruit, kiwi, mango, strawberries, cantaloupe, Brussels sprouts, cabbage, cauliflower, bell peppers and tomato juice. Include at least two vitamin C–rich foods in your daily diet.

Vitamin D

Numerous studies have reported insufficient blood levels of vitamin D in women with lupus. Research has also revealed that the severity of SLE appears to be linked with low levels of vitamin D.[9-11] These findings suggest that vitamin D deficiency may be a risk factor for SLE and the nutrient could play a role in the prevention and/or treatment of the disease. Among its many roles, vitamin D helps regulate the immune system and, in doing so, may help suppress autoimmune conditions such as lupus. An adequate intake of vitamin D may also help reduce the risk of osteoporosis, for which people with lupus have an increased risk.

It's recommended that Canadian adults take 1000 international units (IU) of vitamin D each day in the fall and winter, and year-round if you're over 50, if you have dark-coloured skin or if you don't expose your skin to sunlight in the summer months. (Exposure to sunlight—without the use of sunscreen—

triggers the synthesis of vitamin D in the skin.) People with lupus should take 1000 IU of vitamin D throughout the year, regardless of age, since too much sun exposure can trigger flares. If a blood test has determined you have insufficient vitamin D in your blood, you may be advised to take a higher dose. See Chapter 4, page 51, for more information on vitamin D supplementation.

Vitamin E

Some experts believe that free radical damage may play a role in the development of lupus. Studies have shown that lupus is associated with an increased level of oxidized blood fats and lower levels of circulating vitamin E.[12,13] Treatment with corticosteroid medication can further increase free radical injury. Preliminary animal research has found that supplemental vitamin E can slow the progress of lupus.[14] A small preliminary study conducted in women with SLE found that 150 to 300 IU of vitamin E taken together with prednisone suppressed the formation of lupus autoantibodies.[15] (Autoantibodies are immune compounds that mistakenly target and damage specific tissues or organs of the body.)

The recommended dietary allowance for vitamin E is 22 IU. The best food sources include wheat germ, nuts, seeds, vegetable oils, whole grains and kale. To supplement, take 200 to 400 IU of natural source vitamin E. The upper daily limit is 1500 IU. If you have heart disease or diabetes, don't take high dose vitamin E supplements. See Chapter 4, page 53, to learn about the safety of vitamin E supplementation.

Calcium

Women with SLE have a higher risk of low bone mass and osteoporosis, which are thought to be related to the duration of lupus.[16,17] Corticosteroid drugs used to treat lupus also cause bone loss and are associated with the development of low bone density. To protect your bones, make sure you meet your daily requirements for this essential nutrient.

The recommended dietary allowance (RDA) is 1000 to 1500 milligrams. Best food sources are milk, yogurt, cheese, fortified soy beverages, fortified orange juice, tofu, salmon (with bones), kale, bok choy, broccoli and Swiss chard. If you take calcium supplements, be sure to take them in divided doses during the day; don't take more than 500 or 600 milligrams of calcium at one time. See Chapter 4, page 58, for more information about calcium supplements.

Other Natural Health Products

DHEA (Dehydroepiandrosterone)

The hormone DHEA is produced by the two triangular-shaped adrenal glands, which sit one above each kidney. The secreted DHEA is a building block in the making of estrogen and testosterone. DHEA supplementation seems to change circulating levels of estrogen and progesterone. In women, DHEA increases blood levels of male sex hormones called androgens without increasing blood levels of estrogens. The effects of DHEA on circulating hormone levels may be responsible for its health benefits.

A number of studies have found DHEA supplements, in conjunction with conventional medication, reduce SLE disease activity, the frequency of flares and the dose of corticosteroid medication needed to manage the disease. DHEA may also help SLE symptoms such as muscle ache and oral ulcers. The supplement has also been shown to increase bone mineral density in women being treated with high-dose corticosteroids.[18-25]

DHEA supplements consist of a hormone manufactured from compounds found in soybeans. It's sold as a dietary supplement in the United States but isn't allowed for sale in Canada.

The recommended dose for lupus is 200 milligrams per day as an adjunct to conventional medication. DHEA is considered safe when taken for the short term. However, at doses of 200 milligrams per day, DHEA frequently causes adverse effects such as acne and hirsutism (excessive hair growth on the face or body) in women. For more information on DHEA, see Chapter 8, page 160.

Fish Oil Supplements

Researchers have found that fish oils have anti-inflammatory effects in women with lupus. Studies have found that women with lupus who take fish oil supplements experience symptom improvement, longer periods of remission and a lowering of blood-triglyceride levels.[26-31] Some researchers even suggest that fish oil may reduce free radical damage and help regulate the body's production of antioxidant enzymes.[32]

Fish oil capsules are a concentrated source of two omega-3 fatty acids, DHA (docosahexanaenoic acid) and EPA (eicosapentanoic acid). These acids inhibit the body's production of inflammatory compounds called leukotrienes.

The typical dosage used in lupus studies is 3 grams of fish oil per day. Buy a fish oil supplement that provides both EPA and DHA. Fish oil supplements can cause belching and a fishy taste; taking an enteric-coated product can help prevent these side effects. Because fish oil has a blood-thinning effect, use caution if you're taking blood-thinning medication such as aspirin, warfarin (Coumadin) or heparin.

Nutrition Strategy Checklist for Lupus

☐ Avoid alfalfa
☐ Flaxseed
☐ Vitamin C
☐ Vitamin D
☐ Vitamin E
☐ Calcium
☐ DHEA
☐ Fish oil supplement

Recommended Resources

The Arthritis Society
www.arthritis.ca
393 University Avenue, Suite 1700
Toronto, ON, M5G 1E6
Tel: 416-979-7228
Fax: 416-979-8366
Email: info@arthritis.ca

Lupus Canada
www.lupuscanada.org
590 Alden Road, Suite 211
Markham, ON L3R 8N2
Tel: 905-513-0004 or 1-800-661-1468
Fax: 905-513-9516
Email: info@lupuscanada.org

Lupus Foundation of America, Inc.
www.lupus.org
2000 L Street, NW, Suite 710
Washington, DC, USA 20036
Tel: 202-349-1155
Fax: 202-349-1156

Macular Degeneration (Age-Related Macular Degeneration or AMD)

This chronic eye disease affects 1 million Canadians over the age of 50 and is the leading cause of severe vision loss in older adults.[1] Macular degeneration attacks the central part of the retina called the macula, which controls fine, detailed vision. The condition results in progressive loss of visual sharpness, making it difficult to drive a car, read a book and recognize faces.

The damage caused by macular degeneration interferes with the ability of the eye to process light. As light enters the eye, it passes through the cornea and is focused by the lens onto the retina. The retina sits at the back of the eye and contains over 137 photosensitive cells. These cells, called rods and cones, are essential for black-and-white vision and for detecting movement, colour and pattern. Most of the cells required for perceiving colour and fine detail are located in the centre of the retina, in an area known as the macula. There are two types of macular degeneration.

DRY MACULAR DEGENERATION develops when the tissues of the macula gradually thin as you get older. The light-sensitive cells clustered in the macula slowly break down, blurring central vision and making it difficult to see details. The deterioration of these cells also affects colour vision, causing objects to appear hazy or washed out. Ninety percent of people with macular degeneration have the dry type of this disease.

WET MACULAR DEGENERATION develops when abnormal blood vessels grow under the macula. These blood vessels may leak fluid and blood, causing damage to the sensitive retinal cells. Eventually, scar tissue may form on the retina, creating a central blind spot. Wet macular degeneration is more of a threat to your vision than the dry type: Studies indicate that it's responsible for 90 percent of all cases of blindness associated with this disease. Fortunately, only 10 percent of people with macular degeneration suffer from the wet form of the disease.

What Causes Macular Degeneration?

The exact cause of age-related macular degeneration (AMD) is unclear, but factors such as family history, cigarette smoking, high blood pressure, excessive sunlight exposure, obesity and a diet low in antioxidants are linked with a greater risk of developing the disease. Antioxidants are thought to protect cells in the retina from the harmful effects of free radicals, unstable molecules formed from cigarette smoke, pollution and ultraviolet light. The disease may also develop as a complication of other medical conditions, such as infections, high blood pressure, atherosclerosis, diabetes, myopia (nearsightedness) and eye injuries that lead to retinal detachment.

Because the brain has a unique capability to fill in the vision gaps during the early stages of macular deterioration, many people don't realize that they have a vision problem until the disease is fairly advanced. The damage caused by macular degeneration can't be reversed, but early detection can help reduce the risk of vision loss.

Symptoms

Symptoms of dry macular degeneration may develop quite slowly or very rapidly. There's usually no pain associated with the disease. Blurred vision is the most common early sign; peripheral or side vision remains normal. Gradually, details become hazy and less clear when you look straight ahead. Colours appear dim and grey. Dark, empty areas or a blind spot can also appear in the centre of your vision.

If you have wet macular degeneration, straight objects, such as telephone poles, appear wavy. A dark, empty area or small blind spot may appear in the centre of your vision. Wet macular degeneration usually develops in both eyes, though not always at the same time.

Who's at Risk?

The following are more likely to develop AMD:

- Caucasians over 50 years old
- individuals with a family history of macular degeneration
- women (more susceptible than men)
- people with light-coloured eyes
- people who smoke cigarettes
- people who are obese
- people who have high blood pressure or coronary heart disease
- people who have a low nutrient intake
- people who have long-term exposure to sunlight and environmental pollution

Conventional Treatment

No treatment currently exists for dry macular degeneration. This form of the condition usually progresses slowly and people live normal lives, especially if only one eye is affected. Taking a high dose antioxidant supplement called Vitalux AREDS may reduce the progression of dry macular degeneration to advanced macular degeneration. This vitamin supplement was formulated based on the results of the landmark Age-Related Eye Disease Study (AREDS) published in 2001. The findings revealed that, among 3640 older adults with varying stages of dry macular degeneration, those taking a high-dose combination of antioxidants (25,000 IU of beta carotene, 500 milligrams of vitamin C, 400 IU of vitamin E), 80 milligrams of zinc and 2 milligrams of copper reduced the risk of the disease progressing to its advanced form by 25 percent.[2,3]

Vitalux AREDS is available in drugstores across Canada. Vitalux-S is available for smokers or ex-smokers. Vitalux-S contains the same ingredients as Vitalux AREDS with the exception of beta carotene. The absence of beta carotene is in answer to another major study that linked supplemental beta carotene taken by smokers and recent ex-smokers to an increased incidence of lung cancer and an increased risk of death from lung cancer and cardiovascular disease.

To treat wet macular degeneration in the early stages of the disease, a laser may be used to seal off blood vessels. This can prevent further damage to the retinal cells. However, only 20 percent of people with the disease are good candidates for laser surgery, and the surgery is successful only half of the time. New treatments involving more specialized forms of laser surgery are becoming available; these are most effective at closing leaking blood vessels during the first 3 months of vision loss.

Although you can't avoid the consequences of normal aging, there are certain things you can do to help prevent macular degeneration or to slow the progress of the disease. Eating a low-fat, antioxidant-rich diet (see below), quitting smoking, wearing sunglasses to block out ultraviolet light, controlling your blood pressure and diabetes, and having regular eye examinations to detect early changes in your vision are all important strategies to protect your eyesight.

Managing and Preventing Macular Degeneration

Dietary Strategies

Dietary Fat

Studies have found that people with a high intake of vegetable fats have an increased risk of macular degeneration. This relationship may be due to an individual fatty acid, such as linoleic acid, rather than total fat intake.[4,5] A high fat intake may also increase the risk of disease progression to the advanced stages associated with vision loss.[6,7] In one study of 261 older adults with macular degeneration, a high total-fat intake increased the risk of progression by almost threefold. A high intake of animal fat was associated with a twofold increased risk of disease progression; a high intake of vegetable fat had an even stronger correlation, with nearly a fourfold increased risk of progression. Those who ate the most processed baked goods—a source of vegetable oils and trans fats—had double the risk of macular degeneration progression compared to those who consumed the least.[8]

Researchers speculate that a high-fat diet, which is associated with atherosclerosis (hardening of the arteries), could affect blood vessels in the eye or could be involved in free radical damage that contributes to the development of the advanced stage of macular degeneration. Diets high in fatty foods also increase the risk of obesity, a risk factor for macular degeneration.

Choose lower-fat animal foods such as lean meat, poultry breast and milk and yogurt with 1% or less milk fat. Avoid or limit your intake of processed meats such as sausage, hot dogs, bacon and deli meats, which are high in saturated fat. Use added fats and oils sparingly; aim for no more than 2 to 3 tablespoons (30 to 45 ml) of vegetable oil per day. Read labels on packaged foods to choose products that are free of trans fat. For details on how to reduce your fat intake, see Chapter 3, page 28.

Fish and Omega-3 Fats

Many studies have found that people who eat fish once or twice per week have a lower risk of developing macular degeneration.[9-11] A recent study of 3654 adults who were followed for 10 years found that those who ate fish once per week had a 30 percent reduced risk of developing the eye disease.[12] If you have macular degeneration, adding fish to your weekly menu might reduce the likelihood of the disease progressing to an advanced stage. Studies suggest that higher intakes of baked and broiled fish, and higher intakes of total omega-3 fatty acids, can lower the risk of advanced macular degeneration by as much as 40 percent.[13,14]

Fish is an excellent source of two omega-3 fatty acids, DHA and EPA. DHA is concentrated in the retina where it's thought to exert a number of protective effects. Healthy omega-3 fats reduce inflammation and oxidative damage caused by free radicals and may also help prevent degenerative changes in the eye.

Include oily fish in your diet twice per week. Omega-3–rich choices include salmon, trout, Arctic char, sardines, anchovies, herring and mackerel. Look for foods with added DHA in the grocery store, such as eggs (Naturegg Omega Pro), milk and cheese. Foods that contain ALA (alpha-linolenic acid)—flaxseed and flaxseed oil, salba, canola oil, walnuts and walnut oil, for example—or that are fortified with ALA—such as eggs (Naturegg Omega 3), soy beverages, yogurt and juices—are also sources of omega-3 fats.

Nuts

There's evidence that eating nuts once or twice per week reduces the risk of macular degeneration.[15] Furthermore, nuts may reduce the risk of cardiovascular disease and type 2 diabetes, diseases linked to macular degeneration. Nuts also have antioxidant and anti-inflammatory properties. Include 1 serving (28 grams or 60 ml) of nuts in your diet a few times each week. Enjoy them as a snack or add them to hot cereal, salads and stir-fries.

Lutein- and Zeaxanthin-Rich Foods

These phytochemicals, cousins of beta carotene, are found mainly in fruit and vegetables, especially leafy greens. Once consumed, lutein and zeaxanthin become concentrated in the macula, where they act as a filter, protecting structures of the eye from the damaging effects of the sun's ultraviolet light. Lutein contributes to the density, or thickness, of the macula: the denser the macula, the better they can absorb incoming light. Experimental research has shown that adding lutein-rich foods or a lutein supplement to one's daily diet can increase the density of the macula within 4 weeks, suggesting it can prevent AMD.[16-18] Lutein and zeaxanthin also act as antioxidants, protecting the retina from free radical damage.

Scientists have found that a high dietary intake of carotenoids, especially lutein and zeaxanthin, is associated with a 40 percent to 65 percent lower risk of developing age-related macular degeneration.[19,20] Lutein and zeaxanthin may also reduce the risk of disease progression.

A daily intake of 6 to 15 milligrams of lutein and zeaxanthin combined per day is thought to be optimal for eye health. The best sources are leafy greens, but you'll also get lutein and zeaxanthin from green peas, broccoli, Brussels sprouts, nectarines and oranges. You can't rely on a multivitamin with added lutein to get your daily dose—most provide no more than 0.5 milligrams per daily dose.

Lutein and Zeaxanthin Content of Selected Foods
(Per 1/2 cup [125 ml] unless indicated otherwise)

Food	Lutein and Zeaxanthin (milligrams)
Spinach, frozen, cooked	14.9 mg
Kale, cooked	11.9 mg
Spinach, cooked	10.2 mg
Collard greens, cooked	7.3 mg
Turnip greens, cooked	6.1 mg
Okra, 8 pods	5.8 mg
Red pepper	5.1 mg
Mustard greens, cooked	4.2 mg
Dandelion greens, cooked	2.5 mg
Spinach, raw, 1 cup (250 ml)	1.8 mg
Broccoli, cooked	1.5 mg
Peas, green, cooked	1.4 mg
Beet greens, cooked	1.3 mg
Romaine lettuce, raw, 1 cup (250 ml)	1.3 mg
Brussels sprouts, cooked	1.0 mg
Leaf lettuce, raw, 1 cup (250 ml)	1.0 mg

Source: U.S. Department of Agriculture, Agricultural Research Service, 2007. USDA National Nutrient Database for Standard Reference, Release 21. Nutrient Data Laboratory Home Page, www.ars.usda.gov/nutrientdata.

Lutein and zeaxanthin are fat-soluble compounds, so you'll absorb more of them if you add a small amount of vegetable oil to your green salad or vegetable stir-fry.

Alcohol

Studies suggest that alcohol may increase the risk of macular degeneration. Two studies found that men who drank beer regularly had a higher risk of macular degeneration.[21,22]

Harvard University researchers also found that drinking at least 30 grams of alcohol (two drinks) per day modestly increases the risk of early dry macular degeneration in women.[23] The researchers didn't find that any specific type of alcohol protected the eyes.

Men should aim to consume no more than one to two drinks per day, to a limit of nine per week, and women should consume no more than one drink per day or seven per week. If you're at increased risk for macular degeneration, or you have the disease, avoid beer.

Vitamins and Minerals

Antioxidants

The retina of the eye is particularly vulnerable to oxidative damage from free radicals because of its high consumption of oxygen, its high content of polyunsaturated fats and its exposure to visible light. Research suggests that dietary antioxidants such as vitamins C and E, beta carotene, lycopene and selenium may offer protection from macular degeneration.

A number of studies show that both higher blood levels and higher intakes of these nutrients are associated with a lower risk of macular degeneration.[24-29] When it comes to preventing the development of macular degeneration, it's believed that the combinations of antioxidants found in food—not supplements—are most protective.

VITAMIN C. The recommended dietary allowance (RDA) is 75 and 90 milligrams for women and men, respectively (smokers need an additional 35 milligrams). Best food sources include citrus fruit, citrus juices, cantaloupe, kiwi, mango, strawberries, broccoli, Brussels sprouts, cauliflower, red pepper and tomato juice.

VITAMIN E. The RDA is 22 international units (IU). Best food sources include wheat germ, nuts, seeds, vegetable oils, whole grains and kale.

SELENIUM. The RDA is 55 micrograms. Best food sources are seafood, chicken, organ meats, whole grains, nuts, onions, garlic and mushrooms.

BETA CAROTENE. No RDA has been established. Best food sources are orange and dark-green produce, including carrots, sweet potato, winter squash, broccoli, collard greens, kale, spinach, apricots, cantaloupe, peaches, nectarines, mango and papaya.

LYCOPENE. No RDA has been established. Best food sources are heat-processed tomato products such as tomato juice, tomato paste, pasta sauce and canned tomatoes. Lycopene is also found, in a form less available to the body, in fresh tomatoes, pink grapefruit, watermelon, guava and apricots.

Zinc

This mineral may protect from macular degeneration by nourishing cells in the retina. As well, many enzymes important in the eye use zinc. Studies have found that higher blood levels and higher dietary intakes of zinc are linked with a lower risk of macular degeneration.[30] Findings from studies using high doses of zinc supplements have been contradictory.[31,32]

The evidence does suggest, however, that many years of meeting your daily zinc requirement from food may prevent macular degeneration later in life. Zinc-rich foods include oysters, seafood, red meat, poultry, yogurt, wheat bran, wheat germ, whole grains and enriched breakfast cereals. Most multivitamin and mineral supplements provide 10 to 15 milligrams of zinc. See Chapter 4, page 78, for information on zinc requirements.

If you have dry macular degeneration, it's been demonstrated that taking a daily supplement that combines a high dose of zinc with antioxidants reduces the risk of the disease progressing to an advanced form. The supplement called Vitalux AREDS is formulated for people with dry macular degeneration and is available in drugstores across Canada.

Herbal Remedies

Bilberry (*Vaccinium myrtillus*)

This herb contains anthocyanins, a compound that belongs to the flavonoids family. Anthocyanins help form strong connective tissue and blood capillaries. The anthocyanins in bilberry are thought to improve blood flow in the tiny capillaries of the eye. A small body of evidence suggests that the herb may be useful in preventing macular degeneration.[33,34]

Buy a product standardized to 25 percent to 36 percent anthocyanins. Take 160 milligrams twice daily. Use for 1 to 6 months is usually recommended for improvement in visual disorders. No adverse effects have been reported with bilberry use.

Ginkgo (*Ginkgo biloba*)

Ginkgo is thought to increase blood flow to the eye, thin the blood and act as an antioxidant to protect membranes in the eye from free radical damage. Although the research is very limited, a few preliminary studies have found the herb to have a beneficial effect in macular degeneration.[35-37] The recommended dose is 40 milligrams three times daily. Side effects may include stomach upset and headache.

Because ginkgo acts to thin the blood, the risk of bleeding may be increased if it is combined with blood-thinning drugs such as warfarin (Coumadin), heparin and aspirin.

Other Natural Health Products

Grapeseed Extract

Grapeseed extract is a by-product of wine manufacturing and is a rich source of anthocyanins. Like bilberry, this antioxidant is thought to keep eye capillaries healthy. The recommended supplemental dose for antioxidant protection is 50 milligrams once daily. No adverse effects have been reported with grapeseed extract use.

Lutein

If you're concerned that you aren't getting enough lutein-rich foods in your daily diet, consider taking a lutein supplement. Choose a product made with FloraGlo, a high-quality lutein extract made from marigold petals that has been used in clinical studies. Take 5 to 10 milligrams once daily with a meal.

Nutrition Strategy Checklist for Macular Degeneration

☐ Limit total and saturated fat

☐ Fish and omega-3 fats

☐ Nuts

☐ Lutein and zeaxanthin

☐ Limit alcohol

☐ Vitamin C

☐ Vitamin E

☐ Beta carotene

☐ Lycopene

☐ Zinc

☐ Bilberry OR *ginkgo biloba*

☐ Grapeseed extract

Recommended Resources

Canadian National Institute for the Blind
www.cnib.ca
CNIB National Office
1929 Bayview Avenue
Toronto, ON M4G 3E8
Tel: 1-800-563-2642
Fax: 416-480-7700
Email: info@cnib.ca

Canadian Ophthalmological Society
www.eyesite.ca
610–1525 Carling Avenue
Ottawa, ON K1Z 8R9
Tel: 613-729-6779 or 1-800-267-5763
Fax: 613-729-7209
Email: cos@eyesite.ca

Association for Macular Diseases
www.macula.org
210 E 64th Street
New York, NY, USA 10021
Tel: 212-605-3719

Macular Degeneration Foundation
www.eyesight.org
P. O. Box 531313
Henderson, NV, USA 89053

Tel: 1-888-633-3937
Fax: 702-450-3396

National Eye Institute
U.S. Department of Health and Human Services
National Institutes of Health
www.nei.nih.gov
2020 Vision Place
Bethesda, MD, USA 20892-3655
Tel: 301-496-5248

Migraine Headaches

More than 3 million Canadians suffer from migraine, a type of headache that results from inflammation of the blood vessels and nerves surrounding the brain. Migraine is a chronic condition of recurrent attacks that are usually described as intense, throbbing or pounding pain that involves the temple on one side of the head. Although the exact causes aren't known, migraine headaches seem to be set off by changes in brain activity. Very often, specific substances, actions or stimuli in your body or environment may trigger migraines.

What Causes a Migraine?

Migraine headaches are caused by a combination of vasodilation (enlargement of the blood vessels) and the release of chemicals from nerves that wrap around the blood vessels. During a migraine, the temporal artery, which lies outside the skull just under the skin of the temple, enlarges. This triggers the surrounding nerves to release chemicals that cause inflammation, pain and further enlargement of the artery, which intensifies the pain. Migraine headaches also stimulate your sympathetic nervous system, and that can induce nausea, vomiting, diarrhea and delayed stomach emptying.

Symptoms

The pain of migraine headaches is usually felt on one side of the head, but it can change sides from one attack to the next. About one-third of migraines are bilateral, with pain felt on both sides of the head. The pain is typically aggravated by daily activities such as walking up stairs. It's common for migraine headaches to be accompanied by nausea, vomiting, diarrhea, facial pallor, cold hands, cold feet, and sensitivity to light and sound.

Warning symptoms, which can last hours or days, precede up to 60 percent of migraine attacks. Such symptoms may include fatigue, irritability, depression or food cravings. About 20 percent of migraines are associated with an aura. The aura is a set of neurological symptoms that occur approximately 10 to 30 minutes before the headache starts. During the aura phase, you may experience visual disturbances, such as flashing lights or geometric patterns in front of your eyes, or you may even suffer a brief vision loss. It's not uncommon to feel dizzy and confused or to have some facial tingling and muscle weakness as the aura progresses.

The International Headache Society has recommended a detailed set of criteria for assessing migraine symptoms. It's reasonable to assume you suffer from migraines if your headaches have some of the following characteristics:

- a sequence of at least five attacks that last between 4 and 72 hours
- pain located on one side of your head, sometimes spreading to both sides

- pain that is pulsating or throbbing
- pain that prohibits or limits daily activity
- pain that's aggravated by physical activity
- nausea or vomiting during headache attacks
- sensitivity to light, noise or smell during headache attacks

Most migraines don't conform to a typical pattern. Some people suffer a migraine only once in a while; others are incapacitated by attacks as often as three times a week. The intensity of pain can vary from reasonably mild to completely debilitating. Migraines also vary in length, from a brief 15-minute episode to an attack that can last a week. On average, the duration of a migraine ranges between 4 and 72 hours. For up to 24 hours after an attack, migraine sufferers may feel drained of energy and may continue to be sensitive to light and sound.

Who's at Risk?

Migraine is a universal condition that affects approximately 6 percent of men and 15 percent to 17 percent of women.[1] Migraine generally begins in childhood to early adulthood. Most people who suffer migraine headaches have a family history of the condition, indicating there's a genetic predisposition.

Migraine Triggers

In some cases, certain stimuli or triggers may provoke migraine occurrence within hours or in up to 2 days. Triggers include certain foods, fasting, stress, sleep disturbances, bright lights and cigarette smoke. Although triggers don't actually cause a migraine, they do seem to influence the activities in the brain that stimulate the disease. Often, migraine sufferers are sensitive to the combined effect of more than one trigger.

There are many common migraine triggers, and it's important to determine which ones affect you. Keeping a diary is a good way to identify the circumstances that set off your migraines. Keep in mind, however, that triggers don't always lead to a headache and avoidance of triggers doesn't always prevent a headache from occurring.

1. **Diet.** Certain foods and food additives are well-known migraine triggers. Alcoholic beverages (especially red wine), foods treated with monosodium glutamate (MSG), foods containing tyramine (aged cheeses, soy sauce) or aspartame (NutraSweet), and foods preserved with nitrates and nitrites may provoke migraines. Chocolate, caffeine and dairy products are other known culprits.
2. **Lifestyle.** Changes in your behaviour or your surroundings can encourage migraines. If you alter your eating or sleeping habits, experience high levels of stress or smoke cigarettes, you may find yourself struggling with more frequent migraines.
3. **Environment.** Some people find that bright lights or loud noises bring on a migraine. Weather or temperature changes and physical exertion are common triggers. Even changing time zones may affect your headache frequency. Strong odours, perfume, high altitudes and computer screens are other recognized triggers.
4. **Female hormones.** Women may be more susceptible to migraines because of the estrogen cycles associated with menstruation. Migraines become more prevalent in females after puberty, reaching a peak at age 40 and then declining in frequency as women age. But almost two-thirds of women who suffer migraines experience a worsening of their headaches during their period. Up to 15 percent of women get migraines only during their period. Menstrual migraines are typically without aura and last longer than other migraines. They are also more difficult to treat. To prevent them, it's extremely important for women to avoid migraine triggers during the premenstrual week.

5. **Oral contraceptives and estrogen therapy.** These seem to make migraines worse. Speak to your doctor about alternative contraceptive methods if birth control pills contribute to your migraines.
6. **Pregnancy.** Migraines are more common early in the pregnancy but usually improve by the second trimester. In a small group of women, migraines worsen throughout their pregnancies. During pregnancy, women should pay special attention to avoiding dietary and environmental triggers, sticking to regular sleeping and eating schedules, getting regular exercise and managing stress (as should all women with migraines).

Conventional Treatment
Migraine Relief Medications

These medications target the pain of an attack and should be taken as soon as you sense a headache beginning. General analgesics (painkillers) and NSAIDs (non-steroidal anti-inflammatory drugs) are frequently used to relieve the discomfort of mild and moderate migraine attacks. One of the most effective is sumatriptan (Imitrex), a drug that specifically targets the receptors for serotonin. Some combination medications may be useful in cases where other drug therapies aren't effective.

Because migraines are usually accompanied by extreme nausea, your doctor may also prescribe anti-nausea drugs.

Overuse of these drugs may cause rebound headaches, which aren't migraine- but medication-induced. They may quickly become chronic.

Severe migraine attacks that result in incapacitating pain may be treated with opiates. Although very powerful painkillers, they are also highly addictive and so usually prescribed only in extreme cases.

Migraine Prevention Therapies

As with migraine relief medications, these drugs will work with varying success. The main types of prevention medications are:

- **Beta blockers** to stabilize serotonin levels and reduce the dilation of blood vessels
- **Ergot drugs** to positively affect serotonin levels and blood vessel dilation
- **Calcium channel blockers** to modulate neurotransmitters
- **Antidepressants** to positively affect sero-tonin levels (however, they may have serious interactions with other medications)

Alternative Treatments

A growing body of evidence indicates that alternative therapies have a positive effect on the symptoms and frequency of migraine attacks. Resting in a quiet, dark room and applying ice or pressure often helps relieve pain. Other therapies that have shown some success in alleviating migraine are:

- relaxation therapy
- biofeedback
- acupuncture

- stress-management training
- psychotherapy
- hypnosis
- physiotherapy, osteopathy and chiropractic

Managing Migraines
Dietary Strategies
Food Triggers

A number of foods and beverages have been reported to trigger a migraine attack.[2-7] One study found that when people who suffer migraines eliminate these foods from their diet, about one-third experience fewer headaches and up to 10 percent become headache-free.[8] The following are the most common foods to trigger a migraine, or make one worse:

Cheese, especially aged cheese	Garlic
Chocolate	Hot dogs
Coffee, tea	Milk
Eggs	Wine
Fish	

The following foods and food additives have also been reported to bring on a headache:

Alcoholic beverages	Corn
Artificial sweeteners	Foods with MSG
Citrus fruit	

Foods with nitrites/nitrates (processed meats, smoked fish, some imported cheeses, beets, celery, collards, eggplant, lettuce, radishes, spinach, turnip greens)

Lentils	Red wine
Lima beans	Shellfish
Nuts	Soybeans
Overripe bananas	Tomato
Peanuts, peanut butter	

Some migraine sufferers have actual food allergies. It's thought that certain immune compounds formed in response to an offending food can trigger a migraine headache. If you find that certain foods are triggering migraines, it might be worthwhile to have your doctor refer you to an allergy specialist for food testing.

Elimination/Challenge Diet

A registered dietitian who specializes in food sensitivities (www.dietitians.ca) can plan an elimination/challenge diet for you, a useful tool to identify food triggers. You can also do this on your own. Begin by keeping a food and headache diary. List all foods, beverages, medications and dietary supplements you take. Women should also note the date of their menstrual period, since hormones may precipitate a migraine. Keep this diary for at least 2 weeks or long enough to cover at least three migraine attacks. Once you've completed this exercise, look for patterns. Did you eat the same food before each migraine? Did your migraines hit you after a night of drinking wine?

Once you've identified possible culprits, eliminate those items from your diet for 4 weeks, or longer if you experience migraines less frequently. If you're migraine-free during this period, it's very likely that you've found your triggers. The next step is to confirm if all, or only some, of the foods are the actual culprits. One by one test each food by adding it to your diet. Wait 3 days before testing the next food on your list. Keep in mind that this exercise may not give you clear-cut results. A combination of events may be required to bring on a migraine. For instance, you may get a migraine only when you eat the food at a specific time in your menstrual cycle, or only with the combination of stress and a food trigger.

Vitamins and Minerals

Riboflavin (Vitamin B2)

Your body needs riboflavin to facilitate the release of energy from all body cells. Studies reveal that migraine sufferers have less efficient energy metabolism in their brain cells. It's thought that increasing riboflavin intake (in your diet or in the form of a supplement) and therefore the potential of brain cells to generate energy might prevent migraines. Well-controlled studies have found that a daily 400 milligram supplement of riboflavin was effective at reducing the frequency of headache attacks. One study demonstrated 400 milligrams of riboflavin to be as effective as certain drugs used to treat migraines.[9,10] Although most clinical studies have given patients a 400 milligram dose, one trial found that 25 milligrams of riboflavin taken daily for 3 months significantly reduced the number of migraines and migraine days and the level of migraine pain.[11]

The recommended dietary allowance for riboflavin is 1.1 to 1.3 milligrams per day. Riboflavin is found in many foods, including milk, meat, eggs, nuts, enriched flour and green vegetables. If you take a multivitamin you'll get even more riboflavin, as much as 100 milligrams.

To prevent a migraine, take 400 milligrams of B2 once daily. B2 supplements are available in 25, 50, 100, 500 and 1200 milligram doses. It may take up to 3 months to notice an improvement in your headache frequency. Riboflavin supplements are non-toxic and very well tolerated.

Magnesium

Evidence shows that during a migraine headache, up to 50 percent of people have low magnesium levels in their brain and red blood cells.[12–14] It's thought that a deficiency of magnesium in the brain can cause nerve cells to get overly excited, triggering a migraine attack. (A few medications, including estrogen, estrogen-containing birth control pills and certain diuretics, can deplete magnesium stores.)

German researchers gave eighty-one migraine sufferers either 600 milligrams of magnesium or a placebo pill once daily for 3 months.[15] In the second month of the study, the frequency of migraine attacks was reduced to 42 percent in the magnesium group compared with only 16 percent in the placebo group. As well, both the duration of a migraine and drug use significantly decreased among those people who took magnesium supplements. Another study conducted in children and teenagers found that taking a daily magnesium supplement didn't prevent migraine, but led to a significant reduction in headache days.[16]

The best food sources of magnesium are whole grains, nuts, seeds, legumes, prunes, figs, leafy green vegetables and brewer's yeast.

To prevent a migraine, take 600 milligrams of magnesium per day, in three divided doses. For children, a dose of 9 milligrams per kilogram body weight per day has been used, in three divided doses. Buy a magnesium citrate supplement as the body absorbs this form more readily. Taking more than 350 milligrams of supplemental magnesium per day may cause diarrhea.

Herbal Remedies

Feverfew (*Tanacetum parthenium*)

Since the 1970s, this herbal remedy has been the focus of a number of studies in people with migraines.[17,18] In one study, seventy-six people who experienced migraines were given either whole feverfew leaf or placebo for 4 months.

The treatments were then reversed for another 4-month period. Without knowing which treatment they received, 59 percent of the people identified the feverfew period as more effective compared with 24 percent who chose the placebo period. Feverfew reduced the number of migraines by 32 percent.[19]

The herbal remedy has also been shown to reduce symptoms of migraine including pain, nausea, vomiting and sensitivity to light and noise. It's thought to be more effective in people who suffer more frequent migraine attacks. Feverfew is thought to reduce the frequency and intensity of migraines by preventing the release of substances called prostaglandins, which dilate blood vessels and cause inflammation.

The recommended dose is 50 to 100 milligrams daily of powdered feverfew leaf. You can also try taking the herb at the onset of a migraine to ease the symptoms. Feverfew is considered safe and rarely causes side effects other than mild gastrointestinal upset. The herb may cause an allergic reaction in people sensitive to members of the Asteraceae/Compositae plant family (ragweed, daisy, marigold and chrysanthemum).

Other Natural Health Products

Coenzyme Q10 (CoQ10)

Coenzyme Q10 (CoQ10) is a fat-soluble, vitamin-like substance made by every cell in the body. Like riboflavin, CoQ10 is needed for the production of the body's energy compounds, ATP (adenosine triphosphate), and as such, it might be useful in preventing migraines. Studies have found that taking a daily CoQ10 supplement reduced the frequency of migraine headaches by 30 percent and the number of days with migraine-associated nausea by 45 percent. The supplement has also been shown to lessen the frequency of migraine attacks in children who are deficient in CoQ10.[20-22]

To prevent a migraine, a CoQ10 dose of 100 milligrams taken three times per day is recommended. In children and adolescents, a daily dose of 1 to 3 milligrams per kilogram body weight has been used. It may take up to 3 months for CoQ10 to have a significant benefit.

Nutrition Strategy Checklist for Migraine

☐ Identify food triggers
☐ Vitamin B2
☐ Magnesium
☐ Feverfew
☐ Coenzyme Q10

Recommended Resources

American Headache Society
www.achenet.org
19 Mantua Road
Mt. Royal, NJ, USA 08061
Tel: 609-423-0258 or 1-800-255-2243
Fax: 609-423-0082
Email: achehq@talley.com

National Headache Foundation
www.headaches.org
820 N Orleans, Suite 217
Chicago, IL, USA 60610
Tel: 312-274-2650
Email: info@headaches.org

Motion Sickness

Motion sickness is a common disturbance of the inner ear that causes feelings of nausea and dizziness. It can occur when you're sitting in a speeding car or a rocking boat, on a jerky amusement-park ride or in some other moving vehicle. Although motion sickness is not usually a serious problem, some people suffer so much that they are incapacitated for several days after a trip in a car, airplane or boat. Individuals who are particularly sensitive may even experience nausea and dizziness when riding in an elevator or swaying on a swing. Motion sickness affects your sense of balance and equilibrium, and as a result, your sense of spatial orientation.

What Causes Motion Sickness?

Your sense of balance is maintained by an interaction involving four different parts of the nervous system. The inner ears, eyes, skin pressure receptors and muscle and joint sensory receptors all send messages to the brain, signals that let the brain know if you're turning, bending, standing still or moving in a particular direction. By interpreting these messages, the brain determines where your body is in relation to the world around it.

The symptoms of motion sickness develop when the brain receives conflicting signals from the inner ears, eyes and various sensory receptors. For example, if you read a book in a moving car, your eyes will only see the pages of the book, but your inner ears and your sensory receptors will detect the movement of the car. This conflicting input confuses the brain, upsets your equilibrium and triggers motion sickness. It's thought that levels of certain chemicals in the brain, including histamine, acetylcholine and norepinephrine, are involved in transmitting the conflicting input.

Motion sickness may also develop as a result of excessive stimulation of the fluid-filled semicircular canals inside the inner ear, which are normally accustomed to horizontal movements. The unfamiliar vertical motion of an airplane, elevator or amusement-park ride can disturb the fluid and receptors inside these sensitive canals. Your brain perceives these disturbances as a loss of balance, causing nausea and dizziness. Emotional upset, anxiety, nervousness or poor ventilation inside a moving vehicle can also provoke episodes of motion sickness.

In some cases, motion sickness develops as a result of specific medical conditions that affect the inner ear, including:

- abnormalities in the ear
- viral or bacterial infections of the inner ear
- circulatory problems that reduce the flow of blood to the brain or to the inner ear
- injury to the skull
- allergy
- neurological diseases
- certain medications

Symptoms

For most people, motion sickness is a minor annoyance. Some people, however, can be incapacitated by the condition. Typical symptoms include:

- dizziness (vertigo)
- headache
- facial pallor
- cold sweating
- nausea

- vomiting
- feeling generally unwell

In most instances, the symptoms of motion sickness go away when the motion that caused them stops. However, some people continue to be plagued by symptoms, even for a few days, after a trip is over.

Who's at Risk?

Anyone can experience motion sickness if the motion is turbulent enough and continues long enough, but some people are more sensitive to it than others. Children are more vulnerable to motion sickness than are adults. Infants are very resistant to motion sickness; after infancy, susceptibility increases, peaking at ages 10 to 12, after which it starts to decrease.[1] Females are more prone to motion sickness than males, possibly because of hormonal influences.[2]

Conventional Treatment

Motion sickness is easier to prevent than to treat. The following strategies can help reduce the likelihood of motion sickness:

- Don't read while travelling.
- Don't sit in a seat facing backwards.
- Keep your line of vision as straight ahead as possible.
- Avoid strong odours, tobacco smoke, spicy food, heavy meals or excessive alcohol before you travel.
- Travel in well-ventilated vehicles, wherever possible; keep car windows open slightly or stop frequently for walks in the fresh air.
- Sit or stand where motion is less apparent, such as the front seat of a car, over the wings of an airplane and at the centre of a ship (preferably on deck).

If you suffer from severe motion sickness, you may need to take anti-motion sickness medication to control symptoms. Antihistamines, such as Dramamine (dimenhydrinate), are most commonly used to prevent and treat motion-sickness nausea, vomiting and dizziness. Another type of drug is Scopolamine (hyoscine), a medicated skin patch applied behind the ear at least 4 hours in advance of motion activity. However, this drug may cause some drowsiness. Children under the age of 10 shouldn't use it; antihistamines are used most often for children.

Managing Motion Sickness

Dietary Strategies

Carbohydrates

Some research suggests that people with unexplained dizziness (vertigo) may have difficulties processing sugar (glucose) in the bloodstream. One small study found that more than 80 percent of the patients had abnormal levels of the glucose-clearing hormone insulin, and abnormal glucose-tolerance tests.[3] A low-carbohydrate diet improved symptoms in 90 percent of cases.

If, based on glucose-tolerance tests, your doctor identifies that you have a carbohydrate intolerance, try following a lower-carbohydrate diet, especially when you travel. Limit portions of bread, grains, pasta, rice and potato to only one-quarter of your plate. The remainder of your meal should consist of vegetables and lean protein foods such as poultry breast, lean meat and fish. You may even try avoiding starchy side dishes with your meal and increasing your portion of vegetables. Low-carbohydrate breakfast suggestions include cottage cheese and berries or cantaloupe, or a vegetable omelet with sliced tomato. Low-carbohydrate snacks include nuts, low-carbohydrate energy bars, low-fat cheese and vegetable sticks.

Food Triggers

American researchers studied the relationship of diet to airsickness in pilots and identified possible food triggers.[4] In females, eating high-sodium foods such as preserved meats, potato chips and corn chips as well as thiamin-rich foods like pork, beef, eggs or fish had a significant association with airsickness. In male pilots, there was a connection between airsickness and high-protein foods such as dairy products and meat.

The researchers also found that eating more frequent meals of rich foods the day before travel was linked with a greater risk of airsickness. To prevent motion sickness, try eating two or three light, low-sodium meals the day before air or sea travel.

Herbal Remedies

Ginger (*Zingiber officinale*)

A number of studies have found powdered ginger root effective in treating motion sickness and vertigo. One study found that when taken 25 minutes before subjects were tested in a motor-driven rotary chair, ginger was superior to placebo and drug treatment in reducing symptoms of motion sickness among thirty-six adults susceptible to motion sickness.[5] Another study found that ginger reduced the severity of motion sickness symptoms in naval cadets unaccustomed to sailing on heavy seas.[6] The same researchers also examined the effect of ginger on vertigo and found the herb reduced vertigo symptoms significantly more than the placebo treatment.[7]

Scientists believe that the active components in ginger, gingerol and shogal, ease feelings of motion sickness by increasing the motility of the gastrointestinal tract.[8] Gingerol compounds may also improve appetite and digestion by reducing gastric secretions and increasing the release of important digestive aids. There's some speculation that ginger may also work by influencing the central nervous system.

The recommended dose of powdered ginger root to prevent motion sickness is 500 to 1000 milligrams, taken 4 hours before travel. This is equivalent to 2 to 4 grams of fresh or candied ginger root. To reduce symptoms of vertigo, including nausea, studies have used 1 gram (1000 milligrams) of ginger per day.

Ginger may cause mild intestinal upset. The herb has a slight blood-thinning effect and may possibly interact with blood-thinning medications like warfarin (Coumadin), although no studies have reported this effect. Since ginger may increase bleeding time, it shouldn't be taken before scheduled surgery.

Ginger is a menstrual stimulant and has the potential to induce abortion when taken in doses greater than 250 milligrams four times daily. The use of ginger during pregnancy is controversial; if used, it should be taken for a short period only and limited to 1000 milligrams per day.

Ginkgo (Ginkgo biloba)

A few studies have found this herb effective in reducing motion sickness and vertigo. One study involving sixty-seven people with vertigo found that 47 percent of those taking ginkgo completely recovered after 3 months of treatment compared with only 18 percent of those taking the placebo pill.[9] An Italian study found that ginkgo improved the symptoms of vertigo and dizziness after 1 month of treatment.[10] The study suggests that ginkgo may work by influencing sensory receptors in the eye. The herb also increases blood flow to the brain.

The recommended dose for treating vertigo is 120 to 160 milligrams per day, divided in two or three doses. Choose a product that is standardized to contain 24 percent ginkgo flavone glycosides and 6 percent terpene lactones.

Ginkgo acts to thin the blood and may increase the risk of bleeding if combined with blood-thinning drugs such as warfarin (Coumadin), heparin and aspirin. Ginkgo may also cause bleeding problems if taken with garlic and high dose vitamin E.

Nutrition Strategy Checklist for Motion Sickness

☐ Low-carbohydrate diet
☐ Identify food triggers
☐ Low-fat, low-sodium meals
☐ Ginger OR ginkgo biloba

Recommended Resources

American Academy of Otolaryngology—Head and Neck Surgery
www.entnet.org
1650 Diagonal Road
Alexandria, VA, USA 22314-2857
Tel: 703-836-4444

Mayo Foundation for Medical Education and Research
www.mayoclinic.com
This website is produced by a team of writers, editors, health educators, nurses, doctors and scientists, and is one of the best patient-education sites on the Internet. The information is reliable, thorough and clearly written.

Multiple Sclerosis (MS)

Multiple sclerosis (MS) is a chronic, potentially debilitating and unpredictable disease. It affects the brain and spinal cord, key communication centres that control most body movements by sending messages, in the form of electrical impulses, along nerve fibres to all parts of the body. Each of these nerve fibres is protected by a fatty sheath or covering, called myelin, which ensures that the electrical impulses travel quickly and efficiently along the nerve pathways of the central nervous system.

Multiple sclerosis attacks the myelin sheath around the nerves, destroying it in sections or patches and replacing it with scar tissue. The scar tissue interrupts the electrical impulses as they travel along the nerve fibres, blocking the natural flow of communication throughout the central nervous system. MS can affect every part of your body, eventually interfering with your muscle coordination, vision, emotional responses and intellectual abilities.

There are several different types of MS, each characterized by different patterns of attack and remission.

RELAPSING-REMITTING. This is the most common type of MS; approximately 65 percent to 80 percent of people with MS begin with this form of the disease. Flare-ups occur once or twice every 1 to 3 years, usually followed by periods of remission. It may be weeks to decades between attacks.

BENIGN MS. Up to 25 percent of people with relapsing-remitting MS have this type. The disease has long periods of remission with few attacks and produces little disability.

SECONDARY-PROGRESSIVE. More than half of those people with relapsing-remitting MS move into this stage of continuous deterioration within 10 years. The disease progresses steadily with or without relapses. When attacks do occur, the recovery is usually not complete and disability accumulates over time.

PRIMARY-PROGRESSIVE. This type is relatively rare, affecting 10 percent to 15 percent of people with MS. The disease grows continuously worse from time of diagnosis, with no clearly identifiable periods of attack or remission.

What Causes Multiple Sclerosis?

The cause of MS is still unknown. Most researchers believe that MS is an autoimmune disease. The immune system normally produces antibodies to protect the body from disease, fighting off foreign invaders such as harmful bacteria and viruses. Scientists suspect that a common virus may somehow trigger the immune system to malfunction and develop antibodies against the cells that produce myelin, causing inflammation and damage to the myelin sheath.

Research also seems to indicate that heredity has a role to play in multiple sclerosis. There's evidence that a combination of genes may make certain people more susceptible to MS than others. Approximately 15 percent of people with MS have a close relative who's also affected by the disease.

Environmental conditions may be a factor in multiple sclerosis. MS is five times more common in people who have spent the first 15 years of their lives in a temperate climate such as that in Canada and the northern United States. In fact, Canadians have one of the highest rates of MS in the world. People who live in a tropical climate have a much lower risk of MS, and people who live near the equator almost never develop the disease. There may be a relationship between low levels of sunshine, vitamin D deficiency and MS. Exposure to sun stimulates the production of vitamin D, which is important for regulating your immune system. If you're genetically predisposed to MS, a lack of vitamin D may trigger the immune system to malfunction.

Symptoms

Although the disease tends to progress slowly over time, its symptoms are unpredictable and vary from person to person. Some people have very few attacks and suffer minimal damage to the myelin sheath. Others have severe attacks that leave them with serious and permanent disabilities. Most people with MS find that the disease seems to come and go, with alternating periods of relatively good health (remission) and debilitating flare-ups.

Damage to the myelin sheath produces a wide variety of symptoms, depending on which part of the central nervous system is affected. Symptoms, which may improve during periods of remission, include:

- numbness, weakness, tingling sensations or paralysis in various parts of the body
- extreme fatigue
- blurred or double vision
- loss of balance or coordination, unsteady gait, tremor
- stiffness in muscles, painful muscle spasms
- dizziness or spinning sensation that lasts for a few days
- loss of control over urinary or bowel functions

- sensitivity to heat
- pain on one side of the face
- difficulty in speaking or slurred speech, difficulty swallowing
- difficulty with sexual functions
- problems with short-term memory, concentration, judgment or reasoning

Who's at Risk?

An estimated 55,000 to 75,000 Canadians have MS.[1] As mentioned above, Canada and other countries with a temperate climate are high-risk areas for the disease. MS usually affects men and women between the ages of 20 and 40. MS is more than three times as likely to occur in women as in men and is seen most commonly in people of northern European background.[2]

The risk of MS increases if you have a close relative with the disease, since it seems to run in families. Studies estimate that relatives of people with MS are eight times more likely to develop the condition.[3]

Conventional Treatment

Although there's no cure for MS, it's no longer considered a fatal disease. Medical advances and improvements in the treatment of symptoms with medication now ensure that most people with MS live a normal or near-normal lifespan. Since 1995, Health Canada has approved five medications for the treatment of relapsing-remitting MS, one for the treatment of secondary-progressive MS and one for people at high risk of developing MS. Clinical trials have shown that the medications decrease the frequency and severity of MS attacks and reduce the number of MS lesions in the brain, with several slowing the progression of disability. Treatment early in the disease is recommended. Also important are therapies that help with MS symptoms such as spasticity, bladder problems, pain and fatigue.

Treatment of MS focuses mainly on relieving symptoms and includes the following medications:

- **Corticosteroids** to reduce inflammation in nerve tissue and shorten duration of flare-ups. Side effects of prolonged use include osteoporosis and hypertension.
- **Beta interferons** to help fight viral infection and regulate the immune system. These synthetic copies of proteins that occur naturally in your body are used most often for relapsing-remitting MS, but are prescribed cautiously because long-term effects are unknown.
- **Glatiramer acetate** to block the immune system attack on myelin in those with relapsing-remitting MS.
- **Muscle relaxants** to relieve muscle spasms.

Other medications, such as pain relievers and antidepressants, may ease common symptoms of MS. Physical therapy to strengthen muscles and occupational therapy to learn how to use specialized devices to assist in daily tasks can preserve independence. In addition, counselling helps those suffering from MS, and their families, cope with the emotional and physical stress of the disease.

Certain lifestyle changes may help prevent attacks or reduce the severity of symptoms.

- Get adequate rest to help combat the fatigue associated with MS.
- Exercise regularly to improve strength, muscle tone, balance and coordination, as well as to improve mental attitude.

- Eat a well-balanced diet (see below) to keep your immune system strong.
- Avoid hot tubs, since soaking too long in hot water weakens muscles.
- Have regular massages to improve muscle tone and improve circulation.
- Avoid emotional and physical stress whenever possible.

Managing Multiple Sclerosis
Dietary Strategies

A low-saturated-fat, high-fibre diet that contains plenty of whole grains, fruit and vegetables along with adequate fluids will help you manage your MS. Not only do these foods provide nutrients that may help reduce symptoms of the disease but they can also help prevent the nutrient deficiencies and constipation that often accompany MS. Although weight gain can occur in many people with MS, nutritional wasting is also prevalent.

Fatigue, physical disability and depression can influence food intake and lead to dependence on low-nutrient convenience foods, increased intake of comfort foods, loss of interest in food and a lack of energy to eat a full meal at one sitting. As calorie intake declines, it's very important that the quality of the diet remain high to provide an optimal intake of all nutrients. You'll find a healthy eating guide in Chapter 5, page 111.

Saturated Fat

Animal fat may be directly involved in the development of MS by influencing the immune system. A number of studies have linked high intakes of saturated fat with MS.[4-6] American researchers have found that individuals with MS who followed a low-saturated-fat diet (no more than 20 grams of saturated fat per day) showed significantly less deterioration compared with those who consumed higher-fat diets.[7] The greatest benefit was seen in women and in those with minimum disability at the start of the study.

To reduce your intake of saturated fat, choose lean cuts of meat, poultry breast, skim milk and yogurt with 1% or less milk fat. Avoid or limit processed meats such as sausage, hot dogs, bacon and fatty deli meats. Use little or no added saturated fats such as butter, hard margarines and cream cheese. To achieve an intake of 20 grams of fat per day, you'll need to follow a plant-based diet that contains very little animal food. Choose vegetarian protein foods most often—they contain substantially less saturated fat. Legumes and soy foods are good choices. Eat fish, which is low in saturated fat, at least twice per week. The omega-3 fats found in fish may actually help ease symptoms of MS (see more on fish oil supplements, below).

Polyunsaturated Fat: Linoleic Acid

Polyunsaturated fatty acids are required for growth, development and maintenance of cell membranes, including those of the central nervous system. Polyunsaturated fats are important components of the myelin sheath and are used to produce non-inflammatory immune compounds. It's thought that the metabolism of omega-6 fatty acids is impaired in MS, causing a loss of anti-inflammatory immune compounds, especially during relapses.

Omega-6 polyunsaturated oils, such as sunflower seed, safflower, corn and soybean oils, provide the body with an essential fatty acid called linoleic acid. Some studies, but not all, suggest that supplementing the diet with omega-6 oils appears to slow the progression of MS and reduce the severity and duration of exacerbations. Two large 2-year studies found that diets supplemented with linoleic acid from sunflower seed oil produced a significant reduction in the severity and duration of relapse in MS patients who were treated early in the course of their illness.[8–11]

Since the characteristics of the MS patients studied in each trial differed, and the findings are mixed, it's premature to say that omega-6 oils are an effective treatment for MS. However, there's no evidence that adding polyunsaturated oils to your diet is harmful. The dosage used in the studies ranged from 17 to 20 grams of linoleic acid, the equivalent of 2 tablespoons (30 ml) of sunflower or safflower oil, the best sources of linoleic acid. An oil supplement called Udo's Choice Ultimate Oil Blend, available in health food stores, provides 20 milligrams of linoleic acid per 1.5 teaspoons (7 ml). Some researchers believe that it may take at least 2 years for linoleic acid to exert its effect on the myelin sheath.

Vitamins and Minerals

Antioxidants

Brain and nervous system cells are prone to free radical damage because of their relatively low levels of antioxidant enzymes and high levels of polyunsaturated fats (polyunsaturated fats are easily oxidized by free radicals). Some scientists hypothesize that such free radical damage can promote the progression of MS. Some studies have found that patients with MS have lower levels of antioxidants in their blood and higher levels of oxidized compounds.[12–14]

Although no well-controlled trials have investigated the effects of antioxidant supplements and disease activity, it's prudent to include antioxidant-rich foods in your daily diet.

VITAMIN C. The recommended dietary allowance (RDA) is 75 and 90 milligrams for women and men, respectively (smokers need an additional 35 milligrams). Best food sources include citrus fruit, citrus juices, cantaloupe, kiwi, mango, strawberries, broccoli, Brussels sprouts, cauliflower, red pepper and tomato juice. To supplement, take 500 milligrams of Ester C once or twice daily. The upper daily limit is 2000 milligrams.

VITAMIN E. The RDA is 22 international units (IU). Best food sources include wheat germ, nuts, seeds, vegetable oils, whole grains and kale. To supplement, take 200 to 400 IU of natural source vitamin E. Buy a "mixed" vitamin E supplement if possible. The upper daily limit is 1500 IU.

SELENIUM. The RDA is 55 micrograms. Best food sources are seafood, chicken, organ meats, whole grains, nuts, onions, garlic and mushrooms. Check how much your multivitamin and mineral provides before buying a separate selenium pill. The upper daily limit is 400 micrograms.

BETA CAROTENE. No RDA has been established. Best food sources are orange and dark-green produce, including carrots, sweet potato, winter squash, broccoli, collard greens, kale, spinach, apricots, cantaloupe, peaches, nectarines, mango and papaya. If you smoke, avoid taking beta carotene supplements as they may increase the risk of cancer.

Vitamin B12

Several studies have documented a deficiency of B12 in people with MS.[15-17] Since the formation of myelin and healthy immune function require B12, a deficiency may make you more vulnerable to viral or immune system factors that may cause the disease—and may also impair recovery from MS.

One preliminary study suggests that very high doses of B12 taken for 6 months may improve certain test results; however, improvements in disability were not seen.[18] Other studies have found that B12, taken orally or given by injection, as an adjunct to conventional medication was effective at relieving the symptoms of MS.[19,20]

Since B12 is critical for nerve function, it's important to include good food sources in your daily diet. The vitamin is found naturally in animal foods such as meat, poultry, fish, eggs and dairy products. Fortified soy and rice beverages also supply B12. A multivitamin and mineral supplement will provide additional B12. Single supplements of vitamin B12 are also available and considered very safe. Strict vegetarians should take a single B12 supplement of 500 to 1000 micrograms per day.

Vitamin D

Scientists have been interested in vitamin D's effect on the immune system ever since it was observed that areas with high exposure to sunlight—the principal source of vitamin D—have low rates of MS. It's thought that a vitamin D deficiency associated with a lack of sunshine may influence the immune system in a way that causes MS. Vitamin D has been shown to completely prevent experimental MS in mice, a model used by researchers to study human MS. Vitamin D has also been shown to prevent the progression of the disease in animal research.[21,22]

Studies in humans also support an important role for vitamin D in the prevention of MS. A large study conducted in more than 7 million U.S. military personnel found that, compared to those with the lowest blood levels of vitamin

D, those with the highest levels had a 40 percent lower risk of developing MS.[23] Another study revealed that higher circulating levels of vitamin D were associated with a lower incidence of MS and MS-related disability in women.[24] In 2009, British and Canadian scientists studied a gene mutation that triples the risk of MS and found that the gene is sensitive to vitamin D.[25]

Other studies have hinted that vitamin D supplementation might benefit people with MS. Findings from a Pennsylvania State University study showed that MS patients who took a daily 1000 international unit (IU) vitamin D supplement for 6 months had higher blood levels of the vitamin and changes in blood chemistry that indicated positive effects on their disease. Blood levels of a compound called TGF-beta were increased, which is associated with the remission and suppression of the immune response that produces MS symptoms.[26]

People with MS have also been shown to have significantly reduced bone density and more frequent bone fractures, in part related to low levels of vitamin D in the body.[27,28]

The recommended intake is 1000 IU daily for adults and 400 IU daily for children. Best food sources are fluid milk, fortified soy and rice beverages, oily fish, egg yolks, butter and margarine. However, it's not possible for adults to consume 1000 IU each day from foods alone. For this reason, it's necessary to take a vitamin D supplement in the fall and winter, and year-round if you are over the age of 50, have dark-coloured skin or don't expose your skin to sunshine in the summer months. If you have MS, take 1000 to 2000 IU of vitamin D throughout the year. (See Chapter 4, page 51, to learn about vitamin D supplements.)

Other Natural Health Products

Fish Oil Supplements

Omega-3 fatty acids in fish oil provide the body with EPA (eicosapentaenoic acids) and DHA (docosahexaenoic acid), two fatty acids that may be beneficial in MS. EPA and DHA suppress the body's production of inflammatory cytokines, immune compounds involved in MS. Studies have revealed that people with MS have lower blood levels of omega-3 fats compared with people free of the disease.[29,30] Researchers have also found that fish oil supplements taken for 1 to 2 years by newly diagnosed MS patients produced a significant reduction in exacerbation and disability ratings and reduced relapse rates in those patients with relapsing-remitting MS.[31,32]

Based on the limited research, an optimal fish oil dose for MS is not known. However, a daily dose of 500 to 1000 milligrams of DHA + EPA combined is recommended to help reduce the risk of coronary heart disease, so this is a good starting dose. When buying a fish oil supplement, read labels to determine the amount of DHA and EPA provided in fish oil capsules or liquid supplements. Because fish oil has a blood-thinning effect, use caution if you're taking blood-thinning medication such as aspirin, warfarin (Coumadin) or heparin. See Chapter 8, page 164, for more on fish oil supplements.

Nutrition Strategy Checklist for Multiple Sclerosis

☐ Low-saturated-fat diet
☐ Omega-6 oils
☐ Vitamin C
☐ Vitamin E
☐ Selenium

☐   Beta carotene
☐   Vitamin B12
☐   Vitamin D
☐   Fish oil supplement

Recommended Resources

Multiple Sclerosis Society of Canada
www.mssociety.ca
250 Bloor Street E, Suite 1000
Toronto, ON M4W 3P9
Tel: 416-922-6065 or 1-800-268-7582
Fax: 416-922-7538
Email: info@mssociety.ca

Multiple Sclerosis Foundation
www.msfocus.org
6350 N Andrews Avenue
Fort Lauderdale, FL, USA 33309-2130
Tel: 1-800-441-7055
Fax: 954-351-0630

The National Multiple Sclerosis Society
www.nationalmssociety.org
Tel: 1-800-344-4867

Obesity, Overweight and Weight Loss

Obesity is generally a chronic condition defined by an excess amount of body fat. Although a certain amount of body fat is necessary to store energy, insulate the body from cold and protect our internal organs, excess fat is linked with numerous health problems. Carrying excess body weight increases the risk of type 2 diabetes, high blood pressure, high cholesterol, stroke, heart attack, certain cancers, gallstones, gout, osteoarthritis and sleep apnea.

It's estimated that six out of ten Canadians are overweight or obese and 15 percent are obese. Statistics for overweight among Canadian kids are equally dismal: One-quarter (26 percent) of children aged 2 to 17 are either overweight or obese. What's more alarming is that the number of kids considered obese has tripled over the past 25 years, with a soaring increase from 3 percent in 1984 to 8 percent in 2004.[1]

What Causes Obesity?

Obesity is an excessive accumulation of body fat. The balance between calorie intake and energy expenditure determines your weight: You become overweight or obese when you consume more calories than your body can burn as energy. There's general agreement among doctors and scientists that men who have more than 25 percent body fat and women who have more than 30 percent body fat are considered obese.

Although overeating of foods high in fat, sugar and refined carbohydrates and physical inactivity are the main culprits for obesity, other factors can contribute to the process of excess weight gain. Social, behavioural, cultural, psychological, physiological and genetic factors all play a role. One genetic cause is a deficiency in leptin, a hormone that controls weight by telling the brain to eat less when body fat stores are too high. Certain medications are also associated with weight gain, including antidepressants, anti-convulsants and corticosteroids. Medical conditions such as polycystic ovary syndrome, hypothyroidism and Cushing's syndrome can also contribute to obesity.

Assessing Your Weight

Most people rely on the bathroom scale to tell them whether their weight is healthy or unhealthy. But to get a more accurate picture, there are other numbers you need to consider. The most widely accepted methods used to assess your weight and body fat are body mass index (BMI), waist-to-hip ratio (WHR) and body fat measurements.

Body Mass Index (BMI)

If you're between the ages of 18 and 65, BMI is a height and weight formula that gives a fairly reliable snapshot of your body fat. The easiest and quickest way to determine your BMI is to use an online calculator; you'll find one on my website (www.lesliebeck.com). Your body mass index is calculated by dividing your weight (in kilograms) by your height (in metres squared).

What's Your BMI?

1. Determine your weight in kilograms (kg) (Divide your weight in pounds by 2.2)	Weight (kg)
2. Determine your height in centimetres (cm) (Multiply your height in inches by 2.54)	Height (cm)
3. Determine your height in metres (m) (Divide your height in centimetres by 100)	Height (m)
4. Square your height in metres (m) (Multiply your height in metres by height in metres)	Height (m²)
5. Now, calculate your BMI (Divide #1, your weight in kg, by #4, your height in metres²)	BMI

Doctors and dietitians use the BMI to classify your body weight and assess your risk for disease as follows:

- BMI values less than 18.5 are considered underweight and increase a person's risk for conditions such as osteoporosis, nutrient deficiencies and eating disorders.
- BMI values from 18.5 to 24.9 are defined as healthy or normal weight and linked with a lower risk of health problems.
- If your BMI falls between 25 and 29.9 you're classified as overweight.
- A BMI of 30 or greater is considered obese. As your BMI goes up, so does your risk for type 2 diabetes, heart disease, high blood pressure, gallbladder disease, sleep apnea and some forms of cancer.

Keep in mind, though, that sudden or considerable weight gains or weight losses may also indicate health risk, even if this occurs within the "normal" BMI category.

Body mass index can also be calculated for children and teenagers, but its interpretation depends on age and gender. At each check-up, the doctor should calculate your child's BMI-for-age percentile, which indicates how his or her measurements compare with other children in the same age group. Regular BMI percentile measuring allows you to monitor your child's weight over time.

The BMI is not without drawbacks. It doesn't tell you where you're carrying your body fat, which is important in determining the risk of coronary heart disease. It also doesn't distinguish between body fat weight and muscle weight. Athletes and heavily muscled people may have a high BMI but very little fat because muscle weighs more than fat.

Waist Circumference

To determine where your body fat is located, you'll need to measure your waist. Simply take a measuring tape and, without holding it too tightly or too loosely, measure your waist at the narrowest part of your trunk, about one inch above your belly button. Excess fat around the abdomen (apple shape) is associated with greater health risk than fat located on the hips and thighs (pear shape). When it comes to health, not all fat cells are alike. Whereas body mass index measures overall fat, your waist circumference is a good gauge of abdominal fat. The fat around your middle consists of subcutaneous fat—that's just beneath the skin and that you can pinch—and visceral fat—that's deeper and packs itself around your organs. It's visceral fat that's considered dangerous to your health because it secretes chemicals that increase the body's resistance to insulin and cause inflammation throughout the body.

A waist circumference of 94 cm (37 inches) or greater for men and 80 cm (31.5 inches) or greater for women increases the likelihood of type 2 diabetes, high blood pressure, elevated cholesterol, heart attack, stroke, metabolic syndrome and some cancers. Lower thresholds for waist circumference are recommended for Asian populations. Studies suggest health risk increases among many Asian populations at lower levels of body weight than in Caucasian populations.

Increased girth predicts a person's risk of disease and death better than BMI alone. A number of studies have determined that your waist measurement is a much better predictor of heart attack risk than your BMI.[2-4] The Canadian guidelines to assess body weight now use both BMI and waist circumference.

What's Your Waist Circumference?

	Risk of Heart Disease
Men	
<94 cm (<37 inches)	Lower
≥94 cm (≥37 inches)	Increased
Women	
<80 cm (<31.5 inches)	Lower
≥80 cm (≥31.5 inches)	Increased

Waist-to-Hip Ratio (WHR)

The waist-to-hip ratio is simply your waist measurement divided by your hip measurement. It's another index of body fat distribution used by doctors and researchers. A healthy WHR for women is less than 0.8 and for men, less than 0.9.

What's Your WHR?

1. Using a tape measure, find the circumference of your waist at its narrowest point when your stomach is relaxed.

   Waist = _____ inches

2. Measure the circumference of your hips at their widest point.

   Hips = _____ inches

3. Divide your waist measurement by your hip measurement.

   WHR = _____

Body Fat Measurements

Some health clubs and commercial weight-loss programs estimate body fat by using calipers on folds of skin or by sending harmless electrical impulses through the body. These techniques may provide inaccurate results if performed by untrained individuals.

Who's at Risk?

Most people are at risk for becoming obese if they overeat and lead a sedentary lifestyle. However, research suggests that other risk factors may predispose people to become overweight. A person is more likely to develop obesity if one or both parents are obese. Ethnic background may play a role by influencing the age of onset and speed of weight gain. First Nations Canadians, Hispanics and African Americans are at greater risk of gaining weight earlier in life and developing obesity. Being overweight or obese during childhood and adolescence also increases the risk of adult obesity.

Symptoms

When excess fat is accumulated below the diaphragm and in the chest wall, it may put pressure on the lungs, causing shortness of breath and other breathing difficulties. Difficulty breathing may interfere with sleep, leading to daytime sleepiness and sleep apnea. Overweight and obesity can also worsen a hiatal hernia and cause heartburn and gastrointestinal distress. Excess weight can cause low back pain and other orthopedic problems, particularly in the hips, knees and ankles.

Skin disorders are common in obesity because of increased perspiration and skin folding, which encourage bacterial and fungal growth. Swelling in the feet and ankles is a frequent problem for overweight people. Psychological problems are also common in obesity, including poor self-image, poor motivation and depression.

Conventional Treatment

Safe and *gradual* weight loss is the only effective solution for obesity. Even a modest loss of 10 to 20 pounds (4.5 to 9 kg) can lower blood pressure and cholesterol and reduce the risk of developing serious health problems. The ideal treatment for obesity is a multifaceted program that includes a calorie-reduced diet, physical activity and behaviour therapy. Learning how to make healthy food choices and manage emotions that influence food choices are important components of a successful weight-loss program.

In some cases, prescription drugs may be used to augment diet and exercise therapy. Some medications affect levels of brain chemicals and others affect the absorption of food. Although these medications may improve blood pressure and cholesterol levels and decrease insulin resistance (the body's inability to use blood sugar) over the short term, long-term studies are needed to determine if weight loss from weight-loss medications can improve health. All medications have side effects and risks, which should be discussed with your doctor.

A more drastic treatment is a program that uses a *very low-calorie diet* (VLCD)—commercially prepared formulas of 800 calories or less that replace all food intake. VLCDs are used for moderately obese people who want to lose weight quickly. They are safe only if medically supervised. However, these programs are expensive and people tend to regain weight after going off the diet.

Surgery is reserved only for morbidly obese individuals (those with a BMI greater than 40) with existing physical or medical complications of obesity. Weight-loss surgery (bariatric surgery) is performed in a hospital or a private medical clinic (be sure it has a demonstrated record of efficacy and safety). Bariatric surgeries modify the gastrointestinal tract to reduce food intake and/or nutrient absorption. (The term doesn't include procedures for surgical removal of body fat such as liposuction.) Surgeries such as gastric banding and gastric stapling create a small pouch at the top of the stomach where the food enters from the esophagus. This restricts the amount of food—and calories—that can be eaten at a meal, but food still travels through the normal digestive system. A gastric bypass operation makes the stomach smaller and allows food to bypass part of the small intestine. Because the stomach is smaller, people feel full more quickly and consume fewer calories. Bypassing part of the small intestine also results in fewer calories being absorbed.

Weight-loss surgeries are not without risk. Up to 20 percent of patients require follow-up operations to correct complications. More than one-third of obese patients who have gastric surgery develop gallstones, and nearly 30 percent of patients who have weight-loss surgery develop nutritional deficiencies such as anemia, osteoporosis and metabolic bone disease. These deficiencies can be avoided if vitamin and mineral intakes are maintained.

Choosing a Weight-Loss Program

Ideally, weight loss should occur at a fairly slow and steady pace since rapid weight loss can cause muscle loss and nutrient deficiencies. Weight that's lost rapidly is also difficult to keep off. Losing weight successfully and permanently requires making lifelong changes to your eating and exercise habits.

When researching programs in your community, ask these questions:

- **Is there a nutrition education component? Will you learn healthy-eating skills?** Long-term weight management requires learning and implementing healthy eating skills such as label-reading, navigating restaurant menus and low-fat cooking.
- **Does the program exclude any one food group?** A sound weight loss program should be balanced and include foods from all four food groups. Eliminating one or more food groups omits important nutrients and isn't sustainable over the long term.
- **Does the program rely on specially purchased foods?** Eating pre-packaged meals might require little effort, but you're living in an artificial environment. These programs don't teach you how to eat in the real world—how to shop for and cook healthy foods and how to order in restaurants.
- **Does the program promote and emphasize exercise?** Regular exercise allows you to consume more calories while losing weight and is critical for maintaining a weight loss.
- **Does the program incorporate behavioural therapy and/or stress-management techniques?** If your weight problem stems from eating when bored, stressed, depressed, anxious or angry, you'll need to learn strategies that help you overcome emotional eating.
- **Does the program address social support systems?** It's important to understand the role family, friends and co-workers play in your weight loss success.
- **Does the program offer one-on-one and/or group sessions?** Depending on your personality, you may be more motivated by listening to the successes and challenges of others in a group setting. Or you may prefer the personalized attention that comes from working one-on-one with a counsellor.
- **Does the program emphasize weight maintenance?** Before starting a program,

find out what happens when the program ends. You'll need to learn strategies that will help you keep the weight off permanently, such as dealing with social pressures, vacations and restaurant eating. Only then can you be successful at weight loss.

- **What are the qualifications of the counsellors?** Ask about the training, experience and credentials of the program's counsellors. A reputable person usually has a background or an affiliation with an accredited university offering programs in nutrition or medicine. Beware of the title "nutritionist," since this isn't a licensed designation: Anyone can call himself or herself a nutritionist, so be sure to ask for credentials. The term *registered dietitian* (RD) is a licensed professional designation.

The most difficult part of losing weight is keeping it off by maintaining long-term changes in diet and activity patterns. There's concern among some experts that repeated loss and regain of body weight, known as yo-yo dieting or weight cycling, is harmful to your health. The dietary strategies listed below will help you get started on a safe weight-loss plan.

Managing Weight Loss
Dietary Strategies

- **Set a realistic goal.** You don't have to rely on the bathroom scale when setting a goal. You may prefer to choose a size of clothing, improvements in physical fitness or improvements in blood cholesterol or blood pressure readings. If you do decide to use the scale as your measure of success, choose a realistic 3 to 5 pound (1.5 to 2.5 kg) weight range that you want to aim for.

- **Begin with the right mindset.** Think long-term lifestyle change instead of short-term quick fix. Having the right mindset means being comfortable with slow and steady weight loss. No weight-loss program should cause you to lose much more than 2 to 3 pounds (1 to 1.5 kg) per week.

- **Get social support.** If you need help from a spouse, family member, co-worker or friend, ask for it. It often helps to have a workout partner, especially when you're beginning an exercise program. If your husband pulls out potato chips every night after dinner, ask him to be mindful of your attempt to change your eating habits. If you want positive reinforcement from someone, let that person know.

- **Consider an exercise program** if you're not already active. Calories are burned during exercise, and by building up muscle, exercise helps your body burn more calories at rest. To help you lose body fat, aim to get at least four cardiovascular workouts each week (brisk walking, jogging, stair climbing, swimming, spinning classes, cross-country skiing, aerobics classes). Gradually build up to a minimum of 30 minutes each session. When you're ready, add in weight training two or three times a week. Studies have found that adding a strength workout to a weight-loss program speeds up weight loss.

- **Visit a consulting dietitian** (see www.dietitians.ca). A registered dietitian can develop a nutritious weight-loss diet designed to help you lose weight based on your lifestyle. Weekly visits offer support, encouragement and nutrition education.

- **Reduce calories to 1200 to 1900 calories per day.** A good general target is 1400 to 1600 calories per day for women and 1600 to

1900 calories for men. Men can consume more calories and lose weight because they burn more calories at rest due to their larger muscle mass. The more muscle you have on your body, in relation to fat, the higher your resting metabolism. Your resting metabolism is the amount of energy required to keep your heart beating, your lungs breathing, your brain and liver functioning and your cells alive at complete rest. Research shows that a woman burns 5 percent to 10 percent fewer calories for the body's metabolic needs than a man of the same height and weight.

- **Eat at regular intervals throughout the day.** Eating a meal or snack every 3 to 4 hours will help to boost your metabolism, improve your energy level and maintain a consistent blood-sugar level. Eating regularly prevents hunger and helps eliminate mindless snacking and overeating at the next meal.

- **Don't eat dinner late.** Ideally, sit down to dinner no later than 8 P.M. Remember that as evening approaches, the body's metabolism naturally slows down. Dinnertime is actually when your body needs the smallest meal (despite this being when most of us eat the bulk of our day's calories). If you get home late, tell yourself that you've missed dinner. Just because you walk in the door doesn't mean you have to have dinner. Have a light snack instead—yogurt, a piece of fruit or a bowl of soup.

- **If your meals are more than 5 hours apart, plan for a snack.** Between-meal snacks are important to help keep your energy level up and to prevent snacking on sweets (or some other unhealthy food). Depending on the meal, your blood sugar will drop 3 to 4 hours later. Since your blood sugar is the only source of fuel for your brain, a post-meal dip can make you feel sluggish and tired. And often this is when people go in search of a "pick-me-up." So plan for this energy boost.

But here's my rule: *No snacking on starchy foods* like bagels, pretzels, low-fat cookies, low-fat crackers or fat-free muffins. These foods are quickly converted to blood glucose (remember, they're high-glycemic-index foods), so they're more likely to lead to further hunger and sweet cravings. Better snacks combine low-glycemic carbohydrate with some protein for longer-lasting energy. Good choices include yogurt and fruit, dried fruit and nuts, homemade smoothies, low-fat cheese and whole-grain crackers, or an energy bar. These snacks also contribute more fibre and calcium to your diet.

- **Reduce your portion size of starchy foods.** When you have pasta, no bread. If you have a meal with rice or potato, no bread. Bread adds extra calories to your day. Even though bread on its own is low in fat, it still has calories and these add up. For example, one large bagel is equivalent to four or five slices of bread! If you find you have a tendency to overeat foods like pasta, rice or potatoes, consider skipping the starch at dinner. Instead, enjoy grilled fish, chicken or lean meat with plenty of vegetables.

- **Choose low-glycemic-index carbohydrate foods more often.** These foods tend to be higher in soluble fibre, so they take longer to digest and keep you feeling full longer. A list of low-glycemic-index foods can be found in Chapter 1, page 4.

- **Treat yourself once a week.** Whether it's ice cream, a rich pastry, chicken wings or french fries, enjoy your favourite treat once a week. Make it part of your plan—and don't feel guilty for having it. Keep in mind that any changes you make to lose weight have to be sustainable. It's not realistic to give up sweets forever.

- **Get rid of excess sugar.** A little jam on toast or a teaspoon of sugar in coffee won't affect your weight. But drinks like regular (rather than diet) soft drinks, fruit drinks and fruit juice add extra calories to your diet.

- **Limit alcohol intake to no more than seven to nine drinks per week** (see Chapter 5, page 106). Alcohol calories in beer, wine or liquor add up. Alcohol also tends to lower one's willpower, making it more difficult to stick to a healthy meal plan.

- **Deal with occasional lapses.** The key to long-term weight maintenance is nipping small weight gains in the bud. If you want to stay trim, you've got to catch that 5 pound gain before it becomes 10 pounds. Monitor your weight on a regular weekly basis. Have a plan of action to take off any extra pounds you've gained. You might keep a food diary for a few weeks to help you identify how you gained the weight, and then add an extra workout to your week for a month or give up sweets until the pounds are off.

- **Be consistent.** People who don't give themselves a day or two off to cheat are one and a half times more likely to keep unwanted pounds off. Once you start giving yourself a few breaks on the weekend, you're more likely to ease off on Friday and then Thursday.

- **Keep track.** Journaling what—and how much—you eat provides awareness, focus and motivation. It'll make you think twice about reaching for seconds or those sweets at the office.

- **Step on the scale.** Weighing-in once a week gives you feedback about how well you're maintaining your weight. Frequent weighing allows you to catch small increases in weight very quickly and take corrective action to prevent further weight gain.

If you're serious about losing weight, you'll find more strategies, in addition to four weight-loss plans with accompanying daily and weekly menus, in my book *The No-Fail Diet* (Penguin Canada).

Vitamins and Minerals

Multivitamin and Mineral Supplements

A low-calorie diet (less than 1500 calories per day) may be lacking folate, vitamin D, calcium, iron and zinc. A multivitamin and mineral supplement offers you a little extra nutritional insurance. It provides the recommended daily amounts for vitamins and minerals, with the exception of calcium, magnesium and iron. Take one tablet or capsule daily with a meal. See Chapter 5, page 102, for tips on choosing a multivitamin formula.

Calcium

This important mineral is often missing in a diet designed for weight loss. Unfortunately, it's often lacking in higher-calorie diets, too. If you're consuming less than 3 daily servings of milk, yogurt and/or calcium-fortified beverages, take a 300 milligram supplement of calcium citrate for each serving you're lacking. A list of calcium-rich foods and supplement sources can be found in Chapter 4, page 56.

Iron

A daily multivitamin and mineral supplement will help you meet your iron needs. But it's also important to eat iron-rich foods such as lean red meat, seafood, poultry, eggs, legumes, whole grains, enriched breakfast cereals, dried apricots, raisins and blackstrap molasses. To enhance your body's absorption of iron from plant foods, include a source of vitamin C with your meals; 1/2 cup (125 ml) of citrus juice, red pepper, broccoli, strawberries or tomato juice are a few good choices. Avoid drinking tea with iron-rich meals since tannin compounds in the beverage interfere with iron absorption. Also don't combine an iron-rich meal with large quantities of milk or yogurt, since calcium interferes with iron absorption.

Chromium

This essential mineral is involved in the regulation of carbohydrate and fat metabolism. Chromium has been reported to increase muscle mass and decrease body fat, which could lead to weight loss. Although the majority of studies have not found chromium to be effective in weight loss, a few studies do support its use. In one study, researchers found that chromium supplements taken for 3 months resulted in a significantly greater loss of body fat among overweight adults.[5] Another study found that when chromium was taken in combination with regular exercise, weight loss occurred.[6]

Good food sources of chromium include apples with the skin, green peas, chicken breast, refried beans, mushrooms, oysters, wheat germ and brewer's yeast. Processed and refined starchy foods such as white bread, rice and pasta, sugar and sweets contain very little chromium.

Studies have evaluated chromium picolinate, which is thought to be absorbed better than other forms of the mineral. The dosage used in weight-loss studies, 200 to 400 micrograms per day, is much higher than the recommended dietary allowance. Doses of 600 micrograms can cause cognitive impairment, anemia and kidney damage.

Other Natural Health Products
Conjugated Linoleic Acid (CLA)

This naturally occurring fatty acid is found in dairy products and meat. Because the body doesn't manufacture conjugated linoleic acid (CLA), the only way to get it is through foods or supplements. Although not conclusive, there's some evidence to support the fat-loss claims of CLA. Taking 0.7 to 4.5 grams of CLA per day has been found to significantly reduce body fat and increase muscle mass in some people. (However, the supplement doesn't appear to reduce body weight or body mass index.) In one study, CLA supplements also increased feelings of fullness, but this effect didn't lead to reduced food intake or improved weight maintenance after weight loss.[7-10]

To assist with body fat loss, the recommended dose is 1 gram (1000 milligrams) taken three times a day with meals.

CLA supplements may cause mild stomach upset in some people. There's concern about CLA's long-term safety. Some studies have found increased insulin levels and insulin resistance—risk factors for type 2 diabetes—in people with abdominal obesity taking a specific isomer of CLA.[11] (Isomers are compounds with the same molecular formula but different molecular structures.) Most CLA supplements contain a mixture of CLA isomers; it's unknown whether these mixed CLA products harbour the same risk.

Nutrition Strategy Checklist for Obesity, Overweight and Weight Loss

☐ Calorie-reduced diet

☐ Regular exercise

☐ Multivitamin/mineral
☐ Calcium
☐ Iron
☐ Chromium
☐ CLA

Recommended Resources

Canadian Obesity Network (A network of health professionals and researchers)
www.obesitynetwork.ca
Royal Alexandra Hospital, Room 102,
    Materials Management Centre
10240 Kingsway Avenue
Edmonton, AB T5H 3V9
Tel: 780-735-6764
Fax: 780-735-6763
Email: info@obesitynetwork.ca

Dietitians of Canada
www.dietitians.ca

Merck Frosst/CIHR Research Chair in Obesity
www.obesite.chaire.ulaval.ca
Pav. d'Youville, Room Y-4225
2725 Chemin Sainte-Foy
Hôpital Laval Research Centre
Quebec (Sainte-Foy), QC G1V 4G5
Tel: 418-656-8711 (ext 3392)
Fax: 418-656-4929
Email: Obesity.Chair@crhl.ulaval.ca

International Food Information Council
www.ific.org
1100 Connecticut Avenue NW, Suite 430
Washington, DC, USA 20036
Tel: 202-296-6540
Fax: 202-296-6547

Osteoarthritis

Osteoarthritis, a degenerative disease of the joints, has plagued humans since the earliest days of history. Today, osteoarthritis is the most common form of arthritis and a leading cause of occupational disability. Affecting one in every ten Canadians, osteoarthritis is most prevalent in people over the age of 45.[1] Although not everyone with osteoarthritis has symptoms, those who do find themselves struggling with a pattern of relentless pain, stiffness and swelling that can affect their quality of life.

What Causes Osteoarthritis?

Osteoarthritis is thought to be the result of wear and tear on the joints. Inside each joint is a tough, slippery protein tissue called cartilage, which cushions the ends of bones. Healthy cartilage allows the bones to glide smoothly over one another when we move. It also acts as a shock absorber to protect the joints from the stresses and strains of daily physical activities. With age, the protein content of cartilage degenerates. Small bits of cartilage break off, finding their way into the spaces in the joints, where they irritate the muscle tissue and interfere with joint movement. Once the protective layering of cartilage disintegrates, the bones rub painfully against each other, further restricting joint mobility. Inflammation of the cartilage can also stimulate bones to thicken and grow spurs around the joints. In advanced cases, there's a total loss of cartilage cushion between the bones and joints. Over years of repetitive use, worn joints can irritate and inflame the joints and cause swelling and pain.

As the damage grows more extensive, osteoarthritis causes swelling, stiffness and pain. Eventually, the joint may become enlarged and may even lock in a bent position. The pain associated with osteoarthritis doesn't come from the destruction of the cartilage, which has no nerves and can't sense pain; it's the nerve cells of the muscles, tendons, ligaments and bones that signal pain as they're forced to work in unaccustomed ways.

Osteoarthritis usually targets weight-bearing joints, such as the hips, knees, feet and spine. Although the finger joints and joints at the base of the thumb are not weight bearing, they're also common sites for osteoarthritis.

Scientists think that genetics may play a role in osteoarthritis. One theory is that this type of arthritis might be caused by abnormalities in the cells that manufacture cartilage. Another theory suggests that the disease is actually a disorder of the bone rather than of the cartilage. Failure of the bone to respond to impact may lead to damage of the overlying cartilage.

Osteoarthritis may also develop from known causes such as infection, deformity, injury or diseases such as diabetes and high blood pressure. People working in certain occupational groups, such as movers and workers in manufacturing plants, may be more susceptible to osteoarthritis—for instance, if the job involves repetitive, heavy physical work. High-intensity, high-impact sports may have a similar damaging effect on the joints. Being overweight also contributes to osteoarthritis: Excess body weight puts mechanical stress on the knees and hips and, in addition, may be associated with metabolic abnormalities that can affect cartilage. In fact, the early development of osteoarthritis among weightlifters is thought to be due, in part, to their high body weight. Hormone disturbances, such as diabetes and growth hormone disorders, are also associated with osteoarthritis.

Symptoms

Damage from osteoarthritis progresses slowly and affects only one or two joints in the early stages of the disease. Once symptoms begin, the disease will continue to progress, gradually limiting the motion of the joint and leading to severe disability in many cases. Symptoms of osteoarthritis vary greatly from person to person and may include:

- pain in the joint that may be made worse by exercise
- stiffness in the joint after sleep or periods of inactivity
- swelling in the joint, particularly after use
- reduced range of motion in the joint
- crackle or grind in the joint when moved
- pain when the joint is touched
- pain in the low neck or back (caused by osteoarthritis of the spine)
- bony lumps in the joints of the fingers or at the base of the thumb

Who's at Risk?

Osteoarthritis is more likely to develop in people over age 45. The disease affects men and women in equal numbers. Also at greater risk are people who:

- have a family history of joint disease
- are obese; losing just 10 pounds (4.5 kg) can help prevent knee osteoarthritis
- work in occupations that involve repetitive, heavy physical work
- engage in high-intensity, high-impact sports
- have rheumatoid arthritis and gout
- have medical conditions, such as diabetes and high blood pressure

Conventional Treatment

Although there's no cure for osteoarthritis, there are many things that can be done to control pain and improve joint care. Weight reduction can help relieve the pain of osteoarthritis. Regular exercise can also help lessen the symptoms by increasing flexibility, decreasing pain, improving your overall health and helping you maintain a healthy weight. Be sure to schedule rest in order to avoid overusing joints and to relieve some of the pressure on them. Other treatments to control pain include:

- **Heat.** Applying moist heat reduces pain, stiffness and muscle spasm. It promotes blood circulation, which nourishes and detoxifies muscle fibres. Don't apply heat to an inflamed joint.
- **Cold.** Applying cold helps reduce swelling and lessens pain of inflamed joints by constricting blood flow.
- **Water therapy.** Therapy in a heated pool or whirlpool might ease symptoms.
- **Medications.** NSAIDs (non-steroidal anti-inflammatory drugs), COX-2 inhibitors, acetaminophen, mild narcotic painkillers, corticosteroid injections, topical pain relievers and hyaluronic acid may be used.

Acupuncture may provide temporary pain relief. Research suggests that acupuncture can reduce pain and improve joint functioning in the short term for people with osteoarthritis of the knee. Physical therapy or massage may help ease stiffness and pain in joints.

Surgery may be necessary to relieve pain and disability by removing pieces of cartilage from the joint, or resurfacing or smoothing out bones. Severely damaged joints can be reconstructed or surgically replaced with artificial ones. Joint replacement is major surgery, and is most often performed to replace hip and knee joints.

Managing Osteoarthritis
Dietary Strategies
Weight Control

To help protect your joints from further damage, it's very important to control your weight. Studies have found that higher levels of body fat and obesity are significantly related to osteoarthritis pain.[2,3] Some researchers believe that when it comes to relieving joint pain, losing body fat is more important than losing body weight. Excess body weight puts stress on weight-bearing joints and is also thought to cause metabolic changes in cartilage. Research conducted in obese adults with osteoarthritis has shown that losing excess body weight can decrease inflammatory compounds in the blood and improve joint function.

To determine if you're at a healthy weight, see Obesity, Overweight and Weight Loss, page 569, to calculate your body mass index (BMI). Having a BMI of 25 to 29.9 indicates overweight and a BMI of 30 or greater is defined as obese. If your BMI is greater than 25, use the strategies outlined on page 574 for safe, gradual weight loss.

Soy Protein

There's some evidence that the protein of soybeans can help reduce osteoarthritis pain. In a study of 135 men and women with diagnosed osteoarthritis pain or chronic knee pain, a daily supplement of soy protein (40 grams) reduced knee pain and improved range of motion. What's more, compared to the people taking milk-based protein, those in the soy protein group showed higher blood levels of chemicals that synthesize cartilage. Blood levels of YKL-40, a glycoprotein associated with cartilage breakdown, was significantly decreased. As well, blood levels of insulin-like growth factor-I, linked with cartilage synthesis, was significantly increased. Soy protein was most effective in men.[4] Soy protein contains many different phytochemicals that exert anti-inflammatory, antioxidant and bone-density building actions in the body.

Add 40 grams of soy protein to your daily diet for 3 months to see if your symptoms improve. Use the list below to help you add soy protein–rich foods to your daily diet. Using a soy protein powder is a convenient way to increase your intake. (If you're at high risk for breast cancer, don't use soy protein powder.)

Soy Protein–Rich Foods

Soy Food	Soy Protein (grams)
Soy beverage, 1 cup (250 ml)	9 g
Soy flour, defatted, 1/4 cup (60 ml)	13 g
Soy nuts, 1/4 cup (60 ml)	14 g
Soy protein powder, 1 scoop	25 g
Soybeans, canned, 1/2 cup (125 ml)	14 g
Tempeh, 1/2 cup (125 ml)	16 g
Tofu, firm, 1/2 cup (125 ml)	19 g
Tofu, regular, 1/2 cup (125 ml)	10 g
Veggie burger, 1	11 g
Veggie dog, small, 1	11 g

Vitamins and Minerals

Vitamin C

Since free radical damage may be involved in the progression of osteoarthritis, researchers have hypothesized that higher intakes of antioxidant nutrients might be associated with lower rates of the disease. The best evidence to date supports the use of vitamin C.

One large study conducted among 640 patients with knee osteoarthritis found that those who consumed the most vitamin C in their diet had a threefold reduced risk for the disease progressing compared with people who consumed the least.[5] High intake of vitamin C appeared to protect against cartilage loss. Those with the highest vitamin C intake also had a 70 percent lower risk of developing knee pain.

Vitamin C acts as an antioxidant and also supports collagen synthesis, both of which may be important in slowing the progression of osteoarthritis. The best food sources are citrus fruit, strawberries, kiwi, cantaloupe, broccoli, bell peppers, Brussels sprouts, cabbage, tomatoes and potatoes (see Chapter 4, page 49, for the vitamin C content of selected foods). To supplement, take 500 milligrams of vitamin C once or twice daily.

Vitamin D

Some studies suggest that suboptimal vitamin D levels in the body cause diffuse osteoarthritic pain. Low intakes and low blood levels of vitamin D may impair the response of bone to osteoarthritis, making progression of the disease more likely. In a study of 556 patients with knee osteoarthritis, the risk of disease progression increased threefold in those who had lower vitamin D intakes and reduced blood levels of the nutrient.[6] Reduced vitamin D levels were associated with cartilage loss. Another study also found that low blood–vitamin D was associated with a narrowing of the joint space in elderly women with hip osteoarthritis.[7] Despite these findings, one study conducted in 208 patients concluded that low vitamin D levels were not associated with joint pain and treatment with vitamin D did not reduce pain.[8]

Even if increasing your vitamin D intake doesn't improve osteoarthritis symptoms, it's important to consume enough vitamin D each day to achieve an adequate blood level of the nutrient. Insufficient levels are associated with an increased risk of cancers and possibly heart disease. The recommended intake is 1000 international units (IU) daily for adults and 400 IU daily for children. Best food sources are fluid milk, fortified soy and rice beverages, oily fish, egg yolks, butter and margarine. However, it's not possible for adults to consume 1000 IU each day from foods alone. For this reason, it's necessary to take a vitamin D supplement in the fall and winter, and year-round if you are over the age of 50, have dark-coloured skin or don't expose your skin to sunshine in the summer months. See Chapter 4, page 51, to learn about vitamin D supplements.

Herbal Remedies

Capsaicin Cream

Capsaicin, responsible for the heat of chili peppers, has a long history of use as a topical agent for pain disorders. A number of studies have found capsaicin cream effective in relieving osteoarthritis pain and stiffness.[9-11] When applied to the skin, capsaicin depletes substance P, a compound that transmits feelings of pain from the nerves to the spinal cord.

Capsaicin creams are available with or without a prescription. Zostrix, Capzasin-P and Capsin are all available over the counter. Buy a cream with 0.025 percent to 0.075 percent capsaicin (the higher strength may be more effective). Capsaicin cream produces a burning sensation, which diminishes after several applications. Use a small amount to begin with; when you no longer feel burning upon application, increase the amount of cream you use. Be careful not to touch your eyes or other sensitive tissues after applying capsaicin cream. Wash your hands after using the product.

Devil's Claw

Devil's claw has anti-inflammatory and anti-rheumatic properties and may be helpful in treating osteoarthritis. Research conducted in patients taking devil's claw alone or in conjunction with non-steroidal anti-inflammatory drugs (NSAIDs) found the herb helped decrease osteoarthritis-related pain of the knee and hip. Study participants taking devil's claw also seemed able to decrease use of NSAIDs for pain relief.[12-15]

The active ingredients in devil's claw are known collectively as glycosides. Among them, one called harpagoside is thought to contribute the most to the herb's anti-inflammatory properties.

The dose of devil's claw will depend on the formulation of the product. Buy a supplement standardized to contain a certain amount of harpagoside: Check the ingredient list for the number of milligrams per tablet. For reducing the joint pain of osteoarthritis, 57 to 60 milligrams of harpagoside has been used in clinical studies. See Chapter 7, page 131, for more information on devil's claw.

Other Natural Health Products

Chondroitin Sulphate

This compound belongs to a family of compounds called glycosaminoglycans that are an important part of joint cartilage. Early research from the 1980s until 2001 showed that taking chondroitin sulphate along with conventional painkillers or non-steroidal anti-inflammatory drugs (NSAIDs) significantly reduced pain and improved mobility in patients with osteoarthritis of the hip and knee after several weeks of treatment.[16-21] However, research published since 2005 hasn't been positive. In one large trial, taking chondroitin sulphate alone or in combination with glucosamine hydrochloride didn't reduce pain in most patients with osteoarthritis of the knee; however, the combination did reduce pain in a subgroup of patients with moderate-to-severe osteoarthritis of the knee.[22] These mixed findings could be due to differences in patient populations, products used or study design.

Overall, the evidence shows that some people with osteoarthritis of the knee can experience some benefit from taking chondroitin; however, pain relief is likely to be modest.

Chondroitin supplementation is thought to slow the progression of cartilage degeneration. Taking supplemental chondroitin may offer joints the building blocks they need to repair cartilage. Chondroitin may also increase the amount of hyaluronic acid in the joints and inhibit enzymes that break down cartilage. (Hyaluronic acid is the fluid that keeps the joints lubricated.)

The recommended dose is 200 to 400 milligrams three times daily or 1000 to 1200 milligrams taken once daily. Chondroitin sulphate and glucosamine sulphate are frequently sold together in combination products, but there's no evidence from studies on humans that this combination works better than either product alone. It may take 2 to 4 months of treatment to notice significant improvement in osteoarthritis symptoms.

Occasionally, chondroitin supplements may cause stomach upset and nausea. There's a potential for allergic reaction to chondroitin supplements made from animal sources. See Chapter 8, page 158, for information about chondroitin safety.

Glucosamine Sulphate

Glucosamine, a compound found naturally in the body, is made from glucose and the amino acid glutamine and is essential for the maintenance and repair of cartilage. The body uses glucosamine to make compounds called glycosaminoglycans, which are a major part of joint cartilage. Glucosamine sulphate is the form of glucosamine used in dozens of studies. Studies show that the supplement stimulates the production of glycosaminoglycans. Research suggests that taking glucosamine sulphate may stop and possibly even reverse osteoarthritis.

Findings from studies lasting 1 month to 3 years have shown that glucosamine significantly reduced pain and improved mobility in people with osteoarthritis of the knee.[23-31] The supplement appears to be as effective as ibuprofen and piroxicam (Feldene), two non-steroidal anti-inflammatory drugs (NSAIDs) used to manage osteoarthritis. Whereas conventional medications appear to take 2 weeks to improve symptoms, glucosamine takes 4 to 8 weeks to have an effect. In one study, after 8 weeks of treatment, glucosamine was superior to ibuprofen.

There's also evidence that glucosamine may actually slow joint degeneration in people with osteoarthritis of the knee. Patients taking glucosamine for up to 3 years appear to have significantly less joint degeneration, less joint-space narrowing and significant symptom improvement compared to those taking the placebo. Studies suggest that taking glucosamine sulphate might reduce the risk of disease progression by up to 54 percent.[32]

The recommended dose is 1500 milligrams once daily, or 500 milligrams taken three times daily. Glucosamine sulphate is often combined with chondroitin in supplements; however, it's not known if this combination is any more effective than taking glucosamine or chondroitin alone. Glucosamine supplements may cause nausea, heartburn, diarrhea and/or constipation.

Glucosamine sulphate is made from shellfish, so there's a concern that taking glucosamine supplements can cause a reaction in people with a shellfish allergy. However, that's an allergy to the protein, or meat, not the shell. There have been no documented reports of allergic reaction to glucosamine in people who have a shellfish allergy. See Chapter 8, page 167, for information about glucosamine safety.

SAMe (S-Adenosyl-Methionine)

SAMe is a compound found in virtually all body tissues and fluids. The body makes SAMe from certain amino acids in high-protein foods like fish and meat. In the body, SAMe is used to synthesize hormones, brain neurotransmitters, proteins and cell membranes.

SAMe has analgesic and anti-inflammatory properties, which are thought to be responsible for its beneficial effects in osteoarthritis. Several studies lasting from 2 weeks to 2 years have found SAMe to be significantly better than a placebo and comparable to non-steroidal anti-inflammatory drugs (NSAIDs) for decreasing join pain and improving mobility in osteoarthritis.[33–43] Some evidence even suggests that SAMe might stimulate the growth and repair of cartilage.

Take 200 milligrams three times daily on an empty stomach. Buy an enteric-coated product. SAMe is very well tolerated at the recommended doses, but daily doses greater than 1600 milligrams may cause nausea, gastrointestinal upset and headache. SAMe is sold as a dietary supplement in the United States but hasn't been approved for sale in Canada. See Chapter 8, page 181, for information on SAMe supplementation.

Nutrition Strategy Checklist for Osteoarthritis

☐ Weight control
☐ Soy protein
☐ Vitamin C
☐ Vitamin D
☐ Capsaicin cream
☐ Devil's claw
☐ Chondroitin sulphate OR Glucosamine sulphate*
☐ SAMe

*Best evidence—start here.

Recommended Resources

The Arthritis Society
www.arthritis.ca
393 University Avenue, Suite 1700
Toronto, ON M5G 1E6
Tel: 416-979-7228
Fax: 416-979-8366
Email: info@arthritis.ca

American College of Rheumatology
www.rheumatology.org
1800 Century Place, Suite 250
Atlanta, GA, USA 30345
Tel: 404-633-3777
Fax: 404-633-1870

Arthritis Foundation
www.arthritis.org

P.O. Box 7669
Atlanta, GA, USA 30357-0669
Tel: 1-800-283-7800

**National Institute of Arthritis and
Musculoskeletal and Skin Diseases
Information Clearinghouse
National Institutes of Health**
www.niams.nih.gov
1 AMS Circle
Bethesda, MD, USA 20892-3675
Tel: 301-495-4484 or 1-877-22-NIAMS
  (64267)
Fax: 301-718-6366

Osteoporosis

It's estimated that 2 million Canadians have osteoporosis, a disease resulting in fragile, brittle bones that are more likely to break than normal, healthy bones. Osteoporosis can strike at any age, but it's more likely to occur in later years, affecting one in four women and one in eight men over the age of 50.[1]

Osteoporosis is characterized by low bone mass and deterioration of existing bone tissue. Bones become weaker and more susceptible to fractures, particularly of the hip, spine and wrists. The definition of osteoporosis emphasizes fracture risk, not only low bone density. Although many bone fractures are not life threatening, their impact on health is underappreciated. For instance, hip fractures lead to death in 20 percent of cases. Close to 50 percent of elderly women who fracture a hip lose their ability to live independently.

What Causes Osteoporosis?

Throughout childhood, bones grow in length and density (mass). At some point in adolescence, bones stop growing in length but continue to increase in density, though at a slower rate. Then, by around age 25, bones achieve what's called their peak mass and stop building density. Peak bone mass is determined largely by genetics, but nutrition and other lifestyle factors, such as medications, determine whether you'll achieve your body's genetically programmed peak bone mass.

After achieving peak bone mass, bone density is maintained for about 10 years. After age 35, both men and women normally lose 0.3 percent to 0.5 percent of their bone density per year. For women, though, when estrogen levels drop after menopause, bone loss accelerates and they can lose up to 4 percent of their bone density each year. Ten years after menopause, the rate of bone loss diminishes to about 0.5 percent per year, but during that decade women have the potential to very quickly lose up to 25 percent to 30 percent of their bone density. Accelerated loss of bone density after menopause is a major cause of osteoporosis.

Despite its "dead" appearance, bone is a very active tissue that contains two types of cells. *Osteoclasts* are bone cells that break down bone tissue by removing its mineral content—a process called bone resorption. For example, osteoclasts go to work when your diet lacks calcium; these bone cells release calcium from the bone into the blood for important body functions. *Osteoblasts* are cells that form bone; they're responsible for building the support structure of bones, as well as adding minerals to strengthen bones. Your bones are constantly going through a bone-remodelling cycle: Osteoclast cells resorb bone and osteoblast cells build bone.

Symptoms

Osteoporosis is a silent disease because bone loss occurs without symptoms. You may not know you have the disease until you break a bone. The outward signs of osteoporosis aren't usually apparent until the disease is quite advanced. Signs that you may have osteoporosis include:

- a broken wrist or rib from a slight blow
- a broken hip
- back pain in the mid to lower spine
- loss of more than 1 inch (2.5 cm) of height
- a stooped or hunched-over appearance
- a hump forming in the upper back

Who's at Risk?

The strength of your bones is determined by 1) their bone mineral density, 2) their rate of self-healing and 3) the integrity of their support structures. Any factor that jeopardizes these three factors can increase the odds of getting osteoporosis. Risk factors include:

- older age
- low bone density
- being female
- thin and small body frame
- deficiency of estrogen (early or surgical menopause)
- cigarette smoking
- low intake of calcium
- vitamin D deficiency
- excessive alcohol and caffeine consumption
- lack of exercise
- certain medications (e.g., corticosteroids, chemotherapy)
- prolonged immobilization
- family history of osteoporosis
- previous bone fracture as an adult
- certain health conditions (e.g., kidney failure, hyperthyroidism, rheumatoid arthritis, malabsorption states)

Conventional Treatment

The goal of osteoporosis treatment is to prevent bone fractures by stopping bone loss and increasing bone density and strength. In addition to the medications listed below, lifestyle changes such as quitting smoking, moderating alcohol intake and exercising regularly play important roles in the treatment—and prevention—of osteoporosis. (If you have osteoporosis, speak to your doctor about which types of exercise are safe and won't injure already weakened bones.)

Hormone Replacement Therapy (HRT)

Many studies have shown that hormone replacement therapy (HRT) protects the bones of women. Both estrogen pills and estrogen patches have been found to decrease bone loss, reduce fractures and prevent the loss of height. Estrogen replacement prevents bone loss at any point a woman starts to take it. However, the longer a woman waits after menopause, the greater the chance she'll lose some bone permanently. And once a woman stops taking estrogen, bone loss occurs: Estrogen's protective effect lasts only as long as the estrogen is taken.

Although studies do find that estrogen delays bone loss, recent clinical trials have not found this medication to be effective at preventing bone fractures. The Heart and Estrogen/Progestin Replacement Study (HERS) followed over 2700 post-menopausal women who didn't have osteoporosis and found no significant difference in hip or spine fracture rates among women taking HRT and those not taking the drugs.[2] Experts believe that HRT may reduce bone fractures only in women who have defined osteoporosis when they start on the medication.

Although estrogen therapy might be effective in treating osteoporosis, due to adverse effects such as increased risks of heart attack, stroke, blood clots and breast cancer, HRT is no longer recommended for long-term use in osteoporosis. Rather, it's used in the short term for relief of menopausal hot flashes.

Bisphosphonates

This class of non-hormonal drugs offers an alternative to HRT for both men and women with low bone density or osteoporosis. Bisphosphonate drugs prevent bone breakdown by binding to the bone surface and inhibiting the activity of osteoclasts, the cells that strip down old bone. Studies have demonstrated their ability to reduce the risk of fracture to the hip, wrist and spine in post-menopausal women with osteoporosis. Types of bisphosphonates include Didrocal (etidronate and calcium carbonate), Fosamax (alendronate) and Actonel (risedronate).

Selective Estrogen Receptor Modulators (SERMs)

Often called "designer estrogen," these medications offer all the beneficial effects of estrogen (bone protection, cholesterol lowering) without any of its negative effects (increased breast cancer risk, endometrial bleeding). SERMs such as Evista (raloxifene) have the favourable effects of estrogen on bone and act as an anti-estrogen in the breast and the lining of the uterus. Because of the anti-estrogen effects, hot flashes are a common side effect.

Preventing and Managing Osteoporosis

Dietary Strategies

Soy Foods

Soybeans contain naturally occurring compounds called isoflavones, a type of plant estrogen. Genistein and daidzein are the most active isoflavones in soy and have been the focus of much research. Isoflavones have a chemical structure similar to estrogen and so are able to bind to estrogen receptors in the body—scientists believe that action in relation to bone may be responsible for soy's potential bone-preserving effect.

The interest in soybeans and osteoporosis began when researchers observed that populations that consume soy foods on a regular basis report much lower rates of hip fracture. Since the late 1990s, soy foods and their naturally occurring phytoestrogens have been the focus of many studies. An early 3-month study conducted at Iowa State University found that 40 grams of phytoestrogen-rich soy protein providing 90 milligrams of isoflavones prevented bone loss in perimenopausal women.[3] Women in this study who instead were given whey protein powder (a protein made from milk) showed significant bone loss in the lower spine. Another study published in 1999 from the University of Cincinnati College of Medicine found that 60 to 70 milligrams of soy isoflavones consumed as So Good soy beverage and soy nuts significantly decreased bone turnover in post-menopausal women after 12 weeks.[4]

More recent research has also revealed favourable effects of soy on bone health. A 2008 review of nine studies with a total of 432 participants found that soy isoflavones significantly inhibited bone breakdown and stimulated bone formation.[5] Another combined analysis of ten studies conducted in 608 subjects concluded that soy isoflavones were effective in slowing bone loss of the spine in menopausal women. This effect became more pronounced when more than 90 milligrams of soy isoflavones were consumed each day.[6] However, one recent clinical trial conducted in 237 healthy early post-menopausal women found that consuming 110 milligrams of soy isoflavones each day did not prevent post-menopausal bone loss.[7]

Based on the research to date, a minimum daily intake of 90 milligrams of isoflavones appears to be needed to benefit bones. Soy foods vary in the amount of isoflavones they contain. Even the same type of food made by different manufacturers can differ in isoflavone content.

Isoflavone Content of Selected Soy Foods

Soy Food	Serving Size	Isoflavone Content (milligrams)
Roasted soy nuts	1/4 cup (60 ml)	40–60 mg
Soy beverage, most brands	1 cup (250 ml)	20–25 mg
Soy beverage, So Nice	1 cup (250 ml)	60 mg
Soy flour	1/4 cup (60 ml)	28 mg
Soy hot dog	1	15 mg
Soy protein isolate powder	1 oz (30 g)	30 mg
Soybeans, cooked or canned	1/2 cup (125 ml)	14 mg
Tempeh, cooked	3 oz (90 g)	48 mg
Texturized vegetable protein, dry	1/2 cup (125 ml)	30–120 mg
Tofu, firm	3 oz (90 g)	22 mg
Tofu, soft	3 oz (90 g)	28 mg

Source: USDA Database for the Isoflavone Content of Selected Foods, Release 2.0, September 2008. Available at www.ars.usda.gov/SP2UserFiles/Place/12354500/Data/isoflav/Isoflav_R2.pdf.

Protein-Rich Foods

Protein can be detrimental or beneficial to bone health depending on a number of factors such as the amount consumed each day, the type of protein, calcium intake and acidity of the diet. High levels of dietary protein cause calcium to be excreted by the kidneys. An average increase of 7 grams in dietary protein (1 ounce or 30 g of meat) causes 7 grams of calcium to be lost in the urine. The effect of eating large quantities of protein is rapid, and it appears that the body doesn't correct for this by absorbing more calcium from food. The protein effect may be very important for people who consume very little calcium or for those who, because of intestinal problems, absorb very little calcium.

Although eating very large amounts of protein may not be good for your bones, eating too little isn't healthy either. Protein is an important structural component of bone, and research suggests that a lack of protein increases the risk of hip fracture. The Iowa Women's Health Study found that dietary protein protected post-menopausal women from hip fracture.[8] Another study found that consuming 72 grams of protein each day was associated with high bone densities among women who consumed more than 400 milligrams of calcium daily.[9] Women who ate the most protein had a 69 percent reduced risk of hip fracture compared with women who ate the least. Studies have also found that when protein supplements are given to patients with hip fracture, bone density is increased and the rate of complications and death are reduced immediately after surgery and for 6 months afterward.[10,11]

To determine your protein requirements, see Chapter 2, pages 19, where you'll also find a list of foods and their protein content.

Alcoholic Beverages

Many studies have determined that chronic alcohol abuse depletes bone density. Alcohol acts directly on your bones and suppresses bone formation. Consuming alcohol also increases the risk of falls in post-menopausal women and is associated with an increased incidence of hip fractures. If you drink alcohol, limit your intake to no more than seven drinks per week for women and nine for men.

Caffeine

Drinking caffeinated beverages such as coffee, tea or cola increases the amount of calcium your kidneys excrete in the urine for up to 3 hours after consumption. For every 6 ounce cup of coffee you drink, approximately 48 milligrams of calcium is leached from your bones—an amount that can be fully offset by consuming 3 tablespoons (40 ml) of milk or yogurt. The effects of caffeine are likely most detrimental for women who are not meeting their daily calcium requirements. One study found that 400 milligrams of caffeine caused calcium loss in women whose daily diet had less than 600 milligrams of calcium.[12] Another study, from Tufts University in Boston, found that women who consumed less than 800 milligrams of calcium and 450 milligrams of caffeine (about three small cups of coffee) had

significantly lower bone densities than women who consumed the same amount of caffeine but more than 800 milligrams of calcium.[13] Interestingly, researchers found that habitual caffeine intake was not linked to lower bone densities in young women aged 14 to 40 years.[14]

If you consume caffeinated beverages, the following strategies will help maintain bone density:

- Ensure you're meeting your calcium requirements of 1000 to 1500 milligrams a day.
- Add 3 tablespoons (45 ml) of milk or calcium-fortified soy beverage (58 mg calcium) to each cup of coffee you drink.
- Don't consume more than 450 milligrams of caffeine a day (see Chapter 5, page 110). If you have osteoporosis, aim for no more than 200 milligrams.
- Replace regular coffee with water, tea, herbal tea, vegetable juice, lattes (coffee with milk) or soy beverage. All have substantially less caffeine than coffee.

Vitamins and Minerals

Calcium

The fact that calcium is the most abundant mineral in the body and that 99 percent of it is housed within the bones and teeth underlines the importance of dietary calcium to bone health. During the bone-building process, the osteoblast cells secrete bone mineral, consisting of calcium and phosphorus, which strengthens the bone. By providing structural integrity to bones, dietary calcium plays a critical role in preventing osteoporosis.

The remaining 1 percent of the body's calcium circulates in the bloodstream and is vital to the functioning of the heart, nervous system and muscles. The body keeps this circulating pool of calcium at a constant level. If your diet lacks calcium and your blood-calcium level drops, your body releases parathyroid hormone (PTH), which returns calcium to your blood by taking it from the bones. When you shortchange your diet of calcium, you shortchange your bones too.

Research supports using calcium supplements to lower the risk of osteoporosis. Researchers at the University of Texas Southwestern Medical Center in Dallas found that a 400 milligram calcium citrate supplement taken twice daily increased bone density in healthy post-menopausal women.[15] In contrast, women in the placebo group experienced a 2.38 percent bone-density reduction in the lower spine.

Scientists at the University of Massachusetts studied 98 premenopausal women (average age 39 years) and found that those who received 500 milligrams of calcium carbonate daily increased their bone density by 0.3 percent per year.[16] The women in the placebo group lost bone at a rate of 0.4 percent per year in the hip and 0.7 percent in the neck. A number of studies have also shown that older women and men who take calcium and vitamin D supplements have a lower incidence of non-vertebral fractures.

Calcium supplementation may also reduce the risk of bone fracture among people with osteoporosis. A recent review of twenty-nine studies concluded that taking calcium alone, or in combination with vitamin D, reduced the rate of bone loss and fractures of all types in people aged 50 years and older.[17]

The recommended dietary allowance (RDA) for calcium is 1000 to 1500 milligrams per day depending on your age. The best food sources include milk, yogurt, cheese, fortified soy and rice beverages, fortified orange juice, tofu, salmon (with bones), kale, bok choy, broccoli and Swiss chard. If your diet lacks calcium, as is the case for many Canadians, take a calcium supplement to ensure that you're meeting your daily requirement. See Chapter 4, page 56, for more information on calcium requirements, calcium-rich foods and calcium supplements.

Vitamin D

Experts cite a silent epidemic of vitamin D deficiency, in addition to getting too little calcium, as a contributing factor to osteoporosis. Vitamin D makes calcium and phosphorus available in the blood that bathes the bones, so that they can be deposited as bones harden or mineralize. Vitamin D raises blood levels of calcium in three ways: It stimulates your intestine to absorb more dietary calcium, it tells your kidneys to retain calcium and it withdraws calcium from your bones if your diet is lacking this mineral. A vitamin D deficiency will speed up bone loss and increase the risk of fracture at a younger age.

Vitamin D is different from any other nutrient because the body can synthesize it from sunlight. When ultraviolet light hits the skin, a pre–vitamin D is formed. This compound eventually makes its way to the kidneys, where it's transformed into active vitamin D. However, the long winter months in Canada result in very little vitamin D being synthesized by the skin. Researchers from Tufts University in Boston have demonstrated that blood levels of vitamin D are at their lowest point between February and March and peak in June and July.[18] (Although this is an American study, the findings hold true for Canadians.) But even in the summer, your body might not be making enough vitamin D, since sun protection factor (SPF) in sunscreen blocks production of the vitamin. To help you meet your vitamin D requirements, expose your hands, face and arms to sunlight without sunscreen for 10 to 15 minutes, two or three times a week.

The recommended daily intake is 1000 international units (IU) for adults and 400 IU for children. Best food sources are fluid milk, fortified soy and rice beverages, oily fish, egg yolks, butter and margarine. However, it's not possible for adults to consume 1000 IU each day from foods alone. For this reason, it's necessary to take a vitamin D supplement in the fall and winter, and year-round if you are over the age of 50, have dark-coloured skin or don't expose your skin to sunshine in the summer months. See Chapter 4, page 51, to learn about vitamin D supplements.

Other Nutrients

Although calcium and vitamin D are critical to healthy bones, other nutrients are also important players in bone building. With the exception of sodium (see below), together with calcium and vitamin D, they comprise the nutrient team that orchestrates the continual process of bone building and bone breakdown.

Vitamin A

This vitamin supports bone growth and development. Degradative enzymes in osteoclast cells use vitamin A to break down old bone in order to build new bone. Bone growth relies on this vitamin, as evidenced by children with a vitamin A deficiency who fail to grow properly.

However, although we need some vitamin A for good health, too much may actually decrease bone density and increase the risk of hip fracture.[19,20] Researchers from Harvard University found that among 73,000 post-menopausal women, those who consumed more than 1.5 milligrams (5000 IU) of vitamin A each day, from food and supplements combined, had a significantly higher risk of hip fracture than women who consumed less than 0.5 milligrams (1665 IU) each day.[21] A study from Sweden found similar results with respect to the harmful effects of too much vitamin A. The researchers found that women who consumed more than 1.5 milligrams versus less than 0.5 milligram of vitamin A each day had lower bone densities of the neck and spine and were twice as likely to suffer a hip fracture.[22]

High blood levels of vitamin A stimulate bone breakdown and, based on a growing body of evidence, increase the risk of bone fracture. Vitamin A is found preformed in animal foods such as fortified milk, cheese, butter, eggs and liver. It's absorbed as retinol, the most active form of vitamin A. Unless you eat liver frequently or drink in excess of five glasses of milk each day, your diet is unlikely to cause high levels of vitamin A in your body. Taking vitamin A supplements, however, can result in excessive vitamin A accumulating in the body. Don't take single vitamin A supplements; choose a multivitamin that contains no more than 2500 international units (IU) of vitamin A (as retinol or retinyl palmitate). Beta carotene–rich fruit and vegetables also contribute to our daily vitamin A requirements, since some beta carotene is converted to vitamin A in the body. The best sources of beta carotene include carrots, winter squash, sweet potatoes, spinach, broccoli, rapini, romaine lettuce, apricots, peaches, mango, papaya and cantaloupe. There's no evidence that beta carotene is harmful to bones.

Vitamin C

A number of studies involving post-menopausal women have linked higher intakes of vitamin C with higher bone density. One study revealed that women aged 55 to 64 years who had taken vitamin C supplements for at least 10 years had significantly higher bone mass compared with women who didn't supplement their diet.[23] Vitamin C is important for the formation of collagen, a tissue that lends support to bones. This vitamin may also protect bones by acting as an antioxidant and modifying the negative effect of cigarette smoking on bones. Cigarette smoking inactivates circulating estrogen so that it can't exert its protective effect on bone.

The recommended dietary allowance (RDA) for vitamin C is 75 and 90 milligrams per day for women and men, respectively (smokers need an additional 35 milligrams). Best food sources include citrus fruit, citrus juices, cantaloupe, kiwi, mango, strawberries, broccoli, Brussels sprouts, cauliflower, red pepper and tomato juice. To supplement, take 500 milligrams of vitamin C once or twice daily. The upper daily limit is 2000 milligrams.

Vitamin K

This fat-soluble vitamin is used to make a bone protein called osteocalcin. A high level of osteocalcin in the blood indicates that osteoblast cells are busy making new bone. Without enough vitamin K, the bones produce an abnormal protein that can't bind to the minerals that form the bones.

The large, ongoing Nurses' Health Study from Harvard University found that women with the highest intake of vitamin K had a significantly lower rate of hip fracture compared with women who consumed the least. Eating lettuce was also linked with fewer hip fractures. Lettuce accounted for most of the vitamin K in their diet. Those women who ate 1 or more servings of the leafy green each day (versus 1 or fewer servings a week) had a 45 percent lower risk of hip fractures.[24] A study of elderly men and women also reported low vitamin K intakes were associated with a greater risk of hip fracture.[25]

The best sources of vitamin K are leafy green vegetables including arugula, beet greens, kale, rapini, Swiss chard and spinach. Most of us don't get enough vitamin K in our diet. The recommended daily intake of vitamin K is 90 and 120 micrograms for women and men, respectively. This amount is designed to help our blood clot, not protect our bones. Scientists speculate it takes about 200 micrograms per day to protect bones from thinning—that can be accomplished by eating 1 serving (1/2 cup or 125 ml) of cooked leafy greens each day.

Boron

Although there's no recommended daily intake for boron, research suggests that higher intakes of this trace mineral may slow the loss of calcium, magnesium and phosphorus from the urine. Scientists aren't exactly sure how boron keeps calcium in balance, but they suspect boron is needed for activation of vitamin D.

A daily intake of 1.5 to 3 milligrams of boron is more than adequate to meet your requirements for bone growth and development. The main food sources are fruit and vegetables, but boron content depends on how much of the mineral is in the soil in which they grew. If you want to take a supplement, 3 to 9 milligrams per day is a very safe amount. Intakes greater than 500 milligrams a day can cause nausea, vomiting and diarrhea. However, boron supplements aren't available in Canada (but are in the United States).

Magnesium

One-half of the body's magnesium stores are in the bone. The mineral helps make parathyroid hormone, an important regulator of bone building. Animal studies show that a lack of dietary magnesium causes increased bone breakdown and decreased bone synthesis.

Most of the studies that support the use of magnesium supplements found that osteoporosis is more common in people who have other health problems that cause a magnesium deficiency, such as alcoholism and hyperthyroidism. However, there's preliminary evidence that taking magnesium supplements can prevent bone loss in post-menopausal women. One study also found that among 2,038 men and women age 70 and older, higher magnesium intakes were associated with greater bone densities.[26]

The recommended daily intake for women is 310 to 420 milligrams (see Chapter 4, page 61). The best food sources are wheat bran; whole-grain breads, cereals and pasta; legumes; nuts; seeds and leafy green vegetables.

If you use calcium supplements, buy one with magnesium added—in a 2:1 ratio (two parts calcium for one part magnesium) to avoid gastrointestinal upset. The upper daily limit for magnesium from a supplement is 350 milligrams.

Phosphorus

This mineral is an important component of the bone mineral complex. Indeed, 85 percent of the body's phosphorus is stored in the bones. It appears that both too little and too much dietary phosphorus can result in bone loss.

Scientists believe that a long-standing imbalance of phosphorus and calcium, caused by too much dietary phosphorus and too little dietary calcium, may contribute to bone breakdown. On the other hand, if your diet lacks phosphorus and your blood levels of the mineral become low, your body will release the mineral from your bones in an effort to keep your blood level constant (in the same way that blood-calcium levels remain stable at the expense of your bones). One of the symptoms of a phosphorus deficiency is bone pain. A low blood-phosphorus level can result from poor eating habits, excessive use of phosphorus-binding antacids and intestinal malabsorption.

The recommended daily intake for adults is 700 milligrams of phosphorus. Most of the phosphorus in our diet comes from additives in cheese, bakery products, processed meats and soft drinks. Other food sources include wheat bran, milk, fish, eggs, poultry, beef and pork. Most people don't have a problem getting enough phosphorus. Just make sure you meet your daily calcium requirements so that these two minerals are kept in balance.

Manganese, Zinc and Copper

These trace minerals are important helpers (cofactors) for enzymes that are essential to making bone tissue. Post-menopausal women who received a daily supplement of calcium, manganese, copper and zinc didn't experience any bone loss of the spine at the end of a 2-year study.[27] The placebo group, on the other hand, lost 3.5 percent of their bone mass. Manganese is widely available in foods and deficiencies haven't been seen in humans. Meat and drinking water are your best bets for copper. When it comes to zinc, wheat bran, wheat germ, oysters, seafood, lean red meat and milk are good sources.

Sodium

Like caffeine, sodium causes the kidneys to excrete calcium. This means that you need to limit the amount of sodium you consume each day—and meet daily calcium requirements. In a study of 186 adults aged 23 to 76 years, researchers assigned participants to one of three DASH diets with varying sodium levels. The DASH diet is rich in calcium, magnesium and potassium and has been shown to significantly lower blood pressure. (For more information on the DASH diet, see High Blood Pressure, page 461.) Although the DASH diet reduced bone turnover, reducing sodium intake from the highest (3450 milligrams) to the lowest (1150 milligrams) level was even more effective.[28]

To reduce sodium intake, keep your daily intake less than 2300 milligrams. Read nutrition labels to choose packaged foods that are lower in sodium. Eat more meals prepared at home rather than in restaurants. Avoid the saltshaker at the table and minimize your use of salt in cooking. You'll find additional strategies to help reduce sodium intake in Chapter 5, page 108.

Other Natural Health Products
Fish Oil Supplements
Although preliminary, there's evidence that omega-3 fatty acids in fish oil guard against osteoporosis.[29] Data from animal studies suggest that fish oil may reduce post-menopausal bone loss. Higher intakes of omega-3 fats have been linked with higher bone density. Studies in humans have found that a higher intake of omega-3 fats—and a lower intake of omega-6 fats found in corn and soybean oils—is associated with increased bone densities.[30] Findings from a study conducted in men suggest that high levels of omega-3 fatty acids in the blood—a reflection of one's dietary intake—favourably affect bone health.[31] Supplementation with fish oil reduces

the production of inflammatory immune compounds and helps increase calcium absorption and bone mineral density.

In addition to eating oily fish such as salmon or trout twice per week, take a daily fish oil supplement that supplies 300 to 600 milligrams of DHA + EPA combined, the two omega-3 fatty acids contained in fish oil.

Other Lifestyle Factors
Weight-Bearing Exercise
Until the age of 30, regular exercise helps women get a head start on building peak bone mass. Children who spend the most amount of time being physically active have stronger bones compared with those who are sedentary. But the effect of exercise doesn't stop once you've achieved your peak mass. Bone cells are constantly active, tearing up old bone and laying down new bone. Participating in weight-bearing activities like brisk walking, stair climbing or weight training stimulates bones to increase in strength and density during the pre- and post-menopausal years. One study found that post-menopausal women who worked out three times a week for 9 months actually increased their bone mass by 5.2 percent.[32] Another report revealed that, compared to women who didn't exercise, those who worked out with weights for 1 hour three times a week gained bone mass, to the tune of 1.6 percent. The non-exercisers actually lost 3.6 percent of the bone mass in their spine over the course of the study.[33]

If you have osteoporosis, a safe exercise program can help you slow bone loss, improve posture and balance, and build muscle strength and tone. The benefits of exercise can reduce your risk of falling and fracturing a bone.

Incorporate a mix of activities in your week. If you have never used weights before, consult a certified personal trainer. Personal trainers work in fitness clubs and many will come to your home. They'll design a safe and effective program for you.

Nutrition Strategy Checklist for Osteoporosis

☐ Soy foods
☐ Foods rich in protein
☐ Limit alcohol
☐ Limit caffeine
☐ Calcium
☐ Vitamin D
☐ Vitamin A
☐ Vitamin C
☐ Vitamin K
☐ Boron
☐ Magnesium
☐ Phosphorus
☐ Reduce sodium
☐ Fish oil supplement
☐ Weight-bearing exercise

Recommended Resources

Osteoporosis Canada
www.osteoporosis.ca
1090 Don Mills Road, Suite 301
Toronto, ON M3C 3R6
Tel: 1-800-463-6842
Fax: 416-696-2673

Women's Health Matters Website
Women's College Hospital
www.womenshealthmatters.ca
76 Grenville Street
Toronto, ON M5S 1B2
Email: info@womenshealthmatters.ca

National Institute of Arthritis and
Musculoskeletal and Skin Diseases
National Institutes of Health
www.niams.nih.gov
1 AMS Circle
Bethesda, MD, USA 20892-3675
Tel: 301-495-4484
Fax: 301-718-6366
Email: NIAMSinfo@mail.nih.gov

Parkinson's Disease

Parkinson's disease belongs to a group of conditions called motor system disorders. It's a chronic degenerative disorder that affects the part of the brain that controls muscle movement and it's identifiable by the characteristic tremors that it causes. The disease damages nerve cells, or neurons, in the substantia nigra, an area deep within the brain. These nerve cells produce dopamine, a neurotransmitter that carries messages along nerve pathways from one part of the nervous system to another. These messages enable muscles to make smooth, relaxed, well-controlled movements. In Parkinson's disease, the nerve cells in the substantia nigra begin to degenerate rapidly, resulting in a shortage of dopamine. Without adequate supplies of dopamine, the brain loses the ability to communicate effectively with the nerves and muscles. This loss of communication interferes with the regulation of normal muscle actions, such as walking, sitting and standing.

Parkinson's disease usually begins with a slight tremor or shaking in a limb, often in the hand. The disease progresses quite slowly, but, eventually, the tremor becomes worse, affecting the arms, legs and other parts of the body. Balance deteriorates; automatic movements, such as blinking and smiling, are lost; and daily activities, such as walking, talking and writing, become difficult and time-consuming.

What Causes Parkinson's Disease?

Scientists are working intensively to determine what causes Parkinson's disease. Although we all lose some dopamine-producing cells in the normal course of aging, people with Parkinson's disease lose at least 60 percent of the cells in the substantia nigra.

Researchers believe that the disease might be caused by a combination of genetic and environmental factors. Certain drugs, degenerative diseases and toxins are known to inhibit the action of dopamine in the brain, producing symptoms similar to Parkinson's disease. One theory also holds that free radicals—unstable oxygen molecules created by normal metabolic reactions in the body—may contribute to neuron death, leading to Parkinson's disease. Some researchers also speculate that Parkinson's disease occurs when, for unknown reasons, normal age-related wearing away of dopamine-producing neurons accelerates.

Symptoms

Early symptoms of the disease may be subtle and may occur gradually. People may feel tired or generally unwell. Others may feel shaky, have difficulty getting out of a chair or may notice that their handwriting has changed. In some cases, friends and family members are the first to notice these subtle signs. As the disease progresses, the following symptoms may interfere with daily activities:

- **Tremors.** Tremors begin as a slight shaking in one finger or hand and may spread to other parts of the body, including the head, eyelids and feet. Tremors in the hand may cause the finger and thumb to rub back and forth in a motion known as pill rolling. Fatigue and stress make tremors more noticeable, though they often disappear during sleep.
- **Difficulty moving.** Walking is slow and shuffling, gait is unsteady and posture becomes stooped. Balance problems result in a tendency to fall. Muscles may freeze up, making it difficult to begin moving again. The digestive tract slows down, causing swallowing problems, indigestion and constipation.
- **Rigid muscles.** Muscles become stiff and unresponsive, which limits movement and causes fatigue and aching. Handwriting becomes small and cramped, and daily tasks become difficult.
- **Loss of automatic facial movements.** The face becomes less expressive because facial muscles don't move. A fixed, staring expression with no blinking develops. Arms don't swing while walking and there are no gestures when talking.
- **Impaired speech.** The voice becomes monotonous and soft, and speech becomes slower. Dementia can develop late in the disease.

Other symptoms include depression, lack of energy, difficulty chewing and swallowing, sleep disturbances, constipation, urinary problems and decreased sexual desire.

Who's at Risk?

Parkinson's affects 1 million Canadians and 6.3 million people worldwide.[1] Although the disease typically occurs around the age of 60, it can strike people as young as 30 and 40. Risk factors for Parkinson's disease include:

- **Age.** Symptoms usually appear later in life. The average age of diagnosis is 60, and rates continue to rise as people enter their 70s and 80s.
- **Gender.** Men are slightly more at risk than women. A loss of estrogen levels after menopause may elevate the risk for women.
- **Heredity.** Individuals with a close family relative with Parkinson's disease are three times more likely to develop the disease.
- **Environmental factors.** People exposed to herbicides and pesticides have a higher risk of developing Parkinson's disease.
- **Medications.** Drugs used for psychiatric disorders, epilepsy or nausea may cause symptoms of Parkinson's disease.
- **Toxins.** Manganese dust or the chemical MPTP used in heroin production can trigger symptoms, though these cases are very rare.

Conventional Treatment

At this time, there's no cure for Parkinson's disease. Fortunately, people often need little or no treatment for quite a while after their diagnosis. When symptoms grow more severe, lifestyle changes and medications can provide some relief, including:

- **Physical therapy** to improve mobility, range of motion and muscle tone.
- **Regular weight-bearing exercise** to improve gait, balance and strengthen muscles.
- **Eating a healthy diet** to provide antioxidants to protect against free radical damage (see below).

- **Minimizing stress** to help plan and manage daily tasks at times of peak energy and ability.
- **Medications** to manage symptoms in later stages of the disease:
  - **Levodopa** (Sinemet) is a naturally occurring chemical that's converted into dopamine by nerve cells in the brain. The drug becomes less effective as the disease progresses.
  - **Dopamine agonists** imitate the effects of dopamine on the brain. They're usually used in combination with levodopa.
  - **Selegiline** prevents the breakdown of natural dopamine and dopamine formed from levodopa.
  - **Anticholinergics** help control tremors in the early stages of the disease.
  - **Amantadine** is an antiviral drug prescribed in the later stages of the disease for treatment of involuntary movements.
- **Surgery** to reduce tremors, but it can cause complications and the beneficial effects of the surgery may not last.
- **Deep brain stimulation**, in which a medical device is implanted in the chest and sends electrical impulses to a target area of the brain through a wire. The impulses interrupt signals from the thalamus that may cause symptoms.
- **Fetal cell transplantation**, in which cells from fetuses or embryos are transplanted into the brains of people with Parkinson's disease. This is still an experimental therapy because of the medical, moral and ethical considerations.

Preventing and Managing Parkinson's Disease

Dietary Strategies

It's important to eat a healthy diet that's low in fat and contains plenty of whole grains, vegetables and fruit. These foods provide important vitamins, minerals and antioxidants that help protect from free radical damage to nerve cells. Weight loss can also be a problem for people experiencing difficulty swallowing, loss of appetite or loss of their sense of taste. You'll find dietary guidelines in Chapter 5.

In the later stages of the disease, you may have swallowing problems. To make eating and swallowing easier, take small bites of food and chew each mouthful thoroughly. Swallow each mouthful before putting more food into your mouth. Eat slowly. If your food tends to get cold before you're finished eating, use a warming tray under your plate. Foods that are chopped or puréed in the blender are easier to swallow. Hot cereals, soft bread, scrambled and poached eggs, yogurt, milk, low-fat puddings, applesauce, bananas, baked potatoes without the skin, cooked winter squash, ground meat and poultry are relatively easy to chew and swallow. Avoid nuts and hard candies.

Dietary Fat

Numerous studies report a much higher risk of Parkinson's disease among people who have high intakes of animal fat, with some studies showing as much as a ninefold greater risk.[2-5] Animal fat may increase free radical formation in the brain and, as result, cause oxidative damage to nerve cells in the substantia nigra.

To reduce your intake of animal fat, choose the leanest cuts of meat (flank steak, inside round, pork tenderloin), poultry breast with-out the skin, skim or 1% milk and yogurt, and skim-milk cheese. Avoid processed meats such as bacon, sausage, bologna, hot dogs and salami. Use butter sparingly. More often, substitute animal protein with vegetarian protein foods such as legumes and soy foods.

Eat oily fish such as salmon, trout, sardines and herring at least twice per week. Studies suggest that omega-3 fatty acids found in fish may protect brain cells from free radical damage.

Dietary Protein

Amino acids from high-protein foods such as meat, poultry, fish, eggs and dairy products can affect brain levels of levadopa by competing for entry into the brain. You may need to cut down on high-protein foods, or plan to eat those foods only at times that won't affect your medication. Some studies have found that patients who virtually eliminate protein during the daytime (no more than 10 grams) and have unrestricted intake after 5 p.m. show a more constant response to levadopa and experience symptom improvement.[6-8] Your doctor will advise you if this dietary approach will enhance your treatment.

Redistributing your protein intake may reduce your daily intake of calcium, iron and B vitamins. Consult with a registered dietitian (www.dietitians.ca) to help you develop a meal plan that limits protein during the daytime but provides all essential nutrients.

Dietary Fibre

Because the digestive tract works more slowly in Parkinson's disease, constipation is a common complaint. Constipation may also be a side effect of certain medications. Foods that have a greater proportion of insoluble fibres, such as wheat bran, whole grains, nuts, seeds and certain fruit and vegetables, are used to treat and prevent constipation. One study found that a diet high in insoluble fibre relieved constipation and improved the absorption of levadopa in Parkinson's patients with marked constipation.[9] Psyllium, a type of soluble fibre, also adds bulk to stools and can be used to treat constipation.

Aim to consume 21 to 38 grams of fibre per day, depending on your age. See Constipation, page 320, for a list of high-fibre foods used to treat constipation. Increase your fluid intake to 9 to 13 cups (2.2 to 3.2 L) per day; otherwise constipation may worsen.

Coffee

Drinking coffee and other caffeine-containing beverages may help protect from Parkinson's disease. Researchers from the Mayo Clinic noted that compared with coffee abstaining, coffee drinking was associated with a 65 percent lower risk of Parkinson's disease and a later age of onset. A larger trial that followed 8000 Japanese-American men for 30 years found a similar effect of coffee and caffeine. The more coffee consumed, the lower the risk of Parkinson's disease. Harvard University researchers found that men who consumed the most caffeine reduced their risk for Parkinson's disease by 48 percent. Among women, those who drank one to three cups of coffee per day had a 50 percent reduction in risk.[10-12]

Coffee's protective effects against Parkinson's disease are attributed to caffeine. For men, the protective effect of caffeine appears to be dose related. Men who consume the greatest amount of caffeinated coffee—three or four cups or a total of 471 to 2716 milligrams of caffeine—seem to have the greatest reduction in risk.

These findings don't imply that coffee can delay the progression of Parkinson's disease once you have it—this hasn't been studied. Rather, coffee may prevent the disease from developing in the first place. If your symptoms include difficulty sleeping, limit your intake of caffeine to no more than one cup of coffee per day. See Chapter 5, page 110, for a list of caffeine-containing beverages and foods.

Vitamins and Minerals

B Vitamins: Folate, B6 and B12

Some evidence suggests that an adequate intake of folic acid and vitamins B6 and B12 might reduce the risk of developing Parkinson's disease by preventing elevated blood levels of an amino acid called homocysteine. It's thought that elevated homocysteine—which can occur from a deficiency of B vitamins—may play a role in neurodegenerative disorders, particularly Parkinson's disease. The body produces homocysteine during normal metabolic activities. It's converted to other harmless compounds with the help of folate, B6 and B12.

If you have Parkinson's disease and take levadopa, increasing your intake of these B vitamins can also help prevent rises in homocysteine. Levadopa therapy increases homocysteine levels, which is associated with an increased risk of heart attack, stroke and dementia. Studies have revealed that levadopa-treated patients often have low levels of B vitamins in their bloodstream. One study found that Parkinson's patients with high homocysteine had significantly poorer performance in memory tests.[13]

The best food sources of folate include cooked spinach, lentils, orange juice, asparagus, artichokes and whole-grain breads and cereals. Foods rich in vitamin B6 include meat, poultry, fish, liver, legumes, nuts, seeds, whole grains, green leafy vegetables, bananas and avocados. Vitamin B12 is found in animal foods such as meat, poultry, fish, eggs and dairy products and also in fortified soy and rice beverages.

If you have difficulty eating a varied diet, take multivitamin and mineral supplement to ensure that you're meeting your B vitamin requirements (see Chapter 4, page 35). Avoid taking a high-dose B complex supplement or single supplements of vitamin B6: Vitamin B6 enhances the metabolism of levadopa, reducing its effectiveness. (This drug-nutrient interaction doesn't occur when carbidopa is taken concurrently with levadopa.)

Vitamin E

Free radical damage can cause nerve cell death in the substantia nigra, possibly causing, or worsening, Parkinson's disease. There's evidence of increased free radical damage in the brain tissue of people with Parkinson's disease.[14] Researchers have also noted a higher risk of the disease among people with lower dietary intakes and blood levels of vitamin E.[15-16] Scientists have tested the effects of high-dose vitamin E supplementation on the progression of the disease—with disappointing results. An American study found that vitamin E added no benefit to the treatment of Parkinson's disease.[17] A more recent review of large, well-designed studies concluded there's enough evidence to discourage the use of vitamin E supplements in Parkinson's disease.[18]

If you have Parkinson's disease or you want to reduce your risk of developing the disease, increase your vitamin E intake from foods. The recommended dietary allowance is 22 international units (IU). The best food sources include wheat germ, nuts, seeds, vegetable oils, whole grains and kale.

Other Natural Health Products

Coenzyme Q10 (CoQ10)

This compound is produced by the body and found in every cell. It has a strong antioxidant effect that's thought to buffer the harmful consequences of free radicals on nerve cells. Several animal models of Parkinson's disease have shown beneficial effects from coenzyme Q10 (CoQ10). Preliminary studies have found that high intakes of CoQ10, through supplementation, can slow functional decline in people with early Parkinson's disease.[19,20]

In clinical studies on Parkinson's disease researchers have used doses of 300, 600, 1200 and 2400 milligrams per day, taken in three to four divided doses.

When taken in daily doses of 300 milligrams or more, CoQ10 can interfere with liver enzyme blood tests. Coenzyme Q10 can decrease blood pressure and might have additive blood pressure–lowering effects when used with antihypertensive drugs; if you're taking medication to treat hypertension, use CoQ10 with caution. The supplement may also interfere with the blood-thinning effects of warfarin (Coumadin). Consult your doctor before taking high doses of CoQ10.

Nutrition Strategy Checklist for Parkinson's Disease

☐ Diet low in animal fat
☐ Omega-3 fatty acids
☐ Protein redistribution
☐ Dietary fibre
☐ Coffee

☐ B vitamins
☐ Vitamin E
☐ Coenzyme Q10

Recommended Resources

Parkinson Society Canada
www.parkinson.ca
4211 Yonge Street, Suite 316
Toronto, ON M2P 2A9
Tel: 416-227-9700 or 1-800-565-3000
Fax: 416-227-9600

American Parkinson Disease Association, Inc.
www.apdaparkinson.org
135 Parkinson Avenue
Staten Island, NY, USA 10305
Tel: 1-800-223-2732 or 718-981-8001
Fax: 718-981-4399
Email: apda@apdaparkinson.org

The Michael J. Fox Foundation for Parkinson's Research
www.michaeljfox.org
Church Street Station
P.O. Box 780
New York, NY, USA 10008-0780
Tel: 1-800-708-7644

National Institute of Neurological Disorders and Stroke
National Institutes of Health
www.ninds.nih.gov
P.O. Box 5801
Bethesda, MD, USA 208524
Tel: 301-496-5751
Fax: 301-402-2186

Perimenopause

The signs and symptoms associated with menopause occur over a period of time, called perimenopause, which literally means "around menopause." For many women, the first sign of perimenopause is an erratic menstrual cycle—either skipped, lighter or shorter periods. The hallmark of this countdown to menopause is a fluctuating level of the female sex hormones estrogen and progesterone. Estrogen highs can bring on PMS-like symptoms, including mood swings, fluid retention and headaches, whereas estrogen lows promise hot flashes, vaginal dryness and forgetfulness.

A woman is considered to have reached menopause when a year has passed since her last menstrual period. Although it can vary, the average age a Canadian woman hits menopause is 51. It's at this time that women enter postmenopause, the phase of life in which the risks for heart disease, osteoporosis and breast cancer increase.

Your Menstrual Cycle

In order to understand what happens to your body during menopause, it helps to know how your hormones normally act during the childbearing years. The menstrual cycle is governed by the interaction of four hormones: luteinizing hormone, follicle stimulating hormone (FSH), estrogen and progesterone. By definition, the first day of the menstrual cycle—day one—is the first day bleeding commences. A woman's menstrual cycle lasts 25 to 36 days; most women don't have cycles that last exactly 28 days. The cycle ends just before the next menstrual period.

Bleeding, or menstruation, occurs after estrogen and progesterone levels decrease at the end of the previous cycle. During the early part of your monthly cycle, the ovaries produce estrogen. The brain responds to this increasing estrogen level by telling the pituitary gland to release follicle-stimulating hormone (FSH) and luteinizing hormone (LH). These two hormones, in turn, act on your ovaries. FSH causes egg follicles to develop and release estrogen. When the circulating estrogen rises to a critical level, the pituitary gland releases a surge of LH. This influx of LH causes ovulation by telling the follicle to release a mature egg.

The ruptured egg follicle then turns into something called the corpus luteum, a gland that produces progesterone after ovulation. During the last 14 days of the menstrual cycle, progesterone prepares your body for pregnancy by thickening the lining of your uterus. If conception doesn't occur, the corpus luteum becomes smaller, estrogen and progesterone levels fall and the uterine lining sheds, resulting in the next menstrual period.

What Causes Perimenopause?

For the menstrual cycle to occur regularly, the ovaries must produce enough estrogen and progesterone. As women get older, the supply of eggs and follicles dwindles, resulting in lower levels of estrogen and progesterone. During the years before menopause, declining levels of estrogen and progesterone cause irregular periods—periods may be skipped and they may be lighter. With lower levels of hormones, periods become shorter and eventually cease.

Symptoms
Menstrual Irregularity

As ovulation becomes more erratic, the intervals between periods can become longer or shorter and menstrual flow may become lighter or heavier. Many women also skip periods for a number of months.

Vaginal Changes

The tissues of the vagina and urethra (opening to the bladder) become thinner, less elastic and drier with declining estrogen levels. This can result in decreased lubrication, burning, itching, urinary tract infections and uncomfortable sexual intercourse.

Hot Flashes and Night Sweats

Hot flashes occur in up to 85 percent of North American women.[1,2] It's estimated that 10 percent to 15 percent of women have them severely enough to interfere with their daily life. On average, hot flashes persist for 3 to 5 years, but in 50 percent of women, they last up to 5 years.

A warning signal or aura often precedes a hot flash. A hot flash may begin as a pressure in the head, a headache or a wave of nausea. A sensation of heat then starts in the head and neck and spreads to the torso, arms and entire body. Sweating follows and is most intense in the upper body. Clothing may become soaked, particularly if hot flashes occur during sleep. (Night sweats are another term for hot flashes that occur during sleep.) Chills or shakes may follow as a result of a drop in body temperature. The entire event can last a few seconds to several minutes, and it may take an hour for chills to subside.

Insomnia

Night sweats often cause disrupted sleep. Although many women have no difficulty falling back to sleep, some simply can't. Fatigue caused by lack of sleep can lead to irritability, depression and forgetfulness. Many experts believe that there's something else going on to interrupt sleep, something that's not related to hot flashes during sleep.

Mood Swings

Most women describe the mood swings of perimenopause like those of premenstrual syndrome (PMS). Feelings of depression, anxiety and irritability can be disruptive to personal and work life.

Memory Problems

During perimenopause there are a few things happening to your body that may cause forgetfulness. For one, there's an aging process going on. The older we get, the more short-term memory we lose. Menopausal symptoms such as insomnia and fatigue can also cause memory problems. Evidence suggests that estrogen affects the brain chemistry and structure that's involved in memory, and that the loss of estrogen associated with menopause may be largely responsible for memory decline.

Heavy Bleeding

Most women will experience some change to their monthly cycle. The first sign of perimenopause is irregular menstruation. Your periods may stop suddenly or may become lighter and closer together, and then stop. On the other hand, some women experience heavy bleeding during their periods—usually caused by an imbalance of estrogen and progesterone.

When ovulation doesn't occur, progesterone isn't produced. This means that estrogen continues to build up the uterine lining, which becomes very thick and releases a lot of blood when it sheds in response to a drop in estrogen levels. As estrogen levels decline with approaching menopause, heavy bleeding will become less of an issue.

In some cases, heavy bleeding can be the sign of another health disorder: polyps, a fibroid or, less commonly, cancer. Alert your gynecologist if your periods last more than 7 days, if you bleed between your periods or if your menstrual flow becomes much heavier than usual.

Who's at Risk?

Perimenopausal symptoms can affect women 10 years before actual menopause. Today in Canada, almost 3.5 million women are between the ages of 40 and 54, the phase of life when levels of certain hormones are changing and dwindling. Although perimenopause can start in the late 30s, most women begin noticing symptoms in their 40s.

Not all women experience the uncomfortable symptoms associated with perimenopause. Although research is lacking in this area, there are a few factors that may increase your risk for suffering one or more of the symptoms. Ask yourself the following:

- Are you in your mid- to late 40s?
- Did your mother experience perimenopausal symptoms?
- Do you suffer from premenstrual symptoms, especially mood swings?
- Have you never delivered a baby? (Some research suggests that never having a baby may increase the risk of early menopause.)

- Do you eat a diet that's high in animal fat and lacking fruit, vegetables and fibre?
- Do you drink too much alcohol and coffee?
- Do you smoke cigarettes?
- Is your life full of stress and tension?
- Do you lack adequate sleep on a regular basis?
- Do you lack regular exercise?

Conventional Treatment

Perimenopause itself requires no medical treatment. Instead, treatments focus on relieving symptoms and reducing the risk of osteoporosis and heart disease that may occur during the post-menopausal years. Possible treatments include:

- **Short-term hormone replacement therapy** (estrogen plus progestin) to reduce hot flashes
- **Oral contraceptives** to regulate periods and reduce hot flashes and vaginal dryness
- **Progestin therapy** to regulate periods; used by women who can't take oral contraceptives
- **Endometrial ablation** to provide relief from heavy bleeding; this procedure destroys the lining of the endometrium using a laser, electrical energy or heat

Managing Perimenopause

Maintaining a healthy weight, getting regular exercise and managing stress helps many women ease perimenopausal symptoms. As well, a number of specific nutrition strategies may benefit some women. Although the list of alternative therapies below isn't all-encompassing, it highlights a few important strategies. If you're looking for a more comprehensive guide to managing perimenopausal symptoms, pick up a copy of my book *The Ultimate Nutrition Guide to Menopause* (Penguin Canada).

Dietary Strategies

Trigger Foods and Beverages

Eliminate foods in the diet that can worsen hot flashes, insomnia or mood swings. Caffeine-containing foods and beverages like coffee, tea, dark chocolate and colas trigger hot flashes and can affect the quality of your sleep. Start by avoiding caffeine in the afternoon. Replace these beverages with caffeine-free or decaffeinated beverages like herbal tea, mineral water, fruit and vegetable juice, or decaf coffee. Medications such as Midol, Excedrin and Anacin also provide a fair amount of caffeine. The caffeine content of various beverages, foods and medications can be found in Chapter 5, page 110.

Reduce alcohol intake to no more than one drink a day, preferably none if you're experiencing hot flashes or you're under stress. Drinking alcoholic beverages can bring on a hot flash, interrupt sleep and affect mood. To lessen the effect of alcohol, drink alcohol only with a meal. When alcohol is consumed on an empty stomach, 20 percent is absorbed directly across the walls of your stomach, reaching your brain within a minute. When the stomach is full of food, alcohol is less able to reach the stomach wall and pass through, so its effect on the brain is delayed. When you're socializing, have no more than one drink per hour. Since the liver can't metabolize alcohol any faster than this, drinking slowly will ensure that your blood-alcohol concentration doesn't rise. To slow your pace, alternate one alcoholic drink with a non-alcoholic drink. One drink is equivalent to 5 ounces (145 ml) of wine, 12 ounces (340 ml) of beer, 10 ounces (300 ml) of wine cooler or 1-1/2 ounces (45 ml) of 80-proof (40 percent) distilled spirits.

If you're experiencing hot flashes, avoid spicy foods. Many women complain that certain spices can trigger a hot flash.

Soy Foods and Isoflavones

Diets rich in soy may explain why women living in China and Japan have a 20 percent incidence of hot flashes compared with women in Western countries who have an 85 percent incidence.[3] Well-controlled studies have found that soy foods can modestly ease hot flashes.[4-6] A 12-week Italian study looked at the effects of soy protein and hot flashes in 104 women aged 48 to 61 years. The study found that, compared with the placebo group, the women who consumed 60 grams of soy protein powder reported a 26 percent reduction in the average number of hot flashes by week three and a 33 percent reduction by week four.

Although soy tends to decrease both the frequency and severity of hot flashes, its effects are generally modest or mild. And all the studies found that participating women who received the placebo also experienced some improvement. It's thought that soy isoflavones might be more effective in women who have a higher number of hot flashes.

Soybeans contain naturally occurring compounds called isoflavones, a type of phyto(plant)estrogen. Genistein and daidzein are the most active soy isoflavones and have been the focus of much research. Isoflavones have a similar structure to the hormone estrogen and, as a result, have a weak estrogenic effect in the body. Even though isoflavones in soy are about 50 times less potent than estrogen, they still offer a source of estrogen. When a woman's estrogen levels are low during perimenopause, a regular intake of foods like roasted soy nuts, soy beverages and tofu can help reduce hot flashes.

Experts believe that a daily intake of 40 to 80 milligrams of phytoestrogens is required to help alleviate hot flashes and reduce other health risks.[7] Soy foods vary in the amount of isoflavones they contain, with even the same type of food made by different manufacturers differing in isoflavone content.

Isoflavone Content of Selected Soy Foods

Soy Food	Serving Size	Isoflavone Content (milligrams)
Roasted soy nuts	1/4 cup (60 ml)	40–60 mg
Soy beverage, most brands	1 cup (250 ml)	20–25 mg
Soy beverage, So Nice	1 cup (250 ml)	60 mg
Soy flour	1/4 cup (60 ml)	28 mg
Soy hot dog	1	15 mg
Soy protein isolate powder	1 oz (30 g)	30 mg
Soybeans, cooked or canned	1/2 cup (125 ml)	14 mg
Tempeh, cooked	3 oz (90 g)	48 mg
Texturized vegetable protein, dry	1/2 cup (125 ml)	30–120 mg
Tofu, firm	3 oz (90 g)	22 mg
Tofu, soft	3 oz (90 g)	28 mg

Source: USDA Database for the Isoflavone Content of Selected Foods, Release 2.0, September 2008. Available at: www.ars.usda.gov/SP2UserFiles/Place/12354500/Data/isoflav/Isoflav_R2.pdf.

Carbohydrates

If you're experiencing sleep problems, try eating a small serving of a carbohydrate-rich food—like milk, cereal or a slice of toast—before bedtime. Such foods provide the brain with an amino acid called tryptophan, a building block in the manufacture of serotonin, a brain chemical that has been shown to facilitate sleep, improve mood, diminish pain and even reduce appetite.

This recommendation isn't intended to make you gain weight, so eat something small or drink a glass of low-fat milk or soy beverage. If your insomnia hasn't improved after 1 week, look at other factors that may be disrupting sleep.

If you're feeling depressed or irritable, eat high-carbohydrate meals that contain very little protein. Protein foods such as chicken, meat or fish provide the body with many different amino acids that compete with tryptophan for entry into the brain. Try pasta with tomato sauce, a toasted whole-grain bagel with jam or a bowl of cereal with low-fat milk.

If you're suffering from fuzzy thinking, include carbohydrates in your breakfast. Studies in children and adults have shown that compared with breakfast-skippers, individuals who eat a morning meal score higher on tests of mental performance that same morning.[8–10] The speed of information retrieval (a component of memory) seems to be affected the most by skipping breakfast. Breakfast foods such as whole-grain cereal, fruit, yogurt and whole-grain toast supply brain cells with glucose, their primary energy source. A low blood-glucose level that occurs after a night of fasting needs to be replenished in the morning.

Vitamins and Minerals

Vitamin B12

Many studies have found that vitamin B12 promotes sleep, especially in people with sleep disorders.[11–14] Researchers in Japan have used 1.5 to 3 milligrams of the vitamin each day to restore normal sleep patterns in patients. B12 is thought to restore sleep by working with melatonin, a hormone that's involved in maintaining the body's internal clock. A deficiency of vitamin B12 may cause disturbances in melatonin release.

The recommended dietary intake for vitamin B12 for healthy women is 2.4 micrograms. Vitamin B12 is found in all animal foods: meat, poultry, fish, eggs and dairy products. If you're eating these foods every day, chances are you're meeting your B12 needs. Foods fortified with the vitamin include soy beverages, rice beverages and breakfast cereals (but check labels to be sure).

Strict vegetarians, women who take acid-blocking medication and women over the age of 50 must get B12 from foods fortified with the vitamin or by taking a multivitamin. As we age, we produce less stomach acid, which results in an inability to properly absorb the B12 in foods. Single supplements of vitamin B12 supplements come in 500 or 1000 microgram strengths. See Chapter 4, page 43, for more on vitamin B12.

Choline

Although not an official vitamin, choline is a member of the B vitamin family. It's found in egg yolks, organ meats and legumes, and it's used as a building block for a memory neurotransmitter called acetylcholine. Supplements of choline have been shown to enhance memory and reaction time in animals, particularly aging animals. Researchers believe that choline supplements will improve brain tasks only if you're deficient in the nutrient. Stress and aging can deplete choline levels.

Although it's not known if supplemental choline can improve memory in people who have normal levels of choline, it's important to meet your daily requirements. Healthy women need 425 milligrams of choline each day. The best food sources are egg yolks, liver and other organ meats, brewer's yeast, wheat germ, soybeans, peanuts and green peas.

Supplemental choline is available as lecithin supplements. The maximum safe limit is 3500 milligrams (3.5 grams) of choline a day. High doses of choline can cause low blood pressure and a fishy body odour in some people.

Iron

If you're experiencing heavy menstrual flow, it's extremely important to eat an iron-rich diet. Iron is used by red blood cells to form hemoglobin, the molecule that transports oxygen from your lungs to your cells. If your diet falls short of iron, or if your body loses iron faster than your diet can replace it, red blood cell levels drop and less oxygen is delivered to your tissues. Symptoms of iron deficiency include weakness, lethargy and fatigue on exertion. Iron deficiency is a progressive condition. Even if your iron stores aren't low enough to diagnose anemia, symptoms of iron deficiency can still be felt.

Women who are menstruating require 18 milligrams of iron per day. Post-menopausal women need 8 milligrams. The best iron sources are lean beef, tofu, legumes, enriched breakfast cereals, whole-grain breads, raisins, dried apricots, prune juice, spinach and peas. Iron in food comes in two forms: heme iron in animal foods and nonheme iron in plant foods. Heme iron is the most efficiently absorbed and is found in red meat, chicken, eggs and fish. Nonheme iron is less efficiently absorbed. See Chapter 4, page 70, for tips on how to enhance iron absorption.

A multivitamin and mineral supplement is recommended for women with higher iron requirements. Most formulas provide 10 milligrams, but you can find some that provide up to 18 milligrams. If you're experiencing persistent heavy bleeding, the recommended daily intake might not be enough to meet your needs. Sometimes 100 milligram tablets of supplemental iron are recommended to replenish depleted iron stores. Single iron supplements should be taken only under the supervision of your dietitian or doctor. Take single iron supplements for 3 months and then have your blood retested. Once iron stores are replenished, iron supplements should be discontinued. To prevent constipation associated with high doses of iron, increase your fibre and fluid intake. See Anemia, page 208, for more information about iron supplementation.

Herbal Remedies

Black Cohosh (*Cimicifuga racemosa*) for Hot Flashes

Based on clinical experience and findings from controlled scientific studies, black cohosh is the most promising herbal remedy for treating hot flashes. In studies lasting 6 months to 1 year, black cohosh extracts seemed to modestly reduce symptoms of menopause, such as hot flashes. The most consistent evidence is for a specific commercial extract called Remifemin (Enzymatic Therapy/PhytoPharmica). This extract is standardized to contain 1 milligram triterpene glycosides, calculated as 27-deoxyactein, per 20 milligram tablet. Studies have found that it significantly reduces menopausal symptoms and hot flash frequency compared to placebo. Preliminary evidence suggests that the herbal remedy is comparable to low dose transdermal estradiol (Estraderm) for relieving menopausal symptoms. Research using other formulations of black cohosh is less consistent.[15-17]

Exactly how the herb works is still under scientific debate. It exerts estrogen-like effects, but its active ingredients don't bind to estrogen receptors or influence estrogen levels in the blood. Experiments in animals have demonstrated that black cohosh doesn't stimulate the growth of estrogen-dependent tumours. Instead, the herb—through the naturally occurring triterpene glycosides compounds it contains—may exert its effect by interacting with certain brain receptors.

Buy a product standardized to contain 2.5 percent triterpene glycosides. The typical dose is 40 milligrams taken twice daily. The type of black cohosh used in virtually all the scientific research is sold under the name Remifemin. This product is sold in 20 milligram strength, since a recent study has shown that a lower dose of the herb is equally effective.

Once you start using black cohosh, it may take up to 4 weeks to notice an effect. Mild stomach upset and headache may occur.

Valerian *(Valeriana officinalis)* for Insomnia

Scientists have learned that valerian promotes sleep by weakly binding to two brain receptors, GABA receptors and benzodiazepine receptors. Several small studies conducted among patients with sleep disorders have found valerian reduces the time it takes to fall asleep and improves the quality of sleep. In one double-blind study conducted in Germany, 44 percent of patients taking valerian root reported perfect sleep and 89 percent reported improved sleep compared with those taking the placebo pill. Another small study found that individuals with mild insomnia who took 450 milligrams of

valerian before bedtime experienced a significant decrease in sleep problems. The same researchers studied 128 individuals and found that compared with the placebo, 400 milligrams of valerian produced a significant improvement in sleep quality in people who considered themselves poor sleepers.[18-22]

Unlike commonly prescribed sleeping pills, valerian doesn't lead to dependency or addiction. Nor does it produce a morning drug hangover.

The recommended dose is 400 to 900 milligrams in capsule or tablet form, 2 hours before bedtime for up to 28 days. For tinctures (1:5), take 1 to 3 millilitres (15 to 20 drops) in water several times per day, or try 5 millilitres before bedtime. The herb works best when used over a period of time. Don't take valerian with alcohol or sedative medications.

Nutrition Strategy Checklist for Perimenopause

☐　Avoid alcohol and caffeine
☐　Carbohydrates
☐　Soy foods
☐　Vitamin B12
☐　Choline
☐　Iron
☐　Black cohosh
☐　Valerian

Recommended Resources

National Women's Health Resource Center
www.healthywomen.org
157 Broad Street, Suite 106
Red Bank, NJ, USA 07701
Tel: 1-877-986-9472
Fax: 732-249-4671

The North American Menopause Society
www.menopause.org
P.O. Box 94527
Cleveland, OH, USA 44101
Tel: 440-442-7550
Fax: 440-442-2660
Email: info@menopause.org

Phlebitis

Thrombophlebitis, or phlebitis as it's more commonly known, is an inflammation that develops in a vein, usually accompanied by a blood clot called a thrombus. Phlebitis typically occurs in the veins of the legs, although, rarely, it has also been known to affect the veins in the arms. When the affected vein is close to the surface of the skin, the condition is called *superficial thrombophlebitis*. If the affected vein lies deeper in the body, often within a muscle, the condition is known as *deep vein thrombosis*.

Blot clots that occur in superficial thrombophlebitis don't pose a serious health risk. When phlebitis affects a superficial vein, the inflammatory reaction is sudden and acute, which tends to bind the blood clot firmly to the wall of the vein. Since veins that lie close to the surface of the skin have no surrounding muscles that might squeeze the blood clot and dislodge it, there's little likelihood of a pulmonary embolism (see below). Superficial thrombophlebitis usually resolves by itself in 1 or 2 weeks. The blood clot will be gradually be absorbed by the body, causing no harm.

When a blood clot develops in a deep vein in the leg, however, the condition can be very dangerous as there may not be enough inflammation to make the blood clot adhere to the vein wall. The squeezing action of the calf muscles can dislodge all or part of the blood clot, allowing it to circulate through the bloodstream until it reaches the lungs, where it can block one or more arteries and cause a life-threatening condition called pulmonary embolism.

What Causes Phlebitis?

Phlebitis usually develops because of an irritation or injury to the vein, such as an injection into a vein or a varicose vein that becomes irritated.

Blood clots that form in deeper veins are often the result of poor blood flow or aggregation of cells called platelets that increase the stickiness of the blood. Sluggish blood flow can be caused by:

- extended periods of inactivity, such as sitting during a long car or airplane trip
- long periods of standing in one spot, often job-related
- prolonged bed rest, such as during a lengthy illness or surgical recovery
- restrictive clothing that interferes with circulation
- an inherited blood clotting disorder

Increased stickiness in the blood can be caused by:

- severe infection
- liver disease
- some types of cancer
- recent surgery or childbirth
- estrogen or oral contraceptives

Symptoms

Deep vein thrombosis can be difficult to diagnose because there may be no signs of a problem until the blood clot reaches the lungs. Any symptoms of swelling, pain or warmth in the leg or foot should be considered as possible warning signs of a thrombosis and should receive immediate medical attention. Don't attempt to self-treat phlebitis as it's a potentially fatal disease. Symptoms of deep vein thrombosis include:

- redness, swelling and a feeling of heat in the area of the affected vein
- a vein close to the surface of the skin appearing more noticeable than usual
- a vein that feels hard, like a piece of rope
- pain or discomfort in the area of the affected vein
- discoloration or ulcers on the skin
- swelling in the leg, calf, ankle or foot

Who's at Risk?

The risk of developing phlebitis increases after surgery, childbirth, long periods of illness involving bed rest and long periods of inactivity such as sitting or standing still. People with varicose veins are also more susceptible to phlebitis.

Medical treatments such as injections or insertion of intravenous catheters into a vein may cause irritations that will provoke phlebitis. Medications such as estrogen or oral contraceptives can also increase the likelihood of blood clots. Cigarette smoking, being overweight or obese and having a family history of a blood clotting disorder also increase the risk of phlebitis.

Conventional Treatment

Pain relievers and warm compresses are often used to ease discomfort. Compression bandages or stockings may be recommended to increase blood flow in the veins. More aggressive therapy may be needed for deep vein thrombosis, including:

- anticoagulants (blood-thinning medications) given intravenously or in oral tablets
- restricting activity to prevent the clot from dislodging
- elevating the affected limb
- surgery
- hospitalization

To help prevent blood clots and phlebitis from developing, you should:

- maintain a healthy weight; lose weight, if necessary
- exercise regularly
- limit salt intake
- stop smoking
- when sitting or standing for long periods, take frequent breaks to walk around and get your blood circulating
- avoid wearing tight clothing around your waist during flights or long car rides
- drink plenty of fluids—and avoid alcohol—during long trips to prevent dehydration

Preventing and Managing Phlebitis

Dietary Strategies

Weight Control

A number of studies have identified obesity, especially abdominal obesity, with an increased risk of deep vein thrombosis. Swedish researchers demonstrated that following a healthy diet, getting regular exercise and achieving a healthy weight can improve properties of the blood and reduce the chances that thromboembolism, a blood clot travelling to the lung, will reoccur.[1] Abdominal fat cells are metabolically active and release compounds into the blood that increase inflammation and increase blood clotting.

To determine whether you're at an acceptable weight, turn to Obesity, Overweight and Weight Loss, page 569, to calculate your body mass index (BMI). Having a BMI of between 25 and 29.9 indicates overweight and a BMI of 30 or greater is defined as obese. Measure your waist circumference. Men should strive for a waist size of less than 94 cm (37 inches) and women for less than 80 cm (31.5 inches). Weight loss is best achieved by a combination of reducing calorie intake and increasing physical exercise. See Obesity, Overweight and Weight Loss, page 574, for strategies to help you lose weight safely and permanently.

Fluids and Alcohol

People with phlebitis who travel long distances in an airplane are at increased risk for pulmonary embolism. Scientists speculate that insufficient fluid intake and drinking alcohol can increase the risk of a blood clot dislodging and causing harm.[2] Other risk factors associated with prolonged air travel include low humidity, low oxygen levels, immobilization and the coach or economy-class seat that doesn't allow elevation of the legs.

If you have phlebitis and you travel by air, be sure to drink plenty of water during the flight. Drinking water will keep your circulation efficient and get you out of your seat to use the washroom, allowing you to walk and move your legs.

Research suggests that higher intakes of alcohol are linked with a greater risk of phlebitis.[3] Women should have no more than one drink a day, to a limit of seven per week, and men no more than two drinks per day, to a limit of nine per week. However, it's best to avoid alcoholic beverages altogether, since they cause water to be lost from the body.

Dietary Fibre

Some researchers believe that vein problems in the legs are caused by constipation resulting from a low-fibre diet.[4] Straining to evacuate small, firm stools puts pressure on the abdominal muscles, which can be transmitted to the veins in the leg. To avoid constipation, aim to include 21 to 38 grams of fibre (depending on your age) in your daily diet.

Foods contain varying amounts of insoluble fibres and soluble fibres. Foods that have a greater proportion of insoluble fibres, such as wheat bran, whole grains, nuts, seeds and certain fruit and vegetables, are used to treat and prevent constipation. Once consumed, insoluble fibres make their way to the intestinal tract, where they absorb water, help form larger, softer stools and speed evacuation. Psyllium, a type of soluble fibre, also adds bulk to stools and can be used to treat constipation. See Constipation, page 320, for strategies to increase fibre intake.

Vitamins and Minerals

B Vitamins: Folate, B6 and B12

Elevated blood levels of homocysteine, an amino acid formed during normal metabolism, have been associated with an increased risk of thrombosis.[5] High homocysteine is due to genetic factors as well as a diet lacking folate, B6 and B12. Under normal circumstances, these three B vitamins help break down homocysteine into other harmless amino acids. Some, but not all, studies have shown that taking supplemental folic acid (the synthetic version of food folate), and to a lesser degree B6 and B12, can reduce the risk of deep vein thrombosis, presumably by lowering elevated homocysteine levels.[6]

The best food sources of folate include cooked spinach, lentils, orange juice, asparagus, artichokes and whole-grain breads and cereals. Foods rich in vitamin B6 include meat, poultry, fish, liver, legumes, nuts, seeds, whole grains, green leafy vegetables, bananas and avocados. Vitamin B12 is found in animal foods such as meat, poultry, fish, eggs and dairy products and also in fortified soy and rice beverages.

If you have difficulty eating a varied diet, take a multivitamin and mineral supplement to ensure that you're meeting your B vitamin requirements (see Chapter 4). If a blood test has determined you have elevated homocysteine, a B complex supplement supplying higher doses of folic acid (0.8 milligram) will help lower homocysteine. See Chapter 4, page 35, for more information on B vitamin supplementation.

Herbal Remedies

Horse Chestnut (*Aesculus hippocastanum*)

Many studies have found this herbal remedy to be effective in the treatment of varicose veins and poor circulation in the veins (see Chapter 7, page 147). Although no studies have been conducted in people with phlebitis, this herb is often recommended for the condition.

An active compound in horse chestnut seeds called aesin enhances circulation through the veins. The herb appears to constrict and promote normal tone in the veins so that blood returns to the heart. The compound also has anti-inflammatory properties and may reduce swelling in the legs.

Buy a product standardized to contain 16 percent to 21 percent aescin. Studies have used a 300 milligram horse chestnut seed extract, containing 50 milligrams of aescin, taken twice daily. The safety of horse chestnut during pregnancy and breastfeeding hasn't been established; avoid using the herb at these times. Don't take horse chestnut if you have liver or kidney disease.

Other Natural Health Products

Bromelain

This natural product is a collection of enzymes extracted from the juice and stems of pineapple. Once bromelain is absorbed into the bloodstream, it causes the release of kinin, a substance with anti-inflammatory and blood-thinning properties. Based on its action in the body, bromelain is often recommended for vein problems, including phlebitis.[7,8]

The typical dose of bromelain is 80 to 320 milligrams taken two to three times per day. However, dosage will vary with the form used, so follow the manufacturer's directions. Bromelain may cause diarrhea in some individuals and an allergic reaction in people allergic to pineapple and/or wheat.

Bromelain may increase the risk of bleeding if you take blood-thinning medications and herbs such as aspirin, warfarin (Coumadin), heparin, garlic, ginger, *Ginkgo biloba*, horse chestnut and red clover. Taking zinc supplements concurrently with bromelain can inhibit the enzyme's action.

Nutrition Strategy Checklist for Phlebitis

☐   Weight control

☐   Fluids

☐ Avoid alcohol
☐ Dietary fibre
☐ B vitamins
☐ Horse chestnut
☐ Bromelain

Recommended Resources

Mayo Foundation for Medical Education and Research
www.mayoclinic.com
This website is produced by a team of writers, editors, health educators, nurses, doctors and scientists, and is one of the best patient-education sites on the Internet. The information is reliable, thorough and clearly written.

Polycystic Ovary Syndrome (PCOS)

Sometimes referred to as Stein-Leventhal syndrome, polycystic ovary syndrome (PCOS) is a hormone condition that causes women to have many different symptoms, including irregular menstrual periods, acne and weight problems. The disorder affects 5 percent to 10 percent of all women of reproductive age, and many don't even know they have it.[1] For reasons not fully understood, resistance to the blood sugar–clearing hormone insulin is thought to play a major role in PCOS. Insulin resistance predisposes affected women to increased risk for type 2 diabetes, endometrial and breast cancer, and heart disease.

What Causes Polycystic Ovary Syndrome?

Hormones are produced and regulated by an interrelated series of glands called the endocrine system. Two tiny glands located in the brain, the hypothalamus and the pituitary gland, monitor and balance the normal activity of the endocrine system. The pituitary gland helps control the cycles of the female reproductive system: It secretes luteinizing hormone (LH), which stimulates the ovaries to release mature eggs and to produce the female sex hormones estrogen and progesterone. LH is also necessary for the production of androgens, male sex hormones that are present in small quantities in every woman.

PCOS is thought to develop when the pituitary gland malfunctions and secretes an overabundance of LH, triggering an increase in the production of androgens, which results in a corresponding increase in estrogen levels. PCOS causes the production of these three hormones to remain at high levels, disrupting the natural hormonal balance of the menstrual cycle. Excess production of male hormones may interfere with insulin production.

PCOS usually develops during puberty at the time when menstruation would normally begin. The elevated level of LH in the bloodstream interferes with the normal functioning of the ovaries. The excess hormones prevent eggs from maturing properly, which often results in the failure to ovulate, called anovulation. Failure to release an egg will prevent or delay the onset of menstruation in young girls and may cause mature women to experience irregular periods or skipped periods. PCOS can also cause heavy vaginal bleeding that can lead to iron-deficiency anemia.

The hormonal imbalance seen in women with PCOS also causes cysts (fluid-filled sacs) to accumulate in the ovaries. These cysts are eggs that matured, but were never released because of abnormal hormone levels. Polycystic (meaning "many cysts") ovaries are covered with a tough, thick outer layer and may grow as much as two to five times larger than normal. These cysts interfere with the activity of the ovaries and contribute to the infertility problems associated with PCOS.

Symptoms and Associated Medical Conditions

PCOS progresses fairly slowly, but, unfortunately, the symptoms tend to worsen over time. Although the syndrome affects each woman a little differently, the primary symptoms include:

- abnormal, irregular or absent periods
- infertility
- mood swings
- weight gain or obesity
- elevated blood glucose—30 percent to 40 percent of women with PCOS have high blood-sugar levels
- high blood pressure
- high blood cholesterol
- increased hair growth (hirsutism)
- male-pattern baldness
- acne
- oily skin
- heavy, persistent vaginal bleeding
- iron-deficiency anemia

With the exception of irregular or no menstrual periods, any of the above symptoms can be absent in PCOS. In addition to infertility, women with PCOS face other reproductive concerns. Approximately one-third of all pregnancies in women with PCOS end in miscarriage. There's also an increased risk of pregnancy disorders such as preeclampsia, gestational diabetes, premature labour and stillbirth.

PCOS also disrupts normal physical development by stimulating the production of higher levels of androgens, the male hormones. This causes some women to acquire secondary male characteristics such as frontal balding, deepening of the voice and increased muscle mass. One of the most common symptoms in women with PCOS is hirsutism, a condition that causes body and facial hair to follow a male growth pattern. Women with hirsutism grow excessive amounts of coarse hair on their face, legs, chest and groin.

Obesity affects nearly 50 percent of all women with PCOS and contributes to the already high levels of estrogen associated with this disorder. Androgens are converted to estrogen in body fat, and the greater the amount of body fat a woman has, the higher the level of estrogen. Excess estrogen in the bloodstream can trigger severe acne and is associated with increased risk of endometrial, ovarian and breast cancer.

Women with PCOS have a higher risk of developing insulin resistance, a condition that's further aggravated by obesity. Insulin is a hormone secreted by the pancreas. By attaching to special receptors on body cells, insulin enables cells to take in and store glucose and protein. Insulin resistance is caused by defective insulin receptors so that insulin can't attach properly to these sites. As a result, insulin isn't able to do its job properly and sugar (glucose) is unable to enter the cells where it's needed for energy. Insulin resistance causes a high level of insulin to remain in the bloodstream, causing hyperinsulinemia. These high insulin levels can lead to diabetes and heart disease. High blood insulin can also cause weight gain.

Most women with PCOS have some degree of insulin resistance and many go on to develop type 2 diabetes. It's estimated that by the age of 40, as many as 40 percent of women with PCOS will have type 2 diabetes or impaired glucose tolerance.[2] Treatment directed at reducing insulin resistance can restore ovulation, decrease the levels of male hormones, lower blood fats and elevated blood pressure, and promote weight loss.

Who's at Risk?

Women can develop PCOS as early as their preteens, or the condition may appear at any time throughout their childbearing years. Most women, however, begin to experience symptoms at menarche, the onset of menstruation. PCOS becomes less common as women get older and rarely develops after menopause. But the health consequences of the disorder, such as type 2 diabetes resulting from insulin resistance, persist into the menopausal years.

Although there isn't enough evidence to prove a genetic link to the disease, many women with PCOS have a mother or a sister with similar symptoms.

Conventional Treatment

Since PCOS has no cure, treatment is usually directed at managing the primary symptoms, especially hirsutism, menstrual irregularities and infertility. The choice of treatment will depend on the type and severity of symptoms, a woman's stage of life and her plans regarding pregnancy.

For women not planning to become pregnant, oral contraceptives can control menstrual irregularities. Birth control pills inhibit the production and activity of androgens and therefore help reduce acne, lower the risk of ovarian and endometrial cancer, and slow hair growth for women with hirsutism. Oral contraceptives aren't recommended for menopausal women or for women with risk factors for certain heart or blood diseases.

Antiandrogen drugs (e.g., spironolactone, Diane 35) are also effective in reducing growth of unwanted hair. To further minimize the effects of hirsutism, many women remove excessive hair by shaving, waxing or using depilatories or electrolysis.

For women planning to have children, the treatment of choice is usually the fertility drug clomiphene citrate (Clomid). Clomiphene stimulates the ovaries to release eggs. Studies indicate that 80 percent of women with PCOS ovulate in response to clomiphene, but only 50 percent of these women become pregnant.[3] If clomiphene doesn't work well for you, your physician may try to induce ovulation with a variety of hormone supplements, including follicle-stimulating hormone (FSH) and gonadotropin-releasing hormone (GnRH) drugs such as leuprolide (Lupron) and nafarelin (Synarel).

To lower health risks such as diabetes and heart disease, your doctor may prescribe an insulin-sensitizing drug—such as metformin (Glucophage)—to decrease insulin resistance and delay or prevent the development of type 2 diabetes. These medications also reduce androgen production and restore normal menstrual cycles.

In addition, weight loss can normalize menstrual periods and often increases the likelihood of pregnancy in women with PCOS.

Managing Polycystic Ovary Syndrome

Dietary Strategies

Weight Control

Obesity and overweight, especially abdominal obesity, is present in over half of women with PCOS and has a marked impact on the progression of the syndrome. Excess abdominal fat worsens the symptoms of PCOS by increasing insulin resistance and further elevating levels of male hormones. As a result, weight loss is central to the treatment strategies for PCOS. Research has demonstrated that losing weight if you're obese enhances the body's sensitivity to insulin, normalizes hormone levels and restores menstrual regularity.[4-10] Studies have shown that losing more than 5 percent of body weight can restore fertility in obese women with PCOS.[11,12]

To determine if you're at a healthy weight, see Obesity, Overweight and Weight Loss, page 569, to calculate your body mass index (BMI) and waist circumference. Having a BMI of between 25 and 29.9 indicates overweight and a BMI of 30 or greater is defined as obese. Having a waist circumference greater than 80 cm (31.5 inches) is associated with health risks. Use the strategies outlined in Obesity, Overweight and Weight Loss, page 574, to promote safe, gradual weight loss.

Carbohydrates: Low Glycemic Index

Unfortunately, insulin resistance makes weight loss more difficult to achieve. To help improve insulin resistance and lower blood insulin levels, it's important to eat smaller portions of carbohydrate-rich foods *and* to choose the right types of carbohydrate foods. When you eat a carbohydrate-rich food, whether it's bread, pasta, yogurt, an apple or fruit juice, the carbohydrate is broken down into glucose and absorbed into your bloodstream. Blood sugar (glucose) rises, signalling the pancreas to release insulin into the bloodstream. Insulin then clears sugar from your blood, taking it into your cells, where it's used for energy. If you have insulin resistance, insulin can't perform this task properly and some sugar remains in the blood, causing more insulin to be released. This results in a chronically high insulin level that, over time, increases the risk of type 2 diabetes and heart disease.

Carbohydrate foods are digested and absorbed at different rates. Some foods are digested slowly and result in a steady, slow rise in blood sugar, which means that less insulin is secreted into the blood. Slow carbohydrates have what's called a low glycemic-index (GI) value. Foods with a high glycemic-index value are digested and absorbed more quickly, causing much higher insulin levels.

To prevent an excessive surge of insulin after eating, meals and snacks should emphasize foods with a low GI value. Foods such as whole-grain pumpernickel bread, steel-cut oats, 100% bran cereal, legumes, yogurt and soy milk all have a low GI value. See Chapter 1, page 8, for a list of foods ranked by their glycemic-index value.

Studies have also demonstrated that a calorie-reduced diet that's moderate, not high, in carbohydrates is effective in promoting weight loss in women with PCOS. Studies have assigned participants to weight-loss diets with 40 percent of calories derived from low GI carbohydrates.[13-15] A registered dietitian (www.dietitians.ca) can help design a lower-carbohydrate weight-loss plan for you.

Vitamins and Minerals

Calcium and Vitamin D

Gonadotropin-releasing hormone (GnRH) drugs such as leuprolide (Lupron) and nafarelin (Synarel) improve PCOS symptoms by causing a deficiency of estrogen, a hormone that also prevents bones from losing calcium. As a result, GnRH drugs cause accelerated bone loss, which may be partially irreversible.

A 6-month Italian study of forty-four women with PCOS showed that those women receiving a GnRH medication experienced a significant decrease in bone density.[16] Women given the drug in combination with the antiandrogen drug spironolactone didn't show any change in bone density. Spironolactone offers a bone-sparing effect in this situation. Your doctor may prescribe another medication along with a GnRH drug to offset the bone loss. The jury is still out on whether some of these drug combinations (called add-back regimens) actually prevent bone loss.

To help minimize bone loss if you're taking a GnRH drug, it's very important to meet your recommended daily intakes for calcium and vitamin D, two nutrients critical for bone health.

CALCIUM. The recommended dietary allowance (RDA) is 1000 to 1300 milligrams, depending on your age. The best food sources are milk, yogurt, cheese, fortified soy and rice beverages, fortified orange juice, tofu, salmon (with bones), kale, bok choy, broccoli and Swiss chard. If your diet falls short of calcium, make up the difference by taking a calcium supplement once or twice daily. See Chapter 4, page 58, for more information about calcium supplements.

VITAMIN D. The recommended daily intake is 1000 international units (IU) for adults and 400 IU for children and teenagers. Best food sources are fluid milk, fortified soy and rice beverages, oily fish, egg yolks, butter and margarine. However, it's not possible for adults to consume 1000 IU each day from foods alone. For this reason, it's necessary to take a vitamin D supplement in the fall and winter, and year-round if you are over the age of 50, have dark-coloured skin or don't expose your skin to sunshine in the summer months. See Chapter 4, page 51, to learn about vitamin D supplements.

Chromium

The body uses this mineral to make glucose tolerance factor (GTF), a compound thought to help maintain normal blood-sugar levels by increasing insulin receptor sensitivity. A deficiency of chromium causes impaired glucose tolerance, increased cholesterol and triglyceride levels, and decreased HDL (good) cholesterol levels. Research suggests that when taken as a supplement, chromium can help reduce high blood cholesterol and triglycerides and stabilize blood-sugar levels. A handful of studies have demonstrated that chromium supplementation reduces blood glucose and improves glucose tolerance in women with PCOS. However, taking chromium didn't improve hormone levels or the frequency of ovulation.[17,18]

The recommended dietary intake for women is 25 micrograms of chromium per day. Good food sources include apples with the skin, green peas, chicken breast, refried beans, mushrooms, oysters, wheat germ and brewer's yeast. Processed foods, refined foods with a high glycemic-index value such as white bread, white rice, white potatoes, refined breakfast cereals and cereal bars, sugar and sweets contain very little chromium.

If you're concerned that you're not getting enough chromium in your diet, check your multivitamin and mineral to see how much it contains. Most brands supply 25 to 50 micrograms. If you choose to take a separate chromium supplement, take 200 micrograms per day. Supplements made from chromium picolinate and chromium nicotinate are thought to be absorbed more efficiently than those made from chromium chloride. Don't exceed 400 micrograms per day.

Other Natural Health Products

Inositol

Although not an official vitamin, this natural compound is closely related to the B vitamin family. Inositol is found in foods mainly as phytic acid, a fibrous compound. Good sources include citrus fruit, whole grains, legumes, nuts and seeds. When you eat these foods, intestinal bacteria liberate inositol from phytic acid.

Once in the body, inositol is an essential component of cell membranes. It promotes the export of fat from cells in the liver and intestine. Supplements of inositol are thought to improve insulin sensitivity and have been used to treat symptoms of PCOS. In one study of forty-four obese women, 1200 milligrams of inositol taken once daily for 6 to 8 weeks decreased blood triglycerides and testosterone levels, reduced blood pressure and caused ovulation.[19] Previous studies suggest that people with insulin resistance and type 2 diabetes might be deficient in inositol.

The recommended dose for PCOS is 1200 milligrams per day. When choosing a supplement, look for D-chiro-inositol. No adverse effects of inositol have been reported. Inositol supplements may be difficult to find, since few companies manufacture them (see Chapter 8, page 170).

Nutrition Strategy Checklist for PCOS

☐   Weight control

☐   Low-GI carbohydrate-rich foods

☐   Calcium

☐   Vitamin D

☐   Chromium

☐   Inositol

Recommended Resources

The Hormone Foundation
www.hormone.org
8401 Connecticut Avenue, Suite 900
Chevy Chase, MD, USA 20815-5817
Tel: 1-800-HORMONE
Fax: 1-301-941-0259
Email: hormone@endo-society.org

Polycystic Ovarian Syndrome Association
www.pcosupport.org
P.O. Box 3403
Englewood, CO, USA 80111
Email: info@pcosupport.org

Premenstrual Syndrome (PMS)

Premenstrual syndrome (PMS) is a collection of emotional, psychological and physical symptoms that develop during the 7 to 14 days before the start of your menstrual period and that typically resolve with the onset of menstrual flow.

For some women, the physical and emotional changes caused by PMS are so severe that they interfere with the ability to function at work or interact with family and friends. When PMS symptoms seriously undermine quality of life, the condition is called *premenstrual dysphoric disorder* (PMDD)—a complex medical disorder that affects only a small percentage of women. It's thought to be an excessive reaction to the normal hormonal changes associated with the menstrual cycle.

Your Monthly Cycle

The symptoms of PMS appear during the last 2 weeks of the menstrual cycle, referred to as the luteal phase of your cycle. There are three distinct phases in each menstrual cycle: the follicular phase, ovulation and the luteal phase. Two areas of the brain, the hypothalamus and the pituitary gland, control all the hormonal changes that regulate each of these distinct stages.

The menstrual cycle begins when the hypothalamus produces gonadotropin-releasing hormones (GnRH). These hormones pass into the pituitary gland and trigger the release of luteinizing hormone (LH) and follicle-stimulating hormone (FSH). Working in combination, these two hormones promote the growth of follicles, tiny sac-like structures located in the ovaries. Each follicle surrounds an ovum, or egg. Between ten to twenty follicles will enlarge, but normally only one egg is released during each menstrual cycle. Throughout this time of growth, the follicles produce most of the female sex hormone estrogen, which circulates in your body. This is the follicular phase of your cycle, and it lasts from the first day of your period until you ovulate.

Ovulation occurs in the middle of the menstrual cycle, near day 14, when hormone surges trigger one follicle to burst and release its egg. Over the next 36 hours, the egg will travel through one of your fallopian tubes to reach the uterus.

After ovulation, your body enters the luteal phase: The outer wall of the burst follicle remains in the ovary, transforming into a mass of tissue called the corpus luteum. This tissue begins to secrete another female sex hormone, progesterone, which prepares the uterus for pregnancy. If the egg isn't fertilized and pregnancy doesn't occur, the levels of estrogen and progesterone immediately begin to drop. The lining of the uterus and the unfertilized egg are no longer needed and are eliminated from the body through menstruation. This completes the menstrual cycle and the entire process starts all over again.

What Causes PMS?

Researchers don't know exactly what triggers PMS. One of the most popular theories suggests that PMS is caused by an imbalance in the levels of estrogen and progesterone. Symptoms may develop because you have too much estrogen and not enough progesterone in your system during the last 2 weeks of the menstrual cycle. Estrogen affects the kidneys and causes sodium and water retention. Alterations in estrogen and progesterone can also affect the levels of natural brain chemicals called neurotransmitters. It's thought that deficiencies in serotonin and dopamine, two neurotransmitters that affect mood and emotion, may be responsible for the mood swings typical of PMS.

Excessive levels of a hormone called prolactin may be responsible for breast tenderness and swelling. Prolactin is responsible for stimulating the breast changes and milk production necessary for breastfeeding.

Nutrient deficiencies may account for certain symptoms of PMS. For instance, breast tenderness may also be caused by a lack of essential fats in the diet, which play an important role in regulating pain and inflammation. A deficiency of calcium may cause agitation, irritability and depression. In addition, low calcium levels may stimulate an overproduction of parathyroid hormones, which are believed to influence mood and mental function by interacting with the brain chemical serotonin. Dietary deficiencies of vitamin B6, magnesium and zinc or excessive consumption of caffeine, salt, alcohol and red meat may also trigger PMS.

Symptoms

There are more than 150 documented PMS symptoms, with the most common being depression. Although many can be related to some other condition, the hallmark of PMS is a symptom-free interval from the start of menstruation until ovulation. PMS symptoms tend to fall into two main categories:

1. **Physical symptoms** include breast tenderness and swelling, bloating, fluid retention, weight gain, headaches, food cravings (especially for sweet or salty foods), acne, muscle pain, backaches, fatigue, dizziness, sleep disturbances, constipation or diarrhea. Many women gain an average of 2 to 4 pounds (1 to 2 kg) during the premenstrual week because of fluid retention. Heavier women may gain as much as 8 pounds (3.5 kg).
2. **Emotional or psychological symptoms** include mood swings, depression, irritability,

aggressiveness or hostility, anxiety, crying spells, changes in sex drive, difficulty concentrating and feelings of low self-esteem.

PMS symptoms vary from woman to woman, and they can also be different from one menstrual cycle to the next. PMS symptoms tend to get worse as your menstrual cycle progresses and are then relieved when your period begins.

Who's at Risk?

As many as 80 percent of all North American women experience one or more of the symptoms associated with PMS. Research indicates that 20 percent to 30 percent of women have moderate to severe PMS that interferes with daily functioning. It's estimated that 2 percent to 6 percent of women have PMDD.[1]

PMS can begin any time after puberty. Research suggests that you're more susceptible if you're under a lot of stress, you're younger than 34 years or you drink alcohol.[2] Although heredity may also play a role, PMS symptoms aren't consistent in families and vary considerably among female relatives.

Conventional Treatment

Most treatment approaches are directed at relieving symptoms and improving quality of life. Before you embark on a medication to treat a symptom, try implementing the nutritional approaches suggested below for three consecutive menstrual cycles. If dietary and/or other lifestyle changes don't improve your PMS within 3 months, you may want to talk to your doctor about medications to reduce your symptoms.

Keep in mind that the drugs below can help alleviate symptoms, but some of them have side effects that may cause problems of their own:

- **Diuretics.** The drugs eliminate excess fluid from your body through increased urine production; they're often used to treat premenstrual swelling of hands, feet and face.
- **Analgesics (painkillers).** The most effective of these for headaches, menstrual cramps and pelvic pain are non-steroidal anti-inflammatory medications (NSAIDs) such as ibuprofen (Advil, Motrin) and naproxen (Anaprox).
- **Antidepressants.** Used to treat depression and mood disorders associated with PMS, these drugs increase the level of natural brain chemicals that are affected by the female sex hormones. Selective serotonin reuptake inhibitors (SSRIs) such as fluoxetine (Prozac) and paroxetine (Paxil) are the most effective in reducing the psychological symptoms of PMS.
- **Oral contraceptives.** These are often prescribed to balance hormonal fluctuations. Some women find that birth control pills worsen their symptoms.
- **Ovarian suppressors.** Drugs such as danazol (Danocrine), a synthetic hormone related to the male sex hormone testosterone, may be used to stop the menstrual cycle. Side effects of ovarian suppressors include the development of menopausal symptoms, such as vaginal dryness and hot flashes.

Managing PMS
Dietary Strategies
Meal Timing
Plan to eat three meals and one or two midday snacks. Levels of neurotransmitters in the brain are susceptible to fluctuations in the levels of nutrients in your bloodstream, so any drastic change in normal eating patterns—such as crash dieting, bingeing, or meal or snack skipping—can alter neurotransmitter levels and mood. The hormonal fluctuations of PMS also make you more susceptible to having a low blood-sugar level, which can cause low energy, increased appetite and hunger, irritability and headache.

Carbohydrates
Studies have found that high-carbohydrate meals produce a calming, relaxing effect by influencing the level of serotonin in the brain. Researchers have linked high serotonin levels with happier moods and low levels with mild depression and irritability in women with PMS. One study found that meals high in carbohydrates improved mood in young women within 30 minutes of consumption.[3] Another study found that when women with PMS took a high-carbohydrate drink, their mood improved within 90 minutes.[4]

Carbohydrate-rich foods like whole-grain bread, cereal, rice and pasta contain an amino acid called tryptophan. Eating these foods allows tryptophan, an amino acid that normally competes for entry into the brain with other amino acids found in protein-rich foods, to get into the brain, where it's used to make the neurotransmitter serotonin.

If your mood is affected by PMS, eat high-carbohydrate meals that contain very little protein. High-protein foods like chicken, meat or fish supply the body with other amino acids that compete with tryptophan for entry into the brain. Try pasta with tomato sauce, a toasted whole-grain bagel with jam or a bowl of cereal with low-fat milk.

A liquid dietary supplement called PMS Escape (Enzymatic Therapy), available in the

United States, has been clinically proven to reduce mood swings, irritability and carbohydrate cravings and to increase energy levels. It's thought that it reduces PMS symptoms by increasing the concentration of serotonin in the brain. PMS Escape is a flavoured, powdered drink mix made from a blend of carbohydrates, vitamins and minerals.

You might also consider trying sports carbohydrate-replacement drinks. These are sold at health food stores and sporting good stores as powder mixes or ready to drink and come in a variety of flavours.

Carbohydrates: Low Glycemic Index

Nutritionists classify carbohydrate foods according to their glycemic index (GI) value, or how quickly they cause a rise in blood sugar. Foods with a low GI value raise blood-sugar levels more slowly than do foods with a high GI value. When you eat a food that raises your blood sugar quickly, you'll get a burst of energy—but this spike in sugar also causes your pancreas to release a large amount of insulin into the bloodstream. Since insulin's job is to lower your blood sugar, your quick energy boost will be followed by a crash. That can lead to increased hunger and carbohydrate cravings.

Foods with a low GI value take longer to digest and lead to a gradual, slow rise in blood glucose. You don't get that insulin surge, so the energy from that food lasts longer. The glycemic-index value of a food depends on cooking time, fibre content, fat content and ripeness.

To help reduce hunger and food cravings, emphasize low glycemic-index carbohydrates in your meals and snacks. See Chapter 1, page 8, for a list of low GI foods.

Dietary Fat

A few studies have found that when women with PMS are put on a low-fat diet, they suffer fewer and less-intense PMS symptoms.[5-7] Diets consisting of 15 percent to 20 percent calories from fat are associated with less water retention, less weight gain and fewer menstrual cramps. A low-fat diet may affect PMS symptoms by influencing the levels of hormones in the body, especially estrogen.

To reduce your intake of dietary fat, in particular saturated fat, choose lower-fat animal foods such as lean meat and poultry breast, and milk and yogurt with 1% or less milk fat. Avoid or limit your intake of processed meats such as bacon, sausage, hot dogs and salami. Use added fats and oils sparingly. See Chapter 3, page 24, for foods lower in saturated fat. Include oily fish such as salmon, trout and sardines in your diet twice per week to increase your intake of omega-3 fat, a type of fat that may help ease feelings of depression.

Alcohol and Caffeine

You read earlier that women who drink alcohol are at greater risk for PMS. Alcoholic beverages can trigger or worsen many PMS symptoms, including fatigue, irritability, depression, bowel function, appetite and fluid retention. Alcohol has a dehydrating effect on the body, which can leave you feeling sluggish. Alcohol can also cause fatigue by interfering with the body's ability to sleep soundly. If you suffer with PMS, avoid alcohol completely during the 7 to 14 days before your menstrual period. During the rest of the month, you should consume no more than seven drinks per week (maximum one a day).

Caffeine can also worsen irritability, anxiety, headaches, diarrhea, fatigue and breast tenderness. Drinking too much coffee during the day can overstimulate the body, causing irritability, nervousness, anxiety, insomnia and fatigue. As little as two small cups of coffee in the morning can affect your sleep that same night by blocking the brain's production of a natural sleep-inducing chemical called adenosine.

If your PMS symptoms include irritability, anxiousness or general fatigue, consume no more than 200 milligrams of caffeine daily, and preferably none. Switch to low-caffeine beverages like tea or hot chocolate or caffeine-free alternatives such as decaf coffee, herbal tea, cereal coffee, juice, milk or water. The caffeine content of beverages and foods is outlined in Chapter 5, page 110.

Vitamins and Minerals

Vitamin B6

In 1999, British researchers analyzed the results from nine clinical trials involving 940 women with PMS.[8] They concluded that B6 supplementation was significantly better than the placebo treatment in relieving PMS symptoms, especially depression. A study from the University of Reading in Great Britain that was published after the 1999 review found that 50 milligrams of B6 combined with 200 milligrams of magnesium had a significant but modest effect on reducing anxiety-related PMS symptoms, including nervous tension, mood swings, irritability and anxiety.[9] More recently, a study of sixty females suffering from PMS found that 100 milligrams of B6 taken daily for 3 months led to a significant reduction in overall PMS symptoms, including breast tenderness and depression.[10]

The body needs B6 for the production of two brain chemicals that have a potent effect on mood, serotonin and dopamine. Dopamine

also regulates the secretion of prolactin, a hormone that may be linked to PMS.

To use B6 for PMS, take 50 to 100 milligrams per day. Daily doses over 100 milligrams don't appear to have additional benefit and may increase the risk of adverse effects. Supplementing with too much B6 for a period of time has toxic effects, including irreversible nerve damage. The safe upper daily limit is 100 milligrams.

Vitamin E

Three randomized clinical trials revealed that vitamin E supplements improved PMS-related depression, anxiety, headache, food cravings and insomnia.[11-13] In one study, women with PMS were given either 150 international units (IU), 300 IU or 600 IU of vitamin E. All doses were more effective at relieving symptoms than the placebo pill. How vitamin E works to help ease PMS isn't understood.

The richest sources of vitamin E are vegetable oils, nuts, seeds and wheat germ. Leafy green vegetables (especially kale) are also good sources. But when you consider that 2 tablespoons (30 ml) of grapeseed oil—a cooking oil rich in vitamin E—provides only 11.5 IU, you can see why you must rely on a supplement to increase intake to an effective dose. To supplement, take 200 to 400 IU of vitamin E per day. The upper daily limit is 1500 IU. If you have diabetes or heart disease, don't take high dose vitamin E supplements. See Chapter 4, page 52, for information on the safety of vitamin E.

Calcium and Vitamin D

Research has determined that blood-calcium and blood–vitamin D levels are lower in women with PMS and that calcium supplementation can reduce the severity of PMS symptoms. A well-designed study of 466 women found that those who took 1200 milligrams of supplemental calcium daily for 3 months had a significant reduction in PMS symptoms, especially mood swings, low back pain, food cravings and fluid retention. The majority of women experienced a 50 percent reduction in overall symptoms (compared with a 36 percent improvement among women who took the placebo pill). The strongest improvement was observed during the third menstrual cycle, which implies that the effect of calcium supplements increases with continued use.[14]

Meeting your daily calcium and vitamin D requirements might also reduce the risk of developing PMS in the first place. In a large study of women aged 27 to 44 years who were followed for 10 years, compared to those who consumed the least calcium each day (529 milligrams), women with the highest intake from foods (1283 milligrams) were 30 percent less likely to develop PMS. A high vitamin D intake lowered the risk of PMS by 40 percent.[15]

It's thought that the increasing estrogen levels that occur during the week before the menstrual period cause a decline in circulating levels of calcium and vitamin D, which triggers PMS symptoms. (Interestingly, the symptoms of PMS and hypocalcemia—low calcium in the blood—are strikingly similar.)

CALCIUM. The recommended dietary allowance (RDA) for calcium is 1000 to 1500 milligrams, depending on your age. The best food sources include milk, yogurt, cheese, fortified soy and rice beverages, fortified orange juice, tofu, salmon (with bones), kale, bok choy, broccoli and Swiss chard. If your diet lacks calcium, as is the case for many Canadians, take a calcium supplement to ensure that you're meeting your daily require-

ment. See Chapter 4, page 58, for more information on calcium requirements, calcium-rich foods and calcium supplements.

VITAMIN D. The recommended daily intake is 1000 international units (IU) for adults. Best food sources are fluid milk, fortified soy and rice beverages, oily fish, egg yolks, butter and margarine. However, it's not possible for adults to consume 1000 IU each day from foods alone. For this reason, it's necessary to take a vitamin D supplement in the fall and winter, and year-round if you are over the age of 50, have dark-coloured skin or don't expose your skin to sunshine in the summer months. See Chapter 4, page 51, to learn about vitamin D supplements.

Magnesium

Several studies have reported lower levels of magnesium in women with PMS.[16,17] Research has also determined that increasing your intake of this mineral can improve symptoms of depression, anxiety, fluid retention and breast tenderness. In one study, women who took 250 milligrams of magnesium each day reduced overall PMS symptoms by 35 percent after 3 months.[18-20]

Magnesium is found in all body cells and fluids, where it's needed to maintain fluid balance by pumping sodium and potassium in and out of cells. It's also used by over three hundred enzymes, including those that produce energy and reduce pain. Vitamin D is needed for magnesium absorption, so it's possible that women deficient in vitamin D will also have low levels of magnesium.

The best sources of magnesium are whole foods, including unrefined grains, nuts, seeds, legumes, dried fruit and green vegetables. Studies have determined a daily dose of 200 to

360 milligrams of supplemental magnesium to be effective in easing PMS symptoms. If you take calcium supplements, buy one with magnesium added. A 2:1 calcium citrate supplement will generally give you 300 milligrams of calcium and 150 milligrams of magnesium. Depending on your diet, you might need to take one of these supplements two or three times a day.

If you don't need supplemental calcium, buy a supplement made from magnesium citrate; the body absorbs this form of the mineral more efficiently. The safe upper limit for magnesium is 350 milligrams per day from a supplement— more than this can cause diarrhea, nausea and stomach cramps.

Sodium

High levels of estrogen associated with PMS can cause the kidneys to retain water and sodium. Eliminating table salt and foods high in sodium the week before your period can help prevent swollen hands and feet. Although this is especially important after ovulation, it's prudent to reduce your sodium intake every day of the month. Most women in Canada consume excessive amounts of sodium—which can increase the risk of high blood pressure and osteoporosis.

To help cut back on sodium, read nutrition labels and choose commercial food products that have lower sodium contents. Eating fewer processed foods and restaurant meals is one of the key strategies to desalting your diet. Most of the salt we consume every day comes from processed and prepared foods—only one-fourth comes from the saltshaker. To further reduce your sodium intake, avoid the saltshaker at the table and minimize the use of salt when you cook. Women need only 1500 milligrams of sodium each day for health. Aim for less than

2300 milligrams of sodium each day (that's 1 teaspoon/5 ml worth of table salt). Season your foods with herbs, spices, flavoured vinegars and fruit juices. You'll find strategies to reduce your sodium intake in Chapter 5, page 108.

Herbal Remedies

Chasteberry (Vitex agnus-castus)

For more than 40 years European physicians have been prescribing this herbal remedy to regulate the menstrual cycle and ease PMS symptoms. Taking chasteberry seems to decrease some symptoms of PMS, especially breast pain or tenderness (mastalgia), edema, constipation, irritability, depressed mood or mood alterations, anger and headache in some women.[21-25]

Chasteberry also appears to be effective in treating premenstrual dysphoric disorder (PMDD). In an 8-week study, the herb was comparable to the drug fluoxetine at relieving overall symptoms. However, chasteberry seemed somewhat more effective for physical symptoms such as breast tenderness, swelling, cramps and food cravings, while the medication seemed somewhat more effective for psychological symptoms such as depression, irritability, insomnia, nervous tension and feeling out of control.[26]

Choose a product standardized to contain 6 percent agnuside since this is what has been used in most of the clinical trials. The recommended dose varies and will depend on the formulation of chasteberry. Extracts are typically used in doses of 20 to 240 mg per day. Keep in mind that it takes at least 4 weeks for the herb to start working and several months for it to reach its full effect. Mild side effects may include nausea, headache and skin rash. See Chapter 7, page 128, for more information on chasteberry.

Evening Primrose Oil (*Oenothera biennis*)

Supplements of evening primrose oil are a rich source of gamma-linolenic acid (GLA). GLA is a fatty acid the body uses to make special compounds called prostaglandins that decrease inflammation and pain. Researchers studying women with PMS have focused on a beneficial prostaglandin called PGE_1.

GLA is formed in the body from linoleic acid, an essential fatty acid found in vegetable oils, nuts and seeds. Some experts believe that women with PMS have a reduced ability to make PGE_1 from linoleic acid in the diet and that this can cause symptoms such as breast pain and tenderness, irritability, depression and headache. Many dietary factors, such as animal fat, alcohol and hydrogenated vegetable oils, can also interfere with the conversion of linoleic acid to GLA. The enzyme responsible for this conversion requires zinc, magnesium and vitamins B6 and C to function properly, so a high-fat diet that's missing important vitamins and minerals can hamper GLA production and contribute to low levels of PGE_1.

A number of studies have investigated the effectiveness of evening primrose oil in alleviating PMS symptoms. A handful of studies in the 1980s found that daily supplements of evening primrose oil outperformed the placebo treatment in improving PMS symptoms of breast tenderness, irritability and depression. However, recent studies haven't found evening primrose oil to be an effective treatment for PMS as a whole, possibly because the doses used were too low or the supplement wasn't taken for long enough.

Evening primrose oil does appear to offer promise for treating breast pain and tenderness. Research has shown the supplement to be as effective as certain drugs used to treat cyclic breast pain. Investigators from the University of Wales in Great Britain concluded that evening primrose oil was the best first-line therapy for cyclic breast pain, providing relief with essentially no side effects.[27–29]

Buy a supplement standardized to contain 9 percent GLA. For cyclic breast pain, take 3 to 4 grams per day, split in two equal doses. Start by taking three 500 milligram capsules at breakfast, and repeat at dinner. For PMS, take 2 to 4 grams per day in divided doses. It can take three menstrual cycles to feel the effects of evening primrose oil and up to 8 months for full effectiveness.

Ginkgo (*Ginkgo biloba*)

The finding that ginkgo helped women with PMS occurred by accident. Women who were taking ginkgo for brain health noticed that fluid retention associated with their menstrual cycle lessened while on the herb. Then, in 1993, researchers from France conducted a formal study of 143 women with PMS.[30] They found ginkgo to be significantly more effective than the placebo in treating PMS-related breast tenderness, abdominal bloating and swollen hands, legs and feet. The women in the study took ginkgo on day 16 of their cycle and continued until day 5 of their next cycle, at which time they stopped. They resumed taking the herbal remedy on day 16.

The recommended dose of ginkgo is 80 milligrams twice daily. Start on day 16 (ovulation) and continue until the fifth day of your next period (day 5). Buy a product standardized to contain 24 percent ginkgo flavone glycosides.

A small number of women have reported that the herb caused mild stomach upset. Ginkgo shouldn't be taken with blood-thinning drugs such as warfarin (Coumadin) or heparin unless your doctor is monitoring you.

St. John's Wort (*Hypericum perforatum*)

This yellow-flowered plant has long been heralded for its ability to balance emotions. It's widely used in Europe to treat both mild depression and seasonal affective disorder. A 2008 review of studies conducted in 1200 patients suffering from mild depression concluded that St. John's wort provided a beneficial effect and led to a substantial increase in rates of remission.[31] A small pilot study found that St. John's wort taken daily for 2 months improved symptoms of PMS by roughly 50 percent in some women.[32] However, because the herbal remedy interacts with so many different medications—including oral contraceptives—it might not be a viable option for some women.

Experts believe the herb eases depression by keeping brain serotonin levels high for a longer period of time, the same way that antidepressant drugs Paxil, Zoloft and Prozac do.

Buy a St. John's wort supplement that is standardized to 0.3 percent hyperforin content, the extract used in most clinical studies of mild and moderate depression. The recommended dose is 300 milligrams taken three times daily.

St. John's wort has been reported to cause sensitivity to sunlight in very light-skinned individuals. The herb also has the potential to interact with a number of medications. If you're currently taking a prescription antidepressant drug, don't take it concurrently with St. John's wort. Be sure to consult your physician before stopping any medication.

Other Natural Health Products

Omega-3 Fatty Acid Supplement

The omega-3 fatty acids DHA (docosahexaenoic acid) and EPA (eicosapentaenoic acid) are essential to healthy brain cell function. EPA, in particular, seems more influential on mood. Studies have found that people who are depressed have lower levels of omega-3 fatty acids in their bloodstream. Omega-3 fatty acids also promote the production of anti-inflammatory compounds in the body, which could possibly help reduce menstrual cramping and pain. A preliminary 3-month study conducted in seventy women with PMS found that a daily supplement of krill oil (2 grams) resulted in a significant reduction in both emotional symptoms and the use of painkillers. Although these findings are positive, their validity is limited due to flaws in the study design.[33] (Krill are very small, shrimp-like crustaceans. They serve as a primary food for whales and sharks. Krill oil supplements have a lower DHA and EPA content than supplements made from fish oil.)

If you want to try krill oil, take 2000 milligrams (2 grams) per day. The brand used in the clinical trial was Neptune Krill Oil (Neptune Technologies & Bioresources Inc.).

To improve PMS-related mood swings, you may also consider taking an omega-3 fatty acid supplement that contains a high amount of EPA.

Nutrition Strategy Checklist for PMS

- ☐ Three meals plus two snacks
- ☐ Low-GI carbohydrate-rich foods
- ☐ Low-saturated-fat diet
- ☐ Low-sodium diet
- ☐ Avoid caffeine and alcohol
- ☐ Vitamin B6 OR St. John's wort (if depression is only symptom)
- ☐ Vitamin E

- ☐ Calcium
- ☐ Vitamin D
- ☐ Magnesium
- ☐ Chasteberry (overall symptom relief)
- ☐ Evening primrose oil (cyclic breast pain)
- ☐ Omega-3 fatty acids

Recommended Resources

Mayo Foundation for Medical Education and Research
www.mayoclinic.com
This website is produced by a team of writers, editors, health educators, nurses, doctors and scientists, and is one of the best patient-education sites on the Internet. The information is reliable, thorough and clearly written.

National Association for Premenstrual Syndrome
www.pms.org.uk
41 Old Road East Peckham
Kent, UK TN12 5AP
Tel/Fax: 0870-777-2178

Prostate Cancer

Prostate cancer, a growth of malignant cells in the prostate gland, is now the most commonly diagnosed form of cancer in Canadian men. In 2009, approximately 25,500 men were diagnosed with the disease and 4400 died of it. In fact, one in seven men will develop prostate cancer in his lifetime.[1] Over the past three decades there has been an upward swing in the incidence of prostate cancer, which is likely due to increased early detection and changes in risk factors, including diet and other lifestyle factors. The good news: Since the mid-1990s, death rates from prostate cancer have declined.

What Causes Prostate Cancer?

The prostate is a male sex gland located below the bladder and in front of the rectum. It surrounds the urethra, which is the tube that carries both urine and semen out of the body. The prostate gland contributes to reproductive function by producing a milky fluid that helps to keep the sperm nourished, mobile and healthy. This fluid forms part of the semen, the sperm-carrying fluid released during ejaculation.

Cancer develops when abnormal or mutated cells go out of control, damaging the body's vital organs or tissues. As mutated cells accumulate, they form a mass or clump that is known as a tumour. In the case of prostate cancer, the tumour often remains inside the prostate gland, causing few symptoms until the cancer has reached an advanced stage. Sometimes, however, the cancer cells invade and destroy normal tissue, spreading to other organs and bones, where they can cause life-threatening problems. Very often, prostate cancer spreads to the lymph nodes, to the bones of the pelvis, ribs and spine or to the kidneys, where it causes kidney failure.

The exact cause of prostate cancer is unknown. Theories focus on genetics, hormones, environment and diet as key factors that influence prostate cancer risk. Although your genetic makeup may increase the risk of prostate cancer, your environment and diet can modify such a genetic predisposition. Testosterone, the male sex hormone that stimulates the growth of both healthy and cancerous prostate cells, is also thought to be involved in the development of prostate cancer. Cigarette smoking and exposure to industrial toxins may also play a role.

Screening for Prostate Cancer

A digital rectal exam (DRE) is the most common and simplest diagnostic test for prostate cancer. Starting at age 40, during your annual checkup, your doctor will manually check your prostate, using a gloved finger inserted into the rectum to feel for unusual bumps or hard spots on the gland wall. Although the majority of tumours can be felt this way, approximately one-third of all prostate tumours develop deeper within the gland and cannot be detected during a DRE.

The prostate-specific antigen (PSA) blood test is also used to detect prostate cancer. Normally, the prostate produces PSA, a protein, as part of the fluid production process necessary for healthy semen. A small amount of this substance also circulates in the bloodstream. Elevated blood-PSA levels may indicate prostate cancer, but it can also be caused by less serious conditions such as prostate enlargement, prostate infections and the use of certain drugs or herbal medications.

For men at average risk and with no symptoms of prostate cancer, there are currently no recommended screening guidelines for prostate cancer. Research is ongoing to determine the most effective screening methods. There are varying opinions about prostate cancer screening. The Canadian Task Force on Preventive Health Care recommends against PSA screening. The World Health Organization says it's not clear if PSA testing reduces the number of deaths from prostate cancer. According to Prostate Cancer Canada, a national foundation dedicated to prostate cancer research, education and awareness, men should have a baseline PSA test at the age of 40. Unless your baseline result is a concern to your doctor, the foundation recommends the PSA test be repeated every 5 years until age 50. After the age of 50, PSA testing should be done annually or semi-annually.

Symptoms

Often there are no symptoms for many years in the early stages of the disease. The symptoms that do occur are very similar to those of benign prostatic hyperplasia (BPH), commonly known as prostate enlargement (see page 636), and include:

- chronic, dull pain in the lower pelvis, lower back or upper thighs
- pain during urination
- sudden or intense need to urinate
- frequent urination during the night
- difficulty starting to urinate, dribbling or weak urine flow
- blood in the urine or semen
- a sense of incompletely emptying the bladder
- painful ejaculation
- loss of appetite and weight

Who's at Risk?

- **Older men.** Most cases are diagnosed in men over the age of 65.
- **Certain racial or ethnic groups.** Men of African ancestry have a 60 percent higher incidence of prostate cancer than Caucasian men, and Asian men have the lowest incidence.
- **Men with a family history of the disease.** Having a father or brother with the disease doubles the risk and is associated with developing prostate cancer at an earlier age.
- **Men who eat a high-saturated-fat diet.**

Conventional Treatment

Prostate cancer is very slow growing and is not usually an aggressive type of cancer. Only 3 percent of the men diagnosed with prostate cancer actually die of the disease. Treatment for prostate cancer will vary, depending on how far the cancer has spread, how fast the cancer is growing, your age and your general health.

Older men with early-stage, slow-growing cancer may not need treatment because their risk of dying from the disease is not high. Watchful waiting, or active surveillance, for symptoms and a regular program of PSA tests and rectal exams may be sufficient to monitor the disease. For younger men, the most effective treatment is radical prostatectomy, the surgical removal of the prostate gland. However, research indicates that cancer recurs in 30 percent of all men who have surgery.

Radiation therapy to kill cancerous cells may be used for older men in poor health who may have difficulty withstanding surgery. Cryotherapy, a procedure using liquid nitrogen to freeze and destroy cancerous cells, may also be used. In 90 percent of cases, cryotherapy results in impotence. Hormone therapy may be used to prevent male sex hormones from speeding up the growth of cancer cells.

Prostate cancer and the treatments used to control the disease can cause a number of complications, including incontinence, impotence, reduced libido, breast enlargement and depression.

Preventing and Managing Prostate Cancer

Most of the nutritional recommendations focus on reducing the risk of developing prostate cancer. A few strategies, however, may also prevent the progression of cancer.

Dietary Strategies
A Healthy Diet

SATURATED FAT. Studies comparing the diets of men with prostate cancer with those of men free of the disease have found a number of foods linked to development of the cancer. Most notable is the connection between animal (saturated) fat and prostate cancer. Many studies have found that men who have higher intakes of saturated fat increase their risk for the disease and also have more advanced forms of prostate cancer.[2-7] When mice are injected with human prostate cancer cells and fed a high-fat diet, the cancer grows faster.

It's thought that saturated fat increases production of testosterone, which may promote prostate cancer. Cooking meat at high temperatures produces heterocyclic amines, compounds that may also promote cancer. Research has linked high intakes of meat cooked well done and very well done with a greater risk of prostate cancer.[8,9]

Follow a low-saturated-fat diet by choosing lean cuts of meat (flank steak, inside round, pork tenderloin), poultry breast without the skin, skim or 1% milk and yogurt, and skim-milk cheese. Limit or avoid eating meat cooked well done. Avoid processed meats such as sausage, bacon, hot dogs, salami and fatty deli meats. Use butter and cream cheese sparingly. If you eat meat, consume no more than 3 ounces (90 g) per day.

SOY FOODS. In Asia, where tofu and soy foods are eaten regularly, prostate cancer rates are low. Studies in animals and test tubes have shown soy isoflavones can inhibit the growth of prostate cancer cells. One study, conducted among 12,395 California Seventh-day Adventist men, observed that those who drank more than one glass of soy milk per day were less likely to develop prostate cancer.[10]

Dietary sources of isoflavones, which appear to keep testosterone in check, include soybeans, tofu, tempeh, edamame, miso, soy nuts, soy burgers and soy beverages. Choose unflavoured soy milk to avoid consuming added sugars.

Substitute animal protein more often with vegetarian protein foods such as legumes and soy foods. Eating more legumes, such as kidney beans, chickpeas and lentils, has been associated with a lower risk of prostate cancer.[11,12] Beans, like soy foods, also contain isoflavones that may slow the growth of prostate tumours.

FISH. Eating more fish will help you reduce animal fat in your diet. Fish contains omega-3 fatty acids, compounds that have been shown in the laboratory to inhibit cancer growth. Some evidence suggests that men with higher levels of these fatty acids in their blood have a lower risk of prostate cancer.[13] Aim to eat oily fish such as salmon, trout, Arctic char, herring and sardines at least two times per week.

WHOLE GRAINS AND GROUND FLAXSEED. Consuming plenty of whole-grain breads, cereals, brown rice, whole-wheat pasta and other whole grains has been linked with protection from prostate cancer.[14] These foods offer fibre, phytoestrogens, vitamin E, selenium, flavonoids and antioxidants—all of which may play a role in prostate cancer prevention.

Research from the University of Texas M.D. Anderson Cancer Center suggests that ground flaxseed—a whole grain—may help keep prostate cancer at bay. In men diagnosed with prostate cancer and awaiting surgery, a low-fat diet supplemented with 30 grams (2-1/2 tablespoons) of ground flaxseed reduced serum testosterone, slowed the growth of prostate cancer cells and increased the death rate of cancer cells.[15]

Although more studies are needed, ground flaxseed is a healthy addition to your diet. A 2 tablespoon (30 ml) serving provides fibre, omega-3 fatty acids and phytochemicals. Add ground flaxseed to smoothies, yogurt, hot cereal, applesauce, casseroles, pancake and muffin batters and homemade meat loaf and burgers.

VEGETABLES. The following are particularly important:

- **Cruciferous vegetables.** When it comes to fruit and vegetables, cruciferous vegetables appear to offer the most protection from prostate cancer. One large study found that men with the highest intake of these vegetables had a 39 percent lower risk of the cancer.[16] Another study that followed 29,361 men for 4.2 years found that men who had the highest intake of cruciferous vegetables were 40 percent less likely to be diagnosed with prostate cancer than those who consumed the least. Broccoli and cauliflower were the most protective, possibly because they were consumed more often than other cruciferous vegetables.[17]

  Broccoli, bok choy, cabbage, cauliflower, kale and turnip contain isothiocyanates, natural chemicals that have been shown to help the liver detoxify cancer-causing substances. Include five 1/2 cup (125 ml) servings in your diet each week.

- **Tomatoes.** Lycopene is an antioxidant compound found in red-coloured vegetables and fruit that's thought to lower cancer risk by preventing DNA damage in cells. It's especially abundant in tomatoes. Evidence that lycopene-rich foods help prevent prostate cancer is mixed. A number of studies have found that men with high lycopene intakes from foods such as tomato products have a lower risk of developing prostate cancer compared with men who consume little lycopene. However, one large-scale study found that lycopene in the diet only offered protection to men with a family history of prostate cancer.[18-22]

In a study from Harvard University that followed 47,365 men for 12 years, lycopene was clearly linked with protection from prostate cancer. Men with the highest lycopene intake were 16 percent less likely to be diagnosed with prostate cancer than their peers who consumed the least. Consuming tomato sauce, the primary source of bioavailable lycopene, at least twice per week versus less than once per month was linked with a 23 percent lower risk of prostate cancer. Studies have also related low blood- and tissue-lycopene levels with higher rates of prostate cancer.[23-25]

Tomato sauce and tomato juice offer more lycopene than raw tomatoes, since processing and cooking breaks down cell walls and makes more of the compound available for absorption. Lycopene is fat soluble, so adding a little oil or fat to a tomato-based meal (e.g., spaghetti sauce, pizza) aids in its absorption from the digestive tract into the bloodstream. Studies suggest that a daily intake of 6 to 12 milligrams offers cancer protection. Here's how tomatoes and tomato products compare:

Lycopene Content of Tomatoes and Tomato Products
(Per 1/2 cup [125 ml] serving unless otherwise indicated)

Food	Lycopene (milligrams)
Tomato paste	37.6 mg
Tomato puree, canned	27.2 mg
Pasta sauce, marinara	21.5 mg
Tomato sauce, canned	18.6 mg
Vegetable juice cocktail	11.7 mg
Tomato juice, canned	11.0 mg
Tomato soup, canned	6.3 mg
Tomatoes, stewed, canned	5.1 mg
Vegetable soup, canned	3.5 mg
Tomatoes, red, raw, 1 medium	3.1 mg
Ketchup, 1 tbsp (15 ml)	2.5 mg

Source: U.S. Department of Agriculture, Agricultural Research Service, 2007. USDA National Nutrient Database for Standard Reference, Release 21. Nutrient Data Laboratory Home Page, www.ars.usda.gov/nutrientdata.

- **Vitamin C–rich vegetables.** Some research suggests that vegetables high in vitamin C might also reduce prostate cancer risk. In a study of 1985 men previously exposed to asbestos, a lower risk of prostate cancer was observed with increased intake of vitamin C–rich vegetables, including bell peppers and broccoli.[26] Other vitamin C–rich vegetables include cauliflower, Brussels sprouts, tomatoes and tomato juice. It's interesting to note that these vegetables are also good sources of cruciferous chemicals and lycopene.

POMEGRANATE JUICE. Pomegranate juice is a rich source of antioxidants called polyphenols. Preliminary research suggests that a daily intake of the juice can slow the progression of prostate cancer. A small study found that after treatment for prostate cancer, the length of time it took for prostate-specific antigen (PSA) to double was significantly longer in men who drank 1 cup (250 ml) of pomegranate juice daily for up to 2 years.[27] Findings from studies conducted in test tubes and in animals suggest that pomegranate antioxidants inhibit blood vessel formation in tumours and reduce testosterone production.[28,29]

Although it's too soon to say that drinking pomegranate juice prevents disease, it's certainly a nutritious addition to your diet. Include 1 cup (250 ml) in your daily diet; however, keep in mind that the serving supplies 160 calories. To prevent weight gain, consider cutting an equivalent number of calories from elsewhere in your diet.

GREEN TEA. Drinking green tea may reduce the risk of prostate cancer. Studies have found that populations that drink green tea regularly have lower rates of prostate cancer. Laboratory studies have determined that antioxidants in green tea, called polyphenols, have a number of anti-cancer properties. One study of 49,920 men who were followed for 14 years found that drinking five or more cups of green tea per day—versus less than one—reduced the risk of advanced prostate cancer by 48 percent. Green tea didn't alter the risk of localized (non-aggressive) prostate cancer.[30]

Vitamins and Minerals

Vitamin D

Our requirements for this vitamin are met mainly through exposure to sunlight, when the sun's ultraviolet rays trigger the skin to produce vitamin D. The observation that populations that get little exposure to sunlight have higher rates of prostate cancer has led researchers to speculate that vitamin D is somehow involved. The fact that the prostate can also metabolize vitamin D has opened up investigations into vitamin D and cancer prevention. Laboratory studies have found that vitamin D inhibits the growth of human prostate cancer cells. Despite the plausibility of a link between vitamin D and prostate cancer risk, study findings have been less consistent than for other types of cancer. At the time of writing, there doesn't appear to be a link between the nutrient and the risk of prostate cancer.

Even so, the weight of evidence does suggest that increased vitamin D intake has important health benefits. In fact, vitamin D insufficiency is emerging as a public health concern. The risk of suboptimal blood levels of vitamin D looms particularly large for people with dark-coloured skin, the elderly, the overweight and obese, and those with little sun exposure such as Canadians who live in northern latitudes.

The recommended daily intake is 1000 international units (IU) for adults and 400 IU for children. Best food sources are fluid milk, fortified soy and rice beverages, oily fish, egg yolks, butter and margarine. However, it's not possible for adults to consume 1000 IU each day from foods alone. For this reason, it's necessary to take a vitamin D supplement in the fall and winter, and year-round if you are over the age of 50, have dark-coloured skin or don't expose your skin to sunshine in the summer months. See Chapter 4, page 51, to learn about vitamin D supplements.

Vitamin E and Selenium

Higher intakes of vitamin E have been linked with a lower risk of prostate cancer. Researchers have also observed that men with lower blood levels of this nutrient, especially those who smoke, are at increased risk.[31,32] A number of studies suggest that vitamin E supplements help prevent prostate cancer. One large trial from Finland found that male smokers who took 50 milligrams of vitamin E had a 32 percent lower risk of the cancer than non-supplement-users.[33] Harvard University researchers also learned that 100 international units (IU) of vitamin E protected current smokers and recent quitters from fatal prostate cancer.[34] A 2007 review of randomized controlled trials revealed that vitamin E supplements significantly reduced the risk of prostate cancer, but didn't reduce the risk of any other types of cancer.[35]

Vitamin E is a potent antioxidant and may protect prostate cells from free radical damage, which can lead to cancer. The vitamin may also prevent prostate cancer by altering the levels of sex hormones in the blood. An American study conducted among one hundred older men found that taking 100 IU of vitamin E per day resulted in significantly lower levels of androstenedione and testosterone, two hormones implicated in prostate cancer development.[36]

The protective effects of selenium were discovered by accident when researchers from Arizona investigated the effect of selenium supplement on skin cancer recurrence.[37] Men with a history of skin cancer were given 200 micrograms of selenium or a placebo and followed for 4-1/2 years. Although the risk of skin cancer was unaffected, there was a significant reduction in prostate cancer among the men taking selenium supplements. In areas like northeastern United States and Canada, where the selenium level in the soil is low, rates of prostate cancer are higher. Selenium acts as an antioxidant in the body, protecting cells from the damaging effects of free radicals.

In 2001, the Selenium and Vitamin E Cancer Prevention Trial (SELECT) set out to substantiate these findings. The randomized controlled trial gave 35,000 men aged 50 and older vitamin E (400 IU) and selenium (200 micrograms) together, vitamin E alone, selenium alone or a placebo. In 2008, early findings from SELECT dashed hopes raised by prior studies. Participants were told to stop taking their pills after the data showed no benefit—vitamin E and selenium, taken alone or in combination, didn't prevent prostate cancer. The early analysis also revealed two worrisome trends: a small increase in the number of prostate cancers among vitamin E users and a small rise in type 2 diabetes among those taking selenium. Neither finding was statistically significant, meaning it could be a coincidence. These trends were not observed among men taking vitamin E and selenium supplements together.[38] The SELECT investigators will continue to follow participants for 3 years to determine any long-term effects after stopping the supplements.

In the study, synthetic vitamin E supplements were given. It's possible that other forms of vitamin E may have been more effective. Even so, there's no evidence that taking vitamin E or selenium supplements guards against prostate cancer. Increasing your intake of these antioxidant nutrients from your diet seems to offer the most protection. Numerous studies have also linked a higher intake of selenium-rich foods to less prostate cancer, mainly in men with low blood levels of the mineral (i.e., men whose diets provide little selenium).

The recommended daily intake for vitamin E is 22 IU. Foods rich in vitamin E include avocado, wheat germ, nuts, seeds, vegetable oils, whole grains and kale.

The recommended daily intake for selenium is 55 micrograms, an amount easily obtained from the diet by consuming foods like seafood, chicken, organ meats, whole grains, nuts, onions, garlic and mushrooms.

Calcium

A number of studies have revealed that men with higher calcium and dairy intakes are at increased risk of prostate cancer.[39-41] However, most studies suggest that greater intakes of calcium and dairy increase prostate cancer risk only slightly. A recent study of 29,509 men found that a higher intake of calcium from foods (greater than 2000 milligrams per day), but not supplements, was associated with a modest increase in the risk of non-aggressive prostate cancer. Higher intakes of dietary calcium didn't affect the risk of developing aggressive prostate cancer.[42] It's thought that high intakes of calcium may lower levels of vitamin D in the blood.

Based on this evidence, it's prudent to meet, but not exceed, your daily calcium requirements from food and supplements. Men require 1000 or 1500 milligrams of calcium per day, depending on age. See Chapter 4, page 56, for information on meeting daily calcium needs.

Herbal Remedies

Garlic (Allium sativum)

Eating more garlic and taking garlic supplements may offer protection from prostate cancer. Researchers from the United Kingdom studied 328 men with prostate cancer and found that those who ate garlic at least twice weekly had a 44 percent lower risk of prostate cancer than those who never consumed it.[43] Compared with men who never used garlic supplements, those who used supplements at least twice weekly had a 60 percent lower risk of the cancer.

Studies have shown that garlic's sulphur compounds can slow or prevent the growth of cancer cells. These phytochemicals may also help rid the body of carcinogens by enhancing the action of certain enzymes in the liver and intestinal tract. It's also thought that natural chemicals in garlic have a direct toxic effect on certain types of tumour cells. Garlic's natural sulphur compounds have been shown in the laboratory to enhance the immune system and inhibit the growth of prostate cancer cells. One study found that compounds in aged garlic extract suppressed the growth of hormone-responsive prostate cancer cells.[44,45]

To increase your intake of garlic, reach for it when cooking. Aim to consume two cloves per week. To supplement, buy a product made with aged garlic extract. Take two to six capsules a day, in divided doses. Aged garlic extract is odourless and less irritating to the gastrointestinal tract than other forms of garlic supplements. Garlic (both fresh and supplements) may enhance the effects of blood-thinning medications like warfarin (Coumadin); if you're taking this drug and garlic at the same time, be sure to inform your doctor.

Nutrition Strategy Checklist for Preventing Prostate Cancer

- ☐ Low-saturated-fat diet
- ☐ Fish
- ☐ Soy foods

- [ ] Whole grains and flaxseed
- [ ] Cruciferous vegetables
- [ ] Tomatoes
- [ ] Pomegranate juice
- [ ] Green tea
- [ ] Vitamin D
- [ ] Foods rich in vitamin E
- [ ] Foods rich in selenium
- [ ] Calcium
- [ ] Garlic

Recommended Resources

Canadian Cancer Society
www.cancer.ca
10 Alcorn Avenue, Suite 200
Toronto, ON M4V 3B1
Tel: 416-961-7223
Fax: 416-961-4189

Prostate Cancer Canada
www.prostatecancer.ca
145 Front Street East, Suite 306
Toronto, ON M5A 1E3
Tel: 416-441-2131 or 1-888-255-0333
Fax: 416-441-2325
Email: info@prostatecancer.ca

National Cancer Institute
National Institutes of Health
NCI Public Inquiries Office
www.cancer.gov
6116 Executive Boulevard, Room 3036A
Bethesda, MD, USA 20892-8322
Tel: 1-800-4-CANCER (226237)

Prostate Enlargement (Benign Prostatic Hyperplasia)

Benign prostatic hyperplasia (BPH) is a non-cancerous growth of the prostate resulting in an enlarged prostate gland. Its causes aren't fully understood. The prostate is responsible for making the fluid that nourishes the sperm and helps them move through the reproductive system. The fluid forms part of the semen, which is the milky sperm-carrying substance released during ejaculation. The prostate gland develops steadily throughout childhood and adolescence, growing to the size of a walnut by the time a boy reaches adulthood.

As a man approaches his 40s, the prostate often enters a new growth phase, possibly in response to the natural drop in production of the male hormone testosterone. This reduction in testosterone production allows higher levels of estrogen to circulate in the bloodstream. Researchers speculate that this increase in estrogen may somehow trigger prostate cells to begin growing again. An accumulation of dihydrotestosterone (DHT), a substance derived from testosterone, has also been shown to stimulate new cell growth. The growing tissues of the prostate gland can swell up to three times their normal size, interfering with urine flow.

Because the prostate gland surrounds the urethra, the tube that carries both urine and semen out of the body, changes in the prostate gland almost inevitably affect the urinary tract. As prostate tissues grow, they begin to press on the urethra. This blocks the flow of urine, forcing the bladder muscles to work harder to push the urine out through the tube. The bladder wall thickens and becomes more irritable. Once this happens, the bladder starts to contract more often, leading to frequent urination, especially at night. Eventually, the bladder muscles weaken, preventing the bladder from emptying completely. Urine that remains in the bladder usually becomes stagnant, increasing the risk of bladder infections, incontinence and kidney problems. Sometimes, the prostate can grow so large that it blocks the flow of urine completely, a situation that requires immediate medical attention.

Symptoms

The symptoms of BPH are very similar to those of prostate cancer, and your doctor will suggest diagnostic tests, including a digital rectal exam (DRE) and a prostate-specific antigen (PSA) blood test, to rule out cancer as a cause of your urinary problems. Fortunately, BPH isn't a precursor to prostate cancer. Early diagnosis and treatment does decrease the likelihood of developing the other complications associated with this condition.

Symptoms of prostate enlargement rarely develop before age 40. The size of the swelling or obstruction doesn't determine how severe the symptoms will be. Men with only a small amount of enlargement may have greater problems than men with significant swelling. Symptoms can include:

- difficulty starting to urinate
- more frequent urination, especially at night
- urgent need to urinate
- weak urine stream
- dribbling and leaking at the end of urination
- urinary incontinence
- blocked urination
- painful or bloody urination

Who's at Risk?

BPH is very common. The age at which BPH begins and the amount the prostate grows will vary. Half of all men over 50 develop symptoms of BPH. By age 70, seven out of ten men will have some degree of BPH and one-quarter of these men will require treatment.[1] This condition is more common in North American and European men and less common among Asian men. Married men seem to suffer from prostate enlargement more often than single men. Men with a family history of prostate enlargement appear to have a higher risk of developing the condition themselves.

Conventional Treatment

If symptoms are not bothersome, watchful waiting may be the recommended approach. Lifestyle changes can help control symptoms, including:

- Limit the amount of liquid you drink after 7 P.M. to reduce the need to urinate at night.
- Empty your bladder completely when you urinate.
- Reduce alcohol intake, since alcohol increases urine production.
- Avoid over-the-counter cold medicines and antihistamines, which can cause muscles to tighten, reducing urine flow.
- Exercise regularly.
- Stay warm, since cold temperatures can lead to urine retention.

Various medications may be used to shrink or stop the growth of the prostate. Alpha-blockers relax muscles in the pelvis, making it easier to urinate. Finasteride inhibits the production of DHT, which helps shrink the prostate.

Heat therapy, which sends heat energy to the prostate tissue through the urethra, may also be recommended. It's more effective than drugs in treating moderate to severe symptoms.

Surgery is the most effective treatment for relieving symptoms; however, it's rarely used, given the other treatments now available. Used most often in men who don't respond to medication or who have severe symptoms, surgical procedures are the likeliest to produce side effects which, though usually temporary, include loss of bladder control and impotence.

Managing Prostate Enlargement

Dietary Strategies

A Healthy Diet

SATURATED FAT. Dietary factors that increase the risk of prostate cancer can also increase the risk of prostate enlargement. Studies have revealed that men with the condition have higher intakes of fat, especially animal or saturated fat, and lower intakes of vegetables, fruit and omega-3 fatty acids found in fish.[2-4] For optimal prostate health, follow the dietary guidelines outlined in Prostate Cancer, page 628. Pay particular attention to reducing animal fat and increasing your intake of fruit and vegetables.

SOY FOODS. Foods made from soybeans also play a role in preventing prostate enlargement. Populations that consume soy on a regular basis have much lower rates of prostate disease, including prostate enlargement. Foods made from soybeans contain natural plant estrogens called isoflavones. One of the main isoflavones in soybeans, genistein, has been shown to decrease the growth of prostate tissue. Soy isoflavones may protect the prostate by inhibiting the action of growth-promoting hormones. Include soy foods in your diet at least three times per week, preferably daily. See Chapter 5, page 94, for ways to incorporate a variety of soy foods into your diet.

GROUND FLAXSEED. Flaxseed is a source of plant estrogens called lignans. Although studies have not examined its influence on prostate enlargement, flaxseed is thought to work in the same manner as soy isoflavones. Include 1 to 2 tablespoons (15 to 30 ml) of ground flaxseed in your daily diet. Ground flaxseed can be added to hot cereal, smoothies, yogurt, applesauce, pancake and quick bread batters and homemade burgers and meat loaf.

FRUIT AND VEGETABLES. Research suggests that diets high in beta carotene and vitamin C lower the risk of BPH.[5] Include 7 to 10 daily servings of fruit and vegetables in your diet to increase your intake of these nutrients. Beta carotene–rich foods include orange and dark-green produce such as carrots, sweet potato, winter squash, broccoli, collard greens, kale, spinach, apricots, cantaloupe, peaches, nectarines, mango and papaya. The best sources of vitamin C are citrus fruit, kiwi, strawberries, cantaloupe, red pepper, broccoli, cabbage, cauliflower and tomato juice.

OMEGA-3 FATTY ACIDS. Increasing your intake of polyunsaturated fat from fish and foods rich in an omega-3 fatty acid called alpha-linolenic acid (ALA) has been shown to guard against BPH.[6] Include oily fish such as salmon, trout, sardines, anchovies, herring and Atlantic mackerel in your diet twice per week. To increase your intake of ALA, include 1 teaspoon (5 ml) of flaxseed oil or 1 tablespoon (15 ml) of ground flaxseed in your daily diet.

Other good sources of ALA include walnut oil, hemp oil and canola oil.

STARCHY FOODS. Some research has revealed that high intakes of starchy foods such as bread, crackers, cereals, grains and potatoes increases the likelihood of BPH.[7,8] Moderate your portions of these foods at meals and snacks. Limit your cooked portions of rice to 1 cup (250 ml), pasta to 1-1/2 cups (375 ml), cereal to 1-1/2 cups (375 ml) and bread to two slices. Most often, choose whole-grain starchy foods to increase your intake of vitamins, minerals, fibre and protective phytochemicals.

Weight Control

Obesity has been linked with a higher risk of prostate enlargement.[9,10] In one study of 422 men, the greater the body mass index (BMI), the more likely a man was to have BPH. Men who were overweight (i.e., men who had a BMI of 25 to 29.9) had a 40 percent higher risk of BPH than men whose BMI was between 20 and 25. Men with a BMI of 35 or greater had more than triple the risk. It's thought that obesity somehow stimulates growth of the prostate gland independent of testosterone, possibly through increased blood-glucose levels. This study also revealed that men with elevated fasting blood sugar were three times more likely to have prostate enlargement, and men who had a clinical diagnosis of diabetes were more than twice as likely to have an enlarged prostate as men in the normal weight group.

To determine if you're at a healthy weight, see Obesity, Overweight and Weight Loss, page 569, to calculate your body mass index (BMI). Having a BMI of between 25 and 29.9 indicates overweight and a BMI of 30 or greater is defined as obese. If you determine that your BMI is greater than 25, use the strategies outlined on page 574 to promote safe, gradual weight loss.

Vitamins and Minerals
Zinc

The prostate gland contains more zinc than any other tissue in the body—and it appears to be very important for prostate health, although its exact role in prostate enlargement is still unclear. Researchers do know that the mineral helps many enzymes perform their tasks. Zinc also seems to inhibit male sex hormone metabolism in the prostate.

The recommended dietary intake of zinc for men is 11 milligrams per day. To prevent a deficiency, include zinc-rich foods in your daily diet. Foods such as oysters, seafood, lean red meat, poultry, yogurt, wheat bran, wheat germ, whole grains and enriched breakfast cereals are all good sources. A detailed list of foods and their zinc content can be found in Chapter 4, page 79.

Most adult multivitamin and mineral formulas provide 10 to 20 milligrams of zinc. Single zinc supplements aren't appropriate. In fact, excess zinc, especially from single supplements, can potentially encourage the growth of prostate conditions such as BPH. Large doses of zinc can increase testosterone levels and impair the body's immune system.

Herbal Remedies
Saw Palmetto (*Serenoa repens*)

Of all the herbal extracts found to improve symptoms of prostate enlargement, saw palmetto has been the most heavily studied. Numerous clinical trials lasting up to 1 year have demonstrated that saw palmetto provides mild to moderate improvement in urinary symptoms, including frequent urination, painful urination, hesitancy, urgency and nighttime urination. In a recent review of twenty-one randomized controlled studies, American researchers concluded that, compared with the standard treatment drug Proscar, saw palmetto was equally effective at improving urinary tract symptoms and improving urinary flow.[11-16] And use of the herb was associated with fewer side effects.

Saw palmetto appears to block the conversion of testosterone to DHT and prevents DHT from binding to prostate cells. The herb may also have anti-inflammatory and anti-estrogenic properties.

Buy a product standardized to contain between 80 percent and 90 percent fatty acids. Take 160 milligrams twice daily or 320 milligrams once per day. Significant symptom improvement may take up to 2 months of treatment. The herb is very well tolerated. On rare occasions, saw palmetto may cause stomach upset and headache.

Pygeum *(Pygeum africanum)*

This herb may be used instead of saw palmetto to treat prostate enlargement. Pygeum comes from the bark of an African tree and has a long history of use for urinary problems. A review of eighteen trials conducted among 1562 men found that the herb achieved modestly large improvements in symptoms such as urinary flow and nighttime urination.[17]

Unlike saw palmetto, pygeum isn't thought to affect DHT levels. Rather, it's thought to have anti-inflammatory effects in the prostate and to inhibit the action of growth factors.

The recommended dose is 75 to 200 milligrams taken once daily, or divided in two doses. Buy a product standardized to contain 14 percent triterpenes and 0.5 percent n-docosanol. Pygeum is very safe, although it may cause mild stomach upset in some individuals.

Stinging Nettle *(Urtica dioica)*

This herb is often recommended as a stand-alone treatment for prostate enlargement, despite the limited number of studies evaluating its use. At this time, there's no good evidence that stinging nettle is effective except in combination with saw palmetto.[18] Stinging nettle is thought to affect prostate cell membranes in such a way that cell growth is suppressed. It has also been shown to prevent sex hormones from binding to prostate cell receptors.

If you decide to try stinging nettle, look for a supplement that combines the herb with saw palmetto. Studies have found such a product, containing 120 milligrams of stinging nettle plus 160 milligrams of saw palmetto, taken twice daily, to significantly improve urinary symptoms. However, it's not known if this benefit is from stinging nettle, saw palmetto or both.

Rye Grass Pollen *(Secale cereale)*

Cernilton, a product made from rye grass pollen, has been used in Europe to treat prostate enlargement. A review of two well-controlled trials enrolling 444 men found that rye grass pollen improved overall urinary symptoms, including nighttime urination.[19] In one study, researchers noted that men taking the supplement had significantly reduced prostate size. How rye grass pollen works is unclear. It's thought that it may have anti-inflammatory effects and relieve fluid buildup in the prostate.

The recommended dose of Cernilton is 126 milligrams taken three times per day. (However, this product is available only in Western Europe, Japan, Korea and Argentina.) No side effects have been noted other than occasional stomach upset. This product has been processed to remove allergy-causing proteins, so individuals with an allergy to grass pollen shouldn't have a reaction.

Other Natural Health Products

Beta-Sitosterol

Fruit, vegetables, grains, nuts and seeds contain naturally occurring compounds called sterols. Beta-sitosterol is one plant sterol that has been used to treat symptoms of prostate enlargement. A review of four trials conducted among 519 men found beta-sitosterol effective in improving urinary symptoms and flow measures.[20,21] The supplement hasn't been shown to affect prostate size. Beta-sitosterol binds to prostate cell receptors and appears to exert anti-inflammatory effects in the prostate.

The recommended dose is 60 to 130 milligrams per day, divided in two or three doses. Beta-sitosterol may take up to 4 weeks to have an effect. No significant adverse effects have been reported.

Nutrition Strategy Checklist for Prostate Enlargement

- ☐ Low-saturated-fat diet
- ☐ Soy foods
- ☐ Ground flaxseed
- ☐ Fruit and vegetables
- ☐ Omega-3 fatty acids
- ☐ Moderate starch portions
- ☐ Weight control
- ☐ Zinc
- ☐ Saw palmetto* OR pygeum OR stinging nettle/saw palmetto
- ☐ Beta-sitosterol

*Best evidence—start here.

Recommended Resources

Prostate Cancer Canada
www.prostatecancer.ca
145 Front Street East, Suite 306
Toronto, ON M5A 1E3
Tel: 416-441-2131 or 1-888-255-0333
Fax: 416-441-2325
Email: info@prostatecancer.ca

Mayo Foundation for Medical Education and Research
www.mayoclinic.com
This website is produced by a team of writers, editors, health educators, nurses, doctors and scientists, and is one of the best patient-education sites on the Internet. The information is reliable, thorough and clearly written.

National Kidney and Urologic Diseases Information Clearinghouse
The National Institute of Diabetes and Digestive and Kidney Diseases
National Institutes of Health
Office of Communications and Public Liaison
http://kidney.niddk.nih.gov
31 Center Drive, MSC 2560
Bethesda, MD, USA 20892-2560
Tel: 1-800-622-9010

Psoriasis

Psoriasis is a chronic, inflammatory skin disease that's easily identified by the presence of rough, red, dry patches and thick, silvery scaling on the skin of the elbows, knees, scalp and ears. Psoriasis typically starts to develop during the teenage years and flare-ups may be lifelong. Although some people are only mildly affected by psoriasis, it's a persistent disease that can be the source of considerable discomfort, disability and emotional distress.

What Causes Psoriasis?

Psoriasis is probably caused by a disorder of the immune system that disrupts the activity of the skin cells. The upper layer of the skin, the epidermis, acts as a strong, protective barrier for the body. For most people, the life cycle of the skin is about 28 days. During this 28-day cycle, new skin cells move from the lowest layer of the epidermis to the top layer, where they die and flake off. For people suffering from psoriasis, the cycle progresses much more rapidly. Skin cells multiply nearly ten times faster than necessary, reducing the life cycle to only 4 or 5 days. The rapidly dividing cells accumulate on the outer layer of the epidermis, resulting in the rough scaling and inflammation.

Psoriasis usually occurs on areas of the body that are exposed to irritation, friction or injury. The knees and elbows are common pressure points, but scaling can also develop on the scalp, lower back, hands, feet and nails and may even be found inside the mouth or on the genitals. The red, scaly patches, called plaques, may become cracked and sore, especially on the skin over the joints. Gradually, the skin will heal and return to normal, but the scaling tends to reappear again and again in the same areas.

Some people also experience itching skin or burning sensations when psoriasis develops in the body creases. In more serious cases, pus-filled blisters may develop or inflammation may attack the joints, causing psoriatic arthritis.

Psoriasis isn't contagious. The disease tends to flare up for weeks or months at a time and then subside. During these periods of remission, there are usually no symptoms. Although scientists don't fully understand the causes of this disease, certain factors are known to trigger psoriasis attacks. These include changes in climate, stress, infections, skin injuries, severe sunburn, exposure to household chemicals and reactions to medications. Genetics may also play a role.

Symptoms

The most common type of psoriasis is *plaque psoriasis*, which appears as raised patches of thick, inflamed red skin with silvery flakes or scales (called plaques). The second most common type is called *guttate psoriasis*, which is characterized by small, scaly, pink teardrop patches. It usually appears on the trunk (or torso), arms and legs, but can sometimes cover the entire body. *Pustular psoriasis* appears as small, pus-filled blisters that often occur on the hands and feet, or spread over large areas of the body. This type can be painful, cause fever and may require antibiotics. *Erythrodermic psoriasis* is the least common type and is characterized by widespread reddening and scaling of the skin; it's often accompanied by painful inflammation and may require hospitalization.

Other symptoms of psoriasis include:

- pitted and discoloured finger and toenails; nails may also lift and crack

- itching or burning sensations and minor bleeding, especially on the skin in the body creases
- stiff, swollen joints
- pus-filled blisters

Who's at Risk?

Psoriasis affects at least one in every one hundred Canadians.[1] In one-third of all cases, the skin condition is inherited. Psoriasis usually develops gradually between the ages of 15 and 25 but can occur at any age. Approximately 10 percent to 35 percent of people with psoriasis go on to develop psoriatic arthritis. Psoriatic arthritis causes joint inflammation—pain and swelling of joints in the knees, ankles, fingers and toes—as well as skin rashes.

Conventional Treatment

Treatment usually depends on the severity of the disease, the extent of the areas affected, the type of psoriasis and the disease's response to initial treatment. Over time, affected skin may become resistant to treatments. Some doctors rotate or switch treatments periodically to avoid adverse effects and a resistance. Common treatments include one or a combination of the following:

- **Topical creams or ointments** to improve the patchy areas and remove scales (creams may be derived from vitamins D or A, coal tar, salicylic acid or anthralin, or may contain corticosteroids)
- **Bath oils and moisturizers** to soothe the skin and reduce itching
- **Phototherapy** to reduce the overproduction of skin cells and improve psoriasis

- **Oral medications** to block the rapid growth of cells in more severe cases (drugs include retinoids, derived from vitamin A, or methotrexate) and to suppress the immune system (cyclosporine)

To improve the symptoms of psoriasis, it's also important to eat a nutritionally balanced diet (see below), get adequate rest and exercise regularly. Avoid scratching or rubbing dry patches of skin. Bathe often to soak off scales—mineral or sea salt baths may be beneficial. After bathing, pat skin dry rather than rubbing it with a towel. Use a moisturizer after bathing, but avoid creams with alcohol. In addition, it's helpful to expose your skin to sunlight every day, but avoid sunburn.

Managing Psoriasis
Dietary Strategies
Fish
Oily fish is a rich source of two omega-3 fatty acids: EPA (eicosapentaenoic acid) and DHA (docosahexanaenoic acid). EPA and DHA are used in the body to produce non-inflammatory immune compounds and therefore may be useful in psoriasis. Research suggests that people with psoriatic arthritis have lower levels of these fatty acids in their bloodstream.[2] Although the use of fish oil taken either intravenously or as supplements to treat psoriasis has been the most widely studied (see below), some studies suggest that eating fish can be just as beneficial.

One report found that patients taking medication for their psoriasis who ate a daily 170 gram portion of oily fish for 4 weeks experienced a modest improvement in symptoms.[3] Eating the same amount of white fish (non-oily) had no effect on psoriasis.

Eating fish on a daily basis may not be feasible or desirable for many people. Aim to eat oily fish at least two times per week. Good choices include salmon, trout, herring, Atlantic mackerel, sardines and kipper.

Gluten

Researchers have observed that some people with psoriasis do well on a gluten-free diet. Blood tests have revealed that some people have antibodies to gluten, a protein found in wheat, rye and barley.[4-6] A study from Sweden found that when psoriasis patients with gluten antibodies were placed on a gluten-free diet for 3 months, there was a significant improvement in itching, redness, scaling and the size of plaques.[7] When their ordinary diet was resumed, their psoriasis worsened. Other research has also demonstrated marked improvement of psoriasis symptoms in patients with gluten intolerance.[8]

Gluten is found in wheat, rye, barley and triticale. If your doctor determines that you have gluten antibodies in your bloodsteam, you should eliminate gluten-containing foods, such as bread, cereal, pasta, crackers, cookies and cakes, from your diet. See Celiac Disease, page 269, for detailed information on a gluten-free diet.

Vitamins and Minerals

Folate (Folic Acid)

If you regularly take methotrexate to treat your psoriasis, it's important to supplement your diet with this B vitamin because the drug reduces skin cell division by interfering with the conversion of folic acid to its active form. Long-term use of methotrexate can cause a folate deficiency in the body, which causes side effects, including nausea, mouth ulcers, hair loss, impaired liver function and anemia.

To offset methotrexate's effect on folic acid metabolism, your doctor will recommend a daily folic acid supplement of 1 to 5 milligrams. In addition, ensure your diet includes good sources of folate (the name of the vitamin when it occurs naturally in foods). Folate-rich foods include lentils, black beans, cooked spinach, asparagus, artichokes and avocados.

Beta Carotene

This nutrient is sometimes cited as a remedy for psoriasis. However, there's very little evidence to support such claims, which appear largely based on an Italian study of 316 newly diagnosed psoriasis patients.[9] The researchers found that, compared with healthy controls, the psoriasis sufferers consumed significantly less beta carotene—their diet was low in carrots, tomatoes and fresh fruit.

Based on these findings, a poor intake of beta carotene may increase your risk for developing psoriasis, but it's not known whether the nutrient can improve the condition. Some of the beta carotene you consume is converted to vitamin A in the body; vitamin A is needed to maintain healthy skin and support the immune system.

There's no recommended dietary intake for beta carotene. To increase your intake, reach for orange and dark-green produce. The best sources include carrots, sweet potato, winter squash, broccoli, collard greens, kale, spinach, apricots, cantaloupe, peaches, nectarines, mango and papaya.

Zinc

A handful of studies have found lower levels of zinc in the blood and skin of people with psoriasis.[10,11] This has led researchers to speculate about the benefits of zinc supplements in managing the condition. Unfortunately, two trials found that zinc supplements were ineffective in improving clinical symptoms.[12,13] One study did find, however, that zinc influenced the activity of white blood cells, suggesting that the mineral might help decrease inflammation.

Zinc is essential for a healthy immune system and it also helps the body transport vitamin A. The best food sources include oysters, seafood, red meat, poultry, yogurt, wheat bran, wheat germ, whole grains and enriched breakfast cereals. See Chapter 4, page 79, for a list of zinc content in selected foods.

Most adult multivitamin and mineral formulas provide 10 to 20 milligrams of zinc (children's formulas may or may not contain zinc). Single zinc supplements are rarely appropriate. Too much zinc has toxic effects, including copper deficiency, heart problems, anemia and a reduced immune system.

Herbal Remedies (Herbal Creams)

Aloe Vera

Aloe vera seems to possesses anti-inflammatory, antibacterial and antifungal properties. According to one study conducted among sixty patients with mild to moderate psoriasis, aloe vera cream was effective in reducing symptoms.[14] Patients with psoriasis plaques used the cream three times daily for a maximum of 4 weeks. At the end of the study, the cream had cured 83 percent of the patients, whereas the placebo cream had cured only 6.6 percent.

Use a cream that contains 0.5 percent aloe. Apply liberally as needed three times per day.

Oregon Grape (*Mahonia aquifolium*)

One study found that a cream made from a specific 10 percent Oregon grape root extract modestly decreased the severity of psoriasis symptoms and improved the quality of life of patients.[15] Active components of Oregon grape appear to relieve symptoms of psoriasis by slowing the rate of abnormal cell growth and reducing inflammation.

The specific Oregon grape root extract cream used in research is called Reliéva (Apolla Pharmaceutical Inc., www. relievaforpsoriasis. com). Apply to affected areas two to three times daily.

Other Natural Health Products

Fish Oil Supplements

Most of the studies that show benefits from fish oil have given patients with severe psoriasis fish oil intravenously. However, a few studies suggest that fish oil capsules rich in EPA help reduce psoriasis symptoms.[16,17] Researchers have also found greater improvements when fish oil is taken in combination with medication or phototherapy.[18,19] There's also a possibility that taking fish oil capsules together with cyclosporine may reduce kidney problems associated with that drug's use.[20]

The typical dosage is 2 to 9 grams of fish oil per day, often taken in divided doses. Look for a product rich in EPA. Fish oil supplements can cause belching and a fishy taste; to prevent this, buy an enteric-coated product. Because fish oil has a thinning effect on the blood, use caution if you're taking blood-thinning medication such as aspirin, warfarin (Coumadin) or heparin.

Nutrition Strategy Checklist for Psoriasis

☐ Fish

☐ Gluten

☐ Folic acid (if you use methotrexate)

☐ Beta carotene

☐ Zinc

☐ Aloe vera cream OR Oregon grape root extract cream

☐ Fish oil supplement

Recommended Resources

Psoriasis Society of Canada
www.psoriasissociety.org/index.html
PO Box 25015
Halifax, NS B3M 4H4
Tel: 902-443-8680 or 1-800-656-4494
Fax: 902-457-1664
Email: info@psoriasissociety.org

Psoriasis Support Canada
www.psoriasissupport.ca
Email: info@psoriasissupport.ca

National Institute of Arthritis and Musculoskeletal and Skin Diseases
National Institutes of Health
www.niams.nih.gov
1 AMS Circle
Bethesda, MD, USA 20892-3675
Tel: 301-495-4484
Fax: 301-718-6366
Email: NIAMSinfo@mail.nih.gov

National Psoriasis Foundation
www.psoriasis.org
6600 SW 92nd Avenue, Suite 300
Portland, OR, USA 97223
Tel: 503-244-7404 or 1-800-723-9166
Fax: 503-245-0626
Email: getinfo@psoriasis.org

Rheumatoid Arthritis

One in every one hundred Canadians suffers from arthritis.[1] Arthritis attacks the joints and connective tissue of the body and can lead to immobility and serious disability. There are several types of chronic arthritis, but one of the most severe forms is rheumatoid arthritis, a debilitating and often crippling disease that causes painful inflammation of the joints. At present, there's no cure for rheumatoid arthritis.

What Causes Rheumatoid Arthritis?

Rheumatoid arthritis is an autoimmune disease. An autoimmune disease develops when something in the body triggers the immune system to attack its own tissues. The result is a painful and chronic inflammation that can damage normal tissues.

Rheumatoid arthritis usually begins with an attack on the synovial membrane, a thin layer of tissue that surrounds each joint. It secretes synovial fluid, which helps the joint to move smoothly and carries nutrients to the bones and cartilage. Rheumatoid arthritis inflames the synovial membrane, causing it to grow and thicken. As the disease progresses, the thickening tissue squeezes the bones, cartilage and ligaments, resulting in loss of movement, severe pain and deformity of the joint. The synovial membrane and white blood cells release enzymes and growth factors, which contribute to the destruction of joint function. Rheumatoid arthritis can also affect other parts of the body, such as the eyes, lungs or heart.

Symptoms

Rheumatoid arthritis is considered to be a systemic disease because it affects the body as a whole. And since it triggers an autoimmune response in the body, the impact of the disease isn't limited to the joints. Often, arthritic pain is accompanied by flu-like symptoms, such as fatigue, general aches and pains, and weakness. Weight loss and anemia may also occur. The main symptoms of arthritis are:

- painful, stiff, swollen and tender joints, especially in the hands and feet
- joint pain that's often worse in the morning
- joint pain that occurs all night long
- morning stiffness that lasts longer than 30 minutes
- pain in three or more joints at the same time
- pain in the same joint on both sides of the body

Rheumatoid arthritis may flare up suddenly, affecting many joints at once. More often, it starts slowly. Once the symptoms begin, it may be only a matter of months before there's serious joint destruction. Frequently, affected joints will freeze in one position, which prevents them from opening or extending properly. Cysts may develop behind the knees, causing pain and swelling in the lower legs. You may also develop rheumatoid nodules, small lumps of tissue that form under the skin near the joints.

Rheumatoid arthritis may occasionally go into spontaneous remission, although this is fairly rare. Nearly half of all people diagnosed with this disease develop some pattern of remission and relapse, and experience symptoms that vary from mild to moderate. However, if the symptoms of rheumatoid arthritis are persistent and the disease remains active for a longer period, there's a much greater risk for permanent joint damage and eventual disability.

Who's at Risk?

Arthritis affects twice as many women as men. Although rheumatoid arthritis can strike at any age, it usually affects people between the ages of 25 and 50. Scientists suspect that some people have a genetic predisposition to rheumatoid arthritis. If your parents or siblings suffer from rheumatoid arthritis, there's a greater chance that you'll develop the disease.

Conventional Treatment

Treatment for rheumatoid arthritis may be as simple as rest and following a healthy diet or as complex as drugs and surgery. Usually physicians will start with the most conservative treatment, moving on to more aggressive therapies only when necessary.

There are four main types of drugs used to treat arthritis:

1. **Non-steroidal anti-inflammatory drugs (NSAIDs)** to reduce joint pain and swelling. Non-prescription NSAIDs include aspirin, Motrin and Advil. Prescription NSAIDs include Naprosyn, Relafen, Indocid and Voltaren. These drugs may cause stomach upset, heartburn, ulcers and possibly high blood pressure. COX-2 inhibitors (e.g., Celebrex, Prexige) are another type of NSAID that may be prescribed if traditional NSAIDs are hard on your stomach, or if you've experienced stomach ulcers.
2. **Disease-modifying antirheumatic drugs (DMARDs)** stop arthritis from getting worse by suppressing the immune system, but they don't reverse joint damage. They include

gold salts, methotrexate, hydroxychloro-quine, sulfasalazine, chloroquine and azathioprine. Rashes, suppressed blood-cell production and liver, kidney and eye problems are a few possible side effects.

3. **Corticosteroids** (e.g., prednisone) suppress the activity of the immune system and significantly reduce inflammation anywhere in your body. They may be taken orally or injected directly into your affected joints for fast, short-term relief of pain or may be used intermittently, in combination with other types of treatment. Corticosteroids are recommended only for short-term use. Long-term use of corticosteroids can cause osteoporosis, weight gain, high blood pressure, cataracts and susceptibility to infection.

4. **Biological response modifiers** block specific hormones involved in inflammation. Biologics available and approved by Health Canada for the treatment of rheumatoid arthritis include Enbrel, Humira, Kineret, Orencia, Remicade and Rituxan. These target tumour necrosis factor (TNF), a substance responsible for joint inflamma-tion and pain. By interfering with TNF function, the drugs reduce inflammation and slow joint destruction.

Although drugs may help reduce the symptoms of rheumatoid arthritis, your treat-ment plan should also include regular rest periods, gentle exercise to keep joints from freezing in one position and a healthy diet. Applying heat to affected joints can also ease discomfort. However, to avoid making symptoms worse, heat shouldn't be applied to an already inflamed joint. Cold applied to inflamed joints reduces pain and swelling by constricting blood flow. Applying ice or cold packs appears to decrease inflammation and is recommended when joints are inflamed.

When the disease is severe and drugs aren't effective, you may want to consider surgery. Arthroscopic surgery, for example, uses a scope and instruments inserted through a small incision to clean or remove inflamed or damaged joint tissue. Some kinds of surgery repair bone deformity by realigning joints, fusing joints or rebuilding parts of joints.

Managing Rheumatoid Arthritis
Dietary Strategies
Food Triggers

There's evidence that a small percentage of people with arthritis have food allergies that exacerbate joint symptoms.[2-8] Researchers have found that when allergy-causing foods are removed from the diet, arthritis patients have significantly less pain and stiffness and fewer painful joints. Foods identified as causing problems include milk, wheat, corn, pork and oranges.

There's a widespread belief that nightshade vegetables such as eggplant, bell peppers, tomatoes and potatoes may aggravate arthritis. However, no studies have proven this and the link between nightshade vegetables and arthritis is no longer accepted as true.

If you think a certain food is triggering your joint pain, remove it from your diet for 2 weeks. Keep a diary to document any change in symptoms, along with what you ate and when. After 2 weeks, reintroduce the food and see if your symptoms worsen.

Mediterranean Diet

Some research suggests that people with rheumatoid arthritis can benefit by adopting a Mediterranean-style diet. One study of patients also taking conventional medication found that, compared to a control diet, a Mediterranean diet reduced inflammation, increased physical function and improved vitality.[9]

The Mediterranean diet is followed by people who live in countries that border the Mediterranean Sea. The diet is plentiful in monounsaturated fat, vitamins, minerals and antioxidants, nutrients that can help reduce inflammation in the body.

This healthy pattern of eating is characterized as follows:

• Fruit, vegetables, grains, beans, nuts and seeds are eaten daily.
• Extra-virgin olive is the predominant source of added fat.
• Dairy products, fish and poultry are eaten in moderate amounts.
• Eggs are eaten at most four times weekly.
• Red meat is seldom eaten.
• Wine is consumed in low to moderate amounts and with meals (not on an empty stomach).

Vegetarian Diet

Researchers have found that fasting for 7 to 10 days, followed by a strict vegetarian diet for at least 3 months, can bring about significant long-term improvements in arthritis symptoms.[10–15] This dietary regimen may reduce inflammation in a number of ways. Vegetarian diets are plentiful in vegetables, fruit, legumes and whole grains, foods that supply the body with protective antioxidants (see below). These diets are very low in or free of animal fat, the type of fat that promotes the production of inflammatory immune compounds. It's also thought that vegetarian diets encourage the growth of friendly bacteria in the intestinal tract. Such microbes provide a protective barrier from disease-causing organisms and may also enhance the immune system.

Most of the studies exploring the link between diet and arthritis have used a gluten-free, vegan diet to achieve results. Vegan diets exclude all animal foods, including dairy, fish, poultry and eggs. This may be too extreme for many people. Such a diet also increases the risk of nutrient deficiencies, especially calcium and vitamin D. If you're interested in trying the fasting/vegan diet approach, consult with a registered dietitian for professional guidance (www.dietitians.ca).

You may decide to ease into a vegetarian diet by following a lacto-vegetarian eating plan. This diet includes dairy products but excludes meat, poultry, fish and eggs.

Fish

Fish contains omega-3 fatty acids, which have been shown in many studies to reduce inflammatory compounds in the blood and ease arthritis joint pain and stiffness.[16–18] Omega-3 fats inhibit the body's production of inflammatory immune compounds called leukotrienes. Although the use of fish oil supplements (see below) to treat arthritis has been studied the most, some studies suggest that eating fish can be just as beneficial. An American study found that women who ate at least 2 servings of baked or broiled fish per week were almost half as likely to have rheumatoid arthritis as women who ate fish less than once per week.[19]

Include oily fish in your diet at least twice per week. The best choices include salmon, trout, Arctic char, Atlantic mackerel, herring, sardines and anchovies.

Sodium

Corticosteroid medications, which your doctor may prescribe in order to reduce inflammation, cause the body to retain sodium. To help prevent fluid weight gain and swelling, reduce the amount of sodium in your diet to less than 2300 milligrams per day (about 1 teaspoon/ 5 ml worth of salt). Most of the sodium we consume every day comes from processed and prepared foods and restaurant meals—only one-tenth comes from the saltshaker. Read nutrition labels to choose commercial food products that are lower in sodium. Avoid the saltshaker at the table and minimize the use of salt in cooking. Season your foods with herbs, spices, flavoured vinegars and fruit juices. See Chapter 5, page 108, for strategies to reduce your sodium intake.

Vitamins and Minerals

Many of the drugs that are part of the conventional treatment of rheumatoid arthritis may deplete your body's store of certain vitamins and minerals. It's therefore important to ensure that you're getting adequate amounts of these nutrients in your daily diet or through supplements.

Antioxidants

Free radicals generated by inflammatory immune compounds are thought to cause tissue damage in people with rheumatoid arthritis. When scientists examine the blood and joint fluid of arthritis suffers, they find increased free radical activity and lower levels of antioxidants such as vitamins C and E, beta carotene and selenium.[20-29] A poor intake of these nutrients can contribute to further joint damage. A diet rich in fruit, vegetables and whole grains supplies a wide range of antioxidants that may help fight free radicals.

There's some evidence that vitamin E supplements have anti-inflammatory and pain-relieving properties in addition to their antioxidant properties. One small study of arthritis patients who were given approximately 800 international units (IU) of vitamin E twice daily reported a small improvement in joint pain.[30] However, a 2007 review of twenty randomized controlled trials found no convincing evidence that antioxidant supplements, alone or in combination, were effective in treating rheumatoid arthritis.[31] Despite this, it's important to be meeting your daily requirements by eating an antioxidant-rich diet.

VITAMIN C. The recommended dietary allowance (RDA) is 75 and 90 milligrams per day for women and men, respectively (smokers need an additional 35 milligrams). Best food sources include citrus fruit, citrus juices, cantaloupe, kiwi, mango, strawberries, broccoli, Brussels sprouts, cauliflower, red pepper and tomato juice.

VITAMIN E. The RDA is 22 IU per day. Best food sources include wheat germ, nuts, seeds, vegetable oils, whole grains and kale.

SELENIUM. The RDA is 55 micrograms per day. Best food sources are seafood, chicken, organ meats, whole grains, nuts, onions, garlic and mushrooms.

BETA CAROTENE. No RDA has been established. Best food sources are orange and dark-green produce, including carrots, sweet potato, winter squash, broccoli, collard greens, kale, spinach, apricots, cantaloupe, peaches, nectarines, mango and papaya.

Folic Acid

Methotrexate, a potent DMARD (disease-modifying antirheumatic drug) used to treat arthritis, interferes with the body's metabolism of folic acid. This can lead to side effects such as nausea, mouth ulcers, hair loss, impaired liver function and anemia. Taking a folic acid supplement can help ease gastrointestinal upset associated with methotrexate use. Your doctor will prescribe a folic acid supplement if you take this drug, but you can also find this B vitamin in cooked spinach, lentils, orange juice, whole grains, fortified breakfast cereals, asparagus, artichoke, avocado and seeds. You'll find a list of folate-rich foods in Chapter 4, page 41.

Calcium and Vitamin D

Corticosteroid drugs such as prednisone can thin the bones, and long-term use can lead to osteoporosis. If you're taking such a medication, it's critical that you consume 1000 to 1500 milligrams of calcium and 1000 IU of vitamin D per day to preserve bone health. A 2-year study conducted among ninety-six patients with rheumatoid arthritis who were receiving low-dose corticosteroid therapy found that daily supplements providing 1000 milligrams of calcium and 500 IU of vitamin D prevented bone loss.[32] Patients in the study who didn't supplement their diet lost bone from the spine at a rate of 2 percent per year. The supplement users gained 0.73 percent of bone per year.

Children with juvenile arthritis tend to have lower bone densities and more bone fractures than children who don't have the disease. Studies have also shown calcium and vitamin D supplements increase bone density in children with rheumatoid arthritis.[33,34]

Vitamin D also plays an important role in regulating the body's immune system. Low blood levels of vitamin D have been associated with rheumatoid arthritis disease activity, which is more severe in the winter months when a lack of sunshine prevents vitamin D synthesis in the skin. Some evidence suggests that increasing vitamin D intake may improve arthritis symptoms. A greater intake of vitamin D is also linked with a lower risk of developing rheumatoid arthritis.[35]

Many Canadians don't meet the daily recommended or adequate intakes of calcium and vitamin D from their diet. To learn more about your daily requirements and supplements, see Chapter 4.

Potassium

In addition to causing bone thinning, corticosteroid medications cause the body to lose potassium, a mineral that helps maintain fluid balance. If you're taking such drugs, be sure to increase your intake of potassium by consuming leafy green vegetables, bananas, oranges, orange juice, prune juice, potatoes, avocado, cantaloupe, peaches, tomatoes, low-sodium tomato juice, lima beans, non-fat yogurt and clams.

Herbal Remedies

Boswellia (*Boswellia serrata*)

This herbal product is derived from the resin of the Indian boswellia tree. A few preliminary studies have demonstrated the effectiveness of boswellia in reducing joint pain and swelling when taken for 3 months. However, one study found that the herb offered no improvement.[36] Boswellia is thought to work by reducing inflammation.[37]

The recommended dose is 400 milligrams three times daily. Buy a product standardized to contain 37.5 percent boswellic acids. It may take up to 8 weeks to notice improvement in arthritis symptoms. Boswellia has not been evaluated for safety in children or in pregnant or breastfeeding women.

Capsaicin Cream

Capsaicin, responsible for the heat of chili peppers, has a long history of use as a topical agent for pain disorders of the skin and joints. When applied to the skin surrounding the joint, capsaicin depletes substance P, a compound that transmits feelings of pain from the nerves to the spinal cord. As a result, pain relief is achieved.

Capsaicin creams are available with or without a prescription. Zostrix, Capzasin-P and Capsin are all available over the counter. Buy a cream with 0.025 percent to 0.075 percent capsaicin (the higher strength may be more effective). Capsaicin cream produces a burning sensation, which diminishes after several applications. Use a small amount to begin with; when you no longer feel burning upon application, increase the amount of cream you use. Be careful not to touch your eyes or other sensitive tissues after applying capsaicin cream. Wash your hands after using the product.

Other Natural Health Products

Fish Oil Supplements

There's evidence to support adding a fish oil supplement to your daily nutrition regime. Many studies have found that taking fish oil capsules, alone or in combination with arthritis medications, reduces the number of tender joints and the amount of morning stiffness, improves walking distance and reduces pain.[38-44] Researchers have even found that arthritis patients are able to reduce the dose of or discontinue anti-inflammatory medication while taking fish oil, without experiencing a flare-up of the disease.

Buy a fish oil supplement that contains EPA and DHA, two omega-3 fatty acids responsible for fish oil's anti-inflammatory effect. Most studies have used a dose of fish oil that provides 3.8 grams EPA and 2 grams DHA per day. Fish oil supplements vary in the amounts of EPA and DHA they contain, so read the labels. Take fish oil in divided doses. It may take 3 to 4 months to notice an improvement in symptoms.

Avoid fish *liver* oil capsules. Most are concentrated in vitamin A, which, if consumed for an extended period of time, can decrease bone density. (Some manufacturers make fish liver oil supplements low in vitamin A.) Fish oil supplements can cause belching and a fishy taste; enteric-coated fish oil capsules are better tolerated. See Chapter 8, page 164, for more on fish oil supplements.

Nutrition Strategy Checklist for Rheumatoid Arthritis

☐ Food triggers
☐ Mediterranean diet
☐ Vegetarian diet
☐ Fish
☐ Low-sodium diet
☐ Antioxidants

- ☐ Folic acid
- ☐ Calcium and vitamin D
- ☐ Potassium
- ☐ Boswellia
- ☐ Capsaicin cream
- ☐ Fish oil supplement

Recommended Resources

The Arthritis Society
www.arthritis.ca
393 University Avenue, Suite 1700
Toronto, ON M5G 1E6
Tel: 416-979-7228
Fax: 416-979-8366
Email: info@arthritis.ca

American College of Rheumatology
www.rheumatology.org
1800 Century Place, Suite 250
Atlanta, GA, USA 30345
Tel: 404-633-3777
Fax: 404-633-1870

Arthritis Foundation
www.arthritis.org
P.O. Box 7669
Atlanta, GA, USA 30357-0669
Tel: 1-800-283-7800

National Institute of Arthritis and Musculoskeletal and Skin Diseases
National Institutes of Health,
U.S. Department of Health and Human Services
www.niams.nih.gov
1 AMS Circle
Bethesda, MD, USA 20892-3675
Tel: 301-495-4484 or 1-877-22-NIAMS (64267)
Fax: 301-718-6366

Shingles (Herpes Zoster)

Shingles is a skin rash caused by the same virus that's responsible for chicken pox. Although the symptoms of chicken pox disappear within a week or two, the virus may linger in nerve cells long afterward. Often, the virus remains there for a lifetime without causing any problems. But sometimes the virus reactivates, causing a painful rash of blisters called shingles, or herpes zoster.

Shingles typically begins with a general feeling of illness, a slight fever and a tingling sensation along one side of your body. Within days, a rash of small, fluid-filled blisters appears in the same general area. Unlike chicken pox, which produces itchy spots anywhere on the body, the blisters caused by shingles develop in a limited area only, along the path of the affected nerve root. Typically, this band of blisters occurs on the chest, abdomen, face or back, but it can also affect the neck, limbs or scalp. An outbreak of shingles can be excruciatingly painful, extremely itchy and tender. The blisters usually dry up and heal within a week or two, but while they're active, they carry the varicella-zoster virus and can infect anyone who hasn't been exposed to chicken pox before.

What Causes Shingles?

The cause of shingles isn't clearly understood, but factors such as age, illness, medications, a weakened immune system and stress can trigger the virus to reactivate. Most people recover from the virus in approximately 1 month and never experience another outbreak. However, people with weakened immune systems, such as those with cancer or AIDS, may suffer repeated episodes.

Normally, shingles isn't a serious condition. However, a shingles rash that develops anywhere near the eye could lead to an infection of the cornea and should be treated immediately. In rare cases, the virus may lead to ear damage or encephalitis (inflammation of the brain) or may attack nerves that control muscle movement, resulting in weakness and temporary paralysis.

One of the most common complications of shingles is a condition called postherpetic neuralgia (PHN), an unrelenting, sometimes incapacitating, pain. It affects the areas of the skin that are supplied by the nerves infected with varicella-zoster virus. PHN develops when the shingles virus damages nerve fibres, causing them to carry confused and exaggerated pain messages along the neural pathways connecting the skin to the brain. In some cases, even the touch of clothing, a light breeze or a simple change of temperature can trigger excruciating pain. PHN normally subsides within a few months but it can persist for a year or more. For one in five people who develop shingles, the pain will continue long after the blisters have healed.[1]

Symptoms

Common symptoms of shingles include:

- chills, fever, general feeling of being unwell
- tingling or burning pain along one side of the body before any rash is visible
- red rash with blisters that last 2 to 3 weeks before drying out and scabbing over
- itching, tingling and pain in the area of the rash
- headaches
- stomach upset or abdominal pain

Who's at Risk?

Anyone who has had chicken pox can develop shingles, although it occurs most commonly in people over the age of 60. People with weakened immune systems from HIV/AIDS, those who are receiving medical treatments, such as radiation and chemotherapy, or those who have a history of bone or lymphatic cancer are also more likely to develop shingles.

A person with shingles can pass the varicella-zoster virus to anyone who hasn't had chicken pox, usually through direct contact with the open sores of the rash. Once infected, the person will develop chicken pox, not shingles. The varicella-zoster virus can't be spread to a person with a normal immune system who has already had chicken pox.

Conventional Treatment

Early medical treatment is crucial to minimize the intensity of the outbreak and lower the risk of nerve damage. Treatments may include:

- antiviral drugs (acyclovir, famciclovir and valacyclovir), which are most effective if taken within 72 hours of the rash developing
- aspirin or codeine to provide some pain relief
- cool compresses applied to the blisters to ease the pain and itching
- calamine lotion to relieve itching
- a chicken pox vaccine to help prevent shingles by reactivating the immune system response to varicella-zoster virus in adults

PHN can be very difficult to treat. The following treatments may be used:

- narcotics such as codeine to offer some pain relief (painkillers such as aspirin and ibuprofen are often ineffective)
- creams containing lidocaine or capsaicin (an extract of hot peppers) to help relieve pain *after* the blisters have healed
- antidepressant medications or epilepsy drugs to help calm the brain and blunt the perception of pain
- an injection of local anesthetic directly into the nerve causing the pain to provide relief (relief is very temporary)
- TENS (transcutaneous electrical nerve stimulation) unit to disrupt pain signals by sending a mild electrical current to the affected nerve

Managing and Preventing Shingles

Dietary Strategies

Fruit and Vegetables

A diet low in vitamins and minerals may increase the risk of shingles by compromising the body's immune system. In a study of over 700 adults, those who ate less than 1 serving of fruit per week—versus three servings per day—were three times more likely to contract the varicella-zoster virus. The same study found that among adults over the age of 60, a higher intake of vitamins and minerals and vegetables significantly reduced the risk of developing shingles.[2]

Fruit and vegetables are excellent sources of nutrients and phytochemicals that enhance the immune system. Ensure your daily diet includes 7 to 10 servings of fruit and vegetables combined; aim for at least 3 fruit servings and 4 vegetable servings each day. One serving is equivalent to 1 medium-sized fruit, 1 cup (250 ml) of chopped fruit, 1/2 cup (125 ml) of 100% fruit or vegetable juice, 1/2 cup (125 ml) of cooked or raw vegetables or 1 cup (250 ml) of salad greens. See Chapter 5, page 88, for strategies to increase your fruit and vegetable intake.

Vitamins and Minerals

Vitamins B1 and B12

These two B vitamins have often been suggested as possible treatments for shingles. However, there's very little evidence that high doses speed recovery. Nevertheless, because B1 and B12 are essential to healthy nerve function, be sure to include foods rich in the two vitamins in your daily diet.

Vitamin B1 (thiamin) is found in pork, liver, whole grains, enriched breakfast cereals, legumes and nuts. Vitamin B12 is found in animal foods and foods that have been fortified with the nutrient. Good sources include meat, poultry, fish, eggs and dairy products, as well as fortified soy and rice beverages.

If you're over the age of 50, take a supplement that supplies vitamin B12. One-third of older adults produce inadequate amounts of stomach acid and have lost the ability to properly absorb B12 from food. To boost your intake of both B vitamins, take a multivitamin and mineral supplement. Single supplements of vitamin B12 are available in 500 and 1000 microgram doses and are very safe.

Vitamin C

This nutrient bolsters immunity by enhancing an antiviral agent in the body called interferon. Vitamin C is also needed for proper healing of skin blisters. The recommended dietary allowance (RDA) is 75 and 90 milligrams per day for women and men, respectively (smokers need an additional 35 milligrams). The best food sources include citrus fruit, citrus juices, cantaloupe, kiwi, mango, strawberries, broccoli, Brussels sprouts, cauliflower, red pepper and tomato juice. To supplement, take 500 milligrams vitamin C once or twice daily. The daily upper limit is 2000 milligrams.

Vitamin E
Supplementation with vitamin E is sometimes recommended to reduce the pain associated with postherpetic neuralgia (PHN), but there isn't enough evidence to support its use. However, vitamin E supplements *have* been shown to improve the immune system of older adults by enhancing the action of certain white blood cells called natural killer cells.[3,4] Consuming adequate amounts of the vitamin may help the body fight the varicella-zoster virus.

The RDA is 22 international units (IU) per day. The best food sources include wheat germ, nuts, seeds, vegetable oils, whole grains and kale. To supplement, take 200 to 400 IU of natural source vitamin E. The upper daily limit is 1500 IU. Don't take single vitamin E supplements if you have diabetes or coronary heart disease. See Chapter 4, page 53, to learn more about vitamin E supplements.

Zinc
This mineral is used to make antibodies, immune compounds that fight virus and bacteria. Ensuring a daily intake of zinc-rich foods will help you support your body's immune system. Good food sources include oysters, seafood, red meat, poultry, yogurt, wheat bran, wheat germ, whole grains and enriched breakfast cereals. See Chapter 4, page 79, for a list of zinc-rich foods. Most adult multivitamin and mineral formulas provide 10 to 20 milligrams, which is 100 percent or more of the recommended intake for adults. Single zinc supplements should only be used if your doctor has determined that you're deficient in this mineral. Too much zinc has toxic effects, including copper deficiency, heart problems and anemia.

Herbal Remedies
Capsaicin Cream
Capsaicin, the compound responsible for the heat of chili peppers, is used as a topical agent to relieve the pain of neuralgia that can follow an outbreak of shingles. A number of studies have found that capsaicin cream significantly reduces pain in people with PHN.[5-10] In one study, almost 50 percent of participants experienced a substantial reduction in pain severity and duration when using capsaicin cream. When applied to the skin, capsaicin depletes substance P, a compound that transmits feelings of pain from the nerves to the spinal cord. As a result, pain relief is achieved.

Capsaicin creams are available with or without a prescription. Zostrix, Capzasin-P and Capsin are all available over the counter. Buy a cream with 0.025 percent to 0.075 percent capsaicin (the higher strength may be more effective). Capsaicin cream produces a burning sensation, which diminishes after several applications. Use a small amount to begin with; when you no longer feel burning upon application, increase the amount of cream used. Be careful not to touch your eyes or other sensitive tissues after applying capsaicin cream. Wash your hands after using the product.

Other Natural Health Products
Digestive Enzymes
These enzymes are produced by the pancreas and are released into the intestine after eating.

Once in the gut, digestive enzymes break down protein, carbohydrate and fat into smaller units that can be absorbed into the bloodstream. When taken as a supplement, digestive enzymes are thought to have anti-inflammatory and immune-enhancing effects in the body.

Two studies compared the effects of digestive enzymes versus the standard treatment drug acyclovir in people with shingles. In each study, the enzyme group and the drug group had similar pain relief, but those taking the enzymes reported fewer side effects.[11,12]

When buying digestive enzymes, be aware that the strength is expressed in activity units rather than milligrams and refers to the enzyme's potency. The dosage varies depending on the type of enzymes found in the product, so follow the manufacturer's directions.

Buy an enteric-coated, broad-based enzyme supplement that contains protease (digests proteins), amylase (digests starch) and lipase (digests fat).

Nutrition Strategy Checklist for Shingles

- ☐ Fruit and vegetables
- ☐ Vitamin B1
- ☐ Vitamin B12
- ☐ Vitamin C
- ☐ Vitamin E
- ☐ Zinc
- ☐ Capsaicin cream
- ☐ Digestive enzymes

Recommended Resources

The American Chronic Pain Association
www.theacpa.org
P.O. Box 850
Rocklin, CA, USA 95677

Tel: 916-632-0922
Fax: 916-632-3208
Email: ACPA@pacbell.net

National Institute of Neurological Disorders and Stroke
National Institutes of Health
www.ninds.nih.gov
P.O. Box 5801
Bethesda, MD, USA 20824
Tel: 301-496-5751

National Shingles Foundation
www.vzvfoundation.org
590 Madison Avenue, 12th Floor
New York, NY, USA 10022
Tel: 212-222-3390
Fax: 212-222-8627

Sinusitis (Sinus Infection)

Sinusitis is a persistent infection of the air cavities within the passage of the nose (paranasal sinuses). It's easily mistaken for the common cold. Sometimes, sinusitis clears up in a week or two. But often, sinus infections can linger for months or even years, possibly causing other infections that can have much more serious consequences.

What Causes Sinusitis?

The sinuses are hollow air spaces or cavities located within the bones of the skull. You have four pairs of sinus cavities, called the paranasal sinuses, and they're all located in the vicinity of the nose. The sinuses are designed to lighten the weight of your skull and to add resonance to the sound of your voice. Each sinus opens into the nose for an efficient exchange of air. They're lined with the same type of mucus membrane that's found inside the nasal passages. The sinuses secrete a steady supply of mucus that helps to protect the lungs by trapping dirt and debris inhaled in the air we breathe. This mucus, along with other secretions, normally drains out of the sinuses through the openings into the nose and throat.

Anything that causes inflammation in the nose can also affect the sinuses. Infections, cigarette smoke or allergic reactions to environmental pollens can cause the mucus membranes to swell, interfering with drainage flow from the sinuses to the nose. This forces mucus to back up into the sinuses, creating an ideal environment for bacteria to multiply. As infection and pus build up because of the clogged drainage passages, air also becomes trapped in the sinuses. The combination of swelling, pus and trapped air puts painful pressure on the sinus wall. The swollen mucus membranes can also prevent air from entering the sinuses, creating an unnatural vacuum in the nasal passages. The end result is the characteristic sinus headache.

Acute sinusitis is relatively short-lived, lasting for 3 weeks or less. Although acute sinusitis often mimics the symptoms of a cold, the causes and treatment are quite different. Anything that blocks drainage from the sinuses can ultimately lead to sinusitis. Factors that often lead to acute sinusitis include:

- **Colds.** Acute sinusitis often follows a common cold. The cold virus sets the stage for sinusitis by inflaming the mucus membranes. The drainage openings swell shut because of the inflammation, and bacterial sinusitis quickly takes hold.

- **Allergens.** Breathing in airborne substances can cause allergic reactions that can lead to swollen nasal passages and sinusitis.
- **Smoking.** Tobacco smoke can slow down the drainage action in the sinuses, causing mucus to back up in the sinuses.

Chronic sinusitis is much more persistent. It can linger for weeks or months at a time, despite treatment with antibiotics. It results from many of the same conditions that lead to acute sinusitis. Airborne allergens, such as dust, mould and pollen, are prime causes of chronic sinusitis because they provoke persistent inflammation in the nasal passages. Other factors that trigger chronic sinus infections include:

- **Fungal infections.** Microscopic fungi are normally present in nasal passages. However, people with malfunctioning immune systems may develop allergic reactions to them, leading to allergic fungal sinusitis.
- **Nasal obstructions.** Nasal polyps, tiny tissue growths that sometimes block the nasal passages, can interfere with normal mucus drainage. A deviated septum, a condition that develops when the wall between the nostrils is crooked, can also block the openings to the sinuses.
- **Dental problems.** Bacteria associated with dental infections or tooth problems may trigger sinusitis.

Although most cases of sinusitis do respond to antibiotics, sometimes the infection can spread to other sinus cavities or to the bones surrounding the sinuses. If the infection spreads to the membranes that protect your brain, it can lead to meningitis, a very dangerous condition that can cause brain damage or death. Occasionally, blood clots may develop in the veins around the sinuses, cutting off the blood supply to the brain. This causes symptoms similar to those of a stroke.

Symptoms

Symptoms, which may vary depending on which sinus cavity is affected, include:

- tenderness or swelling over the affected sinus
- fever and chills
- fatigue
- cough that's more severe at night
- nasal congestion
- yellow or green discharge from the nose
- headache, especially in the morning
- pain in your forehead
- swelling or pain around the eyes
- aching in the jaw or teeth, cheeks feel tender to the touch
- earache, neck pain or deep aching at the top of your head

Who's at Risk?

The following people are more susceptible to contracting a sinus infection:

- people who suffer from colds
- cigarette smokers
- people with airborne allergies
- people with asthma
- people with immune deficiencies or abnormalities in mucus production

Conventional Treatment

Pain relievers may help reduce discomfort. Over-the-counter decongestants may help sinuses drain, but these should be used only for a few days, since longer use may lead to even more swelling and congestion. Applying warm facial packs may loosen congestion. Cautiously inhaling steam from a basin of boiling water may reduce swelling.

Antibiotics are prescribed to treat a bacterial infection. They may be required for a longer period to treat chronic sinusitis. (Sinusitis caused by viral infection doesn't require antibiotic treatment.) Nasal sprays containing corticosteroids are often prescribed for severe inflammations. Antifungal medications may be used to treat allergic fungal sinusitis. Surgery may be necessary to remove nasal polyps, correct a deviated septum or manage other nasal obstructions.

Managing Sinusitis

Dietary Strategies

Alcohol and Fluids

Avoid drinking alcoholic beverages while you have sinusitis. Alcohol worsens blockage by causing the nasal and sinus membranes to swell.

Drink at least 9 to 13 cups (2.2 to 3.2 L) of fluid such as water per day. Fluid helps to dilute secretions and promotes drainage of the sinuses.

Probiotics

Fermented milk products, such as yogurt and kefir, contain healthy bacteria called lactic acid bacteria that may help prevent bacterial sinus infection. Once ingested, these microbes take up residence in the gastrointestinal tract, where they exert their health benefits. A number of studies have shown that regular consumption of probiotic foods as well as a probiotic supplement enhances the activity of the immune system.

Include one fermented milk product in your daily diet. To supplement, buy a product that contains 1 billion to 10 billion live cells per dose (capsule). Take one capsule three times daily with food. Children's products are also available. These usually contain one-quarter to one-half of the adult dose.

Vitamins and Minerals

Antioxidants

Damage caused by harmful free radical molecules has been implicated in many chronic inflammatory conditions of the upper respiratory tract. Some evidence suggests that people with chronic sinusitis have reduced levels of antioxidants in the membranes of their sinuses.[1] A reduced antioxidant defence may lead to further inflammation.

Dietary antioxidants include vitamins C and E and selenium. Vitamins C and E are also important for a healthy immune system, and higher doses have been shown to enhance the infection-fighting ability of the body.

VITAMIN C. The recommended dietary allowance (RDA) is 75 and 90 milligrams per day for women and men, respectively (smokers need an additional 35 milligrams). The best food sources include citrus fruit, citrus juices, cantaloupe, kiwi, mango, strawberries, broccoli, Brussels sprouts, cauliflower, red pepper and tomato juice. To supplement, take 500 milligrams of vitamin C once or twice daily. To treat a cold, take 500 milligrams of vitamin C four times daily. The upper daily limit is 2000 milligrams.

VITAMIN E. The RDA is 22 international units (IU) per day. The best food sources include wheat germ, nuts, seeds, vegetable oils, whole grains and kale. To supplement, take 200 to 400 IU of natural source vitamin E. The upper daily limit is 1500 IU. Single supplements of vitamin E aren't recommended for people who have diabetes or heart disease. See Chapter 4, page 53, for more information on the use of vitamin E supplements.

SELENIUM. The RDA is 55 micrograms per day. The best food sources are seafood, chicken, organ meats, whole grains, nuts, onions, garlic and mushrooms. To supplement, take 200 micrograms of selenium per day. The upper daily limit is 400 micrograms.

Zinc

It's important to ensure that your daily diet contains zinc-rich foods, since the mineral is vital to a healthy immune system. Zinc-rich foods include oysters, seafood, red meat, poultry, yogurt, wheat bran, wheat germ, whole grains and enriched breakfast cereals. You'll find a detailed food list in Chapter 4, page 79.

Most adult multivitamin and mineral formulas provide 10 to 20 milligrams. Children's formulas may or may not contain zinc. Single zinc supplements are rarely appropriate. Too much zinc has toxic effects, including copper deficiency, heart problems and anemia.

Herbal Remedies

Echinacea

Many laboratory studies have shown the ability of echinacea to enhance the body's production of white blood cells that fight infection. This herb can be used to treat a cold before sinusitis sets in. Clinical trials in adults taking echinacea to treat a cold suggest that it may help lessen the duration of symptoms.[2] Echinacea may also be helpful in treating acute bacterial sinusitis.

To ensure quality, buy a product standardized to contain 4 percent echinacosides (*Echinacea angustifolia*) and 0.7 percent flavonoids (*Echinacea purpurea*), two of the herb's active ingredients.

You can choose from several forms of the herb to treat active colds and infection:

- **Standardized extracts made from echinacea root:** a total of 900 milligrams three to four times daily
- **Fluid extracts (1:1):** 0.25 to 1.0 millilitres three times daily
- **Tinctures (1:5):** 1 to 2 millilitres three times daily
- **Teas:** 125 to 250 millilitres three to four times daily

Take the herb, in whichever form, until symptoms are relieved, then continue taking it two to three times daily for 1 week. Some experts recommend taking the herb once every 2 hours (300 milligram standardized extract or 3 to 4 millilitre tincture) until symptoms subside, then up to three times daily for a week. Guidelines for doses in children can be found in Chapter 7, page 134. Don't use echinacea if you're allergic to plants in the Asteraceae/Compositae family (ragweed, daisy, marigold and chrysanthemum).

Garlic (*Allium sativum*)

The sulphur compounds in garlic have been shown to stimulate the body's immune system, making garlic a potential agent in the prevention of bacterial sinus infections.[3-5] A number of studies have focused on the specific sulphur compounds in aged garlic extract, a special supplement that's aged for up to 20 months. Whether garlic actually helps treat a cold remains to be proven. However, the herb does have a long history of use in the treatment of infection.

Use one-half to one clove each day in cooking. To supplement, buy a product made with aged garlic extract. Take two to six capsules a day, in divided doses. Aged garlic extract is odourless and less irritating to the gastrointestinal tract than other forms of garlic supplements (garlic oil capsules, garlic powder tablets).

American Ginseng (*Panax quinquefolius*)

A specific extract of American ginseng called COLD-fX (Afexa Life Sciences Inc.) has been shown to reduce cold symptoms. Evidence suggests that taking 200 milligrams of COLD-fX twice daily over a 3 to 4 month period during flu season can reduce the risk of getting a cold or flu. This ginseng extract also seems to reduce symptom severity and the duration of symptoms when infections do occur. COLD-fX might not reduce the chance of getting the first cold of the season, but it seems to reduce the risk of getting repeat colds in a season.[6-8]

For preventing upper respiratory tract infections such as the common cold, take 200 milligrams of COLD-fX twice daily during cold and flu season.

Panax Ginseng

This herbal remedy may help prevent sinus infection by stimulating the immune system. A well-controlled trial from Italy found that 100 milligrams of *Panax ginseng* (G115 extract) taken daily resulted in a significant decline in the frequency of colds and flus.[9]

Take 100 milligrams of ginseng once daily for 3 weeks to 3 months and follow with a 1- to 2-week rest period before you resume taking the herb. In some people, it may cause mild stomach upset, irritability and insomnia. To prevent overstimulation, avoid taking the herb with caffeine. Ginseng shouldn't be used during pregnancy or breastfeeding, or by individuals with poorly controlled high blood pressure.

Other Natural Health Products

Bromelain

This natural product is a collection of enzymes extracted from the juice and stems of pineapple. Based on research demonstrating its effectiveness in reducing swelling of the sinuses caused by injury, it's often recommended for sinusitis. Studies from the 1960s evaluated bromelain's use in the treatment of sinusitis and found favourable results.[10–12] More recently, a trial of 116 children with acute sinusitis found that those treated with bromelain experienced significantly faster recovery than children receiving standard treatment.[13]

Once bromelain is absorbed into the bloodstream, it causes the release of kinin, a substance that has anti-inflammatory properties. It's also been shown to break down mucus and thin nasal secretions. The typical dose of bromelain is 80 to 320 milligrams taken two to three times per day. However, dosage will vary with the form used, so follow the manufacturer's directions.

Bromelain may cause diarrhea in some individuals and an allergic reaction in those people allergic to pineapple and/or wheat. Bromelain may increase your risk of bleeding if you take anti-coagulant medications such as warfarin (Coumadin) or heparin, so consult your doctor before use. Taking zinc supplements concurrently with bromelain can inhibit the enzyme's action, although there have been no reports of this interaction.

Cod Liver Oil

Preliminary evidence suggests that taking cod liver oil in addition to a daily multivitamin may help treat and prevent sinusitis in children. In a 2-year study of ninety-four children with chronic sinusitis aged 6 months to 5 years, those who were given 1 teaspoon (5 ml) of lemon-flavoured cod liver oil per day and one-half of a children's multivitamin tablet had significantly decreased sinus symptoms, fewer episodes of acute sinusitis and fewer doctor visits for acute illness. (The dosage was halved for children younger than 1 year of age.)[14]

Cod liver oil contains omega-3 fatty acids, which have anti-inflammatory effects in the body. The supplement also contains vitamins A and D, nutrients needed for a healthy immune system. If you decide to give your child cod liver oil in addition to a daily multivitamin, be sure to buy a children's product that is lower strength than adult fish oil. Cod liver oil is available in lemon or orange flavours and can be taken alone or added to foods.

Nutrition Strategy Checklist for Sinusitis

☐ Avoid alcohol

☐ Fluids

☐ Probiotics

☐ Antioxidants

☐ Zinc

☐ Echinacea

☐ Garlic

☐ *Panax Ginseng* OR American ginseng

☐ Bromelain

☐ Cod liver oil and multivitamin (children)

Recommended Resources

American Academy of Allergy, Asthma and Immunology
www.aaaai.org
555 E Wells Street, Suite 110
Milwaukee, WI, USA 53202-3823
Tel: 414-272-6071

Asthma and Allergy Foundation of America
www.aafa.org
1233 20th Street NW, Suite 402
Washington, DC, USA 20036
Tel: 1-800-727-8462
Email: info@aafa.org

National Institute of Allergy and Infectious Diseases
National Institutes of Health
NIAID Office of Communications and Government Relations
www3.niaid.nih.gov
6610 Rockledge Drive, MSC 6612
Bethesda, MD, USA 20892-6612
Tel: 301-496-5717
Fax: 301-402-3573

Stress

Contrary to popular belief, stress can be an essential and positive force in our lives. Stress generates the challenges that keep us stimulated, motivated and productive—life without some stress would be monotonous and uneventful, even boring. Many people deliver their best mental and physical performances in response to stressful situations. Stress is the energy associated with change, and it's the way we respond to change that determines whether stress has a positive or negative influence on our lives.

Although a reasonable level of stress can be beneficial, too much stress can be counterproductive. Chronic, continuous stress in our lives can produce negative emotional, behavioural and physical responses. Chronic stress is thought to play a role in a number of illnesses, including high blood pressure, heart attack and digestive disorders, and it has long been considered a factor in certain types of cancer. Stress weakens the immune system, making you more vulnerable to colds, flu and other infections. Excess stress can also lead to overeating and overweight, cigarette smoking, and alcohol and drug abuse.

Because of the strong interaction between mind and body, stress has often been known to produce physical symptoms, even though no physical disease is evident. Many times, doctors find that the causes of back pain, muscle tension and headaches can be traced directly to situations that are emotionally distressing. The psychological effect of prolonged stress can lead to feelings of anxiety, depression, loss of self-esteem, sleep disorders, eating disorders and substance abuse.

The Stress Response

Years of evolution have prepared the body to react to stressful or dangerous situations with a very specific fight-or-flight response. A stress overload triggers a series of involuntary impulses that are initiated in the brain and rapidly involve almost every body system. The adrenal glands pump adrenaline and other stress hormones into the bloodstream. The heart beats faster to send more oxygen to vital organs—blood pressure rises and muscles tense. Muscle and fat tissues release amino acids and fatty acids into the blood for fuel. The liver converts stored starch to sugars for extra energy and digestion slows down. The kidneys retain water to preserve body fluids. All these responses are designed to prepare your body to defend itself, making it swifter, stronger and poised for immediate action.

During an acute bout of stress, these reactions are normal. Once stress is removed, the body enters the adaptation/resistance stage in which energy reserves are adjusted and rebuilt. How well your body adapts to stress depends on the extent of its nutrient stores and your personal coping ability. If stress is ongoing and severe, your body can reach the exhaustion stage, in which its internal resources finally dwindle. At this point, stress can result in many health problems.

It's increasingly difficult to avoid situations that create prolonged stress. Our high-speed lifestyle bombards us with a steady regimen of change. Technological innovations force us to adapt instantly to new developments. Managing the ever-increasing responsibilities of work, home and play often puts excessive pressures on our time and energy. When the demands of our daily environment exceed our ability to cope successfully, stress becomes a problem that can have far-reaching consequences.

Although much is known about the physical pathways of stress in our bodies, studies have indicated that it's actually the *perception* of stress that triggers our emotional and psychological response. And everyone reacts differently. Why do some people cope well with major stressors, such as the death of a loved one or the loss of a job, while others fall apart when they get stuck in a traffic jam or make a simple mistake at work? Whether stress has a negative or positive impact is influenced by an individual's attitude. Those who interpret a stressful situation as an opportunity for personal growth fare much better than those

who view the circumstances as daunting or fraught with tension and concern. The amount of stress that each person can handle is influenced by a number of factors, including:

- **Genetic makeup.** A predisposition to depression, alcoholism or heart problems in the family may make you more vulnerable to stress.
- **Learned behaviours.** Learning problem-solving skills at a young age and cultivating good self-esteem may improve coping abilities.
- **Social support.** Sharing problems with close relatives, friends and colleagues alleviates the pressure of daily stress.
- **A sense of belonging.** Association with a religious, national or ethnic group provides ongoing support and helps with stress management.
- **Lifestyle factors.** People who are undernourished, get inadequate sleep and are physically unwell have a reduced capacity to handle stress.

The workplace is probably the most common source of chronic stress. Job overload, shift work, lack of promotion, role conflicts and thwarted career plans leave most people feeling exhausted, frustrated and even physically ill at the end of a day. And it's not only high-level executives who succumb to the pressures of stress. Often it's the front-line workers, administrative assistants and middle-management employees who have the highest level of stress, mainly because they have so little control over the daily operation of their work environment.

In addition to work problems, a number of life events have been identified and ranked on a stress-rating scale. The highest stress scores were given to major events, such as the death of a spouse, divorce, personal injury or illness, unemployment and marriage. More minor stress factors included Christmas holidays, vacations, traffic tickets and a change in working or social conditions. Although the circumstances that trigger stress may vary from person to person, we all feel the pressures of our demanding lives and must work to develop sensible coping strategies in order to maintain a long and healthy life.

Symptoms of Chronic Stress

There are many warning signs of chronic stress, including:

- feeling tired all the time
- difficulty sleeping
- upset stomach, indigestion, gas pain
- loss of appetite
- muscle tension
- back pain
- headaches
- pounding heart
- anxiety, nervousness
- forgetfulness, difficulty concentrating
- irritability, moodiness
- reduced efficiency, difficulty making decisions
- increased susceptibility to colds and infections
- use of drugs or alcohol to cope

Who's at Risk?

Everyone is at risk for stress, it seems. Approximately one-quarter of Canadians feel really stressed about once a month, 43 percent feel really stressed a few times a week and 9 percent feel really stressed all the time.[1] It's estimated that 75 percent to 90 percent of all visits to family doctors are for stress-related complaints.

Conventional Treatment

A number of simple lifestyle changes will go a long way in helping you cope with stress:

- Learn to recognize stressful situations and avoid situations you know will generate stress, or try to alter the circumstances in some way to create a more positive result.
- Reduce commitments and give up responsibilities that aren't rewarding or positive.
- Simplify your life: Delegate tasks; learn to say no.
- Take a break: Go for a walk, have a bath, go to a movie, take a weekend off work.
- Include regular, moderate exercise in your daily routine.
- Use relaxation techniques such as deep breathing or meditation to help cope with stressful situations.
- Set priorities: Do only those things that you feel are truly important.
- Share problems with friends, colleagues or close relatives.
- Eat a healthy, balanced diet to maintain a high energy level.
- Get a good night's sleep (see Insomnia, page 508, for tips on how to relax before bedtime).
- Take up a hobby or develop new interests—do something you enjoy.
- Consider getting professional help with your efforts to reduce stress.

Managing Stress

The importance of good nutrition during periods of stress cannot be overemphasized. A healthy diet, together with certain nutritional supplements, provides your body with energy, vitamins and minerals for dealing with stress and can offset the negative effects of stress on the body's immune system.

Dietary Strategies

Carbohydrates

Stress affects the concentration of a brain chemical called serotonin, a compound well known for its ability to induce a calming, relaxing effect. Over the years, researchers have learned that high-carbohydrate diets result in a greater amount of serotonin being released in the brain. High-carbohydrate diets that supply little protein provide the brain with trypto-phan, an amino acid that's used as a building block to synthesize serotonin.

When stress-prone individuals are placed on either a high-carbohydrate or a high-protein diet and subjected to stress, those on the high-carbohydrate diet fare better. Studies have found that, among stress-prone individuals, high-carbohydrate, low-protein diets result in increased levels of tryptophan and serotonin, reduced stress hormone levels, improved mood and mental performance, and a decreased stress-induced depression.[2-5]

To help your body respond more positively to stress, include carbohydrate-rich meals and snacks in your daily diet. Pasta, whole-grain breads and cereals, brown rice, legumes, fruit and vegetables should be the focus of your meals rather than meat, poultry, fish or eggs.

Caffeine

Many studies have found that the combination of caffeine and stress has detrimental effects on blood pressure, especially in those who are at high risk for hypertension.[6-10] It appears that the effects of caffeine and stress are additive, leading to greater increases in stress hormones and blood pressure than if measured separately. Regular consumption of caffeine doesn't build up a tolerance for its effects. Both habitual and light caffeine consumers experience negative effects on the body's stress response. Research among healthy individuals has shown that avoidance of coffee decreases heart rate in response to stress.

In general, caffeine is thought to heighten the body's response to mental stress by increasing the release of cortisol, speeding the heart rate, increasing blood pressure and causing inflammation. Some research suggests that caffeine amplifies the effects of mental stress in non-habitual coffee drinkers, but not in habitual consumers.

Individuals who don't drink caffeinated beverages regularly or who have poorly controlled high blood pressure should avoid caffeine, especially when work demands or other stressors are high. See Chapter 5, page 110, to learn the caffeine content of various beverages and foods.

Alcohol

During periods of prolonged stress, it's wise to avoid alcoholic beverages. Although many people drink to relieve stress, alcohol actually induces the body's stress response by stimu-lating the release of various stress hormones.[11-13]

Alcohol has a dehydrating effect and also interferes with sleep, two factors that can cause fatigue and suboptimal physical and mental performance. A study conducted in forty-eight participants found that when placed in a stressful situation, they scored poorly on memory and reaction time tests if alcohol was consumed the night before.[14]

If you must drink during stressful periods, limit yourself to no more than one drink per day.

Vitamins and Minerals

Multivitamin and Mineral Supplements

The body responds to stress by mobilizing its stored energy and converting it into blood glucose for immediate fuel. This requires the help of many different nutrients, most notably the B vitamins. Vitamin B6 is also needed by the brain to synthesize serotonin, a chemical that can help avert psychological stress. Trace minerals such as zinc are needed for the production of many stress hormones.

Studies show that chronically stressed individuals have depressed levels of nutrients in their body and that the extent of these deficiencies is related to the severity and duration of stress. Researchers have found that a multivitamin and mineral supplement can correct nutrient imbalances, resulting in an improved ability to tolerate stress. In one study, a multivitamin in combination with calcium, magnesium and zinc resulted in reduced anxiety and perceived stress among healthy men.[15–20]

To increase your intake of B vitamins during periods of stress, take a multivitamin and mineral supplement once daily. Alternatively, you could use a B complex supplement instead of a standard multivitamin and mineral; choose one with no more than 0.4 milligrams of folic acid. Chapter 4, page 32, outlines food sources for each B vitamin.

Vitamin C

The body's adrenal glands concentrate vitamin C, where it's used to make two hormones involved in the stress response, noradrenaline and thyroxine. These hormones regulate the body's metabolic rate and energy metabolism, which speed up under stress. Animal studies have found that blood–vitamin C levels are decreased during stress.[21,22] Taking daily vitamin C supplements may also reduce the response to stress in humans. In a well-controlled study of sixty healthy young adults who were presented with an acute psychological stress, those taking 1000 milligrams of vitamin C three times daily had lower rises in blood pressure and cortisol and reported less subjective stress than those in the placebo group.[23]

Include plenty of vitamin C–rich foods in your diet each day: Citrus fruit, strawberries, kiwi, cantaloupe, broccoli, bell peppers, Brussels sprouts, cabbage, tomatoes and potatoes are all good sources. A multivitamin supplement will supply additional vitamin C. If you use a B complex supplement, buy one with vitamin C added. If you're experiencing chronic stress, consider taking a separate vitamin C supplement: 1000 milligrams of vitamin C two or three times daily.

Calcium and Magnesium

The body's response to stress includes a decrease in blood levels of calcium and magnesium.[24,25] These two minerals work together to conduct nerve impulses and contract muscles. Magnesium is essential for the production of energy, and your body's needs for this mineral may be increased during prolonged stress. One study conducted in children exposed to a stressful television program found that supplementation with calcium prevented the decline in blood calcium.[26] Another study conducted in adults revealed that taking a daily multivitamin in combination with calcium and magnesium was associated with reduced anxiety, perceived stress and fatigue.[27]

Each day, ensure you're meeting your daily requirements for calcium and magnesium (see Chapter 4, page 56, for RDAs and food sources). If you need to supplement your diet, use a calcium citrate supplement with added magnesium. If you don't take calcium supplements, take 200 to 250 milligrams of magnesium citrate once daily.

Herbal Remedies

Panax Ginseng

Also known as Asian ginseng, this herb is well known for its role as an adaptogen. As such, it's believed to help the body adapt to stress via its effect on the adrenal glands. Studies in animals under stress have shown that ginseng increases endurance and causes chemical changes that may help the body adapt to stress.[28-31] In humans, ginseng has been found to improve mental performance and enhance the immune system, both of which are adversely affected by chronic stress.[32,33]

The typical dosage of a standardized extract is 100 or 200 milligrams once daily. Take ginseng for 3 weeks to 3 months, followed with a 1- to 2-week rest period before you resume taking the herb. In some people, ginseng may cause mild stomach upset, irritability and insomnia. To avoid overstimulation, start with 100 milligrams a day and avoid taking the herb with caffeine. Ginseng shouldn't be used during pregnancy or breastfeeding, or by individuals with poorly controlled high blood pressure.

Siberian Ginseng (Eleutherococcus senticosus)

Unlike Panax ginseng, this herb has a much milder effect and fewer reported side effects. Pregnant and nursing women can safely take Siberian ginseng, and it's much less likely to cause overstimulation in sensitive individuals. To ensure quality, choose a product standardized for eleutherosides B and E. The usual dosage is 300 to 400 milligrams once daily for 6 to 8 weeks, followed by a 1- to 2-week break.

Nutrition Strategy Checklist for Stress

☐ High-carbohydrate diet
☐ Avoid caffeine
☐ Avoid alcohol
☐ Multivitamin/mineral supplement OR B complex
☐ Vitamin C
☐ Calcium
☐ Magnesium
☐ Panax OR Siberian ginseng

Recommended Resources

Canadian Mental Health Association
www.cmha.ca
Phenix Professional Building
595 Montreal Road, Suite 303
Ottawa, ON K1K 4L2
Tel: 613-745-7750
Fax: 613-745-5522
Email: info@cmha.org

The American Institute of Stress
www.stress.org
124 Park Avenue
Yonkers, NY, USA 10703
Tel: 914-963-1200
Fax: 914-965-6267
Email: Stress125@optonline.net

Mayo Foundation for Medical Education and Research
www.mayoclinic.com

This website is produced by a team of writers, editors, health educators, nurses, doctors and scientists, and is one of the best patient-education sites on the Internet. The information is reliable, thorough and clearly written.

Ulcers (Peptic Ulcers)

Once thought to be the inevitable result of a highly spiced diet and a stressful lifestyle, we now know that the majority of stomach ulcers and more than 90 percent of all duodenal ulcers are actually caused by a bacteria called *Helicobacter pylori* (*H. pylori*). This understanding has changed the way ulcers are treated and has allowed many people to enjoy complete recovery.

What Causes Peptic Ulcers?

A peptic ulcer is a hole that develops when the lining of the stomach or the small intestine has been eaten away by stomach acid and digestive juices. The name *peptic* comes from pepsin, an enzyme that helps to break down food for digestion. Normally, the stomach defends itself from acid erosion by secreting mucus that acts as a protective barrier and chemicals that neutralize acids. Blood circulating through the stomach lining promotes new cell growth and repair. Although these defence mechanisms are usually effective, sometimes a particular combination of stomach acids and digestive enzymes can burn right into the delicate tissue of the stomach.

Ulcers are often no bigger than the eraser on the top of a pencil, but the pain that they cause can be unbearable. There are several different types of peptic ulcers:

- **Duodenal ulcers** are the most common type; they develop in the upper small intestine.
- **Gastric ulcers** occur along the upper curve of the stomach.
- **Esophageal ulcers** occur when stomach acid repeatedly flows back up into the esophagus.
- **Marginal ulcers** develop after surgery to remove part of the stomach; they usually appear where the stomach has been reattached to the intestine.

One in every ten people will develop an ulcer.[1] About 80 percent of people with ulcers are infected with the *H. pylori* bacteria. But not everyone infected with *H. pylori* will develop ulcers. This seems to suggest that *H. pylori* infection, by itself, isn't enough to cause a problem. Scientists suspect that the bacteria must work in combination with other factors, such as a genetic predisposition to ulcers, to create the right environment for an ulcer to develop.

Researchers think that *H. pylori* may be transmitted through food or water or by kissing someone who's infected. The bacteria secrete an enzyme that neutralizes stomach acid, then migrate to the stomach lining and burrow into the mucus layer. This weakens the protective coating, allowing acid to irritate the sensitive stomach tissue.

Another major cause of ulcers is the chronic use of non-steroidal anti-inflammatory drugs (NSAIDs) such as ibuprofen and aspirin. Regular use of these drugs irritates the stomach and interferes with the defensive mechanisms that protect the stomach lining. Once the drug use stops, the ulcer usually heals and doesn't recur unless the drugs are taken again. Cigarette smoking is also an important cause of ulcer formation and ulcer-treatment failure.

Ulcers can sometimes cause serious complications that may require surgery:

- **Penetration.** The ulcer can pass right through the wall of the stomach or duodenum and into a nearby organ, such as the liver.
- **Perforation.** Ulcers on the duodenum and sometimes those on the stomach can burn right through the abdominal wall, creating an opening into the abdomen. The abdomen becomes very tender and intense pain spreads rapidly.
- **Bleeding.** Vomiting blood or passing black or bloody stools usually indicates a bleeding ulcer, which may lead to anemia.
- **Obstruction.** Swollen tissue or scarring around the ulcer may narrow the duodenum or the passageway from the stomach. Repeated vomiting, bloating and loss of appetite are symptoms of a blockage.

Symptoms

The symptoms of peptic ulcer disease vary. Many people experience minimal indigestion or no discomfort at all. Unless a complication occurs, ulcers often come and go spontaneously without the individual even knowing it. However, others may report the following symptoms:

- gnawing, burning pain felt anywhere between the breastbone and the navel
- pain that tends to occur when the stomach is empty, often developing 1 to 3 hours after a meal
- moderate or mild pain that may last from a few minutes to many hours
- pain relief from drinking milk, eating or taking antacids, but the pain returns within a few hours
- worsened pain at night

- pain while eating; bloating, nausea or vomiting after eating (gastric ulcer)
- pain while swallowing or lying down (esophageal ulcer)
- poor appetite, weight loss

Who's at Risk?

Duodenal ulcers often occur between the ages of 30 and 50, whereas gastric ulcers are more common after age 60. Duodenal ulcers are twice as common in men, and gastric ulcers are more common in women. Common risk factors for developing an ulcer include:

- daily use of NSAIDs
- exposure to *H. pylori* bacteria
- a family history of peptic ulcer
- cigarette smoking, which doubles the risk of ulcers, increases severity, slows healing and increases risk of recurrence
- drinking caffeinated beverages
- drinking alcohol
- race: blacks and Hispanics are at higher risk

Conventional Treatment

The first step in treating an ulcer involves elimination of risk factors such as use of NSAIDs and cigarette smoking. Usually a combination of antibiotics and acid-blocking medications is used to treat ulcers caused by H. pylori infections. Histamine H2-receptor antagonist drugs, such as Zantac (ranitidine), Pepcid (famotidine) and Tagamet (cimetidine), decrease the production of stomach acid by blocking the action of a protein called histamine, which stimulates gastric acid production. Proton pump inhibitor drugs, such as Losec (omeprazole), Pantoloc (pantoprazole) and Prevacid (lansoprazole), are more potent than histamine H2-receptor antagonists and stop the pumping of acid into the stomach.

Antacids such as Maalox and Rolaids may help relieve symptoms by temporarily neutralizing stomach acids.

Surgery may be necessary if the ulcer fails to heal, keeps recurring or leads to complications. Caffeine, smoking and alcohol should be avoided since they're all known to irritate an ulcer.

Managing Ulcers
Dietary Strategies

The traditional bland diet is no longer recommended for people with peptic ulcers as there's no evidence that it speeds the rate of healing. In view of this, only slight dietary changes are required, many of them based on an individual's tolerance to certain foods. The goal of the peptic ulcer diet is to avoid extreme elevations in stomach acid secretion and irritation of the mucus lining. To help heal an ulcer, implement the following dietary strategies:

• Avoid caffeinated and decaffeinated beverages and alcohol; all stimulate acid secretion.
• Avoid eating frequent meals and bedtime snacks to prevent increased acid secretion.
• Avoid eating large quantities of food at one sitting.
• Avoid spices that may trigger acid secretion and cause indigestion: black pepper, red chili peppers, cloves, garlic and chili powder. You may find that other spices bother you—these should be avoided during the healing process. (Although chili peppers can irritate an active ulcer, they may actually prevent an ulcer from developing in the first place.)

• Citric acid juices, such as apple juice, may cause heartburn and discomfort in some people.
• Carbonated beverages may cause symptoms in some people and should therefore be avoided.

Cranberry Juice

A number of studies have demonstrated the ability of cranberry juice to inhibit the growth of H. pylori in adults and children being treated for the infection.[2-4] Scientists speculate the antioxidants in cranberries, called anthocyanins, prevent H. pylori from adhering to gastric mucus and the lining of the stomach.

If an H. pylori infection is responsible for your peptic ulcer, drink 10 to 16 ounces (300 to 480 ml) of cranberry juice (cocktail) per day. An 8 ounce (250 ml) serving of cranberry cocktail is equivalent to 2 tablespoons (30 ml) of pure cranberry juice. Pure cranberry juice is very tart as it contains no refined sugars or sweeteners. Dilute the beverage with water to decrease its tartness. It's available in natural food stores and many grocery stores. Alternatively, take a 400 milligram cranberry capsule twice daily.

Dietary Fibre

A high-fibre diet may reduce the risk of developing a duodenal ulcer. Research suggests that soluble fibre from fruit and vegetables, legumes, oats, oat bran and pysllium-enriched breakfast cereals offers the most protection.[5] Fibre delays or slows the emptying of the stomach contents into the small intestine, so fibre-rich meals may prevent acids from entering the duodenum quickly.

Adults require 21 to 38 grams of fibre per day, depending on age. To ensure that you're meeting your daily requirement, eat a high-fibre cereal at breakfast, choose 100% whole-grain foods and include 7 to 10 servings of fruit and vegetables (combined) in your daily diet. You'll find the fibre content of selected foods in Chapter 1, page 8.

Fermented Milk Products

There's some evidence that lactic acid bacteria present in yogurt, kefir and acidophilus milk may prevent ulcers from occurring.[6] Such foods are referred to as probiotics, which means "to promote life." Once consumed, these lactic acid bacteria adhere to the lining of the gastrointestinal tract, where they protect the body from disease-causing microbes. In this way, probiotics are thought to reduce the risk of *H. pylori* infections. Research has shown that certain strains of bifidobacteria and lactobacilli can inhibit the growth of *H. pylori* and decrease gastrointestinal symptoms. Using probiotics in conjunction with following standard H. Pylori therapy may also reduce the likelihood of antibiotic-associated diarrhea.[7-9]

Include 1 serving of a fermented milk product in your daily diet. Probiotic supplements are also available (see below).

Polyunsaturated Fat

Laboratory studies suggest that polyunsaturated fats found in fish, vegetable oils, nuts and seeds may prevent a peptic ulcer by inhibiting the growth of *H. pylori*.[10] The body also uses polyunsaturated fats to manufacture prostaglandins, immune compounds that may affect gastric blood flow and acid secretion. Researchers have learned that people with peptic ulcer disease have lower levels of polyunsaturated fats and prostaglandins in their bloodstream.[11-13]

Include 1 to 2 tablespoons (15 to 30 ml) of flaxseed, canola or walnut oil in your daily diet. Other sources of polyunsaturated fat are cooking oils such as grapeseed, safflower, sunflower and sesame seed oils. Eat oily fish such as salmon, trout, herring and sardines two times per week.

Vitamins and Minerals

Antioxidants

Free radical molecules are believed to play an important role in peptic ulcers, in particular gastric ulcers. It's thought that antioxidant nutrients—vitamins C and E, beta carotene and selenium—might protect the lining of the stomach from oxidative damage and speed the healing of ulcers by neutralizing free radicals before they can harm gastric cells. One study found that people with stomach ulcers had markedly lower levels of all antioxidant nutrients compared with healthy people. The degree of antioxidant depletion was similar whether the ulcer was caused by *H. pylori* or NSAID drug use.[14] Use the following as a guide to increase your antioxidant intake:

VITAMIN C. The recommended dietary allowance (RDA) is 75 and 90 milligrams per day for women and men, respectively (smokers need an additional 35 milligrams). Best food sources include citrus fruit, citrus juices, cantaloupe, kiwi, mango, strawberries, broccoli, Brussels sprouts, cauliflower, red pepper and tomato juice. To supplement, take 500 milligrams of vitamin C once daily. The daily upper limit is 2000 milligrams.

VITAMIN E. The RDA is 22 international units (IU) per day. Best food sources include wheat germ, nuts, seeds, vegetable oils, whole grains and kale. To supplement, take 200 to 400 IU of vitamin E. The daily upper limit is 1500 IU. Don't take single vitamin E supplements if you have diabetes or heart disease. See Chapter 4, page 53, for information on vitamin E supplements.

SELENIUM. The RDA is 55 micrograms per day. Best food sources are seafood, chicken, organ meats, whole grains, nuts, onions, garlic and mushrooms. To supplement, take 200 micrograms of selenium-rich yeast per day. The daily upper limit is 400 micrograms.

BETA CAROTENE. No RDA has been established. Best food sources are orange and dark-green produce, including carrots, sweet potato, winter squash, broccoli, collard greens, kale, spinach, apricots, cantaloupe, peaches, nectarines, mango and papaya. Avoid taking high-dose beta carotene supplements if you smoke. The amount of beta carotene added to multivitamins is considered safe for smokers.

Vitamin B12

If you take acid-blocking medication, you need to increase your intake of vitamin B12. In order for vitamin B12 to be absorbed into the bloodstream, it first must be cleaved from protein in foods. Stomach acid performs this task, providing the body with an absorbable form of the vitamin. Acid-blocking drugs have the potential to cause a B12 deficiency, especially in the elderly and in people who don't get enough of the nutrient from their diet.[15–17]

Vitamin B12 is found exclusively in animal foods: meat, poultry, fish, eggs and dairy products. Fortified soy and rice beverages also supply vitamin B12. If you're a strict vegetarian who eats no animal products and you don't drink fortified soy or rice beverages, take a B12 supplement. All adults over the age of 50 are advised to take a multivitamin to get their B12. If you take a single B12 supplement, take 500 to 1000 micrograms once daily. If you're taking a high-dose supplement to correct a deficiency, choose a sublingual (under the tongue) form; it has been shown to be as effective as B12 injections in replenishing vitamin B12 stores.

Herbal Remedies

Licorice (Glycyrrhiza glabra)

A special form of this herb, called deglycyrrhizinated licorice (DGL), may be an effective treatment for healing ulcers. To make DGL, the portion of the herb that causes fluid retention, high blood pressure and potassium loss is removed. Two studies have shown that DGL taken in combination with antacids can heal ulcers as effectively as acid-blocking drugs.[18,19] DGL appears to block the production of inflammatory compounds called prostaglandin E and F2 alpha involved in peptic ulcer.

To treat an ulcer, chew two to four 380 milligram DGL tablets before each meal. The only side effect noted is its unpleasant taste. Licorice as a whole herb (not DGL) may have hormonal activity in the body and shouldn't be used by women with breast cancer, uterine cancer, ovarian cancer, endometriosis or uterine fibroids or by men with low testosterone levels. It's less likely that these effects occur with DGL, but it's prudent to avoid the product if you fall into one of these categories.

Other Natural Health Products

Probiotic Supplements

If you don't eat yogurt or other fermented milk products on a regular basis, consider taking a probiotic supplement. To supplement, buy a product that offers 1 billion to 10 billion live cells per dose (capsule). Take one capsule three times daily with food. See Chapter 8, page 180, for further information on probiotic supplements.

Nutrition Strategy Checklist for Ulcers

- ☐ Avoid caffeine
- ☐ Avoid eating often
- ☐ Avoid spices
- ☐ Cranberry juice
- ☐ High-fibre diet
- ☐ Fermented milk products
- ☐ Polyunsaturated fat
- ☐ Antioxidants
- ☐ Vitamin B12
- ☐ Deglycyrrhizinated licorice (DGL)
- ☐ Probiotic supplements

Recommended Resources

American College of Gastroenterology
www.acg.gi.org
P.O. Box 342260
Bethesda, MD, USA 20827-2260
Tel: 301-263-9000

Mayo Foundation for Medical Education and Research
www.mayoclinic.com
This website is produced by a team of writers, editors, health educators, nurses, doctors and scientists, and is one of the best patient-education sites on the Internet. The information is reliable, thorough and clearly written.

National Digestive Diseases Information Clearinghouse
National Institutes of Health

www.digestive.niddk.nih.gov
2 Information Way
Bethesda, MD, USA 20892-3570
Tel: 301-654-3810
Fax: 703-738-4929
Email: nddic@info.niddk.nih.gov

Urinary Tract Infections (UTIs)

A urinary tract infection (UTI) occurs in the urinary system, which is made up of the kidneys, ureters, bladder and urethra. Although an infection can happen in any part of the tract, the majority of infections arise in the bladder and urethra. Women experience the symptoms of a UTI far more often than men. Although distressing and uncomfortable, UTIs are easily cured and rarely have lasting complications if treated promptly. However, if left untreated, they can lead to potentially life-threatening problems. Early detection and treatment are essential to prevent a serious health risk.

What Causes Urinary Tract Infections?

The role of the urinary system is to help the body eliminate waste products in the form of urine. The urinary process begins with the kidneys, which filter and remove waste products from the bloodstream. These waste products become urine, which flows from the kidneys through small tubes called ureters into the bladder. The bladder serves as a storage tank, collecting the urine until it can be eliminated. During urination, muscles in the bladder push urine out through the urethra, which has an opening on the outside of your body to discharge this fluid waste.

Normally, the urine that flows through the urinary tract system is sterile, which means that it doesn't contain bacteria. UTIs usually begin when bacteria enter the urethra and travel upward through the urinary tract, producing inflammation and irritation. Most UTIs are caused by *Escherichia coli* (*E. coli*) bacteria, which migrate into the urinary tract from the rectum or the vagina. On rare occasions, bacteria may enter the urinary tract through the bloodstream.

Subtle differences in the anatomy of the male and female urinary tract make women more prone than men to develop UTIs. In women, the opening of the urethra is very close to the opening of the rectum, or anus. Because of the close proximity of these two openings, bacteria can be easily transferred from the rectum into the urinary tract, causing infection. Also, the urethra is considerably shorter in women than in men, which allows the bacteria to reach the bladder much more easily. The final difference is that the female urethra is purely a urinary duct, whereas the male urethra also carries semen. It's thought that the male prostate gland secretes a bacteria-killing fluid into the urethra to protect the semen as it travels through this multifunctional passageway. This fluid may help prevent men from contracting UTIs.

The most common type of UTI is *cystitis*, which is an infection of the bladder. Cystitis may be accompanied by an inflammation of the urethra, a condition known as *urethritis*. Sexually transmitted diseases, such as herpes, chlamydia and gonorrhea, often cause urethritis in both men and women. If the infection is left untreated, bacteria will travel farther into the urinary tract. In some cases, the infection

may even attack the kidneys, which can cause permanent kidney damage if not treated promptly.

Symptoms

One of the most recognizable symptoms of a UTI is a burning sensation at the beginning of or during urination. As the infection progresses, the urge to urinate may become stronger and more frequent. The urine may also appear cloudy and/or dark and have a strange odour. Blood may also show up in the urine.

A UTI may produce fever, chills and vomiting or may cause pain in the back or lower abdominal area. Don't ignore these symptoms, because they may indicate the beginning of a kidney infection, a serious complication of a UTI.

Who's at Risk?

Women are at the greatest risk for contracting a urinary tract infection. It's estimated that one-half of all North American women will develop a UTI in their lifetime. Sexually active girls and women are most often at risk. During intercourse, friction can push bacteria from the anus into the urethra, initiating the cycle of infection. Women who use diaphragms or spermicidal agents for birth control are also at increased risk of UTIs.

Pregnant women are at a higher risk for developing UTIs. Pregnancy produces hormonal changes that affect the urinary system, increasing the likelihood of infection. The urinary tract is often dislodged from its normal position by pressure from the growing fetus, which further increases susceptibility.

Urinary tract infections are also a common concern for elderly women. As women approach menopause, falling estrogen levels leave them prone to infections and irritations of the vagina and urinary tract. In rare cases, UTIs may be the result of anatomical problems, causing obstructions within the urinary tract.

Conventional Treatment

In some cases, UTIs will clear up spontaneously, without any treatment. However, most are treated with antibiotics. The drugs may be given in a single, large dose or may be spread over a course of 3 to 7 days. A repeat infection is treated with a second course of antibiotics. Treatment normally continues until symptoms disappear and a urine test shows no bacteria.

Statistics indicate that the vast majority of women who have a UTI will get another in 18 months. Low daily doses of antibiotics for a 6-month period or a single dose of antibiotic after sexual activity may prevent long-term problems. Post-menopausal women with recurrent UTIs may find some relief through estrogen replacement therapy, particularly estrogen creams that are applied to the vagina.

Preventing and Managing Urinary Tract Infections

Personal Hygiene

One of the most important methods of preventing a UTI is to practise good personal hygiene. To avoid spreading bacteria from the rectum into the urethra, wipe gently from front to back whenever you urinate or have a bowel movement. When you feel the urge to urinate, try not to resist. A regular release of fresh, sterile urine will often wash harmful bacteria out of the urethra before it has a chance to travel into the urinary tract.

It's also a wise idea to clean your genital area before having intercourse, as this will remove harmful bacteria that may be accidentally transferred into the urethra. Urinating before and after intercourse will help wash out any bacteria that have migrated into the urinary tract.

Bacteria grow best in a warm, moist environment. Wear cotton underwear or pantyhose with cotton liners for good ventilation. Avoid tight-fitting pants or other types of clothing that may trap heat, irritate tissues and promote bacterial growth. Washing your undergarments in strong soaps or bleach may cause irritations that could lead to a UTI. Avoid chemical irritants such as bubble bath, perfumed soaps, douches, feminine hygiene deodorants and deodorant tampons and pads.

Dietary Strategies

Aggravating Foods

During your recovery period, avoid coffee, alcohol and spicy foods, which may aggravate the urinary tract. You may find that other foods can also exacerbate discomfort. See Interstitial Cystitis, page 514, for a list of condiments and spices that can irritate the bladder; some of these may also aggravate UTIs.

Cranberry Juice

The anti-infective properties of cranberries are attributed to compounds called anthocyanins. These phytochemicals "wrap" around the UTI *Escherichia coli* (*E. coli*) bacteria and prevent them from adhering to the urinary tract wall. However, cranberry doesn't seem to have the ability to release bacteria that have already adhered to urinary tract cells. Studies in the lab suggest that fructose in cranberries might also contribute to the berry's anti-infective action.

Clinical research has demonstrated that, compared to placebo, drinking 300 millilitres of (Ocean Spray) cranberry juice cocktail daily significantly reduced the risk of recurrent urinary tract infections in elderly women. Studies have also found that drinking 16 ounces (500 ml) of cranberry juice cocktail daily reduces the amount of bacteria found in the urine and urinary tract infections in pregnant women.[1-4]

For preventing urinary tract infections, drink 10 to 16 ounces (300 to 500 ml) of cranberry juice cocktail daily. To avoid the extra sugar calories, use 2 tablespoons (30 ml) of cranberry juice once or twice daily. Alternatively, a cranberry capsule can be taken (see below).

Cranberry is usually well tolerated. However, in very large doses, for example, 12 to 16 cups (3 to 4 L) of juice per day, cranberry can cause stomach upset and diarrhea. Nausea, vomiting and diarrhea have also been reported in pregnant women who drank 16 ounces (500 ml) of cranberry juice cocktail daily, the equivalent of about 1/2 cup (125 ml) of pure cranberry juice.

Blueberries

Anthocyanins, the same compounds found in cranberries that prevent E. coli bacteria from adhering to the wall of the urinary tract, are also abundant in blueberries. Reports from Rutgers State University of New Jersey suggest that blueberries also promote urinary tract health. If you don't like cranberry juice, or you want variety, add 1/2 to 1 cup (125 to 250 ml) of fresh, frozen or dried blueberries to your daily diet. Blueberry concentrate is also available in grocery and natural food stores and can be added to water.

Water

Drink at least 9 to 13 cups (2.2 to 3.2 L) of water each day to help flush bacteria out of your system. Women who engage in vigorous exercise should drink 12 to 16 cups (3 to 4 L) per day. Drink 1 to 2 cups (250 to 500 ml) with each meal and snack. Carry a water bottle with you when you travel.

Herbal Remedies

Cranberry Extract

If you don't want to consume the sugar and calories found in cranberry juice, you might consider taking capsules of dried cranberry, available in health food stores and pharmacies. Take one 400-milligram capsule twice a day— the equivalent of a little more than 1 cup (300 ml) of cranberry juice.

Garlic (Allium sativum)

A daily intake of garlic can help the body fight bacterial infection. Studies have shown that garlic, in particular the allyl sulphur compounds in aged garlic extract, stimulate the body's immune system by increasing the activity of white blood cells that fight infection.[5-7]

Scientists agree that one-half to one clove of fresh garlic consumed each day offers health benefits. And most people can take one or two cloves a day without any side effects such as gastrointestinal upset. Add fresh garlic to salad dressings, pasta sauces and stir-fries.

The oil-soluble compounds in fresh garlic account for its odour and its potential to cause stomach upset. If you decide to supplement instead of eating fresh garlic, buy an aged garlic extract. This form of garlic has the highest concentration of the sulphur compounds that boost the immune system. Aged garlic extract is also odourless and gentler on the stomach.

Take two to six capsules per day, in divided doses. Since both fresh garlic and garlic supplements can thin the blood, consult your physician if you're taking blood-thinning medication such as warfarin (Coumadin).

Other Natural Health Products

Probiotic Supplements

Once consumed, friendly bacteria such as *Lactobacillus* and *Bifidobacterium* produce lactic acid and hydrogen peroxide, compounds that suppress the growth of E. coli in the intestinal tract. Research has demonstrated that these bacteria prevent E. coli from attaching to the lining of the intestine and of the vagina.[8–10] Studies have also found that probiotics, especially strains of *Lactobacillus*, can reduce the recurrence of UTIs in women.[11,12] As well, probiotics have been demonstrated to enhance the body's immune system.

If you're taking an antibiotic for your UTI, consider adding a probiotic supplement to your treatment regime. Antibiotics kill all bacteria—friendly and disease-causing. Taking a probiotic supplement while on antibiotic therapy may lessen the chances of a repeat infection and decrease gastrointestinal upset caused by the drug. To prevent antibiotic medication from killing a significant number of probiotic bacteria in the supplement, take antibiotics and probiotic supplements 2 hours apart.

The strength of a probiotic supplement is expressed in the number of live bacteria cells per capsule. To treat a UTI, take 1 billion to 10 billion live cells daily, in three divided doses. Take your supplement with a meal. Probiotic supplements may cause flatulence, which usually subsides as you continue treatment. There are no safety issues associated with taking these supplements.

In addition to taking a supplement, add probiotic foods such as yogurt and kefir to your daily diet.

Nutrition Strategy Checklist for Urinary Tract Infections

☐ Avoid aggravating foods
☐ Cranberry juice OR cranberry supplements
☐ Blueberries
☐ Water
☐ Garlic
☐ Probiotic supplements

Recommended Resources

The Kidney Foundation of Canada
www.kidney.ca
300–5165 Sherbrooke Street W
Montreal, QC H4A 1T6
Tel: 514-369-4806 or 1-800-361-7494
Fax: 514-369-2472
Email: info@kidney.ca

Mayo Foundation for Medical Education
and Research
www.mayoclinic.com
This website is produced by a team of writers, editors, health educators, nurses, doctors and scientists, and is one of the best patient-education sites on the Internet. The information is reliable, thorough and clearly written.

National Kidney and Urologic Diseases
Information Clearinghouse
The National Institute of Diabetes and
Digestive and Kidney Diseases
National Institutes of Health
www.kidney.niddk.nih.gov
3 Information Way

Bethesda, MD, USA 20892–3580
Tel: 1-800-891-5390
Fax: 703-738-4929
Email: nkudic@info.niddk.nih.gov

Varicose Veins

Varicose veins, more common in women than men, occur most often in the legs—on the inside of the leg, at the back of the calf or around the ankles. They can also develop in the vagina during pregnancy, around the anus as hemorrhoids and, occasionally, in other parts of the body. Unfortunately, varicose veins can't be cured, but they can be managed successfully with simple preventative measures and progressive medical treatments.

What Causes Varicose Veins?

To understand how varicose veins develop, it's important to first understand how the body's circulatory system works. Your heart acts like a pump, sending nutrients and oxygen-rich blood to all your cells through a network of arteries. The blood then flows back to the heart along an extensive system of veins. As the blood returns from the lower parts of your body, it must fight against the natural pull of gravity, which constantly draws it backward, away from the heart. To help keep the blood moving upward toward your heart, veins are equipped with a series of tiny, one-way valves. The forward flow of the blood pushes the valves open in the direction of the heart. As gravity exerts its normal pull, the backpressure of the blood causes the valves to close, preventing any blood from flowing backward in the veins.

Varicose veins develop when these important valves become damaged, allowing blood to pool in the veins. This increased blood flow eventually stretches and weakens the veins, causing them to bulge and swell painfully. Over time, these veins lose their elasticity and stretch to become wider and longer. To fit into the same space, the veins begin to twist and bend under the skin, assuming the characteristic snake-like appearance of varicose veins. As the veins become wider, the valves inside them can no longer close tightly. Blood leaks backward into the veins and causes even more stretching and widening. This vicious cycle continues, creating a worsening condition that usually results in large, bulging blue veins that knot the surface of the skin.

Symptoms

Signs of varicose veins include veins that are dark purple or blue in colour; veins can also appear twisted or bulging. Varicose veins usually don't cause any symptoms, but in some cases they can cause swollen feet and ankles, a dull pressure or aching heaviness in the legs, muscle cramps or itchy skin near the affected veins. The discomfort of varicose veins tends to become worse at the end of the day or after prolonged sitting or standing. Women often suffer more during the days immediately before menstruation.

If varicose veins become worse, you may experience some skin changes caused by a slowing of the blood flow through your veins. These changes include dryness, rashes, brown discolorations or ulcers (open sores). The slower blood flow may also cause a painful inflammation known as phlebitis (see page 609). It can also make you more susceptible to dangerous blood clots inside the damaged vein. If these symptoms appear, medical attention is required.

Who's at Risk?

Varicose veins usually begin to appear between the ages of 30 and 60, when veins lose elasticity and begin to stretch. Several factors increase the odds of getting varicose veins, including obesity, prolonged standing and a family history of varicose veins. Women are more susceptible to varicose veins than men because pressure put on the pelvis during pregnancy and hormonal changes associated with menstruation can both interfere with vein function.

Conventional Treatment

Unfortunately, varicose veins don't get better on their own. Treatment may be undertaken for medical or cosmetic reasons and usually works to relieve symptoms, improve appearance and prevent complications.

Elastic stockings (compression or support hose) are often used to slow the progression of varicose veins. These special stockings help keep your veins from stretching and hurting by massaging the legs and stimulating blood flow. They're to be worn daily, from the moment you get out of bed until you retire in the evening.

Elevating your legs by lying down or using a footstool when sitting will also promote blood drainage and help relieve symptoms. Other ways to relieve the symptoms of varicose veins include:

- Exercise regularly—activities such as walking encourage blood circulation in your legs.
- Maintain a healthy weight—shedding excess weight will take unnecessary pressure off your veins.
- Avoid standing or sitting for long periods.
- Don't wear tight clothing or undergarments that restrict your waist, groin or legs.

- When travelling by air or during long car trips, get up from your seat or stop the car once every 45 minutes so that you can stretch and move around.

If a self-care approach doesn't relieve symptoms, your doctor may recommend one of the following medical treatments:

- **Sclerotherapy.** A saline solution is injected into small- or medium-sized veins, causing them to collapse and seal shut. Blood flow is diverted to stronger, healthier veins, and the body gradually reabsorbs the closed veins. The procedure is very effective, relatively painless and can be done in your doctor's office. It may take several injections before each vein is eliminated, and the injections can only be given at 4- to 6-week intervals.
- **Ambulatory phlebectomy.** A series of small incisions are made in the skin in order to grab the vein with a tiny hook and pull it out. This is performed in the doctor's office using local or regional anesthetic.
- **Laser surgery.** A laser is targeted on the blue-coloured, oxygen-deprived blood in the damaged vein. It heats the blood, scalding and sealing the vein, while leaving the surrounding tissue intact. This technique is useful only on veins close to the skin surface.
- **Stripping/ligation.** This surgery is done in an operating room under general anesthetic. An incision at the groin and another at your ankle opens the varicose vein at each end. A fine wire is threaded through the vein and then pulled out again, removing the vein with it. Alternatively, the vein may be tied off and left in place to be absorbed by your body. The stripping/ligation procedure is lengthy and will leave visible scars.

Preventing and Managing Varicose Veins

Dietary Strategies

Dietary Fibre

Eat high-fibre foods such as whole grains, bran cereal and fresh fruit and vegetables to promote regular bowel function. Research suggests that constipation can contribute to varicose veins. Straining to evacuate small, firm stools puts pressure on the abdominal muscles, which can be transmitted to the veins in the leg. To avoid constipation, consume 21 to 38 grams of fibre per day. (For a list of fibre-rich foods, see Chapter 1, page 4.)

Foods contain varying amounts of insoluble fibres and soluble fibres. Foods that have a greater proportion of insoluble fibres, such as wheat bran, whole grains, nuts, seeds and certain fruit and vegetables, are used to treat and prevent constipation. Once consumed, insoluble fibres make their way to the intestinal tract, where they absorb water and help form larger, softer stools and speed evacuation. Psyllium, a type of soluble fibre, also adds bulk to stools and can be used to treat constipation. See Constipation, page 318, for more on psyllium.

Fibre needs plenty of fluid so that it can swell and promote the passage of large, soft stools through the bowel. Drink at least 9 cups (2.2 L) of fluid each day. If you exercise regularly, drink an additional 4 cups (1 L).

Sodium

Reduce your salt intake to prevent swelling that may damage veins. Consume less than 2300 milligrams of sodium per day (about 1 teaspoon/5 ml of table salt). The vast majority of sodium we consume every day comes from processed and prepared foods and restaurant meals. Read nutrition labels on packaged foods to choose brands that contain less sodium. Avoid the saltshaker at the table and minimize the use of salt when you cook. Instead of salt, season your foods with herbs, spices, flavoured vinegars and fruit juices. You'll find strategies to help reduce your sodium intake in Chapter 5, page 108.

Herbal Remedies

Bilberry (Vaccinium myrtillus)

This herb contains anthocyanins, compounds that belong to the flavonoids family of phyto-chemicals. Anthocyanins help form strong connective tissue and blood capillaries. Most research on bilberry has been in eye health, but one controlled study found it to be effective in relieving leg pain and swelling in people with varicose veins. Buy a product standardized to 25 percent to 36 percent anthocyanins. Take 160 milligrams twice daily. No adverse effects have been reported with bilberry use.

Gotu Kola (Centella asiatica)

This herb has long been used in India and Indonesia to promote wound healing and to treat skin diseases. Since the 1970s it has been used in Europe to treat venous insufficiency disorders. Studies have shown that taking the herb for 4 weeks can reduce leg heaviness, discomfort, foot and ankle swelling, and fluid leakage in the veins.[1-5] Gotu kola seems to promote the formation of healthy connective tissue.

Take 60 to 180 milligrams per day of a standardized gotu kola extract, in divided doses. The herb isn't associated with any side effects other than the occasional gastro-intestinal upset and skin rash. People with liver disease shouldn't use gotu kola. Safety in pregnant and breastfeeding women and young children hasn't been established.

Horse Chestnut *(Aesculus hippocastanum)*

Evidence supports the use of horse chestnut in the treatment of varicose veins. Although it doesn't reduce the visible appearance of varicose veins, studies have demonstrated its ability to reduce leg swelling, leg pain and heaviness as well as leg ulcers. One study even found that horse chestnut was as effective as compression stockings, although the herb took longer to have an effect.[6-9]

Aescin, an active compound in horse chestnut seeds, enhances circulation through the veins. The herb appears to constrict and promote normal tone in the veins so that blood returns to the heart. The compound also has anti-inflammatory properties and may reduce swelling in the legs.

Buy a product standardized to contain 16 percent to 21 percent aescin. Studies have used a 300 milligram horse chestnut seed extract containing 50 milligrams of aescin taken twice daily.

In rare instances, horse chestnut seed extract can cause stomach upset, nausea and itching. Use isn't recommended during pregnancy and breastfeeding since there's insufficient information available about its safety at these times. Horse chestnut shouldn't be taken by people with liver or kidney disease.

Other Natural Health Products

Grapeseed Extract

Like bilberry, this supplement is rich in anthocyanins, natural compounds that help keep blood vessels healthy. Grapeseed extract is thought to work by inhibiting the action of enzymes that break down connective tissue. Three studies have

evaluated its use in varicose veins and found that it significantly improved symptoms compared with the placebo treatment.[10-12] Anthocyanins may also help reduce blood clots.

For vein health, many experts recommend taking 75 to 300 milligrams for 3 weeks, followed by a maintenance dose of 40 to 80 milligrams daily. Grapeseed extract is considered extremely safe, although it may have blood-thinning properties when taken in high doses. Consult your doctor if you're taking an anticoagulant medication.

Nutrition Strategy Checklist for Varicose Veins

☐   Dietary fibre
☐   Fluids
☐   Low-sodium diet
☐   Horse chestnut* OR bilberry OR gotu kola
☐   Grapeseed extract

*Best evidence—start here.

Recommended Resources

Mayo Foundation for Medical Education and Research
www.mayoclinic.com
This website is produced by a team of writers, editors, health educators, nurses, doctors and scientists, and is one of the best patient-education sites on the Internet. The information is reliable, thorough and clearly written.

The National Women's Health Information Center
www.womenshealth.gov
U.S. Department of Health and Human Services
Office on Women's Health
Tel: 1-800-994-9662

Notes

Introduction

1. IPSOS-Reid Canadian Nutritional Supplement Review, 2000.
2. The National Institute of Nutrition. *Tracking Nutrition Trends 1989–1994–1997. An Update on Canadians' Attitudes, Knowledge and Reported Actions* (Ottawa, November 1997).

Part One: Nutrition and Diet

3   Dietary Fats and Oils

1. Minister of Health. *Transforming the Food Supply. Report of the Trans Fat Task Force Submitted to the Minister of Health, June 2006.* Available at www.healthcanada.ca/ transfat.

4   Understanding Vitamins and Minerals

1. Cole, BF, JA Baron, RS Sandler, RW Haile, DJ Ahnen, RS Bresalier, G McKeown-Eyssen, RW Summers, RI Rothstein, CA Burke, DC Snover, TR Church, JI Allen, DJ Robertson, GJ Beck, JH Bond, T Byers, JS Mandel, LA Mott, LH Pearson, EL Barry, JR Rees, N Marcon, F Saibil, PM Ueland, ER Greenberg; Polyp Prevention Study Group. Folic acid for the prevention of colorectal adenomas: A randomized clinical trial. *JAMA* 2007, 297(21):2351–2359.
2. Figueiredo, JC, MV Grau, RW Haile, et al. Folic acid and risk of prostate cancer: Results from a randomized clinical trial. *J Natl Cancer Inst* 2009, 101(6):432–435.
3. Lippman, SM, EA Klein, PJ Goodman, et al. Effect of selenium and vitamin E on risk of prostate cancer and other cancers: The Selenium and Vitamin E Cancer Prevention Trial (SELECT). *JAMA* 2009, 301(1):39–51.

5   Elements of a Healthy Diet

1. Montonen, J, P Knekt, R Jarvinen, et al. Whole-grain and fiber intake and the incidence of type 2 diabetes. *Am J Clin Nutr* 2003, 77(3):622–629.
2. Larsson, SC, E Giovannucci, L Bergkvist, A Wolk. Whole grain consumption and risk of colorectal cancer: A population-based cohort of 60,000 women. *Br J Cancer* 2005, 92(9): 1803–1807.
3. Mozaffarian, D, and EB Rimm. Fish intake, contaminants, and human health: Evaluating the risks and the benefits. *JAMA* 2006, 296(15):1885–1899.
4. Kalmijn, S, LJ Launer, A Ott, et al. Dietary fat intake and the risk of incident dementia in the Rotterdam Study. *Ann Neurol* 1997, 42(5): 776–782.
5. Bazzano, LA, J He, LG Ogden, et al. Legume consumption and risk of coronary heart disease in U.S. men and women: NHANES I Epidemiologic Follow-up Study. *Arch Intern Med* 2001, 161(21):2573–2578.

6. Kolonel, LN, JH Hankin, AS Whittemore, et al. Vegetables, fruits, legumes and prostate cancer: A multiethnic case-control study. *Cancer Epidemiol Biomarkers Prev* 2000, 9(8):795–804.
7. Trock, BJ, L Hilakivi-Clarke, and R Clarke. Meta-analysis of soy intake and breast cancer risk. *J Natl Cancer Inst* 2006, 98(7):459–471.
8. Shu, XO, F Jin, Q Dai, W Wen, et al. Soyfood intake during adolescence and subsequent risk of breast cancer among Chinese women. *Cancer Epidemiol Biomarkers Prev* 2001, 10(5):483–488.
9. Huang, HY, B Caballero, S Chang, AJ Alberg, RD Semba, CR Schneyer, RF Wilson, TY Cheng, J Vassy, G Prokopowicz, GJ Barnes 2nd, and EB Bass. The efficacy and safety of multivitamin and mineral supplement use to prevent cancer and chronic disease in adults: A systematic review for a National Institutes of Health state-of-the-science conference. *Ann Intern Med* 2006, 145(5):372–85.
10. Lawson, KA, ME Wright, A Subar, T Mouw, A Hollenbeck, A Schatzkin, MF Leitzmann. Multivitamin use and risk of prostate cancer in the National Institutes of Health–AARP Diet and Health Study. *J Natl Cancer Inst* 2007, 99(10): 754–764.
11. Allen, NE, V Beral, D Casabonne, SW Kan, GK Reeves, A Brown, J Green; Million Women Study Collaborators. Moderate alcohol intake and cancer incidence in women. *J Natl Cancer Inst* 2009, 101(5):296–305.

Part Two: Herbal Remedies and Natural Health Products

6   Herbal Medicine

1. Baseline Natural Health Products Survey Among Consumers, March 2005. Available at www.hc-sc.gc.ca/ dhp-mps/pubs/natur/ eng_cons_survey-eng.php.

7   Popular Herbal Remedies

General

Boon, H, and M Smith. *The Botanical Pharmacy: The Pharmacology of 47 Common Herbs* (Kingston: Quarry Press, 1999).

Chandler, F, ed. *Herbs: Everyday Reference for Health Professionals* (Ottawa: Canadian Pharmacists Association and Canadian Medical Association, 2000).

Schultz, V, R Hansel and VE Tyler. *Rational Phytotherapy: A Physician's Guide to Herbal Medicine*, 3rd ed. (Berlin: Springer-Verlag, 1998).

Bilberry

1. Repossi, P, et al. The role of anthocyanosides on vascular permeability in diabetic retinopathy. *Ann Ottamol Clin Ocul* 1987, 113(4):357–361. [Italian]

2. Scharrer, A, and M Ober. Anthocyanosides in the treatment of retinopathies. *Kiln Monastbl Augenheilkd* 1981, 178 (5):386–9. [German]

3. Perossini, M, G Guidi, S Chiellini, and D Siravo. Diabetic and hypertensive retinopathy therapy with Vaccinium myrtillus anthocyanosides (Tegens). Double-blind, placebo-controlled clinical trial. *Ann Ottalmol Clin Ocul* 1987, 113(2):1173–1177. [Italian]

4. Colombo, D, and R Vescovini. Controlled clinical trial on the use of Vaccinium myrtillus in primary dysmenorrhea. *G Ital Ostet Ginecol* 1985, 7(12):1033–1038. [Italian]

Black Cohosh

1. Liske, E, W Hanggi, HH Henneicke-von Zepelin, et al. Physiological investigation of a unique extract of black cohosh (Cimicifugae racemosae rhizoma): A 6-month clinical study demonstrates no systemic estrogenic effect. *J Women's Health Gend Based Med* 2002, 11(2):163–174.

2. Osmers, R, M Friede, E Liske, et al. Efficacy and safety of isopropanolic black cohosh extract for climacteric symptoms. *Obstet Gynecol* 2005, 105 (5 Pt. 1):1074–1083.

3. Nappi, RE, B Malavasi, B Brundu, and F Facchinetti. Efficacy of Cimicifuga racemosa on climacteric complaints: A randomized study versus low-dose transdermal estradiol. *Gynecol Endocrinol* 2005, 20(1):30–35.

Chasteberry

1. Prilepskaya, VN, AV Ledina, AV Tagiyeva, and FS Revazova. Vitex agnus castus: Successful treatment of moderate to severe premenstrual syndrome. *Maturitas* 2006, 55(1) Suppl 1:S55–63.

2. Loch, EG, et al. Treatment of premenstrual syndrome with a phytopharmaceutical formulation containing Vitex agnus castus. *J Women's Health Gend Based Med* 2000, 9(3):315–320.

3. Schellenberg, R. Treatment for the premenstrual syndrome with agnus castus fruit extract: Prospective, randomized, placebo-controlled study. *Br Med J* 2001, 322(7279): 134–137.

4. Berger, D, W Schaffner, E Schrader, et al. Efficacy of Vitex agnus castus L. extract Ze 440 in patients with premenstrual syndrome (PMS). *Arch Gynecol Obstet* 2000, 264(3): 150–153.

5. Lauritzen, CH, HD Reuter, R Repges, et al. Treatment of premenstrual tension syndrome with Vitex agnus castus: Controlled-double blind versus pyridoxine. *Phytomedicine* 1997, 4:183–189.

6. Atmaca, M, S Kumru, E Tezcan. Fluoxetine versus Vitex agnus castus extract in the treatment of premenstrual dysphoric disorder. *Hum Psychopharmacol Clin Exp* 2003, 18(3):191–195.

Cranberry

1. Avorn, J, M Manone, JH Gurwitz, et al. Reduction of bacteriuria and pyuria after ingestion of cranberry juice. *JAMA* 1994, 27(10)1:751–754.

2. Wing, DA, PJ Rumney, CW Preslicka, and JH Chung. Daily cranberry juice for the prevention of asymptomatic bacteriuria in pregnancy: A randomized, controlled pilot study. *J Urol* 2008, 180(4):1367–1372.

3. Walker, EB, DP Barney, JN Mickelsen, et al. Cranberry concentrate: UTI prophylaxis. *J Fam Pract* 1997, 45:167–168.

4. McMurdo, MET, I Argo, G Phillips, et al. Cranberry or trimethoprim for the prevention of recurrently urinary tract infections? A randomized control trial in older women. *J Antimicrob Chemother* 2009, 63(2):389–395.

Devil's Claw

1. Chantre, P, A Cappelaere, D Leblan, et al. Efficacy and tolerance of Harpagophytum procumbens versus diacerhein in treatment of osteoarthritis. *Phytomedicine* 2000, 7:177–184.

2. Chrubasik, S, J Thanner, O Kunzel, et al. Comparison of outcome measures during treatment with the proprietary Harpagophytum extract doloteffin in patients with pain in the lower back, knee or hip. *Phytomedicine* 2002, 9:181–194.

3. Gagnier, JJ, S Chrubasik, and E Manheimer. Harpagophytum procumbens for osteoarthritis and low back pain: A systematic review. *BMC Complement Altern Med* 2004, 4:13.

4. Wegener, T, and NP Lupke. Treatment of patients with arthrosis of hip or knee with an aqueous extract of devil's claw (Harpagophytum procumbens DC). *Phytother Res* 2003, 17(10):1165–1172.

5. Chrubasik, S, J Thanner, O Kunzel, et al. Comparison of outcome measures during treatment with the proprietary Harpagophytum extract doloteffin in patients with pain in the lower back, knee or hip. *Phytomedicine* 2002, 9(3):181–94.

6. Chrubasik, S, O Kunzel, J Thanner, et al. A 1-year follow-up after a pilot study with Doloteffin for low back pain. *Phytomedicine* 2005, 12(1–2):1–9.

Echinacea

1. Steinmuller, C, et al. Polysaccharides isolated from plant cell cultures of Echinacea pupurea enhance the resistance of immunosuppressed mice against systemic infections with Candida albicans and Listeria monocytogenes. *Int J Immunopharmacol* 1993, 15(5):605–614.

2. Grimm, M, et al. A randomized controlled trial of the effect of fluid extract of Echinacea purpurea on the incidence and severity of colds and respiratory tract infections. *Am J Med* 1999, 106:138–143.

3. Mechart, D, et al. Echinacea root extracts for the prevention of upper respiratory tract infections. *Arch Fam Med* 1998, 7:541–545.

4. Dorn, M, et al. Placebo-controlled, double-blind study of Echinacea pallidae radix in upper respiratory tract infections. *Complement Ther Med* 1997, 5:40–42.

5. Melchart, D, et al. Results of five randomized studies on the immunomodulatory activity of preparations of Echinacea. *J Alt Complement Med* 1995, 1:145–160.

6. Shah, SA, S Sander, CM White, M Rinaldi, and CI Coleman. Evaluation of echinacea for the prevention and treatment of the common cold: A meta-analysis. *Lancet Infect Dis* 2007, 7(7):473–480.

7. Linde, K, B Barrett, K Wölkart, R Bauer, and D Melchart. Echinacea for preventing and treating the common cold. *Cochrane Database Syst Rev* 2006, (1):CD000530.

Evening Primrose

1. Gateley, CA, et al. Drug treatments for mastalgia: 17 years experience in the Cardiff Mastalgia Clinic. *J R Soc Med* 1992, 85(1):12–15.

2. Pye, JK, RE Mansel, and LE Hughes. Clinical experience of drug treatments for mastalgia. *Lancet* 1985, 2(8451): 373–377.

3. Cheung, KL. Management of cyclical mastalgia in oriental women: Pioneer experience of using gamolenic acid (Efamast) in Asia. *Aust N Z J Surg* 1999, 69(7):492–494.

4. Morse, PF, et al. Meta analysis of placebo-controlled studies of the efficacy of Epogram in treatment of atopic eczema: Relationship between plasma essential fatty acid changes and response. *Br J Dermatol* 1989, 121:75–90.

5. Belch, JJ, and A Hill. Evening primrose oil in rheumatologic conditions. *Am J Clin Nutr* 2000, 71(1):352S–356S.

6. Meehan, E, et al. Influence of an n-polyunsaturated fatty acid-enriched diet on the development of tolerance during chronic ethanol administration in rats. *Alcohol Clin Exp Res* 1995, 19(6):1141–1146.

7. Corbett, R, et al. The effects of chronic administration of ethanol on synpatosomal fatty acid composition: Modulation by oil enriched with gamma-linolenic acid. *Alcohol Alcohol* 1992, 27(1):11–14.

8. Vaddadi, KS, and CJ Gilleard. Essential fatty acids, tardive dyskinesia and schizophrenia, in *Omega-6 Essential Fatty Acids: Pathophysiology and Roles in Clinical Medicine*, ed. DF Horrobin (New York: Wiley-Liss, 1990).

Feverfew

1. Murphy, JJ, et al. Randomised double-blind placebo-controlled trial of feverfew in migraine prevention. *Lancet* 1988, 2(8604):189–192.

2. Palevitch, D, G Earon, and R Carasso. Feverfew (tanacetum parthenium) as a prophylactic treatment for migraine: A double-blind, placebo-controlled study. *Phytotherapy Res* 1997, 11:508–511.

3. Pfaffenrath, V, HC Diener, M Fischer, et al. The efficacy and safety of Tanacetum parthenium (feverfew) in migraine prophylaxis: A double-blind, multicentre, randomized placebo-controlled dose-response study. *Cephalalgia* 2002, 22(7):523–532.

4. Diener, HC, V Pfaffenrath, J Schnitker, et al. Efficacy and safety of 6.25 mg t.i.d. feverfew CO2-extract (MIG-99) in migraine prevention: A randomized, double-blind, multi-centre, placebo-controlled study. *Cephalalgia* 2005, 25(11): 1031–1041.

Garlic

1. Steiner, M, et al. A double-blind crossover study in moderately hypercholesterolemic men that compared the effect of aged garlic extract and placebo administration on blood lipids. *Am J Clin Nutr* 1996, 64(6):866–870.

2. Hozgartner, H, et al. Comparison of the efficacy and tolerance of a garlic preparation vs. bezafibrate. *Arzneimittelforschung* 1992, 42(12):1473–1477.

3. Bordia, A. Effects of garlic on blood lipids in patients with coronary heart disease. *Am J Clin Nutr* 1981, 34(10): 2100–2103.

4. Bordia, A, et al. Effect of garlic (Allium sativum) on blood lipids, blood sugar, fibrinogen and fibrinolytic activity in patients with coronary artery disease. *Prostaglandins Leukot Essent Fatty Acids* 1998, 58(4):257–263.

5. Ibid.

6. Ide, N, and BH Lau. Aged garlic extract attenuates intracellular oxidative stress. *Phytomedicine* 1999, 6(2):125–131.

7. Ide, N, and BH Lau. Garlic compounds protect vascular endothelial cells from oxidized low-density lipoprotein-induced injury. *J Pharm Pharmacol* 1997, 49(9):908–911.

8. Steiner, M, et al. A double-blind crossover study in moderately hypercholesterolemic men that compared the effect of aged garlic extract and placebo administration on blood lipids. *Am J Clin Nutr* 1996, 64(6):866–870.

9. Steinmetz, KA, et al. Vegetables, fruit, and colon cancer in the Iowa Women's Health Study. *Am J Epidemiol* 1994, 139(1):1–15.

10. Levi, F, et al. Food groups and colorectal cancer risk. *Br J Cancer* 1999, 79(7–8):1283–1287.

11. Key, TJ, et al. A case-control study of diet and prostate cancer. *Br J Cancer* 1997, 76(5): 678–687.

12. Sivam, GP. Protection against Helicobacter pylori and other bacterial infections by garlic. *J Nutr* 2001, 131(Suppl 3):S1106–S1108.

13. Cellini, L, et al. Inhibition of Helicobacter pylori by garlic extract (Allium sativum). *FEMS Immunol Med Microbiol* 1996, 13(4):273–277.

14. Song, K, and J Milner. The influence of heating on the anticancer properties of garlic. *J Nutr* 2001, 131: 1054S–1057S.

Ginger

1. Grontved, A, et al. Ginger root against seasickness. A controlled trial on the open sea. *Acta Otolaryngol* 1988, 105:45–49.

2. Schmid, R, et al. Comparison of seven commonly used agents for prophylaxis of seasickness. *J Travel Med* 1994, 1:203–206.

3. Stewart, JJ, et al. Effects of ginger on motion sickness susceptibility and gastric function. *Pharmacology* 1991, 42:111–120.

4. Manno, JE, et al. Comparison of efficacy of ginger with various antimotion sickness drugs. *Clin Res Pract Drug Reg Aff* 1988, 6:129–136.

5. Chittumma, P, K Kaewkiattikun, and B Wiriyasiriwach. Comparison of the effectiveness of ginger and vitamin B6 for treatment of nausea and vomiting in early pregnancy: A randomized double-blind controlled trial. *J Med Assoc Thai* 2007, 90(1):15–20.

6. Borrelli, F, R Capasso, G Aviello, et al. Effectiveness and safety of ginger in the treatment of pregnancy-induced nausea and vomiting. *Obstet Gynecol* 2005, 105(4): 849–856.

7. Portnoi, G, LA Chng, L Karimi-Tabesh, et al. Prospective comparative study of the safety and effectiveness of ginger for the treatment of nausea and vomiting in pregnancy. *Am J Obstet Gynecol* 2003, 189(5):1374–1377.

8. Vutyavanich, T, T Kraisarin and R Ruangsri. Ginger for nausea and vomiting in pregnancy: Randomized, double-masked, placebo-controlled trial. *Obstet Gynecol* 2001, 97(4):577–582.

9. Fischer-Rasmussen, W, et al. Ginger treatment of hyper-emesis gravidarum. *Eur J Obstet Gynecol Reprod Biol* 1991, 38:19–24.

10. Ernst, E, and MH Pittler. Efficacy of ginger for nausea and vomiting: A systematic review of randomized clinical trials. *Br J Anaesth* 2000, 84(3):367–371.

11. Grontved, A, and E Hentzer. Vertigo-reducing effect of ginger root: A controlled clinical study. *ORL J Otorhinolaryngol Relat Spec* 1986, 48(5):282–286.

Ginkgo

1. Brautigam, MR, FA Blommaert, G Verleye, et al. Treatment of age-related memory complaints with Gingko biloba extract: A randomized double blind placebo-controlled study. *Phytomedicine* 1998, 5:425–434.

2. Rai, GS, C Shovlin, and KA Wesnes. A double-blind, placebo-controlled study of Ginkgo biloba extract ('tanakan') in elderly outpatients with mild to moderate memory impairment. *Curr Med Res Opin* 1991, 12(6): 350–355.

3. Solomon, PR, F Adams, A Silver, et al. Ginkgo for memory enhancement: A randomized controlled trial. *JAMA* 2002, 288(7):835–840.

4. DeKosky, ST, JD Williamson, AL Fitzpatrick, et al. Ginkgo biloba for prevention of dementia: a randomized controlled trial. *JAMA* 2008, 300(19):2253–2262.

5. Le Bars, PL, et al. A placebo-controlled, double-blind, randomized trial of an extract of Ginkgo biloba for dementia. North American EGb Study Group, *JAMA* 1997, 278(16): 1327–1332.

6. Bauer, U. Six-month double-blind randomised clinical trial of Ginkgo biloba extract versus placebo in two parallel groups in patients suffering from peripheral artery insuffi-ciency. *Arzneimittelforschung* 1984, 34:716–720.

7. Mouren, X, et al. Study of the antiischemic action of Egb 761 in the treatment of peripheral arterial occlusive disease by TcPO2 determination. *Angiology* 1994, 45:413–417.

Ginseng

1. Scaglione, F, et al. Efficacy and safety of the standardized ginseng extract G 115 for potentiating vaccination against influenza syndrome and protection against the common cold. *Drugs Exp Clin Res* 1996, 22(2):65–72.

2. Vuksan, V, et al. American ginseng (Panax quinquefolius L) reduces postprandial glycemia in nondiabetic subjects and subjects with type 2 diabetes mellitus. *Arch Intern Med* 2000, 160(7):1009–1113.

3. Vuksan, V, MP Stavro, JL Sievenpiper, et al. Similar postprandial glycemic reductions with escalation of dose and administration time of American ginseng in type 2 diabetes. *Diabetes Care* 2000, 23(9):1221–1226.

4. McElhaney, JE, S Gravenstein, SK Cole, et al. A placebo-controlled trial of a proprietary extract of North American ginseng (CVT-E002) to prevent acute respiratory illness in institutionalized older adults. *J Am Geriatr Soc* 2004, 52(1):13–19.

5. Predy, GN, V Goel, R Lovlin, et al. Efficacy of an extract of North American ginseng containing poly-furanosyl-pyranosyl-saccharides for preventing upper respiratory tract infections: A randomized controlled trial. *CMAJ* 2005, 173(9):1043–1048.

6. McElhaney, JE, V Goel, B Toane, et al. Efficacy of COLD-fX in the prevention of respiratory symptoms in community-dwelling adults: A randomized, double-blinded, placebo controlled trial. *J Altern Complement Med* 2006, 12(2): 153–157.

Horse Chestnut

1. Guillaume, M, and F Padioleau. Veinotonic effect, vascular protection, antiinflammatory and free radical scavenging properties of horse chestnut extract. *Arzneimittelforschung* 1994, 44(1):25–35.

2. Diehm, C, et al. Medical edema protection—clinical benefit in patients with chronic deep vein incompetence. A placebo controlled double-blind study. *Vasa* 1992, 21(2):188–192.

3. Pittler, MH, and E Ernst. Horse-chestnut seed extract for chronic venous insufficiency. A criteria-based systematic review. *Arch Dermatol* 1998, 134(11):1356–1360.

4. Rehn, D, et al. Comparative clinical efficacy and tolerability of oxerutins and horse chestnut extract in patients with chronic venous insufficiency. *Arzneimittelforschung* 1996, 46(5):483–487.

5. Diehm, C, et al. Comparison of leg compression stocking and oral horse-chestnut seed extract therapy in patients with chronic venous insufficiency. *Lancet* 1996, 347(8997): 292–294.

Milk Thistle

1. Schulz, V, R Hansel and VE Tyler. *Rational Phytotherapy: A Physician's Guide to Herbal Medicine*, 3rd ed. (Berlin: Springer-Verlag, 1998):216.

2. Hikino, H, and Y Kiso. Natural products for liver disease. *Econ Med Plant Res* 1988, 2:39–72.

3. Muzes, G, et al. Effects of silymarin (Legalon) therapy on the antioxidant defense mechanism and lipid peroxidation in alcoholic liver disease. *Orv Hetil* 1990, 131:863–866. [Hungarian]

4. Berenguer, J, and D Carrasco. Double-blind trial of silymarin vs. placebo in the treatment of chronic hepatitis. *Munch Med Wochenschr* 1977, 119:240–260.

5. Buzzelli, G, et al. A pilot study on the liver protective effect of silybin-phosphatidylcholine complex (IdB 1016) in chronic active hepatitis. *Int J Clin Pharmacol Ther Toxicol* 1993, 31:456–460.

6. Lirussi, F, and L Okolicsanyi. Cytoprotection in the nineties: Experience with ursodeoxycholic acid and silymarin in chronic liver disease. *Acta Physiol Hung* 1992, 80:363–367.

7. Salmi, HA, and S Sarna. Effect of silymarin on chemical, functional and morphological alterations of the liver. A double-blind controlled study. *Scand J Gastroenterol* 1982, 17:517–521.

8. Feher, J, et al. Liver protective action of silymarin therapy in chronic alcoholic liver diseases. *Orv Hetil* 1989, 130: 2723–2727. [Hungarian]

9. Fintelmann, V, and A Albert. Proof of the therapeutic efficacy of Legalon® for toxic liver illnesses in a double-blind trial. *Therapiewoche* 1980, 30:5589–5594. [Translated from German]

10. Ferenci, P, et al. Randomized controlled trial of silymarin treatment in patients with cirrhosis of the liver. *J Hepatol* 1989, 9:105–113.

11. Benda, L, et al. The influence of therapy with silymarin on the survival rate of patients with liver cirrhosis. *Wein Klin Wochenschr* 1980, 92:678–683.

12. Brinker, F. *Herb Contraindications and Drug Interactions: With Appendices Addressing Specific Conditions and Medicines*, 2nd ed. (Sandy, OR: Eclectic Medical Publications, 1998):103.

13. Rambaldi, A, B Jacobs, G Iaquinto and C Gluud. Milk thistle for alcoholic and/or hepatitis B or C virus liver diseases. *Cochrane Database Syst Rev* 2005, Apr 18(2): CD003620.

14. Huseini, HF, B Larijani, R Heshmat, et al. The efficacy of Silybum marianum (L.) Gaertn. (silymarin) in the treatment of type II diabetes: A randomized, double-blind, placebo-controlled, clinical trial. *Phytother Res* 2006, 20(12);1036–1039.

St. John's Wort

1. Laakmann, G, et al. St. John's Wort in mild to moderate depression: The relevance of hyperforin for the clinical efficacy. *Pharmacopsychiatry* 1998, 31(Suppl): S54–S59.

2. Schellenberg, R, et al. Pharmacodynamic effects of two different hypericum extracts in healthy volunteers measured by quantitative EEG. *Pharmacopsychiatry* 1998, 31(Suppl): S44–S53.

3. Kasper, S, M Gastpar, WE Müller, HP Volz, A Dienel, M Kieser and HJ Möller. Efficacy of St. John's wort extract WS 5570 in acute treatment of mild depression: A reanalysis of data from controlled clinical trials. *Eur Arch Psychiatry Clin Neurosci* 2008, 258(1):59–63.

Saw Palmetto

1. Wilt, TJ, et al. Saw palmetto extracts for treatment of benign prostatic hyperplasia: A systematic review. *JAMA* 1998, 280(18):1604–1609.

2. Gerber, GS. Saw palmetto for the treatment of men with lower urinary tract symptoms. *J Urol* 2000, 163(5): 1408–1412.

3. Wilt T, A Ishani, and R Mac Donald. Serenoa repens for benign prostatic hyperplasia. *Cochrane Database Syst Rev* 2002, (3):CD001423.

Valerian

1. Lindahl, O, et al. Double-blind study of a valerian preparation. *Pharmacol Biochem Behav* 1989, 32: 1065–1066.

2. Leathwood, PD, et al. Aqueous extract of valerian root improves sleep quality in man. *Pharmacol Biochem Behav* 1982, 17:65–71.

3. Leathwood, PD, et al. Aqueous extract of valerian root reduces latency to fall asleep in man. *Planta Medica* 1985, 51:144–148.

4. Donath, F, S Quispe, K Diefenbach, et al. Critical evaluation of the effect of valerian extract on sleep structure and sleep quality. *Pharmacopsych* 2000, 33(2):47–53.

5. Bent, S, D Padula, Doore et al. Valerian for sleep: A systematic review and meta-analysis. *Am J Med* 2006, 119: 1005–1012.

8 Other Popular Natural Health Products

Alpha Lipoic Acid

1. Konrad, T, P Vicini, K Kusterer, et al. Alpha-lipoic acid treatment decreases serum lactate and pyruvate concentrations and improves glucose effectiveness in lean and obese patients with Type 2 diabetes. *Diabetes Care* 1999, 22(2): 280–287.

2. Jacob, S, EJ Henriksen, AL Schiemann, et al. Enhancement of glucose disposal in patients with type 2 diabetes by alpha-lipoic acid. *Arzneimittelforschung* 1995, 45(8): 872–874.

3. Jacob, S, P Ruus, R Hermann, et al. Oral administration of RAC-alpha-lipoic acid modulates insulin sensitivity in patients with type-2 diabetes mellitus: A placebo-controlled, pilot trial. *Free Rad Biol Med* 1999, 27(3–4):309–314.

4. Ziegler, D, M Hanefeld, K Ruhnau, et al. Treatment of symptomatic diabetic polyneuropathy with the antioxidant alpha-lipoic acid: A 7-month, multicenter, randomized, controlled trial (ALADIN III Study). *Diabetes Care* 1999, 22(8):1296–1301.

5. Reljanovic, M, G Reichel, K Rett, et al. Treatment of diabetic polyneuropathy with the antioxidant thioctic acid (alpha-lipoic acid): A 2-year, multicenter, randomized, double-blind, placebo-controlled trial (ALADIN II). Alpha Lipoic Acid in Diabetic Neuropathy. *Free Radic Res* 1999, 31(3):171–177.

6. Ziegler, D, M Hanefeld, KJ Ruhnau, et al. Treatment of symptomatic diabetic peripheral neuropathy with the antioxidant alpha-lipoic acid: A 3-week, multicenter, randomized, controlled trial (ALADIN Study). *Diabetologia* 1995, 38(12):1425–1433.

7. Ametov, AS, A Barinov, PJ Dyck, et al. The sensory symptoms of diabetic polyneuropathy are improved with alpha-lipoic acid. *Diabetes Care* 2003, 26(3):770–776.

8. Ziegler, D, H Nowak, P Kemplert, et al. Treatment of symptomatic diabetic polyneuropathy with the antioxidant alpha-lipoic acid: A meta-analysis. *Diabet Med* 2004, 21(2): 114–121.

Chondroitin Sulfate

1. McAlindon, TE, et al. Glucosamine and chondroitin for treatment of osteoarthritis: A systematic quality assessment and meta-analysis. *JAMA* 2000, 283:1469–1475.

2. Morreale, P, et al. Comparison of the anti-inflammatory efficacy of chondroitin sulfate and diclofenac sodium in patients with knee osteoarthritis. *J Rheumatol* 1996, 23(8): 1385–1391.

3. Conrozier, T. Anti-arthrosis treatments: Efficacy and tolerance of chondroitin sulfates. *Presse Med* 1998, 27(36): 1862–1865. [French]

4. Mazieres, B, et al. Chondroitin sulfate in the treatment of gonarthrosis and coxarthrosis. 5-months result of a multicenter double-blind controlled prospective study using placebo. *Rev Rhum Mal Osteoartic* 1992, 59(7–8):466–472. [French]

5. Bucsi, L, and G Poor. Efficacy and tolerability of oral chondroitin sulfate as a symptomatic slow-acting drug for

osteoarthritis (SYSADOA) in the treatment of knee osteoarthritis. *Osteoarthritis Cartilage* May 1998, Suppl 6.

6. Leeb, BF, et al. A meta-analysis of chondroitin sulfate in the treatment of osteoarthritis. *J Rheumatol* 2000, 27(1): 205–211.

7. Clegg, DO, DJ Reda, CL Harris, et al. Glucosamine, chondroitin sulfate, and the two in combination for painful knee osteoarthritis. *N Engl J Med* 2006, 354(8):795–808.

8. Reichenbach, S, R Sterchi, M Scherer, et al. Meta-analysis: Chondroitin for osteoarthritis of the knee or hip. *Ann Intern Med* 2007, 146(8):580–590.

Coenzyme Q10

1. Khatta, M, et al. The effect of coenzyme Q10 in patients with congestive heart failure. *Ann Intern Med* 2000, 132(8):636–640.

2. Morisco, C, B Trimarco, and M Condorelli. Effect of coenzyme Q10 therapy in patients with congestive heart failure: A long-term multicenter randomized study. *Clin Investig* 1993, 71(Suppl 8):S134–S136.

3. Hofman-Bang, C, N Rehnqvist, K Swedberg, et al. Coenzyme Q10 as an adjunctive treatment of congestive heart failure. *J Card Fail* 1995, 1:101–107.

4. Baggio, E, R Gandini, AC Plauncher, et al. Italian multi-center study on the safety and efficacy of coenzyme Q10 as adjunctive therapy in heart failure. CoQ10 Drug Surveillance Investigators. *Mol Aspects Med* 1994, (Suppl 15):S287–S294.

5. Soja, AM, and SA Mortensen. Treatment of congestive heart failure with coenzyme Q10 illuminated by meta-analyses of clinical trials. *Mol Aspects Med* 1997, 18 (Suppl):S159–168.

6. Berman, M, A Erman, T Ben-Gal, et al. Coenzyme Q10 in patients with end-stage heart failure awaiting cardiac trans-plantation: A randomized, placebo-controlled study. *Clin Cardiol* 2004, 27(5):295–299.

7. Langsjoen, P, R Willis and K Folkers. Treatment of essential hypertension with coenzyme Q10. *Mol Aspects Med* 1994, 15 Suppl, S265–272.

8. Singh, RB, MA Niaz, SS Rastogi, et al. Effect of hydrosoluble coenzyme Q10 on blood pressures and insulin resistance in hypertensive patients with coronary artery disease. *J Hum Hypertens* 1999, 13(3):203–208.

9. Hodgson, JM, GF Watts, DA Playford, et al. Coenzyme Q10 improves blood pressure and glycaemic control: A controlled trial in subjects with type 2 diabetes. *Eur J Clin Nutr* 2002, 56(11):1137–1142.

10. Rozen, TD, ML Oshinsky, CA Gebeline, et al. Open label trial of coenzyme Q10 as a migraine preventive. *Cephalalgia* 2002, 22(2):137–141.

11. Sandor, PS, L Di Clemente, G Coppola, et al. Efficacy of coenzyme Q10 in migraine prophylaxis: A randomized controlled trial. *Neurology* 2005, 64(4):713–735.

12. Folkers, K, P Langsjoen, R Willis, et al. Lovastatin decreases coenzyme Q levels in humans. *Proc Natl Acad Sci USA* 1990, 87(22):8931.

13. Mortensen, SA, A Leth, E Agner, et al. Dose-related decrease of serum coenzyme Q10 during treatment with HMG-CoA reductase inhibitors. *Mol Aspects Med* 1997, 18(Suppl): S137–S144.

14. Berthold, HK, A Naini, S Di Mauro, et al. Effect of ezetimibe and/or simvastatin on coenzyme Q10 levels in plasma: A randomised trial. *Drug Saf* 2006, 29(8):703–712.

15. Rundek, T, A Naini, R Sacco, et al. Atorvastatin decreases the coenzyme Q10 level in the blood of patients at risk for cardiovascular disease and stroke. *Arch Neurol* 2004, 61(6):889–892.

16. Weis, M, et al. Bioavailability of four oral coenzyme Q10 formulations in healthy volunteers. *Mol Aspects Med* 1994, 15:S273–S280.

17. Heck, AM, BA DeWitt, and AL Lukes. Potential interactions between alternative therapies and warfarin. *Am J Health Syst Pharm* 2000, 57:1221–1227.

18. Spigset, O. Reduced effect of warfarin caused by ubide-carenone. *Lancet* 1994, 334:1372–1373.

Conjugated Linoleic Acid (CLA)

1. Hubbard, NE, et al. Reduction of murine mammary tumor metastasis by conjugated linoleic acid. *Cancer Letter* 2000, 150(1): 93–100.

2. Ip, C, et al. Induction of apoptosis by conjugated linoleic acid in cultured mammary tumor cells and premalignant lesions of the rat mammary gland. *Cancer Epidemiol Biomarkers Prev* 2000, 9(7):689–696.

3. O'Shea, M, et al. Milk fat conjugated linoleic acid (CLA) inhibits growth of human mammary MCF-7 cancer cells. *Anticancer Res* 2000, 20(5B):3591–3601.

4. Ip, C. Review of the effects of trans fatty acids, oleic acid, n-3 polyunsaturated fatty acids, and conjugated linoleic acid on mammary carcinogenesis in animals. *Am J Clin Nutr* 1997, 66(Suppl 6):S1523–S1529.

5. Smedman, A, and B Vessby. Conjugated linoleic acid supple-mentation in humans: Metabolic effects. *Lipids* 2001, 36(8):773–781.

6. Riserus, U, P Arner, K Brismar, and B Vessby. Treatment with dietary trans10cis12 conjugated linoleic acid causes isomer-specific insulin resistance in obese men with the metabolic syndrome. *Diabetes Care* 2002, 25(9):1516–1521.

7. Blankson, H, JA Stakkestad, H Fagertun, et al. Conjugated linoleic acid reduces body fat mass in overweight and obese humans. *J Nutr* 2000, 130(12):2943–2948.

8. Gaullier, JM, J Halse, K Hoye, et al. Conjugated linoleic acid supplementation for 1 y reduces body fat mass in healthy overweight humans. *Am J Clin Nutr* 2004, 79(6):1118–1125.

9. Mougios, V, A Matsakas, A Petridou, et al. Effect of supple-mentation with conjugated linoleic acid on human serum lipids and body fat. *J Nutr Biochem* 2001, 12(10):585–594.

10. Riserus, U, A Smedman, S Basu, and B Vessby. Metabolic effects of conjugated linoleic acid in humans: The Swedish experience. *Am J Clin Nutr* 2004, 79(6 Suppl):1146S–8S.

DHEA

1. Reiter, WJ, G Schatzl, I Mark, et al. Dehydro-epiandros-terone in the treatment of erectile dysfunction in patients with different organic etiologies. *Urol Res* 2001, 29(4):278–281.

2. Reiter, WJ, A Pycha, G Schatzl, et al. Dehydroepiandosterone in the treatment of erectile dysfunction: A prospective, double-blind, randomized, placebo-controlled study. *Urology* 1999, 53(3):590–595.

3. Arlt, W, F Callies, JC van Vlijmen, et al. Dehydroepiandosterone replacement in women with adrenal insufficiency. *N Engl J Med* 1999, 341:1013–1020.

4. Johannsson, G, P Burman, L Wiren, et al. Low dose dehydroepiandrosterone affects behavior in hypopituitary androgen-deficient women: A placebo-controlled trial. *J Clin Endocrinol Metab* 2002, 87(5):2046–2052.

5. Petri, MA, PJ Mease, JT Merrill, et al. Effects of prasterone on disease activity and symptoms in women with active systemic lupus erythematosus. *Arthritis Rheum* 2004, 50(9):2858–2868.

6, Petri, MA, RG Lahita, RF Van Vollenhoven, et al. Effects of prasterone on corticosteroid requirements of women with systemic lupus erythematosus: A double-blind, randomized, placebo-controlled trial. *Arthritis Rheum* 2002, 46(5): 1820–1829.

7. Mease, PJ, JT Merrill, RG Lahita, et al. GL701 (prasterone, dehydroepiandrosterone) improves systemic lupus erythematosus. 2000 American College of Rheumatology Meeting. Philadelphia, 29 October–2 November:1230. [Abstract]

8. van Vollenhoven, RF. Dehydroepiandrosterone in systemic lupus erythematosus. *Rheum Dis Clin North Am* 2000, 26(2):349–362.

9. van Vollenhoven, RF, JL Park, MC Genovese, et al. A double-blind, placebo-controlled, clinical trial of dehydroepiandrosterone in severe lupus erythematosus. *Lupus* 1999, 8:181–187.

10. van Vollenhoven, RF, LM Morabito, EG Engleman, et al. Treatment of systemic lupus erythematosus with dehydroepiandrosterone: 50 patients treated up to 12 months. *J Rheumatol* 1998, 25:285–289.

11. Barry, NN, JL McGuire, and RF van Vollenhoven. Dehydroepiandrosterone in systemic lupus erythematosus: Relationship between dosage, serum levels, and clinical response. *J Rheumatol* 1998, 25:2352–2356.

12. van Vollenhoven, RF, EG Engleman, and JL McGurie. Dehydroepiandrosterone in Systemic Lupus Erythematosus. *Arth Rheum* 1995, 38(12):1826–1831.

13. van Vollenhoven, RF, EG Engleman, and JL McGuire. Dehydroepiandrosterone in Systemic Lupus Erythematosus. *Arth Rheum* 1994, 37(9):1305–1310.

Fish Oil

1. Marchioli, R, F Barzi, E Bomba, et al. Early protection against sudden death by n-3 polyunsaturated fatty acids after myocardial infarction. *Circulation* 2002, 105(16): 1897–1903.

2. Erkkilä, AT, NR Matthan, DM Herrington, and AH Lichtenstein. Higher plasma docosahexaenoic acid is associated with reduced progression of coronary atherosclerosis in women with CAD. *J Lipid Res* 2006, 47(12): 2814–2819.

3. Farmer, A, V Montori, S Dinneen, and C Clar. Fish oil in people with type 2 diabetes mellitus. *Cochrane Database Syst Rev* 2001, (3):CD003205.

4. Prisco, D, R Paniccia, B Bandinelli, et al. Effect of medium-term supplementation with a moderate dose of n-3 polyunsaturated fatty acids on blood pressure in mild hypertensive patients. *Thromb Res* 1998, 1(3):105–112.

5. Toft, I, KH Bonaa, OC Ingebretsen, et al. Effects of n-3 polyunsaturated fatty acids on glucose homeostasis and blood pressure in essential hypertension: A randomized, controlled trial. *Ann Intern Med* 1995, 123(12):911–918.

6. Yosefy, C, JR Viskoper, A Laszt, et al. The effect of fish oil on hypertension, plasma lipids and hemostasis in hypertensive, obese, dyslipidemic patients with and without diabetes mellitus. *Prostaglandins Leukot Essent Fatty Acids* 1999, 61(2):83–87.

7. Maes, M, A Christophe, J Delanghe, et al. Lowered omega3 polyunsaturated fatty acids in serum phospholipids and cholesteryl esters of depressed patients. *Psychiatry Res* 1999, 85(3):275–291.

8. Tiemeier, H, HR van Tuijl, A Hofman, et al. Plasma fatty acid composition and depression are associated in the elderly: The Rotterdam Study. *Am J Clin Nutr* 2003, 78(1):40–46.

9. Su, KP, SY Huang, CC Chiu, and WW Shen. Omega-3 fatty acids in major depressive disorder: A preliminary double-blind, placebo-controlled trial. *Eur Neuropsychopharmacol* 2003, 13(1):267–271.

10. Su, KP, WW Shen, and SY Huang. Are omega3 fatty acids beneficial in depression but not mania? *Arch Gen Psychiatry* 2000, 57(7): 716–717.

11. Burgess, JR, L Stevens, W Zhang, and L Peck. Long-chain polyunsaturated fatty acids in children with attention-deficit hyperactivity disorder. *Am J Clin Nutr* 2000, 71(Suppl 1):S327–S330.

12. Richardson, AJ, and BK Puri. A randomized double-blind, placebo-controlled study of the effects of supplementation with highly unsaturated fatty acids on ADHD-related symptoms in children with specific learning difficulties. *Prog Neuropsychopharmacol Biol Psychiatry* 2002, 26(2): 233–239.

13. Sinn, N, and J Bryan. Effect of supplementation with polyunsaturated fatty acids and micronutrients on learning and behavior problems associated with child ADHD. *J Dev Behav Pediatr* 2007, 28(2):82–91.

14. Navarro, E, M Esteve, A Olivé, J Klaassen, et al. Abnormal fatty acid pattern in rheumatoid arthritis: A rationale for treatment with marine and botanical lipids. *J Rheumatol* 2000, 27(2):298–303.

15. Lau, CS, KD Morley, and JJ Belch. Effects of fish oil supplementation on non-steroidal anti-inflammatory drug requirement in patients with mild rheumatoid arthritis: A double-blind placebo controlled study. *Br J Rheumatol* 1993, 32:982–989.

16. Kjeldsen-Kragh, J, JA Lund, T Riise, et al. Dietary omega-3 fatty acid supplementation and naproxen treatment in patients with rheumatoid arthritis. *J Rheumatol* 1992, 19(10):1531–1536.

17. Astorga, G, A Cubillos, L Masson, and JJ Silva. Active rheumatoid arthritis: Effect of dietary supplementation with omega-3 oils. A controlled double-blind trial. *Rev Med Chil* 1991, 119(3):267–272.

18. van der Tempel, H, JE Tulleken, PC Limburg, et al. Effects of fish oil supplementation in rheumatoid arthritis. *Ann Rheum Dis* 1990, 49(2):76–80.

19. Goldberg, RJ, and J Katz. A meta-analysis of the analgesic effects of omega-3 polyunsaturated fatty acid supplementation for inflammatory joint pain. *Pain* 2007, 129(1–2): 210–223.

Flaxseed

1. Cunnane, SC, MJ Hamadeh, AC Liede, et al. Nutritional attributes of traditional flaxseed in healthy young adults. *Am J Clin Nutr* 1995, 61(1):62–68.
2. Lemay, A, S Dodin, N Kadri, et al. Flaxseed dietary supplement versus hormone replacement therapy in hypercholesterolemic menopausal women. *Obstet Gynecol* 2002, 100(3):495–504.
3. Demark-Wahnefried, W, CN Robertson, PJ Walther, et al. Pilot study to explore effects of low-fat, flaxseed-supplemented diet on proliferation of benign prostatic epithelium and prostate-specific antigen. *Urology* 2004, 63(5):900–904.
4. Bierenbaum, ML, R Reichstein, and TR Watkins. Reducing atherogenic risk in hyperlipemic humans with flaxseed supplementation: A preliminary report. *J Am Coll Nutr* 1993, 12(5):501–504.
5. Jenkins, DJ, CWC Kendall, E Vidgen, et al. Health aspects of partially defatted flaxseed, including effects on serum lipids, oxidative measures, and ex vivo androgen and progestin activity: A controlled, crossover trial. *Am J Clin Nutr* 1999, 69(3):395–402.
6. Lucas, EA, RD Wild, LJ Hammond, et al. Flaxseed improves lipid profile without altering biomarkers of bone metabolism in postmenopausal women. *J Clin Endocrinol Metab* 2002, 87(4):1527–1532.
7. Dodin, S, A Lemay, H Jacques, et al. The effects of flaxseed dietary supplement on lipid profile, bone mineral density, and symptoms in menopausal women: A randomized, double-blind, wheat germ placebo-controlled clinical trial. *J Clin Endocrinol Metab* 2005, 90(3):1390–1397.
8. Thompson, LU, SE Rickard, LJ Orcheson, and MM Seidl. Flaxseed and its lignan and oil components reduce mammary tumor growth at a late stage of carcinogenesis. *Carcinogenesis* 1996, 17(6):1373–1376.
9. Thompson, LU, MM Seidl, SE Rickard, et al. Antitumorigenic effect of a mammalian lignan precurser from flaxseed. *Nutrition and Cancer* 1996, 26(2):159–165.
10. Thompson, LU, JM Chen, T Li, K Strasser-Weippl, and PE Goss. Dietary flaxseed alters tumor biological markers in postmenopausal breast cancer. *Clin Cancer Res* 2005, 11(10):3828–3835.
11. Clark, WF, A Parbtani, HW Huff, et al. Flaxseed: A potential treatment for lupus nephritis. *Kidney Int* 1995, 48(2):475–480.
12. Clark, WF, C Kortas, P Heidenheim, et al. Flaxseed in lupus nephritis: A two-year nonplacebo-controlled crossover study. *J Am Coll Nutr* 2001, 20 (2 Suppl):143–148.

Glucosamine Sulphate

1. Herrero-Beaumont, G, JA Ivorra, M Del Carmen Trabado, et al. Glucosamine sulfate in the treatment of knee osteoarthritis symptoms: A randomized, double-blind, placebo-controlled study using acetaminophen as a side comparator. *Arthritis Rheum* 2007, 56(2):555–567.
2. Towheed, TE, L Maxwell, TP Anastassiades, et al. Glucosamine therapy for treating osteoarthritis. *Cochrane Database Syst Rev* 2005, (2):CD002946.
3. Bruyere, O, K Pavelka, LC Rovati, et al. Glucosamine sulfate reduces osteoarthritis progression in postmenopausal

women with knee osteoarthritis: evidence from two 3-year studies. *Menopause* 2004, 11(2):138–143.
4. Richy, F, O Bruyere, O Ethgen, et al. Structural and symptomatic efficacy of glucosamine and chondroitin in knee osteoarthritis: A comprehensive meta-analysis. *Arch Intern Med* 2003, 163(13):1514–1522.
5. Braham, R, B Dawson, and C Goodman. The effect of glucosamine supplementation on people experiencing regular knee pain. *Br J Sports Med* 2003, 37(1):45–49.
6. Reginster, JY, R Deroisy, LC Rovati, et al. Long-term effects of glucosamine sulfate on osteoarthritis progression: A randomized, placebo-controlled trial. *Lancet* 2001, 357(9252):251–256.
7. Towheed, TE, TP Anastassiades, B Shea, et al. Glucosamine therapy for treating osteoarthritis. *Cochrane Database Syst Rev* 2001, 1:CD002946.
8. McAlindon, TE, MP LaValley, JP Gulin, and DT Felson. Glucosamine and chondroitin for treatment of osteoarthritis: a systematic quality assessment and meta-analysis. *JAMA* 2000, 283:1469–1475.
9. Qiu, GX, SN Gao, G Giacovelli, et al. Efficacy and safety of glucosamine sulfate versus ibuprofen in patients with knee osteoarthritis. *Arzneimittelforschung* 1998, 48:469–474.
10. Poolsup, N, C Suthisisang, P Channark, and W Kittikulsuth. Glucosamine long-term treatment and the progression of knee osteoarthritis: Systematic review of randomized controlled trials. *Ann Pharmacother* 2005, 39(6):1080–1087.

Grapeseed Extract

1. Kiesewetter, H, J Koscielny, U Kalus, et al. Efficacy of orally administered extract of red vine leaf AS 195 (folia vitis viniferae) in chronic venous insufficiency (stages I–II): A randomized, double-blind, placebo-controlled trial. *Arzneimittelforschung* 2000, 50(2):109–117.
2. Freedman, JE, C Parker, L Li, et al. Select flavonoids and whole juice from purple grapes inhibit platelet function and enhance nitric oxide release. *Circulation* 2001, 103(23):2792–2798.
3. Stein, JH, JG Keevil, DA Wiebe, et al. Purple grape juice improves endothelial function and reduces the susceptibility of LDL cholesterol to oxidation in patients with coronary artery disease. *Circulation* 1999, 100(10):1050–1055.
4. Frankel, EN, J Kanner, JB German, et al. Inhibition of oxidation of human low-density lipoprotein by phenolic substances in red wine. *Lancet* 1993, 341:454–457.
5. Chang, WC, and FL Hsu. Inhibition of platelet aggregation and arachidonate metabolism in platelets by procyanidins. *Prostaglandins Leukot Essent Fatty Acids* 1989, 38:181–188.

Inositol

1. Levine, J. Controlled trials of inositol in psychiatry. *Eur Neuropsychopharmacol* 1997, 7:147–155.
2. Levine, J, Y Barak, M Gonzalves, et al. Double-blind, controlled trial of inositol treatment of depression. *Am J Psychiatry* 1995, 152(5): 792–794.
3. Levine, J, Y Barak, O Kofman, and RH Belmaker. Follow-up and relapse analysis of an inositol study of depression. *Isr J Psychiatry Relat Sci* 1995, 32:14–21.

4. Benjamin, J, J Levine, M Fux, et al. Double-blind, placebo-controlled, crossover trial of inositol treatment for panic disorder. *Am J Psychiatry* 1995, 152(7):1084–1086.
5. Palatnik, A, K Frolov, M Fux, and J Benjamin. Double-blind, controlled, crossover trial of inositol versus fluvoxamine for the treatment of panic disorder. *J Clin Psychopharmacol* 2001, 21(3):335–339.
6. Nestler, JE, DJ Jakubowicz, P Reamer, et al. Ovulatory and metabolic effects of D-chiro-inositol in the polycystic ovary syndrome. *N Engl J Med* 1999, 340(17):1314–1320.

Lutein
1. Richer, S, W Stiles, L Statkute, et al. Double-masked, placebo-controlled, randomized trial of lutein and antioxidant supplementation in the intervention of atrophic age-related macular degeneration: The Veterans LAST study (Lutein Antioxidant Supplement Trial). *Optometry* 2004, 75(4):216–230.
2. Landrum, JT, RA Bone, and MD Kilburn. The macular pigment: A possible role in protection from age-related macular degeneration. *Adv Pharmacol* 1997, 38:537–556.
3. Moeller, SM, et al. The role of dietary xanthophylls in cataract and age-related macular degeneration. *J Am Coll Nutr* 2000, 19(Suppl 5):S522–S527.
4. Berendschott, TT, et al. Influence of lutein supplementation on macular pigment, assessed with two objective techniques. *Invest Opthalmol Vis Sci* 2000, 41(11):3322–3326.
5. Dagnelie, G, et al. Lutein improves visual function in some patients with retinal degeneration: A pilot study via the Internet. *Optometry* 2000, 71(3):147–164.
6. Hammond Jr, BR, et al. Dietary modification of human macular pigment density. Invest Opthalmol Vis Sci 1997, 38(9):1795–1801.
7. Hammond Jr, BR, EJ Johnson, RM Russell, et al. *Invest Opthalmol Vis Sci* 1997, 38(9): 1795–1801.
8. Landrum, JT, et al. A one year study of the macular pigment: The effect of 140 days on a lutein supplement. *Exp Eye Res* 1997, 65(1): 57–62.
9. Hankinson, SE, MJ Stampfer, JM Seddon, et al. Nutrient intake and cataract extraction in women: A prospective study. *Br Med J* 1992, 305:335–339.
10. Brown, L, EB Rimm, JM Seddon, et al. A prospective study of carotenoid intake and risk of cataract extraction in U.S. men. *Am J Clin Nutr* 1999, 70(4):517–524.
11. Chasan-Taber, L, WC Willett, JM Seddon, et al. A prospective study of carotenoid and vitamin A intakes and risk of cataract extraction in U.S. women. *Am J Clin Nutr* 1999, 70(4):509–516.

Lycopene
1. Sies, H, and W Stahl. Lycopene: Antioxidant and biological effects and its bioavailability in the human. *Proc Soc Exp Biol Med* 1998, 218:121–124.
2. Rao, AV, and S Agarwal. Bioavailability and in vivo antioxidant properties of lycopene from tomato products and their possible role in the prevention of cancer. *Nutr Cancer* 1998, 31:199–203.
3. Giovannucci, E, A Ascherio, EB Rimm, et al. Intake of carotenoids and retinol in relation to risk of prostate cancer. *J Natl Cancer Inst* 1995, 87(23):1767–1776.

4. Giovannucci, E, EB Rimm, Y Liu, et al. A prospective study of tomato products, lycopene, and prostate cancer risk. *J Natl Cancer Inst* 2002, 94(5):391–398.
5. Lu, QY, JC Hung, D Heber, et al. Inverse associations between plasma lycopene and other carotenoids and prostate cancer. *Cancer Epidemiol Biomarkers Prev* 2001, 10(7): 749–756.
6. Norrish, AE, RT Jackson, SJ Sharpe, and CM Skeaff. Prostate cancer and dietary carotenoids. *Am J Epidemiol* 2000, 151(2):119–123.
7. Etminan, M, B Takkouche, and F Caamano-Isorna. The role of tomato products and lycopene in the prevention of prostate cancer: A meta-analysis of observational studies. *Cancer Epidemiol Biomarkers Prev* 2004, 13(3):340–345.
8. Gann, PH, et al. Lower prostate risk in men with elevated plasma lycopene levels: Results of a prospective study. *Cancer Res* 1999, 59:1225–1230.
9. Nomura, AM, et al. Serum micronutrients and prostate cancer in Japanese Americans in Hawaii. *Cancer Epidemiol Biomarkers Prev* 1997, 6:487–491.
10. Paetau, I, et al. Chronic ingestion of lycopene-rich tomato juice or lycopene supplements significantly increases plasma concentrations of lycopene and related tomato carotenoids in humans. *Am J Clin Nutr* 1998, 68(6):1187–1195.
11. Mohanty, NK, S Saxena, UP Singh, et al. Lycopene as a chemopreventive agent in the treatment of high-grade prostate intraepithelial neoplasia. *Urol Oncol* 2005, 23(6):383–385.
12. Kucuk, O, FH Sarkar, W Sakr, et al. Phase II randomized clinical trial of lycopene supplementation before radical prostatectomy. *Cancer Epidemiol Biomarkers Prev* 2001, 10(8):861–868.
13. Kanetsky, PA, MD Gammon, J Mandelblatt, et al. Dietary intake and blood levels of lycopene: Association with cervical dysplasia among non-Hispanic, black women. *Nutr Cancer* 1998, 31(1):31–40.
14. Sedjo, RL, MR Papenfuss, NE Craft, and AR Guiliano. Effect of plasma micronutrients on clearance of oncogenic human papillomavirus (HPV) infection (United States). *Cancer Causes Control* 2003, 14(4):319–326.

Lysine
1. Griffith, RS, DC DeLong, and JD Nelson. Relation of arginine-lysine antagonism to herpes simplex growth in tissue culture. *Chemotherapy* 1981, 27(3):209–213.
2. Thein, DJ, and WC Hurt. Lysine as a prophylactic agent in the treatment of recurrent herpes simplex labialis. *Oral Surg Oral Med Oral Pathol* 1984, 58(6):659–666.
3. McCune, MA, HO Perry, SA Muller, and WM O'Fallon. Treatment of recurrent herpes simplex infections with L-lysine monohydrochloride. *Cutis* 1984, 34(4):366–373.
4. DiGiovanna, JJ, and H Blank. Failure of lysine in frequently recurrent herpes simplex infection: Treatment and prophylaxis. *Arch Dermatol* 1984, 120(1):48–51.
5. Milman, N, J Scheibel, and O Jessen. Lysine prophylaxis in recurrent herpes simplex labialis: A double-blind, controlled crossover study. *Acta Derm Venereol* 1980, 60(1):85–87.
6. Griffith, RS, A Norins, and C Kagan. A multicentered study of lysine therapy in Herpes simplex infection. *Dermatologica* 1978, 156(5):257–267.

7. Griffith, RS, DE Walsh, KH Myrmel, et al. Success of L-lysine therapy in frequently recurrent herpes simplex infection: Treatment and prophylaxis. *Dermatologica* 1987, 175(4):183–190.

8. Civitelli, R, et al. Dietary L-lysine and calcium metabolism in humans. *Nutrition* 1992, 8(6):400–405.

Melatonin

1. Brzezinski, A. Melatonin in humans. *N Engl J Med* 1997, 336(3):186–195.

2. Buscemi, N, B Vandermeer, N Hooton, et al. The efficacy and safety of exogenous melatonin for primary sleep disorders: A meta-analysis. *J Gen Intern Med* 2005, 20(12): 1151–1158.

3. Ellis, CM, G Lemmens, and JD Parkes. Melatonin and insomnia. *J Sleep Res* 1996, 5(1):61–65.

4. James, SP, DA Sack, NE Rosenthal, and WB Mendelson. Melatonin administration in insomnia. *Neuropsychopharmacol* 1990, 3(1):19–23.

5. Garfinkel, D, et al. Improvement of sleep quality in elderly people by controlled-release melatonin. *Lancet* 1995, 346(8974):541–544.

6. Brusco, LI, I Fainstein, M Marquez, et al. Effect of melatonin in selected populations of sleep-disturbed patients. *Biol Signals Recept* 1999, 8(1–2):126–131.

7. Haimov, I, P Lavie, M Laudon,et al. Melatonin replacement therapy of elderly insomniacs. *Sleep* 1995, 18(7):598–603.

8. Zhdanova, IV, RJ Wurtman, MM Regan, et al. Melatonin treatment for age-related insomnia. *J Clin Endocrinol Metab* 2001, 86(10):4727–4730.

9. Buscemi, N, B Vandermeer, N Hooton, et al. The efficacy and safety of exogenous melatonin for primary sleep disorders: A meta-analysis. *J Gen Intern Med* 2005, 20(12):1151-1158.

10. Palm, L, G Blennow, and L Wetterberg. Long-term melatonin treatment in blind children and young adults with circadian sleep-wake disturbances. *Dev Med Child Neurol* 1997, 39(5):319–325.

11. Skene, DJ, SW Lockley, and J Arendt. Melatonin in circadian sleep disorders in the blind. *Biol Signals Recept* 1999, 8(1–2):90–95.

12. Sack, RL, RW Brandes, AR Kendall, et al. Entrainment of free-running circadian rhythms by melatonin in blind people. *N Engl J Med* 2000, 343(15):1070–1077.

13. Buscemi, N, B Vandermeer, R Pandya, et al. Melatonin for treatment of sleep disorders. Summary, Evidence Report/Technology Assessment #108. (Prepared by the University of Alberta Evidence-based Practice Center, under Contract#290-02-0023.) AHRQ Publ #05-E002-2. Rockville, MD: Agency for Healthcare Research & Quality. November 2004.

14. Suhner, A, P Schlagenhauf, R Johnson, et al. Comparative study to determine the optimal melatonin dosage form for the alleviation of jet lag. *Chronobiol Int* 1998, 15(6):655–656.

15. Petrie, K, AG Dawson, L Thompson, and R Brook. A double-blind trial of melatonin as a treatment for jet lag in international cabin crew. *Biol Psychiatry* 1993, 33(7): 526–530.

16. Claustrat, B, J Brun, M David, et al. Melatonin and jet lag: Confirmatory result using a simplified protocol. *Biol Psychiatry* 1992, 32(8): 705–711.

17. Petrie, K, JV Conaglen, L Thompson, and K Chamberlain . Effect of melatonin on jet lag after long haul flights. *Br Med J* 1989, 298(6675):705–707.

18. Sanders, DC, AK Chaturvedi, and JR Hordinsky. Melatonin: Aeromedical, toxi-copharmacological, and analytical aspects. *J Anal Toxicol* 1999, 23(3):159–167.

19. Herxheimer, A, and KJ Petrie. Melatonin for the prevention and treatment of jet lag. *Cochrane Database Syst Rev* 2002, 2:CD001520.

20. Carman, JS, RM Post, R Buswell, et al. Negative effects of melatonin on depression. *Am J Psychiatry* 1976, 133(10): 1181–1186.

Phosphatidylserine

1. Heiss, WD, J Kessler, R Mielke, et al. Long-term effects of phosphatidylserine, pyritinol, and cognitive training in Alzheimer's disease: A neuropsychological, EEG, and PET investigation. *Dementia* 1994, 5(2):88–98.

2. Crook, T, W Petrie, C Wells, and DC Massari. Effects of phosphatidylserine in Alzheimer's disease. *Psychopharmacol Bull* 1992, 28(1):61–66.

3. Engel, RR, W Satzger, W Gunther, et al. Double-blind crossover study of phospha-tidylserine vs. placebo in patients with early dementia of the Alzheimer type. *Eur Neuropsychopharmacol* 1992, 2(2):149–155.

4. Delwaide, PJ, AM Gyselynck-Mambourg, A Hurlet, and M Ylieff. Double-blind randomized controlled study of phosphatidylserine in senile demented patients. *Acta Neurol Scand* 1986, 73(2):136–140.

5. Amaducci, L. Phosphatidylserine in the treatment of Alzheimer's disease: Results of a multicenter study. *Psychopharmacol Bull* 1988, 24:130–134.

6. Cenacchi, T, T Bertoldin, C Farina, et al. Cognitive decline in the elderly: A double-blind, placebo-controlled multicenter study on efficacy of phosphatidylserine administration. *Aging* (Milano) 1993, 5(2):123–133.

7. Crook, TH, J Tinklenberg, J Yesavage, et al. Effects of phosphatidylserine in age-associated memory impairment. *Neurology* 1991, 41(5):644–649.

8. Villardita, C, S Grioli, G Salmeri, et al. Multicentre clinical trial of brain phosphatidylserine in elderly patients with intellectual deterioration. *Clin Trials J* 1987, 24:84–93.

9. Palmieri, G, R Palmieri, MR Inzoli, et al. Double-blind controlled trial of phosphatidylserine in patients with senile mental deterioration. *Clin Trials J* 1987, 24:73–83.

10. Schreiber, S, O Kampf-Sherf, M Gorfine, et al. An open trial of plant-source derived phosphatydilserine for treatment of age-related cognitive decline. *Isr J Psychiatry Relat Sci* 2000, 37(4):302–307.

Probiotics

1. Colombel, JF, et al. Yoghurt with Bifidobacterium longum reduces erythromycin-induced gastrointestinal effects. *Lancet* 1987, 2:43.

2. Surawicz, CM, et al. Prevention of antibiotic-associated diarrhea by Saccharomyces boulardii: A prospective study. *Gastroenterology* 1989, 96:981–988.

3. McFarland, LV, et al. Prevention of Beta-lactam-associated diarrhea by Saccharomyces boulardii compared with placebo. *Am J Gastroenterol* 1995, 90:439–448.

4. Surawicz, CM, et al. Prevention of antibiotic-associated diarrhea by Saccharomyces boulardii: A prospective study. *Gastroenterology* 1989, 96:981–988.

5. Guandalini, S, et al. Lactobacillus GG administered in oral rehydration solution to children with acute diarrhea: A multicenter European trial. *J Pediatr Gastroenterol Nutr* 2000, 30:54–60.

6. Shornikova, AV, et al. Bacteriotherapy with Lactobacillus reuteri in rotavirus gastroenteritis. *Pediatr Infect Dis J* 1997, 16:1103–1107.

7. Saavedra, JM, et al. Feeding of Bifidobacterium bifidum and Streptococcus thermophilus to infants in hospital for prevention of diarrhoea and shedding of rotavirus. *Lancet* 1994, 344:1046–1049.

8. Scarpignato, C, and P Rampal. Prevention and treatment of traveler's diarrhea: A clinical pharmacological approach. *Chemotherapy* 1995, 41(Suppl 1):S48–S81.

9. Hilton, E, et al. Efficacy of Lactobacillus GG as a diarrheal preventive in travelers. *J Travel Med* 1997, 4:41–43.

10. Oksanen, PJ, et al. Prevention of traveller's diarrhoea by Lactobacillus GG. *Ann Med* 1990, 22:53–56.

11. Kollaritsch, VH, et al. Prevention of traveler's diarrhea with Saccharomyces boulardii: Results of a placebo-controlled double-blind study. *Fortschr Med* 1993, 111:152–156.

12. McFarland, LV. Meta-analysis of probiotics for the prevention of antibiotic associated diarrhea and the treatment of Clostridium difficile disease. *Am J Gastroenterol* 2006, 101(4):812–822.

13. Venturi, A, P Gionchetti, F Rizzello, et al. Impact on the composition of the faecal flora by a new probiotic preparation: Preliminary data on maintenance treatment of patients with ulcerative colitis. *Aliment Pharmacol Ther* 1999, 13(8):1103–1108.

14. Bibiloni, R, RN Fedorak, GW Tannock, et al. VSL#3 probiotic-mixture induces remission in patients with active ulcerative colitis. *Am J Gastroenterol* 2005, 100(7): 1539–1546.

15. Tursi, A, G Brandimarte, GM Giorgetti, et al. Low-dose balsalazide plus a high-potency probiotic preparation is more effective than balsalazide alone or mesalazine in the treatment of acute mild-to-moderate ulcerative colitis. *Med Sci Monit* 2004, 10(11):PI126–31.

16. Halpern, GM, T Prindiville, M Blankenburg, et al. Treatment of irritable bowel syndrome with Lacteol Fort: A random-ized, double-blind, cross-over trial. *Am J Gastroenterol* 1996, 91(8):1579–1585.

17. Kim, HJ, M Camilleri, S McKinzie, et al. A randomized controlled trial of a probiotic, VSL#3, on gut transit and symptoms in diarrhoea-predominant irritable bowel syndrome. *Aliment Pharmacol Ther* 2003, 17(7):895–904.

18. Elmer, GW, CM Surawicz, and LV McFarland. Biotherapeutic agents: A neglected modality for the treat-ment and prevention of selected intestinal and vaginal infections. *JAMA* 1996, 275:870–876.

19. Hilton, E, HD Isenberg, P Alperstein, et al. Ingestion of yogurt containing Lactobacillus acidophilus as prophylaxis for candidal vaginitis. *Ann Intern Med* 1992, 116(5): 353–357.

20. Shalev, E, S Battino, E Weiner, et al. Ingestion of yogurt containing Lactobacillus acidophilus compared with pasteurized yogurt as prophylaxis for recurrent candidal vaginitis and bacterial vaginosis. *Arch Fam Med* 1996, 5(10):593–596.

SAMe

1. Janicak, PG, J Lipinski, JM Davis, et al. S-adenosylmethionine in depression. A literature review and preliminary report. *Ala J Med Sci* 1988, 25(3):306–313.

2. Bressa, GM. S-adenosyl-l-methionine (SAMe) as antidepres-sant: Meta-analysis of clinical studies. *Acta Neurol Scand* 1994, 154(Suppl): S7–S14.

3. Bell, KM, SG Potkin, D Carreon, and L Plon. S-adenosylmethionine blood levels in major depression: Changes with drug treatment. *Acta Neurol Scand* 1994, 154(Suppl):S15–S18.

4. Bell, KM, L Plon, WE Bunney Jr, and SG Potkin. S-adenosylmethionine treatment of depression: A controlled clinical trial. *Am J Psychiatry* 1988, 145(9):1110–1114.

5. Salmaggi, P, GM Bressa, G Nicchia, et al. Double-blind, placebo-controlled study of S-adenosyl-L-methionine in depressed postmenopausal women. *Psychother Psychosom* 1993, 59(1):34–40.

6. De Vanna, M, and R Rigamonti. Oral S-adenosyl-L-methio-nine in depression. *Curr Ther Res* 1992, 52(3):478–485.

7. Rosenbaum, JF, M Fava, WE Falk, et al. The antidepressant potential of oral S-adenosyl-l-methionine. *Acta Psychiatr Scand* 1990, 81(5):432–36.

8. Delle Chiaie, R, P Pancheri, and P Scapicchio. Efficacy and tolerability of oral and intramuscular S-adenosyl-Lmethionine 1,4-butanedisulfonate (SAMe) in the treatment of major depression: Comparison with imipramine in multi-center studies. *Am J Clin Nutr* 2002, 76(5):1172S–1176S.

9. Najm, WI, S Reinsch, F Hoehler, et al. S-adenosylmethio-nine (SAMe) versus celecoxib for the treatment of osteoarthritis symptoms: A double-blind crossover trial. *BMC Musculoskelet Disord* 2004, 5:6.

10. Soeken, KL, WL Lee, RB Bausell, et al. Safety and efficacy of S-adenosylmethionine (SAMe) for osteoarthritis. *J Fam Pract* 2002, 51(5): 425–430.

11. Domljan, Z, B Vrhovac, T Durrigl, and I Pucar. A double-blind trial of ademetionine vs. naproxen in activated gonarthrosis. *Int J Clin Pharmacol Ther Toxicol* 1989, 27(7):329–333.

12. Konig, B. A long-term (two years) clinical trial with S-adenosylmethionine for the treatment of osteoarthritis. *Am J Med* 1987, 83(5a):78–80.

13. Berger, R, and H Nowak. A new medical approach to the treatment of osteoarthritis. Report of an open phase IV study with ademetionine (Gumbaral). *Am J Med* 1987, 83(5A):84–88.

14. Muller-Fassbender, H. Double-blind clinical trial of S-adenosylmethionine versus ibuprofen in the treatment of osteoarthritis. *Am J Med* 1987, 83(5A):81–83.

15. Vetter, G. Double-blind comparative clinical trial with S-adenosylmethionine and indo-methacin in the treatment of osteoarthritis. *Am J Med* 1987, 83(5A):78–80.

16. Maccagno, A, EE Di Giorgio, OL Caston, and CL Sagasta. Double-blind controlled clinical trial of oral S-adenosylmethionine versus piroxicam in knee osteoarthritis. *Am J Med* 1987, 83(5A):72–77.

17. Caruso, I, and V Pietrogrande. Italian double-blind multi-center study comparing S-adenosylmethionine, naproxen, and placebo in the treatment of degenerative joint disease. *Am J Med* 1987, 83(5A):66–71.

18. Glorioso, S, S Todesco, A Mazzi, et al. Double-blind, multi-centre study of the activity of S-adenosylmethionine in hip and knee osteoarthritis. *Int J Clin Pharmacol Res* 1985, 5(1):39–49.

19. di Padova, C. S-adenosylmethionine in the treatment of osteoarthritis: Review of the clinical studies. *Am J Med* 1987, 83(5A):60–65.

20. Jacobsen, S, B Danneskiold-Samsoe, and RB Andersen. Oral S-adenosylmethionine in primary fibromyalgia: Double-blind clinical evaluation. *Scand J Rheumatol* 1991, 20(4):294–302.

21. Tavoni, A, C Vitali, S Bombardieri, and G Pasero. Evaluation of S-adenosylmethionine in primary fibromyalgia: A double-blind cross-over study. *Am J Med* 1987, 83(5A):107–110.

Part Three: The Health Conditions

Acne (Acne vulgaris)

1. Adebamowo, CA, D Spiegelman, CS Berkey, FW Danby, HH Rockett, GA Colditz, WC Willett, and MD Holmes. Milk consumption and acne in adolescent girls. *Dermatol Online J* 2006, 12(4):1.

2. Adebamowo, CA, D Spiegelman, CS Berkey, FW Danby, HH Rockett, GA Colditz, WC Willett, and MD Holmes. Milk consumption and acne in teenaged boys. *J Am Acad Dermatol* 2008, 58(5):787–793.

3. Adebamowo, CA, D Spiegelman, FW Danby, AL Frazier, WC Willett, and MD Holmes. High school dietary dairy intake and teenage acne. *J Am Acad Dermatol* 2005, 52(2):207–214.

4. Downing, DT, et al. Essential fatty acids and acne. *J Am Acad Dermatol* 1986, 14(2 Pt 1):221–225.

5. Akamatsu, H, et al. Suppressive effects of linoleic acid on neutrophil oxygen metabolism and phagocytosis. *J Invest Dermatol* 1990, 95(3):271–274.

6. Smith, R, NJ Mann, H Mäkeläinen, J Roper, A Braue, and G Varigos. A pilot study to determine the short-term effects of a low glycemic load diet on hormonal markers of acne: A nonrandomized, parallel, controlled feeding trial. *Mol Nutr Food Res* 2008, 52(6): 718–726.

7. Smith, RN, A Braue, GA Varigos, and NJ Mann. The effect of a low glycemic load diet on acne vulgaris and the fatty acid composition of skin surface triglycerides. *J Dermatol Sci* 2008, 50(1):41–52.

8. Smith, RN, NJ Mann, A Braue, H Mäkeläinen, and GA Varigos. A low-glycemic-load diet improves symptoms in acne vulgaris patients: A randomized controlled trial. *Am J Clin Nutr* 2007, 86(1):107–115.

9. Smith, RN, NJ Mann, A Braue, H Mäkeläinen, and GA Mäkeläinen. The effect of a high-protein, low glycemic-load diet versus a conventional, high glycemic-load diet on biochemical parameters associated with acne vulgaris:

A randomized, investigator-masked, controlled trial. *J Am Acad Dermatol* 2007, 57(2):247–256.

10. El-Akawi, Z, N Abdel-Latif, and K Abdul-Razzak. Does the plasma level of vitamins A and E affect acne condition? *Clin Exp Dermatol* 2006, 31(3):430–434.

11. Sherertz, EF. Acneiform eruption due to megadose vitamin B6 and B12. *Cutis* 1991, 48(2):119–120.

12. McCarty, M. High-chromium yeast for acne? *Med Hypotheses* 1984, 14(3):307–310.

13. Bruce, A. Swedish views on selenium. *Ann Clin Res* 1986, 18(1):8–12.

14. Michaelsson, G, and LE Edqvist. Erythrocyte glutathione peroxidase activity in acne vulgaris and the effect of selenium and vitamin E treatment. *Acta Derm Venereol* 1984, 64(1):9–14.

15. Michaelsson, G, and K Ljunghall. Patients with herpetiformis acne, psoriasis and Darier's disease have low epidermal zinc concentrations. *Acta Derm Venereol* 1990, 70(4):304–308.

16. Dreno, B, et al. Low dose of zinc gluconate for inflammatory acne. *Acta Derm Venereol* 1989, 69(6):541–543.

17. Verma, KC, et al. Oral zinc sulphate therapy in acne vulgaris: A double-blind trial. *Acta Derm Venereol* 1980, 60(4):337–340.

18. Dreno, B, D Moyse, M Alirezai, P Amblard, N Auffret, C Beylot, I Bodokh, M Chivot, F Daniel, P Humbert, J Meynadier, F Poli; Acne Research and Study Group. Multicenter randomized comparative double-blind controlled clinical trial of the safety and efficacy of zinc gluconate versus minocycline hydrochloride in the treatment of inflammatory acne vulgaris. *Dermatology* 2001, 203(2):135–140.

19. Enshaieh, S, A Jooya, AH Siadat, and F Iraji. The efficacy of 5% topical tea tree oil gel in mild to moderate acne vulgaris: A randomized, double-blind placebo-controlled study. *Indian J Dermatol Venereol Leprol* 2007, 73(1):22–25.

20. Williams, LR, et al. The composition and bacteriocidal activity of oil of Melaleuca alternifolia (tea tree oil). *Int J Aromather* 1988, 1:15–17.

21. Ernst, E, and A Huntley. Tea tree oil: A systematic review of randomized clinical trials. *Forsch Komplemetarmed* 2000, 7(1):17–20.

Alcoholism

1. Alcohol. Alberta Alcohol and Drug Abuse Commission, November 2000. Available at www.gov.ab.ca/aadac/addictions/beyond/beyond_alcohol.html.

2. Biery, JR, et al. Alcohol craving in rehabilitation: Assessment of nutrition therapy. *J Am Diet Assoc* 1991, 91(4):463–466.

3. The American Dietetic Association. *Manual of Clinical Dietetics*, 6th ed. (Chicago, 2000).

4. Pita, ML, et al. Chronic alcoholism decreases polyunsaturated fatty acid levels in human plasma, erythrocytes and platelets: Influence on chronic liver disease. *Thromb Haemost* 1997, 78(2):808–812.

5. Reitz, RC. Dietary fatty acids and alcohol: Effects on cellular membranes. *Alcohol Alcohol* 1994, 28(1):59–71.

6. Hibbeln, JR, and N Salem Jr. Dietary polyunsaturated fatty acids and depression: When cholesterol does not satisfy. *Am J Clin Nutr* 1995, 62(1):1–9.

7. Gloria, L, et al. Nutritional deficiencies in chronic alcoholics: Relation to dietary intake and alcohol consumption. *Am J Gastroenterol* 1997, 92(3):485–489.

8. Fernando, OV, and EW Grimsley. Prevalence of folate deficiency and macrocytosis in patients with and without alcohol-related illness. *South Med J* 1998, 91(8):721–725.

9. Carney, MW, et al. Red cell folate concentrations in psychiatric patients. *J Affect Disord* 1990, 19(3):207–213.

10. Fernandez-Calle, P, et al. Alcoholic cognitive deterioration and nutritional deficiencies. *Acta Neurol Scand* 1994, 89(5):384–390.

11. Harper, C, and J Kril. An introduction to alcohol-induced brain damage and its causes. *Alcohol Alcohol* 1994, 2 (Suppl): 237–243.

12. Tallaksen, CM, et al. Blood and serum thiamin and thiamin phosphate ester concentrations in patients with alcohol dependence syndrome before and after thiamin treatment. *Alcohol Clin Exp Res* 1992, 16(2):320–325.

13. Zubaran, C, et al. Wernicke-Korsakoff syndrome. *Postgrad Med J* 1997, 73(855):27–31.

14. Naidoo, DP, et al. Wernicke's encephalopathy and alcohol-related disease. *Postgrad Med J* 1991, 67(793):978–981.

15. Van Gossum, A, et al. Deficiency in antioxidant factors in patients with alcohol-related chronic pancreatitis. *Dig Dis Sci* 1996, 41(6):1225–1231.

16. Lecomte, E, et al. Effect of alcohol consumption on blood antioxidant nutrients and oxidative stress indicators. *Am J Clin Nutr* 1994, 60(2):255–261.

17. Siest, G, and Y Artur. The relation of alcohol consumption to serum carotenoid and retinal levels: Effects of withdrawal. *Int J Vitam Nutr Res* 1994, 64(3):170–175.

18. Bjorneboe, GA, et al. Diminished serum concentration of vitamin E in alcoholics. *Ann Nutr Metab* 1988, 32(2): 56–61.

19. Bjorneboe, GA, et al. Effect of heavy alcohol consumption on serum concentrations of fat-soluble vitamins and selenium. *Alcohol Alcohol* 1987, (Suppl 1):S533–S537.

20. Altura, BM, and BT Altura. Role of magnesium and calcium in alcohol-induced hypertension and strokes as probed by in vivo television microscopy, digital image microscopy, optical microscopy, 31P-NMR, spectroscopy and a unique magnesium ion-selective electrode. *Alcohol Clin Exp Res* 1994, 18(5):1057–1068.

21. Kim, MJ, MS Shim, MK Kim, et al. Effect of chronic alcohol ingestion on bone mineral density in males without liver cirrhosis. *Korean J Intern Med* 2003, 18(3):174–180.

22. Clark, ML, MF Sowers, F Dekordi, and S Nichols. Bone mineral density and fractures among alcohol-dependent women in treatment and recovery. *Osteoporosis Int* 2003, 14(5):396–403.

23. Abbott, L, et al. Magnesium deficiency in alcoholism: Possible contribution to osteoporosis and cardiovascular disease in alcoholics. *Alcohol Clin Exp Res* 1994, 18(5):1076–1082.

24. Gullstad, L, et al. Oral magnesium supplementation improves metabolic variables and muscle strength in alcoholics. *Alcohol Clin Exp Res* 1992, 16(5):986–990.

25. Poikolainen, K, and L Alho. Magnesium treatment in alcoholics: A randomized clinical trial. *Subst Abuse Treat Prev Policy* 2008, 3:1.

26. Menzano, E, and PL Carlen. Zinc deficiency and corticosteroids in the pathogenesis of alcoholic brain dysfunction: A review. *Alcohol Clin Exp Res* 1994, 18(4):895–901.

27. Feher, J, et al. Liver protective action of silymarin therapy in chronic alcoholic liver diseases. *Orv Hetil* 1989, 130:2723–2727. [Hungarian]

28. Saller, R, R Brignoli, J Melzer, and R Meier. An updated systematic review with meta-analysis for the clinical evidence of silymarin. *Forsch Komplementmed* 2008, 15(1):9–20.

29. Lucena, MI, RJ Andrade, JP de la Cruz, M Rodriguez-Mendizabal, E Blanco, and F Sánchez de la Cuesta. Effects of silymarin MZ-80 on oxidative stress in patients with alcoholic cirrhosis: Results of a randomized, double-blind, placebo-controlled clinical study. *Int J Clin Pharmacol Ther* 2002, 40(1):2–8.

30. Saller, R, R Meier, and R Brignoli. The use of silymarin in the treatment of liver diseases. *Drugs* 2001, 61(14): 2035–2063.

31. Muzes, G, et al. Effects of silymarin (Legalon) therapy on the antioxidant defense mechanism and lipid peroxidation in alcoholic liver disease. *Orv Hetil* 1990, 131:863–866. [Hungarian]

32 Lieber, CS, et al. Attenuation of alcohol-induced hepatic fibrosis by polyunsaturated lecithin. *Hepatology* 1990, 12:1390–1398.

33. Lieber, CS, and E Rubin. Alcoholic fatty liver. *N Engl J Med* 1969, 280:705–708.

34. Schuller-Perez, A, and F Gonzalez San Martin. A controlled study with polyunsaturated phosphatidylcholine compared to placebo in alcoholic steatosis of the liver. *Med Welt* 1985, 36:517–521.

35. Chawla, RK, et al. Biochemistry and pharmacology of S-adenosyl-L-methionine and rationale for its use in liver disease. *Drugs* 1990, 40(Suppl 3):S98–S110.

36. Loguercio, C, et al. Effect of S-adenosyl-L-methionine administration on red blood cell cysteine and glutathione levels in alcoholic patients with and without liver disease. *Alcohol Alcohol* 1994, 29(5):597–604.

Alzheimer's Disease

1. *What Is Alzheimer's Disease?* Alzheimer Society of Canada, September 2000. Available at www.alzheimer.caalz/content/html/disease_en/disease-whatisit-eng.html.

2. Ibid.

3. Poehlman, ET, and RV Dvorak. Energy expenditure, energy intake, and weight loss in Alzheimer disease. *Am J Clin Nutr* 2000, 71(2):650S–655S.

4. Scarmeas N, JA Luchsinger, N Schupf et al. Physical activity, diet, and risk of Alzheimer disease. *JAMA* 2009, 302: 627–637.

5. Freund-Levi, Y, M Eriksdotter-Jonhagen, T Cederholm, et al. Omega-3 fatty acid treatment in 174 patients with mild to moderate Alzheimer's disease: OmegAD study: A randomized double-blind trial. *Arch Neurol* 2006, 63(10):1402–1408.

6. Yehuda, S, et al. Essential fatty acids preparation (SR-3) improves Alzheimer's patients' quality of life. *J Dev Neurosci* 1996, 87(3–4):141–149.

7. Kalmijn, S, et al. Dietary fat intake and the risk of incident dementia in the Rotterdam Study. *Ann Neurol* 1997, 42(5):775–782.

8. Morris, MC, DA Evans, JL Bienias, CC Tangney, DA Bennett, RS Wilson, N Aggarwal, and J Schneider. Consumption of fish and n-3 fatty acids and risk of incident Alzheimer disease. *Arch Neurol* 2003, 60(7):940–946.

9. Meins, W, et al. Subnormal serum vitamin B12 and behavioural and psychological symptoms in Alzheimer's disease. *Int J Geriatr Psychiatry* 2000, 15(5):415–418.

10. Levitt, AJ, and H Karlinsky. Folate, vitamin B12 and cognitive impairment in patients with Alzheimer's disease. *Acta Psychiatr Scand* 1992, 86(4):301–305.

11. Sun, Y, CJ Lu, KL Chien, ST Chen, and RC Chen. Efficacy of multivitamin supplementation containing vitamins B6 and B12 and folic acid as adjunctive treatment with a cholinesterase inhibitor in Alzheimer's disease: A 26-week, randomized, double-blind, placebo-controlled study in Taiwanese patients. *Clin Ther* 2007, 29(10):2204–2214.

12. Sano, M, C Ernesto, RG Thomas, et al. A controlled trial of selegiline, alpha-tocopherol, or both as treatment for Alzheimer's disease. The Alzheimer's Disease Cooperative Study. *N Engl J Med* 1997, 336(17):1216–1222.

13. Petersen, RC, RG Thomas, M Grundman, D Bennett, R Doody, S Ferris, D Galasko, S Jin, J Kaye, A Levey, E Pfeiffer, M Sano, CH van Dyck, LJ Thal; Alzheimer's Disease Cooperative Study Group. Vitamin E and donepezil for the treatment of mild cognitive impairment. *N Engl J Med* 2005, 352(23):2379–2388.

14. Isaac, MG, R Quinn, and N Tabet. Vitamin E for Alzheimer's disease and mild cognitive impairment. *Cochrane Database Syst Rev* 2008 Jul 16, (3):CD002854.

15. Sato, Y, et al. High prevalence of vitamin D deficiency and reduced bone mass in elderly women with Alzheimer's disease. *Bone* 1998, 23(6):555–557.

16. Le Bars, PL, et al. A placebo-controlled, double-blind, randomized trial of an extract of Ginkgo biloba for dementia. North American EGb Study Group. *JAMA* 1997, 278(16):1327–1332.

17. Wettstein, A. Cholinesterase inhibitors and ginkgo extracts: Are they comparable in the treatment of dementia? Comparison of published placebo-controlled efficacy studies of at least six months' duration. *Phytomedicine* 2000, 6(6):393–401.

18. Oken, BS, et al. The efficacy of Ginkgo biloba on cognitive function in Alzheimer disease. *Arch Neurol* 1998, 55(11): 1409–1415.

19. DeKosky, ST, JD Williamson, AL Fitzpatrick, RA Kronmal, DG Ives, JA Saxton, OL Lopez, G Burke, MC Carlson, LP Fried, LH Kuller, JA Robbins, RP Tracy, NF Woolard, L Dunn, BE Snitz, RL Nahin, CD Furberg; Ginkgo Evaluation of Memory (GEM) Study Investigators. Ginkgo biloba for prevention of dementia: A randomized controlled trial. *JAMA* 2008, 300(19)8:2253–2262.

20. Jaggy, H, and E Koch. The chemistry and biology of alkylphenols from Ginkgo biloba L. *Pharmazie* 1997, 52(10):735–738.

21. Mook-Jung, I, et al. Protective effects of asiaticoside derivatives against beta-amyloid neurotoxicity. *J Neurosci Res* 1999, 58:417–425.

22. Hudson, S, and N Tabet. Acetyl-L-carnitine for dementia. *Cochrane Database Syst Rev* 2003, 2:CD003158.

23. Montgomery, SA, LJ Thal, and R Amrein. Meta-analysis of double blind randomized controlled clinical trials of acetyl-L-carnitine versus placebo in the treatment of mild cognitive impairment and mild Alzheimer's disease. *Int Clin Psychopharmacol* 2003, 18(2):61–71.

24. Brooks 3rd, JO, JA Yesavage, A Carta, and D Bravi. Acetyl-L-carnitine slows decline in younger patients with Alzheimer's disease: A reanalysis of a double-blind, placebo-controlled study using the trilinear approach. *Int Psychogeriatr* 1998, 10(2):193–203.

25. Thal, LJ, A Carta, WR Clarke, et al. A 1-year placebo-controlled study of acetyl-L-carnitine in patients with Alzheimer's disease. *Neurology* 1996, 47(3):705–711.

26. Pettegrew, JW, et al. Clinical and neurochemical effects of acetyl-L-carnitine in Alzheimer's disease. *Neurobiol Aging* 1995, 16(1):1–4.

27. Tettamanti, M, et al. Long-term acetyl-L-carnitine treatment in Alzheimer's disease. *Neurology* 1991, 41(11):1726–1732.

28. Rai, G, G Wright, L Scott, et al. Double-blind, placebo controlled study of acetyl-L-carnitine in patients with Alzheimer's dementia. *Curr Med Res Opin* 1990, 11(10): 638–647.

29. Heiss, WD, J Kessler, R Mielke, et al. Long-term effects of phosphatidylserine, pyritinol, and cognitive training in Alzheimer's disease: A neuropsychological, EEG, and PET investigation. *Dementia* 1994, 5(2):88–98.

30. Crook, T, W Petrie, C Wells, and DC Massari. Effects of phosphatidylserine in Alzheimer's disease. *Psychopharmacol Bull* 1992, 28(1): 61–66.

31. Engel, RR, W Satzger, W Gunther, et al. Double-blind cross-over study of phospha-tidylserine vs. placebo in patients with early dementia of the Alzheimer type. *Eur Neuropsychopharmacol* 1992, 2(2):149–155.

Anemia (Iron-Deficiency Anemia)

1. Gardner, EJ, CH Ruxton, and AR Leeds. Black tea—helpful or harmful? A review of the evidence. *Eur J Clin Nutr* 2007, 61(1):3–18.

2. Kuzminski, AM, et al. Effective treatment of cobalamin deficiency with oral cobalamin. *Blood* 1998, 92(4): 1191–1198.

Angina (Angina pectoris)

1. Sesso HD, JE Buring, WG Christen, T Kurth, C Belanger, J MacFadyen, V Bubes, JE Manson, RJ Glynn, and JM Gaziano. Vitamins E and C in the prevention of cardiovascular disease in men: the Physicians' Health Study II randomized controlled trial. *JAMA* 2008, 300(18): 2123–2133.

2. Rimm, EB, MJ Stampfer, A Ascherio, E Giovannucci, et al. Vitamin E consumption and the risk of coronary heart disease in men. *N Engl J Med* 1993, 328(20):1450–1456.

3. Stampfer, MJ, CH Hennekens, JE Manson, GA Colditz, et al. Vitamin E consumption and the risk of coronary disease in women. *N Engl J Med* 1993, 328(20):1444–1449.

4. Lee, IM, NR Cook, JM Gaziano, D Gordon, et al. Vitamin E in the primary prevention of cardiovascular disease and cancer: The Women's Health Study: A randomized controlled trial. *JAMA* 2005, 294(1):56–65.

5. Yusuf, S, G Dagenais, J Pogue, J Bosch, and P Sleight. Vitamin E supplementation and cardiovascular events in high-risk patients: The Heart Outcomes Prevention Evaluation Study Investigators. *N Engl J Med* 2000, 342(3):154–160.

6. Gruppo Italiano per lo Studio della Sopravvivenza nell'Infarto miocardico. Dietary supplementation with n-3 polyunsaturated fatty acids and vitamin E after myocardial infarction: Results of the GISSI-Prevenzione trial. *Lancet* 1999, 354(9177):447–455.

7. Lonn, E, J Bosch, S Yusuf, P Sheridan, J Pogue, JM Arnold, C Ross, A Arnold, P Sleight, J Probstfield, GR Dagenais; HOPE and HOPE-TOO Trial Investigators. Effects of long-term vitamin E supplementation on cardiovascular events and cancer: A randomized controlled trial. *JAMA* 2005, 293(11):1338–1347.

8. Miller 3rd, ER, R Pastor-Barriuso, D Dalal, RA Riemersma, et al. Meta-analysis: High-dosage vitamin E supplementation may increase all-cause mortality. *Ann Intern Med* 2005, 142(1):37–46.

9. Giovannucci, E, Y Liu, BW Hollis, and EB Rimm. 25-hydroxyvitamin D and risk of myocardial infarction in men. *Arch Intern Med* 2008, 168(11):1174–1180.

10. Dobnig, H, S Pilz, H Scharnagl, W Renner, et al. Independent association of low serum 25-hydroxyvitamin D and 1,25-dihydroxyvitamin D levels with all-cause mortality and cardiovascular mortality. *Arch Intern Med* 2008, 168(12):1340–1349.

11. Satake, K, et al. Relation between severity of magnesium deficiency and frequency of anginal attacks in men with variant angina. *J Am Coll Cardiol* 1996, 28(4):897–902.

12. Teragawa, H, et al. The preventative effect of magnesium of coronary spasm in patients with vasospastic angina. *Chest* 2000, 118(6):1690–1695.

13. Shechter, M, CN Bairey Merz, HG Stuehlinger, et al. Effects of oral magnesium therapy on exercise tolerance, exercise-induced chest pain, and quality of life in patients with coronary artery disease. *Am J Cardiol* 2003, 91(5):517–521.

14. Lasserre, B, et al. Should magnesium therapy be considered for the treatment of coronary heart disease? II. Epidemiological evidence in outpatients with and without coronary heart disease. *Magnes Res* 1994, 7(2):145–153.

15. Tran, MT, TM Mitchell, DT Kennedy, and JT Giles. Role of coenzyme Q10 in chronic heart failure, angina, and hypertension. *Pharmacotherapy* 2001, 21(7):797–806.

16. Kamikawa, T, et al. Effects of coenzyme Q10 on exercise tolerance in chronic stable angina pectoris. *Am J Cardiol* 1985, 56(4):247–251.

17. Iyer, RN, et al. L-carnitine moderately improves the exercise tolerance in chronic stable angina. *J Assoc Physicians India* 2000, 48(11):1050–1052.

18. Cacciatore, L, R Cerio, M Ciarimboli, et al. The therapeutic effect of L-carnitine in patients with exercise-induced stable angina: A controlled study. *Drugs Exp Clin Res* 1991, 17:225–235.

19. Cacciatore, L, R Cerio, M Ciarimboli, et al. The therapeutic effect of L-carnitine in patients with exercise-induced stable angina: A controlled study. *Drugs Exp Clin Res* 1991, 17(4):225–235.

20. Cherchi, A, C Lai, F Angelino, et al. Effects of L-carnitine on exercise tolerance in chronic stable angina: A multi-center, double-blind, randomized, placebo-controlled crossover study. *Int J Clin Pharmacol Ther Toxicol* 1985, 23:569–572.

21. Bartels, GL, et al. Effects of L-propionylcarnitine on ischemia-induced myocardial dysfunction in men with angina pectoris. *Am J Cardiol* 1994, 74:125–130.

22. Bartels, GL, et al. Additional anti-ischemic effects of long-term L-propionylcarnitine in anginal patients treated with conventional antianginal therapy. *Cardiovasc Drugs Ther* 1995, 9:749–753.

Asthma

1. *What Is Asthma?* Asthma Society of Canada, April 2005. Available at www.asthma.ca/adults/about/whatIsAsthma. php.

2. Aaron, SD, KL Vandemheen, LP Boulet, RA McIvor, JM Fitzgerald, P Hernandez, C Lemiere, S Sharma, SK Field, GG Alvarez, RE Dales, S Doucette, D Fergusson; Canadian Respiratory Clinical Research Consortium. Overdiagnosis of asthma in obese and non-obese adults. *CMAJ* 2008, 179(11):1121–1131.

3. Barros, R, A Moreira, J Fonseca, JF de Oliveira, L Delgado, MG Castel-Branco, T Haahtela, C Lopes, and P Moreira. Adherence to the Mediterranean diet and fresh fruit intake are associated with improved asthma control. *Allergy* 2008, 63(7):917–923.

4. Castro-Rodriguez, JA, L Garcia-Marcos, JD Alfonseda Rojas, J Valverde-Molina, and M Sanchez-Solis. Mediterranean diet as a protective factor for wheezing in preschool children. *J Pediatr* 2008, 152(6):823–828.

5. Chatzi, L, G Apostolaki, I Bibakis, I Skypala, V Bibaki-Liakou, N Tzanakis, M Kogevinas, and P Cullinan. Protective effect of fruits, vegetables and the Mediterranean diet on asthma and allergies among children in Crete. *Thorax* 2007, 62(8):677–683.

6. Chatzi, L, M Torrent, I Romieu, R Garcia-Esteban, C Ferrer, J Vioque, M Kogevinas, and J Sunyer. Mediterranean diet in pregnancy is protective for wheeze and atopy in childhood. *Thorax* 2008, 63(6):507–513.

7. Monteleonem, CA, and AR Sherman. Nutrition and asthma. *Arch Intern Med* 1997, 157(1):23–34.

8. La Vecchia, C, et al. Vegetable consumption and the risk of chronic disease. *Epidemiology* 1998, 9(2):208–210.

9. Forastiere, F, et al. Consumption of fresh fruit in vitamin C and wheezing symptoms in children. *Thorax* 2000, 55(4):283–288.

10. Lindahl, O, et al. Vegan regimen with reduced medication in the treatment of bronchial asthma. *J Asthma* 1985, 22(1):45–55.

11. Camargo Jr, CA, et al. Prospective study of body mass index, weight change, and risk of adult-onset asthma in women. *Arch Intern Med* 1999, 159(21):2582–2588.

12. Chen, Y, et al. Increased effects of smoking and obesity on asthma among female Canadians. *Am J Epidemiol* 1999, 150(3):255–262.

13. Stenius-Aarniala, B, et al. Immediate and long-term effects of weight reduction in obese people with asthma:

Randomized controlled study. *Br Med J* 2000, 320(7238):827–832.

14. Miyamoto, S, Y Miyake, S Sasaki, K Tanaka, Y Ohya, I Matsunaga, T Yoshida, H Oda, O Ishiko, Y Hirota; Osaka Maternal and Child Health Study Group. Fat and fish intake and asthma in Japanese women: Baseline data from the Osaka Maternal and Child Health Study. *Int J Tuberc Lung Dis* 2007, 11(1):103–109.

15. Medici, TC, et al. Are asthmatics salt-sensitive? A preliminary controlled study. *Chest* 1993, 104(4):1138–1143.

16. Pistelli, R, et al. Respiratory symptoms and bronchial responsiveness are related to dietary salt intake and urinary potassium excretion in male children. *Eur Respir J* 1993, 6(4):517–522.

17. Carey, OJ, et al. Effect of alterations of dietary sodium on the severity of asthma in men. *Thorax* 1993, 48(7): 714–718.

18. Mickleborough, TD, and A Fogarty. Dietary sodium intake and asthma: An epidemiological and clinical review. *Int J Clin Pract* 2006, 60(12):1616–1624.

19. Pogson, ZE, MD Antoniak, SJ Pacey, SA Lewis, JR Britton, and AW Fogarty. Does a low sodium diet improve asthma control? A randomized controlled trial. *Am J Respir Crit Care Med* 2008, 178(2):132–138.

20. Kelly, FJ, et al. Altered lung antioxidant status in patients with mild asthma. *Lancet* 1999, 354(9177):482–483.

21. Bielory, L, and R Gandhi. Asthma and vitamin C. *Ann Allergy* 1994, 73:89–99.

22. Kaur, B, BH Rowe, and E Arnold. Vitamin C supplementation for asthma. *Cochrane Database Syst Rev* 2009 Jan 21, (1):CD000993.

23. Cohen, HA, et al. Blocking effect of vitamin C in exercise-induced asthma. *Arch Pediatr Adolesc Med* 1997, 151(32): 103–109.

24. Caruso, C. Bronchial reactivity and intracellular magnesium: A possible mechanism for the bronchodilating effects of magnesium in asthma. *Clin Sci* 1998, 95(2):137–142.

25. Hashimoto, Y, et al. Assessment of magnesium status in patients with bronchial asthma. *J Asthma* 2000, 37(6): 489–496.

26. Hill, J, et al. Investigation of the effects of short-term change in dietary magnesium intake in asthma. *Eur Respir J* 1997, 10(10): 2225–2229.

27. Gontijo-Amaral, C, MA Ribeiro, LS Gontijo, A Condino-Neto, and JD Ribeiro. Oral magnesium supplementation in asthmatic children: A double-blind randomized placebo-controlled trial. *Eur J Clin Nutr* 2007, 61(1):54–60.

28. Gupta, I, et al. Effects of Boswellia serrata gum resin in patients with bronchial asthma: Results of a double-blind, placebo-controlled, 6-week clinical study. *Eur J Med Res* 1998, 3:511–514.

29. Olsen, SF, ML Østerdal, JD Salvig, LM Mortensen, D Rytter, NJ Secher, and TB Henriksen. Fish oil intake compared with olive oil intake in late pregnancy and asthma in the offspring: 16 y of registry-based follow-up from a randomized controlled trial. *Am J Clin Nutr* 2008, 88(1):167–175.

30. Dunstan, JA, TA Mori, A Barden, LJ Beilin, AL Taylor, PG Holt, and SL Holt. Fish oil supplementation in pregnancy modifies neonatal allergen-specific immune responses and clinical outcomes in infants at high risk of atopy:

A randomized, controlled trial. *J Allergy Clin Immunol* 2003, 112(6):1178–1184.

31. Mickleborough, TD, MR Lindley, AA Ionescu, and AD Fly. Protective effect of fish oil supplementation on exercise-induced bronchoconstriction in asthma. *Chest* 2006, 129(1):39–49.

32. Arm, JP, and TH Lee. The use of fish oil in bronchial asthma. *Allergy Proc* 1989, 10(3):185–187.

33. Dry, J, and D Vincent. Effect of fish oil diet on asthma: Results of a 1-year double-blind study. *Int Arch Allergy Appl Immunol* 1991, 95(2–3):156–157.

34. Villani, F, et al. Effect of dietary supplementation with polyunsaturated fatty acids on bronchial hyperactivity in subjects with seasonal asthma. *Respiration* 1998, 65(4): 265–269.

35. Kalliomäki, M, S Salminen, H Arvilommi, P Kero, P Koskinen, and E Isolauri. Probiotics in primary prevention of atopic disease: A randomised placebo-controlled trial. *Lancet* 2001, 357(9262):1076–1079.

36. Rautava, S, M Kalliomäki, and E Isolauri. Probiotics during pregnancy and breast-feeding might confer immunomodulatory protection against atopic disease in the infant. *J Allergy Clin Immunol* 2002, 109(1):119– 121.

Attention Deficit Hyperactivity Disorder (ADHD)

1. *ADHD Facts and Fiction*. ADHD.ca Eli Lilly and Company, 2008. Available at //www.adhd.ca/portals/adhd/eng/ 1215457001191.html.

2. Ibid.

3. Bornstein, RA, et al. Plasma amino acids in attention deficit disorder. *Psychiatry Res* 1990, 33(3):301–306.

4. Eisenberg, J, et al. Effect of tyrosine on attention deficit disorder with hyperactivity. *J Clin Psychiatry* 1988, 49(5):193–195.

5. Reimherr, FW, et al. An open trial of L-tyrosine in the treatment of attention deficit disorder, residual type. *Am J Psychiatry* 1987, 144(8):1071–1073.

6. Smith, A, et al. Effects of breakfast and caffeine on cognitive performance, mood and cardiovascular functioning. *Appetite* 1994, 22(1):39–55.

7. Joshi, K, S Lad, M Kale, et al. Supplementation with flax oil and vitamin C improves the outcome of Attention Deficit Hyperactivity Disorder (ADHD). *Prostaglandins Leukot Essent Fatty Acids* 2006, 74(1):17–21.

8. Bamforth, KJ, et al. Common food additives are potent inhibitors of human liver 17 alpha-ethinyloestradiol and dopamine sulphotransferases. *Biochem Pharmacol* 1993, 46(10):1713–1720.

9. Weinshilboum, RM. Phenol sulfotransferase in humans: Properties, regulation, and function. *Fed Proc* 1986, 45(8):2223–2228.

10. Harris, RM, and RH Waring. Dietary modulation of human platelet phenolsulphotransferase activity. *Xenobiotica* 1996, 26(12):1241–1247.

11. Rowe, KS. Synthetic food colourings and 'hyperactivity': A double-blind crossover study. *Aust Paediatr J* 1988, 24(2):143–147.

12. Rippere, V. Food additives and hyperactive children: A critique of Conners. *Br J Clin Psychol* 1983, 22(Pt 1):19–32.

13. Adams, W. Lack of behavioural effects from Feingold diet violations. *Percept Mot Skills* 1981, 52(1):307–313.

14. Mattes, JA, and R Gittleman. Effects of artificial food colourings in children with hyperactive symptoms: A critical review and results of a controlled study. *Arch Gen Psychiatry* 1981, 38(6):714–718.

15. Salamay, J, et al. Physiological changes in hyperactive children following the ingestion of food additives. *J Neurosci* 1982, 16(3–4):241–246.

16. Kaplan, BJ, et al. Dietary replacement in preschool-aged hyperactive boys. *Pediatrics* 1989, 83(1):7–17.

17. Egger, J, et al. Controlled trial of oligoantigenic diet treatment in the hyperkinetic syndromes. *Lancet* 1985, 1(8428): 540–545.

18. Wender, DH. The food additive-free diet in the treatment of behaviour disorders: A review. *J Dev Behav Pediatr* 1986, 7(1):35–42.

19. Food Colourings and ADHD in Children. Suite 101.com, July 21, 2008. Available at http://adhd-add-treatments. suite101.com/article.cfm/food_colorings_and_adhd_in_ children.

20. Krummel, DA, et al. Hyperactivity: Is candy causal? *Crit Rev Food Sci Nutr* 1996, 36(1): 31–47.

21. Wolraich, ML, et al. The effect of sugar on behaviour or cognition in children: A meta-analysis. *JAMA* 1995, 274(20):1617–1621.

22. Kanarek, RB. Does sucrose or aspartame cause hyperactivity in children? *Nutr Rev* 1994, 52(5):173–175.

23. Roshon, MS, and RL Hagen. Sugar consumption, task orientation, and learning in preschool children. *J Abnorm Child Psychol* 1989, 17(3):349–357.

24. Wender, EH, and MV Solanto. Effects of sugar on aggressive and inattentive behavior in children with attention deficit disorder with hyperactivity and normal children. *Pediatrics* 1991, 88(5):960–966.

25. Oner, O, OY Alkar, and P Oner. Relation of ferritin levels with symptoms ratings and cognitive performance in children with attention deficit-hyperactivity disorder. *Pediatr Int* 2008, 50(1):40–44.

26. Konofol, E, M Lecendreaux, J Deron, et al. Effects of iron supplementation on attention deficit hyperactivity disorder in children. *Pediatr Neurol* 2008, 38(1):20–26.

27. Konolfol, E, M Lecendreaux, I Arnulf, and MC Mouren. Iron deficiency in children with attention-deficit/ hyperactivity disorder. *Arch Pediatr Adolesc Med* 2004, 158(12):1113–1115.

28. Kozielec, T, and B Starobrat-Hermelin. Assessment of magnesium levels in children with attention deficit hyperactivity disorder (ADHD). *Magnes Res* 1997, 10(2):143–148.

29. Starobrat-Hermelin, B, and T Kozielec. The effects of magnesium supplementation on hyperactivity in children with attention deficit hyperactivity disorder (ADHD): Positive response to a magnesium oral loading test. *Magnes Res* 1997, 10(2):149–156.

30. Bekaroglu, M, et al. Relationships between serum free fatty acids and zinc, and attention deficit hyperactivity disorder: A research note. *J Child Psychol Psychiatry* 1996, 37(2): 225–227.

31. Arnold, LE, et al. Does hair zinc predict amphetamine improvement in ADD/hyperactivity? *Int J Neurosci* 1990, 50(1–2):103–107.

32. Akhondzadhe, S, MR Mohammadi, and M Khademi. Zinc sulfate as an adjunct to methylphenidate for the treatment of attention deficit hyperactivity disorder in children: A double blind and randomized trial. *BMC Psychiatry* 2004, 4:9.

33. Arnold, LE, et al. Gamma-linoleic acid for attention-deficit hyperactivity disorder: Placebo-controlled comparison to D-amphetamine. *Biol Psychiatry* 1989, 25(2):222–228.

34. Aman, MG, et al. The effects of fatty acid supplementation by Efamol in hyperactive children. *J Abnorm Child Psychol* 1987, 15(1):75–90.

35. Richardson, AJ, et al. Reduced behavioural and learning problems in children with specific learning difficulties after supplementation with highly unsaturated fatty acids: A randomized double-blind placebo-controlled trial. Presented at the 2nd Forum of European Neuroscience Societies, July 24–28, 2000, Brighton, United Kingdom.

36. Burgess, JR, et al. Long-chain polyunsaturated fatty acids in children with attention-deficit hyperactivity disorder. *Am J Clin Nutr* 2000, 71(Suppl 1):S327–S330.

37. Stevens, LJ, et al. Essential fatty acid metabolism in boys with attention-deficit hyperactivity disorder. *Am J Clin Nutr* 1995, 62(4):761–768.

38. Mitchell, EA, et al. Clinical characteristics and serum essential fatty acid levels in hyperactive children. *Clin Pediatr* 1987, 26(8):406–411.

39. Vaisman, N, N Kaysar, Y Zaruk-Adasha, et al. Correlation between changes in blood fatty acid composition and visual sustained attention performance in children with inattention: Effect of dietary n-3 fatty acids containing phospholipids. *Am J Clin Nutr* 2008, 87(5):1170–1180.

40. Sorgi, PJ, EM Hallowell, HL Hutchins, and B Sears. Effects of an open label pilot study with high-dose EPA/DHA concentrates on plasma phospholipids and behaviour in children with attention deficit hyperactivity disorder. *Nutr J* 2007, 6: 16.

41. Sinn, N, and J Bryan. Effect of supplementation with polyunsatured fatty acids and micronutrients on learning and behavioural problems associated with child ADHD. *J Dev Behav Pediatr* 2007, 28(2):139–144.

42. Hirayama, S, T Hamazaki, and K Terasawa. Effect of docosahexaenoic acid-containing food administration on symptoms of attention-deficit/hyperactivity disorder: A placebo controlled double-blind study. *Eur J Clin Nutr* 2004, 58(3):467–473.

Breast Cancer

1. Breast cancer stats. The Canadian Cancer Society, April 9, 2009. Available at www.cancer.ca/canadawide/about% 20cancer/cancer%20statistics/stats%20at%20a%20glance/ breast%20cancer.aspx?sc_lang=en.

2. Ibid.

3. Holmes, MD, et al. Association of dietary fat and fatty acids with risk of breast cancer. *JAMA* 1999, 281(10):914–920.

4. Boyd, NF, et al. Effects of a low-fat high-carbohydrate diet on plasma sex hormones in premenopausal women: Results from a randomized controlled trial. Canadian Diet and Breast Cancer Prevention Study Group. *Br J Cancer* 1997, 76(1):127–135.

5. Prentice, RL, B Caan, RT Chlebowski, et al. Low fat dietary pattern and risk of invasive breast cancer: The Women's Health Initiative Randomized Controlled Dietary Modification Trial. *JAMA* 2006, 295(6):629–642.

6. Chlebowski, RT, GL Blackburn, CA Thomson, et al. Dietary fat reduction and breast cancer outcome: Intermin efficacy results from the Women's Intervention Nutrition Study. *J Natl Cancer Inst* 2006, 98(24):1767–1776.

7. Zheng, W, et al. Well-done meat intake and the risk of breast cancer. *J Natl Cancer Inst* 1998, 90(22):1724–1729.

8. Rose, DP, et al. Effect of omega-3 fatty acids on the progression of metastases after surgical excision of human breast cancer cell solid tumors growing in nude mice. *Clin Cancer Res* 1996, 2(10):1751–1756.

9. MacLean, CH, SJ Newberry, WA Mojica, et al. Effects of omega-3 fatty acids on cancer risk: A systematic review. *JAMA* 2006, 295(4):403–415.

10. Silvera, SA, M Jain, GR Howe, et al. Dietary carbohydrates and breast cancer risk: A pro-spective study of the roles of overall glycemic index and glycemic load. *Int J Cancer* 2005, 114(4):653–658.

11. Shu, XO, F Jin, Q Dai, W Wen, JD Potter, LH Kushi, Z Ruan, YT Gao, and W Zheng. Soyfood intake during adolescence and subsequent risk of breast cancer among Chinese women. *Cancer Epidemiol Biomarkers Prev* 2001, 10(5):483–488.

12. Korde, LA, AH Wu, T Fears, AM Nomura, DW West, LN Kolonel, MC Pike, RN Hoover, and RG Ziegler. Childhood soy intake and breast cancer risk in Asian American women. *Cancer Epidemiol Biomarkers Prev* 2009, 18(4):1050–1059.

13. Thompson, LU, et al. Flaxseed and its lignan and oil components reduce mammary tumor growth at a late stage of carcinogenesis. *Carcinogenesis* 1996, 17(6):1373–1376.

14. Thompson, LU, et al. Antitumorigenic effect of a mammalian lignan precurser from flaxseed. *Nutr Cancer* 1996, 26(2):159–165.

15. Flaxseed's role in breast cancer prevention suggested. August 31, 2001. Available at www.nutraingredients-usa.com/news/ng.asp?n=20958-flaxseed-s-role.

16. Thompson, LU, JM Chen, T Li, K Strasser-Weippl, and PE Goss. Dietary flaxseed alters tumor biological markers in postmenopausal breast cancer. *Clin Cancer Res* 2005, 11(10): 3828–3835.

17. Hunter, DJ, et al. A prospective study of intake of vitamin C, E and A and the risk of breast cancer. *N Engl J Med* 1993, 329:234–240.

18. Freudenheim, JL, et al. Premenopausal breast cancer risk and intake of vegetables, fruits and related nutrients. *J Natl Cancer Inst* 1996, 88(6):340–348.

19. Sauerkraut consumption may fight off breast cancer. Dominic Patton, November 4, 2005. Available at www.nutraingredients.com/Research/Sauerkraut-consumption-may-fight-off-breast-cancer.

20. Howe, GR, et al. Dietary factors and risk of breast cancer: Combined analysis of 12 case-control studies. *J Natl Cancer Inst* 1990, 82:561–569.

21. Sun, CL, JM Yuan, WP Koh, and MC Yu. Green tea, black tea and breast cancer risk: A meta-analysis of epidemiological studies. *Carcinogenesis* 2006, 27(7):1310–5. Epub 2005 Nov 25.

22. Nakachi, K, K Suemasu, K Suga, et al. Influence of drinking green tea on breast cancer malignancy among Japanese patients. *Jpn J Cancer Res* 1998, 89(3):254–261.

23. Key, J, S Hodgson, RZ Omar, et al. Meta-analyis of alcohol and breast cancer with consideration of the methodological issues. *Cancer Causes Control* 2006, 17(6):759–770.

24. Allen, NE, V Beral, D Casabonne, SW Kan, GK Reeves, A Brown, J Green; Million Women Study Collaborators. Moderate alcohol intake and cancer incidence in women. *J Natl Cancer Inst* 2009, 101(5):296–305.

25. Hankinson, SE, et al. Alcohol, height, and adiposity in relation to estrogen and prolactin levels in postmenopausal women. *J Natl Cancer Inst* 1995, 87(17):1297–1302.

26. Hirose, K, et al. Effect of body size on breast cancer risk among Japanese women. *Int J Cancer* 1999, 80(3):349–355.

27. Huang, Z, et al. Dual effects of weight and weight gain on breast cancer risk. *JAMA* 1997, 278(17):1407–1411.

28. La Vecchia, C, et al. Body mass index and post-menopausal breast cancer: An age-specific analysis. *Br J Cancer* 1997, 75(3): 441–444.

29. Silvera, SA, M Jain, GR Howe, et al. Energy balance and breast cancer risk: A prospective cohort study. *Breast Cancer Res Treat* 2006, 97(1):97–106.

30. Chang, SC, RG Ziegler, B Dunn, et al. Association of energy intake and energy balance with postmenopausal breast cancer in the prostate, lung, colorectal, and ovarian cancer screening trial. *Cancer Epidemiol Biomarkers Prev* 2006, 15(2):334–341.

31. Reeves, GK, K Pirie, V Beral, et al. Cancer incidence and mortality in relation to body mass index in the Million Women Study: Cohort study. *BMJ* 2007, 335(7630): 1134.

32. Zhang, S, et al. Dietary carotenoids and vitamins A, C, and E and risk of breast cancer. *J Natl Cancer Inst* 1999, 91(6):547–556.

33. Cui, Y, JM Shikany, S Liu, et al. Selected antioxidants and risk of hormone receptor-defined invasive breast cancers among postmenopausal women in the Women's Health Initiative Observational Study. *Am J Clin Nutr* 2008, 87(4):1009–1018.

34. Sato, R, KJ Helzlsouer, AJ Alberg, et al. Prospective study of carotenoids, tocopherols, and retinoid concentrations and the risk of breast cancer. *Cancer Epidemiol Biomarkers Prev* 2002, 11(5):451–457.

35. Robien, K, GJ Cutler, and D Lazovich. Vitamin D intake and breast cancer risk in post-menopausal women: The Iowa Women's Healthy Study. *Cancer Causes Control* 2007, 18(7):775–782.

36. Lappe, JM, D Travers-Gustafson, KM Davies, et al. Vitamin D and calcium supplementation reduces cancer risk: Results of a randomized trial. *Am J Clin Nutr* 2007, 85(6): 1586–1591.

37. Zhang, S, et al. A prospective study of folate intake and the risk of breast cancer. *JAMA* 1999, 281(17):1632–1637.

Bronchitis

1. La Vecchia, C, et al. Vegetable consumption and risk of chronic disease. *Epidemiology* 1998, 9(2):208–210.

2. Mylek, D. ALCAT test results in the treatment of respiratory and gastrointestinal symptoms, arthritis, skin and central nervous system. *Rocz Akad Med Bialymst* 1995, 40(3): 625–629.

3. Morabia, A, et al. Vitamin A, cigarette smoking, and airway obstruction. *Am Rev Respir Dis* 1989, 140(5):1312–1316.

4. Hemila, H, and RM Douglas. Vitamin C and acute respiratory infections. *Int J Tuberc Lung Dis* 1999, 3(9):756–761.

5. Schwartz, J, and ST Weiss. Dietary factors and their relation to respiratory symptoms. *Am J Epidemiol* 1990, 132(1): 67–76.

6. Hunt, C, et al. The clinical and biochemical effects of vitamin C supplementation in short-stay hospitalized geriatric patients. *Int J Vitam Nutr Res* 1984, 54(1):65–74.

7. Britton, J, et al. Dietary magnesium, lung function, wheezing, and airway hyperreactivity in a random adult population sample. *Lancet* 1994, 344(8919):357–362.

8. Schwartz, J, and ST Weiss. Dietary factors and their relation to respiratory symptoms. *Am J Epidemiol* 1990, 132(1): 67–76.

9. Aggarwal, R, J Sentz, and MA Miller. Role of zinc supplementation in prevention of childhood diarrhea and respiratory illnesses: A meta-analysis. *Pediatrics* 2007, 119(6): 1120–1130.

10. Matthys, H, et al. Efficacy and tolerability of myrtol standardized in acute bronchitis: A multi-centre, randomised, double-blind, placebo-controlled parallel group clinical trial vs. cefuroxime and ambroxol. *Arzneimittelforschung* 2000, 50(8):700–711.

11. Meister, R, et al. Efficacy and tolerability of myrtol standardized in long-term treatment of chronic bronchitis: A double-blind, placebo-controlled study. Study Group Investigators. *Arzneimittelforschung*. 1999, 49(4):351–358.

12. Grandjean, EM, et al. Efficacy of oral long-term N-acetylcysteine in chronic bronchopulmonary disease: A meta-analysis of published double-blind, placebo-controlled clinical trials. *Clin Ther* 2000, 22(2):209–221.

13. Holdiness, MR. Clinical pharmacokinetics of N-acetylcysteine. *Clin Pharmacokinet* 1991, 20(2):123–134.

Burns

1. Cunningham, JJ, et al. Calorie and protein provision for recovery from severe burns in infants and young children. *Am J Clin Nutr* 1990, 51(4):553–557.

2. Wolfe, RR. Herman Award Lecture 1996: Relation of metabolic studies to clinical nutrition—the example of burn injury. *Am J Clin Nutr* 1996, 64(5):800–808.

3. Pasulka, PS, and TL Wachtel. Nutritional considerations for the burned patient. *Surg Clin North Am* 1987, 67(1): 109–131.

4. Garrel, DR, et al. Improved clinical status and length of care with low-fat nutrition support in burn patients. *JPEN* 1995, 19(6):482–491.

5. Alexander, JW, and MM Gottschlich. Nutritional immunomodulation in burn patients. *Crit Care Med* 1990, 18(Suppl 2):S149–S153.

6. Gerster, M. The use of n-3 PUFAs (fish oil) in enteral nutrition. *Int J Vitam Nutr Res* 1995, 65(1):3–20.

7. Tashiro, T, et al. N-3 versus n-6 polyunsaturated fatty acids in critical illness. *Nutrition* 1998, 14(6):551–553.

8. Tanaka, H, et al. Reduction of resuscitation fluid volumes in severely burned patients using ascorbic acid administration: A randomized, prospective study. *Arch Surg* 2000, 135(3): 326–331.

9. Zhang, MJ, et al. Comparative observation of the changes in serum lipid peroxides influenced by the supplementation of vitamin E in burn patients and healthy controls. *Burns* 1992, 18(1):19–21.

10. Haberal, M, et al. The stabilizing effect of vitamin E, selenium, and zinc on leucocyte membrane permeability: A study in vitro. *Burns Incl Therm Inj* 1987, 13(2): 118–122.

11. Berger, MM, et al. Trace element supplementation modulates pulmonary infection rates after major burns: A double-blind, placebo-controlled trial. *Am J Clin Nutr* 1998, 68(2):365–371.

12. Berger, MM, et al. Influence of large intakes of trace elements on recovery after major burns. *Nutrition* 1994, 10(4):327–334.

13. Berger, MM, C Binnert, RL Chiolero, et al. Trace element supplementation after major burns increases burned skin trace element concentrations and modules local protein metabolism but not whole body substrate metabolism. *Am J Clin Nutr* 2007, 85(5):1301–1306.

14. Berger, MM, P Eggimann, DK Heyland, et al. Reduction of nosocomial pneumonia after major burns by trace element supplementation: Aggregation of two randomized trials. *Crit Care* 2006, 10(6):R153.

15. Shukla, A, et al. In vitro and in vivo wound healing activity of asiaticoside isolated from Centella asiatica. *J Ethnopharmacol* 1999, 65:1–11.

16. Schmidt, JM, and JS Greenspoon. Aloe vera dermal wound gel is associated with a delay in wound healing. *Obstet Gynecol* 1991, 78:115–117.

17. Klein, AD, and NS Penneys. Aloe vera. *J Am Acad Dermatol* 1988, 18(4 Pt 1):714–720.

18. Visuthikosol, V, et al. Effect of aloe vera gel to healing of burn wound: A clinical and histological study. *J Med Assoc Thai* 1995, 78(8):403–409.

19. Maenthaisong, R, N Chaiyakunapruk, S Niruntrapron, and C Kongkaew. The efficacy of aloe vera used for burn wound healing: A systematic review. *Burns* 2007, 33(6):713–718.

20. Coudray-Lucas, C, et al. Ornithine alpha-ketoglutarate improves wound healing in severe burn patients: A prospective randomized double-blind trial versus isonitrogenous controls. *Crit Care Med* 2000, 28(6):1772–1776.

21. Donati, L, et al. Nutritional and clinical efficacy of ornithine alpha-ketoglutarate in severe burn patients. *Clin Nutr* 1999, 18(5):307–311.

22. De Bandt, JP, et al. A randomized controlled trial of the influence of the mode of enteral ornithine alpha-ketoglutarate administration in burn patients. *J Nutr* 1998, 128(3):563–569.

Candidiasis

1. Pizzo, G, et al. Effect of dietary carbohydrates on the in vitro epithelial adhesion of Candida albicans, Candida tropicalis, and Candida krusei. *New Microbiol* 2000, 23(1):63–71.

2. Samaranayake, YH, et al. The in vitro proteolytic and saccharolytic activity of Candida species cultured in human saliva. *Oral Microbiol Immunol* 1994, 9(4):229–235.
3. Elmer, GW, et al. Biotherapeutic agents. A neglected modality for the treatment and prevention of selected intestinal and vaginal yeast infections. *JAMA* 1996, 275(11): 870–876.
4. Hawes, SE, et al. Hydrogen peroxide-producing lactobacilli and acquisition of vaginal infections. *J Infec Dis* 1996, 174(5):1058–1063.
5. Hilton, E, et al. Ingestion of yogurt containing Lactobacillus acidophilus as a prophylaxis for candidal vaginitis. *Ann Intern Med* 1992, 116(5):353–357.
6. Reid, G, et al. Is there a role for Lactobacilli in prevention of urogenital and intestinal infections? *Clin Microbiol Rev* 1990, 3:335–344.
7. Collins, EB, and P Hardt. Inhibition of Candida albicans by Lactobacillus acidophilus. *J Dairy Scientific* 1980, 63: 830–832.
8. Hatakka, K, AJ Ahola, H Yli-Knuuttila, et al. Probiotics reduce the prevalence of oral candida in the elderly: A randomized controlled trial. *J Dent Res* 2007, 86(2): 125–130.
9. Ankri, S, and D Mirelman. Antimicrobial properties of allicin from garlic. *Microbes Infect* 1999, 1(2):125–129.
10. Ghannoum, MA. Studies on the anticandidal mode of action of Allium sativum (garlic). *J Gen Microbiol* 1988, 134 (Pt 11):2917–2924.
11. Yoshida, S, et al. Antifungal activity of ajoene derived from garlic. *Appl Environ Microbiol* 1987, 53(3):615–617.
12. Adetumbi, M, GT Javor, and BH Lau. Allium sativum (garlic) inhibits lipid synthesis by Candida albicans. *Antimicrob Agents Chemother* 1986, 30(3):499–501.

Canker Sores
1. Nolan, A, PJ Lamey, KA Milligan, and A Forsyth. Recurrent aphthous ulceration and food sensitivity. *J Oral Pathol Med* 1991, 20(10):473–475.
2. Raiha, I, and S Syrjanen. Oral mucosal changes in celiac patients on a gluten-free diet. *Eur J Oral Sci* 1998, 106(5):899–906.
3. McCartan, BE, and DG Weir. Gliadin antibodies identify gluten-sensitive oral ulceration in the absence of villous atrophy. *J Oral Pathol Med* 1991, 20(10):476–478.
4. Porter, SR, et al. Hematologic status in recurrent aphthous stomatitis compared with other oral disease. *Oral Surg Oral Med Oral Pathol* 1988, 66(1):41–44.
5. Weusten, BL, and A Weil. Aphthous ulcers and vitamin B12 deficiency. *Neth J Med* 1998, 53(4):172–175.
6. Haisraeli-Shalish, M, et al. Recurrent aphthous stomatitis and thiamine deficiency. *Oral Surg Oral Med Oral Pathol Oral Radiol Endod* 1996, 82(6):634–636.
7. Nolan, A, et al. Recurrent aphthous ulceration: Vitamin B1, B2 and B6 status and response to replacement therapy. *J Oral Pathol Med* 1991, 20(8):389–391.
8. Porter, S, S Flint, C Scully, and O Keith. Hematologic status in recurrent aphthous stomatitis compared with other oral disease. *Oral Surg Oral Med Pathol* 1988, 66(1):41–44.
9. Das, SK, et al. Deglycyrrhizinated licorice in aphthous ulcers. *J Assoc Physicians India* 1989, 37:647.
10. Martin, MD, J Sherman, P Van der Ven, and J Burgess. A controlled trial of a dissolving oral patch concerning glycyrrhiza (licorice) herbal extract for the treatement of aphthous ulcers. *Gen Dent* 2008, 56(2):206–210.

Cataracts
1. Jacques, PF, SM Moeller, SE Hankinson, et al. Weight status, abdominal obesity, diabetes and early age-related lens opacities. *Am J Clin Nutr* 2003, 78(3):400–405.
2. Hiller, R, et al. Cigarette smoking and the risk of development of lens opacities: The Framingham studies. *Arch Ophthalmol* 1997, 115(9):1113–1118.
3. Christen, WG, et al. Smoking cessation and risk of age-related cataract in men. *JAMA* 2000, 284(6):713–716.
4. Glynn, RJ, et al. Body mass index: An independent predictor of cataract. *Arch Ophthalmol* 1995, 113(9):1131–1137.
5. Schaumberg, DA, RJ Glynn, WG Christen, et al. Relations of body fat distribution and height with cataract in men. *Am J Clin Nutr* 2000, 72(6):1495–1502.
6. Hiller, R, et al. A longitudinal study of body mass index and lens opacities: The Framingham studies. *Ophthalmol* 1998, 105(7):1244–1250.
7. Jacques, PF, SM Moeller, SE Hankinson, et al. Weight status, abdominal obesity, diabetes and early age-related lens opacities. *Am J Clin Nutr* 2003, 78(3):400–405.
8. Tan, J, JJ Wang, V Flood, et al. Carbohydrate nutrition, glycemic index, and the 10-y incidence of cataract. *Am J Clin Nutr* 2007, 86(5):1502–1508.
9. Chiu, CJ, RC Milton, G Gensler, and A Taylor. Dietary carbohydrate and glycemic index in relation to cortical and nuclear lens opacities in the Age-Related Eye Disease Study. *Am J Clin Nutr* 2006, 83(5):1177–1184.
10. Chi, CJ, MS Morris, G Rogers, et al. Carbohydrate intake and glycemic index in relation to the odds of early cortical and nuclear lens opacities. *Am J Clin Nutr* 2005, 81(6):1411–1416.
11. Townend, BS, ME Townend, V Flood, et al. Dietary macronutrient intake and five-year incident cataract: The Blue Mountains Eye Study. *Am J Opthamol* 2007, 143(6):932–939.
12. Brown, L, et al. A prospective study of carotenoid intake and risk of cataract extraction in U.S. men. *Am J Clin Nutr* 1999, 70(4):517–524.
13. Chasan-Taber, L, et al. A prospective study of carotenoid and vitamin A intakes and risk of cataract extraction in U.S. women. *Am J Clin Nutr* 1999, 70(4):509–516.
14. Moeller, SM, R Voland, L Tinker, et al. Associations between age-related nuclear cataract and lutein and zeaxanthin in the diet and serum in the Carotenoids in the Age-Related Eye Disease Study, an Ancillary Study of the Women's Health Inititiative. *Arch Ophthalmol* 2008, 126(3):354–364.
15. Omedilla, B, F Granado, I Blanco, and M Vaquero. Lutein, but not alpha-tocopherol, supplementation improves visual function in patients with age-related cataracts: A 2-y double-blind, placebo-controlled pilot study. *Nutrition* 2003, 19(1):21–24.
16. Cumming, RG, P Mitchell, and W Smith. Dietary sodium intake and cataract: The Blue Mountains Eye Study. *Am J Epidemiol* 2000, 151(6):624–626.

17. Manson, JE, et al. A prospective study of alcohol consumption and risk of cataract. *Am J Prev Med* 1994, 10(3): 156–161.

18. Klein, BE, et al. Incident cataract after a five-year interval and lifestyle factors: The Beaver Dam eye study. *Ophthalmic Epidemiol* 1999, 6(4):247–255.

19. Munoz, B, et al. Alcohol use and risk of posterior subscapular opacities. *Arch Ophthalmol* 1993, 111(1): 110–112.

20. Chasan-Taber, L, et al. A prospective study of alcohol consumption and cataract extraction among U.S. women. *Ann Epidemiol* 2000, 10(6):347–353.

21. Kuzniarrz, M, P Mitchell, RG Cumming, and VM Flood. Use of vitamin supplements and cataract: The Blue Mountains Eye Study. *AM J Ophthalmol* 2001, 132(1): 19–26.

22. Mares-Perlman, JA, et al. Vitamin supplement use and incident cataracts in a population-based study. *Arch Ophthalmol* 2000, 118(11):1556–1563.

23. Leske, MC, et al. Antioxidant vitamins and nuclear opacities: The longitudinal study of cataract. *Ophthalmol* 1998, 105(5):831–836.

24. Seddon, JM, et al. The use of vitamin supplements and the risk of cataract among U.S. male physicians. *Am J Public Health* 1994, 84(5):788–792.

25. Jacques, PF, LT Chylack Jr, SE Hankinson, et al. Long-term nutrient intake and early age-related nuclear lens opacities. *Arch Ophthalmol* 2001, 119(7):1009–1019.

26. Ferrigno, L, R Aldigeri, F Rosmini, et al. Associations between plasma levels of vitamins and cataract in the Italian-American Clinical Trial of Nutritional Supplements and Age-Related Cataract (CTNS): CTNS Report #2. *Ophthalmic Epdiomiol* 2005, 12(2):71–80.

27. Simon, JA, and ES Hudes. Serum ascorbic acid and other correlates of self-reported cataract among older Americans. *J Clin Epidemiol* 1999, 52(12):1207–1211.

28. Tessier, F, et al. Decrease in vitamin C concentration in human lenses during cataract progression. *Int J Vitam Nutr Res* 1998, 68(5):309–315.

29. Taylor, A, PF Jacques, LT Chylack Jr, et al. Long term intake of vitamins and carotenoids and odds of early age-related cortical and posterior subscapular lens opacities. *Am J Clin Nutr* 2002, 75(3):540–549.

30. Rouhianinen, P, et al. Association between low plasma vitamin E concentration and progression of early cortical lens opacities. *Am J Epidemiol* 1996, 144(5):496–500.

31. Christen, WG, S Liu, RJ Glynn, et al. Dietary carotenoids, vitamins C and E, and risk of cataract in women: A prospective study. *Arch Ophthalmol* 2008, 126(1): 102–109.

32. Leske, MC, et al. Antioxidant vitamins and nuclear opacities: The longitudinal study of cataract. *Ophthalmol* 1998, 105(5):831–836.

33. Robertson, JM, et al. Vitamin E intake and risk of cataracts in humans. *Ann N Y Acad Sci* 1989, 570:372–382.

34. Teikari, JM, et al. Long-term supplementation with alpha-tocopherol and beta-carotene and age-related cataract. *Acta Ophthalmol Scand* 1997, 75(6):634–640.

35. Repossi, P, et al. The role of anthocyanosides on vascular permeability in diabetic retinopathy. *Ann Ottamol Clin Ocul* 1987, 113(4):357–361. [Italian]

36. Perossini, M, et al. Diabetic and hypertensive retinopathy with Vaccinium myrtillus. *Ann Ottamol Clin Ocul* 1987, 113(12):1173–1190. [Italian]

Celiac Disease (Gluten Intolerance)

1. Mariani, P, et al. The gluten-free diet: A nutritional risk factor for adolescents with celiac disease? *J Pediatr Gastroenterol Nutr* 1998, 27(5):519–523.

2. Kemppainen, T, et al. Osteoporosis in adult patients with celiac disease. *Bone* 1999, 24(3):249–255.

3. Mora, S, et al. Reversal of low bone density with a gluten-free diet in children and adolescents with celiac disease. *Am J Clin Nutr* 1998, 67(3):477–481.

4. Kemppainen, T, et al. Bone recovery after a gluten-free diet: A 5-year follow-up study. *Bone* 1999, 25(3):355–360.

5. Sategna-Guidetti, C, et al. The effects of 1-year gluten withdrawal on bone mass, bone metabolism and nutritional status in newly-diagnosed adult celiac disease patients. *Aliment Pharmacol Ther* 2000, 14(1):35–43.

6. Rude, RK, and M Olerich. Magnesium deficiency: Possible role in osteoporosis associated with gluten-sensitive enteropathy. *Osteoporos Int* 1996, 6(6):453–461.

Cervical Dysplasia

1. *HPV and Cervical Cancer*. The Canadian Cancer Society, August 21, 2008. Available at www.cancer.ca/Canada-wide/Prevention/Other%20risk%20factors/ Human%20 papillomavirus%20HPV/HPV%20and%20cervical%20cancer. aspx?sc_lang=en.

2. Nagata, C, et al. Serum retinal level and risk of cervical cancer in cases with cervical dysplasia. *Cancer Invest* 1999, 17(4):253–258.

3. Romney, SL, et al. Effects of beta-carotene and other factors on outcome of cervical dysplasia and human papillomavirus infection. *Gynecol Oncol* 1997, 65(3):483–492.

4. Mackerras, D, et al. Randomized double-blind trial of beta-carotene and vitamin C in women with minor cervical abnormalities. *Br J Cancer* 1999, 79(9–10):1448–1453.

5. Keefe, KA, MJ Schell, C Brewer, et al. A randomized, double blind, Phase III trial using oral beta-carotene supplementation for women with high-grade cervical intraepithelial neoplasia. *Cancer Epidemiol Biomarkers Prev* 2001, 10(10):1029–1035.

6. Kantesky, PA, et al. Dietary intake and blood levels of lycopene: Association with cervical dysplasia among non-Hispanic, black women. *Nutr Cancer* 1998, 31(1):31–40.

7. Basu, J, et al. Plasma ascorbic acid and beta-carotene levels in women evaluated for HPV infection, smoking, and cervix dysplasia. *Cancer Detec Prev* 1991, 15(3):165–170.

8. Goodman, MT, et al. The association of plasma micronutrients with the risk of cervical dysplasia in Hawaii. *Cancer Epidemiol Biomarkers Prev* 1998, 7(6):537–544.

9. Whitehead, N, et al. Megaloblastic changes in the cervical epithelium: Association with oral contraceptive therapy. *JAMA* 1973, 226:1421–1424.

10. McPherson, RS. Nutritional factors and the risk of cervical dysplasia. proceedings and abstracts of papers presented at the 22nd annual meeting of the Society for Epidemiological

Research, June 14–16, 1989, Birmingham, AL. *Am J Epidemiol* 1989, 130(4):830. [Abstract]

11. Piyathilake, CJ, M Macaluso, I Brill, et al. Lower red blood cell folate enhances HPV-16-associated risk of cervical intraepithelial neoplasia. *Nutrition* 2007, 23(3):203–210.

12. Butterworth, C, et al. Improvement in cervical dysplasia associated with folic acid therapy in users of oral contraceptives. *Am J Clin Nutr* 1982, 35:73–82.

13. Childers, JM, et al. Chemoprevention of cervical cancer with folic acid: A phase III Southwest Oncology Group Intergroup Study. *Cancer Epidemiol Biomarkers Prev* 1995, 4:155–159.

Chronic Fatigue Syndrome (CFS)

1. Sibbald, B. Chronic Fatigue Syndrome comes out of the closet. *CMAJ* 1998, 159:537–541.

2. U.S. Department of Health and Human Services. *The Facts about Chronic Fatigue Syndrome* (Atlanta, GA: March 1995).

3. Hobday, RA, S Thomas, A O'Donovan, et al. Dietary intervention in chronic fatigue syndrome. *J Hum Nutr Diet* 2008, 21(2):141–149.

4. Gray, JB, and AM Martinovic. Eicosanoids and essential fatty acid modulation in chronic disease and the chronic fatigue syndrome. *Med Hypotheses* 1994, 43(1):32–42.

5. Puri, BK, J Holmes, and G Hamilton. Eicosapentaenoic acid-rich essential fatty acid supplementation in chronic fatigue syndrome associated with symptom remission and structural brain changes. *Int J Clin Prac* 2004, 58(3):297–299.

6. Puri, BK. The use of eicosapentaenoic acid in the treatment of chronic fatigue syndrome. *Prostaglandins Leukot Essent Fatty Acids* 2004, 70(4):399–401.

7. Heap, LC, et al. Vitamin B status in patients with chronic fatigue syndrome. *J R Soc Med* 1999, 92(4):183–185.

8. Regland, B, et al. Increased concentrations of homocysteine in the cerebrospinal fluid in patients with fibromyalgia and chronic fatigue syndrome. *Scand J Rheumatol* 1997, 26(4):301–307.

9. Werbach, MR. Nutritional strategies for treating chronic fatigue syndrome. *Altern Med Rev* 2000, 5(2):93–108.

10. Jacobson, W, et al. Serum folate and chronic fatigue syndrome. *Neurology* 1993, 43(12):2645–2647.

11. Moorkens, G, et al. Magnesium deficit in a sample of the Belgian population presenting with chronic fatigue syndrome. *Magnes Res* 1997, 10(4):329–337.

12. Cox, IM, et al. Red blood cell magnesium and chronic fatigue syndrome. *Lancet* 1991, 337(8744):757–760.

13. Manuel y Keenoy, B, G Moorkens, J Vertommen, et al. Magnesium status and parameters of the oxidant-antioxidant balance in patients with chronic fatigue: Effects of supplementation with magnesium. *J Am Col Nutr* 2000, 19(3):374–382.

14. See, DM, et al. In vitro effects of Echinacea and ginseng on natural killer and antibody-dependent cell cytotoxicity in healthy subjects and chronic fatigue syndrome or acquired immunodeficiency syndrome patients. *Immunopharmacology* 1997, 35(3):229–235.

15. Hartz, AJ, S Bentler, R Noyes, et al. Randomized controlled trial of Siberian ginseng for chronic fatigue. *Psychol Med* 2004, 34(1):51–61.

16. Behan, PO, et al. Effects of high doses of essential fatty acids on the postviral fatigue syndrome. *Acta Neurol Scand* 1990, 82(3): 209–216.

17. Warren, G, et al. The role of essential fatty acids in chronic fatigue syndrome: A case-controlled study of red-cell membrane essential fatty acids (EFA) and a placebo-controlled treatment study with high dose of EFA. *Acta Neurol Scand* 1999, 99(2):112–116.

18. Plioplys, AV, and S Plioplys. Serum levels of carnitine in chronic fatigue syndrome: Clinical correlates. *Neuropsychobiology* 1995, 32(3): 132–138.

19. Kuratsune, H, et al. Acylcarnitine deficiency in chronic fatigue syndrome. *Clin Infec Dis* 1994, 18(Suppl 1):S62–S67.

20. Malaguarnera, M, MP Garganet, E Cristaldi, et al. Acetyl-L-carnitine (ALC) treatment in elderly patients with fatigue. *Arch Gerontol Geriatr* 2008, 46(2):181–190.

21. Vermeulen, RC, and HR Scholte. Exploratory open label, randomized study of acetyl- and propionylcarnitine in chronic fatigue syndrome. *Psychosom Med* 2004, 66(2): 276–282.

22. van Heukelom, RO, JB Prins, MG Smits, and G Bleijenberg. Influence of melatonin on fatigue severity in patients with chronic fatigue syndrome and late melatonin secretion. *Eur J Neurol* 2006, 13(1):55–60.

Cirrhosis of the Liver

1. The American Dietetic Association. *Manual of Clinical Dietetics*, 6th ed. (Chicago, 2000).

2. Jensen, MG. Long-term oral refeeding of patients with cirrhosis of the liver. *Br J Nutr* 1995, 74(4):557–567.

3. Bianchi, GP, et al. Vegetable versus animal protein diet in cirrhotic patients with chronic encephalopathy. *J Intern Med* 1993, 233(5):385–392.

4. Gheorghe, C, R Iacob, R Vadan, et al. Improvement of hepatic encephalopathy using a modified high-calorie high-protien diet. *Rom J Gastroenterol* 2005, 14(3):231–238.

5. Verboeket-van de Venne, WP, et al. Energy expenditure and substrate metabolism in patients with cirrhosis of the liver: Effects of the pattern of food intake. *Gut* 1995, 36(10): 110–116.

6. Marchesini, G, et al. Nutritional treatment with branched-chain amino acids in advanced liver cirrhosis. *J Gastroenterol* 2000, 35(Suppl):S7–S12.

7. Okita, M, et al. Nutritional treatment of liver cirrhosis by branched chain amino acids. *J Nutr Sci Vitaminol* 1985, 31(3):291–303.

8. Maddrey, WC. Branched chain amino acid therapy in liver disease. *J Am Coll Nutr* 1985, 4(6):639–650.

9. Nakaya, Y, K Okita, K Suzuki, et al. BCAA-enriched snack improves nutritional state of cirrhosis. *Nutrition* 2007, 23(2):113–120.

10. Jenkins, DJ, et al. Low glycemic index foods and reduced glucose, amino acid, and endocrine responses in cirrhosis. *Am J Gastroenterol* 1989, 84(7):732–739.

11. Barkoukis, H, KM Fiedler, and E Lerner. A combined high-fiber, low-glycemic index diet normalizes glucose tolerance and reduce hyperglycemia and hyperinsulinemia in adults with hepatic cirrhosis. *J Am Diet Assoc* 2002, 102(10): 1503–1507.

12. Kuiper, J, RA de Man, and HR Buuren. Review article: Management of ascites and associated complications in patients with cirrhosis. *Aliment Pharmacol Ther* 2007, 26(Suppl 2):183–193.

13. Moore, KP, F Wong, P Gines, et al. The management of ascites in cirrhosis: Report on the consensus conference of the International Ascites Club. *Hepatology* 2003, 38(1):258– 266.

14. Gauthier, A, et al. Salt or no salt in the treatment of cirrhotic ascites: A randomized study. *Gut* 1986, 27(6): 705–709.

15. Nalini, G, et al. Oxidative stress in alcoholic liver disease. Ind J Med Res 1999, 110:200– 203.

16. Britton, RS, and BR Bacon. Role of free radicals in liver diseases and hepatic fibrosis. *Hepato-gastroenterology* 1994, 41(4):343–348.

17. Ward, RJ, and TJ Peters. The antioxidant status of patients with either alcohol-induced liver damage or myopathy. *Alcohol Alcohol* 1992, 27(4):359–365.

18. Dufour, JF, CM Oneta, JJ Gonvers, et al. Randomized placebo-controlled trial of ursodeoxycholic acid with vitamin E in nonalcoholic steatohepatitis. *Clin Gastroenerol Hepatol* 2006, 4(12):1537–1543.

19. Harrison, SA, S Torgerson, P Hayashi, et al. Vitamin E and C treatment improves fibrosis in patients with nonalcoholic steatohepatitis. *Am J Gastroenterol* 2003, 98(11): 2485–2490.

20. Ferro, D, et al. Vitamin E reduces monocyte tissue factor expression in cirrhotic patients. *Blood* 1999, 93(9): 2945–2950.

21. Van Gossum, A, and J Neve. Low selenium status in alcoholic cirrhosis is correlated with aminopyrine breath test: Preliminary effects of selenium supplementation. *Biol Trace Elem Res* 1995, 47(1–3):201–207.

22. Muzes, G, et al. Effects of silymarin (Legalon) therapy on the antioxidant defense mechanism and lipid peroxidation in alcoholic liver disease. *Orv Hetil* 1990, 131:863–866. [Hungarian]

23. Ferenci, P, et al. Randomized controlled trial of silymarin in patients with cirrhosis of the liver. *J Hepatol* 1989, 9(1):105–113.

24. Feher, J, et al. Liver protective action of silymarin therapy in chronic alcoholic liver diseases. *Orv Hetil* 1989, 130:2723–2727. [Hungarian]

25. Ferenci, P, et al. Randomized controlled trial of silymarin treatment in patients with cirrhosis of the liver. *J Hepatol* 1989, 9:105–113.

26. Benda, L, et al. The influence of therapy with silymarin on the survival rate of patients with liver cirrhosis. *Wein Klin Wochenschr* 1980, 92:678–683. [German]

27. Mato, JM, et al. S-adenosyl-L-methionine synthetase and methionine metabolism deficiencies in cirrhosis. *Adv Exp Med Biol* 1994, 368(1):113–117.

28. Almasio, P, et al. Role of S-adenosyl-L-methionine in the treatment of intrahepatic cholestasis. *Drugs* 1990, 40(Suppl 3): S111–S123.

29. Loguercio, C, et al. Effect of S-adenosyl-L-methionine administration on red blood cell cysteine and glutathione levels in alcoholic patients with and without liver disease. *Alcohol Alcohol* 1994, 29(5):597–604.

30. Kakimoto, H, et al. Changes in lipid composition of erythrocyte membranes with administration of S-adenosyl-L-methionine in chronic liver disease. *Gastroenterol Jpn* 1992, 27(4):508–513.

31. Mato, JM, et al. S-adenosyl-L-methionine in alcoholic liver cirrhosis: A randomized, placebo-controlled, double-blind, multicenter clinical trial. *J Hepatol* 1999, 30:1081–1089.

32. Rambaldi, A, and C Gluud. S-adenosyl-L-methionine for alcoholic liver diseases. *Cochrane Database Syst Rev* 2006, April 19(2):CD002235.

Colds and Influenza

1. Saketkhoo, K, A Januszkiewicz, and MA Sackner. Effects of drinking hot water, cold water, and chicken soup on nasal mucus velocity and nasal airflow resistance. *Chest* 1978, 74(4):408–410.

2. Kopp-Hoolihan, L. Prophylactic and therapeutic uses of probiotics: A review. *J Am Diet Assoc* 2001, 101(2): 229–238.

3. Isolauri, E, et al. Probiotics: Effects on immunity. *Am J Clin Nutr* 2001, 73(Suppl 2):S444–S450.

4. Lykova, EA, et al. Disruption of microbiocenosis of the large intestine and the immune and interferon status in children with bacterial complications of acute viral infections of the respiratory tract and their correction by high doses of bifidumbacterin forte. *Antibiot Khimioter* 2000, 45(10): 22–27. [Russian]

5. Douglas, RM, EB Chalker, and B Treacy. Vitamin C for preventing and treating the common cold. *Cochrane Database Syst Rev* 2000, 34(2):CD000980.

6. Hemila, H. Vitamin C supplementation and common cold symptoms: Factors affecting the magnitude of benefit. *Med Hypotheses* 1999, 52(2):171–178.

7. Hemila, H, and RM Douglas. Vitamin C and acute respiratory infections. *Int J Tuberc Lung Dis* 1999, 3(9):756–761.

8. Douglas, RM, H Hemial, E Chalker, and B Treacy. Vitamin C for preventing and treating the common cold. *Cochrane Database Syst Rev* 2007 Jul 18, (3):CD000980.

9. Meydani, SN, LS Leka, BC Fine, et al. Vitamin E and respiratory tract infections in elderly nursing home residents: A randomized controlled trial. *JAMA* 2004, 292(7): 828–836.

10. Meydani, SN, et al. Vitamin E supplementation enhances cell-mediated immunity in healthy elderly subjects. *Am J Clin Nutr* 1990, 52(3):557–563.

11. Ravaglia, G, et al. Effect of micronutrient status in natural killer cell immune function in healthy free living subjects aged >/=90 y. *Am J Clin Nutr* 2000, 71(2):590–598.

12. Prasad, AS, FW Beck, B Bao, et al. Duration and severity of symptoms and levels of plasma interleukin-1 receptor antagonist, soluble tumor necrosis factor receptor, and adhesion molecules in patients with common cold treated with zinc acetate. *I Infec Dis* 2008, 197(6):795–802.

13. Prasad, AS, et al. Duration of symptoms and plasma cytokine levels in patients with the common cold treated with zinc actetate: A randomized, double-blind, placebo-controlled trial. *Ann Intern Med* 2000, 133(4):245–252.

14. Petrus, EJ, et al. Randomized, double-masked, placebo-controlled clinical study of the effectiveness of zinc acetate lozenges on common cold symptoms in allergy tested subjects. *Curr Ther Res* 1998, 59:595–607.

15. Mossad, SB, et al. Zinc gluconate lozenges for treating the common cold: A randomized, double-blind, placebo-controlled study. *Ann Intern Med* 1996 15, 125(2):81–88.

16. Marshall, I. Withdrawn: Zinc for the common cold. *Cochrane Database Syst Rev* 2007 Jul 18(3):CD001364.

17. Jackson, JL, et al. Zinc and the common cold: A meta-analysis revisited. *J Nutr* 2000, 139(Suppl 5):S1512–S1515.

18. Eby, GA. Zinc ion availability: The determinant of efficacy in zinc lozenge treatment of common colds. *J Antimicrob Chemother* 1997, 40(4):483–493.

19. Linde, K, B Barrett, K Wolkart, et al. Echinacea for preventing and treating the common cold. *Cochrane Database Syst Rev* 2006 Jan 25, (1):CD000530.

20. Kyo, E, et al. Immunomodulatory effects of aged garlic extract. *J Nutr* 2001, 131(Suppl 3):S1075–S1079.

21. Amagase, H, et al. Intake of garlic and its bioactive components. *J Nutr* 2001, 131(Suppl 3):S955–S962.

22. Salman, H, et al. Effect of a garlic derivative (alliin) on peripheral blood cell immune responses. *Int J Immunopharmacol* 1999, 21(9):589–597.

23. Josling, P. Preventing the common cold with a garlic supplement: A double-blind, placebo-controlled survey. *Adv Ther* 2001, 18(4):189–193.

24. Scaglione, F, et al. Efficacy and safety of the standardized ginseng extract G115 for potentiating vaccination against the influenza syndrome and protection against the common cold. *Drugs Exp Clin Res* 1996, 22:65–72.

25. McElhaney, JE, S Gravenstein, SK Cole, et al. A placebo-controlled trial of a proprietary extract of North American ginseng (CVT-E002) to prevent acute respiratory illness in institutionalized older adults. *J Am Geriatr Soc* 2004, 52(1):13–19.

26. Predy, GN, V Goel, R Lovlin, et al. Efficacy of an extract of North American ginseng containing poly-furanosyl-pyranosyl-saccharides for preventing upper respiratory tract infections: A randomized controlled trial. *CMAJ* 2005, 173(9):1043–1048.

27 McElhaney, JE, V Goel, B Toane, et al. Efficacy of COLD-fX in the prevention of respiratory symptoms in community-dwelling adults: A randomized, double-blinded, placebo controlled trial. *J Altern Complement Med* 2006, 12(2):153–157.

28. de Vrese, M, P Winkler, P Rautenberg, et al. Probiotic bacteria reduced duration and severity but not the incidence of common cold episodes in a double blind, randomized, controlled trial. *Vaccine* 2006, 24(44–46): 6670–6674.

Colorectal Cancer

1. *Colorectal cancer stats.* The Canadian Cancer Society, 2008. Available at www.cancer. ca/canada-wide/about%20cancer/cancer%20statistics/stats%20at%20a%20glance/colorectal%20cancer.aspx?sc_lang=en.

2. Higginbotham, S, ZF Zhang, IM Lee, et al. Dietary glycemic load and risk of colorectal cancer in the Women's Health Study. *J Natl Cancer Inst* 2004, 96(3):229–233.

3. Park, Y, DJ Hunter, D Spiegelman, et al. Dietery fiber intake and risk of colorectal cancer: A pooled analysis of prospective cohort studies. *JAMA* 2005, 294(22): 2849–2857.

4. Jacobs, ET, AR Giuliano, DJ Roe, JM Guillén-Rodríguez, LM Hess, DS Alberts, and ME Martínez. Intake of supplemental and total fiber and risk of colorectal adenoma recurrence in the wheat bran fiber trial. *Cancer Epidemiol Biomarkers Prev* 2002, B11(9):906–914.

5. Alberts, DS, ME Martínez, DJ Roe, JM Guillén-Rodríguez, JR Marshall, JB van Leeuwen, ME Reid, C Ritenbaugh, PA Vargas, AB Bhattacharyya, DL Earnest, and RE Sampliner. Lack of effect of a high-fiber cereal supplement on the recurrence of colorectal adenomas. Phoenix Colon Cancer Prevention Physicians' Network. *N Engl J Med* 2000, 342(16):1156–1162.

6. Schatzkin, A, E Lanza, D Corle, P Lance, F Iber, B Caan, M Shike, J Weissfeld, R Burt, MR Cooper, JW Kikendall, and J Cahill. Lack of effect of a low-fat, high-fiber diet on the recurrence of colorectal adenomas. Polyp Prevention Trial Study Group. *N Engl J Med* 2000, 342(16):1149–1155.

7. Jacobs, ET, E Lanza, DS Alberts, et al. Fiber, sex, and colorectal ademona: Results of a pooled analysis. *Am J Clin Nutr* 2006, 83(2): 343–349.

8. Schatzkin, A, T Mouw, Y Park, et al. Dietary fiber and whole-grain consumption in relation to colorectal cancer in the NIH-AARP Diet and Health Study. *Am J Clin Nutr* 2007, 85(5):1353–1360.

9. Geelan, A, JM Schouten, C Kamphuis, et al. Fish consumption, n-3 fatty acids, and colorectal cancer: A meta-analysis of prospective cohort studies. *Am J Epidemiol* 2007, 166(10):1116–1125.

10. MacLean, CH, SJ Newberry, WA Mojica, et al. Effects of omega-3 fatty acids on cancer risk: A systematic review. *JAMA* 2006, 295(4):403–415.

11. Millen, AE, AF Subar, BI Graubard, et al. Fruit and vegetable intaker and prevalence of colorectal ademona in a cancer screening trial. *Am J Clin Nutr* 2007, 86(6): 1754–1764.

12. van Duijnhoven, F, HB Bueno-De-Mesquita, P Ferrari, et al. Fruits, vegetables, and colorectal cancer risk: The European Prospective Investigation into Cancer and Nutrition. *Am J Clin Nutr* 2009, 89(5):1141– 1152.

13. Larsson, SC, L Bergkvist, J Rutegård, et al. Calcium and dairy food intakes are inversely associated with colorectal cancer risk in the cohort of Swedish men. *Am J Clin Nutr* 2006, 83(3):667–673.

14. Cho, E, SA Smith-Warner, D Spiegelman, et al. Dairy foods, calcium, and colorectal cancer: A pooled analysis of 10 cohort studies. *J Natl Cancer Inst* 2004, 96(13):1015–1022.

15. Norat, T, S Bingham, P Ferrari, et al. Meat, fish, and colorectal cancer risk: The European Prospective Investigation into Cancer and Nutrition. *J Natl Cancer Inst* 2005, 97(12): 906–916.

16. Cross, AJ, MF Leitzmann, MM Gail, et al. A prospective study of red and processed meat intake in relation to cancer risk. *PLoS Med* 2007, 4(12):e325.

17. Larsson, SC, and A Wolk. Meat consumption and risk of colorectal cancer: A meta-analysis of prospective studies. *Int J Cancer* 2006, 119(11):2657–2664.

18. Sinha, R, U Peters, AJ Cross, et al. Meat, meat cooking methods and preservation, and risk for colorectal adenoma. *Cancer Res* 2005, 65(17):8034–8041.

19. Rohrmann, S, S Hermann, and J Linseisen. Heterocyclic aromatic amine intake increases colorectal ademona risk: Findings from a prospective European cohort study. *Am J Clin Nutr* 89(5):1418–1424.

20. Sun, CL, JM Yuan, WP Koh, and MC Yu. Green tea, black tea and colorectal cancer risk: A meta-analysis of epidemiologic studies. *Carcinogenisis* 2006, 27(7):1301–1309.

21. Moskal, A, T Norat, P Ferrari, and E Riboli. Alcohol intake and colorectal cancer risk: A dose-response meta-analysis of published cohort studies. *Int J Cancer* 2007, 120(3): 664–671.

22. Wolin, KY, Y Yan, GA Colditz, and IM Lee. Physical activity and colon cancer prevention: A meta-analysis. *Br J Cancer* 2009, 100(4):611–616.

23. Sanjoaquin, MA, N Allen, E Couto, et al. Folate intake and colorectal cancer risk: A meta-analytical approach. *Int J Cancer* 2005, 113(5):825–828.

24. Zhang, SM, SC Moore, J Lin, et al. Folate, vitamin B6, multivitamin supplements, and colorectal cancer risk in women. *Am J Epidemiol* 2006, 163(2):108–115.

25. Terry, P, M Jain, AB Miller, et al. Dietary intake of folic acid and colorectal cancer risk in a cohort of women. *Int J Cancer* 2002, 97(6):864–867.

26. Giovannucci, E, MJ Stampfer, GA Colditz, et al. Multivitamin use, folate, and colon cancer in women in the Nurses' Health Study. *Ann Intern Med* 1998, 129(7):517–524.

27. Cole, BF, JA Baron, RS Sandler, et al. Folic acid for the prevention of colorectal adenomas: A randomized clinical trial. *JAMA* 2007, 297(21):2351–2359.

28. Bostick, RM, JD Potter, DR McKenzie, et al. Reduced risk of colon cancer with high intake of vitamin E: The Iowa Women's Health Study. *Cancer Res* 1993, 53(18): 4230–4237.

29. Wu, K, WC Willett, JM Chan, et al. A prospective study on supplemental vitamin E intake and risk of colon cancer in women and men. *Cancer Epidemiol Biomarkers Prev* 2002, 11(11):1298–1304.

30. Albanes, D, N Malila, PR Taylor, et al. Effects of supplemental alpha-tocopherol and beta-carotene on colorectal cancer: Results from a controlled trial (Finland), *Cancer Causes Control* 2000, 11(3):197–205.

31. Weingarten, MA, A Zalmanovici, and J Yaphe. Dietary calcium supplementation for preventing colorectal cancer and adenomatous polyps. *Cochrane Database Syst Rev* 2008, (1):CD003548.

32. Peters, U, N Chatterjee, TR Church, et al. High serum selenium and reduced risk of advanced colorectal adenoma in a colorectal cancer early detection program. *Cancer Epidemiol Biomarkers Prev* 2006, 15(2):315–320.

33. Jacobs, ET, R Jiang, DS Alberts, et al. Selenium and colorectal adenoma: Results of a pooled analysis. *J Natl Cancer Inst* 2004, 96(22):1669–1675.

34. Psathakis, D, et al. Blood selenium and glutathione peroxidase status in patients with colorectal cancer. *Dis Colon Rectum* 1998, 41(3):328–335.

35. Reid, ME, AJ Duffiled-Lillico, A Sunga, et al. Selenium supplementation and colorectal adenomas: An analysis of the nutritional prevention of cancer trial. *Int J Cancer* 2006, 118(7):1777–1781.

36. Ngo, SN, DB Williams, L Cobiac, and RJ Head. Does garlic reduce risk of colorectal cancer? A systematic review. *J Nutr* 2007, 137(10): 2264–2269.

37. Steinmetz, KA, et al. Vegetables, fruit, and colon cancer in the Iowa Women's Health Study. *Am J Epidemiol* 1994, 139(1):1–15.

38. Tanaka, S, K Haruma, M Yoshihara, et al. Aged garlic extract has potential suppressive effect on colorectal adenomas in humans. *J Nutr* 2006, 136(3 Suppl):821S–826S.

39. Tanaka, S, K Haruma, M Kunihiro, et al. Effects of aged garlic extract (AGE) on colorectal adenomas: A double-blinded study. *Hiroshima J Med Sci* 2004, 53(3–4):39–45.

Congestive Heart Failure (CHF)

1. Hambrecht, R, et al. Effects of exercise training on left ventricular function and peripheral resistance in patients with chronic heart failure: A randomized trial. *JAMA* 2000, 283(23):3095–3101.

2. Oka, RK, et al. Impact of a home-based walking program and resistance training program on quality of life in patients with heart failure. *Am J Cardiol* 2000, 85(3):365–369.

3. Kiilavuori, K, et al. The effect of physical training on skeletal muscle in patients with chronic heart failure. *Eur J Heart Fail* 2000, 2(1):53–63.

4. Kostis, JB, et al. Nonpharmacologic therapy improves functional and emotional status in congestive heart failure. *Chest* 1994, 106(4):996–1001.

5. Waldenstrom, A. Alcohol and congestive heart failure. *Alcohol Clin Exp Res* 1998, 22(Suppl 7):S315–S317.

6. Singal, PK, et al. Oxidative stress in congestive heart failure. *Curr Cardiol Rep* 2000, 2(3):206–211.

7. Hoeschen, RJ. Oxidative stress and cardiovascular disease. *Can J Cardiol* 1997, 13(11):1021–1025.

8. Ball, AM, and MJ Sole. Oxidative stress and the pathogenesis of heart failure. *Cardiol Clin* 1998, 16(4):665–675.

9. Watanabe, H, et al. Randomized, double-blind, placebo-controlled study of ascorbate on the preventative effect of nitrate intolerance in patients with congestive heart failure. *Circulation* 1998, 97(9):886–891.

10. Chandra, M. Oxy free radical system in heart failure and therapeutic role of oral vitamin E. *J Cardiol* 1996, 57(2): 119–127.

11. Lonn, E, J Bosch, S Yusuf, et al. Effects of long term vitamin E supplementation on cardiovascular events and cancer: A randomized controlled trial. *JAMA* 2005, 293(11): 1338–1347.

12. Brady, JA, et al. Thiamin status, diuretic medications, and the management of congestive heart failure. *J Am Diet Assoc* 1995, 95(5):541–545.

13. Suter, PM, et al. Diuretic use: A risk for subclinical thiamine deficiency in elderly patients. *J Nutr Health Aging* 2000, 4(2):69–71.

14. Seligmann, H, et al. Thiamine deficiency in patients with congestive heart failure receiving long-term furosemide therapy: A pilot study. *Am J Med* 1991, 91(2):151–155.

15. Motro, M, et al. Improved left ventricular function after thiamine supplementation in patients with congestive heart failure receiving long-term furosemide therapy. *Am J Med* 1995, 98(5):485–490.

16. Schleithof, SS, A Zittermann, G Tenderich, et al. Vitamin D supplementation improves cytokine profiles in patients with congestive heart failure: A double-blind, randomized, placebo-controlled trial. *Am J Clin Nutr* 2006, 83(4): 754–759.

17. Crippa, G, et al. Magnesium and cardiovascular drugs: Interactions and therapeutic role. *Ann Ital Med Int* 1999, 14(1):40–45.

18. Douban, S, et al. Significance of magnesium in congestive heart failure. *Am Heart J* 1996, 132(3):664–671.

19. Hix, CD. Magnesium in congestive heart failure, acute myocardial infarction and dysrhythmias. *J Cardiovasc Nurs* 1993, 8(1):19–31.

20. Fuentes, JC, AA Salmon, and MA Silver. Acute and chronic magnesium supplementation: Effects on endothelial function, exercise capacity, and quality of life in patients with symptomatic heart failure. *Congest Heart Fail* 2006, 12(1):9–13.

21. Ceremuzynski, L, et al. Hypomagnesemia in heart failure with ventricular arrhythmias: Beneficial effects of magnesium supplementation. *J Intern Med* 2000, 247(1):78–86.

22. Sueta, CA, et al. Antiarrhythmic action of pharmacological administration of magnesium in heart failure: A critical review of new data. *Magnes Res* 1995, 8(4):389–401.

23. Dorup, I, et al. Oral magnesium supplementation restores the concentrations of magnesium, potassium and sodium-potassium pumps in skeletal muscle of patients receiving diuretic treatment. *J Intern Med* 1993, 233(2):117–123.

24. Pittler, MH, R Guo, and E Ernst. Hawthorn extract for treating chronic heart failure. *Cochrane Database Syst Rev* 2008 Jan 23, (1):CD005312.

25. Upton, R, ed. *Hawthorn Leaf with Flower: Quality Control, Analytical and Therapeutic Monograph* (Santa Cruz: American Herbal Pharmacopoeia, 1999):1–29.

26. Schwinger, RH, et al. Crataegus special extract WS 1442 increases force of contraction in human myocardium camp independently. *J Cardiovasc Pharmacol* 2000, 35(5): 700–707.

27. Miller, AL. Botanical influences on cardiovascular diseases. *Altern Med Rev* 1998, 3(6):422–431.

28. Belardineli, R, A Mucaj, F Lacalaprice, et al. Coenzyme Q10 and exercise training in chronic heart failure. *Eur Heart J* 2006, 27(22):2675–2681.

29. Khatta, M, BS Alexander, et al. The effect of coenzyme Q10 in patients with congestive heart failure. *Ann Intern Med* 2000, 132(8):636–640.

30. Soja, AM, and SA Mortensen. Treatment of congestive heart failure with coenzyme Q10 illuminated by meta-analysis of clinical trials. *Mol Aspects Med* 1997, 18(Suppl 1): S159–S168.

31. Morisco, C, B Trimarco, and M Condorelli. Effect of coenzyme Q10 therapy in patients with congestive heart failure: A long-term multicenter randomized study. *Clin Investig* 1993, 71(Suppl 8):S134–S136.

32. Hofman-Bang, C, et al. Coenzyme Q10 as an adjunctive treatment of congestive heart failure. *J Card Fail* 1995, 1:101–107.

33. Baggio, E, et al. Italian multicenter study on the safety and efficacy of coenzyme Q10 as adjunctive therapy in heart failure. CoQ10 Drug Surveillance Investigators. *Mol Aspects Med* 1994, (Suppl 15):S287–S294.

34. Kuethe, F, A Krack, BM Richartz, and HR Figulla. Creatine supplementation improves muscle strength in patients with congestive heart failure. *Pharmazie* 2006, 61(3):218–222.

35. Therapeutic effects of L-carnitine and propionyl-L-carnitine on cardiovascular diseases: A review. *Ann N Y Acad Sci* 2004 Nov, 1033: 79–91.

36. Arsenian, MA. Carnitine and its derivatives in cardiovascular disease. *Prog Cardiovasc Dis* 1997, 40(3):265–286.

37. Anand, I, et al. Acute and chronic effects of propionyl-L-carnitine on the hemodynamics, exercise capacity, and hormones in patients with congestive heart failure. *Cardiovasc Drugs Ther* 1998, 12(3):291–299.

38. Ferrari, R, and F De Giuli. The propionyl-L-carnitine hypothesis: An alternative approach to treating heart failure. *J Card Fail* 1997, 3(3):217–224.

39. Mancini, M, et al. Controlled study on the therapeutic efficacy of propionyl-L-carnitine in patients with congestive heart failure. *Arzneimittelforschung* 1992, 42(9): 1101–1104.

40. Kobayashi, A, et al. L-carnitine treatment of congestive heart failure: Experimental and clinical study. *Jpn Circ J* 1992, 56(10):86–94.

41. Azuma, J, et al. Double-blind randomized crossover trial of taurine in congestive heart failure. *Curr Ther Res* 1983, 34:543–557.

42. Azuma, J, et al. Double-blind randomized crossover trial of taurine in congestive heart failure. *Clin Cardiol* 1985, 8:276–282.

Constipation

1. Voderholzer, WA, et al. Clinical response to dietary fiber in the treatment of chronic constipation. *Am J Gastroenterol* 1997, 92(1): 95–98.

2. Tramonte, SM, et al. The treatment of chronic constipation in adults: A systematic review. *J Gen Intern Med* 1997, 12(1):15–24.

3. Hillemeier, C. An overview of the effects of dietary fiber on gastrointestinal transit. *Pediatrics* 1995, 96(5 Pt 2):997–999.

4. Jenkins, DJ, et al. Fiber and starchy foods, gut function and implications in disease. *Am J Gastroenterol* 1986, 81(10): 920–930.

5. Muller-Lissne, SA. Effect of wheat bran on weight of stool and gastrointestinal transit time: A meta analysis. *Br J Med* 1988, 296(6622):615–617.

6. Ramkumar, D, and SS Rao. Efficacy and safety of traditional medical therapies for chronic constipation: Systematic review. *Am J Gastroenterol* 2005, 100(4):936–971.

7. Marlett, JA, et al. Comparative laxation of psyllium with and without senna in an ambulatory constipated population. *Am J Gastroenterol* 1987, 82(4):333–337.

8. Ashraf, W, et al. Effects of psyllium therapy on stool characteristics, colon transit and anorectal function in chronic

idiopathic constipation. *Aliment Pharmacol Ther* 1995, 9(6):639–647.

9. McRorie, JW, et al. Psyllium is superior to docusate sodium for treatment of chronic constipation. *Aliment Pharmacol Ther* 1998, 12(5):491–497.

10. Hull, C, et al. Alleviation of constipation in the elderly by dietary fiber supplementation. *J Am Geriatr Soc* 1980, 28(9):410–414.

11. Drouault-Holowacz, S, S Bieuvelet, A Burckel, et al. A double blind randomized controlled trial of a probiotic combination in 100 patients with irritable bowel syndrome. *Gastroeneterol Clin Biol* 2008, 32(2):147–152.

12. Bekkai, NL, ME Bongers, MM Van den Berg, et al. The role of a probiotics mixture in the treatment of childhood constipation: A pilot study. *Nutr J* 2007 Aug 4, 6:17.

13. Dughera, L, C Elia, M Navino, et al. Effects of symbiotic preparations on constipated irritable bowel syndrome symptoms. *Acta Biomed* 2007, 78(2):111–116.

14. Pitkala, KH, TE Strandberg, UH Finne Soveri, et al. Fermented cereal with specific bifidobacteria normalizes bowel movements in elderly nursing home residents: A randomized, controlled trial. *J Nutr Health Aging* 2007, 11(4):305–311.

15. Koebnick, C, I Wagner, P Leitzmann, et al. Probiotic beverage containing Lactobacillus casei Shirota improves gastrointestinal symptoms in patients with chronic constipation. *Can J Gastroenterol* 2003, 17(11):655–659.

Cystic Fibrosis (CF)

1. *What Is Cystic Fibrosis?* The Canadian Cystic Fibrosis Foundation, January 3, 2008. Available at www.cysticfibrosis.ca/page.asp?id=1.

2. Roulet, M, et al. Essential fatty acid deficiency in well nourished young cystic fibrosis patients. *Eur J Pediatr* 1997, 156(12):952–956.

3. Strandvik, B, et al. Effect on renal function of essential fatty acid supplementation in cystic fibrosis. *J Pediatr* 1989, 115(2):242–250.

4. Strandvik, B, and R Hultcrantz. Liver function and morphology during long-term fatty acid supplementation in cystic fibrosis. *Liver* 1994, 14(1):32–36.

5. Christophe, A, et al. Effect of administration of gamma-linolenic acid on the fatty acid composition of serum phospholipids and cholesteryl esters in patients with cystic fibrosis. *Ann Nutr Metab* 1994, 38(1):40–47.

6. Lucarelli, S, et al. Food allergy in cystic fibrosis. *Minerva Pediatr* 1994, 46(12):543– 548.

7. Hill, SM, et al. Cow's milk sensitive enteropathy in cystic fibrosis. *Arch Dis Child* 1989, 64(9):1251–1255.

8. Ansari, EA, et al. Ocular signs and symptoms and vitamin A status in patients with cystic fibrosis treated with daily vitamin A supplements. *Br J Ophthalmol* 1999, 83(6): 688–691.

9. Huet, F, et al. Vitamin A deficiency and nocturnal vision in teenagers with cystic fibrosis. *Eur J Pediatr* 1997, 156(12):949–951.

10. Rayner, RJ, et al. Night blindness and conjunctival xerosis caused by vitamin A deficiency in patients with cystic fibrosis. *Arch Dis Child* 1989, 64(8):1151–1156.

11. Duggan, C, et al. Vitamin A status in acute exacerbations of cystic fibrosis. *Am J Clin Nutr* 1996, 64(4):635–639.

12. Conway, SP, et al. Osteoporosis and osteopenia in adults and adolescents with cystic fibrosis: Prevalence and associated factors. *Thorax* 2000, 55(9):798–804.

13. Donovan, DS, et al. Bone mass and vitamin D deficiency in adults with advanced cystic fibrosis lung disease. *Am J Respir Crit Care Med* 1998, 157(6 Pt 1):1892–1899.

14. Haworth, CS, et al. Low bone mineral density in adults with cystic fibrosis. *Thorax* 1999, 54(11):961–967.

15. Hendersen, RC, and G Lester. Vitamin D levels in children with cystic fibrosis. *South Med J* 1997, 90(4):378–383.

16. Grey, V, et al. Monitoring of 25-OH vitamin D levels in children with cystic fibrosis. *J Pediatr Gastroenterol Nutr* 2000, 30(3):314–319.

17. Haworth, CS, AM Jones, JE Adams, et al. Randomised double blind placebo controlled trial investigating the effect of calcium and vitamin D supplementation on bone mineral density and bone metabolism in adult patients with cystic fibrosis. *J Cyst Fibros* 2004, 3(4):233–236.

18. Dominguez, C, et al. Enhanced oxidative damage in cystic fibrosis patients. *Biofactors* 1998, 8(1–2):149–153.

19. Brown, RK, et al. Pulmonary dysfunction in cystic fibrosis is associated with oxidative stress. *Eur Respir J* 1996, 9(2):334–339.

20. Portal, BC, et al. Altered antioxidant status and increased lipid peroxidation in children with cystic fibrosis. *Am J Clin Nutr* 1995, 61(4):843–847.

21. Sitrin, MD, et al. Vitamin E deficiency and neurologic disease in adults with cystic fibrosis. *Ann Intern Med* 1987, 107(1):51–54.

22. Kelleher, J, et al. The clinical effect of correction of vitamin E depletion in cystic fibrosis. *Int J Vitam Nutr Res* 1987, 57(3):253–259.

23. Winklhofer-Roob, BM, et al. Impaired resistance to oxidation of low density lipoprotein in cystic fibrosis: Improvement during vitamin E supplementation. *Free Radic Biol Med* 1995, 19(6):725–733.

24. Peters, SA, and FJ Kelly. Vitamin E supplementation in cystic fibrosis. *J Pediatr Gastroenterol Nutr* 1996, 22(4): 341–345.

25. Papas, K, J Kalbfleisch, and R Mohon. Bioavailablity of a novel, water-soluble vitamin E formulation in malabsorbing patients. *Dig Dis Sci* 2007, 52(2):347–352.

26. Cornelissen, EA, et al. Vitamin K status in cystic fibrosis. *Acta Pediatr* 1992, 81(9): 658–661.

27. Beker, LT, et al. Effect of vitamin K1 supplementation on vitamin K status in cystic fibrosis patients. *J Pediatr Gastroenterol Nutr* 1997, 24(5):512–517.

28. Rust, P, et al. Effects of long-term oral beta-carotene supplementation on lipid peroxidation in patients with cystic fibrosis. *Int J Vit Nutr Res* 1998, 68(2):83–87.

29. Lepage, G, et al. Supplementation with carotenoids corrects increased lipid peroxidation in children with cystic fibrosis. *Am J Clin Nutr* 1997, 64(1):87–93.

30. Winklhofer-Roob, BM, et al. Response to oral beta-carotene supplementation in patients with cystic fibrosis: A 16-month follow-up study. *Acta Pediatr* 1995, 84(10): 1132–1136.

31. Winklhofer-Roob, BM, et al. Plasma vitamin C concentrations in patients with cystic fibrosis: Evidence of associations with lung inflammation. *Am J Clin Nutr* 1997, 65(6):1858–1866.

32. Lambert, JP. Osteoporosis: A new challenge in cystic fibrosis. *Pharmacotherapy* 2000, 20(1):34–51.

33. Hendersen, RC, and CD Madsen. Bone mineral content and body composition in children and young adults with cystic fibrosis. *Pedatri Pulmonol* 1999, 27(2):80–84.

34. Mocchegiani, E, et al. Role of low zinc bio-availability on cellular immune effectiveness in cystic fibrosis. *Clin Immunol Immunopathol* 1995, 75(3):214–224.

35. Easley, D, et al. Effect of pancreatic enzymes on zinc absorption in cystic fibrosis. *J Pediatr Gastroenterol Nutr* 1998, 26(2):136–139.

36. Safai-Kutti, S, et al. Zinc therapy in children with cystic fibrosis. *Beitr Infusiother* 1991, 27:104–114.

37. Percival, SS, et al. Altered copper status in adult men with cystic fibrosis. *J Am Coll Nutr* 1999, 18(6):614–619.

38. Percival, SS, et al. Reduced copper enzyme activities in blood cells of children with cystic fibrosis. *Am J Clin Nutr* 1995, 62(3):633–638.

39. Abdulhamid, I, FW Beck, S Millard, et al. Effect of zinc supplementation on respiratory tract infections in children with cystic fibrosis. *Pediatr Pulmonol* 2008, 43(3):281–287.

40. Stallings, VA, LJ Stark, KA Robinson, et al. Evidence-based practice recommendations for nutrition-related management of children and adults with cystic fibrosis and pancreatic insufficiency: Results of a systematic review. *J Am Diet Assoc* 2008, 108(5):832–839.

Depression

1. *Mood Disorders.* The Canadian Mental Health Association, 2009. Available at www.cmha.ca/bins/content_page.asp?cid=3-86-92&lang=1.

2. Blum, I, et al. The influence of meal composition on plasma serotonin and norepinephrine concentrations. *Metabolism* 1992, 41(2):137–140.

3. Sayegh, R, et al. The effect of a carbohydrate-rich beverage on mood, appetite, and cognitive function in women with premenstrual syndrome. *Obstet Gynecol* 1995, 86(4 Pt 1): 520–528.

4. Su, KP, SY Huang, TH Chiu, et al. Omega-3 fatty acids for major depressive disorder during pregnancy: Results from a randomized, double-blind, placebo controlled trial. *J Clin Psychiatry* 2008, 69(4): 644–651.

5. Lin, PY, and KP Su. A meta-analytic review of double-blind, placebo-controlled trials of antidepressant efficacy of omega-3 fatty acids. *J Clin Psychiatry* 2007, 68(7):1056–1061.

6. Montgomery, P, and AJ Richardson. Omega-3 fatty acids for bipolar disorder. *Cochrane Database Syst Rev* 2008, Apr 16(2):CD005169.

7. Su, KP, WW Shen, and SY Huang. Are omega3 fatty acids beneficial in depression but not mania? *Arch Gen Psychiatry* 2000, 57(7):716–717.

8. Kinrys, G. Hypomania associated with omega3 fatty acids. *Arch Gen Psychiatry* 2000, 57(7):715–716.

9. Stoll, AL, et al. Omega 3 fatty acids in bipolar disorder: A preliminary double-blind, placebo-controlled trial. *Arch Gen Psychiatry* 1999, 56:407–412.

10. Wyatt, KM, et al. Efficacy of vitamin B6 in the treatment of premenstrual syndrome: Systematic review. *Br J Med* 1999, 318(7195):1375–1381.

11. Morris, DW, MH Trivedi, and AJ Rush. Folate and unipolar depression. *J Altern Complement Med* 2008, 14(3): 277–285.

12. Fava, M. Augmenting antidepressants with folate: A clinical perspective. *J Clin Psychiatry* 2007, 68(Suppl 10):4–7.

13. Young, SN. Folate and depression: A neglected problem. *Rev Psychiatr Neurosci* 2007, 32(2):80–82.

14. Roberts, SH, E Bedson, D Hughes, et al. Folate augmentation of treatment – evaluation for depression (FolATED): Protocol of a randomized controlled trial. *BMC Psychiatry* 2007, Nov 2007, 7:65.

15. Pennix, BW, et al. Vitamin B(12) deficiency and depression in physically disabled older women: Epidemiologic evidence from the Women's Health and Aging Study. *Am J Psychiatry* 2000, 157(5):715–721.

16. Ebly, EM, et al. Folate status, vascular disease and cognition in elderly Canadians. *Age Ageing* 1998, 27(4):485–491.

17. Fava, M, et al. Folate, vitamin B12, and homocysteine in major depressive disorder. *Am J Psychiatry* 1997, 154(3): 426–428.

18. Bell, IR, et al. B complex vitamin patterns in geriatric and young adult inpatients with major depression. *J Am Geriatr Soc* 1991, 39(3):252–257.

19. Docherty, JP, DA Sack, M Roffman, et al. A double-blind, placebo-controlled, exploratory trial of chromium picinolate in atypical depression: Effect on carbohydrate craving. *J Psychiatr Practice* 2005, 11(5):302–314.

20. Davidson, JR, K Abraham, KM Connor, and MN McLeod. Effectiveness of chromium in atypical depression: A placebo-controlled trial. *Biol Psychiatry* 2003, 53(3): 261–264.

21. Marcellini, F, C Giuli, R Papa, et al. Zinc in elderly people: Effects of zinc supplementation on psychological dimensions in dependence of IL-6-174 polymorphisms: A Zincage study. *Rejuvenation Res* 2008, 11(2):479–483.

22. Marcellini, F, C Giuli, R Papa, et al. Zinc status, psychological and nutritional assessment in old people recruited in five European countries: Zincage study. *Biogerontology* 2006, 7(5–6):339–345.

23. Nowak, G, B Szewczyk, and A Pilc. Zinc and depression: An update. *Pharmaceutical Reports* 2005, 57:713–718.

24. Nowak, G, M Siwek, D Dudek, et al. Effect of zinc supplementation on antidepressant therapy in unipolar depression: A preliminary placebo-controlled study. *Pol J Pharamacol* 2003, 55(6):1143–1147.

25. Kasper, S, M Gastpar, WE Müller, HP Volz, A Dienel, M Kieser, and HJ Möller. Efficacy of St. John's wort extract WS 5570 in acute treatment of mild depression: A reanalysis of data from controlled clinical trials. *Eur Arch Psychiatry Clin Neurosci* 2008, 258(1):59–63.

26. Linde, K, et al. St. John's Wort for depression: An overview and meta-analysis of randomized clinical trials. *Br Med J* 1996, 313:253–258.

27. Janicak, PG, J Lipinski, JM Davis, et al. S-adenosylmethionine in depression: A literature review and preliminary report. *Ala J Med Sci* 1988, 25(3):306–313.

28. Bressa, GM. S-adenosyl-l-methionine (SAMe) as antidepressant: Meta-analysis of clinical studies. *Acta Neurol Scand* 1994, 154(Suppl): S7–S14.

29. Bell, KM, SG Potkin, D Carreon, and L Plon. S-adenosylmethionine blood levels in major depression: Changes with drug treatment. *Acta Neurol Scand* 1994, 154(Suppl): S15–S18.

30. Bell, KM, L Plon, WE Bunney Jr, and SG Potkin. S-adenosylmethionine treatment of depression: A controlled clinical trial. *Am J Psychiatry* 1988, 145(9):1110–1114.

31. Salmaggi, P, GM Bressa, G Nicchia, et al. Double-blind, placebo-controlled study of S-adenosyl-L-methionine in depressed postmenopausal women. *Psychother Psychosom* 1993, 59(1):34–40.

32. De Vanna, M, and R Rigamonti. Oral S-adenosyl-L-methionine in depression. *Curr Ther Res* 1992, 52(3): 478–485.

33. Rosenbaum, JF, M Fava, WE Falk, et al. The antidepressant potential of oral S-adenosyl-l-methionine. *Acta Psychiatr Scand* 1990, 81(5):432–436.

34. Delle Chiaie, R, P Pancheri, and P Scapicchio. Efficacy and tolerability of oral and intra-muscular S-adenosyl-Lmethionine 1,4- butanedisulfonate (SAMe) in the treatment of major depression: Comparison with imipramine in multicenter studies. *Am J Clin Nutr* 2002, 76(5):1172S–1176S.

Dermatitis and Eczema

1. *Eczema*. Medline Plus, a service of the U.S. National Library of Medicine, National Institutes of Health, March 2009. Available at www.nlm.nih.gov/medlineplus/eczema.html.

2. *What Is Eczema?* The American Academy of Dermatology, 2009. Available at www.skincarephysicians.com/eczemanet/whatis.html.

3. Saarinen, UM, and M Kajosaari. Breastfeeding as prophylaxis against atopic disease: Prospective follow-up study until 17 years old. *Lancet* 1995, 346(8982):1065–1069.

4. Sampson, HA. Food hypersensitivity and dietary management in atopic dermatitis. *Pediatr Dermatol* 1992, 9(4): 376–379.

5. Bath-Hextall, F, FM Delamere, and HC Williams. Dietary exclusions for established atopic eczema. *Cochrane Database Syst Rev* 2008 Jan 23, (1):CD005203.

6. Lever, R, et al. Randomized controlled trial of advice on egg exclusion diet in young children with atopic eczema and sensitivity to eggs. *Pediatr Allergy Immunol* 1998, 9(1): 13–19.

7. Majamaa, H, et al. Wheat allergy: Diagnostic accuracy of skin prick and patch tests and specific IgE. *Allergy* 1999, 54(8):851–856.

8. Niggemann, B, et al. Outcome of double-blind, placebo-controlled food challenge tests on 107 children with atopic dermatitis. *Clin Exp Allergy* 1999, 29(1):91–96.

9. Yen, CH, YS Dai, YH Yang, et al. Linoleic acid metabolite levels and transepidermal water loss in children with atopic dermatitis. *Ann Allergy Asthma Immunol* 2008, 100(1): 66–73.

10. Horrobin, DF. Essential fatty acid metabolism and its modification in atopic eczema. *Am J Clin Nutr* 2000, 71(Suppl 1):S367–S372.

11. Horrobin, DF. Fatty acid metabolism in health and disease: The role of delta-6-desaturase. *Am J Clin Nutr* 1993, 57(Suppl 5):S732–S736.

12. Wright, S, and TA Sanders. Adipose tissue essential fatty acid composition in patients with atopic eczema. *Eur J Clin Nutr* 1991, 45(10):501–505.

13. Eriksen, BB, and DL Kare. Open trial of omega 3 and 6 fatty acids, vitamins and minerals in atopic dermatitis. *J Dermatolog Treat* 2006, 17(2):83–85.

14. Callaway, J, U Schwab, I Harima, et al. Efficacy of dietary hempseed oil in patients with atopic dermatitis. *J Dermatolog Treat* 2005, 16(2):87–94.

15. Almqvist, C, F Garden, W Xuan, et al. Omega-3 and omega-6 fatty acid exposure from early life does not affect atopy and asthma at age 5 years. *J Allergy Clin Immunol* 2007, 119(6):1438–1444.

16. van Gool, CJ, MP Zeegers, and C Thijs. Oral essential fatty acid supplementation in atopic dermatitis: A meta-anlaysis of placebo-controlled trials. *Br J Dermatol* 2004, 150(4): 728–740.

17. Dunstan, JA, TA Mori, A Barden, et al. Fish oil supplementation in pregnancy modifies neonatal allergen-specific immune responses and clinical outcomes in infants at high risk of atopy: A randomized, controlled trial. *J Allergy Clin Immunol* 2003, 112(6):1178–1184.

18. Kawai, M, T Hirano, S Higa, et al. Flavonoids and related compounds as anti-allergic substances. *Allergol Int* 2007, 56(2):113–123.

19. Tsoureli-Nikita, E, J Hercogova, T Lotti, and G Menchini. Evaluation of dietry intake of vitamin E in the treatment of atopic dermatitis: A study of the clinical course and evaluation of the immunoglobulin E serum levels. *Int J Dermatol* 2002, 41(3):146–150.

20. Sandstead, HH. Zinc deficiency. A public health problem? *Am J Dis Child* 1991, 145(8):853–859.

21. Prasad, AS. Zinc in growth and development and spectrum of human zinc deficiency. *J Am Coll Nutr* 1988, 7(5): 377–384.

22. Di Toro, R, et al. Zinc and copper status of allergic children. *Acta Pediatr Scand* 1987, 76(4):612–617.

23. Aertgeerts, P, et al. Comparison of Kamillosan® cream (2 g ethanolic extract from chamomile flowers in 100g cream) versus steroid (0.25% hydrocortisone, 0.75% flucortin butyl ester) and non-steroid (5% bufexamec) external agents in the maintenance therapy of eczema. *Z Hautkr* 1985, 60:270–277. [German]

24. Patzelt-Wenczler, R, and E Ponce-Poschl. Proof of efficacy of Kamillosan® cream in atopic eczema. *Eur J Med Res* 2000, 5(4):171–175.

25. Isolauri, E, et al. Probiotics in the management of atopic eczema. *Clin Exp Allergy* 2000, 30(11):1604–1610.

26. Majamaa, H, and E Isolauri. Probiotics: A novel approach in the management of food allergy. *J Allergy Clin Immunol* 1997, 99(2):179–185.

27. Betsi, GI, E Papadavid, and ME Falgas. Probiotics for the treatment or prevention of atopic dermatitis: A review of the evidence from randomized controlled trials. *Am J Clin Dermatol* 2008, 9(2):93–103.

Diabetes Mellitus (Type 2 Diabetes)

1. *The Prevalence and Costs of Diabetes.* The Canadian Diabetes Assocation, 2009. Available at www.diabetes.ca/about-diabetes/what/prevalence.

2. The DCCT Research Group. The effect of intensive insulin treatment of diabetes on the development and progression of long-term complications in insulin-dependent diabetes. *N Eng J Med* 1993, 329:977–986.

3. U.K. Prospective Diabetes Study Group. Intensive blood-glucose control with sulphonylureas or insulin compared with conventional treatment and risk of complications in patients with type 2 diabetes (UKPDS 33). *Lancet* 1998, 352(9131):837–853.

4. Bhattacharyya, OK, EA Estey, and AY Chen; Canadian Diabetes Association 2008. Update on the Canadian Diabetes Association 2008 clinical practice guidelines. *Can Fam Physician* 2009, 55(6):613–3.e1–6.

5. The American Dietetic Association. *Manual of Clinical Dietetics,* 6th ed. (Chicago, 2000).

6. Wolever, T, MC Barbeau, S Charron, et al. *Guidelines for the Nutritional Management of Diabetes Mellitus in the New Millennium: A Position Statement by the Canadian Diabetes Association. Canadian Journal of Diabetes Care* 1999, 23(3):56–69. Available at www.diabetes.ca/files/nutritional_guide_eng.pdf.

7. Franz, MJ, et al. Effectiveness of medical nutrition therapy provided by dietitians in the management of non-insulin-dependent diabetes mellitus: A randomized, controlled clinical trial. *J Am Diet Assoc* 1995, 95(9):1009–1117.

8. Livesey, G, R Taylor, T Hulsof, and J Howlett. Glycemic response and health: A systematic review and meta-anlaysis: Relations between dietary glycemic properties and health outcomes. *Am J Clin Nutr* 2008, 87(1):258S–268S.

9. Barclay, AW, P Petocz, J Mitchell-Price, et al. Glycemic index, glycemic load, and chronic disease risk: A meta-analysis of observational studies. *Am J Clin Nutr* 2008, 87(3):627–637.

10. Wolever, TM, AL Gibbs, C Mehling, et al. The Canadian Trial of Carbohydrates in Diabetes (CCD), a 1-y controlled trial of low-glycemic-index dietary carbohydrate in type 2 diabetes: No effect on glycated hemoglobin but reduction in C-reactive protein. *Am J Clin Nutr* 2008, 87(1):114–125.

11. Henry, CJ, HJ Lightowler, EA Tydeman, and R Skeath. Use of low-glycemic index bread to reduce 24-h blood glucose: Implications for dietary advice to non-diabetic and diabetic subjects. *Int J Food Sci Nutr* 2006, 57(3–4):273–278.

12. Kelley, DE. Sugars and starch in the nutritional management of diabetes mellitus. *Am J Clin Nutr* 2003, 78(4):858S–864S.

13. Emanuele, MA, et al. A crossover trial of high and low sucrose-carbohydrate diets in type II diabetics with hyper-triglyceridemia. *J Am Coll Nutr* 1986, 5(5):429–437.

14. Braaten, JT, et al. High beta-glucan oat bran and oat gum reduce postprandial blood glucose and insulin in subjects with and without type 2 diabetes. *Diabet Med* 1994, 11(3):312–318.

15. Del Toma, E, et al. Soluble and insoluble dietary fibre in diabetic diets. *Eur J Clin Nutr* 1988, 42(4):313–319.

16. Vuskan, V, D Whitman, JL Sievenpiper, et al. Supplementation of conventional therapy with the novel grain Salba (Salvia hispanica L.) improves major and emerging cardiovascular risk factors in type 2 diabetes: Results of a randomized controlled trial. *Diabetes Care* 2007, 30(11):2804–2810.

17. Jenkins, DJA, et al. Effect on serum lipids of very high fiber intakes in diets low in saturated fat and cholesterol. *N Eng J Med* 1993, 329:21–26.

18. Lichtenstein, AH, and US Schwab. Relationship of fat to glucose metabolism. *Atherosclerosis* 2000, 150(2):227–243.

19. Thomsen, C, et al. Comparison of the effects on the diurnal blood pressure, glucose and lipid levels of a diet rich in monounsaturated fatty acids with a diet rich in polyunsaturated fatty acids in type 2 diabetic subjects. *Diabet Med* 1995, 12(7):600–606.

20. Lane, JD, MN Feinglos, and RS Surwit. Caffeine increases ambulatory glucose and postprandial responses in coffee drinkers with type 2 diabetes. *Diabetes Care* 2008, 31(2):221–222.

21. MacKenzie, T, R Comi, P Sluss, et al. Metabolic and hormonal effects of caffeine: Randomized, double-blind, placebo-controlled crossover trial. *Metabolism* 2007, 56(12):1694–1698.

22. Bray, GA, KA Jablonski, WY Fujimoto, et al. Relation of central adiposity and body mass index to the development of diabetes in the Diabetes Prevention Program. *Am J Clin Nutr* 2008, 87(5):1212–1218.

23. Meisinger, C, A Doring, B Thorand, et al. Body fat distribution and risk of type 2 diabetes in the general population: Are there differences between men and women? The MONICA/KORA Augsburg cohort study. *Am J Clin Nutr* 2006, 84(3):483–489.

24. Knowler, WC, E Barrett-Connor, SE Fowler, RF Hamman, JM Lachin, EA Walker, and DM Nathan; Diabetes Prevention Program Research Group. Reduction in the incidence of type 2 diabetes with lifestyle intervention or metformin. *N Engl J Med* 2002, 346(6):393–403.

25. Aucot, L, A Poobalan, WC Smith, et al. Weight loss in obese diabetic and non diabetic individuals and long-term diabetes outcomes: A systematic review. *Diabetes Obes Metab* 2004, 6(2):85–94.

26. Bonnefont-Rousselot, D. The role of antioxidant micronutrients in the prevention of diabetic complications. *Treat Endocrinol* 2004, 3(1):41–52.

27. Merzouk, S, A Hichami, S Madani, H Merzouk, et al. Antioxidant status and levels of different vitamins determined by high per-formance liquid chromatography in diabetic subjects with multiple complications. *Gen Physiol Biophys* 2003, 22(1):15–27.

28. Abahusain, MA, et al. Retinol, alpha-tocopherol and carotenoids in diabetes. *Eur J Clin Nutr* 1999, 53(8):630–635.

29. Coyne, T, TI Ibieble, PD Baade, et al. Diabetes mellitus and serum carotneoids: Findings of a population-based study in Queensland, Australia. *Am J Clin Nutr* 2005, 82(3):685–693.

30. Paolisso, G, et al. Plasma vitamin C affects glucose homeostasis in healthy subjects and in non-insulin-dependent diabetics. *Am J Physiol* 1994, 266(2 Pt 1):E261–E268.

31. Cunningham, JJ. The glucose/insulin system and vitamin C: Implications in insulin-dependent diabetes mellitus. *J Am Coll Nutr* 1998, 17(2):105–108.

32. Afkhami-Ardekani, M, and A Shojaoddiny-Ardekani. Effect of vitamin C on blood glucose, serum lipids and serum insulin in type 2 diabetes patients. *Indian J Med Res* 2007, 126(5):471–474.

33. Tousoulis, D, C Antoniades, C Tountas, et al. Vitamin C affects thrombosis/fibrinolysis system and reactive hyperemia in patients with type 2 diabetes and coronary artery disease. *Diabetes Care* 2003, 26(10):2749–2753.

34. Montenen, J, P Knelt. R Jarvinen, and A Reunanen. Dietary antioxidant intake and risk of type 2 diabetes. *Diabetes Care* 2004, 27(2):362–366.

35. Zipitis, CS, and AK Akobeng. Vitamin D supplementation in early childhood and risk of type 1 diabetes: A systematic review and meta-analysis. *Arch Dis Child* 2008, 93(6): 512–517.

36. Palomer, X, JM Gonzalez-Clemente, F Blanco-Vaca, and D Mauricio. Role of vitamin D in the pathogenesis of type 2 diabetes mellitus. *Diabetes Obes Metab* 2008, 10(3): 185–197.

37. Pittas, AG, J Lau, FB Hu, and B Dawson-Hughes. The role of vitamin D and calcium in type 2 diabetes: A systematic review and meta-analysis. *J Clin Endocrinol Metab* 2007, 92(6): 2017–2029.

38. Sugden, JA, JI Davies, MD Witham, et al. Vitamin D improves endothelial function in patients with Type 2 diabetes mellitus and low vitamin D levels. *Diabetes Med* 2008, 25(3):320–325.

39. Song, Y, K He, EB Levitan, et al. Effects of oral magnesium supplementation on glycaemic control in Type 2 diabetes: A meta-analysis of randomized double-blind controlled trials. *Diabetes Med* 2006, 23(10):1050–1056.

40. Paolisso, G, et al. Changes in glucose turnover parameters and improvement of glucose oxidation after 4-week magnesium administration in elderly noninsulin-dependent (type II) diabetic patients. *J Clin Endocrinol Metab* 1994, 78(6):1510–1514.

41. Saggese, G, et al. Hypomagnesemia and the parathyroid hormone–vitamin D endocrine system in children with insulin-dependent diabetes mellitus: Effects of magnesium administration. *J Pediatr* 1991, 118(2):220– 225.

42. Mertz, W. Chromium in human nutrition: A review. *J Nutr* 1993, 123(4):626–633.

43. Ding, W, et al. Serum and urine chromium concentration in elderly diabetics. *Biol Trace Elem Res* 1998, 63(3):231–237.

44. Morris, BW, et al. Chromium homeostasis in patients with type II (NIDDM) diabetes. *I Trace Elem Med Biol* 1999, 13(1–2):57–61.

45. Broadhurst, CL, and P Domenico. Clinical studies on chromium picolinate supplementation in diabetes mellitus: A review. *Diabetes Technol Ther* 2006, 8(6):677–687.

46. Vuskan, V, et al. Similar postprandial glycemic reductions with escalation of dose and administration time of American ginseng in type 2 diabetes. *Diabetes Care* 2000, 23(9):1221– 1226.

47. Vuksan, V, et al. American ginseng (Panax quinquefolius L) reduced postprandial glycemia in nondiabetic subjects and subjects with type 2 diabetes mellitus. *Arch Intern Med* 2000, 160(7):1009–1113.

48. Ziegler, D, M Hanefeld, KJ Ruhnau, et al. Treatment of symptomatic diabetic polyneuropathy with the antioxidant alpha-lipoic acid: A 7-month, multicenter, randomized, controlled trial (ALADIN III Study). *Diabetes Care* 1999, 22(8):1296–1301.

49. Reljanovic, M, G Reichel, K Rett, et al. Treatment of diabetic polyneuropathy with the antioxidant thioctic acid (alpha-lipoic acid): A 2-year, multicenter, randomized, double-blind, placebo-controlled trial (ALADIN II). Alpha Lipoic Acid in Diabetic Neuropathy. *Free Radic Res* 1999, 31(3):171–177.

50. Ziegler, D, M Hanefeld, KJ Ruhnau, et al. Treatment of symptomatic diabetic peripheral neuropathy with the antioxidant alpha-lipoic acid: A 3-week, multicenter, randomized, controlled trial (ALADIN Study). *Diabetologia* 1995, 38(12):1425–1433.

51. Ametov, AS, A Barinov, PJ Dyck, et al. The sensory symptoms of diabetic polyneuropathy are improved with alpha-lipoic acid. *Diabetes Care* 2003, 26(3):770–776.

52. Ziegler, D, H Nowak, P Kemplert, et al. Treatment of symptomatic diabetic polyneuropathy with the antioxidant alpha-lipoic acid: A meta-analysis. *Diabet Med* 2004, 21(2): 114–121.

53. Jacob, S, EJ Henriksen, AL Schiemann, et al. Enhancement of glucose disposal in patients with type 2 diabetes by alpha-lipoic acid. *Arzneimittelforschung* 1995;45(8): 872–874.

54. Jacob, S, P Ruus, R Hermann, et al. Oral administration of RAC-alpha-lipoic acid modulates insulin sensitivity in patients with type-2 diabetes mellitus: A placebo-controlled, pilot trial. *Free Rad Biol Med* 1999, 27(3–4):309–314.

Diarrhea

1. *Diarrhea.* The National Digestive Diseases Information Clearinghouse, March 2007. Available at http://digestive. niddk.nih.gov/ ddiseases/pubs/diarrhea/index.htm.

2. Dennison, BA. Fruit juice consumption by infants and children: A review. *J Am Coll Nutr* 1996, 15(Suppl 5): S4–S11.

3. Hoekstra, JH, et al. Apple juice malabsorption: Fructose or sorbitol? *J Pediatr Gastroenterol Nutr* 1993, 16(1):39–42.

4. Hoekstra, JH, et al. Fluid intake and industrial processing in apple juice induced chronic and non-specific diarrhoea. *Arch Dis Child* 1995, 73(2):126–130.

5. Smith, MM, and F Lifshitz. Excess fruit juice consumption as a contributing factor in nonorganic failure to thrive. *Pediatrics* 1994, 93(3):438–443.

6. Wenus, C, R Goll, EB Loken, et al. Prevention of antibiotic-associated diarrhea by a fermented probiotic milk drink. *Eur J Clin Nutr* 2008, 62(2):299–301.

7. Beausoleil, M, N Fortier, S Guenette, et al. Effect of a fermented milk combining Lactobacillus acidophilus CI1285 and Lactobacillus casei in the prevention of antibiotic-associated diarrhea: A randomized, double-blind, placebo-controlled trial. *Can J Gastroenerol* 2007, 21(11): 732–736.

8. Beniwal, RS, VC Arena, L Thomas, et al. A randomized trial of yogurt for the prevention of antibiotic-associated diarrhea. *Dig Dis Sci* 2003, 48(10):2077–2082.

9. Pedone, CA, CC Arnaud, ER Postaire, et al. Multicentric study of the effect of milk fermented by Lactobacillus casei on the incidence of diarrhea. *Int J Clin Pract* 2000, 54(9):568–571.

10. Rolfe, RD. The role of probiotic cultures in the control of gastrointestinal health. *J Nutr* 2000, 130(Suppl 2): S396–S402.

11. Vanderhoof, JA, et al. Lactobacillus GG in the prevention of antibiotic-associated diarrhea in children. *J Pediatr* 1999, 135(5):564–568.

12. Phuapradit, P, et al. Reduction of rotavirus infection in children receiving bifidobacteria-supplemented formula. *J Med Assoc Thai* 1999, 82(4)(Suppl 1):S43–S48.

13. Guarino, A, et al. Oral bacteria therapy reduces the duration of symptoms and of viral excretion in children with mild diarrhea. *J Pediatr Gastroenterol Nutr* 1997, 25(5): 516–517.

14. Vanderhoof, JA. Food hypersensitivity in children. *Curr Opin Clin Nutr Metab Care* 1998, 1(5):419–422.

15. Ahmed, T, et al. Humoral immune and clinical responses to food antigens following acute diarrhoea in children. *J Paediatr Child Health* 1998, 34(3):229–232.

16. Snyder, JD. Dietary protein sensitivity: Is it an important risk factor for persistent diarrhea? *Acta Paediatr Suppl* 1992, 381(3):78–81.

17. Wapnir, RA. Zinc deficiency, malnutrition and the gastrointestinal tract. *J Nutr* 2000, 130(Suppl 5):S1388–S1392.

18. Faker, PJ, et al. The dynamic link between the integrity of the immune system and zinc status. *J Nutr* 2000, 130(Suppl 5):S1399–S1406.

19. Roy, SK, et al. Impact of zinc supplementation on subsequent growth and morbidity in Bangladeshi children with acute diarrhoea. *Eur J Clin Nutr* 1999, 53(7):529–534.

20. Sazawal, S, et al. Efficacy of zinc supplementation in reducing the incidence and prevalence of acute diarrhea: A community-based, double-blind, controlled trial. *Am J Clin Nutr* 1997, 66(2):413–418.

21. McFarland, LV. Meta-analysis of probiotics for the prevention of antibiotic associated diarrhea and the treatment of Clostridium difficile disease. *Am J Gastroenterol* 2006, 101(4):812–822.

Diverticulosis and Diverticulitis

1. *Diverticulosis and Diverticulitis*. National Digestive Diseases Information Clearinghouse, July 2008. Available at http:// digestive.niddk.nih.gov/ddiseases/pubs/diverticulosis.

2. Strate, LL, YL Liu, S Syngal, et al. Nut, corn, and popcorn consumption and the incidence of diverticular disease. *JAMA* 2008, 300(8):907–914.

3. O'Keefe, SJ. A.R.P. Lecture: Food and the gut. *S Afr Med J* 1995, 85(4):261–268.

4. Cheskin, LJ, and RD Lamport. Diverticular disease: Epidemiology and pharmacological treatment. *Drugs Aging* 1995, 6(1):55–63.

5. Kay, RM. Dietary fibre. *J Lipid Res* 1982, 23(2):221–242.

6. Walker, AR. Diet and bowel diseases: Past history and future prospects. *S Afr Med J* 1985, 68(3):148–152.

7. Leahy, AL, et al. High fibre diet in symptomatic diverticular disease of the colon. *Ann R Coll Surg Eng* 1985, 67(3): 173–174.

8. Aldoori, WH, et al. A prospective study of diet and risk of symptomatic diverticular disease in men. *Am J Clin Nutr* 1994, 60(5):757–764.

9. Tursi, A, G Brandimarte, GM Giorgetti, et al. Balsalazide and/or high-potency probiotic mixture (VSL#3) in maintaining remission after an attack of acute, uncomplicated diverticulitis of the colon. *J Colorectal Dis* 2007, 22(9):1103–1108.

Ear Infections (Otitis Media)

1. *Ear Infection, Middle Ear*. Mayo Foundation for Medical Education and Research, September 19, 2008. Available at www.mayoclinic.com/health/ear-infections/DS00303.

2. Nsouli, TM, et al. Role of food allergy in serious otitis media. *Ann Allergy* 1994, 73(3):215–219.

3. Juntii, H, et al. Cow's milk allergy is associated with recurrent otitis media during childhood. *Acta Otolaryngol* 1999, 119(8):867–873.

4. Hurst, DS. Allergy management of refractory serious otitis media. *Otolaryngol Head Neck Surg* 1990, 102(6):664–669.

5. Bernstein, JM. Role of allergy in eustachian tube blockage and otitis media with effusion: A review. *Otolaryngol Head Neck Surg* 1996, 114(4):562–568.

6. Host, A. Mechanisms of adverse reactions to food: The ear. *Allergy* 1995, 50(Suppl 20):S64–S67.

7. Hatakka, K, K Blomgren, S Pohjavuori, et al. Treatment of acute otitis media with probiotics in otitis-prone children: A double, blind, placebo-controlled study. *Clin Nutr* 2007, 26(3):314–321.

8. Lykova, EA, et al. Disruption of microbiocenosis of the large intestine and the immune and interferon status in children with bacterial complications of acute viral infections of the respiratory tract and their correction by high doses of bifidumbacterin forte. *Antibiot Khimioter* 2000, 45(10): 22–27. [Russian]

9. Roos, K, EG Hakansson, and S Holm. Effect of recolonisation with 'interfering' alpha streptococci on recurrences of acute and secretory otitis media in children: Randomized placebo controlled trial. *Br Med J* 2001, 322(7280):210–222.

10. Karabaev, KE, VF Antoniv, and RU Bekmuradov. Pathogenetic validation of optimal antioxidant therapy in suppurative inflammatory otic diseases in children. *Vestn Otorinolaringol* 1997, (1):5–7. [Russian]

11. Coulehan, JL, et al. Vitamin C and acute illness in Navajo school children. *N Engl J Med* 1976, 295(18):973–977.

12. Yariktas, M, F Doner, H Dogru, H Yasan, and N Delibas. The role of free oxygen radicals on the development of otitis media with effusion. *Int J Pediatr Otorhinolaryngol* 2004, 68(7):889–894.

13. Khakimov, AM, SS Arifov, and FN Faizulaeva. Efficacy of antioxidant therapy in patients with acute and chronic purulent otitis media. *Vestn Otorinolaringol* 1997, (5): 16–19. [Russian]

14. Bondestam, M, T Foucard, and M Gebre-Medhin. Subclinical trace element deficiency in children with undue susceptibility to infections. *Acta Paediatr Scand* 1985, 74(4):515– 520.

15. Mark, JD, KL Grant, and LL Barton. The use of dietary supplements in pediatrics: A study of echinacea. *Clin Pediatr (Phila)* 2001, 40(5):265–269.

16. Klein, JO. Management of acute otitis media in an era of increasing antibiotic resistance. *Int J Pediatr Otorhinolaryngol* 1999, 49(Suppl 1):S15–S27.

17. Uhari, M, et al. A novel use of xylitol sugar in preventing otitis media. *Pediatrics* 1998, 102(4 Pt 1):879–884.

18. Uhari, M, et al. Xylitol chewing gum in prevention of acute otitis media: Double blind randomized trial. *Br Med J* 1996, 313(7066):1180–1184.

Eating Disorders
1. *Understanding Statistics on Eating Disorders.* National Eating Disorder Information Centre, 2008. Available at www.nedic.ca/ knowthefacts/statistics.shtml.

Endometriosis
1. *Endometriosis.* MedicineNet Inc., 2009. Available at www.medicinenet.com/ endometriosis/article.htm2.

2. Sesti, F, A Pietropolli, T Capozzolo, et al. Hormonal suppression treatment or dietary therapy versus placebo in the control of painful symptoms after conservative surgery for endometriosis stage III–IV: A randomized comparative trial. *Fertil Steril* 2007, 88(6):1541–1547.

3. Wu, MY, et al. Increase in the production of interleukin-6, interleukin-10, and interleukin-12 by lipoploysaccharide-stimulated peritoneal macrophages from women with endometriosis. *Am J Reprod Immunol* 1999, 41(1): 106–111.

4. Karck, U, et al. PGE2 and PGF2 alpha release by human peritoneal macrophages in endometriosis. *Prostaglandins* 1996, 51(1):49–60.

5. Nabekura, H, et al. Fallopian tube prostaglandin production with and without endometriosis. *Int J Fertil Menopausal Stud* 1994, 39(1):57–63.

6. Koike, H, et al. Eicosanoids production in endometriosis. *Prostaglandins Leukot Essent Fatty Acids* 1992, 45(4): 313–317.

7. Koike, H, et al. Correlation between dysmenorrheic severity and prostaglandin production in women with endometriosis. *Prostaglandins Leukot Essent Fatty Acids* 1992, 46(2):133– 137.

8. Benedetto, C. Eicosanoids in primary dysmenorrhea, endometriosis and menstrual migraine. *Gynecol Endocrinol* 1989, 3(1):71–94.

9. Parazzini, F, F Chiaffarino, M Surace, et al. Selected food intake and risk of endometriosis. *Hum Reprod* 2004, 19(8): 1755–1759.

10. Ibid.

11. Mojzis, J, L Varinska, G Mojzisova, et al. Antiangiogenic effects of flavonoids and chalcones. *Pharmacol Res* 2008, 57(4):259– 265.

12. Mathias, JR, et al. Relation of endometriosis and neuromuscular disease of the gastrointestinal tract: New insights. *Fertil Steril* 1998, 70(1):81–88.

13. Grodstein, F, et al. Relation of female infertility to consumption of caffeinated beverages. *Am J Epidemiol* 1993, 137(12):1353–1360.

14. Grodstein, F, et al. Infertility in women and moderate alcohol use. *Am J Public Health* 1994, 84(9):1429–1432.

15. Murphy, AA, et al. Endometriosis: A disease of oxidative stress? *Semin Reprod Endocrinol* 1998, 16(4):263–273.

16. Dawood, MY. Hormonal therapies for endometriosis: Implications for bone metabolism. *Acta Obstet Gynecol Scand Suppl* 1994, 159: 22–34.

17. Harel, Z, FM Biro, RK Kottenhahn, and SL Rosenthal. Supplementation with omega-3 polyunsaturated fatty acids in the management of dysmenorrhea in adolescents. *Am J Obstet Gynecol* 1996, 174(4):1335–1338.

18. Sesti, F, A Pietropolli, T Capozzolo, et al. Hormonal suppression treatment or dietary therapy versus placebo in the control of painful symptoms after conservative surgery for endometriosis stage III–IV: A randomized comparative trial. *Fertil Steril* 2007, 88(6):1541–1547.

Fibrocystic Breast Conditions
1. Olawaiye, A, M Withiam-Leitch, G Danakas, and K Kahn. Mastalgia: A review of management. *J Reprod Med* 2005, 50(12):933–939.

2. Boyd, NF, et al. Clinical trial of a low-fat, high-carbohydrate diet in subjects with mammographic breast dysplasia: Report of early outcomes. *J Natl Cancer Inst* 1988, 80(15): 1244–1248.

3. Rose, DP. Effect of a low-fat diet on hormone levels in women with cystic breast disease: I. Serum steroids and gonodotropins. *J Natl Cancer Inst* 1987, 78(4):623–626.

4. Rose, DP, et al. Effect of a low fat diet on hormone levels in women with cystic breast disease. II. Serum radioimmunoassayable prolactin and growth hormone and bioactive lactogenic hormones. *J Natl Cancer Inst* 1987, 78(4): 627–631.

5. Rose, DP, et al. Effects of diet supplementation with wheat bran on serum estrogen levels in the follicular and luteal phases of the menstrual cycle. *Nutrition* 1997, 13:535–539.

6. Rose, D.P, et al. High-fiber diet reduces serum estrogen concentrations in premenopausal women. *Am J Clin Nutr* 1991, 24:520–524.

7. Rosolowich, V, E Saettler, B Szuck, et al. Mastalgia. *J Obstet Gynaecol Can* 2006, 28(1):49–71.

8. Xu, X, et al. Effects of soy isoflavones on estrogen and phytoestrogens metabolism in premenopausal women. *Cancer Epidemiol Biomarkers Prev* 1998, 7:1101–1108.

9. Nagata, C, et al. Decreased serum estradiol concentration associated with high dietary intake of soy products in premenopausal Japanese women. *Nutr Cancer* 1997, 29: 228–233.

10. Cassidy, A, et al. Biological effects of a diet of soy protein rich isoflavones on the menstrual cycle of premenopausal women. *Am J Clin Nutr* 1994, 60:333–340.

11. Petrakis, NL, et al. Stimulatory influence of soy protein isolate on breast secretion in pre and post menopausal women. *Cancer Epidemiol Biomarkers Prev* 1996, 5: 785–794.

12. Bryant, M, A Cassidy, C Hill, et al. Effect of consumption of soy isoflavones on behavioural, somatic and affective symptoms in women with premenstrual syndrome. *Br J Nutr* 2005, 93(5):731–739.

13. Fleming, RM. What effect, if any, does soy protein have on breast tissue? *Integr Cancer Ther* 2003, 2(3):225–228.

14. Russell, LC. Caffeine restriction as initial treatment of breast pain. *Nurse Pract* 1989, 14(2): 36–37.

15. Meyer, EC, et al. Vitamin E and benign breast disease. *Surgery* 1990, 107(5):549–551.

16. Ernster, VL, et al. Vitamin E and benign breast disease : A double-blind, randomized clinical trial. *Surgery* 1985, 97(4):490–494.

17. Pye, JK, et al. Clinical experience of drug treatments for mastalgia. *Lancet* 1985, 2(8451):373–377.

18. Srivastava, A, RE Mansel, N Arvind, et al. Evidence-based management of mastalgia: A meta-analysis of randomized trials. *Breast* 2007, 16(5):503–517.

19. Tamborini, A, and R Taurelle. Value of standardized Ginkgo biloba extract (EGb 761) in the management of congestive symptoms of premenstrual syndrome. *Rev Fr Gynecol Obstet* 1993, 88(7–9):447–457. [French]

Fibromyalgia (FM)

1. *Fibromyalgia.* The Arthritis Society, April 29, 2009. Available at www.arthritis.ca/types%20of%20arthritis/fibromyalgia/default.asp?s=1.

2. Dykman, KD, et al. The effects of nutritional supplements on the symptoms of fibromyalgia and chronic fatigue syndrome. *Integr Physiol Behav Sci* 1998, 33(1):61–71.

3. Swezey, RL, and J Adams. Fibromyalgia: A risk factor for osteoporosis. *J Rheumatol* 1999, 26(12):2642–2644.

4. Warner, AE, and SA Arnspiger. Diffuse musculoskeletal pain is not associated with low vitamin D levels or improved by treatment with vitamin D. *J Clin Rheumatol* 2008, 14(1):12–16.

5. Eisinger, J, et al. Selenium and magnesium status in fibromyalgia. *Magnes Res* 1994, 7(3–4):285–288.

6. Ng, SY. Hair calcium and magnesium levels in patients with fibromyalgia: A case center study. *J Manipulative Physiol Ther* 1999, 22(9):586–593.

7. Russell, IJ, et al. Treatment of fibromyalgia syndrome with Super Malic: A randomized, double blind, placebo controlled, crossover pilot study. *J Rheumatol* 1995, 22(5):953–958.

8. McCarty, DJ, et al. Treatment of pain due to fibromyalgia with topical capsaicin: A pilot study. *Semin Arth Rheum* 1994, 23(Suppl 3):S41–S47.

9. Frerick, H, W Keitel, U Kuhn, et al. Topical treatment of chronic low back pain with a capsicum plaster. *Pain* 2003, 106(1–2):59–64.

10. Keitel, W, H Frerick, U Kuhn, et al. Capsicum pain plaster in chronic non-specific low back pain. *Arzneimittelforschung* 2001, 51(11): 896–903.

11. Russell, IJ, JE Michalek, JD Flechas, and GE Abraham. Treatment of fibromyalgia syndrome with Super Malic: A randomized, double blind, placebo controlled, crossover pilot study. *J Rheumatol* 1995, 22(5):953–958.

12. Citera, G, MA Arias, JA Maldonado-Cocco, et al. The effect of melatonin in patients with fibromyalgia: A pilot study. *Clin Rheumatol* 2000, 19(1):9–13.

13. Jacobsen, S, et al. Oral S-adenosylmethionine in primary fibromyalgia: Double-blind clinical evaluation. *Scand J Rheumatol* 1991, 20:294– 302.

Food Allergies

1. *Food Allergy and Intolerances.* Health Canada, November 2007. Available at www. hc-sc.gc.ca/fn-an/securit/allerg/index-eng.php.

2. Kull, I, M Wickman, G Lilja, et al. Breast feeding and allergic diseases in infants: A prospective birth cohort study. *Arch Dis Child* 2002, 87(6):478–481.

3. Wetzig, H, et al. Associations between duration of breast-feeding, sensitization to hens' egg and eczema infantum in one and two year old children at high risk of atopy. *Int J Hyg Environ Health* 2000, 203(1):17–21.

4. Chandra, RK. Five-year follow-up of high-risk infants with family history of allergy who were exclusively breast-fed or fed partial whey hydrolysate, soy and conventional cow's milk formulas. *J Pediatr Gastroenterol Nutr* 1997, 24(4):380–388.

5. Saarinen, UM, and M Kajosaari. Breastfeeding as prophylaxis against atopic disease: Prospective follow-up study until 17 years old. *Lancet* 1995, 346(8982):1065–1069.

6. Casas, R, et al. Detection of IgA antibodies to cat, beta-lactoglobulin, and ovalbumin allergens in human milk. *J Allergy Clin Immunol* 2000, 105(6 Pt 1):1236–1240.

7. Fiocchi, A, A Assa'ad, S Bahna, et al. Food allergy and the introduction of solid foods to infants: A consensus document. Adverse Reactions to Foods Committee, American College of Allergy, Asthma and Immunology. *Ann Allergy Asthma Immunol* 2006, 97(11):10–20.

Gallstones

1. Kern Jr, F. Effects of dietary cholesterol on cholesterol and bile acid homeostasis in patients with cholesterol gallstones. *J Clin Invest* 1994, 93(3):1186–1194.

2. Narain, PK, et al. Cholesterol enhances membrane-damaging properties of model bile by increasing the intervesicular-intermixed micellar concentration of hydrophobic bile salts. *J Surg Res* 1999, 84(1):112–119.

3. Yago, MD, V Gonzalez, P Serrano, et al. Effect of the type of dietary fat on biliary composition and bile lithogenicity in humans with cholesterol gallstone disease. *Nutrition* 2005, 21(3):339–347.

4. Mendez-Sanchez, N, NC Chavez-Tapia, and M Uribe. The role of dietary fats in the pathogenesis of gallstones. *Front Biosci* 2003, 8:420–427.

5. Caroli-Bosc, FX, et al. Cholelithiasis and dietary risk factors: An epidemiologic investigation in Vidauban, Southeast France. General Practitioner's Group of Vidauban. *Dig Dis Sci* 1998, 43(9):2131–2137.

6. Tsai, CJ, MF Leitzmann, WC Willett, and EL Giovannucci. Prospective study of abdominal obesity and gallstone disease in men. *Am J Clin Nutr* 2004, 80(1):38–44.

7. Festi, D, et al. Gallbladder motility and gallstone formation in obese patients following very low calorie diets: Use it (fat) or lose it (well). *Int J Obes Relat Metab Disord* 1998, 22(6):592–600.

8. Gebhard, RL, et al. The role of gallbladder emptying in gallstone formation during diet-induced rapid weight loss. *Hepatology* 1996, 24(3):544–548.

9. Vezina, WC, et al. Similarity in gallstone formation from 900 kcal/day diets containing 16 g vs 30 g of daily fat: Evidence that fat restriction is not the main culprit of cholelithiasis during rapid weight reduction. *Dig Dis Sci* 1998, 43(3):554–561.

10. Heshka, S, et al. Obesity and risk of gallstone development on a 1200 kcal/d (5025 Kj/d) regular food diet. *Int J Obes Relat Metab Disord* 1996, 20(5):450–454.

11. Syngal, S, et al. Long-term weight patterns and risk for cholecystectomy in women. *Ann Intern Med* 1999, 130(6):471–477.

12. Leitzmann, MF, et al. The relation of physical activity to risk for symptomatic gallstone disease in men. *Ann Intern Med* 1998, 128(6): 417–425.

13. Nair, P, and JF Mayberry. Vegetarianism, dietary fibre and gastro-intestinal disease. *Dig Dis Sci* 1994, 12(3):177–185.

14. Ortega, RM, et al. Differences in diet and food habits between patients with gallstones and controls. *J Am Coll Nutr* 1997, 16(1):88–95.

15. Sichieri, R, et al. A prospective study of hospitalization and gallstone disease among women: Role of dietary factors, fasting period, and dieting. *Am J Public Health* 1991, 81(7): 880–884.

16. Leitzmann, MF, et al. A prospective study of coffee consumption and the risk of symptomatic gallstone disease in men. *JAMA* 1999, 281(22):2106–2112.

17. Simon, JA. Ascorbic acid and cholesterol gallstones. *Med Hypotheses* 1993, 40(2):81–84.

18. Simon, JA, and ES Hudes. Serum ascorbic acid and other correlates of gallbladder disease among U.S. adults. *Am J Public Health* 1998, 88(8):1208–1212.

19. Gustafsson, U, et al. The effect of vitamin C in high doses on plasma and biliary lipid composition in patients with cholesterol gallstones: Prolongation of nucleation time. *Eur J Clin Invest* 1997, 27(5):387–391.

20. Moerman, CJ, et al. Dietary risk factors for clinically diagnosed gallstones in middle-aged men: A 25-year follow-up study (the Zutphen Study). *Ann Epidemiol* 1994, 4(3):248–254.

21. Tsai, CJ, MF Leitzmann, WC Willett, and EL Giovannucci. Long term effect of magnesium consumption on the risk of symptomatic gallstone disease among men. *Am J Gastroenterol* 2008, 103(2):375–382.

Gastroesphageal Reflux Disease (GERD)

1. Corely, DA, and A Kubo. Body mass index and gastroesophageal reflux disease: A systematic review and meta-analysis. *Am J Gastroenerol* 2006, 101(11): 2619–2628.

2. El-Serag, H. The association between obesity and GERD: A review of the epidemiological evidence. *Dig Dis Sci* 2008, 53(9):2307–2312.

3. Jacobson, BC, SC Somers, BC Fuchs, et al. Body-mass index and symptoms of gastroesophageal reflux in women. *N Eng J Med* 2006, 354(22):2340–2348.

4. *Heartburn and Gastroesophageal Reflux Disease*. MediPrimer.com, 2009. Available at www.mediprimer.com/Gastroenterology/heartburn/95.html.

Glaucoma

1. Zang, EA, and EL Wynder. The association between body mass index and the relative frequencies of disease in a sample of hospitalized patients. *Nutr Cancer* 1994, 21(3):247–261.

2. Coleman, AL, KL Stone, G Kodjebacheva, et al. Glaucoma risk and the consumption of fruits and vegetables among older women in the study of osteoporotic fractures. *Am J Opthalmol* 2008, 145(6):1081–1089.

3. Chandrasekaran, S, E Rochthcina, and P Mitchell. Effects of caffeine on intraocular pressure: The Blue Mountains Eye Study. *J Glaucoma* 2005, 14(6):504–507.

4. Avisar, R, E Avisar, and D Weinberger. Effect of coffee consumption on intraocular pressure. *Ann Pharmacother* 2002, 36(6):992–995.

5. Okuno, T, T Sugiyama, M Tominaga, et al. Effects of caffeine in microcirculation of the human ocular fundus. *Jpn J Opthalmol* 2002, 46(2):170–176.

6. Cellini, M, et al. Fatty acid use in glaucomatous optic nerve neuropathy treatment. *Acta Ophthalmol Scand Suppl* 1998, 14(227):41–42.

7. Ritch, R. Neuroprotection: Is it really applicable to glaucoma therapy? *Curr Opin Ophthalmol* 2000, 11(2):78–84.

8. Jampel, HD. Ascorbic acid is cytotoxic to dividing human Tenon's capsule fibroblasts: A possible but contributing factor in glaucoma filtration surgery success. *Arch Ophthalmol* 1990, 108(9):1323–1325.

9. Wendt, MD, et al. Ascorbate stimulates type I and type II collagen in human Tenon's fibroblasts. *J Glaucoma* 1997, 6(6):402–407.

10. Haas, AL, et al. Vitamin E inhibits proliferation of human Tenon's capsule fibroblasts in vitro. *Ophthalmic Res* 1996, 28(3):171–175.

11. Engin, KN, G Engin, H Kucuksahin, et al. Clinical evaluation of the neuroprotective effect of alpha-tocopherol against glaucomatous damage. *Eur J Opthalmol* 2007, 17(4):528–533.

12. Gaspar, AZ, et al. The influence of magnesium in visual field and peripheral vasospasm in glaucoma. *Ophthalmologica* 1995, 209(1):11–13.

13. Ritch, R. Potential role for Ginkgo biloba extract in the treatment of glaucoma. *Med Hypotheses* 2000, 54(2): 221–235.

14. Chung, HS, et al. Ginkgo biloba extract increases ocular blood flow velocity. *J Ocul Pharmacol Ther* 1999, 15(3): 233–240.

15. Quaranta, L, S Bettelli, MG Uva, et al. Effect of Ginkgo biloba extract on preexisting visual field damage in normal tension glaucoma. *Opthalmology* 2003, 110(2):359–362.

Gout

1. *Gout*. The Arthritis Society, April 2009. Available at www.arthritis.ca/types% 20of%20arthritis/gout/default.asp?s=1.

2. Choi, HK, W Willett, and G Curhan. Coffee consumption and the risk of incident gout in men: A prospective study. *Arthritis Rheum* 2007, 56(6):2049–2055.

3. Williams, PT. Effects of diet, physical activity and performance, and body weight on incident gout in ostensibly healthy, vigorous men. *Am J Clin Nutr* 2008, 87(5): 1480–1487.

4. Choi, HK, K Atkinson, EW Karlson, and G Curhan. Obesity, weight change, hypertention, diuretic use, and risk of gout in men: The health professionals' follow-up study. *Arch Intern Med* 2005, 165(7):742–748.

5. Dessein, PH, et al. Beneficial effects of weight loss associated with moderate calorie/carbohydrate restriction, and increased proportional intake of protein and unsaturated fat on serum urate and lipoproprotein levels in gout: A pilot study. *Ann Rheum Dis* 2000, 59(7):539–543.

6. Loenen, HM, et al. Serum uric acid correlates in elderly men and women with special reference to body composition and dietary intake (Dutch Nutrition Surveillance System). *J Clin Epidemiol* 1990, 43(12):1297–1303.

7. Heyden, S. The workingman's diet: II. Effect of weight reduction in obese patients with hypertension, diabetes, hyperuricemia and hyperlipidemia. *Nutr Metab* 1978, 22(3): 141–159.

8. Scott, JT, and RA Sturge. The effect of weight loss on plasma and urinary uric acid and lipid levels. *Adv Exp Med Biol* 1977, 76B(1):274–277.

9. Choi, HK, K Atkinson, EW Karlson, et al. Purine-rich foods, dairy and protein intake, and the risk of gout in men. *N Engl J Med* 2004, 350(11):1093–1103.

10. Ibid.

11. Choi, HK, and G Curhan. Beer, liquor, and wine consumption and serum uric acid levels: The Third National Health and Nutrition Examination Survey. *Arthritis Rheum* 2004, 51(6):1023–1029.

12. Choi, HK, K Atkinson, EW Karlson, et al. Alcohol intake and risk of incident gout in men: A prospective study. *Lancet* 2004, 363(9417):1277–1281.

13. Eastmond, CJ, et al. The effects of alcoholic beverages on urate metabolism in gout sufferers. *Br J Rheumatol* 1995, 34(8):756–769.

14. Gibson, T, et al. Beer drinking and its effect on uric acid. *Br J Rheumatol* 1984, 23(3):203–209.

15. Sharpe, CR. A case-control study of alcohol consumption and drinking behaviour in patients with gout. *Can Med Assoc J* 1984, 131(6):563–567.

16. Gibson, T, et al. A controlled study of diet in patients with gout. *Ann Rheum Dis* 1983, 42(2):123–127.

17. Tofler, OB, and TL Woodings. A 13-year follow-up of social drinkers. *Med J Aust* 1981, 2(9):479–481.

18. Choi, HK, X Gao, and G Curhan. Vitamin C intake and the risk of gout in men: A prospective study. *Arch Intern Med* 2009, 169(5):502–507.

19. Gao, X, G Curhan, JP Forman, et al. Vitamin C intake and serum uric acid concentration in men. *J Rheumatol* 2008, 35(9):1853–1858.

20. Huang, HY, LJ Appel, MJ Choi, et al. The effects of vitamin C supplementation on serum concentrations of uric acid: Results of a randomized controlled trial. *Arthritis Rheum* 2005, 52(6):1843–1847.

Gum Disease

1. Engle, June, ed. "Eye, ear and tooth care" in *The Complete Canadian Health Guide* (Toronto: Key Porter Books, 1993):165.

2. *Brushing up on Gum Disease.* U.S. Food and Drug Administration, May 1990. Available at www.fdc.gov/bbs/topics/CONSUMER/CON0006S.html.

3. Munoz, CA, RD Kiger, JA Stephens, et al. Effects of a nutritional supplement on periodontal status. *Compend Contin Educ Dent* 2001, 22(5):425–428.

4. Requirand, P, et al. Serum fatty acid imbalance in bone loss: Example with periodontal disease. *Clin Nutr* 2000, 19(4): 271–276.

5. Reeves, AF, JM Rees, M Schiff, and P Hujoel. Total body weight and waist circumference associated with chronic periodontitis among adolescents in the United States. *Arch Pediatr Adolesc Med* 2006, 160(9):894–899.

6. Al-Zahrani, MS, NF Bissada, and EA Borawskit. Obesity and periodontal disease in young, middle-aged, and older adults. *J Periodontol* 2003, 74(5):610–615.

7. Al-Zahrani, MS, EA Borawski, and NF Bissada. Periodontitis and three health-enhancing behaviours: Maintaining normal weight, engaging in recommended level of exercise, and consuming a high-quality diet. *J Periodontol* 2005, 76(8): 1362–1366.

8. Amaliya, NI, MF Timmerman, F Abbas, et al. Java project on periodontal diseases: The relationship between vitamin C and the severity of periodontitis. *J Clin Periodontol* 2007, 34(4):299–304.

9. Staudte, H, BW Sigusch, and E Glockmann. Grapefruit consumption improves vitamin C status in periodontitis patients. *Br Dent J* 2005, 199(4):213–217.

10. Nishida, M, et al. Dietary vitamin C and the risk for periodontal disease. *J Periodontol* 2000, 71(8):1215–1223.

11. Rubinoff, AB, et al. Vitamin C and oral health. *J Can Dent Assoc* 1989, 55(9):705–707.

12. Leggott, PJ, et al. Effects of ascorbic acid depletion and supplementation on periodontal health and subgingival microflora in humans. *J Dent Res* 1991, 70(12):1531–1536.

13. Kumpusalo, EA. Periodontal health related to plasma ascorbic acid. *Proc Finn Dent Soc* 1993, 89(1–2):51–59.

14. Holmes, LG. Effects of smoking and/or vitamin C on crevicular fluid flow in clinically healthy gingival. *Quintessence Int* 1990, 21(3):191–195.

15. Leggott, PJ, PB Roberston, DL Rothman, et al. The effect of controlled ascorbic acid depletion and supplementation in periodontal health. *J Periodontol* 1986, 57(8):480–485.

16. Nishida, M, et al. Calcium and risk for periodontal disease. *J Periodontol* 2000, 71(7): 1057–1066.

17. Krall, EA, C Wehler, RI Garcia, et al. Calcium and vitamin D supplements reduce tooth loss in the elderly. *Am J Med* 2001, 111(6): 452–456.

18. Meisel, P, C Schwahn, U Luedemann, et al. Magnesium deficiency is associated with periodontal disease. *J Dent Res* 2005, 84(10): 937–941.

19. Hanioka, T, et al. Effect of topical application of coenzyme Q10 on adult periodontitis. *Mol Aspects Med* 1994, 15(Suppl):S241–S248.

20. Chandra, RV, ML Prabhuji, DA Roopa, et al. Efficacy of lycopene in the treatment of gingivitis: A randomized, placebo-controlled clinical trial. *Oral Health Prev Dent* 2007, 5(4):327–336.

Heart Disease and High Blood Cholesterol

1. Pietinen, P, A Ascherio, P Korhonen, AM Hartman, et al. Intake of fatty acids and risk of coronary heart disease in a cohort of Finnish men: The Alpha-Tocopherol, Beta-Carotene Cancer Prevention Study. *Am J Epidemiol* 1997, 145(10):876–887.

2. Ascherio, A, EB Rimm, EL Giovannucci, D Spiegelman, et al. Dietary fat intake and risk of coronary heart diseae in men: Cohort follow up study in the United States. *BMJ* 1996, 13(7049):84–90.

3. Hu, FB, MJ Stampfer, JE Manson, E Rimm, et al. Dietary fat intake and the risk of coronary heart disease in women. *N Eng J Med* 1997, 337(21):1491–1499.

4. Albert, CM, O Kyungwon, W Whang, JE Manson, et al. Dietary a-linolenic acid intake and risk of sudden cardiac death and coronary heart disease. *Circulation* 2005, 112(21):3232–3238.

5. Herron, KL, IE Lofgren, M Sharman, JS Volek, and ML Fernandez. High intake of cholesterol results in less athero-genic low-density lipoprotein particles in men and women independent of response classification. *Metabolism* 2004, 53(6):823–830.

6. Mutungi, G, J Ratliff, M Puglisi, M Torres-Gonzalez, et al. Dietary cholesterol from eggs increases plasma HDL cholesterol in overweight men consuming a carbohydrate-restricted diet. *J Nutr* 2008, 138(2):272–276.

7. Greene, CM, D Waters, RM Clark, JH Contois, and ML Fernandez. Plasma LDL and HDL characteristics and carotenoid content are positively influenced by egg consumption in an elderly population. *Nutr Metab* (Lond) 2006, 3(6):1–10.

8. Goodrow, EF, TA Wilson, SC Houde, R Vishwanathan, et al. Consumption of one egg per day increases serum lutein and zeaxanthin concentrations in older adults without altering serum lipid and lipoprotein cholesterol concentrations. *J Nutr* 2006, 136(10):2519–2524.

9. Hu, FB, MJ Stampfer, EB Rimm, JE Manson, et al. A prospective study of egg consumption and risk of cardiovas-cular disease in men and women. *JAMA* 1999, 281(15): 1387–1394.

10. Albert, CM, JM Gaziano, WC Willett, and JE Manson. Nut consumption and decreased risk of sudden cardiac death in the Physicians' Health Study. *Arch Intern Med* 2002, 162(12):1382–1387.

11. Hu, FB, MJ Stampfer, JE Manson, EB Rimm, et al. Frequent nut consumption and risk of coronary heart disease in women: Prospective cohort study. *BMJ* 1998, 317(7169): 1341–1345.

12. Ellsworth, JL, LH Kushi, and AR Folsom. Frequent nut intake and risk of death from coronary heart disease and all causes in postmenopausal women: The Iowa Women's Health Study. *Nutr Metab Cardiovasc Dis* 2001, 11(6): 372–377.

13. Fraser, GE, J Sabaté, WL Beeson, and TM Strahan. A possible protective effect of nut consumption on risk of coronary heart disease: The Adventist Health Study. *Arch Intern Med* 1992 Jul, 152(7):1416–1424.

14. Brown, L, B Rosner, WW Willett, and FM Sacks. Cholesterol-lowering effects of dietary fiber: A meta-analysis. *Am J Clin Nutr* 1999, 69(1):30–42.

15. Anderson, JW, LD Allgood, A Lawrence, LA Altringer, et al. Cholesterol-lowering effects of psyllium intake adjunctive to diet therapy in men and women with hypercholes-terolemia: Meta-analysis of 8 controlled trials. *Am J Clin Nutr* 2000, 71(2):472–479.

16. Keenan, JM, JB Wenz, S Myers, C Ripsan, and ZQ Huang. Randomized, controlled, crossover trial of oat bran in hypercholesterolemic subjects. *J Fam Prac* 1991, 33(6): 600–608.

17. Peters, U, C Poole, and L Arab. Does tea affect cardiovas-cular disease? A meta-analysis. *Am J Epidemiol* 2001, 154(6):495–503.

18. Sesso, HD, JM Gaziano, S Liu, and JE Buring. Flavonoid intake and the risk of cardiovascular disease in women. *Am J Clin Nutr* 2003, 77(6):1400–1408.

19. Geleijnse, JM, LJ Launer, DA Van der Kuip, et al. Inverse association of tea and flavonoid intakes with incident myocardial infarction: The Rotterdam Study. *Am J Clin Nutr* 2002, 75(5):880–886.

20. Mukamal, KJ, M Maclure, JE Muller, et al. Tea consumption and mortality after acute myocardial infarction. *Circulation* 2002, 105(21):2476–2481.

21. Simon, JA, et al. Serum ascorbic acid and cardiovascular disease prevalence. *Epidemiology* 1998, 9(3):316–321.

22. Lopes, C, et al. Diet and risk of myocardial infarction. A case-control community-based study. *Acta Med Port* 1998, 11(4):311–317.

23. Giovannucci, E, Y Liu, BW Hollis, and EB Rimm. 25-hydroxyvitamin D and risk of myocardial infarction in men. *Arch Intern Med* 2008, 168(11):1174–1180.

24. Lee, IM, NR Cook, JM Gaziano, D Gordon, et al. Vitamin E in the primary prevention of cardiovascular disease and cancer: The Women's Health Study: A randomized controlled trial. *JAMA* 2005, 294(1):56–65.

25. Yusuf, S, G Dagenais, J Pogue, J Bosch, and P Sleight. Vitamin E supplementation and cardiovascular events in high-risk patients. The Heart Outcomes Prevention Evaluation Study Investigators. *N Engl J Med* 2000, 342(3):154–160.

26. Gruppo Italiano per lo Studio della Sopravvivenza nell'Infarto miocardico. Dietary supplementation with n-3 polyunsaturated fatty acids and vitamin E after myocardial infarction: Results of the GISSI-Prevenzione trial. *Lancet* 1999, 354(9177):447–455.

27. Lonn, E, J Bosch, S Yusuf, P Sheridan, J Pogue, JM Arnold, C Ross, A Arnold, P Sleight, J Probstfield, GR Dagenais; HOPE and HOPE-TOO Trial Investigators. Effects of long-term vitamin E supplementation on cardiovascular events and cancer: A randomized controlled trial. *JAMA* 2005, 293(11):1338–1347.

28. Miller 3rd, ER, R Pastor-Barriuso, D Dalal, RA Riemersma, et al. Meta-analysis: High-dosage vitamin E supplementa-tion may increase all-cause mortality. *Ann Intern Med* 2005, 142(1):37–46.

29. Lopez-Ridaura, R, WC Willett, EB Rimm, S Liu, et al. Magnesium intake and risk of type 2 diabetes in men and women. *Diabetes Care* 2004, 27(1):134–140.

30. Meyer, KA, LH Kishi, DR Jacobs Jr., J Slavin, et al. Carbohydrates, dietary fiber, and incident type 2 diabetes in older women. *Am J Clin Nutr* 1999, 71(4):921–30.

31. Song, V, JE Manson, JE Buring, and S Liu. Dietary magne-sium intake in relation to plasma insulin levels and risk of type 2 diabetes in women. *Diabetes Care* 2003, 27(1):59–65.

32. Larsson, SC, and A Wolk. Magnesium intake and risk of type 2 diabetes: A meta-analysis. *J Intern Med* 2007, 262(2): 208–214.

33. Rodriguez-Moran, M, and F Guerrero-Romero. Oral magne-sium supplementation improves insulin sensitivity and

metabolic control in type 2 diabetic subjects. *Diabetes Care* 2003, 26(4):1147–1152.

34. Shechter, M, CN Bairey Merz, HG Stuehlinger, et al. Effects of oral magnesium therapy on exercise tolerance, exercise-induced chest pain, and quality of life in patients with coronary artery disease. *Am J Cardiol* 2003, 91(5):517–521.

35. Tran, MT, TM Mitchell, DT Kennedy, and JT Giles. Role of coenzyme Q10 in chronic heart failure, angina, and hypertension. *Pharmacotherapy* 2001, 21(7):797–806.

36. Singh, RB, MA Niaz, SS Rastogi, PK Shukla, and AS Thakur. Effect of hydrosoluble coenzyme Q10 on blood pressures and insulin resistance in hypertensive patients with coronary artery disease. *J Hum Hypertens* 1999, 13(3): 203–208.

37. Burke, BE, R Neuenschwander, and RD Olson. Randomized, double-blind, placebo-controlled trial of coenzyme Q10 in isolated systolic hypertension. *South Med J* 2001, 94(11): 1112–1117.

38. Watts, GF, DA Playford, KD Croft, NC Ward, et al. Coenzyme Q(10) improves endothelial dysfunction of the brachial artery in Type II diabetes mellitus. *Diabetologia* 2002, 45(3):420–426.

39. Hill, AM, JD Buckley, KJ Murphy, and PR Howe. Combining fish-oil supplements with regular aerobic exercise improves body composition and cardiovascular disease risk factors. *Am J Clin Nutr* 2007, 85(5):1267–1274.

40. Wang, C, WS Harris, M Chung, AH Lichtenstein, et al. N-3 Fatty acids from fish or fish-oil supplements, but not alpha-linolenic acid, benefit cardiovascular disease outcomes in primary- and secondary-prevention studies: A systematic review. *Am J Clin Nutr* 2006, 84(1):5–17.

41. Becker, DJ, RY Gordon, PB Morris, et al. Simvastatin vs therapeutic lifestyle changes and supplements: Randomized primary prevention trial. *Mayo Clin Proc* 2008, 83(7): 758–764.

42. Liu, J, J Zhang, Y Shi, et al. Chinese red yeast rice (Monascus purpureus) for primary hyperlipidemia: A meta-analysis of randomized controlled trials. *Chin Med* 2006 Nov 23, 1:4.

Hemorrhoids

1. Alonso-Coelle, P, E Mills, D Heels-Ansdell, et al. Fiber for the treatment of hemorrhoids complications: A systematic review and meta-analysis. *Am J Gastroenterol* 2006, 101(1): 181–188.

2. Perez-Miranda, M, et al. Effect of fiber supplements on internal bleeding hemorrhoids. *Hepatogastroenterology* 1996, 43(12):1504–1507.

3. Andersson, H, et al. Colonic transit after fibre supplementation in patients with haemorrhoids. *Hum Nutr Appl Nutr* 1985, 39(2): 101–107.

4. Gupta, PJ. Red hot chilli consumption is harmful in patients operated for anal fissure: A randomized, double-blind, controlled study. *Dig Surg* 2007, 24(5):354–357.

5. Gupta, PJ. Effect of red chili consumption on postoperative symptoms during the post-hemorrhoidectomy period: Randomized, double-blind, controlled study. *World J Surg* 2007, 31(9):1822–1826.

6. Jiang, ZM, and JD Cao. The impact of micronized purified flavonoids fraction on the treatment of acute haemorrhoidal espisodes. *Curr Med Res Opin* 2006, 22(6):1141–1147.

7. Alonso-Coello, P, Q Zhou, MJ Martinez-Zapata, et al. Meta-analysis of flavonoids for the treatment of haemorrhoids. *Br J Surg* 2006, 93(8):909–920.

8. Dimitroulopoulos, D, K Tsamakidis, D Xinopoulos, et al. Prospective, randomized, controlled, observer-blinded trial of combined infrared photocoagulation and micronized purified flavonoids fraction versus each alone for the treatment of hemorrhoidal disease. *Clin Ther* 2005, 27(6): 746–754.

9. Misra, MC, and R Parshad. Randomized clinical trial of micronized flavonoids in the early control of bleeding from acute internal hemorrhoids. *Br J Surg* 2000, 87(7):868–872.

10. Ho, YH, et al. Micronized purified flavonidic fraction compared favorably with rubber band ligation and fibre alone in the management of bleeding hemorrhoids. *Dis Colon Rectum* 2000, 43(1):66–69.

11. Ho, YH, et al. Prospective randomized controlled trial of a micronized flavonidic fraction in reduced bleeding after haemorrhoidectomy. *Br J Surg* 1995, 82(8):1034–1035.

Hepatitis

1. *Hepatitis B.* American Liver Foundation, September 2007. Available at www.liverfoundation.org/education/info/hepatitisb/.

2. Ibid.

3. *Hepatitis C—Quick Facts.* The Public Health Agency of Canada, 2009. Available at www.phac-aspc.gc.ca/hepc/index-eng.php.

4. Imai, K, and K Nakachi. Cross sectional study of effects of drinking green tea on cardiovascular and liver disease. *Br Med J* 1995, 310(6981):693–696.

5. Wada, S, et al. Suppression of D-galactosamine-induced rat liver injury by glycosidic flavonoids-rich fraction from green tea. *Biosc Biotechnol Biochem* 1999, 63(3):570–572.

6. Xu, J, J Wang, F Deng, et al. Green tea extract and its major component, epigallocatechin gallate inhibits heptatis B virus in vitro. *Ativiral Res* 2008, 78(3):242–249.

7. Watanabe, A, K Okada, Y Shimizu, et al. Nutritional therapy of chronic hepatitis by whey protein (non-heated). *J Med* 2000, 31(5–6):283–302.

8. Medina, J, and R Moreno-Otero. Pathophysiological basis for antioxidant therapy in chronic liver disease. *Drugs* 2005, 65(17):2445–2461.

9. Loguercio, C, and A Federico. Oxidative stress in viral and alcoholic hepatitis. *Free Rad Biol Med* 2003, 34(1):1–10.

10. Beck, MA, and OA Levander. Dietary oxidative stress and the potentiation of viral infection. *Annu Rev Nutr* 1998, 18(8):93–116.

11. Yamamoto, Y, et al. Oxidative stress in patients with hepatitis, cirrhosis, and hepoma evaluated by plasma antioxidants. *Biochem Biophys Res Commun* 1998, 247(1): 116–170.

12. Andreone, P, S Fiorino, C Cursaro, et al. Vitamin E as a treatment for chronic hepatitis B: Results of a randomized controlled pilot trial. *Antiviral Red* 2001, 49(2):75–81.

13. Yu, SY, et al. Protective role of selenium against hepatitis B virus and primary liver cancer. *Biol Trace Elem Res* 1997, 56(1):117–124.

14. Look, MP, et al. Interferon/antioxidant combination therapy from chronic hepatitis C: A controlled pilot trial. *Antiviral Res* 1999, 43(2):113–122.

15. Berkson, BM. A conservative triple antioxidant approach to the treatment of hepatitis C: Combination of alpha lipoic acid (thioctic acid), silymarin, and selenium: Three case histories. *Med Klin* 1999, 94(22)(Suppl 3):S84–S89.

16. Kimura, F, H Hayashi, M Yano, et al. Additional effect of low iron diet on iron reduction therapy phlebotomy for chronic hepatitis C. *Hepatogastroenterology* 2005, 52(62):563–566.

17. Berenguer, J, and D Carrasco. Double-blind trial of silymarin vs. placebo in the treatment of chronic hepatitis. *Munch Med Wochenschr* 1977, 119:240–260.

18. Buzzelli, G, et al. A pilot study on the liver protective effect of silybin-phosphatidylcholine complex (IdB 1016) in chronic active hepatitis. *Int J Clin Pharmacol Ther Toxicol* 1993, 31:456–460.

19. Barbieri, B, et al. Coenzyme Q10 administration increases antibody titer in hepatitis B vaccinated volunteers: A single blind placebo-controlled and randomized clinical study. *Biofactors* 1999, 9(2–4):351–357.

20. Yamamoto, Y, et al. Plasma ratio ubiquinol and ubiquinone as a marker of oxidative stress. *Mol Aspects Med* 1997, 18(6)(Suppl): S79–S84.

21. Niederau, C, G Strohmeyer, T Heintges, et al. Polyunsaturated phosphatidyl-choline and interferon alpha for treatment of chronic hepatitis B and C: A multi-center, randomized, double-blind, placebo-controlled trial. *Hepatogastroenterology* 1998, 45(21):797–804.

Herpes (Cold Sores and Genital Herpes)
1. Mostad, SB, et al. Cervical shedding of herpes simplex virus in human immunodeficiency virus-infected women: Effects of hormonal contraception, pregnancy, and vitamin A deficiency. *J Infect Dis* 2000, 181(1):58–63.

2. Terezhalmy, GT, et al. The use of water-soluble bioflavonoid-ascorbic acid complex in the treatment of recurrent herpes labialis. *Oral Surg Oral Med Oral Pathol* 1978, 45:56–62.

3. Syed, TA, et al. Management of genital herpes in men with 0.5% Aloe vera extract in a hydrophilic cream: A placebo-controlled, double-blind study. *J Dermatol Treat* 1997, 8:99–102.

4. Geuenich, S, C Goffinet, S Venzke, et al. Aqueous extracts from peppermint, sage, and lemon balm leaves display potent anti-HVP-1 activity by increasing virion density. *Retrovirology* 2008 Mar 20, 5:27.

5. Koytchev, R, et al. Balm mint extract (Lo-701) for topical treatment of recurring herpes labialis. *Phytomedicine* 1999, 6(4):225–230.

6. Wobling, R, and L Leonhardt. Local therapy of herpes simplex virus with dried extract from Melissa officinalis. *Phytomedicine* 1994, 1(1): 25–31.

7. Dimitrova, Z, et al. Antiherpes effect of Melissa officinalis L. extracts. *Acta Microbiol Bulg* 1993, 29:65–72.

8. Williams, M. Immuno-protection against herpes simplex type II infection by eleutherococcus root extract. *Int J Alt Complement Med* 1995, 13:9–12.

9. McCune, MA, et al. Treatment of recurrent herpes simplex infections with L-lysine monohydrochloride. *Cutis* 1984, 34(4):366–373.

10. Griffith, RS, et al. Success of L-lysine therapy in frequently recurrent simplex infection. Treatment and prophylaxis. *Dermatologica* 1987, 175(4):183–190.

11. Walsh, DE, et al. Subjective response to lysine in therapy of herpes simplex. *J Antimicrob Chemother* 1983, 12(5): 489–496.

Hiatal Hernia
1. Engle, June, ed. "Some specific diseases and disorders" in *The Complete Canadian Health Guide* (Toronto: Key Porter Books, 1993):476.

2. Dutta, SK, M Arora, A Kireet, et al. Upper gastrointestinal symptoms and associated disorders in morbidly obese patients: A prospective study. *Dig Dis Sci* 2009, 54(6): 1243–1246.

3. Lee, HL, CS Eun, OY Lee, et al. Association between GERD-related erosive esophagitis and obesity. *J Clin Gastroenterol* 2008, 42(6):672–675.

4. Wilson, LJ, et al. Association of obesity with hiatal hernia and esophagitis. *Am J Gastroenterol* 1999, 94(10): 2840–2844.

5. Ruhl, CE, and JE Everhart. Overweight, but not high dietary fat intake, increases risk of gastroesophageal reflux disease hospitalization: The NHANES I Epidemiologic Followup Study. First National Health and Nutrition Examination Survey. *Ann Epidemiol* 1999, 9(7):424–435.

6. Stene-Larsen, G, et al. Relationship of overweight to hiatus hernia and reflux oesophagitis. *Scand J Gastroenterol* 1988, 23(4):427–432.

7. Pauwelyn, KA, and M Verhamme. Large hiatal hernia and iron deficiency anaemia: Clinico-endoscopical findings. *Act Clin Belg* 2005, 60(4):166–172.

8. Panzuto, F, E Di Giulio, G Capurso, et al. Large hiatal hernia in patients with iron deficiency anaemia: A prospective study on prevalence and treatment. *Aliment Pharmacol Ther* 2004, 19(6):663–670.

9. Ruhl, CE, and JE Everhart. Relationship of iron-deficiency anemia with esophagitis and hiatal hernia: Hospital findings from a prospective, population-based study. *Am J Gastroenerol* 2001, 96(2):322–326.

10. Moskovitz, M, et al. Large hiatal hernias, anemias, and linear gastric erosion: Studies of etiology and medical therapy. *Am J Gastroenterol* 1992, 87(5):622–626.

High Blood Pressure (Hypertension)
1. Tu, K, C Zhongliang, and LL Lipscombe. Prevalence and incidence of hypertension from 1995 to 2005: A population-based study. *CMAJ* 2008, 178(11):1429–1435.

2. Mertens, IL, and LF Van Gaal. Overweight, obesity and blood pressure: The effects of modest weight reduction. *Obes Res* 2000, 8(3):270–278.

3. Ascherio, A, et al. Prospective study of nutritional factors, blood pressure and hypertension among U.S. women. *Hypertension* 1996, 27(5):1065–1072.

4. Yamori, Y, et al. Nutritional factors for stroke and major cardiovascular diseases: International epidemiological comparison on dietary prevention. *Health Rep* 1004, 6(1):22–27.

5. Mulrow, CD, et al. Dieting to reduce body weight for controlling hypertension in adults. *Cochrane Database Syst Rev* 2000, 23(2): CD000484.

6. Appel, LJ, TJ Moore, E Obarzanek, WM Vollmer, et al. A clinical trial of the effects of dietary patterns on blood pressure. DASH Collaborative Research Group. *N Engl J Med* 1997, 336(16):1117–1124.

7. Sacks, FM, LP Svetkey, WM Vollmer, LJ Appel, GA Bray, D Harsha, E Obarzanek, PR Conlin, ER Miller 3rd, DG Simons-Morton, N Karanja, PH Lin, DASH-Sodium Collaborative Research Group. Effects on blood pressure of reduced dietary sodium and the Dietary Approaches to Stop Hypertension (DASH) diet. DASH-Sodium Collaborative Research Group. *N Engl J Med* 2001, 344(1): 3–10.

8. Resnick, LM, et al. Factors affecting blood pressure responses to diet: The Vanguard study. *Am J Hypertens* 2000, 13(9):956–965.

9. Mori, TA, et al. Dietary fish as a major component of a weight-loss diet: Effect on serum lipids, glucose, and insulin metabolism in overweight hypertensive subjects. *Am J Clin Nutr* 1999, 70(5):817–825.

10. Bao, DQ, et al. Effects of dietary fish and weight reduction on ambulatory blood pressure in overweight hypertensives. *Hypertension* 1998, 32(4):710–717.

11. Pauletto, P, et al. Blood pressure and atherogenic lipoprotein profiles of fish-diet and vegetarian villagers in Tanzania: The Lugalawa Study. *Lancet* 1996, 348(9030):784–788.

12. Nakanishi, N, et al. Association of alcohol consumption with increase in aortic stiffness: A 9-year longitudinal study in middle-aged Japanese men. *Ind Health* 2001, 39(1): 24–28.

13. Nanchahal, K, et al. Alcohol consumption, metabolic cardiovascular risk factors and hypertension in women. *Int J Epidemiol* 2000, 29(1):57–64.

14. Tsuruta, M, et al. Association between alcohol intake and development of hypertension in Japanese normotensive men: 12-year follow-up study. *Am J Hypertens* 2000, 13(5 Pt 1):482–487.

15. Sung, BH, et al. Caffeine elevates blood pressure response to exercise in mild hypertensive men. *Am J Hypertens* 1995, 8(12 Pt 1):1184–1188.

16. Lovallo, WR, et al. Caffeine and behavioural stress effects on blood pressure in borderline hypertensive Caucasian men. *Health Psychol* 1996, 15(1):11–17.

17. Rakic, V, et al. Effects of coffee on ambulatory blood pressure in older men and women: A randomized controlled trial. *Hypertension* 1999, 33(3):869–873.

18. Rachima-Maoz, C, et al. The effect of caffeine on ambulatory blood pressure in hypertensive patients. *Am J Hypertens* 1998, 11(12):1426– 1432.

19. Carr, A, and B Frei. The role of natural antioxidants in preserving the biological activity of endothelium-derived nitric oxide. *Free Radic Biol Med* 2000, 28(12):1806–1814.

20. Frei, B. On the role of vitamin C and other antioxidants in atherogenesis and vascular dysfunction. *Proc Soc Exp Biol Med* 1999, 222(3):196–204.

21. Galley, HF, et al. Combination oral antioxidant supplementation reduces blood pressure. *Clin Sci (Colch)* 1997, 92(4):361–365.

22. Duffy, SJ, N Gokce, M Holbrook, et al. Treatment of hypertension with ascorbic acid. *Lancet* 1999, 354(9195): 2048–2049.

23. Mullan, BA, IS Young, H Fee, and DR McCance. Ascorbic acid reduces blood pressure and arterial stiffness in type 2 diabetes. *Hypertension* 2002, 40(6):804–809.

24. Ward, NC, JM Hodgson, KD Croft, et al. The combination of vitamin C and grapeseed polyphenols increases blood pressure: A randomized, double-blind, placebo-controlled trial. *J Hypertens* 2005, 23(2):427–434.

25. Block, G, AR Mangels, EP Norkus, et al. Ascorbic acid status and subsequent diastolic and systolic blood pressure. *Hypertension* 2001, 37(2):261–267.

26. Allender, PS, et al. Dietary calcium and blood pressure: A meta-analysis of randomized clinical trials. *Ann Intern Med* 1996, 124:825–831.

27. Bucher, HC, et al. Effects of dietary calcium supplementation on blood pressure: A meta-analysis of randomized controlled trials. *J Am Med Assoc* 1996, 275:1016–1022.

28 Ma, J, et al. Associations of serum and dietary magnesium with cardiovascular disease, hypertension, diabetes, insulin, and carotoid arterial wall thickness: The AIRC Study. *J Clin Epidemiol* 1995, 48(7):927–940.

29. Laurant, P, and RM Touyz. Physiological and pathophysiological role of magnesium in the cardiovascular system: Implications in hypertension. *J Hypertens* 2000, 18(9): 1177–1191.

30. Sacks, FM, et al. Combinations of potassium, calcium and magnesium supplements in hypertension. *Hypertension* 1995, 26(6 Pt 1):950–956.

31. Krishna, GG. Role of potassium in the pathogenesis of hypertension. *Am J Med Sci* 1994, 307(2)(Suppl 1): S21–S25.

32. Whelton, PK, et al. Effects of oral potassium on blood pressure: Meta-analysis of randomized controlled clinical trials. *JAMA* 1997, 277(20):1624–1632.

33. Barri, Y, and CS Wingo. The effects of potassium depletion and supplementation on blood pressure: A review. *Am J Med Sci* 1997, 314(1):37–40.

34. Silagy, CA, and HA Neil. A meta-analysis of the effect of garlic on high blood pressure. *J Hypertens* 1994, 12(4): 463–468.

35. McMahon, FG, and R Vargas. Can garlic lower blood pressure? A pilot study. *Pharmacotherapy* 1993, 13(4): 406–407.

36. Steiner, M, et al. A double-blind crossover study in moderately hypercholesterolemic men that compared the effect of aged garlic extract and placebo administration on blood lipids. *Am J Clin Nutr* 1996, 64(6):866–870.

37. Langsjoen, P, P Langsjoen, R Willis, and K Folkers. Treatment of essential hypertension with coenzyme Q10. *Mol Aspects Med* 1994, Vol 15 Suppl:S265–72.

38. Singh, RB, MA Niaz, SS Rastogi, et al. Effect of hydrosoluble coenzyme Q10 on blood pressures and insulin resistance in hypertensive patients with coronary artery disease. *J Hum Hypertens* 1999, 13(3):203–208.

39. Hodgson, JM, GF Watts, DA Playford, et al. Coenzyme Q10 improves blood pressure and glycaemic control: A controlled trial in subjects with type 2 diabetes. *Eur J Clin Nutr* 2002, 56(11):1137–1142.

40. Yosefy, C, JR Viskoper, A Laszt, et al. The effect of fish oil on hypertension, plasma lipids and hemostasis in hypertensive, obese, dyslipidemic patients with and without diabetes

mellitus. *Prostaglandins Leukot Essent Fatty Acids* 1999, 61(2):83–87.

41. Toft, I, KH Bonaa, OC Ingebretsen, et al. Effects of n-3 polyunsaturated fatty acids on glucose homeostasis and blood pressure in essential hypertension: A randomized, controlled trial. *Ann Intern Med* 1995, 123(12): 911–918.

42. Prisco, D, R Paniccia, B Bandinelli, et al. Effect of medium-term supplementation with a moderate dose on n-3 polyunsaturated fatty acids on blood pressure in milk hypertensive patients. *Thromb Res* 1998, 91(3):105–112.

43. Yosevy, C, et al. Repeated fasting and refeeding with 20:5, n-3 eicosapentanoic acid (EPA): A novel approach for rapid fatty acid exchange and its effect on blood pressure. *J Hum Hypertens* 1996, 10(2)(Suppl 3):S135–S139.

Hyperthyroidism (Graves' Disease)

1. *A Major Women's Health Issue.* American Autoimmune Related Diseases Association, Inc., 2001. Available at www.aarda.org/women_health_art.html.

2. *Graves' Disease.* The Thyroid Foundation of Canada, April 23, 2007. Available at www.thyroid.ca/Guides/HG06.html.

3. Yoshiuchi, K, et al. Stressful life events and smoking were associated with Graves' disease in women, but not in men. *Psychosom Med* 1998, 60(2):182–185.

4. Brunova, J, J Bruna, G Joubert, and M Koning. Weight gain in patients after therapy for hyperthyroidism. *S Afr Med J* 2003, 93(7):529–531.

5. Dale, J, J Daykin, R Holder, et al. Weight gain following treatment of hyperthyroidism. *Clin Endocrinol* 2001, 55(2): 233–239.

6. Jansson, S, et al. Overweight: A common problem among women treated for hyperthyroidism. *Postgrad Med* 1993, 69(808):107–111.

7. Abid, M, et al. Thyroid function and energy intake during weight gain following treatment of hyperthyroidism. *J Am Coll Nutr* 1999, 18(2):189–193.

8. Duntas, LH. Oxidants, antioxidants in physical exercise and relation to thyroid function. *Horm Metab Red* 2005, 37(9): 572–576.

9. Guerra, LN, C Rios de Molina Mdel, EA Miler, et al. Antioxidants and methimazole in the treatment of Graves' disease: Effect on urinary malondialdehyde levels. *Clin Chim Acta* 2005, 352(1–2):115–120.

10. Bianchi, G, et al. Oxidative stress and anti-oxidant metabolites in patients with hyperthyroidism: Effect of treatment. *Horm Metab Res* 1999, 31(11):620–624.

11. Costantini, F, et al. Effect of thyroid function on LDL oxidation. *Artherioscler Thromb Vasc Biol* 1998, 18(5):732–737.

12. Goswami, UC, and S Choudhury. The status of retinoids in women suffering from hyper- and hypothyroidism: Interrelationship between vitamin A, beta-carotene and thyroid hormones. *Int J Vitam Nutr Res* 1999, 69(2): 132–135.

13. Mano, T, et al. Vitamin E and coenzyme Q10 concentrations in the thyroid of patients with various thyroid disorders. *Am J Med Sci* 1998, 315(4):230–232.

14. Seven, A, et al. Biochemical evaluation of oxidative stress in propylthiouricil treated hyperthyroid patients: Effect of vitamin C supplementation. *Clin Chem Lab Met* 1998, 36(10):767–770.

15. Vrca, VB, F Skreb, I Cepelak, et al. Supplementation with antioxidants in the treatment of Graves' disease: the effect on glutathione peroxidase activity and concentration of selenium. *Clin Chim Acta* 2004, 341(1–2):55–63.

16. Bacic-Vrca, V, F Skreb, I Cepelak, et al. The effect of antioxidant supplementation on superoxide dismultase activity, Cu and Zn levels, and total antioxidant status in erythrocytes of patients with Graves' disease. *Clin Chem Lab Med* 2005, 43(4):383–388.

17. Uzzan, B, et al. Effects on bone mass of long term treatment with thyroid hormones: A meta-analysis. *J Clin Endocrinol Metab* 1996, 81(12):4278–4289.

18. Yamashita, H, et al. Seasonal changes in calcium homeostasis affect the incidence of postoperative tetany in patients with Graves' disease. *Surgery* 2000, 127(4): 377–382.

19. Solomon, BL, et al. Remission rates with antithyroid drug therapy: Continuing influence of iodine intake? *Ann Intern Med* 1987, 107(4):510–512.

Hypoglycemia

1. Giacco, R, M Parillo, AA Rivellese, et al. Long-term dietary treatment with increased amounts of fibre-rich low-glycemic index natural foods improves blood glucose control and reduces the number of hypoglycemic events in type 1 diabetic patients. *Diabetes Care* 2000, 23(10):1461–1466.

2. Kerr, D, et al. Effect of caffeine on the recognition of and response to hypoglycemia in humans. *Ann Intern Med* 1993, 119(8):799–804.

3. Anderson, RA, et al. Effects of supplemental chromium on patients with symptoms of reactive hypoglycemia. *Metabolism* 1987, 36(4):351–355.

4. Clausen, J. Chromium induced clinical improvement in symptomatic hypoglycemia. *Biol Trace Elem Res* 1988, 17:229–236.

Hypothyroidism

1. *Hypothyroidism.* The Thyroid Foundation of Canada, April 23, 2007. Available at www.thyroid.ca/Guides/HG03.html.

2. Faughnan, M, et al. Screening for thyroid disease at the menopausal clinic. *Clin Invest Med* 1995, 18(1):11–18.

3. Rodondi, N, D Aujesky, E Vittinghoff, et al. Subclinical hypothyroidism and the risk of coronary heart disease: A meta-analysis. *Am J Med* 2006, 119(7):541–551.

4. Pearce, EN. Hypothyroidism and dyslipidemia: Modern concepts and approaches. *Curr Cardiol Rep* 2004, 6(6): 451–456.

5. Pucci, E, et al. Thyroid and lipid metabolism. *Int J Obes Relat Metab Disord* 2000, (Suppl 2): S109–S112.

6. Vierhapper, H, et al. Low-density lipoprotein cholesterol in subclinical hypothyroidism. *Thyroid* 2000, 10(11):981–984.

7. Hak, AE, et al. Subclinical hypothyroidism is an independent risk factor for atherosclerosis and myocardial infarction in elderly women: The Rotterdam Study. *Ann Intern Med* 2000, 132(4):270–278.

8. Bindels, AJ, et al. The prevalence of subclinical hypothyroidism at different total plasma cholesterol levels in middle aged men and women: A need for case-finding? *Clin Endocrinol* 1999, 50(2):217–220.

9. Becerra, A, et al. Lipoprotein(a) and other lipoproteins in hypothyroid patients before and after thyroid replacement therapy. *Clin Nutr* 1999, 18(5):319–322.

10. Oage, A, E Sozmen, and AO Karaoglu. Effect of thyroid function on LDL oxidation in hypothyroidism and hyper-thyroidism. *Endocr Res* 2004, 39(3):481–489.

11. Diekman, T, et al. Increased oxidizability of low-density lipoproteins in hypothyroidism. *J Clin Endocrinol Metab* 1998, 83(5):1752– 1755.

12. Costantini, F, et al. The effect of thyroid function on LDL oxidation. *Arteriosclero Thromb Vasc Biol* 1998, 18(5): 732–737.

13. Teas, J, LE Braverman, MS Kurzer, et al. Seaweed and soy: Companion foods in Asian cusine and their effects on thyroid function in American women. *J Med Food* 2007, 10(1):90–100.

14. Bruce, B, M Messina, and GA Spiller. Isoflavone supple-ments do not affect thyroid function in iodine-replete postmenopausal women. *J Med Fod* 2003, 6(4):309–316.

15. Messina, M, and G Redmond. Effects of soy protein and soybean isoflavones on thyroid function in healthy adults and hypothyroid patients: A review of the relevant litera-ture. *Thyroid* 2006, 16(3):249–258.

16. Ozmen, B, D Ozmen, Z Parlidar, et al. Impact of renal function or folate status on altered plasma homocysteine levels in hypothyroidism. *Endocrin J* 2006, 53(10:119–124.

17. Diekman, MJ, NM van der Put, HJ Blom, et al. Determinants of changes in plasma homocysteine in hyperthyroidism and hypothyroidism. *Clin Endocrinol* (Oxford) 2001, 54(2): 197–204.

18. Nedrebo, BG, et al. Plasma total homocysteine levels in hyperthyroid and hypothyroid patients. *Metabolism* 1998, 47(1):89–93.

19. Tajiri, J, et al. Studies of hypothyroidism in patients with high iodine intake. *J Clin Endocrinol Metab* 1986, 63(2): 412–417.

20. Olivieri, O, et al. Low selenium status in the elderly influ-ences thyroid hormones. *Clin Sci (Colch)* 1995, 89(6): 637–642.

21. Rayman, MP, AJ Thompson, B Bekaert, et al. Randomized controlled trial of the effect of selenium supplementation on thyroid function in the elderly in the United Kingdon. *Am J Clin Nutr* 2008, 87(2):370–378.

22. Negro, R, G Greco, T Mangieri, et al. The influence of selenium supplementation on postpartum thyroid status in pregnant women with thyroid peroxidase autoantibodies. *J Clin Endocrinol Metab* 2007, 92(4):1263–1268.

23. Gartner, R, BC Gasnier, JW Dietrich, et al. Selenium supple-mentation in patients with autoimmune thyroidosis decreases thyroid peroxidase antibodies concentrations. *J Clin Endocrinol Metab* 2002, 87(4):1687–1691.

24. Shakir, KM, et al. Ferrous sulfate-induced increase in requirement for thyroxine in a patient with primary hypothyroidism. *South Med J* 1997, 90(6):637–639.

25. Campbell, NR, et al. Ferrous sulfate reduces thyroxine efficacy in patients with hypothyroidism. *Ann Intern Med* 1992, 117(12):1010–1013.

Impotence (Erectile Dysfunction)

1. *Impotence.* National Kidney and Urologic Diseases Information Clearinghouse, September 1995. Available at www.health/urology/pubs/impotence/ impotence.htm.

2. *Erectile Dysfunction: Learning the Causes and What You Can Do.* The College of Family Physicians of Canada, 2007. Available at www.cfpc.ca/English/cfpc/programs/patient%20 education/erectile%20dysfunction/default.asp?s=1.

3. *Erectile Dysfunction.* National Kidney and Urologic Diseases Information Clearinghouse, December 2005. Available at www.kidney.niddk.nih.gov/kudiseases/pubs/ impotence/index.htm.

4. *What Should I Know about Impotence?* Canadian Health Network, May 1999. Available at www.canadian-health-network.ca/faq-faq/men-hommes/9e.html.

5. *Impotence.* National Kidney and Urologic Diseases Information Clearinghouse, September 1995. Available at www.health/urology/pubs/impotence/impotence.htm.

6. Feldman, HA, et al. Erectile dysfunction and coronary risk factors: Prospective results from the Massachusetts Male Aging Study. *Prev Med* 2000, 30(4):328–338.

7. Larsen, SH, G Wagner, and BL Heitmann. Sexual function and obesity. *Int J Obes* 2007, 31(8):1189–1198.

8. Hammoud, AO, M Gibson, CM Peterson, et al. Obesity and male reproductive potential. *J Androl* 2006, 27(5):619–626.

9. Derby, CA, et al. Modifiable risk factors and erectile dysfunction: Can lifestyle changes modify risk? *Urology* 2000, 56(2):302–306.

10. Feldman, HA, et al. Erectile dysfunction and coronary risk factors: Prospective results from the Massachusetts Male Aging Study. *Prev Med* 2000, 30(4):328–338.

11. Esposito, K, M Ciotola, F Giugliano, et al. Mediterranean diet improves erectile function in subjects with the metabolic syndrome. *Int J Impot Res* 2006, 18(4):405–410.

12. Cakan, M, F Demierl, M Aldemir, and U Altug. Does smoking change the efficacy of combination therapy with vitamin E and colchines in patients with early-stage Peyronie's disease? *Arch Androl* 2006, 52(1):21–27.

13. Inal, T, Z Tokatli, M Akand, et al. Effect of intralesional interferon-alpha 2b combined with oral vitamin E for treat-ment of early stage Peyronie's disease: A randomized and prospective study. *Urology* 2006, 67(5):1038–1042.

14. Khedun, SM, et al. Zinc, hydrochlorothiazide and sexual dysfunction. *Cent Afr J Med* 1995, 41(10):312–315.

15. Sikora, R, et al. Ginkgo biloba extract in the therapy of erectile dysfunction. *J Urol* 1989, 142:188A.

16. Cohen, AJ, and B Bartlik. Ginkgo biloba for antidepressant-induced sexual dysfunction. *J Sex Marital Ther* 1998, 24(2):139–143.

17. Kang, BJ, SJ Lee, MD Kim, and MJ Cho. A placebo-controlled, double blind trial of Ginkgo biloba for antidepressant-induced sexual dysfunction. *Hum Psychopharmacol* 2002, 17(6):279–284.

18. de Andrade, E, AA de Mesquita, J De Almeida Claro, et al. Study of the efficacy of Korean Red Ginseng in the treatment of erectile dysfunction. *Asian J Androl* 2007, 9(2):241–244.

19. Hong, B, YH Ji, JH Hong, et al. A double-blind crossover study evaluating the efficacy of Korean red ginseng in

patients with erectile dysfunction: A preliminary report. *J Urol* 2002, 168(5):2070–2073.

20.   Choi, HK, DH Seong, and KH Rha. Clinical efficacy of Korean red ginseng for erectile dysfunction. *Int J Impot Res* 1995, 7(3):181–186.

21.   Reiter, WJ, et al. Serum dehydroepiandrosterone sulfate concentrations in men with erectile dysfunction. *Urology* 2000, 55(5):755–758.

22.   Reiter, WJ, et al. Dehydroepiandrosterone in the treatment of erectile dysfunction: A prospective, double blind, randomized, placebo-controlled study. *Urology* 1999, 53: 590–595.

23.   Reiter, WJ, G Schatzl, I Mark, et al. Dehydroepiandros-terone in the treatment of erectile dysfunction in patients with different etiologies. *Urol Res* 2001, 29(4):278–281.

24.   Stanislavov, R, and V Nikolova. Treatment of erectile dysfunction with pycnogenol and L-arginine. *J Sex Marital Ther* 2003, 29(3):207–213.

25.   Lebret, T, JM Herve, P Gorny, et al. Efficacy and safety of a novel combination of L-arginine glutamate and yohimbe hydrochloride: A new oral therapy for erectile dysfunction. *Eur Urol* 2002, 41(6):608–613.

26.   Chen, J, et al. Effect of oral administration of high-dose nitric oxide donor L-arginine in men with organic erectile dysfunction: Results of a double blind, randomized placebo-controlled study. *BJU Int* 1999, 83:269–273.

Infertility

1.   Stoppard, Miriam, M.D., and Catherine Younger-Lewis M.D., eds. "Infertility" in *Woman's Body* (Westmount, QC: The Reader's Digest Association [Canada] Ltd., 1995):162.

2.   Hammoud, AO, M Gibson, CM Peterson, et al. Obesity and male reproductive potential. *J Androl* 2006, 27(5):619–626.

3.   Forges, T, P Monneir-Barbarino, JM Alberto, et al. Impact of folate and homocysteine metabolism on human reproduc-tive health. *Hum Reprod Update* 2007, 13(3):225–238.

4.   Gulden, KD. Pernicious anemia, vitiligo and infertility. *J Am Board Fam Pract* 1990, 3(3):217–220.

5.   Sanfilippo, JS, and YK Liu. Vitamin B12 deficiency and infertility: A case report. *Int J Fertil* 1991, 36(1):36–38.

6.   Kumamoto, Y, et al. Clinical efficacy of mecobalamin in treatment of oligozoospermia: Results of a double-blind comparative clinical study. *Acta Urol Jpn* 1998, 34: 1109–1132.

7.   Song, GJ, EP Norkus, and V Lewis. Relationship between seminal ascorbic acid and sperm DNA integrity in infertile men. *Int J Androl* 2006, 29(6):569–575.

8.   Mostafa, T, G Tawadrous, MM Roaia, et al. Effect of smoking on seminal plasma ascorbic acid in infertile and fertile males. *Andrologia* 2006, 38(6):221–224.

9.   Hansen, JC, and Y Deguchi. Selenium and fertility in animals and man: A review. *Acta Vet Scand* 1996, 37(1): 19–30.

10.   Scott, R, et al. The effect of oral selenium supplementation on human sperm motility. *Br J Urol* 1998, 82(1):76–80.

11.   Suleiman, SA, et al. Lipid peroxidation and human sperm motility: Protective role of vitamin E. *J Androl* 1996, 17(5): 530–537.

12.   Geva, E, et al. The effect of antioxidant treatment on human spermatozoa and fertilization rate in an in vitro fertilization program. *Fertil Steril* 1996, 66(3):430–434.

13.   Omu, AE, MK Al-Azemi, EO Kehinde, et al. Indications of the mechanisms involved in improved sperm parameters by zinc therapy. *Med Princ Pract* 2008, 17(2):108–116.

14.   Netter, A, et al. Effect of zinc administration on plasma testosterone, dihydrotestosterone, and sperm count. *Arch Androl* 1981, 7:69–73.

15.   Westphal, LM, ML Polan, and AS Trant. Double-blind, placebo-controlled study of FertilityBlend: A nutritional supplement for improving fertility in women. *Clin Exp Obstet Gynecol* 2006, 33(4):205–208.

16.   Matalliotakis, I, et al. L-carnitine levels in the seminal fluid of fertile and infertile men: Correlation with sperm quality. *Int J Fertil Womens Med* 2000, 45(3):236–240.

17.   Vitali, G, et al. Carnitine supplementation in human idiopathic asthenospermia: Clinical results. *Drugs Exp Clin Res* 1995, 21(4): 157–159.

18.   Zhou, X, F Liu, and S Zhai. Effect of L-carnitine and/or L-acetyl-carnitine in nutrition treatment for male infertility: A systematic review. *Asia Pac J Clin Nutr* 2007, 16(Suppl 1): 383–390.

Inflammatory Bowel Disease (Ulcerative Colitis and Crohn's Disease)

1.   *What Is Inflammatory Bowel Disease?* Crohn's and Colitis Foundation of Canada, 2009. Available at www.ccfc.ca/ English/info/ibd.html.

2.   D'Souza, S, E Levy, D Mack, et al. Dietary patterns and risk for Crohn's disease in children. *Inflamm Bowel Dis* 2008, 14(3): 367–373.

3.   Mishkin, B, et al. Increased prevalence of lactose malabsorp-tion in Crohn's disease patients at low risk for lactose malabsorption based on ethnic origin. *Am J Gastroenterol* 1997, 92(7):1148–1153.

4.   Mishkin, S. Dairy sensitivity, lactose malabsorption, and elimination diets in inflammatory bowel disease. *Am J Clin Nutr* 1997, 65(2):564–567.

5.   Bernstein, CN, et al. Milk intolerance in adults with ulcera-tive colitis. *Am J Gastroenterol* 1994, 89(6):872–877.

6.   Joachim, G. The relationship between habits of food consumption and reported reactions to food in people with inflammatory bowel disease: Testing the limits. *Nutr Health* 1999, 13(2):69–83.

7.   Ben-Ayre, E, E Goldin, D Wenrower, et al. Wheat grass juice in the treatment of active distal ulcerative colitis: A randomized double-blind placebo-controlled trial. *Scand J Gastroenterol* 2002, 37(4):444–449.

8.   Ejderhamn, J, et al. Long-term double-blind study on the influence of dietary fibres on faecal bile acid excretion in juvenile ulcerative colitis. *Scand J Clin Lab Invest* 1992, 52(7):697–706.

9.   Pearson, M, et al. Food intolerance and Crohn's disease. *Gut* 1993, 34(6):783–787.

10.   Buffinton, GD, and WF Doe. Depleted mucosal antioxidant defences in inflammatory bowel disease. *Free Radical Biol Med* 1995, 19(6):911–918.

11.   Lih-Brody, L, et al. Increased oxidative stress and decreased antioxidant defenses in mucosa of inflammatory bowel disease. *Dig Dis Sci* 1996, 41(10):2078–2086.

12.   Reimund, JM, et al. Antioxidant and immune status in active Crohn's disease: A possible relationship. *Clin Nutr* 2000, 19(1):43–48.

13. Hoffenberg, EJ, et al. Circulating antioxidant concentrations in children with inflammatory bowel disease. *Am J Clin Nutr* 1997, 65(5):1482–1488.

14. Rumi, G, et al. Decrease of serum carotenoids in Crohn's disease. *J Physiol Paris* 2000, 94(2):159–161.

15. Sturniolo, GC, et al. Altered plasma and mucosal concentrations of trace elements and antioxidants in active ulcerative colitis. *Scand J Gastroenterol* 1998, 33(6):644–649.

16. Rannem, T, et al. Selenium status in patients with Crohn's disease. *Am J Clin Nutr* 1992, 56(5):933–937.

17. Cravo, ML, et al. Microsatellite instability in non-neoplastic mucosa of patients with ulcerative colitis. *Am J Gastroenterol* 1998, 93(11):2060–2064.

18. *Ulcerative Colitis*. National Disease Information Clearinghouse, April 2000. Available at www.niddk.nih.gov/health/digest/pubs/colitis/colitis.htm.

19. Lashner, BA, et al. The effect of folic acid supplementation on the risk for cancer or dysplasia in ulcerative colitis. *Gastroenterology* 1997, 112(1):29–32.

20. Lashner, BA. Red blood cell folate is associated with the development of dysplasia and cancer in ulcerative colitis. *J Cancer Res Clin Oncol* 1993, 119(9):549–554.

21. Behrend, C, et al. Vitamin B12 absorption after ileorectal anastomosis for Crohn's disease: Effect of ileal resection and time span after surgery. *Eur J Gastroenterol Hepatol* 1995, 7(5):397–400.

22. Delpre, G, et al. Sublingual therapy for cobalamin deficiency as an alternative to oral and parenteral cobalamin supplementation. *Lancet* 1999, 354(9180):740–741.

23. Buchman, AL. Bones and Crohn's: Problems and solutions. *Inflamm Bowel Dis* 1999, 5(3):212–227.

24. Silvennoinen, J, et al. Dietary calcium intake and its relation to bone mineral density in patients with inflammatory bowel disease. *J Intern Med* 1996, 240(5):285–292.

25. Pigot, F, et al. Low bone mineral density in patients with inflammatory bowel disease. *Dig Dis Sci* 1992, 37(9):1396–1403.

26. Bernstein, CN, et al. A randomized, placebo-controlled trial of calcium supplementation for decreased bone density in corticosteroid-using patients with inflammatory bowel disease: A pilot study. *Aliment Pharmacol Ther* 1996, 10(5):777–786.

27. de Silva, AD, E Tsironi, RM Feakins, and DS Rampton. Efficacy and tolerability of oral iron therapy in inflammatory bowel disease: A prospective, comparative trial. *Aliment Pharmacol Ther* 2005, 22(11–12):1097–1105.

28. De Ley, M, R de Vos, DW Hommes, and P Stokkers. Fish oil for induction of remission in ulcerative colitis. *Cochrane Database Syst Rev* 2007, Oct. 17;(4):CD005986.

29. Turner, D, AH Steinhart, and AM Griffiths. Omega 3 fatty acids (fish oil) for maintenance of remission of ulcerative colitis. *Cochrane Database Syst Rev* 2007 July 18, (3):CD006443.

30. Romano, C, S Cucchiara, A Barabino, et al. Usefulness of omega-3 fatty acid supplementation in addition to mesalazine in maintaining remission in pediatric Crohn's disease: A double-blind, randomized, placebo-controlled trial. *World J Gastroenterol* 2005, 11(45):7118–7121.

31. Kim, YI. Can fish oil maintain Crohn's disease in remission? *Nutr Rev* 1996, 54(8):248–252.

32. Loeschke, K, et al. N-3 fatty acids only delay early relapse of ulcerative colitis in remission. *Dig Dis Sci* 1996, 41(10):1087–1094.

33. Hawthorne, AB, et al. Treatment of ulcerative colitis with fish oil supplementation: A prospective 12 month randomized controlled trial. *Gut* 1992, 33(7):922–928.

34. Schultz, M, and RB Sartor. Probiotics and inflammatory bowel disease. *Am J Gastroenterol* 2000, 95(Suppl 1):S19–S21.

35. Shanahan, F. Probiotics and inflammatory bowel disease: Is there a scientific rationale? *Inflamm Bowel Dis* 2000, 6(2):107–115.

36. Rembacken, BJ, et al. Non-pathogenic Escherichia coli versus mesalazine for the treatment of ulcerative colitis: A randomized trial. *Lancet* 1999, 354(9179):635–639.

37. Venturi, A, et al. Impact on the composition of the faecal flora by a new probiotic preparation: Preliminary data on the maintenance treatment of patients with ulcerative colitis. *Aliment Pharmacol Ther* 1999, 13(8):1103–1108.

38. Gionchetti, P, et al. Oral bacteriotherapy as maintenance treatment in patients with chronic pouchitis: A double-blind, placebo-controlled trial. *Gastroenterology* 2000, 119:305–309.

39. Venturi, A, P Gionchetti, F Rizzello, et al. Impact on the composition of the faecal flora by a new probiotic preparation: Preliminary data on maintenance treatment of patients with ulcerative colitis. *Aliment Pharmacol Ther* 1999, 13(8):1103–1108.

40. Bibiloni, R, RN Fedorak, GW Tannock, et al. VSL#3 probiotic-mixture induces remission in patients with active ulcerative colitis. *Am J Gastroenterol* 2005, 100(7):1539–1546.

41. Tursi, A, G Brandimarte, GM Giorgetti, et al. Low-dose balsalazide plus a high-potency probiotic preparation is more effective than balsalazide alone or mesalazine in the treatment of acute mild-to-moderate ulcerative colitis. *Med Sci Monit* 2004, 10(11):PI126– 131.

42. Kanauchi, O, K Mitsuyama, T Homma, et al. Treatment of ulcerative colitis patients by long-term administration of germinated barley foodstuff: Multi-center open trial. *Int J Mol Med* 2003, 12(5):701–704.

Insomnia

1. "Sleep disorders" in *The Merck Manual of Geriatrics*, 1995–2000. Merck and Co. Ltd., 2000. Available at www.merck.com/pubs/mm_ geriatrics/sec6/ch47.htm.

2. *Study: Insomnia.* Statistics Canada, 2002. Available at www.statcan.gc.ca/daily-quotidien/051116/ dq051116a-eng.htm.

3. Curless, R, et al. Is caffeine a factor in subjective insomnia of elderly people? *Age Ageing* 1993, 22(10):41–45.

4. Bliwise, NG. Factors related to sleep quality in healthy elderly women. *Psychol Aging* 1992, 7(1):83–88.

5. Paterson, LM, SJ Wilson, DJ Nutt, et al. A transitional, caffeine-induced model of onset insomnia in rats and healthy volunteers. *Psychopharmacology* 2007, 191(4):943–950.

6. Bonnett, MH, TJ Balkin, DF Dinges, et al. The use of stimulants to modify performance during sleep loss: A review by the sleep deprivation and Stimulant Task Force of the

American Academy of Sleep Medicine. *Sleep* 2005, 28(9): 1163–1187.

7. Bonnett, MH, and DL Arand. Situational insomnia: Consistency, predictors, and outcomes. *Sleep* 2003, 26(8): 1029–1036.

8. Shirlow, MJ, and CD Mathers. A study of caffeine consumption and symptoms: Indigestion, palpitations, tremor, headache and insomnia. *Int J Epidemiol* 1985, 14(2): 239–248.

9. Landolt, HP, et al. Caffeine intake (200 mg) in the morning affects human sleep and EEG power spectra at night. *Brain Research* 1995, 675(1–2):67–74.

10. Landolt, HP, et al. Caffeine reduces low-frequency delta activity in the human sleep EEG. *Neuropsychopharmacology* 1995, 12(3):229–238.

11. Dufour, MC, et al. Alcohol and the elderly. *Clin Geriatr Med* 1992, 8(1):127–141.

12. Stein, MD, and PD Friedmann. Disturbed sleep and its relationship to alcohol use. *Subst Abus* 2005, 26(1):1–13.

13. Okawa, M, et al. Vitamin B12 treatment for sleep-wake rhythm disorders. *Sleep* 1990, 13(1):15–23.

14. Mayer, G, et al. Effects of vitamin B12 on performance and circadian rhythm in normal subjects. *Neuropsychopharmacology* 1996, 15(5):456–464.

15. Lindahl, O, et al. Double blind study of a valerian preparation. *Pharmacol Biochem Behav* 1989, 32:1065–1066.

16. Leathwood, PD, et al. Aqueous extract of valerian root improves sleep quality in man. *Pharmacol Biochem Behav* 1982, 17:65–71.

17. Leathwood, PD, et al. Aqueous extract of valerian root reduces latency to fall asleep in man. *Planta Medica* 1985, 51:144–148.

18. Brzezinski, A. Melatonin in humans. *N Engl J Med* 1997, 336(3):186–195.

19. Buscemi, N, B Vandermeer, N Hooton, et al. The efficacy and safety of exogenous melatonin for primary sleep disorders: A meta-analysis. *J Gen Intern Med* 2005, 20(12): 1151–1158.

20. Ellis, CM, G Lemmens, and JD Parkes. Melatonin and insomnia. *J Sleep Res* 1996, 5(1):61–65.

21. James, SP, DA Sack, NE Rosenthal, and WB Mendelson. Melatonin administration in insomnia. *Neuropsychopharmacology* 1990, 3(1):19–23.

22. Garfinkel, D, et al. Improvement of sleep quality in elderly people by controlled-release melatonin. *Lancet* 1995, 346(8974):541–544.

23. Brusco, LI, I Fainstein, M Marquez, et al. Effect of melatonin in selected populations of sleep-disturbed patients. *Biol Signals Recept* 1999, 8(1–2):126–131.

24. Haimov, I, P Lavie, M Laudon, et al. Melatonin replacement therapy of elderly insomniacs. *Sleep* 1995, 18(7):598–603.

25. Zhdanova, IV, RJ Wurtman, MM Regan, et al. Melatonin treatment for age-related insomnia. *J Clin Endocrinol Metab* 2001, 86(10):4727–4730.

26. Buscemi, N, B Vandermeer, N Hooton, et al. The efficacy and safety of exogenous melatonin for primary sleep disorders: A meta-analysis. *J Gen Intern Med* 2005, 20(12): 1151–1158.

Interstitial Cystitis

1. Pelikan, Z, et al. The role of allergy in interstitial cystitis. *Ned Tijdschr Geneeskd* 1999, 143(25):1289–1292. [Dutch]

2. Whitmore, K, et al. Survey of the effect of Prelief® on food-related exacerbation of interstitial cystitis symptoms. Philadelphia, 1998–1999, unpublished. Available at www.akpharma.com/lcrews/food_survey.htm.

3. Whitmore, K, et al. The Therapeutic Effects of Prelief® in Interstitial Cystitis. Philadelphia, 2000, unpublished. Available at www. akpharma.com/lcrews/food_survey.htm.

4. Smith, SD, et al. Urinary nitric oxide synthase activity and cyclic GMP levels are decreased with interstitial cystitis and increased with urinary tract infections. *J Urol* 1996, 155(4): 1432–1435.

5. Cartledge, JJ, et al. A randomized double-blind placebo-controlled crossover trial of the efficacy of L-arginine in the treatment of interstitial cystitis. *BJU Int* 2000, 85(4): 421–426.

6. Smith, SD, et al. Improvement in interstitial cystitis symptom scores during treatment with oral L-arginine. *J Urol* 1997, 158(3 Pt 1):703–708.

7. Korting, GE, et al. A randomized double-blind trial of oral L-arginine for treatment of interstitial cystitis. *J Urol* 1999, 161(2):558–565.

8. Wheeler, MA, et al. Effect of long term oral L-arginine on the nitric oxide synthase path-way in the urine from patients with interstitial cystitis. *J Urol* 1997, 158(6): 2045–2050.

Irritable Bowel Syndrome (IBS)

1. Niec, AM, et al. Are adverse food reactions linked to irritable bowel syndrome? *Am J Gastroenterol* 1998, 93(11): 2184–2190.

2. Stefanini, GF, et al. Oral cromolyn solution in comparison with elimination diet in the irritable bowel syndrome, diarrheic type: Multicenter study of 428 patients. *Scand J Gastroenterol* 1995, 30(6):535–541.

3. Bischoff, SC, et al. Prevalence of adverse reactions to food in patients with gastrointestinal disease. *Allergy* 1996, 51(11):811–818.

4. Lessof, MH. Food intolerance. *Scand J Gastroenterol* 1985, 109(Suppl):117–121.

5. Freidman, G. Diet and the irritable bowel syndrome. *Gastroenterol Clin North Am* 1991, 20(2):313–324.

6. Isolauri, E, S Rautava, and M Kalliomaki. Food allergy in irritable bowel syndrome: New facts and old fallacies. *Gut* 2004, 53(10):1391–1393.

7. Zar, S, MJ Benson, and D Kumar. Food-specific serum IgG4 and IgE titers to common food antigens in irritable bowel syndrome. *Am J Gastroenterol* 2005, 100(7):1550–1557.

8. Vernai, P, M Di Camillo, and V Marinaro. Lactose malabsorption, irritable bowel syndrome and self-reported milk intolerance. *Dig Liver Dis* 2001, 33(3):234–239.

9. Gupta, D, UC Ghoshal, A Misra, et al. Lactose intolerance in patients with irritable bowel syndrome from northern India: A case-control study. *J Gastroenterol Hepatol* 2007, 22(12): 2261–2265.

10. Gremse, DA, et al. Irritable bowel syndrome and lactose maldigestion in recurrent abdominal pain in childhood. *South Med J* 1999, 92(8):778–781.

11. Bohmer, CJ, and HA Tuynman. The clinical relevance of lactose malabsorption in irritable bowel syndrome. *Eur J Gastroenterol* 1996, 8(10):1013–1016.

12. Vernia, P, et al. Lactose malabsorption and irritable bowel syndrome: Effect of a long-term lactose-free diet. *Ital J Gastroenterol* 1995, 27(3):117–121.

13. Halpern, GM, et al. Treatment of irritable bowel syndrome with Lacteol-Fort: A randomized double-blind, cross-over trial. *Am J Gastroenterol* 1996, 91(8):1579–1585.

14. Fernandez-Banares, F, M Rosinach, M Esteve, et al. Sugar malabsorption in functional abdominal bloating: A pilot study on the long-term effect of dietary treatment. *Clin Nutr* 2006, 25(5):824–831.

15. Goldstein, R, et al. Carbohydrate malabsorption and the effect of dietary restriction on symptoms of irritable bowel syndrome and functional bowel complaints. *Isr Med Assoc J* 2000, 2(8):583–587.

16. Evans, PR, et al. Fructose-sorbitol malabsorption and symptom provocation in irritable bowel syndrome. *Scand J Gastroenterol* 1998, 33(11):1158–1163.

17. Symons, P, et al. Symptom provocation in irritable bowel syndrome: Effects of differing doses of fructose-sorbitol. *Scand J Gastroenterol* 1992, 27(11):940–944.

18. Fernandez-Banares, F, et al. Sugar malabsorption in functional bowel disease: Clinical implications. *Am J Gastroenterol* 1993, 88(12):2044–2050.

19. Symons, P, et al. Symptom provocation in irritable bowel syndrome: Effects of differing doses of fructose-sorbitol. *Scand J Gastroenterol* 1992, 27(11):940–944.

20. Nelis, GF, et al. Role of fructose-sorbitol malabsorption in the irritable bowel syndrome. *Gastroenterology* 1990, 99(4):1016–1020.

21. Shepherd, SJ, and PR Gibson. Fructose malabsorption and symptoms of irritable bowel syndrome: Guidelines for effective dietary management. *J Am Diet Assoc* 2006, 106(10):1631–1639.

22. Simren, M, H Abrahamsson, and ES Bjornsson. Lipid-induced colonic hypersensitivity in the irritable bowel syndrome: The role of bowel habit, sex, and psychological factors. *Clin Gastroenterol Hepatol* 2007, 5(2):201–208.

23. Simren, M, P Agerforz, ES Bjornsson, and H Abrahamsson. Nutrient-dependent enhancement of rectal sensitivity in irritable bowel syndrome (IBS). *Neurogastroenterol Motil* 2007, 19(1):20–29.

24. Serra, J, B Salvioli, F Azpiroz, and JR Malagelada. Lipid-induced intestinal gas retention in irritable bowel syndrome. *Gastroenterology* 2002, 123(3):700–706.

25. Lambert, JP, et al. The value of prescribed 'high fibre' diets for the treatment of irritable bowel syndrome. *Eur J Clin Nutr* 1991, 45(12):601–609.

26. Kruis, W, et al. Comparisons of the therapeutic effect of wheat bran, mebervine and placebo in patients with the irritable bowel syndrome. *Digestion* 1986, 34(3):196–201.

27. Arffmann, S, et al. The effect of wheat bran in the irritable bowel syndrome. A double-blind crossover study. *Scand J Gastroenterol* 1985, 20(3):295–298.

28. Francis, CY, and PJ Whorwell. Bran and irritable bowel syndrome: Time for reappraisal. *Lancet* 1994, 344(8914):39–40.

29. Cappello, G, M Spezzaferro, L Grossi, et al. Peppermint oil (Mintoil) in the treatment of irritable bowel syndrome: A prospective double blind placebo-controlled randomized trial. *Dig Liver Dis* 2007, 39(6):530–536.

30. Vejdani, R, HR Shalmani, M Mir-Fattahi, et al. The efficacy of an herbal medicine, Carmint, on the relief of abdominal pain and bloating in patients with irritable bowel syndrome: A pilot study. *Dig Dis Sci* 2006, 51(8):1501–1507.

31. Pittler, MH, and E Ernst. Peppermint oil for irritable bowel syndrome: A critical review and meta-analysis. *Am J Gastroenterol* 1998, 93(7):1131–1135.

32. Lui, JH, et al. Enteric-coated peppermint-oil capsules in the treatment of irritable bowel syndrome: A prospective, randomized trial. *J Gastroenterol* 1997, 32(6):765–768.

33. Tarpila, S, et al. Ground flaxseed is an effective hypolipodemic bulk laxative. *Gastroenterology* 1997, 112:A836. [Abstract]

34. Bijkerk, CJ, JW Muris, JA Knottnerus, et al. Systematic review: The role of different types of fibre in the treatment of irritable bowel syndrome. *Aliment Pharmacol Ther* 2004, 19(3):245–251.

35. Brenner, DM, MJ Moeller, WD Chey, and PS Schoenfeld PS. The utility of probiotics in the treatment of irritable bowel syndrome: A systematic review. *Am J Gastroenterol* 2009, 104(4):1033–1049.

36. Kim, HJ, M Camilleri, S McKinzie, et al. A randomized controlled trial of a probiotic, VSL#3, on gut transit and symptoms in diarrhoea-predominant irritable bowel syndrome. *Aliment Pharmacol Ther* 2003, 17(7):895–904.

Kidney Stones

1. *Kidney Stones*. The Kidney Foundation of Canada, 2003. Available at www.kidney. ca/page.asp?intNodeID= 22132.

2. Taylor, EN, and GC Curhan. Diet and fluid prescription in stone disease. *Kidney Int* 2006, 70(5):835–839.

3. Straub, M, and RE Hautmann. Developments in stone prevention. *Curr Opin Urol* 2005, 15(2):119–126.

4. Bellizi, V, et al. Effects of water hardness on urinary risk factors for kidney stones in patients with idiopathic nephrolithiasis. *Nephron* 1999, 81(Suppl 1):S66–S70.

5. Caudarella, R, et al. Comparative study of the influence of 3 types of mineral water in patients with idiopathic calcium lithiasis. *J Urol* 1998, 159(3):658–663.

6. Curhan, GC, et al. Beverage use and risk for kidney stones in women. *Ann Intern Med* 1998, 128(7):534–540.

7. Hirvonen, T, et al. Nutrient intake and use of beverages and the risk of kidney stones among male smokers. *Am J Epidemiol* 1999, 150(2):187–194.

8. McHarg, T, A Rodgers, and K Charlton. Influence of cranberry juice on the urinary risk factors for calcium oxalate kidney stone formation. *BJU Int* 2003, 92(7):756–758.

9. Honow, R, N Laube, A Schneider, et al. Influence of grape-fruit-, orange- and apple-juice consumption on urinary variables and risk of crystallization. *Br J Nutr* 2003, 90(2):295–300.

10. Trinchieri, A, R Lizzano, P Bernardini, et al. Effect of acute load of grapefruit juice on urinary excretion of citrate and urinary risk factors for renal stone formation. *Dig Liver Dis* 2002, 34(Suppl 2):S160–163.

11. Seltzer, MA, et al. Dietary manipulation with lemonade to treat hypocitraturic calcium nephrolithiasis. *J Urol* 1996, 156(3):907–909.

12 Penniston, KL, TH Steele, and SY Nakada. Lemonade therapy increases urinary citrate and urine volumes in patients with recurrent calcium oxalate stone formation. *Urology* 2007, 70(5):856–860.

13. Oussama, A, M Touhami, and M Mbarki. In vitro and in vivo study of lemon juice on urinary lithogenesis. *Arch Esp Urol* 2005, 58(10):1087–1092.

14. Laminski, NA, et al. Hyperoxaluria in patients with recurrent calcium oxalate calculi: Dietary and other risk factors. *Br J Urol* 1991, 68(5):454–458.

15. Massey, LK, et al. Effect of dietary oxalate and calcium on urinary oxalate and the risk of formation of calcium oxalate kidney stones. *J Am Diet Assoc* 1993, 93(8):901–906.

16. The American Dietetic Association. *Manual of Clinical Dietetics*, 6th ed. (Chicago, 2000).

17. Giannini, S, et al. Acute effects of moderate dietary protein restriction in patients with idiopathic hypercalciuria and calcium nephrolithiasis. *Am J Clin Nutr* 1999, 69(2): 267–271.

18. Liatsikos, EN, and GA Barbalias. The influence of a low protein diet in idiopathic hypercalciuria. *Int Urol Nephrol* 1999, 31(3):271–276.

19. Rotily, M, et al. Effects of low animal protein or high-fiber diets on urine composition in calcium nephrolithiasis. *Kidney Int* 2000, 57(3):1115–1123.

20. Massey, LK, M Liebman, and SA Kynast-Gales. Ascorbate increases human oxaluria and kidney stone risk. *J Nutr* 2005, 135(7): 1673–1677.

21. Traxer, O, B Huet, J Poindexter, et al. Effect of ascorbic acid on urinary stone risk factors. *J Urol* 2003, 170(2 Pt 1): 397–401.

22. Baxmann, AC, C de OG Mendonca, C Mendonca, and IP Heilberg. Effect of vitamin C supplements on urinary oxalate and pH in calcium stone-forming patients. *Kidney Int* 2003, 63(3):1066–1071.

23. Auer, BL, et al. Relative hyperoxaluria, crystalluria and haematuria after megadose ingestion of vitamin C. *Eur J Clin Invest* 1998, 28(9): 695–700.

24. Urivetszky, M, et al. Ascorbic acid overdosing: A risk factor for calcium oxalate nephrolithiasis. *J Urol* 1992, 147(5): 1215–1218.

25. Curhan, GC, et al. Intake of vitamin B6 and C and the risk of kidney stones in women. *J Am Soc Nephrol* 1999, 10(4): 840–845.

26. Taylor, EN, MJ Stampfer, and GC Curhan. Dietary factors and the risk of incident kidney stones in men: New insights after 14 years of follow-up. *J Am Soc Nephrol* 2004, 15(12): 3225–3232.

27. Martini, LA, and RJ Wood. Should dietary calcium and protein be restricted in patients with nephrolithiasis? *Nutr Rev* 2000, 58(4):111–117.

28. Curhan, CG, et al. Family history and the risk of kidney stones. *J Am Soc Nephrol* 1997, 8(10):1568–1573.

29. Hess, B. Low calcium diet in hypercalciuric nephrolithiasis: First do no harm. *Scanning Microsc* 1996, 10(2):554–556.

30. Curhan, GC. Dietary calcium, dietary protein, and kidney stone formation. *Miner Electrolyte Metab* 1997, 23(3–6): 261–264.

31. Curhan, GC, et al. Comparison of dietary calcium with supplemental calcium and other nutrients as factors affecting risk for kidney stones in women. *Ann Intern Med* 1997, 126(7):497–504.

32. Curhan, GC, et al. A prospective study of dietary calcium and other nutrients and the risk of symptomatic kidney stones. *N Eng J Med* 1993, 328(12):833–838.

33. Taylor, EN, MJ Stampfer, and GC Curhan. Dietary factors and the risk of incident kidney stones in men: New insights after 14 years of follow-up. *J Am Soc Nephrol* 2004, 15(12): 3225–3232.

34. Curhan, GC, WC Willett, EL Knight, and MJ Stampfer. Dietary factors and the risk of incident kidney stones in younger women: Nurses' Health Study II. *Arch Intern Med* 2004, 164(8):885–891.

35. Messa, P, et al. Different dietary calcium intake and relative supersaturation of calcium oxalate in the urine of patients forming renal stones. *Clin Sci (Colch)* 1997, 93(3): 257–263.

36. Lemann Jr, J, et al. Urinary oxalate excretion increases with body size and decreases with increasing dietary calcium intake among healthy adults. *Kidney Int* 1996, 49(1): 200–208.

37. Stitchantraku, W, W Sopassathit, S Prapaipanich, and S Domrongkitchaiporn. Effects of calcium supplements on the risk of renal stone formation in a population with low oxalate intake. *Southeast Asian J Trop Med Public Health* 2004, 35(4):1028–1033.

38. Domrongkitchaiporn, S, W Sopassathit, W Stitchantraku, et al. Schedule of taking calcium supplement and the risk of nephrolithiasis. *Kidney Int* 2004, 65(5):1835–1841.

39. Taylor, EN, MJ Stampfer, and GC Curhan. Dietary factors and the risk of incident kidney stones in men: New insights after 14 years of follow-up. *J Am Soc Nephrol* 2004, 15(12): 3225–3232.

Lactose Intolerance

1. *Lactose Intolerance.* Mayo Foundation for Medical Education and Research, February 16, 2008. Available at www.mayoclinic.com/health/lactose-intolerance/DS00530.

2. Hertzler, SR, et al. Colonic adaptation to the daily lactose feeding in lactose maldigesters reduces lactose intolerance. *Am J Clin Nutr* 1996, 64:1232–1236.

3. Vesa, TH, et al. Tolerance to small amounts of lactose in lactose maldigesters. *Am J Clin Nutr* 1996, 64:197–201.

4. Martini, MC, et al. Reduced intolerance to symptoms from lactose consumed during a meal. *Am J Clin Nutr* 1988, 47:57–60.

5. Hertzler, SR, et al. How much lactose is low lactose? *J Am Diet Assoc* 1996, 96:243–246.

6. Farnworth, ER. The evidence to support health claims for probiotics. *J Nutr* 2008, 138(6):1250S–1254S.

7. Levri, KM, K Ketvertis, M Deramo, et al. Do probiotics reduce adult lactose intolerance? A systematic review. *J Fam Pract* 2005, 54(7):613–620.

8. Hertzler, SR, and SM Clancy. Kefir improves lactose digestion and tolerance in adults with lactose maldigestion. *J Am Diet Assoc* 2003, 103(5):582–587.

Lung Cancer

1. *Lung Cancer Stats*.The Canadian Cancer Society, April 16, 2009. Available at www.cancer.ca/Canada-wide/About%20 cancer/Cancer%20statistics/Stats%20at%20a%20glance/ Lung%20cancer.aspx?sc_lang=en.

2. *Canadian Tobacco Use Monitoring Survey (CTUMS) 2007.* Health Canada, January 19, 2009. Available at www.statcan. gc.ca/cgi-bin/imdb/p2SV.pl?Function=getSurvey&SDDS= 4440&lang=en&db=imdb&adm=8&dis=2.

3. Potter, JD, et al. Alcohol, beer and lung cancer in postmenopausal women: The Iowa Women's Health Study. *Ann Epidemiol* 1992, 2:587–595.

4. Pollack, ES, et al. Prospective study of alcohol consumption and cancer. *N Eng J Med* 1984, 310:617–621.

5. Kvale, G, et al. Dietary habits and lung cancer risk. *Int J Cancer* 1983, 31:397–405.

6. Klatsky, AI, et al. Alcohol and mortality: A ten year Kaiser-Permanente experience. *Ann Inter Med* 1981, 95:139–145.

7. Rohrmann, S, J Linseisen, HC Boshuizen, et al. Ethanol intake and risk of lung cancer in the European Prospective Investigation into Cancer and Nutrition (EPIC). *Am J Epidemiol* 2006, 164(11):1103–1114.

8. Chao, C. Associations between beer, wine, and liquor consumption and lung cancer risk: A meta-analysis. *Cancer Epidemiol Biomarkers Prev* 2007, 16(11):2436–2447.

9. De Stefani, E, et al. Dietary fat and lung cancer: A case-control study in Uruguay. *Cancer Causes and Control* 1997, 8(6):913–921.

10. De Stefani, E, et al. Fatty foods and the risk of lung cancer: A case-control study from Uruguay. *Int J Cancer* 1997, 71(5):760–766.

11. Alavanja, MC, et al. Estimating the effect of dietary fat on the risk of lung cancer in nonsmoking women. *Lung Cancer* 1996, 14(Suppl 1):S63–S74.

12. Alavanja, MC, et al. Saturated fat intake and lung cancer risk among nonsmoking women in Missouri. *J Natl Cancer Inst* 1993, 85(23):1886–1887.

13. Knept, P, et al. Dietary cholesterol, fatty acids, and the risk of lung cancer among men. *Nutr Cancer* 1991, 16:267–275.

14. Goodman, MT, et al. The effect of dietary fat and cholesterol on the risk of lung cancer in Hawaii. *Am J Epidemiol* 1988, 128:1241–1255.

15. Byers, TE, et al. Diet and lung cancer risk: Findings from the Western New York Diet Study. *Am J Epidemiol* 1987, 125:351–363.

16. Smith-Warner, SA, J Ritz, DJ Hunter, et al. Dietary fat and risk of lung cancer in a pooled analysis of prospective studies. *Cancer Epidemiol Biomarkers Prev* 2002, 11(10 Pt 1):987–992.

17. Wu, Y, et al. Dietary cholesterol, fat and lung cancer incidence among older women: The Iowa Women's Health Study. *Cancer Causes and Control* 1994, 5(5):395–400.

18. Zhang, J, et al. Fish consumption is inversely associated with male lung cancer mortality in countries with high levels of cigarette smoking or animal fat consumption. *Int J Epidemiol* 2000, 29(4):615–621.

19. Yam, D, et al. Suppression of tumor growth and metastasis by dietary fish oil combined with vitamins E and C and cisplatin. *Cancer Chemother Pharmacol* 2001, 47(1):34–40.

20. World Cancer Research Fund/The American Institute for Cancer Research. *Food, Nutrition, Physical Activity, and the Prevention of Cancer: A Global Perspective* (Washington DC: AICR, 2007).

21. Miller, AB, HP Altenburg, B Bueno-de-Mesquita, et al. Fruits and vegetables and lung cancer: Findings from the European Prospective Investigation into Cancer and Nutrition. *Int J Cancer* 2004, 108(2):269–276.

22. Kvale, G, et al. Dietary habits and lung cancer risk. *Int J Cancer* 1983, 31:397–405.

23. Feskanich, D, et al. Prospective study of fruit and vegetable consumption and risk of lung cancer among men and women. *J Natl Cancer Inst* 2000, 92(22):1812–1823.

24. Brennan, P, et al. A multicenter case-control study of diet and lung cancer among non-smokers. *Cancer Causes Control* 2000, 11(1):49–58.

25. Nyberg, F, et al. Dietary factors and risk of lung cancer in never-smokers. *Int J Cancer* 1998, 78(4):430–436.

26. Voorrips, LE, RA Goldbohm, DT Verhoeven et al. Vegetable and fruit consumption and lung cancer risk in the Netherlands Cohort Study on Diet and Cancer. *Cancer Causes Control* 2000. 11(2):101–115.

27. Neuhouser, ML, RE Patterson, MD Thornquist et al. Fruits and vegetables are associated with lower lung cancer risk only in the placebo arm of the beta-carotene and retinol efficacy trial (CARET). *Cancer Epidemiol Biomarkers Prev* 2003, 12(4):350–358.

28. Steinmetz, K, et al. Vegetables, fruit, and lung cancer in the Iowa Women's Health Study. *Cancer Res* 1993, 53(3): 536–543.

29. Knekt, P, et al. Dietary flavonoids and the risk of lung cancer and other malignant neoplasms. *Am J Epidemiol* 1997, 146(3):223–230.

30. Le Marchand, L, et al. Intake of flavonoids and lung cancer. *J Natl Cancer Inst* 2000, 92(2): 154–160.

31. Yang, GY, et al. Effect of black and green tea polyphenols on c-jun phosphorylation and H(2)O(2) production in transformed and non-transformed human bronchila cell lines: Possible mechanisms of cell growth inhibition and apoptosis induction. *Carcinogenesis* 2000, 21(11): 2035–2039.

32. Yang, CS, et al. Tea and tea polyphenols inhibit cell hyper-proliferation, lung tumerogenesis, and tumor progression. *Exp Lung Res* 1998, 24(4):629–639.

33. Leanderson, P, et al. Green tea polyphenols inhibit oxidant-induced DNA strand breakage in cultured cell lines. *Free Radic Biol Med* 1997, 23(2):235–242.

34. Shim, JS, et al. Chemopreventive effect of green tea (Camellia sinensis) among cigarette smokers. *Cancer Epidemiol Biomarkers Prev* 1995, 4(4):387–391.

35. Voorrips, LE, et al. A prospective cohort study on antioxidant and folate intake and male lung cancer risk. *Cancer Epidemiol Biomarkers Prev* 2000, 9(4):357–365.

36. Jatoi, A, et al. A cross-sectional study of vitamin intake in postoperative non-small cell lung cancer patients. *J Surg Oncol* 1998, 68(4):231–236.

37. Slatore, CG, AJ Littman, DH Au, et al. Long-term use of supplemental multivitamins, vitamin C, vitamin E, and folate does not reduce the risk of lung cancer. *Am J Respir Crit Care Med* 2008, 177(5):524–530.

38. Woodson, K, et al. Serum alpha-tocopherol and subsequent risk of lung cancer among male smokers. *J Natl Cancer Inst* 1999, 91(20):1738–1743.

39. Knekt, P, et al. Is low selenium status a risk factor for lung cancer? *Am J Epidemiol* 1998, 148(10):975–982.

40. Comstock, GW, et al. The risk of developing lung cancer associated with antioxidants in the blood: Ascorbic acid, carotenoids, alpha-tocopherol, selenium, and total peroxyl radical absorbing capacity. *Cancer Epidemiol Biomarkers Prev* 1997, 6(11):907–916.

41. Goodman, GE, et al. The association between participant characteristics and serum concentrations of beta-carotene, retinal, retinyl palmitate, and alpha-tocopherol among participants in the Carotene and Retinol Efficacy Trial (CARET) for prevention of lung cancer. *Cancer Epidemiol Biomarkers Prev* 1996, 5(10):815–821.

42. Cook, NR, et al. Effects of beta-carotene supplementation on cancer incidence by baseline characteristics in the Physician's Health Study (United States). *Cancer Causes Control* 2000, 11(7):617–626.

43. Omenn, GS, et al. Risk factors for lung cancer and for intervention effects in CARET, the Beta-Carotene and Retinol Efficacy Trial. *J Natl Cancer Inst* 1996, 88(21):1550–1559.

44. Albanes, D, et al. Effects of alpha-tocopherol and beta-carotene supplements on cancer incidence in the Alpha-Tocopherol Beta-Carotene Cancer Prevention Study. *Am J Clin Nutr* 1995, 62(Suppl 6):S1427–S1430.

45. Lee, IM, NR Cook, JM Gaziano, et al. Vitamin E in the primary prevention of cardiovascular disease and cancer: The Women's Health Study: A randomized controlled trial. *JAMA* 2005, 294(1):56–65.

46. Slatore, CG, AJ Littman, DH Au, et al. Long-term use of supplemental multivitamins, vitamin C, vitamin E, and folate does not reduce the risk of lung cancer. *Am J Respir Crit Care Med* 2008, 177(5):524–530.

Lupus

1. *Lupus*. The Arthritis Society, April 29, 2009. Available at www.arthritis.ca/types%20of%20arthritis/lupus/default.asp?s=1.

2. Morimoto, I. A study on immunological effects of L-canavanine. *Kobe J Med Sci* 1989, 35(5–6): 287–298.

3. Alcocer-Varela, J, et al. Effects of L-canavanine on T cells may explain the induction of systemic lupus erythematosus by alfalfa. *Arth Rheum* 1985, 28(1):52–57.

4. Akaogi, J, T Barker, Y Kuroda, et al. Role of non-protein amino acid L-canavanine in autoimmunity. *Autoimmun Rev* 2006, 5(6):429–435.

5. Vasoo, S. Drug-induced lupus: An update. *Lupus* 2006, 15(11):757–761.

6. Philbrick, DJ, and BJ Holub. Flaxseed: A potential treatment for lupus nephritis. *Kidney Int* 1995, 48(2):475–480.

7. Clark, WF, C Kortas, AP Heidenheim, et al. Flaxseed in lupus nephritis: A two-year nonplacebo-controlled crossover study. *J AM Coll Nutr* 2001, 20(2 Suppl):143–148.

8. Minami, Y, T Sasaki, Y Arai, et al. Diet and symptomatic lupus erythematosus: A 4 year prospective study of Japanese patients. *J Rheumatol* 2003, 30(4):747–754.

9. Ruiz-Irastorza, G, MV Egurbide, N Olivares, et al. Vitamin D deficiency in systemic lupus erythematosus: Prevalence, predictors and clinical consequences. *Rheumatology* (Oxford) 2008, 47(6):920–923.

10. Cutolo, M, and K Otsa. Review: Vitamin D, immunity and lupus. *Lupus* 2008, 17(1):6–10.

11. Kamen, DL, GS Cooper, H Bouali, et al. Vitamin D deficiency in systemic lupus erythemaosus. *Autoimmun Rev* 2006, 5(2):114–117.

12. Serban, MG, et al. Lipid peroxidase and erythrocyte redox system in systemic vasculitides treated with corticoids: Effect of vitamin E administration. *Rom J Intern Med* 1994, 32(4):283–289.

13. Comstock, GW, et al. Serum concentrations of alpha tocopherol, beta carotene, and retinal preceding the diagnosis of rheumatoid arthritis and systemic lupus erythematosus. *Ann Rheum Dis* 1997, 56(5):323–325.

14. Weinmann, BJ, and D Hermann. Inhibition of autoimmune deterioration in MRL/lpr mice by vitamin E. *Int J Vitam Nutr Res* 1999, 69(4):255–261.

15. Maeshima, E, XM Liang, M Goda, et al. The efficacy of vtamin E against oxidative damage and autoantibody production in systemic lupus erythematosus: A preliminary study. *Clin Rheumatol* 2007, 26(3):401–404.

16. Compeyrot-Lacassange, S, PN Tyrrell, E Atenafu, et al. Prevalance and etiology of low bone mineral density in juvenile systemic lupus erythematosus. *Arthritis Rheum* 2007, 56(6):1966–1973.

17. Bhattoa, HP, P Bettembuk, A Balogh, et al. Bone mineral density in women with systemic lupus erythematosus. *Clin Rheumatol* 2002, 21(2):135–141.

18. Crosbie, D, C Black, L McIntyre, et al. Dehydroepiandrosterone for systemic lupus erythematosus. *Cochrane Database Syst Rev* 2007 Oct, 17(4):CD005114.

19. Mease, PJ, EM Ginzler, OS Gluck, et al. Effects of prasterone on bone mineral density in women with systemic lupus erythematosus receiving chronic glucocorticoid therapy. *J Rheumatol* 2005, 32(4):616–621.

20. Nordmark, G, C Bengtsson, A Larsson, et al. Effects of dehydroepiandrosterone supplement on health-related quality of life in glucocorticoid treated female patients with systemic lupus erythematosus. *Autoimmunity* 2005, 38(7):531–540.

21. Barry, NN, et al. Dehydroepiandrosterone in systemic lupus erythematosus: Relationship between dosage, serum levels, and clinical response. *J Rheumatol* 1998, 25(12): 2352–2356.

22. van Vollenhoven, RF, et al. A double-blind, placebo-controlled, clinical trial of dehydroepiandrosterone in severe systemic lupus erythematosus. *Lupus* 1999, 8(3): 181–187.

23. van Vollenhoven, RF, et al. Treatment of systemic lupus erythematosus with dehydroepiandrosterone: 50 patients treated up to 12 months. *J Rheumatol* 1998, 25(2):285–289.

24. van Vollenhoven, RF, et al. Dehydroepiandrosterone in systemic lupus erythematosus: Results of a double-blind, placebo-controlled, randomized clinical trial. *Arth Rheum* 1995, 38(12):1826–1831.

25. van Vollenhoven, RF, et al. An open trial of dehydroepiandrosterone in systemic lupus erythematosus. *Arth Rheum* 1994, 37(9):1305–1310.

26. Wright, SA, FM O'Prey, MT McHenry, et al. A randomized interventional trial of omega-3 polyunsaturated fatty acids on endothelial function and disease activity in systemic lupus erythematosus. *Ann Rheum Dis* 2008, 67(6): 841–848.

27. Duffy, EM, GK Meenagh, SA McMillan, et al. The clinical effect of dietary supplementation with omega-3 fish oils and/or copper in systemic lupus erythematosus. *J Rheumatol* 2004: 31(8):1551–1558.

28. Das, UN. Beneficial effect of eicosapentanoic and docosa-hexaenoic acids in the management of systemic lupus erythematosus and its relationship to the cytokine network. *Prostaglandins Leukot Essent Fatty Acids* 1994, 51(3): 207–213.

29. Clark, WF, and A Parbtani. Omega-3 fatty acid supplementation in clinical and experimental lupus nephritis. *Am J Kidney Dis* 1994, 23(5):644–647.

30. Clark, WF, et al. Fish oil in lupus nephritis: Clinical findings and methodological implications. *Kidney Int* 1993, 44(1):75–86.

31. Walton, AJ, et al. Dietary fish oil and the severity of symptoms in patients with systemic lupus erythematosus. *Ann Rheum Dis* 1991, 50(7):463–466.

32. Mohan, IK, and UN Das. Oxidant stress, anti-oxidants and essential fatty acids in systemic lupus erythematosus. *Prostaglandins Leukot Essent Fatty Acids* 1997, 56(3): 193–198.

Macular Degeneration (Age-Related Macular Degeneration)

1. *Age-Related Macular Degeneration (AMD)*. The Canadian National Institute for the Blind, 2009. Available at www.cnib.ca/en/your-eyes/eye-conditions/amd/Default.aspx.

2. Age-Related Eye Disease Study Research Group. A randomized, placebo-controlled, clinical trial of high-dose supplementation with vitamins C and E, beta carotene, and zinc for age-related macular degeneration and vision loss: AREDS report no. 8. *Arch Ophthalmol* 2001, 119(10): 1417–1436.

3. Age-Related Eye Disease Study Research Group. A randomized, placebo-controlled, clinical trial of high-dose supplementation with vitamins C and E and beta carotene for age-related cataract and vision loss: AREDS report no. 9. *Arch Ophthalmol* 2001, 119(10):1439–1452.

4. Cho, S, S Hung, WC Willett, et al. Prospective study of dietary fat and the risk of age-related macular degeneration. *Am J Clin Nutr* 2001, 73(2):209–218.

5. Mares-Perlman, JA, et al. Dietary fat and age-related maculopathy. *Arch Ophthalmol* 1996, 114(2):235–236.

6. Chong, EW, LD Robman, JA Simpson, et al. Fat consumption and its association with age-related macular degeneration. *Arch Ophthalmol* 2009, Vol.127(5):674–680.

7. Seddon, JM, B Rosner, RD Sperduto, et al. Dietary fat and risk of advanced age-related macular degeneration. *Arch Opthalmol* 2001, 119(8):1191–1199.

8. Seddon, JM, J Cote, and B Rosner. Progression of age-related macular degeneration: Association with dietary fat, transunsaturated fat, nuts and fish intake. *Arch Opthalmol* 203, 121)12):1728–1737.

9. Smith, W, et al. Dietary fat and fish intake and age-related maculopathy. *Arch Ophthalmol* 2000, 118(3):401–404.

10. Chong, EW, AJ Kreis, TY Wong, et al. Dietary omega-3 fatty acid and fish intake in the primary prevention of age-related macular degeneration: A systematic review and meta-analysis. *Arch Opthalmol* 2008, 126(6):826– 833.

11. Seddon, JM, S George, and B Rosner. Cigarette smoking, fish consumption, omega-3 fatty acid intake, and associations with age-related macular degeneration: The U.S. Twin Study of Age-Related Macular Degeneration. *Arch Opthalmol* 2006, 124(7):995–1001.

12. Tan, JS, JJ Wang, V Flood, and P Mitchell. Dietary fatty acids and the 10-year incidence of age-related macular degeneration: The Blue Mountains Eye Study. *Arch Ophthalmol* 2009, 127(5):656–665.

13. SanGiovanni, JP, EY Chew, TE Clemons, et al. The relationship of dietary lipid intake and age-related macular degeneration in a case-control study: AREDS Report No. 20. *Arch Opthalmol* 2007, 125(5):671–679.

14. Hodge, WG, D Barnes, HM Schachter, et al. Evidence for the effect of omega-3 fatty acids on progression of age-related macular degeneration: A systematic review. *Retina* 2007, 27(2):216–221.

15. Tan, JS, JJ Wang, V Flood, and P Mitchell. Dietary fatty acids and the 10-year incidence of age-related macular degeneration: The Blue Mountains Eye Study. *Arch Ophthalmol* 2009, 127(5):656–665.

16. Hammond Jr, BR, EJ Johnson, RM Russell, et al. Dietary modification of human macular pigment density. *Invest Opthalmol Vis Sci* 1997, 38(9):1795–1801.

17. Berendschott, TT, et al. Influence of lutein supplementation on macular pigment, assessed with two objective techniques. *Invest Ophthalmol Vis Sci* 2000, 41(11): 3322–3326.

18. Landrum, JT, et al. A one year study of the macular pigment: The effect of 140 days of a lutein supplement. *Exp Eye Res* 1997, 65(1):57–62.

19. Tan, JS, JJ Wang, V Flood, et al. Dietary antioxidants and the long-term incidence of age-related macular degeneration: The Blue Mountains Eye Study. *Ophthalmology* 2008, 115(2):334–341.

20. Seddon, JM, et al. Dietary carotenoids, vitamins A, C and E, and advanced age-related macular degeneration. *JAMA* 1994, 272(18):1413–1420.

21. Moss, SE, et al. Alcohol consumption and the 5-year incidence of age-related maculopathy: The Beaver Dam Eye Study. *Ophthalmology* 1998, 105(5):789–794.

22. Ritter, LL, et al. Alcohol use and age-related maculopathy in the Beaver Dam Eye Study. *Am J Ophthalmol* 1995, 120(2):190–196.

23. Cho, E, et al. Prospective study of alcohol consumption and the risk of age-related macular degeneration. *Arch Ophthalmol* 2000, 118(5):681–688.

24. Delcourt, C, et al. Age-related macular degeneration and antioxidant status in the POLA study. *Arch Ophthalmol* 1999, 117(10):1384–1390.

25. Belda, JI, et al. Serum vitamin E levels negatively correlate with severity of age-related macular degeneration. *Mech Ageing Dev* 1999, 107(2):159–164.

26. VandenLangenberg, GM, et al. Associations between antioxidant and zinc intake and the 5-year incidence of early age-related maculopathy in the Beaver Dam Eye Study. *Am J Epidemiol* 1998, 148(2):204–214.

27. Mayer, MJ, et al. Whole blood selenium and exudative age-related maculopathy. *Acta Ophthalmol Scand* 1998, 76(1): 62–67.

28. Mares-Perlman, JA, et al. Serum antioxidants and age-related macular degeneration in a population-based case-control study. *Arch Ophthalmol* 1995, 113(12): 1518–1523.

29. Eye Disease Case-Control Study Group. Antioxidant status and neovascular age-related macular degeneration, Eye Disease Case-Control Study Group. *Arch Ophthalmol* 1993, 111(1):104–109.

30. Mares-Perlman, JA. Association of zinc and antioxidant nutrients with age-related maculopathy. *Arch Ophthalmol* 1996, 114(8):991–997.

31. Stur, M, et al. Oral zinc and the second eye in age-related macular degeneration. *Invest Ophthalmol Vis Sci* 1996, 37(7):1225–1235.

32. Newsome, DA, et al. Oral zinc in macular degeneration. *Arch Ophthalmol* 1988, 106:192–198.

33 Scharrer, A, and M Ober. Anthocyanosides in the treatment of retinopathies. *Klin Monatsbl Augenheilkd* 1981, 178: 386–389. [German]

34. Caselli, L. Clinical and electroretinographic study on activity of anthocyanosides. *Arch Med Intern* 1985, 37: 29–35.

35. Evans, JR. Ginkgo biloba extract for age-related macular degeneration. *Cochrane Database Syst Rev* 2000, (2): CD001775.

36. Diamond, BJ, et al. Ginkgo biloba extract: Mechanisms and clinical indications. *Arch Phys Med Rehabil* 2000, 81(5): 668–678.

37. Lebuisson, DA, et al. Treatment of senile macular degeneration with Ginkgo biloba extract: A preliminary double-blind, drug versus placebo study. *Presse Med* 1986, 15:1556–1558. [French]

Migraine Headaches

1. William, EM, et al. Guidelines for the diagnosis and management of migraine in clinical practice. *CMAJ* 1997, 156:1273–1287.

2. Wobber, C, J Holzhammer, J Zeitlhofer, et al. Trigger factors of migraine and tension-type headache: Experience and knowledge of the patients. *J Headache Pain* 2006, 7(4): 188–195.

3. Millichap, JG, and MM Yee. The diet factor in pediatric and adolescent migraine. *Pediatr Neurol* 2003, 28(1):9–15.

4. Savi, L, I Rainero, W Valfre, et al. Food and headache attacks: A comparison of patients with migraine and tension-type headaches. *Panminerva Med* 2002, 44(1): 27–31.

5. Littlewood, JT, et al. Red wine as a cause of migraine. *Lancet* 1988, 1(8585):558–559.

6. Monro, J, et al. Food allergy in migraine: Study of dietary exclusion and RAST. *Lancet* 1980, 2(8184):1–4.

7. Grant, EC. Food allergies and migraine. *Lancet* 1979, 1(8123):966–969.

8. Mansfield, LE, et al. Food allergy and adult migraine: Double-blind and mediator confirmation of an allergic etiology. *Ann Allergy* 1985, 55(2):126–129.

9. Boehnke, C, U Reuter, U Flach, et al. High-dose riboflavin treatment is efficacious in migraine prophylaxis: An open study in a tertiary care centre. *Eur J Neurol* 2004, 11(7): 475–477.

10. Schoenen, J, et al. Effectiveness of high-dose riboflavin in migraine prophylaxis: A randomized controlled trial. *Neurology* 1998, 50(2): 466–470.

11. Maizels, M, A Blumenfeld, and R Burchette. A combination of riboflavin, magnesium and feverfew for migraine prophylaxis: A randomized trial. *Headache* 2004, 44(9):885–890.

12. Mauskop, A, and BM Altura. Role of magnesium in the pathogenesis and treatment of migraines. *Clin Neurosci* 1998, 5(1):24–27.

13. Lodi, R, et al. Deficit of brain and skeletal muscle bioenergetics and low brain magnesium in juvenile migraine: An in vivo 31P magnetic resonance spectroscopy. *Pediatr Res* 1997, 42(6):866–871.

14. Aloisi, P, et al. Visual evoked potentials and serum magnesium levels in juvenile migraine patients. *Headache* 1997, 37(6):383–385.

15. Peikert, A, et al. Prophylaxis of migraine with oral magnesium: Results from a prospective, multi-center, placebo-controlled and double-blind randomized study. *Cephalalgia* 1996, 16(4):257–263.

16. Wang, F, SK Van Den Eeden, LM Ackerson, et al. Oral magnesium oxide prophylaxis of frequent migrainous headache in children: A randomized, double-blind, placebo-controlled trial. *Headache* 2003, 43(6):601–610.

17. Diener, HC, V Pfaffenrath, J Schnitker, et al. Efficacy and safety of 6.25 mg t.i.d. feverfew CO_2-extract (MIG-99) in migraine prevention: A randomized, double-blind, multi-centre, placebo-controlled study. *Cephalalgia* 2005, 25(11): 1031–1041.

18. Pitler, MH, and E Ernst. Feverfew for preventing migraine. *Cochrane Database Syst Rev* 2004, (10):CD002286.

19. Murphy, JJ, et al. Randomised double-blind placebo-controlled trial of feverfew in migraine prevention. *Lancet* 1988, 2(8604):189–192.

20. Rozen, TD, ML Oshinsky, CA Gebeline, et al. Open label trial of coenzyme Q10 as a migraine preventive. *Cephalalgia* 2002, 22(2): 137–141.

21. Sandor, PS, L Di Clemene, G Coppola, et al. Efficancy of coenzyme Q10 in migraine prophylaxis: A randomized controlled trial. *Neurology* 2005, 64(4):713–715.

22. Hershey, AD, SW Powers, AL Vockell, et al. Coenzyme Q10 deficiency and response to supplementation in pediatric and adolescent migraine. *Headache* 2007, 47(1):73–80.

Motion Sickness

1. *Motion Sickness in Children*. Medscape.com, 2001. Available at www.medscape.com/adis/DTP/2001/v17.n01/dtp1701.02/dtp1701.02-01.html.

2. Gordon, CR, and A Shupak. Prevention and treatment of motion sickness in children. *CNS Drugs* 1999, 12(5): 369–381.

3. Proctor, CA. Abnormal insulin levels and vertigo. *Laryngoscope* 1981, 91(10):1657– 1662.

4. Lindseth, G, and PD Lindseth. The relationship of diet to airsickness. *Aviat Space Environ Med* 1995, 66(6):537–541.

5. Mowrey, DB, et al. Motion sickness, ginger, and psychophysics. *Lancet* 1982, 1:655–657.

6. Grontved, A, et al. Ginger root against seasickness: A controlled trial on the open sea. *Acta Otolaryngol* 1988, 105(1–2):45–49.

7. Grontved, A, and E Hentzer. Vertigo-reducing effect of ginger root: A controlled clinical study. *ORL J Otorhinolaryngol Relat Spec* 1986, 48(5):282–286.

8. Holtman, S, et al. The anti-motion sickness mechanism of ginger: A comparative study with placebo and dimenhydrinate. *Acta Otolaryngol* 1989, 108(3–4):168–174.

9. Haguenauer, JP, et al. Treatment of balance disorders using Ginkgo biloba extract: A multicentre, double-blind, drug versus placebo study. *Presse Med* 1986, 15:1569–1572. [French]

10. Cesarani, A, et al. Ginkgo biloba (EGb 761) in the treatment of equilibrium disorders. *Adv Ther* 1998, 15(5): 291–304.

Multiple Sclerosis (MS)

1. *Frequently Asked Questions.* Multiple Sclerosis Society of Canada, 2009. Available at www.mssociety.ca/en/information/faq.htm#2.

2. Ibid.

3. Ghadirian, P, et al. Nutritional factors in the aetiology of multiple sclerosis: A case-control study in Montreal, Canada. *Int J Epidemiol* 1998, 27(5):845–852.

4. Esparza, ML, et al. Nutrition, latitude, and multiple sclerosis mortality: An ecologic study. *Am J Epidemiol* 1995, 142(7):733–737.

5. Tola, MR, et al. Dietary habits and multiple sclerosis. A retrospective study in Ferra, Italy. *Acta Neurol* (Napoli) 1994, 16(4):189–197.

6. Sepcic, J, et al. Nutritional factors and multiple sclerosis in Gorski Kotar, Croatia. *Neuroepidemiology* 1993, 12(4): 234–240.

7. Swank, RL, and BB Dugan. Effects of low saturated fat diet in early and late cases of multiple sclerosis. *Lancet* 1990, 336(8706):37–39.

8. Farinotti, M, S Simi, C Di Piertrantonj, et al. Dietary interventions for multiple sclerosis. *Cochrane Database Syst Rev* 2007 Jan 24, (1):CD004192.

9. Schwartz, S, and H Leweling. Multiple sclerosis and nutrition. *Mult Scler* 2005, 11(1):24–32.

10. Bates, D, et al. Polyunsaturated fatty acids in the treatment of acute remitting multiple sclerosis. *Br Med J* 1978, 2: 1390–1391.

11. Millar, JHD, et al. Double-blind trial of linoleate supplementation of the diet in multiple sclerosis. *Br Med J* 1973, 1:765–768.

12. Syburra, C, and S Passi. Oxidative stress in patients with multiple sclerosis. *WMJ* 1999, 71(3):112–115.

13. Glabinski, A, et al. Increased generation of superoxide radicals in the blood of MS patients. *Acta Neurol Scand* 1993, 88(3):174–177.

14. Langemann, H, et al. Measurement of low-molecular-weight antioxidants, uric acid, tyrosine and tryptophan in plaques and white matter from patients with multiple sclerosis. *Eur Neurol* 1992, 32(5):248–252.

15. Sandyk, R, and GI Awerbuch. Vitamin B12 and its relationship to age of onset of multiple sclerosis. *Int J Neurosci* 1993, 71(1–4):93–99.

16. Reynolds, EH, et al. Vitamin B12 metabolism in multiple sclerosis. *Arch Neurol* 1992, 39(6):649–652.

17. Reynolds, EH, et al. Multiple sclerosis associated with vitamin B12 deficiency. *Arch Neurol* 1991, 48(8):808–811.

18. Kira, J, et al. Vitamin B12 metabolism and massive-dose methyl vitamin B12 therapy in Japanese patients with multiple sclerosis. *Intern Med* 1994, 33(2):82–86.

19. Loder, C, J Allawi, and DF Horrobin. Treatment of multiple sclerosis with lofepramine, L-phenylalanine and vitamin B12: Mechanism of action and clinical importance: Role of the locus coeruleus and central noradrenergic systems. *Med Hyptheses* 2002, 59(5):594–602.

20. Wade, DT, CA Young, KR Chaudhuri, and DL Davidson. A randomized placebo controlled exploratory study of vitamin B-12, lofepramine, and L-phenylalanine (the Cari Loder regime) in the treatment of multiple sclerosis. *J Neurol Neurosurg Psychiatry* 2002, 73(3):246–249.

21. Cantorna, MT, et al. 1,25-Dihydroxyvitamin D3 reversibly blocks the progression of relapsing encephalomyelitis, a model of multiple sclerosis. *Proc Natl Acad Sci USA* 1996, 93(15):7861–7864.

22. Brown, SJ. The role of vitamin D in multiple sclerosis. *Ann Pharmacother* 2006, 40(6): 1158–161.

23. Munger, KL, LI Levin, BW Hollis, et al. Serum 25-hydroxyvitamin D levels and risk of multiple sclerosis. *JAMA* 2006, 296(23): 2832–2838.

24. Kragt, J, B van Amerongen, J Killestein, et al. Higher levels of 25-hydroxyvitamin D are associated with a lower incidence of multiple sclerosis only in women. *Mult Scler* 2009, 15(1):9–15.

25. Ramagopalan, SV, NJ Maugeri, L Handunnetthi, et al. Expression of the multiple sclerosis-associated MHC class II Allele HLA-DRB1*1501 is regulated by vitamin D. *PLoS Genet* 2009, 5(2):e1000369. Epub 2009 Feb 6.

26. Mahon, BD, SA Gordon, J Cruz, et al. Cytokine profile in patients with multiple sclerosis following vitamin D supplementation. *J Neuroimmunol* 2003, 134(1–2):128–132.

27. Cosman, F, et al. Fracture history and bone loss in patients with MS. *Neurology* 1998, 51(4):1161–1165.

28. Nieves, J, et al. High prevalence of vitamin D deficiency and reduced bone mass in multiple sclerosis. *Neurology* 1994, 44(9):1687–1692.

29. Nightingale, S, et al. Red blood cell and adipose tissue fatty acids in mild active multiple sclerosis. *Acta Neurol Scand* 1990, 82:43–50.

30. Cunnane, SC, et al. Essential fatty acid and lipid profiles in plasma and erythrocytes in patients with multiple sclerosis. *Am J Clin Nutr* 1989, 50:801–806.

31. Nordvik, I, KM Myhr, H Nyland, and S Bjerve. Effects of dietary advice and n-3 supplementation in newly diagnosed MS patient. *Acta Neurol Scand* 2000, 102(3): 143–149.

32. Weinstock-Guttman, B, M Baier, Y Park, et al. Low fat dietary intervention wth omega-3 fatty acid supplementation in multiple sclerosis. *Prostaglandins Leukot Essent Fatty Acids* 2005, 73(5):397–404.

Obesity, Overweight and Weight Loss

1. Shields, Margot. *Measured Obesity. Overweight Canadian Children and Adolescents.* Statistics Canada, 2005. Available at www.statcan.ca/english/research/82-620-MIE/2005001/pdf/cobesity.pdf.
2. Lakka, HM, TA Lakka, J Tuomilehto, and JT Salonen. Abdominal obesity is associated with increased risk of acute coronary events in men. *Eur Heart J* 2002, 23(9):706–713.
3. De Koning, L, AT Merchant, J Pogue, and SS Anand. Waist circumference and waist-to-hip ratio as predictors of cardiovascular events: Meta-regression of prospective studies. *Eur Heart J* 2007, 28(7):850–856.
4. Canoy, D, SM Boekholdt, N Wareham, R Luben, et al. Body fat distribution and risk of coronary heart disease in men and women in the European Prospective Investigation into Cancer and Nutrition in Norfolk cohort: A population-based prospective study. *Circulation* 2007, 116(25): 2933–2943.
5. Kaats, GR, et al. A randomized, double-masked, placebo-controlled study of the effects of chromium picinolate supplementation on body composition: A replication and extension of a previous study. *Curr Ther Res* 1998, 59: 379–388.
6. Grant, KE, et al. Chromium and exercise training: Effect on obese women. *Med Sci Sports Exerc* 1997, 29(8):992–998.
7. Blankson, H, JA Stakkestad, H Fagertun, et al. Conjugated linoleic acid reduces body fat mass in overweight and obese humans. *J Nutr* 2000, 130(12):2943–2948.
8. Gaullier, JM, J Halse, K Hoye, et al. Conjugated linoleic acid supplementation for 1 y reduces body fat mass in healthy overweight humans. *Am J Clin Nutr* 2004, 79(6): 1118–1125.
9. Mougios, V, A Matsakas, A Petridou, et al. Effect of supplementation with conjugated linoleic acid on human serum lipids and body fat. *J Nutr Biochem* 2001, 12(10):585–594.
10. Riserus, U, A Smedman, S Basu, and B Vessby. Metabolic effects of conjugated linoleic acid in humans: The Swedish experience. *Am J Clin Nutr* 2004, 79(6 Suppl):1146S–8S.
11. Riserus, U, P Arner, K Brismar, and B Vessby. Treatment with dietary trans10cis12 conjugated linoleic acid causes isomer-specific insulin resistance in obese men with the metabolic syndrome. *Diabetes Care* 2002, 25(9):1516–1521.

Osteoarthritis

1. *Osteoarthritis.* The Arthritis Society of Canada, April 29, 2009. Available at www.arthritis.ca/types%20of%20arthritis/osteoarthritis/default.asp?s=1.
2. White-O'Connor, B, and J Sobal. Nutrient intake and obesity in a multidisciplinary assessment of osteoarthritis. *Clin Ther* 1986, 9(Suppl B):S30–S42.
3. Toda, Y, et al. Change in body fat, but not body weight or metabolic correlates of obesity, is related to symptomatic relief of obese patients with knee osteoarthritis after a weight control program. *J Rheumatol* 1998, 25(11): 2181–2186.
4. Arjmandi, BH, DA Khalil, EA Lucas, et al. Soy protein may alleviate osteoarthritis symptoms. *Phytomedicine* 2004, 11(7–8):567–575.
5. McAlindon, TE, et al. Do antioxidant micronutrients protect against the development and progression of knee osteoarthritis? *Arth Rheum* 1996, 39(4):648–656.

6. McAlindon, TE, et al. Relation of dietary intake and serum levels of vitamin D to progression of osteoporosis of the knee among participants in the Framingham Study. *Ann Intern Med* 1996, 125(5):353–359.
7. Lane, NE, et al. Serum vitamin D levels and incident changes of radiographic hip osteoarthritis: A longitudinal study. Study of Osteoporotic Fractures Research Group. *Arth Rheum* 1999, 42(5):854–860.
8. Warner, AE, and SA Arnspiger. Diffuse musculoskeletal pain is not associated with low vitamin D levels or improved by treatment with vitamin D. *J Clin Rheumatol* 2008, 14(1): 12–16.
9. McCleane, G. The analgesic efficacy of topical capsaicin is enhanced by glyceryl trinitrate in painful osteoarthritis: A randomized, double blind placebo controlled study. *Eur J Pain* 2000, 4(4):355–360.
10. Zhang, WY, and A Li Wan Po. The effectiveness of topically applied capsaicin cream: A meta-analysis. *Eur J Clin Pharmacol* 1994, 46(6):517–522.
11. McKay, L, H Gemmell, B Jacobson, and B Hayes. Effect of a topical herbal cream on the pain and stiffness of osteoarthritis: A randomized double-blind, placebo-controlled clinical trial. *J Clin Rheumatol* 2003, 9(3): 164–169.
12. Chantre, P, A Cappelaere, D Leblan, et al. Efficacy and tolerance or Harpagophytum procumbens versus diacerhein in treatment of osteoarthritis. *Phytomedicine* 2000, 7:177–184.
13. Chrubasik, S, J Thanner, O Kunzel, et al. Comparison of outcome measures during treatment with the proprietary Harpagophytum extract doloteffin in patients with pain in the lower back, knee or hip. *Phytomedicine* 2002, 9: 181–194.
14. Gagnier, JJ, S Chrubasik, and E Manheimer. Harpagophytum procumbens for osteoarthritis and low back pain: A systematic review. *BMC Complement Altern Med* 2004, 4:13.
15. Wegener, T, and NP Lupke. Treatment of patients with arthrosis of hip or knee with an aqueous extract of devil's claw (Harpagophytum procumbens DC). *Phytother Res* 2003, 17(10):1165–1172.
16. McAlindon, TE, et al. Glucosamine and chondroitin for treatment of osteoarthritis: A systematic quality assessment and meta-analysis. *JAMA* 2000, 283:1469–1475.
17. Morreale, P, et al. Comparison of the anti-inflammatory efficacy of chondroitin sulfate and diclofenac sodium in patients with knee osteoarthritis. *J Rheumatol* 1996, 23(8): 1385–1391.
18. Conrozier, T. Anti-arthrosis treatments: Efficacy and tolerance of chondroitin sulfates. *Presse Med* 1998, 27(36): 1862–1865. [French]
19. Mazieres, B, et al. Chondroitin sulfate in the treatment of gonarthrosis and coxarthrosis. 5-months result of a multicenter double-blind controlled prospective study using placebo. *Rev Rhum Mal Osteoartic* 1992, 59(7–8):466–472. [French]
20. Bucsi, L, and G Poor. Efficacy and tolerability of oral chondroitin sulfate as a symptomatic slow-acting drug for osteoarthritis (SYSADOA) in the treatment of knee osteoarthritis. *Osteoarthritis Cartilage* 1998 May, (Suppl 6).

21. Leeb, BF, et al. A meta-analysis of chondroitin sulfate in the treatment of osteoarthritis. *J Rheumatol* 2000, 27(1): 205–211.

22. Clegg, DO, DJ Reda, CL Harris, et al. Glucosamine, chondroitin sulfate, and the two in combination for painful knee osteoarthritis. *N Engl J Med* 2006, 354(8):795–808.

23. Herrero-Beaumont, G, JA Ivorra, M Del Carmen Trabado, et al. Glucosamine sulfate in the treatment of knee osteoarthritis symptoms: A randomized, double-blind, placebo-controlled study using acetaminophen as a side comparator. *Arthritis Rheum* 2007, 56(2):555–567.

24. Towheed, TE, L Maxwell, TP Anastassiades, et al. Glucosamine therapy for treating osteoarthritis. *Cochrane Database Syst Rev* 2005, (2):CD002946.

25. Bruyere, O, K Pavelka, LC Rovati, et al. Glucosamine sulfate reduces osteoarthritis progression in postmenopausal women with knee osteoarthritis: Evidence from two 3-year studies. *Menopause* 2004, 11(2):138–143.

26. Richy, F, O Bruyere, O Ethgen, et al. Structural and symptomatic efficacy of glucosamine and chondroitin in knee osteoarthritis: A comprehensive meta-analysis. *Arch Intern Med* 2003, 163(13):1514–1522.

27. Braham, R, B Dawson, and C Goodman. The effect of glucosamine supplementation on people experiencing regular knee pain. *Br J Sports Med* 2003, 37(1):45–49.

28. Reginster, JY, R Deroisy, LC Rovati, et al. Long-term effects of glucosamine sulfate on osteoarthritis progression: A randomized, placebo-controlled trial. *Lancet* 2001, 357(9252):251–256.

29. Towheed, TE, TP Anastassiades, B Shea, et al. Glucosamine therapy for treating osteoarthritis. *Cochrane Database Syst Rev* 2001, 1:CD002946.

30. McAlindon, TE, MP LaValley, JP Gulin, and DT Felson. Glucosamine and chondroitin for treatment of osteoarthritis: A systematic quality assessment and meta-analysis. *JAMA* 2000, 283:1469–1475.

31. Qiu, GX, SN Gao, G Giacovelli, et al. Efficacy and safety of glucosamine sulfate versus ibuprofen in patients with knee osteoarthritis. *Arzneimittelforschung* 1998, 48:469–474.

32. Poolsup, N, C Suthisisang, P Channark, and W Kittikulsuth. Glucosamine long-term treatment and the progression of knee osteoarthritis: Systematic review of randomized controlled trials. *Ann Pharmacother* 2005, 39(6):1080–1087.

33. Najm, WI, S Reinsch, F Hoehler, et al. S-adenosylmethionine (SAMe) versus celecoxib for the treatment of osteoarthritis symptoms: A double-blind crossover trial. *BMC Musculoskelet Disord* 2004, 5:6.

34. Soeken, KL, WL Lee, RB Bausell, et al. Safety and efficacy of S-adenosylmethionine (SAMe) for osteoarthritis. *J Fam Pract* 2002, 51(5):425–430.

35. Domljan, Z, B Vrhovac, T Durrigl, and I Pucar. A double-blind trial of ademetionine vs. naproxen in activated gonarthrosis. *Int J Clin Pharmacol Ther Toxicol* 1989, 27(7):329–333.

36. Konig, B. A long-term (two years) clinical trial with S-adenosylmethionine for the treatment of osteoarthritis. *Am J Med* 1987, 83(5a):78–80.

37. Berger, R, and H Nowak. A new medical approach to the treatment of osteoarthritis: Report of an open phase IV study with ademetionine (Gumbaral). *Am J Med* 1987, 83(5A):84–88.

38. Muller-Fassbender, H. Double-blind clinical trial of S-adenosylmethionine versus ibuprofen in the treatment of osteoarthritis. *Am J Med* 1987, 83(5A):81–83.

39. Vetter, G. Double-blind comparative clinical trial with S-adenosylmethionine and indo-methacin in the treatment of osteoarthritis. *Am J Med* 1987, 83(5A):78–80.

40. Maccagno, A, EE Di Giorgio, OL Caston, and CL Sagasta. Double-blind controlled clinical trial of oral S-adenosylmethionine versus piroxicam in knee osteoarthritis. *Am J Med* 1987, 83(5A):72–77.

41. Caruso, I, and V Pietrogrande. Italian double-blind multi-center study comparing S-adenosylmethionine, naproxen, and placebo in the treatment of degenerative joint disease. *Am J Med* 1987, 83(5A):66–71.

42. Glorioso, S, S Todesco, A Mazzi, et al. Double-blind, multi-centre study of the activity of S-adenosylmethionine in hip and knee osteoarthritis. *Int J Clin Pharmacol Res* 1985, 5(1):39–49.

43. di Padova, C. S-adenosylmethionine in the treatment of osteoarthritis: Review of the clinical studies. *Am J Med* 1987, 83(5A):60–65.

Osteoporosis

1. *What Is Osteoporosis?* Osteoporosis Society of Canada, 2009. Available at www. osteoporosis.ca/index.php/ci_id/ 5526/la_id/1.htm.

2. Cauley, JA, et al. The effect of HRT on fracture risk: Results of a 4-year randomized trial of 2,763 postmenopausal women. *American Society for Bone and Mineral Research* June 1998. [Abstract T394]

3. Alekel, DL, et al. Isoflavone-rich soy protein isolate exerts significant bone sparing effect in the lumbar spine of perimenopausal women. Third International Symposium on the Role of Soy in Preventing and Treating Chronic Disease, October 1999. [Abstract]

4. Schieber, MD, et al. Dietary soy isoflavones favorably influence lipids and bone turnover in healthy postmenopausal women. Third International Symposium on the Role of Soy in Preventing and Treating Chronic Disease, October 1999. [Abstract]

5. Ma, DF, LQ Qin, PY Wang, and R Katoh. Soy isoflavone intake inhibits bone resorption and stimulates bone formation in menopausal women: Meta-analysis of randomized controlled trials. *Eur J Clin Nutr* 2008, 62(2):155–161.

6. Ma, DF, LQ Qin, PY Wang, and R Katoh. Soy isoflavone intake increases bone mineral density in the spine of menopausal women: Meta-analysis of randomized controlled trials. *Clin Nutr* 2008, 27(1):57–64.

7. Brink, E, V Coxam, S Robins, et al. Long-term consumption of isoflavone-enriched foods does not affect bone mineral density, bone metabolism, or hormonal status in early postmenopausal women: A randomized, double-blind, placebo controlled study. *Am J Clin Nutr* 2008, 87(3): 761–770.

8. Munger, RG, et al. Prospective study of dietary protein intake and risk of hip fracture in postmenopausal women. *Am J Clin Nutr* 1999, 69(1):147–152.

9. Rapuri, PB, JC Gallagher, and V Haynatzka. Protein intake: Effects on bone mineral density and the rate of bone loss in elderly women. *Am J Clin Nutr* 2003, 77(6):1517–1525.

10. Schurch, MA, et al. Protein supplements increase serum insulin-like growth factor-I levels and attenuate proximal femur bone loss in patients with recent hip fracture: A randomized, double-blind, placebo-controlled trial. *Ann Intern Med* 1998, 128(10):801–809.

11. Tengstrand, B, T Cederholm, A Soderqvist, and J Tidermark. Effects of protein-rich supplementation and nandrolone on bone tissue after a hip fracture. *Clin Nutr* 2007, 26(4): 460–465.

12. Lloyd, T, et al. Dietary caffeine intake and bone status of postmenopausal women. *Am J Clin Nutr* 1997, 65(6): 1826–1830.

13. Harris, SS, and B Dawson-Hughes. Caffeine and bone loss in healthy menopausal women. *Am J Clin Nutr* 1994, 60(4):573–578.

14. Wetmore, CM, J Ichikawa, AZ LaCroix, et al. Association between caffeine intake and bone mass among young women: Potential effect. *Osteoporos Int* 2008, 19(4): 519–527.

15. Sakhaee, K, et al. The effect of calcium citrate on bone density in the early and mid-postmenopausal period: A randomized, placebo-controlled study. The Second Joint Meeting of the American Society for Bone and Mineral Research and the International Bone and Mineral Society, 1998. Mission Pharmacal Company. [Abstract]

16. Baran, DT, et al. A placebo-controlled study of pre-menopausal women: Calcium supplementation and bone density. Annual Meeting of the American Society for Bone and Mineral Research, 1999. [Abstract]

17. Tang, BM, GD Eslick, C Nowson, et al. Use of calcium or calcium in combination with vitamin D supplementation to prevent fractures and bone loss in people aged 50 years and older: A mata-analysis. *Lancet* 2007, 370(9588):657–666.

18. Harris, SS, and B Dawson-Hughes. Seasonal changes in plasma 25-hydroxyvitamin D concentrations of young American black and white women. *Am J Clin Nutr* 1998, 67(6):1232–1236.

19. Crandell, C. Vitamin A intake and osteoporosis: A clinical update. *J Women's Health* 2004, 13(8):939–953.

20. Jackson, HA, and AH Sheehan. Effect of vitamin A on fracture risk. *Ann Pharmacother* 2005, 39(12):2086–2090.

21. Feskanich, D, V Singh, WC Willett, and GA Colditz. Vitamin A intake and hip fractures among postmenopausal women. *JAMA* 2002, 287(1):47–54.

22. Melhus, H, K Michaëlsson, A Kindmark, et al. Excessive dietary intake of vitamin A is associated with reduced bone mineral density and increased risk for hip fracture. *Ann Intern Med* 1998, 129(10):770–778.

23. Leveille, SG, et al. Dietary vitamin C and bone mineral density: Results from the PEPI Study. *Calcif Tissue Int* 1998, (63)3:183–189.

24. Feskanich, D, et al. Vitamin K intake and hip fractures in women: A prospective study. *Am J Clin Nutr* 1999, 69(1): 74–79.

25. Booth, SL, KL Tucker, H Chen, et al. Dietary vitamin K intakes are associated with hip fracture but not with bone mineral density in elderly men and women. *Am J Clin Nutr* 2000, 71(5):1201–1208.

26. Ryder, KM, RI Shorr, AJ Bush, et al. Magnesium intake from food and supplements is associated with bone mineral density in healthy older white subjects. *J Am Geriatr Soc* 2005, 53(11):1875–1880.

27. Strause, L, et al. Spinal bone loss in postmenopausal women supplemented with calcium and trace minerals. *J Nutr* 1994, 124(7):1060–1064.

28. Lin, PH, F Ginty, LJ Appel, et al. The DASH diet and sodium reduction improve markers of bone turnover and calcium metabolism in adults. *J Nutr* 2003, 133(10): 3130–3136.

29. Salari, P, A Rezaie, B Larijani, and M Abdollahi. A systematic review of the impact of n-3 fatty acids in bone health and osteoporosis. *Med Sci Monit* 2008, 14(3):RA37–RA44.

30. Rousseau, JH, A Kleppinger, and AM Kenny. Self-reported dietary intake of omega-3 fatty acids and association with bone and lower extremity function. *J Am Geriatr Soc* 2008, Aug 22. [Epublication]

31. Högström, M, P Nordström, and A Nordström. N-3 Fatty acids are positively associated with peak bone mineral density and bone accrual in healthy men: The NO2 Study. *Am J Clin Nutr* 2007, 85(3):803–807.

32. Dalsky, GP, et al. Weight-bearing exercise training and lumbar bone mineral content in postmenopausal women. *Ann Intern Med* 1988 Jun, 108(6):824–828.

33. Wolff, I, JJ van Croonenborg, HC Kemper, et al. The effect of exercise training programs on bone mass: A meta-analysis of published controlled trials in pre- and postmenopausal women. *Osteoporosis Int* 1999, 9(1):1–12.

Parkinson's Disease

1. *Parkinson's Disease—Just the Facts*. The Parkinson Society of Canada, 2007. Available at www.parkinson.ca/atf/cf/%7B9EBD08A9-7886-4B2D-A1C4-A131E7096BF8%7D/PSCFactSheetRev1.pdf.

2. Johnson, CC, et al. Adult nutrient intake as a risk factor for Parkinson's disease. *Int J Epidemiol* 1999, 28(6):1102–1109.

3. Anderson, C, et al. Dietary factors in Parkinson's disease: The role of food groups and specific foods. *Mov Disord* 1999, 14(1):21–27.

4. Logroscino, G, et al. Dietary iron, animal fats, and risk of Parkinson's disease. *Mov Disord* 1998, 13(Suppl 1):S13–S16.

5. Logroscino, G, et al. Dietary lipids and antioxidants in Parkinson's disease: A population-based, case-control study. *Ann Neurol* 1996, 39(1):89–94.

6. Karstaedt, PJ, and JH Pincus. Protein redistribution diet remains effective in patients with fluctuating parkinsonism. *Arch Neurol* 1992, 49(2):149–151.

7. Pare, S, et al. Effect of daytime protein restriction on nutrient intakes of free-living Parkinson's disease patients. *Am J Clin Nutr* 1992, 55(3):701–707.

8. Bracco, F, et al. Protein redistribution diet and antiparkinsonian response to levadopa. *Eur Neurol* 1991, 31(2):68–71.

9. Astarloa, R, et al. Clinical and pharmacokinetic effects of a diet rich in insoluble fibre on Parkinson's disease. *Clin Neuropharmacol* 1992, 15(5):375–380.

10. Benedetti, MD, et al. Smoking, alcohol, and coffee consumption preceding Parkinson's disease: A case-control study. *Neurology* 2000, 55(9):1350–1358.

11. Ross, GW, et al. Association of coffee and caffeine intake with the risk of Parkinson disease. *JAMA* 2000, 283(20):2674–2679.

12. Ascherio, A, SM Zhang, MA Hernán, et al. Prospective study of caffeine consumption and risk of Parkinson's disease in men and women. *Ann Neurol* 2001, 50(1):56–63.

13. Ozer, F, H Meral, L Hangogly, et al. Plasma homocysteine levels in patients treated with levadopa: Motor and cognitive associations. *Neurol Res* 2006, 28(8):853–858.

14. Jenner, P, et al. Oxidative stress as a cause of nigral cell death in Parkinson's disease and incidental Lewy body disease. The Royal Kings and Queens Parkinson's Disease Research Group. *Ann Neurol* 1992, 32(Suppl 2):S82–S87.

15. de Rijk, MC, et al. Dietary antioxidants and Parkinson disease: The Rotterdam Study. *Arch Neurol* 1997, 54(6): 762–765.

16. Abbott, RA, et al. Diet, body size, and micronutrient status in Parkinson's disease. *Eur J Clin Nutr* 1992, 46(12): 879–884.

17. Pham, DQ, and R Plakogiannis. Vitamin E supplementation in Alzheimer's disease, Parkinson's disease, tardive dyskineis, and cataract: Part 2. *Ann Pharmacotherap* 2005, 39(12):2065–2072.

18. Etminan, M, SS Gill and A Samii. Intake of vitamin E, vitamin C, and caroteniods and the risk of Parkinson's disease: A meta-analysis. *Lancet Neurol* 2005, 4(6): 362–365.

19. Shults, CW, D Oakes, K Kieburtz, et al. Effects of coenzyme Q10 in early Parkinson disease: Evidence of slowing of the functional decline. *Arch Nerol* 2002, 59(10):1541–1550.

20. Muller, T, T Buttner, AF Gholipur, and W Kuhn. Coenzyme Q10 supplementation provides milk symptomatic benefit in patients with Parkinson's disease. *Neurosci Lett* 2003, 341(3):201–204.

Perimenopause

1. McKinlay, SM, et al. The menopausal syndrome. *Br J Prev Soc Med* 1974, 28:108–115.

2. Thompson, B, et al. Menopausal age and symptomatology in a general practice. *J Biosoc Sci* 1973, 5:71–82.

3. Tang, GWK. The climacteric of Chinese factory workers. *Maturitas* 1994, 19:177–182.

4. Murkies, AL, et al. Dietary flour supplementation decreases postmenopausal hot flushes: Effect of soy and wheat. *Maturitas* 1995, 21:189–195.

5. Brzezinski, A, et al. Short-term effects of phytoestrogens-rich diet on postmenopausal women. *Menopause* 1997, 4:89–94.

6. Albertazzi, P, et al. The effect of dietary soy supplementation on hot flushes. *Obstet Gynecol* 1998, 91(1):6–11.

7. Greenwood, S, et al. The role of isoflavones in menopausal health: Consensus opinion of The North American Menopause Society. *Menopause* 2000, 7(2):215–229.

8. Nicklas, TA, et al. Breakfast consumption with and without vitamin-mineral supplement use favorably impacts daily nutrient intake of ninth-grade students. *J Adolesc Health* 2000, 27(5):314–321.

9. Smith, AP, et al. Breakfast cereal and caffeinated coffee: Effects on working memory, attention, mood, and cardiovascular function. *Physiol Behav* 1999, 67(1):9–17.

10. Benton, D, and PY Parker. Breakfast, blood glucose, and cognition. *Am J Clin Nutr* 1998, 67(4):772S–778S.

11. Akata, T, et al. Successful combined treatment with vitamin B12 and bright artificial light of one case with delayed sleep phase syndrome. *Jpn J Psychiatry Neurol* 1993, 47(2): 439–440.

12. Maeda, K, et al. A multicenter study of the effects of vitamin B12 on sleep-waking rhythm disorders: In Shizuoka Prefecture. *Jpn J Psychiatry Neurol* 1992, 46(1):229–230.

13. Ohta, T, et al. Treatment of persistent sleep-wake schedule disorders in adolescents with methylcobalamin (vitamin B12). *Sleep* 1991, 14(5):414–418.

14. Okawa, M, et al. Vitamin B12 treatment for sleep-wake rhythm disorders. *Sleep* 1990, 13(1):15–23.

15. Liske, E, W Hanggi, HH Henneicke-von Zepelin, et al. Physiological investigation of a unique extract of black cohosh (Cimicifugae racemosae rhizoma): A 6-month clinical study demonstrates no systemic estrogenic effect. *J Womens Health Gend Based Med* 2002, 11(2):163–174.

16. Osmers, R, M Friede, E Liske, et al. Efficacy and safety of isopropanolic black cohosh extract for climacteric symptoms. *Obstet Gynecol* 2005, 105 (5 Pt. 1):1074–1083.

17. Nappi, RE, B Malavasi, B Brundu, and F Facchinetti. Efficacy of Cimicifuga racemosa on climacteric complaints: A randomized study versus low-dose transdermal estradiol. *Gynecol Endocrinol* 2005, 20(1):30–35.

18. Lindahl, O, et al. Double blind study of a valerian preparation. *Pharmacol Biochem and Behav* 1989, 32: 1065–1066.

19. Leathwood, PD, et al. Aqueous extract of valerian root improves sleep quality in man. *Pharmacol Biochem Behav* 1982, 17:65–71.

20. Leathwood, PD, et al. Aqueous extract of valerian root reduces latency to fall asleep in man. *Planta Medica* 1985, 51:144–148.

21. Donath, F, S Quispe, K Diefenbach, et al. Critical evaluation of the effect of valerian extract on sleep structure and sleep quality. *Pharmacopsych* 2000, 33(2):47–53.

22. Bent, S, M Patterson, and D Garvin. Valerian for sleep: A systematic review and meta-analysis. *Altern Ther* 2001, 7:S4.

Phlebitis

1. Schulman, S, et al. Influence of changes in lifestyle on fibrinolytic parameters and recurrence rate in patients with venous thromboembolism. *Blood Coagul Fibrinolysis* 1995, 6(4):311–316.

2. Eklof, B, et al. Venous thromboembolism in association with prolonged air travel. *Dermatol Surg* 1996, 22(7): 637–641.

3. Kozarevic, D, et al. Drinking habits and other characteristics: The Yugoslavia Cardiovascular Disease Study. *Am J Epidemiol* 1982, 116(2):2 87–301.

4. Burkitt, DP. Varicose veins: Facts and fantasy. *Arch Surg* 1976, 111(12):1327–1332.

5. Den Heijer, M, S Lewington, and R Clarke. Homocysteine, MTHFR and risk of venous thrombosis: A meta-analysis of published epidemiologic studies. *J Thromb Haemost* 2005, 3(2):292–299.

6. Hotoleanu, C, M Porojan-Iuga, ML Rusa, and A Andercou. Hyperhomocysteinemia: Clinical and therapeutic involvement in venous thrombosis. *Rom J Intern Med* 2007, 45(2): 159–164.

7. Taussig, SJ, et al. Bromelain: A proteolytic enzyme and its clinical application: A review. *Hiroshima J Med Sci* 1975, 24(2–3):185–193.

8. Seligman, B. Oral bromelains as adjuncts in the treatment of acute thrombophlebitis. *Angiology* 1960, 20(1):22–26.

Polycystic Ovary Syndrome (PCOS)

1. Lau, D. Screening for diabetes in women with polycystic ovary syndrome. *CMAJ* 2007, 176(7):951–952.

2. Legro, RS. Polycystic ovary syndrome: Current and future treatment paradigms. *Am J Obstet Gynecol* 1998, 179(6 Pt 2):S101–S108.

3. Taylor, AE. Systemic adversities of ovarian failure. *J Soc Gynecol Investig* 2001, (1 Suppl Proceedings):S7–S9.

4. Wahrenberg, H, et al. Divergent effects of weight reduction and oral anticonception treatment on adrenergic lipolysis in obese women with the polycystic ovary syndrome. *J Clin Endocrinol Metab* 1999, 84(6):2182–2187.

5. Jakubowicz, DJ, and JE Nestler. 17 alpha-Hydroxyprogesterone response to leuprolide and serum androgens in obese women with and without polycystic ovary syndrome after dietary weight loss. *J Clin Endocrinol Metab* 1997, 82(2):556–560.

6. Andersen, P, et al. Increased insulin sensitivity and fibrinolytic capacity after dietary intervention in obese women with polycystic ovary syndrome. *Metabolism* 1995, 44(5):611–616.

7. Franks, S, et al. The role of nutrition and insulin in the regulation of sex hormone binding globulin. *J Steroid Biochem Mol Biol* 1991, 39(5B):835–838.

8. Hoeger, KM, L Kochman, N Wixom, et al. A randomized, 48-week, placebo-controlled trial of intensive lifestyle modification and/or metformin therapy in overweight women with polycystic ovary syndrome: A pilot study. *Fertil Steril* 2004, 82(2):421–429.

9. Tang, T, J Glanville, CJ Hayden, et al. Combined lifestyle modification and metformin in obese patients with polycystic ovary syndrome: A randomized, placebo-controlled, double-blind multicentre study. *Hum Reprod* 2006, 21(1):80–89.

10. Panidis, D, D Farmakiotis, D Rousso, et al. Obesity, weight loss, and the polycystic ovary syndrome: Effect of treatment with diet and orlistat for 24 weeks on insulin resistance and androgen levels. *Fertil Steril* 2008, 89(4):899–906.

11. Franks, S, et al. Obesity and polycystic ovary syndrome. *Ann NY Acad Sci* 1991, 626:201– 206.

12. Kiddy, DS, et al. Improvement in endocrine and ovarian function during dietary treatment of obese women with polycystic ovary syndrome. *Clin Endocrinol* (Oxford) 1992, 36(10):105–111.

13. Moran, LJ, M Noakes, PM Clifton, et al. Dietary composition in restoring reproductive and metabolic physiology in overweight women with polycystic ovary syndrome. *J Clin Endocrinol Metal* 2003, 88(2):812–819.

14. Douglas, CC, BA Gower, BE Darnell, et al. Role of diet in the treatment of polycystic ovary syndrome. *Fertil Steril* 2006, 85(3):679–688.

15. Qublan, HS, EK Yannakoula, MA Al-Qudah, and FI El-Uri. Dietary intervention versus metformin to improve the reproductive outcome in women with polycystic ovary syndrome: A prospective comparative study. *Saudi Med J* 2007, 28(11):1694–1699.

16. Moghetti, P, et al. Spironolactone, but not flutamide, administration prevents bone loss in hyperandrogenic women treated with gonadotropin-releasing hormone agonist. *J Clin Endocrinol Metab* 1999, 84(4): 1250–1254.

17. Lucidi, RS, AC Thyer, CA Easten, et al. Effect of chromium supplementation on insulin resistance and ovarian menstrual cyclicity in women with polycystic ovary syndrome. *Fertil Steril* 2005, 84(6):1755–1757.

18. Lydic, ML, M McNurlan, S Bembo, et al. Chromium picolinate improves insulin sensitivity in obese subjects with polycystic ovary syndrome. *Fertil Steril* 2006, 86(1): 243–246.

19. Nestler, JE, et al. Ovulatory and metabolic effects of D-chiro-inositol in the polycystic ovary syndrome. *N Engl J Med* 1999, 340(17):1314–1320.

Premenstrual Syndrome (PMS)

1. *Premenstrual Syndrome (PMS)*. MedicineNet, Inc., 2009. Available at www.medicinenet.com/premenstrual_syndrome/article.htm.

2. Deuster, PA, et al. Biological, social, and behavioural factors associated with premenstrual syndrome. *Arch Fam Med* 1999, 8:122–128.

3. Blum, I, et al. The influence of meal composition on plasma serotonin and norepinephrine concentrations. *Metabolism* 1992, 41(2):137–140.

4. Sayegh, R, et al. The effect of a carbohydrate-rich beverage on mood, appetite, and cognitive function in women with premenstrual syndrome. *Obstet Gynecol* 1995, 86(4 Pt 1): 520–528.

5. Jones, DY. Influence of dietary fat on self-reported menstrual symptoms. *Physiol Behav* 1987, 40(4):483–487.

6. Boyd, NF, et al. Effect of a low-fat high-carbohydrate diet on symptoms of cyclical mastopathy. *Lancet* 1988, 2(8603): 128–132.

7. Barnard, ND, et al. Diet and sex-hormone globulin, dysmenorrhea, and premenstrual symptoms. *Obstet Gynecol* 2000, 95(2): 245–250.

8. Wyatt, KM, et al. Efficacy of vitamin B6 in the treatment of premenstrual syndrome: Systematic review. *Br J of Med* 1999, 318(7195):1375–1381.

9. De Souza, MC, et al. A synergistic effect of a daily supplement for 1 month of 200 mg magnesium plus 50 mg vitamin B6 for the relief of anxiety-related premenstrual symptoms: A randomized, double-blind, crossover study. *J Women's Health Gend Based Med* 2000, 9(2):131–139.

10. Sharma, P, S Kulshreshtha, GM Singh, and A Bhagoliwal. Role of bromocriptine and pyridoxine in premenstrual tension syndrome. *Indian J Physiol Pharmacol* 2007, 51(4): 368– 374.

11. London, RS, et al. Efficacy of alpha-tocopherol on premenstrual symptomology: A double-blind study: II Endocrine correlates. *J Am Coll Nutr* 1984, 3:351–356.

12. London, RS, et al. Efficacy of alpha-tocopherol on premenstrual symptomology: A double-blind study. *J Reprod Med* 1987, 32(6): 400–404.

13. London, RS, et al. Efficacy of alpha-tocopherol on premenstrual symptomology: A double-blind study. *J Am Coll Nutr* 1983, 2:115–122.

14. Thys-Jacobs, S, et al. Calcium carbonate and the premenstrual syndrome: Effects on premenstrual and menstrual symptoms. Premenstrual Syndrome Study Group. *Am J Obstet Gynecol* 1998, 179(2):444–452.

15. Bertone-Johnson, ER, SE Hankinson, A Bendich, et al. Calcium and vitamin D intake and risk of incident premenstrual syndrome. *Arch Intern Med* 2005, 165(11): 1246–1252.

16. Posaci, C, et al. Plasma copper, zinc and magnesium levels in patients with premenstrual tension syndrome. *Acta Obstet Gynecol Scand* 1994, 73(6):452–455.

17. Rosenstein, DL, et al. Magnesium measures across the menstrual cycle in premenstrual syndrome. *Biol Psychiatry* 1994, 35(8):557– 561.

18. Walker, AF, et al. Magnesium supplementation alleviates premenstrual symptoms of fluid retention. *J Women's Health* 1998, 7(9):1157– 1165.

19. Facchinetti, F, et al. Oral magnesium successfully relieves premenstrual mood changes. *Obstet Gynecol* 1991, 78(2): 177–181.

20. Quartanta, S, MA Buscaglia, MG Meroni, et al. Pilot study of the efficacy and safety of a modified-release magnesium 250 mg tablet (Sincromag) for the treatment of premenstrual syndrome. *Clin Drug Investig* 2007, 27(1):51–58.

21. Prilepskaya, VN, AV Ledina, AV Tagiyeva, and FS Revazova. Vitex agnus castus: Successful treatment of moderate to severe premenstrual syndrome. *Maturitas* 2006, 55(1) (Suppl) 1:S55–63.

22. Loch, EG, et al. Treatment of premenstrual syndrome with a phytopharmaceutical formulation containing Vitex agnus castus. *J Women's Health Gend Based Med* 2000, 9(3):315–320.

23. Schellenberg, R. Treatment for the premenstrual syndrome with agnus castus fruit extract: Prospective, randomized, placebo-controlled study. *Br Med J* 2001, 322(7279): 134–137.

24. Berger, D, W Schaffner, E Schrader, et al. Efficacy of Vitex agnus castus L. extract Ze 440 in patients with premenstrual syndrome (PMS). *Arch Gynecol Obstet* 2000, 264(3): 150–153.

25. Lauritzen, CH, HD Reuter, R Repges, et al. Treatment of premenstrual tension syndrome with Vitex agnus castus: Controlled-double blind versus pyridoxine. *Phytomedicine* 1997, 4:183–189.

26. Atmaca, M, S Kumru, and E Tezcan. Fluoxetine versus Vitex agnus castus extract in the treatment of premenstrual dysphoric disorder. *Hum Psychopharmacol Clin Exp* 2003, 18(3):191–195.

27. Gateley, CA, et al. Drug treatments for mastalgia: 17 years experience in the Cardiff Mastalgia Clinic. *J R Soc Med* 1992, 85(1):12–15.

28. Pye, JK, RE Mansel, and LE Hughes. Clinical experience of drug treatments for mastalgia. *Lancet* 1985, 2(8451): 373–377.

29. Cheung, KL. Management of cyclical mastalgia in oriental women: Pioneer experience of using gamolenic acid (Efamast) in Asia. *Aust N Z J Surg* 1999, 69(7):492–494.

30. Tamborini, A, and R Taurelle. Value of standardized Ginkgo biloba extract (EGb 761) in the management of congestive symptoms of premenstrual syndrome. *Rev Fr Gynecol Obstet* 1993, 88(7–9):447–457. [French]

31. Kasper, S, M Gastpar, WE Müller, HP Volz, A Dienel, M Kieser, and HJ Möller. Efficacy of St. John's wort extract WS 5570 in acute treatment of mild depression: A reanalysis of data from controlled clinical trials. *Eur Arch Psychiatry Clin Neurosci* 2008, 258(1):59–63.

32. Stevison, C, and E Ernst. A pilot study of Hypericum perforatum for the treatment of premenstrual syndrome. *BJOG* 2000, 107(7):870–876.

33. Sampalis, F, R Bunea, MF Pelland, et al. Evaluation of the effects of Neptune Krill Oil on the management of premenstrual syndrome and dysmenorrheal. *Altern Med Rev* 2003, 8(2):171–179.

Prostate Cancer

1. *Prostate Cancer Stats*. Canadian Cancer Society, April 16, 2009. Available at www.cancer.ca/Canada-wide/About%20 cancer/Cancer%20statistics/Stats%20at%20a%20glance/ Prostate%20cancer.aspx?sc_lang=en.

2. Ramon, JM, et al. Dietary fat intake and prostate cancer risk: A case-control study in Spain. *Cancer Causes Control* 2000, 11(8):679–685.

3. Hayes, RB, et al. Dietary factors and risk for prostate cancer among blacks and whites in the United States. *Cancer Epidemiol Biomarkers Prev* 1999, 8(1):25–34.

4. Deneo-Pellegrini, H, et al. Foods, nutrients and prostate cancer: A case-control study in Uruguay. *Br J Cancer* 1999, 80(3–4):591–597.

5. Bairati, I, et al. Dietary fat and advanced prostate cancer. *J Urol* 1987, 159(4):1271–1275.

6. Barvo, MP, et al. Dietary factors and prostatic cancer. *Urol Int* 1991, 46(2):163–166.

7. West, WD, et al. Adult dietary intake and prostate cancer risk in Utah: A case-control study with special emphasis on aggressive tumors. *Cancer Causes Control* 1991, 2(2):85–94.

8. Cross, AJ, U Peters, VA Kirsh, et al. A prospective study of meat and meat mutagens and prostate cancer risk. *Cancer Res* 2005, 65(24):11779–11784.

9. Koutros, S, AJ Cross, DP Sandler, et al. Meat and meat mutagens and risk of prostate cancer in the Agricultural Health Study. *Cancer Epidemiol Biomarkers Prev* 2008, 17(1):80–87.

10. Jacobsen, BK, et al. Does high soymilk intake reduce prostate cancer incidence? The Adventist Health Study (United States). *Cancer Causes and Control* 1998, 9(6):553– 557.

11. Kolonel, LN, et al. Vegetables, fruits, legumes and prostate cancer: A multiethnic case-control study. *Cancer Epidemiol Biomarkers Prev* 2000, 9(8):795–804.

12. Schuurman, AG, et al. Vegetable and fruit consumption and prostate cancer risk: A cohort study in The Netherlands. *Cancer Epidemiol Biomarkers Prev* 1998, 7(8):673–680.

13. Norrish, AE, et al. Prostate cancer risk and consumption of fish oils: A dietary biomarker-based case-control study. *Br J Cancer* 1999, 81(7):1238–1242.

14. Herbert, JR, et al. Nutritional and socioeconomic factors in relation to prostate cancer mortality: A cross-national survey. *J Natl Cancer Inst* 1998, 90(21):1637–1647.

15. Demark-Wahnefried, W, TJ Polascik, SL George, et al. Flaxseed supplementation (not dietary fat restriction) reduces prostate cancer proliferation rates in men presurgery. *Cancer Epidemiol Biomarkers Prev* 2008, 17(12):3577–3587.

16. Kolonel, LN, et al. Vegetables, fruits, legumes and prostate cancer: A multiethnic case-control study. *Cancer Epidemiol Biomarkers Prev* 2000, 9(8):795–804.

17. Kirsh, VA, U Peters, ST Mayne, et al. Prospective study of fruit and vegetable intake and risk of prostate cancer. *J Natl Cancer Inst* 2007, 99(15):1200–1209.

18. Giovannucci, E, A Ascherio, EB Rimm, et al. Intake of carotenoids and retinol in relation to risk of prostate cancer. *J Natl Cancer Inst* 1995, 87(23):1767–1776.

19. Giovannucci, E, EB Rimm, Y Liu, et al. A prospective study of tomato products, lycopene, and prostate cancer risk. *J Natl Cancer Inst* 2002, 94(5):391–398.

20. Lu, QY, JC Hung, D Heber, et al. Inverse associations between plasma lycopene and other carotenoids and prostate cancer. *Cancer Epidemiol Biomarkers Prev* 2001, 10(7): 749–756.

21. Norrish, AE, RT Jackson, SJ Sharpe, and CM Skeaff. Prostate cancer and dietary carotenoids. *Am J Epidemiol* 2000, 151(2):119–123.

22. Etminan, M, B Takkouche, and F Caamano-Isorna. The role of tomato products and lycopene in the prevention of prostate cancer: A meta-analysis of observational studies. *Cancer Epidemiol Biomarkers Prev* 2004, 13(3):340–345.

23. Gann, PH, et al. Lower prostate risk in men with elevated plasma lycopene levels: Results of a prospective study. *Cancer Res* 1999, 59:1225–1230.

24. Nomura, AM, et al. Serum micronutrients and prostate cancer in Japanese Americans in Hawaii. *Cancer Epidemiol Biomarkers Prev* 1997, 6:487–491.

25. Paetau, I, et al. Chronic ingestion of lycopene-rich tomato juice or lycopene supplements significantly increases plasma concentrations of lycopene and related tomato carotenoids in humans. *Am J Clin Nutr* 1998, 68(6): 1187–1195.

26. Ambrosini, GL, NH de Klerk, L Fritschi, et al. Fruit, vegetable, vitamin A intake, and prostate cancer risk. *Prostate Cancer Prostatic Dis* 2008, 11(1):61–66.

27. Pantuck, AJ, JT Leppert, N Zomorodian, et al. Phase II study of pomegranate juice for men with rising prostate-specific antigen following surgery or radiation for prostate cancer. *Clin Cancer Res* 2006, 12(13):4018–4026.

28. Sartippour, MR, NP Seeram, JY Rao, et al. Ellagitannin-rich pomegranate extract inhibits angiogenesis in prostate cancer in vitro and in vivo. *Int J Oncol* 2008, 32(2):475–480.

29. Hong, MY, NP Seeram, and D Heber. Pomegranate polyphenols down-regulate expression of androgen-synthesizing genes in human prostate cancer cells overexpressing the androgen receptor. *J Nutr Biochem* 2008, Vol.19(12): 848–855.

30. Kurahashi, N, S Sasazuki, M Iwasaki, et al. Green tea consumption and prostate cancer risk in Japanese men: A prospective study. *Am J Epidemiol* 2008, 167(1):71–77.

31. Hlezlsouer, KJ, et al. Association between alpha-tocopherol, gamma-tocopherol, selenium, and subsequent prostate cancer. *J Natl Cancer Inst* 2000, 92(24):2018–2023.

32. Eichholzer, M, et al. Smoking, plasma vitamins C, E, retinal, and carotene, and fatal prostate cancer: Seventeen-year follow-up of the prospective Basel Study. *Prostate* 1999, 38(3):189–198.

33. Heinonen, OP, et al. Prostate cancer and supplementation with alpha-tocopherol and beta-carotene: Incidence and mortality in a controlled trial. *J Natl Cancer Inst* 1998, 90(6):440–446.

34. Chan, JM, et al. Supplemental vitamin E intake and prostate cancer risk in a large cohort of men in the United States. *Cancer Epidemiol Biomarkers Prev* 1999, 8(10): 893–899.

35. Alkhenizan, A, and K Hafez. The role of vitamin E in the prevention of cancer: A meta-analysis of randomized controlled trials. *Ann Saud Med* 2007, 27(6):409–414.

36. Hartman, TJ, et al. Effects of long-term alpha-tocopherol supplementation on serum hormones in older men. *Prostate* 2001, 46(1):33–38.

37. Clark, LC, et al. Decreased risk of prostate cancer with selenium supplementation: Results of a double-blind cancer prevention trial. *Br J Urol* 1998, 81(5):730–734.

38. Lippman, SM, EA Klein, PJ Goodman, et al. Effect of selenium and vitamin E on risk of prostate cancer and other cancers: The Selenium and Vitamin E Cancer Prevention Trial (SELECT). *JAMA* 2009, 301(1):39–51.

39. Chan, JM, MJ Stampfer, J Ma, et al. Dairy products, calcium and prostate cancer risk in the Physicians' Health Study. *Am J Clin Nutr* 2001, 74(4):549–554.

40. Gao, X, MP LaValley, and KL Tucker. Prospective studies of dairy product and calcium intakes and prostate cancer risk: A meta analysis. *J Natl Cancer Inst* 2005, 97(23): 1768–1777.

41. Kesse, E, S Bertrais, P Astorg, et al. Dairy products, calcium and phosphorus intake, and the risk of prostate cancer: Results of the French prospective SU.VI.MAX (Supplementation en Vitamines et Minéraux AntioXydants) Study. *Br J Nutr* 2006, 95(3):539–545.

42. Ahn, J, D Albanes, U Peters, et al. Dairy products, calcium intake, and risk of prostate cancer in the prostate, lung, colorectal, and ovarian cancer screening trial. *Cancer Epidemiol Biomarkers Prev* 2007, 16(12): 2623–2630.

43. Key, TJ, et al. A case-control study of diet and prostate cancer. *Br J Cancer* 1997, 76(5):678– 687.

44. Sigounas, G, et al. S-allylmercaptocysteine inhibits cell proliferation and reduces the viability of erythroleukemia, breast, and prostate cancer cell lines. *Nutr Cancer* 1997, 27(2):186–191.

45. Pinto, JT, et al. Effects of garlic thioallyl derivatives on growth, glutathione concentration, and polyamine formation of human prostate carcinoma cells in culture. *Am J Clin Nutr* 1997, 66(2):398–405.

Prostate Enlargement (Benign Prostatic Hyperplasia)

1. *Benign Prostatic Hyperplasia (BPH).* Prostate Cancer Canada, 2009. Available at www.prostatecancer.ca/Prostate-Cancer/About-the-Prostate/BPH.aspx.

2. Lagiou, P, et al. Diet and benign prostatic hyperplasia: A study in Greece. *Urology* 1999, 54(2):284–290.

3. Gu, F. Changes in the prevalence of benign prostatic hyper-plasia in China. *Chin Med J* (Engl) 1997, 110(3):163–166.

4. Yang, YJ, et al. Comparison of fatty acid profiles in the serum of patients with prostate cancer and benign prostatic hyperplasia. *Clin Biochem* 1999, 32(6):405–409.

5. Tavani, A, E Longoni, C Bosetti, et al. Intake of selected micronutrients and the risk of surgically treated benign prostatic hyperplasia: A case-control study from Italy. *Eur Urol* 2006, 50(3):549–554.

6. Bravi, F, C Bosetti, L Dal Maso, et al. Macronutrients, fatty acids, cholesterol, and risk of benign prostatic hyperplasia. *Urology* 2006, 67(6):1205–1211.

7. Ibid.

8. Bravi, F, C Bosetti, L Dal Maso, et al. Food groups and risk of benign prostatic hyperplasia. *Urology* 2006, 67(1):73–79.

9. Xie, LP, Y Bai, XZ Zhang, et al. Obesity and benign prostatic enlargement: A large observational study in China. *Urology* 2007, 69(4):680–684.

10. Parson, JK. Modifiable risk factors for benign prostatic hyperplasia and lower urinary tract symptoms: New approaches to old problems. *J Urol* 2007, 178(2):395–401.

11. Wilt, TJ, et al. Saw palmetto extracts for treatment of benign prostatic hyperplasia: A systematic review. *JAMA* 1998, 280(18):1604–1609.

12. Gerber, GS. Saw palmetto for the treatment of men with lower urinary tract symptoms. *J Urol* 2000, 163(5): 1408–1412.

13. Wilt, T, A Ishani, and R MacDonald. Serenoa repens for benign prostatic hyperplasia. *Cochrane Database Syst Rev* 2002, (3):CD001423.

14. Hizli, F, and MC Uygur. A prospective study of the efficacy of Serenoa repens, tamsulosin, and Serenoa repens plus tamulson in treatment for patients with benign prostatic hyperplasia. *Int Urol Nephrol* 2007, 39(3):879–886.

15. Ulbricht, C, E Basch, S Bent, et al. Evidence-based system-atic review of saw palmetto by the National Standard Research Collaboration. *J Soc Integr Oncol* 2006, 4(4): 170–186.

16. Gerber, GS, and JM Fitzpatrick. The role of lipido-sterolic extract of Serenoa repens in the management of lower urinary tract symptoms associated with benign prostatic hyperplasia. *BJU Int* 2004, 94(3):338–344.

17. Wilt, T, A Ishani, R MacDonald, et al. Pygeum africanum for benign prostatic hyperplasia. *Cochrane Database Syst Rev* 2002, (1):CD001044.

18. Lopakin, N, A Sivkov, S Schlafke, et al. Efficacy and safety of a combination of Sabal and Uritca extract in lower urinary tract symptoms: Long term follow-up of a placebo-controlled, double-blind, multicenter trial. *Int Urol Nephrol* 2007, 39(4):1137–1146.

19. Wilt, T, R MacDonald, A Ishani, et al. Cernilton for benign prostatic hyperplasia. *Cochrane Database Syst Rev* 2000, (2):CD001042.

20. Wilt, T, et al. Beta-sitosterols for benign prostatic hyper-plasia. *Cochrane Database Syst Rev* 2000, (2):CD001043.

21. Berges, RR, A Kassen, and T Senge. Treatment of sympto-matic benign prostatic hyperplasia with beta-sitosterol: An 18-month follow-up. *BJU Int* 2000, 85(7):842–846.

Psoriasis

1. *Psoriasis*. Veteran Affairs Canada, May 4, 2006. Available at www.vac-acc.gc.ca/clients/sub.cfm?source=dispen/elguide/ psoriasis.

2. Azzini, M, et al. Fatty acids and antioxidant micronutrients in psoriatic arthritis. *J Rheumatol* 1995, 22(1):103–108.

3. Collier, PM, et al. Effect of regular consumption of oily fish compared with white fish on chronic plaque psoriasis. *Eur J Clin Nutr* 1993, 47(4):251–254.

4. Abenavoli, A, I Proietti, A Leggio, et al. Cutaneous manifes-tations in celiac disease. *World J Gastroenterol* 2006, 12(6): 843–852.

5. Michaelsson, G, et al. Patients with psoriasis have elevated levels of serum eosinophil cationic protein and increased numbers of EG2 positive eosinophils in the duodenal stroma. *Br J Dermatol* 1996, 135(3):371–378.

6. Michaelsson, G, et al. Patients with psoriasis often have increased serum levels of IgA antibodies to gliadin. *Br J Dermatol* 1993, 129(6):667–673.

7. Michaelsson, G, et al. Psoriasis patients with antibodies to gliadin can be improved by a gluten-free diet. *Br J Dermatol* 2000, 142(1):44–51.

8. Addoralorato, G, A Parente, G de LOrenzi, et al. Rapid regression of psoriasis in a celiac patient after gluten-free diet: A case report and review of the literature. *Digestion* 2003, 68(1):9–12.

9. Naldi, L, et al. Dietary factors and the risk of psoriasis: Results of an Italian case-control study. *Br J Dermatol* 1996, 134(1):101–106.

10. Tasaki, M, et al. Analyses of serum copper and zinc levels and copper/zinc ratios in skin diseases. *J Dermatol* 1993, 20(1):21–24.

11. Michaelsson, G, and K Ljunghall. Patients with dermatitis herpetiformis, acne, psoriasis and Darier's disease have low epidermal zinc concentrations. *Acta Derm Venereol* 1990, 70(4):304–308.

12. Burrows, NP, et al. A trial of oral zinc supplementation in psoriasis. *Cutis* 1994, 54(2):117–118.

13. Leibovici, V, et al. Effect of zinc therapy on neutrophil chemotaxis in psoriasis. *Isr J Med Sci* 1990, 26(6):306–309.

14. Syed, TA, et al. Management of psoriasis with Aloe vera extract in a hydrophilic cream: A placebo-controlled, double-blind study. *Trop Med Int Health* 1996, 1(4): 505–509.

15. Gieler, U, et al. Mahonia aquifolium: A new type of topical treatment for psoriasis. *J Dermatol Treat* 1995, 6:31–34.

16. Kojima, T, et al. Long-term administration of highly purified eicosapentaenoic acid provides improvement for psoriasis. *Dermatologica* 1991, 182(4):225–230.

17. Lassus, A, et al. Effects of dietary supplementation with polyunsaturated ethyl ester lipids (Angiosan) in patients with psoriasis and psoriatic arthritis. *J Int Med Res* 1990, 18(1):68–73.

18. Danno, K, and N Sugie. Combination therapy with low-dose etretinate and eicosapentaenoic acid for psoriasis vulgaris. *J Dermatol* 1998, 25(11):703–705.

19. Gupta, AK, et al. Double-blind, placebo-controlled study to evaluate the efficacy of fish oil and low-dose UVB in the treatment of psoriasis. *Br J Dermatol* 1989, 129(6): 801–807.

20. Stoof, TJ, et al. Does fish oil protect renal function in cyclosporin-treated psoriasis patients? *J Intern Med* 1989, 226(6):437–441.

Rheumatoid Arthritis

1. *Rheumatoid Arthritis*. The Arthritis Society of Canada, January 2001. Available at www.arthritis.ca/types%20of%20arthritis/ra/default.asp?s=1.

2. Kjeldsen-Kragh, J, et al. Antibodies against dietary antigens in rheumatoid arthritis patients treated with fasting and a one-year vegetarian diet. *Clin Exp Rheumatol* 1995, 13(2):167–172.

3. van de Laar, MA, et al. Food intolerance in rheumatoid arthritis: II. Clinical and histological aspects. *Ann Rheum Dis* 1992, 51(3): 303–306.

4. van de Laar, MA, et al. Food intolerance in rheumatoid arthritis: I. A double blind, controlled trial of the clinical effects of elimination of milk allergens and azo dyes. *Ann Rheum Dis* 1992, 51(3):298–302.

5. Denman, AM, et al. Joint complaints and food allergic disorders. *Ann Allergy* 1983, 51(2 Pt 2):260–263.

6. Felder, M, et al. Food allergy in patients with rheumatoid arthritis. *Clin Rheumatol* 1987, 6(2):181–184.

7. Karaty, S, T Erdem, A Kiziltunc, et al. General or personal diet: The individualized model for diet challenges in patients with rheumatoid arthritis. *Rheumatol Int* 2006, 26(6):556–560.

8. Hvatum, M, L Kanerud, R Hallgren, and P Brandtzaeg. The gut-joint axis: Cross reactive food antibodies in rheumatoid arthritis. *Gut* 2006, 55(9):1240–1247.

9. Skoldastam, L, L Hagfors, and G Johansson. An experimental study of a Mediterranean diet intervention for patients with rheumatoid arthritis. *Ann Rheum Dis* 2003, 62(3):208–214.

10. Muller, H, et al. Fasting followed by vegetarian diet in patients with rheumatoid arthritis: A systematic review. *Scand J Rheumatol* 2001, 30(1):1–10.

11. Hanninen, NI, K Kaartinen, et al. Antioxidants in vegan diet and rheumatic disorders. *Toxicology* 2000, 155(1–3): 45–53.

12. Kjeldsen-Kragh, J. Rheumatoid arthritis treated with vegetarian diets. *Am J Clin Nutr* 1999, 70(Suppl 3): 594S–600S.

13. Peltonen, R, et al. Faecal microbial flora and disease activity in rheumatoid arthritis during a vegan diet. *Br J Rheumatol* 1997, 36(1):64–68.

14. Kjeldsen-Kragh, J, et al. Vegetarian diet for patients with rheumatoid arthritis—status: Two years after introduction of the diet. *Clin Rheumatol* 1994, 13(3):475–482.

15. Elkan, AC, B Sjöberg, B Kolsrud, et al. Gluten-free vegan diet induced decreased LDL and oxidized LDL levels and raised atheroprotective natural antiobodies against phosphorylcholine in patients with rheumatoid arthritis: A randomized study. *Arthritis Res Ther* 2008, 10(2):R34. Epub 2008 Mar 18.

16. Galarraga, B, M Ho, HM Youssef, et al. Cod liver oil (n-3 fatty acids) as an non-steroidal anti-inflammatory drug sparing agent in rheumatoid arthritis. *Rheumatology* (Oxford) 2008, 47(5):665–669.

17. Stamp, LK, MJ James, and LG Cleland. Diet and rheumatoid arthritis: A review of the literature. *Semin Arthritis Rheum* 2005, 35(2):77–94.

18. Sundrarjun, T, S Komindr, N Archararit, et al. Effects of n-3 fatty acids on serum interlueukin-6, tumour necrosis factor-alpha and soluble tumour necrosis factor receptor p55 in active rheumatoid arthritis. *J Int Med Res* 2004, 32(5): 443–454.

19. Shapiro, JA, et al. Diet and rheumatoid arthritis in women: Possible protective effect of fish consumption. *Epidemiology* 1996, 7(3):256–263.

20. Comstock, GW, et al. Serum concentrations of alpha tocopherol, beta carotene, and retinal preceding the diagnosis of rheumatoid arthritis and systemic lupus erythematosus. *Ann Rheum Dis* 1997, 56(5):323–325.

21. Gambhir, JK, et al. Correlation between blood antioxidant levels and lipid peroxidation in rheumatoid arthritis. *Clin Biochem* 1997, 30(4):351–355.

22. Kose, K, et al. Plasma selenium levels in rheumatoid arthritis. *Biol Trace Elem Res* 1996, 53(1–3):51–56.

23. Azzini, M, et al. Fatty acids and antioxidant micronutrients in psoroiatic arthritis. *J Rheumatol* 1995, 22(1):103–108.

24. Heliovaara, M, et al. Serum antioxidants and the risk of rheumatoid arthritis. *Ann Rheum Dis* 1994, 53(1):51–53.

25. O'Dell, JR, et al. Serum selenium concentrations in rheumatoid arthritis. *Ann Rheum Dis* 1991, 50(6):376–378.

26. Situnayake, RD, et al. Chain breaking antioxidant status in rheumatoid arthritis: Clinical and laboratory correlates. *Ann Rheum Dis* 1991, 50(2):81–86.

27. Tarp, U, et al. Glutathione peroxidase activity in patients with rheumatoid arthritis and in normal subjects: Effects of long-term selenium supplementation. *Arth Rheum* 1987, 30(10):1162–1166.

28. Peretz, A, et al. Selenium status in relation to clinical variables and corticosteroids treatment in rheumatoid arthritis. *J Rheumatol* 1987, 14(6):1104–1107.

29. Lunec, J, and DR Blake. The determination of dehydroascorbic acid and ascorbic acid in the serum and synovial fluid of patients with rheumatoid arthritis (RA). *Free Rad Res Commun* 1985, 1(1):31–39.

30. Edmonds, SE, et al. Putative analgesic activity of prepared oral doses of vitamin E in the treatment of rheumatoid arthritis: Results of a prospective placebo controlled double blind trial. *Ann Rheum Dis* 1997, 56(11):649–655.

31. Canter, PH, B Wider, and E Ernst. The antioxidant vitamins A, C, E and selenium in treatment of arthritis: A systematic review of randomized controlled trials. *Rheumatology* (Oxford) 2007, 46(8):1223–1233.

32. Buckley, LM, et al. Calcium and vitamin D3 supplementation prevents bone loss in the spine secondary to low-dose corticosteroids in patients with rheumatoid arthritis: A randomized, double-blind, placebo-controlled trial. *Ann Intern Med* 1996, 125(12):961–968.

33. Thornton, J, D Ashcroft, T O'Neill, et al. A systematic review of the effectiveness of strategies for reducing fracture risk in children with juvenile idiopathic arthritis with additional data on long-term risk of fracture and cost of disease management. *Health Technol Assess* 2008, 12(3):iii–ix, xi–xiv, 1–208.

34. Lovell, JJ, D Glass, J Ranz, et al. A randomized controlled trial of calcium supplementation to increase bone mineral density in children with juvenile rheumatoid arthritis. *Arthritis Rheum* 2006, 54(7):2235–2242.

35. Cutolo, M, K Otsa, M Uprus, et al. Vitamin D in rheumatoid arthritis. *Autoimmun Rev* 2007, 7(1):59–64.

36. Etzel, R. Special extract of Boswellia serrata (H 15) in the treatment of rheumatoid arthritis. *Phytomedicine* 1996, 3:91–94.

37. Sander, O, et al. Is H15 (resin extract of Boswellia serrata, incense) a useful supplement to established drug therapy of chronic polyarthritis? Results of a double-blind pilot study. *Z Rheumatol* 1998, 57:11–16. [in German, English abstract]

38. James, MJ, and LG Cleland. Dietary n-3 fatty acids and therapy for rheumatoid arthritis. *Semin Arth Rheum* 1997, 27:85–97.

39. Volker, D, P Fitzgerald, G Major, and M Garg. Efficacy of fish oil concentrate in the treatment of rheumatoid arthritis. *J Rheumatol* 2000, 27(10):2343–2346.

40. Fortin, PR, et al. Validation of a meta-analysis: The effects of fish oil in rheumatoid arthritis. *J Clin Epidemiol* 1995, 48(11):1379–1390.

41. Geusens, P, et al. Long-term effect of omega-3 fatty acid supplementation in active rheumatoid arthritis: A 12-month, double-blind, controlled study. *Arth Rheum* 1994, 37(6): 824–829.

42. Berbert, AA, CR Kondo, CL Almendra, et al. Supplementation with fish oil and olive oil in patients with rheumatoid arthritis. *Nutrition* 2006, 21(2):131–136.

43. Adam, O, C Beringer, T Kless, et al. Anti-inflammatory effects of a low arachidonic acid diet and fish oil in patients with rheumatoid arthritis. *Rheumatol Int* 2003, 23(1): 27–36.

44. Kremer, JM, et al. Effects of high dose fish oil on rheumatoid arthritis after stopping nonsteroidal anti-inflammatory drugs: Clinical and immune correlates. *Arth Rheum* 1995, 38(8):1107–1114.

Shingles (Herpes Zoster)

1. *Shingles*. Mayo Foundation for Education and Research, May 21, 2008. Available at www.mayoclinic.com/health/shingles/DS00098/DSECTION=complications.

2. Thomas, SL, JG Wheeler, and AJ Hall. Micronutrient intake and the risk of herpes zoster: A case-control study. *Int J Epidemiol* 2006, 35(2):307–314.

3. Meydani, SN, et al. Vitamin E supplementation enhances cell-mediated immunity in healthy elderly subjects. *Am J Clin Nutr* 1990, 52(3):557–563.

4. Ravaglia, G, et al. Effect of micronutrient status in natural killer cell immune function in healthy free living subjects aged >/=90 y. *Am J Clin Nutr* 2000, 71(2):590–598.

5. Frucht-Pery, J, et al. The use of capsaicin in herpes zoster opthalmicus neuralgia. *Acta Opthalmol Scan* 1997, 75(3): 311–313.

6. Watson, CP, et al. A randomized vehicle-controlled trial of topical capsaicin in the treatment of postherpetic neuralgia. *Clin Ther* 1993, 15(3):510–526.

7. Peikert, A, et al. Topical 0.025% capsaicin in chronic post-herpetic neuralgia: Efficacy predictors of response and long-term course. *J Neurol* 1991, 238(8):452–426.

8. Watson, CP, et al. The prognosis with postherpetic neuralgia. *Pain* 1991, 46(2):195–199.

9. Hempenstall, K, TJ Nurmikko, RW Johnson, et al. Analgesic therapy in postherpetic neuralgia: A quantitative systematic review. *PLoS Med* 2005, 2(7):e164, Epub 2005 Jul 26.

10. Douglas MW, RW Johnson, and AL Cunningham. Tolerability of treatments for postherpetci neuralgia. *Drug Saf* 2004, 27(15):1217–1233.

11. Kleine, MW, et al. The intestinal absorption of orally administered hydrolytic enzymes and their effects in the treatment of acute herpes zoster as compared with those of oral acyclovir therapy. *Phytomedicine* 1995, 2:7–15.

12. Billigmann, P. Enzyme therapy—an alternative in treatment for herpes zoster: A controlled study of 192 patients. *Fortschr Med* 1995, 113:43–48. [German]

Sinusitis (Sinus Infection)

1. Westerveld, GJ, et al. Antioxidant levels in the nasal mucosa of patients with chronic sinusitis and healthy controls. *Arch Otolaryngol Head Neck Surg* 1997, 123(2):201–204.

2. Shah, SA, S Sander, CM White, M Rinaldi, and CI Coleman. Evaluation of echinacea for the prevention and treatment of the common cold: A meta-analysis. *Lancet Infect Dis* 2007, 7(7):473–480.

3. Kyo, E, et al. Immunomodulatory effects of aged garlic extract. *J Nutr* 2001, 131(Suppl 3): 1075S–1079S.

4. Amagase, H, et al. Intake of garlic and its bioactive components. *J Nutr* 2001, 131(Suppl 3):955S–962S.

5. Salman, H, et al. Effect of a garlic derivative (alliin) on peripheral blood cell immune responses. *Int J Immunopharmacol* 1999, 21(9):589–597.

6. McElhaney, JE, S Gravenstein, SK Cole, et al. A placebo-controlled trial of a proprietary extract of North American ginseng (CVT-E002) to prevent acute respiratory illness in institutionalized older adults. *J Am Geriatr Soc* 2004, 52(1):13–19.

7. Predy, GN, V Goel, R Lovlin, et al. Efficacy of an extract of North American ginseng containing poly-furanosyl-pyranosyl-saccharides for preventing upper respiratory tract infections: A randomized controlled trial. *CMAJ* 2005, 173(9):1043–1048.

8. McElhaney, JE, V Goel, B Toane, et al. Efficacy of COLD-fX in the prevention of respiratory symptoms in community-dwelling adults: A randomized, double-blinded, placebo controlled trial. *J Altern Complement Med* 2006, 12(2): 153–157.

9. Scaglione, F, et al. Efficacy and safety of the standardized ginseng extract G115 for potentiating vaccination against the influenza syndrome and protection against the common cold. *Drugs Exp Clin Res* 1996, 22:65–72.

10. Selzer, AP. Adjunctive use of bromelains in sinusitis: A controlled study. *Eye Ear Nose Throat Mon* 1967, 46(10): 1281–1288.

11. Ryan, RE. A double-blind clinical evaluation of bromelains in the treatment of acute sinusitis. *Headache* 1967, 7(1): 13–17.

12. Taub, SJ. The use of bromelains in sinusitis: A double-blind clinical evaluation. *Eye Ear Nose Throat Mon* 1967, 46(3): 361–362.

13. Braun, JM, B Schneider, and HJ Beuth. Therapeutic use, efficacy and safety of the proteolytic pineapple enzyme

Bromelain-POS in children with acute sinusitis in Germany. *In Vivo* 2005, 19(2):417–421.

14. Linday, LA, JN Dolitsky, and RD Shindledecker. Nutritional supplements as adjunctive therapy for children with chronic/recurrent sinusitis: Pilot research. *Int J Pediatr Otorhinolaryngol* 2004, 68(6):785–793.

Stress

1. *Full Compass Survey.* Canadian Mental Health Association. April 20, 2001. Available at www.cmha.ca/bins/content_page.asp?cid=5-34-212-213&lang=1#_Toc 512618117.

2. Markus, R, et al. Effects of food on cortisol and mood in vulnerable subjects under controllable and uncontrollable stress. *Physiol Behav* 2000, 70(3–4):333–342.

3. Markus, CR, et al. Carbohydrate intake improves cognitive performance of stress-prone individuals under controllable and uncontrollable laboratory stress. *Br J Nutr* 1999, 82(6):457–467.

4. Markus, CR, et al. Does carbohydrate-rich, protein-poor food prevent a deterioration of mood and cognitive performance of stress-prone subjects when subjected to a stressful task? *Appetite* 1998, 31(1):49–65.

5. Markus, CR. Effects of carbohydrate on brain tryptophan availability and stress performance. *Biol Psychol* 2007, 76(1–2):83–90.

6. Shepard, JD, et al. Additive pressor effects of caffeine and stress in male medical students at risk for hypertension. *Am J Hypertens* 2000, 13(5 Pt 1):475–481.

7. al'Absi, M, et al. Hypothalamic-pituitary-adrenocortical responses to psychological stress and caffeine in men at high and low risk for hypertension. *Psychosom Med* 1998, 60(4):521–527.

8. Lovallo, WR, et al. Hypertension risk and caffeine's effect on cardiovascular activity during mental stress in young men. *Health Psychol* 1991, 10(4):236–243.

9. Lane, JD, et al. Caffeine effects on cardiovascular and neuroendocrine responses to acute psychological stress and their relationship to level of habitual caffeine consumption. *Psychosom Med* 1990, 52(3):320–336.

10. van Dusseldorp, M, et al. Effects of coffee on cardiovascular responses to stress: A 14-week controlled trial. *Psychosom Med* 1992, 54(3):344–353.

11. Eskay, RL, et al. The effects of alcohol on selected regulatory aspects of the stress axis, in *Alcohol and the Endocrine System*, ed. Zakhari S. (Bethesda, MD: National Institute of Alcohol Abuse and Alcoholism Research Monograph No. 23, 1993).

12. Waltman, C, et al. The effects of mild ethanol intoxication on the hypothalamic-pituitary-adrenal axis in nonalcoholic men. *J Clin Endocrin Met* 1993, 77(2):518–522.

13. Spencer, RL, and ES McEwen. Adaptation of the hypothalamic-pituitary-adrenal axis in chronic ethanol stress. *Neuroendocrinology* 1990, 52(5):481–489.

14. McKinney, A, and K Coyle. Next-day effects of alcohol and an additional stressor on memory and psychomotor performance. *J Stud Alcohol Drugs* 2007, 68(3):446–454.

15. Earle, R. *The Third Wave of Stress Science: Controlling Future Shock Trauma in Workplace Hyperchange.* The Canadian Institute of Stress, 2007. Available at www.stress canada.org/research.html.

16. Gruenwald, J, HJ Graubaum, and A Harde. Effect of a probiotic multivitamin compound on stress and exhaustion. *Adv Ther* 2002, 19(3):141–150.

17. Schlebusch L, BA Bosch, G Polglase, et al. A double-blind, placebo-controlled, double-centre study of the effects of an oral multivitamin-mineral combination on stress. *S Afr Med J* 2000, 90(12):1216–1223.

18. McCarty, MF. High dose pyridoxine as an 'anti-stress' strategy. *Med Hypotheses* 2000, 54(5):803–807.

19. Baldewicz, T, et al. Plasma pyridoxine deficiency is related to increased psychological distress in recently bereaved homosexual men. *Psychosom Med* 1998, 60(3):297–308.

20. Carroll, D, et al. The effects of an oral multi-vitamin combination with calcium, magnesium, and zinc on psychological well-being in healthy young male volunteers: A double-blind placebo-controlled trial. *Psychopharmacology* 2000, 150(2):220–225.

21. Desole, MS, et al. Analysis of immobilization stress-induced changes of ascorbic acid, noradrenaline, and dopamine metabolism in discrete brain areas of the rat. *Pharmacol Res* 1990, 22(Suppl 3):43–44.

22. Tverdokhlip, P, et al. Effect of emotional and pain stress on the level of antioxidant vitamins in the blood of rats. *Vopr Pitan* 1987, (6):52–54. [Russian]

23. Brody, S, R Preut, K Schommer, and TH Schurmeyer. A randomized controlled trial of high dose ascorbic acid for reduction of blood pressure, cortisol, and subjective responses to psychological stress. *Psychopharmacology* (Berlin) 2002, 159(3):319–324.

24. Cernak, I, et al. Alterations in magnesium and oxidative status during chronic emotional stress. *Magnes Res* 2000, 13(1):29–36.

25. Fujita, T, et al. Fall of blood ionized calcium on watching a provocative TV program and its prevention by active absorbable algal calcium (AAA Ca). *J Bone Miner Metab* 1990, 17(2):131–136.

26. Ibid.

27. Carroll, D, C Ring, M Suter, and G Willemsen. The effects of an oral multivitamin combination with calcium, magnesium, and zinc on psychological well-being in healthy young male volunteers: A double-blind placebo-controlled trial. *Psychopharmacology* (Berlin) 2000, 150(2):220–225.

28. Kim, DH, et al. Inhibition of stress-induced plasma corticosterone levels by ginsenosides in mice: Involvement of nitric oxide. *Neuroreport* 1998, 9(10):2261–2264.

29. Bittles, AH, et al. The effect of ginseng on the lifespan and stress responses in mice. *Gerontology* 1979, 25(3):125–131.

30. Dua, PR, et al. Adpatogenic activity of Indian Panax pseudo-ginseng. *Ind J Exp Biol* 1989, 27:631–634.

31. Hiai, S, et al. Features of ginseng saponin induced corticosterone secretion. *Endocrinol Jpn* 1979, 26:737–740.

32. Scaglione, F, et al. Efficacy and safety of the standardized ginseng extract G115 for potentiating vaccination against the influenza syndrome and protection against the common cold. *Drugs Exp Clin Res* 1996, 22:65–72.

33. Sorenson, H, and J Sonne. A double-masked study of the effects of ginseng on cognitive functions. *Curr Ther Res* 1996, 57:959–968.

Ulcers (Peptic Ulcers)

1. *H. pylori and Peptic Ulcer.* National Digestive Diseases Information Clearinghouse, October 2004. Available at http://digestive.niddk.nih.gov/ddiseases/pubs/hpylori/index.htm.
2. Gotteland, M, M Andrews, M Toledo, et al. Modulation of Helicobacter pylori colonization with cranberry juice and Lactobacillus johnsonii La1 in children. *Nutrition* 2008, 24(5):421–426.
3. Shmuely, H, J Yahav, Z Samra, et al. Effect of cranberry juice on eradication of Helicobater pylori in patients treated with antibiotics and a proton pump inhibitor. *Mol Nutr Food Res* 2007, 51(6):746–751.
4. Zhang, L, L Ma, K Pan, et al. Efficacy of cranberry juice on Helicobacter pylori infection: A double-blind, randomized placebo-controlled trial. *Helicobacter* 2005, 10(2):139–145.
5. Ryan-Harshman, M, and W Aldoori. How diet and lifestyle affects duodenal ulcers: Review of the evidence. *Can Fam Physician* 2004, 50:727–732.
6. Elmstahl, S, et al. Fermented milk products are associated to ulcer disease: Results from a cross-sectional population study. *Eur J Clin Nutr* 1998, 52(9):668–674.
7. Miki, K, Y Urita, F Ishikawa, et al. Effect of Bifidobacterium bifidum fermented milk on Helicobacter pylori and serum pepsinogen levels in humans. *J Dairy Sci* 2007, 90(6): 2630–2640.
8. de Bortoli, N, G Leonardi, E Ciancia, et al. Helicobacter pylori eradication: A randomized prospective study of triple therapy versus triple therapy plus lactoferrin and probiotics. *Am J Gastroenterol* 2007, 102(5):951–956.
9. Canducci, F, F Cremonini, A Armuzzi, et al. Probiotics and Helicobacter pylori eradication. *Dig Liver Dis* 2002, 34(Suppl 2):S81–S83.
10. Thompson, L, et al. Inhibitory effect of polyunsaturated fatty acids on the growth of Helicobacter pylori: A possible explanation of the effect of diet on peptic ulceration. *Gut* 1994, 35(11):1157–1161.
11. Manjari, V, and UN Das. Oxidant stress, anti-oxidants, nitric acid and essential fatty acids in peptic ulcer disease. *Prostaglandins Leukot Essent Fatty Acids* 1998, 59(6): 401–406.
12. Hollander, D, and A Tarnawski. Is there a role for essential fatty acids in gastroduodenal mucosal protection? *J Clin Gastroenterol* 1991, 13(Suppl 1):S72–S74.
13. Hawley, CJ. Prostaglandins: Mucosal protection and peptic ulceration. *Methods Find Exp Clin Pharmacol* 1989, 11(Suppl 1):24–51.
14. Nair, S, et al. Micronutrients antioxidant in gastric mucosa and serum in patients with gastritis and gastric ulcer: Does Helicobacter pylori infection alter the results? *J Clin Gastroenterol* 2000, 30(4):381–385.
15. Force, RW, and MC Nahata. Effect of histamine H2-receptor antagonists on vitamin B12 absorption. *Ann Pharmacother* 1992, 26(10):1283–1286.
16. Dharmarajan, TS, MR Kanagala, P Murakonda, et al. Do acid-lowering agents affect vitamin B12 status in older adults? *J Am Med Dir Assoc* 2008, 9(3):162–167.
17. Valuck, RJ, and JM Ruscin. A case-control study on adverse effects: H2 blocker or proton pump inhibitor use and risk of vitamin B12 deficiency in older adults. *J Clin Epidemiol* 2004, 57(4):422–428.

18. Kassir, ZA, et al. Endoscopic controlled trial of four drug regimens in the treatment of chronic duodenal ulceration. *Ir Med J* 1985, 78:153–156.
19. Morgan, AG, et al. Maintenance therapy: A two-year comparison between Caved-S and cimetidine treatment in the prevention of symptomatic gastric ulcer recurrence. *Gut* 1985, 26:599–602.

Urinary Tract Infections (UTIs)

1. Avorn, J, M Manone, JH Gurwitz, et al. Reduction of bacteriuria and pyuria after ingestion of cranberry juice. *JAMA* 1994, 27(10)1:751–754.
2. Wing, DA, PJ Rumney, CW Preslicka, and JH Chung. Daily cranberry juice for the prevention of asymptomatic bacteriuria in pregnancy: A randomized, controlled pilot study. *J Urol* 2008, 180(4):1367–1372.
3. Kontiokari, T, et al. Randomised trial of cranberry-lingonberry juice and Lactobacillus GG drink for the prevention of urinary tract infections in women. *Br Med J* 2001, 322(7302):1571.
4. Avron, J, et al. Reduction of bacteriuria and pyuria after ingestion of cranberry juice. *JAMA* 1994, 271:751–754.
5. Kyo, E, et al. Immunomodulatory effects of aged garlic extract. *J Nutr* 2001, 131(Suppl 3):1075S–1079S.
6. Amagase, H, et al. Intake of garlic and its bioactive components. *J Nutr* 2001, 131(Suppl 3):955S–962S.
7. Salman, H, et al. Effect of a garlic derivative (alliin) on peripheral blood cell immune responses. *Int J Immunopharmacol* 1999, 21(9):589–597.
8. Reid, G. Potential preventative strategies and therapies in urinary tract infection. *World J Urol* 1999, 17(6):359–363.
9. Velraeds, MM, et al. Inhibition of initial adhesion of uropathogenic Enterococcus faecalis by biosurfactants from Lactobacillus isolates. *Appl Environ Micorbiol* 1996, 62(6): 1958–1963.
10. Hawthorn, LA, and G Reid. Exclusion of uropathogen adhesion to polymer surfaces by Lactobacillus acidophilus. *J Biomed Mater Res* 1990, 24(1):39–46.
11. Reid, G, et al. Is there a role for lactobacilli in prevention of urogenital and intestinal functions? *Clin Microbiol Rev* 1990, 3(4):335–344.
12. Falagas, ME, GI Betsi, T Tokas, and S Athanasiou. Probiotics for prevention of recurrent urinary tract infections in women: A review of the evidence from microbiological and clinical studies. *Drugs* 2006, 66(9): 1253–1261.

Varicose Veins

1. Cesarone, MR, et al. Activity of Centella asiatica in venous insufficiency. *Minerva Cardioangiol* 1992, 42:137–143.
2. Belcaro, GV, et al. Improvement of capillary permeability in patients with venous hypertension after treatment with TTFCA. *Angiology* 1990, 41:533–540.
3. Belcaro, GV, et al. Capillary filtration and ankle edema in patients with venous hypertension treated with TTCFA. *Angiology* 1990, 41:12–18.
4. Pointel, JP, et al. Titrated extract of Centella asiatica (TECA) in the treatment of venous insufficiency of the lower limbs. *Angiology* 1987, 38:46–50.
5. Lohr, E, et al. Anti-edemic therapy in chronic venous insufficiency with tendency to formation of edema. *Munch Med Wsch* 1986, 128(34):579–581. [German]

6. Rudofsky, G, et al. Antiedematous effects and clinical effectiveness of horse chestnut seed extract in double bind studies. *Phlebologie und Proktologie* 1986, 15:47–54. [German]

7. Neiss, A, et al. Proof of the efficacy of horse chestnut seed extract in the treatment of varicose veins. *Munch Med Wsch* 1976, 118(7):213–216. [German]

8. Leach, MJ, J Pincombe, and G Foster. Clinical efficacy of horse chestnut seed extract in the treatment of venus ulceration. *J Wound Care* 2006, 15(4):159–167.

9. Diehm, C, et al. Comparison of leg compression stocking and oral horse-chestnut seed extract therapy in patients with chronic venous insufficiency. *Lancet* 1996 Feb 3, 347(8997):292–294.

10. Tixier, JM, et al. Evidence by in vivo and in vitro studies that binding of pycnogenols to elastin affects its rate of degradation by elastases. *Biochem Pharmacol* 1984, 33:3933–3939.

11. Masquelier, J, et al. Stabilization of collagen by procyanidolic oligomers. *Acta Therap* 1981, 7:101–105.

12. Schwitters, B, et al. *OPC in Practice: Bioflavonols and Their Applications* (Rome: Alfa Omega, 1993).

Index